UNDERGROUND

Travel Information 0171-222-1234
Travelcheck 0171-222-1200

© London Regional Transport

LRT Registered User No. 97/2726

D0255511

Diary 1A 4. 96

Key to lines

Bakerloo	
Central	
Circle	
District	
East London	
Hammersmith & City	
Jubilee	
Metropolitan	
Northern	
Piccadilly	
Victoria	
Waterloo & City †	
Docklands Light Railway	
British Rail	

● Interchange stat
○ Connections wit
   Connections wit
   walking distanc
⊖ Airport interch
+ Closed Sundays
++ Closed Saturday

xxxxxx Restricted service
xxxxxx Peak Saturday mornings
   Peak hours only
|||||||| Under construction

† For opening times see poster journey planners
‡ Certain stations are closed during public holidays

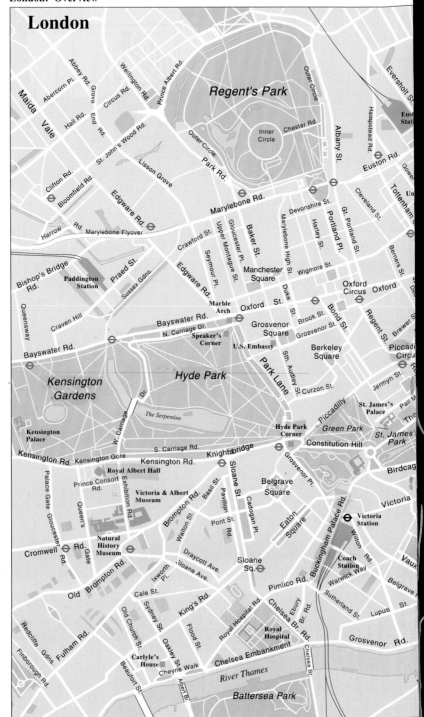

London

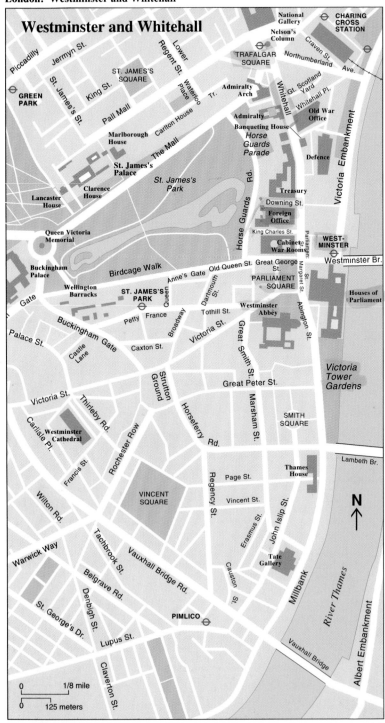

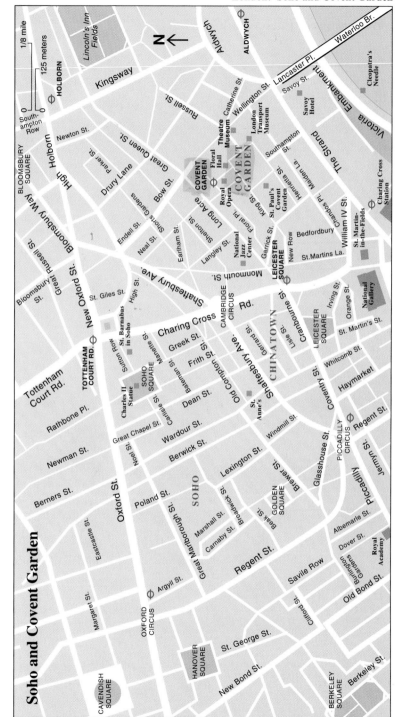

Soho and Covent Garden

London: Soho and Covent Garden

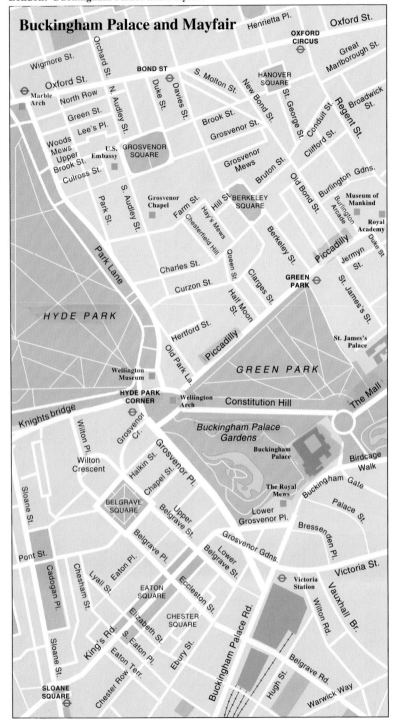

Buckingham Palace and Mayfair

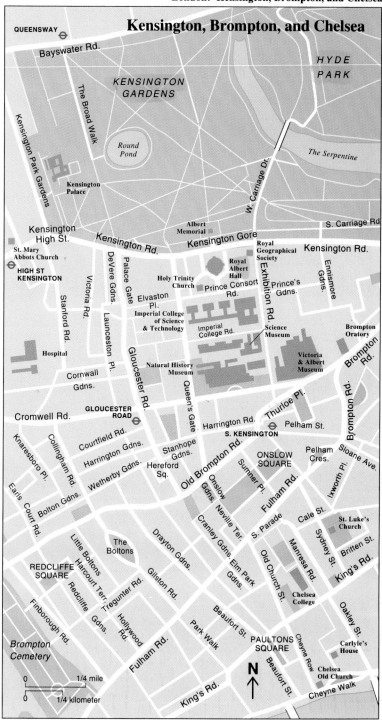

Kensington, Brompton, and Chelsea

QUEENSWAY

Bayswater Rd.

HYDE PARK

KENSINGTON GARDENS

The Broad Walk

Kensington Park Gardens

Round Pond

The Serpentine

Kensington Palace

Kensington High St.

St. Mary Abbots Church

HIGH ST KENSINGTON

Albert Memorial

Kensington Rd.

Kensington Gore

Royal Geographical Society

Kensington Rd.

W. Carriage Dr.

S. Carriage Rd.

DeVere Gdns.

Palace Gate

Victoria Rd.

Stanford Rd.

Launceston Pl.

Holy Trinity Church

Royal Albert Hall

Prince Consort Rd.

Elvaston Pl.

Imperial College of Science & Technology

Imperial College Rd.

Exhibition Rd.

Prince's Gdns.

Ennismore Gdns.

Science Museum

Brompton Oratory

Hospital

Cornwall Gdns.

Gloucester Rd.

Natural History Museum

Victoria & Albert Museum

Brompton Rd.

Cromwell Rd.

GLOUCESTER ROAD

Queen's Gate

Thurloe Pl.

Harrington Rd.

Pelham St.

S. KENSINGTON

Knaresboro Pl.

Collingham Rd.

Courtfield Rd.

Harrington Gdns.

Stanhope Gdns.

Hereford Sq.

Old Brompton Rd.

ONSLOW SQUARE

Pelham Cres.

Sloane Ave.

Earls Court Rd.

Bolton Gdns.

Wetherby Gdns.

Onslow Gdns.

Neville Ter.

Sumner Pl.

Fulham Rd.

Ixworth Pl.

Little Boltons

Drayton Gdns.

Cranley Gdns.

Elm Park Gdns.

S. Parade

Cale St.

Sydney St.

St. Luke's Church

Britten St.

REDCLIFFE SQUARE

The Boltons

Harcourt Terr.

Redcliffe Gdns.

Tregunter Rd.

Gilston Rd.

Hollywood Rd.

Old Church St.

Manresa Rd.

King's Rd.

Finborough Rd.

Fulham Rd.

Park Walk

Beaufort St.

Chelsea College

Oakley St.

Brompton Cemetery

PAULTONS SQUARE

Cheyne Row

Carlyle's House

Chelsea Old Church

0   1/4 mile

0   1/4 kilometer

N

King's Rd.

Beaufort St.

Cheyne Walk

London: City of London

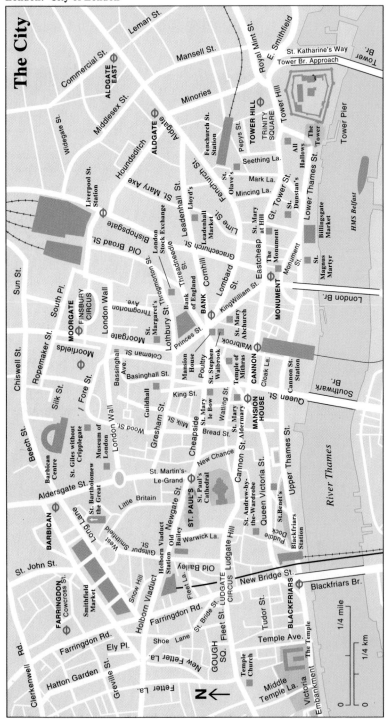

LET'S GO
Britain & Ireland

■ Let's Go writers travel on your budget.

"Guides that penetrate the veneer of the holiday brochures and mine the grit of real life."
—The Economist

"The writers seem to have experienced every rooster-packed bus and lunar-surfaced mattress about which they write."
—The New York Times

"All the dirt, dirt cheap."
—People

■ Great for independent travelers.

"The guides are aimed not only at young budget travelers but at the independent traveler, a sort of streetwise cookbook for traveling alone."
—The New York Times

"Flush with candor and irreverence, chock full of budget travel advice."
—The Des Moines Register

"An indispensable resource. *Let's Go*'s practical information can be used by every traveler."
—The Chattanooga Free Press

■ Let's Go is completely revised each year.

"Only *Let's Go* has the zeal to annually update every title on its list."
—The Boston Globe

"Unbeatable: good sight-seeing advice; up-to-date info on restaurants, hotels, and inns; a commitment to money-saving travel; and a wry style that brightens nearly every page."
—The Washington Post

■ All the important information you need.

"*Let's Go* authors provide a comedic element while still providing concise information and thorough coverage of the country. Anything you need to know about budget traveling is detailed in this book."
—The Chicago Sun-Times

"Value-packed, unbeatable, accurate, and comprehensive."
—Los Angeles Times

Let's Go Publications

Let's Go: Alaska & the Pacific Northwest 1999
Let's Go: Australia 1999
Let's Go: Austria & Switzerland 1999
Let's Go: Britain & Ireland 1999
Let's Go: California 1999
Let's Go: Central America 1999
Let's Go: Eastern Europe 1999
Let's Go: Ecuador & the Galápagos Islands 1999
Let's Go: Europe 1999
Let's Go: France 1999
Let's Go: Germany 1999
Let's Go: Greece 1999 **New title!**
Let's Go: India & Nepal 1999
Let's Go: Ireland 1999
Let's Go: Israel & Egypt 1999
Let's Go: Italy 1999
Let's Go: London 1999
Let's Go: Mexico 1999
Let's Go: New York City 1999
Let's Go: New Zealand 1999
Let's Go: Paris 1999
Let's Go: Rome 1999
Let's Go: South Africa 1999 **New title!**
Let's Go: Southeast Asia 1999
Let's Go: Spain & Portugal 1999
Let's Go: Turkey 1999 **New title!**
Let's Go: USA 1999
Let's Go: Washington, D.C. 1999

Let's Go Map Guides

Amsterdam	Madrid
Berlin	New Orleans
Boston	New York City
Chicago	Paris
Florence	Rome
London	San Francisco
Los Angeles	Washington, D.C.

Coming Soon: Prague, Seattle

Let's Go Publications

Let's Go
Britain &
Ireland
1999

Olivia Choe
Editor

Alexandra M. Leichtman
Associate Editor

Researcher-Writers:
Christa Franklin
Nick Grandy
Daryl Sng

with

Adriane N. Giebel   **Ben Jackson**   **Justine Sadoff**

St. Martin's Press ✹ New York

HELPING LET'S GO

If you want to share your discoveries, suggestions, or corrections, please drop us a line. We read every piece of correspondence, whether a postcard, a 10-page email, or a coconut. Please note that mail received after May 1999 may be too late for the 2000 book, but will be kept for future editions. **Address mail to:**

Let's Go: Britain & Ireland
67 Mount Auburn Street
Cambridge, MA 02138
USA

Visit Let's Go at **http://www.letsgo.com**, or send email to:

feedback@letsgo.com
Subject: "Let's Go: Britain & Ireland"

In addition to the invaluable travel advice our readers share with us, many are kind enough to offer their services as researchers or editors. Unfortunately, our charter enables us to employ only currently enrolled Harvard-Radcliffe students.

About Let's Go

THIRTY-NINE YEARS OF WISDOM

Back in 1960, a few students at Harvard University banded together to produce a 20-page pamphlet offering a collection of tips on budget travel in Europe. This modest, mimeographed packet, offered as an extra to passengers on student charter flights to Europe, met with instant popularity. The following year, students traveling to Europe researched the first, full-fledged edition of *Let's Go: Europe*, a pocket-sized book featuring honest, irreverent writing and a decidedly youthful outlook on the world. Throughout the 60s, our guides reflected the times; the 1969 guide to America led off by inviting travelers to "dig the scene" at San Francisco's Haight-Ashbury. During the 70s and 80s, we gradually added regional guides and expanded coverage into the Middle East and Central America. With the addition of our in-depth city guides, handy map guides, and extensive coverage of Asia and Australia, the 90s are also proving to be a time of explosive growth for Let's Go, and there's certainly no end in sight. The maiden edition of *Let's Go: South Africa,* our pioneer guide to sub-Saharan Africa, hits the shelves this year, along with the first editions of *Let's Go: Greece* and *Let's Go: Turkey.*

We've seen a lot in 39 years. *Let's Go: Europe* is now the world's bestselling international guide, translated into seven languages. And our new guides bring Let's Go's total number of titles, with their spirit of adventure and their reputation for honesty, accuracy, and editorial integrity, to 44. But some things never change: our guides are still researched, written, and produced entirely by students who know first-hand how to see the world on the cheap.

HOW WE DO IT

Each guide is completely revised and thoroughly updated every year by a well-traveled set of over 200 students. Every winter, we recruit over 160 researchers and 70 editors to write the books anew. After several months of training, researcher-writers hit the road for seven weeks of exploration, from Anchorage to Adelaide, Estonia to El Salvador, Iceland to Indonesia. Hired for their rare combination of budget travel sense, writing ability, stamina, and courage, these adventurous travelers know that train strikes, stolen luggage, food poisoning, and marriage proposals are all part of a day's work. Back at our offices, editors work from spring to fall, massaging copy written on Himalayan bus rides into witty yet informative prose. A student staff of typesetters, cartographers, publicists, and managers keeps our lively team together. In September, the collected efforts of the summer are delivered to our printer, who turns them into books in record time, so that you have the most up-to-date information available for your vacation. Even as you read this, work on next year's editions is well underway.

WHY WE DO IT

We don't think of budget travel as the last recourse of the destitute; we believe that it's the only way to travel. Living cheaply and simply brings you closer to the people and places you've been saving up to visit. Our books will ease your anxieties and answer your questions about the basics—so you can get off the beaten track and explore. Once you learn the ropes, we encourage you to put *Let's Go* down now and then to strike out on your own. You know as well as we that the best discoveries are often those you make yourself. When you find something worth sharing, please drop us a line. We're Let's Go Publications, 67 Mount Auburn St., Cambridge, MA 02138, USA (email: feedback@letsgo.com). For more info, visit our website, http://www.letsgo.com.

HAPPY TRAVELS!

Contents

ABOUT LET'S GO—V
HOW TO USE THIS BOOK—IX
LIST OF MAPS—XI
LET'S GO PICKS—XVII

ESSENTIALS I
    PLANNING YOUR TRIP—I
    When to Go, Climate, Resources at Home, Internet Resources, Documents and
    Formalities, Money, Safety and Security, Health, Insurance, Alternatives to Tourism,
    Specific Concerns, Packing
    GETTING THERE—25
    Budget Travel Agencies, By Plane, By Train, By Bus, By Boat
    ONCE THERE—31
    Diplomatic Missions, Getting About, Accommodations, Longer Stays, Camping and
    the Outdoors, Keeping in Touch

GREAT BRITAIN 52
    History, Literature, Art, The Media, Music, Food, Pubs and Beer, Sports

LONDON. 70
    GETTING IN AND OUT—70
    GETTING ABOUT—74
    PRACTICAL INFORMATION—76
    ACCOMMODATIONS—78
    FOOD AND DRINK—84
    SIGHTS—94
    Central London, West London, North London, East London, South London, Greater
    London
    MUSEUMS—126
    ENTERTAINMENT—131
    SHOPPING—138
    BISEXUAL, GAY, AND LESBIAN LONDON—140

SOUTH ENGLAND 142
    KENT—142
    Canterbury, Sandwich, Deal, Dover
    SUSSEX—155
    Rye, Brighton, Arundel, Chichester
    HAMPSHIRE—169
    Portsmouth, Isle of Wight, Winchester, South Downs Way

SOUTHWEST ENGLAND 185
    THE DORSET COAST—188
    Dorchester, Weymouth, Lyme Regis
    DEVON—193
    Exeter, Exmoor National Park, Dartmoor National Park, Plymouth
    CORNWALL—205
    Bodmin Moor, Falmouth, Penzance, Land's End to St. Ives, St. Ives, Newquay

HEART OF ENGLAND 219
    OXFORDSHIRE—219
    Oxford, Salisbury, Stonehenge
    AVON AND SOMERSET—236
    Bath, Bristol, Wells, Glastonbury
    SOUTHERN MIDLANDS—250
    Cheltenham, The Cotswolds, Worcester, Stratford-upon-Avon, Birmingham

EAST ANGLIA 271
    CAMBRIDGESHIRE—272
    Cambridge, Ely
    NORFOLK AND SUFFOLK—285
    Norwich, King's Lynn, Bury St. Edmunds

CENTRAL ENGLAND 297
    Shrewsbury, Nottingham, Lincoln, Sheffield, Peak District National Park, Manches-
    ter, Chester, Blackpool, Liverpool, Leeds

NORTH ENGLAND **337**
*Pennine Way, Yorkshire Dales National Park, York, North York Moors National
Park, Durham City, Newcastle-Upon-Tyne, Northumberland, Carlisle, Hadrian's
Wall, Lake District National Park*

WALES **388**
Getting There and Getting About
LIFE AND TIMES—390
History, Lliterature and Music, Ffood, Llanguage, Ffestivals

SOUTH WALES **396**
*Cardiff (Caerdydd), Wye Valley, Brecon Beacons National Park, Swansea (Abertawe),
Gower Peninsula, Tenby (Dinbych-y-pysgod), Pembrokeshire Coast National Park*

NORTH WALES **425**
*Aberystwyth, Cardigan (Aberteifi), Machynlleth, Harlech, Llqn Peninsula (Penrhyn
Llyn), Snowdonia National Park, Caernarfon, Bangor, Isle of Anglesey (Ynys Môn),
Conwy, Vale of Conwy and Betws-y-Coed, Llangollen*

SCOTLAND **455**
Getting There, Getting About
LIFE AND TIMES—458
History, Language, Literature and Music, Food and Drink, Festivals

SOUTHERN SCOTLAND **464**
Edinburgh, The Borders, Dumfries and Galloway, Glasgow, Arran

CENTRAL SCOTLAND AND ARGYLL **505**
*Stirling, Inveraray, Loch Lomond, St. Andrews, Fife Seaside , Perth, Pitlochry, Oban,
Isle of Islay, Isle of Mull*

HIGHLANDS AND ISLANDS **529**
*Aberdeen, East Grampian Coast and Mountains, Elgin, Cairngorm Mountains and
Aviemore, Inverness, Glen Coe, Fort William and Ben Nevis, Road to the Isles and
Mallaig, The Small Isles, Isle of Skye, Outer Hebrides, The Northwest, Inverness to the
Ferry Ports, Orkney Islands, Shetland Islands*

ISLE OF MAN **573**
Douglas

NORTHERN IRELAND **579**
Essentials, History and Politics
BELFAST—585
COS. DOWN AND ARMAGH—594
Newcastle and the Mourne Mountains, Armagh Town
CO. ANTRIM—597
Larne, Glens of Antrim, Causeway Coast, Portrush
COS. DERRY AND FERMANAGH—603
Derry City, Enniskillen

REPUBLIC OF IRELAND **609**
History, Literary Traditions, Music, Media and Popular Culture, Sports, Food and Drink
CO. DUBLIN—621
Dublin
COS. WICKLOW, MEATH, AND LOUTH—640
Boyne Valley, Athlone
COS. WEXFORD, WATERFORD, KILKENNY, AND TIPPERARY—644
Wexford City, Waterford City, Kilkenny City
COS. CORK AND KERRY—651
*Cork City, Beara Peninsula, Killarney, Ring of Kerry, Dingle, The Dingle Peninsula,
Tralee*
COS. LIMERICK AND CLARE—666
Limerick City
COS. GALWAY AND MAYO—670
Galway City, Aran Islands, Connemara, Westport, Achill Island, Ballina
COS. SLIGO AND DONEGAL—683
Sligo Town, Donegal Town, Letterkenny, Inishowen Peninsula

APPENDIX **690**
Holidays, Telephone Codes, Time Zones, Measurements, Language

INDEX **695**

RESEARCHER-WRITERS—714
ACKNOWLEDGMENTS—715
THANKS TO OUR READERS—716

How to Use This Book

"Bonjour! Welcome to the wonderful world of **Britain and Ireland!** My name is William the Conqueror. This earth, this realm, this rain-driven plot o' land is my kingdom. I have invaded and subjugated these meek peoples and built a great many Norman castles. I am a royal bastard! And look at what you're holding—that, my friends, is a copy of *Let's Go: Britain & Ireland 1999,* the most comprehensive budget travel guide ever to be written about my property!

"I began my invasion of this barbaric land with a longsword and a boat. You, on the other hand, are armed with a handy-dandy yellow guide! This thing is a marvel of modern alchemy. The **Essentials** section is full of publications, organizations, and travel guilds that will smooth your journey and perhaps save you gold. If my soldiers could read, I'd make them read it. Hold on, Mathilda, there's more! Learn something of this strange and sheep-strewn land and its strange and sheep-strewn people in the next section—**History and Literature,** and so on and so forth—featuring myself and all of my historical friends, from the great Caesar to the pretty and well-named Prince William. Armed with this cultural knowledge, you'll be the life of the ale house!

"The remainder of the book is divided into places that I conquered and places that I didn't. For example, **England,** mother country of lush valleys, majestic castles, and adorable little villages, I crushed. **Wales,** home to windy, sand beaches and sexpot Tom Jones, I defeated. **Scotland,** birthplace of haggis, I postponed. **Ireland,** land of bogs, Irish people, and *crubeen* (tasty pig's feet), I ignored.

"I have arranged the towns in an elegant, easy-to-conquer order, for your plundering pleasure. **Getting There** shows you the best ways to get from hamlet to hamlet. **Orientation** gives you a plan of attack for each city, and often includes direction to the nearest Norman castle. *Mi casa, su casa, amigos!* **Practical Information** provides the lowdown on tourist offices, post offices, bike rental, and phone codes! **Accommodations** suggests where to lay down your hauberk and park your steed. **Food**—there's nothing William the Conqueror likes better after a hard day of pillaging than *naan* and vegetarian curry! **Sights** details Norman castles...and other lesser sights! **Entertainment** sections list enough minstrels, fayres, and dance clubs to keep even rowdy soldiers content. **Near** sections make good day-conquers.

"Feeling overwhelmed by the massive size of this tome? Think you don't have enough time because *my* royal spawn took a millennium to subdue this territory? Don't worry! I have compiled a number of useful lists for you! **Let's Go Picks** (p. xvii) set out the best of the best, including the best toilets in all the land. **Highlights of the Region,** at the beginning of each chapter, give you the most bang for your travel shilling. These are the absolute do-not-miss sights of the region like Norman castles. Finally, a **thumb** in the margin identifies places fit for a king.

"I hope this little chat was helpful. If not, write me! William the Conqueror, 67 Mt. Auburn St., Cambridge, MA, 02138 (email: fanmail@letsgo.com). Happy plundering!"

A NOTE TO OUR READERS

The information for this book was gathered by *Let's Go*'s researchers from May through August. Each listing is derived from the assigned researcher's opinion based upon his or her visit at a particular time. The opinions are expressed in a candid and forthright manner. Other travelers might disagree. Those traveling at a different time may have different experiences since prices, dates, hours, and conditions are always subject to change. You are urged to check beforehand to avoid inconvenience and surprises. Travel always involves a certain degree of risk, especially in low-cost areas. When traveling, especially on a budget, always take particular care to ensure your safety.

Maps

Britain & Ireland: Points of Interest .... xii-xiii
Britain & Ireland: Transport Map .... xiv-xv
Britain & Ireland: Regional xvi
Central London: Major Street Finder 72-73
South England 144
Canterbury 146
Brighton 158
Portsmouth 170
Winchester 176
Southwest England 186
Exeter 194
Heart of England 220
Oxford 222
Salisbury 232
Bath 237
Stratford-upon-Avon 263
East Anglia 271
Cambridge 273
Norwich 286
Central England 297
Lincoln 303
Peak District National Park 308
Manchester 316
Chester 323
Liverpool 330
North England 337
Yorkshire Dales National Park 344

York 349
North York Moors National Park 356
Durham 363
Newcastle-Upon-Tyne 366
Lake District National Park 374
Wales 389
Cardiff (Caerdydd) 397
Brecon Beacons National Park 410
Scotland 456
Southern Scotland 464
Edinburgh 466-67
Glasgow 490
Central Scotland and Argyll 505
St. Andrews 512
Highlands and Islands 530
Inverness 538
Isle of Man 574
Northern Ireland 579
Central Belfast 584
Derry 602
Ireland: Republic of Ireland & Northern Ireland 610-611
Central Dublin 622-623
Dublin Pub Crawl 631
Cork 652
Limerick 667
Galway 671

Color Maps

London: Underground .... color inset
London: Overview: .... color inset
London: Westminster and Whitehall .... color inset
London: Buckingham Palace and Mayfair .... color inset
London: Kensington, Brompton, and Chelsea .... color inset
London: City of London .... color inset

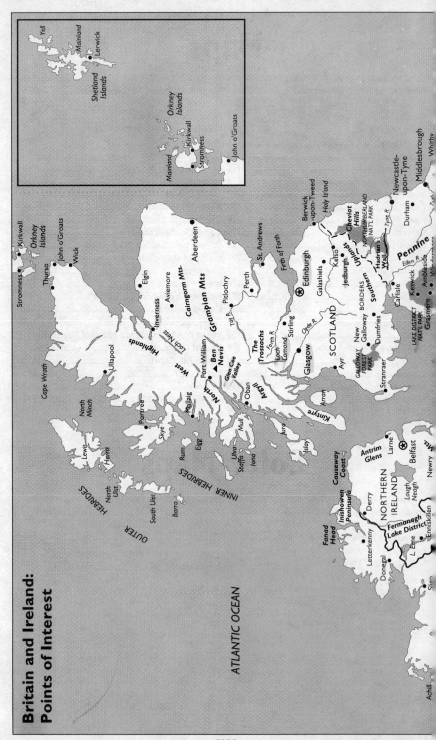

Britain and Ireland: Points of Interest

Shetland Islands
Yell
Mainland
Lerwick

Orkney Islands
Mainland
Kirkwall
Stromness
John o'Groats

Whitby
Middlesbrough
Newcastle-upon-Tyne
Durham

Berwick-upon-Tweed
Holy Island
Cheviot Hills
NORTHUMBERLAND NATL PARK
Pennine
Tyne R.
Kelso
Jedburgh
Uplands
Southern
BORDERS
Hadrian's Wall
Eden R.
Carlisle
Keswick
LAKE DISTRICT NATL PARK
Ambleside
Grasmere
Windermere

Kirkwall
Orkney Islands
John o'Groats
Stromness
Thurso
Wick

Aberdeen
Cairngorm Mts.
Aviemore
Elgin
Grampian Mts
Pitlochry
Perth
St. Andrews
Firth of Forth
Edinburgh
Galashiels
SCOTLAND
New Galloway
Dumfries
GALLOWAY FOREST PARK
Stranraer
Ayr
Glasgow
Stirling
Loch Lomond
The Trossachs
Forth R.
Clyde R.
Tay R.
Inverness
Highlands
Loch Ness
West
North
Fort William
▲ Ben Nevis
Glen Coe Valley
Oban
MULL
Kintyre
Arran
Cape Wrath
Ullapool
North Minch
Portree
Mallaig
Skye
Rum
Eigg
Staffa
Iona
Urva
Mull
Jura
Islay

Lewis
Harris
North Uist
South Uist
Barra
OUTER HEBRIDES
INNER HEBRIDES

Larne
Antrim Glens
Causeway Coast
Belfast
Mts
NORTHERN IRELAND
Derry
Inishowen Peninsula
Fanad Head
Lough Neagh
Newry
L. Erne
Lough
Fermonagh Lake District
Enniskillen
Letterkenny
Donegal
Sligo
Achill

ATLANTIC OCEAN

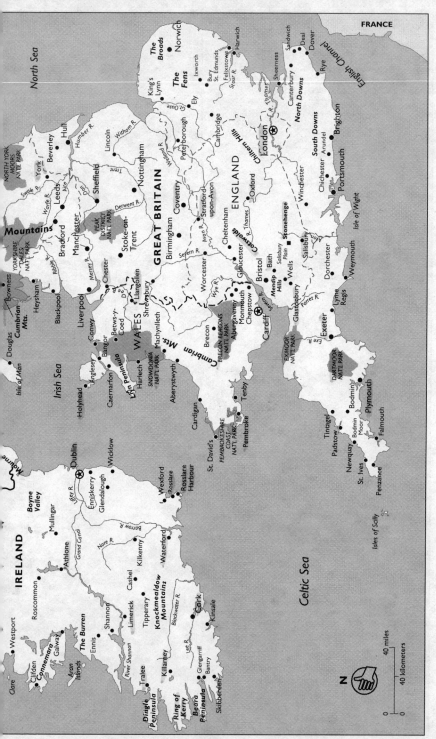

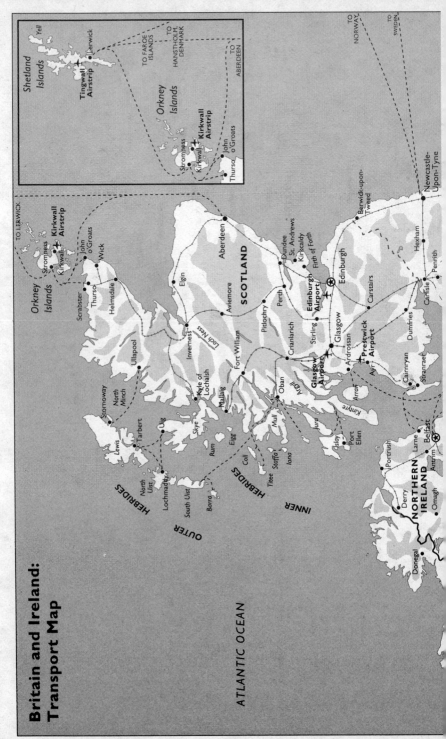

Britain and Ireland: Transport Map

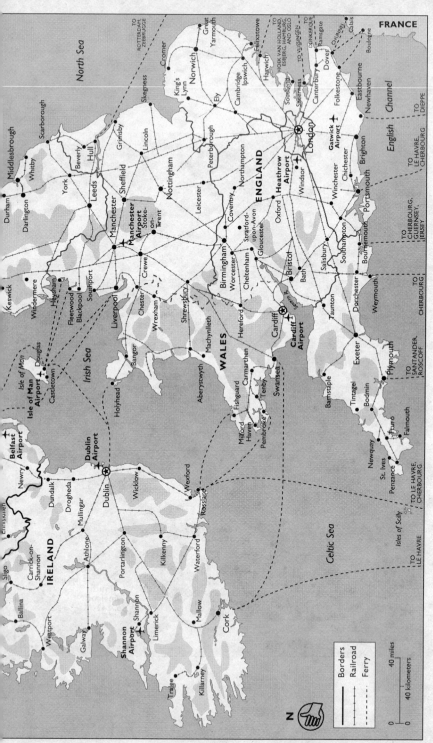

xv

TO SHETLANDS & ORKNEYS (SEE INSET)

Shetland Islands

Orkney Islands

HEBRIDES

OUTER

Thurso

Ullapool

Skye

Inverness

HEBRIDES

Highlands & Islands
pp. 529-572

Aberdeen

INNER

Mull

Fort William

Oban

Central Scotland & Argyll
pp. 505-528

St. Andrews

Glasgow

Edinburgh

Arran

Southern Scotland
pp. 464-504

Derry

Larne

Northern Ireland
pp. 574-608

Belfast

Dumfries

Newcastle-Upon-Tyne

Stranraer

Carlisle

Durham

Sligo

Isle of Man
pp. 573-578

North England
pp. 337-387

Galway

Dublin

York

Leeds

Liverpool

Manchester

Holyhead

Sheffield

Lincoln

Republic of Ireland
pp. 609-689

Bangor

Central England
pp. 297-336

Limerick

Shrewsbury

Norwich

Rosslare Harbour

Aberystwyth

Birmingham

Cambridge

East Anglia
pp. 271-296

Cork

Fishguard

Stratford-upon-Avon

Wales
pp. 388-454

Heart of England
pp. 219-270

Oxford

London
pp. 70-141

N

Britain and Ireland: Regional

Swansea

Cardiff

Bristol

Bath

Salisbury

South England
pp. 142-184

Dover

0 100 miles

Southwest England
pp. 185-218

Portsmouth

Plymouth

Isle of Wight

FRANCE

0 100 kilometers

Penzance

Let's Go Picks

Of all the trails we've hiked, of all the clubs we've crashed, of all the castles we've coveted, these are the walks, the sights, and the attractions that *B&I '99* loved the most. Check 'em out or discover your own; either way, post us some mail—"e" or snail—and let us know what you think.

Killer Castles and Cathedrals: The regal polygonal towers of **Caernarfon Castle** (p. 443). Gorgeous views of water and...sheep from **Castle Howard's** Temple of the Four Winds (p. 355). **Blenheim Palace,** not quite a castle, but the largest private home in England (p. 231). The gut-wrenching views of the sea from *Mel*-ancholy **Dunnotar Castle** (p. 533). Warwick Castle **York Minster**—Britain's biggest Gothic cathedral and more medieval stained glass than anywhere else in the world (p. 349). Getting sent to **Coventry** isn't quite so bad if you take in its two fantastic cathedrals, one bombed in World War II, the other rebuilt from it (p. 267).

Best Nightlife: London, duh (p. 131). **Newcastle,** because it's mad! It's brilliant, baby (p. 368)! Gorge on chocolate and dance all night in **Birmingham** (p. 269). Feel the hipness in the air on Canal St. in **Manchester's Gay Village** (p. 321). Drink and be merry amidst **Blackpool** Vegas-style lights (p. 326). **Liverpool's Cream:** people travel for miles to wave their hands in the air like trash-talking semaphorists (p. 329). The entire **Derry** pick-up scene (p. 605). **Haltwhistle**—just kidding.

Best Hikes: Stunning ocean views in **Pembrokeshire Coast National Park** (p. 419). Windy walks on the cliffs of **Whitby** (p. 359). The wily Ways of **Yorkshire Dales National Park** (p. 343). Dramatic peaks, flower-filled valleys, and water, water everywhere in the **Lake District National Park** (p. 375). Dashing up the U.K.'s highest peak, **Ben Nevis,** for a glimpse of Ireland (p. 543). **Giant's Causeway**—County Antrim's "eighth wonder of the world" (p. 600). Killarney Park, offering gorgeous hiking and biking (p. 659). The 5000 ft. drop at **Benbulben** (p. 683).

Best Pubs: The **Lamb and Flag** offers music and madness near Covent Garden (p. 92). The terraces of **Turf Tavern** in the heart of Oxford (p. 225). **Ye Olde Trip to Jerusalem,** a pub carved into the sandstone base of Nottingham Castle (p. 300). **The Stag's Head** in Dublin, so good looking it's been featured in Guinness ads (p. 630). The best trad in Ireland plays at **The Liverpool Bar** in Belfast (p. 589).

Best Toilets: The naturally **self-flushing** toilet of Kisimul Castle in Barra (p. 559). The **stained-glass** portrayal of a toilet in Christ Church Cathedral's windows in Oxford (p. 226). The sleek **space-pod** toilet in Worcester (p. 260). The **two-seater** in Cardoness Castle—for you and a very special friend (p. 488).

Most Indescribable: The eerie subterranean boat trips in **Speedwell Cavern** in Castleton (p. 313). The shadowed, carved interior of **Bryn Celli Ddu** on Anglesey (p. 445). Risqué teapots and vicious butterflies in **Conwy** (p. 448). **Fair Isle,** at the farthest tip of the Shetlands and Britain's most northern point (p. 568). The "whistling sands" of the beaches at **Aberdaron,** one of Wales's lovely unspoiled hamlets. The **Murals of Belfast.** Hallucinating from lack of sleep at **St. Paul's.** First day in Scotland, first **haggis** experience.

Most Unforgettable: Mellowing at a midnight bonfire under the misty peaks of **Glen Coe.** Phone calls from J. in **Cambridge.** Driving the **Cornwall** coast. A spontaneous daytrip to **Ireland.** Learning how to drive in **Dublin.** Coke cans and Altoids hiding a multitude of **sins.** A Saturday night sojourn along **Keats Walk** by the River Itchen. Tightening the thumbscrews in **Inverary's Jail**—wait, what were we thinking? London **shopping** sprees.

ESSENTIALS

PLANNING YOUR TRIP

■ When to Go

July and August are considered the tourist "high season." Hostels, B&Bs, and sights will be packed. The shoulder months directly before and after provide some of the best experiences; the weather is hospitable and flights are less expensive. Traveling during the off-season (mid-Sept. to May) will further reduce the damage to your bank account. Airfares will be less expensive and you won't have to compete with gaggles of garrulous tourists pulling up prices and ruining the view. However, sights, accommodations (particularly hostels), and tourist offices may close in the off-season. In some rural areas, local transportation slows to a crawl, or shuts down altogether, especially on Sundays or on holidays (see p. 690). The infamous climate of the British Isles may have some bearing on your plans as well.

■ Climate

The **weather** in **Britain** and **Ireland** is subject to frequent changes but few extremes, with an average temperature in the low to mid-60°s Fahrenheit in the summer and in the low 40°s Fahrenheit during the winter. Throughout the islands, you can expect unstable weather patterns; a bright and cloudless morning frequently precedes outright downpour in the afternoon. The period of May through August brings the best weather; temperatures can reach the 70°s Fahrenheit, even in Scotland. A recent warming trend has brought hotter springs, lower rainfalls, and hayfever to Brits.

Scotland is generally soggy; you should be prepared with warm, waterproof clothing at all times. Northern Scotland stretches into the same latitudes as parts of Siberia, and temperatures are often below freezing, even in summer. August and September, the hottest months of the year, bring brilliant purple heather and, unfortunately, midges (gnats). Though Ireland gets the most publicity for its wet weather, **Wales** also suffers 200 rainy days a year. April is the driest month in Ireland, especially on the east coast near Dublin. May and June are the sunniest months, particularly in the south and southeast, and July and August are the warmest. December and January have the most insufferable weather of the year—wet, cold, and cloudy.

To convert from °C to °F, multiply by 1.8 and add 32. For an approximation, double the Celsius and add 25. To convert from °F to °C, subtract 32 and multiply by 0.55.

°C	-5	0	5	10	15	20	25	30	35	40
°F	23	32	41	50	59	68	77	86	95	104

■ Resources at Home

NATIONAL TOURIST BUREAUS

British Tourist Authority (BTA). In **Australia,** Level 16, Gateway Bldg., 1 Macquarie Pl., Sydney NSW 2000 (tel. (02) 9377 4400). In **Canada,** 111 Avenue Rd., Ste. 450, Toronto, Ont. M5R 3J8 (tel. (888) VISIT UK (847-4885) or (416) 925 6326). In **New Zealand,** Dilworth Bldg., Ste. 305, Corner Customs and Queen St., Auckland 1 (tel. (09) 303 1446). In **South Africa,** Lancaster Gate, Hyde Ln. Manor, Hyde Park, Sandton 2196 (tel. (011) 325 0343; fax 325 0344). In the **U.S.,** 551 Fifth Ave., Ste. 701, New York, NY 10176-0799 (tel. (800) GO2 BRIT (462 2748) or (212) 986 2200). On the **Internet,** http://www.visitbritain.com.

Irish Tourist Board (Bord Fáilte). In **Australia,** Level 5, 36 Carrington St., Sydney NSW 2000 (tel. (02) 9299 6177; fax 9299 6323). In **Canada** and the **U.S.,** 345 Park Ave., New York, NY 10154 (tel. (800) 223 6470 or (212) 418 0800; fax 371 9052). In **New Zealand,** 87 Queen St., Auckland (tel. (09) 302 2867). In **South Africa,** Everite House, 20 DeKorte St., Braamfontein, P.O. Box 30615, Johannesburg (tel. (011) 339 4865; fax 339 2474). In the **U.K.,** 150 New Bond St., London W1Y 0AQ (tel. (0171) 518 0800; fax 493 9065). On the **Internet,** http://ireland.travel.ie.

Northern Ireland Tourist Board. Head Office: 59 North St., Belfast BT1 1NB, Northern Ireland (tel. (01232) 246609; fax 312424). In **Canada,** 111 Avenue Rd., Ste. 450, Toronto, Ont. M5R 3J8 (tel. (416) 925 6368; fax 925 6033). In **Ireland,** 16 Nassau St., Dublin 2 (tel. (01) 679 1977; CallSave (01850) 230230; fax (01) 679 1851). In the **U.K.,** 24 Haymarket, London SW1Y 4DG (tel. (0171) 766 9920; fax 766 9929). In the **U.S.,** 551 Fifth Ave., Ste. 701, New York, NY 10176-0799 (tel. (800) 326 0036 or (212) 922 0101; fax 922 0099). On the **Internet,** http://www.ni-tourism.com.

USEFUL ORGANIZATIONS

Council on International Educational Exchange (Council), 205 E. 42nd St., New York, NY 10017-5706 (tel. (888) COUNCIL (268 6245); fax (212) 822 2699; email info@ciee.org; http://www.ciee.org). A private, nonprofit organization, Council administers work, academic, volunteer, and internship programs around the world. They also offer identity cards, including the ISIC and the GO25, and a range of publications, including the magazine *Student Travels* (free).

Federation of International Youth Travel Organizations (FIYTO), Bredgade 25H, DK-1260 Copenhagen K, Denmark (tel. (45) 33 33 96 00; fax 33 93 96 76; email mailbox@fiyto.org; http://www.fiyto.org), is an international organization promoting educational, cultural, and social travel for young people. Member organizations include language schools, educational travel companies, national tourist boards, accommodation centers, and other suppliers of travel services to youth and students. FIYTO sponsors the GO25 Card (http://www.go25.org).

International Student Travel Confederation, Herengracht 479, 1017 BS Amsterdam, The Netherlands (tel. (31) 20 421 2800; fax 20 421 2810; email istcinfo@istc.org; http://www.istc.org). A nonprofit confederation of student travel organizations whose focus is to develop and facilitate travel among young people and students. Member organizations include International Student Surface Travel Association (ISSA), Student Air Travel Association (SATA), IASIS Travel Insurance, the International Association for Educational and Work Exchange Programs (IAEWEP), and the International Student Identity Card Association (ISIC).

PRESERVATION SOCIETIES

If you plan to do visit numerous castles and historical sites, a membership to one or both of the following historical preservation societies will pay off. They offer free admission to certain castles, cathedrals, and monuments around Britain. The **National Trust** is a British charity dedicated to preserving sites in England, Wales, and Northern Ireland. Members receive free entry to over 300 Trust sites in Britain (membership US$45; families US$70). U.S. and Canadian residents should contact The Royal Oak Foundation, 285 W. Broadway, #400, New York, NY 10013-2299. All others should contact the National Trust Membership Department, P.O. Box 39, Bromley, Kent BR1 3XL, England (tel. (0181) 315 1111; http://www.ukindex.co.uk/nationaltrust). **English Heritage,** English Heritage Membership Department, Freepost 31 (WD214), London, W1E 5EZ (tel. (0171) 973 3434; http://www.english-heritage.org.uk) offers admission to over 400 historical sites around England, including Stonehenge (membership UK£25, young persons £16, seniors £15.50, families £43, single-parent families £25). They also offer Overseas Visitors Passes good for 7 or 14 days of sightseeing (adults £13.30, £17.30; families £27.30, £35.30). Allow one month for membership and pass processing.

Historic Scotland maintains over 300 properties including Edinburgh and Stirling Castles. Membership includes free admission to Historic Scotland sites as well as half price admission to English Heritage and Welsh Cadw properties (£22, students and seniors £16, families £40, single-parent families £26). Apply over the phone, on-line or in person at any manned Historic Scotland site. For more information, contact Historic Scotland, Longmore House, Salisbury Pl., Edinburgh, EH9 1SH (tel. (0131) 668 8800 or 668 8999; http://www.historic-scotland.gov.uk). **The National Trust for Scotland,** Membership Services, 5 Charlotte Sq., Edinburgh (tel. (0131) 243 9589; http://www.nts.org.uk) offers admission to hundreds of historical sites, including Culzean and Fyvie Castles (£25, under 26 £10, seniors £17, families £42).

USEFUL PUBLICATIONS

Blue Guides, published in Britain by A&C Black Ltd., 35 Bedford Row, London WC1R 4JH; in the U.S. by W.W. Norton & Co. Inc., 500 Fifth Ave., New York, NY 10110; in Canada by Penguin Books Canada Ltd., 10 Alcorn Ave., #300, Toronto, Ont. N47 3B2. Blue Guides provide invaluable and unmatched historical and cultural information as well as sight-seeing routes, maps, tourist information, and listings of pricey hotels.

Bon Voyage!, 2069 W. Bullard Ave., Fresno, CA 93711-1200 (tel. (800) 995 9716 or (209) 447 8441; fax 266 6460; email 70754.3511@compuserve.com). Annual mail order catalog offers a range of products for every kind of traveler, lowest prices guaranteed.

The College Connection, Inc., 1295 Prospect St., Ste. B, La Jolla, CA 92037 (tel. (619) 551 9770; fax 551 9987; email eurailnow@aol.com; http://www.eurail-pass.com). Publishes *The Passport,* a booklet listing hints about traveling and studying abroad. Free for *Let's Go* readers; send your request by email or fax only. The College Rail Connection, a division of The College Connection, also sells rail-passes with student discounts.

Forsyth Travel Library, 1750 E. 131 St., P.O. Box 480800, Kansas City, MO 64148 (tel. (800) 367 7984; fax (816) 942 6969; email forsyth@avi.net; http://www.for-syth.com). A mail-order service that stocks a range of maps and guides for rail and ferry travel in Europe; also sells and reserves rail tickets and passes. Call or write for a free catalogue, or visit their website.

Wide World Books and Maps, 1911 N. 45th St., Seattle, WA 98103 (tel. (206) 634-3453; fax 634-0558; email travel@speakeasy.org; http://www.ww-books.com). A good selection of travel guides, travel accessories, and maps.

■ Internet Resources

Along with everything else in the '90s, budget travel is moving rapidly into the information age. Today, you can make airline, hotel, hostel, or car rental reservations on the Internet, and connect personally with others abroad. **NetTravel: How Travelers Use the Internet,** by Michael Shapiro, is a very thorough and informative guide to all aspects of travel planning through the Internet (US$25).

THE WORLD WIDE WEB

As a travel resource, the World Wide Web is unmatched; where else could you find the exact exchange rate between the British pound and the Mongolian tugrik at 3am on a Sunday? Unfortunately, the volume of information on the Web can make it daunting to navigate; it is sometimes hard to distinguish between good information and marketing. **Search engines** can significantly aid the process. **Alta Vista** (http://www.altavista.digital.com) and **Excite** (http://www.excite.com) are among the most popular. **Yahoo!** is a slightly more organized search engine; check out its travel links (http://www.yahoo.com/Recreation/Travel). Check out **Let's Go's web site** (http://www.letsgo.com) and find our newsletter, information about our books, an always-current list of links, and more. Web sites specific to certain aspects of travel appear throughout the Essentials chapter, but here are a few to get you started.

Microsoft Expedia (http://expedia.msn.com). Everything you need to make travel plans on the web—compare flight fares, look at maps, make reservations. Fare-Tracker, a free service within Expedia, sends you monthly emails about the cheapest fares to any destination.

Shoestring Travel (http://www.stratpub.com). An alternative to Microsoft's monolithic site. This budget travel e-zine features listings of home exchanges, links, and accommodations.

Cybercafe Guide (http://www.cyberiacafe.net/cyberia/guide/ccafe.htm). Information about cybercafes worldwide.

Britain and Ireland Websites

British Tourist Authority (http://www.visitbritain.com) is a good place to start. Lots of specialized pages (cycling, shopping, Millennium) and links abound.

Ireland's National Tourism Database (http://www.touchtel.ie). Information on hostels, castles, and camping. Also covers Northern Ireland.

Official Guide to Northern Ireland (http://www.interknowledge.com/northern-ireland). Regional information on sights, accommodations, transportation, and other travel tips. Accessible by city or county.

Scotland (http://www.scotland.org). Truly a directory of all Scots, with 4185 links at last count. Also information on education, society, politics, culture, tourism, ecology, and the arts.

United Kingdom Camping and Caravanning (http://www.rscom.com/ccuk). Lists recommended campsites, links, and tips and hints for campers and caravanners.

NEWSGROUPS

Another popular source of information are **newsgroups,** which are forums for discussion of specific topics. One user posts a written question or thought, to which other users respond. There is information available on almost every imaginable topic. In some cases this proliferation has become burdensome; the quality of discussion is often poor, and you have to wade through piles of nonsense to come to useful information. Still, there are still a number of useful newsgroups for the traveler.

Usenet, the name for the family of newsgroups, can be accessed easily from most Internet gateways. In UNIX systems, type "tin" at the prompt. Most commercial providers offer access to Usenet, and often have their own version of Usenet. For Web-based access to newsgroups check out Deja News (http://www.dejanews.com). Try **soc.culture.british, rec.travel.airalt.politics.britain, uk.politics,** and **clari.world.europe.british-isles.uk.**

■ Documents and Formalities

All applications should be filed several weeks or months in advance of your planned departure date. Remember that you are relying on government agencies to complete these transactions. Demand for passports is highest between January and August, so try to apply as early as possible. A backlog in processing can spoil your plans.

When you travel, always carry on your person two or more forms of identification, including at least one photo ID. A passport combined with a driver's license or birth certificate usually serves as adequate proof of your identity and citizenship. Many establishments, especially banks, require several IDs before cashing traveler's checks. Never carry all your forms of ID together, however; you risk being left entirely without ID or funds in case of theft or loss. Also carry several extra passport-size photos that you can attach to the sundry IDs or railpasses you will eventually acquire. If you plan an extended stay, register your passport with the nearest embassy or consulate.

U.S. citizens seeking information about documents, formalities, and travel abroad should request the booklet *Your Trip Abroad* (US$1.25) from the **Superintendent of Documents,** U.S. Government Printing Office, P.O. Box 371954, Pittsburgh, PA 15250-7954 (tel. (202) 512-1800; fax 512-2250; email gpoaccess@gpo.gov; http://www.access.gpo.gov/su_docs; open M-F 7:30am-5pm).

DIPLOMATIC MISSIONS

Britain: In **Australia,** British High Commission, Commonwealth Ave., Yarralumla, Canberra, ACT 2600 (tel. (02) 6270 6666). In **Canada,** British Consulate-General, British Trade & Investment Office, 777 Bay St., Ste. 2800, Toronto, Ont. M5G 2G2 (tel. (416) 593-1290). In **Ireland,** British Embassy, 29 Merrion Rd., Ballsbridge, Dublin 4 (tel. (01) 205 3700; fax 205 3885). In **New Zealand,** British Consulate-General, 17th fl., Fay Richwhite Bldg., 151 Queen St., Auckland 1 (tel. (09) 303 2973). In **South Africa,** British High Commission, Liberty Life Pl., Glyn St., 0083 Hatfield, Pretoria. In the **U.S.,** British Consulate, 19 Observatory Circle NW, Washington, D.C. 20008 (tel. (202) 588-7800; fax 588-7850). British Embassy, 3100 Massachusetts Ave. NW, Washington, D.C. 20008 (tel. (202) 462-1340).

Ireland: In **Australia,** Irish Embassy, 20 Arkana St., Yarralumla ACT 2600 (tel. (02) 6273 3022; fax 6273 3741). In **Canada,** 130 Albert St., Ste. 1105, Ottawa, Ont. K1P 5G4 (tel. (613) 233-6281; fax 233-5835). In **New Zealand,** Honorary Consul, Dingwall Bldg., 2nd fl., 87 Queen St., P.O. Box 279, Auckland 1 (tel. (09) 302 2867). In **South Africa,** Tubach Center, 1234 Church St., 0083 Colbyn, Pretoria (tel. (012) 342 5062). In the **U.K.,** 17 Grosvenor Pl., London SW1X 7HR (tel. (0171) 235 2171). In the **U.S.,** Irish Embassy, 2234 Massachusetts Ave. NW, Washington, D.C. 20008 (tel. (202) 462-3939).

ENTRANCE REQUIREMENTS

Citizens of Australia, Canada, New Zealand, South Africa, and the U.S. all need valid **passports** to enter Britain and Ireland and to re-enter their own country. Some countries do not allow entrance if the holder's passport expires in under six months; returning home with an expired passport is illegal, and may result in a fine. *Know Before You Go* tells you everything you need to know (published by **U.S. Customs Service,** P.O. Box 7407, Washington, D.C. 20044; tel. (202) 927-0316; http://www.customs.ustreas.gov).

Upon entering Britain or Ireland, you must declare certain items from abroad and must pay a duty on the value of those articles that exceed the allowance established by that country's **customs** service (see p. 7). Keeping receipts for purchases made abroad will help establish values when you return. It is wise to make a list, including serial numbers, of any valuables that you carry with you from home; if you register this list with customs before your departure and have an official stamp it, you will avoid import duty charges and ensure an easy passage upon your return. Be especially careful to document items manufactured abroad.

When you enter Britain or Ireland, dress neatly and carry **proof of your financial independence,** such as a visa to the next country on your itinerary, an airplane ticket to depart, money to cover the cost of your living expenses, etc. Admission as a visitor does not include the right to work for pay, which is authorized only by a work permit. (See **Longer Stays,** p. 41.) Entering to study requires a special visa, and immigration officers may also want to see proof of acceptance from a school and proof that the course of study will take up most of your time in the country, as well as proof that you can support yourself (see **Study,** p. 18).

PASSPORTS

Before you leave, photocopy the page of your passport that contains your photograph, passport number, and other identifying information. Carry one copy in a safe place apart from your passport, and leave another at home. These measures will help prove your citizenship and facilitate the issuing of a new passport if you lose the original. Consulates recommend that you carry an expired passport or an official copy of your birth certificate in a part of your baggage separate from other documents.

If you do lose your passport, immediately notify the local police and the nearest embassy or consulate of your home government. To expedite its replacement, you will need to know all information previously recorded and show identification and proof of citizenship. A replacement may take weeks to process, and it may be valid only for a limited time. Some consulates can issue new passports within 24 hours if you give them proof of citizenship. Any visas stamped in your old passport will be irretrievably lost. In an emergency, ask for immediate temporary traveling papers that will permit you to re-enter your home country.

Your passport is a public document belonging to your nation's government. You may have to surrender it to a foreign government official, but if you don't get it back in a reasonable amount of time, inform the nearest mission of your home country.

Australia: Apply for a passport in person, at a post office, a passport office, or an Australian diplomatic mission overseas. An appointment may be necessary. Passport offices are located in Adelaide, Brisbane, Canberra City, Darwin, Hobart, Melbourne, Newcastle, Perth, and Sydney. Adult passports cost AUS$120 (32-page) or $180 (64-page), children AUS$60 (32-page) or $90 (64-page). For more info, call toll-free (in Australia) 13 12 32, or visit http://www.austemb.org.

Canada: Application forms are available at all passport offices, Canadian missions, and many travel agencies. Citizens may apply in person at any regional Passport Office. Passports cost CDN$60, plus a $25 consular fee, are valid for 5 years, and are not renewable. For additional info, contact the Canadian Passport Office, Dept. of Foreign Affairs and International Trade, Ottawa, Ont. K1A 0G3 (tel. (613) 994-3500; http://www.dfait-maeci.gc.ca/passport). Travelers may also call the 24hr. line (tel. (800) 567-6868), Toronto (tel. (416) 973-3251), Vancouver (tel. (604) 775-6250), or Montréal (tel. (514) 283-2152). Further help is available in the booklet *Bon Voyage, But...* (free at any passport office) or by calling InfoCentre (Canada tel. (800) 267-8376 or (613) 944-4000).

Ireland: Citizens can apply for a passport by mail to either the Dept. of Foreign Affairs, Passport Office, Setanta Centre, Molesworth St., Dublin 2 (tel. (01) 671 1633; fax 671 1092), or the Passport Office, Irish Life Bldg., 1a South Mall, Cork (tel. (021) 272525; fax 275770). Obtain an application at a local Garda station or request one from a passport office. The new Passport Express Service, available through post offices, allows citizens to get a passport in 2 weeks for an extra IR£3. Passports cost IR£45 and are valid for 5 years.

New Zealand: Application forms for passports are available in New Zealand from travel agents and Dept. of Internal Affairs Link Centres in the main cities and towns. Applications may also be forwarded to the Passport Office, P.O. Box 10526, Wellington, New Zealand. Standard processing time 10 working days for correct applications. Adults NZ$80, children $40. Urgent passport services also available for an extra NZ$80. An adult passport is valid for 10 years. More information is available on the Internet (http://www.govt.nz/agency_info/forms.shtml).

South Africa: Citizens can apply for a passport at any Home Affairs Office or South African Mission. Tourist passports, valid for 10 years, cost SAR80. Current passports less than 10 years old (from the date of issuance) may be renewed until December 31, 1999; citizens whose passport does not extend far beyond this date are urged to renew it as soon as possible to avoid the expected glut of applications. Renewal is free, and processing usually takes 2 weeks. For further information, contact the nearest Dept. of Home Affairs Office.

United States: Citizens may apply for a passport at any federal or state courthouse or post office authorized to accept passport applications. Passports are valid for 10 years (5 years if under 18) and cost US$65 (under 18 $40). Passports may be renewed by mail or in person (US$55). Report a passport lost or stolen in the U.S. in writing to Passport Services, 1425 K St., N.W., U.S. Dept. of State, Washington D.C. 20524 or to the nearest passport agency. For more info, contact the U.S. Passport Information's 24hr. recorded message (tel. (202) 647-0518). Additional information (including publications) about documents, formalities and travel abroad is available through the Bureau of Consular Affairs homepage (http://travel.state.gov), or through the State Department site (http://www.state.gov).

CUSTOMS: ENTERING

Britain: Citizens or visitors arriving in the U.K. from outside the EU must declare any goods in excess of the following allowances: 200 cigarettes, 100 cigarillos, 50 cigars or 250g tobacco; 2L still table wine; 1L strong liquors over 22% volume, or 2L fortified or sparkling wine or other liquors; 60mL perfume; 250mL toilet water; and UK£145 worth of all other goods including gifts and souvenirs. You must be over 17 to import liquor or tobacco. These allowances also apply to duty-free purchases within the EU, except for the last category, other goods, which then has an allowance of UK£75. Goods obtained duty- and tax-paid for personal use (regulated according to set guide levels) within the EU do not require any further customs duty. For more info about U.K. customs, contact Her Majesty's Customs and Excise, Wayfarer House, Great Southwest Rd., Feltham, Middlesex, TW14 8NP (tel. (0181) 910 3744; fax 910 3765).

Ireland: Citizens must declare everything in excess of IR£34 (£15 per traveler under 15 years of age) obtained outside the EU or duty- and tax-free in the EU above the following allowances: 200 cigarettes, 100 cigarillos, 50 cigars, or 250g tobacco; 2L still table wine; 1L strong liquor or 2L of liquor under 22% volume; 50mL perfume; and 250mL toilet water. Goods obtained duty- and tax-paid in another EU country up to a value of IR£460 (£115 per traveler under 15) will not be subject to additional customs duties. You must be over 17 to import tobacco or alcohol. For more information, contact The Revenue Commissioners, Dublin Castle, Dublin 1 (tel. (01) 679 2777; fax 671 2021; email taxes@iol.ie; http://www.revenue.ie), or The Collector of Customs and Excise, The Custom House, Dublin 1 (tel. (01) 873 4555).

CUSTOMS: GOING HOME

Upon returning home, you must declare all articles you acquired abroad and pay a **duty** on those articles that exceed the allowance established by your country's customs service. Goods and gifts purchased at **duty-free** shops abroad are not exempt from duty or sales tax at your point of return; you must declare these items as well. "Duty-free" merely means that you need not pay a tax in the country of purchase.

Australia: Citizens may import AUS$400 (under 18 AUS$200) of goods duty-free, in addition to 1.125L alcohol and 250 cigarettes or 250g tobacco. You must be over 18 to import alcohol or tobacco. Amounts of cash of AUS$10,000 or more, or the equivalent in foreign currency, must be reported. All foodstuffs and animal products must be declared on arrival. For information, contact the Regional Director, Australian Customs Service, GPO Box 8, Sydney NSW 2001 (tel. (02) 9213 2000; fax 9213 4000; http://www.customs.gov.au).

Canada: Citizens who remain abroad for at least 1 week may bring back up to CDN$500 worth of goods duty-free any time. Citizens or residents who travel for a period between 48 hours and 6 days can bring back up to CDN$200. Both of these exemptions may include tobacco and alcohol. You are permitted to ship goods except tobacco and alcohol home under the CDN$500 exemption as long as you declare them when you arrive. Goods under the CDN$200 exemption, as well as all alcohol and tobacco, must be in your hand or checked luggage. Citizens of legal age (which varies by province) may import in-person up to 200 cigarettes, 50 cigars or cigarillos, 200g loose tobacco, 1.14L wine or alcohol, and 24 355mL cans/bottles of beer; the value of these products is included in the CDN$200 or CDN$500. For more information, write to Canadian Customs, 2265 St. Laurent Blvd., Ottawa, Ont. K1G 4K3 (tel. (613) 993-0534; 24hr. Automated Customs Information tel. (800) 461-9999; http://www.revcan.ca).

New Zealand: Citizens may import up to NZ$700 worth of goods duty-free if they are intended for personal use or are unsolicited gifts. The concession is 200 cigarettes (1 carton) or 250g tobacco or 50 cigars or a combination of all 3 not to exceed 250g. You may also bring in 4.5L of beer or wine and 1.125L of liquor. Only travelers over 17 may import tobacco or alcohol. Contact New Zealand Customs, 50 Anzac Ave., Box 29, Auckland (tel. (09) 377 3520; fax 309 2978).

South Africa: Citizens may import duty-free: 400 cigarettes, 50 cigars, 250g tobacco, 2L wine, 1L of spirits, 250mL toilet water, 50mL perfume, and other consumable items up to a value of SAR500. Goods up to a value of SAR10,000 over and above this duty-free allowance are dutiable at 20%; such goods are also exempted from payment of VAT. Items acquired abroad and sent to the Republic as unaccompanied baggage do not qualify for any allowances. You may not export or import South African bank notes in excess of SAR25,000. For more information, consult the free pamphlet *South African Customs Information,* available in airports or from the Commissioner for Customs and Excise, Private Bag X47, Pretoria 0001 (tel. (12) 314 9911; fax 328 6478).

United States: Citizens may import US$400 worth of accompanying goods duty-free and must pay a 10% tax on the next US$1000. You must declare all purchases, so have sales slips ready. The US$400 personal exemption covers goods purchased for personal or household use (this includes gifts) and cannot include more than 100 cigars, 200 cigarettes (1 carton), and 1L of wine or liquor. You must be over 21 to bring liquor into the U.S. If you mail home personal goods of U.S. origin, you can avoid duty charges by marking the package "American goods returned." For more information, consult the brochure *Know Before You Go,* available from the U.S. Customs Service, Box 7407, Washington, D.C. 20044 (tel. (202) 927-6724; http://www.customs.ustreas.gov).

YOUTH, STUDENT, AND TEACHER IDENTIFICATION

The **International Student Identity Card (ISIC)** is the most widely accepted form of student identification. Flashing this card can procure you discounts for sights, theaters, museums, accommodations, meals, train, ferry, bus, and airplane transportation, and other services. Present the card wherever you go, and ask about discounts even when none are advertised. It also provides insurance benefits, including US$100 per day of in-hospital sickness for a maximum of 60 days, and US$3000 accident-related medical reimbursement for each accident (see **Insurance,** p. 18). In addition, cardholders have access to a toll-free 24-hour ISIC helpline whose multilingual staff can provide assistance in medical, legal, and financial emergencies overseas (tel. (800) 626-2427 in the U.S. and Canada, (0181) 666 9025 in the U.K.; elsewhere call collect (44) 181 666 9025).

Many student travel agencies around the world issue ISICs, including STA Travel in Australia and New Zealand; Travel CUTS and via the web (http://www.isic-canada.org) in Canada; USIT in Ireland and Northern Ireland; SASTS in South Africa; Council Travel, Campus Travel and STA Travel in the U.K.; Let's Go Travel, STA Travel, and via the web (http://www.ciee.org/idcards/index.htm) in the U.S.; and any of the other organizations under the auspices of the International Student Travel Confederation (ISTC). The card is valid from September to December of the following year and costs US$20, CDN$15 or AUS$15. Applicants must be at least 12 years old and degree-seeking students of a secondary or post-secondary school. Because of the proliferation of phony ISICs, many airlines and some other services require other proof of student identity, such as a signed letter from the registrar attesting to your student status and stamped with the school seal or your school ID card. The **International Teacher Identity Card (ITIC)** offers the same insurance coverage, and similar but limited discounts. The fee is US$20, UK£5, or AUS$13. For more information on these cards, consult the organization's web site (email isicinfo@istc.org; http://www.istc.org).

Federation of International Youth Travel Organizations (FIYTO) issues a discount card to travelers who are under 26 but not students. Known as the **GO25 Card,** this one-year card offers many of the same benefits as the ISIC, and most organizations that sell the ISIC also sell the GO25 Card. To apply, you will need a passport, valid driver's license, or copy of a birth certificate; and a passport-sized photo with your name printed on the back. The fee is US$20. Information is available on the web (http://www.ciee.org), or by contacting Travel CUTS in Canada, STA Travel in the U.K., Council Travel in the U.S., or FIYTO headquarters in Denmark (see **Useful Organizations,** p. 3).

DRIVING PERMITS AND CAR INSURANCE

You can use an American or Canadian driver's license for six months in the U.K., if you've had it for one year. If you plan on staying longer, you will need an **International Driving Permit (IDP).** Be forewarned that many car rental agencies in the U.K. may require an IDP. Your IDP, valid for one year, must be issued in your own country before departure. You must be 18 years old to receive the IDP and a valid driver's license from your home country must always accompany the IDP. An application for an IDP usually needs to include one or two photos, a current local license, an additional form of identification, and a fee. **Australians** can obtain an IDP by contacting their local **Royal Automobile Club (RAC), the National Royal Motorist Association (NRMA)** if in NSW or the ACT, where a permit can be obtained for AUS$15. Call to obtain an application (tel. (08) 9421 4271; fax (08) 9221 1887; http://www.rac.com.au). Canadian license holders can obtain an IDP (CDN$10) through any **Canadian Automobile Association (CAA)** branch office in Canada, by writing to CAA, 1145 Hunt Club Rd., Ste. 200, Ontario K1V 0Y3 (tel. (613) 247-0117, ext. 2025; fax 247-0118; http://www.caa.ca). Citizens of **Ireland** should drop into their nearest **Automobile Association (AA)** office (tel. (01) 283 3555; fax 283 3660) where an IDP can be picked up for IR£4. In **New Zealand,** contact your local **Automobile Association (AA),** or their main office at P.O. Box 5, Auckland (tel. (9) 377 4660; fax 302 2037; http://www.nzaa.co.nz). IDPs cost NZ$8, plus $2 for return postage if mailed from abroad. In South Africa visit your local **Automobile Association of South Africa,** P.O. Box 596, 2000 Johannesburg (tel. (11) 799 1000; fax 799 1010), where IDPs can be purchased for SAR28.50. **U.S.** license holders can obtain an IDP (US$10) at any **American Automobile Association (AAA)** office or by writing to AAA Florida, Travel Agency Services Department, 1000 AAA Dr. (mail stop 28), Heathrow, FL 32746 (tel. (407) 444-4245; fax 444-4247). You do not have to be a member of AAA to receive an IDP.

Most credit cards cover standard **insurance.** If you rent, lease, or borrow a car, you will need a **green card,** or **International Insurance Certificate,** to prove that you have liability insurance. Obtain it through the car rental agency; most include coverage in their prices. If you lease a car, you can obtain a green card from the dealer. Some travel agents offer the card; it may also be available at border crossings. Verify whether your auto insurance applies abroad; even if it does, you will still need a green card to certify this to foreign officials. If you have a collision abroad, the accident will show up on your domestic records if you report it to your insurance company.

■ Money

CURRENCY AND EXCHANGE

US$1 = British pounds £0.61	£1 = US$1.63
AUS$1 = £0.37	£1 = AUS$2.74
CDN$1 = £0.41	£1 = CDN$2.47
NZ$1 = £0.31	£1 = NZ$3.24
SAR1 = £0.10	£1 = SAR10.39
UK£1 = IR£0.86	IR£1 = UK£1.16
US$1 = Irish Pounds IR£0.71	IR£1 = US$1.41
AUS$1 = IR£0.43	IR£1 = AUS$2.36
CDN$1 = IR£0.47	IR£1 = CDN$2.14
NZ$1 = IR£0.36	IR£1 = NZ$2.80
SAR 1 = IR£0.11	IR£1 = SAR8.95

> The information in this book was researched during the summer of 1998. Due to inflation and the invisible hand, actual prices may be higher or lower than those we list. In the chapters on England, Wales, Scotland, and Northern Ireland, the symbol "£" denotes British pounds. In the chapter on the Republic of Ireland, it denotes Irish pounds.

The **pound sterling** (£) is the main unit of currency in **Great Britain.** It is divided into 100 pence (p), issued in standard denominations of 1p, 2p, 5p, 10p, 20p, 50p, £1, and £2 in coin, and £5, £10, £20, and £50 in notes. (Scotland uses a £1 note.) A pound is often called a "quid," as in "ten quid" (not "quids"). Northern Ireland and Scotland have their own bank notes, which are identical in value to other British notes and can be used interchangeably with standard currency, though you may have difficulty using Scottish £1 notes outside Scotland. The monetary unit of **Irish currency** is the Irish pound or "punt." Irish and British currencies are issued in the same denominations but are not interchangeable.

If you stay in hostels and prepare your own food, expect to spend anywhere from US$20-60 per person per day, depending on the local cost of living and your needs. Transportation will increase these figures. Don't sacrifice your health or safety for a cheaper tab. No matter how low your budget, if you plan to travel for more than a couple of days, you will need a larger amount of cash than usual. Carrying it around with you, even in a moneybelt, is risky; personal checks from home will probably not be acceptable no matter how many forms of identification you have.

It is more expensive to buy foreign currency than to buy domestic. In other words, British pounds are less expensive in Great Britain than in the U.S. However, it's always a good idea to bring enough British or Irish currency to last for the first 24-72 hours of a trip, especially for those arriving on weekends or bank holidays. Observe commission rates closely and check newspapers to get the standard rate of exchange. A good rule of thumb is to go only to banks or bureaux de change which have a 5% margin or less between their buy and sell prices. Anything more, and they are making too much profit. Since you lose money with every transaction, convert in large sums (unless the currency is depreciating rapidly), but don't convert more than you need.

If you are using traveler's checks or bills, be sure to carry some in small denominations (US$50 or less), especially for times when you are forced to exchange money at disadvantageous rates. However, it is a good idea to carry a range of denominations since charges are sometimes levied on each check cashed.

TRAVELER'S CHECKS

Traveler's checks are one of the least troublesome means of carrying funds, and they can be refunded if stolen. Several agencies and many banks sell them, usually for face value plus a small percentage commission. (Members of the American Automobile Association, and some banks and credit unions, can get American Express checks commission-free; see **Driving Permits and Insurance,** p. 9). **American Express** and **Visa** are the most widely recognized, though other major checks are sold, exchanged, cashed, and refunded with almost equal ease. Virtually all banks in the U.K. cash traveler's checks; you can also cash them at street bureaux de change for a small commission fee. In most parts of Britain and Ireland, checks are accepted as readily as cash and can be used in paying for accommodations, food, and various goods. Keep in mind that in small towns, traveler's checks are less readily accepted than in cities with large tourist industries. Nonetheless, there will probably be at least one place in every town where you can exchange them for local currency.

Each agency provides refunds **if your checks are lost or stolen,** and many provide additional services. (You may need a police report verifying the loss or theft.) You should expect a fair amount of red tape and delay in the event of theft or loss of traveler's checks. To expedite the refund process, keep your check receipts separate from your checks, record check numbers when you cash them and leave a list of check numbers with someone at home, and ask for a list of refund centers when you buy your checks (American Express and Bank of America have over 40,000 centers worldwide). Keep a separate supply of cash or traveler's checks for emergencies. Never countersign your checks until you're prepared to cash them, and always bring your passport with you when you plan to use the checks.

American Express: in **Australia** (tel. (800) 251902); in **New Zealand** (tel. (0800) 7282). Elsewhere, call the U.S. collect (tel. (801) 964 6665). American Express traveler's checks are available in pounds sterling and are the most widely recognized worldwide, as well as the easiest to replace if lost or stolen. Checks can be purchased for a small fee (1-4%) at American Express Travel Service Offices, banks, and American Automobile Association offices (AAA members can buy the checks commission-free). Cardmembers can also buy checks at American Express Dispensers at Travel Service Offices at airports, or order them by phone (U.S. tel. (800)

ORDER-TC (673 3782)). American Express offices cash their checks for free, although they often offer slightly worse rates than banks. Visit their online travel offices (http://www.aexp.com).

Citicorp: in the **U.S. and Canada** (tel. (800) 645 6556); in **Europe, the Middle East, or Africa** (tel. (44) 171 508 7007); from elsewhere call the U.S. collect (tel. (813) 623 1709). Sells both Citicorp and Citicorp Visa traveler's checks in pounds sterling. Commission is 1-2% on check purchases. Citicorp's World Courier Service guarantees hand-delivery of checks when a refund location is not convenient.

Thomas Cook MasterCard: For 24hr. cashing or refund assistance: in the **U.S., Canada,** or **Caribbean** (tel. (800) 223 7373); in the **U.K.** (toll-free tel. (0800) 622101, collect tel. (01733) 318950); from anywhere else call collect (tel. (44) 1733 318950). Offers checks in pounds sterling. Commission 2% for purchases. Thomas Cook offices will cash checks commission-free; banks will make a commission charge.

Visa: in the **U.K.** (tel. (0800) 895078); in the **U.S.** (tel. (800) 227 6811); from anywhere else call (tel. (44) 1733 318949) and reverse the charges. Any of the above numbers can tell you the location of their nearest office. Any type of Visa traveler's checks can be reported lost at the Visa number.

CREDIT CARDS

Major credit cards—**MasterCard** and **Visa** are the most welcomed—can be used to extract cash advances in local currency from associated banks and teller machines throughout the U.K. and at certain Irish banks. Credit card companies get the wholesale exchange rate, which is generally 5% better than the retail rate used by banks and even better than that used by other currency exchange establishments. However, you will be charged ruinous interest rates if you don't pay off the bill quickly, so be careful when using this service. **American Express** cards also work in some ATMs, as well as at AmEx offices and major airports. All such machines require a **Personal Identification Number (PIN),** which credit cards in the United States do not usually carry. You must ask your credit card company to assign you a PIN before you leave; without it, you will be unable to withdraw cash with your credit card outside the U.S.

American Express (U.S. tel. (800) 843-2273) has a hefty annual fee (US$55) but offers a number of services. AmEx cardholders can cash personal checks at AmEx offices. U.S. Assist, a 24-hour hotline offering medical and legal assistance in emergencies, is also available (from Britain and Ireland call U.S. collect (301) 214-8228). Cardholders can take advantage of the Travel Service. **MasterCard** (U.S. tel. (800) 307-7309, accepts collect calls; http://www.mastercard.com) and **Visa** (U.S. tel. (800) 336-8472; http://www.visa.com) are issued in cooperation with individual banks and other organizations; ask the issuer about services which go along with the cards. Keep in mind that MasterCard and Visa sometimes have different names ("EuroCard" or "Access" for MasterCard; "Carte Bleue" or "Barclaycard" for Visa).

CASH CARDS

ATM cards, called "cashpoint cards" in Britain, are welcomed widely in the U.K. and Ireland. Depending on the system that your bank at home uses, you will probably be able to access your own personal bank account whenever you need to. (Keep all receipts—even if an ATM won't give you your cash, it may register a withdrawal on your statement.) Happily, ATMs (called "cashpoints" in Britain) get the same wholesale exchange rate as credit cards. Despite these perks, do some research before relying too heavily on automation. There is often a limit on the amount of money you can withdraw per day (usually about US$500, depending on the type of card and account), and computer network failures are common. Memorize your PIN code in numeral form since machines outside the U.S. and Canada often don't have letters on the keys. If your PIN is longer than four digits, ask your bank whether the first four digits will work, or whether you need a new number.

The two major international money networks are **Cirrus** (U.S. tel. (800) 4-CIRRUS (424 7787)) and **PLUS** (U.S. tel. (800) 843 7587). Carrying two cards, one linked to each network, will leave you covered in all but the most remote regions. However, convenience does have its price: both networks can charge up to US$5 for each transaction. Call the card issuer (not the network) for details.

GETTING MONEY FROM HOME

One of the easiest ways to get money from home is to bring an **American Express** card. AmEx allows its cardholders to draw cash from their checking accounts at any of its major offices and many of its representatives' offices, up to US$1000 every 21 days (no service charge, no interest). AmEx also offers Express Cash, with over 100,000 ATMs located in airports, hotels, banks, office complexes, and shopping areas. Express Cash withdrawals are automatically debited from the Cardmember's checking account or line of credit. Green card holders may withdraw up to US$1000 in a seven-day period. There is a 2% transaction fee for each cash withdrawal, with a US$2.50 minimum/$20 maximum. To enroll in Express Cash, Cardmembers may call (tel. (800) CASH-NOW (227 4669)). Outside the U.S. call collect (tel. (336) 668 5041). Unless you are using the AmEx service, avoid cashing checks in foreign currencies; they usually take weeks and a US$30 fee to clear.

Money can also be wired abroad through international money transfer services operated by **Western Union** (U.S. tel. (800) 325-6000). In the U.S., call Western Union any time (tel. (800) CALL-CASH (225 5227)) to cable money with your Visa, Discover, or MasterCard within the U.S. and the U.K. The rates for sending cash are generally US$10-11 cheaper than with a credit card, and the money is usually available in the country you're sending it to within an hour, although this may vary.

Some people also choose to send cash abroad via **FedEx** to avoid transmission fees and taxes. FedEx is reasonably reliable; however, this method may be illegal and somewhat risky, and you must remain at a legitimate address for a day or two to wait for the money's arrival. In general, it is safer to swallow the cost of wire transmission and preserve your peace of mind.

In emergencies, U.S. citizens can have money sent via the State Department's **Overseas Citizens Service, American Citizens Services,** Consular Affairs, Room 4811, U.S. Department of State, Washington, D.C. 20520 (tel. (202) 647-5225; nights, Sundays, and holidays tel. (202) 647-4000; fax (on demand only) 647-3000; email ca@his.com; http://travel.state.gov). For a US$15 fee, the State Department will forward money within hours to the nearest consular office. The office serves only Americans in the direst of straits abroad; non-American travelers should contact their diplomatic missions for information on wiring cash.

VAT (VALUE-ADDED TAX)

Both Britain and Ireland charge value-added tax (VAT), a national sales tax on most goods and some services. The British rate is 17.5% on many services and on all goods except books, medicine, and food. In Ireland, VAT ranges from nothing on most food and children's clothing to 17% in restaurants and 21% on clothing, jewelry, appliances, and cameras. Prices stated in *Let's Go* include VAT unless otherwise specified. Visitors to the United Kingdom can get a **VAT refund** on goods taken out of the country through the **Retail Export Scheme.** Look for signs like "Tax Free Shopping" or "Tax Free for Tourists" ("Cashback" in Ireland) and ask the shopkeeper about minimum purchases (usually £50-100) as well as for the appropriate form. Keep purchases in carry-on luggage so a customs officer can inspect the goods and validate refund forms. To receive a refund, mail the stamped forms back to the store in the envelope provided. Refunds can take up to three months to be processed. Heathrow and Gatwick airports both offer on-site cash refunds; look for signs and leave at least an extra hour at the airport, as lines can be long.

TIPPING

Most restaurants in Britain and Ireland figure a service charge into the bill. The menu almost always indicates whether or not gratuity is included. Ask when in doubt. In restaurants that do not include a tip in the bill, leave 10-15%, *only if satisfied with the service,* with the percentage varying according to the quality of service. Remember, though, that no tip should be less than 50p. Note that citizens of countries where tipping is customary (such as the U.S.) are often expected to tip.

Tipping is less common for other services, especially in rural areas, but always welcome. Porters, parking lot attendants, and hairdressers are usually tipped, cab drivers less so. Hotel housekeepers will gladly accept a show of appreciation, but B&B owners may actually be insulted. At cafes, tip only if you have been served at the table. Many pubs have a container for tips, and while tipping the bartender is sometimes seen as a come-on, it is usually appreciated. The standards vary by pub and tipping the bartender is more acceptable in a large city than a rural one.

■ Safety and Security

SAFETY

Tourists are vulnerable to crime for two reasons: they carry large amounts of cash and they are not as street savvy as locals. Be alert about your belongings, surroundings, and companions. Britain and Ireland are safer for the traveler than many other European countries; still, exercise caution, particularly in the larger cities. To avoid unwanted attention, try to blend in as much as possible.

Muggings are usually unplanned; nervous, over-the-shoulder glances can be a tip that you have something valuable to protect. If you feel uncomfortable, walking purposefully into a cafe or shop and checking your map is better than doing it on a street corner. **Stay near busy and well-lit areas** and don't try to cross through parks, parking lots, or any large, deserted areas, especially after dark. When exploring a new city, find out about unsafe areas from tourist information, from the manager of your hotel or hostel, or from a local whom you trust. Especially if traveling alone, be sure that someone at home knows your itinerary. You may want to carry a small whistle to scare off attackers or attract attention; memorize the emergency number: **999** throughout Britain and Ireland.

If you are using a **car,** learn local driving signals. Be sure to park your vehicle in a garage or well-traveled area. **Wear a seat belt at all times. Use carseats for children under 40 lbs.** Study route maps before you hit the road. **Sleeping in your car** is one of the most dangerous (and often illegal) ways to get your rest. If your car breaks down, wait for the police to assist you.

A good self-defense course will give you more concrete ways to react to aggression, but often carries a steep price tag. **Impact, Prepare,** and **Model Mugging** can refer you to local self-defense courses in the United States (tel. (800) 345-KICK— to get you in the mood (345-4525)). Course prices vary from $50-400. Women's and men's courses are offered. Community colleges frequently offer inexpensive self-defense courses.

The **Australian Department of Foreign Affairs and Trade** (tel. (2) 6261 9111; http://www.dfat.gov.au) offers travel information and advisories, as does the **Canadian Department of Foreign Affairs and International Trade** (DFAIT; tel. (800) 267-8376; http://www.dfait-maeci.gc.ca). Their free publication, *Bon Voyage*, offers travel tips to Canadian citizens; to order, call (613) 944-4000. For official **United States Department of State** travel advisories, call the 24-hour hotline (tel. (202) 647-5225; http://travel.state.gov). Publications like *A Safe Trip Abroad* can be obtained for a small fee by calling the Superintendent of Documents (tel. (202) 512-1800).

SECURITY

Don't put a wallet with money in your back pocket. Women should sling **purses** over the shoulder and under the opposite arm. Carry all your treasured items (including your cash, passport, railpass, traveler's checks, and airline ticket) either in a **moneybelt** or **neck pouch** stashed securely *inside* your clothing. A small combination padlock slipped through the two zippers of a backpack will give you peace of mind. Never count your money in public, and carry as little as possible. Also, be alert in public telephone booths. If you must say your calling card number to the operator, do so very quietly; if you punch it in, make sure no one can look over your shoulder. Don't use a fanny pack; it's a ridiculously visible invitation to thieves, and marks you definitively as a tourist.

Try to keep your valuables on your person at all times. Consider this an ironclad rule in the dorm rooms of some hostels. Even a trip to the shower can cost you a wallet or a camera. You may want to sleep with your valuables under your pillow, and put the straps of your bag around the leg of your bed. Be particularly careful on trains and buses; secure your luggage to the rack with a lock. Label all your belongings with your name, address, and home phone number, and keep a record of all serial numbers on valuables. *Let's Go* lists locker availability in hostels and train stations, but you'll need your own padlock. Lockers are useful but not impregnable. Safes are fine in higher-quality hotels of international repute, but in guest houses, beware of leaving your possessions with the owner.

Almost half of all Americans who land in foreign jails are brought up on drug charges. If you are caught with any quantity of illegal or controlled drugs in Britain or Ireland, one of two things may happen: you may be arrested and tried under British or Irish law, or you may be immediately expelled from the country. Penalties for possession, use, or dealing are strict and your home government is powerless to shield you from the judicial system of a foreign country. If you are imprisoned, consular officers can visit you, provide you with a list of local attorneys, and inform your family and friends, but that's it. London-based **Release** (tel. (0171) 729 9904, 24hr. hotline (0171) 603 8654) advises people who have been arrested on drug charges; that's about all they can do.

■ Health

Common sense is the simplest prescription for good health while you travel: eat well, drink and sleep enough, and don't overexert yourself. Drinking lots of fluids will help prevent dehydration and constipation, and wearing sturdy shoes and clean socks, and using talcum powder can help keep your feet dry. To minimize the effects of jet lag, "reset" your body's clock by adopting the time of your destination immediately upon arrival.

BEFORE YOU GO

For minor health problems, bring a compact **first-aid kit,** including bandages, aspirin or other pain killer, antibiotic cream, a thermometer, a Swiss Army knife with tweezers, moleskin, a decongestant for colds, motion sickness remedy, medicine for diarrhea or stomach problems, sunscreen, insect repellent, and burn ointment.

In your **passport,** write the names of any people you wish to be contacted in case of a medical emergency, and also list any allergies or medical conditions of which doctors should be aware. **Allergy** sufferers should find out if their conditions are likely to be aggravated in the regions they plan to visit, and obtain a full supply of any necessary medication before the trip, since matching a prescription to a foreign equivalent is not always easy, safe, or possible. Carry up-to-date, legible **prescriptions** or a statement from your doctor, especially if you use insulin, a syringe, or a narcotic. While traveling, keep all medication with you in carry-on luggage.

Check your **immunization** records before you go. Travelers over two years old should be sure that the following vaccines are up to date: Measles, Mumps, and Rubella (MMR); Diptheria, Tetanus, and Pertussis (DTP or DTap); Polio (OPV); Haemophilus Influenza B (HbCV); and Hepatitus B (HBV). A booster of Tetanus-diptheria (Td) is recommended once every 10 years.

While there are no restrictions for **HIV-positive** travelers in Britain, paying for emergency treatment can be phenomenally expensive and your insurance may not cover it. Consult your provider for details or call the U.K. Department of Health Clinical Services Division (tel. (0171) 972 4839). Those with medical conditions (like diabetes, allergies to antibiotics, epilepsy, and heart conditions) can obtain a stainless steel **Medic Alert** identification tag (US$35 the first year, and $15 annually thereafter), which identifies the disease and gives a 24-hour collect-call information number. Contact Medic Alert Foundation, 2323 Colorado Ave., Turlock, CA 95382 (tel. (800) 825-3785). Diabetics can contact the **American Diabetes Association**, 1660 Duke St., Alexandria, VA 22314 (tel. (800) 232-3472), for copies of the article "Travel and Diabetes" and a diabetic ID card, which carries messages in 18 languages explaining the carrier's diabetic status.

Global Emergency Medical Services (GEMS), 2001 Westside Dr., #120, Alpharetta, GA 30201 (tel. (800) 860-1111; fax (770) 475-0058), offers *MedPass,* a service that provides 24-hour international medical assistance through registered nurses who have online access to your medical info, your primary physician, and a world-wide network of screened, credentialed English-speaking doctors and hospitals.

ONCE THERE

The general police and medical **emergency** number for most of Britain and Ireland is **999,** a free call from any phone. Late-night pharmacies are scarce, even in cities. Good medical services are widely available, but free care is not. Doctors and hospitals often expect immediate cash payment for services. Check with your private or government insurance provider for details about overseas coverage.

While on the road, remember that traveling—no matter how comfy the beds or tasty the food, is a strenuous change for your body. Eat well, drink lots of (safe) **fluids,** get enough sleep, and don't overexert yourself. You may feel fatigue and discomfort not because of any specific illness, but because your body is adapting to a new climate, food, water quality, or pace when you arrive. If symptoms persist or worsen, of course, they may be signs of an illness. You'll need plenty of protein and carbohydrates, so bring quick-energy foods with you as you travel. And remember to take care of your **feet:** bring moleskin for blisters, wear comfortable shoes with arch support, and change your socks often.

Many diseases are transmitted by insects—mainly mosquitoes, fleas, ticks, and lice. Be aware of insects in wet or forested areas, while hiking, and especially while camping. **Ticks** can be particularly dangerous in rural and forested regions. Brush off ticks periodically when walking, using a fine-toothed comb on your scalp. Do not try to remove ticks by burning them or coating them with nail polish remover or petroleum jelly. If you find a tick on your skin, grasp its head with tweezers as close to the skin as possible and apply slow, steady traction.

Visiting foreign countries means eating foreign foods, which can make travelers susceptible to the aptly named **Traveler's Diarrhea.** The most dangerous side effect of diarrhea is dehydration; the simplest and most effective anti-dehydration formula is 8 oz. of (clean) water with a half-teaspoon of sugar or honey and a pinch of salt. Also try soft drinks without caffeine, and salted crackers. Down several of these remedies a day, rest, and wait for the disease to run its course. If you develop a fever, or if your symptoms don't go away after four or five days, consult a doctor. Also consult a doctor if children develop traveler's diarrhea, since treatment is different. To ensure that your food is safe, make sure that everything is cooked properly. Don't order meat "rare." Eggs should be thoroughly cooked, not served sunny-side up. Campers and hikers should guard against **Giardia,** which is acquired by drinking untreated water from streams or lakes. It can stay with you for years. Symptoms of parasitic infections in general include swollen glands or lymph nodes, fever, rashes, digestive problems, eye problems, and anemia. Boil your water—your body will thank you.

You wouldn't think that heat-related health problems would be an issue in Great Britain. The summer of 1995, however, saw record high temperatures that sent fair-skinned Brits to the emergency room with **heat-stroke** and sunburn. Those traveling in Britain and Ireland during the summer months should take precautions: relax in hot weather, drink lots of non-alcoholic fluids, and if necessary, stay indoors. Wear a hat, sunglasses, and a lightweight longsleeved shirt to avoid heatstroke. Victims of heatstroke must be cooled off with wet towels and taken to a doctor immediately.

Always drink enough liquids to keep your urine clear. Alcoholic beverages are dehydrating, as are coffee, strong tea, and caffeinated sodas. If you'll be sweating a lot, be sure to eat enough salty food to prevent electrolyte depletion, which causes severe headaches. Less debilitating is **sunburn.** Bring sunscreen and apply it liberally.

Extreme cold poses a serious risk to travelers in Britain, particularly hikers—overexposure to cold brings the risk of **hypothermia.** Body temperature drops rapidly, resulting in the failure to produce body heat. Warning signs are easy to detect: shivering, poor coordination, exhaustion, slurred speech, sleepiness, hallucination, or amnesia. *Do not let hypothermia victims fall asleep*—their body temperature will drop further, and if they lose consciousness they may die. Seek medical help as soon as possible. To avoid hypothermia, keep dry and stay out of the wind. In wet weather, wool and most synthetics, such as pile, will keep you warm but most other fabric, especially cotton, will make you colder. Avoid smoking and consuming alcohol and caffeine. Dress in layers, and watch for **frostbite** when the temperature is below freezing. Look for skin that has turned white, waxy, and cold, and if you find frostbite do not rub the skin. Get dry and slowly warm the area with dry fabric or steady body contact. Seek medical attention for serious cases.

BIRTH CONTROL AND ABORTION

Reliable contraceptive devices may be difficult to find while traveling. Women on the pill should bring enough to allow for possible loss or extended stays. Bring a prescription, since forms of the pill vary a good deal. The sponge is probably too bulky to be worthwhile on the road. Women who use a diaphragm should have enough contraceptive jelly on hand. Though condoms are increasingly available, you might want to bring your favorite national brand before you go; availability and quality vary.

Abortion and emergency post-coital contraceptive pills are legal in Britain; visitors should go to the nearest Family Planning clinic for emergency contraception and abortion counseling. For more information contact the **U.K. Family Planning Association,** 2-12 Pentonville Rd., London N1 9FP (tel. (171) 837 5432; fax 837 3026), or the **International Planned Parenthood Federation,** European Regional Office, Regent's College Inner Circle, Regent's Park, London NW1 4NS (tel. (0171) 487 7900; fax 487 7950).

AIDS, HIV, AND STDS

Acquired Immune Deficiency Syndrome (AIDS) is a growing problem around the world. The Public Health Laboratory Service AIDS Centre estimates that over 45,000 people in the U.K. are infected with the **Human Immunodeficiency Virus (HIV).**

The easiest mode of HIV transmission is through direct blood-to-blood contact with an HIV-positive person; *never* share intravenous drug, tattooing, or other needles. The most common mode of transmission is sexual intercourse. Health professionals recommend the use of latex condoms; follow the instructions on the packet. A major British brand is Mates. Casual contact (including drinking from the same glass or using the same eating utensils as an infected person) is not believed to pose a risk.

For more information on AIDS, call the **U.S. Center for Disease Control's** (24hr. hotline tel. (800) 342-2437). In the U.K. call the 24-hour National AIDS Helpline (tel. (0800) 567123), or write to the **National AIDS Trust,** New City Cloisters, 188-196 Old St., London EC1 9FR (tel. (0171) 814 6767). In Europe, write to the **World Health Organization,** Attn: Global Program on AIDS, 20 Avenue Appia, 1211 Geneva 27, Switzerland (tel. (41) 22 791 2111; fax 22 791 0746). Council's brochure, *Travel Safe: AIDS and International Travel,* is available at all Council Travel offices.

Sexually transmitted diseases (STDs), such as gonorrhea, chlamydia, genital warts, syphilis, hepatitis B, and herpes, can be permanent and difficult to treat. Warning signs for STDs include: swelling, sores, bumps, or blisters on sex organs, rectum, or mouth; burning and pain during urination and bowel movements; itching around sex organs; swelling or redness in the throat, flu-like symptoms with fever, chills, and aches. If these symptoms develop, see a doctor immediately. Condoms may protect you from certain STDs, but direct oral or tactile contact can lead to transmission.

■ Insurance

Beware of buying unnecessary travel coverage—your regular insurance policies may well extend to many travel-related accidents. **Medical insurance** (especially university policies) often cover costs incurred abroad; check with your provider. **Medicare's** "foreign travel" coverage is valid only in Canada and Mexico. Canadians are protected by their home province's health insurance plan for up to 90 days after leaving the country; check with the provincial Ministry of Health or Health Plan Headquarters for details. Australia has a Reciprocal Health Care Agreement (RHCA) with Great Britain, which entitles Australians to many of the services that they would receive at home. Your **homeowners' insurance** (or your family's coverage) often covers theft during travel. Homeowners are generally covered against loss of travel documents (passport, plane ticket, railpass, etc.) up to US$500.

ISIC and **ITIC** provide basic insurance benefits, including US$100 per day of in-hospital sickness for a maximum of 60 days, and US$3000 of accident-related medical reimbursement (see **Youth, Student, and Teacher Identification,** p. 9). Cardholders have access to a toll-free 24-hour helpline whose multilingual staff can provide assistance in medical, legal, and financial emergencies overseas (tel. (800) 626-2427 in the U.S. and Canada; elsewhere call the U.S. collect (713) 267-2525). **Council** and **STA** offer a range of plans that can supplement your basic insurance coverage, with options covering medical treatment and hospitalization, accidents, baggage loss, and even charter flights missed due to illness. Most **American Express** (tel. (800) 528-4800) cardholders receive automatic car rental (collision and theft, but not liability) insurance and travel accident coverage (US$100,000 in life insurance) on flight purchases made with the card.

Remember that insurance companies usually require a copy of the police report for thefts, or evidence of having paid medical expenses (doctor's statements and receipts) before they will honor a claim, and they may have time limits on filing for reimbursement. Always carry policy numbers and proof of insurance. Check with each insurance carrier for specific restrictions and policies.

Campus Travel, 105-106 St. Aldates, Oxford OXI IDD (tel. (01865) 258000; fax 792378). Available only to travelers under 35 years old or with ISIC cards. Offers various per trip packages, both Europe and worldwide, that cover medical costs, property loss, trip cancellation/interruption, personal liability, and extreme activities (e.g. bungee jumping). 24hr. hotline.

Travel Assistance International, by Worldwide Assistance Services, Inc., 1133 15th St. NW, Ste. 400, Washington, D.C. 20005-2710 (tel. (800) 821-2828 or (202) 828-5894; fax 828-5896; email wassist@aol.com; http://www.worldwide-assistance.com). TAI provides its members with a 24hr. free hotline for travel emergencies and referrals in over 200 countries. Their Per-Trip (starting at US$21) and Frequent Traveler (starting at US$88) plans include medical (evacuation and repatriation), travel, and communication services.

■ Alternatives to Tourism

STUDY

It's not difficult to spend a summer, term, or year studying in Britain or Ireland under the auspices of a well-established program. Enrolling as a full-time student, however, is somewhat more difficult; the requirements for admission can be hard to meet unless you attended a British secondary school, and often only a limited number of foreign students are accepted each year. For information on studying in Britain, contact the British Council office in your country. Most American undergraduates enroll in programs sponsored by U.S. universities, and many colleges give academic information about study abroad programs. Local libraries and bookstores are also helpful sources for current information on study abroad.

American Institute for Foreign Study, College Division, 102 Greenwich Ave., Greenwich, CT 06830 (tel. (800) 727-2437, ext. 6084; http://www.aifs.com). Organizes programs for high school and college study in universities. Summer, fall, spring, and year-long programs available. Scholarships available. Contact Yesenia Garcia with questions (ygarcia@aifs.com).

Association of Commonwealth Universities, John Foster House, 36 Gordon Sq., London WC1H OPF (tel. (0171) 387 8572; fax 387 2655; email info@acu.ac.uk; http://www.acu.ac.uk). Administers scholarship programs such as the British Marshall scholarships and publishes information about Commonwealth universities.

Coláiste Dara, Indreabhän, Co. Galway, Ireland (tel. (091) 553480). 3-week intensive Irish-language summer courses for students 10-18 in the Connemara gaeltacht, 14mi. west of Galway City (IR£290). Homestays with Irish-speaking families and boating included.

Council on International Educational Exchange sponsors over 40 study abroad programs throughout the world. Contact them for more information (see **Useful Organizations,** p. 3).

Peterson's, P.O. Box 2123, Princeton, NJ 08543-2123 (tel. (800) 338-3282; fax (609) 243-9150; http://www.petersons.com). Their comprehensive Study Abroad annual guide lists programs in countries all over the world. Purchase a copy at your local bookstore (US$27) or call their toll-free number in the U.S.

Universities and Colleges Admissions Services, Fulton House, Jewssop, Cheltenham GL50 3SH (tel. (01242) 227788). Provides information and handles applications for admission to all full-time undergraduate courses at universities and their affiliated colleges in the United Kingdom. Write to them for an application and the extremely informative *U.C.A.S. Handbook.*

UKCOSA/United Kingdom Council for International Education, 9-17 St. Albans Pl., London N1 0NX (tel. (0171) 226 3762; fax 226 3373; http://www.britcoun.org/web_site/ukcosa/index.htm). Advises prospective and current students on immigration, finance, and more.

WORK

There's no better way to immerse yourself in a foreign culture than to become part of its economy. It's easy to find a **temporary job,** but it will rarely be glamorous and may not even pay for your plane fare, let alone your living costs. Officially, you can hold a job in Britain only with a **work permit** (see **Longer Stays,** p. 41). Once you find a job, your employer must apply for a permit on your behalf. However, a prospective employer must prove that you are more skilled than a resident applicant, and many prospective employers are reluctant to jump through administrative hoops. EU residents and Commonwealth residents with a parent or grandparent born in the U.K. do not need a work permit.

If you are a U.S. citizen and a full-time student at a U.S. university, the simplest way to get a job abroad is through work permit programs run by **BUNAC** and its member organizations. For a US$225 application fee, BUNAC can procure six-month work permits (and a handbook to help you find work and housing, and other perks). BUNAC also administers programs for residents of Australia, New Zealand, and South Africa. For more information contact BUNAC, 16 Bowling Green Ln., London EC1 0BD (U.K. tel. (0171) 251 3472, U.S. tel. (800) GO-BUNAC (462-8622); http://www.bunac.org.uk). Another helpful resource is *Summer Jobs: Britain 1999* (US$17), published by **Peterson's Guides** (see **Study,** p. 18), which lists roughly 30,000 jobs in England, Scotland, Wales, and Northern Ireland.

Childcare International, Ltd., Trafalgar House, Grenville Pl., London NW7 3SA (tel. (0181) 959 3611 or 906 3116; fax 906 3461; email office@child-int.demon.co.uk; http://www.ipi.co.uk/childint), offers *au pair* positions in the United Kingdom and provides information on qualifications required. UK£60 application fee. The organization prefers a long placement but does arrange summer work. Member of the International *Au Pair* Association.

International Schools Services, Educational Staffing Program, 15 Roszel Rd., P.O. Box 5910, Princeton, NJ 08543 (tel. (609) 452-0990; fax 452-2690; email edustaffing@iss.edu; http://www.iss.edu). Recruits teachers and administrators for schools. All instruction in English. Applicants must have a bachelor's degree and two years of relevant experience. Nonrefundable US$100 application fee. The *ISS Directory of Overseas Schools* (US$35) is also helpful.

Transitions Abroad, P.O. Box 1300, 18 Hulst Rd., Amherst, MA 01004-1300 (tel. (800) 293-0373; fax 256-0373; email trabroad@aol.com; http://www.transa-broad.com). Magazine lists resources for overseas study, work, and volunteering (US$20-42 per 6 issues, depending on location). Also publishes *The Alternative Travel Directory,* a comprehensive guide to living, learning, and working overseas (US$20 plus $4 postage).

Vacation Work Publications, 9 Park End St., Oxford OX1 1HJ (tel. (01865) 241978; fax 790885). Publishes a wide variety of guides and directories with job listings and info for the working traveler, including *Teaching English Abroad* (UK£10, postage UK£2.50, £1.50 within U.K.) and *The Au Pair and Nanny's Guide to Working Abroad* (UK£9, £2.50 and £1.50 postage). Opportunities for summer or full-time work in numerous countries. Write for a catalogue.

VOLUNTEERING

Volunteer jobs are readily available almost everywhere. **Council** has a Voluntary Services Dept., 205 E. 42nd St., New York, NY 10017 (tel. (888) COUNCIL (268-6245); fax (212) 822-2699; email info@ciee.org; http://www.ciee.org), which offers two- to four-week environmental or community services projects in over 30 countries. Participants must be at least 18 years old (US$255 placement fee). Listings in Vacation Work Publications' *International Directory of Voluntary Work* (UK£9; postage £2.50, £1.50 within U.K.) can be helpful; contacting volunteer organization directly may help you avoid the hefty fees levied by Council and BUNAC.

■ Specific Concerns

WOMEN TRAVELERS

Women exploring on their own inevitably face additional safety concerns, but these warnings and suggestions should not discourage women from traveling alone. Be adventurous, but avoid unnecessary risks. Trust your instincts: if you'd feel better somewhere else, move on. Always carry extra money for a phone call, bus, or taxi. You might consider staying in hostels which offer single rooms that lock from the inside or in religious organizations that offer rooms for women only. Communal showers in some hostels are safer than others; check them before settling in. Stick to centrally located accommodations and avoid solitary late-night treks or rides. **Hitching** is never safe for lone women, or even for two women traveling together. Choose train compartments occupied by other women or couples.

The less you look like a tourist, the better off you'll be. Look as if you know where you're going (even when you don't) and consider approaching women or couples for directions if you're lost or feel uncomfortable. In general, dress conservatively, especially in rural areas. Your best answer to verbal harassment is no answer at all (a reaction is what the harasser wants). In crowds, you may be pinched or squeezed; wearing a conspicuous **wedding band** may help prevent unwanted overtures. Facial expressions are the key to avoiding unwanted attention.

Don't hesitate to seek out a police officer or a passerby if you are being harassed. *Let's Go* lists emergency numbers (including rape crisis lines) in the Practical Information listings of most cities. The emergency number is **999** for Britain and Ireland. Carry a **whistle** on your keychain, and don't hesitate to use it in an emergency.

A Foxy Old Woman's Guide to Traveling Alone, by Jay Ben-Lesser (Crossing Press, US$11), gives informal advice, and a resource list on solo travel on a low-to-medium budget.

A Journey of One's Own: Uncommon Advice for the Independent Woman Traveler, by Thalia Zepatos (US$17). Interesting and full of good advice, with a bibliography of books and resources. **Adventures in Good Company: The Complete Guide to Women's Tours and Outdoor Trips** (US$17) on group travel by the same author.

Active Women Vacation Guide, by Evelyn Kay (US$17.95; shipping is free for *Let's Go* readers). Includes listings of 1,000 trips worldwide offered by travel companies for active women and stories of women's traveling adventures. Blue Panda Publications, 3031 Fifth St., Boulder, CO 80304 (tel. (303) 449-8474; fax 449-7525).

Women travelers are often vulnerable to urinary tract and bladder infections, common and severely uncomfortable bacterial diseases which cause a burning sensation and painful and sometimes frequent urination. Untreated, these infections can lead to kidney infections, sterility, and even death. Drink tons of vitamin-C-rich juice, plenty of clean water, and urinate frequently, especially right after intercourse. If symptoms persist, see a doctor.

OLDER TRAVELERS

Senior citizens are eligible for a wide range of discounts on transportation, museums, movies, theaters, restaurants, and accommodations. If you don't see a senior citizen price listed, ask, and you may be delightfully surprised. Agencies for senior group travel are growing in enrollment and popularity. Try **ElderTreks,** 597 Markham St., Toronto, Ont. M6G 2L7 Canada (tel. (800) 741-7956; fax (416) 588-9839; email passages@inforamp.net; http://www.eldertreks.com), or **Walking the World,** P.O. Box 1186, Fort Collins, CO 80522 (tel. (970) 498-0500; fax 498-9100; email walktworld@aol.com).

AARP (American Association of Retired Persons), 601 E St. NW, Washington, D.C. 20049 (tel. (202) 434-2277). Members receive benefits, including discounts on lodging, car rental, cruises, and sight-seeing. Annual fee US$8 per couple, $20 per 3yr., lifetime membership US$75.

Elderhostel, 75 Federal St., 3rd fl., Boston, MA 02110-1941 (tel. (617) 426-7788; fax 426-8351; email Cadyg@elderhostel.org; http://www.elderhostel.org). Travelers over 55 (and their spouses) can participate in 1-4 week programs at colleges, universities, and other learning centers in over 70 countries.

Unbelievably Good Deals and Great Adventures That You Absolutely Can't Get Unless You're Over 50, by Joan Rattner Heilman, with some great tips on senior discounts (Contemporary Books, US$10).

BISEXUAL, GAY, AND LESBIAN TRAVELERS

As is true elsewhere, people in rural areas of Britain and Ireland may not be as accepting as those in big cities. Public displays of affection in Ireland and most of Britain may bring you verbal harassment. The gay scene varies from extremely low-key to flashy. The sections on Brighton, Liverpool, London, Manchester, Belfast, and Dublin reflect the relatively sizable gay scenes in those places. In larger cities, look for the national publication *Pink Papers* at information centers, gay venues, and newsagents. In the summer of 1998, the age of consent for homosexual sex was lowered from 18 to 16, to match the heterosexual age of consent. In Ireland, the age of consent for both heterosexual and homosexual sex is 17. Listed below are contact organizations and publishers which offer materials addressing possible concerns.

Gay's the Word, 66 Marchmont St., London WC1N 1AB (tel. (0171) 278 7654). Tube: Russell Sq. The largest gay and lesbian bookshop in the U.K. Mail order service available. No catalogue of listings, but they will provide a list of titles on a given subject. Open M-Sa 10am-6:30pm, Th 10am-7pm, Su 2-6pm.

International Gay and Lesbian Travel Association, 4331 N. Federal Hwy., Ste. 304, Fort Lauderdale, FL 33308 (tel. (800) 448-8550 or (954) 776-2626; fax 776-3303; email IGLTA@aol.com; http://www.iglta.org). An organization of over 1350 companies serving gay and lesbian travelers worldwide. Call for lists of travel agents, accommodations, and events.

Spartacus International Gay Guides (US$32.95), published by Bruno Gmunder, Verlag GMBH, Leuschnerdamm 31, 10999 Berlin, Germany (tel. (49) 030 615 0030; fax 030 615 9007; email bgvtravel@aol.com). Lists bars, restaurants, hotels, and bookstores around the world catering to gays. Also lists hotlines for gays in various countries and homosexuality laws for each country. Available in bookstores and in the U.S. by mail from Lambda Rising, 1625 Connecticut Ave. NW, Washington, D.C. 20009-1013 (tel. (202) 462-6969).

DISABLED TRAVELERS

Transportation companies in Britain and Ireland are conscientious about providing facilities and services for travelers with disabilities. Advance booking is strongly recommended; if you notify the bus or coach company of your plans ahead of time, they will usually have staff ready to assist you and assure room for a wheelchair. **Rail** is probably the most convenient form of travel in Europe. Large stations in Britain are equipped with wheelchair facilities. Unfortunately, disabled person's railcards are generally offered to U.K. citizens only. But any traveler who is blind and traveling with a companion, or in a wheelchair, is eligible for a 34-50% discount. Guide dogs are always conveyed free, but both the U.K. and Ireland impose a six-month quarantine on all animals entering the country and require that the owner obtain an import license eight weeks in advance. In 1998 Parliament was considering modifying animal passports for guide dogs; consult a British or Irish Consulate for the latest information. Ireland is much less wheelchair-accessible than Britain. Write to the British Tourist Authority or the Bord Fáilte for free handbooks and access guides. For travel by **Underground,** pick up the free booklet *Access to the Underground* from Tourist Information Centres and London Transport Information Centres, or by post from the Unit for Disabled Passengers, London Transport, 172 Buckingham Palace Rd., London SW1W 9TN (tel. (0171) 918 3312). Consult the **Disability Net** (http://www.disabilitynet.co.uk/info/transport) for tips for disabled travelers in Britain.

Access Project (PHSP), 39 Bradley Gdns., West Ealing, London W13 8HE. Contact Gordon Couch at gordon.couch@virgin.net. Distributes access guides to London and Paris for a donation of UK£7.50. Researched by persons with disabilities. They cover traveling, accommodations, and access to sights and entertainment. Includes a "Loo Guide" with a list of wheelchair-accessible toilets.

Disabled Drivers' Motor Club, Cottingham Way, Thrapston, Northamptonshire NN14 4PL (tel. (01832) 734724); fax 733816; email ddmc@ukonline.co.uk). Membership (£8 per year) includes arrangements with specialized insurance brokers and discounts on ferries and other transportation in the U.K.

Graphic Language Press, P.O. Box 270, Cardiff-by-the-Sea, CA 92007 (tel. (760) 944-9594; email niteowl@cts.com; contact person A. Mackin). Publishes Wheelchair Through Europe, a guide covering accessible hotels, transportation, sightseeing and resources for disabled travelers in many European cities. Available for $12.95 (includes S&H) check payable to Graphic Language Press.

Society for the Advancement of Travel for the Handicapped (SATH), 347 Fifth Ave., #610, New York, NY 10016 (tel. (212) 447-1928; fax 725-8253; email sathtravel@aol.com; http://www.sath.org). Advocacy group publishing a quarterly color travel magazine *OPEN WORLD* (free for members or on subscription US$13 for nonmembers). Also publishes a wide range of information sheets on disability travel facilitation and accessible destinations. Annual membership US$45)

Tripscope, Evelyn Rd., London W4 5JL (tel. (0181) 994 9294; fax 994 3618; email tripscope@cableinet.co.uk). Offers advice on the practical details of travel tailored to individual budgets and levels of mobility. Primarily for travelers in Britain, but also helpful for travel in Ireland and Europe.

MINORITY TRAVELERS

In the 1991 census, 3 million Britons (roughly 5.5% of the total population) did not categorize themselves as white. Ian McAuley's *Passport's Guide to Ethnic London* (US$15) details immigrant contributions to English culture. Ethnic minorities are generally concentrated in the larger, English cities, and more remote regions tend to be homogenous. Minority travelers should steel themselves for reduced anonymity in these regions, but this should not be an impediment to travel plans. On the whole, the Irish have never had to address racial diversity on a large scale. Darker-skinned travelers may be the subjects of unusual attention, especially in rural areas, but comments or stares are more likely to be motivated by curiosity than ill-will. There are few resources specifically oriented toward minority travelers in Britain; in cases of harassment or assault, contact the police or the Commission for Racial Equality, Elliot House, 10-12 Allington St., London SW1E 5EH (tel. (0171) 828 7022; http:// www.open.gov.uk/cre/crehome.htm

Go Girl! The Black Woman's Book of Travel and Adventure, Elaine Lee, ed. The Eighth Mountain Press, 624 SE 29th Ave., Portland, OR 97214. (tel. (503) 233-3936; fax 233-0774; US$18). Includes travelers' tales, advice on how to travel inexpensively and safely, and a discussion of issues of specific concern to black women. With essays from Maya Angelou, Alice Walker and Gwendolyn Brooks, it's a good read for any traveler.

The Jewish Traveler, Alan M. Tigay, editor. Published by *Hadassah Magazine* (US$30). Covers Jewish history of cities worldwide. Also includes accommodations, kosher restaurants, synagogues, and sights of interest. Available for purchase on the web (http://www.amazon.com).

TRAVELERS WITH CHILDREN

Family vacations are recipes for disaster—unless you slow your pace and plan ahead. When deciding where to stay, remember the special needs of young children; if you pick a B&B, call ahead and make sure it's child-friendly. If you rent a car, make sure the rental company provides a car seat for younger children. Consider using a papoose-style device to carry your baby on walking trips. Be sure that your child carries some sort of ID in case of an emergency, and arrange a meeting place in case of separation when sight-seeing.

Restaurants often have children's menus and discounts. Virtually all museums and tourist attractions also have a children's rate. Children under two generally fly for 10% of the adult airfare on international flights (this does not necessarily include a seat). International fares are usually discounted 25% for children from two to eleven. BritRail offers special rates for children under 15 and youths under 26 (see **By Train,** p. 32). **Backpacking with Babies and Small Children,** Wilderness Press (tel. (800) 443-7227; US$10) provides friendly advice. **Take Your Kids to Europe,** by Cynthia W. Harriman, Globe-Pequot Press (tel. (800) 285-4078; US$17), is a budget travel guide geared towards families.

DIETARY CONCERNS

Vegetarians should have no problem finding suitable cuisine. Vegetarian and wholefood restaurants and markets are fairly common in large cities in Britain; and Ireland is, after all, the land of the potato. *Let's Go* often notes restaurants with good vegetarian selections in city listings, and most restaurants have vegetarian selections on their menus. **The International Vegetarian Travel Guide** (UK£2) was last published in 1991. Order back copies from the Vegetarian Society of the U.K. (VSUK), Parkdale, Dunham Rd., Altringham, Cheshire WA14 4QG (tel. (0161) 928 0793; fax 926 9182). VSUK also publishes other titles, including *The European Vegetarian Guide to Hotels and Restaurants.* Call or send a self-addressed, stamped envelope for a copy.

Travelers who keep **kosher** should contact synagogues in larger cities for information on kosher restaurants; your own synagogue or college Hillel should have access to lists of Jewish institutions. If you are strict in your observance, consider preparing your own food on the road. For listings of synagogues, kosher restaurants, and Jewish institutions, consult the **The Jewish Travel Guide,** from Vallantine Mitchell Publishers, Newbury House 890-900, Eastern Ave., Newbury Park, Ilford, Essex IG2 7HH (tel. (0181) 599 8866; fax 599 0984). Available in the U.S. from Sepher-Hermon Press, 1265 46th St., Brooklyn, NY 11219 (tel. (718) 972-9010; US$15 plus $2.50 shipping).

TRAVELING ALONE

Greater independence and challenge, better opportunities to meet and interact with natives, and the chance to write a great travel log (in the grand tradition of Mark Twain, John Steinbeck, and Charles Kuralt) are among the benefits of traveling alone. But you are also a more visible target for robbery and harassment. Be well-organized and look confident at all times. Try not to stand out as a tourist. If questioned, never admit that you are traveling alone. Maintain regular contact with someone at home who knows your itinerary. **Connecting: News for Solo Travelers,** P.O. Box 29088, 1996 W. Broadway, Vancouver, BC V6J 5C2 (tel. (800) 557-1757 or (604) 737-7791), is a bi-monthly newsletter which features solo traveling tips and lists singles looking for travel companions (US$25). **A Foxy Old Woman's Guide to Traveling Alone,** by Jay Ben-Lesser, encompasses practically every specific concern, offering anecdotes and tips for anyone interested in solitary adventure (see **Women Travelers,** p. 20). Single parents and others will find a useful list of resources in Eleanor Berman's **Traveling On Your Own,** Crown Publishers, Inc., 201 E. 50th St., New York, NY 10022 (US$13).

■ Packing

Plan your packing according to the type of travel (multi-city backpacking tour, week-long stay in one place, etc.) and the ever-present British damp. The larger your pack, the more cumbersome it is to carry and store safely. Before you leave, pack your bag, strap it on, and imagine yourself walking uphill on hot asphalt for three hours. Then imagine losing it on the train. Pack only essentials. A good general rule is to lay out only what you absolutely need, then take half the clothes and twice the money.

LUGGAGE

Backpack: If you plan to cover most of your itinerary by foot, a sturdy backpack is unbeatable. Many packs are designed specifically for travelers, while others are for hikers; consider how you will use the pack before purchasing one or the other. In any case, get a pack with a strong, padded hip belt to transfer weight from your shoulders to your hips. Be wary of excessively low-end prices, and don't sacrifice quality. Good packs range in cost US$150-420. See also p. 45.

Suitcase or trunk: Fine if you plan to live in 1 or 2 cities, but a bad idea if you're going to be moving around a lot. Make sure it has wheels and consider how much it weighs even when empty. Hard-sided luggage is more durable, but it is also heavier. Soft-sided luggage should have a PVC frame, a strong lining to resist bad weather and rough handling, and seams triple-stitched for durability.

Duffel bag: If you are not backpacking, an empty, lightweight duffel bag packed inside your luggage will be useful: once abroad you can fill your luggage with purchases and keep your dirty clothes quarantined.

Daypack, rucksack, or courier bag: Bringing a smaller bag in addition to your pack or suitcase allows you to leave your big bag behind while you go sight-seeing. It can be used as an airplane carry-on to keep essentials with you.

CLOTHING AND FOOTWEAR

Clothing: When choosing your travel wardrobe, aim for versatility and comfort. As a general rule, dress is more conservative in Britain than in other English-speaking countries; slacks are more appropriate than shorts, especially in rural areas. heavy cottons, which soak up water and can literally take days to dry.

Walking shoes: Well-cushioned **sneakers** are good for walking, though you may want to consider a good water-proofed pair of **hiking boots.** A double pair of socks—light silk or polypropylene inside and thick wool outside—will cushion feet, keep them dry, and help prevent blisters. Talcum powder in your shoes and on your feet can prevent sores, and moleskin is great for blisters. Break in your shoes before you leave and bring a pair of flip-flops for protection in the shower.

Rain gear: A waterproof jacket and a backpack cover will take care of you and your stuff at a moment's notice. Gore-Tex® is a miracle material that's both waterproof and breathable; it's all but mandatory if you plan on hiking.

MISCELLANEOUS

Sleepsacks: If you plan to stay in **youth hostels,** don't pay the linen charge; make the requisite sleepsack yourself. Fold a full-size sheet in half, then sew it closed along the open long side and one of the short sides.

Washing clothes: *Let's Go* attempts to provide information on laundry in the **Practical Information** listings for each city, but sometimes it may be easiest to use a sink. Bring a small bar or tube of detergent soap, a rubber squash ball to stop up the sink, and a travel clothesline.

Electric current: In the U.K. and Ireland, electricity is 220 volts AC, enough to fry any 110V North American appliance. 220V appliances don't like 110V current, either. Travel and hardware stores sell **adapters** (which change the shape of the plug) and **converters** (which change the voltage). Don't make the mistake of using only an adapter (unless instructions explicitly state otherwise), or you'll melt your radio. Even with adapters and converters, British outlets can overload appliances. If you smell burning hair, *for goodness' sake turn off your dryer*.

Other useful items: first-aid kit; umbrella; sealable plastic bags (for damp clothes, soap, food, shampoo, and other spillables); alarm clock; waterproof matches; sun hat; moleskin (for blisters); needle and thread; safety pins; sunglasses; a personal stereo (Walkman) with headphones; pocketknife; plastic water bottle; compass; string (makeshift clothesline and lashing material); towel; padlock; whistle; rubber bands; toilet paper; flashlight; cold-water soap; earplugs; insect repellent; electrical tape (for patching tears); clothespins; maps and phrasebooks; tweezers; garbage bags; sunscreen; vitamins.

GETTING THERE

■ Budget Travel Agencies

Students and people under 26 ("youth") with proper ID qualify for enticing reduced airfares. These are rarely available from airlines or travel agents, but instead from student travel agencies which negotiate special reduced-rate bulk purchase with the airlines, then resell them to the youth market. Return-date change fees also tend to be low (around US$35 per segment through Council or Let's Go Travel). Most flights are on major airlines, though in peak season some agencies may sell seats on less reliable chartered aircraft. Student travel agencies can also help non-students and people over 26, but probably won't be able to get the same low fares.

Campus Travel, 52 Grosvenor Gdns., London SW1W 0AG (http://www.campus-travel.co.uk). 46 branches in the U.K. offer discount and ID cards for students and youths, as well as cheap fares on plane, train, boat, and bus travel. Skytrekker, flexible airline tickets. Travel insurance for students and those under 35. Maps, guides, and travel suggestion booklets. Call the U.K., from Europe (tel. (44) 171 730 3402); from North America (tel. (44) 171 730 2101); worldwide (tel. (44) 171 730 8111); in Manchester (tel. (0161) 273 1721); in Scotland (tel. (0131) 668 3303).

Council Travel (http://www.ciee.org/travel/index.htm), the travel division of Council, is a full-service travel agency specializing in youth and budget travel. They offer discount airfares on scheduled airlines, railpasses, hosteling cards, low-cost accommodations, guidebooks, budget tours, travel gear, and international student (ISIC), youth (GO25), and teacher (ITIC) identity cards. U.S. offices include: Emory Village, 1561 N. Decatur Rd., **Atlanta,** GA 30307 (tel. (404) 377 9997); 2000 Guadalupe, **Austin,** TX 78705 (tel. (512) 472 4931); 273 Newbury St., **Boston,** MA 02116 (tel. (617) 266 1926); 1153 N. Dearborn, **Chicago,** IL 60610 (tel. (312) 951 0585); 10904 Lindbrook Dr., **Los Angeles,** CA 90024 (tel. (310) 208 3551); 1501 University Ave. SE, #300, **Minneapolis,** MN 55414 (tel. (612) 379 2323); 205 E. 42nd St., **New York,** NY 10017 (tel. (212) 822 2700); 530 Bush St., **San Francisco,** CA 94108 (tel. (415) 421 3473); 1314 NE 43rd St., #210, **Seattle,** WA 98105 (tel. (206) 632 2448); 3300 M St. NW, **Washington, D.C.** 20007 (tel. (202) 337 6464). **For U.S. cities not listed,** call (800) 2-COUNCIL (226 8624). In the U.K., 28a Poland St. (Oxford Circus), **London** W1V 3DB (tel. (0171) 287 3337).

Council Charter, 205 E. 42nd St., New York, NY 10017 (tel. (212) 661-0311; fax 972-0194). Offers a combination of inexpensive charter and scheduled airfares from a variety of U.S. gateways to most major European destinations. One-way fares and open jaws (fly into one city and out of another) are available.

Let's Go Travel, Harvard Student Agencies, 17 Holyoke St., Cambridge, MA 02138 (tel. (617) 495-9649; fax 495-7956; email travel@hsa.net; http://hsa.net/travel). Railpasses, HI-AYH memberships, ISICs, ITICs, FIYTO cards, guidebooks (including every *Let's Go* at a substantial discount), maps, bargain flights, and a complete line of budget travel gear. All items available by mail; call or write for a catalogue (or see the catalogue in center of this publication).

STA Travel, 6560 Scottsdale Rd., #F100, Scottsdale, AZ 85253 (nationwide tel. (800) 777-0112; fax (602) 922-0793; http://sta-travel.com). A student and youth travel organization with over 150 offices worldwide offering discount airfares for youths, railpasses, accommodations, tours, insurance, and ISICs. Sixteen offices in the U.S. including: 297 Newbury St., **Boston,** MA 02115 (tel. (617) 266-6014); 429 S. Dearborn St., **Chicago,** IL 60605 (tel. (312) 786-9050); 7202 Melrose Ave., **Los Angeles,** CA 90046 (tel. (213) 934-8722); 10 Downing St., Ste. G, **New York,** NY 10003 (tel. (212) 627-3111); 4341 University Way NE, **Seattle,** WA 98105 (tel. (206) 633-5000); 2401 Pennsylvania Ave., **Washington, D.C.** 20037 (tel. (202) 887-0912); 51 Grant Ave., **San Francisco,** CA 94108 (tel. (415) 391-8407), University of Miami, 100 Whitten Univ. Ctr., 1306 Stanford Dr., **Coral Gables,** FL 33146 (tel. (305) 284-1044). In the U.K., 6 Wrights Ln., **London** W8 6TA (tel. (0171) 938 4711 for North American travel). In New Zealand, 10 High St., **Auckland** (tel. (09) 309 9723). In Australia, 222 Faraday St., **Melbourne** VIC 3050 (tel. (03) 349 6911).

Travel CUTS (Canadian Universities Travel Services Limited), 187 College St., Toronto, Ont. M5T 1P7 (tel. (416) 979-2406; fax 979-8167; email mail@travelcuts.com). Canada's national student travel bureau and equivalent of Council, with 40 offices across Canada. Also in the U.K., 295a Regent St., **London** W1R 7YA (tel. (0171) 637 3161). Discounted domestic and international airfares open to all; special student fares to all destinations with valid ISIC. Issues ISIC, FIYTO, GO25, and HI hostel cards, as well as railpasses. Offers free *Student Traveller* magazine, as well as information on the Student Work Abroad Program (SWAP).

USIT Youth and Student Travel, 19-21 Aston Quay, O'Connell Bridge, **Dublin** 2 (tel. (01) 677 8117; fax 679 8833). In the U.S., New York Student Center, 895 Amsterdam Ave., **New York,** NY, 10025 (tel. (212) 663-5435; email usitny@aol.com). Additional offices in Cork, Galway, Limerick, Waterford, Maynooth, Coleraine, Derry, Athlone, Jordanstown, Belfast, and Greece. Specializes in youth and student travel. Offers low-cost tickets and flexible travel arrangements all over the world. Supplies ISIC and FIYTO-GO 25 cards in Ireland only.

■ By Plane

The price you pay for airfare varies widely depending on where (and when) you purchase your ticket and how flexible your travel plans are. Understanding the airline industry's byzantine pricing system is the best way of finding a cheap fare. Very generally, courier fares (if you can deal with restrictions) are the cheapest, followed by tickets bought from consolidators and stand-by seating. However, last-minute specials, airfare wars, and charter flights can often beat these fares. Always get quotes from different sources; an hour or two of research can save you hundreds of dollars. Call every toll-free number and don't be afraid to ask about discounts, as it's unlikely they'll be volunteered. Knowledgeable **travel agents,** particularly those specializing in the region to which you will be traveling, can provide excellent guidance. Be warned: some travel agents may not want to spend time finding the cheapest fares (for which they receive the lowest commissions). If you are unsatisfied with an agent's quotes; it doesn't hurt to call again and speak to a different agent.

Students and others under 26 need never pay full price for a ticket. Seniors can also get great deals; many airlines offer senior traveler clubs or airline passes with few restrictions and discounts for their companions as well. Sunday papers often have travel sections that list bargain fares from the local airport. Outsmart airline reps with the phone-book-sized *Official Airline Guide* (check your local library; at US$359 per yr., the tome costs as much as some flights), a monthly guide listing nearly every scheduled flight in the world (with fares, US$479) and toll-free phone numbers for all the airlines which allow you to book reservations directly. More manageable is Michael McColl's *The Worldwide Guide to Cheap Airfare* (US$15).

There is also a wealth of travel information to be found on the Internet. The **Air Traveler's Handbook** (http://www.cs.cmu.edu/afs/cs.cmu.edu/user/mkant/Public/Travel/airfare.html) is an excellent source of general information on air travel. **TravelHUB** (http://www.travelhub.com) provides a directory of travel agents that includes a searchable database of fares from over 500 consolidators (see **Ticket Consolidators**, below). Edward Hasbrouck maintains a **Consolidators FAQ** (http://www.travel-library.com/air-travel/consolidators.html) that provides great background on finding cheap international flights. Groups such as the **Air Courier Association** (http://www.aircourier.org) offer information about traveling as a courier and provide up-to-date listings of last-minute opportunities. **Travelocity** (http://www.travelocity.com) operates a searchable online database of published airfares, which you can reserve online.

Most airfares peak between mid-June and early September. Midweek (M-Th morning) round-trip flights run about US$40-50 cheaper than on weekends; weekend flights, however, are generally less crowded. Traveling from hub to hub (for example, New York to London) will win a more competitive fare than from smaller cities. Return-date flexibility is usually not an option for the budget traveler; traveling with an "open return" ticket can be pricier than fixing a return date and paying to change it. Whenever flying internationally, pick up your ticket well in advance of the departure date, confirm the flight within 72 hours of departure, and arrive at the airport at least three hours before your flight.

COMMERCIAL AIRLINES·

The commercial airlines' lowest regular offer is the **Advance Purchase Excursion Fare (APEX);** specials advertised in newspapers may be cheaper, but have more restrictions and fewer available seats. APEX fares provide you with confirmed reservations and allow "open-jaw" tickets (landing in and returning from different cities). Generally, reservations must be made 7 to 21 days in advance, with 7- to 14-day minimum, and up to 90-day maximum stay limits, and hefty cancellation and change penalties (fees rise in summer). Book APEX fares early during peak season; by May you will have a hard time getting the departure date you want.

The major carriers flying in and out of London include **British Airways, Continental, United,** and **Virgin Atlantic.** However, look into flights to less-popular destinations or on smaller carriers. Some of the best fares to Britain can be found on **IcelandAir** or **KLM.** Even **El Al Israel Airlines** and **Iberia** sometimes offer cheap flights between North America and Britain.

TICKET CONSOLIDATORS

Ticket consolidators resell unsold tickets on commercial and charter airlines at unpublished fares. Consolidator flights are the best deals if you are traveling on short notice (you bypass advance purchase requirements), or in the peak season, when published fares are jacked way up. Fares sold by consolidators are generally much cheaper; a 30-40% price reduction is not uncommon. Also ask about accommodations and car rental discounts. There are rarely age constraints or stay limitations, but unlike tickets bought through an airline, your tickets won't be valid for another flight if you miss yours, and you will have to go back to the consolidator to get a refund. Keep in mind that these tickets are often for coach seats on connecting (not direct) flights on foreign airlines, and that frequent-flyer miles may not be credited. Not all consolidators deal with the general public; many only sell tickets through travel agents. **Bucket shops** are retail agencies that specialize in getting cheap tickets. Although ticket prices are marked up slightly, bucket shops generally have access to a larger market than is available to the public and can get tickets from wholesale consolidators. Look for bucket shops' tiny ads in the travel section of weekend papers, such as the *Sunday New York Times.* In London, call the **Air Travel Advisory Bureau** (tel. (0171) 636 5000) for names of reliable consolidators and discount flight specialists. Kelly Monaghan's *Consolidators: Air Travel's Bargain Basement* (US$7 plus $2 shipping) from the Intrepid Traveler, P.O. Box 438, New York, NY 10034 (email intreptrav@aol.com), is an invaluable source for more information and lists of consolidators by location and destination.

Check out the competition. Among the many reputable and trustworthy companies are, unfortunately, some sketchy dealers. Contact the local Better Business Bureau to find out how long the company has been in business and its track record. Although not necessary, it is preferable to deal with consolidators close to home so you can visit in person, if necessary. Ask to receive your tickets as quickly as possible so you have time to fix any problems. Get the company's policy in writing: insist on a **receipt** that gives full details about the tickets, refunds, and restrictions, and record who you talked to and when. It may be worth paying with a credit card (despite the 2-5% fee) so you can stop payment if you never receive your tickets. Beware the "bait and switch" gag: disreputable firms will advertise a super-low fare and then tell a caller that it has been sold. Although this is a viable excuse, if they can't offer you a price near the advertised fare on *any* date, it is a scam to lure in customers—report them to the Better Business Bureau.

To the **U.K.** or destinations **worldwide,** try **Cheap Tickets** (tel. (800) 377-1000), which has offices in Los Angeles, San Francisco, Honolulu, Seattle, and New York. **Travel Avenue,** Chicago, IL (tel. (800) 333-3335; fax (312) 876-1254; http://www.travelavenue.com) will search for the lowest airfare available, including consolidated prices, and will even give you a 5% rebate on fares over US$350.

STAND-BY FLIGHTS

Airhitch, 2641 Broadway, 3rd fl., New York, NY 10025 (tel. (800) 326-2009 or (212) 864-2000; fax 864-5489) and Los Angeles, CA (tel. (310) 726-5000), will add a certain thrill to the prospects of when you will leave and where exactly you will end up. Complete flexibility on both sides of the Atlantic is necessary; flights cost about US$159 each way when departing from the Northeast, $189 from the Southeast, $209 from the Midwest, and $239 from the West Coast or Northwest. Travel within the U.S. and Europe is also possible, with rates ranging from $79-139. The snag is that you buy not a ticket, but the promise that you will get to a destination near where you're intending to go within a window of time (usually 5 days) from a location in a region you've specified. You call in before your date-range to hear all of your flight options for the next seven days and your probability of boarding. You then decide which flights you want to try to make and present a voucher at the airport which grants you the right to board a flight on a space-available basis. This procedure must be followed again for the return trip. Be aware that you may only receive a monetary refund if all available flights which departed within your date-range from the specified region are full, but future travel credit is always available. There are several offices in Europe, so continental travelers can register there for their return, but **there are no offices in the U.K.** The closest one is in Paris (tel. (33) 47 00 16 30).

Air-Tech.Com, 588 Broadway, #204, New York, NY 10012 (tel. (212) 219-7000; fax 219-0066), offers a very similar service. Their Travel Window is one to four days. Rates between the U.S. and Europe (continually updated; call and verify) are: Northeast US$169; West Coast US$229; Midwest/Southeast US$199. Upon registration and payment, Air-Tech.Com sends you a FlightPass with a contact date falling soon before your Travel Window, when you are to call them for flight instructions. You must go through the same procedure to return—and no refunds are granted unless the company fails to get you a seat before your Travel Window expires. Air-Tech also arranges courier flights and regular confirmed-reserved flights at discount rates.

Be sure to read all the fine print in your agreements with either company—a call to the **Better Business Bureau** (tel. (212) 533-6200) may be worthwhile. Be warned that it is difficult to receive refunds, and that clients' vouchers will not be honored if an airline fails to receive payment in time.

CHARTER FLIGHTS

Charters are flights a tour operator contracts with an airline (usually one specializing in charters) to fly extra loads of passengers in the peak season. Charters are often cheaper than flights on scheduled airlines, although fare wars, consolidator tickets, and small airlines can beat charter prices. Some charters operate nonstop, and restrictions on minimum advance-purchase and minimum stay are more lenient. However, charter flights fly less frequently than major airlines, make refunds particularly difficult, and are almost always fully booked. Schedules and itineraries may also change or be cancelled at the last moment (as late as 48 hours before the trip, and without a full refund), and check-in, boarding, and baggage claim are often much slower. As always, pay with a credit card if you can; consider traveler's insurance against trip interruption.

Eleventh-hour **discount clubs** and **fare brokers** offer members savings on European travel, including charter flights and tour packages. Research your options carefully. **Last Minute Travel Service,** 100 Sylvan Rd., Woburn, MA 01801 (tel. (800) 527-8646 or (617) 267-9800) is among the few travel clubs that don't charge a membership fee. **Travelers Advantage,** Stamford, CT (tel. (800) 548-1116; http://www.travelersadvantage.com) specializes in European travel and tour packages, but charges a US$49 annual fee. As with all travel arrangements, study contracts carefully; you don't want to be stuck with an unwanted overnight layover.

COURIER COMPANIES

If you travel light, consider flying internationally as a **courier.** The company hiring you will use your checked luggage space for freight; you're usually only allowed to bring carry-ons. You are responsible for the safe delivery of the baggage claim slips (given to you by a courier company representative) to the representative waiting for you when you arrive—don't screw up or you will be blacklisted as a courier. You will probably never see the cargo you are transporting—the company handles it all—and airport officials know that couriers are not responsible for the baggage checked for them. You must be over 21 (18 in some cases), have a valid passport, and procure your own visa (if necessary); most flights are round-trip only with short fixed-length stays (usually 1 week); only single tickets are issued (but a companion may be able to get a next-day flight); and most flights are from New York. Round-trip fares to Western Europe from the U.S. range from US$100-400 (off-season) to US$200-550 (summer). For an annual fee of US$45, the **International Association of Air Travel Couriers,** 8 South J St., P.O. Box 1349, Lake Worth, FL 33460 (tel. (561) 582-8320; http://www.courier.org), informs travelers (via email, fax, and mailings) of courier opportunities worldwide.

Check your bookstore or library for handbooks such as *Air Courier Bargains* (US$15 plus $3.50 shipping from the Intrepid Traveler, P.O. Box 438, New York, NY 10034; email intreptrav@aol.com), and *The Courier Air Travel Handbook* (US$10 plus $3.50 shipping) from Bookmasters, Inc., P.O. Box 2039, Mansfield, OH 44905 (tel. (800) 507-2665).

■ By Train

In 1994, the **Channel Tunnel** (Chunnel) was completed, physically connecting England and France (the horror!/*l'horreur!*). Eurostar operates rather like an airline with similar discounts, reservations, and restrictions. Return tickets start at US$150, and 12 trains per day run from London and Paris. While France, Brit, BritFrance, Eurailpass, and Europasses are not tickets to ride, they are tickets to a discount, as is being a youth. From the U.S. call (800) EUROSTAR (387-6782) to purchase your ticket. In the U.K., call (01233) 617575 for more information. Or contact **Rail Europe** (see p. 32).

■ By Bus

Supabus (run by **Bus Éireann,** the Irish national bus company) offers connecting service from Bristol and London to Cork, Waterford, Tralee, Killarney, Ennis, and Limerick, and from Cardiff and Birmingham to Cork, Waterford, Ennis, and Limerick. Prices range from UK£10 to £25. Tickets can be booked through USIT, any Bus Éireann office, Irish Ferries, Stena Line, or any Eurolines (tel. (01582) 404511) or National Express (tel. (0990) 808080) office in Britain. Inconvenient arrival and departure times mean you won't be sleeping very well. Supabus connects in London to the immense Eurolines network, which in turn connects with many European destinations. Contact the Bus Éireann General Inquiries desk in Dublin (tel. (01) 836 6111) or a travel agent. Take an **express bus** to London from over 270 destinations in Europe with Eurolines (U.K.) Ltd., 52 Grosvenor Gdns., Victoria, London SW1W OAU (tel. (0171) 730 8235); London-Paris UK£34, return £49).

■ By Boat

> *Don't you understand? The water is freezing and there aren't enough boats...not enough by half. Half the people on this ship are going to die.*
> Rose DeWitt Bukater, Titanic

Ferry travel is dependable, inexpensive, and slow. Almost all sailings in June, July, and August are controlled sailings, which means that you must book the crossing at least a day in advance. If you're traveling with a car in July or August, reserve through a ferry office or travel agency. Arrive an hour in advance, and remember your passport. Ask ahead where to board the ferry. Unlike train or air travel, ferries lack the convenience of location; you must arrange connections to larger cities at additional cost.

Prices vary greatly by ports, season, and length of stay. In the summer expect to pay at least £25 per foot passenger to cross from France and £60 from Northern Europe. Limited-day returns (usually 3 or 5 nights including travel) are generally not much more than the single fare. Always ask about reduced fares—flashing an HI/YHA card or ISIC with TravelSave stamps might win a discount on your fare. Children under 4 usually travel free and bicycles can be carried for a small fee, if any. Some travelers ask car drivers to let them travel as one of the four or five free passengers allotted to a car. This can reduce costs considerably, but consider the risks before getting into a stranger's car. The main ferry companies operating between Britain and France or Northern Europe are listed below; call or write for brochures with complete listings of routes and fares.

Brittany Ferries: Millbay, Plymouth, Devon PL1 3EW (tel. (0990) 360360 or (01705) 838836; fax (01752) 255065; http://www.brittany-ferries.com). Caen, St. Malo, and Roscoff, France to Portsmouth; Cherbourg and St. Malo, France to Poole; Santander, Spain to Plymouth.

Color Line: International Ferry Terminal, Royal Quays, North Shields, Tyne and Wear NE29 6EE (tel. (0191) 296 1313; fax 296 1540; http://www.colorline.com). Bergen/Haugesund/Stravanger, Norway to Newcastle.

Hoverspeed: International Hoverport, Marine Parade, Dover, Kent CT17 9T (tel. (0990) 240241; fax (01304) 212673; http://www.hoverspeed.co.uk). Calais, France and Ostend, Belgium to Dover; Boulogne, France to Folkestone.

P&O European Ferries: Penninsular House, Wharf Rd., Portsmouth PO2 8TA (tel. (0845) 980555; fax (01705) 864611; http://www.poef.com). Cherbourg and Le Havre, France and Bilboa, Spain to Portsmouth.

P&O North Sea Ferries: King George Dock, Hedon Rd., Hull HU9 5QA (tel. (01482 377177; fax 706438; http://www.ponsf.com). Rotterdam, Netherlands and Zeebrugge, Belgium to Hull.

P&O Stena Line: Channel House, Channel View Rd., Dover, Kent CT17 9TJ (tel. (0990) 980111; http://www.posl.com). Calais, France to Dover; Dieppe, France to Newhaven.

Scandanavian Seaways: Scandinavia House, Parkeston Quay, Harwich, Essex CO12 4QG (tel. (0990) 333000 or (01255) 240240; fax 244370; http://www.scansea.com). Ijmuiden (Amsterdam), Netherlands and Esbjerg, Denmark to Harwich; Gothenberg, Sweden and Hamberg, Germany to Newcastle.

Stena Line: Charter House, Park St., Ashford, Kent TN24 8EX (tel. (0990) 707070 or (01233) 647047; fax 202231; http://www.stenaline.co.uk). Hook of Holland to Holyhead, Wales.

ONCE THERE

■ Diplomatic Missions

Australia: Fitzwilton House, Wilton Terr., **Dublin** 2 (tel. (01) 676 1517). Australian Embassy, 18 Belgrade Mews W., **London** SW1 (tel. (0171) 235 3731).

Canada: Canadian Embassy, Canada House, 65 St. Stephens Green, **Dublin** 2 (tel. (01) 478 1988). Canada House, Trafalgar Sq., **London** SW1Y 5BJ (tel. (0171) 258 6600; fax 258 6533).

Ireland: Irish Embassy, 17 Grosvenor Pl., **London** SW1X 7HR (tel. (0171) 235 2171).

New Zealand: New Zealand, New Zealand House, 80 Haymarket, **London** SW1Y 4TQ (tel. (0171) 930 8422).

South Africa: South African Embassy, Alexandra House, Earlsfort Terr., **Dublin** 2 (tel. (01) 661 5590). South African High Commission, South Africa House, Trafalgar Sq., **London** WC2N 5DP (tel. (0171) 451 7299; fax 451 7283).

U.K.: British Embassy, 31 Merrion Rd., **Dublin** 4 (tel. (01) 259 5211).

U.S.: American Embassy, 42 Elgin Rd., Ballsbridge, **Dublin** 4 (tel. (01) 668 7122). American Embassy, 24 Grosvenor Sq., **London** W1AE (tel. (0171) 499 9000; fax 629 9124). Consulate General, Queens House, 14 Queens St., **Belfast** BT1 6EQ (tel. (01232) 328239).

■ Getting About

In general, fares on all modes of public transportation in Britain and Ireland are either **single** (one-way) or **return** (round-trip). *Let's Go* lists prices for a single trip, unless otherwise noted; note that return fares, especially day returns, can be more economical, as they often cost only a little more than a single. Prices for most fares tend to rise on Friday and Saturday. **Period returns** require you to return within a specific number of days; **day return** means you must return on the same day. A **supersaver** (return) won't allow you to travel on Fridays or most Saturdays and often not before 9am, but is often cheaper. An **APEX** (return) is a cheaper rate and must be purchased at least a week beforehand; a **Super APEX** (return) is the cheapest (up to 60% off standard return) and must be purchased at least two weeks before traveling, usually 21 days in advance. Always keep your ticket when you travel, as it will sometimes be inspected on the journey or collected at the station when you arrive.

Roads between cities and towns have official letters and numbers ("N" and "R" in the Republic, "M," "A," and "B" in Britain), though in Ireland most locals refer to them by destination ("the Kerry Road"). In Ireland, most signs are in English and Irish; some destination signs are only in Irish. Road signs in Britain generally use the metric system; additional white signs in Ireland show distances in miles.

BY PLANE

If you're traveling between the Isles, look into the many **flights** between Gatwick, Heathrow, Luton, Manchester, Birmingham, Liverpool, Edinburgh, and Glasgow (Britain); Dublin, Shannon, Cork, Knock, and Waterford (Ireland); Belfast and Derry (Northern Ireland); and Ronaldsway (Isle of Man). Aer Lingus, British Airways, and British Midlands are some of the companies offering service to Ireland. **Aer Lingus** offers flights hourly from London to Dublin (from £90), and from other airports (tel. (800) 223-6537). **British Airways** (tel. (800) 247-9297; Belfast (01232) 899131; London (0181) 759 8181) offers 4-5 flights per day starting at £80. **British Midland** (U.S. tel. (800) 788-0555; Belfast (01232) 241188; Dublin (01) 283 0700; London (0345) 554554) also flies between Britain and Ireland; **Manx Airlines** (tel. (01) 260 1588) zips between the Isle of Man and destinations in Britain, Ireland, and Jersey. They also offer service from Cardiff to Dublin.

BY FERRY

Ferry service connecting ports in England, Scotland, Wales, and Ireland is inexpensive and usually the best way to make day trips to another island. Ferry companies advertise low special rates for day returns in local papers; otherwise, expect to pay £20-30 depending on ports, season, and length of stay. Ferry companies often offer special discounts in conjunction with bus or train companies; a little advance research can save you, and your wallet, much angst.

Caledonian MacBrayne: The Ferry Terminal, Gourock, Rentfrewshire PA19 1QP (tel. (01475) 650100; fax 637607; http://www.calmac.co.uk). Routes in the Hebrides and the west coast of Scotland.

Irish Ferries: Reliance House, Water St., Liverpool L2 8TP (tel. (0990) 171717 or (0151) 236 5507; fax 236 0562, http://www.irish-ferries.ie). Dublin, Ireland to Holyhead, Wales; Rosslare, Ireland to Pembroke, Wales.

P&O European Ferries: Peninsular House, Wharf Rd., Portsmouth PO2 8TA (tel. (0845) 980555; fax (01705) 864611; http://www.poef.com). Larne, Ireland to Cairnryan, Scotland.

P&O Scottish Ferries: P.O. Box 5, P&O Ferries Terminal, Jamieson's Quay, Aberdeen AB11 5NP (tel. (01224) 589111 or 572615; fax 574411; http://www.poscottishferries.co.uk/posf/index.htm). Routes between Aberdeen, Lerwick, Stromness, and Scrabster.

SeaCat Scotland: 34 Charlotte St., Stranraer, Wigtownshire DG9 7EF (tel. (01232) 313543; fax (01776) 702355; email info@seacontainers.com). Belfast, Northern Ireland to Stranraer, Scotland.

Stena Line: Charter House, Park St., Ashford, Kent TN24 8EX (tel. (0990) 707070 or (01233) 647047; fax 202231; http://www.stenaline.co.uk). Belfast, Northern Ireland to Stranraer, Scotland; Rosslare, Ireland to Fishguard, Wales; Dun Laoghaire, Ireland to Holyhead, Wales.

Swansea Cork Ferries: Ferry Port, King's Dock, Swansea SA1 8RU (tel. (01792) 456116; fax 644356). Swansea, Wales to Cork, Ireland.

Isle of Man Steam Packet Company: P.O. Box 5, Imperial Bldg., Douglas, Isle of Man (tel. (01624) 661661; fax 661065; http://www.steam-packet.com/index.htm#contents). Belfast, Northern Ireland and Dublin, Ireland and Liverpool to Douglas, Isle of Man.

BY TRAIN

Rail Europe, 226 Westchester Ave., White Plains, NY 10604 (tel. (800) 438-7245; fax 432-1329; http://www.raileurope.com), is the North American distributor of Eurailpass, Europass, Eurostar, and BritRail products and services. If you plan to travel a great deal within Britain, the **BritRail Pass** can be a good buy. (Eurailpasses are *not* valid in Britain.) BritRail Passes are only available in the U.S. and Canada; *you must buy them before traveling to Britain.* They allow unlimited travel in England, Wales, and Scotland. Passes are not valid for ferry, jetfoil, or catamaran transport, although British Rail does offer **fare packages** for rail service combined with one or more of these options. British Rail also offers passes which connect to the Irish rail system (both Northern Ireland and the Republic of Ireland) and include ferry crossing (US$359 for 5 days, $511 for 10 days). In 1998, BritRail Standard Class Passes cost US$259 for eight days, $395 for 15 days, $510 for 22 days, and $590 for one month. Senior citizens are offered a discount for first-class at US$319, $489, $630, and $730, respectively. Those between 16 and 25 pay US$205, $318, $410, or $475. One child (age 5-15) travels free with each adult or senior pass; ask for the Family Pass. Additional children pay half the standard adult fare. BritRail Travel also offers **Flexipasses,** which allow travel on a limited number of days within a set time period (4, 8, or 15 per month; 16-25-year-olds can also buy a special 15 days per 2 month pass). Passes and additional details on discounts are available from most travel agents or **BritRail Travel International's Reservation Centre,** 1500 Broadway, New York, NY 10036-4015 (tel. (888) BRITRAIL (274-7245); fax (212) 575-2542). You can also try **Rail Pass Express** (tel. (800) 722-7151). While in Britain, call National Rail Inquiries (tel. (0345) 484950).

The **Young Person's Railcard** (£18, valid for 1yr.) offers 33% off most fares and discounts on Holyman Sally Ferries. Buy this pass at major British Rail Travel Centres in the U.K. You must prove you're either between 16 and 25 (with a birth certificate or passport), or a full-time student over 25 at a "recognised educational establishment," and submit a passport-sized photo. Those 60 and over can purchase a **Senior Railcard** (£16), taking up to 33% off most fares; these are also available at major British Rail Travel Centres. Families have their own Railcard, as do travelers in wheelchairs.

While the **Eurailpass** is *not* accepted in Britain, it *is* accepted in Ireland. However, Eurailpasses are not economical for use solely in Ireland, since rail routes in the Republic of Ireland are not extensive enough to make the cost of the pass pay off. If you plan to visit other countries in Europe that use Eurailpass, limit your pass use to the Continent—you'll get more for your money. If anything, get a **Flexipass, Youthpass,** or **Youth Flexipass;** you can use the Eurailpass on Irish Ferries from Rosslare to Cherbourg or Le Havre.

Trains run by **Iarnród Éireann** (Irish Rail) branch out from Dublin to larger cities, but there is limited service between these cities. For schedule information, pick up an *InterCity Rail Travellers Guide* (50p), available at most train stations. By far the most useful travel pass for students on trains and buses in Ireland is the **TravelSave stamp** (IR£8), available at any USIT with an ISIC card. Affixed to your ISIC card, this stamp decreases single fares by 50% on national rail and allows you to break your journey to visit at any stop on the way to your final destination. It also provides 15% discounts on bus fares over IR£1. A **Faircard** (IR£8) can get anyone under 26 up to 50% off the price of any inter-city trip. Those over 26 can get the less potent **Weekender card** (IR£5) which allows up to 33% off (F-Tu only). Both are valid through the end of the year. Information is available from the Irish Rail information office, 35 Lower Abbey St., Dublin 1 (tel. (01) 836 6222).

Northern Ireland Railways (tel. (01232) 899411, inquiries 230671) service is not extensive, but covers the northeastern coastal region well. British Rail passes aren't valid here, but Northern Ireland Railways offers its own discounts. A Northern Ireland **TravelSave stamp** (UK£6) gets 50% off all trains and 15% discounts on bus fares over £1 for those with ISIC cards. The **Freedom of Northern Ireland** ticket allows unlimited travel by train and Ulsterbus for seven consecutive days (UK£35), three consecutive days (UK£25), or a single day (UK£10).

BY BUS AND COACH

The British and Irish distinguish between **buses,** which cover short local routes, and **coaches,** which cover long distances with few stops. For practical purposes, *Let's Go* usually uses the term "buses" to refer to both. Long-distance coach travel in Britain is more extensive than in most European countries, and is the cheapest option. **National Express** (tel. (0990) 808080), the principal operator of long-distance coach services in Britain, can be booked through Eurolines (U.K.) Ltd., 4 Cardiff Rd., Luton, Bedfordshire LU1 1PP (tel. (01582) 404511). Each region also has local companies. Some coaches require advance reservation. **Seniors'** (over 50), **Students'**, and **Young Persons' Discount Coach Cards** (ages 16-25) are £8 and reduce standard fares on National Express by about 30%.

Stray Travel by **Slow Coach,** 171 Earl's Court Rd., London SW5 9RF (tel. (0171) 373 7737; fax 373 7739), offers a service aimed at rambling hostelers: £119 buys a ticket on a clockwise circuit of London, Bath, Manchester, the Lake District, Edinburgh, and York; three coaches per week stop at hostels along the way. Tickets are good for six months, so travelers can move at any rate they wish. In Scotland, **Go Blue Banana Bus** and **Haggis Backpackers** run similar deals; consult **Scotland: Getting About,** p. 455, for details.

Ireland's national bus company, **Bus Éireann** (tel. (01) 836 6111), operates both long-distance **Expressway** buses, which link larger cities, and **Local** buses, which serve the countryside and smaller towns. The timetable (IR£1) is available at Busáras Station in Dublin and at many tourist offices. A number of **private bus services** are faster and cheaper than Bus Éireann.

It is difficult to make Bus Éireann's discount **Rambler** tickets pay off; individual tickets are a better bet. The **Rambler** ticket offers unlimited bus travel within Ireland for three out of eight consecutive days (IR£28), eight out of 15 days (IR£68), or 15 out of 30 days (IR£98). A combined **Irish Explorer Rail/Bus** ticket (IR£90) good for unlimited travel for eight out of 15 consecutive days on rail and bus lines is also available. Buy the ticket from Bus Éireann at the main tourist office in Dublin, Store St., Dublin 1 (tel. (01) 836 6111); Cork (tel. (021) 508188); Waterford (tel. (051) 879000); Galway (tel. (091) 562000). You can also contact the Irish Rail information office, 35 Lower Abbey St., Dublin 1 (tel. (01) 836 6222).

Ulsterbus, Laganside, Belfast (tel. (01232) 320011), runs throughout **Northern Ireland,** where there are no private bus services. Coverage expands in the summer. Pick up a regional timetable (25p) at any station. Again, the bus discount passes won't save you much money: a **Freedom of Northern Ireland** bus pass offers one day (UK£10), and seven consecutive days (UK£35). The **Emerald Card** offers travel for eight out of 15 consecutive days (UK£105; under 16 £53), or 15 out of 30 consecutive days (UK£180).

Intra-city services (mostly fast and frequent minibuses) in both Britain and Ireland are provided by local companies together with county councils. In towns where two or three intra-city, rural-service companies link up, the confusion can be incredible, so head for the local tourist office or bus station for help. Be on the lookout for regional coach passes, which offer unlimited travel in a certain area for a certain number of days; these are usually known as **Rovers, Ramblers,** and **Explorers,** and we usually list them in relevant sections.

BY CAR

The advantages of car travel speak for themselves. Disadvantages include high gasoline prices (petrol), villainous exhaust, and the fact that **they drive on the left.** Be particularly cautious at roundabouts (rotary interchanges); give way to traffic from the right. In both countries, the law requires drivers and front-seat passengers to wear seat belts; in Britain, rear-seat passengers are also required to buckle up when belts are provided. In Ireland, children under 12 may not sit in the front seat.

Britain is covered by a skeletal but adequate system of limited-access **highways** ("M-roads" or "motorways"), connecting London with Birmingham, Liverpool, Manchester, Cardiff, and Southern Scotland. The M-roads are supplemented by a tight web of "A-roads" and "B-roads" in England, Scotland, Wales, and Northern Ireland. **Speed limits** are 60mph (97km/h) on single carriageways (non-divided highways), 70mph (113km/h) on motorways (highways), and dual carriageways (divided highways), and usually 30mph (48km/h) in urban areas. (Speed limits are always marked at the beginning of town areas; upon leaving, you'll see a circular sign with a slash through it, signaling the end of the speed restriction.) Speed limits aren't rabidly enforced, but note that many British roads are sinuous and single-track; use common sense, especially in rural or mountainous areas.

In **Ireland,** roads numbered below N50 are primary routes that connect all major towns; roads numbered N50 and above are secondary routes, similar to Britain's A-roads; regional R-roads are comparable to Britain's B-roads. Most of these are two-lane. The general **speed limit** is 55mph (90km/h) on the open road and either 30mph (50km/h) or 40mph (65km/h) in town. Signs on roadways are usually in both English and Irish, sometimes only Irish for destination signs.

Hiring (renting) an automobile is the least expensive option if you drive for a month or less. For more extended travel, you might consider **leasing.** Major rental companies with agencies almost everywhere in Britain and Ireland include **Avis** (U.S. tel. (800) 331-1084, U.K. tel. (0181) 899 1000), **Budget Rent-A-Car** (U.S. tel. (800) 472-3325, U.K. tel. (0181) 75922; http://www.budgetrentacar.com), and **Hertz** (U.S. tel. (800) 654-3001, U.K. tel (0990) 996699; http://www.hertz.com). Prices start at UK£130 a week (plus VAT) with unlimited mileage; for insurance reasons, renters are required to be over 21 and under 70 (those 18-21 should consider leasing). In Ireland, you won't get anything cheaper than IR£30 per day. All plans require sizable deposits unless you pay by credit card. Make sure you understand insurance before you rent; some agreements make you pay for damages you may not have caused. Automatics are generally more expensive than stick shifts.

Several U.S. firms offer rental or leasing plans for Britain and Ireland; try **Kemwel Holiday Autos,** 106 Calvert St., Harrison, NY 10528-3199 (tel. (800) 678-0678); **Auto Europe,** 39 Commercial St., P.O. Box 7006, Portland, ME 04112 (tel. (800) 223-5555; http://kemwel.com); or **Europe by Car,** 1 Rockefeller Plaza, New York, NY 10020 (tel. (800) 223-1516; fax (212) 426-1458; http://www.europebycar.com; 5% student and faculty discounts available). In Ireland, those under 23 generally cannot rent (see **Driving Permits and Insurance,** p. 9).

BY BICYCLE

Today, biking is one of the key elements of the classic budget voyage. With the prolif-eration of mountain bikes, you can do some serious natural sight-seeing. Remember that touring involves pedaling both yourself and whatever you store in **panniers** (bags which strap to your bike). Take some reasonably challenging day-long rides at home to prepare yourself before you leave, and have your bike tuned up by a reputable shop. Wear reflective clothing, drink plenty of water (even if you're not thirsty), and ride on the same side as the traffic. Learn the international signals for turns, and use them. Know how to fix a modern derailleur-equipped mount and change a tire, and practice on your own bike. A few simple tools and a good bike manual will be invalu-able. Cyclists should consult tourist offices or books on cycling in Britain and Ireland for touring routes. **The Mountaineers Books,** 1001 SW Klickitat Way, #201, Seattle, WA 98134 (tel. (800) 553-4453 or (206) 223-6303; fax 223-6306; mbooks@mountain-eers.org) offers several nation-specific tour books (especially France, Germany, Ire-land, and the U.K.). Send for a catalogue. **Michelin road maps** are clear and detailed.

If you are nervous about striking out on your own, **CBT Bicycle Tours** offer one- to seven-week tours, priced around US$95 per day, including all lodging and breakfasts, one-third off all dinners, complete van support, airport transfers, three staff members, and extensive route notes and maps each day. Tours run May through August, with departures every seven to 10 days. In 1999, CBT will visit England, Scotland, and Ire-land. Contact CBT Bicycle Tours, 415 W. Fullerton, #1003, Chicago, IL 60614 (tel. (800) 736-BIKE (2453) or (773) 404-1710; fax 404-1833; http://www.cbttours.com).

Many airlines will count your bike as your second free piece of luggage; a few charge. The additional or automatic fee runs about US$60-110 each way. Bikes must be packed in a cardboard box with the pedals and front wheel detached; airlines sell bike boxes at the airport (US$10). A better option is to buy a bike in Britain and Ire-land and sell it before you leave. A bike bought new overseas is subject to customs

duties if brought into your home country; used bikes, however, will not be taxed. According to British law, your bike must carry a white light at the front of the cycle and a red light and red reflector at the back, but these laws aren't strictly observed.

Riding a bike with a frame pack strapped on it or your back is about as safe as pedaling blindfolded over a sheet of ice; **panniers are essential.** The first thing to buy, however, is a suitable **bike helmet.** At about US$25-50, they're a much better buy than head injury or death. U-shaped **Citadel** or **Kryptonite locks** are expensive (starting at US$30), but the companies insure their locks against theft of your bike for one to two years. Much of Britain's countryside is well-suited for cycling; many roads are not heavily traveled. Ireland is largely similar, although one *Let's Go* reader points out that after a while it seems that the country is all uphill. Even well-traveled routes will often cover highly uneven terrain.

If you plan to explore several widely separated regions, you can combine cycling with train travel. Depending upon the route you are traveling, many trains allow you to put your bike in the luggage compartment free and store your bike at most stations for a nominal fee; call (0171) 928 5151 to inquire about the specific route you are traveling. In addition, bikes often ride free on ferries leaving Britain and Ireland.

Renting (or **hiring**) a bike is preferable to bringing your own if your touring will be confined to one or two regions. Consult the British Tourist Authority pamphlet, *Britain for Cyclists* (free) for more details. In **Ireland,** you can rent bikes from **Raleigh Rent-a-Bike** shops almost anywhere in the country (IR£7 per day, £30 per week, plus £40 deposit). The **One-Way Rental** plan allows you to rent a bike at one shop and return it at another for IR£12. Make **reservations** at C. Harding for Bicycles, 30 Bachelors' Walk, Dublin 1 (tel./fax (01) 873 3622). A list of Raleigh dealers is available at most tourist offices and bike shops, or by calling Raleigh Ireland Limited (tel. (01) 626 1333). Tourist offices sell *Cycling Touring Ireland* (IR£7).

BY HIKING TRAIL

The British maintain an extensive system of long-distance paths that range from the gently rolling footpaths of the **South Downs Way** to the rugged mountain trails of the **Pennine Way.** These paths are well-marked and maintained, and in many cases are a day's walk between hostels. Explorers will enjoy the Ordnance Survey 1:25,000 Second Series maps, which mark almost every house, barn, standing stone, graveyard, and pub. Less ambitious hikers will want the 1:50,000 scale maps. The **Ramblers' Association,** 1-5 Wandsworth Rd., London SW8 2XX (tel. (0171) 339 8500; fax 339 8501), publishes a *Yearbook* on walking and places to stay, as well as free newsletters and color magazines (membership UK£17, families £21).

There are many long-distance rural paths in the **Republic of Ireland,** though they lack the sophisticated infrastructure of England's. **Wicklow Way,** a popular trail through mountainous County Wicklow, is an exception, with hostels within a day's walk of each other. Bord Fáilte publishes numerous brochures describing the trails. The best hill-walking maps are the Ordnance Survey series, which cost IR£4.20 each.

The **Ulster Way** encircles **Northern Ireland** with 560 mi. of marked trail. For detailed leaflets on various trails, contact **Sports Council for Northern Ireland,** House of Sport, Upper Malone Rd., Belfast BT9 5LA (tel. (01232) 381222).

BY THUMB

Let's Go strongly urges you to consider seriously the risks before you choose to hitchhike. We do not recommend hitching as a safe means of transportation, and none of the information presented in this book is intended to do so.

No one should hitch without careful consideration of the risks involved. Not everyone can be an airplane pilot, but any bozo can drive a car. Hitching means entrusting your life to a random person who happens to stop beside you on the road and risking theft, assault, sexual harassment, and unsafe driving. In spite of this, there can be gains to hitching. Favorable hitching experiences allow you to meet local people and get where you're going, especially in Ireland, where public transportation can be sketchy. The choice, however, remains yours.

Depending on the circumstances and the norms of the country, men and women traveling in groups and men traveling alone might consider hitching (called "autostop" in much of Europe) beyond the range of bus or train routes. If you're a woman traveling alone, don't hitch. It's just too dangerous. A man and a woman are a safer combination, two men will have a harder time, and three will go nowhere.

If you do decide to hitch, Britain and Ireland are probably the easiest places in Western Europe to get a lift. Experienced hitchers pick a spot outside of built-up areas, where drivers can stop, return to the road without causing an accident, and have time to look over potential passengers as they approach. Hitching (or even standing) on super-highways is usually illegal: one may only thumb at rest stops or at the entrance ramps to highways. In the Practical Information section of many cities, we list the tram or bus lines that take travelers to strategic points for hitching out.

Finally, success will depend on what one looks like. Successful hitchers travel light and stack their belongings in a compact but visible cluster. Most Europeans signal with an open hand, rather than a thumb; many write their destination on a sign in large, bold letters and draw a smiley-face under it. Drivers prefer hitchers who are neat and wholesome. No one stops for anyone wearing sunglasses.

Safety issues are important, even for those who are not hitching alone. Safe hitchers avoid getting in the back of a two-door car, and never let go of their backpacks. They will not get into a car that they can't get out of again in a hurry. If they ever feel threatened, they insist on being let off, regardless of where they are. Acting as if they are going to open the car door or vomit on the upholstery will usually get a driver to stop. Hitching at night is particularly dangerous; experienced hitchers stand in well-lit places, and expect drivers to be leery of nocturnal thumbers (or open-handers).

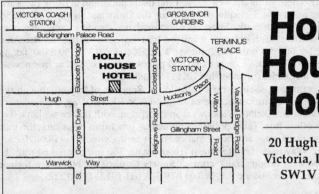

■ Accommodations

Tourist offices can provide invaluable aid. These offices often have free or inexpensive lists of vacancies, which they will post on their doors after hours. For about £2, most offices will book a place to stay. Calling direct can pay off in your pocket, since some proprietors inflate prices in response to finder's fees. Most offices also offer a book ahead service; for about £2.50, they'll reserve a room in the next town you visit. In many places, tourist offices only list proprietors who have paid a hefty fee to belong to the tourist board organization; other owners who may have chosen to remain independent are less visible.

Securing advance reservations with a deposit will greatly lessen the anxiety of arrival, especially in the summer. Write to a hotel or hostel specifying the date of arrival and the length of your stay (commit yourself only to a minimum stay, since you may wish to switch lodgings). The proprietor will write back to confirm availability, whereupon you should send a deposit of one night's rent, preferably a signed traveler's check in pounds. Some places accept personal checks or money orders in U.S. dollars (possibly for a fee). You may want to phone before leaving home to confirm. A few hostels accept credit card reservations over the phone. A room referred to as "en suite" has a private bathroom.

HOSTELS

A Hosteler's Bill of Rights

There are certain standard features that we do not include in our hostel listings. Unless we state otherwise, you can expect that every hostel has: no lockout, no curfew, a kitchen, free hot showers, secure luggage storage, and no key deposit.

For tight budgets and those lonesome traveling blues, hostels can't be beat. Hostels are generally dorm-style accommodations, often in large single-sex rooms with bunk beds, although some hostels do offer private rooms for families and couples. They sometimes have kitchens and utensils for your use, bike or moped rentals, storage areas, and laundry facilities. There can be drawbacks: some hostels close during certain daytime "lock-out" hours, have a curfew, impose a maximum stay, or, less frequently, require that you do chores. Fees are US$5-30 per night and hostels associated with one of the large hostel associations often have lower rates for members. Check out the **Internet Guide to Hostelling** (http://hostels.com), which includes hostels from around the world in addition to tons of information about hostelling and backpacking worldwide. **Eurotrip** (http://www.eurotrip.com/accommodation/accommodation.html) also has information on budget hostels and several international hostel associations. The major hostelling organization worldwide, **Hostelling International (HI),** offers the International Booking Network (IBN), which allows you to make reservation months in advance or from the road. In Ireland, **Independent Holiday Hostels (IHH)** operates 160 hostels with no lockout or curfew (with a few exceptions), which accept all ages, require no membership card, and have a mellow atmosphere; all are Bord Fáilte-approved. Write IHH at the **IHH Office,** 67 Lower Garginer St., Dublin (tel. (01) 836 4700; fax 836 4710). Pick up a free booklet with complete descriptions of each at any IHH hostel. Independent hostels in Britain have no distinct organization, but may present a better deal and friendlier quarters than their associated counterparts. If you plan to stay in hostels, consider joining one of these associations:

An Óige (Irish Youth Hostel Association), 61 Mountjoy St., Dublin 7 (tel. (01) 830 4555; fax 830 5808; email anoige@iol.ie; http://www.irelandyha.org). 1yr. membership is IR£7.50, under 18 £4, families £7.50 for each adult with children under 16 free. Prices from IR£4-9.50 a night. 37 locations.

Australian Youth Hostels Association (AYHA), Level 3, 10 Mallett St., Camperdown NSW 2050 (tel. (02) 9565 1699; fax 9565 1325; email YHA@yha.org.au; http://www.yha.org.au). Memberships AUS$44, renewal $27, under 18 $13.

Hostelling International-American Youth Hostels (HI-AYH), 733 15th St. NW, Ste. 840, Washington, D.C. 20005 (tel. (202) 783-6161, ext. 136; fax 783-6171; email hiayhserv@hiayh.org; http://www.hiayh.org). 1yr. membership US$25, under 18 $10, over 54 $15, families $35.

Hostelling International-Canada (HI-C), 400-205 Catherine St., Ottawa, Ontario K2P 1C3 (tel. (613) 237-7884; fax 237-7868; email info@hostellingintl.ca; http://www.hostellingintl.ca). 1yr. membership CDN$25, under 18 $12, 2yr. $35, lifetime $175.

Youth Hostels Association of England and Wales (YHA), Trevelyan House, 8 St. Stephen's Hill, St. Albans, Hertfordshire AL1 2DY, England (tel. (01727) 855215; fax 844126; email yhacustomerservices@compuserve.com; http://www.yha.org.uk). Enrollment fees UK£10, under 18 £5; families £20 for both parents with children under 18 enrolled free (single parents pay only £10); lifetime membership £140. Overnight prices UK£5.85-21.30, under 18 UK£4-17.90.

Hostelling International Northern Ireland (HINI), 22-32 Donegall Rd., Belfast BT12 5JN, Northern Ireland (tel. (01232) 324733 or 315435; fax 439699; email info@hini.org.uk; http://www.hini.org.uk). 1 yr. membership packages UK£7, under 18 £3; families £14 (up to 6 children); lifetime £50.

Youth Hostels Association of New Zealand (YHANZ), P.O. Box 436, 173 Cashel St., Christchurch 1 (tel. (643) 379 9970; fax 365 4476; email info@yha.org.nz; http://www.yha.org.nz). Annual membership fee NZ$24.

Hostelling International South Africa, P.O. Box 4402, Cape Town 8000 (tel. (021) 242511; fax 244119; email info@hisa.org.za; http://www.hisa.org.za). Membership SAR50, group SAR120, family SAR100, lifetime SAR250.

Scotland Youth Hostels Association (SYHA), 7 Glebe Crescent, Stirling FK8 2JA (tel. (01786) 891400; fax 891333; email syha@syha.org.uk; http://

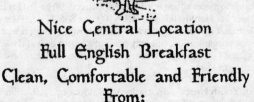

www.syha.org.uk). 80 hostels all over Scotland. You can also call their Centralised Booking Service (tel. (0541) 553255). Annual membership £6, under 18 £2.50, families £16 for each parent with children under 18 free, lifetime £60.

BED AND BREAKFASTS

For a cozy alternative to impersonal hotel rooms, B&Bs (private homes with rooms available to travelers) range from the acceptable to the sublime. Hosts will sometimes go out of their way to be accommodating by accepting travelers with pets, giving personalized tours, or offering home-cooked meals. On the other hand, many B&Bs do not provide phones, TVs, or private bathrooms.

Expect to pay £16-60 per person in London (often in advance) and £10-24 in the rest of Britain. Some proprietors grant rate reductions to guests who pay in advance or by the week and will grant discounts between September and May. **Bed and Breakfast (GB),** 94-96 Bell St., Henley-on-Thames, Oxon, England RG9 1XS (tel. (01491) 578803; fax 410806), is a reservation service which covers London, England, Scotland, Wales, and Ireland and books for a minimum deposit of £30 (not refundable, but can be deducted from the total price of your stay).

Singles in Irish B&Bs run IR£12-20, doubles £20-34. The breakfasts are often filling enough to get you through to dinner. B&Bs displaying a shamrock are officially approved by the Irish Tourist Board (Bord Fáilte). In Northern Ireland, check the *Where to Stay in Northern Ireland* (UK£4), available at most tourist offices.

DORMS

Many **colleges and universities** open their residence halls to travelers when school is not in session—some do so even during term-time. Dorms are often clean and you may find listings of places to stay or a ride out of town. *Let's Go* lists colleges which rent dorm rooms among the accommodations for appropriate cities. College dorms are popular with many travelers, especially those looking for long-term lodging, so reserve ahead. For information, write to **British Universities Accommodation Consortium,** University Park, P.O. Box Bn 25, Nottingham NG7 2RD (tel. (0115) 950 4571; fax 942 2505; email buac@nottingham.ac.uk).

▓ Longer Stays

If you're looking for a **job,** it's likely you'll have better luck in cities. Once you've got yourself a source of funds, **housing** will probably be the most pressing concern. In this we can only suggest looking around the town of your choice for some real estate agencies who may be able to arrange rentals or leases for you. Check the larger city papers for employment and apartment listings. Also, you might try college campus noticeboards. **BUNAC** will help with job placement and permits (see **Alternatives to Tourism,** p. 18). Renting a room is also a very common housing solution for the ex-pat. **Food** shopping and the other details of living should not be difficult to arrange. *Let's Go* attempts to list the most significant markets and supermarkets in the towns we visit to give you a good start.

HOME EXCHANGE AND RENTALS

Home exchange offers the traveler with a home the opportunity to live like a native, and to dramatically cut down on accommodation fees—usually only an administration fee is paid to the matching service. Once the introductions are made, the choice is left to the two hopeful partners. Visit http://www.aitec.edu.au/~bwechner/Documents/Travel/Lists/HomeExchangeClubs.html for a list of exchange companies.

Europa-Let/Tropical Inn-Let, 92 N. Main St., Ashland, OR 97520 (tel. (800) 462-4486 or (541) 482-5806; fax 482-0660; email europalet@wave.net), offers private rental properties with fully equipped kitchens in Ireland and the U.K. Customized computer searches allow clients to choose properties according to specific needs and budget.

Hometours International, Inc., P.O. Box 11503, Knoxville, TN 37939 (tel. (800) 367-4668; email hometours@aol.com; http://thor.he.net/~hometour/), offers lodging in apartments, houses, villas, and castles in the U.K. They are also the U.S. representative for Bed & Breakfast (GB) and for HF Holidays, which gives walking tours in the U.K. Brochures are US$5 for each country. 10 vouchers at $45 each for 10 nights in over 2000 B&Bs in the U.K.

FINDING A JOB

While casual jobs are readily available in larger cities, wages are unlikely to be more than £3-4 per hour. Advice can be found at a local university's work abroad resource center (see **Alternatives to Tourism**, p. 18).

Unless you're a citizen of a European Economic Area nation or British Commonwealth nation, you'll have a tough time finding a legal paying job. Citizens of British Commonwealth nations (including Australia, Canada, New Zealand, and South Africa) ages 17-27 may work in Britain during a visit if the employment they take is "incidental to their holiday" by obtaining a working holiday visa. Commonwealth citizens 17 years or older with a U.K.-born grandparent may apply for entry clearance, which will allow them to work for four years without a work permit. Commonwealth citizens with a U.K.-born parent can apply for the right of abode, which allows them to live and work in Britain. Students at American universities can apply for a Blue Card Permit which exempts them from further entry clearance and allows them to work up to six months; permits are available from BUNAC or Council.

Officially, you can hold a job in European countries only with a work permit, applied for by your prospective employer (or by you, with supporting papers from the employer). The real catch-22 is that normally you must physically enter the country in order to have immigration officials validate your work permit papers and note your status in your passport. This means that if you can't set up a job from afar and have the work permit sent to you, you must enter the country to look for a job, find an employer and have them start the permit process, then *leave* the country until the permit is sent to you (up to six weeks), and finally return and start work.

OPENING A BANK ACCOUNT

An English **sterling bank account** is a convenient way to manage funds. If you're planning on working for a year, you should have no problems. The head branches of the five big U.K. banks are in London: **Barclays Bank,** 54 Lombard St. EC3P 3AH (tel. (0171) 699 5000); **Lloyd's Bank,** 71 Lombard St. EC3P 3BS (tel. (0171) 626 1500); **Midland Bank,** 10 Lower Thames St. EC3R 6AE (tel. (0171) 260 8000); and **National Westminster Bank,** 41 Lothbury EC2P 2BP (tel. (0171) 606 6060). (Tube: Bank for all.) **Abbey National,** head office at 201 Grafton Gate East, Central Milton Keynes, MK9 1AN (tel. (01908) 343000), will refer you to your nearest branch or a special branch set up to deal with short-term customers. Contact your home bank a few months before coming to London, and find out if it can make arrangements in advance for an account to be opened at a bank in the U.K. Once in the U.K., it may be harder to have your home bank help you open an account.

Be sure to obtain a **letter of introduction** from your bank; when opening an account, you will need to show this letter, a **letter from an employer** confirming the tenure of employment in Britain and a regular salary, or a **letter from your school** (in Britain) confirming your status as a full-time student. Students are screened rigorously. American college students studying abroad should contact their home school's bursar's office, which may have a special arrangement with a bank in London. Banks sometimes require a large deposit to be placed in the account, which could ideally support the student for the full period of study. Alternatively, they may accept proof that regular payments would be made into the account (e.g., from parents).

Once you have made your way through all the red tape, the bank will generally issue you a checkbook, a check guarantee card (vouching for checks of up to £50 or £100), and a cash machine card. They may be rather reticent about handing out credit cards to temporary visitors—which should not matter as long as you can arrange to have your own credit card bills paid back home. Note that Barclaycard acts as both a Visa card and a check guarantee card for Barclay's checks. If the obstacles prove too great, try a **building society,** the British version of a savings and loan—building societies are less likely to require proof of employment.

■ Camping and the Outdoors

USEFUL PUBLICATIONS

A variety of publishing companies offer hiking guidebooks to meet the educational needs of novice or expert. For information about camping, hiking, and biking, write or call the publishers listed below to receive a free catalogue.

Automobile Association, AA Publishing. Orders and enquiries to TBS Frating Distribution Centre, Colchester, Essex, CO7 7DW (tel. (01206) 255678; fax 255916; http://www.theaa.co.uk). Publishes a wide range of maps, atlases, and travel guides, including *Camping and Caravanning: Britain & Ireland* (UK£8).

The Caravan Club, East Grinstead House, East Grinstead, West Sussex RH19 1UA, (tel. (01342) 326944; fax 410258; http://www.caravanclub.co.uk), produces one of the most detailed English-language guides to campsites in Europe and the U.K.

Stanfords Ltd., 12-14 Long Acre, London WC2E 9LP (tel. (0171) 836 2260; fax 379 4776), supplies maps of just about anywhere, but especially continental Europe and the British Isles.

The Mountaineers Books, 1001 SW Klickitat Way, #201, Seattle, WA 98134 (tel. (800) 553-4453 or (206) 223-6303; fax 223-6306; email mbooks@mountaineers.org; http://www.mountaineers.org). Many titles on hiking (the *100 Hikes* series), biking, mountaineering, natural history, and conservation.

CAMPING AND HIKING EQUIPMENT

Purchase **equipment** before you leave. This way you'll know exactly what you have and how much it weighs. Spend some time examining catalogs and talking to knowledgeable salespeople. Whether buying or renting, finding sturdy, light, and inexpensive equipment is a must.

Sleeping bags: Most good **sleeping bags** are rated by "season," or the lowest outdoor temperature at which they will keep you warm ("summer" means 30-40°F, "3-season" usually means 0°F, and "4-season" or "winter" often means below -50°F and are rarely necessary). Sleeping bags are made either of down (warmer and lighter, but more expensive, and miserable when wet) or of synthetic material (heavier, more durable, and warmer when wet). Prices vary, but might range from US$65-100 for a summer synthetic to $250-550 for a good down winter bag. **Sleeping bag pads,** including foam pads (US$15 and up) and air mattresses ($25-50) cushion your back and neck and insulate you from the ground. Another good alternative is the **Therm-A-Rest,** which is part foam and part air-mattress and inflates to full padding when you unroll it.

Tents: The best **tents** are free-standing, with their own frames and suspension systems; they set up quickly and require no staking (except in high winds). Tents are also classified by season, which should be taken into account to avoid baking in a winter tent in the middle of the summer. Low profile dome tents are the best all-around. When pitched, their internal space is almost entirely usable, which means little unnecessary bulk. Tent sizes can be somewhat misleading: 2 people *can* fit in a 2-person tent, but will find life more pleasant in a 4-person. If you're traveling by car, go for the bigger tent; if you're hiking, stick with a smaller tent that weighs no more than 3-4 lbs. Good 2-person tents start at US$150, 4-person tents at $400, but you can sometimes find last year's model for half the price. Be sure to seal the seams of your tent with waterproofer, and make sure it has a rai- fly.

Backpacks: If you intend to do a lot of hiking, you should have a **frame backpack. Internal-frame packs** mold better to your back, keep a lower center of gravity, and can flex adequately to allow you to hike difficult trails that require a lot of bending and maneuvering. **External-frame packs** are more comfortable for long hikes over even terrain since they keep the weight higher and distribute it more evenly. Whichever you choose, make sure your pack has a strong, padded hip belt, which transfers the weight from the shoulders to the legs. Any serious backpacking requires a pack of at least 4000 cubic inches. Allow an additional 500 cubic inches for your sleeping bag in internal-frame packs. Sturdy backpacks cost anywhere from US$125-500. It doesn't pay to economize—cheaper packs may be less comfortable, and the straps are more likely to fray or rip. Before you buy any pack, try it on and imagine carrying it, full, a few miles up a rocky incline.

Boots: Be sure to wear hiking boots with good **ankle support** which are appropriate for the terrain you are hiking. Your boots should fit snugly and comfortably over one or two wool socks and a thin liner sock. Be sure that the boots are broken in—a bad blister will ruin your hiking for days.

Other necessities: Rain gear should come in two pieces, a top and pants, rather than a poncho. **Synthetics,** like polypropylene tops, socks, and long underwear, along with a pile jacket, will keep you warm even when wet. When camping in autumn, winter, or spring, bring along a **"space blanket,"** which helps you to retain your body heat and doubles as a groundcloth (US$5-15). Plastic **canteens** or water bottles keep water cooler than metal ones do, and are virtually shatter- and leak-proof. Large, collapsible **water sacks** will significantly improve your lot in primitive campgrounds and weigh practically nothing when empty, though they can get bulky. Bring **water-purification tablets** for when you can't boil water. Though most campgrounds provide campfire sites, you may want to bring a small **metal grate** or **grill** of your own. For those places that forbid fires or the gathering of firewood (this includes virtually every organized campground in Europe), you'll need a **camp stove.** The classic Coleman starts at about US$30. Campers should also look into buying an **International Camping Carnet.** Similar to a hostel membership card, it's required at a few campgrounds and provides discounts at others. It's available from **The Caravan Club** (see **Useful Publications,** p. 44). A **first aid kit, swiss army knife, insect repellent, calamine lotion,** and **waterproof matches** or a **lighter** are essential camping items. Other items include: a **battery-operated lantern,** a **plastic groundcloth,** a **nylon tarp,** a **waterproof backpack cover** (although you can also store your belongings in plastic bags inside your backpack), and a **"stuff sack"** or plastic bag to keep your sleeping bag dry.

The mail order firms listed below offer lower prices than those you'll find in many stores, but shop around locally first in order to determine what items actually look like and weigh. Many of these firms have online shopping available from the web. Keep in mind that camping equipment is generally more expensive in Australia, New Zealand, and the U.K. than in North America.

Campmor, P.O. Box 700, Saddle River, NJ 07458-0700 (tel. (888) CAMPMOR (226-7667), outside the U.S. call (201) 825-8300; email customer-service@campmor.com; http://www.campmor.com), has a wide selection of name brand equipment at low prices. One-year guarantee for unused or defective merchandise.

Eastern Mountain Sports (EMS), 1 Vose Farm Rd., Peterborough, NH 03458 (tel. (603) 924-7231; email emsmail@emsonline.com; http://www.emsonline.com), has stores throughout the U.S. Though slightly higher-priced, they provide excellent service and guaranteed customer satisfaction on most items sold. They don't have a catalogue, and they generally don't take mail or phone orders; call the above number for the branch nearest you.

Recreational Equipment, Inc. (REI), 222 Yale Ave. N., Seattle, WA 98109-5429 (tel. (800) 426-4840); http://www.rei.com), stocks a comprehensive selection of REI brand and other leading brand equipment, clothing, and footwear for the activities of travel, camping, cycling, paddling, climbing, and winter sports. In addition to mail-order and an Internet commerce site, REI has 49 retail stores, including a flagship store in Seattle, WA.

L.L. Bean, Freeport, ME 04033-0001 (in Canada or the U.S. tel. (800) 441-5713; in the U.K. (0800) 962954; elsewhere (207) 552-6878; fax 552-4080; http://www.llbean.com). This monolithic equipment and outdoor clothing supplier offers high quality and loads of information. Call or write for their free catalogue.

Mountain Designs, P.O. Box 1472, Fortitude Valley, Queensland 4006, Australia (tel. (07) 3252 8894; fax 3252 4569), is a leading Australian manufacturer and mail-order retailer of camping and climbing gear.

YHA Adventure Shop, 14 Southampton St., London WC2E 7HY (tel./fax (0171) 836 8541). Main branch of one of Britain's largest outdoor equipment suppliers.

CAMPERS AND RVS

European RVs are smaller and more economical than the 40 ft. Winnebagos of the American road. Renting an RV will always be more expensive than tenting or hostelling, but the costs compare favorably with the price of renting a car and staying in hotels, and the convenience of bringing along your own bedroom, bathroom, and kitchen makes it an attractive option for some, especially older travelers and families with small children.

It is not difficult to arrange an RV rental from overseas, although you will want to begin gathering information several months before your departure. Rates vary widely by region, season (July and August are the most expensive months), and type of RV. It always pays to contact several different companies to compare vehicles and prices. **Avis** (tel. (800) 331-1084) and **Hertz** (tel. (800) 654-3001) are U.S. firms which can arrange RV rentals in Europe. **Auto Europe** (tel. (800) 223-5555) and **National Car Rentals** (tel. (800) 227-3876; in Canada (800) 227-7368) are European firms with branches in North America. *Camping Your Way through Europe,* by Carol Mickelsen (Affordable Press, US$15), and *Exploring Europe by RV,* by Dennis and Tina Jaffe (Globe Pequot, also US$15), are good resources for planning this type of trip.

WILDERNESS AND SAFETY CONCERNS

Stay warm, stay dry, and **stay hydrated.** The vast majority of life-threatening wilderness problems stem from a failure to follow these rules. On any hike, however brief, you should pack enough equipment to keep you alive should disaster strike. This includes **rain gear, hat** and **mittens,** a **first-aid kit, a reflector, a whistle, high energy food,** and **water.** Dress in warm layers of **synthetic materials** designed for the outdoors, or **wool.** Pile fleece jackets and Gore-Tex® raingear are excellent choices (see **Camping and Hiking Equipment,** p. 45). Never rely on **cotton** for warmth. This "death cloth" will be absolutely useless should it get wet. When camping, be sure to bring a proper tent with rain-fly and warm sleeping bags.

Check **weather forecasts** and pay attention to the skies when hiking. Weather patterns can change instantly. Remember that rain is always likely in the British Isles and that the northernmost reaches of Scotland can rival arctic temperatures at night. If on a day hike, turn back if the weather starts to look nasty. If on an overnight, begin looking for shelter immediately. Whenever possible, let someone know when and where you are going hiking, either a friend, your hostel, a park ranger, or a local hiking organization. Do not attempt a hike beyond your ability—you may be endangering your life. A good guide to outdoor survival is *How to Stay Alive in the Woods,* by Bradford Angier (Macmillan, US$8). See **Health,** p. 15, for information about outdoor dangers such as giardia and insects, as well as basic medical concerns and first aid.

■ Keeping in Touch

MAIL

Mail can be sent internationally through **Poste Restante** (the international phrase for General Delivery) to any city or town; it's well worth using, generally without any surcharges, and much more reliable than you might think. Mark the envelope

REGENCY
HOUSE HOTEL
— JVM HOTELS —

A GEORGIAN TOWN HOUSE IN
THE HEART OF LONDON'S
HISTORIC BLOOMSBURY
A SHORT STROLL AWAY FROM
THE BRITISH MUSEUM,
WEST END THEATRES
AND OXFORD STREET SHOPS.

Rooms available both with and without
full size showers and toilets.
All rooms have colour T.V,
direct dial telephones,
tea and coffee making facilities.
Room rates are inclusive of all taxes
and English breakfast.

71 GOWER STREET
LONDON WC1 E6HJ
TEL: 0171 6371804
FAX: 0171 3235077

"HOLD" and address it, for example, "William V. <u>WINDSOR</u>, *Poste Restante*, London, England." The last name should be capitalized and underlined. The mail will go to a special desk in the central post office, unless you specify a post office by street address or postal code. It's best to use the largest post office in the area; when possible, it's usually safer and quicker to send mail express or registered.

When picking up your mail, bring your passport or other ID. If the clerks insist that there is nothing for you, have them check under your first name as well. *Let's Go* lists post offices in the **Practical Information** section for each city and most towns.

Aerogrammes, printed sheets that fold into envelopes and travel via airmail, are available at post offices. Most post offices will charge exorbitant fees or simply refuse to send Aerogrammes with enclosures. Airmail from Europe and the U.S. averages one to two weeks. Allow two weeks from Australia and New Zealand.

If regular airmail is too slow, there are faster, more expensive, options. **FedEx** (U.S. tel. (800) 463-3339; Ireland tel. (1800) 535800; U.K. tel. (0800) 123800) can get a letter from New York to London in two days for a whopping US$25.50. By U.S. Express Mail, the same letter would arrive in two to three days and would cost US$16.50.

Surface mail is by far the cheapest and slowest way to send mail. It takes one to three months to cross the Atlantic and two to four for the Pacific—appropriate for sending large quantities of items you won't need to see for a while. It is vital, therefore, to distinguish your airmail from surface mail by explicitly labeling "airmail." When ordering books and materials from abroad, always include one or two **International Reply Coupons (IRCs)**—a way of providing the postage to cover delivery. IRCs should be available from your local post office as well as abroad (US$1.05).

American Express offices throughout the world will act as a mail service for cardholders if they are contacted in advance. Under this free **"Client Letter Service,"** they will hold mail for 30 days, forward upon request, and accept telegrams. Just like *Poste Restante,* the last name of the person to whom the mail is addressed should be capitalized and underlined. Some offices will offer these services to non-cardholders (especially those who have purchased AmEx Travellers' Cheques), but call ahead to make sure. Check the Practical Information section of the cities you plan to visit; *Let's Go* lists AmEx office locations for most large cities. A complete list is available free from AmEx (U.S. tel. (800) 528-4800) in the booklet *Traveler's Companion,* or online (http://www.americanexpress.com).

TELEPHONES

In Britain and Northern Ireland
Operator: 100
Directory inquiries: 192
International operator: 155
International directory assistance: 153

In the Republic of Ireland
Operator (not available from card phones): 10
Directory inquiries (including Northern Ireland): 1190
British inquiries: 1197
Telecom Éireann information: (1800) 330330
International operator: 114

Calling Britain and Ireland
You can place **international calls** from most telephones. Remember time differences so as not to wake B&B proprietors in the wee hours (see **Time Zones,** p. 690). Dial your country's international access code (0011 from Australia, 011 from Canada or the U.S., 00 from Ireland, New Zealand, and the U.K., and 09 from South Africa); then the country code (see **Telephone Codes,** p. 690); then the regional "telephone code," *dropping the initial zero;* and, finally, the local number. In small villages, you may have to go through the operator. *Let's Go* lists telephone codes at the end of **Practical Information** sections, though when covering rural areas where more than

one telephone code may apply we list the telephone code, in parentheses, together with the number. Thus, when calling from the U.S. to order silver glitter pumps from Harrods in London (telephone code 0171), dial 011 44 171 730 1234. Regional telephone codes range from two to seven digits, and local numbers range from three to seven digits. Wherever possible, use a **calling card** (see below) for international phone calls, as the long distance rates for national phone services are often unpredictable and exorbitant.

Calling from Britain and Ireland

To make international direct calls from Britain or the Republic of Ireland, dial the international access code (00 for both countries); then the country code (see **Telephone Codes,** p. 690); area code (dropping the initial zero); and local number.

The newly remodeled **British pay phone** charges 10p for local calls. A series of harsh beeps will warn you to insert more money when your time is up. For the rest of the call, the digital display ticks off your credit in suspenseful 1p increments. Unused coins are returned (if you're lucky). You may use all remaining credit on a second call by pressing the "follow on call" button (often marked "FC"). Phones don't accept 1p, 2p, or 5p coins. The dial tone is a continuous purring sound; a repeated double-purr means the line is ringing. Some phones have a button for international assistance. If you can find a Mercury phone, use it, and replace "1 800" with "1 500."

If you'll be making more than a few calls during your stay in Britain, pick up a handy **Phonecard,** available in denominations of UK£2, £5, £10, and £20. They're available at post offices, newsagents, or John Menzies stationery shops. Many phones only accept Phonecards. Phone booths that take cards are labeled in green and are common except in rural areas; coin booths are labeled in red. Mercury phones are cheaper than the ubiquitous BT phones.

Irish pay phones are similar. Most people use **callcards;** they're essential for international calls. When the unit number on the digital display starts flashing, you may push the eject button on the card phone; you can then pull out your expired card and replace it with a fresh one (don't wait for the units to fall to zero or you'll be disconnected). Callcards have grown in popularity, and most people prefer using them to coins. **Public coin phones** will sometimes make change, but private pay phones in hotels and restaurants do not. In any pay phone, do not insert money until you are asked to, or until your call goes through. The frightening "pip-pip" noise that the phone makes before it starts ringing is normal and can last up to 10 seconds. Local calls cost 20p for four minutes on standard phones.

Operators in most countries will place **collect calls** for you. It's cheaper to find a pay phone and deposit just enough money to be able to say "Call me" and give your number (though some pay phones can't receive calls). Some companies, seizing upon this "call-me-back" concept, have created callback phone services. Under these plans, you call a specified number, ring once, and hang up. The company's computer calls back and gives you a dial tone. You can then make as many calls as you want, at rates about 20-60% lower than you'd pay using credit cards or pay phones. This option is most economical for loquacious travelers, as services may include a US$10-25 minimum billing per month. For information, call **America Tele-Fone** (tel. (800) 321-5817) or **Telegroup** (tel. (800) 338-0225).

Another option is **direct access** to an operator in the country you're dialing—calling card rates are often cheaper than those for direct calls, and service a bit speedier. Long-distance companies in your home country may have economical arrangements for their clients calling home from overseas. By calling a toll-free number in Britain or Ireland, you can access an operator who will help you place a **collect** or **calling card** call to the country of your choice. **From Britain,** call **Australia Direct** (0800 890061), **Canada Direct** (0800 890016), **Ireland Direct** (0800 890353), **New Zealand Direct** (0800 890064), **South Africa Direct** (0800 890027), or the **U.S.** (AT&T USA Direct: 0800 890011; MCI 0800 890222; Sprint Express: 0800 890877). **From Ireland,** call **Australia Direct** (1 800 550061), **Canada Direct** (1 800 555001), **Telecom New Zealand** (1 800 550064), **Telekom South Africa** (1 800 550027), **BT Direct** (1 800 550144), and **AT&T USA Direct** (1 800 550000); or **Sprint Express** (1 800 552001).

A **calling card** is probably your best bet; your local long-distance service provider will have a number for you to dial while traveling (either toll-free or charged as a local call) to connect instantly to an operator in your home country. The calls (plus a small surcharge) are then billed either collect or to the calling card. For more information, call your home country's calling card provider: **Australia Direct** (tel. 132200), **Canada Direct** (tel. (800) 565 4708), **Ireland Direct** (tel. (800) 250250), **Telecom New Zealand** (tel. 123), **Telkom South Africa** (tel. 09 03), **BT Direct** in the **U.K.** (tel. (800) 345144), or **AT&T** about its **USADirect** and **World Connect** services (tel. (888) 288-4685; from abroad call collect (810) 262-6644), **Sprint** (tel. (800) 877-4646; from abroad, call collect (913) 624-5335), or **MCI WorldPhone** and **World Reach** (tel. (800) 444-4141; from abroad dial the country's MCI access number). MCI's WorldPhone also provides access to MCI's **Traveler's Assist,** which gives legal and medical advice, exchange rate information, and translation services. Many other long distance carriers and phone companies provide such travel information; contact your phone service provider.

Reduced rates for most international calls from Britain apply from 6pm to 8am Monday through Friday and all day and night on Saturday and Sunday; calls are slightly more expensive from 1pm to 6pm Monday through Friday, and most expensive on weekday mornings (8am-1pm).

OTHER COMMUNICATION

Domestic and international **telegrams** offer an option slower than phone but faster than post. Fill out a form at any post or telephone office; cables arrive in one or two days. Telegrams can be quite expensive; **Western Union** (tel. (800) 325-6000), for example, adds a surcharge to the per-word rate depending on the country. You may wish to consider **faxes** for more immediate, personal, and cheaper communication. Major cities have bureaus where you can pay to send and receive faxes.

Between May 2 and Octoberfest, **EurAide,** P.O. Box 2375, Naperville, IL 60567 (tel. (630) 420-2343; fax 420-2369; http://www.cube.net/kmu/euraide.html), offers **Overseas Access,** a service useful to travelers without a set itinerary. The cost is US$15 per week or US$40 per month plus a US$15 registration fee. To reach you, people call, fax, or use the internet to leave a message; you receive it by calling Munich whenever you wish, which is cheaper than calling overseas. You may also leave messages for callers to pick up by phone.

If you're spending a year abroad and want to keep in touch with friends or colleagues, **electronic mail (email)** is an attractive option. With a minimum of computer knowledge and a little planning, you can beam messages anywhere for no per-message charges. **Traveltales.com** (http://www.traveltales.com) provides free, web-based email for travelers, as do **Hotmail** (http://www.hotmail.com) and **USANET** (http://www.usa.net). See **Internet Resources,** p. 4, for travel sites. *Let's Go* tries to list local internet providers in the **Practical Information** section of cities.

If you're already hooked up at home, you should be able to find access numbers for your destination country; check with your internet provider before leaving. If you're not connected, one comparatively cheap, easy-to-use provider is **America Online,** 8615 Westwood Center Dr., Vienna, VA 22070 (tel. (800) 827-6364), which offers **"GLOBALnet,"** making it possible for American net-junkies to access the internet, sexy chat rooms, and, of course, email through their home accounts while travelling in 70 countries. The US$6-12 per hour surcharge and the fact that GLOBALnet only works on computers with AOL software already installed, however, pose problems. Travelers who have the luxury of a laptop with them can use a **modem** to call an internet service provider. Long-distance phone cards specifically intended for such calls can defray normally high phone charges. Check with your long-distance phone provider to see if they offer this option; otherwise, try a **C.COM Internet PhoneCard** (tel. (888) 464-2266), which offers Internet connection calls for 15¢ per minute, minimum initial purchase of US$5.

GREAT BRITAIN

English, a language of many dialects created by invaded and colonized peoples, is today the true *lingua franca*. One need only review the history of Britain to appreciate this paradox. Once considered too common for real scholarship, the tongue was later forced upon the people of Wales, Scotland, and Ireland, in an attempt to assimilate them into the British Empire. With the rise of mercantilism and later Empire, English went global.

"England" originally referred to a group of Anglo-Saxon principalities united in the 9th century, though it came to mean the areas of most centralized power. By 1603, the English had established control over Ireland, Scotland, and Wales; the "United Kingdom of Great Britain and Ireland" was proclaimed in 1801. But in the 20th century, this union began to disintegrate, foreshadowing the collapse of the overseas Empire. Most of Ireland won independence in 1921; Scotland and Wales were promised regional autonomy in 1975. As the ongoing troubles in Northern Ireland reflect, questions of union and nationalism will be contested for years to come—just as they are in Britain's former colonies. The Union Jack no longer flies over two-fifths of the earth's surface, but the Empire's heirs have retained a proud, occasionally even arrogant, detachment from the rest of the world. In spite of it all, the British can be acutely aware of the inequalities in their own land.

Names, like language, hold a certain political force. Deciding just what to call this part of the world can incite local tempers and fuel debates. "Great Britain" refers to England, Scotland, and Wales (and don't call a Scot or Welshman "English"—it's neither accurate nor polite); the political term "United Kingdom" refers to these nations in addition to Northern Ireland and the Isle of Man. Because of distinctions in law and currency, Let's Go uses "Britain" to refer to England, Scotland, Wales, the Isle of Man, and Northern Ireland, and "Ireland" to refer to the Republic of Ireland.

HISTORY

CELTS, ROMANS, ANGLES, AND SAXONS

Ages before the much-maligned Chunnel finally linked England to the rest of the world, foreign tourists had scattered throughout the Isle of Britain. Stonehenge and the stone circles of Avebury bear mute witness to the Isles' earliest inhabitants, but recorded history began with the Celts, who battled Julius Caesar's army in the first century BC. Caesar was ultimately victorious, and the Romans occupied southern Britain until AD 410. The Pictish tribes to the north, described fancifully in Roman histories as having blue skin, fought imperial rule and sent the Roman armies scuttling southward. Their fierce resistance inspired the Romans to construct Hadrian's Wall—an edifice 73 mi. long and 12 ft. high—in an effort to contain the northern threat (see **Hadrian's Wall**, p. 373). The 4th century brought the decline of the Roman Empire, leaving Britain vulnerable to raids from northern Europe by hordes of **Angles, Saxons,** and **Jutes.** These tribes established settlements and kingdoms alongside those of the resilient Celts (or Britons) in Wales and Cornwall; the name "England" is in fact derived from "Anglaland," the land of the Angles.

CHRISTIANITY AND THE NORMANS BUST IN

Roman Christianity officially arrived in 597 when eager missionary **Augustine** successfully converted King Æthelbert of Kent and founded England's first church at Canterbury. Even though subsequent kings were not as receptive to the new religion, **Christianity** was all the rage soon enough. By the end of the 7th century, the religion had a solid foothold in England: its spread was immortalized by the Venerable Bede in

731 with his *Ecclesiastical History of the English People.* In the late 9th century, **King Alfred** of Wessex sought to unify the different regions of England against the threat of invasion by Vikings (who did *not* wear horns on their helmets—trust us). Alfred repelled the onslaught, politically and economically unified southern England, and established centers of learning throughout his kingdom. The English and the Danes maintained an uneasy truce until 1066, when William I (better known as William the Conqueror) of Normandy invaded England in order to seize the throne from Harold, Earl of Wessex; William slaughtered Harold and, for good measure, his two brothers.

William promptly set about cataloguing his new English acquisitions in the epic sheepskin *Domesday Book,* a compilation of all landholders and their possessions, which has come to serve as the starting point of the written history of most English towns. Norman French became the language of the educated and elite, while the English language was marginalized, splitting into 14 main dialects, each with its own spelling and grammar. The English people were likewise subjugated, galvanizing class division between those who owned and those who worked the land.

MEDIEVAL TIMES AND THE TUDOR RENAISSANCE

Henry II ascended to the throne in 1154 and initiated the conquest of Ireland. His son, Richard I (better known as the Lion-Heart), led the Third Crusade to Jerusalem, where he won access to the Holy Shrines. Soon after that expansion of power, noblemen, tired of royal abuses of authority, forced his brother King John to sign the **Magna Carta** in 1215. The document, credited with laying the groundwork for modern democracy, was, in fact, a reassertion and codification of feudal rights. The first **Parliament** convened 50 years later in 1265, and Wales became a principality of the English crown in 1282. The **Black Plague** ravaged Britain in the 14th century, killing one-third of the population. Many more fell in the **100 Years' War** (or the 116 Years' War to be more precise), which started in 1337 with Edward III's invasion of France.

While King Richard II was on an Irish holiday in 1399, Henry Bolingbroke invaded Britain and snatched the throne. This bold move put the Lancasters in control, and gave Shakespeare something decent to write about (the Henriad plays). Henry V defeated the French in the **Battle of Agincourt** (1415), a victory for the British underdogs that soon became legendary. But his son Henry VI (despite being crowned King of France in 1431) blew it and was executed in the Tower of London. Child-king Edward V ascended to the throne in 1483 and descended the same year, deposed by his loving uncle Richard III who might have had him murdered in the Tower.

After the turmoil of the **Wars of the Roses,** Henry VII emerged victorious and inaugurated the rule of the **House of Tudor,** a dynasty that survived until 1603. His successor, **Henry VIII,** waged wars against France and Scotland, and proclaimed himself king of Ireland in 1542. In his infamous battle with the Pope over multiple marriages, that same Henry converted Britain from Roman Catholicism to Protestantism, establishing the Anglican Church and placing himself at its head. During the reign of Henry's daughter, **Elizabeth I,** the British defeated the Spanish Armada to become the leading Protestant power in Europe.

QUESTIONS OF LOYALTY: RELIGION AND ROYALTY

The union of England, Wales, and Scotland effectively took place in 1603, when Protestant **James VI** of Scotland ascended to the throne as **James I** of England. James and successive fellow members of the house of Stuart/Stewart (depending on the monarch's degree of Francophilia) began to irk Parliament with their Catholic sympathies and their firm belief in the "divine right" of kings. Tensions erupted in the **English Civil War** (1642-48). In the aftermath the monarchy was abolished when Parliament saw to it that Charles I and his head parted ways, and a Puritan Commonwealth was founded in 1649. **Oliver Cromwell** emerged as a rebellious and adept military leader of this new Commonwealth. His massacre of nearly half of the indigenous Irishmen earned him temporary submission and eternal bitterness from Britain's neighbors. Cromwell's son Richard succeeded him as Lord Protector, but lacked the qualities that allowed his father to maintain a grasp on the republic. Much to the relief of the masses, Charles II was brought to power unconditionally in 1660, restoring stability to the British throne. But the **Restoration** did not signal the end of the troubles with the Stuarts: although Charles II was pliant enough to suit Parliament, there was much debate about whether to exclude Charles II's fervently Catholic brother James II from the succession. Debate during the **Exclusion Crisis** spawned the establishment of two political parties, the Whigs (who were firmly Protestant) and the Tories (who likened their opponents to the lately discredited Puritans).

PARLIAMENT AND THE CROWN

The relatively bloodless **Glorious Revolution** erupted in 1688 to prevent James II from establishing a Catholic dynasty; Dutch Protestant William of Orange and his wife Mary were crowned when they agreed to the Bill of Rights. The ascension of William and Mary marked the end of a century of violent upheaval. Supporters of James II (Jacobites) remained a distant threat, and became only less so in 1745 when James II's grandson, "Bonnie Prince Charlie," failed in his attempt to invade and recapture the throne. But the Bill of Rights did far more than simply end debate about who would hold the Crown; it also quietly revolutionized the relationship between Crown and Parliament, bringing a triumphant Parliamentary leadership to the fore. Over the 18th century, the office of Prime Minister, held at the beginning of the century by the master negotiator Robert Walpole and at the end by the astute politician William Pitt the Younger, gradually eclipsed the monarch as the seat of power in British government.

The 18th century witnessed one of the greatest social changes in British history: massive portions of the rural populace migrated to towns, pushed off the land by the **Enclosure Acts** and lured by rapidly growing opportunities in industrial employment. Over the next hundred years, industrialization irreversibly altered the texture of British and global society as Britain expanded into an Empire. The gulf between workers and owners that began as early as the 11th century was replaced by a wider gap between factory owners and their laborers.

THE VICTORIAN ERA: LIBERALISM AND LABOUR

By the 1830s, the combined force of class divisions and often frightening workplace conditions spurred the beginnings of domestic industrial regulation. A century of reform was inaugurated in 1832 by a moderate expansion of enfranchisement through the ambitiously titled Great Reform Bill. At the same time, some morally stringent Victorian Liberals, such as **William Gladstone,** picked up where free-traders like **Robert Peel** left off, extending the economic notion of a free market to encompass a more open attitude toward different religions. The **Chartist Movement** of the mid-19th century dramatically pressed for universal manhood suffrage regardless of class, but modest reforms and a boom in the 1840s effectively curbed more radical reform until later in the century. The 40s also brought the Irish famine, which killed over a million people and caused twice that many to emigrate. **The Great Exhibition of 1851,** a fair celebrating British and imperial products, as well as Queen Victoria's Golden and Diamond Jubilees, were symbols of the pinnacle of Britain's technological and imperial prowess.

By the end of the century, trade-union organization had strengthened, assuming its modern form during the 1889 strike of the East London dockers and finding a political voice in the **Labour Party** at the turn of the century. Despite the gains of organized labor, the quality of urban life declined alarmingly. Perched comfortably on divans, the Victorian elite took up aid to the poor as its pet project. This paved the way for a slew of welfare programs established by the Liberal government in 1910. The peers drew the line at Lloyd George's "people's budget" and provoked a constitutional crisis. Meanwhile, pressures to alter the position of different marginalized groups just before the war proved largely ineffectual. **Suffragettes'** attempts to win women the vote by disrupting Parliament and staging hunger strikes unfortunately alienated political support for their cause.

Britain was at the height of its economic and political power in the second half of the 19th century. By Victoria's death in 1901, Britain controlled a significant portion of the world's land and the sun truly never set on the British **Empire**. Britian was also an economic leader, contolling most of the world's finance. However, the death of the Queen, whose reign lasted over 60 years (40 of those without her beloved husband Albert), for many marked the beginning of the end of Empire.

Increasing troubles with Ireland had plagued the nation for half a century and Prime Minister **William Gladstone's** attempt to introduce a Home Rule Bill for Ireland had splintered the Labor Party. Herbert Asquith traded support for Irish Home Rule for the votes of the Home Rule party, only to face the possibility of civil war in Ireland—a threat interrupted by the explosion of **World War I** (see **History,** p. 609).

WORLD WAR I AND AFTERMATH

The Great War, Britain's first continental military action in a century, scarred the British spirit with the loss of a generation and dashed Victorian dreams of a peaceful, progressive society. The war demoralized the nation; 750,000 men died and another 1.5 million were left wounded, and Britain had to suffer the further indignity of America's growing prominence in the Allied effort, in the international economy, and in world affairs, all areas that Britain had ruled without equal less than a decade before. Hope for a new beginning *within* England was generally lost—though women gained **suffrage** at this time—as a sense of aimlessness overtook the nation's politics. A succession of amusing mediocrities came to political power. The 1930s brought **depression** and mass unemployment (inertially presided over by Baldwin's National government). In December 1936, King Edward VIII shocked the world with the announcement of his abdication of kingship and empire. His decision was prompted by his desire to marry Wallace Simpson, a twice-divorced Baltimore socialite. The decade came to a close with the appeasement of **Hitler,** led by Neville "peace in our time" Chamberlain.

WORLD WAR II AND THE POST-WAR CONSENSUS

WWI, which posed little domestic threat, failed to prepare Britain for the utter devastation of Hitler's onslaught. The British were forced to face German air attacks as early as the summer of 1940, when the prolonged **Battle of Britain** began. Although the British were the ultimate victors, London and other British cities were demolished by the fiery **"Blitzkriegs"** of the early 40s. The fall of France precipitated the end of the Chamberlain government and the creation of a war cabinet led by the determined and eloquent **Winston Churchill.** After the war, the Empire made one last gasp and immediately lost its power: the British took control of parts of the old Ottoman Empire, only to lose them to the forces of democracy, nationalism and self-determinism, which the Allies themselves had unleashed.

The growing affluence and diversity of the postwar era propelled Britain to the center stage of international popular culture, and gave rise and fall to countless subcultures clustered around pop music and fashion. At the same time, Harold Wilson's Labour government introduced a number of liberal reforms, including changes of divorce and homosexuality laws and the abolition of capital punishment. Wilson also sought to drive the nation forward with technological advance, but toward the end of the 60s he became mired in the government's increasingly strained relationship with organized labor, which now represented middle-class clerical workers as much as railwaymen and Durham miners.

Britain had gradually relinquished the majority of its colonial holdings in Africa, the Middle East, and South Asia, and retreated tail-between-legs from the Suez Canal crisis. Conservative **Harold Macmillan** paved the way for the denouement of the **Empire,** hoping to win Britain its place in the **European Community,** a task completed in 1971 by Edward Heath.

Increasing economic problems that stemmed from Britain's colonial retreat led to a boom in the 70s of the theorization of "decline." Conservative and Labour governments alike floundered in attempts to curtail unemployment while maintaining 0a base level of social welfare benefits. The discovery of oil in the North Sea lifted hopes briefly, but plummeting prices hobbled its market value. Government after government wrangled with labor unions, culminating in a series of public-service strikes in early 1979, the **"Winter of Discontent,"** which stymied the Labour government.

THE THATCHER YEARS AND BEYOND

It was against this backdrop that Britain grasped at what looked like a chance for change: the admonishing "Victorian values" and nationalism of **Prime Minister Margaret "The Iron Lady" Thatcher.** Her term seemed hexed by painful economic recession, but by 1983, victory in Argentina in the **Falkland Islands** (smelling of former British imperialism) and embarrassing disarray in the Labour Party clinched her second term. Thatcher turned from the war in the islands to "the enemy within," referring to the bitter miners' strikes, while denationalizing and dismantling the welfare state with legislation and quips like, "There is no such thing as society."

Unlike her Tory and Labour predecessors, Thatcher neither believed in nor succumbed to the long-standing view that the government should focus its economic policies on reducing unemployment. The first prime minister to break with the postwar consensus, she preferred to control inflation using monetarist economic policies, rather than pursuing the means and ends of Keynesian economics. By 1987, the Tories had won over a contented sector of the affluent working class with such popular policies as the sale of public housing to its occupants, though some shuddered at the mention of "that bloody woman's" name. Thatcher's policies brought dramatic prosperity to many, but sharpened the divide between rich and poor.

Thatcher prided herself on "politics of conviction," but her stubbornness was her undoing, as she clung to the unpopular poll tax and resisted European integration. A 1990 Conservative party vote of no-confidence led to her resignation and the intraparty election of **John Major** as prime minister. The softspoken Major quietly jettisoned the poll tax and stepped more carefully around Europe. His **"Citizen's Charter"** tried to continue the reform of public services, though less radically, by gently speaking of Health Service "customers" and promising refunds to delayed rail passengers. But Major's cabinet became more occupied with predicting the end to a deep recession resulting partly from the credit-fueled 80s boom. In 1993, the British pound toppled out of the EC's monetary regulation system, embarrassing Major's government and casting doubt on Britain's place in the Community. Finally, in August of the same year, after severe division between Major and anti-treaty rebels within the Conservative Party, Britain became the last member of the EC to ratify the **Maastricht Treaty** on a closer **European Union (EU).**

Even with these Conservative debacles, Labour failed again to shed the image gained in the 70s, and the Tories under John Major won another five years in April 1992. Labour's defeat spurred the election of a new leader, Scotsman **John Smith,** and the pursuit of reform, but the beloved Smith's untimely death in May 1994 dashed Labour hopes once more. Major struggled with unpopularity; by 1995, Major's ratings were so low that he resigned as leader of the Party in order to force a leadership election. Major won the election, restoring some semblance of authority, but as the Conservatives began to lose parliamentary seats and continued to languish in the polls, the Labour Party, under the leadership of charismatic **Tony Blair,** cut ties with the labor unions, refashioned itself into the alternative for discontented voters and finally began to rise in popularity.

POLITICS TODAY

Despite tense relations with unions, the Labour Party claimed a clear victory in the May 1997 elections, garnering the biggest Labour majority ever. Labour began by announcing radical welfare and budget reform programs, but its broad popularity has been largely attributed to newly adopted centrist economic policies. In 1998, Blair has nurtured closer relations with the EU, maintained a moderate economic and social position, and was named one of *People Magazine's* 50 Most Beautiful People. All in all, not a bad year for Tony.

ROYALTY TODAY

It's not easy being Queen. Lots of money, to be sure, but no end of unabashedly publicized disaster. In 1992 (on the Queen's 45th wedding anniversary, no less) over a hundred rooms in Windsor Palace burned, and in 1993, the Queen began to pay income tax. The sad spectacle of royal life took a tragic turn in 1997 as a car carrying Princess Diana crashed in a tunnel in Paris. The princess, her companion Dodi Fayed, and the driver (later declared drunk at the time of the accident), were killed. In an ironic twist, it appears that the accident occurred as the princess was fleeing press paparazzi—the same tabloid reporters and photographers whose screaming headlines and shocking photographs have tormented the Royal family for years.

However, the fate of the royals in the coming years will depend on whether the monarchy embraces Diana's fervent populism or retreats to the private realm with traditional composure and aloofness. Though the Queen Mother is extremely well-loved, and Prince Charles' popularity is gradually increasing, royal watchers and teen magazines have turned to the young Prince William as the savior of the ailing, aging monarchy. Admired by throngs of screaming pre-pubescent girls and *Let's Go* editors alike, His Royal Sighness (actual nickname, no joke) is second in line for the throne after his father, Charles, Prince of Wales.

LITERATURE

An understanding of Britain comes more easily when accompanied by a familiarity with legends and literature. To attempt a three-page summary of British literature is, of course, absurd, but we'll give it a shot. Pick a couple titles and bring them along; the well-chosen novel or collection of poems will illuminate any sojourn into the countries of Britain.

OLD ENGLISH AND THE MIDDLE AGES

Beowulf is a triumph of Old English literature. Dated tenuously at the beginning of the 7th century, the work provides a sonorous, rhythmic testament of 5th- and 6th-century Danish culture as seen through Anglo-Saxon eyes. **Geoffrey Chaucer,** writing centuries later, tapped into the spirited and musical side of Middle English; his *Canterbury Tales* (c. 1387) remain some of the funniest—and sauciest—stories in the English canon. The anonymously authored *Gawain and the Green Knight,* another Middle English masterwork (c. 1375), plays out a simple tale of chivalry and courtliness in a mysterious and magical landscape. A more recondite medieval masterpiece is **William Langland's** *Piers Plowman* (1367-86), which turned the theme of pilgrimage into an intense, often tortured allegory. Much of the best work of this period deals with the injustice of the burgeoning class stratification.

The 14th century saw the first translation of the Bible into English by **John Wycliffe** and his followers in the 1380s. Edition after edition of the authoritative word emerged, followed by hurly-burly over exactly how authoritative that word really was. The translator **William Tyndale** fled to the Continent to finish his Biblical work, but loyalists of Henry VIII soon martyred him for his pains. A Geneva English edition rose in the mid-16th century as a steadfastly Protestant version of the Bible, prompting **King James** to set 47 translators to bring forth a Word of God the King could tolerate. The result, completed in 1611, rumbles with magnificent pace and rhetoric, and remains a literary monument to this day.

THE ENGLISH RENAISSANCE: BARDS AND BRAWLS

The 16th century also provided Britain with its most famous literary figure. Those who equate **William Shakespeare** with an English-class avalanche of whithers and wherefores would do well to know that the Bard held one of the filthiest feathers ever to scrawl the English language. An entire town bustles year-round in tribute to Shakespeare (see **Stratford-upon-Avon,** p. 262), but his inimitable plays remain the truest monuments to his genius.

Christopher Marlowe and **Ben Jonson** tag-teamed their way through the end of the 16th century: Marlowe lost his life to a dagger in a pub brawl and Jonson spent spells in jail for acts as varied as insulting Scotland and killing an actor in a sword-fight. None of this prevented Marlowe from guiding *Dr. Faustus* and *Tamburlaine* into the world of British letters or Jonson from lashing some of the most arcane Greek and Latin forms to an admirably spare, plain-spoken verse. **John Donne** (1572-1631), the pastor of London's St. Paul's Cathedral, wrote dramatic, devotional poetry; and penned erotic verse on the side. The quintessential work of this period isn't *Hamlet* (considered inferior until the 18th century), but **Robert Burton's** *Anatomy of Melancholy* (1621), which gives insight into Renaissance intellectual life.

Shakespeare Made Easy	
To have sex	*To make the* "beast with two backs."
This guy's a fat pain-in-the-ass!	"This sanguine coward, this bed-presser, this horse-back-breaker, this huge hill of flesh."
You suck!	"The devil damn thee black, thou cream-faced loon."
This guy from Iceland's a moron, and I hate him.	"Pish for thee, Iceland dog! Thou prick-ear'd cur of Iceland!"
A guy in a bar wants to fight you.	"Brass, cur! Thou damned and luxurious mountain goat, thou offer'st me brass?"
You kicked his butt and want to tell your friends all about it	"I took by the throat the circumcised dog, and smote him, thus."

THE 17TH AND 18TH CENTURIES: GODS AND MEN

The British Puritans, like their American counterparts, produced a huge volume of obsessive and beautiful literature. Blind **John Milton** in *Paradise Lost* gave Satan, Adam, and Eve a complexity the Bible did not grant them, allowing Milton "to justify the ways of God to man," as he put it. Another Puritan vision came from **John Bunyan,** a self-taught Nonconformist pastor whose *Pilgrim's Progress* charts the Christian's quest for redemption in a world awaiting the apocalypse. After the monarchy regained full power, British writers such as **Alexander Pope** and **John Dryden** led a Neoclassical revival, which yielded a new keen satire of English social and political life. Setting the tone for the second half of the 18th century, **Samuel Johnson** wrote the first definitive English dictionary, *A Journey to the Western Islands of Scotland, The Lives of the Poets,* and many philosophical essays, including the influential *Rambler* series. **Daniel Defoe,** appealing to the adventurous capitalist in us all, inaugurated the era of the English novel with his popular island-bound *Robinson Crusoe.*

THE 19TH CENTURY: BLUSH AND BITTERNESS

William Blake's mock-evangelical "proems" seem to prophesy both the rise and fall of British might; the soaring spirit of "Jerusalem" (which became an anthem of the Victorian era) coexists with the dark, grimy reality of "London." **William Wordsworth's** immense blank-verse poem *The Prelude* contains some of the greatest word-painting in the language, and helped make Wordsworth the leader of the Romantic literary movement in England. One of the finer Romantic poets, **John Keats,** died at the age of 26 of tuberculosis contracted while nursing his brother. **Alfred, Lord Tennyson** spun gorgeous verse for over a half-century. **Jane Austen** in *Pride and Prejudice* (1813) slyly criticized human self-importance, while **Matthew Arnold** (1822-88) rebelled against the industrialization of literature, trying to reinforce elitist culture against the anarchy of mass rule.

Charles Dickens's often biting, sometimes sentimental works, like *A Christmas Carol,* draw on the bleakness of his childhood as well as the more severe destitution of others. In *Wuthering Heights,* **Emily Brontë** matches the noble but limp pancake of a man, Edgar Linton, against the exquisitely ferocious, socially unmanageable Heathcliff. Her sister Charlotte, not to be outdone, created Bertha, our favorite madwoman in the attic, in *Jane Eyre.*

Thomas Hardy (1840-1928) brought the Victorian Age to an end on a dark note with the fate-ridden Wessex landscapes of *Jude the Obscure* and *Tess of the d'Urbervilles.* Like Hardy, **George Eliot (Mary Ann Evans)** lost her religious faith; her skepticism drew her to the security of traditional village life. Eliot's depictions in *Middlemarch* sweep into the entangled lives of an entire town; the novel is majestic in scope and powerful in its realization of human tragedy. **Gerard Manley Hopkins** (1844-89) revolutionized English poetry with his "sprung rhythm" verses; he is considered the chief forerunner of poetic modernism.

THE 20TH CENTURY: THE MODERN AGE

English audiences, willing or no, experienced the poignant outrage of war poets like **Siegfried Sassoon** and **Wilfred Owen.** After World War I, London became the home of artistic movements like *Blast!* and the **Bloomsbury Group,** pulling the world's intellects into its midst. **T. S. Eliot** was a Missouri boy, though he relocated to Britain later in life. It didn't help—*The Waste Land* (1922), one of the most important poems of this century, is a picture of a fragmented, motionless, precious world waiting for the end. In *To the Lighthouse,* **Virginia Woolf** explores British culture and the private, ineffable yearnings of the individual mind; *Orlando* unsettles not only language but also history and gender. **Evelyn Waugh** declined, fell, and tuned a critical eye on English society. **E. M. Forster's** half-critical, half-abashedly romantic works, among them *A Passage to India* and *Howards End,* make obvious the links between British repression, class hypocrisy, and dreams of Empire. Language and politics take on a frightening obscurity in **George Orwell's** World War II-era writing: in *1984,* fascism and communism have converged into a ravenous totalitarian state which strives to strip the world of memory and words of meaning.

The contemporary British temper has yet to emerge clearly in literature, leaving other media, including film and pop music, to pick up the slack. Instead, British literature has splintered in a thousand brilliant directions. **W.H. Auden** emerged as Eliot's successor in the mainstream of British literature, yet his disjointed and ironic meditations belong outside the broad literary current. The minimally furnished poems of **Philip Larkin** explore the aftermath of modernism, questioning the value of its psychic destruction and searching for a new home for the tired spirit. **Tom Stoppard,** originally Czech, pushes Pirandellian comedy to new limits; grim yet hysterical plays like *Rosencrantz and Guildenstern are Dead* and *Travesties* challenge the very idea of theater and communication in a post-certainty age. **Jeanette Winterson's** wry, nimble voice vaults across the 1980s, touching on topics as far-flung as Deuteronomy, lesbianism, and Napoleon's chicken-eating.

OUTSIDE THE CLASSROOM

Britain has produced a great number of less prestigious yet still influential writers whose works give expression to contemporary trends and values. **Sir Arthur Conan Doyle** immortalized London's Baker St. and fired the detective story craze. The hilarious stories of **P.G. Wodehouse** (often featuring Bertie Wooster and his butler Jeeves), and the elegant mystery novels of **Dorothy L. Sayers** and **Agatha Christie** affectionately satirize the figure of the useless British aristocrat. **James Herriot** (Alf Wight), author of *All Creatures Great and Small,* faced backlash from a flock of steadfastly unanthropomorphized sheep: they trampled him and broke his leg. **Sue Townsend's** *Diaries of Adrian Mole* sets brilliant adolescence in Thatcherite Britain. The allegories of **Richard Adams** (such as *Watership Down*) depict Britain as a wondering nation searching for new myths and new heroes, while **J.R.R. Tolkien's** engrossing fantasies prove that old British myths remain vibrant sources for the present. **C.S. Lewis's** Narnia and **Lewis Carroll's** Alice continue to enchant generations. **Ian Fleming** and **John LeCarré** perfected the Cold War espionage novel. Recently, the British literary scene has seen an influx of Booker prize-winning foreign authors; **Salman Rushdie** gives a moving, if controversial, voice to Indian migrants; **Kazuo Ishiguro** captured the nuances of a butler's life in *The Remains of the Day*; **Ben Okri,** born and educated in Nigeria, draws on the myths of Africa and Europe; and **Arundhati Roy** travels through India in *The God of Small Things*. Other prominent modern authors include **Martin Amis, Julian Barnes** and **Will Self.**

ART

British art has long been dominated by continental influences, first in the religious art of the Middle Ages, and later by artists such as **Hans Holbein** in the court of Henry VIII, and **Anthony Van Dyck** in the court of Charles I. In the 18th century, however, English artists came into their own. **William Hogarth** (1723-92) concocted his own blend of satirical didacticism in series of paintings (later released as engravings), such as "A Rake's Progress," where small dogs mimic the human drama depicted. **Thomas Gainsborough** (1727-88), versatile and prolific, produced portraits and landscapes influenced by Rubens and Van Dyck. His contemporary **Sir Joshua Reynolds** (1723-92), perhaps the most prominent portraitist of the 18th century, helped found the Royal Academy. His *Discourses Delivered at the Royal Academy* was the most important art criticism of the time.

In the 19th century, **J.M.W. Turner** (1775-1851) and **John Constable** (1776-1837) vied in glorifying the English countryside with their magnificent landscape paintings. **Sir Edwin Landseer** (1802-73) did the same for animals, crowning his achievement by sculpting the four lions at the base of Nelson's Column in Trafalgar Sq., London (see p. 102). Together with **Sir John Everett Millais** and **William Holman Hunt,** poet and artist **Dante Gabriel Rossetti** (1828-82) founded the Pre-Raphaelite Brotherhood, an artistic movement devoted to the treatment of moral and religious themes in a manner which, while supposedly unsullied by the corrupt influence of all art beginning with the Italian Renaissance, occasionally lapsed into the worst excesses of Victorian sentimentality. The art of illustration flourished in this period, typified by the output of **Sir John Tenniel** (1820-1914), who furnished the brilliant illustrations for Lewis Carroll's *Alice's Adventures in Wonderland* and produced biting cartoons for the massively popular weekly, **Punch.**

Today, non-natives seeking to typify British art may think of the sweet, pallid watercolors of Prince Charles (some of whose paintings were, appropriately, recently reproduced as postage stamps). However, the 20th century has seen such luminaries as painters **Francis Bacon** (1909-1992), German-born **Lucian Freud** (b. 1922), and **David Hockney** (b. 1937), as well as the sculptor **Henry Moore** (1898-1986), whose reclining nudes typify the humanist tradition in art. More recently, the multimedia artist **Damien Hirst** has shocked, fascinated, and appalled audiences worldwide with such installations as a shark suspended in a formaldehyde solution.

THE MEDIA

PRINT

In a culture not yet completely addicted to the telly, the influence of papers is enormous. **The Sun,** a daily Rupert Murdoch-owned tabloid better known for its page-three pin-up than for its reporting, surprisingly withdrew support from the Conservatives (*The Sun* has been credited with helping Margaret Thatcher claim victory in her re-election campaign) and backed Labour's **Tony Blair** in the May 1997 elections.

The Financial Times, printed on orange paper, does more elegantly for the City what the *Wall Street Journal* does for Manhattan. **The Times,** for centuries a model of thoughtful discretion and mild infallibility, has turned Tory under the leadership of Rupert "Buy It" Murdoch. **The Daily Telegraph** (dubbed "Torygraph") is fairly conservative and old-fashioned; **The Independent** lives up to its name. Of the tabloids, *The Daily Mail, The Daily Express,* and *The Standard* (the only evening paper) make serious attempts at popular journalism, while the *Daily Mirror, News of the World,* the *Star,* and *Today* are as shrill and lewd as *The Sun.* The best international news is in *The Times, The Manchester Guardian,* and *The Independent.*

On Sundays, *The Sunday Times, The Sunday Telegraph, The Independent on Sunday,* and the highly polished *Observer* publish multi-section papers with glossy magazines. Sunday editions offer detailed arts, sports, and news coverage, together with a few more "soft bits" than their daily counterparts. Although they share close association with their sister dailies, they're actually separate newspapers, with a subtly distinctive look and style.

The popular *Viz* parodies modern prejudices and hypocrisies with unashamedly outrageous comic strips. World affairs are covered with a refreshing candor and surreptitious wit by **The Economist. The New Statesman** on the left and **The Spectator** on the right cover politics and the arts with verve and sense. *Private Eye* is subversive, hilarious, and overtly political. Britain also boasts some of the best music mags in the world: *Melody Maker* and *New Musical Express* trace the latest trends with often hilarious wit (check these for concert news). *Q* covers a broader spectrum in excellent detail, while *Gramophone* focuses on classical music. The indispensable London journal **Time Out** is the most comprehensive calendar guide to the city and features fascinating pieces on British life and culture. If you're curious to see who'll be gracing the cover of *Rolling Stone* next year, pick up *The Face,* the U.K.'s ultimate scene mag.

RADIO AND TELEVISION

The **BBC** established its reputation for fairness and wit with its radio services: BBC1 has ceded responsibilities of news coverage to its cousin BBC4, but continues to feature rock-and-roll institution John Peel. BBC2 has easy listening and light talk shows; BBC3 broadcasts classical music. AM is called Medium Wave (MW) in Britain. Each town and region in the country is equipped with a variety of local commercial broadcasting services.

Soaps and Suds

Like their American compatriots, the British are addicted to a number of soaps broadcast over the airwaves. Britain pioneered the soap opera on radio with *The Archers,* the longest-running soap in the world. Set in the idyllic fictional village of Ambridge, *The Archers* chronicles the escapades of a farming family in its weekday broadcasts at on Radio 4. It is television, however, that has become the preferred purveyor of soaps. Most popular in Britain are *Eastenders* on BBC and *Coronation Street* on ITV. They chronicle the lives of rough-and-tumble working-class neighborhoods in London and Manchester, respectively. The public enthusiasm for these TV soaps has infected even the once-pastoral *Archers,* who now boast their own share of disasters and illicit love-affairs.

Television owners in England pay a tax to support the advertisement-free activities of BBC TV. Close association with the government has not hampered innovation. Once home of **Monty Python's Flying Circus,** BBC TV broadcasts on two national channels. BBC1 carries news at 1, 6, and 9pm as well as various Britcoms and popular Australian soaps. Sheep-dog trials are telecast on **BBC2,** along with cultural programs. **ITV,** Britain's established commercial network and the only all-night channel, carries drama and comedy, along with its own news. Channel 4 has highly respected arts programming and a fine news broadcast at 7pm on weeknights; they also broadcast popular American shows (including *Friends, Frasier,* and *ER*). Channel 5, the newest channel, features late-night sports shows. This web of national programming is supplemented by local stations. Parliament was introduced to television in late 1989: try to catch a session of Question Time, the refreshingly hostile parliamentary interrogation of the prime minister. The BBC alternative is Murdoch's **Sky TV** which shows a selection of American shows as well as some uniquely British programs like *Dream Team,* a football-based drama.

FILM

British film has endured an uneven history, marked by cycles of confidence and expansion followed by decline and stagnation. The early dominance of the American studio system lured British talent to Hollywood. Charlie Chaplin left the English vaudeville scene to produce some of the world's greatest comedy. Some of his best are *The Kid* (1921), *The Gold Rush* (1925), and *City Lights* (1931). Sir Laurence Olivier directed and starred in a screen version of *Hamlet* (1948), which is still without parallel. Cary Grant and Vivien Leigh, two of America's biggest stars, were British by birth. The indigenous British film industry was once generously subsidized by the government, but the conservative upsurge in the late 70s and 80s led to a decrease in production and a another drain of talent to America. Nevertheless, British film, whether assisted by outside investors and talent, has had a formidable impact on world cinema.

Early British film was heavily influenced by two directors and one incomparable actor. Master of suspense Alfred Hitchcock snared audiences with his *39 Steps* (1935) and *The Lady Vanishes* (1938), made in Britain, as well as a slew of memorable American films, including *Vertigo* (1958), *Psycho* (1960), and *The Birds* (1963). David Lean's meticulous attention to detail in *Brief Encounter* (1945) and *Oliver Twist* (1948) made him the preeminent British director of the 40s. The brilliant pre-*Star Wars* **Sir Alec Guinness** made a string of wickedly funny films including *Kind Hearts and Coronets* (1950), *The Man in the White Suit* (1951), and *The Lavender Hill Mob* (1951). Later he would win an Oscar for David Lean's *Bridge on the River Kwai,* star along with Peter O'Toole in David Lean's *Lawrence of Arabia,* and play the narrator Zhivago in *Dr. Zhivago* (1965), a film by David Lean.

The New Wave movement in the 1960s focused on the contemporary working-class experience, producing such cinematic adaptations as John Osborne's play *Look Back in Anger* (1959), directed by Tony Richardson. Around the same time, **John Schlesinger** directed a series of films, including *Billy Liar* (1963), deflecting working class angst into fantastical comedy. With the success of **Tony Richardson's** *Tom Jones* (1963), starring Albert Finney, the New Wave movement ended, eclipsed by the phenomenon of "Swingin' London," and an upsurge in international interest in British culture. American director Richard Lester made rock stars into film stars in the **Beatles'** *A Hard Day's Night* (1963), Michael Caine shagged his way to the top in Lewis Gilbert's *Alfie* (1966), and Scot **Sean Connery** drank the first of many martinis, shaken not stirred, as **James Bond** in *Dr. No* (1962). As the hopes and promises of the decade began to look a little tarnished, elements of British cinema took on a darker edge. Expatriate **Stanley Kubrick** went beyond the infinite without leaving England in *2001* (1969)—but descended into mayhem in *A Clockwork Orange* (1971). Along with Lindsay Anderson, director of *If...* (1968), Kubrick exposed the restlessness of British youth and their discontent with society.

After stagnating through the 1970s, British film returned with a vengeance on Oscar night, 1982, seizing Best Picture for **Hugh Hudson's** *Chariots of Fire.* The next year **Richard Attenborough's** *Gandhi* swept the Oscars and British film was again thrust to the forefront of international cinema. More recently, actor-director-writer-producer **Kenneth Branagh** has focused his talents on adapting Shakespeare. His critically acclaimed films include *Henry V* (1989), *Much Ado About Nothing* (1993), *Othello* (1995), and the lengthy *Hamlet* (1996). Often co-star and former wife, **Emma Thompson,** has been apotheosized for her own version of Jane Austen's *Sense and Sensibility.* Most of Austen's novels, along with those of E.M. Forster, have made their way onto the big screen in recent years. Director-producer team **Merchant Ivory** has put out several Forster films, including *A Room with a View* (1986) and *Howard's End* (1993). In 1996, the thick Scottish brogues and heroin escapades of *Trainspotting* were all the rage. The most notable British films of the 1990s seems to fall into two genres: historical Merchant-Ivory-ish epics like **Anthony Minghella's** *The English Patient,* and small touching comedies like Anthony Minghella's *Truly, Madly, Deeply.* In the non-Minghella category, recent comedies include Mike Newell's *Four Weddings and a Funeral* (1994) and Peter Catteneo's *The Full Monty* (1997) which bared the comedic underbelly of the Sheffield unemployed.

The British are also noted for their small offbeat, independent films. A few directors to get you started are **Michael Apted** whose documentary series *7 Up, 14 Up, 21 Up, 28 Up,* and *35 Up* has followed a group of Britons from childhood to the present, recording their expectation and the often sad results. If he films it, the next installment (you guess the title) is due out around the millenium. **Peter Greenaway** brings a disconcerting feel to British cinema; his *The Cook, The Thief, His Wife and Her Lover* (1990) is cutting edge and definitely not family fare. **Mike Leigh,** whose arresting *Secrets and Lies* (1995) was nominated for an Oscar, is perhaps the most inventive of the indie filmmakers; he casts actors, works with them to create characters in rehearsal, then crafts a plot around them.

In the 80s and 90s a pack of British actors have ascended to worldwide cultural preeminence. Welshman **Sir Anthony Hopkins** has played psychopaths, presidents and psychopathic presidents, while dimpled **Hugh Grant** remains popular in remarkably homogenous roles, despite notorious traffic violations. **Helena Bonham Carter** reigns as the queen of the period drama and **Kristen Scott Thomas** exudes a remote grace, no matter what the setting. The next generation of British actors are led at the box office by the unsinkable **Kate Winslet** and Scot **Ewan MacGregor,** the next Obi-Wan. As yet unsullied by big Hollywood (and big paychecks) are indie faves Gary Oldman, Tim Roth, Minnie Driver and Kate Beckinsale.

MUSIC

CLASSICAL

Britain was long called "a land without music," a tag not entirely deserved. Reflecting the court-centered English Renaissance, Queen Elizabeth I pitched in not merely by writing a bit of poetry, but also by funding art of various sorts, including music. **William Byrd** wrote magnificent pieces for both Anglican and Roman churches. **Morley, Weelkes,** and **Wilbye** revamped madrigals; **John Dowland** wrote lachrymose works for lute. **Henry Purcell** was Britain's best-known composer for centuries—his opera *Dido and Aeneas* is still performed. British hospitality welcomed Handel, Mozart (who wrote his first symphony in Chelsea), and Haydn (whose last cluster of symphonies is named "London"). **Gilbert and Sullivan's** operettas have been loved since the late 19th century for their puns, social satire, farce, and pomp. Though the pair were rumored to hate each other, they produced such gems as *The Mikado, H.M.S. Pinafore,* and *The Pirates of Penzance.* Serious music began a "second renaissance" under **Edward Elgar,** whose bombast is outweighed by moments of quiet eloquence, like "Nimrod" in his *Enigma Variations.* **Delius** had his own take on musical impressionism, while **Gustav "The Planets" Holst** adapted Neoclassical methods and folk materials to Romantic moods.

William Walton and **Ralph Vaughan Williams** brought musical modernism to Britain in the 20th century; Walton's *First Symphony,* Vaughan Williams's *Sixth Symphony,* and Havergal Brian's *Gothic* are arguably three of this century's finest scores. **Benjamin Britten's** *Young Person's Guide to the Orchestra* continues to introduce classical music to young and old alike. **Michael Tippett** wrote operas, four symphonies, and the oratorio *A Child of Our Time,* for which he asked T. S. Eliot to pen the words; Eliot told Tippett he could do a better job himself. Peter Maxwell Davies, Harrison Birtwistle, Brian Ferneyhough, and Robert Simpson are all important British postwar composers.

GREAT BRITAIN

GREAT BRITAIN

THE GOLDEN AGE: CLASSIC ROCK

After World War II, imported American rock and jazz provided musical inspiration for the first wave of "British Invasion" bands. The **Beatles** spun out the songs everyone seems to know and appeared to be at the front of every musical and cultural trend. **The Rolling Stones** became their nastier, harder-edged answer, while **The Kinks** voiced horror at the American vulgarity that seemed, to them, to have crushed Little England. **The Who** began as Kinks-like popsters, then expanded into "rock operas" like *Tommy* (lately a Broadway hit) and the better *Quadrophenia,* which chronicled the fights in Brighton between "rockers" (who liked leather jackets and America) and "mods" (who liked scooters, speed, androgyny, and the Who).

Psychedelic drugs and high hopes produced a flurry of great tunes by bands like the short-lived **Creation** from '66 to '68. White British adapters of the blues—most famously the **Yardbirds**—spawned guitar heroes such as **Eric Clapton** (Cream) and **Jimmy Page** (Led Zeppelin), who dominated mass markets in the early 70s. The same period's "art-rock" (Yes, **Pink Floyd,** Roxy Music) was at times exciting, at times dreadful. British staples like **Queen** and **Elton John** found an international audience. Working-class "skinheads" adopted the sounds and aggression of Jamaican reggae and ska; later skins would split into socialist/anti-racist and right-wing/neo-fascist factions, both propelled by stripped-down rock called "oi."

THE SILVER AGE: PUNK AND POP

While **David Bowie** flitted through personae, "pub rock" groups tried to return rock to the people—and in London, a King's Road entrepreneur organized the **Sex Pistols** to get publicity for his boutique, "Sex." With "Sex's" clothes and Johnny Rotten's snarl, the Pistols indelibly marked music and culture. **The Clash** made their punk explicit, anti-Thatcherite, political; the all-female **Slits** mixed theirs with reggae. "Do it yourself" was the order of the day: untouched, and often untouchable, by the big corporations, the second wave of punks started their own clubs, record labels, and studios, creating the **International Pop Underground** that persists to this day.

Unemployment gave Northerners the time to form bands and the dire straits to inspire them. The fans who sent it up the charts were surprised to learn that the Buzzcocks' **Pete Shelley** wrote "Ever Fallen in Love?" about a man. **Joy Division** (which became New Order) and Factory Records made Manchester echo with gloomily poetic rock and graphic design. Leeds' Mekons stayed true to punk's roots, and Gang of Four's *Entertainment!* chewed up funk and reggae to spit out a profound Marxist critique of capital, work, and sex. Birmingham's **Au Pairs** asked feminist questions over a hokey backbeat, and that grim city's leftist ska bands, like the Selecter and the Specials, took their "two-tone" style to the people. **Elvis Costello,** Squeeze, and the Jam found that punk and ska had cleared the ground for smart pop, which stayed bitingly British even as it took over world charts.

Melancholy stylishness like **Felt** and **Eyeless in Gaza** passed unnoticed through the 80s, but **The Smiths** of Manchester and **The Cure** shook teens everywhere. Bristol's Subway Records sent **Flatmates, Razorcuts,** and **Rosehips** spinning winsomely across the land. **King of the Slums** bowed and scraped before the electric violin; sweetly loud **My Bloody Valentine** were much-copied in '91-92. Oxford's **Tallulah Gosh** idealized childhood in million-mile-an-hour pop; regrouped as Heavenly, they and Bristol-based Sarah Records inspired self-proclaimed "boys" and "girls" to cast aside volume and swagger for clean tunes and last-chance tries at innocence.

THE MODERN AGE: SYNTH-POP, DANCE AND RAVE

Alas, punk went mainstream and died an angry death with Sid Vicious, leaving the British club scene increasingly receptive to the burgeoning field of electronic music. Prompted by the keyboard swagger of Germans Kraftwerk and Einstürzende Neubaten, a swarm of bubbly New Romantics, such as **The Human League,** A Flock of Seagulls, and Kajagoogoo, took to the English stage. While Brits **Duran Duran** and **Eurythmics** dominated the American charts through the 80s, synth-pop bands like

Erasure, Depeche Mode, New Order, and The Pet Shop Boys refined the electronic message and kept the home crowds dancing through the night.

In the late 80s, a crop of guitar noise bands from Manchester helped to create the early rave movement. Mop-topped, sweaty youths dropped ecstasy and danced maniacally to the Stone Roses, Primal Scream, and The Charlatans. The sound was soon copied, and innovative British acts like Curve and Ride were overshadowed by toss-off one-hit wonders like EMF and Jesus Jones. The much-hyped, much-adored London Suede rose and fell (and rose and fell), replaced by the "Brit-pop" sounds of Blur, Pulp, James, The Verve, and the Beatles-esque Oasis. The Spice Girls have taken Brits by storm. The spunky, leggy, (dare we say) spicy girls have exploded onto the music scene, selling more albums than any other U.K. group, save the Beatles. To the dismay of fine music lovers everywhere, Ginger Spice (née Sexy Spice) has announced her intention to pursue a solo career, but never fear, the spicy 1997 movie *Spiceworld*, is now available on video. Brits are equally in love with spicy boy-bands like Take That and East 17, also sadly defunct. Also ravaging the London music scene are several Scottish groups, including Texas, Mogwai, and Arab Strap.

Although bands abound in the U.K., many listen mostly to dance and electronic music. The wildly successful rave scene (and the synthetic drugs that accompanied it) exploded across Europe. In Britain, as elsewhere, DJs replaced traditional artists as the primary music messenger, though groups such as Orbital, the Orb, and The Future Sound of London still managed to rack up hits. Originating from the repetitive rhythms of techno, rave music exploded into numerous toe-tappin' subcultures; house, jungle, breakbeat, trance, ambient, drum 'n' bass, and trip-hop rule much of the club scene. Trip-hop in particular has become distinctively British, with artists like Massive Attack and Portishead trickling into the mainstream. Similarly popular are electronic music demigods The Prodigy and the Chemical Brothers. Despite the fleeting fame of one-hit-wonder bands like Right Said Fred and Chumbawamba, Tricky and his trip-hop/electronic brethren are primed to lead the next invasion.

FOOD

> English cooking, like the English climate, is a training for life's unavoidable hardships.
>
> —R. P. Lister

British cuisine's deservedly modest reputation redeems itself in the few specialties without which the world's palate would be sadly incomplete. Chances are you may well leave the island addicted to rice pudding (a creamy dessert), Yorkshire pudding (not a creamy dessert), British-style baked beans, shortbread, digestive biscuits, or the inestimable Hobnob (plain or chocolate-covered).

Britain is a nation of carnivores, and the best native dishes are roasts—beef, lamb, and Wiltshire hams. Many proprietors will prepare vegetarian meals on request, if the incessance of meat is too much for you. Vegetables—often boiled into a flavorless, textureless, colorless mass—are generally the weakest part of the meal; ask for a salad instead (though remember that the word "salad" often means a mixture of mayonnaise and something else, the equivalent of American "tuna salad" or "egg salad"). Meat isn't just for dinner, either; the British like their breakfasts meaty and cholesterol-filled. The famous English breakfast, served in most B&Bs across Britain, consists of orange juice, cereal, eggs, bacon, sausage, toast (and/or fried bread), butter,

Flakes and Smarties

British food has character (of one sort or another), and the traditional menu is a mad hodgepodge of candy, crisps, yeasts, and squashes. Britain has a greater variety of **candy** for sale than most countries. Brands to watch out for include Flake by Cadbury, Crunchies (which are made out of honeycombed magic), and the ever-popular Smarties. Watch out for the orange ones—they're made of orange chocolate. Potato chips, or **crisps** as they are known in England, are not just salted, but come in a range of flavors, including Prawn Cocktail, Beef, Chicken, Fruit 'n' Spice, and the more traditional Salt & Vinegar. All this sugar and salt can be washed down with pineapple and grapefruit flavored soda Lilt or a can of Ribena, a red currant syrup which has to be diluted with water. This latter beverage belongs to a family of drinks known as **squash,** all of which are diluted before consumption. But the food that expatriate Britons miss most is **Marmite,** a yeast extract which is spread on bread or toast. If you weren't fed Marmite as a baby, you'll never appreciate it; most babies don't either.

marmalade, grilled tomatoes (and/or mushrooms), and (in winter) porridge. You will probably want tea to wash all this down; unlike its French and Italian counterparts, British coffee is far from exceptional.

The British like their desserts exceedingly sweet, but even if you shy from sugar, try one of the glorious British puddings, which are nothing like American pudding."Boiled in a pail, tied in the tail of an old bleached shirt, so hot that they hurt," some of the best varieties are bread pudding, **Christmas pudding,** treacle tart, Spotted Dick, and steamed castle pudding, all served with thick jams and syrups. Perhaps the most blatant misnomer in the English language is **trifle,** a wondrous combination of the best things in life—cake, custard, jam, whipped cream, and fresh fruit (strawberries are best). Scones, Jaffa cakes, and rich Dundee fruitcake are all tasty side-effects of the British sweet tooth.

Pub grub (food served in bars; lunch and dinner only, and often only during certain hours) is fast, filling, and a fine option when all else is closed or vandalishly expensive. Hot meals vary from Cornish **pasties** (PAH-stee; meat and vegetable wrapped in pastry) to **steak and kidney pie** with vegetables. The inexpensive "ploughman's lunch" is simply cheese, bread, pickle, chutney, and a tomato; contrary to common belief, it is not traditional British country fare but the product of a 1960s advertising campaign. **Fish and chips** (American "french fries"), a perennial favorite, are traditionally served in newsprint, dripping with grease, salt, and vinegar.

In **restaurants,** watch the fine print: a perfectly inexpensive entree may be only one item on a bill supplemented with side dishes, shamefully priced drinks, VAT, minimum per-person charges, and an occasional 50p–£2 cover charge.

Outdoor markets and **supermarkets** (such as Safeway, Sainsbury, the Co-op, and Tesco) sell suitable fare for picnics. Excellent options include cheese (Stilton—very, very sharp; Double Gloucester—very sharp; or Cheddar—sharp and cheap), apples (Cox's pippins are tasty), and a package of Hobnobs (oaty biscuits). Find a suitably picturesque view. As an alternative to British food, try Chinese, Greek, and especially Indian cuisines—Britain offers some of the best *tandoori* food outside of India, particularly in London and the larger northern cities.

TEA

British "tea" refers both to a drink and a **social ritual.** The drink (various blends include **Earl Grey,** Darjeeling, Lapsang Suchong, and Special Swamp Water) is served strong and milky; if you want it any other way, say so. The social ritual centers around a meal. Afternoon **high tea** includes cooked meats, salad, sandwiches, and pastries. Fans of Victorianism will appreciate the **dainty cucumber sandwiches** served at classy tea joints like Harrods and the Savoy Hotel in London. Outside the capital, dinner moves to noontime and tea becomes the evening meal, often served with a huge pot of the liquid. **Cream tea,** a specialty of Cornwall and Devon, includes toast, shortbread, crumpets, scones, and jam, accompanied by clotted cream (a cross between whipped cream and butter). Most Brits take short tea breaks each day, mornings ("elevenses") and afternoons (around 4pm). Sunday takes the cake for best tea day; the indulgent can while away a couple of hours over a pot of Earl Grey, a pile of buttered scones, and the Sunday supplements.

PUBS AND BEER

> What three things does drink especially provoke?—Marry, sir, nose-painting, sleep, and urine.
>
> —The Porter in *Macbeth*

"As much of the history of England has been brought about in public houses as in the House of Commons," said Sir William Harcourt. You may not witness history in the making, but you will certainly absorb the spirit of the land with a stop at a local tavern. The pub's importance as a social institution is reflected in its careful furnishings. Mahogany walls appear ancient and are often intricately carved; velvet-covered benches face a crackling fireplace under brass ceiling fans and chandeliers. Indeed, such establishments resemble the private living rooms they have come to replace. Many pubs are centuries old, and each has a distinctive history, ambience, and clientele. Pub crawls are the British equivalent of bar hopping.

Beer is the standard pub drink, and it is "pulled" from the tap at room temperature into pint glasses (nearly 20oz.) or the more modest half-pints. A request for "a beer" will get you a full pint, and it won't be the blond fizzy lager to which Americans are accustomed. **Bitter** is the staple of British beer, named for its sharp, hoppy aftertaste. Fullers and Youngs are slightly fruity on the palate, while Abbot and Ruddles are dark and full-bodied. Other worthy brews include Courage, Directors, Tetleys, John Smith, and Samuel Smith. "Real ale," naturally carbonated (unlike most beers) and drawn from a barrel, retains a die-hard cult of connoisseurs in the shadow of giant corporate breweries. Brown, pale, and India pale ales—less common varieties—all have a relatively heavy flavor with noticeable hop. **Stout** is rich, dark, and creamy; try standing a match on the silky foam head of the Irish **Guinness.** Most draught ales and stouts are served at room temperature, so if you can't stand the heat, try a **lager,** the European equivalent of American beer. German, Dutch, American, and even Mexican imports are steadily gaining acceptance, especially among trendier crowds. **Cider,** a fermented apple juice served sweet or dry, is one potent, cold and tasty alternative to beer. Especially succulent brands include Strongbow, Blackthorn, Bulmer's Woodpecker, Red Rock, and Diamond White. Other options include the **shandy,** a refreshing combination of beer and fizzy lemonade; **black velvet,** a mating of stout and champagne; **black and tan,** stout and beer (layered like a parfait); and **snakebite,** a murky mix of lager and cider.

Those who don't drink alcohol should savor the pub experience all the same; Cidona, a non-alcoholic cider, and BritVic fruit juices are served. Along with food and drink, pubs also often host games. Traditional pub games include darts, pool, and snooker (billiards played on a larger table with smaller balls). More recently, a brash and bewildering army of video games, fruit (slot) machines, and extortionate CD jukeboxes has invaded many pubs.

Visitors will learn to their dismay that pubs close relatively early, especially in England. Generally, drinks are served 11am-11pm Monday to Saturday, noon-10:30pm on Sunday (though most take a closing break from about 3-7pm on Sundays). A bell 10 minutes or more before closing time signifies "last orders." T.S. Eliot knew the special agony of pub closings: many a drunkard has argued that the most painful words in all *The Waste Land* come in its second part, with the publican-god's cry, "HURRY UP PLEASE IT'S TIME." Whether or not patrons consider the existential implications of the call, it does signal that just a few minutes remain for them to finish their beers before chairs go up and lights go down. The drinking age in Britain is (a recently more enforced) 18.

SPORTS

Many evils may arise which God forbid.
—*King Edward II, banning football in London, 1314*

Football (soccer) is the national game in Britain. Pitches (fields) are everywhere; tiny grounds dot the countryside, and grand, storied stadiums dominate cities. The English Football Association (FA), formed in 1863, is divided into a number of leagues. At the top, the 20 teams in the Premier League are populated with world-class players from Britain and abroad. At the end of the season, the teams with the worst records in the Premiership face "relegation," or demotion to the First Division whose top teams are "promoted." The same process affects the teams of the Second Division, Third Division, and non-league clubs.

Perennially at the top of the table (standings) are Manchester United, Liverpool, and Arsenal. British teams have traditionally suffered at the hands of their more polished European counterparts in Germany and Italy. However, English football seems to be on the upswing. Despite poor national team performances in recent World Cups, in 1998, Chelsea, a British team, was able to capture the prestigious Winners Cup, defeating the best teams in Europe.

British soccer culture is truly unique. British football draws huge crowds—over half a million people attend professional matches in Britain every Saturday from mid-August to May. Though there are almost 100 professional teams in England alone, each club commands fierce fan loyalty; supporters routinely traverse the length and breadth of the island to watch their local teams play. Fans sporting painted faces and dressed in team colors make themselves heard with uncanny synchronized cheering. Immense popularity and excessive enthusiasm have, however, proved problematic: mass violence and vandalism at stadiums have dogged the game for years. In a particularly horrific incident in 1989, 95 people were crushed to death in Sheffield after a surge of fans tried to push their way into the grounds. The atmosphere in the stands has become a bit tamer now that most stadiums sell only seats rather than spaces in the once infamous "terraces."

According to legend, **rugby** was born one glorious day in 1823 when an inspired (or slightly confused) Rugby College student picked up a soccer ball and ran it into the goal. Since then, rugby has evolved into a complex and subtle game. The first Rugby Union was formed in 1871, and professional play started in 1895. **Rugby League,** a professional sport using modified rules and played by teams of 13 was soon formed. Now, the rugby world is separated into the Union (amateurs) and the League (professionals). A *melée* of blood, mud, and drinking songs, "rugger" is exciting to watch. The game is played by teams of 15 with no non-injury substitutions and little stoppage of play. An oval shaped ball, slightly larger than an American football, is carried, kicked or passed backward until the team is able to touch the ball down past the goal line or kick it through the uprights. The most striking play in rugby is the scrum which resembles a woven knot of large, sweaty men seething around a ball. Both teams' "forwards" (the big guys) try to kick the ball to the "backs" who grab it and run like hell before Hugh, the bloke with half his teeth knocked out, breaks free to flatten him. The season runs from September to May. The culmination of international rugby is the Rugby World Cup, set to be played in Cardiff, Wales, in 1999.

Cricket remains a confusing spectacle to most North Americans. Though played with a ball and a bat (a larger, flatter version of its American counterpart), the game is only a very, very distant cousin of the American favorite, baseball. The impossibility of explaining its rules to an American has virtually become a national in-joke in England, and though cricket often seems incomprehensible to those not raised on Marmite, crumpets, and full English breakfasts, its rules are actually quite simple. Teams are composed of 11 players. The game is played on a 22 yd. green, marked by two **wickets** at each end. (Wickets consist of three vertical stumps and two bails.) One team acts as **batsmen** and the other as **fielders.** The batting team sends up its first two batsmen. Their goal is to make as many runs as they can while protecting their wicket; as the fielders run for the ball, the two batsmen switch places. If they switch once, they score a single; twice a double; and so on. The goal of the fielders is to try to get the batsmen out by hitting or **taking** the wickets with the ball or by catching the ball while it is in the air. A good pitcher or **bowler** will force the batsmen to protect his wicket. Once the batsmen is knocked out, the next one in the batting order replaces him until the whole team has been up to bat. Then the teams switch places. Innings can take a long time: teams have been known to score 500 runs during one inning. In a normal match, both teams bat only twice. Once a synonym for civility, cricket's image has been dulled. Purists disdain one-day matches; "first class" matches amble on rather ambiguously for days, often ending in draws.

The **Henley Royal Regatta,** the most famous annual crew race in the world, conducts itself both as a proper social affair (like Ascot) and a popular corporate social event (like Wimbledon). The event transpires on the last weekend in June and the first in July. Saturday is the most popular and busiest day, but some of the best races are the Sunday finals. The **Boat Race** (tel. (0171) 379 3234), between eights from Oxford (p. 219) and Cambridge (p. 272), enacts the traditional rivalry between the schools. Old-money alums, fortified by strawberries and champagne, will sport their crested blazers and college ties to cheer the teams on April 3, 1999.

When **tennis** was just becoming popular at the end of the 15th century, Henry VII played in black velvet. As the game developed, white became the traditional color for players to wear on the court (better to sweat in, cooler). Today, the era of wearing exclusively white on the court is over, but the fun continues. For two weeks starting in late June (June 21-July 4 in 1999), tennis buffs all over the world focus their attention on **Wimbledon,** tennis's only Grand Slam event played on grass.

Prized for their impressive speed and their astonishing grace, **horses** have pleased riders and observers alike in several arenas. Princess Anne competed in the 1976 Olympics in **eventing,** which involves three days of competition in dressage, cross country and show-jumping. Competitions take place frequently; ask at a local stable. In late June, **polo** devotees flock to the **Royal Windsor Cup.**

Even those who aren't too fond of the four-legged beasts agree that watching a troupe of horses clamber down the track can get almost anyone's adrenaline pumping. The **Royal Gold Cup Meeting** at **Ascot** occurs each summer in the second half of June. An important society event, some see it as essentially an excuse for Brits of all strata to indulge in drinking and gambling while wearing silly hats. The Queen takes up residence at Windsor Castle to lavish her full attentions on this socio-political vaudeville act. In July, the George VI and Queen Elizabeth Diamond Stakes are run here; during the winter Ascot hosts steeplechase meetings. Top hats, gypsies, and Pimms also distinguish the **Derby** (DAR-bee; tel. (01483) 202050, tickets tel. (01372) 470047), to be run on June 5, 1999 at **Epsom** Racecourse, Epsom, Surrey. **Greyhound racing**—a.k.a. "the dogs"—is the second most popular spectator sport in Britain, after football. It's a quick and reliable way to lose money—races last all of 20 seconds. Almost all races start at 7:30pm.

All the King's Horses

Questions of social class are always close at hand. Horse racing's epithet—the "Sport of Kings"—is hardly hyperbolic; the sport has long enjoyed royal patronage. Newmarket was established as a major racing center under James I; Edward VII liked nothing better than a day spent relishing what he called "the glorious uncertainty of the turf," and watching his famed wonder-horse, Diamond Jubilee. Tennis has long been accorded a similar position, with the Duke and Duchess of Kent participating in the winner's ceremony. Those who frequent such events, sipping Pimms and indulging in strawberries at Ascot, are known as "toffs." The word is of uncertain origin, perhaps derived from the tassels worn by well-to-do students. Sports like football, by contrast, are often preferred by people known as "yobs." "Yob" comes from the word "boy" spelled backwards, a reversing process known as backslang, used to obfuscate a word's meaning.

ENGLAND

London

A man who is tired of London is tired of life; for there is in London all that life can afford.

—Samuel Johnson

Those who journey to London expecting friendly, rosy-cheeked, frumpy, tea-drinking, Queen-loving gardeners may be astounded to find that London is equally the province of slinkily dressed, buff young things who spend their nights lounging around shadowy Soho cafes. London is an irrepressibly international city, the center of rave culture, the Britpop explosion, and countless other ripples which float swingers the world over. At the same time, those expecting non-stop hedonism may run headlong into an exquisitely British sense of propriety, morality, and culture. Pubs close at eleven, MPs resign over the smallest sexual peccadillos, and some of the hottest pick-up scenes are at the bookstores. Drunken revelers returning from a late night may pass fur-hatted guards on their way to work wearing the blazing scarlet coats which American colonial militiamen found such easy targets in 1775.

GETTING IN AND OUT

■ From the Airport

With planes landing every 47 seconds, **Heathrow Airport** (tel. (0181) 759 4321) in Hounslow, Middlesex, is the world's busiest international airport. The bureaux de change in each terminal are open daily. The cheapest way to reach central London from Heathrow is by **Underground** (Piccadilly line; about 45min. to central London), with one stop for terminals 1, 2, and 3, and another for terminal 4. To reach **Victoria Station,** transfer at Gloucester Rd. or South Kensington to a District Line or Circle Line train heading east. At Victoria, you'll find a blue **Tourist Information Centre** with an accommodations service, currency exchange, and help with transportation connections. Introduced in the summer of 1998, the **Heathrow Express** travels between Heathrow and Paddington Station every 15 minutes (15min., 5:10am-11:40pm, £10); the express train departs from Heathrow terminal #1, 2, 3, and 4.

London Regional Transport's **Airbus** (tel. 222 1234) makes the one-hour trip from Heathrow to central points in the city. The Airbus A1 runs to Victoria, stopping at Hyde Park Corner, Harrods, and the Earl's Ct. tube station (daily 5am-9pm). Airbus A2 runs to Russell Sq. and King's Cross stations, with stops at Euston, Baker St., Marble Arch, Paddington, Bayswater, Queensway, Notting Hill Gate, Holland Park, and Shepherd's Bush (to King's Cross daily 6:40am-10:40pm, to Russell Sq. daily 5:20am-10:50pm). (Prices for both buses £6, return £10; children £4 and £6.) **Airbus Direct** is a faster bus service (same prices as Airbus) that stops only in the center of the City and at Hyde Park Corner.

Gatwick Airport in West Sussex (tel. (01293) 535353) is London's second-busiest airport. Heathrow is not close to the city and Gatwick is even farther. A number of 24-hour restaurants and bureaux de change are located in both the North and South Terminals. From Gatwick, take the **BR Gatwick Express** (tel. (0345) 484950) train to Victoria Station (daily 5am-midnight every 15min., midnight-5am approx. every 30min.; one-month open return £19). **National Express coaches** run between Gatwick and Victoria (1hr., 5:05am-8:20pm every hr., £8.50, return £11).

Taxis that congregate outside the terminals charge a fee based upon distance. Fares from central London to Heathrow run at least £30; from central London to Gatwick, around £50-60. Travelers also should consider using **Airport Transfers,** a private chauffeur service (tel. 403 2228). For a flat rate, London Airways will take up to four people from either airport to any central London destination (£20-30 per car from Heathrow, £47 per car from Gatwick).

International flights are now arriving in **Stansted Airport,** northeast of London in Essex (tel. (01279) 680500). Stansted is served by British Rail's **Stansted Express** to Liverpool St. Station (40min., 3 per hr., M-Sa 5am-11pm, Su 7am-11pm, £10.40).

■ From the Train and Bus Stations

British Rail (BR) trains leave London from the major stations (see chart below for details). Confirm prices and London stations at the new, centralized **British Rail information number,** which functions 24 hours, is (0345) 484 950. **To Europe,** try (0990) 848848, or for **Eurostar** (through the Chunnel), call (0345) 881881.

All mainline stations sell British Rail's various Railcards, which offer regular discounts on train travel (see **By Train,** p. 32). A **Network Card** gives the same discount for travel in the Network Southeast area. The **Network Rover** allows unlimited travel on Network Southeast for the daytripper (3 weekend days £47; 7 days £69; children half-price). Ask at any mainline station.

Station	Destinations
Euston	Bangor, Birmingham, Carlisle, Chester, Coventry, Glasgow, Holyhead, Inverness, Liverpool, Llandudno, Manchester, Perth, Preston, Shrewsbury
King's Cross	Aberdeen, Bradford, Cambridge, Dundee, Durham, Edinburgh, Ely, Glasgow, Inverness, King's Lynn, Leeds, Newcastle, Perth, York
Liverpool Street	Colchester, Ipswich, Norwich
Paddington	Bath, Bristol, Cardiff, Exeter, Gloucester, Newton Abbot, Oxford, Penzance, Plymouth, Stratford-upon-Avon, Swansea
St. Pancras	Derby, Leicester, Nottingham, Sheffield
Victoria	Brighton, Canterbury, Dover, Hastings
Waterloo	Eurostar trains (to Paris and the Continent), Hampton Court, Penzance, Portsmouth, Salisbury, Southampton

To arrive in or depart from London by bus, you'll travel through **Victoria Coach Station** (tube: Victoria), on Buckingham Palace Rd., the hub of Britain's coach network. The coach station is centrally located, and easily accessible by the Victoria tube station. Much of the commuting area around London is served by **Green Line** coaches, which leave frequently from Eccleston Bridge behind Victoria Station. (For information, call (0181) 668 7261 M-F 8am-8:30pm, Sa-Su 9am-5pm; or try the information kiosk on Eccleston Bridge.)

BY THUMB

Anyone who values safety will take a train or bus out of London. Hitching can be difficult within central London. Ask at hostels for other travelers heading in your direction. *Let's Go* does not recommend hitching.

■ Orientation

London is a colossal aggregate of distinct villages and anonymous suburbs, of ancient settlements and modern developments. As London grew, it swallowed adjacent cities and nearby villages, and chewed up the counties of Kent, Surrey, Essex, Hertford-

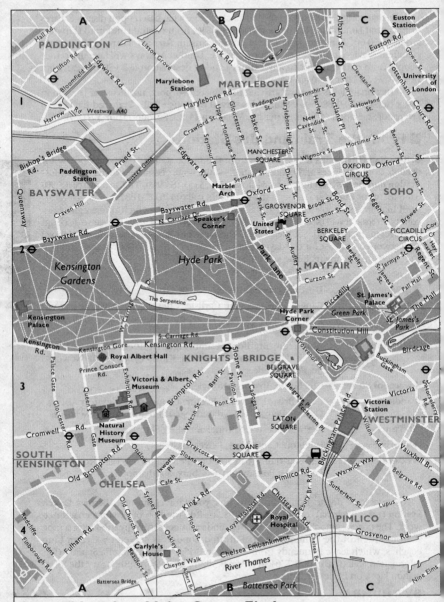

Central London: Major Street Finder

Albert Embankment **D4**	Berkeley St **C2**	Buckingham Palace Rd **C3**	Clerkenwell Rd **E1**
Aldersgate **E1**	Birdcage Walk **C3**	Cannon St **F2**	Constitution Hill **C3**
Aldwych **D2**	Bishops Br. Rd **A1**	Chancery Ln **D1**	Cornhill/Leadenhall St **F2**
Audley(N&S) **B2**	Bishopsgate **F1**	Charing Cross Rd **D2**	Coventry/Cranbourne **D2**
Baker St **B1**	Blackfriars Rd **E2**	Charterhouse St **E1**	Craven Hill Rd/Praed St **A2**
Bayswater Rd **A2**	Bloomsbury Way **D1**	Cheapside **E2**	Cromwell Rd **A3**
Beech St/Chiswell St **E1**	Bond St (New&Old) **C2**	Chelsea Br. Rd **B4**	Curzon St **C2**
Belgrave Pl **B3**	Bow St/Lancaster Pl **D2**	Chelsea Embankment **B4**	Drury Ln **D2**
Beaufort **A4**	Brompton Rd **B3**	Cheyne Walk **B4**	Eastcheap/Great Tower **F2**
Belgrave Rd **C4**	Buckingham Gate **C3**	City Rd **F1**	Eccleston Pl **C3**

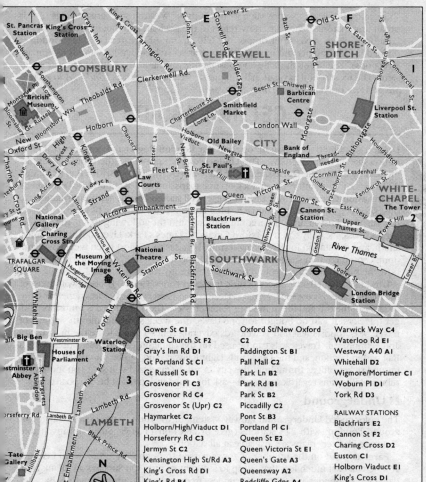

Gower St **C1**
Grace Church St **F2**
Gray's Inn Rd **D1**
Gt Portland St **C1**
Gt Russell St **D1**
Grosvenor Pl **C3**
Grosvenor Rd **C4**
Grosvenor St (Upr) **C2**
Haymarket **C2**
Holborn/High/Viaduct **D1**
Horseferry Rd **C3**
Jermyn St **C2**
Kensington High St/Rd **A3**
King's Cross Rd **D1**
King's Rd **B4**
Kingsway **D2**
Knightsbridge **B3**
Lambeth Palace Rd **D3**
Lisson Grove **A1**
Lombard St **F2**
London Wall **E1**
Long Acre/Grt Queen **D2**
Long Ln **E1**
Ludgate Hill **E2**
Marylebone High St **B1**
Marylebone Rd **B1**
Millbank **D4**
Montague Pl **D1**
Moorgate **F1**
New Bridge St **E2**
New Cavendish **C1**
Newgate St **E1**
Nine Elms Ln **C4**
Oakley St **B4**
Old St **F1**
Old Brompton Rd **A4**
Onslow Sq/St **A3**

Oxford St/New Oxford **C2**
Paddington St **B1**
Pall Mall **C2**
Park Ln **B2**
Park Rd **B1**
Park St **B2**
Piccadilly **C2**
Pont St **B3**
Portland Pl **C1**
Queen St **E2**
Queen Victoria St **E1**
Queen's Gate **A3**
Queensway **A2**
Redcliffe Gdns **A4**
Regent St **C2**
Royal Hospital Rd **B4**
St. James's St **C2**
Seymour Pl **A1**
Seymour St **A2**
Shaftesbury Ave **C2**
Sloane/Lwr Sloane **B3**
Southampton Row **D1**
Southwark Bridge Rd **E2**
Southwark Rd **E2**
St. Margarets/Abingdon **D3**
Stamford St **E2**
Strand **D2**
Sydney St **A4**
Thames St(Upr&Lwr) **F2**
The Mall **C2**
Theobald's Rd **D1**
Threadneedle St **F2**
Tottenham Ct Rd **C1**
Vauxhall Br. Rd **C4**
Victoria Embankment **D2**
Victoria St **C3**

Warwick Way **C4**
Waterloo Rd **E1**
Westway A40 **A1**
Whitehall **D2**
Wigmore/Mortimer **C1**
Woburn Pl **D1**
York Rd **D3**

RAILWAY STATIONS
Blackfriars **E2**
Cannon St **F2**
Charing Cross **D2**
Euston **C1**
Holborn Viaduct **E1**
King's Cross **D1**
Liverpool St **F1**
London Bridge **F2**
Marylebone **B1**
Paddington **A2**
St Pancras **D1**
Victoria **C3**
Waterloo East **E3**
Waterloo **D3**

BRIDGES
Albert **B4**
Battersea **A4**
Blackfriars **E2**
Chelsea **C4**
Hungerford Footbridge **D2**
Lambeth **D3**
London Bridge **F2**
Southwark **E2**
Tower Bridge **F2**
Waterloo **D2**
Westminster **D3**

Edgware Rd **A1**
Euston Rd **C1**
Exhibition Rd **A3**
Farringdon Rd **E1**
Fenchurch/Aldgate **F2**
Fleet St **E2**
Fulham Rd **A4**
Gloucester Pl **B1**
Gloucester Rd **A3**
Goswell Rd **E1**

shire, and Middlesex. Names such as the "City of Westminster" are vestiges of this urban imperialism. "The City" now refers to the ancient, and much smaller, "City of London," which covers but one of the 620 sq. mi. of Greater London. London is divided into boroughs and into postal code areas (whose letters stand for compass directions). The borough name and postal code appear at the bottom of most street signs. The most useful navigational aids are street atlases, such as *London A to Z, ABC Street Atlas,* or Nicholson's *London Streetfinder* (from £4).

GETTING ABOUT

London's public transit system, operated by **London Regional Transport (LRT),** is impressively comprehensive. The **Underground** (known as "the tube") is supplemented by **buses,** the **Docklands Light Railway (DLR),** and by **British Rail (BR).** Call 222 1234 for 24hr. information. Pick up free maps and guides at **London Transport's Information Centres.** You can find these well-staffed booths with information on buses, Underground trains, the DLR, BR's London routes, and night buses at Heathrow airport, Euston and Victoria rail stations, and the following major tube stops: King's Cross, Piccadilly Circus, Oxford Circus, St. James's Park, Liverpool St., Hammersmith, and the station for Heathrow terminals 1, 2, and 3 (most open weekdays 8am-6pm; central London stations also have weekend hours). For 24-hour information on how the buses and Underground trains are currently running, call 222 1200.

London is divided into six concentric transport zones. Central London, with most of the major sights, is covered by zone 1; Heathrow Airport is zone 6. Fares depend on the distance of the trip and the number of zones crossed. The **Travelcard** is a must for budget travelers. It can be bought for one day's, one week's, or one month's worth of travel. Most tourists will find Travelcards covering zones 1 and 2 to be the most useful and economical. Travelcards can be used on the Underground, regular buses, British Rail within London, and the Docklands Light Railway, and can be purchased at Underground ticket offices throughout the city. A valid Travelcard will save you money on tube and BR trains regardless of zone—ask for an extension ticket before boarding.

■ Underground

The color-coded **Underground** railway system, or the **tube,** is the easiest way to get around London, with 273 stations (give or take) on 11 lines. Small but invaluable "Journey Planner" maps are available at all stations.

Fares depend on the number of zones passed through—a journey within central zone 1 will cost much less than a trip to a distant suburb. On Sundays and Bank Holidays (see **Appendix,** p. 690), trains run less frequently. All transfers are free. Bicycles are allowed on the above-ground sections of the Circle, District, Metropolitan, and Piccadilly lines for a child's fare except during morning and evening rush hours. A single adult ticket will cost between £1.60 and £3.30, with most central London trips costing £1.60 to £1.80. Return tickets cost exactly double the price of a single ticket. If you plan to make more than two trips in a day, a Travelcard will save you money (see above). You may also consider buying a **Carnet** (£10), which is a booklet entitling you to 10 one-way trips within Zone 1, if you'll be using the tube sporadically.

You can buy your ticket either from the ticket window or from a machine. The ticket allows you to go through the automatic gates; keep it until you reach your final destination, where the exit gates will collect it. Be aware that inspectors are becoming strict about enforcing the tube's on-the-spot £10 fine for travel without a valid ticket. Acting the befuddled foreigner may not get you off the hook.

Most tube lines' **last trains** leave Central London between midnight and 12:30am; service resumes around 6am. The gap is bridged by Night Buses (see **Buses** below). Some distant stations close on Sundays and other off-peak periods.

Many stations feature labyrinthine tunnels and steep staircases; if you're carrying a lot of luggage, you might fare better on a longer route that requires fewer transfers. And remember to stand to the right and walk on the left on escalators, or risk a rude tumbling from commuters in full stride.

■ Buses

If you're in a hurry, don't take a bus. Take the tube; it's faster, easier, and generally more consistent. However, riding the buses is a great way to orient yourself to the city's layout and to soak up its atmosphere and sights. Buses #11 and 14 offer excellent sight-seeing at discount rates. Unfortunately, double-decker **Routemaster** buses, with their conductors and open rear platforms, are being replaced to save money. On modern double-deckers and single-deck "hoppa" buses, you pay your fare to the driver as you board, and you must have exact change. On Routemasters, take a seat and wait for the conductor to tell you the fare and let you know when to get off.

Bus stops are marked with route information; at busy intersections or complicated one-way systems, maps tell where to board each bus. A warning: each stop is marked with route numbers and only those buses stop there. On stops marked "request," buses stop only if you flag them down (to get on) or pull the bell cord (to get off). While waiting, you must form a queue (line up); bus conductors may refuse some passengers at the stop with looks of scorn during busy periods. Service is sporadic during the day; it is common to wait 20 minutes only to be greeted by a procession of three identical buses in a row. Regular buses run from about 6am to midnight.

Night buses (the "N" routes) now run frequently throughout London from 11:30pm until the first day buses get going. When the tube sleeps (last trains run between midnight and 12:30am), night buses provide an inexpensive and convenient alternative to taxis. All Night bus routes pass through Trafalgar Sq. and many stop at Victoria as well. London Transport's information offices put out a free brochure about Night buses, which includes times of the last British Rail and Underground trains. One-week and one-month Travelcards (see above) are valid on night buses, while one-day Travelcards are not.

The bus network is divided into four zones. In and around central London, one-way **fares** range from 50p to about £1.20, depending on the number of zones through which you pass. Travelcards purchased for the Underground are valid on buses.

London Transport issues a free bus map for London called the *All-London Bus Guide,* which is available at most tube stations and LRT information offices. The *Central Bus Guide* describes only routes in zone 1. To find out whether buses are running on schedule or whether routes have changed, call 222 1200. Wheelchair accessible **Mobility Bus** routes, numbered in the 800s and 900s, service most of outer London. **Stationlink,** a wheelchair accessible bus, travels hourly between the major train stations. For information on either service, call 918 3312.

■ Docklands Light Railway

The **Docklands Light Railway (DLR;** 24hr. hotline 918 4000), London's newest transport system, connects the flashy developments of the old docks with the City of London. The tube's zone system applies to the DLR, and DLR lines appear on all tube maps. Fares are the same as for the tube, and Travelcards are valid. The **red line** runs north-south (connecting with the tube at Bow Church and Stratford); the **green line** runs west-east to merge with the red line (connecting with the tube at Bank, Shadwell, and Tower Hill/Gateway); and the new **Beckton** line, starts at Poplar Station on the red line and extends 5 mi. to the east. The area is also served by a network of buses that have similar prices to the DLR rail cars. The N50 Night bus serves the Docklands area late at night.

■ British Rail

Most of London is fully served by buses and the tube. Some districts, however, notably southeast London, are most easily reached by train. The BR is speedy and runs frequently to suburbs and daytrip areas around London, functioning as a commuter rail that is often cheaper than the tube. The North London Link, stretching across north London from North Woolwich to Richmond, often deposits travelers closer to sights (such as Keats's House) than the tube. Trains (every 20min.) scoot from Hampstead Heath to Kew in 25 minutes. However, BR is used by most visitors for its service from Gatwick Airport to Victoria (see **Getting In and Out,** p. 71).

■ Taxicabs

In order to earn a license, London taxicab drivers must pass a rigorous exam called "The Knowledge" to demonstrate that they know the city's streets by heart; the route taken by a cabbie is virtually certain to be the shortest and quickest. A taxi is available if its yellow light is aglow. You can catch a cab yourself or call a radio dispatcher for one (tel. 272 0272 or 253 5000); beware that you may be charged extra for ordering a cab by phone. Drivers are required to charge according to the meter for trips within London. A 10% tip is expected, with a surplus charge for extra baggage or passengers. Taxis in London are notoriously expensive. If you believe that you have been overcharged, get the driver's number.

Apart from the licensed cabs, there are many **"minicab"** companies, listed in the Yellow Pages. Ladycabs (tel. 241 4780) has only female cabbies. (Open M-Th 7:30am-12:30am, F 7:30am-1am, Sa 9am-2am, Su 10am-midnight.) Be sure to ask the price when you order a minicab. Reclaim **lost property** (tel. 833 0996) you have left in a taxi at 15 Penton St., N1 (tube: Angel; open M-F 9am-4pm).

The cheapest way to get to and from the airports (besides public transportation of course) is to call a cab company that will dispatch an ordinary car (not the snazzy and distinctive London cabs) for a set fee (see **Getting In and Out,** p. 70).

■ Boats

The **River Thames** no longer commands as much traffic as in the Middle Ages, but if you venture out in a boat you can still sense the pulse of a major lifeline. **Catamaran Cruisers** (tel. 839 3572) offers cruises with commentary. Tours run from Charing Cross to Greenwich pier (every 30min., 10:30am-5:15pm; £6, return £8, day pass £8.50, children £3, £4, £4.25). **Westminster Pier** (tube: Westminster) serves **Greenwich** (tel. 930 4097), **Hampton Court, Kew,** and **Richmond** (tel. (0181) 940 3891), and the **Thames Barrier** (tel. 930 3373). Call the London Tourist Board's **help line** for details on boat tours and transportation at (0839) 12 34 32.

PRACTICAL INFORMATION

■ Tourist Offices

London Tourist Board Information Centre, Victoria Station Forecourt, SW1 (tel. (0839) 123432; recorded message only, 39-49p per min., available within U.K. only). Tube: Victoria. Information on London and England, a well-stocked bookshop, theater and tour bookings, and an accommodations service (a hefty £5 booking fee, plus 15% refundable deposit; tel. 932 2020; fax 932 2021; MC, Visa only). Expect long waits around noon. Their cheapest rooms cost £22, most run £25-30. **Victoria Station** center open Apr.-Nov. daily 8am-7pm; Dec.-Mar. M-Sa 8am-7pm, Su 8am-5pm. Additional tourist offices located at **Heathrow Airport** (open daily Apr.-Nov. 9am-6pm; Dec.-Mar. 9am-5pm), **Liverpool St. Underground Station** (open M 8:15am-7pm, Tu-Sa 8:15am-6pm, Su 8:30am-4:45pm), and **Selfridges** department stores during store hours (see **Department Stores,** p. 138).

British Travel Centre, 12 Regent St., SW. Tube: Piccadilly Circus. Down Regent St. from the Lower Regent St. tube exit. Run by the British Tourist Authority (tel. (0181) 846 9000) and ideal for travelers bound for destinations outside of London. Combines the services of the BTA, British Rail, and a Traveler's Exchange with an accommodations service. £5 surcharge for booking and a required deposit (either 1 night's stay or 15% of the total stay depending on the place; does not book for hostels). Also sells maps, theater tickets, books, and pamphlets translated into many languages. Long queues. Open M-F 9am-6:30pm, Sa-Su 10am-4pm.

City of London Information Centre, St. Paul's Churchyard, EC4 (tel. 606 3030). Tube: St. Paul's. Specializes in information about the City of London but answers questions on all of London. Helpful, knowledgeable staff. Open daily 9:30am-5pm.

London Transport Information Offices, (24hr. tel. 222 1234). At Euston (open M-Sa 7:15am-6pm, Su 8:30am-5pm); Victoria (open M-Sa 7:45am-9pm, Su 8:45am-9pm); King's Cross (open M-Sa 8am-6pm, Su 8:30am-5pm); Liverpool St. (open M-Sa 8am-6pm, Su 8:45am-5:30pm); Oxford Circus (open M-Sa 8:45am-6pm); Piccadilly (open daily 8:45am-6pm); St. James's Park (open M-F 8am-5:30pm); Heathrow Central station (open M-Sa 6:30am-7pm, Su 7:15am-7pm); Heathrow Terminal 1 (open daily 7:15am-10pm); Heathrow Terminal 2 (open M-Sa 7:15am-5pm, Su 8:15am-5pm); Heathrow Terminal 4 (open M-Sa 6am-3pm, Su 7:15am-3pm); Hammersmith (open M-F 7:15am-6pm, Sa 8:15am-6pm); and West Croydon Bus Station (open M-F 7:30am-6pm, Sa 8:15am-5pm). Helpful agents offer advice on travel by underground or bus. Free maps. Booths sell helpful brochures, guidebooks, and the museum Whitecard (see **Museums,** p. 126).

Greenwich Tourist Information Centre, 48 Greenwich Church St., SE10 (tel. (0181) 858 6376). Offers information on sights in Greenwich and surrounding areas. Open daily 10am-5pm.

Southwark Tourist Information Centre, Hay's Galleria, Tooley St., SE1 (tel. 403 8299). Helpful advice in navigating the newly dynamic areas south of the muddy Thames. Open daily 10am-5pm.

■ Emergency, Social, and Sundry Services

Emergency medical care, psychological counseling, crash housing, and sympathetic support can often be found in London free of charge.

AIDS: National AIDS Helpline (24hr. tel. (0800) 567123). Toll-free for information on testing, health care, or to simply answer questions and listen.

Alcoholics Anonymous: London Helpline (tel. 352 3001) daily 10am-10pm.

Automobile Breakdown: Members can call the 24hr. AA breakdown service (tel. (0800) 887 766) or RAC Breakdown Service (tel. (0800) 828282).

British Diabetic Association: (tel. 323 1531). Information on diabetic services.

Dental Care: Eastman Dental Hospital (tel. 915 1000; fax 915 1012). Phone for emergency treatment availability and times.

Domestic Violence/Rape: Women's Aid, 52-54 Featherstone St., EC1 (tel. 392 2092). 24hr. helpline provides aid, advice, and emergency shelter for victims of domestic and sexual abuse. **The London Rape Crisis Centre's Rape Crisis Hotline,** P.O. Box 69, WC1 (tel. 837 1600) allows you, emergency or not, to talk to a woman, receive legal or medical information, or obtain referrals. They'll send someone to accompany you to the police, doctor, clinic, and court upon request. Hours vary—call for more information.

Emergency (Medical, Police, and Fire): Dial 999; no coins required.

Family Planning Association: 2-12 Pentonville Rd., N1 (tel. 837 4044). Tube: Angel. Informational services: contraception, pregnancy tests, and abortion referrals.

Hospitals: In an emergency, you can be treated at no charge in the Accidents and Emergencies (A&E) ward of a hospital. You have to pay for routine medical care unless you work legally in Britain, in which case NHS tax is deducted from your wages, and care is free. Socialized medicine has lowered fees here, so don't ignore any health problem merely because you are low on cash. The following have 24hr. walk-in A&E (also known as casualty) departments: **Royal London Hospital,** Whitechapel Rd., E1 (tel. 377 7000; tube: Whitechapel); **Royal Free Hospital,** Pond St., NW3 (tel. 794 0500; tube: Belsize Park or BR: Hampstead Heath); **Charing Cross Hospital,** Fulham Palace Rd. (entrance St. Dunstan's Rd.), W6 (tel. (0181) 846 1234; tube: Baron's Ct. or Hammersmith); **St. Thomas' Hospital,** Lambeth Palace Rd., SE1 (tel. 928 9292; tube: Westminster); **University College Hospital,** Gower St. (entrance on Grafton Way), WC1 (tel. 387 9300). Tube: Euston or Warren St. For others, look in the gray Businesses and Services phone book.

Narcotics Anonymous: Call 730 0009. Hotline answered daily 10am-10pm.

Pharmacies: Every police station keeps a list of emergency doctors and chemists in its area. Listings under "Chemists" in the Yellow Pages. **Bliss Chemists** (5 Marble Arch, W1; tel. 723 6116) is open daily, including public holidays, 9am-midnight.

LONDON

Police: Stations in every district of London, including: Headquarters, New Scotland Yard, Broadway, SW1 (tel. 230 1212; tube: St. James's Park); West End Central, 10 Vine St., W1 (tel. 437 1212; tube: Piccadilly Circus); Islington (tel. 704 1212). For emergencies, dial 999.

Samaritans: (tel. 734 2800). 24hr. crisis hotline.

Sexual Health: Jefferiss Wing Centre for Sexual Health, St. Mary's Hospital, Praed St., W2 (tel. 725 6619). Tube: Paddington. Free, confidential sexual health services.

ACCOMMODATIONS

Landing in London with no place to stay is a bit like landing on a bicycle and finding that it has no seat. Plan ahead to nab one of the more desirable rooms, particularly in July and August. The **Tourist Information Centre Accommodations Service** is the source for official bureaucratic room-finding (see **Tourist Offices,** p. 76).

TYPES OF ACCOMMODATIONS

London offers a wide range of accommodation types to suit different travelers. There are three major categories of accommodation in the following listings: Hostels, B&Bs, and Halls of Residence. **Hostels** are definitely your cheapest option if traveling alone. Rates in private hostels vary significantly; most of London's HI/YHA hostels tend to cost more than private ones (around £15-20 per night), but are usually cleaner and often have spectacular locations. For more general information on hostels and Bed and Breakfasts, see **Accommodations,** p. 39

London's universities rent out rooms in their **Halls of Residence** over the summer. These are generally the cheapest single rooms available, particularly if you have a student ID. Rooms tend to be spartan—standard student digs—but clean. Generally the halls offer rooms to individuals for two or three months over the summer, and during the long Easter Break in the spring, so calling or writing ahead is advisable. The **King's Campus Vacation Bureau,** 127 Stanford St., SE1 (tel. 928 3777), controls bookings for a number of University of London residence halls. All are available from early June to mid-September. Some halls reserve a few rooms for travelers year-round.

ACCOMMODATION DISTRICTS

When contemplating where to stay, tourists should take into consideration what sorts of fun they'll be having in London. Some districts are better for those interested in being close to the sights, others are more geared toward those who love the night-life, baby. What follows is a thumbnail sketch of the areas in which tourists are most likely to bunk down. London is not very well served by public transportation after midnight, so if you're staying in the sticks you'll have to swallow a huge wait for a night bus or an expensive cab ride.

Bloomsbury: Quiet residential streets lined with B&Bs, a few halls of residence, and a few hostels. Close to the massive British Museum, the outstanding Indian restaurants of Drummond St. to the north, and the nightlife, shopping, and theater of Covent Garden to the south. Budget hotels line Gower St., Russell Sq., Cartwright Gdns., and Argyle Sq.

Near Victoria Station: A variety of B&Bs and a few hostels near the Big Sights: Buckingham Palace, Westminster Abbey, Parliament, and Whitehall. Theater and nightlife districts aren't very far. Forage on Belgrave Rd., St. George's Dr., Warwick Way, or historic Ebury St. Take advantage of fierce competition by haggling.

Paddington and Bayswater: No major sights, but within a reasonable distance from nearly all of them. Bayswater/Queensway sustains a raucous, touristy pub scene, and a few decent restaurants. Lovely Hyde Park and Kensington Gardens are just to the south, but nightlife districts like Soho and Covent Garden are quite a distance. B&Bs, some a bit decrepit, cluster around Norfolk Sq. and Sussex Gdns.

Earl's Court: This is the destination of choice for backpackers looking for dirt-cheap hostels. Vibrant gay and lesbian scene, and a large number of Aussie pubs. Close to the sights around Victoria, the museums of South Kensington, and the commercial district of High Street Kensington. The police have recently installed closed-circuit video cameras around the neighborhood, but be careful at night. Also beware over-eager guides willing to lead you from the station to a hostel. Their "hostel" may turn out to be a crowded, ramshackle affair.

Kensington and Chelsea: Elegant and pricey, but a few B&Bs and hostels offer out-standing value. Hyde Park and Kensington Gardens are just to the north, as are the fantastic museums (V&A, Natural History, and Science) which line the Park's south-ern border. Some of the city's best, and priciest, shopping is nearby.

North London and Belsize Park: This huge area contains a few pleasant B&Bs, a few hostels, and a number of residence halls. The prices offer outstanding value even though the long, expensive commute diminishes the savings.

■ HI/YHA Hostels

Each of the Hostelling International/YHA hostels in London requires a Hostelling International or Youth Hostel Association **membership card.** Overseas visitors can buy one at YHA London Headquarters or at the hostels themselves for £10.20, under 18 £5. An **International Guest Pass** (£1.70) permits residents of places other than England and Wales to stay at hostel rates without joining the hostel association. After you purchase six Guest Passes, you attain full membership. The cheerful staff mem-bers, often international travelers themselves, keep London HI/YHA hostels clean and refreshingly well managed. Plan ahead, since London hostels are exceptionally crowded. During the summer, beds fill up months in advance. But hostels frequently hold some beds free until a few days before—it's always worth checking. To secure a place, show up as early as possible and expect to stand in line. With a Visa or Master-Card, you can book in advance by phone. The **central reservations number** for all London hostels is 248 6547 (open M-Sa 9am-5pm).

All hostels are equipped with large **lockers** that require a padlock. Bring your own or purchase one from the hostel for £3. London hostels do not charge for a sheet or sleeping bag. Most have laundry facilities and some kitchen equipment.

Oxford Street, 14-18 Noel St., W1 (tel. 734 1618; fax 734 1657). Tube: Oxford Cir-cus. Walk east on Oxford St. and turn right on Poland St.; the hostel stands next to a blue and green nature mural. As close as you can possibly get to the Soho action. Spacious TV lounge, clean **kitchen** with microwave, **laundry** facilities and cur-rency exchange. Small, clean 2- to 4-bed rooms. Rooms have large **storage lock-ers,** but you must bring your own padlock. 3-4 bed dorm £18.70, under 18 £15.25; double £40.60. Packed breakfast £2.10. Book at least 3-4 weeks in advance—very few walk-ins accepted. Full payment required to secure a reservation. No children. Reception open 7am-11pm. 24hr. security; no curfew.

Hampstead Heath, 4 Wellgarth Rd., NW11 (tel. (0181) 458 9054 or 458 7096; fax 209 0546). Tube: Golders Green, then bus #210 or 268 toward Hampstead, or on foot by turning left from the station onto North End Rd., then left again onto Wellgarth Rd. (10min.). A beautiful, sprawling hostel. **Kitchen** and **laundry** facilities. Video games and outdoor foosball. Internet and fax access. 200 beds in 2- to 6-bed dorms £15.60, under 18 £13.35. Family rooms: doubles £38.50; triples £55; quads £71; quints £87; 6-bed £103.50 (breakfast included). 24hr. security and reception. No curfew. Book in advance.

City of London, 36 Carter Ln., EC4 (tel. 236 4965; fax 236 7681). Tube: St. Paul's. From the City Information Centre on the opposite side of St. Paul's Cathedral, go left down Godliman St., then take the 1st right onto Carter Ln. (a helpful sign out-side the Centre points you in the right direction). A stone's throw from St. Paul's. Scrupulously clean, with secure luggage storage, currency exchange, **laundry** facil-ities, and theater box office. Rooms contain between 1 and 15 beds; average room has 5 beds. Some triple-decker bunk beds. Single-sex rooms only. Dorms £19, under 18 £17; 5- to 8-bed dorms £21.30, £17.90. Singles £25, under 18 £21.50; dou-bles £49, £41; triples £67.50, £90; quads £57, £76. 24hr. security. Reception open 7am-11pm. Call at least a week in advance. Make bookings for other UK hostels at reception. Canteen offers inexpensive set lunches and dinners.

Earl's Court, Earl's Ct., 38 Bolton Gdns., SW5 (tel. 373 7083; fax 835 2034). Tube: Earl's Ct. Exit from the tube station onto Earl's Ct. Rd. and turn right; Bolton Gdns. is the 5th street on your left. Townhouse in a leafy residential neighborhood. 4- to 16-bed rooms. Lounge has TV and a soft drink machine. Currency exchange. Meals 5-8pm. **Kitchen** and **laundry** access. Very clean. All rooms single-sex. £18.70, under 18 £16.45. Non-members £1.70 extra. Student discount £1. Continental or full English breakfast. Reception open 7am-11pm. 24hr. security. No curfew.

Holland House, Holland Walk, W8 (tel. 937 0748; fax 376 0667). Tube: High St. Ken. Jacobean mansion nestled in Holland Park. Rooms are clean and relatively spacious, with built-in **storage lockers**—bring a padlock. **Laundry** and **kitchen** facilities. Daytime luggage storage. HI membership required. Dorms £18.70, under 18 £16.45. Cooked breakfast included. 24hr. access. Set dinner £4.45 (served 5-8pm).

King's Cross/St. Pancras, 79-81 Euston Rd., N1 (tel. 388 9998; fax 388 6766). Tube: King's Cross/St.Pancras or Euston. New 8-story hostel located between 2 major train stations. New beds, sparkling bathrooms. Some rooms with air-conditioning. "Premium" rooms include bathroom, TV, and coffee/tea facilities. **Laundry** and **kitchen** facilities. Game room lounge. Meals £5 (served 6-9pm). Family rooms available. 4-5 bed dorm £21.30, under 18 £17.90; 2-bed rooms £22.50, £19.40, with bath £24.30, under 18 £20.90; 4-bed family rooms £80; 5-bed £97.50. Luggage storage. No curfew. Book in advance. Max. stay 1 week.

Rotherhithe, Island Yard, Salter Rd., SE1 (tel. 232 2114; fax 237 2919). Tube: Rotherhithe. A 15-min. walk down Brunel Rd., then onto Salter. In the Docklands—transportation into the city takes around 30min. Restaurant, a lounge, and bar. No curfew. 6- to 10-bed dorms £21.30, under 18 £17.90; 4-bed dorms £21.75, £18; 2-bed dorms £24.50, £20.50. Breakfast included. Wheelchair accessible.

Epping Forest, Wellington Hall, High Beach, Loughton, Essex IG10 (tel./fax (0181) 508 5161). Tube: Loughton (zone 6, 45min. from central London), then a brisk 35-min. walk. Follow Station Rd. as it crosses Epping High Rd. and becomes Forest Rd. Continue along Forest Rd. as it becomes Earl's Path, straight through the roundabout, keep right until the King's Oak pub, turn left and then right at the "Wellington Hall" sign; the hostel will be on your left. Cab from the station costs £3 per carload. Remote woodland setting. Large **kitchen.** Dorms £8, students £7, under 18 £5.40; 4-bed family rooms (2 adults, 2 children) £30.50; 6-bed family rooms £42. **Camping** (tents not supplied) £4 per person. Reception open 7:30-10am. 5-11pm lockout. Curfew 11pm. Call ahead. Open Mar.-Nov.

■ Private Hostels

Private hostels don't require an HI card, have a youthful clientele and usually have single-sex rooms. Some have kitchen facilities. Few have curfews, so get on down. Almost all accept major credit cards.

Bloomsbury

Ashlee House, 261-65 Gray's Inn Rd., WC1 (tel. 833 9400; fax 833 6777; email ashleehouse@tsnxt.co.uk). Tube: King's Cross. From King's Cross, turn right onto Pentonville Rd. and then right again onto Gray's Inn Rd.; the hostel is a few blocks up the road on the right. Newly opened, Ashlee House offers clean, bright rooms within easy walking distance of King's Cross. 140 beds. Offers a range of facilities, including **laundry, kitchens,** and secure luggage room. Small but functional rooms. all have washbasins and central heating. Dorms £13; 4- and 6-bed rooms £17; twins £22. Generous breakfast (served M-F 7:30-9:30am, Sa-Su 8-10am). Spacious reception area open 24hr. No curfew or lockout. Check-out 10am.

Central University of Iowa Hostel, 7 Bedford Pl., WC1 (tel./fax 580 1121). Tube: Holborn or Russell Sq. From Holborn Rd., head right on Southampton Rd. Walk 2 blocks, take the 2nd street on the left (Bloomsbury Pl.), then take the first right. From Russell Sq., head left and turn left onto Southampton Row, then turn right onto Russell Sq.; Bedford Pl. is the 1st left. On a quiet street near the British Museum. Spartan rooms with bunk beds. Wood bunks are superior to the metal variety. **Laundry** facilities, towels and linen, TV lounge. Singles £21; twins £19; 4-5 bed room £17. £10 key deposit. Continental breakfast. Reception 9am-1pm and 3-8:30pm. No curfew. Open May 20-Aug. 20.

Tonbridge School Clubs, Ltd. (tel. 837 4406), Judd and Cromer St., WC1. Tube: King's Cross/St. Pancras. Follow Euston Rd. to the site of the new British Library and turn left onto Judd St.; the hostel is 3 blocks down. Students with non-British passports only. A clean, no-frills place to sleep and shower. Men sleep in basement gym, women in karate-club hall. Blankets and foam pads provided. Pool tables, TV, video games. Floor space £5. Daytime storage space. Lockout 9am-9pm; lights-out 11:30pm; midnight curfew. Use caution when walking in the area at night.

Paddington and Bayswater

Hyde Park Hostel, 2-6 Inverness Terr., W2 (tel. 229 5101; fax 229 3170). Tube: Bayswater or Queensway. New, conveniently located hostel. Clean rooms with high ceilings and red bunks. Pool room/lounge. Color TV lounge, and plans for addition of a bar. **Kitchen, laundry** facilities. 10-bed dorms £12.50; 6- to 8-bed dorms £14; 4-bed dorms £15. £5 key deposit. Continental breakfast. 24hr. reception.

Quest Hotel, 45 Queensborough Terr., W2 (tel. 229 7782). Tube: Queensway. From the tube, turn right onto Bayswater; walk along Bayswater for 2 blocks and then turn left onto Queensborough Terr. The hostel, a terraced house, is on your left. 60-70 beds. Communal, clean, and sociable, with one theme party per month. Pool room and **kitchen** available. Satellite TV in lounge. 4- to 8-bed dorms (co-ed and 1 women-only) £15; 2-bed dorm £18. Ask about weekly rates during winter. Continental breakfast (served 8-9:45am) and sheets included (changed daily). Check-out 10am. No curfew or lockout. Key deposit £3.

Kensington, Chelsea, and Earl's Court

☻**Albert Hotel,** 191 Queens Gate, SW7 (tel. 584 3019; fax 823 8520). Tube: Gloucester Rd., or Bus #2 or 70 from South Kensington. A long walk from the tube; take a right on Cromwell and a left on Queen's Gate. Approximately ¼ mi. up Queen's Gate on your right, near Hyde Park. The bus, which stops near the Royal Albert Hall on Kensington Gore, is much quicker. Seems more like a quality hotel. Rooms range from large dorms to intimate doubles, most with bath. **Laundry.** Dorm (single-sex or co-ed) £12; 4- to 6-bed dorm £15; singles or doubles £40. Weekly: dorm only, £72. Continental breakfast and sheets provided. 24hr. reception. No lockout or curfew. Luggage storage £1 per day. Reserve with 1 night's deposit.

Curzon House Hotel, 58 Courtfield Gdns., SW5 (tel. 581 2116; fax 835 1319). Tube: Gloucester Rd. Turn right onto Gloucester Rd., right again on Courtfield Rd., and right on Courtfield Gdns. TV lounge features groovy, plush, velour-checked couches. No bunk beds. Bathrooms are basic, but functional. **Kitchen.** 4-bed dorm (single-sex) £17. Singles £30; doubles £44; triples £39. Weekly and seasonal discounts as low as £70 per week in winter. Breakfast included. MC, Visa.

Court Hotel, 194-196 Earl's Ct. Rd., SW5 (tel. 373 0027; fax 912 9500). Tube: Earl's Ct. Sister hostel at 17 Kempsford Gardens (tel. 373 2174). All single, double, and twin rooms have TV and tea/coffee set. Full **kitchen** facilities and spacious TV lounge. Safe available for valuables. 3- to 4-bed dorm (single-sex) £15; singles £26; doubles £35. Weekly: dorm £91; singles £165; doubles £210. Linen provided. Key deposit £10. No curfew. Reservations not accepted; call for availability.

O'Callaghan's Hotel, 205 Earl's Ct. Rd., SW5 (tel. 370 3000; fax 370 2623). Tube: Earl's Ct. A bare-bones place to hit the hay; guests like the relaxed atmosphere as well as the prices. 32 beds in neat, blue rooms. Friendly management will pick you up from Victoria and drive you to two other branches if first hostel is full. Rooms have big windows and bunk beds. Dorms £10; doubles £24. Weekly: dorms £60; doubles £140. Winter discounts. 24hr. reception.

Near Victoria Station

Victoria Hotel, 71 Belgrave Rd. SW1 (tel. 834 3077; fax 932 0693). Tube: Pimlico. From the station, take the Bessborough St. (south side) exit and go left along Lupus St., then take a right at St. George's Sq. Belgrave Rd. starts on the other side. Clean, friendly, bohemian hostel with pool room and TV. 70 beds. **Kitchen.** 6-8 bed dorm rooms £12.50-15. Continental breakfast. Luggage storage. 24hr. reception.

North London

◉**International Student House,** 229 Great Portland St., W1 (tel. 631 8300, -8310; fax 631 8315). Tube: Great Portland St. At the foot of Regent's Park, across the street from the tube station's rotunda. 60s exterior hides network of events and activities. Lockable cupboards in dorms, **laundry** facilities. Dorms (without breakfast) £10; singles £28; doubles £20; triples £16.50. Rooms with W.C. and telephones £4 extra. Continental breakfast. No curfew. Reserve at least 1 month ahead.

■ Halls of Residence

◉**Hampstead Campus,** 23 Kidderpore Ave., NW3 (tel. 435 3564; fax 431 4402). Tube: Finchley Rd. or West Hampstead, then Bus #13, 28, 82, or 113 to the Platt's Ln. stop on Finchley Rd. Turn onto Platt's Ln. then take an immediate right on Kidderpore Ave. Beautiful residential surroundings. **Kitchen,** TV lounge, game rooms. Singles £15.50; twins £26.50. 10% off 7 nights or more. 24hr. security.

◉**Stamford Street Apartments,** 127 Stamford St., SE1 (tel. 873 2960; fax 873 2962). Tube: Waterloo. From the station, take the exit marked "Waterloo Bridge." Take the pedestrian subway marked "Subway to York Road," and follow it around the circle to reach Stamford St. Spacious singles with wood furniture, refrigerators, and an attached bathroom. **Kitchen,** TV lounge, and **Laundry** facilities. Singles with bath £32.50. 24hr. reception. Disabled access. Open July-Sept.

High Holborn Residence, 178 High Holborn, WC1 (tel. 379 5589; fax 379 5640). Tube: Holborn. 10min. walk down High Holborn. Spacious, well-furnished rooms with incoming calls and voice mail. Lounge and bar. **Laundry** and **kitchen** facilities. Singles £27; twins £45, with bath £52. Continental breakfast. Reception daily 7am-11pm. Excellent disabled access. Book in advance. Open July to mid-Sept.

Wellington Hall, 71 Vincent Sq., Westminster, SW1 (tel. 834 4740; fax 233 7709). Tube: Victoria. Walk 1 long block along Vauxhall Bridge Rd.; turn left on Rochester Row. Convenient to Westminster, Big Ben, Buckingham Palace, and the Tate Gallery. Spacious rooms. English breakfast. Singles £25; doubles £38.50. Book in advance. Rooms generally available June-Sept. and Easter.

Queen Alexandra's House, Kensington Gore, SW7 (tel. 589 3635; fax 589 3177). Tube: South Kensington, or Bus #9, 10, or 52 to Royal Albert Hall; the hostel is just behind the Royal Albert Hall to the left. Women only. Beautiful Victorian building. **Kitchen, laundry,** sitting room, and music rooms. Cozy singles £25. Continental breakfast. Write in advance for a booking form. Fax is best.

University of North London, The Arcade, 385-401 Holloway Rd., N7 (tel. 607 5415; fax 609 0052; email summerlets@unl.ac.uk). Tube: Holloway Rd. Head left from the tube station. Above the Hogshead Pub right before Parkhurst Rd. Single rooms in 4- to 6-person flats with own **kitchen** and bathroom. Single beds £11, with linen £16; £70 per week with linens. Book months in advance. Open July 6 to mid-Sept.

John Adams Hall, 15-23 Endsleigh St., WC1 (tel. 387 4086; fax 383 0164). Tube: Euston. Head right on Euston Rd., take 1st right onto Gordon St. and 1st left onto Endsleigh Gdns.; Endsleigh St. is the 2nd right. Elegant Georgian building. Small, simple singles with desks, wardrobes, and sinks. **Laundry** facilities, TV lounge, ping-pong, and reading room. Singles £22; doubles £38. English breakfast. Reception daily 8am-1pm and 2-10pm. Open July-Aug. and Easter.

■ Bed and Breakfasts

Bloomsbury

◉**Arosfa Hotel,** 83 Gower St., WC1 (tel./fax 636 2115). The name is Welsh for "place to rest," and the charming couple who have turned this B&B around over the last 2 years ensure that it lives up to its name. All furnishings and fixtures are close to new, the rooms are spacious, and the facilities are immaculate. Singles £31; doubles £44, with bath £58; triples £59, £70. MC, Visa.

Mentone Hotel, 54-55 Cartwright Gdns., WC1 (tel. 387 3927; fax 388 4671). Pleasantly decorated and newly renovated, with a bright, cheery atmosphere. Rooms with color TV and tea/coffee makers. Singles £42, with bath £60; doubles £60, with £75; triples with bath £85; quads with bath £90. English breakfast.

Alhambra Hotel, 17-19 Argyle St., WC1 (tel. 837 9575; fax 916 2476). Sparkling clean, modest singles in the main building; refurbished annex is pricier and posher. TVs in all rooms. Cozy dining room. Singles £30, with shower £40; doubles £40, with shower £45, with bath £55; triples £55, with shower £60, with bath £70; quads with bath £90. English breakfast.

Ruskin Hotel, 23-24 Montague St., WC1 (tel. 636 7388; fax 323 1662). From Holborn tube station, take Southampton Row, then the 2nd left onto Great Russell St.; Montague St. is the 2nd right. Across from the British Museum. Meticulously clean, well-kept rooms sport hot pots and hair dryers. TV lounge. Pretty back garden. Singles £42; doubles £60, with bath £75; triples £75, with bath £85. English breakfast.

Euro Hotel, 51-53 Cartwright Gdns., WC1 (tel. 387 4321; fax 383 5044). Large rooms with cable TV, radio, hot pot, phone, and sink. Immaculate bathrooms. Free **email** at reception. Singles £46, with bath £68; doubles £63, with bath £82.50; triples £76, with bath £96; quads £84, with bath £104. Under 13 £9.50. 10% discount for stays over 1 week. Flexible winter discounts. Full English breakfast.

Near Victoria Station

⊛**Melbourne House,** 79 Belgrave Rd., SW1 (tel. 828 3516; fax 828 7120). Past Warwick Sq. Closer to Pimlico than Victoria; from Pimlico station take the Bessborough St. (south side) exit and go left along Lupus St. Turn right at St. George's Sq.; Belgrave Rd. starts on the other side of the square. Extraordinary cleanliness and recently refurbished. Sparkling rooms with TV, phone, and hot pot. Singles £30, with bath £50; doubles or twins with bath £70; triples with bath £95; family quad with bath £110. English breakfast. Book ahead. No credit cards.

⊛**Luna and Simone Hotel,** 47-49 Belgrave Rd., SW1 (tel. 834 5897; fax 828 2478), past Warwick St. Tube: Victoria or Pimlico. Immaculate and well-maintained. The rooms, decorated in shades of blue, all come with TV, phones, hair dryers, and firm mattresses. Singles £25; doubles £50, with bath £60; triples with shower £75. English breakfast. Luggage storage.

Georgian House Hotel, 35 St. George's Dr., SW1 (tel. 834 1438; fax 976 6085). Terrific discounts on "student rooms" on the 3rd and 4th floors (you don't even need to be a student; just be willing to walk up the long flights of stairs). Spacious rooms come with TV, phone, and hot pot. Older, but cheaper rooms in the annex (about a block away). Reception 8am-11pm. Singles £29, students £19, with bath £36-39; doubles with bath £49-55, students £32; triples with bath £63-68, students £45; quads £69-75, students £54. Huge English breakfast.

Oxford House, 92-94 Cambridge St., SW1 (tel. 834 6467; fax 834 0225), close to the church. From St. George's Dr. (see directions above to St. George's), turn right onto Clarendon St., then take the 1st left onto Cambridge St. Set in a quiet residential area. Clean rooms with flowered wallpaper. Singles £36; doubles £46-48; triples £56-59; quads £76-80. Fabulously well-prepared English breakfast. Reserve 3-4 weeks ahead. Reservations only and 5% surcharge with credit card.

Paddington and Bayswater

⊛**Hyde Park Rooms Hotel,** 137 Sussex Gdns., W2 (tel. 723 0225 or 723 0965). Large, airy rooms with TVs and washbasins. The baths are spic and span. There are only 14 rooms—book in advance. Singles £26, with bath £38; doubles £38, with bath £48; triples £57, with bath £72. English breakfast.

Dean Court Hotel, 57 Inverness Terr., W2 (tel. 229 2961; fax 727 1190). Tube: Bayswater or Queensway. From Queensway, make a right onto Bayswater Rd., walk left along Bayswater, and Inverness is your 1st left. This hotel offers clean, functional rooms with firm mattresses, English breakfast, full-pressure showers, and a friendly atmosphere. **The New Kent** next door offers the same rooms and management. Dorms £14 per night, £79 per week; doubles £38; twins £49; triples £54.

Earl's Court

York House Hotel, 27-28 Philbeach Gdns., SW5 (tel. 373 7519; fax 370 4641). Mod, 60s-style TV lounge and a lovely garden. Extraordinarily clean. Friendly staff, surroundings, and low prices. Singles £30; doubles £47, with bath £66; triples £58, with bath £79; quads £67. English breakfast.

Mowbray Court Hotel, 28-32 Penywern Rd., SW5 (tel. 373 8285 or 370 3690; fax 370 5693; email mowbraycrthot@hotmail.com). Staff this helpful is a rarity in London; wake-up calls, tour arrangements, taxicabs, theater bookings, and dry cleaning are all available. Rooms with towels, shampoo, hair dryers, TV, radio, telephone. In-room safes cost £2 per day. A lift serves all floors. Singles £40, with bath £48; doubles £50, with bath £60; triples £63, with bath £72; family rooms for 4 people £76, with bath £85; for 5 £90, with bath £100; for 6 £106, with bath £110. Continental breakfast. Reserve ahead.

Kensington and Chelsea

ⓜ**Abbey House Hotel,** 11 Vicarage Gate, W8 (tel. 727 2594), off Kensington Church St. Tube: High St. Kensington. The owners will spend 20min. giving you an introduction to London. Newly renovated. 24hr. tea, coffee, and ice room. Palatial rooms with color TVs, washbasins, towels, and soap. Singles £40; doubles £65; triples £78; quads £90; quints £100. English breakfast. Book ahead.

Vicarage Hotel, 10 Vicarage Gate, W8 (tel. 229 4030; fax 792 5989). Tube: High St. Kensington. The stately breakfast room is only surpassed by the comfortable, immaculate bedrooms and spotless bathrooms. TV room for guests to watch or deposit daytime luggage. Singles £40; doubles £63; triples £80; quads £88. English breakfast. No credit cards.

Swiss House, 171 Old Brompton Rd., SW5 (tel. 373 2769; fax 373 4983; email recep@swiss-hh.demon.co.uk). Beautiful B&B with airy, spacious rooms. 14-channel cable TV, telephone, towels, shampoo, and soap included. Singles £42, with bath £59; doubles with bath £75, with third person £87. Extra bed £12. Continental breakfast included, as well as coffee and snacks, which are available all day. English breakfast £5. 10% discount if staying over 1 week.

North London

Dillons Hotel, 21 Belsize Pk., NW3 (tel. 794 3360; fax 431 7900). Tube: Belsize Pk. or Swiss Cottage. Or head right on Haverstock Hill and take the 2nd left onto Belsize Ave., which becomes Belsize Pk. 15 large, well-furnished, and bright rooms. TV lounge. Singles £26, with shower £34; doubles £38, with bath £46; triples £44, with shower £52; quads with shower £58. Continental breakfast. For stays over a week, they accommodate with a fridge and microwave for the room. Book in advance. One-night deposit required for reservation.

FOOD AND DRINK

■ Restaurants

Savoring the booty of imperialism needn't be a guilty pleasure; imports from former colonies have spiced up London kitchens considerably. The city is perhaps most famous for its **Indian restaurants;** the cheapest cluster around Westbourne Grove (tube: Bayswater), Euston Sq., and Brick Ln. in the East End.

London's wealth of international restaurants shouldn't deter you from sampling Britain's own infamous cuisine. **Pubs** are a solid choice for meat pastries (Cornish pasties and pies), potatoes, and shepherd's pie (a meat mixture topped with mashed potatoes and baked). **Fish-and-chip shops** and **kebab shops** can be found on nearly every corner. They vary little in price but can be miles apart in quality. Look for queues out the door and hop in line. Budget travelers should remember that it is always cheaper to eat **take-away,** rather than having a sit-down meal.

THE WEST END

Soho, Piccadilly, and Covent Garden offer an inexhaustible world of dining options. The sandwich bars and cafes here will gladly send you off with a substantial meal for under £3. The entire West End is easily accessed by the Piccadilly Circus, Leicester Sq., Covent Garden, Tottenham Ct. Rd., and Charing Cross tube stations.

Soho and Piccadilly Circus

Scads of unimpressive pizza and fast food joints cluster around Piccadilly Circus. A trip a few blocks down Shaftesbury Ave. and left onto Wardour or Dean St. rewards the hungry with the smart cafes and cheaper sandwich shops of Soho. **Old Compton St.**, Soho's main drag, lies off Wardour St. one block north of and parallel to Shaftesbury Ave. For fresh fruit, check out **Berwick Market** on Berwick St.

⊛**Mandeer,** 8 Bloomsbury Way (tel. 242 6202). Tube: Tottenham Ct. Rd. A few streets off New Oxford St., Mandeer offers some of the best Indian food around and the chance to learn about owner Ramesh Patel's Ayurvedic Science of Life. Food is fresh, organic, and vegetarian. Lunch buffet options begin at a mere £3.50. Open M-Sa for lunch (self-service) noon-3pm, dinner 5-10pm.

⊛**The Stockpot,** 18 Old Compton St., W1 (tel. 287 1066), by Cambridge Circus. Tube: Leicester Sq. or Piccadilly Circus. The cheapest place in Soho to soak up some style. Menus are handwritten daily. Entrees £2.20-4. Fresh strawberries and cream in season £1.65. Open M-Tu 11:30am-11:30pm, W-Sa 11:30am-11:45pm, Su noon-11pm. Also at 40 Panton St. (Tube: Leicester Sq.). No credit cards.

⊛**West End Kitchen,** 5 Panton St., SW1 (tel. 839 4241). Tube: Picadilly Circus. Taste a variety of ethnic and English dishes while relaxing in cozy wooden booths. A 3-course set lunch £3.50, spaghetti bolognese £1.85, and moussaka £3. The place to come for "good food at great value." Open daily 7am-11:45pm.

⊛**The Wren Café at St. James's,** 35 Jermyn St., SW1 (tel. 437 9419). Tube: Piccadilly Circus or Green Park. Whole food delights in the shadow of a Wren church. Casserole of the day with brown rice £4. Open M-Sa 8:30am-6pm, Su 9am-5pm.

Café Emm, 17 Frith St., W1 (tel. 437 0723). Tube: Leicester Sq. Large portions served in a soothing atmosphere. All dishes, from vegetarian casseroles to sausages and mash, are £5. Last order 30min. before closing. Open M-Th noon-3pm and 5:30-11pm, F noon-3pm and 5:30pm-1am, Sa 5pm-1am, Su 5:30-11pm.

Govinda's Vegetarian Restaurant, 9 Soho St., W1 (tel. 437 3662). Tube: Tottenham Ct. Rd. Next to their Radha Krishna Temple, the International Society for Krishna Consciousness serves wholesome, vegetarian Indian food for very little money. No eggs, meat, or seafood used, though some dishes contain milk or cream. The cafeteria-style buffet fills stomachs for a mere £5. Open M-Sa 7am-8pm.

Chinatown

Dozens of traditional, inexpensive restaurants are crammed into London's Chinatown (tube: Leicester Sq.), which occupies the few blocks between Shaftesbury Ave. and Leicester Sq. Gerrard St., the pedestrian-only backbone of Chinatown, is one block south of Shaftesbury Ave. Because of the pre-1997 Hong Kong connection, Cantonese cooking and language dominate. In this sea of seemingly identical restaurants, **Lok Ho Fook,** 4-5 Gerrard St., W1 (tel. 437 2001), with its welcoming atmosphere and low prices (open daily noon-11:45pm), and **Kowloon Restaurant,** 21-22 Gerrard St., W1 (tel. 437 0148), with its grand portions of noodles (£2.50-6) and bakery, are the standouts (open daily noon-11:45pm). If you want to splurge, **Golden Dragon,** 28-29 Gerrard St., W1 (tel. 734 2763), serves the finest *dim sum* outside of Hong Kong (open M-F noon-11:30pm, Sa noon-midnight, Su 11am-11pm).

Covent Garden

Covent Garden offers an enticing array of eateries to playgoers and tourists in the heart of London's theater district (tube: Covent Garden). Don't let expensive looks deceive you; good food at reasonable prices can be found. Tucked away from the tourist labyrinth, **Neal's Yard** (off Neal St.) overflows with sumptuous vegetarian joints. These restaurants close relatively early; late at night, keep an eye out for the inconspicuous brasseries that dot the area.

⊛**Neal's Yard Salad Bar,** 2 Neal's Yard, WC2 (tel. 836 3233). Take-away or sit outside at this simple vegetarian's nirvana. Get a plateful of the hearty and wholesome hot vegetable dishes for £4.50-5 (take-away discount 50p). Tempting mix 'n' match salads from £2. Open daily 11am-9pm.

◉**Neal's Yard Bakery Co-op,** 6 Neal's Yard, WC2 (tel. 836 5199). Only organic flour and filtered water are used in the delicious breads here. A small open-air counter offers a plethora of baked goods, sandwiches, and salads—all vegetarian with many vegan options. Large loaf £1.90. Bean burger £2.20, take-away £1.80. 50% discount on day-old breads. No smoking. Open M-Sa 10:30am-4:30pm.

◉**Belgo Centraal,** 50 Earlham St., WC2 (tel. 813 2233). Second branch called **Belgo Noord** in Camden Town on 72 Chalk Farm Rd., NW1 (tel. 267 0718; tube: Chalk Farm Rd.). Waiters in monk's cowls, bizarre 21st-century beerhall interior, and great specials make this one of Covent Garden's most popular restaurants. During "lunchtime" (daily noon-5pm), £5 buys you wild boar sausage, Belgian mash, and a BEER (the inimitable *Hoegaarten*). Weekday specials 5-6:30pm. Open M-Sa noon-11:30pm, Su noon-10:30pm. Wheelchair access.

Café Sofra, 26 Wellington St., WC2 (tel. 836 4726). This Turkish cafe serves fresh meat and vegetarian dishes. The mouth-watering quiche (£2.50) and wide array of Mediterranean dishes will satiate the palate. Take-away discount 50p-£2. Finish your meal with some of the best *baklava* (60p) in the city. Open M-Sa 7am-11pm (take-away 7am-10pm), Su 8am-10pm.

Food for Thought, 31 Neal St., WC2 (tel. 836 0239). Verdant foliage decorates this tiny restaurant, which offers excellent vegetarian food at moderate prices. Soups, salads, and stir-fries. Tasty daily specials like chick pea ratatouille from £3.40. Take-away discount 40-50p. Open M-Sa 9:30am-9pm, Su noon-4:30pm.

BLOOMSBURY AND EUSTON

Superb Greek, Italian, and vegetarian restaurants line Goodge St., conveniently close to the British Museum. Northwest of Bloomsbury, around Euston Sq., a vast number of what many Londoners consider the city's best and most traditional Indian restaurants ply their trade. Try to avoid the restaurants on Woburn Pl., Southampton Row, and Great Russell St., which cater to swarms of tourists.

Near Goodge St.

Goodge St. (to the right of the Goodge St. station) and Tottenham St. (to the left of the station) are the main culinary areas, but those who meander down side streets will make delicious discoveries.

The Coffee Gallery, 23 Museum St. (tel. 436 0455). Tube: Tottenham Ct. Rd. or Holborn. Sandwich prices (mozzarella, tomato, and basil £2.90) are comparable to the other cafes flanking the British Museum, but the crowd here is less touristy and the atmosphere miles ahead. Within the bright blue walls lies a gallery of ceramics and paintings, in which delicious, fresh, Italian garden food is served. Menu changes daily. Open M-F 8am-5:30pm, Sa 10am-5:30pm.

Crank's Restaurant/Take-Away, 9-11 Tottenham St., W1 (tel. 631 3912). Another branch of London's original health food restaurant, founded in 1961. Enjoy the art exhibits, which are also for sale. Large vegetarian dishes made with fresh ingredients, including free-range eggs and organic flour. Entrees ranging from vegetarian lasagna to polenta with roast vegetables (£5). Healthy yogurt drinks. No smoking. Open M-Sa 8am-7:30pm, Su 11-5pm.

Near Euston

◉**Diwana Bhel Poori House,** 121 Drummond St., NW1 (tel. 387 5556). Tube: Warren St. Tasty Indian vegetarian food in a clean and airy restaurant. Spicy sauces and chutneys make for creative use of vegetables. The specialty is *thali* (an assortment of vegetables, rices, sauces, breads, and desserts; £3.80-4.10). Lunch buffet includes 4 vegetable dishes, rice, savories, and dessert (served noon-2:30pm; £4). Open daily noon-11:30pm.

Chutney's, 124 Drummond St., NW1 (tel. 338 0604). Tube: Warren St. A cheerful cafe serving vegetarian dishes from western and southern India. Delicious chutneys. All-you-can-eat lunch buffet (served M-Sa noon-2:45pm; £5). Su buffet (served noon-10:30pm; £5). *Dosas* (filled pancakes; £3.50-4.30). Take-away available 6-11:30pm. Open M-Sa noon-2:45pm and 6-11:30pm, Su noon-10:30pm.

Great Nepalese Restaurant, 48 Eversholt St., NW1 (tel. 338 6737). Tube: Euston Sq. From the station, head left up Eversholt St. Try Nepalese specialties like *bhutuwa* chicken, prepared with ginger, garlic, spice, and green herbs (£4.60). Delicious vegetarian dishes. Don't miss Nepalese Rum (£1.65), poured from the bottle shaped like the *khukuri* knife—the national weapon of Nepal. 10% take-away discount. Open M-Sa noon-2:45pm and 6-11:45pm, Su noon-2:30pm and 6-11:15pm.

Around Russell Sq.

⊛**Wagamama,** 4A Streatham St., WC1 (tel. 323 9223). Tube: Tottenham Ct. Rd. Go down New Oxford St. and left onto Bloomsbury St. Streatham St. is the first right. "Positive Eating+Positive Living." Strangers slurping happily from their massive bowls of ramen sit elbow-to-elbow at long tables, like extras from *Tampopo.* Pan-fried noodles, rice dishes, and vegetarian soup bases also available. Noodles in various combinations and permutations (£4.50-5.70). Try the raw juice (£2). No smoking. Open M-Sa noon-11pm, Su 12:30-10pm. MC, Visa. Another **branch** has opened in Soho at 10a Lexington St., W1 (tel. 292 0990; fax 734 1815). Tube: Piccadilly Circus. From Piccadilly, head down Shaftesbury Ave., turn left on Great Windmill St. which turns into Lexington. Open M-Sa noon-11pm, Su 12:30-10pm.

Woolley's Salad Shop and Sandwich Bar, 33 Theobald's Rd., WC1 (tel. 405 3028). Tube: Holborn. Healthy and delicious picnic fare for take-away, mostly vegetarian. Mix and match their 10 fresh salads in a variety of sizes (70p-£6.30 for a huge party pot). The sandwich shop offers everything from chicken *saag* to smoked salmon lovingly swaddled in fresh rolls (90p-£2.30). Open M-F 7am-3:30pm.

VICTORIA, KENSINGTON, AND CHELSEA

Victoria

Restaurants abound around Victoria Station, but many charge a queen's ransom. Follow the suits to find the cheapest lunch spots.

Ciaccio, 5 Warwick Way, SW1 (tel. 828 1342). An intimate Italian eatery whose handsome portions make for an unbeatable value. Pick a container of pasta and one of about 10 sauces (pesto, veggie, tomato and meat), and they'll heat it up in the microwave for £1.69-2.85. Open M-F 10am-7pm, Sa 9:30am-6pm.

The Well, 2 Eccleston Pl., SW1 (tel. 730 7303). A large open eatery dispensing sandwiches (£1.55-1.80) and good cheer (free). Breakfast especially cheap. All profits and tips go to good works and charity. Open M-F 9am-6pm, Sa 9:30am-5pm.

Knightsbridge and Hyde Park Corner

Epicurean stomachs-on-a-budget enticed by the sumptuous outlay of the Harrods food court may growl with disappointment at the dearth of affordable eateries near Knightsbridge. Knightsbridge Green, northwest of Harrods off Brompton Rd., offers several sandwich shops, in addition to fresh fruit and vegetable stands where you can procure provisions for a picnic.

Mima's Café, 9 Knightsbridge Green, SW1 (tel. 589 6820). Practically every sandwich under the sun (£2.70 or less), including delicious chicken and sweet corn. Huge salads £4.40-6. Take-away discount. Open M-Sa 6am-5:30pm.

Knightsbridge Express, 17 Knightsbridge Green, SW1 (tel. 589 3039). Crowds pack this eatery during lunch hours. Most sandwiches £1.50-2.40. Pasta platters £3.80. Hearty omelette sandwich (£2.80). Take-away discount. Open M-Sa 6am-5pm.

Arco Bars, 46 Hans Crescent, SW1 (tel. 584 6454). Cheap, hearty Italian food. Large portions of pasta or eggs are all £4 take-away. Generously filled sandwiches on excellent bread £1.30-2.20 take-away. Open M-F 7am-6pm, Sa 8am-6pm.

Hard Rock Cafe, 150 Old Park Ln., W1 (tel. 629 0382). Tube: Hyde Park Corner. This little-known neighborhood restaurant serves burgers and fries (£7.25) to a small local crowd in an intimate and quiet atmosphere. The perfect eatery for those wishing to avoid lines, loud music, and rock 'n' roll memorabilia. The madness first began here in 1971. Open Su-Th 11:30am-12:30am, F-Sa 11:30am-1am.

South Kensington

The unofficial French quarter of London, South Kensington is one of the ritziest areas in the city. As one would expect, South Ken (as it's called by those in the know) is not brimming with bargains. For budget dining, **Old Brompton Rd.** and **Fulham Rd.** are the main thoroughfares. The South Ken tube station lies closest, but some of the restaurants below require a substantial hike from there; others can be easily reached from the Earl's Ct. tube station. Old Brompton Rd. is served by buses #74 and C1; Fulham Road by buses #14, 45A, and 211.

Café Floris, 5 Harrington Rd., SW7 (tel. 589 3276). A bustling cafe offering large, fresh sandwiches (£1.50-2) and filling breakfasts. Colossal breakfast special for £3.50 is a better value than anything for miles. Open daily 7am-7pm.

Jules Rotisserie, 6-8 Bute St., SW7 (tel. 584 0600; fax 584 0614). This lively, pleasant restaurant with indoor and outdoor seating serves roasted free-range poultry. Quarter chicken with potatoes and green salad £6.25. Free delivery (tel. 221 3331). Open M-Sa noon-11:30pm, Su noon-10:30pm.

Luigi's, 359-361 Fulham Rd., SW10 (tel. 351 7825). Chaotic and tasty, enjoy this Italian deli-style restaurant's authentic salads, pastas, and desserts at one of its large outdoor tables. The wafting scent of the flower stand next door transports you to the south of Italy. Amazingly large pizzas for around £5. Open daily 8am-11pm.

Chelsea

When hunger pangs strike during a promenade down **King's Rd.,** you can either sate your desires and suck dry your wallet on the spot, or jaunt down a neighboring thoroughfare, where affordable restaurants abound. Buses #11 and 22 run the length of King's Rd. from the Victoria or Sloane Sq. tube stations. Almost every destination along King's Rd. requires a bus ride or a considerable walk. As an alternative, turn right onto Sydney St. or Edith Grove and head towards Fulham Rd., which runs parallel to King's Rd. and provides access to a cornucopia of culinary delights.

Chelsea Kitchen, 98 King's Rd., SW3 (tel. 589 1330). 7min. walk from the tube. Locals rave about the eclectic menu of cheap, filling, and tasty food: turkey and mushroom pie, spaghetti bolognese, and a Spanish omelette are each £2.80 or less. Cozy booth seating. When the weather is amenable, grab one of the front tables and watch the Sloane Rangers pass you by. Set menu £5. Breakfast served 8-11:25am. Open M-Sa 8am-11:30pm, Su 9am-11:30pm.

SWTen, 488 King's Rd., SW10 (tel. 352 4227), near the World's End. A hike from the tube. Cosmopolitan, sun-filled French atmosphere at budget prices. Tremendously sized portions despite the chic atmosphere. Huge sandwiches on crusty bread £1.20-3. Salads £2.80-3.50. Specials (around £3) are a phenomenal value. Take-away discount. Open M-F 8am-4pm.

New Culture Revolution, 305 King's Rd., SW3 (tel. 342 9281). Also at 43 Parkway, NW1 (tel. 267 2700; tube: Camden Town). China's cultural revolution finally hits Chelsea with this clean, friendly restaurant that is a favorite among locals. Highlights include the vegetarian *guo tei* (dumplings filled with vegetables and noodles, £4.90). Healthy, large portions leave you satisfied. Open daily noon-11pm.

Earl's Court

Earl's Court, a take-away carnival, revolves around cheap, palatable food. Groceries abound and shops stay open late and on Sunday. Look for coffee shops and Indian restaurants on Gloucester Rd. north of Cromwell Rd. (especially by Elvaston Pl.). The Troubadour Coffee House (see **Folks and Roots,** p. 135) serves a vast selection of coffee drinks and assorted snacks, soups, and sandwiches for under £4.

Troubador Coffee House, 265 Old Brompton Rd., SW5 (tel. 370 1434), near Earl's Ct. and Old Brompton Rd. junction. Copper pots, pitchforks, and mandolins are suspended from the ceiling, and whirring espresso machines steam up the windows in this enjoyable community cafe. Assorted snacks, soups, and sandwiches under £4. Special breakfasts £3-4. Vast selection of coffee drinks. Open M-Sa 9:30am-12:30am, Su 9:30am-11pm.

Perry's Bakery, 151 Earl's Court Rd., SW5 (tel. 370 4825). Amiable Bulgarian-Israeli management prides itself on a somewhat eclectic menu and phenomenal fresh baked goods. Flaky *borekas* (pastry filled with cheese) make a filling snack (with spinach £1.40). For breakfast, enjoy their croissant plus all-you-can-drink tea or coffee for £2. Challah loaves £1.50. For dinner enjoy a combo plate of the day's special for less than £3. Min. charge £2 to eat in. Open daily 5:30am-midnight.

NOTTING HILL AND BAYSWATER

The many restaurants dotting the streets that radiate from the Notting Hill Gate and Ladbroke Grove stations exude a certain "goodness" not readily found elsewhere. Dishes from around the globe can be found in the area's restaurants. Stylish coffeehouses and pastry shops cluster near the Ladbroke Grove station.

Manzara, 24 Pembridge Rd., W11 (tel. 727 3062). Tube: Notting Hill Gate. Ostensibly a take-away shop, Manzara actually seats 40 people. In the afternoon, pizzas are £3.50, sandwiches £2. In the evenings, they offer a £6 all-you-can-eat array of Greek and Turkish specialties, including grilled-while-you-watch kebabs. Try the mixed *meze* (£4.25). Take-away discount. Open daily 7:30am-midnight.

The Grain Shop, 269a Portobello Rd., W11 (tel. 229 5571). Tube: Ladbroke Grove. The line of customers often reaches halfway into the streets. Organic whole grain breads baked daily on the premises (80p-£1.40 per loaf), as well as excellent sourdough loaves (£1.80). Try any combination of the 6 hot vegetarian dishes—large £4.10, medium £3, small £2. Huge vegan brownies £1. Open M-Sa 9:30am-6pm.

Royal China, 13 Queens Way, W2 (tel. 221 2535). Tube: Bayswater or Queensway. The best and most exotic *dim sum* served outside of Chinatown. A huge meal of freshly made dumplings averages £10 per person, but one can easily get by on less. Try the steamed duck's tongue (£1.80) or the marinated chicken feet (£1.80). Entrees £10-15. Open daily noon-11pm.

THE CITY

This area is splendid for lunch (when food is fresh for the options traders) and disastrous for dinner (when the expense accounts go home and the food goes stale). Pick up some fresh fruit from a vendor in **Leadenhall Market** on Gracechurch St.

The Place Below (tel. 329 0789), in St. Mary-le-Bow Church crypt, Cheapside, EC2. Tube: St. Paul's. Generous vegetarian dishes served in an impressive church basement. Menu changes daily. Quiche and salad £6, take-away £3. £2 discount when you sit in from 11:30am-noon. Serves as a cafe with a doughy collection of muffins, scones, etc., until lunch at 11:30am. Open M-F 7:30am-2:30pm.

Futures!, 8 Botolph Alley, EC3 (tel. 623 4529). Tube: Monument. Off Botolph Ln. Fresh take-away vegetarian breakfast and lunch prepared in a petite kitchen open to view! Daily main dishes, like quiche, £3.40! Spinach pizza £1.85! Open M-F 7:30-10am and 11:30am-3pm!!! Stop by their snazzy, more expensive Futures! branch in Exchange Sq. (behind Liverpool Station)*!!!!!*

St. John, 26 St. John St., EC1 (tel. 251 0849). Tube: Farringdon. This airy, classically designed establishment is a strange hybrid of restaurant, bar and bakery. There is an idiosyncratic, but nonetheless excellent, selection of food available, including smoked eel (£6.70) and winkles and *samphire* (£4). Bar menu. Fresh bread from the bakery is £1.20. Restaurant open M-F noon-3pm and 6-11:30pm, Sa 6-11:30pm. Bar open M-F 11am-11pm, Sa 6-11pm.

Tinseltown 24 Hour Diner, 44-46 St. John St., EC1 (tel. 689 2424; fax 689 7860). Tube: Clerkenwell. The interior of this restaurant features pictures of movie stars and 15 TV screens. The food selection is eclectic and titled with puns: "The Breakfast Club" offers a breakfast from £2, and "Full Metal Jackets," or potatoes, start at £3. All beer £1.50, house wine £5. Best of all, it's open 24hr.

THE EAST END

⊛**Lahore Kebab House,** 2 Umberston St., E1 (tel. 481 9738). Tube: Whitechapel or Shadwell DLR. Off Commercial Rd. Some of the best and cheapest Indian and Pakistani cuisine in the city. The *seekh* kebab (50p) is wrapped in freshly baked *roti* (50p) and dipped in a surprisingly spicy yoghurt dip. There's no dish over £4.50 and, if you're thirsty, feel free to bring your own beer. Open daily noon-midnight.

⊛**Brick Lane Beigel Bake,** 159 Brick Ln., E1 (tel. 729 0616). Tube: Aldgate East. At the top of Brick Ln. perches a lonely vestige of the Jewish East End of yore. But this inexpensive, authentic bakery tries to pick up the slack in the wake of the exodus, not only by offering perfect bagels (60p for 6), but by staying open 24hr.

The Cherry Orchard Café, 247 Globe Rd., E2 (tel. (0181) 980 6678). Tube: Bethnal Green. Walk down Roman Rd., then turn left onto Globe. A fabulous restaurant run by Buddhists. The outdoor garden is lovely in warm weather. The strictly vegetarian menu changes daily. Delicious hot entrees (spinach lasagna £4) served in large portions. Hot food served from noon. Open M 11am-3pm, Tu-F 11am-7pm.

ISLINGTON

⊛**Café Olé,** 119 Upper St., N1 (tel. 226 6991). A hip Italian-Spanish bar-cafe adorned with colorful playbills and painted floral borders on the salmon walls. Endless breakfast £4.20. Variety of generously sized paellas £4.20-5. Lunch menu offers pasta (£3.80-4.80) and salads (£4-4.70), in addition to sandwiches (£1-2.50). Evening dinner specials around £6. Open M-Sa 8am-11pm.

LeMercury, 140a Upper St., N1 (tel. 354 4088; fax 359 7186). Tube: Angel or Highbury and Islington. This French restaurant has the quintessential Islington candlelit effect, with outstanding prices to boot. All main courses, including honey-roasted breast of duck, £5.85. Lunch and dinner 3-course *prix fixe* 11am-7:15pm, £5.50. Kids eat Sunday Roast free. Open M-Sa 11am-1am, Su noon-11:30pm.

Indian Veg Bhelpoori House, 92-93 Chapel Market, N1 (tel. 837 4607 or 833 1167). One of the best bargains in London. All-you-can-eat lunch (£3.25) or dinner buffet (£3.50) of 30 vegetarian dishes and chutneys. Open daily noon-11:30pm.

CAMDEN TOWN

Camden Town can be a bit grotty, especially in the wake of the weekend markets; however, glamourous cafes and international restaurants are magnetically attracted to **Camden High St.,** which runs south from the Camden Town tube station to Mornington Crescent, and north to Chalk Farm, becoming **Chalk Farm Rd.**

Le Petit Prince, 5 Holmes Rd., NW5 (tel. 267 0752). Tube: Kentish Town. French-Algerian cuisine served in a cafe-bar-restaurant decorated with illustrations from Saint-Exupéry's *Le Petit Prince.* Generous plantain sauté starter £3.45, vegetarian couscous £5.45. Lamb, chicken, and fish dishes are slightly more expensive, but come with unlimited couscous and vegetable broth. Open daily 5:30pm-late.

Captain Nemo, 171 Kentish Town Rd., NW1 (tel. 485 3658). Tube: Kentish Town. *Let's Go* would not blithely send you all the way to Kentish Town for "good chips." This seemingly unassuming Chinese-chippie take-away combo rocks your world with their tangy, delicious, great chips in curry sauce (£1.40). Open M-F noon-2:45pm and 5:30-11:30pm, Sa-Su 5:30-11:30pm.

Nontas, 14-16 Camden High St., NW1 (tel. 387 4579). Tube: Mornington Crescent or Camden Town. One of the best Greek venues in the city. The incomparable *meze* (£8.75) offers a seemingly endless selection of dips, meats, and cheeses. Ouzerie in front serves luscious pastries, like *baklava* (£1.05) and Turkish coffee (85p). Open M-Sa noon-2:45pm and 6-11:30pm. Ouzerie open M-Sa 8am-11:30pm.

HAMPSTEAD

This affluent North London district has an artsy bent. The food of local restaurants is almost as important as the area they provide for the ritzy young crowd. The station (tube: Hampstead) is on the corner of Heath and Hampstead High St.

◉**Le Crêperie de Hampstead,** 77 Hampstead High St., NW3. Outside the King William IV pub. This Hampstead institution is guaranteed nirvana. Brittany crepes made before your eyes in a tiny van. Sweet fillings (including Belgian chocolate, bananas, and Grand Marnier) and savory (spinach and garlic cream, mushroom, and cheese) £2-3. Open M-Th 11:45am-11pm, F-Su 11:45am-11:30pm.

Paris-London Cafe, 3 Junction Rd., NW3 (tel. 561 0330). *Le tube:* Archway. *De l'autre côté de la station, ce petit restaurant serve la haute cuisine française directement de belle Paris. En général les plats coûtent £5. Les denrées principales, comme moules marinières (£4), escargots en beurre d'ail (£5.25), ou soupe à l'oignon (£2.10). Menu à 3 plats £10. Silly frogs. Ouvert M-Sa 9am-10:30pm.*

SOUTH OF THE THAMES

Renovation has made dining cheaply near Waterloo Station (tube: Waterloo) difficult. Nonetheless the dinner specials Monday through Saturday 6-7pm at **The Fire Station,** 150 Waterloo Rd., SE1 (tel. 620 2226), allow for affordable gourmet dining (two courses for £10; open M-Sa noon-11pm, Su noon-10:30pm). **Lower Marsh** has escaped the development fracas, and the **Freshly Maid Café,** 79 Lower Marsh (tel. 928 5426; open M-F 6am-7pm), and **Marie's Café,** 90 Lower Marsh (tel. 928 1050; open M-F 7am-5pm, Sa 7am-3pm), serve cheap and exotic fare.

■ Notable Chains

As prices rise in London's central areas, the high streets are becoming congested with inexpensive, semi-gourmet franchises. So, before you order another Big Mac Meal, *Let's Go* recommends you check out the following chains. The establishments listed have locations all over the city, but hours and prices may vary.

Prêt à Manger. In 10 years, this bustling chrome-and-metal sandwich shop has grown to dominate the London franchise scene. Everything Pret serves is made of the freshest ingredients. The chicken breast and avocado (£2.35) and hummus, pepper, and onion sandwich (£1.85) will sate the most discerning palates. The deluxe sushi pack (£5) is inexpensive and satisfying. For dessert, try the freshly baked *pain au chocolat* or almond croissant (85p) and wash it all down with a cappuccino, mocha, or hot chocolate (£1). Eat-in prices are slighly more expensive (the few pence aren't worth the ambience). Many branches are closed for dinner.

Café Dôme. The star of this Parisian chain is its 3-course *prix fixe* for £5, which changes daily. On the day it was reviewed, the *prix fixe* started with a parmesan and artichoke filo, continued with grilled smoked mackerel and mussels with seasonal vegetables marinated in a tomato and Rosemary oil, and concluded with white chocolate cheesecake. *C'est magnifique!* Fresh salads £5-7.

Cafe Pasta. Generally found in rather ritzy areas, this chain serves healthy portions of Italian food at reasonable prices to the beautiful people. The atmosphere matches the fresh, light fare. Pastas start around £5.

Pierre Victoire. Popular brasserie chain offers inexpensive Parisian fare in expensive London neighborhoods. French staples like seafood *pot au feu* and smoked mackerel pâté. Menu changes daily. *Prix fixe* 2-course lunch £4.90.

GROCERIES AND SUPERMARKETS

Tesco and **Sainsbury's** are the two largest chains of supermarkets. Other chains include **Europa, Spar,** and **Asda.** If you're willing to spend a bit more, then you might consider **Marks and Spencer,** which introduced baby tomatoes, potatoes, and other cute produce to Britain. If you're willing to splurge, then the foodhalls of **Harrods** and **Fortnum and Mason's** are attractions in their own right.

■ Pubs and Bars

The atmosphere and clientele of London's 7000 pubs vary considerably from one neighborhood to the next. Avoid pubs within a half-mile radius of an inner-city train station (Paddington, Euston, King's Cross/St. Pancras, and Victoria). Some prey upon tourists by charging an extra 20-40p per pint. For the best prices, head to the East End. Stylish, lively pubs cluster around the fringes of the West End. Many historic ale-houses lend an ancient air to areas swallowed by urban sprawl, such as Highgate and Hampstead. Some of the oldest pubs cluster in the City. Buy drinks at the bar; a pint should set you back £1.80-2.35.

THE WEST END

The Dog and Duck, 8 Bateman St., W1 (tel. 437 4447). Tube: Tottenham Ct. Rd. Frequent winner of the Best Pub in Soho award. Crowds pile in at lunch for the cheap pints (£2-2.20). Evenings bring locals, actors on the way home, and, yes, some tourists. Open M-F noon-11pm, Sa 6-11pm, Su 7-10:30pm.

The Three Greyhounds, 25 Greek St., W1 (tel. 287 0754). Tube: Leicester Sq. This tiny, medieval-styled pub provides personality and a welcome respite from the endless posturing of Soho. 1996 winner of the Best Pub in Soho award. Good food as well. Open M-Sa 11am-11pm, Su noon-10:30pm.

Riki Tik, 23-24 Bateman St., W1 (tel. 437 1977). Tube: Leicester Sq., Tottenham Ct. Rd., or Piccadilly Circus. A hyped, hip, and tremendously swinging bar specializing in flavored vodka shots; chocolate is a house favorite (£2.60). During happy hour (W-Sa noon-8pm) and the deliciously fruity cocktails are a near-bargain at £6.50 per pitcher. Open M-Sa noon-1am. £3 cover after 11pm.

Crown and Anchor, 22 Neal St., WC2 (tel. 836 5649). Tube: Covent Garden. One of Covent Garden's most popular pubs. The crowd perches on kegs or sits on the cobblestones outside, forming a mellow oasis in the midst of Neal St.'s bustling pedestrian zone. Open M-Sa 11am-11pm, Su noon-10:30pm.

Lamb and Flag, 33 Rose St., WC2 (tel. 497 9504), off Garrick St. Tube: Covent Garden or Leicester Sq. Rose St. is off Long Acre, which runs between the 2 tube stops. Traditional old English pub, separated into 2 sections—the public bar and the saloon bar. Open M-Th 11am-11pm, F-Sa 11am-10:45pm, Su noon-10:30pm.

KENSINGTON, CHELSEA, AND EARL'S COURT

The Scarsdale, 23a Edward Sq., W8 (tel. 937 1811). Tube: High St. Kensington. Walk down High St. and turn left onto Edward Sq. When you see people sitting outside in a sea of flowers and ivy, contentedly throwing back a few pints, well, you've found it. Don't be thrown off by the fact that it looks like a house. Good food during meal times. Open M-Sa noon-11pm, Su noon-10:30pm.

World's End Distillery, 459 King's Rd. (tel. 376 8946), near World's End Pass before Edith Grove. Tube: Sloane Sq. This classy pub dates back to 1689 when it became renowned for its tea garden. Now a variety of ages enjoy pints in the comfy bookshelf-lined booths. Open M-Sa 11am-11pm, Su noon-10:30pm.

The Chelsea Potter, 119 King's Rd., SW3 (tel. 589 0262). Tube: Sloane Sq. Walk up Kings Rd. At the Safeway, turn onto Tryon St. and walk up a few blocks. This pub's name reflects its history as a haven for Chelsea artists throwing pots and living on their trust funds. Pints of Foster's £2.15. Open M-Sa 11am-11pm, Su noon-10:30pm.

The Goat in Boots, 333 Fulham Rd. Tube: South Kensington. Take Onslow to Fulham and walk for about 20min. Multi-level bar attracts a young, fun-loving crowd. Drink specials each night. Open M-Sa 11:30am-11pm, Su noon-10:30pm.

Cadogan Arms, 218 King's Rd., SW3 (tel. 352 1645), near Old Church St. Tube: Sloane Sq. or Victoria, then bus #11 or 22. Country feel is a retreat from King's Rd. TV and pool table. Open M-Sa 11am-11pm, Su noon-10:30pm.

The King's Head and Eight Bells, 50 Cheyne Walk, SW3 (tel. 352 1820). Tube: Sloane Sq. or South Kensington. Take any bus down King's Rd., get off at Oakley St., walk toward the river, and turn right on Cheyne Walk. Wide selection of beers on tap, including heavenly Hoegaarden (£3.30 per delicious pint). Open M-Sa 11am-11pm, Su noon-10:30pm.

BLOOMSBURY

The Old Crown, 33 New Oxford St., WC1 (tel. 836 9121). Tube: Tottenham Ct. Rd. A thoroughly untraditional pub. The lively crowd spills out into the outdoor seating, creating a babble of voices above the cool jazz playing in the background. Homemade food from £2.75. Open M-Sa 10am-11pm.

Cittie of Yorke, 22 High Holborn, WC1 (tel. 242 7670). Tube: Holborn. Built in 1430, the clock and half-timbered facade of this watering hole conceal a cavernous interior replete with enormous ale casks and intimate booths. Standard pub fare from £4.25. Open M-Sa 11:30am-11pm. AmEx, MC, Visa.

Lord John Russell Pub, 91 Marchmont St., WC1 (tel. 388 0500). Tube: Russell Sq. The exact point where the bustle of Marchmont St. flows into the residential calm of nearby Cartwright Gardens. Calm and pleasant. Ploughman's lunch £3.75. Open M-Sa 11:30am-11pm, Su noon-11pm.

The Lamb, 94 Lamb's Conduit St., WC1 (tel. 405 0713). Tube: Russell Sq. E.M. Forster and other Bloomsbury luminaries used to tipple here. Limited outdoor seating and a no-smoking room tastefully decorated with old *Vanity Fair* caricatures. Food served noon-5pm. Open M-Sa 11am-11pm, Su noon-10:30pm. MC, Visa.

The Water Rats, 328 Grays Inn Rd., WC1 (tel. 837 7269). Tube: King's Cross/St. Pancras. This used to be one of Marx and Engels's favorite haunts. Tu-F venue for indie rock and punk. Cover £5, concessions £3.50. Bands start at 9pm. Closed from 7:30-8:30pm during music nights. Open daily 8:30am-midnight.

THE CITY AND EAST END

Black Friar, 174 Queen Victoria St., EC4 (tel. 236 5650). Tube: Blackfriars. Directly across from the station. One of the most exquisite and fascinating pubs in all of London. Arches, mosaics, and reliefs line the pub's walls. See the "side chapel" (located in back). Prices unfortunately reflect the pub's popularity. Average pint £2.10. Lunch 11:30am-2:30pm. Open M-W 11:30am-10pm, Th-F 11:30am-11pm.

Ye Olde Cheshire Cheese, Wine Office Ct. by 145 Fleet St., EC4 (tel. 353 6170). Tube: Blackfriars or St. Paul's. On Fleet St., watch out for Wine Office Ct. on the right; small sign indicates the alley. Classic 17th-century bar where Dr. Johnson and Dickens as well as little-known Americans Mark Twain and Theodore Roosevelt hung out. One of the few London pubs with the original wood interior intact. Open M-Sa 11:30am-11pm, Su noon-3pm.

The Shakespeare, 2 Goswell Rd., EC1 (tel. 253 6166). Tube: Barbican. Upstairs flooded with hip student crowd and businesspeople getting soused during and after work. Lunch served 11:30am-2:45pm, dinner 6:30-10pm. Pint of Bard's Brew £1.60. Open M-F 11am-11pm, Sa 11am-3pm.

CAMDEN TOWN AND ISLINGTON

Filthy MacNasty's Whiskey Café, 68 Amwell St. (tel. 837 6067). Tube: Angel. Exit the station left, then right onto Pentonville Rd., and turn left at Claremont Sq., which turns into Amwell. Celtic drawings line the fire-colored walls; former Pogues singer Shane MacGowan frequently appears for last call. Traditional Irish music on Sunday nights. A pint of Guinness £2.10. Runner-up in the Time Out 1997 Best Bar in London Award. Open daily noon-11pm. Wheelchair accessible.

The Engineer, 65 Gloucester Ave., NW1 (tel. 722 0950; fax 483 0592). Tube: Chalk Farm. Bright, flowery atmosphere and a sumptuous back garden that makes everybody feel relaxed. Pints £2.25. Open daily noon-11pm. Wheelchair accessible.

THE EAST END

The Blind Beggar, 337 Whitechapel Rd., E1 (tel. 247 6195). Tube: Whitechapel. You may be sitting where George Cornell sat when he was gunned down by rival Bethnal Green gangster Ronnie Kray in 1966. Keep your head low. Spacious pub with conservatory and garden. Open M-Sa 11am-11pm, Su noon-10:30pm.

HAMPSTEAD AND HIGHGATE

King of Bohemia, 10 Hampstead High St., NW3 (tel. (0181) 435 6513). Tube: Hampstead. Traditional-looking pub serves up techno music to a young, upscale clientele that swarms to the outdoor seating in summer. Library-like seating in back is a pleasant place to down a pint. Open M-Sa 11am-11pm, Su noon-10:30pm.

The Holly Bush, 22 Holly Mount, NW3 (tel. (0181) 435 2892). Tube: Hampstead. From the tube climb Holly Hill and watch for the sharp right turn. Quintessential snug Hampstead pub in a quaint cul-de-sac. Pints from £1.55. Open M-F noon-3pm and 5:30-11pm, Sa noon-4pm and 6-11pm, Su noon-10:30pm.

■ Tea

London hotels serve afternoon set teas, often hybrids of the cream and high varieties, which are expensive and sometimes disappointing. You might order single items from the menu instead of the full set to avoid a sugar overdose. Cafes often serve a simpler tea (pot of tea, scone, preserves, and butter) for a lower price.

The Savoy, Strand, WC2 (tel. 836 4343). The elegance of this music-accompanied tea is well worth the splurge. Graciously wolf down the delicious tarts, scones, and sandwiches as the bemused waitstaff refills your tray time after time. Strict dress code—no jeans or shorts, neckties preferred for gentlemen. If gentlemen "forget" their jacket, they'll be forced to borrow a garish red number from the cloakroom. Set tea £18.50. Tea served daily 3-5pm. Sa and Su book ahead.

Georgian Restaurant, Harrods, Knightsbridge, SW1 (tel. 225 6800). Tube: Knightsbridge. A carefully staged event. Revel in bourgeois satisfaction as you enjoy your expensive repast inside or on the terrace (£15.50). Beautiful view of downtown Knightsbridge. Tea served M-Sa 3:45-5:15pm.

The Muffin Man, 12 Wrights Ln., W8 (tel 937 6652). Tube: High St. Kensington. Everything you dreamed a tearoom could be. Set cream tea £4.50. Min. £1.50 from noon-3:30pm. Open M-Sa 8am-5:30pm.

The Orangery Tea Room, Kensington Palace, Kensington Gdns., W8 (tel. 376 0239). Tube: High St. Kensington. Light meals and tea served in the marvelously airy Orangery built for Queen Anne in 1705. Scones with clotted cream and jam £3.75. Tea £1.70. Trundle through the gardens afterward. Open daily 10am-6pm.

SIGHTS

The landmarks of London that attract those on foot and in ever-lengthening coaches face an onslaught of up to five million visitors a year. These stampedes thicken from the late morning onwards, so try to get started as early as possible. Pacing any assault will allow a much more thorough exploration of the districts that make up the city. Sightseers (particularly couples) who don't qualify for student or senior discounts may want to consider the **London for less** card, issued by Metropolis International (order by phone (0181) 964 4242), which offers discounts for major attractions, theaters, restaurants, and hotels. The card is endorsed by the British Tourist Authority, and is available at all BTA offices (see p. 76; 2-person, 4-day card £13).

TOURS

You can begin to familiarize yourself with the eclectic wonders of London through a good city tour. Most tour buses stop at Marble Arch and do not require reservations. The **Original London Sightseeing Tour** (tel. (0181) 877 1722) provides a convenient, albeit cursory, overview of London's attractions from a double-decker bus. *(Tours daily in summer 9am-7pm; winter 9:30am-5:30pm. £12, under 16 £6.)* Two-hour tours depart from Baker St., Haymarket (near Piccadilly Circus), Marble Arch, Embankment, and near Victoria Station. Route includes views of Buckingham Palace, the Houses of Parliament, Westminster Abbey, the Tower of London, St. Paul's, and Piccadilly Circus. A ticket allows you to ride the buses for a 24-hour period—permitting visitors to hop off at major sights and hop on a later bus to finish the tour. Other companies have a hop-on hop-off policy, but be sure to ask how often buses circle through the route—Original London coaches come every five to ten minutes.

Walking tours can fill in the specifics of London that bus tours run right over. With a good guide, a tour can be as entertaining as it is informative. Among the best are **The Original London Walks** (tel. 624 3978), which cover a specific topic such as Legal London, Jack the Ripper, or Spies and Spycatchers. *(Tours £4.50, students £3.50, accompanied children under 15 free.)* The two-hour tours are led by well-regarded guides; many consider this company to be the best in London. **Historical Tours of London** (tel. (0181) 668 4019) also leads popular tours. *(£4.50, students, seniors, and children £3.50.)* Leaflets for these and others are available in hotels and tourist information centers. For meeting times, see the "Around Town" section of *Time Out* magazine.

If glancing at London from the top of a bus is unsatisfactory and hoofing it seems daunting, a tour led by **The London Bicycle Tour Company** (tel. 928 6838) may be the happy medium. They offer a Saturday tour of the East End and a Sunday tour of Middle London and Royal West. *(Easter-Oct. Sa-Su 2pm. Approximately 3½hr. £10; independent bike £2 per hour, £10 per day, £30 per week. Tube: Blackfriars or Waterloo. Tours depart from Gabriel's Wharf, 56 Upper Ground, SE1.)*

✍ HIGHLIGHTS OF LONDON

- **London is packed with first-rate attractions. Here are some suggested itineraries to help you make the most of a short visit:**
- **One Day**—Take in the Houses of Parliament and Westminster Abbey. Tour Buckingham Palace, then stroll down the Mall toward Trafalgar Sq. to visit the National Gallery. Wander around Picadilly Circus, sip a pint at a nearby pub, and enjoy a late dinner in Soho or Chinatown.
- **Three Days**—first day as above. The second day, see the City of London: climb St. Paul's Cathedral for a stunning view, then take a Beefeater tour of the Tower of London. Dine in the East End for some of the best Indian food in the city. On the third day, head to Bloomsbury and visit the British Museum, followed by the British Library and Madame Tussaud's. Stroll through Regent's Park and dine in chic Islington. Finish off the evening with theater and coffee in Covent Garden.
- **One Week**—first three days as above. Spend a day exploring the museums of Kensington and Knightsbridge. Head over to Harrods department store and take-away a picnic meal to Hyde Park and Kensington Gardens. Visit the Tate Gallery, the Wallace Collection, and the Courtauld Gallery. Stroll through the greenery of Hampstead Heath and see Highgate Cemetery. Explore the South Bank: visit the HMS Belfast, Southwark Cathedral, and the London Dungeon and enjoy a show at Shakespeare's Globe Theatre. To learn more about the history of Britain and London itself, tour the Museum of London, the London Transport Museum, and the Imperial War Museum. Don't miss the vibrant ethnic neighborhoods of London, including Brixton, Golders Green, and the East End.

■ Central London

■ Westminster

The old city of Westminster was once a seething nest of criminals, and is now the U.K.'s center of political and religious power. And they say some things never change.

St. Margaret's has served as the parish church of the House of Commons since 1614, when Protestant MPs feared Westminster Abbey was about to become Catholic. John Milton, Samuel Pepys, and Winston Churchill were married here. Beneath the high altar lies the headless body of Sir Walter Raleigh, who was executed across the street in 1618. The inscription on his memorial respectfully asks readers not to "reflect on his errors." *(Open daily 9:30am-5pm when services are not being held.)*

On the south side of the abbey cluster the buildings of the hoity-toity **Westminster School,** founded as a part of the Abbey. References to the school date as far back as the 14th century, but Queen Elizabeth officially founded it in 1560. The arch in Dean's Yard is pitted with the carved initials of England's most privileged schoolboys, among them Ben Jonson, John Dryden, John Locke, and Christopher Wren.

The **Victoria Tower Gardens,** a narrow spit of land along the Thames immediately south of the Houses of Parliament, offers a pleasant view of the river. Four assertive corner towers distinguish former church **St. John the Evangelist,** now a chamber music concert hall in nearby Smith Sq., off Millbank at the south end of the Victoria Tower Gardens. *(Box office tel. 222 1061; call ahead for details and concert times.)* Any flurry of activity around the square is likely to be connected with no. 31, where the **Central Office of the Conservative Party** lurks, ready to swing into (re)action down the road in Parliament.

WESTMINSTER ABBEY

> Think how many royal bones
> Sleep within this heap of stones;
> For here they lie, had realms and lands,
> That now want strength to stir their hands.
>
> —*Francis Beaumont*

Tel. 222 5152. **Tube:** Westminster. **Open** M-F 9am-4:45pm, last admission 3:45pm, some Wednesdays until 7:45pm (call 222 7110), Sa 9am-2:45pm. **Admission** £5, concessions £3, ages 11-18 £2, family £10, children under 11 free. **Photography** permitted W 6-7:45pm only. **Tours** (tel. 222 7110) last 1½hr. £3. Depart from the Enquiry Desk in the nave. Apr.-Oct. M-F 10, 10:30, 11am, 2, 2:30, and 3pm, F no 3pm tour, Sa 10, 11am, and 12:30pm. Nov.-Mar. M-F 10, 11am, 2, and 3pm, F no 3pm tour, Sa 10, 11am, and 12:30pm. Book tours by calling or inquiring at the Abbey desk. Portable, **tape-recorded tours** in assorted languages £2.

Neither a cathedral nor a parish church, **Westminster Abbey** is a "royal peculiar," controlled directly by the Crown and outside the jurisdiction of the **Church of England.** As both the site of every royal coronation since 1066 and the final resting place for an imposing assortment of sovereigns, politicians, poets, and artists, the Abbey's significance extends far beyond religion. Westminster today functions as a hybrid national church and honor roll. Burial in the abbey is the greatest and rarest of honors in Britain,—over the last 200 years, space has become so limited that many coffins stand upright under the pavement.

Although the Abbey was consecrated by King Edward the Confessor on December 28, 1065, only the Pyx Chamber and the Norman Undercroft (now the Westminster Abbey Treasure Museum; see below) survive from the original structure. Most of the present Abbey was erected under the direction of Henry III during the 13th century. What we see today, however, is not Henry's legacy either—most of the stone visible in the Abbey is actually refacing that dates from the 18th century. The stones that make the two **West Front Towers,** designed and built by Sir Christopher Wren and his Baroque pupil, Nicholas Hawksmoor, are of similar vintage. The North Entrance, completed after 1850, is the youngest part of the Abbey, whose entrance's Victorian stonework includes carved figures of dragons and griffins. Work on the cathedral continued into this decade—1995 witnessed the conclusion of over 22 years of cleaning the Abbey's soot-stained stones.

The cluttered **Statesmen's Aisle,** in the early Gothic north transept, has the most eclectic group of memorials. Prime Ministers Disraeli and Gladstone couldn't stand each other in life, but in death their figures symmetrically flank a large memorial to Sir Peter Warren, alongside Peel, Castlereagh, Palmerston, and others. Sir Francis Vere's Elizabethan tomb in the southeast corner of the transept features the cracked shells of his armor held above his body. A strange paving stone in front of the memorial bears no exalted name, only the strange inscription, "Stone coffin underneath."

The **High Altar,** directly south of the north transept, has been the scene of coronations and royal weddings since 1066. Anne of Cleves, Henry VIII's fourth wife, lies in a tomb on the south side of the sanctuary, just before the altar. A series of crowded choir chapels fills the space east of the north transept.

Beyond these chapels stands the **Chapel of Henry VII** (built 1503-12), perhaps England's most outstanding piece of the period. Every one of its magnificently carved wooden stalls, reserved for the Knights of the Order of the Bath, features a colorful headpiece bearing the chosen personal statement of its occupant. The lower sides of the seats, which fold up to support those standing during long services, were the only part of the design left to the carpenters' discretion; they feature cartoon-like images of wives beating up their husbands and other pagan stories. Lord Nelson's stall was no. 20, on the south side. Latter-day members of the order include Americans Ronald Reagan and Norman Schwarzkopf. The walls sport 95 saints, including the once-lovely Bernadette, who grew a beard overnight after praying to be saved from a multitude of suitors. The chapel's elaborate ceiling was hand-carved after it had been erected. Henry VII and his wife Elizabeth lie at the very end of the chapel. Nearby is the stone that once marked Oliver Cromwell's grave. Protestant Elizabeth I (in the north aisle) and the Catholic cousin she had beheaded, Mary, Queen of Scots (in the south aisle), are buried on opposite sides of the Henry VII chapel.

The **Royal Air Force (RAF) Chapel,** at the far east end, commemorates the Battle of Britain. A hole in the wall in the northeast corner of the Air Force memorial, damage from a German bomb, has deliberately been left unrepaired. Many may find themselves a little choked up when surrounded by the stained glass panels celebrating the few to whom so many owe so much.

Behind the High Altar, in the **Chapel of St. Edward the Confessor,** rests the Coronation Chair, on which all but two (Edward V and Edward VIII) English monarchs since 1308 have been crowned. Those who look closely will notice that much of the chair's surface is covered in graffiti; when schoolchildren were allowed to sit in the chair, they carved their names into the wood. The chair used to rest on the ancient **Stone of Scone** ("skoon"). The legendary stone (some say it was the biblical Jacob's pillow) was used in the coronation of ancient Scottish kings; James I took it to London to represent the Union, and in the 1950s it was reclaimed for months by daring Scottish nationalists (see **Stoned,** p. 98). During WWII, it was hidden from possible capture by Hitler—rumor has it that only Churchill, Roosevelt, the Prime Minister of Canada, and the two workers who moved the stone knew of its whereabouts. The chair sits next to the 7 ft. State Sword and the shield of Edward III. On July 4, 1996 Prime Minister Major announced that—700 years after being taken from Scotland— the stone would return home and visit the Abbey only for coronations (see p. 516).

Numerous monarchs are interred in the chapel, from Henry III (d. 1272) to George II (d. 1760). Edward I had himself placed in an unsealed crypt here, in case he was needed again to fight the Scots; his mummy was carried as a standard by the English army as it tried to conquer Scotland. An engraving by William Blake commemorates the moment in 1774 when the Royal Society of Antiquaries opened this coffin in order to assess the body's state of preservation. Sick persons hoping to be cured would spend nights at the base of the Shrine of St. Edward the Confessor, at the center of the chapel. The king purportedly wielded healing powers during his life and dispensed free medical care to hundreds.

Visitors uninterested in the graves of English monarchs may find the names on the graves and plaques in the **Poets' Corner** more compelling. This shrine celebrates those who have died, been canonized, and later anthologized. It begins with Geoffrey Chaucer, who was originally buried in the abbey in 1400—the short Gothic tomb you see today in the east wall of the transept was not erected until 1556. The lower classes of the dead poets' society, and those leading "unconventional" lifestyles, often had to wait a while before getting a permanent spot in the Abbey; even the Bard remained on the waiting list until 125 years after his mortal coil was shuffled off. Oscar Wilde was honored with a long overdue monument in Poets' Corner in 1995, the centenary of his conviction for homosexual activities. Floor panels commemorate

Tennyson, T.S. Eliot, Dylan Thomas, Henry James, Lewis Carroll, Lord Byron, W.H. Auden, and WWI poets, all at the foot of Chaucer's tomb. Each one bears an appropriate description or image for puzzle solvers: D.H. Lawrence's publishing mark (a phoenix) or T.S. Eliot's symbol of death.

The south wall bears tributes to Edmund Spenser and John Milton. A partition wall divides the south transept, its east side graced with the graves of Samuel Johnson and actor David Garrick, its west side with busts of William Wordsworth, Samuel Taylor Coleridge, and Robert Burns, in addition to a full-length William Shakespeare that overshadows the tiny plaques memorializing the Brontë sisters. On the west wall of the transept, Handel's massive memorial looms over his grave next to the resting place of prolific Charles Dickens. On this side of the wall, you'll also find the grave of Rudyard Kipling and a memorial to that morbid Dorset farm boy, Thomas Hardy. Among the writers and poets lie two outsiders: Old Parr, who reportedly lived to the age of 152, and "Spot" Ward, who once healed George II of a thumb injury.

At the foot of the **Organ Loft,** found in the crossing, a memorial to Sir Isaac Newton sits next to the grave of Lord Kelvin. Franklin Roosevelt, David Lloyd George, Lord and Lady Baden-Powell of Boy Scout fame, the presumptive David Livingstone, and the heretical Charles Darwin are remembered in the nave. "Rare Ben Jonson" is buried upright; on his deathbed he proclaimed, "Six feet long by two feet wide is too much for me. Two feet by two feet will do for all I want."

Stoned

On Christmas Day, 1950, daring Scottish patriot Ian Hamilton broke into Westminster Abbey with three of his friends and pulled the 555 lb. Stone of Scone out of its wooden container, accidentally breaking it into two pieces. Hamilton's girlfriend Kay drove to Scotland with the smaller piece, while he stowed the larger piece in his car. The car's engine could not handle the weight, however, and the stone was abandoned in a field. Returning to the spot two weeks later, Hamilton found it guarded by gypsies; he joined their troupe to take the stone to Scotland.

The stone was repaired in a Glasgow workyard, but the patriots were frustrated that they could not display their national symbol in public. On April 11, 1951, Hamilton & Co. carried the stone to the altar at Arbroath Abbey where it was discovered and returned to England. Now-deceased Glasgow councilor Bertie Gray claimed, before he died, that the stone was copied and that the stone in Westminster Abbey was a fake. The British authorities dispute his claim. The questionable stone has since been returned to Scotland by Prime Minister Major (see p. 516).

THE HOUSES OF PARLIAMENT

The Houses of Parliament (tube: Westminster), oft-imagined in foggy silhouette against the Thames, have become London's visual trademark. For the classic view captured by Claude Monet, walk about halfway over Westminster Bridge, preferably at dusk. Like the government offices along Whitehall, the Houses of Parliament occupy the former site of a royal palace. Only Jewel Tower (see **Westminster,** p. 95) and Westminster Hall (to the left of St. Stephen's entrance on St. Margaret St.) survive from the original palace, which was destroyed by a fire on October 16, 1834. **Sir Charles Barry** and **A.W.N. Pugin** won a competition for the design of the new houses. From 1840 to 1888, Barry built a hulking, symmetrical block that Pugin ornamented with tortured imitations of late medieval decoration—"Tudor details on a classic body," Pugin later sneered, before dying of insanity.

The immense complex blankets eight acres and includes more than 1000 rooms and 100 staircases. Space is nevertheless so inadequate that Members of Parliament (MPs) cannot have private offices or staff, and the archives—the original copies of every Act of Parliament passed since 1497—are stuffed into **Victoria Tower,** the large tower to the south. A flag flown from the tower (a signal light after dusk) indicates that Parliament is in session.

Although you can hear **Big Ben,** you can't see him; he's actually neither the northernmost tower nor the clock but the 14-ton bell that tolls the hours. Ben is most likely named after the robustly proportioned Sir Benjamin Hall, who served as Commissioner of Works when the bell was cast and hung in 1858. The familiar 16-note tune that precedes the top-of-the-hour toll is a selection from Handel's *Messiah.*

Unfortunately, access to Westminster Hall and the Houses of Parliament has been restricted since a bomb killed an MP in 1979. To get a **guided tour** (M-Th) or a seat at **Question Time** when the Prime Minister attends (W 3-3:30pm), you need to obtain tickets—available on a limited basis from your embassy—or an introduction from an MP. Because demand for these tickets is extremely high, the most likely way of getting into the building is to queue for a seat at a debate when Parliament is in session. As a rough guide, the Houses are not in session during Easter week, summer recess (late July to mid-Oct.), and a three-week winter recess during Christmas time. Tours for overseas visitors can be arranged by sending a written request to the Public Information Office, 1 Derby Gate, Westminster, SW1. The **House of Commons Visitors' Gallery** (for "Distinguished and Ordinary Strangers") holds extraordinary hours. *(Open M-Tu and Th 2:30-10pm, W 9:30am-2pm, F 9:30am-3pm.)* The **House of Lords Visitors' Gallery** is often easier to access, though the Lords perform less important work. *(Open M-W 2:30pm-late, Th 3pm-late, occasionally F 11am-4pm.)* These hours are very rough guidelines—MPs leave when they're done with business and begin when they feel like it. Visitors should arrive early and be prepared to wait by St. Stephen's Gate (on the left for Commons, on the right for Lords; free). To view smaller, more focused business, visitors can attend meetings of any of the various committees by jumping the queue and going straight up to the entrance. For times of committee meetings, call the **House of Commons Information Office** (tel. 219 4272).

After entering St. Stephen's Gate and submitting to an elaborate security check, you will be standing in **St. Stephen's Hall.** This chapel is where the House of Commons used to sit. In the floor are four brass markers where the Speaker's Chair stood. Charles I, in his ill-fated attempt to arrest five MPs, sat here in the place of the Speaker in 1641. No sovereign has entered the Commons since.

To the left from the Central Lobby are the **Chambers of the House of Commons.** Most traditional features still remain, such as two red lines fixed two sword-lengths apart, which (for safety's sake) debating members may not cross. The Government party (the party with the most MPs in the House) sits to the Speaker's right, and the Opposition sits to his left. Members vote by filing into **division lobbies** parallel to the chamber: ayes to the west, nays to the east.

To enter the Lords' Gallery, go back through the Central Lobby and pass through the Peers' corridor. The ostentatious **House of Lords,** dominated by the sovereign's Throne of State under a gilt canopy, contrasts with the sober, green-upholstered Commons' Chamber. The Lord Chancellor presides over the House from his seat on the **Woolsack,** stuffed with wool from all nations of the Kingdom and Commonwealth—harking back to a time when wool, like the Lords, was more vital to Britain.

Outside the Houses is the **Old Palace Yard,** site of the untimely demises of Sir Walter Raleigh and the Gunpowder Plotter Guy Fawkes (the palace's cellars are still ceremonially searched before every opening of Parliament). To the north squats **Westminster Hall** (rebuilt around 1400), where high treason trials, including those of Thomas More, Fawkes, and Charles I, were held until 1825.

■ Whitehall

Whitehall was born in 1245 as York Place, residence for the Archbishops of York. Cardinal Wolsey enlarged it into a palace for Henry VIII in 1530. William II, however, resented a diplomat's description of Whitehall as "the biggest, most hideous place in all Europe," and relocated to Kensington Palace. Since the original palace burned down in 1698, "Whitehall" has become a synonym for the British civil service.

10 Downing St., which serves as the Prime Minister's headquarters, lies just steps up Parliament St. from the Houses. Sir George Downing, ex-Ambassador to The Hague, built this house in 1681. Prime Minister Sir Robert Walpole made it his official residence in 1732. The exterior of "Number Ten" is decidedly unimpressive, but behind the famous door spreads an extensive political network, including the Chancellor of the Execchequer at No. 11 Downing St., and the Chief Whip of the House of Commons at No. 12. The public has long been banned from entering Downing St.

The **Cabinet War Rooms** lurk at the end of King Charles St., near Horse Guards Rd. The formal **Cenotaph,** which honors the war dead, usually decked with wreaths, stands where Parliament St. turns into Whitehall. **New Scotland Yard** is unremarkable no matter how many mystery novels you've read.

The 1622 **Banqueting House** (tel. 930 4179), at the corner of Horse Guards Ave. and Whitehall, opposite Horse Guards Hall, is one of the few intact masterpieces of Inigo Jones, dripping with beauty and irony that recall the tumultuous times of the Stuart monarchy. James I and Charles I held feasts and staged elaborate masques (thinly-disguised pieces of theatrical propaganda) in the main hall. The 60 ft. ceiling was commissioned by Charles I; the scenes Rubens painted are allegorical representations of the divine strength of the English monarch. The party ended on January 27, 1649, when King Charles I, draped in black velvet, stepped out of a first floor window to the scaffold where he was beheaded by Cromwell's men. The weather vane on the roof tells another tale of Stuart misfortune—James II placed it there to see if the wind was favorable for his rival to the throne William of Orange's voyage from the Netherlands. From 1724 to 1890, the Banqueting House served as a Chapel Royal. These days the hall sees no executions, just harmless state dinners (behind bulletproof glass) and the occasional concert. *(Open M-Sa 10am-5pm, last admission 4pm. Closed for government functions. Admission £3.50, students and seniors £2.70, children £2.30.)*

For folks who can't get enough of mounted, betassled guards, another battery of the **Queen's Life Guard** mark time on the west side of Whitehall north of Downing St. Monday to Saturday at 11am and Sunday at 10am. The arrival of more mounted troops, and lots of barking in incoherent English mark Whitehall's **Changing of the Guard,** a less crowded and impressive version of the Buckingham Palace spectacle. Daily at 4pm, the barking is accompanied by dismounting and strutting, and is called the **Inspection of the Guard.** The Changing and Inspection don't occur on June Saturdays, when the Guard is gearing up for **Trooping the Colour,** a celebration of the Queen's birthday.

■ The Mall and St. James's

Just north of Buckingham Palace and the Mall, up Stable Yard or Marlborough Rd., stands **St. James's Palace,** the residence of the monarchy from 1660 to 1668 and again from 1715 to 1837 (tube: Green Park). The scene of many a three-volume novel and Regency romance, over the years this palace has hosted tens of thousands of the young girls whose families "presented" them at Court. Ambassadors and the elite set of barristers known as "Queen's Counsel" are still received "into the Court of St. James's." You can visit Inigo Jones's **Queen's Chapel,** built in 1626. (Open for Sunday services Oct.-July 8:30 and 11am.)

Henry VIII declared **St. James's Park** London's first royal park in 1532. The fenced-off peninsula at the east end of the park's pond, **Duck Island,** is the mating ground for thousands of waterfowl. St. James's is also a good place to discover that lawn chairs in England are not free—chairs have been hired out here since the 18th century. *(Chairs 70p for a 4hr. sit—don't find the attendants, just sit and they'll find you.)*

The high-rent district around the palace has also taken the moniker St. James's. Bordered by St. James's Park and Green Park to the south and Piccadilly to the north, it begins at an equestrian statue of notorious madman George III on Cockspur St. off Trafalgar Sq. **St. James's St.,** next to St. James's Palace, runs into stately **Pall Mall** (both rhyme with "pal"). Lined with double rows of plane trees, the Mall grandly traverses the space from Trafalgar Sq. to Buckingham Palace (tube: Charing Cross).

Along the north side of the Mall lie the imposing facades of grand houses, starting with **Carlton House Terr.,** erected by John Nash as part of the 18th-century Regent's Park route; the terrace statue memorializes the "Grand Old Duke of York." It now contains the Royal Society of Distinguished Scientists and the area's newest and most attention-grabbing neighbor, the avant-garde **Institute of Contemporary Arts (ICA)**, established in 1947 to provide resources and facilities to British artists.

Pall Mall and St. James's St., together with **Jermyn St.**, parallel to Pall Mall to the north, flank the traditional stomping grounds of the upper-class English clubman. Revel in the patrician solemnity of the area at the quintessential men's store **Alfred Dunhill**, 30 Duke Street (tel. 838 8000; entrance on Jermyn)—lurking upstairs above the staid merchandise is a riotously sublime collection of smoking vessels from the world over. *(Open M-F 9am-6pm.)*

These Regency storefronts rub elbows with a number of famous London coffee-houses-turned-clubs. The coffeehouses of the early 18th century, whose political life was painted vividly by Addison and Steele in their journal *The Spectator*, were trans-formed by the 19th century into exclusive clubs for political and literary men of a par-ticular social station. The chief Tory club, the **Carlton**, 69 St. James's St., was bombed by the IRA not long ago. The chief Liberal club, the **Reform**, 104 Pall Mall, served as a social center of Parliamentary power.

Around the corner from St. James's Palace stand royal medalists Spink's, and Christie, Manson, and Wodds Fine Art Auctioneers—better known as **Christie's**, 8 King St. (tel. 839 9060; tube: Green Park). Auctions, open to the public, are held most weekdays at 10:30am.

Between aristocratic Jermyn St. and Piccadilly, you can enter **St. James's Church** (tube: Green Park or Piccadilly Circus), a postwar reconstruction by Sir Albert Rich-ardson of what Wren considered his best parish church.

BUCKINGHAM PALACE

> I must say, notwithstanding the expense which has been incurred in building the palace, no sovereign in Europe, I may even add, perhaps no private gentleman, is so ill-lodged as the king of this country.
> —Duke of Wellington, 1828

Tel. 799 2331; www.royal.gov.uk. **Tube:** Victoria, and walk up Buckingham Palace Rd.; Green Park and St. James's Park are also convenient. **Open** daily Aug.-Sept. **Admission** £9.50, seniors £7, under 17 £5. **Tours** may be available; call for details.

When a freshly crowned Victoria moved from St. James's Palace in 1837, Bucking-ham Palace, built in 1825 by John Nash, had faulty drains and a host of other leaky dif-ficulties. Home improvements were made, and now, when the flag is flying, the Queen is at home—and you can visit her home.

After a recent debate about the proper way to subsidize the monarchy's senselessly posh existence (spurred by the need for funds to rebuild Windsor castle, which went up in flames in November 1992), Buckingham Palace finally opened to the public. The doors have been open for the past couple years—at press time it was unknown as to the exact opening dates for 1999. Not all of the Palace is laid open, but visitors are able to stroll through the Blue Drawing Room, the Throne Room, the Picture Gal-lery, and the Music Room, as well as other stately rooms.

If you happen to visit the palace during an off month, try to catch the chart-topping Kodak Moment for London tourists—the **Changing of the Guard,** which takes place daily from April to late August, and only on alternate days from September to March. The "Old Guard" marches from St. James's Palace down the Mall to Buckingham Pal-ace, leaving at approximately 11:10am. The "New Guard" begins marching as early as 10:20am. When they meet at the central gates of the palace, the officers of the regi-ments then touch hands, symbolically exchanging keys, *et voilà*, the guard is offi-cially changed. In wet weather or on pressing state holidays, the Changing of the Guard does not occur. To witness the spectacle, show up well before 11:30am and stand directly in front of the palace. You can also watch along the routes of the troops prior to their arrival at the palace (10:40-11:25am) between the Victoria Memorial and St. James's Palace or along Birdcage Walk.

LONDON

In the extravagant **Trooping the Colour** ceremony, held on the Queen's official birthday in the middle of June, the colors of a chosen regiment are paraded ceremonially before her and her family. The actual ceremony takes place at Horse Guards Parade, followed by a procession down the Mall to the palace, where she reviews her Household Cavalry and appears on the balcony for a Royal Air Force fly-by. Tickets for the event must be obtained through the mail. Write well in advance to the Household Division HQ, Horse Guards, SW1. If you don't get a ticket for the event, you should ask for tickets to a rehearsal (without the Queen) on a preceding Saturday.

Down the left side of the palace, off Buckingham Gate, an enclosed passageway leads to the **Queen's Gallery.** The exhibition changes every few months, but you can usually catch a few of Charles I's Italian masters, George IV's Dutch still-lifes, Prince Albert's primitives, and occasionally a couple of Leonardo da Vinci drawings. *(Open daily 9:30am-4:30pm, last admission 4pm. Admission £4, seniors £3, under 17 £2.)*

Also off Buckingham Gate stands the curious **Royal Mews Museum,** which houses the royal coaches and other historic royal riding implements. *(Open Oct.-Mar. W noon-4pm; Apr.-July Tu-Th noon-4pm; Aug.-Sept. M 10:30am-4:30pm, Tu-Th noon-4pm. £4, seniors £3, under 17 £2, family of 4 £10.)* A combined pass for the Gallery and Mews may be purchased. *(Admission £6.50, seniors £4.50, under 17 £3.50.)*

Nearby is the **Guards Museum** at Wellington Barracks on Birdcage Walk, off Buckingham Gate. *(Open M-Th and Sa-Su 10am-4pm. £2, students, seniors, and children £1.)*

■ Trafalgar Square and Charing Cross

Unlike many squares in London, **Trafalgar Sq.** (tube: Charing Cross), which slopes down from the National Gallery into the center of a vicious traffic roundabout, has been public land since the razing of hundreds of houses made way for its construction in the 1830s. **Nelson's Column,** a fluted granite pillar, commands the square, with four majestic, beloved lions guarding the base. The monument and square commemorate Admiral Horatio Nelson, killed during his triumph over Napoleon's navy.

At the head of the square squats the ordering facade of the **National Gallery,** Britain's collection of Old Masters. The church of **St. Martin-in-the-Fields,** on the northeastern corner of the square opposite the National Gallery, dates from the 1720s. St. Martin, which has its own world-renowned chamber orchestra, sponsors lunchtime and evening concerts, as well as a summer festival in mid-July. *(Lunchtime concerts M-Tu and F 1:05pm. Box office in the bookshop open M-W 10am-6pm and Th-Sa 10am-7:30pm. Phone bookings (tel. 839 8362) M-F 10am-4pm.)* Across the street from St. Martin's, half obscured by the mammoth buildings that ring Trafalgar Sq., sits the **National Portrait Gallery,** wherein lie busts, caricatures, photos, and paintings of everyone who is or was anyone in the U.K.

The original **Charing Cross,** last of 13 crosses set up to mark the stages of Queen Eleanor's royal funeral procession in 1291, was actually located at the top of Whitehall, immediately south of the present Trafalgar Sq. Like many things, it was destroyed by Cromwell, and a replica now stands outside Charing Cross Station, just uphill from the Victoria Embankment. While the spot is still the geographical center of the city (all distances to London are measured from it), it is no longer the pulsing heart of London life it once was. "Why, Sir, Fleet Street has a very animated appearance," Samuel Johnson once remarked, "but I think the full tide of human existence is at Charing Cross."

■ Piccadilly

All of the West End's major arteries—Piccadilly, Regent St., Shaftesbury Ave., and The Haymarket—merge and swirl around **Piccadilly Circus,** the bright, gaudy hub of Nash's 19th-century London. Today, the Circus earns its place on postcards with lurid neon signs, hordes of tourists, and a fountain topped by a statue everyone calls "Eros," though it was intended to be the Angel of Christian Charity in memory of the Earl of Shaftesbury. Piccadilly overflows with glam, glitz, and commerce, and is undergoing a high-profile incursion by American corporations.

The Circus was ground zero for Victorian popular entertainment, but only the facades of the great music halls remain, propped up against contemporary tourist traps. **London Pavilion,** 1 Piccadilly Circus, is a historic theater recently converted into a mall (across the street from the Lillywhite's and Sogo stores). Inside the Pavilion lurks **Madame Tussaud's Rock Circus** (tel. 734 7203), an ultra-cheesy waxwork museum and revolving theatre dedicated to the history of rock 'n' roll. *(Open Su-M and W-Th 11am-9pm, Tu noon-9pm, F-Sa 11am-10pm; July 9-Sept. 3 Tu 11am-10pm, Su-M and W-Sa 10am-10pm. £8, students and seniors £7, children £6.50, family £20.)* The massive, laser-decorated arcade and mall **Trocadero,** 13 Coventry St. (tel. 439 1791), holds the entrance to Segaworld, a "virtual amusement park," in which access to each new floor of "rides" costs £3 and video games range from 30p-£1. Featured alongside the Trocadero's other many delights is an IMAX theater (tel. 494 4153). *(Tickets £7, students, seniors, and children £5.50.)*

For an escape from the world of the gaudy and the touristy, check out **Piccadilly,** a broad, mile-long avenue once lined with aristocratic mansions stretching from Regent St. in the east to Hyde Park Corner in the west. The only remnant of Piccadilly's stately past is the showy **Burlington House** (across from 185 Piccadilly), built in 1665 for the Earls of Burlington and redesigned in the 18th century by Colin Campbell to accommodate the burgeoning **Royal Academy of Arts.**

An easily overlooked courtyard next to the Academy opens onto the **Albany,** an 18th-century apartment block renowned as one of London's most prestigious addresses. Built in 1771 and remodeled in 1812 to serve as "residential chambers for bachelor gentlemen," the Albany evolved into an exclusive enclave of literary repute. Lord Byron wrote his epic "Childe Harold" here.

Piccadilly continues past imperious Bond St., the Ritz Hotel and its distinctive lightbulb sign, the Green Park tube station, and a string of privileged men's clubs on the rim of Green Park. The avenue merges into Hyde Park corner at the gateway of the **Wellington Museum** in **Apsley House,** built by Robert Adam in the 1780s as the home of the Duke of Wellington.

Running north from Piccadilly Circus are the grand facades of (upper) **Regent St.,** built by John Nash in the early 19th century as part of a processional route for the Prince Regent. The facades have changed since Nash's time, and today the street is known for the crisp cuts of Burberry raincoats and Aquascutum suits.

■ Soho, Leicester Square, and Chinatown

For centuries, **Soho** was London's red-light district of prostitutes and sex shows. Today, however, the sex industry adds merely one small ingredient to the cosmopolitan stew that is Soho. It's a young and vibrant area with narrow streets lined by cool cafes, classic pubs, unpretentious shops, and theaters.

Loosely bounded by Oxford St. to the north, Shaftesbury Ave. to the south, Charing Cross Rd. to the east, and Regent St. to the west (tube: Leicester Sq., Piccadilly Circus, or Tottenham Ct. Rd.), Soho first emerged as a discrete area in 1681 with the laying out of **Soho Sq.** (tube: Tottenham Ct. Rd., just off Oxford St.). Grand mansions quickly sprang up as the area became popular with the fashionable set, famous for throwing extravagant parties. By the end of the 18th century, however, the leisured classes had moved out, replaced by the leisure industries. Today, the square is a center of the filmmaking industry.

Soho has a history of welcoming all colors and creeds to its streets. The district was first settled by French Huguenots fleeing religious persecution after the revocation of the Edict of Nantes in 1685. In more recent years, an influx of settlers from the New Territories of Hong Kong have built London's Chinatown south of Soho. A strong Mediterranean influence can also be detected in the aromas of espresso, garlic, and sizzling meats wafting through the area's maze of streets.

Perhaps contemporary Soho's most salient feature, especially on sunny days, is its vibrant **sidewalk cafe culture,** a recent development marking an intentional departure from the pornographic past. An *al fresco* mecca, today's Soho overflows with media types, artists, writers, club kids, and posers. The area has a significant and visible gay presence; a concentration of gay-owned restaurants and bars has turned **Old Compton St.** into the gay heart of London.

The ruins of **St. Anne's Church** (tel. 437 5006) provide an eerie backdrop to Wardour St., which runs north from Shaftesbury Ave. *(Church gardens open M-Sa 8am-dusk, Su 9am-dusk.)* Since the 1840s, **Berwick Street Market** (parallel to the north end of Wardour St.) is famous for the widest and cheapest selection of fruits and vegetables in central London. *(Open M-Sa 9am-6pm.)*

Running parallel to Regent St. is **Carnaby St.,** a notorious hotbed of 1960s sex, fashion, and Mods. It witnessed the rise of youth culture and became the heart of what *Time* magazine termed "Swingin' London." Many of the chic boutiques and parading celebrities have long since left the area, which has lapsed into a lurid tourist trap. **Leicester Sq.,** just south of Shaftesbury Ave., between Piccadilly Circus and Charing Cross Rd. is an entertainment nexus. Amusements range from very expensive, mammoth cinemas to the free performances provided by street entertainers.

On the north side of the square, at Leicester Pl., the French presence in Soho manifests itself in **Notre-Dame de France** (tel. 437 9363). This church may not be architecturally distinguished, but those who venture inside will be rewarded with the exquisite Aubusson tapestry lining the inner walls. On the south side of the square, a large queue marks the **half-price ticket booth,** where theater tickets are sold for half price on the day of the show.

Cantonese immigrants first arrived in Britain as cooks on British ships, and London's first Chinese community formed around the docks near Limehouse. Today, however, London's primary **Chinatown** (known in Chinese as *Tong Yan Kai,* "Chinese Street") lies off the north side of Leicester Sq. Between theaters on Shaftesbury Ave and cinemas on Leicester Sq., the streets sprout Chinese language signs and pagoda-capped telephone booths. **Gerrard St.,** the main thoroughfare, runs closest to the Leicester Sq. tube station. Chinatown is most vibrant during the year's two major festivals: the **Mid-Autumn Festival,** at the end of September, and the **Chinese New Year Festival,** during the beginning of February. For further information on festivals or Chinatown call the **Chinese Community Centre,** 44 Gerrard St., 2nd floor (tel. 439 3822). *(Open M-Th and Sa-Su 11am-5pm.)*

■ Covent Garden

The outdoor cafes, upscale shops, and slick crowds animating Covent Garden today belie the square's medieval beginnings as a literal "convent garden" where the monks of Westminster Abbey grew their vegetables. When Henry VIII abolished the monasteries in 1536, he granted the land to John Russell, first Earl of Bedford. The Earl's descendants developed it into a fashionable *piazza* (designed by Inigo Jones) in the 1630s, giving London its first planned square.

Jones's **St. Paul's Church** now stands as the sole remnant of the original square, although the interior had to be rebuilt after bring gutted by a fire in 1795. Known as "the actor's church," St. Paul's is filled with plaques commemorating the achievements of Boris Karloff, Vivien Leigh, Noel Coward, and Tony Simpson ("inspired player of small parts"), among others. The connection to the theater dates back to the mid-17th century when this was the center of London's theatrical culture. *(Open M 10am-2:30pm, Tu 9am-4pm, W 9:30am-4pm, Th 8:30am-4pm, F 9:30am-4pm, Su 9am-12:30pm. Services M 8:30am. Holy Communion services Su 11am, W 1:10pm, and Th 8:30am. Evensong sung on the 2nd Su of each month at 4pm.)* The Victorian Flower Market building in the southeast corner of the piazza now contains the **London Transport Museum** (see **Museums,** p. 129).

The **Theatre Royal** and the **Royal Opera House** lend a sense of civility to the area, adding pre-theater and pre-concert goers to the throng of visitors. The Theatre Royal (entrance on Catherine St.) was first built in 1663 as one of two legal theatrical venues in London. The Royal Opera House (on Bow St.) began as a theater for concerts and plays in 1732 and now houses the Royal Opera and Royal Ballet companies. The **Theatre Museum** sits to the south, on the corner of Russell and Wellington streets.

The **Photographers' Gallery** holds its reputation as one of London's major venues for contemporary photographic exhibitions. Further along, Neal St. leads to **Neal's Yard,** where the adventurous can come face to face with wild vegetarians and peruse their stores and restaurants, which sell wholesome foods, cheeses and yogurts, herbs, and fresh-baked breads. At the northern section of St. Martin's Ln., six streets converge at the **Seven Dials** monument (the 7th dial is the monument itself, a sundial).

■ Holborn and the Inns of Court

There's no law like English law. The historical center of English law lies in an area straddling the precincts of Westminster and the City and surrounding long and litigious precincts of High Holborn, Chancery Ln., and Fleet St. The Strand and Fleet St. meet at the **Royal Courts of Justice** (tel. 936 6000; tube: Temple), a wonderfully elaborate Gothic structure designed in 1874 by architect G.E. Street for the Supreme Court of Judicature. The biggest draw for tourists who sit in on proceedings are the **wigs** the justices and barristers wear. *(Courts and galleries open to the public M-F 9am-4:30pm. Court cases start at 10-10:30am, but they break for lunch 1-2pm.)*

Barristers in the City are affiliated with one of the famous **Inns of Court** (Middle Temple, Inner Temple, Lincoln's Inn, and Gray's Inn), four ancient legal institutions that provide lectures and apprenticeships for law students and regulate admission to the bar. Inside, the Inns are organized like Oxford colleges, each with its own gardens, chapel, library, dining hall, common rooms, and chambers. Most were founded in the 13th century when a royal decree barred the clergy from the courts of justice, giving rise to a new class of professional legal advocates. Most inns do not allow visitors but are still worth seeing from the outside.

South of Fleet St., the labyrinth of the **Temple** (tube: Temple) encloses the prestigious and stately Middle and Inner Temple Inns. They derive their name from the clandestine, crusading Order of the Knights Templar, who embraced this site as their English seat in the 12th century. The secretive order dissolved in 1312 (although some claim it still exists in the form of the Masons and Skull & Bones) and this property was eventually passed on to the Knights Hospitallers of St. John, who leased it to a community of common-law scholars in 1338.

Held in common by both the Middle and Inner Temples, the **Temple Church** is made of an older round church (built in 1185) and a newer addition of a rectangular nave (1240). The older portion is the finest of the few round churches left in England. It contains gorgeous stained-glass windows, a handsome 12th-century Norman doorway, an altar screen by Wren (1682), and 10 arresting, armor-clad stone effigies of sinister Knights Templar dating from the 12th and 14th centuries. Be sure to note the grotesque heads lining the circular wall surrounding the effigies.

Back across Fleet St., on the other side of the Royal Courts, **Lincoln's Inn** (tube: Holborn) was the only Inn to emerge unscathed from the Blitz. **New Sq.** and its cloistered churchyard (to the right as you enter from Lincoln's Inn Fields) appear today much as they did in the 1680s. The **Old Hall**, east of New Sq., dates from 1492; here the Lord High Chancellor presided over the High Court of Chancery from 1733 to 1873. **Gray's Inn** (tube: Chancery Ln.), dubbed "that stronghold of melancholy" by Dickens, stands at the northern end of Fulwood Pl., off High Holborn. The **Hall,** to your right as you pass through the archway, retains its original stained glass (1580) and most of its ornate screen. The first performance of Shakespeare's *Comedy of Errors* took place here in 1594.

Of the nine Inns of Chancery, only **Staple Inn's** building survives (located where Gray's Inn Rd. meets High Holborn; tube: Chancery Ln.). The half-timbered Elizabethan front, with its easily recognized vertical striping, dates from 1586. **Walking tours** are available (see **Touring,** p. 94).

■ The Strand And Fleet Street

Hugging the embankment of the River Thames, **The Strand** (tube: Charing Cross or Temple) has fared ill throughout London's growth. Once lined with fine Tudor houses, today this major thoroughfare curves from Trafalgar Sq. through a jumbled assortment of dull commercial buildings.

Somerset House, a magnificent Palladian structure built by Sir William Chambers in 1776, stands on the site of the 16th-century palace where Elizabeth I resided during the brief reign of her sister Mary. Formerly the administrative center of the Royal Navy, the building now houses the exquisite and intimately-housed **Courtauld Gallery** (see **Museums,** p. 129).

Just east of the Courtauld, **St. Mary-le-Strand's** (tel. 836 3205), slender steeple and elegant portico rise above an island of decaying steps in the middle of the modern roadway. Designed by James Gibbs and consecrated in 1724, the church overlooks the site of the original Maypole, where London's first hackney cabs assembled in 1634. Inside, the Baroque barrel vault and altar walls reflect not only the glory of God but also Gibbs' architectural training in Rome. *(Open M-F 11am-3:30pm.)* Across the street, newsreaders intone "This is London" every hour from Bush House, the nerve center of the BBC's radio services.

To the east stands handsome **St. Clement Danes** (tel. 242 8282), whose melodious bells get their 15 seconds of fame in the nursery rhyme "Oranges and lemons, say the bells of St. Clement's." *(Open daily 8am-5pm.)* The bells still ring daily. Designed by Wren in 1682, the church was built over the ruins of an older Norman structure reputed to be the tomb of Harold Harefoot, leader of a colony of Danes who settled the area in the 9th century. Today it is the official church of the Royal Air Force—evident in the plaques and monuments which honor these bold airmen. Samuel Johnson worshipped here—a statue of the Doctor strikes a bizarre pose outside the church.

Twining's Teas, 216 The Strand (tel. 353 3511), near the Fleet St. end of the road, honors the leaf which started a war. *(Open M-F 9:30am-4:30pm.)* It is the oldest business in Britain and the narrowest shop in London. Just east stands the only Strand building to avoid the Great Fire, the **Wig and Pen Club,** 229-230 The Strand, which was constructed over Roman ruins in 1625. Frequented by the best-known barristers and journalists in London, the Wig and Pen is open to members only, though a traveler dressed in a coat and tie can peek upstairs.

As you stroll away from the Courts of Justice, two of London's top educational institutions heave into view. **King's College,** an unremarkable concrete building, is on the left; straight across the road stands the **London School of Economics,** the setting for feisty student radicalism in the 1960s, now newly installed as Prime Minister Tony Blair's favorite generator of political ideas.

The **Temple Bar Monument** stands where The Strand meets Fleet St., marking the boundary between Westminster and the City. The Sovereign must obtain ceremonial permission from the Lord Mayor to enter the City here.

Fleet Street (tube: Blackfriars or St. Paul's) was until recently the hub of British journalism. Nowadays, Fleet St. is just a celebrated name and a few (vacated) famous buildings. Following a standoff with the printing unions in 1986, *The Times,* under the command of infamous media mogul Rupert Murdoch, moved to cheaper land at Wapping, Docklands, initiating a mass exodus from the street. The *Daily Telegraph* soon abandoned its startling Greek and Egyptian Revival building in favor of the delights of Canary Wharf, and others followed.

The tiered spire of Wren's **St. Bride's** (1675), near 89 Fleet St., became the inspiration for countless wedding cakes thanks to an ingenious local baker. Dubbed "the printers' cathedral" because England's first moveable-type printing press was housed here in 1500, it has long had a connection with newspapermen. The current church is sparkling clean and quite beautiful inside. *(Open M-F 8am-6pm, Sa 9am-5pm.)* Next door stands Reuters, one of the last remaining media powerhouses left on Fleet St.

A few blocks down the street, opposite 54 Fleet St., a large white sign labels the alleyway entrance (through Hind Ct.) to Johnson's Ct. Inside the alley, more discreet signs point the way to **Samuel Johnson's House,** 17 Gough Sq. (tel. 353 3745), a self-described "shrine to the English language" that was Dr. Johnson's abode from 1748-1759. Here Johnson completed his *Dictionary,* the first definitive English lexicon, even though rumor falsely insists that he omitted "sausage." He compiled this amazing document by reading all the great books of the age and marking the words he wanted included in the Dictionary with black pen. The knowledgeable curator is eager to supplement your visit with anecdotes about the **Great Cham** and his hyperbolic biographer, James Boswell. *(Open May-Sept. M-Sa 11am-5:30pm; Oct.-Apr. M-Sa 11am-5pm. Admission £3, students and seniors £2, children £1. Audio tour 50p.)*

A few blocks down Fleet St., the neo-Gothic **St. Dunstan-in-the-West** (tel. 405 1929) holds its magnificent lantern tower high above the banks surrounding it. The chimes of its curious 17th-century clock are sounded on the quarter hour by a pair of hammer-wielding mechanical giants. *(Open Tu and F 9:30am-3pm, Su 10am-4pm.)*

■ The City of London

Until the 18th century, the **City of London** was London; all other boroughs and neighborhoods now swallowed up by "London" were neighboring towns or outlying villages. Today, the 1 sq. mi. City of London is the financial center of Europe. Each weekday 350,000 people surge in at 9am and rush out again unfailingly at 5pm, leaving behind a resident population of only 6000. At the center of the City, the massive **Bank of England** controls the country's finances, and the **Stock Exchange** makes (or breaks) the nation's fortune (see **City: Bank to Tower,** p. 108). International banks proliferate around them, bowing in homage to these great temples of mammon. Towering cranes, office building sites, and rising share indices bore witness to the British "economic resurgence" of the late 1980s. Panic in such City stalwarts as Lloyd's of London is testimony to the precariousness of the early 1990s.

The City owes much of its graceful appearance to Sir Christopher Wren, who was the chief architect working after the **Great Fire of 1666** almost completely razed the area. Wren's studio designed 52 churches to replace the 89 destroyed in the fire, and the surviving 24 churches are some of the only buildings in the City from the period immediately following the Great Fire. The original effect of a forest of steeples surrounding the grand dome of St. Paul's is perhaps his greatest contribution to London's cityscape; unfortunately, modern skyscrapers now obscure that effect.

Perhaps the most important secular structures of the City are the buildings of the **Livery Companies.** The companies began as medieval guilds representing specific trades and occupations, such as the Drapers and the Fishmongers. New guilds, such as the Information Technologists, have formed to keep up with changing times. The 84 **livery halls** are scattered around the square mile. Most halls do not open to the public; those that do require tickets.

The **City of London Information Centre,** St. Paul's Churchyard, EC4 (tel. 332 1456; tube: St. Paul's), specializes in information about the City, but answers questions on all of London. The helpful, knowledgeable staff is worth speaking to before exploring this part of the city. *(Open Apr.-Sept. daily 9:30am-5pm; Oct.-Mar. M-F 9:30am-5pm, Sa 9:30am-12:30pm.)* The **Lord Mayor's Show,** on the second Saturday of November, is a glittering parade of pomp and red velvet to the Royal Courts of Justice in celebration of London citizens' right to elect their Lord Mayor. A newer tradition is July's **City of London Festival,** which fills the churches, halls, squares, and sidewalks of the area with music and theater.

CITY (WESTERN SECTION): BANK TO ST. PAUL'S

The few remaining stones of the Roman **Temple of Mithras,** Queen Victoria St. (tube: Bank or Mansion House), dwell incongruously in the shadow of the Temple Court building. Down Queen Victoria St., **St. Mary Aldermary** (tel. 248 4906), towers over its surroundings. A rare Gothic Wren creation, it is especially notable for its delicate fan vaulting. *(Open W-F 11am-3pm.)* The bells that recalled Mayor Dick Whittington to London rang out from St. Marie de Arcubus, replaced by Wren's **St. Mary-le-Bow** (tel. 248 5139) Cheapside, in 1683. *(Open M-Th 6:30am-6pm, F 6:30am-4pm.)*

St. James Garlickhythe (tel. 236 1719), on Upper Thames St., gets its name from the garlic once sold nearby. *(Open M-F 10qm-4pm.)* To the west on Queen Victoria St. stands a rare red-brick Wren church with an elegant cupola, **St. Benet's.** Just across the street, the **College of Arms** (tel. 248 2762) rests on its heraldic authority behind ornate gates. The College regulates the granting and recognition of coats of arms. The officer-in-waiting can assess your claim to a British family coat of arms. *(Open M-F 10am-4pm.)* Farther west, **St. Andrew-by-the-Wardrobe,** 146 Queen Victoria (tel. 248 7546; tube: Blackfriars), was originally built next to Edward III's Royal Stores. Now the church cowers beneath the Faraday building, the first building allowed to exceed the City's previously strict height limit. *(Open Sept.-July M-F 8:30am-6pm.)*

Queen Victoria St. meets New Bridge St. in the area known as **Blackfriars,** named in reference to the darkly-clad Dominican brothers who built a monastery there in the Middle Ages. A peaceful haven is offered by **St. Martin Ludgate** (tel. 248 6054), a Wren church on Ludgate Hill featuring some fine Grinling Gibbons woodwork. *(Open M-F 11am-3pm.)*

If you begin to tire of churches, the **Old Bailey** (tel. 248 3277; tube: St. Paul's) is just around the corner. Technically the Central Criminal Courts, but infamous as the site of Britain's grimiest prison, it crouches under a copper dome and a wide-eyed figure of justice on the corner of Old Bailey and Newgate St. Trial-watching persists as a favorite occupation, and the Old Bailey fills up during scandalous cases. You can enter the public Visitors' Gallery and watch bewigged barristers at work. Even women wear wigs so that they too may look like wise old men. *(Open M-F 10am-1pm and 2-5pm; entrance in Warwick Passage off Old Bailey.)* The Chief Post Office building, off Newgate to the north, envelops the stimulating **National Postal Museum.**

CITY: BARBICAN AND NORTHERN SECTION

Housing some of England's greatest cultural treasures, the **Barbican Centre** (tube: Barbican or Moorgate) is a maze of apartment buildings, restaurants, gardens, and exhibition halls, described at its 1982 opening as "the city's gift to the nation." **The Royal Shakespeare Company,** the **London Symphony Orchestra,** the **Museum of London,** the **Guildhall School for Music and Drama,** and the **Barbican Art Gallery** call this complex home, as do the many politicians and actors who reside in the Barbican's distinctive apartments. The complex's unexpectedly verdant central courtyard, with artificial lakes and planned gardens, tempers the Barbican's urbanity.

In order to reach **St. Bartholomew the Great** (tel. 606 5171), continue past the Barbican tube on Beech St. and make a left on Little Britain. Parts of the church date from 1123, although 800 years of alteration have much embellished it. *(Open M-F 8:30am-5pm, Sa 10:30am-1:30pm, Su 8am-8pm.)* For an early pint, try one of the pubs around **Smithfield Market,** an ancient meat and poultry trade market—the pubs around here are licensed to serve ale starting at 7am.

Just north of the square, up St. John's St. and off Clerkenwell Rd., **St. John's Gate** (tel. 253 6644), holds the headquarters of the British Order of the Hospital of St. John, the last vestiges of the medieval crusading order of Knights Hospitallers. *(Open M-F 10am-5pm, Sa 10am-4pm. 1 hr. tours Tu and F-Sa 11am and 2:30pm; £2.50 donation.)*

CITY (EASTERN SECTION): BANK TO THE TOWER

The massive windowless walls and foreboding doors of the **Bank of England** enclose four full acres (tube: Bank). The present building dates from 1925, but the 8 ft. thick outer wall is the same one built by eccentric architect Sir John Soane in 1788. The only part open to the public is the plush **Bank of England Museum.** Its neighbors, the Greek-columned Royal Exchange, Stock Exchange, and Lloyd's financial building are closed to visitors.

The 1986 **Lloyd's** building and **Leadenhall Market,** off Leadenhall St., supply the most startling architectural clash in the City. The ducts, lifts, and chutes of Lloyd's are straight out of the 21st century. This futuristic setting houses the **Lutine Bell,** which is still occasionally rung—once for bad insurance news, twice for good. In contrast, across a narrow alley behind Lloyd's stretch the ornate red canopies and dazzling gargoyles of Victorian **Leadenhall Market.**

Behind the imposing **Mansion House,** home of the Lord Mayor, stands **St. Stephen Walbrook** (tel. 283 4444), on Walbrook St. Arguably Wren's finest, and allegedly his personal favorite, the church combines four major styles: the old-fashioned English church characterized by nave and chancel; the Puritan hall church, which lacks any separation between priest and congregation; the Greek Cross-plan church; and the domed church, a study for St. Paul's. The Samaritans, a social service group that advises the suicidal and severely depressed, was founded here in 1953 by rector Chad Varah. *(Open M-Th 10am-4pm, F 10am-3pm.)*

The church of **St. Mary Woolnoth** (tel. 626 7901), at King William and Lombard St., may look odd without a spire, but the interior and the black and gilt reredos confirm the talents of Wren's pupil Nicholas Hawksmoor. The only City church untouched by the Blitz, it "kept the hours" in T.S. Eliot's *The Waste Land. (Open M-F 7:45am-5pm.)* **St. Mary Abchurch** (tel. 626 0306), off Abchurch Ln., provides a neat domed comparison to St. Stephen's—its mellow, dark wood and Baroque paintings contrast with St. Stephen's bright, airy interior. *(Open M-Th 10am-2pm.)*

Before even the most basic rebuilding of the city, Wren designed a tall Doric pillar. Completed in 1677, the simply-named **Monument** (tube: Monument) lies at the bottom of Monument St. Supposedly, the 202 ft. pillar stands exactly that many feet from where the Great Fire broke out in Pudding Ln. on September 2, 1666. High on Fish St. Hill, the column offers an expansive view of London. Bring stern resolution and £1.50 (child 50p) to climb its 311 steps. Upon successfully descending the tower, you'll be given a free certificate announcing your feat, signed by the City Secretary. *(Open Apr.-Sept. M-F 10am-5:40pm, Sa-Su 2-5:40pm; Oct.-Mar. M-Sa 10am-5:40pm.)*

Over the river near the Monument, the **London Bridge** succeeds a slew of ancestors. The famed version stood from 1176 until it burned in 1758. The most recent predecessor didn't fall; in 1973 it was sold to an American millionaire for £1.03 million and shipped, block by block, to Lake Havasu City, Arizona.

St. Mary-at-Hill, Lovat Ln. (tel. 626 4184), is a typical Wren church with a surprisingly convincing reworking of the old interior by early Victorian craftsmen, and an even more convincing contemporary reconstruction project. *(Open M-F 10am-3pm.)* **St. Dunstan-in-the-East,** St. Dunstan's Hill, suffered severe damage in the Blitz; only Wren's amazing spire remains. The ruins have been converted into a gorgeous little garden that makes a fine picnic spot.

Pepys witnessed the spread of the Great Fire from atop **All Hallows by the Tower,** at the end of Great Tower St. Just inside the south entrance is an arch from the 7th-century Saxon church, discovered in 1960. Brass rubbings cost a mere £1.20. At the tiny **St. Olave's** on Hart St., an annual memorial service is held for Pepys, who is buried here with his wife. *(Open M-F 9am-5pm.)*

ST. PAUL'S CATHEDRAL

Tube: St. Paul's. *Open* M-Sa 8:30am-4pm. *Galleries and ambulatory open M-Sa 8:45am-4:15pm.* **Admission** *to cathedral, ambulatory, and crypt £4.50, students £3.50, children £2; with galleries £7.50, £6.50, £3.50.* **Tours** *depart at 11, 11:30am, 1:30, and 2pm; £3, students £2.* **Audio tours** *(45min.) £3, students £2.50, families £7; available from opening until 3pm in various languages.*

St. Paul's is arguably the most stunning architectural sight in London. It dominates its surroundings, even as modern usurpers sneak up around it. Prince Charles and Lady Diana broke a 200-year tradition of holding royal weddings in Westminster Abbey so they could celebrate their ill-fated nuptials here. The first cathedral to stand on the site was founded in 604 and destroyed by fire in 1089. The second was a medieval structure, one of the largest in Europe, topped by a spire ascending 489 ft. Falling into almost complete neglect in the 16th century, the cathedral burned in the Great Fire of 1666, giving Wren the opportunity to build from scratch.

Both the design and the building of the cathedral were dogged by controversy. Like his Renaissance predecessors, Wren preferred an equal-armed Greek Cross plan, while ecclesiastical authorities insisted upon a traditional medieval design with a long nave and choir for services. Wren's final design compromised by translating a Gothic cathedral into Baroque and Classical terms: a Greek Cross floor plan with medieval detailing. Wren's second model received the King's warrant of approval (and is thus

A City with a View

When you've had enough of urban smog and chaos, consider climbing above the city to gain a little perspective.

Monument, King William St. Tube: Monument. A fantastic 311-step view of the Thames, Tower of London, and St. Paul's from one of Wren's most famously ramrod structures. Right in the middle of the Bank District. £1

St. Paul's. Tube: St. Paul's. Set in the heart of the City of London, this cathedral's inner elegance can only be matched by the view from its 271-step dome. Unrivalled views of ye olde City, the Docklands, and the West End.

Primrose Hill, Regent's Park. Tube: Camden Town, Great Portland Baker St. and Baker St. You're up to your head in urban slime, and suddenly, by the grace of grassy Primrose Hill you rise above the city to a wonderful view of London. On a good day you can see past the Surrey Downs.

Anywhere along the South bank of the Thames at night. Tube: Tower Hill or Tower Gateway. Cross Tower Bridge and look upon the city's skyscrapers floodlit in evening colors. A wonderful place for dinner or an evening walk.

known as the "Warrant Model"), but still differed from today's St. Paul's. The cathedral was topped off in 1710; at 365 ft. above the ground, the huge classical dome is the second largest free-standing dome in Europe (St. Peter's in the Vatican is the largest). Queen Victoria, believing the cathedral's cream and wooden interior to be too dull, flooded it with gold before her death in 1901.

In December 1940, London burned once again. On the night of the 29th, at the height of the Blitz, St. Paul's was engulfed by a sea of fire. Fifty-one firebombs landed on the cathedral, all swiftly put out by the heroic volunteer St. Paul's Fire Watch; a small monument in the floor at the end of the nave honors them. Two of the four high-explosive bombs that landed did explode, wrecking the north transept; the clear glass there bears silent testimony.

Dotted with sculptures, bronzes, and mosaics, St. Paul's makes a rewarding place for a wander. Above the choir, three neo-Byzantine glass mosaics by William Richmond, done in 1904, tell the story of Creation. The stalls in the **Choir,** carved by Grinling Gibbons, narrowly escaped a bomb, but the old altar did not. It was replaced with the current marble **High Altar,** covered by a St. Peter's-like *baldacchino* of oak, splendidly gilded. Above looms the crowning glory, the ceiling mosaic of Christ Seated in Majesty. A trial mosaic adorns the east wall of **St. Dunstan's Chapel,** on the left by the entrance. On the other side of the nave in the **Chapel of St. Michael and St. George** sits a richly carved throne by Grinling Gibbons, made for the coronation of William and Mary in 1710. Along the south aisle hangs Holman Hunt's third version of *The Light of the World.*

The **ambulatory** contains a statue of poet John Donne (Dean of the Cathedral 1621-1631) in shrouds, one of the few monuments to survive from old St. Paul's. Also in the ambulatory is a modern, abstract sculpture of the Virgin Mary and Baby Jesus by Henry Moore, entitled *Mother and Child.* Britain restored the former **Jesus Chapel** after the Blitz and dedicated it to U.S. soldiers who died during WWII. The graceful and intricate choir gates were executed by Jean Tijou early in the 18th century.

The **crypt,** saturated with tombs and monuments, forms a catalogue of Britain's officially "great" figures of the last two centuries, including Florence Nightingale and sculptor Henry Moore. (A few remnants made it through the Great Fire, including a memorial to Francis Bacon's father Nicolas.) The massive tombs of Wellington and Nelson dominate the crypt. A bust of George Washington stands opposite a memorial to Lawrence of Arabia. Around the corner lounges Rodin's fine bust of poet W.F. Henley (1849-1903). **Painter's Corner** holds the tombs of Sir Joshua Reynolds, Sir Lawrence Alma-Tadema, and J.M.W. Turner, along with memorials to John Constable and the revolutionary William Blake. Nearby, a black slab in the floor marks Wren's grave, with his son's famous epitaph close by: *Lector, si monumentum requiris circumspice* (roughly, "Reader, if you seek his monument, look around you").

The display of **models** of St. Paul's details the history of the cathedral in all of its incarnations, displaying how the upper parts of the exterior walls are mere facades, concealing the flying buttresses which support the nave roof. *(Audiovisual presentations every 30min. 10:30am-3pm. Crypt open M-Sa 8:45am-4:45pm; last admission at 4pm.)*

The best place to head in St. Paul's is straight up. A visitor may ascend to whichever of three different levels in the dome his or her legs, heart, and courage will allow. Two-hundred fifty-nine steps lead to the vertiginous **Whispering Gallery,** on the inside base of the dome. A further 119 steps up, the first external view glitters from the **Stone Gallery,** only to be eclipsed by the uninterrupted and incomparable panorama from the **Golden Gallery,** 152 steps higher at the top of the dome. Before descending, take a peek down into the cathedral through the glass peephole in the floor; Nelson lies buried more than 400 ft. directly below.

THE TOWER OF LONDON

Tel. 709 0765. Tube: Tower Hill. Open M-Sa 9am-5pm, Su 10am-5pm (last ticket sold at 4pm). Admission £9.50, students and seniors £7.15, children £6.25, families £28.40. Yeomen lead 1hr. tours every 30min. For tickets to the Ceremony of the Keys, the nightly ritual locking of the gates, write six weeks in advance to the Ceremony of the Keys, Waterloo Block, HM Tower of London, EC3 N4AB, with the number and date of tickets and enclosing a stamped addressed envelope or coupon-response international.

The **Tower of London,** palace and prison of English monarchs for over 500 years, is soaked in blood and history. Its intriguing past and striking buildings attract over two million visitors per year. The oldest continuously occupied fortress in Europe, "The Tower" was founded by William the Conqueror in 1066 to provide protection for and from his subjects. Not one but 20 towers stand behind its walls, though many associate the image of the **White Tower,** the oldest one, with the Tower of London. Completed in 1097, it overpowers all the fortifications that were built around it in the following centuries. Originally a royal residence, the last monarch it housed was James I. Since then it has served as a wardrobe, storehouse, public records office, mint, armory, and prison.

Two rings of defenses surround the White Tower. On the **Inner Ward,** the **Bell Tower** squats on the southwest corner. Since the 1190s, this tower has sounded the curfew bell each night. Sir Thomas More, "the king's good servant but God's first," spent some time here, courtesy of his former friend Henry VIII, before he was executed on **Tower Hill,** the scaffold site just northwest of the fortress where thousands gathered to watch the axe fall.

Along the curtain wall hovers the **Bloody Tower,** arguably the most famous, and certainly the most infamous, part of the fortress. Once pleasantly named the Garden Tower, due to the officers' garden nearby, the Bloody Tower supposedly saw the murder of the Little Princes, the uncrowned King Edward V and his brother (aged 13 and 10), by agents of Richard III. The murder remains one of history's great mysteries; some believe that Richard was innocent and that Henry VII arranged the murders to ease his own ascent. Two children's remains found in the grounds in 1674 (and buried in Westminster Abbey) have never been conclusively identified as those of the Princes. Sir Walter Raleigh did some time in the prison here off and on for 13 years and occupied himself by writing a voluminous *History of the World Part I.* Before he got around to writing Part II, James I had him beheaded.

Henry III lived in the adjacent **Wakefield Tower,** largest after the White Tower. The crown kept its public records and its jewels here until 1856 and 1967 respectively, although Wakefield also has its own gruesome past. Lancastrian Henry VI was imprisoned by Yorkist Edward IV during the Wars of the Roses and was murdered on May 21, 1471, while praying here. Students from King's College, Cambridge—founded by Henry—annually place lilies on the spot of the murder.

Counterclockwise around the inner **Wall Walk** come the **Lanthorn, Salt, Broad Arrow, Constable,** and **Martin** towers. In 1671, the self-styled "Colonel" Thomas Blood nearly pulled off the heist of the millennium. Blood befriended the ward of Martin tower, where the crown jewels were kept, and visited him late at night with some "friends." They subdued the guard and stuffed their trousers with booty, only to be caught at the nearby docks. Surprisingly, Blood wasn't executed, and was later awarded a privileged spot in the court of Charles II, the moral being, of course, that crime does pay (*Let's Go* does not endorse the theft of state treasures). The inner ring is completed by the **Brick, Bowyer, Flint, Devereux,** and **Beauchamp** towers.

Within the inner ring adjoining the Bell Tower lurks the Tudor **Queen's House** (which will become the King's House when Prince Charles ascends the throne). The house has served time as a prison for some of the Tower's most notable guests: both Anne Boleyn and Catherine Howard were incarcerated here by charming hubby Henry VIII; Guy Fawkes was interrogated in the Council Chamber on the upper floor; and in 1941, Hitler's henchman Rudolf Hess was brought here after parachuting into Scotland. The only prisoners remaining today are the clipped **ravens** hopping around on the grass outside the White Tower. Legend has it that without the ravens the Tower would crumble and a great disaster would befall the monarchy; the ravens even have a tomb and gravestone of their own.

Although more famous for the prisoners who languished and died here, the Tower has seen a handful of spectacular escape attempts. The Bishop of Durham escaped from Henry I out a window and down a rope. The Welsh Prince Gruffydd ap Llewelyn, prisoner of Henry III in 1244, had a less successful escape attempt—his rope of knotted sheets broke and he fell to his death. Prisoners of special privilege sometimes received the honor of a private execution, particularly when their public execution risked escape or riot. A block on the Tower Green, inside the Inner Ward, marks the spot where the axe fell on Queen Catherine Howard, Lady Jane Grey, Anne Boleyn, and the Earl of Essex, Queen Elizabeth's rejected suitor. All these and More (Sir Thomas) were treated to unconsecrated burial in the nearby **Chapel of St. Peter ad Vincula** (St. Peter in Chains; entrance to the chapel by Yeoman tour only).

For many, a visit to the Tower climaxes with a glimpse of the **Crown Jewels.** In the queue at the **Jewel House** (about 15-30min.) the crowd is ushered into the vault and onto "people-movers" which whisk them past the dazzling crowns and ensure that no awestruck gazers hold up the queue. Oliver Cromwell melted down much of the original royal booty; most of the collection dates from after Charles II's Restoration in 1660. The **Imperial State Crown** and the **Sceptre with the Cross** feature the Stars of Africa, cut from the Cullinan Diamond. **St. Edward's Crown,** made for Charles II in 1661, is only worn by the monarch during coronation.

The Tower is still guarded by the **Yeomen** of the Guard Extraordinary, popularly known as the "Beefeaters," who live in the fortress. Visitors enter the Tower through the **Byward Tower** on the southwest of the **Outer Ward,** which sports a precariously hung portcullis. The password, required for entry here after hours, has been changed every day since 1327. Along the outer wall, **St. Thomas's Tower** (after Thomas à Becket) tops the evocative **Traitors' Gate,** through which boats once brought new captives. The whole castle used to be surrounded by a broad **moat** dug by Edward I. Cholera epidemics forced the Duke of Wellington to drain the stagnant pond in 1843. The filled land became a vegetable garden during World War II but has since sprouted a tennis court and bowling green for the Yeomen who live and work in the Tower. Yeoman **tours** provide an amusing and dramatic introduction to the Tower, but are by no means comprehensive. Signs are posted inside the tower for similar free tours highlighting other points of interest. Come early (the biggest crowds come in the afternoon, particularly on Sundays) and stay long; the Tower is one of London's priciest sights, so don't go if you're pressed for time.

Tower Bridge, a granite-and-steel structure reminiscent of a castle with a drawbridge, is a familiar sight. The **Tower Bridge Experience** (tel. 403 3761), an exhibition nearly as technologically elaborate as the bridge itself, explains the bridge's genesis through the eyes of its painters, designers, and ghosts in cute but expensive 75-minute tours. The view from the upper level, hampered by steel bars, is far less panoramic than it seems from below. (*Open Apr.-Oct. daily 10am-6:30pm; Nov.-Mar. 9:30am-6pm. Last entry 1¼hr. before closing. £5.70, children £3.90.*)

■ West London

■ Mayfair

The center of London's blue-blooded *beau monde* was—in a delightful twist of fate—named for the 17th-century May Fair, held on the site of Shepherd's Market, a notorious haunt of prostitutes. Modern Mayfair has a distinctly patrician atmosphere; it is the most expensive property in the British version of *Monopoly*. In the 18th and 19th centuries, the aristocracy kept houses in Mayfair where they lived during "the season" (the season for opera and balls), retiring to their country estates in the summer. Mayfair is bordered by Oxford St. to the north, Piccadilly to the south, Park Ln. to the west, and Regent St. to the east. *(Tube: Green Park, Bond St., or Piccadilly Circus.)*

Near what is now the Bond St. tube station, Blake saw mystical visions for 17 years on S. Molton St. On busy Brook St., home to the ritzy **Claridge's Hotel** (tel. 629 8860), Handel wrote the *Messiah*. *(Singles £255; 2-bedroom penthouse £2450; no student discounts.)*

Bond St. is the traditional address for the oldest and most prestigious shops, art dealers, auction houses, and hair salons in the city. Starting at the New Bond St. end, **Sotheby's**, 34 Bond St. (tel. 493 5000), displays everything from Dutch masters to the world's oldest condom before they're put on the auction block. *(Open for viewing M-F 9am-4:30pm, Su noon-4pm.)* Modern art aficionados should note the rugged Henry Moore frieze high up on the crest of the **Time-Life Building,** corner of Bruton St. At the **Marlborough Fine Arts** (tel. 629 5161), the biggest contemporary names are sold; **Agnew's** and **Colnaghi's,** 43 and 14 Old Bond St., deal in Old Masters.

Running west off Bond St., Grosvenor St. ends at **Grosvenor Sq.,** one of the largest in central London. The square, occasionally called "little America," has gradually evolved into a U.S. military and political enclave since future President John Adams lived at No. 9 while serving as the first American ambassador to England in 1785. From here you can see the humorless and top-heavy **U.S. Embassy** rising to the west. The metal eagle atop the building is as long as a double-decker bus.

In the opposite (northeast) corner of Mayfair (tube: Oxford Circus), tiny Hanover Square provides a gracious residential setting for **St. George's Hanover Church,** where the *crème de la crème* of London society have been married. To the south, off Conduit St., the name **Savile Row** is synonymous with the elegant and expensive "bespoke" tailoring that has prospered there for centuries.

■ Kensington, Knightsbridge, and Belgravia

Kensington, a gracious, sheltered residential area, reposes between multi-ethnic Notting Hill to the north and chic Chelsea to the south. **Kensington High St.,** which pierces the area, has become a locus for shopping and scoping. Take the tube to High St. Kensington, Notting Hill Gate, or Holland Park to reach **Holland Park,** a peacock-peppered swath of green full of small pleasures. **Holland House** (see **Accommodations,** p. 74), a Jacobean mansion built in 1607, lies on the park's grounds and contains a youth hostel, rose gardens, an open-air amphitheater (box office tel. 602 7856), an ecology center, and a number of playgrounds, as well as cricket pitches, public tennis courts, and traditional Japanese Kyoto Gardens. *(Open daily 7:30am-9:30pm.)* Two petite exhibition galleries, the **Ice House** and the **Orangery** (tel. 361 3204) blossom in the middle of the park. *(Open daily 11am-7pm. Free.)*

The curious **Leighton House,** 12 Holland Park Rd. (tel. 602 3316), lies a block west of the Institute, and is a presumptuous yet pleasant pastiche. The thoroughly blue Arab Hall, with inlaid tiles, a pool, and a dome, is an attempt to recreate the wonders of the Orient in thoroughly Occidental Kensington. Now a center for the arts, Leighton House features concerts, receptions, and other events in the evenings, as well as frequent art exhibitions and competitions. *(Open M-Sa 11am-5:30pm. Free.)*

To reach the grandiose South Kensington museums, take the tube to the South Kensington station or bus #49 from Kensington High St. The **Victoria and Albert**

Museum, the **Natural History Museum** (both on Cromwell Rd.), and the **Science Museum** (on Exhibition Rd.) all testify on a grand scale to the Victorian mania for collecting, codifying, and cataloging.

Patrician **Knightsbridge** is wealthy, groomed, and sometimes forbidding. The neighborhood is defined most of all by London's premier department store, **Harrods.** Extravagance is its specialty. Its dominating five-story megastructure might easily be mistaken for a fortress, except for the giant flag proclaiming "sale." *(Open M-Tu and Sa 10am-6pm, W-F 10am-7pm; see **Shopping,** p. 138.)*

Belgravia was first constructed to billet servants after the building of Buckingham Palace in the 1820s, but it soon became the bastion of wealth and privilege it is today. Belgravia lies south of Hyde Park, ringed by stately Sloane St. to the west, Victoria Station to the south, and Buckingham Palace Gardens to the east. The spacious avenues and crescents of the district surround **Belgrave Sq.,** 10 acres of park surrounded by late-Georgian buildings that were the setting for *My Fair Lady.*

HYDE PARK AND KENSINGTON GARDENS

Totalling 630 acres, **Hyde Park** (tel. 298 2100) and the contiguous **Kensington Gardens** constitute the largest open area in the center of the city, thus earning their reputation as the "lungs of London." *(Park open daily 5am-midnight; gardens open daily dawn-dusk. Both free.)* At the far west of the Gardens, you can drop your calling card at **Kensington Palace** (tel. 376 0198; tube: Kensington High St. or Queensway), originally the residence of King William III and Queen Mary II and recently of Princess Margaret. *(Open May-Sept. for tours only. Hourly tours M-Sa 10am-5pm. £7.50, students and seniors £5.90, children £5.35, families £23. Allow 1¼ hr. for the tour; reserve through Ticketmaster at tel. 344 4444.)* Be sure to seek out the lovely, cloistered **Sunken Garden** as well.

The statue of **Peter Pan** stands near the **Italian Fountains** on the Serpentine's west bank. The **Serpentine,** a lake carved in 1730, runs from these fountains in the north, near Bayswater Rd., south toward Knightsbridge. Harriet Westbrook, Percy Bysshe Shelley's first wife, numbers among the famous people who have drowned in this human-made "pond."

On the southern edge of Kensington Gardens, the Lord Mayor had the **Albert Memorial** built to honor Victoria's beloved husband. The extravagant monument has now spent years under scaffolding. Across the street, the **Royal Albert Hall,** with its ornate oval dome, hosts the Promenade Concerts (Proms) in summer (see **Music,** p. 234). As always, exercise caution at night.

On summer evenings and Sundays from late morning to dusk, proselytizers, politicos, and flat-out crazies assemble to dispense the fruits of their knowledge to whoever's biting at **Speakers' Corner,** in the northeast corner of Hyde Park (tube: Marble Arch, not Hyde Park Corner), the finest example of free speech in the world.

■ Chelsea

Now quiet and expensive, **Chelsea** has historically been one of London's flashiest districts—Thomas More, Oscar Wilde, and the Sex Pistols have all been residents at one time or another. It used to be that few streets in London screamed louder for a visit than **King's Rd.** Mohawked UB40s (a reference to the unemployed: it's the form they must fill out to get benefits) and pearl-necklaced Sloane Rangers (the awfully loose English equivalent of preppies) gazed at trendy window displays and at each other. While the hordes still flock here on Saturday afternoons to see and be seen, the ambience is drastically muted; most current scenesters look like they are desperately trying to recapture a past they have only read about.

Any proper exploration of Chelsea begins at **Sloane Sq.** The square takes its name from Sir Hans Sloane (1660-1753), whose collection comprised the whole of the first British Museum. Be aware that the tube is practically nonexistent around here, so you'll have to rely on **buses** (#11, 19, 22, 211, and 319).

Off King's Rd., Chelsea becomes cozier, the closest thing to a village that central London now possesses. Totally immune to the ever-changing world of King's Rd. are the commandingly militaresque buildings of Wren's **Royal Hospital,** founded in 1691 by Charles II for retired soldiers and still inhabited by 400 army pensioners. *(Grounds open daily Apr.-Sept. 10am-8pm. Museum open daily Apr.-Sept. 10am-noon and 2-4pm. Call ahead.)* East of the Hospital lie the **Ranelagh Gardens.** Here 18th-century pleasure-seekers spent their evenings watching pageants and fireworks and imbibing to excess. *(Usually open until dusk. Free.)* The **Chelsea Flower Show** blooms here during the third week in May (Tu-F), but even Royal Horticultural Society members have trouble procuring tickets for the first two days. The lovely **Chelsea Physic Garden** (tel. 352-5646) is next door. *(Open W 2-5pm, Su 2-6pm. £3.50, students, seniors, and children £1.80. Wheelchair accessible.)*

   Cheyne (pronounced "CHAY-nee") **Walk, Cheyne Row,** and **Tite Street** formed the heart of Chelsea's artist colony at the turn of the century. Watch for the blue plaques on the houses; J.M.W. Turner moved into a house in Cheyne Walk, and Edgar Allan Poe lived nearby. Mary Ann Evans (a.k.a. George Eliot) moved into No. 4 just before her death. Dante Gabriel Rossetti kept his disreputable *ménage* (which included peacocks and a kangaroo) in No. 16, where he doused himself with chloral hydrate. Nos. 19 to 26 cover the ground that used to be Chelsea Manor, where Queen Elizabeth I once lived. Both Mick Jagger and Keith Richards got satisfaction on the Walk in the 1960s. The area's arbiter of the aesthetic, Oscar Wilde, reposed stylishly at 34 Tite St. from 1884-1895 and was arrested for homosexual activity at Chelsea's best-known hotel, the Cadogan (75 Sloane St.). John Singer Sargent, James MacNeill Whistler, Radclyffe Hall, and Bertrand Russell also lived on Tite St. Today, fashionable artists' and designers' homes line the street, though the area is too expensive to remain a true bastion of bohemian culture.

   Chelsea's famed resident Thomas Carlyle crafted his magnificent prose on Cheyne Row. On this miraculously quiet street colored by flowers and tidy houses, **Carlyle's House,** 24 Cheyne Row (tel. 352 7087), has remained virtually unchanged since the Sage of Chelsea expired in his armchair. Family portraits and sketches ornament the walls—which he had doubled in thickness, vainly hoping to keep out noise. *(Open Apr.-Oct. W-Su 11am-5pm. Last admission 4:30pm. Admission £3.20, children £1.60.)*

■ Notting Hill

Notting Hill is one of London's most diverse neighborhoods—a variety of racial, ethnic, and socioeconomic groups call this area home. On the lively streets, trendy places to eat and shop ply their trade among dilapidated stores, wafts of incense, and Bob Marley posters, while MPs mingle cautiously with hipsters. The region explodes with exuberant festivity every summer during the **Notting Hill Carnival,** Europe's biggest outdoor festival (every Aug. bank holiday weekend). Steel drummers, fantastic costumes, entranced followers, and dancing policemen parade down the street, to the beat of Afro-Caribbean music.

   Commercial Portobello Rd., the area's lively main thoroughfare, runs parallel to Ladbroke Grove. The **Portobello Market** (see p. 257) makes this already lively commercial district downright vivacious every Saturday. The name "Portobello" may evoke childhood memories, even if you've never been to London—one of the market's most famed patrons is **Paddington Bear,** whose purchases here always landed his paws in a pot of trouble.

   The area has a checkered past of racial conflict that it is gradually putting to rest. Irish and Jewish immigrants were the first to occupy the poor areas of "Notting Dale" in the late-19th century, but the 1930s saw the arrival of Fascist demonstrations against Jews and local immigrant groups. Inter-ethnic tension re-emerged in the 1950s when Teddy-Boy gangs engaged in open warfare against Afro-Caribbean immigrants—the devastating riots that ensued are depicted in Colin MacInnes's novel *Absolute Beginners* (later made into a movie musical starring David Bowie). Amy Garvey (widow of Marcus Garvey, famed black separatist) helped the black community on Notting Hill survive various onslaughts. Today the multi-ethnic area sees little racial animosity.

■ North London

■ Marylebone and Regent's Park

Located between Regent's Park and Oxford St., the grid-like district of **Marylebone** (MAR-lee-bun) is dotted with elegant late-Georgian town houses. The name derives from "St. Mary-by-the-bourne," the "bourne" referring to the Tyburn or the Westbourne stream, both now underground. The eternally dammed Westbourne now forms the Serpentine in Hyde Park.

There's little to see in this well-kept, well-bred region of residences and office buildings. The area's most fondly remembered resident is **Sherlock Holmes** who, although fictitious, still receives about 50 letters per week addressed to his 221b Baker St. residence. The **Sherlock Holmes Museum,** 239 Baker St. (marked "221b"), will thrill Holmes enthusiasts with its re-creation of the detective's lodgings.

Ever since the redoubtable **Madame Tussaud,** one of Louis XVI's tutors, trekked from Paris in 1802 carrying wax effigies of French nobles decapitated in the Revolution, Madame Tussaud's Wax Museum, on Marylebone Rd. (tel. 935 6861), with an adjacent Planetarium, has been a London landmark and popular tourist attraction. *(Open M-F 9am-5:30pm, Sa-Su 9:30am-5:30pm; in winter opens 1 hr. later. Museum £9.75, seniors £7.45, children £6.50; Both museum and planetarium £12, seniors £9.25, children £8.)*

Oxford St., the southern border of Marylebone, passes through Oxford Circus, Bond St., and Marble Arch tube stations. Arguably London's major shopping boulevard, it's jam-packed with shops (ranging from cheap chain stores to the posh boutiques around Bond St.), crowds, and fast-food stands. Off Oxford St., pleasant **James's St.** (tube: Bond St.) lures passersby with several cafes—a good place for people-watching from a sidewalk table. Manchester Sq. holds the lavish (and free) **Wallace Collection,** a must-see for fans of Dutch art and medieval armor (see p. 130).

Five-hundred-acre **Regent's Park** (tube: Regent's Park, Great Portland St., Baker St., or Camden Town) is full of lakes, promenades, and open spaces, and has become a popular spot for family cricket and football matches. Within the park's Inner Circle, the delightful **Queen Mary's Gardens** erupt in color in early summer. The rose garden dazzles with 20,000 blooms. The park is also home to the animals of the **London Zoo.** North of Regent's Park stands **Primrose Hill,** long a favorite spot for picnics and kite-flying. On a clear day you can see as far as the Surrey Downs. *(Open 5am-dusk.)*

■ Bloomsbury

During the first half of the 20th century, Bloomsbury gained its reputation as an intellectual and artistic center, due largely to the presence of the famed Bloomsbury Group, which included biographer Lytton Strachey, novelist E.M. Forster, economist John Maynard Keynes, art critic Roger Fry, painter Vanessa Bell (sister of Virginia Woolf), and hovering on the fringe, T.S. Eliot, the eminent British poet from St. Louis. Very little of the famed intellectual gossip and high modernist argot currently emanates from 51 Gordon Sq., where Virginia Woolf lived with her husband.

Today, the British Museum, the British Library, and the University of London guarantee a continued concentration of cerebral, as well as tourist, activities in the area. The **British Museum** makes an appropriate Bloomsbury centerpiece; forbidding on the outside but quirky and amazing within, it contains the remains of thousands of years' worth of world history and civilization.

To the north, close by Strachey and Keynes's former homes, stands the **Percival David Foundation of Chinese Art,** 53 Gordon Sq. (tel. 387 3909; tube: Russell Sq. or Goodge St.), a connoisseur's hoard of fabulously rare ceramics. The top floors offer eccentric delights. *(Open M-F 10:30am-5pm. Free.)* The sprawling new **British Library,** next to St. Pancras Station, is Bloomsbury's latest addition; the library is home to thousands of books and manuscripts of the past millennium.

Up St. Pancras Rd., **St. Pancras Old Church** sits serenely in its large and leafy garden. Parts of the church date from the 11th century. Mary Godwin first met Shelley here in 1813 by the grave of her mother, Mary Wollstonecraft. Rumor has it that believing her mum died during her birth, Godwin insisted that Shelley make love with her on the grave.

Directly northeast of the British museum, **Russell Sq.** squares off as central London's second-largest, after Lincoln's Inn Fields. T.S. Eliot, the "Pope of Russell Square," hid from his emotionally ailing first wife at No. 24 while he worked as an editor and later director of the Faber and Faber publishing house.

Bernard St. leads east to Brunswick Sq., sight of the **Thomas Coram Foundation for Children,** 40 Brunswick Sq. (tel. 278 2424; tube: Russell Sq.). Thomas Coram, a retired sea captain, established the Foundling Hospital for abandoned children here in 1747. Although the hospital was torn down in 1926, its art treasures remain, displayed in a suite of splendidly restored 18th-century rooms (call for information).

Across from the Foundation lies **Coram's Fields,** 93 Guilford St. (tel. 837 6138), seven acres of old Foundling Hospital grounds that have been preserved as a children's park, complete with a menagerie of petting animals, an aviary, and a paddling pool for tykes under five. *(Open daily Easter-Oct. 9am-dusk; Nov.-Mar. 9am-5pm. Free. No dogs allowed—no adults, either, unless accompanied by a child.)*

Charles Dickens lived at 48 Doughty St. (east of Russell Sq., parallel to Gray's Inn Rd.) from 1837 to 1839, working on *The Pickwick Papers, Nicholas Nickleby, Barnaby Rudge,* and *Oliver Twist.* The **Dickens House** (tel. 405 2127; tube: Russell Sq. or Chancery Ln.) holds prints, photographs, manuscripts, letters, and personal effects. *(Open M-Sa 10am-5pm, last entry 4:30pm. £3.50, students £2.50, children £1.50, families £7.)*

To the south of the British Museum, the shrapnel-scarred Corinthian portico of Hawksmoor's 18th-century church, **St. George's, Bloomsbury** looms in Bloomsbury Way. A statue of George I crowns the heavy steeple, which was modeled on the tomb of King Mausolus in Turkey. Inside, novelist Anthony Trollope was baptized before the gilded mahogany altar, where Dickens set his "Bloomsbury Christening" in *Sketches by Boz. (Open M-Sa 9:30am-5:30pm.)*

■ Camden Town

Camden Town started to develop with the opening of the Regent's Canal in 1820. By the 19th century, Camden Town was a solid working-class district, spliced with railways and covered in soot. Charles Dickens spent his childhood here, crowded in a four-room tenement with his extended family at No. 16 (now No. 141) Bayham St. Irish, Cypriot, Greek, Italian, and Portuguese immigrants have all settled here.

Contemporary Camden Town is a stomping ground for trendy youth of all subcultural affiliations. Trends are initiated and abandoned at the **Camden Markets,** drawing swarms of bargain-seeking Londoners and curious, often bewildered, tourists each weekend (tube: Camden Town; see **Shopping,** p. 140). Though the area is renowned for its shoes and boots, anything and everything can be found here, and the clientele reflects the diversity of the goods.

■ Islington

Islington became "trendy" during the late 17th century, when its ale houses and cream teas made it popular for wealthy scene-makers. In more recent times, Islington was one of London's first areas to undergo regentrification; it established itself as an academic and artistic haven by the 1930s, serving as home to writers such as George Orwell, Evelyn Waugh, Douglas Adams, and Salman Rushdie.

Today, Islington is one of the hottest neighborhoods in London. The area is favored by trendy, style-conscious, and well-to-do Londoners. Many of the more stylish University of London students and professors live here, alongside several ethnic communities including Turkish, Irish, Italian, and Bengali residents. As the number of gay pubs in the area attests, Islington is also home to a large gay community.

A refurbished 19th-century chapel now houses the **Crafts Council,** 44a Pentonville Rd. (tel. 806 2500; tube: Angel), the national organization for the promotion of contemporary crafts. Exit the station to the left and take the first right onto Pentonville Rd. *(Open Tu-Sa 11am-6pm, Su 2-6pm. Wheelchair accessible.)*

The **Business Design Centre,** 52 Upper St. (tel. 359 3535 or 288 8666), is hard to miss. The modern-looking glass facade belies its origin as the Royal Agricultural Hall, completed in 1861. Known as "the Aggie," the Hall's large, enclosed space served as the site for a wide range of crafts exhibitions, animal shows, meetings, Christmas fêtes, military tournaments, circuses, and the World's Fair. Annual exhibits include Fresh Art, a showcase for recent fine arts graduates, and New Designers, a spring-board for design students. Many exhibitions charge admission—call for details.

■ Hampstead and Highgate

Foliage in London traditionally pulls in well-heeled and artistic residents, and the twin villages of "Ham and High," surrounding the gorgeous Hampstead Heath, are no exception. Keats, Dickens, and more recently, Emma Thompson and Kenneth Branagh have all called the area home. The tidy streets lined with Jaguars, boutiques, and Georgian townhouses provide a window on the theory and practice of being idly rich, which may explain Karl Marx's, Jinnah's (the founder of Pakistan), and former Labour leader Michael Foot's past residences. *(To get to Hampstead, take the tube to Hampstead or British Rail to Hampstead Heath. To reach Highgate, take the tube to Archway, then Bus #210 to Highgate Village. Either trip takes around 30 min. from the center of London.)*

This dual legacy of art and wealth shines through in the area's many restored houses, most notably the **Keats House,** Keats Grove (tel. 435 2062), one of London's finest literary shrines. To get there from the Hampstead tube station, head left down High St. for several blocks, turn left down Downshire Hill, and then take the first right onto Keats Grove. (The BR Hampstead Heath station is much closer.) The decor and furnishings stay true to the Regency style of the early 19th century, providing an evocative showcase for manuscripts, letters, and contemporary pans of Keats' works by critics dead and forgotten. *(Open Apr.-Oct. M-F 10am-1pm and 2-6pm, Sa 10am-1pm and 2-5pm, Su 2-5pm; Nov.-Mar. M-F 1-5pm, Sa 10am-1pm and 2-5pm, Su 2-5pm. Free.)* The **Keats Memorial Library** (tel. 794 6829) next door contains 8500 books on the poet's life, family, and friends. *(Open by appointment to accredited researchers only.)*

Among the delicate china, furniture, and early keyboard instruments exhibited in the **Fenton House,** Hampstead Grove (tel. 435 3471), sits a prototype 18th-century "double guitar," proving that Britain's fascination with excessively stringed instruments predates the meaty guitar hooks of the young Jimmy Page. *(Open Apr.-Nov. W-F 2-5pm, Sa-Su 11am-5pm. £4, children £2.)*

Hampstead Heath (tube: Hampstead or BR Hampstead Heath) separates Hampstead and Highgate from the rest of London. Stroll through acres of lush greenery and forget the hustle and bustle of the city among the carefree picnickers, kite flyers, and anglers. But don't stay too late—it's inadvisable to wander the heath alone at night.

The southeastern tip of the heath is called **Parliament Hill,** but rather deceptively—no Parliament, no hill. It was toward this "hill" that Guy Fawkes and his accomplices fled after planting explosives under the House of Commons in 1605, hoping for a good view of the explosion. He was later caught and tortured in the Tower of London (see p. 111). On a hot day, take a dip in the murky waters of **Kenwood Ladies' Pond, Highgate Men's Pond,** or the *outré* **Mixed Bathing Pond.** The ponds are a refreshing, free way to escape the rare sunny London days.

To get from Hampstead to Highgate, walk across the heath (an easy way to get lost, but very scenic) or up Hampstead Ln. Both take about 45 minutes. You can also take Bus #210 from Jack Straw's Castle junction, or take the tube to Archway. **Highgate Cemetery** (tel. (0181) 340 1834), on Swains Ln., is a remarkable monument to the Victorian fascination with death. The most famous resident is Karl Marx, buried in the **Eastern Cemetery** in 1883. *(Open M-F 10am-6pm, Sa-Su 11am-6pm. £1.)* Herbert Spencer, who vehemently opposed socialism, shares Highgate with socialism's most influential proponent, Marx. On a more harmonious note, Spencer's bones lie near those of his reputed lover, the novelist George Eliot (Mary Ann Evans, buried in the western section). Though its guest list lacks the same notoriety, the **Western Cemetery** provides rest for Michael Faraday, the Dickens family, and ornate tombs and mausolea worth seeing regardless of their occupants. *(Access by guided tour only M-F noon, 2, and 4pm, Sa-Su every hr. 11am-4pm. Around £3. Camera permit £1, valid in both sections.)*

■ East London

■ The East End

Today's East End eludes the simple characterization that earlier times would have allowed. Once it was the Jewish center of London, then the Huguenot center, and later the center for a number of more recent immigrant groups—Irish, Somalis, Chinese, and Muslim Bangladeshis. Marked today by an invisible line across Bishops Gate St., London's East End nonetheless continues to serve, as it always has, as a refuge for both those who aren't welcome in the City and those who don't want to be subject to the City's jurisdiction. A large working-class English population moved into the district during the Industrial Revolution, followed by a wave of Jewish immigrants fleeing persecution in Eastern Europe who settled around **Whitechapel.** In 1978, the latest immigration wave brought a large Muslim Bangladeshi community to the East End. On Sundays, vibrant market stalls selling books, bric-a-brac, leather jackets, and salt beef sandwiches flank **Brick Ln.** and Middlesex St., better known as **Petticoat Ln.** (see **Shopping,** p. 140). The towering minarets, grand scale, and large congregation of the **East London Mosque,** 82-92 Whitechapel Rd. (tel. 247 1357; tube: Aldgate East), testify to the size of London's Muslim community.

Christ Church, Commercial St., E1 (tel. 247 7202; tube: Aldgate East; left on leaving the station, left again onto Commercial St.), is an island of Anglicanism amid a diverse spectrum of other traditions. *(Open to visitors M-F noon-2:30pm.)*

Most of the Jewish community has moved on to suburbs; one of the only notable remnants is the city's oldest standing synagogue, **Bevis Marks Synagogue,** Bevis Marks and Heneage Ln., EC3 (tel. 626 1274; fax 283 8825; tube: Aldgate; from Aldgate High St. turn right onto Houndsditch; Creechurch Ln. on the left leads to Bevis Marks). *(Organized tours Su-W and F noon; call in advance. Building open Su-M, W, and F 11:30am-1pm, Tu 10:30am-4pm. Donation £1.)*

The most recent wave of immigrants to join this cultural milieu consists of City artists. Some of their work, much of which focuses on the experience of the East End's nonwhite population, occasionally hangs on the high white walls of the **Whitechapel Art Gallery** (tel. 522 7888) on Whitechapel High St.

An overdramatized aspect of the East End's history is its association with London's notorious criminals. Jack the Ripper's six murders took place in Whitechapel; tour his trail with a guided walk, offered every evening (see **London Walks,** p. 94). Along Cambridge Heath Rd. lies the delightful **Bethnal Green Museum of Childhood.**

■ Docklands

London Docklands, the largest commercial development in Europe, is the only section of London built wholly anew—a total break from the city's typically slow architectural evolution. Developers have poured tons of steel, reflective glass, and money onto the banks of the Thames east of London Bridge.

The 800 ft. **Canary Wharf** building, Britain's tallest edifice and the jewel of the Docklands, is visible to the east from almost anywhere in London. The pyramid-topped structure, which contains shops, restaurants, and a concert hall, is the emblem of the new Docklands.

Docklands proper covers a huge expanse (55 mi. of waterfront to be exact), from the Tower of London to Greenwich. The best way to see the region is via the **Docklands Light Railway (DLR)** (tel. 918 4000 or 363 9700), a driverless, totally automatic elevated rail system. The DLR's smooth ride affords a panoramic view that helps you put the huge expanse of the Docklands into perspective. All tickets, Travelcards, and passes issued by London Transport, London Underground, and Britrail are valid on the DLR, provided they cover the correct zones.

The **Docklands Visitor Centre** (tel. 512 1111; DLR: Crossharbour, then left up the road) should be the first stop for any tour of the Docklands. Loads of brochures hide behind the reception, the most useful being the *DLR Tourist Guide,* which includes a map, points of interest, and DLR info. *(Open M-F 8:30am-6pm, Sa-Su 9:30am-5pm.)*

On the southern end of the Isle of Dogs, the pastoral expanses of **Mudchute Park** (DLR: Crossharbour or Mudchute), come as a relief after the human-made modernity of Canary Wharf. At **Mudchute City Farm,** Pier St., E14 (tel. 515 5901) there are 32 acres of grassy heath, plus horses to ride and farm animals to pet. *(Open daily 9am-5pm, Tu and Th later—call for details.)* For a sweeping view of Greenwich, follow the DLR southern line to its endpoint at Island Gardens. You can walk through the chilly foot tunnel and take in some of the sights.

Many of the ancient Dockland wharfs have now been turned into major leisure spots. Six sailing centers, three pools, a go-karting racetrack, and an artificial ski mountain currently stand where ships and toxic waste used to rest. For general information and bookings for all of the above activities, call 476 2134. The Docklands Visitor Centre also has a list of all sport and leisure facilities.

The year-round **Beckton Alps Ski Centre** (tel. 511 0351; DLR: Beckton, zone 4), is a one-run hillock rising 45m above the surrounding supermarkets and electronics superstores. It is covered with a specially designed carpet upon which water is sprayed to make it slippery. The 200m run is served by a rope tow. The slope is open most days, but call to check on conditions—cold rainy days are the best. Pants, long sleeves, and gloves are required. *(£6 per 3hr. M-F £7 per 3hr. including equipment rental.)*

■ South London

■ The South Bank and Lambeth

A hulk of worn concrete and futuristic slate, the **South Bank** gestures defiantly at the center of London from across the Thames. Housing the British terminus of the Channel Tunnel, this region is currently becoming one of London's most dynamic, as major commercial development is currently underway. The massive **South Bank Centre** is the predominant architectural eyesore; yet behind this hulking facade lurks artistic and cultural activity (tube: Waterloo, then follow signs for York Rd.; or Embankment and cross the Hungerford footbridge).

Contemporary development began in 1951 during the Festival of Britain, the centenary of the Great Exhibition of 1851, when the **Royal Festival Hall** was built. A veritable eruption of construction ensued, producing the **National Film Theatre,** the **Hayward Gallery** and **Queen Elizabeth Hall** complex, and the **Royal National Theatre.** The **Jubilee Gardens,** planted for the Queen's Silver Jubilee in 1977, stretch along the Embankment.

The 3000-seat **Royal Festival Hall** and its three auditoriums (Olivier, Lyttleton, and Cottlesoe) are home to the Philharmonia and London Philharmonic orchestras, the English National Ballet, and host to countless others; its chamber-musical sibling is the **Queen Elizabeth Hall. The National Theatre** promotes "art for the people" through platform performances, foyer concerts, lectures, tours, and workshops. The **Hayward Gallery,** on Belvedere Rd., houses contemporary art exhibitions. The Film Theatre operates the incredible **Museum of the Moving Image** (see p. 129).

Gabriel's Wharf (tel. 401 3610) is a great place to watch original crafts being fashioned while grabbing a snack after a visit to the National Theatre. During the summer, take advantage of sporadic free festivals. *(Crafts workshops Tu-Su 11am-6pm; call the Wharf for information on festivals.)* The **OXO Tower,** adjacent to Gabriel's Wharf, boasts a meticulously planned potpourri of rooftop cafes, retail outlets, designer workshops, performance spaces, and flats that will make it a hub of London activity.

Numerous pedestrian pathways will make it easier to get to the jumbled stalls of the **Cut Street Market** near Waterloo station. Farther along Waterloo Rd., the magnificently restored **Old Vic,** former home of Olivier's National Repertory Theatre, now hosts popular seasons of lesser-known classics and worthy revivals.

■ Southwark

Historically a hotbed of prostitution, incarceration, and bear-baiting, **Southwark** (across London Bridge from the city) seems an unlikely location for a new cradle of London high culture (tube: London Bridge). The area around the **Borough High St.,** "the Borough," has survived—with a few minor changes—for nearly 2000 years. Until 1750, London Bridge was the only bridge over the Thames in London, and the inns along the highway leading to it hosted many travelers. The neighborhood has also been associated with entertainment from the days of the frost fairs (the old London Bridge used to cause the Thames to freeze over during the winter) to the more vicious pleasures of Defoe's *Moll Flanders.* Shakespeare's and Marlowe's plays were performed at the **Rose Theatre,** built in 1587 and rediscovered during construction in 1989. A project spearheaded by the late actor/director Sam Wanamaker built a "new" **Shakespeare's Globe Theatre** (tel. 902 1400) on the riverbank. The theater held its first full season in the summer of 1997 (see **Entertainment,** p. 132), featuring Shakespeare's *The Winter's Tale* and *Henry V,* as well the Womad Acoustic Concert and other non-Bardic performances. *(1hr. tours available May-Sept. M 9am-4pm, Tu-Sa 9am-12:30pm, Su 9am-2:30pm; Oct.-Apr. daily 10am-5pm. £5, seniors and students £4, under 15 £3, families £14.)*

Around the corner from the Globe, the new **Golden Hinde** offers landlubbers the chance to board a rebuilt 16th-century galleon. Attendants clad as pirates lead tours through the five levels of the vessel, seemingly geared especially toward the kiddies. *(Yar. Open daily 10am-4pm. £2.30, seniors £1.90, children £1.50, families £6.)*

The **Liberty of the Clink,** which operated for more than six centuries, was the Bishop's private prison for London's criminals. The **Clink Prison Museum,** 1 Clink St. (tel. 378 1558), recreates the "glory days" of the prison with an eerie choral soundtrack and restraining and torture devices. *(Open June-Sept. M-F 10am-6pm, Sa-Su 10am-9pm; Oct.-May daily 10am-6pm. £4, students and seniors £3, children £3, families £9.)*

The **Southwark Cathedral** (tel. 407 2939) is a more endearing remnant of ecclesiatical power. Probably the most striking Gothic church in the city after Westminster Abbey, it is certainly the oldest—having been the site of a nunnery as early as 606. Mostly rebuilt in the 1890s, only the church's 1207 choir and retro-choir survive. *(Open M-F 9am-6pm. Evensong Su 3pm. Free. Photo permit £1, video permit £5.)*

If your appetite for the macabre is not sated by the minutiae of early medicine, the **London Dungeon** awaits buried beneath the London Bridge Station at 28 Tooley St. (see **Museums,** p. 224). Not for the squeamish, this dark maze of more than 40 exhibits recreates horrifying historical scenarios of execution, torture, and plague.

Just upstream from Tower Bridge, the WWII warship **HMS Belfast** (tel. 407 6434) once led the bombardment of the French coast during D-Day landings and still looks as if it would enjoy nothing better than blowing 100 Golden Hindes to smithereens. *(Open daily Mar. 1-Oct. 31 10am-6pm, last admission 5:15pm; Nov. 1-Feb. 28 10am-5pm, last admission 4:15pm. £4.70, students and seniors £3.60, children £2.40. Pool of London ferries run between five destinations along the river including the HMS Belfast; all-day pass adults £2, students, seniors, and children £1.)* The labyrinth of the engine house and the whopping great guns make it a fun place to play sailor. Mind your head, matey. You can take the ferry that runs from Tower Pier on the north bank to the Belfast whenever the ship is open, or take the tube to London Bridge. Follow Tooley St. from London Bridge, past the London Dungeon, and look for the signs. East of Tower Bridge, the bleached Bauhaus box perching on the Thames is the **Design Museum,** around the corner from which hides the **Bramah Tea and Coffee Museum.**

The **Southwark Tourist Information Centre** (tel. 403 8299), in the lower level of Hay's Galleria, Tooley St., SE1, books rooms and provides information on the area's sights. Ask for the handy list of conveniently located accommodation. *(Open M-Sa 10am-5pm, Su 11am-5pm.)* Galleria also inexplicably possesses a free petanque court—ask for rules and boules inside Balls Brothers Wine Bar. Across Tooley St. from the Galleria lies **Winston Churchill's Britain At War Museum.**

■ Greater London

■ Greenwich

London's love affair with the Thames and Britain's love affair with the sea climax in **Greenwich** (GREN-idge), at a point where the Thames runs wide and deep. Charles II authorized the establishment of a small observatory here in 1675 "for perfecting navigation and astronomy," and successive royal astronomers perfected their craft to such a degree that they were blessed with the Prime Meridian in 1884.

The splendid **Greenwich Park,** used as a burial ground during the 1353 plague, contains most of the major sights. At the top of the hill in the middle of the park stands the **Old Royal Observatory** (tel. (0181) 312 6565), designed by Sir Christopher Wren. *(Open daily 10am-5pm; last admission 4:30pm. Admission to the Old Royal Observatory, National Maritime Museum, and the Queen's House: £5, students and seniors £4, children 5-16 £2.50, families £15. Admission to the Observatory alone: £4, students and seniors £3, children £2, families £12. Planetarium usually features a show M-Sa every ½hr. 11:30am-4pm; tickets £2, concessions and children £1.50. 45min. audio guide to the observatory £2.)* Flamsteed House, remarkable for its unique octagonal top room, contains Britain's largest refracting telescope and an excellent collection of early astronomical instruments displayed with nearly comprehensible explanations. The **Prime Meridian** is marked by a brass strip in the observatory courtyard and a laser beam inside; play the "now I'm west, now I'm east" game for as long as you're amused. At the foot of the hill is the highly informative **National Maritime Museum** (see **Museums,** p. 129).

The museum forms the west addition to **Queen's House** (tel. (0181) 858 4422), the 17th-century home that was started for James I's wife, Anne of Denmark, who unfortunately died before construction was completed. *(Open daily 10am-5pm; no separate entry, see prices for observatory.)* The **Children's Boating Pool** next to the playground gives kids a chance to unleash pent-up seafaring energy accumulated in the nearby museums. *(Open Apr.-Oct. daily 9am-dusk. £1.50 per person for 20min., or £2.50 per 2-3 child boat for 20min.)*

Charles II commissioned Wren to tear down the Royal Palace of Placentia and to construct the **Royal Naval College** (tel. (0181) 858 2154) in its place. *(Open daily 2:30-4:30pm. Free. Services Su 8:30am holy communion, 11am sung eucharist.)* By the River Thames in Greenwich, the **Cutty Sark** (tel. (0181) 858 2698), one of the last great tea clippers, anchors in dry dock. *(Open M-Sa 10am-6pm, Su noon-6pm; last entry 30min. before close. £3.50, students, seniors, and children £2.50, families £8.50.)* The ship (whose name, meaning "short shift," comes from Burns's poem "Tam O'Shanter") carried 1.3 million pounds of tea on each 120-day return trip from China. The **Gipsy Moth IV** rests nearby.

In the run up to year 2000, no description of Greenwich would be complete without mentioning **The Millennium Experience,** or as it is more popularly known, the Millennium Dome. Not due to open until December 31, 1999, this huge structure, covering some 80,000 square meters of floor space, is intended to provide an international focus for the arrival of the new millennium.

Trains leave from Charing Cross, Waterloo East, and London Bridge for Greenwich (less than 20min., day return £3). The friendly **Greenwich Tourist Information Centre,** 46 Greenwich Church St., SE10 (tel. (0181) 858 6376) will arrange a variety of afternoon tours. *(Open daily in summer 10:15am-5pm; in winter usually 11am-4pm. Tours £4, students and seniors £3, under 14 free. 1-1½hr.; call (0181) 858 6169 for info.)*

■ Richmond

Ever since Henry I came up the Thames in the 12th century, **Richmond** has preened its royal pedigree. Although Henry VII's Richmond Palace, built in 1500, was demolished during Cromwell's Commonwealth, the town has not lost its dignified sheen—the 18th-century riverside houses and pathways beneath Richmond Hill make this area possibly the most serene in or around London. The **Richmond Tourist Informa-**

tion Centre (tel. (0181) 940 9125), in the old Town Hall on Whittaker Ave., has complete information on Richmond and surrounding areas. *(Open June-Sept. M-F 10am-6pm, Sa 10am-5pm, Su 10:15am-4:15pm; Oct.-May same hours, but closed Sundays.)*

Richmond Park, atop Richmond Hill, is Europe's largest city park, with 2500 acres. Descend Richmond Hill and follow Bridge St. across the Thames. The **Marble Hill House** (tel. (0181) 892 5115; bus #33, 90B, 290, H22, R68, or R70 from the station) is a 10-minute walk left along the river (follow the signs and the tourists) from here. *(Open daily Apr.-Oct. 10am-6pm; Nov.-Mar. W-Su 10am-4pm. £3, students, seniors, and children £2.30.)* Perched on the Thames amid vast trimmed lawns, this Palladian house was built in 1729 for Henrietta Howard, George II's mistress.

KEW GARDENS

Tel. (0181) 940 1171. Tube: Kew Gardens (zone 3). BR North London line: Kew Gardens. Boats travel daily between Kew and Westminster pier. From Westminster 10:15, 10:30, 11:15am, noon, 2pm; from Kew 3:30, 4:30, and 5:30pm; call 930 2062 beforehand, as trip times may vary according to fluctuations in the Thames. £6, return £10, discounts for seniors and children. Parking available outside of the gardens. Open M-F 9:30am-6:30pm, last admission 6pm, Sa-Su and bank holidays 9:30am-7:30pm, last admission 7pm. Conservatories close at 5:30pm. Call to confirm closing times, as they may vary by season. Admission £5, students and seniors £3.50, ages 5-16 £2.50, under 5 free, late admission from 4:45pm £3.50. Tours leave Victoria Gate daily at 11am and 2pm, £1; sign up early as tours fill quickly. Kew also hosts summer jazz concerts—tickets run £18-25. Call Ticketmaster at 344 4444 for details.

The perfect complement or antidote to days of sightseeing in central London, the **Royal Botanic Gardens** at Kew provide a restorative breath of fresh air. Yet another example of the Empire's collecting frenzy, the Gardens were originally intended to recreate Eden by bringing together plants from all over the world. Today the park displays thousands of flowers, plants, bushes, fruits, trees, and vegetables from throughout the globe, spread over 300 perfectly maintained acres. Founded in 1759 by Princess Augusta, Kew gradually grew in size until it became a royal park in 1841.

The wonders of the gardens comprise several sections, and demand several hours to be viewed properly. The steamy, tropical **Palm House,** a unique masterpiece of Victorian engineering built in 1848, will stun you with the revelation that bananas are in fact giant herbs. Downstairs, the beautifully lit aquariums of the **Marine Display** let you watch batfish and porcupine puffer fish interact with colorful sea kelp.

Although replete with voluptuous fronds, the Palm House is dwarfed by its younger Victorian sibling, the **Temperate House.** The cooler climate here nurtures 3000 species, arranged over 50,000 sq. ft. according to geographical origins. Across from the Temperate House, the **Evolution House** leads you through 3.5 billion years of floracentric history, from the primordial ooze (recreated with relish) to the exciting moment when flowering plants appeared. Its misty waterfalls and dinosaur footprints play like a cross between "Land of the Lost" and Biosphere II.

On the opposite side of the park from William Chambers's 1762 **pagoda,** the **Princess of Wales Conservatory** allows a browse through 10 different tropical climates; it's just a few steps from a rainforest to an arid desert. Its award-winning pyramidal design allows it to both remain innocuous among the foliage and conserve energy.

In the northeastern section of the gardens stands **Kew Palace.** Built in 1631 but leased as a royal residence since 1730, this inconspicuous summer home of King George III and Queen Charlotte is closed until further notice. Instead, visitors may wish to visit **Queen Charlotte's Cottage,** a small, picturesque structure given by George to Charlotte as a picnic site. The cottage's distinctly Bavarian feel may speak to the King's Teutonic roots. *(Open Sa-Su and holidays 10:30am-4pm.)*

Other points of interest at the gardens include the **Marianne North Gallery,** a small but interesting collection of 19th-century paintings, the **Rhododendron Dell** (built by Capability Brown), and the **Waterlily House.**

HAMPTON COURT PALACE

Open *Mar. to late Oct. M 10:15am-6pm, Tu-Su 9:30am-6pm; late Oct. to Mar. M 10:15am-4:30pm, Tu-Su 9:30am-4:30pm; last admission 45min. before closing. Privy gardens and maze open and close with palace. Gardens open at the same time as the palace, but close at 9pm or dusk, whichever comes first (admission free). All-encompassing* **admission** *£9.25, students and seniors £7, under 15 £6.10, under 5 free, families £27.65; only to maze or Privy Garden £2.10, under 16 £1.30; only to tennis court 50p, children 20p. Wheelchair accessible.*

Although a monarch hasn't lived here since George II packed it in over 200 years ago, **Hampton Court Palace** (tel. (0181) 781 9500) continues to exude regal charm. Cardinal Wolsey built it in 1514, showing Henry VIII by his example how to act the part of a splendid and all-powerful ruler. Henry learned the lesson well—he confiscated the Court in 1525 when Wolsey fell out of favor. Today, the palace stands in three distinct parts, each bearing the mark of one of its strong-willed inhabitants.

To help tourists make sense of the chaos of the chaotic and schizophrenic arrangement of the palace, it is divided into six "routes" through which tourists may meander. Fans of Henry VIII have a myriad options for discovering how the king lived, reigned, and ate his way to a size 54 waist. **Henry VIII's State Apartments,** the first of the palace routes, allows would-be sycophants a chance to reenact some Tudor brown-nosing. Every morning, courtiers would gather in the **Great Watching Chamber.** If the style of Henry's rooms strikes you as a bit vulgar, you're not alone. When William III (of William and Mary fame) sailed up from the Netherlands to ascend to the throne with his wife, he declared the palace a "gothic monstrosity," and commissioned Wren to demolish it and build a palace to rival Louis XIV's Versailles. Wren's work can be seen in the opulent **King's and Queen's Apartments,** two complementary palace routes. Along the ceiling of the **King's Guard Chamber,** almost 3000 guns and weapons arranged in six repeating patterns along the upper wall reminded visitors that the man they were about to see, no matter which throne they found him on, was not to be trifled with.

The legacies of all the palace's past residents can be felt in the **Wolsey Rooms,** which house **tapestries** woven from the Raphael cartoons in the Victoria and Albert Museum (see **Museums,** p. 128).

The **maze** (open Mar.-Oct.), a hedgerow labyrinth first planted in 1714 that inspired the hedges a crazed Jack Nicholson dashed through at Stanley Kubrick's Overlook Hotel. "Solve" the maze by getting to the benches in the middle, and back.

The walls of the palace are steeped in more royal lore and anecdotes than can possibly be discovered during a quick stroll through—tours and audio guides are available. By tube, take the district line to Richmond (zone 3); Bus #R68 runs from the station to Hampton court (80p). BR runs trains from Waterloo to Hampton Court every 30 minutes (day return £4).

WINDSOR AND ETON

Windsor Castle (tel. (01753) 868286 or 831118 for 24hr. information), proves beyond a doubt that, to borrow from Mel Brooks, it's good to be the Queen. *(Open daily Apr.-Oct. 10am-5:30pm, last entry 4pm; Nov.-Mar. 10am-4pm, last entry 3pm. £8.80, over 60 £6.20, under 17 £4.60, families £20.50. Most of the castle is wheelchair accessible—call (01753) 868 286, ext. 2235 for details.)* Within these ancient stone walls lie some of the most sumptuous rooms in Europe and some of the rarest artworks in the Western world. But beyond the velvet and fine art, this castle's essence is its strategic location high in the hills above the Thames and the thousands of hauberks, swords, pistols, rifles, and suits of armor that bedeck its walls. The castle now dominates this cutesy river town of cobbled lanes and tea shops surrounded by the 4800-acre Great Park, far away from London in the farming country of Surrey. Built by William the Conqueror as a fortress rather than as a residence, it has grown over nine centuries into the world's largest inhabited castle. Saunter blithely in and out of its labyrinthine terraces and enjoy dreamlike views of the Thames Valley.

Be aware that Windsor is a working castle, which may sound a little strange in this day and age, but only means that various members of the Royal Family reside here on weekends and for various special ceremonies. The practical consequence of the Royals' residence is that, often without warning, large areas of the castle will be unavailable to visitors. The steep admission prices will be lowered, but it is wise to call before visiting to check that the areas you want to see are open.

The 13 acres covered by the castle are organized into the lower, middle, and upper wards. The **Round Tower** dominates the middle ward. The **Moat Garden,** filled not with water but with roses and well-attended grass, surrounds the tower.

You can visit the elegantly furnished **state apartments,** which are mostly used for ceremonial occasions and official entertainment. The rooms are richly decorated with artwork from the massive Royal Collection, including works by Holbein, Rubens, Rembrandt, and an entire room of Van Dycks. In the same wing is **Queen Mary's Doll House,** an exact replica of a palace on a tiny scale.

A stroll down to the lower ward will bring you to **St. George's Chapel,** a sumptuous 15th-century building with delicate fan vaulting and an amazing wall of stained glass dedicated to the Order of the Garter. Here, Henry VIII rests in a surprisingly modest tomb near George V, Edward IV, Charles I, and Henry VI. A ceremonial procession of the Knights of the Garter, led by the Queen, takes place here in June. Windsor's **Changing of the Guard** takes place in front of the Guard Room at 11am. *(In summer M-Sa; in winter alternate days M-Sa.)*

Windsor is notorious to contemporary visitors as the site of a fire that helped make 1992 an *annus horribilis* for the royal family. The fierce conflagration blazed for nine hours on November 20, 1992, and was only extinguished through the efforts of 225 firefighters and 39 fire engines. Six rooms and three towers were destroyed or badly damaged by smoke and flames, although 80% of the state rooms escaped harm. Refurbishments following the fire are now completed, and the redesigned St. George's Hall, Lantern Lobby, and Grand Reception Room are all now available for viewing. To see Queen Mary's doll house, pay an extra pound, which, according to Queen Mary's original 1924 request, is still donated to charity.

Follow the road that bears left around royal grounds to reach the entrance to **Windsor Great Park,** a huge expanse of parkland where deer graze and royals ride. The park follows the 3 mi. **Long Walk,** which passes by a couple of former hunting lodges, one of which houses the Queen Mum (on weekends). The town of Royal Windsor is directly across the road from the castle gate. Built up around the castle during the Middle Ages, it is filled with specialty shops, tea houses, and pubs.

Eton College (tel. (01753) 671177), England's preeminent public (i.e., private) school, was founded by Henry VI in 1440. Eton boys still wear tailcoats to every class and solemnly raise one finger in greeting to any teacher on the street. Despite its position at the apex of the British class system, Eton has molded some notable dissidents and revolutionaries—Percy Bysshe Shelley, Aldous Huxley, George Orwell, and even former Liberal Party leader Jeremy Thorpe. The Queen is the sole (honorary) female Old Etonian. Wander around the schoolyard, a central quad where Eton boys have frolicked for centuries. *(Open daily July-Aug. and late Mar. to mid-Apr. 10:30am-4:30pm; other times 2-4:30pm. £2.50, under 16 £2. Tours £3.50, under 16 £3. Tours depart daily 2:15pm and 3:30pm.)*

Legoland Windsor (tel. (0990) 040 404), offers superbly detailed buildings and sights from European cities, including Miniland, a replica of the City of London. *(Open daily Mar. 14-Nov. 1 and Oct. weekends 10am-6pm; July 18-Aug. 31 10am-8pm. £16, children £13, seniors £10; additional £1 for the shuttle from the BR: Windsor and Eton Riverside stations.)*

MUSEUMS

A couple of centuries as capital of one of the world's richest and most powerful countries, and a decidedly English penchant for collecting, have given London a spectacular set of museums. Admission is often free, but many museums now charge or request a £1-2 donation. Most charge for special exhibits and offer student and senior citizen discounts. The London **White Card** is a discount card which allows you unlimited access to participating museums for a period of three or seven days. The card is available at any of the participating museums, including the V&A, the Science Museum, the Natural History Museum, and the Courtauld Institute (3-day card £15, families £30; 7-day card £25, families £50).

BRITISH MUSEUM

*Located at Great Russell St., WC1. **Tel.** 323 8299 for information desk. **Tube:** Tottenham Ct. Rd., Goodge St., Russell Sq., or Holborn. **Open** M-Sa 10am-5pm, Su 2:30-6pm. **Admission** free; suggested donation £2. **Guided tours** depart M-Sa 10:30, 11am, 1:30, 2:30pm; Su 3, 3:20, 3:45pm; £7, students £4, under 16 £3; 1½hr. **Highlights** of the Museum tour departs M-Sa 1pm from upstairs, 3pm downstairs; cost £5, students £3; 1hr. Larger, **special exhibits** £4, students, seniors, and children £3. Rear entrance on Montague St. Visually-impaired should enquire about tactile exhibits; a **touch tour** of Roman and Egyptian sculpture is offered in room 84 in the basement—ask at the main desk for details.*

The sheer volume of the British Museum's collections is a fascinating document of the political, military, and economic power of the British Empire. Founded in 1753, the museum began with the personal collection of the physician Sir Hans Sloane. Today the British museum's national archaeological collections recapitulate the glory days of Egypt, Asia, Greece, Rome, and prehistoric and medieval Europe. The museum also houses superb temporary exhibitions of its coin and medal and its print and drawing collections.

The outstanding **ancient Egypt** collection occupies rooms on the ground and upper floors. Entering the ground floor gallery, the **Rosetta Stone,** discovered in 1799 by French soldiers, rests to the left. Its Greek text enabled Champollion to finally crack the Egyptian hieroglyphic code. The head of Ramses II, famed for his arrogance towards Moses and higher beings in Exodus, dominates the northern section of Room 25. In the side gallery 25a, don't miss three of the finest and best known Theban tomb paintings. The upstairs Egyptian gallery contains brilliant sarcophagi and grisly mummies. Delicate papyri include the *Book of the Dead of Ani.*

The **Greek antiquities** exhibits are dominated by the **Elgin Marbles,** 5th-century BC reliefs from the Parthenon, now residing in the spacious Duveen Gallery. In 1810, Lord Elgin "procured" the statues and pieces of the Parthenon frieze while serving as ambassador to Constantinople. The marbles comprise three main groups: the frieze, which portrays the most important Athenian civic festivals, the *metopes,* which depict incidents from the battle of the Lapiths and Centaurs (symbolizing the triumph of "civilization" over "barbarism"), and the remains of large statues that stood in the east and west pediments of the building.

Other Greek highlights include two of the Seven Wonders of the Ancient World. Once crowded by a four-horse chariot, the **Mausoleum at Halicarnassus** and the **Temple of Artemis,** were built to replace the one buried by Herostratus in 356 BC.

Among the many sculptures of the **Roman antiquities,** the dark blue glass of the **Portland Vase,** the inspiration for ceramic designer Josiah Wedgewood, stands out. The **Roman Britain** section includes the **Mindenhall Treasure,** a magnificent collection of 4th-century silver tableware. Nearby crouches **Lindow Man,** an Iron Age Celt supposedly sacrificed in a gruesome ritual and preserved by peat-bog. The **Sutton Hoo Ship Burial,** an Anglo-Saxon ship buried in Suffolk complete with an unknown king, is the centerpiece of the **Middle Ages** galleries.

The majority of the museum's **Oriental Collections** reside in the recently refurbished Gallery 33. The gallery's eastern half is dedicated to the Chinese collection, and the western half is filled by Indian and Southeast Asian exhibits, which include the largest collection of Indian religious sculpture outside of India. Upstairs, the collection continues with a series of three galleries displaying Japanese artifacts, paintings, and calligraphy. The most recent gallery additions are **Renaissance to the 20th Century,** featuring housewares from Bach to *Bauhaus,* and the **Mexican Gallery,** highlighted by exquisite masks and weapons coated with a mosaic of turquoise.

NATIONAL GALLERY

*Located in Trafalgar Sq., WC2. **Tel.** 839 3321 or 747 2885. **Tube:** Charing Cross, Leicester Sq., Embankment, or Piccadilly Circus. **Open** M-Tu and F-Sa 10am-6pm, W 10am-8pm, Su noon-6pm. **Admission** free. **Tours** depart from the Sainsbury Wing M-F 11:30am and 2:30pm, evening tour W 6:30pm, Sa 2 and 3:30pm; tours also in sign language the 1st Saturday of each month 11:30am. The Orange St. and Sainsbury Wing entrances are **wheelchair accessible.***

The National Gallery maintains one of the world's finest collections of Western art, especially strong in works by Rembrandt, Rubens, and Italian Renaissance painters. The Berggruen Collection of works from the turn of this century has been temporarily loaned to the National. You can spend days in this recently renovated maze of galleries. The **Micro Gallery,** a computerized catalogue, guides you to the works you want to see and offers astounding and amusing facts. *(Open M-Tu and F-Sa 10am-5:30pm, W 10am-7:30pm, Su noon-5:30pm.)*

The National's collection is divided into four sections; paintings within these sections are arranged by school. The collection starts in the new **Sainsbury Wing,** to the west of the main building, with works painted from 1260 to 1510. Paintings from 1510 to 1600 are found in the **West Wing,** to the left of the Trafalgar Sq. entrance. Titian's *Bacchus and Ariadne* and Holbein's *The Ambassadors* are worth a peek. Impressive collections of Rembrandt and Rubens adorn the **North Wing.** Van Dyck's *Equestrian Portrait of Charles I* headlines the State Portrait room.

The **East Wing,** right of the main entrance, is devoted to painting from 1700 to 1920, including a well-respected English collection. The natural light provides the perfect setting for viewing the paintings, such as Turner's *Rain, Steam, and Speed.* Impressionist works include a number of Monet's near-abstract waterlilies, Cézanne's *Old Woman with Roses,* and Rousseau's rainswept *Tropical Storm with a Tiger.* Picasso's *Fruit Dish, Bottle, and Violin* (1914), the National Gallery's initial foray into the abstract, has since been joined by another room of Picasso's work.

The National Gallery holds frequent special exhibitions in the basement galleries of the Sainsbury Wing, which sometimes cost up to £6 but are often free. In 1999, look for "Luca Signorelli in British Collections" (Nov. 11, 1998-Jan. 31, 1999), "Portraits by Ingres" (Jan. 27, 1998-Apr. 25, 1999), and "Rembrandt Self Portraits" (June 9-Sept. 5, 1999), among others. The National shows free films about art every Monday at 1pm in the Sainsbury Wing, and lectures take place in the afternoons (Tu-F at 1pm, Sa at noon; for more info, call 747 2885). Linger on Wednesday nights and admire the musuem's treasures against music performed by students of the Royal College of Music in the Sainsbury Wing Foyer. (Free.)

NATIONAL PORTRAIT GALLERY

*Located at St. Martin's Pl., WC2, just opposite St.-Martin's-in-the-Fields. **Tel.** 306 0055. **Tube:** Charing Cross, Leicester Sq., Piccadilly Circus, or Embankment. **Open** M-Sa 10am-6pm, Su noon-6pm. **Admission** free, excluding temporary exhibits. Informative 1hr. lectures, Tu and Th 1:10pm, Sa-Su 3pm. Check the monthly schedule for topics and locations. Orange St. entrance is **wheelchair accessible** and there is a lift to all floors. For more information, call ext. 216.*

This unofficial *Who's Who* began in 1856 as "the fulfillment of a patriotic and moral ideal"—namely to showcase Britain's noteworthy citizens. The museum's principle of looking "to the celebrity of the person represented, rather than to the merit of the artist," has not affected the quality of the works—Reynolds, Holbein, Sargent, and Gainsborough portraits that stare up from countless history books segue into Warhol's Elizabeth II and Annie Leibovitz's photos of John Lennon and Yoko Ono.

The 9000 paintings have been arranged more or less chronologically, from the top floor down. Follow the flow of British history through the galleries: from the War of the Roses (Yorks and Lancasters), to the Civil War (Cromwell and his buddies), to the American Revolution (George Washington), to imperial days (Florence Nightingale), and on to modern times (Margaret Thatcher).

The gallery often mounts temporary displays and has planned exhibits of "British Sporting Heroes" (Oct. 16, 1998-Jan. 24 1999), the Raeburn (Jan.-Feb. 1999), the "John Kobal Photographic Portrait Award 1998 (Oct. 30, 1998-Feb. 14, 1999), and "Millias: Portraits" (Feb. 19-June 6, 1999), in addition to others. *(£4, students, seniors, and children £3.)* The annual British Petroleum Portrait Award features works from England's most promising portrait artists (June-Oct.).

TATE GALLERY

Located at Millbank, SW1. Tel. 887 8000 for recorded information or tel. 887 8725 for assistance. Tube: Pimlico. Open daily 10am-5:50pm. Admission free. Tours run M-F 11am for British Old Masters: Van Dyck to the Pre-Raphaelites, noon for the Turner Collection, 2pm for Early Modern Art, 3pm for Conceptual Art, and only Sa 3pm for the General Tour: The Essential Tate. Audio guides (£3, students, seniors, and children £2, for the main collection, the Clore galleries, or the Turner galleries; £4, students, seniors, and children £3, for 2; £5, students, seniors, and children £4 for all 3) feature a 5-10min. discussion on major works.

The Tate Gallery opened in 1897 expressly to display contemporary British art. Since then, the gallery has widened its scope, obtaining a superb collection of British works from the 16th century to the present and a distinguished ensemble of international modern art. The highly recommended audio guides (£2-3, students and seniors £1.50-2) make modern art comprehensible.

The Tate's **British collection** starts at the far end of the gallery with 16th- and 17th-century painting. The parade of Constables includes the famous views of Salisbury Cathedral, and Hampstead scenes. George Stubbs's landscapes and sporting scenes lead to Gainsborough's landscapes and Sir Joshua Reynolds's portraits. Don't miss the visionary works of poet, philosopher, and painter William Blake.

The Tate's outstanding **modern collection** of international 20th-century art features sculptures by Henry Moore, Epstein, Eric Gill, and Barbara Hepworth, in addition to Rodin's **The Kiss.** The works of Monet, Degas, Van Gogh, Beardsley, Matisse, and the Camden Town Group hang to the left of the entrance. Paintings by Picasso, Dalí, Francis Bacon, and members of the Bloomsbury Group, sculptures by Modigliani and Giacometti, and samples of modern art lie to the right of the central hall. The Tate's 300-work J.M.W. Turner collection resides in the **Clore Gallery.**

The Tate hosts a series of temporary exhibits in the downstairs galleries. In 1999 the Tate will host exhibitions on Jackson Pollock (Mar. 11-June 6), and the Bloomsbury group (Nov. 1999-Jan. 2000). Admission varies.

VICTORIA & ALBERT MUSEUM

The V&A is located on Cromwell Rd., SW7. Tel. 938 8500, 938 8441 for 24hr. recorded info, or 938 8349 for current exhibitions. Tube: South Kensington. Buses C1, 14, and 74. Open M noon-5:50pm, Tu-Su 10am-5:50pm. Admission £5, concessions £3, students and those under 18 free. Admissions free 4:30-6pm. Most of the museum is wheelchair accessible; wheelchair users are advised to use the side entrance on Exhibition Rd. and to call ahead at 938 8638. Gallery tours and taped tours are available for the visually impaired. One-hour introductory museum tours meet at the Cromwell entrance information desk daily 12:30, 1:30, 2:30 and 3:30pm, Tu-Su additional 10:30 and 11:30am tours. On Wednesday evenings during the summer, the V&A hires a few musicians, sets up a wine bar, and opens a few galleries for museum patrons from 6:30-9:30pm (£3). Experts give lectures on select pieces during these open gallery evenings (£5). Call 938 8500 for more info *or to make (required) **reservations**. The V&A also offers scores of special events. Free gallery talks on a wide array of topics are given throughout the summer Tu-Sa 2pm.*

Housing the best collection of Italian Renaissance sculpture outside Italy, the greatest collection of Indian art outside India, and the international center for John Constable studies, the mind-bogglingly inclusive V&A has practically perfected the display of fine and applied arts.

The stars of the **Renaissance collection** are the famed *Raphael Cartoons*—seven of the 10 large, full-color sketches made by Raphael and his apprentices as tapestry patterns for the Sistine Chapel. The endless galleries of Italian sculpture include Donatello's *Ascension* and *Madonna and Child*. The **Medieval Treasury,** in the center of the ground floor, features stained glass and illuminations. Plaster cast reproductions of European sculpture and architecture occupy rooms 46A-B on the ground floor. Next door, test your perception in the **Fakes and Forgeries gallery.**

The V&A's formidable **Asian collections** have recently been supplemented by the Nehru Gallery of Indian Art and the T.T. Tsui Gallery of Chinese Art. The **Nehru gallery** contains splendid examples of textiles, painting, Mughal jewelry and decor, and revealing displays on European imperial conduct. The elegant **Tsui gallery** divides its 5000-year span of Chinese art into six areas of life: Eating and Drinking, Living, Worship, Ruling, Collecting, and Burial. Treasures include the Sakyamuni Buddha and an Imperial Throne. The **Toshiba Gallery of Japanese Art** has a prime collection of lacquer art, as well as armor and contemporary sculpture. The V&A's **Islamic Art** is punctuated by the intricacies of Persian carpets and Moroccan rugs.

The first floor holds **British art and design.** International design classics—mostly chairs—grace "Twentieth Century Design." The **jewelry collection** (rooms 91-93— actually a pilfer-proof vault!) includes pieces dating from 2000 BC. The **National Art Library,** located on the first floor, houses Beatrix Potter originals as well as first editions of Winnie the Pooh. The new **Frank Lloyd Wright gallery,** on the second floor of the Henry Cole Wing, displays the Wright-designed interior of the Kauffmann Office, the V&A's first 20th-century period room. The exquisitely redesigned **Glass Gallery** recently reopened in room C-131. Photography aficionados will want to visit the **Print Room** (503 in the Henry Cole Wing). The print collection encompasses both the incipient stages of the medium and contemporary products.

■ Recommended Collections

The Courtauld Gallery, Somerset House, the Strand, WC2 (tel. 873 2526), across from the corner of Aldwych and the Strand. Tube: Temple, Embankment, Charing Cross, or Covent Garden. Eleven-room gallery in Somerset House with Impressionist and post-Impressionist works, including pieces by Cézanne, Degas, Gauguin, Seurat, and Renoir, plus Van Gogh's *Portrait of the Artist with a Bandaged Ear,* and Manet's *Bar aux Folies Bergère.* The Institute's other collections include early Italian religious paintings—works by Botticelli, Rubens (*Descent from the Cross*), Bruegel, Cranach *(Adam and Eve)*, and Modigliani. Open M-Sa 10am-6pm. £4, students, seniors, and children £2. M half-price. Wheelchair accessible.

London Transport Museum, Covent Garden, WC2 (tel. 379 6344, recorded info 565 7299). Tube: Covent Garden. On the east side of the Covent Garden plaza. The museum boasts 2 new mezzanine floors, 2 new galleries, and a variety of interactive video displays. Low-tech exhibits provide a thought-provoking cultural history: see how the expansion of the transportation system fed the growth of suburbs. High-tech simulators allow you to recklessly endanger the lives of scores of cyber-commuters as you take the helm of a subway train. Open M-Th and Sa-Su 10am-6pm, F 11am-6pm, last admission 5:15pm. £4.95, students, seniors, and children £2.95, families (2 adults, 2 kids) £12.85, under 5 free. Wheelchair accessible.

Museum of London, 150 London Wall, EC2 (tel. 600 3699, 24hr. info tel. 600 0807; email info@museum-london.org.uk). Tube: St. Paul's or Barbican. Comprehensive is an understatement: this fabulously engrossing museum tells the story of the metropolis from the beginning of time, from its origins as Londinium up through the 1996 European Soccer Championships hosted here. Exhibits including reconstructed industrial-age streets and 17th-century royal carriages outline London's domestic, political, religious, cultural, industrial, sartorial, and natural histories. Open Tu-Sa 10am-5:50pm, Su noon-5:50pm, last entry 5:30pm. £4, students, seniors, and children £2, families £9.50, free after 4:30pm. Wheelchair accessible.

Museum of the Moving Image (MOMI), South Bank Centre, SE1 (tel. 401 2636, or 24hr. info 401 2636). Tube: Waterloo; or Embankment (cross the Hungerford footbridge). The entertaining museum charts the development of image-making with light, from shadow puppets to film and telly. Costumed actor-guides are stationed at interactive exhibits—act out your favorite western, read the TV news, or watch your own superimposed image fly over the River Thames. Open daily 10am-6pm; last entry 5pm, but allow around 2hr. £6.25, students £5.25, handicapped, seniors, and children £4.50, families £17. MC, Visa.

National Maritime Museum, Romney Rd., Greenwich, SE10 (tel. (0181) 858 4422, recorded info (0181) 312 6565; fax (0181) 312 6632). BR: Greenwich or DLR: Island Gardens and use the pedestrian foot tunnel under the Thames. A documentation of the history of British sea power. The highlight is the hands-on gallery, where visitors can play modern sailor, tracking and destroying enemy ships using sophisticated radar. Open 10am-5pm, last admission 4:30. £5, students and seniors £4, ages 5-16 £2.50, families £15.

Natural History Museum, Cromwell Rd., SW7 (tel. 938 9123). Tube: South Kensington. See whales, volcanoes, and dinosaurs all in one day in this former Victorian cathedral. The museum's personality is split between glorious, encyclopedic explanations and high-tech, more hands-on exhibits (buttons, levers, and microscopes galore). Open M-Sa 10am-5:50pm, Su 11am-5:50pm. £6, students and seniors £3.20, ages 5-17 £3, families (up to 2 adults and 4 children) £16. Free M-F 4:30-6pm, Sa-Su, and Bank holidays 5-5:50pm. Wheelchair accessible.

Royal Academy, Piccadilly, W1 (tel. 439 7438, fax 434 0837), across from no. 185. Tube: Green Park or Piccadilly Circus. The academy hosts traveling exhibits of the highest order. The whopping annual summer exhibition (June-Aug.) is a London institution—works of contemporary artists cover every inch of wall space and are for sale (at non-budget prices). Open daily M-Sa 10am-6pm, Su 10am-8:30pm. Admission varies by exhibition; average £6, students, seniors, and children £4.

Royal Air Force Museum, Grahame Park Way, NW9 (tel. (0181) 205 6867 or (0181) 205 2266 for 24hr. information). Tube: Colindale. Exit left and head straight for about 15min., or take the Bus #303 from the tube station. The RAF has converted this former WWI airbase into a hangarful of the country's aeronautic greatest hits. Along with displays of the dignified history of the RAF, Gulf War footage and high-tech weapons exhibits hint at the future of Britain's air defense. Open daily 10am-6pm, last admission 5:30pm. £6.50, students £3.25, families £16.60. Wheelchair accessible.

Science Museum, Exhibition Rd., SW7 (tel. 938 8008 or 938 8080). Tube: South Kensington. Closet science geeks will be outed by their ecstatic cries as they enter this wonderland of diagrammed motors, springs, and spaceships. The museum's introductory exhibit romps through a "synopsis" of science since 6000 BC, lingering (a bit self-indulgently) over the steam-powered Industrial Revolution that vaulted Britain to world domination. The 3-floor Wellcome Museum of Medical History confronts visitors with a glut of fascinating information. Open daily 10am-6pm. £6.50, students, seniors, and children £3.50, under 5 and people with disabilities free. Free daily 4:30-6pm.

Sir John Soane's Museum, 13 Lincoln's Inn Fields, WC2 (tel. 405 2107). Tube: Holborn. Soane was an architect's architect, but the idiosyncratic home he designed for himself will intrigue even laypersons. Artifacts on display include Hogarth paintings, the massive sarcophagus of Seti I, and casts of famous buildings and sculptures from around the world. Open Tu-Sa 10am-5pm. Free. Tours (restricted to 22 people) leave Sa 2:30pm; tickets sold from 2pm on day of tour.

The Wallace Collection, Hertford House, Manchester Sq., W1 (tel. 935 0687). Tube: Bond St. This unassuming mansion defines the adjective "sumptuous." Outstanding works include Hals's *The Laughing Cavalier,* Delacroix's *Execution of Marino Faliero,* Fragonard's *The Swing,* and Rubens's *Christ on the Cross.* Works by Major Dutch Golden Age artists hang near a number of Rubens oil sketches (drafts of some of his most famous works). This is perhaps the best free collection in London outside of the British Museum. Open M-Sa 10am-5pm, Su 11am-5pm. Guided tours M-Tu 1pm, W 11:30am and 1pm, Th-F 1pm, Sa 11:30am, Su 3pm. Free.

ENTERTAINMENT

On any given day or night, Londoners and visitors can choose from the widest range of entertainment a city can offer. Suffering competition only from Broadway, the West End is the world's theater capital, supplemented by an adventurous "fringe." Music scenes range from the black ties of the Royal Opera House to Wembley mobs and nightclub raves. The work of British filmmakers like Derek Jarman, Sally Potter, and Mike Leigh—often available in the States only on video—is shown in cinemas all over the city. Dance, comedy, sports, and countless unclassifiable happenings can leave you poring in bewilderment over the listings in *Time Out* (£1.70) and *What's On* (£1.20). **Kidsline** (tel. 222 8070) answers queries on children's events (M-F 4-6pm). **Artsline** (tel. 388 2227) provides information about disabled access at entertainment venues across London (M-F 9:30am-5:30pm).

■ Theater

The stage for a national dramatic tradition dating from Shakespeare's day, London is for theater. The Royal Academy for the Dramatic Arts draws students from around the globe. Playwrights such as Tom Stoppard and Alan Ayckbourn premier their works in the West End; class-conscious dramatists, younger writers, and performance artists uphold a vibrant "fringe" scene; Shakespearean and Jacobean revenge tragedies are revived everywhere. Tickets are relatively inexpensive; the cheapest seats in most theaters cost about £8, rising to £30 for orchestra seats. Previews and matinees cost a few pounds less, and many theaters offer dirt-cheap **student/senior standbys** (indicated by "concs," "concessions," or "S" in newspaper and *Time Out* listings)—around £7 with ID just before curtain (arrive 2hr. early to ensure a seat). **Day seats** are sold 9-10am on the day of the show at a reduced price, but you must come even earlier to snag one. If a show is sold out, returned tickets may be sold (at full price) just before curtain. Most theaters also offer senior citizen discounts on advance ticket purchases for weekday matinees. For the latest on West End standbys, call **Student Theatreline** (tel. 379 8900; updated from 2pm daily).

Stalls are orchestra seats. **Upper Circle** and **Dress Circle** refer to balcony seats above the stalls. **Slips** are seats along the top edges of the theater; usually the cheapest, they often have restricted views of the stage. The **interval** is the intermission. Programs are never free; they cost £1.50 to £2. Matinees are on weekdays and Saturday between 2 and 3pm. Evening shows start between 7:15 and 8pm.

The **Leicester Square Half-Price Ticket Booth** sells tickets at half-price (plus £1.50-2 booking fee) on the day of the performance, but carries tickets only for the West End, Barbican (and Pit), and National Theatres. Tickets are sold from the top of the pile, which means you can't choose a seat, and the priciest seats are sold first. Lines are the worst on Saturday. *(Open M-Sa noon-6:30pm; cash only; max. 4 per person.)* Accept no imitations: the peculiar structure with the small tower on the south side of Leicester Sq. is the only discount booth sanctioned by the **Society of London Theater** (tel. 836 0971), but doesn't offer tickets to the huge musicals (*Cats, Phantom,* etc.). Your next best bet for the lowest prices is to schlep to a theater's box office and select your seats from their seating plan. Reserve seats by calling the box office and then paying by post or in person within three days.

Barbican Theatre, Barbican Centre, EC2 (tel. 382 7272 for 24hr. information or call 638 8891 for reservations; http://www.barbican.org.uk). Tube: Barbican or Moorgate. London home of the Royal Shakespeare Company. Tickets for the main stage £7.50-24; weekday matinees £6-13; Saturday matinees and previews £8-18. Student and senior citizen standbys bookable in person or by telephone from 9am on the day of the performance, £6 (1 per person). Fascinating futuristic auditorium showcases the Bard's work in style; each row of seats has its own side door (there are no aisles). Forward-leaning balconies guarantee that none of the 1100 seats sit farther than 65ft. from center stage, and every seat gives a clear view. Stick around at the interval to watch the shiny metal safety curtain seal off the stage. The Pit—the 200-seat 2nd theater—showcases Jacobean, Restoration, and experimental contemporary works in a more intimate setting. Evenings and Saturday matinees £14-17; previews £11-13; midweek matinees £13-16. Student and senior citizen standbys available from 9am the day of the performance for £6.50. There are always several sign language and audio-described performances during the run of each show. Box office (Level 0 of the Centre) open daily 9am-8pm. AmEx, MC, Visa.

Royal National Theatre, South Bank Centre, SE1 (tel. 452 3400). Tube: Waterloo, or Embankment (cross the Hungerford footbridge). The brilliant repertory companies in the Olivier and Lyttleton theaters (£10-27) put on classics from Shakespeare to Ibsen, as well as mainstream contemporary drama. The smaller Cottesloe theater (£12 or 18) plays with more experimental works like Kushner's *Angels in America.* All 3 theaters are well ranked and have widely spaced rows, so even the rear balcony seats offer an unobstructed view of the stage. 40 day seats in each of the 3 theaters reduced to £10-12 at 10am on day of performance. General standby seats sold 2hr. before performance (£10-14); student and senior standby 45min. before show £7.50; senior citizens can book any show in advance for £10.50. The complex features live music, exhibitions, and other activities. The National's outstanding bookshop (tel. 452 3456; ask for the bookstore), has the widest selection in London for plays and books about theater. (Open M-Sa 10am-10:45pm.) Backstage tours M-Sa £4, students, seniors, and children £3.50. Book in advance; call 452 3400 for times. Box office open M-Sa 10am-8pm.

Shakespeare's Globe Theatre, New Globe Walk, Bankside, SE1 (tel. 401 9919 or Ticketmaster at 316 4703). Tube: London Bridge. This meticulous reconstruction of the Globe began its inaugural 1997 season with *Henry V* and *The Winter's Tale,* among others. Patrons may either purchase spots on the benches in the 3-tier space or stand through a performance as "groundlings." The groundling option may actually be the preferable one, not only because it costs less and allows a historical communion with the Elizabethan peasantry, but because it puts you much closer to both the stage and the roaming wine vendors. However, groundlings should prepare for the possibility of rain without the use of umbrellas (which impede sight lines). For information on educational workshops and "walkshops," call 902 1400. Groundling tickets for any performance £5. Box office open M-Sa 10am-8pm, until 6pm by phone.

The Lottery

George Orwell's apocalyptic *1984* predicted that the lottery would be the one event that would continue to delight the masses even when all else had been eradicated by Big Brother. Following the introduction of the National Lottery, many fear that Orwell has been proved right. The choosing of the winning numbers has become the most watched television program in Britain. The first multi-million pound pay-outs brought joy, then ruin, to families not able to bear the glare of the tabloids and the stress that large, unearned bounty seems to induce.

The lottery has created a furor not just because of its brashness, but because it represents a radical departure from how taxes used to be raised in Britain. Surplus funds are to go to the *Millennium Fund,* to oversee a program of beautification and public works to prepare Britain for the year 2000. The administration of the funds, however, has also been controversial, with some suggesting that subsidies to the opera are unwarranted when it is the poorest and least-educated Britons who are contributing most to this *fin-de-siècle* project.

■ Film

The degenerate heart of the celluloid monster is Leicester Square, where the most recent hits premiere a day before hitting the chains around the city. Other cinemas have one screen only, and you may find yourself in a converted theater, complete with gilt boxes. *Time Out* includes unbeatable guides both to commercial films and to the vast range of cheaper, more varied alternatives—including late-night films, free films, and repertory cinema clubs. Many reduce prices all day Monday and for matinees Tuesday through Friday. The city's best repertory cinemas:

The Prince Charles, Leicester Pl., WC2 (tel. 437 8181 or 437 7003). Tube: Leicester Sq. A Soho institution: 4 shows per day; generally second runs and a sprinkling of classics for £2-2.50. Every Friday the **Rocky Horror Picture Show** struts in, complete with a live troupe for £6, students, seniors, and children £3.

Gate Cinema, Notting Hill Gate, W11 (tel. 727 4043). Tube: Notting Hill Gate. Art house films, with a repertory on Sun. Featured directors include Wim Wenders, Jane Campion, and Derek Jarman. £6.50, M-F before 6pm and late shows £3.50, Su matinee £4, students, seniors, and children £3.

National Film Theatre (NFT), South Bank Centre, SE1 (tel. 928 3232 for box office). Tube: Waterloo, or Embankment and cross the Hungerford footbridge. One of the world's leading cinemas, with an array of film, TV, and video in its 3 auditoria. Program changes daily but is arranged in seasonal series. For ticket availability, call 633 0274. Most main screenings £5, students, seniors, and children £3.50.

The Ritzy Cinema, Brixton Oval, Coldharbour Ln., SW2 (tel. 737 2121, reservations 733 2229). Tube: Brixton. This classy old-style picture house shows a combination of artsy and mainstream films. Tickets £6, students, seniors, and children £3.

■ Music

London doesn't produce many musicians, but its abundant venues showcase them by the score. Unparalleled classical resources include five world-class orchestras, two opera houses, two huge arts centers, and countless concert halls. Additionally, London serves as the port of call for popular music: any rocker hoping to storm the British Isles, or conquer the world from Liverpool, Dublin, or Manchester, must first gig successfully in the one of the capital's numerous clubs. Check the listings in *Time Out.* Keep your eyes open for special festivals or gigs posted on most of the city's surfaces and for discounts posted on student union bulletin boards. Many of the most famous troupes take the summer off.

CLASSICAL

London's world-class orchestras provide only a fraction of the notes that fill its major music centers. London has been the professional home of some of the greatest conductors of the century—Sir Thomas Beecham, Otto Klemperer, and Andre Previn.

The venerable **London Symphony Orchestra** inhabits **Barbican Hall** in the **Barbican Centre** (tube: Barbican; tel. 638 4141 for information; box office tel. 638 8891). *(Tickets £6-30; student standbys, when available, are sold shortly before the performance at reduced prices.)* The **London Philharmonic** and the **Philharmonia Orchestra** play in the vast **Royal Festival Hall** in the grim labyrinth of the **South Bank Centre** (box office tel. 928 8800; tube: Waterloo, or Embankment and cross the Hungerford footbridge). *(Open daily 10am-9pm. Tickets £4-28; student standbys sold 2hr. before performance at lowest price.)* Vladimir Ashkenazy's **Royal Philharmonic Orchestra** performs at the Barbican and the South Bank, and the **BBC Symphony Orchestra** periodically pops up around town.

Exuberant and skilled, the **Proms** (BBC Henry Wood Promenade Concerts) never fail to enliven London summers. Every day for eight weeks from July to September, an impressive roster of musicians performs outstanding programs including annually commissioned new works in the **Royal Albert Hall** (box office tel. 589 8212; tube: South Kensington). The last night usually steals the show, with the massed singing of "Land of Hope and Glory," and closing with a rousing chorus of "Jerusalem"; a lottery of thousands determines who will be allowed to paint their faces as Union Jacks and "air-conduct" in person. *(Box office open daily 9am-9pm. Gallery £2, arena £3—join the queue around 6pm; £4-18, up to £30 for special performances.)*

Small, elegant, and Victorian, **Wigmore Hall,** 36 Wigmore St., W1 (tel. 935 2141; tube: Bond St. or Oxford Circus), leans to chamber groups and soloists (tickets £6-20; 1hr. standbys at lowest price) as does **St. John's,** Smith Sq. (box office tel. 222 1061; tube: Bond St. or Oxford Circus), a converted church just off Millbank. *(Tickets £6-20, usually reduced for seniors and students.)*

Outdoor concerts and festivals in summer are phenomenally popular and relatively cheap. The **Kenwood Lakeside Concerts** at Kenwood, on Hampstead Heath present top-class performances, often graced by firework displays (tel. 973 3427; booking 344 4444; tube: Golders Green, Archway, or East Finchley). From Golders Green or Archway, take bus #210, or from East Finchley, take the free shuttle bus to Kenwood. Every summer Saturday (mid-June to early Sept.) at 7:30pm and sporadic Sundays at 7pm, music floats to the audience from a performance shell across the lake. *(£1 booking fee. Reserved deck chairs £11-25, students and seniors £8-12. Grass admission £8.50-15, students and seniors £8.50-12.)* If the outdoors are more important to you than the concert, you can listen from afar for free. The **City of London Festival** (tel. 377 0540), stirs even the stuffiest stuffed shirts (June 23-July 16, 1998; events free-£25); the **Greenwich and Docklands International Festival** (tel. (0181) 305 1818) packs music and fireworks (July 10-19; up to £14); Bach fans go for Baroque at the **Lufthansa Festival of Baroque Music** (tel. 437 5053; June-July; £5-15).

OPERA AND BALLET

The **Royal Opera House,** at Covent Garden, Box St., (box office at 48 Floral St., WC2; tel. 304 4000, fax 497 1256; tube: Covent Garden), is going to be closed for refurbishment until 1999, but both the opera and ballet will be touring around London. Tickets for the resident companies, the Royal Opera and the Royal Ballet, come in a bewildering variety of prices and flavors. Since both companies are touring, it's best to call the box office for ticket prices (open M-Sa 10am-7pm).

All works at the **English National Opera** are sung in English. Seats in the Opera's London Coliseum (tel. 632 8300; tube: Charing Cross or Leicester Sq.), on St. Martin's Ln. £6.50-£55. One-hundred balcony day seats (£5) are available from 10am. If all tickets have been sold, standing room only tickets might be sold on the day of the performance. *(Box office open M-Sa 10am-8pm.)*

ROCK AND POP

The capital offers a wide, strange, and satisfying variety of musical entertainment. Often, thrash metallists play the same venue as Gaelic folk singers: check listings carefully. *Time Out* and *What's On* have extensive listings and information about bookings and festivals. You can make credit card reservations for major events by calling **Ticketmaster** (tel. 344 4444), though you may be charged a booking fee.

Apollo Hammersmith, Queen Caroline St., W6 (tel. 416 6080). Tube: Hammersmith. Mainstream rock. Tickets £17.50, 22.50, 27.50, or 32.50. Box office phones answered M-Sa 8am-9:30pm, Su 10am-8pm.

Brixton Academy, 211 Stockwell Rd., SW9 (tel. 924 9999). Tube: Brixton. Time-honored, rowdy venue for a wide variety of music, including rock, reggae, rap, and alternative. 4300 capacity. £8-25. Box office takes cash only—book ahead with a credit card. MC, Visa.

Dublin Castle, 94 Parkway St. (tel. 485 1773). Tube: Camden Town. Irish pub facade hides one of London's most infamous indie clubs. A no-holds-barred joint. 3-4 bands a night, usually starting at 9pm. £3.50-9.

Hackney Empire, 291 Marc St., E8 (tel. (0181) 985 2424). Tube: Bethnal Green then bus #253 north or BR: Hackney Central. Comedy theater hosts popular routines like the Caribbean duo Bello and Blacka. £3-12. Prices and hours vary by show.

Half Moon Putney, 93 Lower Richmond Rd., SW15 (tel. (0181) 780 9383). Tube: Putney Bridge. Rocking pub with a mix of rock, jazz, and folk. £3-7. Music starts at 8:30-9:45pm.

Mean Fiddler, 24-28 Harlesden High St., NW10 (tel. (0181) 963 0940). Tube: Willesden Junction. Night Bus #N18. Cavernous club with good bars, mixing country & western, folk, and indie. Tu-Th 8pm-2am, F-Sa 8:30pm-3am, Su 8pm-1am. £10-15.

Rock Garden, The Piazza, Covent Garden, WC2 (tel. 240 3961). Tube: Covent Garden. A variety of great new bands play nightly £5—rock, indie, acid jazz, soul. Happy hour daily 5-8pm, cover £2, all drinks £1. Th pop, F live music, Su 70s disco. Open M-Th 5pm-3am, F 5pm-6am, Sa 4pm-4am, Su 7-3am.

Shepherd's Bush Empire, Shepherds Bush Green, W12 (tel. (0181) 740 7474). Tube: Shepherds Bush. Hosts dorky cool musicians like David Byrne, the Proclaimers, and Boy George. 2000 capacity, with 6 bars. Concerts £6-20.

The Venue, 2a Clifton Rise, New Cross, SE14 (tel. (0181) 692 4077). Tube: New Cross, Night Bus #N77. Getting to be a big indie scene. Dancing goes late into the night. Cover £5-6, £3 before 9pm. Open F-Sa 8pm-4am; music starts 8pm.

Wembley Stadium and **Wembley Arena,** Empire Way, Wembley (tel. (0181) 902 0902). Tube: Wembley Park or Wembley Central. A football (soccer) stadium. Take a pair of binoculars. Open M-Sa 8am-9pm, Su 9am-8pm. £25-65. The **Arena** is the largest indoor venue in London, serving high-priced refreshments. Open 6:30-11pm selected nights. £16-30.

JAZZ

In the summer, hundreds of jazz festivals appear in the London area, including July's **City of London Festival** (tel. 377 0540) and the **JVC Capital Radio Jazz, Funk, and Soul Festival** (Royal Albert Hall, box office tel. 589 8212). Ronnie Scott's, Bass Clef, and Jazz Café are the most popular clubs. Jazz clubs stay open later than pubs.

100 Club, 100 Oxford St., W1 (tel. 636 0933). Tube: Tottenham Ct. Rd. A melange of traditional modern jazz, swing, and blues hidden behind a battered doorway. Fridays are indie dance nights and Saturdays welcome big band jazz. £5-8. Open Su-Th 7:30pm-midnight, F 7:30pm-3am, Sa 7:30pm-1am.

606 Club, 90 Lots Rd., SW10 (tel. 352 5953). Tube: Fulham Broadway. New talent along with household names in diverse styles. Open M-Sa 8:30pm-2am, Su 8:30pm-midnight. Music begins M-W 9:30pm, Th-Sa 10pm, Su 9:30pm. Non-members are not allowed on the weekend without eating dinner. Cover Su-Th £4, F-Sa £4.50.

Jazz Café, 5 Parkway, Camden Town, NW1 (tel. 344 0044). Tube: Camden Town. Night Bus #N93. Top new venue in a converted bank. Classic and experimental jazz with threads of Latin, soul, and African. Tickets for shows £6-18, cover £3. Open M-Th 7pm-midnight, F-Sa 7pm-2am, Su noon-5pm and 7-11pm.

Jazz at Pizza Express, 10 Dean St., W1 (tel. 439 8722). Tube: Tottenham Ct. Rd. or Leicester Sq. Packed, dark club hiding behind a pizzeria. Fantastic groups and occasional greats; get there early. Cover £10-20. Music daily 9pm-midnight; doors open at 7:45pm. Restaurant open daily 11:30am-12:30am.

Ronnie Scott's, 47 Frith St., W1 (tel. 439 0747; fax 437 5081). Tube: Leicester Sq. or Piccadilly Circus. The most famous jazz club in London and one of the oldest in the world; saw the likes of Ella Fitzgerald and Dizzy Gillespie. Open fabulously late—the music just keeps going. Cover £15, 26 and under £8. Book ahead or arrive by 9:30pm. Box office open M-F 11am-6pm, Sa 12:30pm-6pm. Music 9:30pm-2am. Open M-Sa 8:30pm-3am.

FOLK AND ROOTS

Folk music in London usually means Irish music. Celtic aside, the term "folk" covers a host of musical hybrids including acoustic rock, political tunes, folksy blues, and even English country & western. Africa Centre (see **Nightclubbing,** below), offers music and dance from Africa. Some of the best are free, but welcome donations.

Bunjie's, 27 Litchfield St., WC2 (tel. 240 1796). Tube: Covent Garden. Packed vegetarian restaurant with folk and almost-folk groups; lively, dancing audience. Cover £3-3.50, students £2. Open M-Sa noon-11pm. Intimate venue for folk music, featured M-W and Sa 8:30-11pm. Poetry night F 8-11pm. Comedy Th 8-11pm.

Troubadour Coffee House, 265 Old Brompton Rd., SW5 (tel. 370 1434). Tube: Earl's Ct. Acoustic entertainment in a warm cafe. Bob Dylan and Paul Simon played here early in their careers. On W, cafe becomes "Institute for Acoustic Research"; M attracts some of the best poets around. F-Sa folk and jazz. Now offers classical music—call for info. Cover £4.50, students and seniors £3.50. Open 8pm-11pm.

■ Nightclubbing

London pounds to 100% Groovy Liverpool tunes, ecstatic Manchester rave, home-town soul and house, imported U.S. hip-hop, and Jamaican reggae. Black is eternally in, and dress codes (denoted by "DC") are rarely more elaborate than standard Londonwear. To save money, show up early (before pubs close), party during the week (London has enough slackers and party people to make even Tuesdays slammin'), and figure out where you're going before you get too drunk to care. Many clubs host a variety of provocative one-nighters (like "Get Up and Use Me") throughout the week. Keep your eyes and ears peeled.

Remember that **the tube** shuts down two or three hours before most clubs and that taxis can be hard to find in the wee hours of the morning. Some late-night frolickers catch "minicabs," little unmarked cars that sometimes wait outside clubs. Arrange transportation in advance or acquaint yourself with the extensive network of night buses (tel. 222 1234 for info). Listings include some of the night bus routes that connect to venues outside of central London, but routes change. Double-check to keep yourself from getting stranded, late at night, in those silver satin pants. As always, check the extensive listings in *Time Out* and *What's On*. Record stores in Brixton and Soho (on Berwick St.) often post flyers and handbills advertising dance-club events.

Africa Centre, 38 King St., WC2 (tel. 836 1973). Tube: Covent Garden. Art center by day, psychedelic, blacklit den of funk by night. Live African music at the "Limpopo Club" most Fridays, but Saturday's "Funkin' Pussy" lets Funkateers shake booty to vintage funk and hip-hop. Open F 9pm-3am, cover £5 in advance, £6 at the door; Sa 9pm-3am, cover before 11pm £3, after 11pm £7, students and seniors £5.

Bar Rumba, 36 Shaftesbury Ave., W1 (tel. 287 6933). Tube: Piccadilly Circus. ¡Muy caliente! At Tuesday's excellent "Salsa Pa'Ti," a seemingly random crowd of all ages and nationalities are fused into one nation under a salsa groove. The dancing is somewhat formal, so if you can't tango, cha-cha, or pachanga, arrive at 7pm for instruction (£6, cover included). Dancing is informal other nights, but the Latin flavor persists, the bar serves 'til 3am, and the cover's low. £6-12. Open most nights 5pm-3:30am, F 'til 4am, Sa 'til 6am. Call ahead.

The Hanover Grand, 6 Hanover St., W1 (tel. 499 7977). Tube: Oxford Circus. Big, big fun in large, loud, funkified atmosphere. Where swingers go to get down. Underground garage and hip-hop. Don't be afraid to dress all out. Cover £5-15, on W before 11pm only £3. Open Tu for venues only, W-F 10:30pm-4am, Sa 10:30pm-5am.

Iceni, 11 White Horse St., W1 (tel. 495 5333). Tube: Green Park. Off Curzon St. 3 beautiful floors of deep funk entertainment in this stylish Mayfair hotspot. Often wildly different beats between floors, from swing to 80s to techno. Cover £10-12. Open F 11pm-3am, Sa 10pm-3am.

Ministry of Sound, 103 Gaunt St., SE1 (tel. 378 6528). Tube: Elephant and Castle. Night buses #N12, N62, N65, N72, N77, or N78. Mega-club with long queues, beefy covers, beautiful people, and pumping house tunes, but beware—bouncers concoct the "most appropriate" crowd, so without the right look you'll be eternally stuck in the queue. One of the first major rave spots. Cover F £10, Sa £15. Open F 10:30pm-6:30am, Sa midnight-9am.

The Underworld, 174 Camden High St., NW1 (tel. 482 1932). Tube: Camden Town. Across the street from the tube. Huge, fire station-like pub leads into soul center and techno training camp downstairs. Thursday night is "Stardust County," with indie DJ and moshers. Cover £2-5.

Velvet Underground, 143 Charing Cross Rd. (tel. 439 4655). Tube: Tottenham Ct. Rd. Velvet-soaked bar and leisure lounge combined with pumping house and techno dance club after 10pm. Particularly cheap and juicy during the week; various promotions attract the young and foreign. F-Sa free before 10pm. Cover varies from £6-10. Open M-Th 5pm-3am, F 5pm-4am, Sa 8pm-4am.

The Wag Club, 35 Wardour St., W1 (tel. 437 5534). Tube: Piccadilly Circus. Known as "The Wag," this funky, multi-level complex features bars and an eatery among the carefully coifed clientele. Two dance floors and a wild variety of beats guarantee some groove for everyone's taste. Cover M-Th £4, F £9, Sa £10; £1 less with flier before 11pm. Open M-Th 10pm-3:30am, F 10:30pm-4am, Sa 10:30pm-5am.

■ Spectator Sports

Association Football

London has 13 of the 92 professional teams in England. The big two are **Arsenal,** Arsenal Stadium, Avenell Rd., N5 (tel. 704 4000; tube: Arsenal) and **Tottenham Hotspur,** White Hart Ln., 748 High Rd., W17 (tel. (0181) 365 5000; BR: White Hart Ln.). *(Tickets £10-35. Available in advance from each club's box office.)* England plays international matches at Wembley Stadium (tel. (0181) 900 1234; tube: Wembley Park), usually on Wednesday evenings.

Rugby

The most significant contests, including the springtime five nations championship (featuring England, Scotland, Wales, Ireland, and France) are played at **Twickenham** (tel. (0181) 892 8161; BR: Twickenham). Other venues include **Saracens,** Dale Green Rd., N14 (tel. (01923) 496 200; tube: Oakwood), and **Rosslyn Park,** Priory Ln., Upper Richmond Rd., SW15 (tel. (0181) 876 1879; BR: Barnes).

Cricket

London's two grounds stage both county and international matches. **Lord's,** St. John's Wood Rd., NW8 (tel. 289 1300, ext. 1611; tube: St. John's Wood), is *the* cricket ground. **Middlesex** plays here. *(Tickets £7 for summer matches, international matches £15-37.)* **Foster's Oval,** Kennington Oval, SE11 (tel. 582 6660; tube: Oval), houses the **Surrey** cricket club. *(Tickets £7-8, internationals £21-36.)*

Tennis

It's all about **Wimbledon** (late-June to early-July): If you want to get in, arrive early (6am); the gate opens at 10:30am (get off the tube at Southfields). Entrance to the grounds costs £7-8, £5-6 after 5pm. If you arrive early enough, you can buy one of the few show court tickets available. Depending on the day, center court tickets cost £21-47, No. 1 court tickets £12-33, No. 2 court tickets £14-22. Other courts have first-come, first-served seats or standing-room-only. If you fail to get center or No. 1 court tickets in the morning, try to find the resale booth (usually in Aorangi Park), which sells tickets handed in by those who leave early. *(Open from 2:30pm; tickets only £2.)* Also, on the first Saturday of the championships, 2000 extra center court tickets are put up for sale for £25. Call (0181) 946 2244 for ticket information.

Horses

The **Royal Gold Cup Meeting** at **Ascot** (tel. (01344) 22211) takes place each summer in the second half of June. An "important" society event, it is essentially an excuse for Brits of all strata to indulge in the twin pastimes of drinking and gambling while wearing silly hats. *(Grandstand tickets £24, Silver Ring £6.)* More accessible, less expensive summer evening races are run at **Royal Windsor Racecourse,** Berkshire (tel. (01753) 865 234; BR: Windsor Riverside; tattersalls and paddock £8), and **Kempton Park Racecourse,** Sunbury-on-Thames (tel. (01932) 782292; BR: Kempton Park). *(Grandstand £12, Silver Ring £6.)*

Greyhound Racing

The dogs race year-round at **Walthamstow** (tel. (0181) 531 4255), and **Wembley** (tel. (0181) 902 8833). In late June, Wimbledon hosts the **Greyhound Derby,** (tel. (0181) 944 1066). Admission starts at £2.50.

SHOPPING

London Transport's handy *Shoppers' Bus Wheel* instructs Routemaster shoppers on the routes between shopping areas (available free from any London Transport Information Centre). *Nicholson's Shopping Guide and Streetfinder* (£3), and *Time Out's* massive *Directory to London's Shops and Services* (£6) are also excellent resources. Sales happen in July and January. Check *Time Out's* "Sell Out" section.

Tourists who have purchased anything over £50 should ask about getting a refund on the 17.5% VAT. Another option is to save receipts and to send off for a refund at the airport. Each shopping area has a late night of shopping. Kings Rd. and Kensington High St., for example, stay open late on Wednesdays, while the West End shops open their doors to the night on Thursdays. Many stores may be closed on Sunday.

DEPARTMENT STORES

Fortnum & Mason, 181 Piccadilly, W1 (tel. 734 8040). Tube: Green Park or Piccadilly Circus. Liveried clerks vend expensive foods in red-carpeted and chandeliered halls at this renowned establishment. Look out for free samples of the food court's wares. Expensive but fun to sniff around. Open M-Sa 9:30am-6pm.

Harrods, 87-135 Brompton Rd., SW3 (tel. 730 1234). Tube: Knightsbridge. Simply put, this is *the* store in London, perhaps the world—English gentlemen keeping a stiff upper lip elsewhere dream of the Harrods food court. Their humble motto *Omnia Omnibus Ubique* ("All things for all people, everywhere") says it all. Harrods's sales (mid-July and after Christmas) get so crazy that the police bring out a whole detail and combat operations truck to deal with the shoppers. Shorts, ripped clothing, and backpacks are forbidden in this quasi-museum of luxury—nevertheless, the downstairs sometimes seems like a tourist convention. Open M-Tu and Sa 10am-6pm, W-F 10am-7pm.

Harvey Nichols, 109-125 Knightsbridge, SW3 (tel. 235 5000). Tube: Knightsbridge. The trendiest of London's huge department stores, also one of the most expensive. Wacky and avant-garde window displays which change frequently. Stupendous sale in early July. Open M-Tu and Th-Sa 10am-7pm, W 10am-8pm, Su noon-6pm.

John Lewis, 278-306 Oxford St. (tel. 629 7711). Tube: Oxford Circus. Giant department store offering merchandise in various price ranges. Open M-W and F 9:30am-6pm, Th 10am-8pm, Sa 9am-6pm. Sister shop **Peter Jones** (tel. 730 3434) at Sloane Square is equally wide-ranging (tube: Sloane Sq.). Open M-Tu and Th-Sa 9:30am-6pm, W 9:30am-7pm. Only accepts its own credit card.

Liberty's of London (tel. 734 1234), south of Oxford Circus on Regent St. and Great Marlborough St. Tube: Oxford Circus. Home of the famous Liberty prints—from entire bolts of fabric to silk ties. Giant sales (early July and Dec.). Open M-W and F-Sa 10am-6:30pm, Th 10am-7:30pm, Su noon-6pm.

Marks & Spencer, 458 Oxford St., W1 (tel. 935 7954). Tube: Bond St. Also at 113 Kensington High St. (tel. 938 3711); 85 Kings Rd. (tel. 376 5634; tube: Sloane Sq.) and literally hundreds of other locations. Brits know it as Marks & Sparks or M&S. Sells British staples in a classy but value-conscious manner. Open M-F 9am-8pm, Sa 9am-7pm, Su noon-6pm (weekend hours vary).

Selfridges, 400 Oxford St. (tel. 629 1234). Tube: Bond St. An immense pseudo-Renaissance building with fashions, homewares, foods, and a tourist office. The food hall is amazing, with a deli, a bakery, and an oyster bar. Mid-July sale. Open M-W 10am-7pm and Th-F 10am-8pm, Sa 9:30am-7pm, Su noon-6pm.

CLOTHING

Jigsaw, 31 Brompton Rd., SW3 (tel. 584 6226). Tube: Knightsbridge. Also at 21 Long Acre, WC2 (tel. 240 3855; tube: Covent Garden); 124 Kings Rd., SW3 (tel. 589 5083; tube: Sloane Sq.); and others. Purveyors of rather expensive women's threads in a variety of luscious fabrics and subtle, muted colors. Some stores have a smallish men's department as well. Open M-Tu and Th-F 10:30am-7pm, W 10:30am-7:30pm, Sa 10am-7pm, Su noon-5pm.

The Story of Airwear

Dr. Marten shoes were originally called Dr. Maerten. Although the omnipresent cultural clodhoppers are identified with the U.K., they were born a half-century ago in Munich, when Dr. Klaus Maerten designed them after a skiing accident so that he might walk more comfortably. Marketed first to elderly German women with foot trouble, the air-cushioned shoes gained in popularity and soon production was extended to Britain. The "e" in the name was dropped, and what was once a healing sole became a youth icon. The shoes have been spotted on everyone from Pete Townsend and The Clash to Madonna and Pope John Paul II.

Kookai, 5-7 Brompton Rd., SW3 (tel. 581 9633). Tube: Knightsbridge. Also at 362 Oxford St., W1 (tel. 499 4564; tube: Bond St.). Also at 123 Kensington High St., W8 (tel. 938 1427); 27a Sloane Sq., SW1 (tel. 730 6903); 124 King's Rd., SW1 (tel. 589 0120; tube: Sloane Sq.). Sexy, slinky women's clothes at almost reasonable prices. Open M-Tu and Th-Sa 10am-7pm, W 10am-8pm, Su noon-5pm.

Sam Walker, 41 Neal St., WC2 (tel. 240 7800). Tube: Covent Garden. A wonderful, if expensive, collection of immaculately restored men's vintage clothing. True, the prices here are higher than other vintage clothing shops, but so is quality, and a restored vintage corduroy blazer is still much cheaper than a new one. Also sells its own line of dress shoes. Open M-Sa 10am-7:30pm, Su noon-7pm.

Top Shop/Top Man, 214 Oxford St., W1 (tel. 636 7700). Tube: Oxford Circus. An absolute *must-visit* for the wannabe club kid on a budget. First-floor sales racks for aspiring Topmen; racks for aspiring Topwomen in the basement. Open M-W and F-Sa 10am-7pm, Th 10am-8pm, Su noon-6pm.

BOOKSTORES

In London, even the chain bookstores are wonders. An exhaustive selection of book-shops lines Charing Cross Rd. between Tottenham Ct. Rd. and Leicester Sq., and many vend secondhand paperbacks. Cecil Ct., near Leicester Sq., is a treasure trove of tiny shops with specialty bookstores for dance, Italy, travel, and other topics. Establishments along Great Russell St. stock esoteric and specialized books on any subject from Adorno to the Zohar. The best places to look for maps and travel books is **Stanford's,** 12 Long Acre (tel. 836 1321; tube: Covent Garden; open M 10am-6pm, Tu-F 9am-7pm, Sa 10am-7pm); also try Harrods and the YHA shop.

Dillons, Trafalgar Sq., Grand Bldg., WC2 (tel. 839 4411). Tube: Charing Cross or Leicester Sq. This is the branch open latest; the largest is at 82 Gower St., WC2 (tel. 636 1577). Numerous other branches. One of London's best. Strong on academic subjects. Fair selection of reduced-price and secondhand books, plus classical CDs and tapes. Open M-Sa 9:30am-9pm, Su noon-6pm.

Foyles, 119 Charing Cross Rd., WC1 (tel. 437 5660). Tube: Tottenham Ct. Rd. or Leicester Sq. Giant warehouse. Open M-W and F-Sa 9am-6pm, Th 9am-7pm.

Hatchards, 187 Piccadilly, W1 (tel. 439 9921). Tube: Green Park. Oldest of London's bookstores. Open M and W-Sa 9am-6pm, Tu 9:30am-6pm, Su noon-6pm.

Skoob Books, 15-17 Sicilian Ave., Southampton Row and Vernon Pl., WC1 (tel. 405 0030). Tube: Holborn. The best used bookstore in Bloomsbury; academic and general interest. 10% student discount. Open M-Sa 10:30am-6:30pm.

Waterstone's, 121-125 Charing Cross Rd., WC1 (tel. 434 4291), next door to Foyles. Tube: Leicester Sq. A good chain bookstore. Many branches, including 193 Kensington High St., W8 (tel. 937 8432) and 101 Old Brompton Rd., SW7 (tel. 581 8522). Open M-Sa 9am-8pm, Su noon-6pm.

RECORD STORES

The best bargains are found in vinyl, though the record market is frustratingly efficient. At **Camden Town, Brixton, Ladbroke Grove,** or Soho's **Hanway St.,** record stores tempt collectors and intimidate browsers with rare vinyl and memorabilia at rock-star prices. The shops surrounding the intersection of **D'Arblay** and **Berwick St.** in Soho provide listening booths for sampling the latest 12" singles. Early LPs and singles by British bands aren't as rare and dear here as they are elsewhere.

Black Market, 25 D'Arblay St., W1 (tel. 437 0478). Tube: Oxford Circus. This Soho institution flirts with "Hard Rock Cafe" tourist trap oblivion by hawking logoed merchandise, but if you're looking for the latest hip-hop, techno, house, or garage 12 in., they've got the goods. Open M-Sa 11am-7pm, Su 11:45am-7pm.

Honest Jon's, 276-8 Portobello Rd., W10 (tel. (0181) 969 9822). Tube: Ladbroke Grove. Newly refurbished but still fonkay. No. 276 holds an impressive jazz collection—Blakey, Parker, and Mingus are only the tip of the iceberg. 278 sports a selection of hip-hop LP's and decent 12 in. singles, as well as funk holdings from A to Zapp. Collector prices, sadly. Open M-Sa 10am-6pm, Su 11am-5pm.

Music and Video Exchange, 229 Camden High St., NW1 (tel. 267 1898). Tube: Camden Town. Branch at 95 Berwick St., W8 (tel. 434 2939). Dirt-cheap 70s stuff in the basement. Strong offerings in rap (esp. old-school), acid jazz, and trip-hop. If your head is still throbbing from some house or techno groove, you can scratch that itch in the recently renovated house room. Open M-F 11am-6pm, Sa-Su 11am-7pm.

STREET MARKETS

Brick Lane, E1. Tube: Aldgate East. Market with a South Asian flair: food, rugs, bolts of fabric, and sitar strains. Open Su 6am-1pm (see **East End,** p. 119).

Brixton Market, Electric Ave., Brixton Station Rd. and Popes Rd., SW2. Tube: Brixton. Covered market halls and outdoor stalls sprawl out from the station. The wide selection of African and West Indian fruit, vegetables, fabrics, and records make Brixton one of the most vibrant and hippest markets. Open M-Tu and Th-Sa 8:30am-5:30pm, W 8:30am-1pm.

Camden Markets, by Regent's Canal and along Camden High St., NW1. Tube: Camden Town. One of the most popular, and crowded, places to find almost anything old or funky at discount prices. The best collection of stalls crops up on Sundays. Open W-Su 9:30am-5:30pm (see **Camden Town,** p. 117).

Camden Passage, Islington High St., N1. Tube: Angel. Right from the tube, then right on narrow, pedestrian-only Islington High St. Big antique market, plus prints and drawings. Open W and Sa 8:30am-3pm, but many start to pack up around 2pm.

Greenwich Market, Covered Market Sq., SE10, near the Cutty Sark. BR: Greenwich. A popular crafts market in a pastoral setting frequented by London lawyers on day-trips down the river. On Greenwich High Rd., the Open-Air Second-hand Market sells vintage dresses. Open Sa-Su 9am-6pm (see **Greenwich,** p. 122).

Petticoat Lane, E1. Tube: Liverpool St., Aldgate, or Aldgate East. A London institution—street after street of stalls, mostly cheap clothing and household appliances. The real action begins at about 9:30am. Open Su 9am-2pm; starts shutting down around noon (see **The East End,** p. 119).

Portobello Road, W11. Tube: Notting Hill Gate or Ladbroke Grove. Popular and old antique market, immortalized by Paddington Bear. *Watch your wallet.* Antique market Sa 7am-5pm. Clothes market F-Sa 8am-3pm (see **Notting Hill,** p. 115).

BISEXUAL, GAY, AND LESBIAN LONDON

London's gay scene ranges from the flamboyant to the campy to the cruisy to the mainstream. The 24-hour **Lesbian and Gay Switchboard** (tel. 837 7324) is an excellent source of info; the **Bisexual Helpline** (tel. (0181) 569 7500) has more limited hours (Tu-W 7:30-9:30pm). If you can't find what you need here, consult *Gay Times, Capital Gay, Pink Paper, Diva,* and others at **Gay's the Word,** 66 Marchmont St., WC1 (tel. 278 7654), Britain's largest gay bookstore (open M-Sa 10am-6:30pm, Su 2-6pm). The **Clone Zone,** 64 Old Compton St., W1 (tel. 287 3530; tube: Leicester Sq.) sells books and t-shirts.

Soho's most famous gay pub is **Comptons of Soho,** 53 Old Compton St., W1 (tel. 437 4445; tube: Leicester Sq.). The more hardcore **Substation Soho,** Falconberg Ct., W1 (tel. 287 9608), is a cruisy, late-night testosterone fest. Drag 'til you drop at **The Black Cap,** 171 Camden High St., NW1 (tube: Camden Town). On Sunday nights, the ever-popular "Girl Bar" takes over at the **The Box,** Seven Dials, 32-34 Monmouth St., WC2 (tel. 240 5828). **The Candy Bar,** 16 Chenies St., WC1 (tube: Goodge St.) is London's first lesbian bar.

The thumping dance clubs of London bring together a spicy mix of gays, lesbians, bisexuals, and folks who just want to shake it down.

Heaven, Villiers St., WC2 (tel. 930 2020; tube: Embankment) is still the oldest and biggest gay disco in Europe. Open F-Sa 10pm-3am. Cover F £6, after 11:30pm £7; Sa £7; after 11:30pm £8.

The Fridge, Town Hall Parade, Brixton Hill, SW2 (tel. 326 5100; tube: Brixton) is home to the biggest gay one-nighter, known as "Love Muscle." Open Sa 10pm-6am; Cover £12, £10 before midnight with flyer or after 3am.

"G.A.Y." at London Astoria 1 (Sa), and 2 (Th and M), 157 Charing Cross Rd., WC2 (tel. 734 6963; tube: Tottenham Ct. Rd.) is the most frequent one-nighter. Open M 10:30pm-3am, Th 10:30pm-4am, Sa 10:30pm-5am. Cover M £3, if student or with flyer, £1, Th £3, free with flyer, Sa £6, with flyer £5.

"Popstarz," Leisure Lounge, 121 Holborn, EC1 (tel. 738 2336; tube: Chancery Ln.) is the most popular weekly event. The Friday indie party proved so popular during its 1996 inception that it moved to this larger venue. Open 10pm-5am. Cover £5, after 11pm £6, students £1 off.

South England

Sprawling its greenery eastward toward the continent, the landscape of South England simultaneously asserts Britain's island heritage and belies a continental link that runs deeper than the Chunnel. Early Britons settled the counties of Kent, Sussex, and Hampshire by hopping a stream that would later be known as the English Channel. Later European visitor William the Conqueror left his mark upon the downsland in the form of awe-inspiring cathedrals, many built around settlements begun by Julius Caesar. More recently, buried evidence of Caesar's invasion was uncovered by the German bombings of the World War II.

Victorian mansions lining Channel shores, rivers lapping medieval town walls, and majestic cathedrals summon a chorus of past voices, many of them literary. Geoffrey Chaucer's pilgrims colored the way to Canterbury with tales both spiritual and bawdy. Jane Austen's pen made its masterful strokes in the archipelago of named houses near the southern downs and borders. Charles Dickens drew mammoth novels from his early experiences in Portsmouth. E.M. Forster, Virginia Woolf, and other Bloomsburyites vacationed and lived near the South Downs, where the "idea of England" is as timeless as the land itself.

GETTING ABOUT

Public transportation pampers the area within 90 mi. of London. **British Rail** offers cheap day-return tickets, and you can easily make short hops from one town to another, especially on the coast. The **Network Away Break** ticket allows five days of cheap fares for specific destinations on British Rail Network Southeast. Most local **bus** companies offer special passes as well. The **Explorer** ticket (£5.40, seniors and children £4.10), available from any local ticket office, allows one day of unlimited travel on all **Stagecoach** bus routes in East Kent, Maidenstone, Hastings, and Southdown. The **Freedom** and **Bus Ranger** tickets available for periods of one, four, and 13 weeks, allow travel on most buses within a defined zone. You can best enjoy the scenic terrain on foot, bike, or moped. The region's many good youth hostels, particularly along the South Downs Way (p. 180), provide respite for weary walkers. Tourist offices have camping directories.

🖐 HIGHLIGHTS OF SOUTH ENGLAND

- Ride on horseback to the **Canterbury Cathedral** (see p. 147), which has inspired pilgrims since the 12th century. Visit the Altar of the Sword's Point and find purity in ancient enmity.
- Stroll through the carnival madness of the beach at **Brighton** (see p. 159), and take a tour of Brighton's pan-Asian Royal Pavilion.
- Don't miss the famous chalk-white cliffs of **Dover** (see p. 152), one of the first glimpses of England for ferry travelers. Climb the Grand Shaft, carved into the rock in Napoleonic times, and visit Shakespeare's Cliff, featured in *King Lear*.
- Hike the salty slopes of the **South Downs Way** (see p. 180), and sleep surrounded by Bronze-Age burial mounds.

KENT

■ Canterbury

Whan Zephyrus eek with his sweete breeth
Inspired hath in every holt and heeth

The tendre croppes, and the yonge sonne
Hath in the Ram his halve cours yronne...
Thanne longen folk to goon on pilgrimages...
—Geoffrey Chaucer, Prologue to *The Canterbury Tales*

With pilgrims coming and going for nearly a millennium, the soul of Canterbury is a flighty thing, tossed somewhere between a cathedral and the open road. Once surpassed only by Jerusalem and Rome as a pilgrimage site, the city has been vending food, rooms, and souvenirs to visitors since the murder of a bishop in his own cathedral—for innkeepers, local priests, and medal-makers, a most fortunate fall. Archbishop Thomas à Becket met his demise after an irate Henry II asked, "Will no one rid me of this troublesome priest?" and a few of his henchmen took the hint. Subsequent healings and miracles were attributed to "the hooly blisful martir," and thus "to Canterbury they wende." Chaucer saw enough irony in tourist flocks to capture them in his ever-bawdy *Canterbury Tales*. Visitors today can admire the soaring, grand cathedral and look for the city's nomad charms; amidst all of Canterbury's careful cultivation dwell friendly souls and warm welcomes.

GETTING THERE

Not everyone can travel to Canterbury on horseback with a group of verbally gifted pilgrims. **Trains** (tel. (0345) 484950) run hourly from London's **Victoria Station** to Canterbury **East Station** (the stop nearest the youth hostel), and from **Charing Cross** and **Waterloo** stations to Canterbury's **West Station** (1½hr., £15.70, day return £15.80). Ask everyone in your compartment to tell one story each way. **National Express buses** (tel. (0990) 808080) to Canterbury leave London's Victoria Bus Station hourly (2hr., £6-8). Canterbury, on the rail and bus lines from the Dover and Folkestone hovercraft terminals, is almost as easy to reach from the Continent as from the rest of England.

ORIENTATION

Canterbury is roughly circular, its slowly eroding city wall ringed by a road. An unbroken street crosses the circle from west to east, taking the names **St. Peter's, High,** and **St. George's St.** The cathedral rises in the northeast quadrant. To reach the tourist office from East Station, cross the footbridge, take a left down the hill onto Station Rd. East, bear right into the roundabout onto Castle St., which becomes St. Margaret's St. From West Station, make a right onto Station Rd. West, turn left onto St. Dunstan's St., walk through Westgate Tower onto St. Peter's St. (which becomes High St.), and after about six blocks, make a right onto St. Margaret's St.

PRACTICAL INFORMATION

Transportation
  Trains: East Station, Station Rd. East, off Castle St., southeast of town. Open M-Sa 6:10am-8pm, Su 6:30am-9pm. **West Station,** Station Rd. West, off St. Dunstan's St. Open M-F 6:15am-8pm, Sa 6:30am-8pm, Su 7:15am-9:30pm.
  Buses: St. George's Ln. (tel. 472082). Open M-Sa 8:15am-5:15pm. Get there by 5pm to book National Express tickets.
  Taxis: Longport (tel. 458885). Open daily 6am-4am.
  Bike Rental: Byways Bicycle Hire, 2 Admiralty Walk (tel. 277397). Owner delivers. £10 per day, £50 per week, plus a £50 deposit.

Tourist and Financial Services
  Tourist Office: 34 St. Margaret's St., CT1 2TG (tel. 766567; fax 459840). Book-a-bed-ahead for £2.50 and 10% deposit. Free mini-guide. Wide range of maps, guides, and walks of Canterbury and the rest of Kent. Open daily Apr.-June 9:30am-5:30pm; July-Aug. 9am-6pm; Sept.-Mar. 9:30am-5pm.

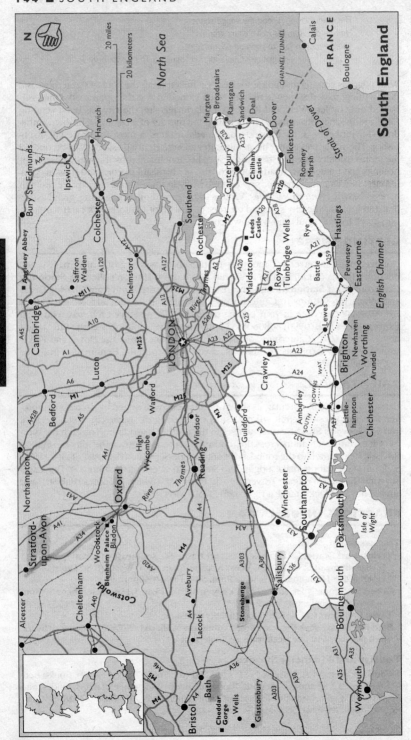

Tours: Guided tours of the city (1½hr.) depart from the tourist office Apr.-Nov. daily at 2pm; additional tour July-Aug. M-Sa at 11:30am. £3, students, seniors, and children £2.50, family ticket £7.50, under 14 free.
Financial Services: Lloyds, 49 High St. (tel. 451681). Open M-Tu and Th-F 9am-5pm, W 9:30am-5pm, Sa 9:30am-12:30pm. **National Westminster,** 51 St. George (tel. 780087). Open M-Tu and Th-F 9am-5:30pm, W 9:30am-5:30pm, Sa 9:30am-3:30pm. **Thomas Cook,** 14 Mercery Ln. (tel. 767656). Open M-Sa 9am-5:30pm. Many **ATMs.** *Radix malorum est cupiditas.*

Local Services

Launderette: 36 St. Peter's St. (tel. 786911), near Westgate Towers. Open M-Sa 8:30am-5:45pm. Soap available.
Bi-Gay-Lesbian Organizations: Kent Gay Information Line, tel. (01233) 625395, ext. 2. Open Tu 7:30-10pm.
Market: W 9am-2pm, in the center of town outside Marks and Spencer.

Emergency and Communications

Emergency: Dial 999; no coins required.
Police: Old Dover Rd. (tel. 762055), outside the eastern city wall.
Hotlines: Samaritans (crisis; tel. 457777), on the corner of Love and Ivy Ln. Open 24hr. **AIDS advice and counseling,** Chaucer Hospital, Mackington Rd. (tel. 452552).
Hospital: Kent and Canterbury Hospital (tel. 766877), off Ethelbert Rd.
Post Office: 28 High St. (tel. 475280), across from Best Ln. Accepts *Poste Restante.* Open M-F 9am-5:30pm, Sa 9am-12:30pm. **Postal Code:** CT1 2BA.
Internet Access: Blockbuster Internet Bar, 1 New Dover Rd. (tel. 472745), across from Safeway. £3 per hr., 10% student discounts.
Telephone Code: 01227.

ACCOMMODATIONS

Book ahead in summer or arrive by mid-morning to secure recently vacated rooms. B&Bs bunch by both train stations and on London and Whitstable Rd., just beyond West Station. If desperate, head for the more costly B&Bs (£18-20) along New Dover Rd., a half-mile walk from East Station, near the youth hostel. Singles are scarce.

YHA Youth Hostel, 54 New Dover Rd. (tel. 462911; fax 470752), ¾mi. from East Station and ½mi. southeast of the bus station. Turn right as you leave the station and continue up the main artery, which becomes Upper Bridge St. At the second rotary, turn right onto St. George's Pl., which becomes New Dover Rd. It's on the right. £9.75, under 18 £6.55. 86 beds. Breakfast £3, packed lunch £3.35, evening meal £4.45. Showers and laundry. Lockers £1 plus deposit. Bureau de change. Doors open 7:30-10am and 1-11pm. In summer book a week in advance. Open daily Feb.-Dec.; call for off-season openings.
Hampton House, 40 New Dover Rd. (tel. 464912). Luxurious house boasts comfortable, quiet, Laura Ashley-esque rooms. Lovely proprietors provide tea and coffee room service and a traditional English breakfast. £20 per person, varies off-season.
Kingsbridge Villa, 14-15 Best Ln. (tel. 766415). Refurbished rooms a few steps off the main street; breakfast room moonlights as an Italian restaurant. Full English breakfast. £18 per person; doubles with bath £45. Rates negotiable off-season.
The Tudor House, 6 Best Ln. (tel. 765650), off High St., in the town center. Eat breakfast in front of a Tudor fireplace in this 16th-century house. Guests can rent bikes and boats (£5 per day). Singles £18; doubles £32, with bath £42.
Let's Stay, Mrs. Connolly, 26 New Dover Rd. (tel. 463628), on the way to the hostel. Hostel-style accommodation in Irish hostess's immaculate home. 2 rooms with 2 wooden bunks each; 2 bathrooms. Backpackers get preference. £10. Full English breakfast; vegetarian options available and delightful conversation included. Ask about the origin of the name! Closed Jan.-Feb. 1999.
London Guest House, 14 London Rd., near West Station (tel. 765860). Walk 10-15min. from city center. Spacious Victorian house with floral rooms in immaculate condition. Singles from £17.50; doubles £36.

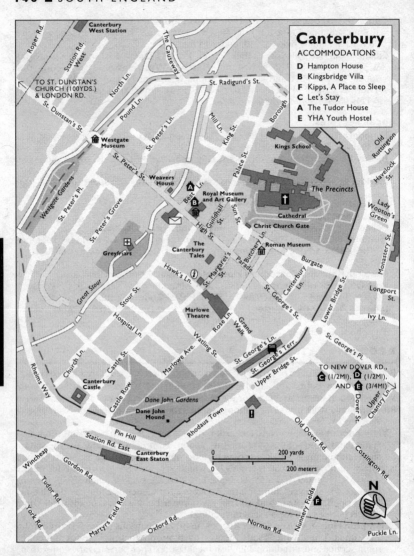

Canterbury

ACCOMMODATIONS

D Hampton House
B Kingsbridge Villa
F Kipps, A Place to Sleep
C Let's Stay
A The Tudor House
E YHA Youth Hostel

Milton House, Mrs. Wright, 9 S. Canterbury Rd. (tel. 765531). A 20min. walk from town center. Two tidy rooms and a warm welcome on a quiet street. Doubles £30-33. Singles usually available off-season for £18.

Kipps, A Place to Sleep, 40 Nunnery Fields (tel. 786121; fax 766992). 10min. walk from the city center, 15min. from East Station. Friendly place featuring a variety of accommodations and a terrific self-catering kitchen. Dorms £10; singles £14; doubles £26; weekly rates available. Towels £1.

Camping: St. Martin's Touring Caravan and Camping Site, Bekesbourne Ln. (tel. 463216), off the A257 (Sandwich Rd.), 1½mi. east of city center. Take Longport Rd. from the city wall. Good facilities and 210 pitches for tents. £3 pitch fee; £4.25 per person, under 18 £1.50. Open year-round.

FOOD AND PUBS

Bakeries and sweet shops please the palates of weary pilgrims around the cathedral. Pubs, restaurants, and fast-food dens crowd High St. **Safeway,** St. George's Pl. (tel. 769335), is four minutes from the town center, 10 if you can't navigate the subway tunnels under the roundabout (open M-Th and Sa 8am-8pm, F 8am-9pm, Su 10am-4pm). At 53-54 Castle St., **Gambell's Farmshop** (tel. 453196) deals in fresh fruits and vegetables. Request sophisticated pizzas and pasta at **Ask,** 24 High St. (tel. 767617), at surprisingly decent prices (main dishes about £5; open daily 11:30am-11pm). **Marlowe's,** 55 St. Peter's St. (tel. 462194), presents an eclectic mix of vegetarian and beefy English, American, and Mexican food in a friendly setting. Choose from eight toppings for 8 oz. burgers (£6.60), or stuff down a burrito for 15p more (open daily 11:30am-10:30pm). Near the cathedral, **Café Venezia,** 60-61 Palace St. (787786), serves cheap Italian (pizza £1 per slice, entrees about £5) inside handpainted walls (open daily July-Aug. 9am-11pm, Sept.-June 9am-6pm). **The Famous Sandwich Shop,** 16 St. Dunstans St. (tel. 765554), creates fresh sandwiches and homemade vegetable lasagna for £1.80 (open M-Sa 8:15am-4pm). **The White Hart,** Worthgate Pl. (tel. 765091), near East Station, is a congenial pub with homemade luncheon specials (£3-6). Ask to eat in the rose garden (open for lunch M-Sa noon-2pm).

The **Miller's Arms,** Mill Ln. off Radigund St., offers 6 draught beers, while nearby **Simple Simon's,** 3-9 Church Ln. (tel. 762355), draws in students from the university (open daily 11am-11pm). **Alberry's,** 38 St. Margaret's St., a snazzy wine bar, pours for chic crowds. (M-Th until 11pm, F-Sa 2am. Happy hour daily 5-7pm., 25% discount.)

SIGHTS

An amazingly quiet and blissful Canterbury greets the early riser; by all means, get up and enjoy the city before the daytrippers arrive. **Canterbury Cathedral** has drawn the faithful (and the morbidly curious) since 1170, when Archbishop Thomas à Becket was beheaded here with a strike so forceful it broke the blade of the axe. *(Open Easter-Oct. M-Sa 8:45am-7pm, Su 11am-2:30pm and 4:30-5:30pm; Nov.-Easter daily 8:45am-5pm. Evensong M-F 5:30pm, Sa-Su 3:15pm. Cathedral closed for 2 days around the 3rd week of July for the University of Kent's graduation. Admission £2.50, students, seniors, children £1.50. Visitors are charged at the gate; after hours you may be able to wander into the precincts for free, but probably not into the building, unless you happen to be an Anglican bishop.)* Little information about the building is posted, presumably to encourage you to take a guided tour. *(4 per day, fewer off-season. Check the nave or visitors center for times. £3, students and seniors £2, children £1.20. Self-guide booklet £1.25. Audio tour £2.50.)* The murder site today is closed off by a rail—a kind of permanent police line—around the **Altar of the Sword's Point.** Travelers with a taste for the gruesome can view a 15-minute audio-visual recreation of the heinous deed, just off the cloisters. *(Shown continuously 10am-4pm. £1, students and seniors 70p, children 50p.)* Money collected from pilgrims built many of the cathedral's splendors—including the early Gothic nave, constructed mostly between the 13th and 15th centuries on a site allegedly first consecrated by St. Augustine 700 years earlier. Among the nave's entombed inhabitants are Henry IV, his wife Joan of Navarre, and the Black Prince. A solitary candle marks the spot in adjacent Trinity Chapel where Becket's body lay until 1538, when Henry VIII burned his remains and destroyed the shrine to show how he dealt with bishops who crossed the monarch.

In a building beset with fire and rebuilt again and again, the **Norman crypt,** a huge, 12th-century chapel, remains intact. The **Corona Tower,** 105 steps above the easternmost apse, offers obstructed views of treetops. *(60p, children 30p.)* Under the **Bell Harry tower**—at the crossing of the nave and western transepts—perpendicular arches support intricate 15th-century fan vaulting. The cathedral's **welcome center** cum gift shop dispenses information and pamphlets. *(20p-£2.50. Open M-Sa 9am-4pm.)*

After atoning for that night in Brighton by a cathedral pilgrimage, progress over to **The Canterbury Tales,** St. Margaret's St. (tel. 454888), where a gap-toothed Wife of Bath and her waxen companions enact an abbreviated version of the stories—complete with the smells of sweat, hay, and general grime. As if your bus/rail/hitchhiking/ car trip to the town weren't enough, the exhibit simulates the journey all over again, only this time with headsets, and in several different languages. *(Open July-Aug. daily 9am-6pm; Mar.-June and Sept.-Oct. daily 9:30am-5:30pm; Nov.-Feb. Su-F 10am-4:30pm, Sa 9:30am-5:30pm. £4.95, students and seniors £4.25, children £3.95.)*

The remainder of Chaucer's medieval Canterbury crowds around the branches of the River Stour on the way to the **West Gate,** through which pilgrims entered the city, and the only one of the city's seven medieval gates to survive the wartime blitz. The **West Gate Museum** (tel. 452747, ext. 129), formerly a prison, keeps armor and prison relics, and commands broad views of the city. *(Open M-Sa 11am-12:30pm and 1:30-3:30pm. 90p, students and seniors 60p, children and disabled 45p.)* Alongside the museum and the peaceful River Stour sit the well-tended **West Gate Gardens,** the perfect place for a picnic. Several rickety monastic houses perch precariously along the banks of the river, which is now a small stream. For a quiet break, walk over to Stour St. and visit the riverside gardens of the **Greyfriars,** the first Franciscan friary in England. Greyfriars was built over the river in 1267 by Franciscans who arrived in England in 1224, two years before Francis of Assisi died. A small museum and chapel can be found inside the simple building. *(Open in summer M-F 2-4pm. Free.)* The medieval **Poor Priests' Hospital,** also on Stour St., now houses the **Canterbury Heritage Museum** (tel. 452747), featuring a large collection of pilgrim badges from medieval souvenir shops as well as reconstructions of the city in various stages, from the Romans to Rupert. *(Open June-Oct. M-Sa 10:30am-5pm, Su 1:30-5pm; Nov.-May M-Sa 10:30am-5pm. £2.20, students and seniors £1.25, children £1.10.)*

At 1 St. Peter's St. stands the famous **Weaver's House,** where Huguenots lived during the 15th century. Walk into the garden to see an authentic witch-dunking stool swinging above the river. **Weaver's River Tours** (tel. 464660) runs cruises from here several times daily, except in time of drought. *(30min. £4, children £3.)* The recently opened **Roman Museum,** Butchery Ln. (tel. 785575), houses hairpins, building fragments, and other artifacts from Canterbury's Roman inhabitants in a hands-on exhibit. *(Open M-Sa 10am-5pm, last admission 4pm; £1.90, students and seniors £1.25, children and disabled 95p.)* The **Royal Museum and Art Gallery,** 18 High St. (tel. 452747) showcases new local talents. The museum recounts the history of the "Buffs," one of the oldest regiments of the British Army. *(Open M-Sa 10am-5pm in the public library building; free.)*

Near the medieval city wall lie the **Dane John Mound and Gardens** and the massive, solemn remnants of the Norman **Canterbury Castle,** built for Conquering Bill himself. To the north on St. Dunstan's St., the vaults of **St. Dunstan's Church** contain a relic said to be the head of Sir Thomas More. Legend has it that his daughter bribed the executioner at the Tower and buried the head beside the altar. Little remains of **St. Augustine's Abbey** (tel. 767345), built in AD 598, but older Roman ruins and the site of St. Augustine's first tomb (AD 605) can be viewed outside the city wall near the cathedral. *(Open Apr.-Nov. daily 10am-6pm; Dec.-Mar. 10am-4pm. £2.50, students £1.90, children £1.30.)* In 1997, the 1400th anniversary of Augustine's arrival in Canterbury to re-establish Christianity in southern England brought with it a bevy of improvements to the abbey. Just around the corner from St. Augustine's on North Holmes St. stands the **Church of St. Martin,** the oldest parish church in England. Pagan King Ethelbert was married here to the French Christian Princess Bertha in 562. Joseph Conrad's heart sleeps in darkness inside the church.

ENTERTAINMENT

Around Canterbury provides an up-to-date calendar of events in Canterbury; *What, Where, When,* published biweekly, describes entertainment in all its urban guises; both are free from the tourist office. Call 767744 for the recorded "Leisure Line." Buskers (street musicians) blend in with the crowds, especially along St. Peter's and High St. Budding streetside string quartets almost succeed with Vivaldi while young bands of impromptu players ramble from corner to corner, acting out the most absurd of Chaucer's scenes. The occasional Fool can be found performing juggling tricks.

The task of regaling pilgrims with stories today falls upon the **Marlowe Theatre,** The Friars (tel. 787787), which stages London productions and variety shows. *(Tickets £6.50-22. Discounts available for students, seniors, and children.)* The **Gulbenkian Theatre,** at the University of Kent, University Rd. (tel. 769075), west of town out St. Dunstan's St., past St. Thomas' Hill, stages a range of productions. *(Box office open Sept.-Dec. M noon-4pm, Tu-F 10:30am-6pm, until 8pm performance evenings. Tickets £5-21; ask about student and senior discounts.)*

For information on summer arts events and the **Canterbury Festival**—two full October weeks of drama, opera, cabaret, chamber music, dance, and exhibitions inspired by French culture—call 452853, or write to Canterbury Festival, Christ Church Gate, The Precincts, Canterbury, Kent CT1 2EE. The **Chaucer Festival Spring Pilgrimage** in late April ushers in a medieval fair and period-costumed performers. Call the Chaucer Centre (tel. 470379) for more information.

∎ Near Canterbury

The **Stour Music Festival,** a celebration of Renaissance and Baroque music, lasts for 10 days at the end of June in Ashford, 5 mi. southwest of Canterbury. Wildly popular, the festival takes place in and around **All Saint's Boughton Aluph Church,** accessible by rail from West Station and situated on the A28. Call the Canterbury tourist office at 766567 for tickets (£3-15); reserve at least a month in advance.

Leeds Castle, 23 mi. southwest of Canterbury on the A20 London-Folkestone road, near Maidstone (tel. (01622) 765400), was named after the fun-loving chief minister of Ethelbert IV. Henry VIII transformed it into a lavish dwelling whose 500 acres of woodlands and gardens host unusual waterfowl, including black swans; lose yourself in a maze of 2400 yew trees. The castle houses an alarming collection of medieval dog collars. From Canterbury, take the train from West Station and change at Ashford. *(Open Mar.-Oct. daily 10am-5pm; Nov.-Feb. daily 10am-3pm. Admission to castle and grounds £8.80, students and seniors £6.80, children £5.80, families £24; grounds only £6, students and seniors £4.80, children £3.70, families £16. Wheelchair access.)*

▨ Sandwich

Less of a meal and more of a light snack, Sandwich (pop. 5500) was the northernmost of the Cinque Ports (a defensive system of coastal towns), and thus received special privileges from the King in exchange for a pledge to provide ships should war arise on the coast, until silt encroached on Kent, drawing the seas a few miles away, and leaving Sandwich useless to the King's Navy. Streets almost narrow enough to prohibit car traffic make this village of medieval gateways and half-timbered houses worth further exploration for an afternoon.

GETTING THERE Sandwich slices in 5 mi. north of Deal and 11 mi. east of Canterbury; trains and buses run regularly between these three points. **Trains** (tel. (0345) 484950) depart at least hourly for **Deal** (£1.80), **Dover** (£3.50), and London's **Charing Cross** Station (£17). **Buses** make the trip to **Deal** several times daily. **National Express** (tel. (0990) 808080) heads to London once a day (£11).

ORIENTATION AND PRACTICAL INFORMATION Sandwich's **tourist office,** Old Police Waiting Room, Guildhall, New St. (tel. 613565), hands out a free leaflet outlining a self-guided **tour** of town (open May-Sept. daily 11am-3pm). When the office is closed, the information center at Deal (tel. (01304) 369576) will answer questions. Also available at the tourist office is the free packet entitled *Sandwich Walks,* which details short, pleasant jaunts about the town and countryside. The **train station** lies just off St. George's Rd. To reach the center of town, bear left on Delfside, turn left on St. George's, then right onto New St. **Buses** stop across from Guildhall on Cattlemarket. A small **police** station rests on Cattlemarket, but unless the crime is committed in the morning, better give nearby Dover a call (tel. 240055). Sandwich's **post office,** 16-20 Market St. (tel. 615327), is open M-Sa 8:30am-6pm. The **postal code** is CT13 9DA; the **telephone code** is 01304.

ACCOMMODATIONS AND FOOD Sandwich lacks a youth hostel. Those with an itch to spend the night should call in advance. Check with the tourist office for newly sprouted B&B and self-catering options. Six minutes from the train station you'll hit **Mrs. Rogers'** neighborhood, 57 St. George's Rd. (tel. 612772; 2 bedrooms; £16). For hidden decadence, **The B&B Above the Sandwich Golf Shop,** 38 King St. (tel. 620141), is worth the £20. Bubble bath, down blankets, fresh fruit and chocolate croissants for breakfast will spoil you in this 700-year-old-house. Or try the **New Inn,** 2 Harnet St. (tel. 612335), near the Guildhall, and enjoy a complete English breakfast (£25). Campers walk along Moat Sole behind Guildhall and across train tracks to the **Sandwich Leisure Park Campsite,** Woodnesborough Rd. (tel. 612681), one half-mile from town (100 pitches; electric hook-up; £7.50-9.50; open Mar.-Oct.).

Food hasn't been the same since the Earl of Sandwich munched his masterwork. Pick up the makings for your own at the neighborhood grocery **Spar,** 16-20 Market St. (tel. 612233; open M-F 8am-11pm, Su 8:30am-10:30pm). Have a hearty pub lunch at **The Red Cow,** 12 Moat Sole (tel. 613243), behind the Guildhall Museum (£3.50-5; meals served M-Sa 11am-2:30pm and 6-11pm, Su noon-3pm and 7-10:30pm). At the **16th-Century Tea House,** 9 Cattlemarket (tel. 612392), across from Guildhall, enjoy lunch (£3.50-5), a pot of tea with an immense fruit scone for £1.50 (open daily 8am-6pm). **Sandwich Continental,** 6 Market St. (tel. 617151), is an upbeat, family-run restaurant that serves a creative selection of (could it be?) sandwiches from £1.60 (open M-Sa 8:30am-10:30pm).

SIGHTS Strand St. boasts perhaps the largest concentration of half-timber Tudor buildings in England. The elevated Butts, Rope Walk, and Mill Wall that once provided fortification, now make for an enjoyable stroll. The River Stour, dominated by the **Barbican,** was built by Henry VIII as part of his coastal defense scheme. The **Guildhall Museum** (tel. 617197), beside the tourist office on Cattle Market, contains detailed histories of every possible point of interest in Sandwich's geography and history—except the origins of its culinary offspring. *(Open Apr.-Sept. Tu-W and F 10:30am-12:30pm and 2-4pm, Th and Sa 10:30am-4pm, Su 2-4pm; Oct.-Mar. Tu-W, F, and Su 2-4pm, Th and Sa 10:30am-4pm. £1, children 50p, family £2.)* For an irreverent taste of the town, and one last pun on its name, take a **Bite of Sandwich** theatrical tour. *(July-Aug. F 7:30pm; £3. Call the tourist office for details.)* The **Gazen Salts Nature Reserve** (tel. 617341, evenings only) graces the northwest of town; from the Butts, follow signs across Gallows Field, the former execution site. The reserve hosts numerous birds and animals and just borders the marshland which silted over and separated Sandwich from the sea. *(Free.)*

▨ Deal

Julius Caesar came ashore with an invasion force at Deal in 55 BC. The three 16th-century castles represent Henry VIII's effort to prevent a repeat. Quiet and serene today, Deal deals in subtle pleasures and reserved charm. Inland visitors will find it almost quiet enough to hear the waves lapping at the pebbly shore.

ORIENTATION AND PRACTICAL INFORMATION Deal lies 8 mi. north of Dover and 12 mi. southeast of Canterbury; trains and buses stop here on their way to these cities. **Trains** run at least every hour to **London** (£17) via **Dover** (£2.70) and **Sandwich** (£1.80). The **train station** stands just west of town off Queen St.; to reach Deal's center, turn left onto Queen St. and follow it until you reach the pedestrian precinct of High St. **National Express buses** (tel. (0990) 808080) attack Deal from London's **Victoria Station** (£11). The **bus station** (tel. 374088) is on South St., one block south of Broad St. (open M-W and F-Sa 9:20am-1pm and 1:30-4:45pm). The town extends north to south along the coast; main arteries **Beach, High,** and **West St.** all parallel the coast. Deal's **tourist office,** Town Hall, High St. (tel. 369576), pulls in a good catch of leaflets, including the indispensable *Deal Walks,* which details 10 walks (3-8½mi.) in the area. For £5 or a 10% deposit, they'll reserve you a room (open M-F

9am-12:30pm and 1:30-5pm; mid-May to mid-Sept. also Sa 9am-2pm). **Banks** dwell on High St.; **Lloyd's,** 2 High St. (tel: (01303) 851181), is at the corner of High and South St. (open M-Tu and Th-F 9am-5pm, W 9:30am-5pm), while **National Westminster,** 31 High St. (tel. 372126), guards the corner of High and Queen St. (Open M-Tu and Th-F 9am-4:30pm, W 9:30am-4:30pm, Sa 9:30am-1pm). Rent some wheels at **Deal Pram and Cycle Hire Centre** (tel. 366080) rear of 42 High St. (£10 per day, £40 per week, deposit from £50; open M-Sa 9am-5:30pm, Su 10am-4pm). A **launderette** (tel. 360926) bubbles at 5 Queens St. (Open M-F 8am-8pm, last wash 6:45; Sa-Su 8am-6pm, last wash 4:45pm. Change and soap available.) The **post office,** 17-19 Queen St. (tel. 374216), is open M-F 8:30am-5:30pm, Sa 9am-5:30pm. The **postal code** is CT14 6BB; the **telephone code** is 01304.

ACCOMMODATIONS AND FOOD Daytrips to Deal are the norm; the nearest youth hostels are in Dover and Canterbury. If you plan to stay in town, phone B&Bs in advance, especially in summer. Hefty **Cannongate,** 26 Gilford Rd. (tel. 375238), fires a full English breakfast (singles £13, with bath £15; doubles £26, with bath £30). **Sondes Lodge,** 14 Sondes Rd. (tel. 368741), is a pebble's toss from the peaceful beach with showers in every room (doubles £45).

Greengrocers glisten on High St. **Tesco** sells the usual stuff at 2 Queen St. (open M-F 8am-8pm, Sa 8am-6pm, Su 10am-4pm). Enjoy the Channel view and photos of motley locals with their catches at the **Lobster Pot,** 81 Beach St. (tel. 374713; all-day English breakfast; take-away fish and chips £3.60; open daily 7am-9:45pm). **Ronnie's,** 1b Stanhope Rd. (tel. 374300), revels in plush chairs (cream tea £2.50; open M-Sa 9am-5pm). **Dunkerley's,** 19 Beach St. (tel. 375016), overlooking the sea, has an elegant two-course lunch deal for £7.50 (open M 6-10pm, Tu-F noon-3pm and 6-10pm).

SIGHTS **Deal Castle** (tel. 372762) is the largest of Henry VIII's coastal constructions. Originally meant to serve as an imposing bulwark, rather than an elegant palace, the castle successfully warded off continental invaders. Check out the medieval subliminal advertising: the castle's six buttresses form the distinctive shape of the Tudor Rose, Henry's family symbol. The castle stands south of town at the corner of Deal Castle Rd. and Victoria Rd. *(Free audio tour available. Open Apr.-Nov. daily 10am-6pm; Dec.-Mar. W-Su 10am-4pm. £3, students and seniors £2.30, children £1.50. Limited wheelchair access.)* **Walmer Castle** (tel. 364288) rests south of Deal on the A258 to Dover (around ½mi. from town). The best preserved and most elegant of Henry VIII's citadels, Walmer has been gradually transformed into a country estate. Since the 1700s, it's been the official residence of the Lords Warden of the Cinque Ports, a defensive system of coastal towns. Notable Lords Wardens include the Duke of Wellington (whose famed Wellington boots are on display) and Winston Churchill. The post is currently filled by the best preserved and most elegant Queen Mum. *(Open Apr.-Oct. daily 10am-6pm; Nov.-Mar. W-Su 10am-4pm. £4, students and seniors £3, children £2. Wheelchair access to gardens and courtyard.)*

Along the Coast to Deal Pier ticks the **Timeball Tower** (tel. 201200), a fascinating contraption connected by electric current to Greenwich Observatory. When ships used the Downs as a makeshift port before crossing the Channel, the ball atop the tower was lowered at precisely 1pm each day to indicate the time. Today, the ball drops every hour on the hour. *(Open July-Aug. Tu-Su 10am-5pm. Tours in winter by arrange-*

Gays and the Government

British attitudes towards sexuality can be baffling: tabloids sport topless girls, national television channels think little of having a series of "Out" films, London Underground is quite happy to supply transsexuals with one male and one female ID while they undergo conversion—yet this is also a country with strict laws regulating sexuality. Section 28 of the criminal code, for example, bans local authorities from promoting homosexuality. Gays have yet to be welcomed in the military. In recent years, however, the judiciary has made its distaste for both policies quite clear and only rarely applies Section 28.

ment. £1.20, seniors and children 80p.) The **Maritime and Local History Museum,** 22 St. George's Rd. (tel. 372679), located behind the tourist office, delves into Deal's past with such maritime relics as figureheads and stern boards. *(Open late May to late Sept. 2-5pm. £1.50, students and seniors £1, children 50p.)*

A **street theater tour,** the "Deal Trail of Blood," brings to life the town's smuggling past and includes a pinch of pub-crawling in Old Deal (1½hr.; reserve tickets at the tourist office; £3). For a more relaxing tour of the town, amble through Deal's old footpaths, along the town streets and over beachfront property. Refer to the tourist office's free pamphlet, *Deal Walks.* Late-July unleashes the **Deal Summer Music Festival** and a score of musical acts ranging from classical to modern music. For more information, call 612292 (tickets £5-12).

■ Dover

> The sea is calm tonight.
> The tide is full, the moon lies fair
> Upon the straits;—on the French coast the light
> Gleams and is gone; the cliffs of England stand
> Glimmering and vast, out in the tranquil bay.
> —Matthew Arnold, "Dover Beach"

The crashing tide of the English Channel has been drowned out by the puttering of ferries, the hum of hovercraft, and the chatter of French families *en vacances.* The Chunnel, completed in 1994, has altered the identity of Dover—an even greater stream of cars and new international rail lines invade the town, supplementing the usual parade of ferries journeying to Calais, and reinforcing its long-standing political and economic significance. But despite the clamor, Dover has retained its dignified maritime identity. The beach often seems a darkling plain of lighthouses and Norman ruins, but on a clear day, you may glimpse the far-off specter of France.

GETTING THERE

Trains (tel. (0345) 484950) roll to Dover's **Priory Station** from London's **Victoria, Waterloo East, London Bridge,** and **Charing Cross** stations about every 45 minutes (2hr., £17). Many trains branch off en route; check schedules to see which trains split. **National Express buses** (tel. (0990) 808080) run regularly (15 per day, £13) from London's **Victoria Station;** they continue to the Eastern Docks after stopping at the Pencester Rd. bus station (2¾hr.). Buses also make hourly trips to **Canterbury** (45min., £4), Deal (40min., £2.50), and **Sandwich** (50min.; £3.40); a bus to **Folkestone,** the actual termination point for the Chunnel trains, runs every half-hour (30min., £2.10).

Major **ferry** companies operate ships from Dover to Calais, and the Dover tourist office offers a ferry booking service. Ferries sail to Calais and to Oostend, Belgium. **Hovercrafts** leave from the Hoverport at the Prince of Wales Pier for Calais. Free bus service leaves Priory Station for the docks 45 minutes to 1 hour before sailing time. (See **By Boat,** p. 30, for complete ferry and hovercraft information.) The **Channel Tunnel (Chunnel)** offers passenger service on **Eurostar** and car transport on **Le Shuttle** to and from the Continent (see **By Train,** p. 30).

ORIENTATION

To reach the tourist office from the railway station, turn left onto **Folkestone Rd.** Continue until **York St.;** turn right and follow it to the end, where you turn left onto **Townwall St.;** the tourist office is on the left. From the bus station, turn left from Pencester onto **Cannon St.** Proceed through the pedestrian-friendly city to Townwall St. and turn left. York St., which becomes **High St.** and eventually **London Rd.,** borders the center of town. **Maison Dieu Rd.** graces the town's other side.

PRACTICAL INFORMATION

Trains: Priory Station, on aptly named Station Approach Rd. Ticket office open M-Sa 4:15am-11:20pm, Su 6:15am-11:20pm.

Buses: Pencester Rd. (tel. (01304) 240024), which runs between York St. and Maison Dieu Rd. Purchase tickets on the bus or in the ticket office. Open M-F 8:30am-5:30pm, Sa 8:30am-noon.

Tourist Office: Townwall St. (tel. 205108; fax 225498), a block from the shore. The friendly folk greet a slew of international arrivals and sell ferry and hovercraft tickets; after hours call for a list of accommodations. Open daily July-Aug. 8am-7:30pm; Sept.-June 9am-6pm.

Financial Services: Several **banks** bump elbows in Market Sq. **Thomas Cook,** 3 Cannon St. (tel. 204215). Open M-Tu and Th-Sa 9am-5:30pm, W 10am-5:30pm.

Launderette: Cherry Tree Ave. (tel. 242822), right off London Rd., beyond the hostel. Change machine and soap available. Open daily 8am-8pm; last wash 7:15pm.

Emergency: 999; no coins required.

Police: Ladywell St. (tel. 240055), right off High St.

Hospital: Buckland Hospital (tel. 201624), on Coomb Valley Rd. northwest of town. Take bus #D9 or D5 from outside the post office.

Post Office: 68 Pencester Rd. (241747), by bus station. Open M-F 9am-5:30pm, Sa 9am-12:30pm. **Postal Code:** CT16 1PB.

Telephone Code: 01304.

ACCOMMODATIONS

At the height of tourist season, rooms can be difficult to find. Plan ahead—the ferry terminal makes an ugly and unsafe campground. Several of the hundreds of B&Bs on **Folkestone Rd.** (by the train station) stay open all night; if the lights are on, ring the bell. During the day, try the B&Bs near the center of town on **Castle St.** The cheapest places are generally on Folkestone Rd. past the train station—quite a walk from the center of town. Look for "White Cliffs Association" plaques outside homes for quality, moderately-priced rooms. Most B&Bs ask for a deposit.

YHA Charlton House, 306 London Rd. (tel. 201314; fax 202236), with overflow at **14 Goodwyne Rd.** (closer to town center). A ½mi. walk from the train station; turn left onto Folkestone Rd., left onto Effingham St., past the gas station onto Saxon St., and left at the bottom of the street onto High St., which becomes London Rd. Be prepared to rub elbows with families. £9.75, under 18 £6.55. 69 beds; 2-10 beds per room. Lounge and game room with pool table. Breakfast £2.95, 3-course dinner £4.40. Kitchen, forceful showers, and lockers available. Lockout 10am-1pm, curfew 11pm. Overflow building has 60 beds, some with bath; kitchen and lounge area. You may have to wait a bit after ringing for staff at the overflow hostel; same prices as main hostel, but bring exact change.

YMCA, 4 Leyburne Rd. (tel. 206138), turn right off Goodwyne Rd. Men and women accepted. Basic accommodations. 47 mattresses (sheets and blankets provided) in a co-ed room on a dance floor. Separate rooms for women also available. £5. Reception open M-F 8:30am-noon and 6-10pm, Sa-Su 6-10pm. Curfew 10pm. Reservations recommended; call ahead during summer months.

Victoria Guest House, 1 Laureston Pl. (tel./fax 205140). The well-traveled hosts extend a friendly welcome to their international guests. Think twice about complaining of sore muscles; your neighbor might have just swum the Channel. Gracious Victorian rooms in an excellent location. Doubles £28-40; family room £48-54. Special 5-day rates available.

Amanda Guest House, 4 Harold St. (tel. 201711). Bathrooms in the hall are a small price to pay for the elegant Victorian light fixtures and marble fireplaces. Twins £24-34; family room £38-46.

Gladstone Guest House, 3 Laurelston Pl. (tel. 208457). Tastefully decorated pale rooms with cherry finish. Ask for a room with views of the lovely rolling hills and fish ponds below. Singles £25; doubles £38-40.

Dover's Restover Bed & Breakfast, 69 Folkestone Rd. (tel. 206031), across from
the train station. Comfortable B&B offers well-equipped rooms, pleasant service,
and a full English breakfast. Singles £16-18; doubles £28-42.

Camping: Harthorn Farm (tel. 852658), at Martin Mill Station off the A258 between
Dover and Deal. Close to the railway. 250 pitches. Electricity hook-up £2. Car-and-
tent fee June to mid-Sept. £11 for 2 people, mid-Sept. to Oct. and Mar.-May £8.50.
£2 per extra person. Without car £3.50 per person.

FOOD

Despite the proximity of the Continent, Dover's cuisine remains staunchly English.
Grease fires rage dawn to dusk in the fish and chip shops on London Rd. and Biggin
St., and a decent pub lunch can be had almost anywhere in the city center. If you're
looking to dine and dance, head to **Images** (locally known as "Damages"), Castle St.
(tel. 207518), Dover's sordid semblance of a happening nightclub (cover £3; open
8pm-2am). Be cautious: Dover can be unsafe at night.

Chaplin's, 2 Church St. (tel. 204870). Pictures of Charlie complement the classic feel
of this Dover diner. Shoe leather is (sadly) not on the menu, but you won't miss it
with specials like roast chicken, vegetables, and potatoes (£4.50). Open M-Sa 9am-
9pm, Su 9:30am-8:30pm.

The Lighthouse Café and Tea Room (tel. 242028), at the end of Prince of Wales
Pier. Basic English chips fare, but not a basic location: a view of Dover castle,
beaches, and the White Cliffs as you sip tea from ½mi. off shore. Open Mar.-Aug.
M-F 9am-6pm, Sa-Su 9am-7pm, Sept.-Feb. Sa-Su 9am-5pm.

Pizza Pronto, 7 Ladywell (tel. 214234). Mouth-watering smells of take-away pizza
waft down the street. Cheese pizza £3.70. Open daily 5pm-midnight.

Moonflower, 32-34 High St. (tel. 212198). Chinese take-away in full spicy splendor.
Set meals £5.80, chicken dishes £3.30-4.10. Open M-Th noon-2:30pm and 6pm-
midnight, F-Sa noon-2:30pm and 5pm-midnight, Su 5pm-midnight.

Curry Garden, 24 High St. (tel. 206357). Aching for a change from Dover's British
diners? Tandoori chicken £4.20. Open daily noon-3pm and 6pm-midnight.

SIGHTS

The view from Castle Hill Rd., on the east side of town, reveals why **Dover Castle** is
famed both for its magnificent setting and for its impregnability. Many have launched
assaults on it by land, sea, and air: the French tried in 1216, the English themselves
during the Civil War in the 17th century, and the Germans in World Wars I and II; all
efforts failed. Look down the well shaft to discover how sophisticated the castle's
(unfortunately lead-piped) plumbing system was. The **castle keep** has an odd medley
of trivia and relics from the 12th century to the present. Boulogne, 22 mi. across the
Channel, can (barely) be seen on clear days from the castle's top; it was from that
coast that the Germans launched rocket bombs in World War II. These "doodle-bugs"
destroyed the **Church of St. James,** the ruins of which crumble at the base of Castle
Hill. The empty **Pharos,** built in 43 BC, sits alongside **St. Mary's,** a tiled Saxon church.
The only Roman lighthouse still in existence and certainly the tallest remaining
Roman edifice in Britain, the Pharos's gaping keyhole windows testify to its original
purpose. **Hell Fire Corner** is a 3½ mi. labyrinth of secret **tunnels** only recently declas-
sified. Originally built in the late 18th century to defend Britain from attack by Napoleon, the graffiti-covered tunnels served as the base for the evacuation of Allied troops
from Dunkirk in World War II. *(Hourly buses from the town center run daily Apr.-Sept.; 45p.
Castle and complex open Apr.-Sept. daily 10am-6pm. Oct.-Mar. daily 10am-4pm. £6.60, students and seniors £5, children £3.30, families £15. Partial wheelchair access.)*

Relatively recent excavation has unearthed a remarkably well-preserved **Roman
painted house,** New St. (tel. 203279), off Cannon St. near Market Sq. It's the oldest
Roman house in Britain, complete with an under-floor central heating system. *(Open
Apr.-Sept. Tu-Su 10am-5pm. £2, seniors and children 80p.)* **The White Cliffs Experience**
(tel. 214566) in Market Sq. employs costumed Roman soldiers, videos, and a rebuilt

ferry deck to illustrate Dover's nearly two millennia of history. On the third floor note the painted figure of Michael Jackson next to Charles II and Richard the Lionheart—all famous channel crossers. *(£5.50, students and seniors £4.25, children £3.75.)* Check the White Cliffs Experience brochure, free at the tourist office, for discount coupons. Tickets purchased at White Cliffs include a tour of the **Dover Museum,** Market Sq. (tel. 201066), which similarly displays curious bits of Dover history. *(Open daily Apr.-Oct. 10am-6pm; Nov.-Mar. 10am-5:30pm. £1.65, students, seniors, and children 85p. Wheelchair access.)*

A few miles west of Dover (25min. by foot along Snargate St.) sprawls the whitest, steepest, and most famous of the cliffs. Known as **Shakespeare Cliff** (look for the signs), it is traditionally identified with eyeless Gloucester's battle with the brink in *King Lear.* Closer to town on Snargate St. is the **Grand Shaft** (tel. 201200), a 140 ft. triple spiral staircase shot through the rock in Napoleonic times to link the army on the Western Heights and the city center. The first stairwell was for "officers and their ladies," the second for "sergeants and their wives," the last for "soldiers and their women." *(Ascend July-Aug. W-Su 2-5pm; on bank holidays 10am-5pm. £1.20, seniors and children 70p.)* For more startling views, take the A20 toward Folkestone to **Samphire Hoe,** a well-groomed park planted in the summer of 1997 from material dug to create the Chunnel. There are dozens of walks within a short distance of the center of town; consult the tourist office for more information.

SUSSEX

■ Rye

Settled before the Roman invasion, Rye's port flourished until the waterways choked with silt and the sea retreated, leaving the village like a marshy ship nestled on top of a rock. Throughout the 18th century, the town was best known for its bands of smugglers, who darted past royal authorities to stash contraband in an elaborate network of cellars, secret passageways, and attics. According to local myth, Rye's name derives from the French *la rie,* the waste spot. Alas, marsh and law-breakers are no more to be found in this handsome village. Green, rolling hills studded with sheep lie outside the town, while in Rye (pop. 4400), sloping cobblestone streets and tea shops await visitors looking for the archetypal English village experience.

GETTING THERE Trains (tel. (0345) 484950) roll to London's **Charing Cross** and **Cannon St.** stations (1½hr., £15.30), to **Brighton** (1¾hr., £10.30), and **Eastbourne** (1hr., £5.80) via **Ashford,** and to **Dover** (1¾hr., £8.60) **via Ashford.** You can also go via **Tunbridge Wells,** changing at **Hastings. National Express** (tel. (0990) 808080) runs from London to Rye (£12). Regular bus service runs to points all around southeast England and beyond; schedules flap in the train station's parking lot.

ORIENTATION AND PRACTICAL INFORMATION Pinned in by waterways on three sides, Rye sits at the mouth of the River Rother. To reach the tourist office from the **train station** (tel. (0345) 484950), off Cinque Port St., turn right on Cinque Port St. (it becomes Wish St.). Turn left onto the Strand Quay; the office is on the left. **Buses** (tel. 223343) stop in front of the train station. To reach the oldest part of town, hike up Market Rd. to High St., Lion St., and Mermaid St. The **tourist office,** Rye Heritage Centre, The Strand Quay (tel. 226696), distributes the free *Rye: 1066 Country* guide, which lists points of interest, accommodations, and restaurants. (Open mid-Mar. to Oct. daily 9am-5:30pm; Nov.-Dec. M-F 10am-1pm, Sa-Su 10am-4pm; Jan. to mid-Mar. M-F 10am-3pm, Sa-Su 10am-4pm.) The office also shows a "laser and light film" (a movie, in big-city lingo) about Rye's smuggling past (£2, students, seniors, and children £1.50). **Lloyds, Barclays,** and **National Westminster** line High St. **Cyclonic** and the **Surf Shack,** Market Rd. rent bikes (around £2 per hr., £10 per day). The town **market** takes place on Thursdays (8:30am-3pm). A **launderette** spins in

Ropewalk Arcade (open daily 8:30am-6pm). Call the **emergency** number 999, or find **police** at Cinque Port St. (tel. 222112). **Post office** workers eat their favorite kind of bread at 22-24 Cinque Port St. (tel. 224711; open M-Sa 9am-5:30pm). Rye's **postal code** is TN31 7AA; its **telephone code** is 01797.

ACCOMMODATIONS Rye's many fine, inexpensive B&Bs are often far from town. Call ahead, and you may get picked up. To go to **Glencoe Farms,** West Undercliff (tel. 224347), exit right from the station and take a right on Ferry Rd. across the tracks; after Ferry Rd. becomes Udimore Rd., West Undercliff comes up on the left; follow the signs to the farm. Friendly proprietors, animals to pet, and three airy rooms overlooking sheep fields (£15). The **YHA Youth Hostel** is at Hastings (see p. 157). Rockin' Richard and Jane McGowan run the delightful **Amberley Bed and Breakfast,** 51 Winchelsea Rd. (tel. 225693; £12-16, with breakfast £16-20, pastoral views free). To get to **Mrs. Jones,** 2 The Grove (tel. 223447), take a left through the train station car park and another left onto Rope Walk, which becomes The Grove just past the train tracks (3min.). Features comfortable rooms let by a classical music and Virginia Woolf aficionado (£16.50). The clean and friendly **Riverhaven Guest House** is at 60 New Winchelsea Rd. (tel. 223267; £15).

FOOD AND PUBS For standard pub grub, several places to gorge line High St. **Jempson's Coffee House and Bakery** (tel. 223986), Cinque Port St. and Market Rd., features a mouthwatering assortment of pastries and lunch dishes (open M-Sa 8am-6pm). **Fletcher's House,** Lion St. (tel. 223101) serves morning coffee, lunch, and tea in the house where dramatist John Fletcher was born in 1579. (filling lunches £3-6, cream tea with cucumber sandwich £3.50. Open weekends only 10am-5:15pm.) **The Mariners,** High St. (tel 223480), is a classic tea shop that offers cream or farmer's tea for £2.90. (Open daily 10am-5pm.) For whisky, buy a drink at the **Mermaid Inn** (see below) and sit above old smuggling tunnels. At Rye's only nightclub, **Horizon,** 48 Ferry Rd. (tel. 222343), Spice Girls reign (cover about £3.50).

SIGHTS AND ENTERTAINMENT Well-preserved half-timber homes cover the hill on which much of the town sits, and recall the days when smugglers stole through a sleepy Rye. Henry James wrote his later novels while living in **Lamb House,** at the corner of West and Mermaid St. *(Open Apr.-Oct. W and Sa 2-6pm. £2.20.)* Before descending the hill, check out **St. Mary's Church** (tel. 222430) at the top of Lion St., a huge 12th-century parish church which houses one of the oldest functioning clocks in the country. A climb up the tower steps reveals a terrific view of the river valley, but avoid the ascent when the bell is about to ring…your ears may never forgive you. *(£2, students and seniors £1.)* Around the corner from the church rises the **Ypres Tower** (c. 1350) above the **Rye Museum.** Originally built to fortify the town against invaders from the sea, the tower has served as a jail, and now contains a museum. A walk down Mermaid St. leads you to the famed **Mermaid Inn** (tel. 223065), where smugglers once cavorted until dawn. *(Open M-Sa 11am-11pm, Su noon-10:30pm.)* Not many cavort in Rye these days, though some brush close to it during the **festival** of art, theater, and music for two weeks at the start of September. *(Festival booking office tel. 227338. Tickets £2-12.)*

Dirty Dancing

Long before the lambada or the Macarena, dancing hand-to-hand or cheek-to-cheek was considered improper by meddling British prudes. When the **waltz** appeared in 1812, it was deemed indecorous because the dancers embraced while dancing, and Mr. Theodore Hook accused the waltz of leading to "the most licentious consequences." A century later the **Argentine tango** crossed the Atlantic; its suggestive movements prompted mothers to forbid their daughters from accepting invitations to dances. The **Charleston,** which followed soon after, sparked dissension in temperance societies, and **twisters** of the 1950s were chided for allowing an all-too titillating glimpse of their knees.

■ Near Rye: Hastings, Battle and Penvensey

Hastings

Many sights of interest surround Rye, but transportation to them runs from the larger, burg of **Hastings,** where **Hastings Castle** (tel. 781111) guards the town from atop a cliff. *(£2.90, students and seniors £2.30, children £1.90.)* **Trains** between Rye and Hastings run daily (20min., departs every 30min.). The **tourist office** (tel. 781111) neighbors the Town Hall on Queen's Parade, and the **post office** stamps at 13-15 Cambridge Rd. (tel. 464243; open M-F 9am-5:30pm, Sa 9am-7pm). The **phone code** is 01424. Hastings is home to the only **YHA Youth Hostel** (tel. 812373), Rye Rd., in the area. From **Rye,** the hostel is a grueling 7 mi. hike down the A259 past Winchelsea and Icklesham (look for the sign on the right). Take bus #711 from Rye to the White Hart in Guestling (M-Sa roughly 2 per hr., summer also Su every 2hr., last bus around 7:45pm, £1.85). From the White Hart, the hostel is downhill on the left. You can also take the train to Three Oaks (£1.90) and walk 1½ mi. (55 beds with 4-12 per room. Breakfast £2.85. £8.80, under 18 £5.95. Open July-Aug. daily; mid-Feb. to June and Sept.-Oct. 6 days per week—but the one day it's closed varies, so call ahead; Nov.-Dec. F-Sa; closed Jan to mid-Feb.) The hostel also has **camping** pitches (£4.40 per pitch).

Battle

Appropriately named after the decisive fight between William of Normandy and King Harold of England that took place here in 1066, the town of **Battle** makes a fine expedition from Rye. To commemorate his victory in the Battle of Hastings, William the Conqueror had **Battle Abbey** (tel. 773 7921) built in 1094, spitefully positioning its high altar upon the very spot where Harold was felled by an arrow in the eye (see p. 52). The town grew prosperous enough to survive Henry VIII's closing of the abbey in 1538. Little remains of the abbey apart from the gate and a handsome series of 13th-century common quarters. *(Open daily Easter-Oct. 10am-6pm; Nov.-Easter 10am-4pm. £3.50, students and seniors £2.60, children £1.80.)* The battlefield where Harold's troops were taken by surprise is now a pasture trampled only by sheep. In summer, you can take a tour of the abbey and walk the **battlefield trail** (tel. (01634) 832666), a 1 mi. jaunt up and down the green hillside. Bus #5 runs directly to the Abbey from Hastings, every hour during opening hours Monday to Saturday (20min., Su every 2hr., £4.40). **B&Bs** in Battle charge £15-20 and can be booked through the **tourist office,** 88 High St. (tel. 773721; fax 773436), opposite Battle Abbey (open Apr.-Sept. daily 10am-6pm; Oct.-Mar. M-Sa 10am-4pm, some Su 1-4pm). Battle shares its **phone code,** 01424, with Hastings.

Pevensey

This town owes its existence to Norman fraternal devotion. William the Conqueror's march to Battle began from the Roman fortress Anderita, located here. Will then gave it to his brother, who added a keep. The castle (tel. 762604) now lies at the center of town. *(Open Apr.-Oct. daily 10am-6pm; Nov.-Mar. W-Su 10am-4pm. £2, students and seniors £1.50, children £1.)* The religious legacy of the Norman conquest is immortalized in **St. Mary's** (tel. 762294), in nearby Westham, which claims to be the first church built by the Normans in England.

The best part of Pevensey owes its origins to commerce rather than conquest. The **Mint House,** High St. (tel. 762337), begun as a mint under the Normans, was transformed by Henry VIII's physician into a country retreat, and eventually became a smugglers' den, complete with sliding ceiling panels. It now teems with Victorian miscellany, stuffed birds, grandfather clocks, and other fascinating oddities themselves worth the price of admission (open M-Sa 9:30am-5pm; 80p). **Trains** run from Rye via Hastings to Pevensey (every hr., £5.60). Pevensey's **tourist office** stands guard in Pevensey Castle Car Park, High St. (tel./fax 761444; open Easter-Oct. M-F 10am-5:15pm, Sa-Su 10am-5pm). Pevensey's **phone code** is 01323.

ENGLAND

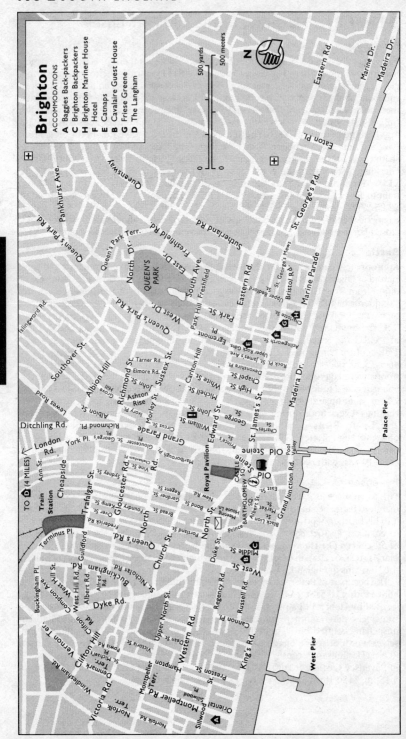

Brighton

ACCOMMODATIONS

A Baggies Back-packers
C Brighton Backpackers
H Brighton Mariner House
F Hotel
E Catnaps
B Cavalaire Guest House
G Friese Greene
D The Langham

500 yards
500 meters

N

TO D (4 MILES)
Train Station

Palace Pier
West Pier

■ Brighton

In Lydia's imagination, a visit to Brighton comprised every possibility of earthly happiness.

—Jane Austen, *Pride and Prejudice*

The undisputed home of the "dirty weekend," Brighton (pop. 250,000) sparkles with a risqué, tawdry luster all its own. According to legend, the future King George IV sidled into Brighton for some hanky-panky around 1784. Having staged a fake wedding with a certain "Mrs. Jones" (Maria Fitzherbert), he headed off to the farmhouse known today as the Royal Pavilion, and the royal rumpus began. Brighton turns a blind eye to some of the more outrageous activities which occur along its shores; holiday-goers and locals alike peel it off—all off—at England's first bathing beach. Kemp Town (jokingly called Camp Town), among other areas of Brighton, thrives with one of the largest gay and lesbian populations in Britain, while the Lanes—narrow ventricled streets which line the pebble-coated beaches—witness much of the action. Foreign students flock to the southern coast (ostensibly to learn English) and join an already immense student population in setting the town abuzz with mayhem and frivolity. Although the city is slowly becoming a mini-metropolis (it recently merged with nearby Hove), Brighton remains Britain's version of a pumping seaside resort. Lovingly known as "London-by-the-Sea," Brighton's open, welcoming demeanor and youthful spirit make for a memorable sojourn for adventurous travelers.

GETTING THERE

Trains (tel. (0345) 484950) ease on down the road from **London** to Brighton (1¼hr., at least 6 per hr., £13.70). They depart Brighton for other southern locales, including **Arundel** via **Ford** (50min., 2 per hr., day return £5.90) and **Portsmouth** (1½hr., 1 per hr., day return £11.10). **National Express** (tel. (0990) 808080) heads to Brighton from **London** (2hr., 15 per day, £9 return).

ORIENTATION AND PRACTICAL INFORMATION

The train is at least 10 minutes from the town center and waterfront. To reach the tourist office in **Bartholomew Sq.,** opposite the town hall, walk south along **Queen's Rd.** towards the water. Turn left onto **North St.** (not to be confused with North Rd. or North "Laine") and continue until you reach **Ship St.;** then turn right onto Ship and proceed along to **Prince Albert St.,** which leads to the tourist office.

Transportation

Trains: (tel. (0345) 484950), at the end of Queen's Rd. heading north. Ticket office open 24hr. Travel Centre open M-Sa 8:15am-6pm.

Buses: National Express (tel. (01273) 383744) stops at Pool Valley, at the southern angle of Old Steine. Tickets and info at **One Stop Travel,** Old Steine (tel. 700406). Open M-F 8:30am-5:45pm, Sa 9am-5pm; June-Sept. also Su 11am-4:30pm.

Local Transportation: Most local buses are operated by **Brighton and Hove** (tel. (01273) 886200). To get to **Hove** hop on any of the buses traveling westward along Western Rd. (just a few blocks off the beach, the continuation of North St., running parallel to the waterfront). The tourist office can give route and price information for most buses. All carriers in the central area charge 70p; travel to the YHA costs £1.25.

Bike Rental: Freedom Bikes, 108 St. James's St. (tel. 681698). £8 per day for a snazzy mountain bike, £24 per week, £50 per month. Open M-Sa 9:30am-5:30pm. Vendors also rent small watercraft, bikes, and in-line skates on the waterfront, although prices are higher, and quality somewhat lower.

Tourist and Financial Services

Tourist Office: 10 Bartholomew Sq. (tel. 292599). Enthusiastic staff vends materials on practically any subject and books National Express tickets and beds (£1 per adult plus 10% deposit). Free street maps available. Open M-F 9am-5pm, Sa 10am-5pm, Su 10am-4pm; June-Sept. longer hours. **Walking tours** leave the tourist office June-Aug. Th 11am (£3).

Budget Travel: Campus Travel, 61 Ditchling Rd. (tel. 570226). Open M and W-F 9:30am-6pm, Tu 10am-6pm, Sa 10am-5pm. **STA,** 38 North St. (tel. 728282). Open M-W and F 9:30am-5:30pm, Tu 10am-5:30pm, Sa 10am-4pm.

Financial Services: Banks along North St., between West St. and Old Steine, including **Thomas Cook,** 58 North St. (tel. 325711). Open M-Tu and Th-Sa 9am-5:30pm, W 10am-5:30pm.

American Express: 82 North St., BN1 1ZA (tel. 321242 or 203766). Open M-Tu and Th-Sa 9am-5:30pm, W 9:30am-5:30pm.

Local Services

Library: Church St. (tel. 290800), on the Royal Pavilion's grounds, in a fantastic Victorian building. Intriguing exhibits and a good cafe. Open M-Tu and Th-F 10am-7pm, Sa 10am-4pm.

Launderette: 5 Palace Rd. (tel. 327972). Soap available. Open daily 8am-8pm.

Women's Center: 10 St. George's Mews (tel. 600526). Services include pregnancy testing. Open M and W-Th 10:30am-3:30pm, Sa 11:30am-1:30pm.

Disabled Information: Snowdon House, 3 Rutland Gdns., Hove BN3 5PD (tel. 203016). Open daily 10am-4pm. **Tourist office** has a phenomenal printout.

Emergency and Communications

Emergency: Dial 999; no coins required.

Police: John St. (tel. 606744).

Hotlines: Samaritans (crisis; tel. 772277). Open 24hr.; drop-in 10am-10pm. **Gay and Lesbian Switchboard** (tel. 690825). Referral point for other gay groups. Open M-Sa 6-10pm, Su 8-10pm. **Sussex AIDS Helpline** (tel. 571660). Open daily 8-10pm.

Hospital: Royal Sussex County, Eastern Rd. (tel. 696955), parallel to Marine Parade.

Post Office: 51 Ship St. (tel. 573209), off Prince Albert St. in the Lanes. Bureau de change. Open M-Sa 9am-5:30pm **Postal Code:** BN1 1BA.

Internet Access: Cybar, 9-12 Middle St. (tel. 384280; http://www.cybar.co.uk). Oh-so-trendy restaurant and bar complete with internet hookups. £2.50 per 30min. Open M-W 10:30am-11pm, Th-Sa 10:30am-1pm, Su noon-10:30pm.

Telephone Code: 01273.

ACCOMMODATIONS

Brighton's best bets for budget lodging are its three hostels. B&Bs and cheaper hotels begin at £18. Shabbier B&Bs and hotels collect west of West Pier and east of Palace Pier. There is a huge number of B&Bs in **Kemp Town,** the neighborhood which runs perpendicular to the sea, east of Palace Pier, and a bit farther from the center of town. Test the beds and smell for dust before signing your night away. Frequent conventions make rooms hard to come by—book early or consult the tourist office immediately upon arrival. Luckily, the high concentration of accommodations means that a little legwork and some hard bargaining can go a long way. Inquire at the tourist office for a list of guest houses owned and operated by gays or lesbians. Rooms may be cheaper in **Hove,** just west of Brighton (see **Local Transportation,** p. 159).

⊛**Brighton Backpackers Hostel,** 75-76 Middle St. (tel. 777717). Unforgettably painted independent hostel that bubbles with international flavor. *The* place to meet other backpackers in Brighton. Clean rooms overlook the ocean. Innovative artwork—courtesy of previous guests—graces most of the walls. Great location, and no curfew. Friendly Miles offers advice and tunes from his guitar against the chirp of resident parakeets. TV lounge, pool table, and internet access (free!). Sunday-night *Simpsons* ritual in lounge. The quieter **annex** faces the ocean. 4- to 8-bed coed and single-sex dorms £9; less in winter. Weekly: £50. Annex £10-12.50. Inexpensive breakfast and dinner. Sheets £1. Kitchen and laundry.

Baggies Back-packers, 33 Oriental Pl. (tel. 733740), near West Pier. Go west of West Pier along King's Rd.; Oriental Pl. will be on your right. Jazz, exquisite murals, and a mosaic floor of world maps set the tone for this mellow, international hostel. Spacious and clean. Try to keep the music down after midnight. Coed and single-sex dorms as well as an assortment of doubles. Coed dorms £9, single-sex dorms £10, weekly £45; doubles £23. Laundry facilities. Video collection and kitchen facilities. Key deposit £5. No lockout or curfew.

YHA Youth Hostel, Patcham Pl. (tel. 556196), 4mi. north on the main London Rd. Take Patcham bus #5 or 5A (from stop E) from Old Steine in front of the Royal Pavilion to the Black Lion Hotel (5A gets you closer). Georgian-style country house filled with friendly staff. Rooms (6-16 beds each) look new, although they're 400 years old. Good jumping-off point for the South Downs Way (see p. 180). Not the place to stay if you want to party late. £9.75, under 18 £6.30. Breakfast £3. Laundry facilities. Reception closed 10am-1pm. Curfew 11pm. Call ahead in July-Aug. or show up around breakfast time—often full; closed Jan.

Catnaps, 21 Atlingworth St. (tel. 685193; fax 622026). Guest house in Kemp Town for gays and lesbians. Malcolm and his adorable pair of spaniels keep 7 immaculate rooms with elegant high ceilings. TV lounge, free map, and safe sex packet in each room. Connecting balconies are a favorite. Full English breakfast; will cater to vegetarians—phone requests ahead. Singles £18; doubles £34-36.

Cavalaire Guest House, 34 Upper Rock Gdns. (tel. 696899; fax 600504). TV and assorted electrical appliances in each room. Wonderful breakfast; clean and tidy rooms. Singles £19-20; doubles £40-52.

Friese Greene, 20 Middle St. (tel. 747551). Bohemian, family-run hostel situated in the heart of Brighton's nightlife. Great location attracts serious partiers and seasoned travelers looking for a cheap place to crash. Clean, decent rooms are comfortable. £9; weekly £45. Sheets £1. Laundry, kitchen, pool, and TV.

Brighton Marina House Hotel, 8 Charlotte St., Marine Parade (tel./fax 605349 or 679484). Gracious, clean guest house with showers in rooms (except for singles) and phones for incoming calls. Convenient location. Restaurant serves English, Indian, and Chinese cuisine on request and specializes in vegetarian dishes (starting at £10 for a complete meal). Singles £15-39.

The Langham, 16 Charlotte St. (tel./fax 682843). 9 tidy, inexpensive rooms in pastels. Like other Kemp Town guest houses, a 10min. walk to the Lanes. £18-20.

FOOD AND PUBS

The area around the Lanes is full of trendy and expensive places waiting to gobble up tourist dollars. For cheaper fare, try the fish and chip shops along the beach and north of the Lanes. As always, the best deal is to cook for yourself. Brighton has several large supermarkets, near the center of town. Try **Safeway,** 5-8 St. James's Pl. (tel. 570363; open M-Sa 8am-9pm, Su 10am-4pm), or **Waitrose,** 131 Western Rd. (tel. 326549; open M-Tu and Sa 8:30am-7pm, W-Th 8:30am-8pm, F 8:30am-9pm, Su 10am-4pm).

Food for Friends, 17a Prince Albert St. (tel. 202310). Cheap, well-cooked, well-seasoned vegetarian food in a breezy, youthful atmosphere. Daily specials—the salads send the taste buds straight to heaven (£2-3.25); entrees £3-6. Get the "Taster" special: £5.20 for a portion of all the day's entrees. Open daily 8am-10pm.

Donatello, 3 Brighton Pl. (tel. 775477). Open-air Italian restaurant on the fringe of the Lanes. Hot spot to people-watch during the day. Salads (£3.20), pasta (£4.40), and the specialty Donatello pizza (£5.35). Open daily 11:30am-11:30pm.

Terre à Terre, 71 East St. (tel. 729051). If you want to splurge, this is the place to do it. Well-prepared vegetarian dishes cheerfully dispensed. Entrees £8. Open Tu-Su noon-10:30pm.

Piccolo, 52 Ship St. (tel. 203701). Busy even on late nights, Piccolo specializes in homemade pasta and pizza. Take-away lunch pizza £2.50; pastas £4-5. Open daily 11:30am-11pm. Wheelchair access.

Noori's, 70-71 Ship St. (tel. 329405 or 747109). Spicy tandoori and curry dishes. Tandoori chicken for £5; vegetarians will take a shine to Noori's *dal* (£3.75). Open M-Th noon-2:15pm and 6-11:30pm, F-Sa noon-2:15pm and 6pm-midnight, Su 1-11pm.

SIGHTS

Brighton's transformation from the sleepy village of Brighthelmstone to England's "center of fame and fashion" was catalyzed by the scientific efforts of one man and the whimsical imagination of another. In 1750, Dr. Richard Russell wrote a treatise on the merits of drinking and bathing in sea water to treat glandular disease. Before then, sea-swimming was thought nearly suicidal. The treatment received universal acclaim, and seaside towns began to prosper. Although recession hit Brighton hard, the city has nearly completed a revitalization of the waterfront, and tourism is booming.

John Nash's transformation of a plain-Jane farmhouse into the **Royal Pavilion** (tel. 290900) from 1815 to 1822 also brought about Brighton's rise to fashion and popularity. Rejecting Henry Holland's initial classically inspired villa, George IV (then Prince of Wales) had Nash, his favorite architect, embellish the estate in a loosely Oriental, unabashedly ornate fashion, mixing Chinese, Indian, and even Gothic decorations. "Opulence" doesn't do the place justice. Rumor has it George wept tears of joy upon first entering it, proving that wealth does not give one taste. Queen Victoria was less thrilled. *(Open daily June-Sept. 10am-6pm; Oct.-May 10am-5pm. £4.50, students and seniors £3.25, children £2.50. Partial wheelchair access.)* You can also enjoy the palace from the large shady parks surrounding it. Rent deck chairs for £1 per day.

Around the corner from the Pavilion stands the **Brighton Museum and Art Gallery,** Church St. (tel. 603005). Featuring paintings, English pottery, and Art Deco and Art Nouveau collections wild enough to make viewers spontaneously dance the Charleston, the museum occupies the same buildings as the fantastic public library (see p. 160). Leer at Salavador Dalí's incredibly sexy, red, pursing sofa, *Mae West's Lips.* At the fine **Willett Collection of Pottery,** avant-garde art and antique Brighton relics simultaneously reflect the varied faces of this seaside escape. *(Open M-Tu and Th-Sa 10am-5pm, Su 2-5pm. Free. Limited wheelchair access.)*

Before heading to the seafront, see where small fishermen's cottages once thrived in the **Lanes.** A jumble of 17th-century streets—some no wider than 3 ft.—stretches south of North St. and constitutes the heart of Old Brighton. Though now filled with antique jewelry shops, cafes, and overpriced knick-knack vendors, the Lanes' trendiness is rooted in the past.

The main attraction in Brighton is, of course, the **beach.** Those who associate the word "beach" with visions of sand and sun may be sorely disappointed—the weather can be quite nippy even in June and July, and the closest thing to sand on the beach are the fist-sized brown rocks. At least, as one optimistic hostel owner observes, no one tracks sand into her room at night. In fact, the whole town seems to revolve around this sort of glass-is-half-full spirit. Even in 70°F weather with overcast skies, beach-goers gamely strip to bikinis and lifeguards don sunglasses. During the peak of the summer, visitors have to fight for a spot on the beach. Hang loose just west of Brighton Marina at the **nude bathing** areas. Be sure to stay within the limits. **Telescombe Beach,** nearly 4½ mi. to the east of Palace Pier, is frequented by a mostly gay crowd. Look for a sign before Telescombe Tavern marked "Telescombe Cliffs." Numerous sailing opportunities crop up in summer; check at the tourist office.

The heavily promoted **Palace Pier,** a century old and recently repainted, offers a host of amusements, including a museum of slot machines, between the piers under King's Road Arches. This vision of futuristic videogames (some of which top £1 per play) is the fourth largest tourist attraction in England. The pier's toilets have condom machines dispensing an array of colors and flavors, just in case. And the deck chairs are free. **Volk's Railway** (tel. 681061), Britain's first 3 ft. gauge electric train, shuttles along the waterfront. *(Runs Apr.-Sept. daily 11am-6pm. £1, children 50p.)* Although England's largest aquarium, **Brighton Sea Life Centre** (tel. 604234), has freed its dolphins, Missie and Silver, many other sea creatures remain trapped in glass tanks for your viewing pleasure. *(Open daily in summer 10am-7pm; in winter 10am-6pm. Last admission 1hr. before close. £5.50, seniors £4.25, children £3.95. Wheelchair access.)* The **Grand Hotel,** on the front on King's Rd., has been substantially rebuilt since a 1984 IRA bombing that killed five but left then-Prime Minister Margaret Thatcher unscathed.

Farther along, the ghostly **West Pier** lies abandoned out in the sea. Full-scale renovation is set to begin in the spring of 1999. Tours available for £10 (tel. 321499). A short walk along the coast past West Pier leads to **Hove.** Casual walkers will find many examples of Regency architecture in lovely **Brunswick Sq.**

Several churches add a bit of holiness to Brighton's shores. **St. Nicholas' Church,** Dyke Rd., dates from 1370 and treasures a 12th-century baptismal font some consider to be the most beautiful Norman carving in Sussex. **St. Bartholomew's Church,** on Ann St., was originally called "The Barn" or "Noah's Ark." This little-known spurt of Victorian genius rises higher than Westminster Abbey, to 135 ft. To get there, take bus #5, 5A, or 5B. In the same elaborate tradition as the Pavilion, **Preston Manor** (tel. 603005), a grand house 2 mi. north of Brighton on the A23, portrays the life of Edwardian gentry. *(Open M 1-5pm, Tu-Sa 10am-5pm, Su and bank holidays 2-5pm. £2.85, students £2.35, children £1.75. Some wheelchair access; call ahead. Take bus #5, 5A, 770, or 773.)*

ENTERTAINMENT

Brighton brims with nightlife options, earning it the nickname "London-by-the-Sea." And as surely as the tide turns, clubs and venues go in and out of fashion. The local monthly, *The Punter,* details evening events and can be found at pubs, newsagents, and record stores. *What's On,* a poster-sized flysheet, points the hedonist toward hot-and-happening scenes. Pub-crawling in the Lanes is a good bet on any night. Gay and lesbian venues can be found in the latest issues of *Gay Times* (£2.20) or *Capital Gay.*

Summer brings outdoor concerts and assorted entertainment (mimes, jugglers) to the pavilion lawn, the beach deck, and around the Lanes. Although the Lanes are the most vibrant part of town at night, they are not necessarily the safest. The City Council spent £5 million installing surveillance equipment along the seafront and major streets to ensure safety during late-night partying, but it is still a good idea to avoid walking alone late at night through Brighton's spaghetti-style streets.

Brighton is a student town, and where there are students there are cheap drinks. Many pubs and clubs offer fantastic drink specials during the week—some budget-minded backpackers find no reason to go out on weekends, when most places are crowded and expensive. **Fortune of War,** 157 King's Rd. Arches (tel. 205065), is always a lucky choice. *(Open M-Th 10pm-2am, F 10pm-3am, Sa 10pm-4am.)* **Cuba,** 160 King's Rd. Arches (tel. 770505), is close by. *(Cover £3-6. Open M-Sa 11am-11pm, Su 11am-10:30pm.)* Revelers congregate in front of these two pubs—on the beach between West and Palace Pier—and drink until about 11pm. Also popular is **Squid and Starfish,** 77 Middle St. (tel. 727114), next door to the Backpacker's Hostel. Brightly colored walls and a vodka mural make this pub a popular place to begin an evening. *(Open M-F 5-11pm, Sa noon-11pm, Su 5-10:30pm.)* Bedsteads and vodka bottle chandeliers make **Smugglers,** on Ship St., a raucous place to drink. Pints go for £1.60. *(Happy hour(s) M-F noon-8pm.)* Fantastic outdoor and balcony seating await at **Beiderbeck's,** Clarence Yard, Meeting House Ln. (tel. 326778), an "American" pub flooded by Europeans. **The King and Queen,** Marlborough Pl. (tel. 607207), hosts jazz lunches on Wednesday, Thursday, and Sunday, in a lovely Tudor building.

Most clubs are open 10pm-2am every day except Sunday. The most technically armed and massively populated are **Paradox** (tel. 321628) and **Event II** (tel. 732627), both on West St. Paradox gets a bit dressy towards the end of the week. The monthly "Wild Fruit" gay night is popular among people of all persuasions. Event II spent over £1 million adding all of the electric trimmings to its already immense dance floor. The arches of old-WWII-tunnels-turned-**Zap Club,** King's Rd. (tel. 821588), provide space for dark rendezvous and dirty dancing; come here for hard-core grinding to rave and house music. The club is open into the wee hours of the morn. **Gloucester,** Gloucester Plaza (tel. 699068), provides good cheap fun with music varying nightly. Slightly unsightly **Casablanca,** Middle St. (tel. 321817), plays live jazz to a largely student crowd. Get ready to sweat it again, Sam (discount for Backpackers hostelers, see p. 160). Gay clubbers flock to zany **Zanzibar,** St. James St. (tel. 622100), or **Revenge,** on Old Steine, Brighton's largest gay dance club. **Queen's Arms,** 8 George St. (tel. 696873), packs an enthusiastic gay and lesbian crowd into its Saturday night cabaret.

Who's Afraid of Vanessa Bell?

"It has a charming garden, with a pond and fruit trees and vegetables, all now rather wild, but you could make it lovely." So Virginia Woolf described **Charleston Farmhouse** in 1916 to her sister, Vanessa Bell, when Vanessa sought a remote spot in which to relocate her household. Though originally lacking amenities such as electricity and a telephone, Charleston soon became a center for literary, artistic, and intellectual life in Britain. Frequent guests included members of the Bloomsbury Group: economist John Maynard Keynes, art theorist Clive Bell, Roger Fry, Lytton Strachey, and Leonard and Virginia Woolf. Keynes was notorious at the Farmhouse for his inexplicable experiment with time, when he set all the house's clocks back one hour. The servants retaliated by refusing to wind the kitchen clock. Charleston was nearly abandoned in the late 1970s, but in 1980 the Charleston Trust Fund purchased the estate and refurbished the property.

Brighton Centre, King's Rd., and the **Dome,** 29 New Rd.(tel. 709709), host Brighton's biggest rock and jazz concerts and events ranging from Chippendales shows to Brighton youth orchestra concerts. Tickets can be purchased from Ticketmaster (24hr. tel. (0870) 900 9100), or at the Dome booking office. *(Open M-Sa 10am-5:30pm.)* The tourist office also sells tickets. Plays and touring London productions take the stage at the **Theatre Royal,** New Rd. (tel. 328488), a Victorian beauty with red plush interior. *(Tickets £6-18. Open M-Sa 10am-8pm.)* **Komedia** (tel. 277772), on Gardner St., houses a cafe, bar, theater, and cabaret. *(Tickets £5-8, discounts available. Stand-by tickets sold 15min. before showtime. Box office open Tu-Sa noon-8pm; Su-M only 1hr. before listed event. Cafe bar open M-F 5-11pm, Sa-Su 11am-11pm.)*

The **Brighton Festival** (tel. 292961; box office tel. 709709), held each May, is the largest festival in England; it celebrates music, film, and all the arts. Gays and lesbians celebrate the concurrent **Brighton Pride Festival** (tel. 730562).

■ Near Brighton

If you are inclined to leave the urban attractions and distractions of Brighton in search of more relaxed pursuits, take a 10-minute train ride to the historic town of **Lewes** (return £1.90), hometown of Thomas Paine, author of *Rights of Man* and *Common Sense.* The Norman **Lewes Castle** (tel. 486290) merits a visit. *(Castle open M-Sa 10am-5:30pm or dusk, Su 11am-5:30pm or dusk. £3.40, students and seniors £2.90, children £1.80.)* The 15th-century **Anne of Cleves House Museum** (tel. 474610) celebrates the clever woman who got the house from Henry VIII in their divorce settlement *without* losing her head. *(Open Apr.-Oct. M-Sa 10am-5:30pm, Su noon-5:30pm; Nov.-Mar. Tu, Th, and Sa 10am-5:30pm. £2.20, students and seniors £2, children £1.10.)* Just south of Lewes off the A27 is **The Charleston Farmhouse** (tel. (01323) 811265), the intellectual and artistic country home of the Bloomsbury Group, which highlights the domestic decorative art of Vanessa Bell (see p. 164) and Duncan Grant. *(Open July-Aug. W-Sa 11:30am-5pm, Su 2-5pm; Apr.-June and Sept.-Oct. W-Su 2-5pm. £5.)* Three miles east of Brighton rests **The Grange** (tel. (01273) 301004), in the village of **Rottingdean.** Now taken up largely by an art gallery and museum, the house once sheltered Rudyard Kipling, after whom its gardens are named. *(Open M-Sa 10am-4pm, Su 2-4pm. Free.)* The popular **South Downs Way** attracts hikers (see p. 180).

■ Arundel

Minding its quiet, stony spot on a downsland hillside, Arundel (pop. 3200) is a great base for exploring the beautiful country side along the River Arun. Home to a romantic castle, a number of English Catholics, and a host of tea rooms and antique shops, Arundel sits in the shadow of towers, ramparts, and cathedral spires.

ORIENTATION AND PRACTICAL INFORMATION

Trains (tel. (0345) 484950) leave London's **Victoria Station** for Arundel (1¼hr., 1 per hr., £15.50). Trains to **Chichester** (£5.50) and **Portsmouth** (£8.80) also run often. Most other train and bus routes require connections at Littlehampton to the south or Barnham to the east. Bus #11 goes to **Littlehampton** (M-Sa 1 per hr., Su 6 per day), picking up passengers across from the Norfolk Arms on High St. Arundel doesn't offer local bike rentals, but two-wheelers can be found at **Cycle Hire** (tel. (01903) 770649), in nearby Angmering. The **tourist office,** 61 High St. (tel. 882268), hands out the free *Town Guide.* (Open in summer M-F 9am-5pm; Sa-Su 10am-5pm; off-season M-F 9am-3pm, Sa-Su 10am-3pm.) Banks with **ATMs** include **Lloyds,** 14 High St. (tel. 717221; open M-F 9:30am-4:30pm). Sort things out at the **post office,** 2-4 High St. (tel. 882113; open M-F 9am-5:30pm, Sa 9am-12:30pm); the **postal code** is BN18 9AA. The **telephone code** is 01903.

ACCOMMODATIONS

A glut of tourists takes its toll on accommodations during summer; savvy travelers plan ahead to avoid anxiety and a severe gouging of the wallet. Situated 1½ mi. out of town, **YHA Warningcamp** (tel. 882204; fax 870615) awaits at the end of a potentially pleasant walk: turn left out of the train station and turn right at the "Public Footpath" sign, making another right onto the path. Follow the trail and the River Arun until you reach the railroad tracks; cross them, go through the gate, and make a left, which leads to the hostel. Cyclists should make a right from the train station onto the A27 and take the first left; after 1 mi., turn left at the sign and then follow the second set of signs (two right turns). Note: the footpath is shorter than the A27 route and features magnificent castle views. The hostel is a Georgian house with aqua-green interior. (£8.80, under 18 £6. Camping £3.85. Breakfast £3, evening meal £4.50. Single-sex and coed showers with private changing booths. Huge kitchen and laundry facilities. Lockout 10am-5pm. Curfew 11pm. Open July-Aug. daily; Apr.-June M-Sa; Sept.-Oct. Tu-Sa; Nov.-Dec. F-Sa; Jan.-Mar. closed.)

The tourist office maintains an up-to-date list of vacancies in town just outside the entrance; make it your first stop if you haven't booked ahead. B&Bs are consistent with Arundel's elegance, and priced accordingly. Those in search of twins and doubles should first try **Castle View,** 63 High St. (tel./fax 883029), where Mr. and Mrs. Overy incubate three rooms with private facilities directly across from the castle walls. The Overys have a family of vegetarians and know how to make them happy (from £44 per room). **Arden House,** 4 Queens Ln. (tel. 882544), keeps eight immaculate rooms, some with wood-beamed ceilings, convenient to town center and station (doubles or twins £35, with bath £39; singles available off-season and occasionally during the summer for £20). **The Bridge House and Cottage,** 18 Queen St. (tel. 882142), offers comfortable rooms and a great location in a hotel atmosphere. The adjacent cottage has lovely gardens complete with bridges and a koi-filled pond (singles £22-28; doubles £32-40; twins £34-42). Campers can claim a pitch at the **Ship and Anchor Site** (tel. (01243) 551262), 2 mi. from Arundel on Ford Rd. along the River Arun, with pub and shops. (£3.25 per person, children £1.50. £1.25 per vehicle. Showers. Open Apr.-Sept.)

FOOD

Arundel's pubs and tea shops are generally a bit expensive. A variety of fruit and bread peddlers line High and Tarrant St. Locals frequent **Belinda's,** 13 Tarrant St. (tel. 882977), a 16th-century tea room with a large selection of wines. Linger over cream teas (£3.50) and delicious homemade jam (open Tu-Sa 6am-5:30pm, Su 11am-5:30pm). **The Castle View,** 63 High St. (tel. 883029), bakes lasagna (£4.30). Munch to your heart's content while gazing at the castle walls (open daily in summer 10am-5:30pm; in winter 10:30am-5pm). For pub grub, try the **White Hart,** 12 Queen St. (tel. 882374), whose entrees, though a bit pricey, are tasty; seek out the summer specials (food served daily 11am-2:30pm and 6-9pm). For picnics and late-night snacks, **Alldays,** 17 Queen St., honors its name (open M-Sa 6:30am-11pm, Su 7:30am-11pm). More refined customers can stop by **Pallant Wines,** 17 High St. They please your palate with fresh salads and vino (open M-Sa 9am-6pm, Su 11am-1pm).

SIGHTS

Poised above the town like the backdrop of a fairy-tale, **Arundel Castle** (tel. 883136) is lord of the skyline. The castle, seat of the Duke of Norfolk, was built in the 11th century but heavily damaged during the Civil War because the Duke was, like his successors, the highest-ranking Catholic in all British aristocracy. The castle was restored piecemeal by the dukes who called it home in the 18th and 19th centuries. Portraits by Van Dyck, Overbech, and others stare from the **Barons' Hall.** The many photographs of the current Duke and his family lend the place a comfortable air of "home-sweet-castle." The 122 ft. library, meticulously carved in the late 18th century, and the family chapel will make you want to marry nobility. Among the Duke's treasures on display are the rosary beads supposedly clutched by Mary, Queen of Scots at her execution. Don't overlook the graphically defined death warrant served against one of the Duke's ancestors by agreeable Elizabeth I. *(Castle open Apr.-Oct. Su-F noon-5pm, last entry 4pm. £5.70 and worth it, seniors £5, children £4.)* In late August, the castle is the glorious centerpiece of the **Arundel Festival** (tel. 883690; box office tel. 883474), ten days of symphonic concerts, jousting, and art exhibitions. *(Tickets £4-20.)* The **Festival Fringe** simultaneously offers free or inexpensive concerts and events. Tickets go on sale 6-8 weeks before the festivals begin.

Along the River Arun across from the castle are the remains of **Blackfriars,** a Dominican priory. A nearby placard recounts the troubled past of a group of monks who lived there. Atop the same hill as Arundel Castle sits the **Cathedral of Our Lady and St. Philip Howard** (tel. 882297). A Catholic cathedral, the French Gothic building was designed by Joseph Hansom, inventor of the hansom cab, and is decidedly more impressive from the outside. Though executed for cheering on the Spanish Armada in 1588, St. Philip occupies an honored place in the north transept. *(Open daily in summer 9am-6pm; in winter 9am-dusk. Free.)*

The **Arundel Museum and Heritage Center,** 61 High St. (tel. 882344), chronicles over two millennia of the town in a collection highlighted by a history of the castle. The "Do Not Touch" signs outnumber the things you'd want to grab. *(Open Easter-Sept. M-Sa 10:30am-5pm, Su 2-5pm. £1, students, seniors, and children 50p.)* Concealed observation enclosures at the **Wildfowl and Wetlands Trust Centre** (tel. 883355), less than 1 mi. past the castle on Mill Rd., permit visitors to "come nose to beak with nature." Just make sure nature doesn't nip back. Over 12,000 birds roost on 60 acres. *(Open daily in summer 9:30am-5:30pm; in winter 9:30am-4:30pm; last admission 1hr. before closing. £4, students and seniors £3, children £2.)*

■ Near Arundel: Petworth and The Body Shop

Petworth House (tel. (01798) 342207), 10 mi. from Arundel, showcases the talents of Capability Brown and J.M.W. Turner, among other artists. Brown landscaped the gardens; Turner painted the landscape. Some of Turner's best works hang in the library of the Third Earl of Egremont, an early 19th-century patron of arts and letters. Petworth now retains the artwork produced 1802-1812 and 1827-1831; the ground floor visitors' gallery contains 71 other sculptures and 59 paintings, including works by William Blake and Van Dyck. *(House open Apr.-Oct. Sa-W 1-5:30pm, last admission 4:30pm; extra rooms shown M-W. Grounds open daily July-Aug. 11am-6pm; Apr.-June and Sept.-Oct. noon-6pm. Ground-floor wheelchair access. House and grounds £4.50, under 17 £2.50, families £12; deer park free.)* Take the train to Pulborough (10min. from Arundel); walk the 2 mi. to the house or catch bus #1 or 1A. Ask for directions at the tourist office.

In the nearby town of **Littlehampton, The Body Shop Tour** (tel. (01903) 844044) takes visitors behind the scenes at the retail chain's factory, explaining how the Maori people of New Zealand crushed coconuts specifically for your shampoo. Ask to speak with an ethnobotanist, and buy your discount Body Shop goodies. *(Tours M-F* *throughout the day; special tours can be arranged on Sa. £4, students, seniors, and children £2.95. Reservations required.)* From Arundel, bus #11 runs hourly to Littlehampton; from there Chauffeur Taxis (tel. (01903) 715117) offers discounted fares for the rest of the voyage; walking can be risky on the main road.

■ Chichester

Despite centuries of confinement within the remains of Roman walls, the citizens of Chichester (pop. 30,000) seem content with their lot. The town still thrives on its bevy of markets (cattle, corn, and others), and its roads all still lead to the ornate Market Cross, a gift of kindly Bishop Storey in 1501 to "help the poore people of the citye." Today, Chichester hosts one of the country's best theaters, a summer arts festival, a host of gallery exhibits, and a nearby summer motor racing spectacular.

GETTING THERE Chichester is 45 mi. southwest of London and 15 mi. east of Portsmouth. **Trains** (tel. (0345) 484950) run to and from London's **Victoria Station** (1½hr., 2 per hr., £17.20), **Brighton** (1hr., 2-3 per hr., £8.70), and **Portsmouth** (40min., 2-3 per hr., £6). **National Express buses** (tel. (0990) 808080) run less frequently to **London** (2 per day, period return £10). Stagecoach Coastline buses serve **Brighton** (#700 and 701, 2hr., 2 per hr., £4.40) and **Portsmouth** (#700 or 701, 1hr., 2 per hr., £3.90). If you plan forays into the local area by bus, ask about the **Explorer** ticket: £4.40 buys a day's unlimited travel on buses servicing the south of England from Kent to Salisbury (seniors £3.30, children £2.20, families £8.80).

ORIENTATION AND PRACTICAL INFORMATION Four Roman streets named for their compass directions divide Chichester into quadrants that converge at **Market Cross**. The **bus station** (tel. (01903) 237661) lies diagonally across from the **train station** on Southgate. To reach the well-stocked **tourist office** (tel. 775888; fax 539449) from the train station, turn left as you exit onto Southgate, which then turns into South St. (Open July-Aug. M-Sa 9:15am-5:15pm, last booking 5pm, Su 10am-4pm; Sept.-June M-Sa 9:15am-5:15pm. 24hr. computer info.) **Guided tours** of the city depart from the tourist office (June-Sept. M 2:30pm and Sa 11am; £2). Several **banks** reside on East St. Change currency at **Thomas Cook,** 40 East St. (tel. 536733; open M and W-Sa 9am-5:30pm, Tu 10am-5:30pm). Wednesday and Saturday are **market days** in Chichester, in the parking lot just off Market Ave. Spruce up at the **launderette,** 11 Eastgate (open daily 8am-8pm, last wash 7pm). The **police** (tel. 536733) are on Kingsham Rd. The **post office,** 10 West St. (tel. 784251), is across from the cathedral (open M and Th 8:45am-5:30pm, Tu-W and F 9am-5:30pm, Sa 9am-4pm). The **postal code** is PO19 1AB; the **telephone code** is 01243.

ACCOMMODATIONS AND FOOD Cheap rooms are rare; plan on paying £16-20, and expect a 15-minute walk. **Hedgehogs,** 45 Whyke Ln. (tel. 780022), reasonably close to the town center, offers cozy rooms and happy hedgehog paraphernalia (singles £18-20; doubles £24-26; no smoking). Colorful geraniums, fresh-squeezed OJ, and grapefruit welcome guests to **Bayleaf,** 16 Whyke Rd. (tel. 774330; £22). Campsites lie at **Southern Leisure Centre,** Vinnetrow Rd. (tel. 787715), a 15-minute walk southeast of town. (£2 per person; pitch fee £8-10. Showers and laundry. Open Apr.-Oct.)

The hot scent of yeast flows from bakeries on North St., while groceries await at **Tesco** (tel. 227500), on East St., next to Lloyd's (open M-W and Sa 8am-6pm, Th-F 8am-6:30pm). The town's most notable eateries congregate around the cathedral and tend to gouge the pocket. **The Medieval Crypt,** 12a South St. (tel. 537033), is actually housed in an 800-year-old undercroft. It's a bit dear for dinner (£10-12), but has excellent lunch specials and salads (£5.50) ranging from mozzarella and tomato to chicken livers (open M-F noon-3pm and 6-9:30pm, Sa noon-3pm and 6-10:30pm, Su noon-3pm). **Maison Blanc Boulangerie and Patisserie,** 56 South St. (tel. 539292), is sure to make even the most resolute Francophobe's mouth water with a fantastic selection of cakes and coffees. *Pain au chocolat* is 75p; have a dozen. (Open M-F 8:45am-5:30pm, Sa 8:45am-6pm; June-Sept. also Su 9am-5pm; service closes 30min. early.) The **Pasta Factory,** 6 South St. (tel. 785764), rolls out fresh pasta twice daily; its *cannelloni sorentina* will give you pleasant dreams for weeks (£6).

SIGHTS Begun in 1091, **Chichester Cathedral** stands just west of the town's 15th-century market cross and is a hybrid of Norman remains and later additions. A glorious **Marc Chagall** stained-glass depiction of Psalm 150 ("let everything that hath breath praise the Lord") brings worshipers from all walks of the animal kingdom into one coherent pattern. Even Lizard Boy gets into the act. The carved effigies of 14th-century Earl Richard Fitzalan and his wife inspired Philip Larkin's "An Arundel Tomb," now displayed on a nearby pillar. *(Open daily in summer 7:30am-6:30pm; in winter 7:30am-5pm. £2 donation encouraged. Tours from the West Door Apr.-Oct. M-Sa 11am and 2:15pm. Evensong M-Sa 5:30pm, Su 3:30pm. Wheelchair access.)*

Chichester's other attractions include the Pallants, a quiet area with elegant 18th- and 19th-century houses in the southeast quadrant. The **Pallant House,** 9 North Pallant (tel. 774557), a restored Queen Anne building complete with period furniture, has been optimistically attributed to Sir Christopher Wren and contains a small gallery of mainly 20th-century British art. Familiar foreign faces in the crowd are Picasso and Cézanne, though displays rotate. *(Open Tu-Sa 10am-5:45pm, last admission 4:45pm. £2.80, students £1.50, seniors £2.20, children £1.)*

ENTERTAINMENT Unexpectedly emerging in a residential neighborhood north of town, the **Chichester Festival Theatre** (tel. 781312) is the cultural center of Chichester. Founded by Sir Laurence Olivier, the venue has attracted such artists as Dame Maggie Smith, Peter Ustinov, Kathleen Turner, and Julie Christie. The newer **Minerva Studio Theatre** is a smaller space for more intimate productions, including theater in the round. *(Box office open M-Sa 10am-8pm, or until 6pm if there is no performance. Tickets £14-25. 60 seats available at the box office on day of show at 10am; £6-8; only 2 tickets per person. Wheelchair access and special arrangements made for the visually and hearing impaired— phone ahead.)* The **Theatre Restaurant and Café** caters to patrons from 12:30pm on matinee days and from 5:30pm for evening shows. During the first two weeks in July, the **Chichester Festivities** enliven the quiet town. Artists and musicians collaborate to produce one of the finest spells of concentrated creativity in all of England. Obtain a schedule by writing to Chichester Festivities, Canon Gate House, South St. Chichester PO19 1PU (tel. 785718); a full program is published in April. *(Tickets from £2. Open mid-May to the festival's end M-Sa 10am-5:30pm; or check at the tourist office.)*

■ Near Chichester

The **Fishbourne Roman Palace** (tel. (01243) 785859), built in AD 75 as a home for local chieftains, is the largest Roman residence excavated in Britain. More than three-quarters of the building remains buried under the houses along Salthill Rd. The *Cupid on a Dolphin* is the most exceptional of a collection of amazing mosaics. *(Open daily Aug. 10am-6pm; Mar.-July and Sept.-Oct. 10am-5pm; Feb. and Nov.-Dec. 10am-4pm; Jan. Su only 10am-4pm. £3.80, students and seniors £3.20, children £1.80, families £9.50.)* Fishbourne is an easy 2 mi. walk from the Avenue de Chartres roundabout in Chichester; go west along Westgate, which becomes Fishbourne Rd. (the A259) for 1½ mi., or take bus #700 or 701 from Chichester center. Buses stop at Salthill Rd., five minutes from the palace, and the Fishbourne rail station.

Three miles northeast of Chichester stands **Goodwood House** (tel. (01243) 774107), ancestral home of the Duke of Richmond and Gordon. Splendid Canalettos, Reynoldses, and Stubbs vie for attention in the 18th-century country abode. *(Open Aug. Su-Th 2-5pm; Apr.-July and Sept. Su-M 2-5pm. £5.50, children 12-18 £2. Take bus #268, then walk about 1mi.)* For a leisurely wander through a village unlike any other you'll find in England, head to the **Weald and Downland Open Air Museum** (tel. (01243) 811348), in Singleton, 6 mi. north of Chichester. Over the past 25 years, 40 buildings representing different eras in British history have been removed from their original sites and reconstructed here. Visitors can skip from a medieval farmstead to a Tudor market hall to a Victorian rural school. *(Open Mar.-Oct. daily 10:30am-6pm, last admission 5pm; Nov.-Feb. W and Sa-Su 10:30am-4pm. £5.20, children £2.50, families £14.)*

HAMPSHIRE

■ Portsmouth

Don't talk to me about the naval tradition. It's nothing but rum, sodomy, and the lash.

—*Winston Churchill*

Set Victorian prudery against prostitutes, drunkards, and a lot of bloody cursing sailors, and an image of 900-year-old Portsmouth (pop. 190,500) will emerge. Henry VIII's *Mary Rose,* which sank in 1545 and was raised 437 years later, epitomizes an incomparable naval heritage in a city that will appeal most to those fascinated by the storied history of the Royal Navy. On the seafront, older visitors relive a thousand D-Days while fresh faces explore the warships and learn of the days when Britannia truly ruled the waves.

GETTING THERE

Portsmouth is easily accessible by land or by sea. **Trains** (tel. (0345) 484950) from London **Waterloo** stop at both Portsmouth and Southsea station (town station) and Portsmouth Harbor station (1½hr., 3 per hr., £19.40). They also arrive from nearby **Chichester** (40min., 2-3 per hr., £4.30). **National Express buses** (tel. (0990) 808080) rumble from **London** every hour (2½hr., £12.50) and **Salisbury** every two hours (2hr., £7). **Passenger ferries** (tel. 827744) chug to the **Isle of Wight** from Portsmouth Harbour station (15-20min., in summer 2 per hr., in winter 1 per hr., day return £6.75, return £9.90). Isle of Wight **Hovercraft** (tel. 811000) departs from Clarence Esplanade every half-hour (9min., return £7.90, children £3.95). For continental services, consult **By Boat,** p. 30.

ORIENTATION AND PRACTICAL INFORMATION

Portsmouth sprawls along the coast for miles—Portsmouth, Old Portsmouth, and the resort community of Southsea can seem like altogether different cities. Major sights in Portsmouth cluster at **The Hard, Old Portsmouth** (near the Portsmouth and Southsea train station), and **Southsea Esplanade.** A reliable and comprehensive bus system connects the outstretches of the city. For those with little time to spare, the ubiquitous **Guide Friday** bus tour may be a worthy investment—buses stop every half-hour at many major areas of the city, and a ticket entitles you to get on and off as you please for one full day (runs 10am-6pm; £6, students and seniors £5, children £2).

Trains: Portsmouth and Southsea Station, Commercial Rd. Travel Centre open M-F 8:40am-6pm, Sa 8:40am-4:30pm, Su 9:25am-4:30pm. Office open M-Sa 5:40am-8:30pm, Su 6:40am-8:40pm. **Portsmouth Harbour Station,** The Hard, ¾mi. away at the end of the line. Office open M-F 5:50am-7:30pm, Sa 6am-7:30pm, Su 6:40am-8:10pm. Trains run to Cosham hostel (5 per hr., £1.60) between to the harbor (return £1.20). Call Brighton (tel. (01703) 229393) for rail info.
Buses: The Hard Interchange, The Hard, next to the Harbour station. National Express services (tel. (0990) 808080). Office open M-F 8am-5pm, Sa 8am-4pm. Local services (tel. 498894 or 650967).
Taxi: Streamline Taxis (tel. 811111). **Mainline Taxis** (tel. 751111).
Tourist Office: The Hard (tel. 826722), by the entrance to historic ships. Open daily 9:30am-5:45pm. Another **branch** at 102 Commercial Rd. (tel. 838382), next to the train station. Open M-Sa 9:30am-5:30pm. Bureau de change. Accommodations booking service. **Seasonal offices** (in summer) near the Sea Life Centre, Clarence Esplanade (tel. 832464; open daily Apr.-Sept. 10am-4:45pm).

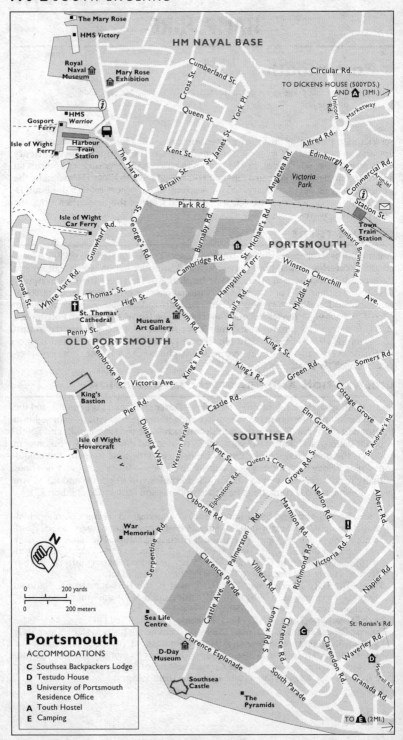

The Mary Rose

HMS Victory

HM NAVAL BASE

Royal Naval Museum

Mary Rose Exhibition

Cumberland St.

Circular Rd.

TO DICKENS HOUSE (500YDS.) AND A (3MI.)

Cross St.

Queen St.

York Pl.

St. James St.

Marketway

Gosport Ferry

HMS Warrior

Isle of Wight Ferry

Harbour Train Station

Kent St.

The Hard

Britain St.

Alfred Rd.

Edinburgh Rd.

Anglesea Rd.

Victoria Park

Commercial Rd.

Arundel St.

Park Rd.

Isle of Wight Car Ferry

Gunwharf Rd.

St. George's Rd.

Burnaby Rd.

Cambridge Rd.

St. Michael's Rd.

PORTSMOUTH

Station St.

Town Train Station

Isambard Brunel Rd.

White Hart Rd.

Broad St.

St. Thomas' St.

High St.

St. Thomas' Cathedral

Penny St.

Pembroke Rd.

Museum Rd.

Museum & Art Gallery

OLD PORTSMOUTH

Hampshire Terr.

St. Paul's Rd.

Winston Churchill Ave.

Middle St.

King's St.

King's Terr.

King's Rd.

Green Rd.

Somers Rd.

Victoria Ave.

King's Bastion

Pier Rd.

Castle Rd.

Elm Grove

Cottage Grove

St. Andrew's Rd.

SOUTHSEA

Isle of Wight Hovercraft

Dusburg Way

Western Parade

Kent St.

Queen's Cres.

Grove Rd. S.

Nelson Rd.

War Memorial

Serpentine Rd.

Osborne Rd.

Elphinstone Rd.

Palmerston Rd.

Marmion Rd.

Richmond Rd.

Villiers Rd.

Victoria Rd. S.

Albert Rd.

Napier Rd.

Clarence Parade

Castle Ave.

Clarence Rd. S.

Lennox Rd. S.

St. Ronan's Rd.

Waverley Rd.

Clarendon Rd.

Granada Rd.

Mitchell Rd.

Sea Life Centre

D-Day Museum

Clarence Esplanade

South Parade

Southsea Castle

The Pyramids

TO E (2MI.)

N

0   200 yards
0   200 meters

Portsmouth

ACCOMMODATIONS

C Southsea Backpackers Lodge
D Testudo House
B University of Portsmouth Residence Office
A Touth Hostel
E Camping

Budget Travel: Travel Shop, University of Portsmouth Union, Alexandra House, Museum Rd. (tel. 816645). Purchase bus, train, and plane tickets here. Open during term M-F 9:30am-3pm; all other times M-F 10am-3pm.

Financial Services: Major banks clump around the Commercial Rd. shopping precinct, just north of Portsmouth and Southsea Station, including Lloyds (open M-Tu and Th-F 9am-5pm, W 9:30am-5pm, Sa 9:30am-12:30pm).

American Express: 110 Commercial Rd. (tel. 865865). Open M-F 9am-5:30pm, Sa 9am-5pm.

Emergency: Dial 999; no coins required.

Police: Winston Churchill Ave., Cosham (tel. 839333).

Hotlines: AIDS, Keswick House (tel. 650704). **Alcohol Advisory Service** (tel. 296467). **Lesbian Line** (tel. 876999).

Hospital: St. Mary's Hospital, Milton Rd. (tel. 822331).

Post Office: Slindon St. (tel. 835201), near the town station. Open M and Th 8:45am-5:30pm, Tu-W and F 9am-5:30pm, Sa 9am-7pm. **Postal Code:** PO1 1AB.

Telephone Code: 01705.

ACCOMMODATIONS

Moderately priced B&Bs clutter Southsea, Portsmouth's contiguous resort town, 1½ mi. east of the Hard along the coast. Many are located along Waverly Rd., Clarendon Rd., and South Parade. Take bus #1C, 3, 5, 24A, 27B, 40, X40, or 41 to Southsea Parade. Cheaper lodgings lie two or three blocks inland—Whitwell, Granada, St. Roman's, and Malvern Rd. all have a fair sprinkling.

Southsea Backpackers Lodge, 4 Florence Rd. (tel. 832495). Take any Southsea bus and get off at The Strand. Very clean hostel with private rooms spreading over a 4-story home. Pan-European crowd and energetic, agreeable owners. 2 kitchens, laundry facilities, comfy lounge, wooden bunks, ample showers. Well-stocked, inexpensive grocery counter. Dorms £9; singles £15; doubles or twins £25.

YHA Youth Hostel, Wymering Manor, Old Wymering Ln., Medina Rd., Cosham (tel. 375661). Take any bus to Cosham (#1, 3, 40, and others) to police station and follow the signs. By train, make a right and walk up High St. from Cosham Station; turn left on Wayte St. and cross the roundabout to Medina Rd. After 6 blocks, Old Wymering Ln. will be on your right; the hostel is across from the church. The former home of Catherine Parr, sixth wife of Henry VIII, the hostel features exquisitely detailed woodwork and architecture, preserved better than a National Trust property; Queen Mary took tea here. Sleep in a Tudor drawing room. 58 beds. £8.80, under 18 £6. Lockout 10am-5pm. Curfew 11pm. Open Feb.-Aug. daily; Sept.-Nov. F-Sa; closed Dec.-Jan.

Testudo House, 19 Whitwell Rd., Southsea (tel. 824324). Lovely Mrs. Parkes fluffs the pillows and tickles the ivory in her spotless, agreeably decorated home. Beautiful china on breakfast room walls. Singles £17.50; doubles £34. No smoking.

University of Portsmouth Halls of Residence, Nuffield Centre, St. Michael's Rd. (tel. 843178), overlooking Southsea common, 15min. from the Hard. Singles and twins available mid-July through Sept. Small, modern rooms in **Burrel House, Rees Hall,** or **Harry Law Hall,** all reasonably convenient. £16.45. Booking ahead is highly recommended, but last minute arrivals should contact Rees Hall directly.

Camping: Southsea Caravan Park, Melville Rd., Southsea (tel. 735070). At the eastern end of seafront, 5-6mi. from The Hard. 2-person tent £8-9 per night; after Sept. from £7. Toilets, showers, laundry facilities, shop, restaurant-bar, and pool. Open year-round; call ahead.

FOOD AND PUBS

Restaurants that transcend pub grub purgatory reside along Osbourne, Palmerston, and Clarendon Rd. in the Southsea shopping district. **Country Kitchen,** 59a Marmion Rd., is a hardwood wholefood restaurant with excellent veggie specials hovering around £3. Fat-free fruit bars go for 80p (open M-Sa 9:30am-5pm, last order 4:45pm). At **Fabio's,** 108 Palmerston Rd. (tel. 811139), pizzas and pasta romance the air. Prices start at £5, with a 25% discount for take-away (open daily noon-3pm and 5pm-midnight). The coffee will keep you wide-eyed for days at **Brown's,** 9 Clarendon Rd. (tel. 822617), where solid English food is served in relaxed surroundings (omelettes £3-4; open M 9:30am-9pm, Tu-Sa 9:30am-9:30pm, Su 11am-3pm). **Tesco** also awaits on Craswell St. (tel. 839222), just off the town center, and defeats its neighbor in the freshly squeezed orange juice challenge (open M-Th 8am-8pm, F 8am-9pm, Sa 8am-7pm, Su 10am-4pm). A **Waitrose** lives in Southsea on Marmion Rd. (open M-W 8:30am-7pm, Th-F 8:30am-8pm, Sa 8:30am-7pm, Su 10am-4pm).

There is no drought of pubs to provide the weary sailor with galley fare and a bottle of gin, especially near the Hard; for a more family-oriented pub, try **The Ship & Castle,** 1-2 The Hard (tel. 832009), which boasts an extensive if slightly pricy menu that includes steaks, veggies, and Indian fare (open M-Sa 11am-11pm, Su noon-10:30pm).

SIGHTS AND ENTERTAINMENT

Portsmouth overflows with magnificent ships and seafaring relics. The bulk of sights worth seeing anchor near The Hard, delighting war buffs, intriguing historians, and looking like some pretty big boats to the rest of the world. If you fall into one of the first two categories, plunge head-first into the unparalleled **Naval Heritage Centre** (tel. 861512 or 861533), in the Naval Base. The entrance is next to the Hard tourist office—follow the brown signs to Portsmouth Historic Ships. Henry VIII's best-loved ship, the **Mary Rose** (tel. 812931), set sail from Portsmouth in July 1545 only to keel over and sink before the monarch's eyes. Not until 1982 was she raised from her watery grave. On display in a special **ship hall,** the skeletal hulk, now being continuously sprayed with a waxy preservative mixture designed to slowly dry the timber over the next 20 years, is an eerie sight. An enthralling collection of Tudor artifacts, displayed in a separate exhibition hall, gives a revealing look at 16th-century naval life. (£5.75, students and seniors £5, children £4.25.)

Two 100 ft. masts lead the way to Admiral Horatio Nelson's flagship **HMS Victory** (tel. 722351), the oldest surviving Ship of the Line. The ship won the decisive Battle of Trafalgar against the French and Spanish in 1805. *Victory* vividly portrays the dismal, cramped conditions for press-ganged recruits and contains Nelson's venerated death-bed—now a veritable shrine among members of the Royal Navy. (Only on view via a guided tour—be sure to check your admission ticket for your time slot. £5.75, students and seniors £5.25, children £4.25.) **HMS Warrior** (tel. 291379), though eclipsed by its neighbor, provides an intriguing companion to the *Victory.* The pride and joy of Queen Victoria's navy and the first iron-clad battleship in the world, *Warrior* has never seen battle. Nonetheless, a respectful Napoleon III called it "The Black Snake among the Rabbits in the Channel." (Same prices as HMS Victory.) The five galleries of the **Royal Naval Museum** (tel. 727562) fill in the historical gaps between the three ships.

The new **Dockyard 500 Exhibition** is an assemblage of fairly interesting factoids posted on the walls of a boat warehouse. Experience naval humor at its best: count the puns on the word "dock." (Open July-Aug. 10am-7pm; Mar.-June and Sept.-Oct. 10am-6pm; Nov.-Feb. 10am-5:30pm. £2.50, students and seniors £2, children £1.50. Historic Dockyard area only free.) An **All-In Supersaver** is by far the best value if you plan to see more than two attractions in Portsmouth—it includes admission to all three ships, the museum, the Dockyard 500 exhibit, the dockyard acoustaguide and a harbor water tour. (£13, students and seniors £11, children £10.) Allow about 1½ hours for each ship if you're studying to build an empire. (Ships open July-Aug. 10am-5pm; Mar.-June and Sept.-Oct. 10am-4:30pm; Nov.-Feb. 10am-4pm; last admission 1hr. before closing.)

Show up at the jetty by the tourist office for a 45-minute **guided ride.** (£3, seniors £2.50, students and children £2, families £10.) Vessels frequent **Spitbank Fort,** which has protected Portsmouth through two World Wars and remains relatively unscathed. Boats depart from the Historic Dockyard. (25min. crossing. Runs Easter-Oct.—weather permitting—Sa 1:30pm and 2:45pm, Su 2pm. £5.75, seniors £4.75, students and children £4.) At The Hard, consider taking **Portsmouth Harbour Tours' Waterbus** (tel. 822584), a more scenic way to make the trek to Southsea Esplanade. (Runs daily Easter-Oct. 10:30am-5pm. 50min. Return £3, students and children £2.) It's fun with fission at **Royal Navy Submarine Museum** (tel. 529217), at the docksite of the *HMS Alliance.* A passenger ferry (included in ticket) crosses from the Harbour continuously; or take bus #9 to Haslar Hospital. *(£5, seniors £4.75, students and children £4.)*

You may want to continue along the water's edge to Clarence Esplanade for the other side of Portsmouth's seaside sights. In the **D-Day Museum** (tel. 827261), the impressive Overlord Embroidery, a latter-day Bayeux Tapestry, recounts the invasion of France. *(Open Apr.-Oct. daily 10am-5:30pm; Nov.-Mar. M 1-5pm, Tu-Su 10am-5pm. £4.50, seniors £3.40, students and children £2.70, families £11.70. Wheelchair access.)* Don't let the garish exterior of the **Sea Life Centre** (tel. 875222) fool you—the insides reveal a finful of verve. "Don't touch the catfish. They bite!" *(Open daily in summer 10am-7pm; in winter 10am-5pm. £5.50, seniors £4.25, students and children £4.)* Also at Clarence Esplanade is **Southsea Castle** (tel. 827261), yet another coastal fortification built by Henry VIII in 1544. He could hardly bring forth a son, but God Almighty could he fortress away the sea. It's said that poor ol' Hank saw his beloved *Mary Rose* take the dive here. *(Open Apr.-Oct. daily 10am-5:30pm; Nov.-Mar. Sa-Su 10am-4:30pm. £1.70, seniors £1.40, students and children £1, under 13 free. Partial wheelchair access.)* The **Royal Marines Museum** (tel. 819385), chronicles various battles and includes a prodigious display of medals, a jungle room, and a marine in drag. *(Open daily June-Aug. 10am-5pm; Sept.-May 10am-4:30pm. £3.75, seniors £2.75, students and children £2.)* The **Natural History Museum,** in Cumberland House on East Parade, shelters bears, badgers, and, from April to September, a collection of live butterflies. *(Open daily Apr.-Oct. 10am-5:30pm; Nov.-Mar. 10am-4:30pm. Apr.-Oct. £1.60, seniors £1.30, students and children £1.15, under 13 free, families £4.35; Nov.-Mar. £1.10, 80p, 65p, and £2.85.)*

Charles Dickens was born and lived in Portsmouth briefly, and returned much later to derive inspiration for *Nicholas Nickleby.* His birthplace at 393 Old Commercial Rd., ¾ mi. north of the town station, is today an uninspired **museum** (tel. 827261). Morbidly enough, the only authentic Dickens artifacts in the Regency-style house are the couch on which he died and a lock of his precious hair. *(Open daily Apr.-Oct. 10am-5:30pm; Dec. 10am-4:30pm. £2, seniors £1.50, students and children £1.20, families £5.20.)* If Dickens disappoints, drown your sorrows at the aptly named **Oliver Twist,** a pub located at the end of Old Commercial Rd. Drink your pint and then ask for more. Feel the heat and inhale the chlorine at the **Pyramids** (tel. 799977), a series of water slides and fun pools all housed in pinnacles of power. *(Open June-July Sa-M 10am-6pm, Tu and Th 10am-7pm, W 11am-6pm, F 10am-8pm; Aug.-Sept. Sa-M 10am-8pm, Tu and Th 10am-7pm, W 11am-8pm, F 10am-8pm. £4, seniors and children £3.20, families £12.)*

Both **Southsea Common** and the well-groomed **Victoria Park** offer better opportunities for pleasant reclining than Portsmouth's be-pebbled beachfront.

■ Isle of Wight

> She thinks of nothing but the Isle of Wight and she calls it the Island, as if there were no other island in the world.
>
> —Jane Austen, Mansfield Park

Far more tranquil and sun-splashed than its mother island to the north, the Isle of Wight offers travelers dramatic scenery, beautiful sandy beaches, and relaxing family holidays. The quiet life the Isle offers has softened the hardest of hearts through the centuries, from Karl Marx, who exclaimed that "the island is a little paradise!", to Queen Victoria, who reportedly found much amusement here (and little elsewhere). Although best known for its lovely shores of stone and sand, the Isle of Wight also boasts much inland beauty.

GETTING THERE AND GETTING ABOUT

The Isle of Wight can only be reached by ferry or hovercraft. Several companies whisk travelers from the mainland. **Wight Link** ferries drift from **Lymington** to **Yarmouth** (return £7.90, children £4; day return £6.40, children £3.20), splash from **Portsmouth** and **Southsea** to **Fishbourne** (return £7.90, children £4), or sail from

Portsmouth Harbour to **Ryde** Pier (return £9.90, children £5; day return £6.75, children £3.40; half-day return £5.60, children £2.80). **Red Funnel** ferries (tel. (01703) 334010; http://www.redfunnel.co.uk) steam out of **Southampton** and dock at **West Cowes** (8-10 per day, return £6.50, children £3.90). **Hovertravel** (tel. (01705) 811000 and (01983) 811000) sails from **Southsea** to **Ryde** (9min.; 50 per day; return £9.90, children £5; day return £8.20, children £4.10).

Trains and Buses

The **train station** (tel. (0345) 484950) is located at Ryde Pier. Train service operated by British Rail covers the eastern end of the island only. **Island Line** service is limited to **Ryde, Shanklin, Sandown, Brading,** and a few points in between. **Southern Vectis** buses (tel. 827005) cover the entire island. **Travel Centres** (tel. 827005) in **Cowes, Freshwater, Ventnor, Sandown, Shanklin, Ryde,** and **Newport,** sell the complete service timetable (50p). Most people buy their tickets on board. If you plan to explore more than one island town, invest in the **Island Rover** ticket, which gives you unlimited travel on both the regular and Island Explorer open-top buses (1 day £6.25, children £3.15; 2 days £9.95, children £5; week £25.50, children £12.75).

Car and Bike Rentals

Self-Drive Minibus and Car Hire, 10 Osborne Rd., Shanklin (tel. 864263) offers free drop-off and pick-up service (open daily 8:30am-5:30pm; from £22.50 per day). **Solent Self Drive,** Marghams Garage, Crocker St., Newport and Red Funnel Terminal, West Cowes (tel. 282050 or (0800) 724734), offers daily, weekend, and weekly rates (from £27.50 per day, £48 per weekend, £165 per week). Solent also rents **mountain bikes** (£9 per day, £49 per week; £40 deposit). In Sandown stop by **Island Cycle Hire,** 17 Beachfield Rd. (tel. 407030), which rents bikes, including helmets and locks. (£5.50 per ½ day, £10 per day, £50 per week; £25 deposit plus ID. Open Apr.-Sept. daily 9am-5pm; Oct.-Mar. M-Sa 10am-5:30pm.)

ORIENTATION AND PRACTICAL INFORMATION

The Isle of Wight is shaped like a diamond, with towns clustering along its shores. The towns of **Ryde, Cowes, Sandown, Shanklin, Ventnor, Yarmouth,** and, in the center (at the origin of the River Medina), **Newport,** offer the best places to find tourist offices, accommodations, and bus service. Each **tourist office** offers an individual town map as well as the Isle of Wight "Official Pocket Guide" (free). Isle of Wight Tourism has a **general inquiry service** (tel. 862942 or 813818; fax 863047), which directs you to one of the seven regional offices listed below; call this number first. All offer accommodations services (tel. 813813).

Ryde: (tel. 562905), at the corner of Western Esplanade and Union St., opposite Ryde Pier. Open July-Aug. daily 9am-7pm; Easter-June and Sept.-Oct. daily 9am-6pm; Nov.-Easter F-M and W 10am-4pm.

Sandown: 8 High St. (tel. 403886), across from Boots Pharmacy. Open July-Aug. daily 9am-8:45pm; Easter-June and Sept.-Oct. 9am-6pm; Nov.-Mar. M-Sa 9am-5pm.

Shanklin: 67 High St. (tel. 862942). Same hours as Sandown.

Ventnor: 34 High St. (tel. 853625). Open daily Easter-Oct. 9:15am-5:15pm; call central line for winter hours.

Yarmouth: The Quay (tel. 813818). Follow the signs from the ferry stop. Open Easter-Oct. daily 9:30am-6pm; Nov.-Dec. Th-Su 10am-4pm; Jan.-Easter F-M 10am-4pm.

Newport: South St. (tel. 525450), near the bus station. Open daily July-Aug. 9:30am-6pm; Easter-June and Sept.-Oct. 6am-5:30pm; call central line for winter hours.

Cowes: Fountain Quay (tel. 291914). In the alley way next to the ferry terminal for RedJet (to Southampton). Open July-Aug. daily 9am-6pm; Apr.-June daily 9am-5pm; Jan.-Feb. Tu-Sa 10am-4pm; Cowes week (1st week in Aug.) daily 8am-8pm.

Financial Services, Emergency, and Communications

Banks and **ATMs** can be found in all of the major town centers. Make sure you stock up on cash, as banks with ATMs are rare in the smaller towns. For recorded **weather** information, call (01705) 552100. The **police** can be reached at 528000. For crisis advice, call **Samaritans** (tel. 521234). Disabled travelers seek assistance from **Disability Info** (tel. 522823). **St. Mary's Hospital** (tel. 524081) lies in Newport. There is a **post office** in every town center; the **telephone code** is 01983 for the entire island.

ACCOMMODATIONS

Accommodations on the Isle of Wight tend to stick to a 2-night-minimum rule. Prices range from decent to absurd. Budget travelers should try one of the **YHA Youth Hostels** on either end of the island or look into less-visited areas. Lodgings are also occasionally offered above **pubs**.

> **YHA Sandown,** The Firs, Fitzroy St., Sandown (tel. 402651). Offers clean, new, pleasant respite from a hard day's sunbathing. Extensive menu comes with a friendly welcome. £8.80, under 18 £6. Breakfast £3. Luggage storage available. Lockout 10am-5pm. Open June-Aug. daily; Apr.-May Tu-Su; Sept.-Oct. W-Su.
>
> **YHA Totland Bay,** Hurst Hill, Totland Bay (tel. 752165), on the west end of the island. Take Southern Vectis bus #7/7A to Totland War Memorial; turn left up Weston Rd., and take the 2nd left onto Hurst Hill. Hostel is on the left. Comfortable hostel in a fantastic location. Cliffs, walking trails, and Alum Bay are all close by. £9.75, under 18 £6.55. Open July-Aug. daily; mid-Feb. to June and Sept.-Oct. M-Sa.
>
> **Union Inn,** Cowes. Offers reasonable budget B&B in a non-budget town. Rooms have TVs and tea-making facilities. £23-25. Evening meals available £4-8.
>
> **Camping:** Check the free *Isle of Wight Camping and Touring Guide*, available from all tourist information centers; sites are plentiful. **Beaper Farm Camping Site,** Ryde (tel. 615210). £7 per tent and 2 people. Shower and laundry facilities.

SIGHTS

The image of Queen Victoria as a stern, aging monarch, perpetually in mourning, is shattered by the airy splendor and romantic dreams that still fill **Osborne House** (tel. 281784), featured in the recent film *Mrs. Brown.* Completed in 1846 under the direction of Thomas Cubitt and Victoria's husband Prince Albert himself, the house was meant to provide a family refuge from affairs of the state. Victoria used it as a long-term retreat after the Prince's death in 1861. Visitors are able to see the bedroom where she died in 1901. The house and grounds are filled with Italian sculptures and paintings, many of which portray Victoria and Albert's nine children and many grandchildren. Take a turn on the grounds that lead to the sea. A **horse-and-carriage ride** takes you to the children's **Swiss Cottage.** *(Open Apr.-Nov. daily 10am-5pm; Feb.-Mar. and Nov. to mid-Dec. by pre-booked tours only. £6.50, students and seniors £4.90, children £3.30. Grounds only, but missing the best of the site, £3.50, children £2.)* To reach Osborne House, take bus Southern Vectis bus #4 or 5 from Ryde or Newport.

In the inland town of Newport, **Carisbrooke Castle** (tel. 522107), a former Norman fortress, harkens back to the Civil War period. The castle was the 1647 prison of Charles I; see the ancient chapel where the lonely king awaited his fate. The castle museum offers a range of exhibits, including the **Tennyson Room,** which contains the poet's hat, desk, cloak, and—for the morbid—his funeral pall. *(Open daily Apr.-Oct. 10am-6pm; Nov.-Mar. 10am-4pm. £4, students and seniors £3, children £2.)*

Some of the Isle of Wight's most charming sights pre-date both Victorians and Normans. On the western tip of the island, the white chalk **Needles** jut into the dark blue sea. The third rock sports a lighthouse that was manned until 1997. A good view of the Needles can be had from **Alum Bay;** check for local cruises to see the chalk cliffs around the bay. The **Pleasure Park** may distract you from the natural beauty of the bay, but a chairlift runs down to the base of the cliffs and back. The famous colored sands, used by Victorians as pigment for painting, can now be yours in cheesy, but cute, glass ornaments. Walkers and cyclists will enjoy the coastal path stretching from nearby Totland, past lighthouses both modern and medieval at St. Catherine's Point, to St. Lawrence at the southern end of the island.

ENGLAND

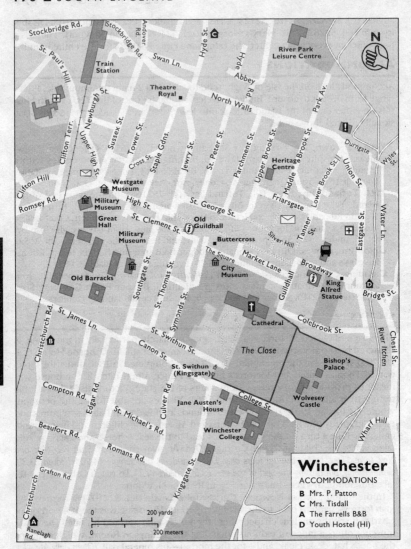

Winchester

ACCOMMODATIONS

B Mrs. P. Patton
C Mrs. Tisdall
A The Farrells B&B
D Youth Hostel (HI)

■ Winchester

Winchester's glory stretches back to Roman times when it was a walled city known as "Venta Belgarum." Both William the Conqueror and Alfred the Great deemed the town the center of their kingdoms, and monks painstakingly prepared the *Domesday Book* for William here (see **Christianity and the Normans Bust In**, p. 52). During the Great Plague of 1665, Charles II moved his court to Winchester, where he checked. up frequently on the well-being of his London properties and occasionally on the death of a third of his subjects. In the more recent past, Jane Austen and John Keats both lived and wrote in town, and Winchester was the site of inspiration for Keats's much-adored "To Autumn." Yet while its grandest days may have passed, Winchester is intent on dusting itself off. The town's 905-year-old cathedral, which has been under painstaking renovation for years, is finally ready for show. Meanwhile, newly hooked moviegoers and readers pack the Austen sights, hoping to relive the romance and intrigue of a century gone by.

GETTING THERE

Just north of Southampton, Winchester makes an excellent daytrip from **Salisbury** (25mi.) or **Portsmouth** (27mi.). **Trains** (tel. (0345) 484950) run from London's **Waterloo** Station (1hr., 2 per hr., £16, return £37.40), and leave for **Chichester** (change at Fareham; 50min., 1 per hr., £9-10), **Portsmouth** (1hr., 1 per hr., £7), and **Brighton** (1½hr., 1 per hr., £17). **National Express** (tel. (0990) 808080) runs buses to **Oxford** (2½hr., 3 per day, £9) and to **London via Heathrow** (1½hr., 7 per day, £9-13). **Hampshire** bus #68 heads to **Salisbury** (1½hr., 7 per day, return £4), #69 to **Portsmouth** (1½hr., 12 per day, return £4), and #47 to **Southampton** (50min., 2 per hr., return £3). **Explorer** tickets are available for travel in Hampshire and Wiltshire (£4.40, seniors £3.30, children £2.20, families £8.80). **Hitchers** heading to Winchester tend to approach along the A34 and M3 from north; the A33 from south; the A31, A272 or A3090 from east; and the A272 from west.

ORIENTATION

Winchester proper consists of a rough, disjointed square bounded by the **North Walls, Eastgate St.** (which runs along the River Itchen), **College St.** (which turns into Canon St.), and **Southgate St.** (which becomes Jewry St.). The **train station,** Station Hill, is northwest of the city center near the intersection of **City Rd.** and **Sussex St.** The city center is an easy 10-minute walk (down City Rd., right on Jewry St., then left on High St.). Winchester's major axis, **High St.,** is reserved for pedestrians until it passes the huge statue of Alfred the Great and transforms into **Broadway.**

PRACTICAL INFORMATION

Trains: Winchester Station, Station Hill (tel. (0345) 484950), northwest of the city center near the intersection of City Rd. and Sussex St. **Travel Centre** open M-F 9am-6pm, Sa 9am-5pm, Su 9am-4:30pm. **Ticket counter** open M-F 6am-8:30pm, Sa 6am-7:30pm, Su 7am-8:30pm.

Buses: Local buses stop at Broadway (Basingstoke tel. (01256) 464501), across from the Guildhall. National Express (tel. (0990) 808080) buses stop just outside at Alfred the Great's Statue, right down the street from the hostel. Open M 7:30am-8:30pm, Tu-F 8:30am-5:30pm.

Taxi: City Cars (tel. 853000) and **Francis Taxis** (tel. 884343) collect by the market.

Tourist Office: The Guildhall, Broadway (tel. 840500 or 848180; fax 850348), near King Alfred. Stocks free maps, seasonal *What's On* guides (10p), guides to wheelchair accessible city attractions, and city guides (£1). Helpful multilingual staff will book accommodations for £2.50 plus a 10% deposit. Open June-Sept. M-Sa 10am-6pm, Su 11am-2pm; Oct.-May M-Sa 10am-5pm. Also offers **guided tours** (May-Sept. M-Sa 2 per day, Su 1 per day; Oct. M-F 2 per day, Sa 1 per day; £2.50, children free).

Financial Services: Major banks, including **Barclays** and **Lloyds,** cluster around the junction of Jewry and High St. **ATMs** wallpaper High St. **Thomas Cook,** 30 High St. (tel. 841661 for travel information). Bureau de change. Open M-Tu and Th-Sa 9am-5:30pm, W 10am-5:30pm.

Market: Vegetables and fruits are sold by vendors on Middle Brook St. behind Marks and Spencer and across from the town library. Open W-Sa 8am-6pm.

Emergency: Dial 999; no coins required.

Police: North Walls (tel. 868100), near the intersection with Middle Brook St.

Hotlines: Samaritans (crisis), 10 Parchment St. (tel. 860633), off the pedestrian area of High St. 24hr. phone service; walk-in 8am-10pm. **Gay and Lesbian Hotline** (tel. (01703) 637363).

Hospital: Royal Hampshire County, Romsey Rd. (tel. 863535), at St. James Ln. If you find yourself here, take a peek around. Florence Nightingale helped design it.

Post Office: Middle Brook St. (tel. 854004). Turn off High St. at Marks and Spencer. Open M-Sa 9am-5:30pm. **Postal Code:** SO23 8WA.

Telephone Code: 01962.

ACCOMMODATIONS

Winchester's B&Bs cluster half a mile southwest of the tourist office, near Ranelagh Rd., on Christchurch and St. Cross Rd. Buses #29 and 47 make the journey from town center to Ranelagh Rd. (2 per hr.). Bus #69 runs the same route less frequently (1 per hr.). Many pubs also offer accommodations, but try to book early, especially in the summer. A steady stream of Londoners drives up prices all over town, making Winchester's youth hostel particularly attractive.

YHA Youth Hostel, 1 Water Ln. (tel. 853723). If you're Itchen for a river view, pass the statue of Alfred the Great, cross the bridge, and turn left before Cricketers Pub. Located in an 18th-century watermill perched atop rushing water of the River Itchen. All single-sex rooms. Expect a quick chore or two. £8.80, under 18 £6. Kitchen available. Lockout 10am-5pm. Stringent 11pm curfew. Call ahead for reservations. Open July-Aug. daily; mid-Feb. to June and Sept.-Oct. Tu-Sa; Nov. to mid-Feb. open only for groups with advance booking.

The Farrells B&B, 5 Ranelagh Rd. (tel. 869555), 10min. walk from town off Christchurch Rd. Furniture a mother would rave over in a well-kept home. The phrase "English hospitality" could have been coined for Mrs. Farrell. Tell 'em *Let's Go* sent you. Singles £18-20; doubles £18-42.

Mrs. Tisdall, 32 Hyde St. (tel. 851621), a 5min. walk from town on Jewry St., which becomes Hyde St. Conveniently located between the train station and the town center. 18th-century home with friendly proprietors. Large, comfortable rooms, and a filling breakfast, vegetarian or omnivorous. Doubles £32 (can be booked as a single for £20); 10% discount for *Let's Go* users. Laundry services available.

Mrs. P. Patton, 12 Christchurch Rd. (tel. 854272), between St. James Ln. and Beaufort Rd., 5min. from the Cathedral on a silent street of stately houses. Breakfast served near a pool in a magnificent conservatory. Graceful doubles, newly repainted and refurbished. Look for the partridge-in-a-pear-tree curtains in the bedroom on the right. Doubles £28-32; singles may be available for £20-24.

Mrs. Brett, 3 St. Michael's Rd. (tel. 861450). From High St., with your back to the cathedral, turn left onto Southgate St. and continue as it turns into St. Cross (about 10min.). Turn left onto St. Michael's Rd. Mrs. Brett's is the second on the left. Large, comfortable rooms with views of watchrabbit Theo scampering about in the greenery below. Plenty of Dick Francis mysteries to choose from. Doubles £36; singles £19 for longer stays.

Mrs. Winn, 2 N. Hill Close (tel. 864926). Comfortable, cheap rooms just up the road from the train station. The price of proximity is the dull rumble of coaches en route. Mind the teddy bears as you climb the stairs. All rooms £15.

FOOD

High St. and St. George's St. are home to several food markets, fast food venues, and tea and coffee houses. More substantial restaurants line Jewry St. **Sainsbury** (tel. 861792), at Middle Brook St. off High St., hawks groceries (open M-W 8am-6:30pm, Th 8am-7pm, F 8am-8pm). An upscale, local clientele fills **The Wykeham Arms,** 75 Kingsgate St. (tel. 853834), near the Cathedral Close. Beer mugs festoon the walls. Check out their renowned wines (lunches from £5 available M-Sa noon-2:30pm, sandwiches noon-6pm). **Chompers,** Southgate St. (tel. 860752), makes amazingly cheap and fresh sandwiches. The home-cooked turkey beats holiday leftovers, hands down (open M-F 8am-3pm). Winchester's smallest public house, the **Eclipse Inn,** The Square (tel. (01962) 865676), offers entrees from around £3.50 in a 16th-century rectory which claustrophobics should avoid (open daily 11am-11pm; food served noon-2:30pm and Su-Th 6-8:30pm). Located next to the Godbegot House off High St., **Royal Oak** (tel. 861136), despite its refurbished gleam, is another of the countless English pubs that claim fame as the kingdom's oldest. Descend into the 900-year-old subterranean foundations and enjoy several locally brewed beers (open daily 11am-11pm; food served noon-5pm; Monday night jazz in summer). Before leaving High St., fill your pack with nine crusty rolls for 99p at the **Baker's Oven. The Exchange,** 9 Southgate, boasts a wild menu, with crocodile, vegan nut, and (for the truly adventurous) beef burgers (open M-Sa 10am-11pm, Su noon-10:30pm; discounts for students and seniors). You won't care how long it rains once you step into **Noah's** (tel. 862828), on Jewry St., which features ice cream sundaes and blackboard tables for drawing (open M 9:30am-5:30pm, Tu-Sa 9:30am-10:30pm).

SIGHTS

The **Buttercross,** 12 High St., is a good starting point for a walking tour of the town. This statue of St. John, William of Wykeham, and King Alfred derives its name from the shadow it cast over the 15th-century open markets—a shadow that kept the butter cool. Duck through the archway (note the stones from William the Conqueror's palace), pass through the square, and behold the 900-year-old **Winchester Cathedral,** 5 The Close (tel. 853137). Famed for its nave, the 556 ft. long cathedral is the longest medieval building in Europe. Magnificent tiles, roped off for preservation, cover much of the floor near the chancel. **Jane Austen's tomb** rests in the northern aisle of the nave; while staring at her memorial plaque, don't walk past (or over) Jane herself buried in the floor. The stained glass window in the rear seems oddly Cubist—Cromwell's soldiers smashed the original window in the 17th century, and though the original glass pieces have been reinserted, the pattern got lost in the shuffle. *(Cathedral open daily 7:15am-6:30pm, visiting encouraged after 8:30am, East End closes at 5pm. £2.50 voluntary donation, students £2. Wheelchair access.)*

The **Norman crypt,** one of the finest (and supposedly the oldest) in England, can only be viewed in the summer by **guided tour.** *(M-Sa 10:30am, 12:30pm, and 2:30pm, water level permitting. Meet at north transept. Free.)* The crypt contains the statues of two of Winchester's most famous figures: Bishop William of Wykeham, founder of Winchester College, and St. Swithun, patron saint of weather. St. Swithun was interred inside the cathedral against his will; in retaliation, the saint brought torrents down on the culprits for 40 days. Supposedly, if it rains July 15 (St. Swithun's Day), it will rain for the next 40 days, and it might anyway.

The **Triforium Gallery** at the south transept contains several relics, including 14th-century altar-screen figures. The 12th-century *Winchester Bible* resides in the library. *(Open Easter-Oct. M 2-4pm, Tu-Sa 10am-noon and 2-4pm; Nov.-Feb. W 11am-2:30pm and Sa 11am-3:30pm; book before arriving—gallery subject to unannounced closures. £1, students 50p.)*

The **West Gate Museum** (tel. 869864), at the top of High St., was the medieval gateway to the city and, more recently, a prison. The museum houses a painted wooden Tudor ceiling and prisoners' inscriptions. Look for the bitter epitaph: "Here lies Thomas, an example of the terrible inconstancy of human things." *(Open Apr.-Sept. M-F 10am-5pm, Sa 10am-1pm and 2-5pm, Su 2-5pm; Feb.-Mar. and Oct. Tu-Su; closed Nov.-Jan. 30p, seniors and children 20p. No wheelchair access.)* Beside the close, the **Winchester City Museum** (tel. 863064) flaunts Roman relics and mannequins of Winchester tobacconists. *(Open Apr.-Sept. M-Sa 10am-5pm, Su 2-5pm; Oct.-Mar. Tu-Sa. Free. Limited wheelchair access.)* Southward, tiny **St. Swithun's Chapel,** rebuilt in the 16th century, nestles above **King's Gate,** one of two surviving city gates (the other is West Gate).

King's Gate leads to prestigious **Winchester College** (tour booking tel. 621217), founded in 1382 as England's first "public" school. Most of the 14th-century buildings remain intact. *(Tours £2.50, seniors and children £2.)* Across from the YHA begins a beautiful walk along the **River Itchen** visited by poet John Keats; directions and his poem "To Autumn" are available at the tourist office for 50p. Further along the walk lies St. Cross's Hospital. The Norman bishop used to live in **Wolvesey Castle** (tel. 854766), down College St. You can see most of the ruins from the entrance without paying, although the guides inside the site are informative. *(Open daily Apr.-Oct. 10am-6pm. £1.80, students and seniors £1.40, children 90p.)*

At the end of High St. atop Castle Hill, Henry III built his castle on the remains of an earlier fortress sponsored by William the Conqueror. The fortress was a haunt for royals, including Henry V who lodged here with his happy few en route to Agincourt. What remains is the **Great Hall,** containing a Round Table, modeled after King Arthur's and dated six centuries after his legendary reign. Henry VIII tried to pass it off as such to Holy Roman Emperor Charles V, and had the table painted with an

"Arthur" resembling Henry himself. *(Open daily Mar.-Oct. 10am-5pm. Free.)* Just through **Queen Eleanor's Garden,** in the Peninsula Barracks, five **military museums** detail the story of the city and the country's military power. The **Royal Greenjackets Museum** (tel. 863846) features a 10 by 20 ft. diorama and audio presentation of the Battle of Waterloo; for 10p, fire a couple more shots into the diorama. *(Open M-Sa 10am-1pm and 2-5pm, Su noon-4pm; hours for the other military museums vary. £2.)*

ENTERTAINMENT

Weekend nights attract hordes of artists and teenagers to bars along Broadway and High St. **Muswell's,** Jewry St., draws the 18-30 crowd on Fridays and Saturdays. *(Open daily 11am-11pm.)* **Mash Tun** (tel. 861440), on Eastgate St., packs in the youngsters with shagadelic paintings and funky music. *(Open daily noon-11pm.)* **Barringtons** (tel. 855111), at Colebrook St. and High St. across from the hostel, filters hundreds of students indoors and onto a riverside patio. *(Open M-Sa 11am-midnight, Su noon-10:30pm.)*

If the British weather won't let you stay dry anyway, go aquatic at **River Park Leisure Center** (tel. 869525). The park offers a huge pool and **Twister the Water Slide,** free with the price of a swim. *(£1.80, students, seniors, children, and disabled 95p.)* Twister will make you rue the day you left your bathing suit at home.

With its Edwardian glory, the **Theatre Royal,** Jewry St., hosts regional theatrical companies and concerts; the theater should reopen in new-found splendor in early 1999. A **Folk Festival** comes in the last weekend of April. In early July, the **Hat Fair** fills a weekend with theater, street performances, and peculiar headgear.

■ Near Winchester

Jane Austen lived in the meek village of **Chawton,** 15 mi. northeast of Winchester, from 1809 to 1817. Here she penned *Pride and Prejudice, Emma, Northanger Abbey,* and *Persuasion.* The number of visitors to her former **cottage** (tel. (01420) 83262), which displays many of her belongings, has supposedly quadrupled since the recent release of film versions of several of Austen's novels. The door was purposefully left creaky to warn Jane so she could hide her manuscript in her needlework basket. *(Open Mar.-Dec. daily 11am-4:30pm; Jan.-Feb. Sa-Su 11am-4:30pm. £2.50, under 18 50p. Wheelchair access.)* Take **Hampshire** bus #X64 (tel. (01256) 464501; M-Sa 11 per day, return £4.50). On Sundays take **London and Country** bus #65. Ask to be let off at Chawton roundabout and follow the brown signs.

Just outside Romsey, a small town southwest of Winchester along the A31, lies the Palladian mansion **Broadlands** (tel. (01794) 505010), once home to the Victorian Prime Minister Lord Palmerston and the late Lord Mountbatten—the philandering last Viceroy of India, uncle of Prince Philip. You can experience the uncanny sensation of being inside a piece of china in the Wedgewood room. *(Open mid-June to mid-Sept. noon-5:30pm; last admission 4pm. £5, students and seniors £4.25, under 12 £3.50.)*

The **New Forest,** 20 mi. southwest of Winchester, was William the Conqueror's 145 sq. mi. personal hunting ground. The **Rufus Stone** (near Brook and Cadnam) marks the spot where his son, William Rufus, was accidentally slain. Today ponies, donkeys, cows, and deer frolic freely. During the week, take bus #66 to Romsey (1 per hr.) and change from there; on Sundays take bus #X66 (mid-May to mid-Sept 3 per day, return £4.10). The New Forest also has a **Museum and Visitor Centre,** High St., Lyndhurst (tel. (01703) 282269). Contact the center for a list of campsites. *(Open daily 10am-6pm. £2.50, seniors £2, children £1.50, families £6.50. Wheelchair access.)*

■ South Downs Way

The windswept slopes and chalk cliffs of the South Downs Way hide the footprints of millennia. Once stretching through to the Continent, the sparse soil and light vegetation of the Downs provided the only land prehistoric tribes could cultivate. Forts and settlements dot the paths of Bronze and Iron Age tribes, who were followed by Celts,

Romans, Saxons, and Normans. This is fertile ground for legend; from *Domesday* to A.A. Milne, the Downs have borne words as prodigiously as downland flowers.

The South Downs Way stretches from Eastbourne west towards Portsmouth and Winchester, never far from coastal metropoles yet rarely crossing civilization's edge. Robbed of some of its pastoral innocence during the air raids of World War II, the Way nonetheless remains a ribbon of salt-sprayed, sheep-watched timelessness.

GETTING THERE AND GETTING ABOUT

Trains (tel. (0345) 484950) run every hour from London's **Victoria** (£16.90) to **Eastbourne.** Trains also connect London's **Waterloo** to **Petersfield,** at the intersection of Forty Acre Ln. and the B2146 (every 2hr., £14.50). From other cities in the east, change at **Ashford** (ticket counter open M-F 6:15am-9pm, Sa-Su 6:50am-9pm). From the west, take a train to **Amberly** (via Horsham), where the Way greets the River Arun. Eastbourne's helpful **Bus Stop Shop** (tel. 416416), Arndale Centre, dispenses information on local services to get you to the Way. From the train station, turn left onto the crowded Terminus Rd.; the Centre is on the left (open M-Sa 9am-5pm).

Walking the entire path takes about 10 days, but public transportation makes it possible to walk just a segment of the trail. Catch a bus or train to one of the major southeastern towns, such as Eastbourne, where local buses #3 or 8 will drop you off at the foot of the way. **County Bus** #126 runs (5 per day, £2.20) from Eastbourne to **Alfriston** (35min.) and **Wilmington** (25min.). You can take a **train** to **Lewes,** where frequent rail service (about 3 per hr.) will connect you to **Southease;** or take a bus from Lewes to **Kingston** (#123, 10min., 6 per day) or **Rodmell** (#123, 20min., 1 per day). All local bus fares are under £2 return. For bus schedules, call Eastbourne Buses (tel. 416416) or East Sussex County Busline (tel. (01273) 474747).

Cycling has long been a popular alternative means of seeing the downlands: D.H. Lawrence cycled the Way in 1909, visiting his friend Rudyard Kipling. Except for a brief section of the way stretching from Alfriston to Eastbourne, and the western section between Brighton and Winchester, cycling and horseback riding are permitted. **Winton Street Farm Stables,** Winton St., Alfriston (tel. 870089), and **Audiburn Riding Stables,** Ashcombe Ln., Kingston, Lewes (tel. 474398), conducts guided one-hour horseback tours (£10 per person). Both farms run several tours daily. If you plan to cycle, gear up in one of the larger towns, as cycle rentals along the Way are rare (£18 per day). Beware of chalk dust.

PRACTICAL INFORMATION

Serious hikers will want to begin their exploration of the Way in **Eastbourne,** the official start of the Way, which offers accommodations and local services. Travelers looking for a shorter excursion along the Way may choose to base themselves in the larger cities of **Brighton** (see p. 159) and **Chichester** (see p. 167).

Tourist Offices
Eastbourne: Cornfield Rd. (tel. 411400). Provides vague maps (free) and detailed Ordnance Survey 1:50,000 Maps (#16, 17, 198, and 199 are the most useful; around £5). Also sells a number of guides (see below). Open M-Sa 9am-6pm, Su 10am-1pm.
Lewes: 187 High St. (tel. 483448). Books rooms, and provides leaflets and Ordnance Survey maps. Open M-F 9am-5pm, Sa 10am-5pm; summer also Su 10am-2pm.

Financial Services
Eastbourne: All major banks are located in the town center, and **ATMs** are numerous. Be sure to pick up your sterling before hitting the trail. **Thomas Cook,** 101 Terminus Rd. (tel. 725431). Open M-Tu and Th-Sa 9am-5:30pm, W 10am-5:30pm.

Guidebooks and Printed Information
Eastbourne tourist office: *On Foot in East Sussex* (£3.20) and *Along the South Downs Way* (£5) are most useful for trekkers; *Exploring East Sussex* (£2) lists various guided walks and cycle rides (many walks and rides are free; some ask for a £1-

ENGLAND

2 donation); *The South Downs Way* photocopied edition (£2) offers information on accommodations.

Waterstone's Booksellers, 120 Terminus Rd., Eastbourne (tel. 735676), around the corner from the tourist office. Offers a comprehensive, if slightly pricey, selection of books about the Way. Open M-Sa 9am-5:30pm.

Eastbourne Central Library (tel. 434206). Stocks Ordnance Survey Maps, but they circulate, so you may not find the one you want. Open M-Tu and Th-F 9:30am-6:30pm, Sa 9:30am-5pm.

Camping and Hiking Supplies

Safeway, High St., Eastbourne. Conveniently located about halfway between the hostel (see **Accommodations,** p. 182) and the center of town. Open M-Th 8am-8pm, F 8am-9pm, Sa 8am-7pm, Su 10am-4pm.

Millets Leisure, 151 Terminus Rd., Eastbourne (tel. 728340). Stocks last-minute camping supplies. Open M-Sa 9am-5:30pm.

Telephone Codes

Eastbourne and Alfriston: 01323
Lewes: 01273

ACCOMMODATIONS

The tourist offices in **Brighton, Chichester, Lewes,** and **Eastbourne** can supply information on accommodations and points of interest. There are few towns along the Way, and B&Bs fill quickly, especially in the summer. (One wedding in Lewes can fill all rooms within a 12mi. radius.) Consider making daytrips along parts of the Way, especially from Brighton. If you're looking for B&B in one of the larger towns, try Brighton or Southcliff Ave. in Eastbourne. **Camping** on the Way is permitted with the landowner's permission. Fortunately, the following four **YHA Hostels** lie along or near the Way, each within a day's walk of the next. Be sure to call at least a week ahead; the hostels are often full at the same time. For other hostels near the Way, check the **Accommodations** sections in Brighton (p. 160), or Arundel (p. 165).

Eastbourne: East Dean Rd., Eastbourne, East Sussex BN20 8ES (tel./fax 721081). Converted golf clubhouse on the A259 between South Downs Way and the Seven Sisters, about 3mi. from Beachy Head. From Eastbourne Station, turn right and follow the A259 (marked Seaford/Brighton) for 1½mi.; even pro cyclists gasp at the steep hill leading to the hostel. Buses #711 and 712 depart from Shelter H on Terminus Rd., just left of the station (return £1.40). Spare, clean rooms with bunks. £8, under 18 £5.40. Breakfast only. Lockout 10am-5pm. Curfew 11pm. Open July-Sept. daily; Apr.-June W-M; closed Oct.-Mar. **Camping** in the woods.

Alfriston: Frog Firle, Alfriston, Polegate, East Sussex BN26 5TT (tel. 870423; fax 870615). 1½mi. from the Way and from Alfriston, 8mi. from Eastbourne. At the market cross, turn left at the sign marking "South Downs Way" and pass the village green toward the White Bridge. Follow the overgrown riverside path to Litlington footbridge and turn right along the path; the hostel is at the end of the path in a stone house with bovine neighbors. Authentic Tudor wood. £8.80, under 18 £6. Lockout 10am-5pm. Curfew 11pm. Open July-Aug. daily; Feb.-June and Sept.-Oct. M-Sa; Nov.-Dec. F-Sa; closed Jan.

Telescombe: Bank Cottages, Telescombe, Lewes, East Sussex BN7 3HZ (tel. 301357). 2mi. from Way, 12mi. from Alfriston. 18th-century house. £7.20, under 18 £5. Lockout 10am-5pm. Curfew 11pm. Open July-Aug. daily; Easter-June Th-M.

Truleigh Hill: Tottington Barn, Truleigh Hill, Shoreham-by-Sea, West Sussex BN43 5FB (tel. (01903) 813419; fax 812016). At the center of the Way, 10mi. from Brighton. Modern building on 4½ acres. £8.80, under 18 £6. Breakfast £2.85, dinner £4.25. Curfew 11pm. Open June-Sept. daily; Apr.-May M-Sa.

HIKING THE SOUTH DOWNS WAY

Eastbourne to Alfriston

The best place to begin walking the Way is the Victorian seaside city of **Eastbourne,** which lives in the shelter of **Beachy Head,** the official starting point of the path. If you plan to start hiking immediately, the open-topped bus #3, from Terminus Rd. in Eastbourne, will bring you to the top of **Beachy Head,** for a pricey £1.80 (Su-F 7 per day). You can save money and gain scenic vistas by asking to be let off at the bottom of Beachy Head and climbing it yourself. (No beach here: *beau chef* means "fine headland.") Make the strenuous ascent and follow the fields ever upward past some inquisitively bent trees and an inordinate amount of bunny doo-doo to reach the cliffs. South Downs Way officially begins at a marker just past the cliff-observing fences. Beachy Head itself, 543 ft. above the sea, is reputed by mountaineers to have the same vertiginous effects as Alpine ridges. Visible from Beachy Head is the west-ward coterie of the **Seven Sisters,** a series of chalk ridges surpassing the Head in maj-esty. The queenly sisters hold court about 4½ mi. away, over a windswept series of hills. The path winds past a number of *tumuli*—the burial mounds of Bronze Age peoples constructed around 1500 BC—but the overgrown bush makes them impos-sible to distinguish. To reach **Alfriston,** follow the Way 4 mi. over a path reputedly used by smugglers who docked among the cliffs. You can also take bus #711 or 712 from Terminus Rd. (35min., M-Sa 6 per day, £2).

If the salt air tends to get you seasick, try the shorter **bridleway path** to Alfriston (8mi., as opposed to the 11mi. coastal jaunt). The bridleway can be joined from a path just below the hostel and passes through the village of **Wilmington** and by its famous **Long Man,** a 260 ft. earth sculpture of mysterious origins. Attributed to pre-historic peoples, Romans, 14th-century monks, and aliens, the Long Man is best viewed from a distance and is almost invisible when you first come over his hillside on the Way. It is rumored that Victorian prudes robbed the fellow of male attributes that might have elucidated his name. Proceeding back through the Long Man's gate and onto the South Downs Way path over Windover Hill will lead you to **Alfriston,** a sleepy one-road village called "the last of the old towns." The center of this one-time smuggler's den features a **market cross**—a stone marker erected in Henry IV's day as a symbol of fair trading.

Alfriston to Forty Acre Lane

From Alfriston town center you can pick up the Way behind the Star Inn, on High St. (the *only* street), and continue 7 mi. to **Southease** among hills so green and vast, one might fear Julie Andrews lurks tunefully over the next ridge. The Way directly crosses **Firle Beacon,** with a mound at the top which is said to contain a giant's silver coffin. Reaching Southease, proceed north ¾ mi. to **Rodmell.** A Merchant-Ivory set of a town, Rodmell's single street contains **Monk's House,** home of Leonard and Virginia Woolf from 1919 until each of their deaths. Thanks to the National Trust, the house retains its intimacy and most of the original furnishings. Virginia's bedroom contains a fireplace with tiles painted by Vanessa Bell. The faithful can retrace the writer's last steps to the River Ouse (1mi.), where she committed "the one experience I shall never describe"; her ashes nourish a fig tree in the garden. *(House open Apr.-Oct. W and Sa 2-5:30pm; £2.50, children £1.25, families £15.)* For information, call the regional National Trust office (tel. (01892) 890651). The **Telescombe Youth Hostel** (see **Accommodations,** p. 182) lies 1 mi. south of Rodmell.

The closest that the Way actually comes to **Lewes** (LOO-iss) is at the village of **Kingston** to the southwest. A stone at the parish boundary, called **Nan Kemp's corner,** feeds one of the more macabre Downs legends: townspeople whisper that a woman named Nan Kemp, jealous of her husband's affection for their newborn, roasted it for him to eat, then killed herself at the site of the present stone. From here, continue on a long stretch of the Way from Kingston to **Pyecombe** (8mi.), which will bring you to **Ditchling Beacon,** the highest point in East Sussex's Downs. The hill was one in a series that relayed the message of the defeat of the Spanish Armada to Elizabeth I.

Ambling from Pyecombe to **Upper Beeding** (another 8mi.) brings you to **Devil's Dyke,** a dramatic chalk cliff that looks like a cross-section cut out of a hillside. Local legend says that the Dyke was built by Lucifer himself to let the sea into the Weald and float away all Christian churches. The Prince of Darkness was interrupted by the light of an old woman's candle, which—in a moment of diabolic weakness—he thought was the sun. On the path from Upper Beeding to **Washington** lies the grove of **Chanctonbury Ring**—trees planted in the 18th century around a 3rd-century Roman template, built on a previous Celtic one. The ring is visible from miles around.

Completing the 6½ mi. trek from Washington to **Amberly** brings you to a path leading to **Burpham,** from which the **YHA Warningcamp** (see **Accommodations,** p. 165) is accessible by a 3 mi. walk. The 19 mi. of orchids and spiked rampion fields from Amberly to **Buriton,** passing through **Cocking,** complete the Way to the northwest. Southward, across the River Arun to **Littleton Down** are views of the Weald and occasionally the North Downs. The spire of Chichester Cathedral marks the beginning of **Forty Acre Lane,** the final arm of the Way which reaches out to touch the West Sussex/Hampshire border. ·

Southwest England

Mists of legend shroud the counties of Dorset, Devon, and Cornwall in England's **West Country.** King Arthur was allegedly born at Tintagel on Cornwall's northern coast and is said to have battled Mordred on Bodmin Moor. One hamlet purports to be the site of Camelot, another village claims to be the resting place of the Holy Grail, and no fewer than three small lakes are identified as the final resting place of Arthur's sword, Excalibur. The ghost of Sherlock Holmes still pursues the Hound of the Baskervilles across Dartmoor and St. Michael's Mount at Marazion is believed to have held the terrible giant Cormoran hostage in its well.

It is easy to lose the spirit of legend among "King Arthur" parking lots, "Mayflour" bake shops, and the smoke of industrial cities like Bristol and Plymouth. Still, the terrain is unfailingly beautiful. Stretches of sand blend with pointed cliffs along the Cornwall coastline, while the heathered moors of Devon softly capture the eye.

Legends aside, the West Country's hills have been a place of refuge for several distinct peoples, all of whom left their mark on land and culture. Bronze Age barrows (burial mounds), Stone Age quoits (chamber tombs), and megaliths of unknown purpose litter the countryside. The Celts maintained a stronghold in Cornwall even as the Saxons and Normans overran the rest of the country. Their language, Cornish, held out tenaciously against English for years. Though the last native speaker of Cornish died several decades ago, a few committed souls are attempting a revival. Today, this fabled region often seems overrun by sheep and tourists, but its lazily rolling hills and salty sea air provide a refreshing change from fast-paced city rhythms.

🐚 HIGHLIGHTS OF SOUTHWEST ENGLAND

- Don't miss **Exeter,** Southwest England's most vibrant city. The local citizenry maintains with an energetic university lifestyle amid a slew of historical attractions (see p. 193).
- King Arthur is said to have lived in Cornwall, and tales of Camelot and the Knights of the Round Table still echo across **Bodmin Moor** (p. 206). See the site of Arthur's death near Camelford, or take a trip back in time at **Tintagel** (p. 207).
- Slip through salt water at **Newquay** (p. 216), Britain's most terrifically trashy surf resort. The international backpacker crowd hits the beach harder than the waves by day, and parties harder still by night.

GETTING THERE AND GETTING ABOUT

Unfortunately, no single rail or bus pass covers all of the worthwhile spots in the region, and many of the more remote towns are accessible only by local buses. Select a pass that best suits your itinerary, but realize that at times you may find yourself taking a local bus (usually under £3), renting a bike, or walking to a spot of interest. Buses are few and far between, so plan carefully.

Trains and Buses

British Rail (tel. (0345) 484950) offers fast and frequent service from London and the North. The region's primary east-west line from London's **Paddington** Station passes through **Taunton, Exeter** (2½hr., 2 per hr., £41), **Plymouth** (3½hr., 1 per hr., £52), and **Truro,** ending at **Penzance** (5½hr., 6 per day, £53). The north-south line from **Glasgow** and **Edinburgh** (M-Sa 1 per day) passes through Bristol, Taunton, and Exeter before ending at Plymouth; it may be easier to travel through London. Branch lines connect St. Ives, Newquay, Falmouth, and Barnstaple to the network.

Special fares make rail travel competitive with bus travel; ask about cheap day-return fares which, as elsewhere in Britain, are often only marginally more expensive than single fares. British Rail offers a variety of **Rail Rover passes** in the West Country: the **Freedom of the Southwest Rover** allows 8 days of unlimited travel within a 15

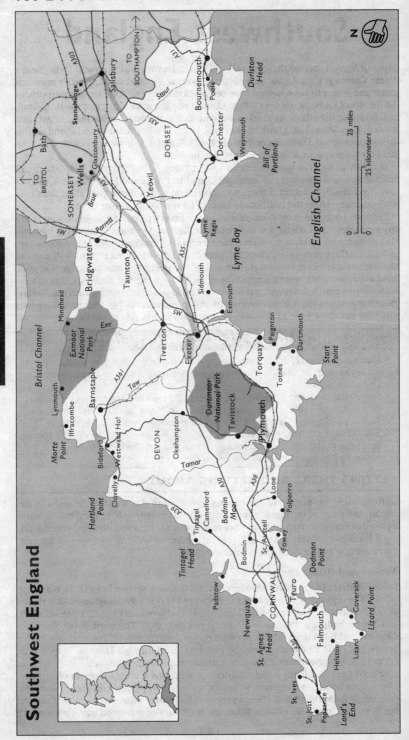

Southwest England

day period in the area from Bristol Parkway through Salisbury and down to Weymouth, covering all of Cornwall, Devon, Somerset, and part of Avon and Dorset (£59). The **Devon Rail Rover** is bounded by and includes the Taunton-to-Exmouth line on the east and the Gunnislake-Plymouth line in the west (£23 for 3 days of travel in 7, £38 for 8 days in 15). The **Cornish Rail Rover** is bounded by and includes the Gunnislake-Plymouth line (£17.50 3 days in 7, £32 for 8 days in 15). For information, call **National Rail Inquiries** (tel. (0345) 484950).

National Express buses (tel. (0990) 808080) run to major points along the north coast via Bristol and to points along the south coast (including **Penzance**) via **Exeter** and **Plymouth.** For journeys within the region, local bus service is less expensive and more extensive than the local trains, and passes through towns too small to have train stations. All the large regional bus companies—**Western National** (in Cornwall and south Devon; tel. (01752) 222666 in Plymouth, (01209) 719988 in Camborne), **Southern National** (in Somerset and West Dorset), **Devon General,** and the **Badgerline** (in Avon and Somerset; tel. (0117) 955 3231)—offer **Explorer** or **Day Rambler** tickets, which allow a full day's travel on any bus within their region for £4-6. The aptly named **Key West** ticket (£22.65) is good on all Devon and Cornwall routes for a week; there is also a three-day ticket for £13.40. Phone ahead in the off season; branch-line rail service on Sundays shuts down for the winter, and many bus lines don't run between September and March.

Hiking and Biking

In southwestern England, distances between towns are so short that it is feasible to travel through the region on your own steam. The narrow roads and hilly landscape can make biking difficult, but hardy cyclists will find the quiet lanes and countryside rewarding terrain. If you're walking or cycling, on- or off-road, bring along a large-scale Ordnance Survey map and an impregnable windbreaker to shield you from foul weather. If you'll be hiking through countryside, it is important to respect the property of local residents whose livelihood depends on the land you're crossing.

The longest coastal path in England, the **South-West Peninsula Coast Path,** originates in Dorset and passes through South Devon, Cornwall, and North Devon, ending in Somerset. The path, which takes several months to walk in its entirety, winds past cliffs, caves, beaches, ports, and resort colonies. Walkers should expect to run into herds of sheep and hordes of tourists. Many rivers intersect the path on their way to the sea, so you will have to take a ferry or wade through the crossings. Check times carefully to avoid being stranded. Some sections of the trail are difficult enough to dissuade all but the most ambitious; check your route with a tourist official before you set out to make sure that the area you want to visit is well-marked.

The path is divided into four parts based on the national parks and counties through which it passes. The **Dorset Coast Path,** stretching from Lyme Regis to Poole Harbor, can be negotiated in a few days, and accommodations and eats can be found along the way. Ordnance Survey Maps 1:50,000: 193, 194, 195 and *Purbeck Outdoor Leisure Map* will enable you to plan your route. The **South Devon Coast Path** picks up near Paighton and continues through Plymouth, winding around spectacular cliffs, wide estuaries, and remote bays set off by lush vegetation and wildflowers. The **Cornwall Coast Path,** which includes some of the most rugged stretches of the route, starts in Plymouth (a ferry service takes you on to Cremyll), rounds the southwestern tip of Britain, and continues up the northern Atlantic coast to Bude. The magnificent Cornish cliffs in this stretch of the path harbor a vast range of birds and sea life. The final section, the **Somerset and North Devon Coastal Path,** extends from Bude through Exmoor National Park to Minehead (p. 199). The least arduous of the four sections, it still offers magnificent coastal scenery in North Devon and the highest seaside cliffs in southwestern England.

Most of the path is smooth enough to cover on a bike; often bike rental shops will suggest three-day to week-long routes along the coast. Journeys of any length are possible along all parts of the path, as buses serve most points along the route, and youth hostels and B&Bs are spaced at 5 to 25 mi. intervals along it. The Countryside Commission and most tourist offices sell extremely useful guides and Ordnance Survey maps covering each section of the path (see **By Hiking Trail,** p. 37).

ENGLAND

THE DORSET COAST

■ Dorchester

Every city has its favorite children, but in Dorchester, Thomas Hardy is an only son. Those who live here indulge his spirit, perhaps to the point of spoiling it. Before draining a pint, grayed gentlemen in pubs will tell you handed-down stories about the author whose statue soberly overlooks the town's main street. It seems every business here—from inns to shoe stores—manages to incorporate "Hardy" into its name. Those travelers not Hardy-hooked will hardly be hooked on Dorchester. Today, the inspiration for the novelist's "Casterbridge" is a sleepy city that has seen more prosperous times. But Dorchester *is* far from the madding crowd; ramblers and cyclists will enjoy the sloping hills, and the Neolithic and Roman oddities outside of town.

GETTING THERE

The county seat of Dorset, Dorchester is 120 mi. southwest of London. **Trains** (tel. (0990) 808080) leave **South Station** for points north and east, including London's **Waterloo** (2½hr., 14 per day, £32, return £33). Trains from **West Station** leave for **Weymouth** (15min., 20 per day, £2.40, return £3). The **Wilts & Dorset bus** (tel. 673555) connects Dorchester with Salisbury (change at Blandsford; 4 per day with the first bus leaving Salisbury Station at 8:50am, £4.50). **Dorchester Coachways**, Grove Trading Estate (tel. 262992), provides service within the local perimeter. **National Express** (tel. (0990) 808080) sends buses to London's **Waterloo** (£17.50-21) and Exeter (£8-10); tickets sold at the tourist office. Those **hitching** from Salisbury to Dorchester take the A354 to the A35; from Exeter, the A30 to the A35. From Dorchester to London, most walk down High West St. and over Greys Bridge.

ORIENTATION AND PRACTICAL INFORMATION

The intersection of **High West** with **South St.** (which eventually becomes Cornhill St.) serves as the unofficial center of town. The main **shopping district** extends southward along South St. **Trains** (tel. (0345) 484950), which stop at **Dorchester South** (information and ticket agent open M-Sa 6am-8pm) and **Dorchester West** (buy your tickets on the train), are located off Weymouth Ave., which runs southwest from the bottom of South St. Rent a bike at **Dorchester Cycles**, 31a Great Western Rd. (tel. 268787; open M-Sa 9am-5:30pm; £7.50 per day, £37.50 per week; deposit £50).

To reach the **tourist office**, 11 Antelope Walk (tel. 267992), from South Station, walk straight out of the station onto Weymouth Ave. Cross Great Western Rd. onto South St. and continue up almost until the top of the street, where you'll see a leaping antelope. Make a left onto Antelope Walk; the office is at the end, on the left. To reach the tourist office from West Station, turn right onto Great Western Rd. and then left onto South St. The office sells helpful maps and walking tour guides for 10p-£5 (open Apr.-Oct. M-Sa 9am-5pm, Su 10am-3pm; Nov.-Mar. M-Sa 9am-4pm). Guided walking **tours** leave from the tourist office (mid-June to mid-Sept. M 3pm; £2, students and seniors £1.75, under 16 free).

Sightsee and **change currency** at the same time: **Barclays,** 10 South St., operates in a house where Hardy's Mayor of Casterbridge supposedly lived (open M-F 9:30am-5pm, Sa 9:30am-noon). **ATMs** are scattered along High St. **Market Day** extravaganza is Wednesday, in the parking lot near Dorchester South rail station (open 8am-3pm). The **police** (tel. 251212) can be found on Weymouth Ave. The local **West Dorset Hospital** (tel. 251150) is on Dames Rd. The **post office**, 43 South St. (tel. 251093), changes currency and accepts *poste restante* (open M-Sa 9am-5:30pm). Dorchester's **postal code** is DT1 1DH; the **telephone code** is 01305.

ACCOMMODATIONS AND FOOD

Dorchester has no youth hostels. The nearest **YHA Hostel** is several miles away at **Litton Cheney** (tel. (01308) 482340; £7.20, under 18 £5; open Apr.-Aug. Tu-Su). Lodging in Dorchester is pricey (£15-18) at the town's scattered boarding houses and pubs. Try the **Royal Oak** (tel. 269440), on High West St. (£19.50), or inquire at the tourist office. None is especially plush, and most have only two rooms. Try to call ahead, especially for scarce singles.

Maumbury Cottage, 9 Maumbury Rd. (tel. 266726). Close to Dorchester West station and 5min. from Dorchester South station, kind Mrs. Wade keeps 1 cozy single, 1 double, and 1 twin. Lucky guests will hear personal Hardy stories and get a free tour of town. "Jolly good breakfasts." £16.

The Old House at Home, Salisbury St. (tel. 268909). Just off High East St. by the Jehovah's Witness building, the Stephensons greet guests in their historic home, which operated as a pub for well over 200 years. Enjoy an outstanding breakfast (they cater on the side). Immaculate, but few rooms. 2 doubles, 1 with bath. £30-38; rooms can be booked as singles for £18-20.

Mountain Ash, 30 Mountain Ash Rd. (tel. 264811). Head up High West St. through the roundabout, turn right onto St. Thomas Rd. at the Sidney Arms, and take your first left onto Mountain Ash Rd.; it's on the left. Mrs. Priddle owns a well-kept home with recently refurbished rooms. 1 single and 2 doubles. £15-18 per person.

Camping: Giant's Head Caravan and Camping Park, Old Sherborne Rd., Cerne Abbas (tel. (01300) 341242), 8mi. north of Dorchester. Head out of town on The Grove, bear right onto Old Sherborne Rd. 2 people and tent £5-7, depending on the season. Open Apr.-Oct.

The eateries along High West and High East St. provide a range of options. An unusually large number of bakeries also lurk in the alleys off South St. **Mount Stevens** on High St. offers 8 kinds of fruit scones for £1.10. Heed the warning to "duck or grouse" when entering the **King's Arms,** 30 High East St., then sit and have a pint in this historic inn, featured in Hardy's *Mayor of Casterbridge.* If dainty tea is more to your liking, head in the opposite direction on High West St. **The Old Tea House** makes delicious lunches and teas for under £3. Also in the area, the **Potter In** (it's a pun, not a typo), 19 Durngate St. (tel. 260312), serves tasty treats, including homemade ice cream, ranging in flavor from gooseberry to turtle. Enjoy your snack while sunning on the secluded patio (open M-Sa 9:30am-5pm; July-Aug. also Su 11am-4pm). **Waitrose Supermarket** rests in the Tudor Arcade off South St. (open M-W and Sa 8:30am-6pm, Th-F 8:30am-8pm; in summer also Su 10am-4pm).

SIGHTS AND ENTERTAINMENT

Dorchester's half-dozen Hardy attractions can't quite compete with the compelling sights in the hills just outside of town. Two vastly different periods collide in the countryside, Roman Britain and Hardy's Wessex. The traveler with a taste for adventure and, preferably, a bike, can negotiate both in a day. In town, at the **Dorset County Museum,** 66 High West St. (tel. 262735), a replica of Hardy's study shines among the relics of Dorchester's other keepers—the Druids, Saxons, and Romans. *(Open M-Sa 10am-5pm; July-Aug. also Su; £3, students and seniors £2.50, children £1.50.)* Before hitting the high road to visit the more pastoral sites of Hardy's youth, take a walk to **Max Gate** (tel. 262538), a home that Hardy, who studied to be an architect, designed and occupied at Arlington Ave. and Syward Rd. *Tess of the D'Urbervilles* and *Jude the Obscure* were written here. *(Drawing room and garden open Apr.-Sept. Su-M and W 2-5pm. £2, children £1.)*

Next stop on the Hardy adventure is the ever-so-small **Stinsford Church** to the northeast of town in Stinsford Village. Follow the London Rd. which eventually becomes Stinsford Hill. At the roundabout, proceed straight ahead, and after crossing to the continuation of Stinsford Rd., take the first right. Follow the road over the hill; the churchyard will be straight ahead. Hardy was christened in the church and his

ENGLAND

family plot can be found in the yard. Oddly, Hardy's desire to be entombed in the shadow of the tiny church was satisfied only in part—his heart alone is buried there, for his ashes rest in Westminster Abbey (see p. 96). Alongside the Hardy heart rests the poet Cecil Day Lewis, who asked to be buried near the beloved author.

Scattered ruins outside of town testify to Dorchester's status as a former Roman stronghold. Just past the entrance to the Dorchester South railway station on Weymouth Ave. sprawl the **Maumbury Rings,** a Bronze Age monument with a gaping, grassy maw used as an amphitheater by the Romans. The complete foundation and mosaic floor of a **Roman Town House** are at the back of the County Hall complex, near the Top o' Town roundabout. *(Enter the parking lot and walk all the way back; the gate—marked by black signs—is unlocked during daylight hours.)* The only remaining fragment of the **Roman Wall** is on Albert Rd., a short walk to the south. Look sharp, or you'll walk right by. The most significant of Dorchester's ancient ruins is **Maiden Castle,** a fortification dating from 3000 BC which was seized by the Romans in AD 44. The "castle" is really a fortified hilltop patrolled by sheep. There is no bus transport, but the local shuttle to Vespasian Way goes halfway (every 15min. from Trinity St.). Or you can take a scenic 2 mi. hike from the center of town down Maiden Castle Rd.

Dorchester barely dabbles in nightlife, though weekends bring respectable crowds to the pubs. **Stationmasters** by South Station packs the largest crowds for pints and pool. *(Open M-Sa 11am-11:30pm, Su 3-10:30pm.)* **The Sun Inn** (tel. 250445), at the junction of Old Sherbourne Rd. and Lower Burton, has wonderful pub grub. *(Open M-Sa 11am-3pm and 5:30-11pm. Food served M-Sa noon-2pm and 6:30-11pm, Su noon-2pm and 6:30-10:30pm.)* Ring the **Dorchester Arts Centre,** School Ln., The Grove (tel. 266926), for information on regional theater and local musicians.

■ Weymouth

Pasty legs have been all the fashion in Weymouth ever since King George III dipped his in these waters to cure his madness. Even from its beginnings, Weymouth seemed an occasional thing, a port of call for voyaging ships and mentally adrift royalty. Weymouth was one of the cities where the Black Plague first reached England's shores, carried by seafaring rats who decided to step off board and have a look at the city. Today a resort town with a sandy beach—deemed spectacular by English Channel standards—Weymouth pulls droves of daytrippers to its welcoming waters, ice cream huts, and roadside trampolines. Every other housefront advertises "B&B," and the pulse of life is marked by the turning of the "Vacancy" sign.

GETTING THERE

Trains (tel. (0345) 484950) connect Weymouth with London's **Waterloo** Station (3hr., 18 per day, £33-35, return £35). There's also hourly service to **Chichester** (2½hr., £24, return £32), **Brighton** (3½hr., £31, return £34), and **Dorchester** (15min., £2.20). **National Express** (tel. (0990) 808080) runs buses to **London** (2 per day, £18-21, return £22-26), **Brighton** (1 per day, £15-18, return £19-22), **Chichester** (1 per day, £13), and other destinations.

PRACTICAL INFORMATION

The **train station** (tel. (0345) 484950) is at Ranelagh Rd. You can purchase tickets by phone (tel. (0345) 125625); the **Travel Centre** is open M-Sa 10am-5pm. **National Express bus** (tel. (0990) 808080) tickets can be bought at the tourist office or at the **Southern National** office on the Esplanade, across from George III's brightly painted statue (open M-F 8:45am-5:15pm, Sa 9am-4:45pm). The Weymouth **tourist office** (tel. 785747) is on the Esplanade at the King's Statue (open daily Apr.-Sept. 9:30am-5pm; Oct.-Mar. 10:30am-3pm). Their helpful map runs 25p, and their *Guide to Weymouth* is £1. The Weymouth **market** sells sundries near the train station (open Th 8am-3pm). The **hospital** is on Melcombe Ave. (tel. 772211). The **post office** is at 67 St. Thomas St. (tel. 784828; open M-F 9am-5:30pm, Sa 9am-5pm). Weymouth's **postal code** is DT4 8HA, and its **telephone code** is 01305.

ACCOMMODATIONS AND FOOD

Sunbathing crowds soak up all the rooms in summer; try to make reservations early. B&Bs on the Esplanade cost a pretty penny and fill up quickly. Side streets provide the best B&B bargains; most offer breakfast and color TV for about £15, all just steps from the beach. **Wilton Guest House,** 5 Gloucester St. (tel. 783317), only two blocks from the tourist office and the Esplanade, has clean rooms with comfortable beds and extra fluffy pillows (£14 per person). Right across the street, **Melcombe Villa** (tel. 783026) opens its attractive, modern rooms (£15 per person). **Seaways** (tel. 771646) has centrally located rooms at 5 Turton St., which runs parallel to the Esplanade (the second right off Gloucester Terr.; from £15). Various **pubs** provide high quality accommodations starting at £16.

Restaurants and sandwich shops crowd into the Old Town area, surrounding St. Thomas St. **Ye Olde Sally Lunne Shoppe,** 9 Upper St. at Albans St., offers a variety of bak'd goodes to take out to the beach (open M-Sa 8:30am-5pm). **Brunches,** 27 Maiden St. (tel. 788900), serves up good seafood and pasta lunches (£3-4) in a relaxed and youthful atmosphere (senior and children's menu available; open M-Sa 8am-5:30pm). Three pubs surround **Brewers' Quay,** once the site of the local brewery and now the bustling home to a variety of shops, cafes, and the local museum. Near the bridge leading to the Quay, **The Marlboro Restaurant** (tel. 785700) offers take-away and dine-in. Generous servings of fish and chips for £3.50. You'll Roo the day you don't stop at **The House on Pooh Corner,** 50 St. Mary St. (tel. 770472), which serves pasta and Piglet. Lasagna costs £4.65; Piglet is priceless. Veggie items are available. (Open M-F 9:30am-4pm, Sa 9:30am-5pm, Su 11am-5pm; last order 15min. before closing.) Everything else can be purchased at the **Tesco** supermarket, on St. Thomas St. next to the post office (open M-F 8am-8pm, Sa 8am-6:30pm).

SIGHTS AND ENTERTAINMENT

Weymouth's most popular attraction is the **English Channel** and the lively beach it maintains. The east side of the beach is a bit pebbly, but the sand smooths as you walk south toward the more protected cove. *(Open daily 9am-dusk. Free.)* Landlubbers in Weymouth can expect less promising recreational fare. The **Time Walk,** Hope Sq., Brewer's Quay (tel. 777622), provides a Disney-esque journey through Weymouth's history. Surprisingly well constructed and fitted with Broadway-quality lighting, the Time Walk is narrated by animated cats. A real microbrewery is also on site, depicting the building's former inhabitant, the Devenish Brewery, and providing free samples. Don't miss King George's **bathing machine,** a floating circle that brought His Highness sufficiently far out to sea that he could bathe modestly in the buff. *(Open daily July-Aug. 10am-8:30pm; Sept.-June 10am-5:30pm; last Time Walk 1hr. before closing. £3.75, students and seniors £3.25, children £2.50.)* For more traditional gadgets, head to **The Tudor House,** 3 Trinity St. (tel. 812341), a furnished early 17th-century merchant's home. *(Open June-Sept. Tu-F 11am-3:45pm; Oct.-May the first Su of each month and bank holidays only 2-4pm. £1.50, students £1, children 50p.)* A 15-minute walk along the harbor takes you to **Nothe Gardens,** a well-manicured park with breathtaking views of Weymouth and the Dorset coastline.

In the old harbor, the **Deep Sea Adventure and Sharky's Playground,** 9 Custom House Quay (tel. 760690), reel in three floors of exhibits tracing the development of diving and sea salvage techniques from the 17th century. The cavernous interior offers respite (albeit kitschy respite) from the bustle of the beach. *(Museum and playground open daily July-Aug. 9:30am-8pm, Sept.-June 9:30am-7pm; last entry 5:30pm. Deep Sea Adventure £3.50, students and seniors £3, children £2.50; Sharky's mazes and slides free for adults, children £2.75.)* Along the same quay, various boats advertise **fishing trips,** which start at about £4. For a land trip, check out the **horse and buggy rides** pulled by weary-looking beasts of burden. From the quieter south side, a 4 mi. peaceful cliffside stroll along the **Underbarn Walk** leads to the island town of **Portland.** Every 10 minutes buses run to Portland from the King's Statue (stop K5) near the Weymouth tourist office. Visitors to the **Portland Bill Conservation Area** at the south tip of the island can climb up the steps of the lighthouse for an eye-popping view and a morsel of peace from the screaming ninnies on the **Esplanade,** the site where Kazuo Ishiguro's butler Stevens waited for the pier lights to come on and considered the remains of the day. Also keep an eye out for **Veasta,** the mythical 12 ft. seahorse-monster believed to inhabit the waters off Chesil beach. **Portland Castle** (tel. 820539), built by Henry VIII to stave off French and Spanish attacks, overlooks the harbor. World War II soldiers used the site as a base. *(Open Apr.-Oct. daily 10am-6pm. £2.30, students and seniors £1.70, children £1.20.)*

As daytrippers roll out of town, the quay rocks at the **Rendezvous,** St. Thomas St., Town Bridge (tel. 761343), with live music every Tuesday and occasional strippers of both sexes. Dress sharp. *(Open until 2am.)* Down Bond St., a young crowd packs **Malibu** for flowing drafts and throbbing beats (entrance on New St.). According to some locals, crowds can be raucous, even a little rough. For a touch of higher culture, visit the **Pavilion Theatre,** the Pavilion Complex, the Esplanade (tel. 783225), which provides a stage for shows ranging from children's performers and craft fairs to drama and ballet. *(Tickets about £5-10.)* From the last week of July to the end of August, Monday night skies are filled with **fireworks** exploding over the sea

■ Lyme Regis

Known as the "Pearl of Dorset," Lyme Regis (pop. 3500) perches precariously on the face of a hillside on the Dorset coast. Steep climbs, startling views, and stunning natural beauty entice both budget travelers and would-be beach bums to this quiet hamlet, where you can hear the sigh of waves from the main road. Though the town retains many of the rugged characteristics of an 18th-century fishing village, the 19th-century intellectuals who clambered down the steep streets of Lyme Regis to palatial beachfront cottages also made an impression. It was here that Jane Austen worked and vacationed and Whistler painted *The Master Smith* and *The Little Rose.* More recently, native John Fowles set his neo-Victorian novel *The French Lieutenant's Woman* in Lyme Regis, and part of the movie was filmed on location.

ORIENTATION AND PRACTICAL INFORMATION Lyme Regis makes a fine daytrip from Exeter, and is also accessible from Weymouth. The easiest way to reach Lyme from Exeter is by **train** (tel. (0345) 484950). To get to **Axminster** (5mi. north of Lyme on A35), take the **London-Exeter** rail line (from **Exeter** St. David's and Central Stations; 14 per day, £5.50). **Sewards Coaches bus** #896 runs once a day in the summer from Exeter (1¾hr., Tu and Th-Sa, £9). Then take **Southern National** bus #31/X31 (1 per hr.) from Axminster to Lyme (£1.50).

The **tourist office** (tel. 442138) sits on Church St. at Guildhall St. Walk down the hill from the bus stop, turn left onto Bridge St. and walk straight ahead (open M-F 10am-6pm; in summer also Sa-Su 10am-5pm). Three **banks,** including **Midland Bank** and **Lloyd's,** have **ATMs** outside on Broad St. The **police** debate *habeas corpus* on Hill Rd. (tel. 442603). The **post office** sits at 37 Broad St. (open M-F 8:30am-5:30pm, Sa 8:30am-7pm); the **postal code** is DT7 3QF. Lyme's **telephone code** is 01297.

ACCOMMODATIONS AND FOOD The **Newhaven Hotel** (tel. 442499), at the beginning of Pound St., tempts with glimpses of ocean and a cheerful hostess. Impressive breakfasts to order (in summer £20-26; in winter £17). **Camping** costs £2 per person (additional £1 each for tent and car) at **Hook Farm** (tel. 442801), a 25-minute walk from the coast along the River Exe footpath.

Coffee shops and greengrocers line Broad St., the town's main strip, and fish and chips sizzle where the Cobb meets Marine Parade. Pubs along Broad St. offer generous portions of traditional English food in dark-wooded decor; try **The Volunteer Inn,** 31 Broad St., or the **Royal Lion** (tel. 445622). For excellent seafood and location, stroll down to the **Cobb Arms** (tel. 443242) on Marine St. (fresh cooked crab £6.50). **Lyme's Fish Bar,** 34 Coombe St. (tel. 442375), offers fish and chips (£2) and neighborhood fun (open daily noon-2:30pm and 5-10pm, F-Sa 5-11:30pm). Sneak vegetarian delights and quality pub grub at **Smuggler's Restaurant,** 30 Broad St. (tel. 442795; open M-F 6-9:30pm, Sa noon-10pm, Su noon-9pm).

SIGHTS AND ENTERTAINMENT Lyme's stone **Cobb,** a large rock seawall, curves out from the land to cradle the small harbor. Austen's Louisa Musgrove suffered an unfortunate fall here and brightened Anne Elliot's prospects in *Persuasion.* A few years ago, a man who fell off the Cobb evoked a national scandal by suing the government for £96,000, presumably charging that the sea-dwelling rocks were negligent for getting wet. A cartoon in the *Telegraph* pictured financially strapped MPs standing on the Cobb, trying to fall off to get money. Footpaths wind along the coast towards Seaton and over clifftops to Charmouth. Navigate down to the beach itself to enjoy the abundant rock pools. The **Marine Aquarium** (tel. 443678), on the Cobb, features local catches such as luminescent, frighteningly magnified models of plankton. Ask them to show you the sea mice (look, furry!). *(Open May-Oct. daily 10am-5pm; later in July-Aug. £1.30, students and seniors £1, children 80p, under 5 free. Wheelchair access.)*

Chalkboard notices on the Cobb advertise **fishing trips.** *(Afternoon and night deep-sea angling for about £9.)* Call the *Predator* (tel. 442397) or *Neptune* (tel. (0468) 570437) for details. History buff Richard J. Fox, former world-champion town crier, conducts **tours** dressed in 17th-century military regalia on Tuesdays in July and August at 3pm Inquire at Country Stocks, 53 Broad St. (tel. 443568), or meet at the Guildhall. *(1½hr. £1.50, children £1.20.)* Luxuriate in **Langmoor Gardens,** accessible from Pound St. The green expanse looks down upon the ocean and includes lonely palm trees, standing like exiles from across the sea. Follow the signs and turn off Coombe St. to the left to reach the **Riverside Walk,** a short path with lovely garden views and the Lym hurrying past on both sides. Look for the small stone memorial to the Lepers' Hospital which once stood along the Lym. In the summer, along with hordes of tourists, several festivals visit Lyme Regis. Popular among these are the **Jazz Festival** (early July) and the **Regatta Carnival** (early August).

DEVON

■ Exeter

In 1068, the inhabitants of Exeter earned the respect of William the Conqueror, holding their own against his forces for 18 days in their besieged city. When the wells within the city ran dry, the Exonians used wine for cooking, bathing, and (of course) drinking, which might explain why the city finally fell to the Normans. Exeter gradually and proudly developed over centuries as the county seat of Devon, only to be flattened in a few days of Nazi bombing in 1942. Frantic rebuilding has made the city an odd mixture of the venerable and the banal: Roman and Norman ruins poke from delicatessen parking lots, and the cash registers of a bustling department store stand atop a medieval catacomb. But this jigsaw cityscape—along with a large university community—has helped foster the diversity of Exeter's population, noteworthy in the homogeneous hills of Devon.

GETTING THERE

Frequent trains and buses travel from London and Bristol and transfer here for trips to the rest of Devon and Cornwall. **Trains** (tel. (0345) 484950) leave for Exeter from London (3hr., 16 per day, **Paddington** and **Waterloo Stations,** £36 and £40, respectively). **National Express buses** (tel. (0990) 808080) are the least expensive way to Exeter, especially if you take advantage of a discount student coach card (from London's **Victoria Coach** Station 4hr., 8 per day, £22-25). Buses also run from **Bristol** (2¾hr., 7 per day, £9-11) and from **Bath** (2¾hr., 3 per day, £11.50-14).

ORIENTATION

To reach the town center from St. David's Station, where most **trains** (tel. (0345) 484950) unload, follow the footpath in front of the station and turn right onto **St. David's Hill,** which becomes **Iron Bridge** and then **North St.** The trip is all uphill

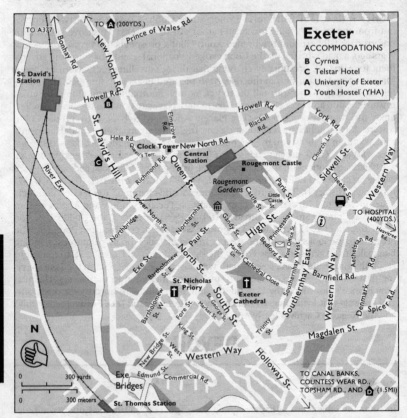

from here. Turn left after the Guildhall Shopping Centre onto **High St.** From Central Station, take **Queen St.** up to High St. **Buses** stop in the station on **Paris St.;** walk through the arcade to Sidwell St. and turn left to reach High St.

PRACTICAL INFORMATION

Trains: Exeter St. David's Station, St. David's Hill, lies several blocks from the center of town (information office open M-F 8:45am-7:40pm, Sa 8:45am-6:30pm, Su 10am-5:30pm). Some trains from London's **Waterloo** (9 per day) go through **Exeter Central Station,** located on Queen St. next to Northernhay Gardens (office open M-F 7:50am-6pm, Sa 8:50am-5:40pm).

Buses: Paris St. (tel. 256231), off High St. just outside the city walls. Open M-Sa 8:30am-6pm, Su 9am-5pm. 24 hr. **lockers** (50p-£2). **Minibuses** shuttle between city areas. An **Exeter Freedom Ticket** allows unlimited travel (£2.50 per day, £8.25 per week; 2 passport-sized photos needed for week passes). Stops are frequent, especially around High St., but the minibuses will skip stops unless hailed.

Tourist office: Extremely friendly staff helps at the Civic Centre in the City Council Bldg., Paris St. (tel. 265700), across the street from the rear of the bus station. Accommodations service available for 10% deposit. Open M-F 9am-5pm, Sa 9am-1pm and 2-5pm. Wheelchair accessible.

Tours: A local institution for over a decade, the Exeter City Council's **themed walking tours** (tel. 265212) are frequented as often by locals as tourists and are the best way to explore this idiosyncratic city. The "Forgotten Exeter" tour will acquaint you with the Exeter exploits of Henry VII while pointing out many of the city's lesser-known nooks and crannies. "Ghosts and Legends of Exeter" frights huge local crowds each Hallowe'en. Most walks leave from the front of the Royal Clarence Hotel, but a few depart from the Quay. Tours run 1½hr.; Apr.-Oct. 5-8 per day; Nov.-Mar. 11am and 2pm; free.

Financial Services: Barclays sits at 20 High St. and **Thomas Cook** on Princesshay nearby on Bedford St. **ATMs** are plentiful.

Emergency: Dial 999; no coins required.

Police: Heavitree Rd. (tel. (0990) 777444), 3 blocks past the junction of Heavitree Rd., Western Way, and Paris St.

Post Office: Bedford St. (tel. 423401). Open M-F 9am-5:30pm, Sa 9am-7pm. The city's **postal code** is EX1 1AA.

Internet Access: Travel cyberspace, coffee in hand, at **Internet Express,** 1b Queen St. (tel. 201544), in the Central Train Station building. £2.50 per 30min., £2.25 with student ID. Open M-F 9am-8pm, Sa 10am-6pm, Su noon-6pm.

Telephone code: 01392.

ACCOMMODATIONS

Exeter's less expensive B&Bs flourish on St. David's Hill between the train station and the center of town, as well as on Howell Rd. closer to the Central Station.

YHA Youth Hostel, 47 Countess Wear Rd. (tel. 873329; fax 876939), 2mi. southeast of the city center off Topsham Rd. Take minibus #K, T, or J from High St. to the Countess Wear Post Office (£1). Follow Exe Vale Rd. to the end and turn left. Spacious, cheery hostel with a self-catering kitchen. £9.80, under 18 £6.60. English breakfast £3. Evening meal £4.50. About 10 **campsites** at half-price.

Telstar Hotel, 77 St. David's Hill (tel. 272466), between downtown and St. David's rail station and next to the **Fort Williams Hotel** (run by the same family). Eager-to-please but sometimes-overwhelmed owners and comfortable rooms. Book a week ahead during the summer. Singles from £16; doubles from £28.

Cyrnea, 73 Howell Rd. (tel. 438386). From St. David's, follow Hele Rd. to New North Rd. Turn left at the clock onto Elm Grove and right onto Howell; Cyrnea is on the right. Central location and friendly atmosphere. If Mr. Budge is home when you call, he may chauffeur you from the station. £14.

University of Exeter (tel. 211500). Accommodations at St. Luke's campus buildings during school vacations. Call ahead and directions will be given for the particular residence hall. Profit from other people's pain and do not follow the signs to the main campus; take Minibus H or U to Cowley Bridge to save the trek from High St. Clean, simple rooms, £12.50. Breakfast included. Call for availability.

FOOD AND PUBS

St. George's Market, 91 High St., holds several stalls selling produce and meats (most stalls open M-Tu and Th-Sa 8am-5pm, W 8am-3pm). Exeter's largest supermarket by far is **Sainsbury's** (tel. 217129), across the River Exe at Cowick St. (open M-Th 8:30am-8pm, F 8:30am-9pm, Sa 8am-7pm, Su 10am-4pm). **Marks and Spencer** on High St. will save you the walk. At **Herbies,** 15 North St. (tel. 58473), as in herbivorous, you'll find leafy delights (£3-4; open M 11am-2:30pm, Tu-F 11am-2:30pm and 6-9:30pm, Sa 10:30am-4pm and 6-9:30pm). Some less expensive eateries lie just outside the town center near Central Station along Queen St. To escape the crowds on High St., duck into **Cripes!,** 21 Gandy St. (tel. 491411), for crepes (from £4) and lunchtime specials (open daily noon-11:30pm, last order 10:30pm). **Porter Black's,** 7 North St. (tel. 410680), offers cheap yet fantastic English and Irish fare (open M-F noon-9pm, Sa noon-6pm, Su noon-2pm).

Pubs abound in Exeter, and many hide in the alleys off High St. A skeleton guards the medieval well in the basement of the **Well House Tavern** (tel. 495365) on Cathedral Close (annexed to the ancient and blue-blood-haunted **Royal Clarence Hotel**), while hearty ale flows upstairs. When Sir Francis Drake was not aboard his own craft, he preferred no place to the **Ship Inn** (tel. 72040), on St. Martin's Ln. off High St. Beef and veggie burgers cost less in the pub and snack bar downstairs; upstairs is more plush and expensive. Duck into **Coolings** on Gandy St. for a relaxed atmosphere and a young local crowd (open M-Sa 11am-11pm, Su 7-10:30pm).

SIGHTS

Exeter Cathedral (tel. 255573; fax 498769), low-slung and lovely, overlooks the commercial clutter of High St. The west front holds hundreds of stone figures in sundry states of mutilation, crowned by a statue of St. Peter as a virile naked fisherman. Inside, effigy tombs (including cadavers) line the walls, and shattered flagstones mark the chapel where a German bomb landed in 1942. When the intricate 15th-century clock strikes one, look for the tiny hole in the wooden door beneath, where the bishop's cat once ran in after mice (hence, perhaps, "Hickory Dickory Dock"). The building has been extensively (and expensively) restored, thanks to a staunch campaign by locals and the patronage of Prince Charles. The 60 ft. **Bishop's Throne,** made without nails, was disassembled in 1640 and again during WWII to save it from destruction. A collection of manuscripts, donated to the cathedral in the 11th century by the munificent Bishop Leofric and known to modern scholars as the **Exeter Book,** is the richest treasury of early Anglo-Saxon poetry in the world. The book is on display in the library. Ask at the information desk about the shortcut. *(Cathedral open daily 7am-6:30pm; library open M-F 2-5pm. £2 donation requested. Free choral Evensong services M-F 5:30pm, Sa-Su 3pm. Free guided tours Apr.-Oct. M-F 11:30am and 2:30pm, Sa 11am.)*

After his siege, William the Conqueror built **Rougemont Castle** to keep the natives in check. The ruins between High St. and Central Station include a gatehouse dating from 1070. The immaculate flower beds of the Regency-era **Rougemont Gardens,** on Castle St., surround the remaining castle walls. Due to security at the adjacent court building, tourists can only view the ruins from a non-photogenic angle below; no good views unless you're a criminal. (*Let's Go* does not recommend crime.) The expansive 17th-century **Northernhay Gardens** unfold just beyond Rougemont and the preserved **Roman city walls.**

To bring water into the city, medieval authorities dug subterranean ducts and adjacent tunnels to maintain them; today the **underground passages** (tel. 265887) are the only public ancient city passages in Britain, and are accessible from Romangate Passage next to Boots on High St. The passages, which are 2 by 6 ft., contain doors built by Cavaliers from 1642 to 1646 to keep out besieging Roundheads—not for the claustrophobic. *(Open July-Sept. M-Sa 10am-5:30pm; Oct.-June Tu-F 2-5pm, Sa 10am-5pm. 2 tours per hr.; last tour at 4:45pm. Book tickets by noon during July and Aug. £3.50, students, seniors, and children £2.50, families £9.50.)* The 900-year-old **St. Nicholas Priory** (tel. 265858) has a medieval guest hall and kitchen, along with a timeworn toilet seat young Arthur himself couldn't lift. Take the alleyway next to The Mint at 154 Fore St. *(Open Easter-Oct. M, W, and Sa 3-4:30pm. £1.25, students, seniors, and children 75p.)* **The Royal Albert Museum,** Queen St. (tel. 265858), houses such treasures as a blackened skull from New Guinea and a large elephant from Kenya. *(Open M-Sa 10am-5pm. Free.)*

ENTERTAINMENT

Exeter's newest watering hole is more like an ocean: the bright, airy **Imperial** (tel. 434050), a pub on New North Rd. just up from St. David's station, graces a Georgian mansion. *(2 dinners for £5.)* Exeter's students hang at the **Double Locks** (tel. 256947), Canal Banks towards Topsham from the Exe Bridges. A boat leaves hourly from the Quay during the day. *(Open M-Sa 11am-11pm, Su noon-10:30pm.)* **The Cavern,** in a brick cellar at 83-84 Queen St. (tel. 495370), hosts live bands every night. *(Open M-Tu 11am-11pm, W-Sa 11am-midnight, Su 6:30-11pm. Check the kiosks on High St. for details.)*

The professional **Northcott Theatre** company (tel. 493493), based on Stocker Rd. at the University of Exeter, performs throughout the year. *(Tickets £7-15, student standbys £6.)* The **Exeter and Devon Arts Centre** (tel. 421111), at Bradninch Pl. on Gandy St., and the **Arts Booking and Information Centre** (tel. 211080), opposite Boots just off High St., supply monthly listings of cultural events in the city. The **Exeter Festival** features concerts, opera, talks, and an explosion of theater for three weeks in July. *(Ticket prices vary. Call the Arts Centre for details.)*

■ Exmoor National Park

Once the English royal hunting preserve, Exmoor is among the smallest of Britain's 11 National Parks, covering 265 sq. mi. on the north coast of England's southwestern peninsula. Dramatic sea-swept cliffs fringe woodlands and moors where sheep and cattle graze in purple heather. Countless ancient bridges span over 300 mi. of rivers full of trout and salmon, and thatched hamlets dot the valleys. Wild ponies still roam, and the last great herds of red deer graze in woodlands between the river valleys. Though over 80% of Exmoor is privately owned (as in most British National Parks), the territory is accommodating to respectful hikers and bikers.

GETTING THERE

Exmoor is accessible by bus and train from Exeter, Plymouth, Bristol and London, often via Taunton. Exmoor's western gateway, **Barnstaple**, is easily accessible at the end of a branch **rail** (tel. (0345) 484950) line from **Exeter** (1hr., 12 per day, £9.70). Trains also run from **Bristol** to **Barnstaple** (change at Exeter St. David's, 10 per day, £19). Take **British Rail** from **London** (3hr., 8 per day, £42), or **Plymouth** (change at Exeter St. David's, 2hr., 9 per day, £18.60). **Stagecoach** bus #315 rolls from **Exeter** to **Ilfracombe;** Barnstaple is near the end of the line (2¼hr., M-Sa 2 per day, £5.60). One **National Express** (tel. (0990) 808080), another bus chugs from **Bristol** (2½hr., 2 per day, £14). National Express also runs from **London** (5hr., from Victoria Station 3 per day, £25.50). From **Plymouth**, catch the **Western National** (#86, 2½hr., 2 per day, £4.10) For more information, call the bus station in Plymouth (tel. (01752) 222666), or Exeter (tel. (01392) 427711).

From **Taunton,** you can reach **Minehead**, Exmoor's eastern gateway, by the hourly **Southern National** (tel. (01935) 476233) bus #28 (1¼hr., M-Sa 12 per day, Su 4 per day, £3.20) or by **West Somerset Railway** (tel. (01643) 704996), a private line that runs to **Minehead** from **Bishops Lydeard**, a town 4 mi. from Taunton (1¼hr., July-Aug. 4-7 per day, May-June and Sept.-Oct. 4 per day, £5.40, return £8.20). Buses shuttle to Bishops Lydeard from the Taunton rail station. Bus service to both Minehead and Taunton is erratic; call ahead to confirm routes and times. Alternative routes include **Southern National** from **Minehead** to **Porlock** (7 per day, £1.45), and by rail from **Exeter** to **Taunton** (25min., £7), or via **Tortes** (45min. from Exeter, £7.80).

GETTING ABOUT

Although getting to the outskirts of Exmoor by public transport is relatively easy, bus service is erratic. Picking up a copy of the detailed *Exmoor and West Somerset Public Transportation Guide* will make your life much simpler.

The park is best toured on foot or by bike. Two long-distance paths are the **Somerset and North Devon Coast Path** for hikers and the **coastal path,** which follows the ghost of the Barnstaple railroad, for bikers. Both routes pass through or near the towns of (west to east) Barnstaple, Ilfracombe, Combe Martin, Lynton, Porlock Weir, Minehead, and Williton (see **Food, Sights, and Activities,** p. 199). The **Tarka Trail** traces a 180 mi. figure-eight (starting in Barnstaple), 31 mi. of which are bicycle-friendly. The following buses may help cut down on coastal travel time: **Southern National** from Minehead to Ilfracombe (#300, 2hr., M-F 2 per day, £4.70), Williton (#28, 30min., M-Sa 1 per hr., £1.10), and Dunster (#28, M-Sa 1 per hr., 65p). **North Devon Bus** (tel. (01271) 45444) runs from Barnstaple to Ilfracombe (M-Sa 2 per hr., £1.60) and from Ilfracombe to Combe Martin (1 per day, 80p).

PRACTICAL INFORMATION

The National Park Information Centres listed below supply detailed large-scale Ordnance Survey maps of the region (about £5), bus timetables, and the invaluable *Exmoor Visitor*. The centers offer themed guided walks from 1½ to 10 mi. Always be prepared for a sudden rainstorm. Sea winds create volatile weather, and thunderstorms blow up without warning. Be sure to stock up on food and equipment in the larger towns, as stores in the tiny coastal villages have a smaller selection of goods.

National Park Information Centres

Combe Martin: Seacot, Cross St. (tel./fax (01271) 883319), 3mi. east of Ilfracombe. Open Easter-Oct. daily 10am-1:15pm and 1:45-5pm; open until 7pm in peak times.

County Gate: A39 Countisbury (tel. (01598) 741321), 7mi. east of Lynton. Open daily Apr.-Sept. 10am-1:15pm and 1:45-5pm; Oct. 10am-4pm.

Dulverton: Dulverton Heritage Centre, the Guildhall, Fore St., Dulverton, Somerset (tel. (01398) 323841). Open daily Apr.-Oct. 10am-5pm; Nov.-Mar. 10am-3pm.

Dunster: Dunster Steep Car Park (tel. (01643) 821835), 2mi. east of Minehead. Open Apr.-Oct. daily 10am-5pm; in winter, usually weekends only.

Lynmouth: The Esplanade (tel. (01598) 752509). Open daily Apr.-June and Oct. 10am-5pm; July-Sept. 10am-6pm.

Tourist Offices

Barnstaple: 36 Boutport St., EX31 1RX (tel. (01271) 375000). Open Easter-Oct. M-Sa 9:30am-5pm; July-Aug. stays open later.

Ilfracombe (Il-fra-COOM): The Landmark Seafront, in the Landmark Theatre, EX34 9BX (tel. (01271) 863001). Open Easter-Sept. M 9:30am-showtime, Tu-F 10am-showtime, Sa 11am-7pm, Su 10am-8:15pm; Nov.-Easter M-F 10am-5pm.

Lynton: Town Hall, Lynton, EX35 6BT (tel. (01598) 752225). Also offers information on Lynmouth. Open Easter-Oct. daily 9:30am-6pm; Nov.-Mar. M-Sa 9:30am-1:30pm.

Minehead: 17 Friday St., TA24 5UB (tel. (01643) 702624). Open July-Aug. M-Sa 9:30am-5:30pm; Apr.-June and Sept.-Oct. 9:30am-5pm; Nov.-Mar. M-Sa 10am-4pm.

ACCOMMODATIONS AND CAMPING

Rain or shine, hostels and B&Bs (£14-16) fill up quickly; check listings and the *Exmoor Visitor* at the tourist office. At busy times, camping may be the easiest way to see the park. The *Exmoor Visitor* lists several caravan parks that accept tents, but campsites that don't advertise are easy to find, especially near coastal towns. Before pitching a tent, ask the landowner's permission; most of Exmoor is private property.

Hostels

The quality of YHA hostels varies widely according to proprietor and location. In general, you can expect smaller accommodations with a self-catering kitchen, a day lockout (usually 10am-5pm), a curfew (around 11pm-midnight), and no laundry facilities. Hostel schedules change frequently; check the accommodations guide, or call (tel. (01722) 337494; open M-F 9am-5pm) for current schedules.

Crowcombe Heathfield: Denzel House, Crowcombe Heathfield, Taunton, Somerset TA4 4BT (tel. (01984) 667249), on the Taunton-Minehead Rd., 2mi. from the village below Quantock Hills. Turn onto the road marked "Crowcombe Station & Lydeard St. Lawrence. The hostel is about 1mi. down the road, on the left. Large house in the woods. £7.20, under 18 £5. Open Apr.-Sept.; schedule varies from open daily to open only weekends; call far in advance.

Exford: On Withypoole Rd., Exe Mead, Exford, Minehead, Somerset TA24 7PU (tel. (01643) 831288). Take Exmoor bus #280 or 285 from Minehead, next to the River Exe bridge, first road on the left. Superior grade, in the center of the park's moorland. £8.80, under 18 £6. Laundry facilities. Open July-Aug. daily; mid-Feb. to June and Sept.-Oct. M-Sa; closed Nov. to mid-Feb.

Elmscott: Elmscott, Hartland, Bideford, Devon EX39 6ES (tel. (01237) 441367). Extremely difficult to find—get a map before you go. 4mi. southwest of Hartland village by footpath. On weekends bus #119 goes to Bideford. £7.20, under 18 £5. Call for off-season times.

Quantox: Sevenacres, Holford, Bridgwater, Somerset (tel. (01278) 741224). 1½mi. past the Alfoxton Park Hotel in Holford—keep right after passing through gate by hotel stables. From Kilze, take Pardlestone Ln. opposite post office for 1mi., then follow signs. Country house in forest overlooking Bridgewater Bay, with riding stables nearby. £7.20, under 18 £5. Open Apr.-Aug. M-Sa

Ilfracombe: Ashmour House, 1 Hillsborough Terr., Ilfracombe, Devon EX34 9NR (tel. (01271) 865337; fax 862652). Take Red bus #3, 6, 30 or 300 or Filer's bus #301/303 from Barnstaple, just off the main road. Georgian terrace house with view of the Welsh coast. Family rooms available. £8.80, under 18 £6. Open July-Aug. daily; Apr.-June and Sept. M-Sa; closed Oct.-Mar.

Instow: Worlington House, New Rd., Instow, Bideford, Devon EX39 4LW (tel. (01271) 860394). Take Filer's bus #301 or Red bus #1, 2, or B from Barnstaple and get off at the Quay in Instow. The Victorian house is an exhausting mile-long uphill climb from the bus stop. Must be a YHA member. £8.80, under 18 £6. Breakfast £3, 3-course evening meal £4.50; laundry facilities available. Open Apr.-Sept. daily; mid-Feb. to Mar. and Oct.-Nov. Tu-Sa; closed Dec. to mid-Feb.

Lynton: Lynbridge, Lynton, Devon EX35 6AZ (tel. (01598) 753237). Take Filer's bus #311 from Barnstaple to Castle Hill Car Park, Lynton. Small former hotel in valley of River Lyn West. £8.80, under 18 £6. Breakfast £3, dinner £4.40. Open daily July-Aug.; call for other times.

Minehead: Alcombe Combe, Minehead, Somerset TA24 6EW (tel. (01643) 702595), 2mi. from town center. Follow Friday St. as it becomes Alcombe Rd., turn right on Brook St. and follow to Manor Rd. From Taunton, take Minehead bus to Alcombe stop (1mi. from hostel). Spacious grounds. £8.80, under 18 £6. Open July-Aug. daily; Apr.-June Tu-Su; Sept.-Oct. W-Su; closed Nov.-Mar.

FOOD, SIGHTS, AND ACTIVITIES

Although **Barnstaple** is not the only suitable hiking base for the coastal path or the Tarka Trail, it is the largest town in the region, a transport center, and the best place to get camping and hiking gear and a hearty pre-trip meal. **La Pizzeria,** 35 Boutport St. (tel. 321274), serves up Italian fare. There are also daily markets at the **Pannier Market.** Inexpensive camping equipment can be bought at **Cassie's Surplus,** 19 Tuly St. (tel. (01271) 46198), across from the tourist office (open M-Sa 9am-5pm). **Tarka Trail** (tel. (01271) 24202), conveniently located at the head of the coastal bike path, will rent you a nice set of (bike) wheels. From the center of town, cross the bridge, take the second left after the bridge at the roundabout; Tarka is by the railroad station (open daily 9am-5pm; £6-8 per day). The path provides level cycling for 15 mi. on the coast, where the old Barnstaple railroad tracks used to run.

Two good places to begin traipsing into the forest close to Barnstaple are **Blackmoor Gate,** 9 mi. northwest of Barnstaple, and **Parracombe,** 2 mi. farther northwest along the road. Both are on Filer's Barnstaple-Lynton bus line.

Minehead is only a mile from the park's eastern boundary. The town boasts a **nature trail,** designed for disabled visitors, that winds past labeled vegetation. Other well-marked paths weave through North Hill, an easy walk from the town center. The **South West Coast Path,** Britain's longest National Trail, begins in Minehead.

The village of **Dunster** lies 3 mi. east of Minehead. **Dunster Castle** (tel. (01643) 821314) thrives over the former 17th-century yarn market. Home to the Luttrell family for 600 years, the castle has seen its share of battles, especially during the English civil wars. The elaborate interior includes a not-to-be-missed 16th-century portrait of Sir John Luttrell wading buck-naked through the surf. *(Open Apr.-Sept. Sa-W 11am-5pm; Oct. Sa-W 11am-4pm. Subtropical gardens open daily Apr.-Sept. 10am-5pm; Oct.-Mar. 11am-4pm. £5.20, children £2.70; garden and grounds only £2.80, children £1.30, families £6.70.)* Buses from Minehead stop at the base of Dunster Village every hour in the summer.

■ Dartmoor National Park

Much of Dartmoor National Park's 367 sq. mi. (south of Exmoor, 10 mi. west of Exeter, and 7 mi. east of Plymouth) is scattered with remnants of the past, from oddly balanced granite tors to rock forms arranged by the hand of Neolithic man. Ramblers among the standing stones and chambered tombs littered across the park may also come across the skeleton of a once-flourishing tin-mining industry and the heavily guarded Princetown prison. Because of its rough terrain and harsh climate, Dartmoor has been largely untouched for centuries, except by sheep and native wild ponies. Today, many spirits linger, perhaps the most famous being the canine immortalized by Sir Arthur Conan Doyle's *Hound of the Baskervilles.*

GETTING THERE AND GETTING ABOUT

Buses are infrequent and often erratic: plan ahead. In the summer months, the **Transmoor Link** (Devon bus #82, 3 per day) cuts through the middle of the park on its southwest-northeast route between **Plymouth** and **Exeter,** passing through **Yelverton** (at the southwest corner of the park), **Princetown, Postbridge, Moretonhampstead,** and at the park's northeast corner **Steps Bridge** (late May to Sept. 3 per day). **Devon General** #X38/39 also binds **Exeter** and **Plymouth,** stopping in **Buckfastleigh** and **Ashburton** along the park's southern edge (M-Sa 8 per day, Su 7 per day). **Plymouth** runs 14 buses to **Ivybridge** (service #X80 or **Western National** #88 or X88, 30min., 1 per hr.); to **Tavistock,** north of Yelverton on the park's western edge (#83, 84, or 86, 1hr., M-F 1-3 per hr.; #98A Tavistock to Plymouth); and to **Okehampton,** on the park's northern edge (#86, M-F 7 per day, Su 2 per day). Services and prices change seasonally and routes are not permanent; check schedules at the bus station and with tourist offices (a guide to services is available).

For more information, contact the **Exeter bus station** (tel. (01392) 427711), the **Devon County Council's Public Transportation Helpline** (tel. (01392) 382800; open M-F 8:30am-5pm), or any National Park Information Centre (see below). The invaluable *Dartmoor Public Transportation Guide,* in any nearby bus station or tourist information center contains listings of relevant bus routes and useful phone numbers, and suggests walking routes. A 30 mi. drive across the park takes three hours; the bus stops every time a sheep crosses its path. Once you've reached the park's perimeter, make your way on bike or foot, as bus connections require careful planning. In the winter, snow often renders the park and its tortuous roads virtually inviolable. **Hitchers** report that rides are frequent.

ORIENTATION AND PRACTICAL INFORMATION

Visitors should not underestimate Dartmoor's moody weather or treacherous terrain. An Ordnance Survey Map scaled 1:50,000 (£4.25) or 1:25,000 (£6), a compass, and truly waterproof garb are essential; mists come down without warning, and there is no shelter away from the roads. Footpaths marked on the map are usually not signposted on the high moor; invest in the better (1:25,000) Ordnance Survey Map with terrain markings. Tourist offices also offer very detailed guides to walks, some with map supplements (50p-£9). The official **Dartmoor Rescue Group** (tel. (01837) 86333) is on call through the police. See **Wilderness and Safety Concerns,** p. 47, for more information.

Most of Dartmoor's roads are hilly but good for cycling. Fishing, canoeing, and climbing are also popular. For canoeing arrangements, contact Mr. K. Chamberlain, **Mountain Stream Activities,** Hexworthy (tel. (01364) 646000). For horseback riding, contact **Sherberton Stables,** Hexworthy, Princetown (tel. (01364) 631276; £7.50 per hr.); **Cholwell Farm and Riding Stables,** Mary Tavy, Tavistock (tel. (01822) 810526; £5 per hr.); or **Skaigh Stables,** Skaigh Ln., Sticklepath (tel. (01837) 840429; £9 per hr., £30 per day). Call ahead for reservations and directions.

> **Warning:** The Ministry of Defense uses much of the northern moor for target practice; consult the *Dartmoor Visitor* or an Ordnance Survey map for the boundaries of the danger area, and check the weekly **firing timetable** (available in park and tourist offices, hostels and campsites, police stations, local pubs, and the Friday papers), or call (01837) 52241 ext. 3210 from Okehampton, (01752) 501478 from Plymouth, or (01392) 270164 from Exeter, for information.

National Park Information Centres
The Dartmoor National Park Authority offers guided walks (2-6hr., £2-4) departing from many locations in the park. Check the *Dartmoor Visitor* (available at any tourist office); also check the publication's back page for an updated list of Information Centres and a map showing their locations.

Tavistock: Town Hall, Bedford Sq., Tavistock PL19 0AE (tel. (01822) 612938). Books accommodations £3-3.50. Open Easter-Oct. M-Sa 10am-5pm; Nov.-Easter M-Tu and F-Sa 10am-4pm.

Ivybridge: (tel. (01752) 897035). Books beds for free within 10mi., about £3 elsewhere. Open July-Aug. M-Sa 9am-5pm, Su 10am-4pm; Sept.-June M-Sa 9am-5pm.

Okehampton: 3 West St. (tel. (01837) 53020), in the courtyard adjacent to the White Hart Hotel. Books beds for £3 (you must be there in person). Open June-Aug. daily 10am-5pm; Apr. and Sept.-Oct. M-Sa 10am-5pm.

Newbridge: (tel. (01364) 631303), in Riverside car park. Will book accommodations for £2 deposit. Open Easter-Oct. daily 10am-5pm.

Postbridge: (tel. (01822) 880272). In a car park off the B3212 Moretonhampstead-Yelverton Rd. Open Apr.-Oct. daily 10am-5pm; Nov.-Mar. Sa-Su 10am-4pm. Hours may vary.

Princetown (High Moorland Visitor Centre): (tel. (01822) 890414). In the former Duchy Hotel. Includes a small museum. Disabled access. Open daily in summer 10am-5pm; winter 10am-4pm.

ACCOMMODATIONS AND CAMPING

B&B signs are often displayed on pubs and farmhouses along the roads. The Dartmoor National Park Information Centres will give you a free accommodations list and post notices in the window. The Tavistock, Ivybridge, and Okehampton offices will book you a room for £2-3. The following YHAs offer accommodations in the park:

YHA Steps Bridge, Dunsford, Exeter EX6 7EQ (tel. (01647) 252435; fax 252948), 1mi. southwest of Dunsford village on the B3212, near the eastern edge of the park. Take the Exeter-Moretonhampstead bus #359 and get off at Steps Bridge. The warden creates vegetarian delights and fosters a homey atmosphere in this cabin in the woods. £7.20, under 18 £5. Open Apr.-Sept.; closed Oct.-Mar.

YHA Bellever, Postbridge, Yelverton, Devon PL20 6TU (tel. (01822) 880227), 1mi. southeast of Postbridge village on bus #359 from Exeter. Also bus #82 from Plymouth or Exeter to Postbridge. Ask to be let off as close to the hostel as possible. In the heart of the park and very popular. £8.80, under 18 £6. Showers. Open July-Aug. daily; Apr.-June M-Sa; Sept.-Oct. Tu-Sa.

Camping

Although official campsites exist, many travelers camp on the open moor. Dartmoor land is privately owned, so ask permission before crossing or camping on land whose owner is evident. Backpack camping is permitted on the non-enclosed moor land more than 100 yd. away from the road or out of sight of inhabited areas and farmhouses. Campers may only stay for one night in a single spot. Hikers shouldn't climb fences or walls unless signs are posted that they may do so or build fires in the moors; stick to the marked paths. Call ahead for reservations, especially in the summer.

Ashburton Caravan Park, Waterleat, Ashburton (tel. (01364) 652552). 1½mi. from town; head north on North St. and follow the signs. July-Aug. £9 for a 2-person tent, £2.25 each additional person; Easter-June and Sept.-Oct. £7 and £1.50. Open Easter-Sept.

River Dart Country Park, Holne Park, Ashburton (tel. (01364) 652511). £4.60-5.70, children £3.75-4.50. Open Apr.-Sept.

Okehampton: Yertiz Caravan and Camping Park, Exeter Rd. (tel. (01837) 52281). 1mi. east of Okehampton on the brow of a hill near the Esso Garage. July-Aug. £2.75 per person; Sept.-June £2.25; additional campers 50p. Open year-round.

Tavistock: Higher Longford Farm, Moorshop, Tavistock (tel. (01822) 613360). 2mi. from Tavistock toward Princetown on B3357. £5.50 per person, with car £6.50; 2 people with car £7.50; electricity £1.75. Office open daily 10am-5pm. Open year-round.

SIGHTS

Postbridge and **Princetown** hover at the southern edge of the park's north-central plateau. Dartmoor's forbidding maximum-security prison looms over Princetown, the larger of the two towns. A walking tour with a view of the prison is available. Frenchmen from the Napoleonic Wars and Americans who fought to annex Canada

ENGLAND

in 1812 once languished within the prison's walls. Prehistoric remains lurk on a nearby moor, the setting of one of the most famous of Sir Arthur Conan Doyle's Sherlock Holmes tales, *The Hound of the Baskervilles*, which emerged from an ancient Dartmoor legend of a gigantic, glowing pooch. Several peaks crown the northern moor, the highest of which is **High Willhays** (2038ft.).

The rugged eastern part of the park gathers around **Hay Tor** village. Two mile north lie Dartmoor's celebrated medieval ruins at **Hound Tor,** where excavations unearthed the remains of 13th-century huts and longhouses. Check the *Dartmoor Visitor* for guided walks on the mound and bus routes.

Sir Francis Drake was born west of Hay Tor at **Tavistock.** South of Hay Tor lies **Yelverton,** where Cistercian monks in 1273 built **Buckland Abbey** (tel. (01822) 853607), off Milton Combe Rd. Drake later bought the abbey and transformed it into his private palace. The exterior and grounds, including the huge **Tithe Barn,** make for an interesting wander, but you may not want to bother with the lusterless Tudor and Georgian interior. Sir Francis himself wanders about on summer Sundays. *(Open Apr.-Oct. M-W and F-Su 10:30am-5:30pm; last admission 4:45pm; Nov.-Mar. Sa-Su 2-5pm. £4.30, students and seniors £2.10; grounds only £2.10 and £1.10. Wheelchair accessible.)*

The last castle to be built in England isn't Norman, Tudor, or Georgian. It's **Castle Drogo** (tel. (01647) 433306), built between 1910 and 1930 by Indian tea baron Julius Drewe. Convinced that he was a direct descendant of a Norman baron who had arrived in the 11th century with William the Conqueror, Drewe constructed this granite fortress in his predecessor's style. *(Open Apr.-Oct. Sa-Th 11am-5:30pm; grounds open daily 10:30am-5:30pm. £5; grounds only £2.30.)*

■ Plymouth

Fifty-nine air raids during World War II left Plymouth a cracked shell of a city. In the spaces once occupied by ancient streets and buildings, a new urban plan emerged—identical, rectilinear rows of buildings and awkward thoroughfares. The resulting bus-station atmosphere of new Plymouth is perhaps appropriate: this has long been a city of departures and arrivals. Sir Francis Drake, Captain Cook, the Pilgrims, Lord Nelson, and millions of emigrants to the United States and New Zealand have immortalized Plymouth in their haste to sail away from it. Heed their age-old message: this is the starting point of great journeys, but seek your destination elsewhere.

GETTING THERE

Plymouth lies on the southern coast between Dartmoor National Park and the Cornwall peninsula, on the east-west rail line between London and Penzance. **Trains** (tel. (0345) 484950) run at least every hour to London **Paddington** (3½hr., £53), **Bristol** (3½hr., £25), and **Penzance** (1¾hr., £10). **National Express buses** (tel. (0990) 808080) serve London's **Victoria Coach Station** (4½hr., £27) and **Bristol** (2½hr., £18). **Stagecoach Devon** buses connect Plymouth and **Exeter** by running around Dartmoor (#X38, 1¼hr., £4.15), while **Transmoor Link** #82 goes through the park during the summer and on weekends. Sit on the right-hand side of the #X38 for a supreme view of Dartmoor. **Ferries** (tel. (0990) 360360) go to **Roscoff, France** (6hr., 12 per week, £20-58, depending on season and length of stay), and **Santander, Spain** (24hr., 1-2 per week, return £80-145, depending on season and length of stay). Check in an hour before departure; disabled travelers should arrive two hours in advance.

ORIENTATION

Plymouth's center, wedged between the River Tamar and Plymouth Sound, sprouts half lush grass and half bleak buildings. Almost all the attractions and shops are scattered in a rough semicircle around the city's crown jewel, the **Hoe** (or "High Place"; the area along the coastal road and overlooking the harbor). This area, which stretches from the rim of the blocky, metropolitan corridors of the **Royal Parade** and **Armada Way,** is home to a wide, grassy park topped by twin monuments.

PRACTICAL INFORMATION

Transportation

Trains: Plymouth Station, North Rd. (tel. (0345) 484950), north of the city center. Ticket office open M-F 5:30am-8:30pm, Sa 5:30am-7pm, Su 9:30am-8:30pm. Take Western National bus #14, 72, or 83/84 to the city center at Royal Parade.

Buses: Bretonside Station Western National Office (tel. 222666), near St. Andrew's Cross at the eastern end of Royal Parade. Look for stairs down to the station. **Lockers** on the downstairs platform 50p-£2. Information office open M-Sa 7am-7pm, Su 9am-5pm; bank holidays 8am-5pm.

Ferries: Millbay Docks, Brittany Ferries (tel. (0990) 360360). Take city bus #34 to the docks (to the west of the city center at the mouth of the River Tamar) and follow signs to the ferry stand, a 15min. walk from the bus stop. Or avoid the walk and take a taxi (£3). Book tickets at least 24hr. in advance, though foot passengers may need to come only 2hr. ahead. Check in 1hr. before departure.

Local Transportation: Hoppa and **Citybus** buses shuttle from Royal Parade (70p-£1.80).

Taxis: Plymouth Taxis (tel. 606060) won't leave you stranded.

Bike Rental: Cycle Scene, 52b Mutley Plain (tel. 257701). Mountain bikes £10 per day, £50 deposit. Open M-Sa 9am-6pm.

Tourist and Financial Services

Tourist Office: Island House, 9 The Barbican (tel. 264849; fax 257955). On Sutton Harbour, south of the bus station. Helpful staff can book accommodations. Free map available. The building is said to have housed the Pilgrims just before their departure on the *Mayflower*. A list of those on the boat can be found on the side of the building. Open M-Sa 9am-5pm, Su 10am-4pm.

Tours: Daily **bus tours** operated by **Guide Friday** leave every 20min. from stations near the Barbican and the Hoe (tel. 222221; £5, students and seniors £4, children £1). **Boat cruises** around the harbor depart sporadically from spots near the *Mayflower* shrine on the Barbican; check boards there for times and prices.

Financial Services: Thomas Cook, 9 Old Town St. (tel. 667245; fax 252299), across from the post office. Open M-W and F-Sa 9am-5:30pm, Th 10am-5:30pm. **ATMs** are plentiful along Royal Parade and Armada Way.

American Express: 139 Armada Way (tel. 228708; fax 260747), in the plaza formed by New George St. and Armada Way. Open M and W-Sa 9am-5pm, Tu 9:30am-5pm.

Local Services

Launderette: Hoegate Laundromat, 55 Noltte St. (tel. 223031). Bring change; soap available. Open M-Th 8am-8pm, F-Su 8am-7pm. Last wash 1hr. before closing.

Emergency and Communications

Emergency: Dial 999; no coins required.

Police: Charles St. (tel. (0990) 777444), near Charles Cross bus station.

Hotlines: Samaritans (crisis), 20 Oxford Pl., Western Approach (tel. 221666), off North Rd. 24hr. hotline. Doors open daily 9am-10pm. **AIDS Line** (tel. (01392) 411600). **Rape Crisis Center** (tel. 223584 or 263600). Open W and F 7-9:30pm. **Virginia House,** 40 Looe St. (tel. 662778). Drop-in counseling services and information on numerous other support groups and services. Open M-F 9am-8pm.

Hospital: Derriford Hospital, Derriford (tel. 777111). About 5mi. north of the city center. Take bus #10, 11 or 15 from Royal Parade in front of Dingles.

Post Office: 5 St. Andrew's Cross (tel. 222450). Open M-F 9am-5:30pm, Sa 9am-5:30pm. **Postal Code:** PL1 1AB.

Telephone Code: 01752.

ACCOMMODATIONS

Inexpensive B&Bs grace Citadel Rd. and Athenaeum St. between the west end of Royal Parade and the Hoe. Rooms tend to be small, but prices are usually reasonable (£12-15). Consult the tourist office for accommodation listings in *Welcome to Plymouth* or for B&B availability.

ENGLAND

YHA Youth Hostel, Belmont House, Belmont Pl., Stoke (tel. 562189), 2mi. from city center. Take bus #15 or 81 to Stoke; the hostel is on your left. Space and elegance in a mansion with beautiful 2½-acre grounds. £9.75, under 18 £6.55. Breakfast £3, evening meals £4.50. Lockout 10am-5pm. Curfew 11pm. Book in advance.

Plymouth Backpackers Hotel, 172 Citadel Rd. (tel. 225158), 2 blocks from the west end of the Hoe. Basic dorms, laid-back atmosphere. From £8. Free showers; baths £1.50. Laundry service. No curfew. Smoking allowed downstairs.

YWCA, 9-13 Lockyer St. (tel. 660321), a pebble's toss from the Hoe and the Royal Parade. Women only. Basic, mostly single bedrooms. Feel the tropics—tanning bed only £1.45 for 25 min.! Game room and laundry facilities. £6.50 per person, £10 key deposit. Reception open M-F 8am-noon and 4-9:30pm, Sa 9am-noon and 4-9:30pm, Su 10am-8:30pm.

Camping: Riverside Caravan Park, Longbridge Rd., Marsh Mills (tel. 344122). Take bus #21 or 51 from city center toward Exeter. July-Aug. £3 per person; £3 per pitch; Sept.-June £2.50 per person, £3.50 per pitch, £3 per car.

FOOD AND PUBS

The city center and cobbled streets of the **Barbican** quake with tourists and shoppers. The largest supermarket in town is **Sainsbury's** (tel. 674767), in the Armada Shopping Centre (open M-Sa 8am-8pm, Su 10am-4pm). Pick up picnic fixings at **Plymouth Market** (tel. 264904), an indoor bazaar at the west end of New George St. (open M-Tu and Th-Sa 8am-5:30pm, W 8am-4:30pm).

The Tudor Rose, 36 New St., The Barbican (tel. 255502). An elegant little cafe covered with floral chintz indoors and with flowers in the quiet outdoors garden. Conveniently sandwiched between Barbican sites, serving "traditional English fayre," including Devon cream teas from £2.70. Open daily 10am-5:30pm.

Cap'n Jaspers, a stand by the Barbican side of the Harbor. Sells local catch to schools of tourists. Gobble sandwiches on picnic tables guarded by seagulls. Burgers from £1.10. Open M-Sa 6:30am-11:45pm, Su 10am-11:45pm.

Plymouth Arts Centre Restaurant, 38 Looe St. (tel. 202616), at Kinterbury St. up the hill from St. Andrew's Cross. Homemade for herbivores. Catch a flick downstairs (tickets £2.50-3.50). Unique, healthy dishes served in colorful surroundings. Meals served Tu and Th noon-2pm and 5-9pm, W and F-Sa noon-2pm and 5-8pm; coffee and snacks in between.

Heart and Soul Vegetarian Café, 37 New St. (tel. 263590). Vegetarian treats. Spinach rolls, pasties, and soups, all for under £2. Open M-Sa 10am-5:30pm.

Crawl through pubs on Southside St. on the way to the Barbican; **The Ship** and **The Navy,** almost at the end of Southside St., serve seaside spirits with some fishing nets hanging about. A thirtysomething crowd frequents the **Queen's Arms** on Southside at Friar's Lane, while the younger set sips at **The Bank** near the cinema.

SIGHTS AND ENTERTAINMENT

The Hoe watched battles with the Spanish Armada and boasts its own landmarks. Climb the spiral steps and leaning ladders to the balcony of **Smeaton's Tower** for ferocious blasts of wind from the Channel and a magnificent view of Plymouth and the Royal Citadel. Originally a lighthouse 14 mi. offshore, the 72 ft. tower was moved to its present site in 1882. Legend has it that Sir Francis Drake was playing bowls on the Hoe in 1588 when he heard that the Armada had entered the Channel. Classically British, Drake finished his game before hoisting sail. *(Open Easter-Sept. 10:30am-5pm. 75p, seniors 55p, children 40p, free with admission ticket to the Plymouth Dome.)*

A plaque and weathered American flag on The Barbican marks the spot where the **Pilgrims** set off in 1620 for their historic voyage to America. Subsequent departures have been marked as well, including Sir Humphrey Gilbert's voyage to Newfoundland, Sir Walter Raleigh's attempt to colonize North Carolina, and Captain Cook's voyage to Australia and New Zealand. Behind the former 13th-century **St. Andrews Church,** which was bombed in 1941, sits the 15th-century **Prysten House** containing an 11th-century tapestry and the **New World Tapestry,** which narrates the story of North American settlement and which—when finished—will be the longest in the world. Add your own stitch for £1. *(Open Apr.-Oct. M-Sa 10am-4pm. 50p, seniors and children 25p.)* In 1762, the local Jewish community built a **synagogue** on Catherine St. behind St. Andrew's Church. Still active today, it is the oldest Ashkenazi synagogue in the English-speaking world. The building is not clearly labeled; from St. Andrew's, make a right into the alley behind the Eyeland Express store.

The blackened shell of **Charles Church,** destroyed by a bomb in 1941, stands in the middle of the Charles Cross traffic circle half a block east of the bus station. The roofless walls are Plymouth's memorial to her citizens killed in the Blitz; grass grows where the altar used to stand. Keys to the ruin are available from the chief inspector's office at the Bretonside Bus Station.

The **Theatre Royal** (tel. 267222), on Royal Parade, offers perhaps the best stage in the West Country, featuring ballet, opera and West End touring companies, including the Royal National. Discount tickets available for limited shows, usually mid-week performances. Call the box office for details. *(Tickets from £12, student standby tickets purchased 30min. before the show from £10.)* The newly-opened **National Marine Aquarium,** The Barbican (tel. 220084), offers elaborate, attractive marine life exhibits like a tank of sharks and an immense re-creation of a deep-sea coral reef. *(Open daily 10am-6pm. £6.50, students and seniors £5, children £4.)*

CORNWALL

You know you've hit the Cornish "Riviera" when every cottage has a name like "Shore Enuf" or "Beachy Keen." England's southwest tip has some of the broadest, sandiest beaches in northern Europe, and the surf is up year-round whether or not the sun decides to break through. But the peninsula's riches are no secret. Every year hundreds of thousands of British and foreign tourists jockey for rays on the beaches of Penzance, St. Ives, and Newquay. Cornwall is also home to a rich collection of Stone Age and Iron Age monuments—the region has apparently attracted partially naked people for thousands of years.

GETTING ABOUT

By far the best base for exploring the region is Penzance, the terminus of **British Rail's Cornish Railways** service (tel. (0345) 484950) and of **Western National's** bus service from Plymouth. The main rail line from **Plymouth** to **Penzance** bypasses the coastal towns, but there is connecting rail service to **Newquay** (change at Par; 5-8 per day, return £10), **Falmouth** (change at Truro; M-Sa 13 per day, Su 9 per day, £7.30), and **St. Ives** (direct or with a change at St. Erth; 1-2 per hr., £2.70). Trains are frequent and distances short enough that you can easily make even Newquay a daytrip.

The **Western National** network is similarly thorough, although the interior is not served as well as the coast. **Buses** run frequently from **Penzance** to **Land's End** (#1 or 1A; M-F 12 per day, Sa 7 per day, £3.20) and **St. Ives** (#16 or 17, M-Sa 3 per hr., £2.30), and from **St. Ives** to **Newquay** (#57 or X2, M-Sa 2 per day), stopping in the smaller towns along these routes. Pick up a set of timetables at any Cornwall bus station (20p). Many buses don't run on Sundays, and many run only May through September; call the Camborne bus station (tel. (01209) 719988) to check. **Explorer tickets** are an excellent value for those making long-distance trips or hopping from town to town (£5 per day, seniors £3.50). Also potentially money-saving are three- and seven-day **Key West** tickets (£13 and £22; seniors £10 and £17). Cyclists may not relish the narrow roads, but the cliff paths, with their evenly spaced hostels, make for easy hiking.

■ Bodmin Moor

Bodmin Moor, like Dartmoor and Exmoor to the east, is high country, containing Cornwall's loftiest points—Rough Tor (1311ft.; rhymes with "chow-tor") and Brown Willy (1377ft.). Unlike Exmoor and Dartmoor, however, Bodmin Moor is not a national park, and so technically *any* hiking and camping in this scenic area requires permission from the private owners of these wind-battered lands. In practice, hikers keep to designated paths and the sheep don't prosecute. The region is rich with remains of ancient history: Bronze Age Cornishmen littered stone hut circles at the base of Rough Tor. Some maintain that Camelford, at the moor's northern edge, is the site of King Arthur's Camelot, and that Arthur and his illegitimate son Mordred fought each other at Slaughter Bridge, 1 mi. north of town.

GETTING THERE AND GETTING ABOUT

Bodmin Moor spreads north of Bodmin town towards Tintagel (on the coast), Camelford, and Launceston (both inland). Bodmin is the park's point of entry, accessible from all directions; however, it is not a good place to start hiking. **Trains** (tel. (0345) 484950) stop at the Bodmin Parkway Station on the **Plymouth-Penzance** line (from Plymouth 45min., single £6, return £11.10). The town is served directly (M-Sa) by **buses** from Padstow on the north coast (10 per day) and St. Austell on the southern shore (12 per day). **National Express** (tel. (0990) 808080) buses arrive from farther afield: Plymouth in the southeast (1½hr., 3 per day afternoons only, £3.75; book in advance). **Western National** (tel. (01208) 79898) #X4 service departs from the Mt. Folly bus stop by the Bodmin post office for **Camelford** and **Tintagel** (1hr., 1 per hr., £2.50). The #X5 leaves from **Plymouth** for the same towns (2hr., 1 per day, £3.40).

Since Bodmin is not a national park, it lacks information centers dedicated to the area; ask at the tourist office instead. **Hiking** is convenient, especially from Camelford, and is the only way to reach the tors, which give grand views of the boulder-strewn expanse. **Bikes** can be hired in Bodmin and surrounding towns.

ACCOMMODATIONS

B&Bs may be spotted across the moor or booked for a 10% deposit through the Bodmin tourist office (tel. (01208) 76616). The 13th-century monk's fishery, **St. Anne's Chapel Hayes** (tel. (01208) 72797), next to the River Camel just outside of Bodmin on the Camel Trail, provides B&B for £13.50. **Colliford Tavern** (tel. (01208) 821335), in the middle of the moorland, offers B&B accommodations (£19-25; open Easter-Sept.; tavern open noon-2pm and 7-11pm). The nearest youth hostels are on the beautiful, rugged northern coast of Cornwall, a few miles northwest of the moor. Both cost £8.80 (under 18 £6) and have a 10am-5pm lockout and an 11pm curfew.

> **YHA Boscastle Harbour,** Palace Stables, Boscastle Harbor PL35 0HD (tel. (01840) 250287); take Western National from Bodmin or Wadebridge. Beautiful hostel among steep green hills and flowery riverbanks. Open daily mid-May to Sept.; closed Oct.-Mar.
>
> **YHA Tintagel,** Dunderhole Point, Tintagel PL34 0DW (tel. (01840) 770334). From Tintagel, walk ¼mi. past the 900-year-old St. Materiana's Church; then bear left through the cemetery and keep as close to the shore as possible. After 300m look closely for the hostel's chimney, located in a hollow by the sea. Clean, self-catering kitchen, spectacular views, 26 beds, and 1 happy owner. Open May-Sept. daily; Mar.-Apr. Th-Tu; closed Oct.-Feb.

■ Bodmin

The remarkably unremarkable town of **Bodmin** (pop. 14,500) is the last supply stop before venturing onto Arthurian stomping grounds. Hidden in the quiet forests and farmlands that surround Bodmin is the stately mansion **Lanhydrock** (tel. 73320), 17th-century Gothic on the outside and plush Victorian on the inside. Built in the

(take in a rock show)

and use **AT&T Direct**^{SM} Service
to tell everyone about it.

It's all within **AT&T** your reach.

Exploring lost cultures? You better have an

AT&T Direct^{SM} Service wallet guide.

It's a list of access numbers you need to call home fast and clear from

around the world, using an AT&T Calling Card or credit card.

What an amazing planet we live on.

For a list of **AT&T Access Numbers,**
take the attached wallet guide.

It's all within  your reach.

www.att.com/traveler

For your
calling
convenience
tear off
and take
with you!

AT&T Direct℠ Service

WALLET GUIDE

Inside you'll find simple instructions on how to use AT&T Direct Service to place calling card or collect calls from outside the U.S.

All you need are the AT&T Access Numbers when you travel outside the U.S. because you can access us quickly and easily from virtually anywhere in the world. And if you need any further help, there's always an AT&T English-speaking Operator available to assist you.

www.att.com/traveler

Calling From Specially Marked Telephones

Throughout the world, there are specially marked phones that connect you to AT&T Direct℠ Service. Simply look for the AT&T logo. In the following countries, access to AT&T Direct Service is *only* available from these phones: Ethiopia, Mongolia, Nigeria, Seychelles Islands.

Public phones in Europe displaying the red 3C symbol also give you quick and easy access to AT&T Direct Service. Just lift the handset and dial ✱60 (in France dial M60) and you'll be connected to AT&T.

Pay phones in the United Kingdom displaying the New World symbol provide easy access to AT&T. Simply lift the handset and press the pre-programmed button marked AT&T.

Customer Care

If you have any questions, call 800 331-1140, Ext. 707.

When outside the U.S., dial the AT&T Access Number for the country *you are in* and ask the AT&T Operator for Customer Care.

108-25   © AT&T 6/98

Printed in the U.S.A.
on recycled paper.

To Call the U.S. and Other Countries Using Your AT&T Calling Card* or credit card∞, Follow These Steps:

1. Make sure you have an outside line. (From a hotel room, follow the hotel's instructions to get an outside line, as if you were placing a local call.)

2. If you want to call a country other than the U.S., make sure the country *you are in* is highlighted in blue on the chart like this: [   ]

3. Enter the AT&T Access Number listed in the chart for the country *you are in.*

4. When prompted, enter the telephone number you are calling as follows:

   • For calls to the U.S., dial the Area Code (no need to dial 1 before the Area Code) + 7-digit number.

   • For calls to other countries,† enter 01 + the Country Code, City Code, and Local Number.

5. After the tone, enter your AT&T Calling Card* or credit card number (not the international number). If you need help or wish to call the U.S. collect, hold for an AT&T Operator.

* You may also use your AT&T Corporate Card, AT&T Universal Card, or most U.S. local phone company cards.
† The cost of calls to countries other than the U.S. consists of basic connection rates plus an additional charge based on the country you are calling.
∞ Credit card billing subject to availability.

Special Features

Just dial the AT&T Access Number for the country *you are in* and follow the instructions listed below.

● To call U.S. 800 numbers: Enter the 800 number you are calling. (Note: Based upon the 800 number dialed, calls may be toll-free or AT&T Direct℠ Service charges may apply for the duration of the call; some numbers may be restricted.)

● To set up conference calls: Dial AT&T TeleConference Services at 800 232-1234. (Note: One conferee must be in the U.S.)

● To access language interpreters: Dial AT&T Language Line® Services at 408 648-5871.

● To record and deliver messages: Dial #123 if you get a busy signal or no answer, or dial AT&T True Messages® Service at 800 562-6275.

Here's a time-saving tip for placing additional calls: When you finish your conversation, or if there is a busy signal or no answer, don't hang up – press # and wait for the voice prompt or an AT&T Operator.

AT&T

AT&T Access Numbers

(Refer to footnotes before dialing.) From the countries highlighted in blue below, like this ☐, you can make calls to virtually any location in the world; and from *all* the countries listed, you can make calls to the U.S.

It's all within your reach.

AT&T

Albania ●	00-800-0010
American Samoa	633 2-USA
Angola	0199
Anguilla ▲	1-800-872-2881
Antigua ✦	1-800-872-2881
(Public Card Phones)	#1
Argentina	0-800-54-288
Armenia ●▲	8✦10111
Aruba	800-8000
Australia	1-800-881-011
Austria ○	022-903-011
Bahamas	1-800-872-2881
Bahrain	800-001
Bahrain ✦	800-000
Barbados ✦	1-800-872-2881
Belarus ✕ —	8✦800101
Belgium ●	0-800-100-10
Belize ▲	811
(From Hotels Only)	555
Benin ●	102
Bermuda ✦	1-800-872-2881
Bolivia ●	0-800-1112

Bosnia ▲	00-800-0010
Brazil	000-8010
British V.I. ✦	1-800-872-2881
Brunei ●	800-1111
Bulgaria ▲●	00-800-0010
Cambodia ✳	1-800-881-001
Canada	1 800 CALL ATT
Cape Verde Islands	112
Cayman Islands ✦	1-800-872-2881
Chile	800-800-311
or	800-800-288
China, PRC ▲	108-11
(Easter Island)	
Colombia	980-11-0010
Cook Island	09-111
Costa Rica	0-800-0-114-114
Croatia ▲	99-385-0111
Cyprus ●	080-90010
Czech Rep. ●	00-42-000-101
Denmark	8001-0010
Dominica ✦	1-800-872-2881

Dom. Rep. ✱✦ □	1-800-872-2881
Ecuador ▲	999-119
Egypt ● (Cairo)	510-0200
(Outside Cairo)	02-510-0200
El Salvador ○	800-1785
Estonia ●	8-00-800-1001
Fiji	004-890-1001
Finland ●	0800 99 00 11
France	0800 99 0011
French Antilles	0800 99 00 11
French Guiana	0800 99 0011
Gabon ○	00✦001
Gambia ●	00111
Georgia ▲	8✦0288
Germany	0130-0010
Ghana	0191
Gibraltar	8800
Greece ●	00-800-1311
Grenada ✦	1-800-872-2881
Guadeloupe ✦ ✳	0800 99 00 11
(Marie Galante)	

Guam	1 800 CALL ATT
Guantanamo Bay ↑ (Cuba)	935
Guatemala ○ ✱	99-99-190
Guyana ✱	165
Haiti	183
Honduras	800-0-123
Hong Kong	800-96-1111
Hungary	00✦800-01111
Iceland ●	800 9001
India ✱▲	000-117
Indonesia ↦	001-801-10
Ireland ✓	1-800-550-000
Israel	1-800-94-94-949
Italy ●	172-1011
Ivory Coast ▲	00-111-11
Jamaica ○	1-800-872-2881
Jamaica □	872
Japan IDC ●▲	0066-55-111
Japan KDD ●	005-39-111
Kazakhstan ●	8✦800-121-4321
Korea ●✱	0072-911 or 0030-911
Korea ✱	550-HOME or 550-2USA

Kuwait	800-288
Latvia (Riga)	7007007
(Outside Riga)	8✦27007007
Lebanon ○ (Beirut)	426-801
(Outside Beirut)	01-426-801
Liechtenstein ●	0-800-89-0011
Lithuania ✱ —	8✦196
Luxembourg †	0800-0111
Macao	0800-111
Macedonia, F.Y.R. of ●○	99-800-4288
Malaysia ○	1800-80-0011
Malta	0800-890-110
Marshall Isl.	1 800 CALL ATT
Mauritius	73120
Mexico ∇[1]	01-800-288-2872
Micronesia	288
Monaco ●	800-90-288
Montserrat	1-800-872-2881
Morocco	002-11-0011
Netherlands Antilles ✦	001-800-872-2881

Netherlands ●	0800-022-9111
New Zealand	000-911
Nicaragua	174
Norway	800-190-11
Pakistan ▲	00-800-01001
Palau	02288
Panama	109
(Canal Zone)	281-0109
Papua New Guinea	0507-12880
Paraguay ▲ (Asuncion City)	008-11-800
Peru ▲	0-800-50000
Philippines ●	105-11
Poland	0✦0-800-111-1111
Portugal ▲	05017-1-288
Qatar	0800-011-77
Reunion Isl.	0800 99 0011
Romania ●	01-800-4288
Russia ●✱▲ (Moscow)	755-5042
(Outside Moscow)	8-095-755-5042

Russia ●✱▲ (St. Petersburg)	325-5042
(Outside St. Petersburg)	8-812-325-5042
St. Kitts/Nevis & St. Lucia ✦	1-800-872-2881
St. Pierre & Miquelon	0800 99 0011
St. Vincent △▲	1-800-872-2881
Saipan ▲	1 800 CALL ATT
San Marino ▲	172-1011
Saudi Arabia ◇	1-800-10
Senegal	3072
Sierra Leone	1100
Singapore ■	800-0111-111
Slovakia ●	00-42-100-101
Solomon Isl.	0811
So. Africa	0-800-99-0123
Spain	900-99-00-11
Sri Lanka ■	430-430
Sudan	800-001
Suriname △	156

Sweden	020-795-611
Switzerland ●	0-800-890011
Syria	0-801
Taiwan	0080-10288-0
Thailand <	001-999-111-11
Trinidad/Tob.	1-800-872-2881
Turkey ●	00-800-12277
Turks & Caicos ✦	1-800-872-2881
Uganda	8✦100-11
Ukraine ▲	8✦100-11
U.A. Emirates	800-121
U.A. Emirates ◇	0800-89-0011 or 0500-89-0011
U.K. ▲✦	
U.S. ▲	1 800 CALL ATT
Uruguay ■	000-410
Uzbekistan 8✦	641-7440010
Venezuela	800-11-120
Vietnam ●	1-201-0288
Yemen	00 800 101
Zambia	00-899
Zimbabwe ▲	110-98990

● Public phones require coin or card deposit. ✱ Press red button. ‡ Additional charges apply when calling outside of Moscow. ■ AT&T Direct® calls cannot be placed to this country from outside the U.S. ✳ Not available from pay phones in Phnom Penh and Siem Reap only. ✕ Not available from public phones. ✦ From St. Maarten or phones at Bobby's Marina, use 1-800-872-2881.

◇ From this country, AT&T Direct® calls terminate to designated countries only. ↦ From U.S. Military Bases only. — Not yet available in all areas. ○ Select hotels. ✓ May not be available from every phone/public phone. † Collect calling from public phones. ▲ Available from phones with international calling capabilities or from most Public Calling Centers. ✓ From Northern Ireland use U.K. access code.

◇ Collect calling only. ○ Public phones require local coin payment through the call duration. ✦ Await second dial tone. ▼ When calling from public phones, phones marked 'Lenftel.' *If call does not complete, use 001-800-462-4240. ▲ Available from public phones only. ✦ Public phones and select hotels. ✓ When calling from public phones use phones marked Lenso.

□ Calling Card calls available from select hotels. ✦ Use phones allowing international access. ▼ Including Puerto Rico and the U.S. Virgin Islands. ▼ AT&T Direct® Service only from telephone calling centers in Hanoi and post offices in Da Nang, Ho Chi Minh City and Quang Ninh. ✦ If call does not complete, use 0800-013-0011.

WE GIVE YOU THE WORLD...AT A DISCOUNT

LET'S GO®

TRAVEL

MERCHANDISE CATALOG FOR 1999

LET'S GO
Travel Gear

World Journey

Equipped with Eagle Creek Comfort Zone Carry System which includes Hydrofil nylon knit on backpanel and lumbar pads. Parallel internal frame. Easy packing panel load design with internal cinch straps. Lockable zippers. Detachable daypack. Converts into suitcase. 26x15x9", 5100 cu. in., 6 lbs. 12 oz. Black, Evergreen, or Blue. $30 discount with railpass. **$225.00**

Security Items

Undercover Neckpouch Ripstop nylon with a soft Cambrelle back. Three pockets. 5 1/2" x 8 1/2". Lifetime guarantee. Black or Tan. **$10.50**

Undercover Waistpouch Ripstop nylon with a soft Cambrelle back. Two pockets. 12" x 5" with adjustable waistband. Lifetime guarantee. Black or Tan. **$10.50**

Continental Journey

Carry-on size pack with internal frame suspension. Comfort Zone padded shoulder straps and hip belt. Leather hand grip. Easy packing panel load design with internal cinch straps. Lockable zippers. Detachable daypack. Converts into suitcase. 21x15x9", 3900 cu. in., 4 lbs. 5 oz. Black, Evergreen, or Blue. $20 discount with railpass. **$175.00**

Travel Lock Great for locking up your World or Continental Journey. Two-dial combination lock. **$5.25**

Hostelling Essentials

Hostelling International Membership

Cardholders receive priority, discounts, and reservation privileges at most domestic and international hostels.

Youth (under 18)..................... free
Adult (ages 18-55)................**$25.00**
Senior (over 55)...................**$15.00**

European Hostelling Guide

Offers essential information concerning over 2500 European hostels. **$10.95**

Sleepsack

Required at many hostels. Washable polyester/cotton. Durable and compact. **$14.95**

International ID Cards
1999

Provide discounts on airfares, tourist attractions and more. Includes basic accident and medical insurance. **$20.00**

International Student ID Card (ISIC)
International Teacher ID Card (ITIC)
International Youth ID Card (GO25)

1-800-5LETSGO
http://www.hsa.net/travel

— Prices are in US dollars and subject to change.—

Eurailpass Unlimited travel in and among all 17 countries: **Austria, Belgium, Denmark, Finland, France, Germany, Greece, Holland, Hungary, Italy, Luxembourg, Norway, Portugal, Republic of Ireland, Spain, Sweden, and Switzerland.**

	15 days	21 days	1 month	2 months	3 months	10 days	15 days
First Class	*consecutive days*					*in two months*	
1 Passenger	$554	$718	$890	$1260	$1558	$654	$862
2 or More Passengers	$470	$610	$756	$1072	$1324	$556	$732
Youthpass (Second Class)							
Passengers under 26	$388	$499	$623	$882	$1089	$458	$599

Europass Travel in the five Europass countries: **France, Germany, Italy, Spain, and Switzerland.** Up to two of the four associate regions (Austria and Hungary; Benelux (Belgium, Netherlands, and Luxembourg); Greece; Portugal) may be added.

	5 days	6 days	8 days	10 days	15 days	first	second
First Class	*in two months*					*associate country*	
1 Passenger	$348	$368	$448	$528	$728	+$60	+$40
2 to 5 Passengers traveling together	$296	$314	$382	$450	$620	+$52	+$34
Youthpass (Second Class)							
Passengers under 26	$233	$253	$313	$363	$513	+$45	+$33

Pass Protection For an additional $10, insure any railpass against theft or loss.

Discounts *with the purchase of a railpass*
- $30 off a World Journey backpack
- $20 off a Continental Journey backpack
- Any *Let's Go* Guide for 1/2 Price
- Free 2-3 Week Domestic Shipping

Call about Eurostar–the Channel Tunnel Train–and other country-specific passes.

Airfares & Special Promotions

Call for information on and availability of standard airline tickets, student, teacher, and youth discounted airfares, as well as other special promotions.

Publications & More

Let's Go Travel Guides—
The Bible of the Budget Traveler

USA • India and Nepal • Southeast Asia............22.99
Australia • Eastern Europe • Europe.................21.99
Britain & Ireland • Central America • France •
Germany • Israel & Egypt • Italy • Mexico •
Spain & Portugal..19.99
Alaska & The Pacific Northwest • Austria &
Switzerland • California & Hawaii • Ecuador
& The Galapagos Islands • Greece • Ireland.....18.99
South Africa • Turkey....................................17.99
New York City • New Zealand • London •
Paris • Rome • Washington D.C. 15.99

Let's Go **Map Guides**
Know your destination inside and out!
Great to accompany your Eurailpass.

Amsterdam, Berlin, Boston, Chicago, Florence, London, Los Angeles, Madrid, New Orleans, New York, Paris, Rome, San Francisco, Washington D.C. **8.95**

Michelin Maps

Czech/Slovak Republics • Europe • France • Germany • Germany/Austria /Benelux • Great Britain & Ireland • Greece • Italy • Poland • Scandinavia & Finland • Spain & Portugal **10.95**

LET'S GO® Order Form

| Last Name* | First Name* | Home and Day Phone Number* (very important) |

| Street* | (Sorry, we cannot ship to Post Office Boxes) |

| City* | State* | Zip Code* |

| Citizenship‡§¤ (Country) | School/College§ | Date of Birth‡§ | Date of Travel* |

Qty	Description	Color	Unit Price	Total Price

Shipping and Handling

2-3 Week Domestic Shipping
Merchandise value under $30	$4
Merchandise value $30-$100	$6
Merchandise value over $100	$8

2-3 Day Domestic Shipping
Merchandise value under $30	$14
Merchandise value $30-$100	$16
Merchandise value over $100	$18

Overnight Domestic Shipping
Merchandise value under $30	$24
Merchandise value $30-$100	$26
Merchandise value over $100	$28

| All International Shipping | $30 |

Total Purchase Price	
Shipping and Handling	+
MA Residents add 5% sales tax on gear and books	+
TOTAL	

☐ Mastercard   ☐ Visa

Cardholder name:

Card number:

Expiration date:

When ordering an International ID Card, please include:
1. Proof of birthdate (copy of passport, birth certificate, or driver's license).
2. One picture (1.5" x 2") signed on the reverse side.
3. (ISIC/ITIC only) Proof of current student/teacher status (letter from registrar or administrator, proof of tuition, or copy of student/faculty ID card. FULL-TIME only).

* Required for all orders
‡ Required in addition for each Hostelling Membership
§ Required in addition for each International ID Card
¤ Required in addition for each railpass

Prices are in US dollars and subject to change.

Make check or money order payable to:
Let's Go Travel
17 Holyoke Street
Cambridge, MA 02138
(617) 495-9649

1-800-5LETSGO

Hours: Mon.-Fri., 10am-6pm ET

1600s and gutted by a disastrous fire in 1881, the mansion retains few original features except the magnificent gallery ceiling, decorated with scenes from the Old Testament in delicate plasterwork (wow, Goliath was big!). The numerous benches across the 1000-acre estate's elaborate gardens make for pleasant picnics. *(Open Apr.-Oct. Tu-Su 11am-5:30pm, last entry 5pm. £6.20, children £3.10. Grounds only open daily Apr.-Oct. £3.10, children £1.55; family pass £15 for house and gardens.)* Walk 2½ mi. southeast of Bodmin on the A38, or take Western National #55 from Bodmin.

To get to the center of town from the **Bodmin Parkway Station,** 5 mi. out of town on the A38, hop bus #55 (£1.20), or take a taxi (£4). If you miss the bus to the train station, call **ABTaxis** (tel. 75000). The helpful **tourist office** (tel. 76616), in Bodmin at the Mount Folly Car Park, carries Ordnance Surveys maps of the area (£5; open M-Sa 10am-5pm). The major banks on Fore St. have **ATMs** which accept Cirrus and Plus. Find two-wheeled transport at **The Bike Shop** (tel. 72557), in Church Sq. at the bottom of Mt. Folly and Fore St. (mountain bikes £8 per day; deposit £25; open M-Sa 9am-6pm). The **police station** (tel. (0990) 777444) is up Priory Rd., past the ATS car parks. The **post office** (tel. 72638) is situated just beyond the tourist office up Crinnicks Hill (open M-F 9am-5:30pm, Sa 9am-12:30pm). Bodmin's **postal code** is PL3 1AA; its **telephone code** is 01208.

For accommodations in the town itself, try **Elmsleigh,** 52 St. Nicholas St. (tel. 75976), which provides large, pastel-wallpapered rooms and breakfasts with rose-shaped butter pats (£14). The closest camping to Bodmin is a mile north of the town at the **Camping and Caravanning Club,** Old Callywith Rd. (tel. 73834), with laundry, showers, and a shop. (July-Aug. £3.80 per person, children £1.45, £4 per pitch; Sept.-June prices lower; electricity £1.50.) For food, head to Fore St., where grocers and bakers hawk edibles. **Pots Coffee Shop and Restaurant,** 55 Fore St. (tel. 74601), offers a huge variety of fillings for sandwiches or jacket potatoes, and makes blackcurrant milkshakes as thick as yogurt (open M-Sa 9am-5:30pm, Su 11:30am-2pm).

■ Camelford and Tintagel

Thirteen miles north of Bodmin, **Camelford** seems not to have grown much since the days when it was Arthur's Camelot (if the legend is to be believed). Tiny **Slaughter Bridge,** a mile north of town, crudely inlaid with hunks of petrified wood, marks the site where Arthur fell. Folks at the Camelford **tourist office** (tel. (01840) 212954), in the North Cornwall Museum, can tell you how to find the inscribed stone marking his grave (open Apr.-Sept. M-Sa 10am-5pm). From the center of town, **Rough Tor** is a 1¼ hour walk through mist and nervous sheep. Take Rough Tor Rd. to the end; the summit looms ahead. The climb is not arduous until the 300 ft. ascent at the top of the tor, where stacked granite boulders form steps and passageways, offering a wind-ravaged lookout above the moor.

Tintagel, 6 mi. northwest of Camelford, is the promontory fortress of Arthurian legend. Roman and medieval ruins cling to a headland besieged by the Atlantic; some have collapsed into the sea. If you climb through the debris to Merlin's cave below, check for low tide times and be careful on the steep cliffs. The site is dominated by a building that is unfortunately not a ruin: the King Arthur's Castle Hotel and the attached Excali-Bar (ouch!) loom on a neighboring cliff. Still, it's possible to imagine a mythical figure stepping forth from this brittle castle hacked into the hillside. *(Castle open daily Apr.-Sept. 10am-6pm; Oct.-Mar. 10am-4pm. £2.80, students £2.10, seniors £1.40, children £1.90, under 5 free.)* Inland lies the one-road village, lined with Arthur bistros and Pendragon gift shops. On Fore St. in the center of town stands **King Arthur's Great Hall of Chivalry** (tel. (01840) 770526). An antechamber tells Arthur's story with spotlights, a pulsing red laser, and a "mist of time" laid down by a humidifier; beyond, the great hall houses not one, not two, but *three* Round Tables. *(Open daily 10am-5pm. £2.50, children £1.75.)* Down the street toward the castle is the **Old Post Office** (tel. 01840) 770024), a medieval manor house (mind your head) used as a post office in the 19th century. *(Open May-Oct. daily 11am-5:30pm. £2, children £1.)* Tintagel has no tourist office; a **YHA Youth Hostel** at Dunderhole Point provides seaside lodgings (see **Accommodations,** p. 206), or try the **B&Bs** on Bossiney Rd.

■ Falmouth

Seven rivers flow into the town of Falmouth (pop. 18,300), which maintains its maritime routes even while reaching for urban vitality. Two spectacular castles guard this historically divisive port. In the 16th and 17th centuries, Falmouth's ruthless Killigrews built a name on piracy and murder. The Killigrews were loyal to none but themselves; a particularly faithless one sold Pendennis Castle to the Spanish. Though only souvenir shops now skirmish in Falmouth, the magnificent 450-year-old fortresses of Pendennis and St. Mawes still eye each other across the narrow harbor, like two retired soldiers in seafront beach chairs, occasionally awakening to welcome modern-day armadas sailing sedately through their harbor.

GETTING THERE

About 60 mi. west of Plymouth along England's southern coast, Falmouth is accessible by **rail** (tel. (0345) 484950) from any stop on the **London-Penzance** line (including **Exeter** and **Plymouth**); change at **Truro** and go three stops (30min., Plymouth-Falmouth M-Sa 17 per day, in summer Su 9 per day, £9.50). From Truro, **Western National buses** #X89, 89, 88A, and X90 run to Falmouth (M-Sa 2 per hr., Su 1 per hr., £2.20). From London, **National Express** (6½hr., 2 per day, £34.50) stops in **Newquay, Plymouth,** and **Penzance.** From Penzance, **Western National** buses #2 and 2A rumble to **Helston** (7 per day, £3.50).

ORIENTATION

Falmouth has three train stations, all stops on the Truro-Falmouth line and all platforms in the grass. **Penmere Halt** is a 10-minute walk from town, though it's the closest stop to the tourist office; the **Dell-Falmouth Town** is east of the center and close to budget B&B-land; **Falmouth Docks** is nearest the hostel and Pendennis Castle. Out-of-town buses and local **Hoppa** buses stop just outside the tourist office at **The Moor,** a large traffic island on Killigrew St., which runs perpendicular to the harbor. As elsewhere in Cornwall, streets are narrow; hug a wall if a car comes by. The narrow streets make **hitching** difficult, since there's no room to pull over. Hitchers generally head 1½ mi. out of town to Dracaena Ave.

PRACTICAL INFORMATION

Trains: None of the stations sell tickets; get 'em at **Newell's Travel Agency,** 26 Killigrew St., The Moor (tel. 315066 for bus and train reservations), next door to the tourist office. Open M-F 9am-5:30pm, Sa 9am-4pm.

Buses: Buses stop next to the tourist office at The Moor. Call **Western National** (tel. (01209) 719 9880. For **National Express** schedules and tickets, contact Newell's Travel Agency (see above).

Boats and Ferries: Check signs on Prince of Wales Pier and Custom House Quay. **St. Mawe's Ferry Co.** (tel. 313201 or 313813) runs cruises around the bay (2 per day) and ferries to St. Mawes (M-Sa 2 per hr., Su 1 per hr., return £4, children £2).

Taxis: Falmouth & Penryn Radio Taxi (tel. 315194).

Bike Rental: Aldridge Cycles (tel. 318600), opposite Quay Side Inn on Swanpool St. £5 per day, £20 deposit. Open M-Tu and Th-Su 9am-5:30pm, W 9am-1pm.

Tourist Office: 28 Killigrew St., The Moor (tel. 312300). From inland, follow signs to Killigrew Rd. or Kimberley Park Rd., then go downhill toward the river. Offers accommodations service and has information on the Lizard Peninsula. Open Apr.-Sept. M-Th 9am-5pm, F 9am-4:45pm; July-Aug. also Su 10am-4pm; Oct.-Mar. M-Th 9am-1pm and 2-5pm, F 9am-1pm and 2-4:45pm.

Financial Services: Barclays, 6 Killigrew St. (tel. 78341), The Moor. Open M and W-F 9am-5:30pm, Tu 9:30am-5:30pm, Sa 9:30am-noon. **Lloyds,** 11-12 Killigrew St., The Moor (tel. 212600). Open M-Tu and Th-F 9am-5pm, W 9:30am-5pm. Both are equipped with **ATMs.**

Emergency: Dial 999; no coins required.

Police: (tel. (0990) 700400 daytime or 777444 24hr.) Unfortunately, the nearest station is in Penryn (tel. 372231).

Hotlines: Samaritans (crisis; tel. (01872) 77277). Open 24hr. **Cornwall AIDS Helpline** (tel. (01872) 42520). Open M-F 10am-4pm. **Gay and Lesbian Switchboard Cornwall** (tel. (01209) 314449). Open M and F 7:30-10:30pm. **Women's Aid** (tel. (01736) 350319). Open M-F 10am-4pm.

Hospital: Falmouth Hospital, Trescobeas Rd. (tel. (01872) 74242).

Post Office: The Moor (tel. 312525). Open M-F 9am-5:30pm, Sa 9am-12:30pm. **Postal Code:** TR11 3RB.

Telephone Code: 01326.

ACCOMMODATIONS

The B&Bs on Cliff Rd. and Castle Dr. have spectacular views of the foliage and cliffs that touch the water; reserve ahead and expect to pay for the thrill. Ask about the ghost. B&Bs closer to town are cheaper, but lack beach access and views. The especially accommodating tourist office will book a bed within your budget.

YHA Youth Hostel, Pendennis Castle, Falmouth (tel. 311435; fax 315473). A 30min. walk from town ending with an uphill hike by the sea. Guests can savor the sunset beyond this star-shaped castle after tours end at 6pm. Some upstairs rooms have startling views. The hostel is rather small and often occupied by school groups; book at least 3 weeks ahead in summer. Guests also get into summer concerts held on the castle grounds for free. £8.80, under 18 £6. Breakfast £3, packed lunch £2.45, dinner £4.50. Reception open 8:30-10am and 5-10:30pm. Curfew 11pm. Open Feb.-Sept. daily; Oct.-Nov. Tu-Sa; closed Dec.-Jan.

Engleton House, 67 Killigrew St. (tel. 315447). Large rooms with comfortable beds and cheery floral decorations. Twins and doubles £30-34.

Castleton Guest House, 68 Killigrew St. (tel. 311072), next door to Engleton House. Comfortable accommodations with adorable vanity tables in a 200-year-old house. Vegetarians may request alternatives to the English breakfast. Doubles £30.

Dolvean Hotel, 50 Melvill Rd. (tel. 313658; fax 313995). Offers a luxurious view of the beach and a short walk to the shore. Paul makes sure you have everything you need, including biscuits by your bedside in the morning. Mid-June to Oct. and bank holidays £23; Nov. to mid-June £20.

Camping: Tremorvah Tent Park, Swanpool Rd. (tel. 318311), just past Swanpool Beach and reachable by Hoppa bus #6 (every 30min.). A lovely hillside spot with laundry and showers. £3 per night, car 50p extra; £18 per week, July-Aug. £20.

FOOD

You won't escape Falmouth without picking up a pasty (PAH-stee; the frighteningly omnipresent Cornish stuffed turnover) filled with meat or vegetables, about £1 at any bakery, coffeehouse, barbershop, or pet store on the waterfront. ("Welcome to the bank. Pasty?") The town's supermarket is **Tesco,** on The Moor (open M-Tu 8:30am-5:30pm, W-F 8am-8pm, Sa 8am-5:30pm, Su 10am-4pm). **De Wynn's 19th Century Coffee House,** 55 Church St. (tel. 319259), delivers exotic teas and baked specialties in a dainty antique-shop setting (open M-Sa 10am-5pm, Su 11am-4pm). **Bon Ton Roulet,** 18 Church St. (tel. 319290), features racy turn-of-the-century 'toons and jacket potatoes for £2-3; entrees are more pricey. (Open M-Sa 11am-2:15pm and 6:30-10:15pm; in summer also Su noon-2:15pm and 7-10:15pm.) The various bistros and small restaurants that line Church St. offer hidden deals on their blackboard menus.

SIGHTS AND ENTERTAINMENT

Pendennis Castle (tel. 316594), built by Henry VIII to keep French frigates out of Falmouth, now features a walk-through diorama that assaults the senses with waxen gunners bellowing incoherently and a dry ice machine. Better views and ventilation are on the battlements. *(Open daily July-Aug. 9am-6pm; Apr.-June and Sept.-Oct. 10am-6pm; Nov.-Mar. 10am-4pm. £3, students and seniors £2.30, children £1.50.)* Across the channel

ENGLAND

from Pendennis stands the magnificently preserved **St. Mawes Castle** (tel. 270526), built by Henry VIII to blow holes through any Frenchman the gunners of Pendennis spared. An occasionally wet 20-minute ferry ride from Falmouth ends among the thatched roofs and aspiring tropical gardens of St. Mawes village. *(Ferries depart from Town Pier and the Quay every 30min., return £3.50.)* Henry's stone minion is now a six-story playset where English schoolboys try to froth enough spit to make scary cannon sound effects. The tower is worth climbing, but Pendennis wins the battle for superior views. *(Open daily Apr.-Oct. 10am-6pm; Nov.-Mar. F-Tu 10am-4pm. £2.50, students and seniors £1.90, children £1.30. 1hr. cassette tour with admission. Regardless of what the tourist brochure might say, there is not a whit of wheelchair access to the castle.)*

For a small town, Falmouth has a surprisingly vibrant social scene. Falmouth's hottest club, **Paradox** (tel. 314453), on The Moor, puts in a few good hours spinning rock and chart music before heading off to bed. *(Open daily 7pm-1am.)* Swill your rum and sail for booty at the **Pirate Inn** on Grove Place, opposite the Killigrew Monument and the Quay. Local live bands perform every night. *(Open M-Th 7pm-midnight, F-Sa 7pm-1am, Su 7-10:30pm.)* On Friday and Saturday nights, the crowd at **The Cork and Bottle** vies to match that of **The Grapes Inn** (tel. 314704), directly across the road at 64 Church St. *(Open M-Sa 11am-11pm, Su noon-10:30pm.)* The **Falmouth Arts Centre,** Church St. (tel. 212300), holds art exhibitions, concerts, theater, and films. *(Theater tickets around £5.)* Mid-July heralds the **Cutty Sark Tall Ships Race.** The town itself throws a tizzy over the first two weeks of August with **Carnival** and **Regatta Weeks.**

To taste the surf, head to one of the three beaches on Falmouth's southern shore. If the skies look gray in the morning, hold a sun vigil until noon, and the Cornish weather might surprise you. **Castle Beach,** on Pendennis Head, is too pebbly for swimming or sunbathing, but low tide reveals a labyrinth of seaweed and tidepools writhing with life. **Gyllyngvase Beach** is the sandiest and has the best facilities, making it popular with both windsurfers and families.

■ Near Falmouth: Lizard Peninsula

Once a leper's colony, the **Lizard Peninsula** between Falmouth and Penzance sits in relative isolation, untrampled by tourists. Though the peninsula's name does not help the tourist office corner the herpephobic market, visitors will likely not encounter reptilia. "Lizard" is a corruption of Old Cornish "Lys ardh," meaning "the high place." A scaly line of cliffs and caves striped with serpentine paths leads to **Lizard Point,** the most southerly prong of England—where the Atlantic becomes the English Channel. Inland, the heath of **Goonhilly Downs** is riven by slices of purple rock: the Lizard's rare minerals produce soil that yields exotic flora. While traveling through Goonhill Downs, pay a visit to **Earth Station Goonhilly** (tel. (0800) 679593), the world's largest satellite station. Exhibits, films, and a shuttle tour through the satellites' perimeter are offered, as well as a free "Internet Zone." One and a half miles from Mullion, a village on the west coast of the Lizard, waves swirl around rocks at **Mullion Cove,** lined with steep but grassy and climbable cliffs. Hundreds of seabirds nest on **Mullion Island,** 300m off the cove.

Take **Western National** bus #2 or 2A from Falmouth or Penzance to Helston (1hr., 2 per hr., £3) and one of the **Truronian** (tel. (01872) 273453) lines down to Mullion and the Lizard (1hr., 6 per day, £2.25 and £2.50 respectively). The Penzance and St. Ives bus stations provide guided tours of town on Tuesdays (leaves Penzance 11am, St. Ives at 11:30am; £5.70, children £3.80). For information on **bus service** into the peninsula, call Camborne (tel. (01209) 719988). **Driving** access is via the A30383 from the A394. The tiny town of **The Lizard** has capitalized handily on its unique claim to fame, enjoying a roaring (or at least hissing) trade in "serpentine sales and gifts." Snaking out of the town is the path to **Lizard Point,** where perilous cliffside paths wind past wildflowers, clinging to the rocks above the waves. A small information booth near the car park vends walking maps for a small fee.

If you'd like to stay the night and claim front-row seats for the sunset, contact the **Helston tourist office** (tel. 565431), in front of the Coinagehall bus stop (open M-Sa 10am-1pm and 2-5pm, may close 15min. early). A variety of **short walks** exploring the rocky cliffs, sandy beaches, and flaming flora of the peninsula radiate from The Lizard; check the maps and the free *Guide to the Lizard Peninsula* from the Helston tourist office. Pick up cash in Helston if you need it—ATMs are not native. Access to the peninsula is tedious; everything runs through Helston. **YHA Coverack** (tel. 280687), in the southeast, is the only YHA hostel on the peninsula (£8.80, under 18 £6; breakfast £3, dinner £4.50; open Apr.-Oct. daily). Take Truronian bus #T3 from Helston to Coverack Village. Shetland ponies share their digs with campers on the farm at **Henry's Campsite** (tel. 290596; £3 per 1-person tent, £5 per 2-person, 50p each additional person).

■ Penzance

Penzance is the very model of an ancient English pirate town. Fresh, bracing, salty air makes the city seem as timeless as the sea itself: old pirate hangouts choke its streets, smugglers' tunnels run beneath its alleys, and buildings still bear the scorch marks of 16th-century raids. But the ghost galleons that visit the city's harbor each night are accompanied by an armada of ship-in-a-bottle booty raids on tourist doubloons. Countless souvenir shops can make Penzance feel as authentic as the wooden pirates on a Disney ride. In any case, the city's most valuable treasure shines in the sky, not buried underground—the sun smiles on Penzance like a knowing conspirator.

GETTING THERE

Just 10 mi. from England's southwesternmost point, Penzance is the last stop on a long **train** ride (tel. (0345) 484950) from **London** (£53) via **Plymouth** (1½hr., £10, return £12) and **Exeter** (2½hr., £24.50, return £31). Change at **St. Erth** for **St. Ives** (£3); change at **Par** for **Newquay** (£10-11). A **Regional Railways** timetable at the tourist office longs to share its wisdom; don't forget about the many long-term Southwest England rail passes (see **Trains,** p. 185).

Eight **National Express Rapide buses** (tel. (0990) 808080) travel to **London** daily (8hr., £35.50; stops at **Heathrow**). Buses run to **Plymouth** via **Truro** (3hr., 2 per hr., £6). Local service runs to **St. Ives** (#16 or 17, 40min., 5 per hr., £2.40), **Land's End** (#1 or 4, 50min., 1 per hr., £3), **Mousehole** (MUZ-zle; 20min., 2 per hr., £1.20), **Falmouth** (Western National bus #2/2X, 1½hr., 2 per hr., £4.80), and **Helston** (Hoppa bus #2, 45min., 1 per hr., £3, change here for **Lizard Peninsula**).

National Express, Western National, and Cornwall buses offer **guided tours** of the area and bargain Explorer passes. **Western National** guided tours (tel. (01209) 719988) include weekly trips from Penzance to King Arthur's Country (Boscastle and Tintagel; Th 9:30am; £7.20, children £4.80), fishing villages (W 9:30am; £6, children £4), and the Lizard Peninsula (M 11am; £6, children £4).

ORIENTATION

Penzance's rail station, bus station, and tourist office stand conveniently together in the same square, adjacent to both the harbor and the town. **Market Jew St.** rises up from the harbor, laden with well-stocked bakeries and ill-stacked bookstores (the street's name is a corruption of the Cornish "Marghas Yow," meaning "Market Thursday"). **Chapel St.,** the cobblestone row of antique shops and pubs, descends from the town center into a welter of alleys near the algaed docks.

PRACTICAL INFORMATION

Trains: Wharf Rd. (tel. (0345) 484950), at the head of Albert Pier. Office open M-Sa 6:15am-6:15pm, Su 8:15am-5:15pm.

Buses: Wharf Rd. (Camborne tel. (01209) 719988), at the head of Albert Pier. Information and ticket office open M-F 8:30am-4:45pm, Sa 8:30am-3pm. Don't pay 5p to use the bus station's toilets—they're free across the road at the rail station.

Bike Rental: Bike Bitz (tel. 333243), on Albert St. Mountain bikes £6 per day, £10 overnight; deposit £50 or ID. Open M-Sa 9am-5pm.

Tourist Office: Station Rd. (tel. 362207), between the train and bus stations. Books beds for a 10% deposit. Free map of Penzance. Open in summer M-F 9am-5pm, Sa 9am-4pm, Su 10am-1pm; in winter M-F 9am-5pm, Sa 10am-1pm. Arranges mini-coach **tours** of attractions in west Cornwall, led by the mirthful Harry Safari (Su-F 1 per day; £12.50).

Financial Services: Barclays, 8-9 Market Jew St. (tel. 362271; fax 364297). Open M-Tu and Th-F 9am-5pm, W 10am-5pm.

Launderette: Polyclean, on the corner of Leskinnick and Market Jew St. Soap available. Open daily 9am-9pm; last wash 7:45pm.

Emergency: Dial 999; no coins required.

Police: Penalverne Dr. (central regional tel. (0990) 777444), off Alverton St.

Hotlines: Samaritans (crisis; tel. (01872) 277277). Open 24hr. **Women's Aid** (tel. 350319). Open M-F 10am-4pm.

Hospital: West Cornwall Hospital, St. Clare St. (tel. 362382). Bus #10, 10A, 11, 11A, 11D to St. Clare St.

Post Office: 113 Market Jew St. (tel. 363284). Open M-F 9am-5:30pm, Sa 9am-12:30pm. **Postal Code:** TR18 2LB.

Telephone Code: A booty-calling 01736.

ACCOMMODATIONS

Penzance's fleet of B&Bs occupies the hills above the Esplanade and beach, primarily Morrab Rd. between Alverton St. and Western Promenade Rd. Also check out the side streets off Chapel St. and, further out, on Alexandra Rd. Prices range £13-16. Camping areas blanket the west Cornwall peninsula.

YHA Youth Hostel, Castle Horneck (tel. 362666). A 30min. stroll up Market Jew St. and then Alverton St. (Hoppa B and hop off at Pirate Inn, or Albert's taxi from the train or bus station for £2.30). Turn right onto Castle Horneck and take the left fork up the hill; follow the signs across the road. An 18th-century mansion restored to its former glory amidst rich foliage. The loquacious warden Paul keeps the cappuccino and conversation flowing. Classy lounge, self-catering kitchen, and laundry facilities. £9.75, under 18 £6.55. Breakfast £3, cafeteria dinner £2-5. Reception open daily 5-11pm. Lockout 10am-5pm. No curfew. Open year-round. **Campsites** in the backyard for £5, including use of hostel facilities.

Cornerways, 5 Leskinnick St. (tel. 364645), a block from the rail station. You're in luck—you'll get a warm B&B welcome from the entire royal family, past and present, and on porcelain. Book weeks ahead. Friendly proprietress offers vegetarian options as well; call ahead. *Let's Go* readers £14; student doubles £22; optional evening meal £6.50.

YMCA, The Orchard Alverton (tel. 365016), past the Alexandra Rd. roundabout on the left. Co-ed dorm accommodations in linoleum-floored rooms, some of which have washbasins. No smoking. £9.35. Light breakfast £2.70. Lockout 9:30am-2pm, Sa-Su 10am-6pm. No curfew.

Trelawney, 28 Chapel St. (tel. 367658). Next door to the home of Maria and Elizabeth Branwell, mother and aunt of the infamous Brontë siblings. Large, comfortable rooms with a bidet for your, uh…laundry. £15.

Camping: Bone Valley, Heamoor, Penzance (tel. 360313). Family-run site 2mi. from town center. July-Aug. £5 per person; Sept.-June £4 per person; £1 per car.

FOOD AND PUBS

Expect to pay at least £7 for Penzance's excellent seafood dinners along the Quay. Market Jew St. fare is unexciting and expensive. The best buys are in coffee shops and local eateries on smaller streets and alleys, far from the hustle-bustle of town. **The Turk's Head,** 46 Chapel St., serves delicious food in a 13th-century pub—Penzance's oldest—sacked by Spanish pirates in 1595. In the 17th century a smuggler's tunnel allegedly wound from the harbor to the inn. (Lunch £4-5, seafood dinners from £5. Open M-Sa 11am-2:30pm and 6-10pm, Su noon-2:30pm and 6-10pm.) **The Hungry Horse** (tel. 363446), hidden in an alley off Chapel St., is a bit of a splurge, but worth every penny. Try gourmet pizzas from £4 and chargrilled specialties from about £7 (open M-Sa 7-10:30pm). For a great deal, head to **Snatch-a-Bite,** 45 New St. (tel. 366866), off Market Jew St. at Lloyds Bank, where you'll find sumptuous salads (under £3.50), sandwiches (under £2), and that rarity in Britain, a *mug* of coffee (60p; open M-Sa 9am-4pm). The **Market House Café** (tel. 366656), across from Abbey National, offers veggie specials in an environmentally friendly atmosphere for under £3.50 (open M-F 9:30am-4:30pm, Sa 9am-5pm). On the waterfront, the **Dolphin Tavern,** The Quay (tel. 364106), is haunted by an old sea captain's ghost and was the first place tobacco was smoked in Britain. On Chapel St., you can spit and cuss as smugglers once did in the nautical chambers of the 400-year-old **Admiral Benbow,** or swill elderberry wine and Cornish mead by candlelight in the medieval dungeon of **The Regent Meadery Restaurant** (tel. 362946; open daily 6:30-10pm).

SIGHTS AND ENTERTAINMENT

Most of the town's few sights lie on Chapel St. between Market Jew St. and the docks. The bizarre and gaudily painted facade of the **Egyptian House,** near the top of the street, pokes fun at itself and the 1830s craze for Egyptian ornamentation. A stoned sailor greets visitors to the **Maritime Museum,** 19 Chapel St., which simulates the life of an 18th-century seaman with 5 ft. ceilings and scant lighting. The maritime quiz challenges would-be old salts—just what is a *binnacle? (Open May-Oct. M-Sa 10:30am-4:30pm. £2, seniors £1.50, children £1. Arrrr!)* A few blocks west, nestled in the Penlee Gardens, the recently renovated **Penzance and District Museum and Art Gallery** (tel. 363625) houses, as the name suggests, a joint regional art gallery. Look for the 18th-century Scold's Bridle—a menacing discouragement for loose lips. *(Open M-F 10:30am-4:30pm, Sa 10:30am-12:30pm. £2, students and seniors £1, children free.)*

In AD 495, the archangel St. Michael supposedly appeared to some fishermen on a small island across the bay from Penzance at Marazion. A Benedictine monastery was built on the spot, and today **St. Michael's Mount** (tel. 710507) sits like an offshore apparition, with a church and castle at its peak and a village at its base. The castle's interior is unspectacular; the grounds are more textured, and the 30-story views are captivating. Joachim von Ribbentrop, Hitler's foreign minister, had the mountain picked out as his personal residence after the conquest of England. *(Open Apr.-Oct. M-F 10:30am-5:45pm, most weekends during summer, and clement days during winter; last admission at 4:45pm. Island admission £3.90, children £1.95; families £10.)* Take bus #2 or 2A from Penzance to Marazion, and turn right at the post office, toward the harbor (M-Sa 3 per hr., return 80p). Access to the monastery is by ferry when the seaweed-strewn causeway to the island is submerged during high tide (return £1.40, children 80p). Walkers beware—the sea-shaped pathway is painfully uneven.

In the wasteland of B&Bs back on shore near Morrab Rd., **Morrab Gardens** is a mirage of palms and grassy lawns. Bacchus visits the city in June during the pagan **Golowan Festival,** including St. John's Eve featuring bonfires, fireworks, and the election of the mock Mayor of the Quay. For seven weeks during the summer, natives and tourists flock to the **Minack Theatre** (visitor center tel. (01736) 381081), an open-air auditorium, 9 mi. from Penzance, with offerings from Shakespeare to the inevitable *Pirates of Penzance.* Hacked into a cliffside at Porthcurno, the theatre reportedly

Are You Chicken?

Before automobiles allowed life-threatening games, Brits were letting out their aggression in cock-fights, a long-established popular sport introduced by the Romans. Cocks were bred and trained to don steel spurs and fight to the death in a small round area called the "cockpit." Battles—known as "mains"—were fought between teams of birds, and the last surviving chicken was named champion. During the Middle Ages, schoolboys brought pet cocks to school and their masters arranged matches. The bird-bloodbaths were prohibited in 1849, but scattered cock-fights are secretly carried on to this day.

ENGLAND

appeared in a dream of Victorian Rowena Cade, who enlisted the help of some sympathetic souls and constructed the amphitheatre "with her own hands." *(Open daily Apr.-Oct. 9:30am-5:30pm; Oct.-Dec. 10am-4pm; closed noon-4:30pm during matinees. Performances £5-6, children £2.50-3. Matinees £2, seniors £1.50, ages 12-18 £1, under 12 free.)* On Wednesdays, a bus runs from the Penzance tourist office. *(£9.50, children £6, including tickets.)* For other buses, call Western National (tel. (01209) 719988), Mount's Bay Coaches (tel. (01736) 363320) or Oates Travel (tel. (01736) 795343). Access by **car** is via the B3283.

■ Near Penzance: The North Devon Coast Path

Although this coastal stretch is the highest of England's Cliff Walks, it's the least arduous of the four sections of the Southwest Peninsula Coast Path, which hugs cliffs and shore all the way around Cornwall and back to South Devon. The path runs 87 mi. from Minehead west through Porlock, Lynmouth, Ilfracombe, and Marshland Mouth at the Devon-Cornwall border, passing within 2 mi. of the YHA youth hostels at Minehead, Lynton, Ilfracombe, Instow, and Hartland. The hostels are about 20 mi. apart, an ambitious but not impossible day's walk. On the way, the path passes **Culbone** and England's smallest church, the 100 ft. dunes of **Saunton Sands,** and the steep cobbled streets of **Clovelly Village** on Hartland Point, with pubs dating back to the 1500s. Pick up the Countryside Commission's leaflet on the path at any tourist office, and bring a large-scale Ordnance Survey map, also available at tourist offices—some stretches of the path are not clearly marked.

■ Land's End to St. Ives

The Penwith Peninsula scrolls into the Celtic Sea at **Land's End** with dramatic granite cliffs. Unfortunately, protective efforts could not prevent the area from being sold and transformed into an area of outlandish commercial booty. Land's End is now a tourist holiday park of rides, historic displays, and other plastic phenomena, but a look out to the cliffs and sea will remind you why you came. **Buses** run to Land's End from Penzance (1hr., 1 per hr., return £3.20) and St. Ives (35min., 3 per day, £2). If the Atlantic winds are chill, the water's-edge **First and Last House** (tel. (01736) 871680) will provide you with a cup of coffee for 60p.

Buses #10, 10A, 10B, or 11 from Penzance will take you to **St. Just** (pop. 2700), just north of Land's End on Cape Cornwall. This craggy coast, strewn with cows and cottages, remains unexploited and remarkably beautiful. Short (2-4mi.) day hikes are outlined in leaflets in most tourist offices, but the dramatic cliff path winding around the entire coast unveils the best of Cornwall. The **YHA St. Just,** at Letcha Vean (tel. (01736) 788437), is set on three pristine acres with a view of the sea from many rooms. From the bus station's rear exit, turn left and follow the lane to its end, past the chapel and farm. (£8.80, under 18 £6. Daytime bedroom lockout. Open Apr.-Oct. daily; mid-Feb. to Mar. Tu-Sa; Nov. Su-Th.) Just 1½ mi. from Land's End (9 mi. from Penzance) in the tiny hamlet of Sennon, **Land's End Backpackers and Guest House,** White Sands Lodge (tel. (01736) 871776), will dazzle with its Crayola-bright walls, communal spirit, and a wholefood cafe (£9; private guest house rooms £12.50, with breakfast £15.) Give 'em a ring and they may pick you up from the Penzance bus or train station; or take Western National #1 or 1A from Penzance or Land's End (1hr., 12 per day) or #15 from Land's End to Sennon (5min., 1 per day).

The tiny village of **Zenner** (accessible by bus from St. Ives) hosts **The Old Chapel** (tel. (01736) 798307), a beautiful and immaculate independent hostel. Rest your weary soul with a free welcome of tea and conversation (£9). Hiking is nearby and all meals are available in the hostel's cafe—try the "best chocolate cake in England."

Inland on the Penwith Peninsula, some of the best-preserved Stone and Iron Age monuments in England lie along the Land's End-St. Ives bus route. Once covered by mounds of earth, the *quoits* (also called cromlechs or dolmens) are believed to be burial chambers dating back to 2500 BC. The **Zennor Quoit** is named for the town where a mermaid, drawn by the singing of a young man, happily returned to the sea with him in tow. On misty evenings, locals claim to see and hear the happy pair. The **Lanyon Quoit,** off the Morvah-Penzance road about 3 mi. from each town, is one of the best-preserved megaliths in the area.

The famous stone near Morvah (on the Land's End-St. Ives bus route), with a hole through the middle, has the sensible Cornish name **Mên-an-Tol,** or "stone with a hole through the middle." The big bagel is allegedly endowed with magical, curative powers. Climbing through the aperture supposedly remedies backache, assures easy childbirth, or induces any alteration in physiology your heart desires. Who needs Viagra? The best-preserved Iron Age village in Britain is at **Chysauster** (tel. (0831) 757934), between Penzance and Zennor, about 4 mi. from each. *(Open daily Apr.-Oct. 10am-6pm. £1.50, students and seniors £1.10, children 80p.)* Take the footpath off the B3311 near Gulval (2½mi.) or Western National bus #16 (4 per day, £1.60). For those unafraid of hills and hell-bent drivers, **biking** is the best way to tour the region, affording glimpses of sparkling coastlines.

■ St. Ives

Like a finger curved and beckoning, the tiny town of St. Ives perches on a spit of land lined by pastel beaches and azure waters 10 mi. north of Penzance. The town's cobbled medieval alleyways, splashed with the color of overflowing flowerpots and nearby turquoise seas, have drawn visitors for more than a century. In the 1920s, a colony of painters and sculptors moved here; today their legacy fills the windows of the countless local galleries. Virginia Woolf too was bewitched by the energy of the Atlantic at St. Ives: her masterpiece of motion and stasis, *To the Lighthouse,* is thought to be based on the Godrevy Lighthouse which distantly watches the city, disappearing and reappearing in the morning fog. Whether one seeks to find the perfect subject or the perfect strip of sand, St. Ives has it, if hidden beneath a veneer of postcards, waist packs, and ice cream cones.

PRACTICAL INFORMATION Trains (tel. (0345) 484950) run during the summer between **St. Erth** and St. Ives (10min., 2 per hr., £2.80-4.20), and St. Erth connects to both **Penzance** and **Truro. Buses** run from **Penzance** (3 per hr., off-season M-Sa only, £1.80), and **National Express** (tel. (0990) 808080) buses between **Plymouth** and **Penzance** stop in St. Ives year-round (6 per day).

The **tourist office** (tel. 796297) is in the Guildhall on Street-an-Pol. From the bus and train stations, walk down to the foot of Tregenna Hill and turn right on Street-an-Pol. The helpful staff book beds for 10% of the first night's bill (B&B proprietor pays the fee, but beware of price inflation) and sell maps of this medieval maze (10p)—trust us, you'll need one (open M-Sa 9:30am-5:30pm, Su 10am-1pm; closed Sa-Su in winter). On Wednesday evenings at 6pm (July-Aug. only), weave up one alley and down another on a **walking tour** (1¼hr., £2.50), leaving from the Tate Gallery. **ATMs** wallpaper Fore St. **Luggage** can be stored at the St. Ives Travel Agency for (£1-1.50; M-F 9am-5:30pm, Sa 9am-5pm), or at the nearby Western National Office, at the Malakoff (£1-2; open M-Sa 9am-5pm; Su 9am-2pm). Bikes and surfboards can be hired or repaired at **Windansea Surf Shop,** 11 Fore St. (tel. 796560; open daily 9:30am-6pm; surfboard or wetsuit £5 per day, £25 per week; £5 deposit.) The **post office** (tel. 795004) is on Tregenna Pl. at High St. (open M-F 9am-5:30pm, Sa 9am-1pm). The **postal code** is TR26 1AA. **Internet access** at the St. Ives Library, Gabriel St. (tel. (01736) 796408; £2 per 30min., £4 per hour; open Tu-Th 10:30am-4:30pm, F 10:30am-5:30pm). The **telephone code** is 01736.

ACCOMMODATIONS Although the closest youth hostel to St. Ives rests in Penzance, **B&Bs** line every alley in town (from £14). A bevy awaits on **Park Ave.** and **Tregenna Terr.;** for fine sea views, try **Clodgy View** and **West Pl.** Note that prices usually dip for rooms farther from the water and higher up on the gusty hillside. **Harbour Lights,** Court Cocking, Fore St. (tel. 795525), occupies a 536-year-old building on one of the city's oldest streets and offers cheap, bustling moorings with canopies above the beds just 30 ft. from the sea (£16-17). In a more tranquil setting is **Downlong Cottage,** 95 Backroad East (tel. 798107). Ask for an upstairs room where glimpses of the glimmering sea will get you up and going faster than a fire alarm on the Empire State Building, and friendly kitties will cuddle you back to sleep (£15-18). If you can't find a room in summer, seek one of the £15 guest houses in **Carbis Bay** (a 20min. coastal walk or a 3min. ride on the St. Ives-Penzance rail, return £1, but there's often no time to collect the fare). Places to camp are abundant in nearby **Hayle** (check the tourist office for listings), including **Trevalgan Camping Park** (tel. 796433), with laundry and cooking facilities, and access to the coastal path, and **Ayr Holiday Park** (tel. 795855), at the top of Bullans Ln.

FOOD Fore St. is packed with small bakeries, each with its own interpretation of the Cornish pasty. Storefront blackboards will tempt you with a phenomenon called **Cornish cream tea** (a delicious pot of tea with scones, jam, and Cornish clotted cream). Try one (£2.50) at **Bumble's Tea Room** (tel. 797977), at Digey Sq., near the Tate (open M-Sa 10am-4:30pm, Su 11am-4:30pm; in winter closed Su). Minuscule **Ferrell's Bakery,** 64 Fore St. (tel. 797703), bakes a delicious pasty as well as a lovely saffron bun rumored to be Cornwall's best (open M-Sa 9am-5pm). If your appetite for pasties remains unsatiated, go for the extremely tasty chocolate and banana pasty at **Granny's Pasties,** 9 Fore St. (open daily 9:30am-5:30pm). For the pasty-weary, **The Café** (tel. 793621), on Island Sq., has vegetarian meals like spinach and feta pasta for around £7 (open daily 10am-3pm and 7-10pm). Stock up on groceries at **Co-op Supermarket,** Royal Sq., or at **Spar,** Tregenna Pl. (open daily 7am-10pm). Beer has flowed on the wharf at **The Sloop** (tel. 796584), on the corner of the Wharf and Fish St., since 1312 (drinks daily 11am-11pm; victuals daily noon-3pm and 6-8:45pm). A younger pub with a younger clientele is **The Three Ferrets,** 17 Chapel St. (tel. 795364; open M-Sa 11am-11pm, Su noon-10:30pm).

SIGHTS The sun god accepts offerings of roast leg of Briton at a number of beaches in St. Ives. **Porthgwidden Beach** and **Porthminster Beach** (near the train station) cater to family-oriented sunbathing, while twentysomething surfers and their groupies lounge around **Porthmeor Beach** a bit north. You can go to the lighthouse if it is fine: **Our Liz** (tel. 794051) operates two-hour trips to Hell's Mouth which happen to pass within yards of the **Godrevy Lighthouse;** check the blackboards on The Wharf; a sunset cruise usually departs at 6:30pm during low tides. Other cruises, including sea-lion watching, are available. *(£6, children £4.)*

The modernist fruits of this art colony by the sea are on display at the **Tate Gallery,** (tel. 796226) Porthmeor Beach, the younger sister of the larger Tate Gallery in London (see p. 128). The collection focuses on abstract art (mainly local, in constantly shifting displays), and its seafront location is fairly successful at integrating art and the environment that inspired it. *(Open Apr.-Sept. M and F-Sa 11am-7pm, Tu-Th 11am-9pm, Su 11am-5pm; Oct.-Mar. Tu-Su 11am-5pm; closed for 2 weeks in early Nov. £3.50, students, seniors, and disabled £2. Free gallery tours M-Sa 2:30pm. Wheelchair accessible.)* Also under the protective wing of the Tate is the nearby **Barbara Hepworth Museum and Sculpture Garden,** where Hepworth's works, which helped set the standard for 20th-century abstract sculpture, are set within their native environment: her former studio and lush garden. *(Open same hours and dates as the Tate. £3, students and seniors £1.50; same-day admission to both museums £5.50, students and seniors £3.)*

■ Newquay

At the edge of King Arthur's legendary realm, black-suited knights ride white horses. Newquay (NEW-key) (pop 20,000) is the outpost for Britain's surfer subculture, a trippy enclave of neon youth and blue-haired bus tours on the otherwise wall-flowered Cornish coast. Newquay's world-class shores represent a tweaked cross-section of Aussie, Kiwi, Californian, and Continental surfer culture that is somehow universal:

visitors to Newquay are classified as English, international, or *surfer*. Charged by a nightlife that sweeps the town like gale-force Fistral winds, Newquay's water-lovers ride the crest of world counterculture.

GETTING THERE

Getting to or from Newquay by rail from the main London-Penzance line requires a quick stopover in the small town of Par. **Trains** (tel. (0345) 484950) go to **Par** (50min., 5 per day, £4.10), **Plymouth via Par** (2hr., 1 per hr., £7.80), or **Penzance via Par** (2hr., 1 per hr., £9.60). You can buy rail tickets from **LSA Travel** (tel. 877180) at the station (open M-F 9am-5pm, Sa 9am-4pm). **Luggage** may be left at the station (£1 per item; open daily 8:30am-3pm). By **bus**, catch **Western National** to Newquay via **Bodmin** (2hr., 3 per day, £3.10), **St. Austell** (45min., 2 per hr., £2.60; off-season M-Sa only), or **St. Ives** (2hr., June-Sept. 3 per day, £3.30). **National Express** also runs directly to Newquay from **London**. The **bus station**, 1 East St., has a helpful Western National office. (Open M-Th 9am-5:30pm and 6:30-9pm, F 9am-5:30pm, Sa 8:30am-5:30pm, Su 9am-1pm and 5-9pm.) For bus info, call Bodmin at (01208) 79898.

PRACTICAL INFORMATION

The **tourist office** (tel. 871345), on Marcus Hill, four blocks from the train station, sells street guide maps for 50p as well as a £1 "What's On in Newquay" guide (open M-Sa 9am-6pm, Su 10am-5pm; shortened hours in winter). **Cycle Revolutions,** 7 Beach Rd. (tel. 872364), rents mountain bikes (£5-8 per day, £50 per week; ID deposit). Also try **Cycle Extreme** (tel. 874888). Get hold of a board at **Fistral Surf,** 1 Beacon Rd. (tel. 850520), which rents all the surf paraphernalia one needs to bust the rippingest British tubes, mate (£5 per day, £12 per 3 days, £25 per week; open daily 9am-6pm, until 10pm in the summer). Up-to-the-minute surf condition updates will cost 50p per min. when you make a **surf call** (tel. (0891) 360360). **Newquay Hospital** (tel. 893600) heals bang-ups at St. Thomas Rd. The **post office,** 31-33 East St. (tel. 873364), is open M-F 9am-5:30pm, Sa 9am-12:30pm. Newquay's **postal code** is TR7 1BU. **Internet access** is available at the Newquay Backpackers International (see below). Newquay's **telephone code** is 01637.

ACCOMMODATIONS

Newquay's surfer subculture has created its own system of residential life in **independent backpacker's hostels.** The local YHA hostel closed a few years ago, partly because its curfew was incompatible with Newquay's nocturnal habits. Be wary of choosing a place to stay based solely on proximity to the beach: while some of Newquay's hostels are well-kept and offer initiation into the ways of the wetsuited, others are dark, dirty, and do not welcome those not already into the scene. Hordes of B&Bs manifest themselves near Fistral Beach, and closer to town between Mt. Wise and East St., averaging about £14 per night.

Fistral Backpackers, 18 Headland Rd. (tel. 873146). Clean, somewhat cramped rooms, just seconds from Britain's best surfing beach. More waves on the walls than in your dreams. £6.50-8. Book far in advance.

Seagull Cottage, 98 Fore St. (tel. 875648; email backpacker@dial.pipex.com). Cozy rooms close to Fistral and a scone's throw from town. Breakfast with a jungle of china parrot plates. £11-14.

Newquay Backpackers International, 69-73 Tower Rd. (tel. 879366). Welcomes surf bunnies and those who'd as soon be caught in their birthday suit as in a wetsuit. Dine amongst the waves. Ray is your ticket to Newquay nightlife. £6-9. **Internet access** available 10am-8pm for 10p per min.

Quebec Hotel, 34 Grosvenor Ave. (tel. 874430). Simple rooms close to the bus and train stations. No singles. £12-14.

Camping: Trevelque Caravan and Camping Park (tel. 851851), in Porth. £4.80-5.50, depending on season. Or, try **Hendra Tourist Park** (tel. 875778), about 1½mi. east of town beyond the Lane Theatre. From Trenance Gardens, go under the viaduct and past the boating lake; then turn left. Bus #58 also runs directly to Hendra from the town center every 30min. Families and couples only; £3-5 per person, electricity £2.75.

FOOD

The restaurants in Newquay pour tea and squish pasties into tourists who clamor for a quick, bland, and costly fill-up. **Somerfield** supermarket (tel. 876006), off Fore St., offers a huge selection, especially for Cornwall (open M-Th and Sa 8am-8pm, F 8am-9pm, Su 10am-4pm). **Food for Thought,** 33a Bank St. (tel. 871717), at the corner of Bank St. and Beachfield Ave., prepares take-away "Californian" salads, sandwiches, and subs for £2-3 (open daily 8:30am-10pm). Up the road at 28-30 East St., **Boston's** (tel. 852626) fires up its ovens to create tasty pizzas (from £3) and chocolate chip cookies (open Su-Th 8:30am-10pm, F-Sa 8:30am-2am). For a spot of tea and scrumptious homemade baked goods, call on **Wilbur's Cafe** (tel. 877805), on Fore St. (open daily 10am-5:30pm). Pub grubbers should try **Corker's** on Beach Rd. for £4 specials.

SIGHTS AND ENTERTAINMENT

All but the heartiest should avoid Newquay on bank holidays, when a sea of young Britons descend upon the town to surf, cruise, and party. By far, Newquay's biggest attraction is its beach life. After a 3000 mi. trip across the Atlantic, winds descend on **Fistral Beach** with a vengeance, creating what most consider the best surfing conditions in all of Europe. On the bay side, **Towan Beach** and **Great Western Beach** offer safer bathing and are popular with families. Nearby, enticing **Lusty Glaze Beach** attracts beachgoers of all ages.

Even on ordinary nights, Newquay nightlife rises like the Kraaken. The beast stirs at about 9pm and reigns almost until daybreak; clubs are open until 1am. Surfers and a young international crowd jam **The Red Lion** (tel. 872195), on North Quay Hill at Tower Rd. and Fore St., where the pilgrimage trail of **surfer bars** begins. From the Lion, head to **The Sailor's Arms,** Fore St. (tel. 872838), for more beer to cruise. Next door to the pub is **Sailors,** a club that features two levels, four bars, 24 video screens, a disco night on Thursday, and no dearth of tanned flesh. Cover is usually £4-6 before 11pm. Dress is smarter, but still casual, like everything in Newquay. Following the town center to Bank St. will bring you to **The Newquay Arms,** which completes the immediate surfer-scoping perimeter. All of these spots exceed critical density at the end of July and the beginning of August. If surfing and clubbing wear you out, **The Lane Theatre** (tel. 876945), the stage for the Newquay Dramatic Society, presents a midsummer night's drama. *(Book tickets M-W 9:30am-2:30pm. £5-6.)* Comedians and musicians also often entertain by the beach for free, or your largesse.

Heart of England

After London, the Heart of England contains the largest number of "must-sees" in the country. Extending from London west to Salisbury and Bath and north to the Cotswolds and Stratford-upon-Avon, the Heart of England centers on Oxford, England's oldest university town. The region is warm and inviting, brightened by light yellow Cotswolds stone. Saved from the threat of industrialization by Shakespeare's pre-eminence, Stratford-upon-Avon still looks like a village, though the tranquil country scenery and groomed flowerbeds peek out from under crowds of tourists. Bath and Stonehenge, though similarly overrun in the summer months, retain an air of ancient and unshakable dignity. When possible, spend more than just a day in these towns and roam free from the glut of daytrippers. Only an overnight can provide the wonder of twilight at an English river's edge.

🅰 HIGHLIGHTS OF THE HEART OF ENGLAND

- The university city of **Oxford** (p. 219) is one of Britain's true must-sees. Layered with architectural fantasies, historical relics, and traditions bizarre enough to befuddle an anthropologist, Oxford bears the legacy of eight centuries of brilliance.
- Visitors are welcomed to the cheerful city of **Salisbury,** which still rallies around its cathedral, England's tallest and one of its most beautiful (p. 231).
- Puzzle over the ancient rocks at **Stonehenge,** one of the greatest engineering feats of the second millenium BC, and one of the world's great mysteries (see p. 235).
- Eighteenth-century pleasure-seekers paved the old Roman spa town of **Bath** with their glorious buildings and uproarious behavior, Bath still offers visitors a chance to escape from the ordinary, if not from other tourists (see p. 236).
- Strut into Shakespeare's hometown of **Stratford-upon-Avon,** where historic buildings try to honor Shakespeare's footsteps and the world-renowned Royal Shakespeare Company venerates his every syllable (see p. 262).

OXFORDSHIRE

▓ Oxford

Towery city and branchy between towers;
Cuckoo-echoing, bell-swarmèd, lark-charmèd, rook-racked, river-
rounded...

Gerard Manley Hopkins, "Duns Scotus's Oxford"

Oxford—originally named as the place where oxen could ford the Thames—has naturally inspired stories of crossings. Oxford's three favorite sons—Lewis Carroll, C.S. Lewis, and J.R.R. Tolkien—sat near the stone-bridged waters dreaming of crossings through mirrors, through wardrobes, through mountain passes. Today, trucks rumble, bus brakes screech, and bicycles crush the toes of pedestrians shoving past each other in Oxford's streets. Though half a millenium of scholarship lies behind Oxford, two centuries of industrial bustle have certainly left their mark. The spires of the University still inspire, but are in some places black with soot. Still, there are pockets of respite to charm and edify the academic pilgrim: the basement room of Blackwell's Bookshop, the impeccable galleries of the Ashmolean Museum, the reflective canopies of Addison's Walk. Despite the crush of tourists and the speeding bicycles of students, Oxford has an irrepressible grandeur.

Heart of England

GETTING THERE

Local trains run every 30 minutes from London. **Thames Trains** leave from **Paddington** (1hr., £11.80 day return). The **Oxford Tube** (tel. 772250) sends buses from **Victoria Station** in London (1½hr., 1-6 per hr., £7 next-day return, £6 students, seniors, and children). **Oxford CityLink** (tel. 785400) also sends buses from **Victoria Station** (1¾hr., 4 per hr., £7 next-day return, £6 students, seniors, and children), from **Gatwick Airport** (2hr., departs every 2hr., £17 next-day return, £8.50 children), and from **Heathrow Airport** (2 per hr., £10 day return, £5 children).

ORIENTATION

Queen, High, St. Aldates, and **Cornmarket St.** meet at right angles at **Carfax,** the town center. Oxford extends some three miles around Carfax, though the colleges are all within a mile; they lie mainly to the east of Carfax along High and **Broad St.** The bus and **train** stations and **tourist information** center lie to the northwest. Past the east end of High St. over Magdalen Bridge, the neighborhoods of **East Oxford** stretch along **Cowley Rd.** and **Iffley Rd. Abingdon Rd.** leads off to **South Oxford,** while more upscale residential areas surround **Woodstock Rd.** and **Banbury Rd.** to the north.

When walking around Oxford, especially near Carfax, beware the perils of the "pedestrian zone," into which bikes and buses mercilessly intrude. College parks and quads remain sacrosanct, untroubled by so much as a solitary cyclist. The *Cycle into Oxford* pamphlet, with excellent cycling maps of the city and its hinterland, is free at the tourist office.

PRACTICAL INFORMATION

Transportation

Trains: Park End St. (tel. (0345) 484950; recording 794422), west of Carfax. Ticket office open M-F 6am-8pm, Sa 6:45am-8pm, Su 7:45am-8pm.

Buses: Gloucester Green (follow arrows up Cornmarket St. from Carfax). Three major companies operate. **Stagecoach Oxford** (tel. 772250; desk open M-F 7:15am-6:30pm, Sa-Su 9am-noon and 12:30-2:45pm) and **National Express** (tel. (0990) 808080; desk open M-F 8am-5:30pm and Sa 8am-5pm, Su 9:45am-3:15pm) both offer national routes. **Oxford CityLink** (tel. 785400 or 772250 for timetable; desk open daily 6:30am-6:30pm) runs direct to Heathrow, Gatwick, London and elsewhere.

Public Transportation: The **Oxford Bus Company** (tel. 785400) and **Stagecoach** (tel. 772250) compete vigorously for your patronage, making for swift and frequent service. The Oxford Bus Company operates **Park & Ride** (mostly for commuters) and **Cityline.** Cityline buses #3 and 4 go down Iffley Rd.; buses #13 and 14 go up Marston Rd.; the #20s go up Banbury Rd.; the #30s go down Abingdon Rd.; and the #50s go down Cowley Rd. Most local services board on the streets around Carfax. Fares are low (most 60p single). Day and week passes are available and well worth the purchase; buy them from the bus driver or at the bus station.

Taxi: Radio Taxi (tel. 242424). **ABC** (tel. 770077).

Tourist and Financial Services

Tourist Office: The Old School, Gloucester Green (tel. 726871; fax 240261). From Carfax, follow signposts up Cornmarket St., left onto George St., and right into Gloucester Green. Located beside the bus station. A pamphleteer's paradise, with an extremely busy staff which books rooms for £2.50 and a 10% deposit. Accommodations list 50p. The 70p street map and guide includes a valuable index. Open M-Sa 9:30am-5pm, Su 10am-3:30pm.

Tours: A 2hr. walking tour focusing on the history of Oxford University leaves the tourist office 2-5 times daily 11am-2pm (£4, children £2.50). It provides access to some colleges which are otherwise inaccessible. The tourist office also offers special interest tours (e.g., walk in Lewis Carroll's footsteps). Ubiquitous **Guide Friday** (tel. 790522) runs bus tours from the train station with live guides (£8, students and seniors £6.50, children £2.50). **The Oxford Classic Tour** (tel. 240105), yet another bus service, charges less and will hand you earphones in the language of your choice (£7, students and seniors £5, children £2). Both bus tours allow hop on/hop off access all day. **Student groups** also offer tours; some will regale you with stories you won't hear on the official tours and will give you your money back if you're dissatisfied. Others won't. Prices and times vary; look for the signs.

Budget Travel: Campus Travel, 105 St. Aldates St. (tel. 242067). Eurotrain tickets, ISICs, railcards, discount airfare, bus tickets, and insurance. Open M-Tu and Th-F 9am-5:30pm, W 10am-5:30pm, Sa 10am-5pm. **STA Travel,** 36 George St. (tel. 792800). Open M-W and F 9am-5:30pm, Th 10am-5:30pm, Sa 11am-5pm.

Banks: Banks crowd in on Carfax. **Barclays,** 54 Cornmarket St. Open M-Tu and Th-F 9:30am-4:30pm, W 9:30am-5pm, Sa 10am-noon. **ATMs** easy to find.

American Express: 4 Queen St. (tel. 792066). Open M-Tu and Th-F 9am-5:30pm, W 9:30am-5:30pm, Sa 9am-5pm; foreign currency exchange also open Su 11am-3pm in summer.

Local Services

Camping and Hiking Supplies: YHA Adventure Shop, 9-10 St. Clements (tel. 247948), on Magdalen Bridge roundabout. Open M-Tu and F 9:30am-5:30pm, W 10am-5:30pm, Th 9:30am-6pm, Sa 9am-6pm; summer also Su 11am-5pm.

Luggage storage: Pensioners' Club in Gloucester Green (tel. 242237), by the bus station. £1-2 donation requested. Open M-Sa 9am-4:45pm.

Bookstores: Blackwell's, 48-51 Broad St. (tel. 792792; fax 794143; email blackwells.extra@blackwell.co.uk; http://www.blackwell.co.uk/bookshops). Oxford's biggest, and one of the world's best. Open M-Sa 9am-6pm, Su 11am-5pm. See **Sights,** p. 226.

ENGLAND

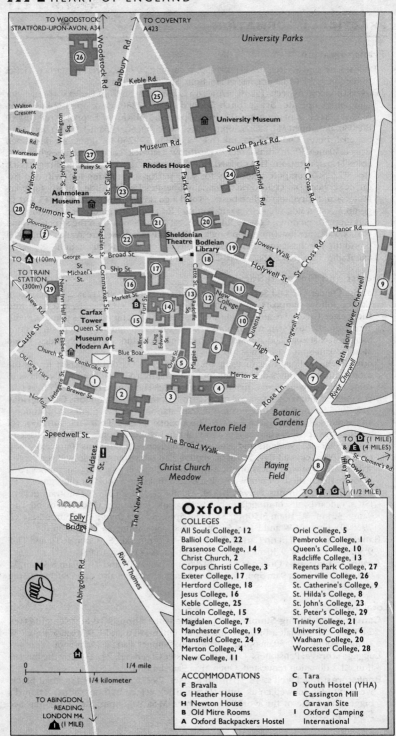

TO WOODSTOCK
STRATFORD-UPON-AVON, A34

TO COVENTRY
A423

University Parks

Woodstock Rd.

Banbury Rd.

Keble Rd.

26

25

Walton
Crescent

Richmond
Rd.

Worcester
Pl.

University Museum

Museum Rd.

South Parks Rd.

St. Cross Rd.

Wellington
Sq.

St. John's Ln.

Pusey St.

27

Rhodes House

Parks Rd.

Mansfield Rd.

Ashmolean
Museum

St. Giles St.

23

Alfred

Beaumont St.

28

Gloucester St.

Magdalen St.

22

21

Sheldonian
Theatre

20

Bodleian
Library

24

19

Jowett Walk

Manor Rd.

TO A (100m)

George St.

Broad St.

18

Holywell St.

St. Michael's
St.

Ship St.

Carte St.

9

TO TRAIN
STATION
(300m)

New Rd.

New Inn Hall St.

Cornmarket St.

29

Market St.

16

17

13

12

New
College Ln.

11

Queens Ln.

Longwall St.

Path along River Cherwell

Castle St.

Bonn Sq.

Turl St.

14

Radcliffe
Sq.

10

High St.

Carfax
Tower

B

15

6

Church St.

Museum of
Modern Art

Queen St.

King Edward
St.

Alfred
St.

Magpie Ln.

Oriel St.

5

Merton St.

Rose Ln.

7

Blue Boar
St.

Pembroke St.

1

2

3

4

River Cherwell

Old Grey Friars
St.

Norfolk
St.

Littlegate St.

St. Ebbes St.

Brewer St.

Botanic
Gardens

Merton Field

TO D (1 MILE)
& E (4 MILES)

Speedwell St.

The Broad Walk

St. Clement's Rd.

Cowley Rd.

Iffley Rd.

St. Aldates St.

Christ Church
Meadow

Playing
Field

8

TO F, G (1/2 MILE)

N

The New Walk

River Thames

Folly
Bridge

Oxford

COLLEGES

All Souls College, 12
Balliol College, 22
Brasenose College, 14
Christ Church, 2
Corpus Christi College, 3
Exeter College, 17
Hertford College, 18
Jesus College, 16
Keble College, 25
Lincoln College, 15
Magdalen College, 7
Manchester College, 19
Mansfield College, 24
Merton College, 4
New College, 11

Oriel College, 5
Pembroke College, 1
Queen's College, 10
Radcliffe College, 13
Regents Park College, 27
Somerville College, 26
St. Catherine's College, 9
St. Hilda's College, 8
St. John's College, 23
St. Peter's College, 29
Trinity College, 21
University College, 6
Wadham College, 20
Worcester College, 28

ACCOMMODATIONS

F Bravalla
G Heather House
H Newton House
B Old Mitre Rooms
A Oxford Backpackers Hostel

C Tara
D Youth Hostel (YHA)
E Cassington Mill
  Caravan Site
I Oxford Camping
  International

0   1/4 mile
0   1/4 kilometer

TO ABINGDON,
READING,
LONDON M4.
(1 MILE)

ENGLAND

Launderette: Clean-o-Fine, 66 Abingdon Rd., South Oxford. Open M-F 8am-9:30pm, Sa-Su 7:30am-9:30pm, last wash 8:30pm. Wash and dry £1.40, soap 70p.

Public Toilets: Underneath Gloucester Green Bus Station. Changing room and disabled access (open 24hr.).

Emergency and Communications

Emergency: Dial 999; no coins required.

Police: St. Aldates and Speedwell St. (tel. 266000).

Hotlines: Samaritans (crisis), 123 Iffley Rd. (tel. 722122). 24hr.; drop-in daily 8am-10pm. **Gay Switchboard,** Oxford Friend (tel. 793999). Open daily 7am-9pm. **Vita Clinic Health Line** (women's health issues; tel. 246036). Open alternate Fridays 9:15-10:30am. **Rape Crisis** (tel. 726295). Open M and Th 7-9pm, W 4-6pm, Su 6-8pm. In emergency call **London Rape Crisis Center** at (0171) 837 1600 or dial 999.

Pharmacy: Boots, 6-8 Cornmarket St. (tel. 247461). Open M-F 8:45am-6pm and Su 11am-5pm.

Hospital: John Radcliffe Hospital, Headley Wy. (tel. 741166). Bus #13B or 14A.

Post Office: 124 St. Aldates St. (tel. 202863). Open M-F 9am-5:30pm, Sa 9am-6pm. Bureau de change. **Postal Code: OX1 1ZZ.**

Internet Access: Daily Information, 31 Warnborough Rd. (tel. 310011). £6 per hr., £1 minimum. Open M-W 9am-9pm, Th-Sa 9am-6pm. If possible, call beforehand.

Telephone Code: 01865.

ACCOMMODATIONS

Oxford abounds with accommodations, but completely fills up in the summer. **Book at least a week ahead** in the summer, especially for singles, and be prepared to mail in a deposit or give a credit card number. **B&Bs** line the main roads out of town and are reachable by bus (or a 15-45min. walk for the energetic). The 300s on **Banbury Rd.** stand north of town and are reachable by all Cityline buses in the #20s. Cheaper B&Bs lie in the 200s and 300s on **Iffley Rd.** (take Cityline bus #3 or 4), 250-350 on **Cowley Rd.** (take Cityline Buses in the #50s), and on **Abingdon Rd.** in South Oxford (take Cityline buses in the #30s). Wherever you go, expect to pay £18-22 per person. The tourist office provides a same-day bed-finding service for £2.50 plus a 10% deposit. If it's late and you're homeless, call the **Oxford Association of Hotels and Guest Houses** at one of the following numbers: 774083 (East Oxford), 862138 (West Oxford), 510327 (North Oxford), or 244268 (South Oxford).

YHA Youth Hostel, 32 Jack Straw's Ln., Headington (tel. 762997; fax 769402). Catch Citylink bus #13 or 14 heading away from Carfax on High St. and ask the driver to stop at Jack Straw's Ln. (at least 4 per hr., last bus 11:10pm; 60p, return £1 return). The hostel is an 8min. walk up the hill. One of England's largest hostels (114 beds), with generous facilities to match: kitchen, laundry, lockers, and food shop. Most rooms have wooden beds with 6-8 bunks. Close quarters and large lounges promote multilingual chatter. £10.25, under 18 £7.05, student ID £1 off. Cafeteria serves breakfast (£3) and dinner (£4.40). June-Aug. book 2 weeks ahead and expect to send a deposit or give a credit card number.

Newton House, 82-84 Abingdon Rd. (tel. 240561), ½mi. from town center; take any Abingdon bus across Folly Bridge. Affable proprietor and dark wardrobes await Narnia fans; don't get lost. Doubles £36-46, with bath £46-56; varies with season.

Bravalla, 242 Iffley Rd. (tel. 241326; fax 249757). Six sunny rooms (all doubles or twins) with soothing floral patterns and pastels. Breakfast in a conservatory. Guests sign breakfast board the previous night; good vegetarian options. Singles £25; doubles with bath £38-44. TV. Reserve several weeks ahead.

Old Mitre Rooms, 4b Turl St. (tel. 279800), next to Past-Times. Recently refurbished Lincoln College dorms with shaggy green carpet. Some Quad views. Singles £23; doubles £42, with bath £46; triples £55, with bath £60. Open July to early Sept.

Heather House, 192 Iffley Rd. (tel./fax 249757). Walk 20min. or take the bus marked "Rose Hill" from the bus station, train station, or Carfax Tower (65p). Vibrant Australian proprietor and sparkling, modern rooms. Vivian's matchless repository of advice and information will remind you why you love to travel. Private facilities. Dorms £18-20; singles £22; doubles £46.

◉**Tara,** 10 Holywell St. (call *Typetalk* (free) at (04451) 494 2022; within the U.K. (0800) 515152; give the operator Tara's phone number (01865) 202953; fax 200297). A lark-charmed dream among the spires on Oxford's oldest medieval street. Framed paperback covers hang in the bathroom, including *Gone with the Wind* (hence the name). Kind, hearing-impaired proprietors Mr. and Mrs. Godwin lip-read well and speak clearly. Many rooms overlook a college; others peek out at Mr. Godwin's budding garden. Singles £28; doubles £55. Desk, basin, and TV in each room. Guest kitchen. Reserve at least 2 weeks ahead.

Oxford Backpackers Hotel, 9a Hythe Bridge St. (tel. 721761). Right between the bus and train stations, this independent hostel combines good prices and a great location. Music enlivens the common room, hallways, and bathroom nonstop; make friends in an extremely social atmosphere. As for the decor, the colors are *not* meant to go together. £9-11 per night, depending on season and availability. Photo ID required. Breakfast £1. Laundry facilities and kitchen.

Camping: Oxford Camping International, 426 Abingdon Rd. (tel. 246551; after 5:30pm call 725646), behind the Touchwoods camping store. 129 sites. £2.80 per tent; £1.65 per person; 90p per child; caravan plots £8.50. Toilet and laundry facilities. Showers 20p. **Cassington Mill Caravan Site,** Eynsham Rd., Cassington (tel. 881081), about 4mi. northwest on the A40. 85 pitches and hot showers. £7 for 2 people, a car and a tent. The **YHA Hostel** may offer limited camping; call ahead.

FOOD

The swank, bulging swagger of Oxford's eateries seduces students fed up with fetid college food. For fresh produce, deli goods, breads, and shoe leather, visit the **Covered Market** between Market St. and Carfax (open M-Sa 8am-5:30pm). The Wednesday **market** at Gloucester Green (all day, by the bus station) offers deals on produce, pies, meats, clothing, and more. The closest supermarket to Carfax is the **Co-op** on Cornmarket St. (open M-F 8am-7pm, Sa 8am-6pm). If you're across Magdalen Bridge, try **Uhuru Wholefoods,** 48 Cowley Rd. (tel. 248249) for vegetarian and vegan specialties as well as organic wines and beers (open M-F 10am-6pm, Sa 9:30am-5:30pm).

Eat and run at one of the better take-aways: **Harvey's of Oxford,** 58 High St. (tel. 723152) near Magdalen College, recognizable by the line out the door (cherry-apple flapjacks 85p, great chunks of carrot cake £1.25, mighty sandwiches £1.50-2.75; open M-F 8:30am-5:30pm, Sa 8:30am-6pm, Su 9am-6pm). **Fasta Pasta** in the covered market hawks cheap, gourmet sandwiches and bagels, as well as an impressive selection of olives; check out the cookie shop as well.

For those staying at B&Bs across Magdalen Bridge, there are a number of cheap and tasty restaurants along the first four blocks of Cowley Rd. The funky **Hi-Lo Jamaican Eating House,** 70 Cowley Rd. (tel. 725984), **Dhaka,** 186 Cowley Rd. (tel. 202011), and **The Pak Fook,** 100 Cowley Rd. (tel. 247958), are all good bets. Those exiled near Somerville should seek **Jamal's Tandoori Restaurant,** 108 Walton St. (tel. 310102). Keep an eye out for the legendary **kebab vans** that fuel students after hours—usually at Broad, High, Queen, and St. Aldates St. **Vegetarians** might wish to consult the *Green Pages* (£3), available at the tourist office.

◉**Café CoCo,** Cowley Rd. (tel. 200232), offers a lively atmosphere and a great Mediterranean menu. Populated by students and thirtysomethings, CoCo's is a bargain not to be missed. Entrees £4.65-7.50 ("Greek Messe"). Open daily 10am-11pm.

The Nosebag, 6-8 St. Michael's St. (tel. 721033). More wholesome than the name suggests. A different gourmet-grade menu each night, served cafeteria-style. Good vegetarian options available. Lunch under £5.50, dinner under £7. **The Saddlebag Café** downstairs sells sandwiches, salads, and cakes during the day. Open M 9:30am-5:30pm, Tu-Th 9:30am-10pm, F-Sa 9:30am-10:30pm, Su 9:30-9pm.

Chiang Mai, 130a High St. (tel. 202233). Spicy Thai food (we mean *spicy*) in half-timbered surroundings. Victorian fireplaces. Extensive vegetarian menu; entrees £5.50-9. Try the sticky rice dessert for £3.50. Book 2 days or more in advance, especially on weekends. In the summer, go at lunchtime to avoid crowds. Open M-Sa noon-2:30pm and 6-11pm.

Heroes, 8 Ship St. (tel. 723459). Student clientele feeds on sandwiches, freshly baked breads, and a super selection of stuffings (£1.70-3.30). Potted homemade pâté for the adventurous. Open M-F 8am-5pm, Sa 8:30am-6pm, Su 10am-5pm.

⊗Cherwell Boathouse, Bardwell Rd. (tel. 552746), off Banbury Rd., 1mi. north of town; make a right at the sign for the boathouse. All Citylink Buses in the 20s go up Banbury (or take a taxi). Perched on the leafy bank of the Cherwell, the romantic Boathouse offers two 3-course meals—one vegetarian, both unorthodox, often cooked with wine from the well-loved cellar of the amiable young proprietors. Book well in advance and expect to spend the entire evening. Lunch £17.50, dinner £18.50, and worth every pence. When you're finished, rent a punt next door (£8, £10 on weekends; £40 deposit) and drift into the night. Open Tu-Sa noon-2pm and 6-10pm, Su noon-2pm only.

PUBS

Pubs far outnumber colleges in Oxford; many even consider them the city's prime attraction. Most pubs are open by noon, begin to fill up around 5pm, and close at 11pm (10:30pm on Sundays). Food is served during lunch and dinner hours (roughly noon-2pm and 6-8pm). Be ready to crawl—some pubs are so small that a single band of merry students will squeeze out other patrons. *Good Pubs of Oxford* (£3 at bookstores and tourist office) is an indispensable guide to the town's beer dungeons. Buy it, use it, keep it dry.

⊗Turf Tavern, 4 Bath Pl. (tel. 243235), off Holywell St. This sprawling, cavernous 13th-century pub is nestled deep in an alleyway against the ruins of the city wall. Features 2 secluded terraces and many rooms. Intimate and relaxed until the student crowd turns it into a mosh pit. Many, many drinks: beers, punches, ciders, and country wines—mead, elderberry, apple, and red-and-white currant. Open M-Sa 11am-11pm, Su noon-10:30pm. Hot food served in back room noon-8pm.

The Eagle and Child, 49 St. Giles St. (tel. 310154). Known as the Bird and Baby, this archipelago of paneled alcoves moistened the tongues of C.S. Lewis and J.R.R. Tolkien for a quarter-century. *The Hobbit* and *The Chronicles of Narnia* were first read aloud here, as the many photos of the Inklings Club testify. Settle into a dim alcove and observe distinguished dons—and students—still rolling in. Open M-Sa 11am-11pm, Su noon-10:30pm.

The Kings Arms, Holywell St. (tel. 242369). Oxford's unofficial student union draws a trendy crowd. A cafe lurks in the large interior. And you can withdraw from the merry masses in the front to quieter rooms at the back. Open M-Sa 10:30am-11pm, Su 10:30am-10:30pm.

The Bear, Alfred St. Over 5000 ties from England's brightest cover every flat surface but the floor. You can buy your own "The Bear 1242-1992" tie for £10. Basketball players beware: the ceiling droops at just over 6ft. During the day, the clients are older than the yellowed neckwear, and the young sit out back. Open M-Sa noon-11pm, Su noon-3pm.

The Perch, Binsey Village (tel. 240386). From Walton St. in Jericho, walk down Walton Well Rd. and straight through Port Meadow. Cross Rainbow Bridge and head north along the Thames Path, then follow the trail west when you see a few buildings several hundred yards across a field. Half-hour walk from the tourist center. Just off the Thames, this picturesque pub boasts a thatched roof, children's play area, and a huge garden with weeping willows and picnic tables. Open M-Sa 11:30am-11pm and Su noon-10:30pm. Food served daily noon-2pm and 7-9pm except Sunday night.

The Jolly Farmers, 20 Paradise St. (tel. 793759). Take Queen St. from Carfax, turn left on Castle St., then right on Paradise St. Oxfordshire's only gay and lesbian pub, featuring occasional comedy, female impersonators, and male strippers. The pub is significantly more sedate in the summer, without its student crowds. Open M-Sa noon-11pm, Su 12:30-10:30pm.

The Elm Tree, 95 Cowley Rd. (tel. 244706). The best Irish pub in town. Popular with the student crowd. Chronicles of Irish history (interspersed with the occasional Bob Marley poster) are plastered colorfully on the walls. Charming owner will dance a few steps with the regulars as he collects empty glasses. Live Irish music Friday and Saturday nights, traditional music on Wednesday and Sunday. Open daily 11am-11pm.

ENGLAND

SIGHTS

King Henry II founded Oxford, Britain's first university, in 1167. Until then, the English had traveled to Paris to study, a fact that never sat well with the Francophobic English king. After his tiff with Thomas à Becket, Archbishop of Canterbury, Henry ordered the return of English students studying in Paris, so that "there may never be wanting a succession of persons duly qualified for the service of God in church and state." Christ Church alone has produced 13 prime ministers, and Prime Minister Tony Blair hails from St. John's College.

Summer brings hordes of international students, many younger than college age, to programs on the University's campus. During recess months the chatter on the campuses is a thousand-tongued Babel of anything but British English. Actual University students are likely to be found not lounging in verdant quads, but behind cash registers. The tourist office guide *Welcome to Oxford* (£1) lists the colleges' public visiting hours (usually for a few hours in the afternoon; often curtailed without prior notice or explanation), and the tourist office map costs 20p. Some colleges charge admission; others may impose mercenary fees during peak tourist times. At Christ Church, don't bother trying to sneak in (even after cleverly hiding your backpack and bright yellow *Let's Go*): elderly bouncers sporting bowler hats and stationed 50 ft. apart will squint at you and kick you out. Other colleges have been known to be less vigilant near the back gates. Coddle the porters or you will get nowhere.

Two museums near Carfax attempt to synthesize Oxford's history. The **Museum of Oxford** on St. Aldates St. (tel. 815559), across from the post office, might be the most comprehensive local history collection in Britain. The exhibit is staid, save for the skeleton of a murderer dissected at Christ Church, which is simply stale. *(Open Tu-F 10am-4pm, Sa 10am-5pm. £1.50, students and seniors £1, children 50p, families £3.50.)* The **Oxford Story,** 6 Broad St. (tel. 790055), hauls visitors around on medieval-style "desks" through self-congratulatory dioramas recreating Oxford's past. Share the simple pleasures of a 13th-century student making merry with a wench; hear the cries of the bishops burned a few feet away on Broad St. *(Open July-Aug. 9:30am-6pm; Apr.-June and Sept.-Oct. 9:30am-5pm; Nov.-Mar. 10am-4:30pm. £5, students and seniors £4.25, children £3.95, families £14.95.)* Better yet, stay outside and see stone, not fiberglass, quads.

Carfax and South of Queen and High Streets

Start your walking tour at Carfax, the "four-forked" center of activity, with a hike up the 99 spiral stairs of **Carfax Tower** (tel. 792653) for a view of the city. Admire the bell-ringing chamber as you climb. *(Open daily Apr.-Oct. 10am-5:30pm; Nov.-Mar. 10am-3:30pm. £1.20, under 16 60p.)*

Just down St. Aldates St. stands **Christ Church** (tel. 276492), an intimidating pile of stone dwarfing the other colleges. "The House" has Oxford's grandest quad and its most socially distinguished, obnoxious students. In June, (you'd bloody well better) hush while navigating the narrow strip open to tourists lest you be rebuked by irritable undergrads prepping for exams. King Charles I made Christ Church his capital for three and a half years during the Civil War, escaping the college dressed as a servant when the city was besieged. *(Open M-Sa 9am-5pm, Su 1-5pm. Services Su 8, 10, 11:15am, 6pm; weekdays 7:30am, 6pm. Admission is a scandalous £3, students, seniors, and children £2, families £6.)* Christ Church's chapel is also Oxford's **cathedral,** the smallest in England. In AD 730, Oxford's patron saint, St. Frideswide, built a nunnery on this site in honor of two miracles: the blinding of an annoying suitor, and his subsequent recovery. The cathedral contains a stained glass window (c. 1320) depicting Thomas à Becket kneeling in supplication just before being hacked apart in Canterbury Cathedral. A rather incongruous toilet floats in the background of an 1870 stained glass window depicting St. Frideswide's death. The Reverend Charles Dodgson (better known as **Lewis Carroll**) was friendly with Dean Liddell of Christ Church—and friendlier with his daughter Alice—and used to visit the family in the gardens of the Dean's house. From the largest tree in the garden (which is private but visible from the cathedral), the Cheshire Cat first grinned and vanished; the White Rabbit can be spotted fretting in the stained glass of the hall.

The adjoining **Tom Quad** sometimes becomes the site of undergraduate lily-pond-dunking. The quad takes its name from **Great Tom,** the seven-ton bell in Tom Tower, which has faithfully rung 101 strokes (the original number of students) at 9:05pm (the original undergraduate curfew) every evening since 1682. Sixty coats of arms preside over the ceiling under the tower. Nearby, the fan-vaulted **college hall** bears imposing portraits of some of Christ Church's most famous alums—Charles Dodgson, Sir Philip Sidney, William Penn, John Ruskin, John Locke, and a bored-looking W.H. Auden in the corner by the kitchen.

Through an archway (to your left as you face the cathedral) lies **Peckwater Quad,** encircled by the most elegant Palladian building in Oxford. Look here for faded rowing standings chalked on the walls and for Christ Church's library (closed to visitors). The adjoining **Canterbury Quad** houses the **Christ Church Picture Gallery** (tel. 276172; enter on Oriel Sq. and at Canterbury Gate), a fine collection of Italian, Dutch, and Flemish paintings, starring Tintoretto and Vermeer. Leonardo and Michelangelo come out of hiding on occasion. *(Open Apr.-Sept. M-Sa 10:30am-1pm and 2-5:30pm, Su 2-5:30pm; Oct.-Mar. closes at 4:30pm. £1, students and seniors 50p. Visitors to gallery only should enter through Canterbury Gate off Oriel St.)* Spreading east and south from the main entrance, **Christ Church Meadow** compensates for Oxford's lack of "backs" (the riverside gardens in Cambridge). A fenced portion of the meadow contains a herd of American longhorn cattle, given by Bill Clinton on a visit to the city. Across St. Aldates at 30 Pembroke St., is the **Museum of Modern Art** (tel. 722733), which will house a Hitchcock exhibit in the summer of 1999. *(Open Tu-W and F-Su 11am-6pm, Th 11am-9pm. £2.50, students and seniors £1.50, children free. Free for all W 11am-1pm and Th 6-9pm. Wheelchair access.)* Right before Folly Bridge stands the **Bates Collection of Musical Instruments,** Faculty of Music, St. Aldgates (tel. 276139). *(Open M-F 2-5pm. Free.)*

Oriel College (a.k.a. "The House of the Blessed Mary the Virgin in Oxford") is wedged between High and Merton St. (tel. 276555; not open to the public) and was once the turf of Sir Walter Raleigh. Just south of Oriel, **Corpus Christi College** (tel. 276700) surrounds a quad with a sundial in the center, crowned by a golden pelican. The garden wall contains a gate built to facilitate visits between Charles I and his queen, residents at adjacent Christ Church and Merton during the Civil War. *(Open daily 1:30-4:30pm.)* Next door, **Merton College** (tel. 276310), off Merton St., features a fine garden and a 14th-century library holding the first printed Welsh Bible. Philologist J.R.R. Tolkien lectured here, inventing Elvish in his spare time. *(£1.)* The college is also home to the **Mob Quad,** Oxford's oldest and least impressive, dating from the 14th century. Nearby **St. Alban's Quad** has some of the University's best gargoyles; Japanese tourists visit daily and try to identify the rooms Crown Prince Narahito inhabited in his Merton days. *(Open M-F 2-4pm, Sa-Su 10am-4pm.)*

The soot-blackened **University College** (tel. 276619), on High St., up the crooked Logic Ln. from Merton St., dates from 1249 and vies with Merton for the title of oldest college, claiming Alfred the Great as its founder. Percy Bysshe Shelley was expelled from University for writing the pamphlet *The Necessity of Atheism,* but has since been immortalized in a prominent godless monument inside the college (to the right as you enter from High St.). Bill Clinton spent his Rhodes days here; his rooms at 46 Leckford Rd. are an endless source of smoked-but-didn't-inhale jokes for tour guides. *(Open July-Aug. daily 10am-6pm.)* Down High St. on the right lies the **Botanic Garden,** a sumptuous array of plants that have flourished for three centuries. *(Open daily Apr.-Sept. 9am-5pm; Oct.-Mar. 9am-4:30pm; glasshouses open daily 2-4pm. Late June to early Sept. £1.50, children free; free the rest of the year.)* The path connecting the Botanic Garden to the Christ Church Meadow provides a beautiful view of the Thames as well as the cricket and tennis courts on the opposite bank.

North of Queen and High Streets

Across High St. from the Botanic Garden, extensive verdant grounds surround the flower-laced quads of **Magdalen College** (MAUD-lin; tel. 276000), traditionally considered Oxford's handsomest. The college also boasts a deer park with the river watering its flank, and Addison's Walk (a circular path) framing a meadow at one edge. A cowled monk allegedly paces through Magdalen's oft-photographed clois-

ENGLAND

ters. The college's spiritual patron is alumnus Oscar Wilde—the place has always walked on the flamboyant side. Marking a personal decline and fall, Edward Gibbon declared the 14 months he spent here "the most idle and unprofitable of my whole career." *(Open daily July-Sept. noon-6pm; Oct.-June 2-5pm. Apr.-Sept. £2, students, seniors, and children £1; Oct.-Mar. free.)*

Up High St. toward Carfax, a statue of Queen Caroline (wife of George II) crowns the front gate of **Queen's College** (tel. 279121). Wren and Hawksmoor went to the trouble of rebuilding Queen's in the 17th and 18th centuries, with a distinctive Queen Anne style, in glorious orange, white, and gold. A trumpet call summons students to dinner; a boar's head graces the Christmas table. The latter tradition supposedly commemorates an early student of the college who, attacked by a boar on the outskirts of Oxford, choked his assailant to death with a volume of Aristotle. Alumni include starry-eyed Edmund Halley and the more earthly Jeremy Bentham. The College is closed to the public, except for those on authorized tours.

Next to Queen's stands **All Souls** (tel. 279379), a graduate college with a prodigious endowment. Candidates who survive the terribly difficult admission exams get invited to dinner, where it is ensured that they are "well-born, well-bred, and only moderately learned." All Souls is reputed to have the most heavenly wine cellar in Oxford. **The Great Quad,** with its fastidious lawn and two spare spires, may be Oxford's most serene, ordered space. *(Open Apr.-Oct. M-F 2-4:30pm; Nov.-Mar. 2-4pm; closed in August.)*

Turn up Catte St. to the **Bodleian Library** (tel. 277165), Oxford's principal reading and research library with over five million books and 50,000 manuscripts. Sir Thomas Bodley endowed the library's first wing in 1602 on a site that had housed university libraries since 1488; the institution has since grown to fill the immense **Old Library** complex, the round **Radcliffe Camera** next door, and two newer buildings on Broad St. As a copyright library, the Bodleian receives a copy of every book printed in Great Britain—*gratis.* Admission to the reading rooms is by ticket only. If you can prove you're a scholar (a student ID may be sufficient, but a letter of introduction from your college is encouraged), present two passport photos (which can be taken on the spot), and promise not to light any fires, the Admissions Office will issue a two-day pass for £3. No one has ever been permitted to take out a book, not even Cromwell. Well, especially not Cromwell. *(Library open M-F 9am-6pm, Sa 9am-1pm. Tours in summer M-F 4 per day, Sa-Su 2 per day; in winter 2 per day. £3.50. Tours leave from the Divinity School, across the street.)* The **Sheldonian Theatre** (tel. 277299), set beside the Bodleian, is a Roman-style auditorium designed by Wren when he was a teenager. Graduation ceremonies, conducted in Latin, take place in the Sheldonian and can be witnessed with permission from one of the "bulldogs" (bowler-hatted university officers). The cupola of the theatre affords an inspiring view of the spires of Oxford. The ivy-crowned stone heads on the fence behind the Sheldonian do not represent ancient emperors; they are a 20th-century study of beards. *(Open M-Sa 10am-12:30pm and 2-4:30pm, subject to change. £1.50, children £1.)* Next to the Sheldonian, the Broad St. **Museum of the History of Science** (tel. 277280) contains a radiant collection of sundials, as well as ancient navigational instruments and countless clocks. *(Open Tu-Sa noon-4pm. Free.)*

Oxford Made Easy

Oxford undergraduates study for three years, each year consisting of three eight-week terms; at times it seems as if more time is spent on holiday than at school. The university itself has no official, central campus. Though central facilities—libraries, laboratories, and faculties—are established and maintained by the university, Oxford's 40 independent colleges, where students live and learn simultaneously (at least in theory), are scattered throughout the city. Students must dress in formalwear called **subfuse** for all official University events, including exams; carnations are obligatory. At the end of their last academic year, students from all the colleges assemble for degree examinations, a grueling three-week ordeal that takes place in the Examination Schools on High Street in late June and early July. Each year, university authorities do their best to quell the vigorous post-examination celebrations in the street. Each year they fail. The authorities, that is.

On Broad St., across from the Museum of the History of Science, you can browse at **Blackwell's,** the famous bookstore. The basement room dwarfs the building and undermines the foundations of Trinity College next door; Guinness lists it as the largest room devoted to bookselling anywhere in the world. Ask for help if you need it—the staff won't offer (see **Bookstores,** p. 221).

Trinity College, Broad St. (tel. 279900), founded in 1555, has a splendid Baroque chapel, including a limewood altarpiece, a cedar lattices, and angel-capped pediments, with cherubim everywhere. Trinity's series of eccentric presidents includes Ralph Kettell, who used to come to dinner with a pair of scissors and chop at any person's hair he deemed too long. *(Open daily 10:30-11:45am and 2-5pm. £2, students, seniors, and children £1.)* Students at **Balliol College** (tel. 277777) preserve a semblance of tradition by hurling bricks over the wall at their conservative Trinity College rivals. The interior gates of Balliol College, up Broad St. from Blackwell's, still bear scorch marks from the immolations of 16th-century Protestant martyrs (the pyres were built a few yards from the college, where a small cross set into Broad St. rattles cyclists today). A mulberry tree planted by Queen Elizabeth still shades napping students. Matthew Arnold, the poet Swinburne, Gerard Manley Hopkins, Aldous Huxley, and Adam Smith were all sons of Balliol's spires. *(Open daily 2-5pm. £1, students and children free.)*

Across Catte St. from the Bodleian, New College Ln. leads inevitably to **New College** (tel. 279555). So named because of its relative anonymity at the time of its founding by William of Wykeham in 1379, New College has become one of Oxford's most prestigious colleges. The layers of the front quad—compare the different stones of the first and second stories—reveal the architectural history of the college. Look for the exquisitely detailed misericords, carved by sympathetic carpenters into the pews to support monks' bottoms. A croquet garden is encircled by part of the **old city wall,** and every three years the mayor of the City of Oxford visits the college for a ceremonial inspection to ascertain the wall's repair. The bell tower has Seven Deadly Sins gargoyles on one side, and Seven Virtues on the other, all equally grotesque. A former head of the college, Rev. Warden Spooner, is now remembered as the unintentional inventor of "spoonerisms." This stern but befuddled academic would raise a toast to "our queer old dean" or rebuke a student who had allegedly "hissed all the mystery lectures" and "tasted the whole worm." *(Open daily Easter-Oct. 11am-5pm; Nov.-Easter 2-4pm, use the Holywell St. Gate. £1.50.)*

Up St. Giles from Broad St., the imposing **Ashmolean Museum,** Beaumont St. (tel. 278000), was Britain's first public museum when it opened in 1683. Leonardo, Monet, Manet, Van Gogh, Michelangelo, Rodin, and Matisse convene for the permanent collection. *(Open Tu-Sa 10am-4pm, Su 2-4pm. Free.)* Ashmolean's **Cast Gallery,** behind the museum, stores over 250 casts of Greek sculptures. While the museum undergoes renovation, the entire collection is on display—the finest classical collection outside London. *(Open Tu-Sa 10am-4pm, Su 2-4pm. Free.)*

A few blocks up St. Giles, as the street becomes Woodstock Rd., stands **Somerville College** (tel. 270600), Oxford's most famous women's college. (The oldest is Lady Margaret Hall.) Somerville's alumnae include Dorothy Sayers, Indira Gandhi, Margaret Thatcher, Ena Franey, and Shirley Williams. Women were not granted degrees until 1920—Cambridge held out until 1948—and they comprise only about 38% of Oxford's student body today. *(Open daily 2-5:30pm.)* **Keble College** (tel. 272727), at the corner of Keble and Park St., was designed by architect William Butterfield to stand out from the Museum's sandstone background; the intricate, multi-patterned red brick, known as "The Fair Isle Sweater," was deemed "actively ugly" by Sir Nikolaus Pevsner. *(Open M-Sa 2-5pm.)* Through a passageway to the left, the **Hayward** and **deBreyne Buildings** squat on the tarmac-like black plexiglass spaceships. Across Park St. from Keble College, you can walk through the iron and stone temple of the **University Museum** (tel. 272950), Parks Rd. *(Open M-Sa noon-5pm. Free.)* At **Pitt Rivers Museum** (tel. 270949), behold an eclectic ethnography and natural history collection that includes shrunken heads and rare butterflies. *(Open M-Sa 1-4:30pm. Free.)*

ENTERTAINMENT

Public transit ends between 11pm and midnight, but nightlife can last until 3am. Pick up *This Month in Oxford* from the tourist office, or check out the posters plastered around town advertise upcoming events. *Daily Information*, posted in the tourist office and most colleges, provides some pointers, and pubs often have their own brochures. The university itself offers marvelous entertainment. College theatre groups often stage productions in gardens or in cloisters.

Music is a cherished art at Oxford; attend a concert or an Evensong service at one of the colleges, or a performance at the **Holywell Music Rooms,** the oldest in the country. **City of Oxford Orchestra** (tel. 744457), the city's professional symphony orchestra, plays a subscription series in the Sheldonian and college chapels in the summer. *(Shows at 8pm. Tickets £12-15; 25% student discount.)* They also have Sunday coffee concerts. Get tickets from **Blackwell's Music Shop,** 38 Holywell St. (tel. 261384). *(Open M and W-Sa 9am-6pm, Tu 9:30am-6pm, Su noon-5pm.)*

The **Apollo Theatre,** George St. (tel. 244544), presents a wide range of performances, ranging from lounge-lizard jazz to the Welsh National Opera, which visits at the end of May and in October. *(Open M-Sa 10am-6pm. Tickets from £6, discounts for students and seniors.)* The **Oxford Playhouse,** 11-12 Beaumont St. (tel. 798600), is a venue for bands, dance troupes, and the Oxford Stage Company. *(Tickets from £6, students and seniors £4, standby tickets for seniors and students on day of show.)* The **Oxford Union,** St. Michael's St. (tel. (0171) 385 8993), shows solid student productions. *(Tickets £8, students, seniors, and children £5.)* The **Old Fire Station,** 40 George St. (tel. 794490) features more avant-garde work. It turns into a club called OFS from Wednesday through Saturday. *(Cover £4-5.)* On Friday and Saturday nights, "eat till 2, drink till 2:20, be merry till 3" to funk, jazz, or 80s music; 70s night on Thursday. *(Open M-Tu 11am-11pm, W-Sa 11am-3pm.)*

The **Westgate Pub** (tel. 250099), on Park End St., blasts techno until 2am (F-Sa), offering jazz on Monday and comedy on Tuesday. Otherwise head up Walton St. or down Cowley Rd. (by far the most self-indulgent of Oxford's neighborhoods)—both areas provide late-night clubs, as well as a fascinating jumble of ethnic restaurants, exotic shops, used bookstores, and alternative lifestyles. The **Zodiac,** 193 Cowley Rd., has the best bands around, for a hefty cover of £5 and up. Try **Rats,** 182 Cowley Rd. (tel. 245999), for intimate late nights and cheap drinks. *(Open till midnight, doors close 11pm.)* **Freud's,** 119 Walton St. (tel. 311171), in an old church building (stained-glass windows included), is cafe by day and club by night. The **Phoenix Picture House** (tel. 554909), on Walton St., shows a range of matinees and late-night movies.

A more traditional pastime in Oxford is **punting** on the River Thames (known in Oxford as the Isis) or on the River Cherwell (CHAR-wul). Before venturing out in boats that look like shallow gondolas, punters receive a tall pole, a small oar, and an advisory against falling into the river. Try to avoid creating an obstacle course for irate rowers. Don't be surprised if you suddenly come upon **Parson's Pleasure,** a small riverside area where men sometimes sunbathe nude. Female passersby may open their parasols and tip them at a discreet angle to obscure the view. **Oxford Boat Hire,** Folly Bridge, south of Carfax and behind the Head of the River pub, rents from June to September. *(£6-8 per hr., £15-20 deposit.)* **Riverside Boating Co.,** Folly Bridge, across St. Aldates from the Head of the River pub, rents from April to September. *(£6 per hr., £20 deposit. Open daily 10am-dusk.)* **Magdalen Bridge Boat Co.,** Magdalen Bridge (tel. 202643), east of Carfax along High St., rents from March to October. *(£10 per hr., deposit £20 plus ID. Open daily 10am-9pm.)* Around Magdalen Bridge, students offer chauffeured punts plus a glass of wine for you and three friends. (1hr., £18.) Call **Salter Brothers,** Folly Bridge (tel. 243421), for cruises to Abingdon. *(2hr., 2 per day. £9.45, children £6.40. Open May-Oct. daily 9am-5:30pm.)*

The university celebrates **Eights Week** at the end of May, when all the colleges enter crews in the bumping races and beautiful people gather on the banks to nibble strawberries and sip champagne. In early September, **St. Giles Fair** invades one of Oxford's main streets with an old-fashioned carnival, complete with Victorian roundabout and whirligigs. Daybreak on May 1 brings one of Oxford's loveliest moments: the Magdalen College Choir greets the summer by singing madrigals from the top of the tower to a crowd below, and the town indulges in morris dancing, beating the bounds, and other age-old rituals of merrymaking—pubs open at 7am.

■ Near Oxford: Blenheim

The largest private home in England (and one of the loveliest) and birthplace of Winston Churchill, **Blenheim Place** (BLEN-em; tel. (01993) 811325) was built in appreciation of the Duke of Marlborough's victory over Louis XIV at the Battle of Blenheim in 1704, and as a token of Queen Anne's friendship with the Duke's wife, Sarah. The palace's rent is a single French franc, payable each year to the Crown. Blenheim's 2100 gorgeous acres include fantastic gardens and a lake, all designed by landscaper "Capability" Brown. While attending a party here, Churchill's mother gave birth to the future Prime Minister; his baby curls are on display. In September, Blenheim hosts the **International Horse Trials.** *(Palace open daily mid-Mar. to Oct. 10:30am-5:30pm; grounds open year-round 9am-5pm. £7.80, students and seniors £5.80, children £3.80, includes a boat trip on the lake.)* **Stagecoach Express** (tel. 772250) runs to Blenheim Palace from Gloucester Green bus station (20min., £3 return, concessions £2.25). The same bus also goes to Stratford and Birmingham. Another service, **Blenheim Palace Shuttle** (tel. (01993) 813888), offers hourly buses from George St. The £10 ticket includes transport, palace admission, and a guided tour. Blenheim sprawls in **Woodstock,** 8 mi. north of Oxford on the A44. Geoffrey Chaucer once lived in Woodstock, and Winston Churchill rests in the nearby village churchyard of **Bladon.**

▓ Salisbury

When the spire of Salisbury Cathedral was built in the early 14th century, the supporting pillars underneath began to buckle from the strain. Today the city itself seems to crouch under the weight of its cathedral-town roots. Salisbury revolves around the axis of the Salisbury Stake—the highest spire in England—visible throughout the city. Children play in the vast cathedral close, while elderly, grocery-bag-laden women hustle by. That all roads in the city seem to lead to the cathedral gates is no accident. Salisbury's small grid of streets (five running north to south and six east to west) was carefully charted by Bishop Poore in the early 13th century. Seven hundred years later, the town retains the imprint of its medieval origins as a bustling center for exchange of goods and ideas. This is perhaps most vividly demonstrated by the scores of inviting pubs scattered through the town, beckoning to road-weary travelers just as they did in the old Bishop's day.

GETTING THERE

Salisbury lies 80 mi. southwest of London. **Trains** (tel. (0345) 484950) depart for most major towns in the region, including **Winchester** (change at **Southampton;** 1½hr., 1 per hr., £10), **Southampton** (40min., 2 per hr., £7), **Portsmouth** and Southsea (1½hr., 1 per hr., £11-13), and **London** (1½hr,. 1 per hr., £22-30). **National Express buses** (tel. (0990) 808080) run from London's **Victoria** Station (2¾hr., 3 per day, £9.25, return £12.50). For £4.80 (seniors £3.15, children £2.10, families £8.50) you can buy an **Explorer** ticket good for a day's worth of travel on **Wilts** and some **Hampshire, Provincial,** and **Solent Blue** buses. Take **Wilts and Dorset** bus #X4 (tel. (01722) 336855) from **Bath** (2hr., 6 per day, £3) or use their service to get to **Stonehenge** (40min., M-Sa 10 per day, Su 4 per day, £4.60).

ORIENTATION AND PRACTICAL INFORMATION

You'll find the Salisbury bus station in the center of town; the train station is a 10- to 15-minute walk from there. To reach the tourist office from the train station, turn left out of the station onto **South Western Rd.,** bear right onto **Fisherton St.** (later called Bridge St.), pass over the bridge, and cross **High St.** Walk straight ahead onto **Silver St.,** which becomes **Butcher Row** and then **Fish Row.**

ENGLAND

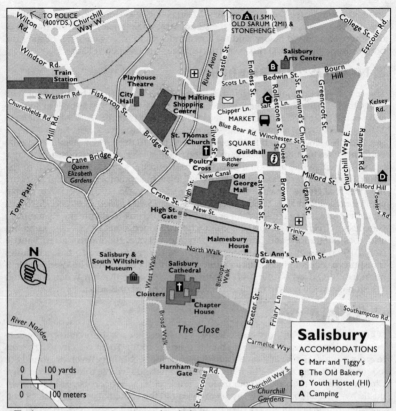

Salisbury

ACCOMMODATIONS

C Marr and Tiggy's
B The Old Bakery
D Youth Hostel (HI)
A Camping

Trains: S. Western Rd. (tel. (0345) 484950), west of town across the river. Ticket office open M-Sa 5:20am-8pm, Su 7:30am-8:45pm.

Buses: 8 Endless St. (tel. 336855). Open M-F 8:15am-5:45pm, Sa 8:15am-5:15pm.

Taxis: A and B Taxis (tel. 744744). Wheelchair facilities available. Taxis cruise from the train station and New Canal (by the cinema).

Bike Rental: Hayball Cycles, 26-30 Winchester St. (tel. 411378), just beyond McDonalds. £9 per day, £2.50 overnight, £55 per week; cash deposit £25. Open M-Sa 9am-5:30pm.

Tourist Office: Fish Row (tel. 334956; fax 422059), in the Guildhall in Market Sq. Extremely helpful staff. National Express ticket service. Books rooms with a deposit, deducted from your accommodations bill. Open July-Aug. M-Sa 9:30am-7pm, Su 10:30am-5pm; June and Sept. M-Sa 9:30am-6pm, Su 10:30am-4:30pm; May M-Sa 9:30am-5pm, Su 10:30am-4:30pm; Oct.-Apr. M-Sa 9:30am-5pm. Also offers **guided tours** (1½hr., Apr.-Oct. 11am and 6pm, £2, children £1).

Financial Services: Thomas Cook, 5 Queen St. (tel. 412787). Open M-Tu and Th-Sa 9am-5:30pm, W 10am-5:30pm.

Market: Market Sq. (go figure). Everything from peaches and plums to posters and pants. Open Tu and Sa roughly 7am-4pm.

Launderette: Washing Well, 28 Chipper Ln. (tel. 322899). Bring change and soap. Open daily 8am-9pm.

Emergency: Dial 999; no coins required.

Police: Wilton Rd. (tel. 411444).

Hotlines: Samaritans (crisis), 42 Milford St. (tel. 323355). Open 24hr. **Rape Crisis,** Southampton (tel. (01703) 701213). Open M 7-10pm, Tu 10am-1pm, Th 1-4pm, Su 7-10pm.

Post Office: 24 Castle St. (tel. 413051), at Chipper Ln. *Poste Restante,* bureau de change. Open M-Sa 9am-5:30pm. **Postal Code:** SP1 1AB.
Telephone Code: 01722.

ACCOMMODATIONS

Salisbury's proximity to much-frequented Stonehenge breeds many B&Bs, mostly well-appointed and reasonably priced (around £18-20). Guesthouses aplenty, with rates hovering around £17, are scattered throughout the town; check with the tourist office, or the listings outside it. Many pubs take overnight guests as well (look for signs), but their rates tend to be higher.

YHA Youth Hostel, Milford Hill House, Milford Hill (tel. 327572). From the tourist office, turn left on Fish Row, right on Queen St., left on Milford St., and walk ahead a few blocks under the overpass. The hostel will be on the left, up a hilly driveway. 74 beds. Smell the cedar from your window or tent. £9.75, under 18 £6.55. Lock-out 10am-1pm. Curfew 11:30pm. Definitely phone ahead, especially in peak season. **Camping** is also available in the 2-acre garden; £4.70 per person.

Matt and Tiggy's, 51 Salt Ln. (tel. 327443), just up from the bus station; remarkably convenient. A welcoming 450-year-old house with warped floors and ceiling beams and an overflow house located nearby. Mellow, hostel-style, 2-, 3-, and 4-person bedrooms. Young and *très* cool proprietors and their *très* cooler babies will lodge you cheerfully. £9.50, in winter £9. Breakfast £2. Sheets 80p. Tiny cafe next door, boasting cheap sandwiches and baked goods (open daily 11am-5pm).

The Old Bakery, 35 Bedwin St. (tel. 320100), from the bus station head 2 blocks up Rollestone St., turn left onto Bedwin St. and go about 2 doors down. The friendly proprietors have turned this 15th-century building into a comfortable, environmentally friendly resting spot. Scrumptious breakfast featuring gourmet coffee. Singles £18; doubles £17-21; £3 less without breakfast. Prices lower off-season.

Camping: Hudson's Field of the **Camping Club of Great Britain,** Castle Rd. (tel. 320713). On the way to Old Sarum, with showers and 100 pitches. Curfew (for vehicles only) 11pm. July-Aug. £5 per person, May-June £4, Mar.-Apr. and Sept. £3.50, plus £5 pitch per night.

FOOD AND PUBS

Carbon dating has unequivocally determined that Salisbury's cafeteria steaks existed millennia before Stonehenge was even a twinkle in the eyes of the Old People. Other sorts of food, though, are eons fresher. From 7am to 4pm on Tuesdays and Saturdays the town center resounds with vendors hawking clothes, fresh local produce, and homemade jams. **Reeve the Baker** (main branch next to the tourist office, between the town square and Fish Row) stocks all the strolling sightseer could crave, from Cornish pasties to caterpillar meringues (8 currant buns for £1.05). **Salisbury Health Foods,** 15 Queen St., vends scrumptious frozen yogurt with exotic fruit toppings (open M-Sa 9am-5:30pm). **Tesco supermarket,** on Castle St. at Chipper Ln. (open M-Th 8am-8pm, F 8am-9pm, Sa 8am-7pm, Su 10am-4pm), battles **Sainsbury's** (tel. 332282), one block east at The Maltings (open M-Th 8am-8pm, F 8am-9pm, Sa 8am-7pm, Su 10am-4pm) for supermarket supremacy. Though your best bet is pub food, there are reasonably priced restaurants on the way to the train station offering various forms of ethnic cuisine. Try **The Asia Restaurant,** 90 Fisherton St. (tel. 327628), where a friendly staff serves up Indian food at fair prices.

Even the most jaded pub dweller will find a pleasing venue among Salisbury's 60-odd watering holes. Most serve cheap food (£3-5), and many offer drink specials and live music. **The Old Mill,** located atop the river at the end of a 10-minute scenic stroll along Town Path, is *the* setting for an outdoor drink on a summer's evening. The **New Inn,** 41-47 New St. (tel. 327679), forged the way for non-smoking pubs in Britain and offers a warm atmosphere. Sip your brew with a view in the garden, facing the cathedral. **Coach & Horses,** Winchester St. (tel. 336254), serves meals and drinks all day in what is reputed to be Salisbury's oldest pub. Jam with locals the second Wednesday of every month (open M-Sa 10am-10pm; veggie meals available). Or you can share your pint closer to town at **The Bishop's Mill,** over the creatively named Bridge St. Bridge. **The Pheasant,** Salt Ln. (tel. 320675), serves lunch in the quintessential pub. Locals are still adjusting to the transformation of the **Avon Brewery Inn,** 75 Castle St., from a traditional pub to a genteel Victorian saloon, but the food remains tasty and well-priced (open M-Sa 11am-11pm, Su noon-3pm and 7-10:30pm).

SIGHTS AND ENTERTAINMENT

Salisbury Cathedral (tel. 555120) rises from its grassy close to a neck-breaking height of 404 ft. The bases of the marble pillars literally bend inward under the strain of 6400 tons of limestone; if a pillar rings when you knock on it, you should probably move away. Nearly 700 years have left the cathedral in need of structural and aesthetic repair (Sir Christopher Wren once calculated that the spire leaned 29.5 in.). Scaffolding will shroud parts of the spire, tower, and west front of the cathedral for years to come. Once inside, head to the wooden tomb of William Longespee, Earl of Salisbury (d. 1226), rare indeed in a universe of stone sarcophagi. A tiny stone figure rests in the nave. Legend has it either that a boy bishop is entombed on the spot or that it covers the heart of Richard Poore, bishop and founder of the cathedral. The incongruously abstract stained-glass window at the eastern end, gleaming in rich, jewel-like hues, is dedicated to prisoners of conscience, for whom a prayer is said each day. *(Cathedral open daily May to Aug. 8am-8:15pm, Sept.-Apr. 8am-6:30pm. Voluntary donation £3, students and seniors £2, children £1, families £6. General tours M-Sa 11:15am and 2:15pm; more in summer, hours vary. Free. Roof and tower tours M-Sa 11am, 2pm, 3pm, and 6:30pm, Su 4:30pm. £2. Evensong M-Sa 5:30pm, Su 3pm.)*

Much to King John's chagrin, one of four surviving copies of the *Magna Carta* rests in the **Chapter House.** Named for the practice of reading a chapter of the Bible at meetings there, the Chapter House is surrounded by detailed medieval friezes. On one favorite, Noah fills his ark and releases the dove while Cain bludgeons his fair brother's head with what looks like a hammer. Ask a guide for a complete list of the figures in relief. *(Open Mar.-Oct. M-Sa 9:30am-4:45pm, Su 1-4:45pm; Nov.-Feb. M-Sa 11am-3pm, Su 1-3:15pm. Free.)* The **cloisters** adjoining the cathedral somehow grew to be the largest in England, although the cathedral never housed any monks. The open lawns of the **cathedral close** flank some beautifully preserved old homes, including **Malmesbury House,** where Handel once lived and where the ghost of a cavalier now haunts forever. And ever. Hallelujah. Shhh! (It's a private residence.) Tours are available every half hour. *(Open Apr.-Sept. Tu-Sa noon-5:30pm. £4.)*

The **Salisbury and South Wiltshire Museum,** King's House, 65 The Close (tel. 332151), houses a potpourri of artwork (including Turner's exquisite watercolors of the nearby cathedral), handicraft, and random oddities. Exhibits trace the development of Salisbury and present the latest crackpot theories on Stonehenge. The museum boasts the bizarre 12 ft. Giant and his companion Hobnob, a stuffed behemoth of obscure origins. Purchased in 1873 for 30 shillings, the absurd figure has numerous times greeted royalty; he enjoyed the procession of George V and Queen Elizabeth's coronation, as well as Victoria's Diamond Jubilee. *(Open July-Aug. M-Sa 10am-5pm, Su 2-5pm; Sept.-June M-Sa 10am-5pm. £3, students and seniors £2, children 75p.)*

See shows by Salisbury's repertory theater company at the **Playhouse,** Malthouse Ln. (tel. 320333), over the bridge off Fisherton St. *(Tickets £8.50-14, £2 discount for students, seniors, and children. Half-price tickets available on the day of the show. Wheelchair access.)* The **Salisbury Festival** features dance exhibitions, music at venues throughout the city, and a wine-tasting festival at the Salisbury library for two weeks in mid- to late May. Contact the Festival Box Office, Salisbury Playhouse, Malthouse Ln., Salisbury SP2 7RA (tel. 320333). *(Tickets from £2.50.)* The **Salisbury Arts Centre,** Bedwin St. (tel. 321744), offers music, theater, and exhibitions throughout the year. *(Tickets from £5.)* In the summer there are free Sunday concerts in various parks. Call the tourist office for further information.

■ Near Salisbury

The germ of Salisbury, **Old Sarum** (tel. (01722) 335398), lies 2 mi. north of town. Here, an Iron Age fort evolved into a Saxon town, then a Norman fortress. In the 13th century, church officials moved the settlement and built a new cathedral. Old Sarum was the most notorious of the "rotten boroughs" eliminated by the Reform Act of 1832. Now a lonely windswept mound, it is still an atmospheric place to visit. Look for the **crop circle,** a finely detailed wheatfield imprint supposedly left by celestial visitors which appears annually. *(Open daily Apr.-Oct. 10am-6pm; Nov.-Mar. 10am-4pm. £2, students and seniors £1.50, children £1.)* Old Sarum is off the A345, the road to Stonehenge. Buses #3 and #5-9 run every 15 minutes from Salisbury.

Declared by James I to be "the finest house in the land," **Wilton House** (tel. (01722) 746720 or 746729), 3 mi. west of Salisbury on the A30 and home to the Earl of Pembroke, showcases paintings by Van Dyck, Rembrandt, Rubens, and others, and has an impressive, almost outrageous interior designed partly by Inigo Jones. The Tudor kitchen and Victorian laundry room shed a whole new light on the domestic arts. *(Open Apr.-Oct. daily 11am-6pm. House and grounds £6.75, students and seniors £5.75, children £4; grounds only £3.75, children £2.50.)* Catch bus #60 or 61 outside Marks and Spencer (M-Sa every 10min., Su 1 per hr.).

■ Stonehenge

> *You may put a hundred questions to these rough-hewn giants as they bend in grim contemplation of their fellow companions; but your curiosity falls dead in the vast sunny stillness that shrouds them and the strange monument, with all its unspoken memories, becomes simply a heart-stirring picture in a land of pictures.*
>
> —Henry James

Perhaps the gentle giants on Salisbury's windswept plain will remain fascinating for millennia to come, both for their mystery and for their sheer longevity. A submerged colossus amid swaying grass and indifferent cows, Stonehenge stands unperturbed by 50mph whipping winds and the legions of people who have been by its side for over 5000 years.

The present stones—22 ft. high—comprise the fifth temple constructed on the site. The first probably consisted of an arch and circular earthwork, and was in use for about 500 years. Its relics are the Aubrey Holes (white patches in the earth) and the Heel Stone (the isolated, rough block standing outside the circle). The next monument consisted of about 60 stones imported up the River Avon from Wales around 2100 BC, used to mark astronomical directions. This monument may once have been composed of two concentric circles and two horseshoes of megaliths, both enclosed by earthworks. The present shape, once a complete circle, dates from about 1500 BC; Stonehenge seemed old even to the ancient Saxons and Normans.

The monument is even more impressive considering that its stones—some of which weigh 45 tons—were erected by an infinitely tedious process of rope-and-log leverage. Many generations persevered to complete each temple in this spot, leaving us to marvel at the religious dedication inspired by the site. The most famous Stonehenge legend holds that the circle was built of Irish stones magically transported by Merlin. Other stories attribute the monument to giants, Phoenicians, Mycenaean Greeks, Druids, Romans, Danes, and aliens. In any case, whether they traveled by land, water, or flying saucer, the Bronze Age builders (c. 2800-1500 BC) seem to have possessed more technology than we can explain. The giants keep their ageless secret from archaeologists and supermarket tabloids alike.

Many peoples have worshipped at the Stonehenge site, from late Neolithic and early Bronze Age chieftains to contemporary mystics. In 300 BC, Druids arrived from the Continent and claimed Stonehenge as their shrine. The 1998 Summer Solstice saw the return of Druids, absent since a confrontation with police 10 years earlier.

GETTING THERE

Getting to Stonehenge takes little effort—as long as you don't have a 45-ton rock in tow. **Wilts & Dorset** (tel. (01722) 336855) runs several **buses** daily from Salisbury center and from the train station (40min., return £4.60). The first bus leaves Salisbury at 8:45am (Su 10:35am, though times vary seasonally), and the last leaves Stonehenge at 6pm (Su 5:45pm). **Guide Friday**, with Wilts and Dorset, runs a **tour bus** from Salisbury (3 per day, £6-12.50)

For the same price as a trip to Salisbury, get an **Explorer ticket** which allows you to travel all day on any bus and use it to stop by **Avebury** (tel. (01672) 539425), a cousin of Stonehenge which is less crowded by tourists and more crowded by residents of the tiny village situated within the largest stone ring in Britain. Take bus #5 or 6 to Swindon (viewing free; wheelchair access).

PRACTICAL INFORMATION

Admission to Stonehenge includes a 40-minute English Heritage audio tour that makes use of handsets resembling cellular telephones. The effect may be more haunting than Stonehenge itself—a bizarre march of tourists who seem to be engaged in business calls. Nonetheless, the tour is helpful, and includes arguments between a shepherd and his mother about the stones' origins. For those who don't want to press "9" at the sound of the tone, English Heritage (tel. (01980) 625368) also offers guided personal tours throughout the day. *(Open daily June-Aug. 9am-7pm; mid-Mar. to May and Sept. to mid-Oct. 9:30am-6pm; mid-Oct. to mid-Mar. 9:30am-4pm. £3.90, students, seniors, and unemployed £2.90, children £2. Wheelchair access.)* If you'd rather not get stoned by the price of admission, admire the stones from the roadside or from Amesbury Hill, 1½ mi. up the A303. Even if you do see Stonehenge up close, it's worth the walk to view the coterie of giants looming in the distance.

The most scenic walking or cycling route to Stonehenge follows the **Woodford Valley Route** through Woodford and Wilsford. Go north from Salisbury on Castle Rd., bear left just before Victoria Park onto Stratford Rd., and follow the road over the bridge through Lower, Middle, and Upper Woodford. After about 9 mi., turn left onto the A303 for the last mile. If Stonehenge doesn't provide enough rock for you, keep your eyes peeled when you reach Wilsford for the Jacobean mansion that belongs to singer **Sting,** on the right-hand side in the fields of gold (actually fields of flowering mustard plants). Don't go inside the gates or you'll meet the police, not the Police.

AVON AND SOMERSET

■ Bath

A visit to the elegant Georgian city of Bath (pop. 83,000) remains *de rigueur*, even though it is now more of a museum—or perhaps a museum's gift shop—than a resort. But expensive trinkets can't conceal Bath's sophistication. Immortalized by Fielding, Smollett, Austen, and Dickens, Bath once stood second only to London as the social capital of England. Queen Anne's visit to the natural hot springs here in 1701 established Bath as one of the great meeting places for 18th-century British artists, politicians, and intellectuals. Heavily bombed in World War II, Bath has been painstakingly restored so that today, too, every thoroughfare is fashionable, though more hair salons than literary salons grace its fair streets.

Legend ascribes the founding of Bath to King Lear's leper father Bladud, who wandered the countryside bemoaning his banishment from court. He became a swineherd, but his pigs soon caught the affliction. The devoted and decomposing animals led their king to a therapeutic spring. Out of gratitude, Bladud founded a city on the site. The Romans built an elaborate complex of baths to house the curative waters here early in their occupation of Britain. The baths (coed during Roman times) have

ENGLAND

Bath

ACCOMMODATIONS

G International Backpackers Hostel
B Lynn Shearn
D Mrs. Guy
H Mrs. Rowe
F White Guest House
E YHA Youth Hostel
C YMCA International House
A Camping

North Rd.

Sham Castle Ln.

TO **E** (200YDS.)

Cleveland Walk

Sydney Buildings

Beckford Rd.

Sydney Rd.

Sydney Gardens

Holburne Museum

Sydney Pl.

Raby Pl.

D

Pulteney Gdns.

Pulteney Rd.

Broadway

F

Bathwick St.

Henrietta Rd.

Henrietta Park

Garden for the Blind

Great Pulteney St.

Laura Pl.

County Cricket Grounds

North Parade Rd.

Ferry Ln.

Rossiter Rd.

Train Station

St. John's Rd.

River Avon

Victoria Art Gallery Pl.

Pulteney Bridge

Orange Grove

Abbey

Pierrepont St.

S. Parade

Book Museum

Manvers St.

Claverton St.

The Building of Bath Museum

Assembly Rooms & Museum of Costume

Julian Rd.

Lansdown Rd.

Bennett St.

Walcot St.

C

Broad St.

Royal Photographic Society

Octagon

George St.

Milsom St.

Upper Borough Walls

Borough Walls

Cheap St.

High St.

Guildhall

i

Pump Room & Roman Baths

Stall St.

Southgate St.

Westgate St.

St. James Parade

Corn St.

G

TO **H** (1/4 MILE)

Museum of East Asian Art

THE CIRCUS

Gay St.

QUEEN SQUARE

Theatre Royal

Charlotte St.

James St. West

Green Park Rd.

River Avon

Wells Rd.

Crescent Ln.

Royal Crescent

Brock St.

Royal Ave.

Upper Bristol Rd.

Charles St.

Herschel House and Museum

Bridge Rd.

Green Park

Lower Bristol Rd.

Marlboro Buildings

Marlboro Ln.

B

Midland Rd.

Lower Oldfield Park

TO A36 AND **A** (2 MILES)

TO A4

Royal Victoria Park

N

0   200 yards

0   200 meters

traditionally been a site of eyebrow-raising behavior. After one look around, Queen Victoria would discreetly pull the shade of her carriage when passing through.

GETTING THERE

Bath is served by direct Intercity **rail** service (tel. (0345) 484950) from London's **Paddington Station** (1½hr., 1 per hr., £27) and **Waterloo Station** (2¼hr., 2 per day, £19.90), **Exeter** (1¾hr., 15 per day, £19), and **Bristol** (15min., 32 per day, £4.40). **National Express** (tel. (0990) 808080) operates **buses** from London's **Victoria coach station** (3hr., 9 per day, £10.75-18.50 return), **Oxford** (2hr., 6 per day, £12). **Badgerline** buses offer a **Day Rambler** ticket (£4.80, seniors and children £3.50) for unlimited travel in the region. The **Slow Coach** stops here on its circuit of England (consult **By Bus and Coach,** p. 33, for details).

ORIENTATION AND PRACTICAL INFORMATION

The **Pulteney** and **North Parade Bridges** span the **River Avon,** which bends around the city from the east. **The Roman Baths,** the **Abbey,** and the **Pump Room** are all in the city center. The **Royal Crescent** and the **Circus** lie to the northwest. The train and bus stations are near the south end of **Manvers St.,** at the bend in the river. From either terminal, walk up Manvers St. to the Terrace Walk roundabout and turn left onto York St. to reach the tourist office in the Abbey Churchyard.

Transportation

Trains: Railway Pl., at the south end of Manvers St. Booking office open M-F 5:30am-8:30pm, Sa 6am-8:30pm, Su 7:45am-8:30pm. Travel Centre open M-F 8am-7pm, Sa 9am-6pm, Su 9:30am-6pm.

Buses: Manvers St. (tel. 464446). Ticket office open M-Sa 8:30am-5:30pm. Information Centre open M-Sa 9am-5:30pm. **National Express** (tel. (0990) 808080) is the main carrier. Luggage storage available during ticket office hours (£2 per 2 days).

Taxis: Taxis near stations and throughout the city, or call **Abbey Radio** (tel. 465843) or **Orange Grove Taxis** (tel. 447777).

Bike Rental: Avon Valley Bike Hire (tel. 461880), behind the train station. £9 per ½ day, £14 per day; £250 deposit by cash, credit card, or debit card. Open Apr.-Oct. daily 9am-5:30pm; Nov.-Mar. M-Sa 9am-5:30pm, Su 10am-5pm.

Boat Rental: Bath Boating Station (tel. 466407), at the end of Forester Rd., about ½mi. north of town. Punts and canoes £4 per person per hr., £1.50 each additional hr. Open daily summer 9am-9pm, winter 9am-5:30pm.

Tourist and Financial Services

Tourist Office: Abbey Chambers (tel. 477101; fax 477787). Efficient staff with a computerized booking system and a booking fee of £2.50 plus 10% deposit. Office gets crowded in summer. Map and mini-guide 25p. Pick up *This Month in Bath* (free). Open June-Sept. M-Tu and F-Sa 9:30am-6pm, W-Th 9:45am-6pm, Su 10am-4pm; Oct.-May M-Sa 9am-5pm, Su 10am-4pm.

Tours: Free guided **walking tours** given by the Mayor's Honorary Guides depart from the Abbey Churchyard daily at 10:30am and 2pm. Tours are very popular and range from good to excellent, depending on your guide. Open-topped, narrated 1hr. **bus tours** by **Guide Friday** (tel. 444102) depart from the bus station every 15min. between 9:30am and 5pm, and can be joined at various points on the route. £7, students and seniors £5.50, children £3. Young hordes eager for a day away use **Mad Max Tours** (tel. 465674) for a day-long trip to Wiltshire (Stonehenge, Avebury Stone Circle, the Cotswolds). Departs at 8:45am from "the statue" on Cheap St., stops at the YHA hostel at 8:50am, and returns at 4:30pm. £14. Try to book ahead through Mad Max or the Bath Youth Hostel.

Financial Services: Barclays, 37 Milsom St. (tel. (0800) 400100). Open M-F 9am-5pm, Sa 9:30am-12:30pm. **Lloyds** (B3, tel. 310256). Open M-Tu and Th-F 9am-5:30pm, W 9:30am-5:30pm, Sa 9:30am-12:30pm. **Thomas Cook,** 20 New Bond St. (C4; tel. 463191). Open M-W and F-Sa 9am-5:30pm, Th 10am-5:30pm.

American Express: 5 Bridge St. (tel. 444757), just before Pulteney Bridge. Open M-Tu and Th-F 9am-5:30pm, W 9:30am-5:30pm, Sa 9am-5pm. Also in the tourist office (tel. 424416).

Local Services

Luggage Storage: At the bus station during ticket office hours (M-Sa 8:30am-5:30pm) and at **Bath International Backpackers Hostel** (see **Accommodations**).

Lost Property: at the Police Station, Manvers St. (tel. 824434). Open M-F 10am-3pm.

Gay and Lesbian Information: Gay West (tel. (0117) 942 0842).

Launderette: Spruce Goose, Margaret's Buildings (off Brock St.). £3 per load, soap 60p. Open daily 8am-9pm, last wash 8pm.

Emergency and Communications

Emergency: Dial 999; no coins required.

Police: Manvers St. (tel. 444343), just up from the train and bus stations.

Crisis Line: Samaritans (crisis), 10 Newbridge St. (tel. 429222).

Hospital: Royal United Hospital, Coombe Park, in Weston (tel. 428331). Take bus #14, 16, or 17 from the rail or bus station.

Post Office: New Bond St. (tel. 445358), across from the Podium Shopping centre. Bureau de change. Open M-Sa 9am-5:30pm. **Postal Code:** BA1 1A5.

Internet Access: Midnight Express Café at the **Bath International Backpackers Hostel** (see **Accommodations**). 2 computers. £3 per 30 min., £5 per hr. Open daily 5-7pm and 9-11pm, though hours may vary. Call 446787 for info.

Telephone Code: 01225.

ACCOMMODATIONS

Bath's well-to-do visitors drive up the prices of the B&Bs—don't try to find a bargain basement room (some are quite frightening). Instead, expect to pay £18 and up, and enjoy Bath's gracious style. B&Bs cluster on **Pulteney Rd.** and **Pulteney Gdns.** From the stations, walk up Manvers St., which becomes Pierrepont St., right onto N. Parade Rd. and past the cricket ground to Pulteney Rd. For a more relaxed setting, continue past Pulteney Gdns. (or take the footpath from behind the rail station) to **Widcombe Hill.** The steep climb has prices to match (from £17). A walk west toward Royal Victoria Park on **Crescent Gdns.** will reveal another front of B&Bs.

YHA Youth Hostel, Bathwick Hill (tel. 465674; fax 482947). From N. Parade Rd., turn left onto Pulteney Rd., then right onto Bathwick Hill. A footpath takes the hardy up the ever-ascending hill to the hostel (a steep 20min. walk). Save your energy for the city: Badgerline "University" bus #18 (6 per hr. until midnight; £1 return) runs to the hostel from the bus station or the Orange Grove roundabout. Secluded and graciously clean Italianate mansion overlooking the city. Don't underestimate the hill; you'll regret it. £9.75, under 18 £6.55. Breakfast £3, dinner £4.40. 117 beds. Showers, TV, laundry (£2.10 per load), lockers. No lockout, no curfew. In summer reserve a week in advance.

International Backpackers Hostel, 13 Pierrepont St. (tel. 446787; fax 446305). Extremely convenient location; up the street from the stations and 3 blocks from the baths. A self-proclaimed "totally fun-packed mad place to stay." Each room and bed is identified by a music genre and artist ("I'm sleeping in Rap"). Bordello-esque bar and lounge in the basement. £8-10, depending on season. Breakfast £1.

⊛**Lynn Shearn,** Prior House, 3 Marlborough Ln. (tel. 313587). Convenient location on the west side beside the arbor of Royal Victoria Park. Easy 12min. walk, or take bus #14 from the station (6 per hr., get off at Hinton Grange). Look for the *Let's Go* sign in the window; among Bath's best values. Warm proprietors welcome you as friends. Doubles with full English breakfast £30, with bath £35. No smoking.

YMCA International House, Broad St. Pl. (tel. 460471). From Walcott St. across from the Hilton Hotel, walk under the arch and up the steps. Men and women accepted. More central than the YHA hostel (3min. from tourist office); clean, but no abundance of bathrooms. 180 beds. Dorms £10; singles £14.50; doubles and triples £13 per person; prices drop after 2 nights. Continental breakfast included. Dinner £4. Laundry. Key deposit £5. No curfew. Heavily booked in summer.

Mrs. Guy, 14 Raby Pl. (tel. 465120; fax 465283). From N. Parade Rd., turn left onto Pulteney Rd., then right up Bathwick Hill; Raby Pl. is the first row of buildings on the left. Luxuriate in this elegant Georgian home. TV/VCR lounge. Fresh seasonal fruits, yogurt, and homemade jams in Wedgwood dishes complement a generous English breakfast. Doubles £42-45, all with bath. No smoking.

Mrs. Rowe, 7 Widcombe Crescent (tel. 422726). Proceed up Widcombe Hill and turn right; in the southeastern area, uphill from the stations. The height of grandfather-clock elegance with a view to match. 10min. from town center. Singles £20; twins £36; doubles with bath £42.

The White Guest House, 23 Pulteney Gdns. (tel. 426075). From North Parade make a right at the traffic light, Pulteney Gdns. is the 2nd left. A homey B&B with a patio filled with flowers. All rooms with TV, all but one with bath. Kind proprietors will knock £2 off if you tell them *Let's Go* sent you. Singles £20-22; doubles £36-40; triples £50; prices lower Nov.-Apr.

Camping: Newton Mill Camping, Newton Rd. (tel. 333909; fax 461556; email newtonmill@hare2.demon.co.uk), 2½mi. west of city center off the A36. Take bus #5 from bus station (5 per hr.; £1.60 return) to Twerton and ask the bus driver to let you off at the campsite. 105 car and caravan sites in an idyllic stream-side setting. Walk-on campers use meadow across the stream. £3.50 per person for walk-on campers; no reservation necessary. £9.95 for tent, car and 2 people; book a week in advance. Shop, laundry (£3 per load), bar, restaurant, and free showers.

FOOD AND PUBS

For fruits and vegetables, visit the **Guildhall Market**, between High St. and Grand Parade (open M-Sa 8am-5:30pm). **Harvest Natural Foods,** 27 Walcot St. (tel. 465519), stocks a tremendous selection of organic produce (open M-Sa 9:30am-5:30pm). Grab picnic fare from the excellent salad bar at **Waitrose supermarket** in the Podium on High St. across from the post office. So many fresh fruit juices, so little time (open M-F 8:30am-8pm, Sa 8:30-7pm, Su 11am-5pm). On Sundays, when food is hard to come by, hit the pubs; many offer 3-course Sunday lunches at bargain prices. For a quick take-away bite, stop by **Viva Mexico,** 19 Barton St. (tel. 316316) and try the chocolate and banana chimichanga for £1 (open M-Th 6-10pm, F 6-11pm, Sa noon-midnight, Su 5-10pm). Tasty sandwiches abound at **La Baguette** near the Roman Baths on Stall St. Airy french bread sandwiches (around £1.60)—*c'est fantastique!* (open M-Sa 8:30am-5:30pm, Su 9am-5pm).

For history and food, head to **The Pump Room,** Abbey Churchyard (tel. 444477), which elegantly exercises its scandalous monopoly over Bath Spa drinking water in a palatial Victorian ballroom. Cream tea (£5.25) is served from 2:30pm until closing; weekend reservations are essential. Handel plays in the background; once you've paid the check you may be Baroque as well (open daily Apr.-Sept. 9am-6pm; Oct.-Mar. 9:30am-5pm).

Demuths Restaurant, 2 North Parade Passage (tel. 446059), off Abbey Green. Creative vegetarian and vegan dishes even the most devoted carnivore would enjoy. Fresh, colorful vegetables match the brightly colored paintings and fresh flowers; the lemon yellow walls may inspire you to try the luscious lemon sponge (£2.50). Entrees around £8. Open daily 10-11:30am, noon-4pm and 6:30-10pm.

Tilleys Bistro, 3 N. Parage Passage (tel. 484200). Salivate over Tilleys' impressive Frenchie creations. Meat and veggie menus. Mushroom crepes under £5. Open M-Sa noon-2:30pm and 6:30-11pm, Su 6:30-10:30pm.

The Walrus and The Carpenter, 28 Barton St. (tel. 314684), uphill from the Theatre Royal. Basic bistro dishes served alongside candle-stuffed wine bottles. Good burgers with creative toppings (£6-9); vegetarian entrees as well (£5-8). Try the famed veggie nut-roast. Open M-Sa noon-2:30pm and 6-11pm, Su noon-11pm.

The Canary, 3 Queen St. (tel. 424846). Airy tea house serving tasty twists on light meals. Try the Somerset rabbit from an 18th-century recipe or the honey-spiced chicken; dishes £5-6. Open M-F 10am-5pm, Sa 9am-5:30pm, Su 11am-5:30pm.

Scoff's, Kingsmead Sq. (tel. 462483), corner of Monmouth and Westgate St. Memorable, freshly baked wholefood and filling lunches served in a woody dining room. Wonderful cold vegetable pizza (£2.90; take it out for a picnic in the square and it's £1.90). Open M-Sa 8am-8pm.

Café Retro, 18 York St. (tel. 339347). Not particularly retro. Café Retro offers near-gourmet dishes and wonderful specials (Moroccan lamb tajine £10.50). It's pricy, but worth the splurge. Hit it for lunch—after 6pm prices rise as steeply as Bathwick Hill. Open daily 10am-11pm.

The Crystal Palace, 11 Abbey Green, behind Marks and Sparks. A sprawling, 18th-century pub and restaurant with an outdoor patio. Ploughman's lunch (bread with salad and pickles) served 6 different ways (£3.80-4.30). Open for meals daily noon-2:30pm and 6-8:30pm.

If you're looking for a drink, **The Boater,** 9 Argyle St. (tel. 464211), overlooks the river with outdoor seating and a view of the lit-up Pulteney Bridge (open M-Sa 11am-11pm, Su noon-10:30pm). **The Garrick's Head,** St. John's Pl. (tel. 448819), is a scoping ground for the stage door of the Theatre Royal. For a late night, **The Huntsman,** North Parade (tel. 331367), at the Terrace Walk roundabout, is open M-Sa until 2am.

SIGHTS

The **Roman Baths** (tel. 477759), once the spot for naughty sightings, are now a must-see for all. (*Open Apr.-July and Sept. daily 9am-6pm; Aug. 9am-6pm and 7-9pm; Oct.-Mar. 9am-5pm. Partial wheelchair access. £6.30, seniors £5.60, children £3.80, families £16.50; or buy a joint ticket to the Museum of Costume, £8.40, seniors £7.50, children £5, families £22. Avoid crowds by arriving when the museum opens, or 1½hr. before closing.*) In 1880, sewer diggers inadvertently uncovered the first glimpse of what recent excavation has shown to be a splendid model of advanced Roman engineering. Long before the age of Hanoverian refinement, Bath flourished for nearly 400 years as the Roman spa city of Aquae Sulis. Most of the visible complex is not Roman, but a Victorian dream of what Romans might have built. Even so, the architectural bits and pieces of Roman possessions are impressive. On a cold day, the hot springs give off a surreal mist that has bewitched hordes ever since the Celtic tribes settled here. Read the various recovered curses (in Latin or in English) that Romans cast into Minerva's spring. Tradition said that if the written curse floated on the water, it would be visited back upon the curser, but Romans neatly avoided this by writing their ill wishes on lead. Guided tours run hourly from the main pool. Audio tours are also available. Penny-pinching travelers can view one of the baths in the complex by entering (for free) through the **Pump Room** on Stall St.; look for explanatory posters. But the Roman Baths Museum is worth the price.

Situated next door to the Baths, on a site that once contained a Saxon cathedral three times as large, the 15th-century **Bath Abbey** (tel. 477752) towers over its neighbors, beckoning to visitors across the skyline (*open daily 9am-4:30pm; £1.50 donation requested*). An anomaly among the city's first-century Roman and 18th-century Georgian sights, the abbey saw the crowning of King Edgar, "first king of all England," in AD 973. The whimsical west facade sports angels climbing ladders up to heaven—and two angels climbing down. Tombstones cover every possible surface in the church save the sanctuary and ceiling. Peruse the protruding markers—they reveal the eerie and often mysterious ways various Brits and Yanks met their ends. A stone just inside the entrance remembers Reverend Dr. Thomas "Dismal Science" Malthus (1766-1834), founder of modern demographics and inspiration to family planners everywhere. Play "Trivial Pursuit: New Testament Edition" with the 56 stained-glass scenes of Jesus' life at the east end. The Abbey's **Heritage Vaults** (tel. 422462) below detail the millennia-spanning history of the stone giant. (*Open M-Sa 10am-4pm. £2, students, seniors, and children £1; wheelchair access.*) Among the exhibits are statues from the original facade (including an angel in a nosedive) and a disappearing diorama that we believe must be magic.

The **Museum of Costume,** Bennett St. (tel. 477752), houses a dazzling fashion parade of 400 years of catwalks. (*Open daily 10am-5pm. £3.80, seniors £3.50, children £2.70; or by joint ticket with Roman Baths; wheelchair access.*) Phenomenal collection of wedding gowns, as well as a "generously cut" number worn by Queen Victoria. The clothes are closeted in the basement of the **Assembly Rooms** (tel. 477789), which staged fashionable social events in the late 18th century. *(Open daily 10am-5pm. Free.)* Although World War II ravaged the rooms, renovations duplicate the originals in fine detail. They provide the glowing crystal chandelier, you supply the swirling ladies and gentlemen. A few blocks over on the Paragon, the **Building of Bath Museum** (tel. 333895) recounts in precise detail (8 scale models!) how this Georgian masterpiece progressed from the drawing board to the drawing room. *(Open mid-Feb. to Nov. Tu-Su 10:30am-5pm. £3, students and seniors £2, children £1.50.)*

In the city's residential northwest corner, Nash's contemporaries John Wood, father and son, made the Georgian rowhouse a design to be reckoned with. Among notable inhabitants of the rowhouses, Jane Austen lived at 13 Queen Sq. ("Oh, what a dismal sight Bath is!"). From Queen Sq., walk up Gay St. to **The Circus,** which has attracted illustrious residents for two centuries. Blue plaques mark the houses of Thomas Gainsborough, William Pitt, and David Livingstone. Proceed from there up Brock St. to Royal Crescent, stopping at the oasis of book, art, and antique stores at **Margaret's Building** on the way. The interior of **One Royal Crescent** (tel. 428126) has been painstakingly restored by the Bath Preservation Trust to a near-perfect replica of a 1770 townhouse, authentic to the last teacup and butter knife. *(Open Mar.-Oct. Tu-Su 10:30am-5pm; Nov. to mid-Dec. Tu-Su 10:30am-4pm. £3.80, students, seniors, and children £3.)* **Royal Victoria Park,** next to Royal Crescent, contains one of the finest collections of trees in the country, and its **botanical gardens** nurture 5000 species of plants from all over the globe. For bird aficionados, there's also an aviary. *(Park open M-Sa 9am-dusk, Su 10am-dusk. Free.)*

Amble back down the hill to **Beckford's Tower,** Lansdowne Rd. (tel. 338727), for 156 steps and stupendous views *(£2, students, seniors, and children £1).* The tower is under renovation until late 1999, but may be open to visitors on weekends and bank holidays. The **Victoria Art Gallery,** Bridge St. (tel. 477772), will please those with a discerning eye. *(Open Tu-F 10am-5:30pm, Sa 10am-5pm, Su 2-5pm. Free. Wheelchair access.)* The gallery holds a diverse collection of works including Old Masters and contemporary British art, such as Thomas Barker's "The Bride of Death"—Victorian melodrama at its sappiest. The museum sits next to the Pulteney Bridge—a work of art in its own right.

Up Milsom St., away from the tourist-trafficked abbey and baths, rests the **Royal Photographic Society Octagon Galleries** (tel. 462841), where visitors can view well-executed contemporary exhibits, trace the history of photography, and purchase that disturbing black-and-white print for their bedrooms. *(Open daily 9:30am-5:30pm. £2.50, students, seniors, and children £1.75, free for disabled visitors.)* The **Museum of East Asian Art,** 12 Bennett St. (tel. 464640), displays objects from 5000 BC. *(Open Apr.-Oct. M-Sa 10am-6pm, Su noon-5pm. £3.50, students £2.50, seniors £3, children 6-12 £1, children under 6 free, families £8.)* Amazing collections of jade and rhino horn carvings.

Homesick Yankees and those who want to visit the United States vicariously (but haven't yet found a McDonald's) should stop by the **American Museum** (tel. 460503), perched above the city at Claverton Manor. *(Museum open late Mar. to early Nov. Tu-Su 2-5pm. Gardens open Tu-F 1-6pm, Sa-Su noon-6pm. House, grounds, and galleries £5, students and seniors £4.50, children £2.50; grounds, Folk Art, and New Galleries only £2.50, children £1.25.)* Inside is a fascinating series of furnished rooms transplanted from historically significant American homes. Among the most impressive are a 17th-century Puritan Keeping Room, a Shaker Meeting House, and a cozy Revolutionary War-era tavern kitchen with a working beehive oven. Climb Bathwick Hill to reach the manor, or let bus #18 (£1.20) save you the steep 2 mi. trudge.

Throughout the city lie stretches of green cultivated to comfort weary limbs (consult a map or inquire at the tourist office for the *Borders, Beds, and Shrubberies* brochure). **Henrietta Park,** laid out in 1897 to celebrate the Diamond Jubilee, was redesigned as a garden for the blind—only the most olfactory pleasing flowers and shrubs were chosen for its tranquil grounds. Relax in the **Public Gardens** as the waters of the River Avon sweep by *(open daily 10am-8pm; £1, children 50p).*

ENTERTAINMENT

Classical and jazz concerts enliven **The Pump Room** (see **Food and Drink,** p. 240) during morning coffee (daily 9:30am-noon) and afternoon tea (2:30-5pm). In summer, buskers (street musicians) perform in the Abbey Churchyard, and a brass band often graces the Parade Gardens. Beau Nash's old haunt, the magnificent **Theatre Royal,** Sawclose (tel. 448844), at the south end of Barton St., produces opera, ballet, and pre- and post-London theater. *(Tickets £8-22; £1 student tickets available M-Th. Box office open M-Sa 10am-8pm, Su noon-8pm.)*

The **Bizarre Bath Walking Tour** (tel. 335124; no advance booking required) begins at the Huntsman Inn at North Parade Passage nightly at 8pm. Punsters lead locals and tourists alike around, pulling pranks for about 1¼ hours. Tours vary from mildly amusing to hysterically funny and include absolutely no historical or architectural content. *(£3.50, students £3.)*

A night on the town could begin and end at cafe-bar **P.J. Peppers** (tel. 465777), on George St. The Bold and the Beautiful prance about, revealing more flesh in 15 minutes than the baths saw in all their years. *(Open daily 8am-11pm.)* A couple notches down on the pretty-boy meter, **The Pig and Fiddle** pub, on the corner of Saracen and Broad St., packs in a rowdy young crowd for pints around their large picnic table patio area. Bath nights wake up at **The Bell,** 103 Walcot St. (tel. 460426), an artsy pub which challenges its clientele to talk over the live jazz, blues, funk, and reggae. *(Open M-Sa 11am-11pm, Su 11am-3pm and 6:30-11pm.)* **The Hat and Feather** (tel. 425672), farther down Walcot St. at London St., rocks with 2 levels of funk and rave. *(Open daily 11am-11pm.)* For later nightlife, try **Cadillacs** on Walcot St. for the standard top-of-the-charts nightclub experience (located just below the Bell). At 14 George St., **Moles** (tel. 404445) burrows underground and pounds out techno and house music. Dress sharp and act smart. The club is "members only," but you might get in… if you can find it. *(Cover £5. Open M-Sa 9pm-2am.)* A final nightlife staple is **The Hush** (tel. 446288), on the Paragon at Lansdowne Rd. Head to this late-night pub before 10pm. *(Cover after 10pm £1-3 depending on the night. Open M-Sa 9:30pm-2am.)*

The renowned **Bath International Festival of the Arts,** over two weeks of concerts and exhibits, induces merriment all over town from late May to early June. Book well in advance for the **Bath International Music Festival** (box office tel. 463362; http://Bathfestivals.com) and its world-class maestri. *(Open M-Sa 9:30am-5:30pm.)* The **Contemporary Art Fair** (tel. 463362) opens the festival by bringing together the work of over 700 British artists. Musical offerings range from major symphony orchestras and choruses to chamber music, solo recitals, and jazz. For a complete festival brochure and reservations, write to the Bath Festivals Office, 2 Church St., Abbey Green, Bath BA1 1NL. The concurrent **Fringe Festival** (tel. 480097) celebrates music, dance, and liberal politics.

■ Bristol

The Anglo-Saxons called it "Brigstow" (the place of a bridge), and since then Bristol has served as a place of great comings and goings. Bristol's fame, wealth, and one-time status as a "second city" to London grew mostly from its once-bustling slave and sugar cane trade with the West Indies and America. Working business center by day, Bristol becomes a newer, younger city at night. Local pubs, clubs, and late-night eateries cluster near the educational and commercial districts. Although much of Bristol's architectural might was felled by the bombs of World War II, its rebuilt city center, parks, and majestic bridges entice many a traveler to a pleasant sojourn.

GETTING THERE

Trains (tel. (0345) 484950) link Bristol with London **Paddington Station** (£31.50), nearby **Cardiff,** Wales (£8.70), neighboring **Bath** (£4.50), and **Manchester** (£36). Most trains stop at **Bristol Temple Meads Station**; (the Parkway Station is rather far out). **Buses** trundle from the Marlborough St. Bus Station, with **National Express** run-

ENGLAND

ning to **London** (18 per day, £9, return £12-17), **Cardiff** (£4, return £5-8), **Birmingham** (£14), and **Manchester** (£21.25).

ORIENTATION AND PRACTICAL INFORMATION

Bristol is a sprawling mass of neighborhoods stretching for miles in several directions. The majority of shopping and commerce occurs in the **Broadmead** district while the oldest part of the city can be found in the **Corn, Baldwin, Quay, St. Augustine's Parade** and **Broad St.** area. **St. Michael's Hill** takes you to Cotham, while **Park St.** (which becomes **Queens Rd.**) offers nighttime entertainment and takes you into the tiny **Clifton** neighborhood.

Trains: Bristol Temple Meads Station (tel. 929 4255).
Buses: Marlborough St. Bus Station (tel. 955 3231). Information shop open M-F 7:30am-6pm and Sa 10am-5:30pm.
Ferries: Bristol Ferryboat Company (tel. 927 3416).
Taxis: Yellow Cab Company (tel. 923 1515).
Tourist Office: St. Nicholas Church, St. Nicholas St. (tel. 926 0767). Books theatre tickets as well as accommodations. Sells National Express and local bus passes, and a wide selection of city maps and books. Open July-Sept. daily 9:30am-5:30pm; Oct.-June M-Sa 9:30am-5:30pm, Su 11am-4pm.
Financial Services: Barclays, Lloyds, and **Midland Banks** can be found in the Broadmead area as well as closer to the city center. **Midland Bank** open M, W-F 9am-5pm, Th 9am-7pm, and Sa 9:30am-3:30pm.
American Express: 31 Union St. (tel. 927 7788). Open M, W-F 9am-5:30pm, Tu 9:30am-5:30pm, Sa 9am-5pm.
Emergency: Dial 999; no coins required.
Police: Nelson St. (tel. 927 7777).
Hospital: Bristol Royal Infirmary, Upper Maudlin St. (tel. 923 0000).
Post Office: The Galleries, Wine St. (tel. 925 2322). **Postal Code:** BS1 3XX.
Internet Access: Net Gates Café, 51 Broad St. (tel. 907 4000), offers yummy food as well as deliciously quick connections. £2.50 per 30min., students with ID £1.50. Open M-Sa 9:30am-6:30pm.
Telephone Code: 0117.

ACCOMMODATIONS

Budget accommodations are nearly impossible to find in Bristol. The **University of Bristol** (tel. 926 5698) offers accommodations in the heart of the city. If the YHA is fully booked, budget travelers should hop over to nearby Bath where cheaper accommodations are more plentiful. Pricier accommodations can be found in **Clifton** and nearby **Cliftonwode,** and **Cotham.** While a few B&B's are in the St. Paul's neighborhood, travelers should note that the area is difficult to navigate and perhaps unsafe.

YHA Youth Hostel, Hayman House, 14 Narrow Quay (tel. 922 1659; fax 927 3789). 30-bed hotel inhabiting a beautifully renovated warehouse in the city center. Bureau de change, free luggage storage (bring a padlock), laundry and games facilities, and full meals. £11.80, under 18 £8. Reception open 7am-midnight (arrange late-night entry beforehand). Book ahead, especially in summer. Open year-round.
St. Michael's Guest House, 145 St. Michael's Hill (tel. 907 7820), above St. Michael's Café. Book in advance and expect a walk. Cable TV in every room is your reward. Singles £25; doubles £35; triples £45.
Wellington Park Hotel, 13-15 Wellington Park Rd. (tel. 974 3293). A hefty walk from the city center, but in a beautiful, historic (and expensive) neighborhood. Singles £25-35; doubles £40-50. Call ahead.

FOOD

◉**Boston Tea Party,** 75 Park St. (tel. 929 8601), offers a deliciously diverse international selection of teas and coffee, as well as gourmet sandwiches (around £3). Vegetarian and vegan cakes. Open M 7am-6pm, Tu-Sa 7am-10pm, Su 9am-7pm.

Three Sugar Loaves, 2 Christmas Steps (tel. 929 2431), the former hangout of actors like Lilly Langtry, offers delicious food in a friendly and comfortable pub. Entrees range £2-4 throughout all three buildings that comprise the restaurant (the oldest part dates back to 1648). Karaoke (!) is endured by locals the first Thursday of each month. Meals served M-F 11:30am-2pm; pub open M-F 11:30am-2pm and 5-11pm, Sa noon-3pm and 6-11pm.

Le Château, 32 Park St. (tel. 926 8654), woos lunch guests as well as late-night revelers with its comfy interior, stained glass, and reasonable prices. Entrees £5-7 and daily specials £4-6. Open M-W 11am-11pm, Th 11am-1am, F-Sa noon-1am.

St. Michael's Café, 145 St. Michael's Hill (tel. 907 7820), boasts a wide-selection of vegetarian foods as well as yummy milkshakes. Most dishes under £4 with Elvis and the Beatles. Open M-F 7:30am-7pm, Sa 8am-4pm, and Su 9am-3pm.

SIGHTS AND ENTERTAINMENT

Bristol Cathedral (tel. 926 4879), positioned on the expansive College Green, was begun in 1298, and in 1542 was named the Cathedral Church of the Holy and Undivided Trinity. Remnants of both Saxon and Norman architecture linger in the South Transept and chapter house. Elizabeth I termed the medieval church of **St. Mary Redcliffe,** 10 Redcliffe Parade W. (tel. 929 1487), the "fairest, goodliest, and most famous Parish Church in England." It sits above the once-bustling "floating harbour" and burial site of Admiral William Penn (father of the founder of Pennsylvania). *(Open in summer M-Sa 8am-8pm, Su 7:30am-8pm; in winter M-Sa 8am-5;30pm, Su 7:30am-8pm.)*

The architecture of **Isambard Kingdom Brunel,** including the famous **Clifton Suspension Bridge** over the Avon Gorge, can be found throughout the city. The bridge can be reached after a lovely walk through the heart of Clifton neighborhood. A display at nearby **Bridge House,** Sion Pl. (tel. 974 4664), documents its history. *(£1, seniors 80p, under 16 50p.)* Be sure to visit **S.S. Great Britain,** Great Western Ferry Dock (tel. 929 1843), the first "ocean-going propeller ship" ever built, on the way back to the city center. *(Open daily Apr.-Oct. 10am-5:30pm, last entrance 5pm; Nov.-Mar. 10am-4:30pm, last entrance 4pm. £4.50, seniors £3.50; children £3.)*

If city walking has worn you out, try the well-stocked **Bristol City Museum and Art Gallery,** Queen's Rd. (tel. 922 3571), which holds rolling exhibitions, sculpture, and paintings. *(Free admission on Su.)* Also worth a visit is **Harvey's Wine Cellars,** 12 Denmark St. (tel. 927 5036), where the famous Harvey's Bristol Cream sherry was born. *(Open M-Sa 10am-5pm. £4, students and seniors £3.)* Last but not least, be sure not to miss **John Wesley's Chapel,** the oldest Methodist building in the world.

Home to hundreds of university students, Bristol offers its own fair share of nightlife. **The Sedan Chair,** 4-11 Broad Quay (tel. 926 4676), is usually filled with university students and twentysomethings. *(Pint specials. Occasional cover. Open M and Th-Sa noon-2am.)* **Po-Na-Na,** 67 Queens Rd. (tel. 904 4445), offers imitation North African decor and well-mixed music. Monday is Casino Night. *(Cover £3-5. Open M-Sa 9pm-2am.)* **Lakota,** 6 Upper York St. (tel. 942 6208), is the hippest place in the area for dancing and people-watching, with a cover charge to match. Weekends only.

▓ Wells

The cathedral at Wells (pop. 10,000) guards its city like a staid but approving father. Named for the five natural springs at its center, Wells truly is a cathedral's child, with its main streets leaning affectionately toward their parent's stony shoulders. The cathedral and the Bishop's Palace (haunt of such weighty figures as Cardinal Wolsey) retain an opulence not found elsewhere. The Cathedral Music School brings world-renowned musicians to teach and play. Lined with petite Tudor buildings and golden sandstone shops, the streets of Wells fade elegantly into the Somerset meadows surrounding them.

GETTING THERE

Rail routes leave Wells well enough alone, but **Badgerline** bus #173 runs regularly to **Bath** (tel. (01225) 464446; 1¼hr., M-Sa 1 per hr., Su every 3hr., £2.85, return £4.20), and buses #376 and 676 head to **Bristol** (tel. (0117) 955 3231; 1hr., 1 per hr., Su every 3hr., £2.70). Buses #163 and 376 make frequent, short hops to **Glastonbury** (purchase tickets on board, return £2.55). If you'll be skipping from place to place, buy a **Day Rambler** (£5.10, seniors £3.60). **Bakers Dolphin** coach travel service (tel. 679000) offers inexpensive—and fast—buses to **London** (2hr., 1 per day, £14).

ORIENTATION AND PRACTICAL INFORMATION

Buses stop at the **Princes Rd. Depot.** To reach the tourist office, turn left onto **Priory Rd.** from Princes. Proceed along Priory, which becomes **Broad St.** and eventually merges with **High St. Market Pl.** rests at the top of High St.

> **Buses:** (tel. 673084). Badgerline buses from Avon and Somerset stop at the Princes Rd. depot. Office open M-Tu and Th-F 9am-5pm, W and Sa 9am-1pm.
>
> **Cycle Hire: Bike City,** 31 Broad St. (tel. 671711). £4.50 per half day, £8 per day, £38 per week; deposit £50-75. Open M-Sa 9am-5:30pm.
>
> **Tourist Office:** Town Hall (tel. 672552; fax 670869), in Market Pl., to the right as you face the cathedral grounds. Books rooms; 10% deposit payable to proprietor. Free area bus timetables. Open daily Apr.-Oct. 9:30am-5:30pm; Nov.-Mar. 10am-4pm.
>
> **Tours:** Call the fashionably attired town crier, Freddy Gibbons (tel. 676139), or his cohort Mrs. Spincer (tel. (01934) 832350).
>
> **Financial Services: Thomas Cook,** 8 High St. (tel. 677747) and entrance to the Cathedral, near Market Pl. Open M-Th and Sa 9am-5:30pm, F 10am-5:30pm.
>
> **Launderette: Wells Laundrette,** 39 St. Cuthbert St. Bring change; soap available. Open daily 8am-8pm; last wash 7pm.
>
> **Emergency:** Dial 999; no coins required.
>
> **Police:** Glastonbury Rd. (tel. (01823) 363966).
>
> **Hospital: Wells District Hospital,** Bath Rd. (tel. 673154).
>
> **Post Office:** Market Pl. (tel. 677825). Open M and W-F 9am-5:30pm, Tu 9:30am-5:30pm, Sa 9am-12:30pm. **Postal Code:** BA5 2RA.
>
> **Telephone Code:** 01749.

ACCOMMODATIONS

B&Bs are lovely but expensive, and most offer only doubles and prefer longer stays. When in doubt about staying overnight, daytrip to Wells from Bath. One of the closest **YHA Youth Hostels** and **campgrounds** are 10 mi. away in Cheddar (like the cheese; in fact, it is the cheese; see **Near Wells: Wookey Hole and Cheddar,** p. 247).

> **Richmond House,** 2 Chamberlain St. (tel. 676438). Brass mirrors, lace curtains, an antique fireplace—and that's just the bathroom. Fresh flowers in large rooms a breath away from the cathedral and town. Vegetarian breakfast available. Expect world-class musicians from the Cathedral School at breakfast. You may very well want to live here forever. First night £20, subsequent nights £18. Non-smoking.
>
> **Number Nine,** Chamberlain St. (tel. 672270). Tasteful and immaculate Georgian house with a rose garden growing from an ancient convent wall. Enormous airy rooms and baths. Ask the proprietress to show you her artwork. Doubles £36; July-Aug. singles £21-23.
>
> **The Old Poor House,** 7a St. Andrew St. (tel. 675052). One need not be a pauper to stay here. Mrs. Wood is perfectly charming and she'll give you a clean room right up the street from the cathedral. £18-20.

FOOD

Assemble a picnic at the **market** behind the bus stops (open W and Sa 8:30am-4pm), or purchase tasty breads, cheeses, and other provisions at **Laurelbank Dairy Co.,** 14 Queens St. (tel. 679803; open M-Sa 9am-5:30pm). Greengrocers straddle busy Broad and High St., and a grand **Tesco** feeds the town at Princes Rd., across from the bus depot (open M-Th 8:30am-8pm, F 8:30am-9pm, Sa 8am-8pm, Su 10am-4pm).

For great home-cooked pizzas and quiches travel to **The Good Earth,** 4 Priory Rd. (tel. 678600). There's an adjoining shop as well (soups £1-1.65, salads £1.55-2.75; open M-Sa 9:30am-5:30pm). **Cloisters Restaurant** (tel. 676543), in the cathedral cloisters, serves salads (£2.50), soups (£1.80), and desserts (about £1) in the lacework shadows of Gothic arches (open M-Sa 10am-5pm). **Da Luciano Expresso Bar,** 14 Broad St., serves some of the best lasagna in England (£4.65) as well as cappuccino (95p). Fish take their final swim—in batter—at **Raso's Fish and Chips,** 17 Broad St. (tel. 672340), which serves you know-what-for £2.50. (Open M-Th noon-2:30pm and 5-10:30pm, F noon-2:30pm and 5pm-midnight, Sa noon-midnight.) The **Crown Hotel,** near Market Pl., serves pub food with an original twist until 9pm. Try the warm chicken salad for £4.75.

Drink from **The Fountain,** 1 St. Thomas St. (tel. 672317), behind the cathedral, located in a building that once housed the cathedral's artisans; today it's a pub that shares a kitchen with the nationally renowned restaurant upstairs. A local crowd frequents the **King's Head,** High St. (tel. 672141), for liquid refreshment.

SIGHTS

The 13th-century **Cathedral Church of St. Andrew** (tel. 674483), in the center of town, anchors a fantastically preserved cathedral complex, with a bishop's palace, vicar's close, and chapter house. Atop the fanciful 14th-century astronomical clock in the north transept, a pair of jousting, mechanical knights spur on their chargers and strike at each other every 15 minutes—the same unfortunate rider is unseated every time. Walter Raleigh, Dean of Wells and nephew to the Sir, was murdered in the deanery where he had been imprisoned for his Royalist ways. M.C. Escher would be inspired by the swerving steps to the Chapter House, though the house itself is a Gothic dream of symmetry. *(Open in summer daily 7:15am-8:30pm if there's no concert; until 6pm in winter. Suggested donation £3, students and seniors £2, children £1. Tours 10:15, 11:15am, 12:15, 2:15, and 3:15pm. Evensong M-Sa 5:15pm, Su 3pm. Photo permits £1.)* The renowned **Wells Cathedral School Choir** performs September to April; visiting choirs assume the honor through summer break. Pick up the leaflet *Music in Wells Cathedral* at the cathedral or tourist office for concert details and ticket information.

The 13th-century **Bishop's Palace** (tel. 678691), to the right of the cathedral (entrance from Market Pl.), is a humble parish priest's abode in the tradition of the country cottage at Versailles. Prince of the Church Ralph of Shrewsbury (1329-63), alarmed by village riots in the 14th century, built the moat and walls to protect himself. The mute swans in the moat have been trained to pull a bell-rope when they want to be fed. The palace **gardens** offer Arcadian ecstasy, with lush springs that give the city its name—the ideal setting for a strawberry and champagne picnic. *(Open Easter-Oct. Tu-F 10am-6pm, Su 2-6pm. Palace and gardens £3, students £1.50, seniors £2, children free.)* **Vicar's Close,** behind the cathedral, is reputedly the oldest street of houses in Europe; the houses date from 1363, their chimneys from 1470.

North of the cathedral green and left of the cathedral's entrance, the refurbished **Wells Museum,** 8 Cathedral Green (tel. 673477), enshrines an above-average collection, including views of cathedral statuary. The statues look ill-proportioned but are designed to appear normal when viewed from below. Also on display are an alabaster "crystal ball" and the bones of two goats and an elderly woman, found in nearby Wookey Hole Caves, supposedly those of the legendary "Witch of Wookey Hole." *(Open daily July-Aug. 10am-8pm; Easter-June and Sept.-Oct. 10am-5:30pm; Oct.-Easter W-Su only 11am-4pm. £2, students and seniors £1.50, children and disabled £1, families £5.)*

■ Near Wells: Wookey Hole and Cheddar

You need only venture a short distance from the simplicity and serenity of Wells to encounter a fantastic vale of cheese, in every sense of the word. If you plan to see both Wookey Hole and Cheddar, buy a **Day Rambler** in Wells (see p. 245).

Disappointing some and delighting few, **Wookey Hole,** only 2 mi. northwest of Wells and **Wookey Hole Caves and Papermill** (tel. 672243) hold some weird prehistoric animal mutations. Admission includes the subterranean caves, a tour of the working paper mill, and a spectacular collection of wooden carousel animals. The gold lion is worth over £75,000. *(Open daily May-Sept. 9:30am-5:30pm; Oct.-Apr. 10:30am-4:30pm. £6.70, £4.50 from Wells tourist office.)* **Camp** at **Homestead Park** (tel. 673022), beside a babbling brook (£9 per tent, car, and 2 people; £2 per additional person). Lunch at the **Wookey Hole Inn** (open daily 10:30am-2pm and 7-10:30pm).

The **Cheddar Gorge,** formed by the River Yeo (YO!) in the hills just northeast of town of **Cheddar,** is a popular daytrip and may be worth a visit, depending on your sensibilities and toleration for an overcrowded melange of touristy tea shops and cheezwizardry. Take bus #126 from Wells (20min., M-Sa 1 per hr., £1.60) and follow the signs to **Jacob's Ladder,** a 322-step stairwell to the top. The unsullied view of the hills to the north and the broad expansive plain to the south rewards the intrepid climber. *(£2, seniors and children £1.50.)*

At the foot of the cliffs huddle the **Cheddar Showcaves** (tel. (01934) 742343), the finest showcaves in England. Note the different mineral colors of the stalagmites and stalactites: rust-red is iron, green manganese, gray lead. Feast your eyes on the Cheddar Man, a 9000-year-old skeleton typical of the Stone-Agers who settled in the Gorge. *(Caves open daily Easter-Sept. 10am-5pm; Oct.-Easter 10:30am-4:30pm. All caves, Jacob's Ladder, museum, and open-top bus ride around the Gorge £6.90, students and children £4; discount tickets available from Wells tourist office.)*

In 1170 Henry II declared Cheddar cheese the best in England. Today, wine and cheese enthusiasts nibble away at **Chewton Cheese Dairy** (tel. (01761) 241666), just north of Wells on the A39. *(Open Apr.-Dec. M-Sa 9am-5pm, Su 10am-4pm; Jan.-Mar. M-Sa 8:30am-4pm. Best time to view cheese-making 11:30am-2pm. Not for the lactose intolerant.)* Take the bus toward Bristol and get off at Cheddar Rd., just outside Wells.

The town's **tourist office** is located at the base of Cheddar Gorge (tel. (01934) 744071; open Feb.-Nov. daily 10am-5pm; off-season, leave a message). The town's **YHA Youth Hostel,** Hillfield (tel. (01934) 742494), is located in a stone Victorian house off the Hayes, 3 blocks from the Cheddar bus stop (walk up Tweentown Rd.), and half a mile from Cheddar Gorge. (£8.80, under 18 £6. Breakfast £3, packed lunch £2.55, dinner £4. No lockout for those spending more than one night. Curfew 11pm. Open July-Aug. daily; Apr.-June and Sept.-Oct. M-Sa; Feb.-Mar. and Nov.-Dec. Sa-Su.) The hostel is served by frequent buses from Wells (#126, 826, 827, M-Sa 1 per hr. until 5:40pm, £1.20). Camping is available at **Bucklegrove Caravan and Camping Park** (tel. 870261), in Rodney Stoke, near Cheddar (£5-9.50 for tent and 2 persons; open Mar.-Oct. daily).

▓ Glastonbury

The reputed birthplace of Christianity in England and the seat of Arthurian myth, Glastonbury has evolved into an intersection of Christianity, mysticism, and granola. According to one legend, Jesus, Joseph of Arimathea, and Saints Augustine and Patrick all came here. Other myths hold that the area is the resting place of the Holy Grail, that Glastonbury Tor is the Isle of Avalon—with the bones of Arthur and Guinevere safe beneath Glastonbury Abbey—and that the Tor contains a passage to the underworld. Today the site of the infamous Glastonbury Festival, Glastonbury's streets bustle in the morning with old women buying curative herbs and Osiris candles, not milk and vegetables. Grow your hair, suspend your disbelief, and join hands with Glastonbury's subculture of hippies, spiritualists, and mystics.

GETTING THERE **Baker's Dolphin** swims speedily from London (3¼hr., 1 per day, return £5). Frequent **Badgerline** buses run from **Bristol** (#376, 1½hr., 1 per hr., Su every 3 hr., £2.55) and from **Wells** (#163, 167, 168, 378, or 379, return £2.70). From **Bath,** change at Wells (return £3.90). For information on other Badgerline services, call Bristol (tel. (0117) 955 3231), Bath (tel. (01225) 464446), or Wells (tel. (01749)

673084). **Southern National** (tel. (01823) 272033) buses take travelers to points south, such as **Lyme Regis** and **Weymouth. Explorer Passes** enable you to travel a full day to various locales (£5, seniors £3.80, children £2.75).

ORIENTATION AND PRACTICAL INFORMATION Glastonbury finds its center 6 mi. southwest of Wells on the A39 and 22 mi. northeast of Taunton on the A361. The compact town is bounded by **Manor House Rd.** in the north, **Bere Ln.** in the south, **Magdalene St.** in the west, and **Wells Rd.** in the east. Most **buses** stop in front of the town hall. To get to the **tourist office,** The Tribunal, 9 High St. (tel. 832954 or 832949), from the bus stop, turn right onto High St.; the office is on the left through the alleyway. They'll book rooms for a 10% deposit; after hours find the B&B list behind the building in St. John's carpark (open Easter-Sept. Su-Th 10am-5pm, F-Sa 10am-4:30pm; Oct.-Easter daily 10am-4pm). Numerous **ATMs** and **banks,** including Barclays, sit on High St. (most open M-F 9:30am-4:30pm). The **police** (tel. (01823) 337911) have chosen a pad in the less mellow nearby town of **Street** at 1 West End. The **post office** (tel. 831536) accepts *Poste Restante* at 35-37 High St. (open M-F 9:30am-5:30pm, Sa 9am-1pm). The **postal code** is BA6 9HG. **Internet access** is available at Café Galatea (see below). The **telephone code** is 01458.

ACCOMMODATIONS While singles are rare beasts in Glastonbury, the tourist office can give you a list of their favorite haunts. The **YHA Youth Hostel,** The Chalet, Ivythorn Hill St. (tel. 442961), sits off the B3151 in Street. Take Badgerline bus #376 to Loythorn Rd., and walk 1 mi. The hostel is a Swiss-style chalet with views of Glastonbury Tor, Sedgemoor, and Mendip Hills. (£7.70, under 18 £5.15. Lockout 10am-5pm. Curfew 11pm. Open July-Aug. daily; Apr.-June W-M; Sept.-Oct. Th-M.) The newly-opened **Glastonbury Backpackers** (tel. 833353) is in the **Crown Hotel,** Market Pl. A rainbow of brightly colored rooms, the attached restaurant and friendly staff only improve the hostel's great location. Check out the "Bridal Suite" with jungle-print sheets and ceiling mirror (£9; doubles £26-30). For glorious private bathrooms, lovely gardens, and lovelier proprietors, call upon the Hankins at **Blake House,** 3 Bove Town (tel. 831680). Chat about your travels and immortalize your visit with a pin on their world map (£17; continental breakfast only). Mrs. Talbot's modern house on a central residential street, **Tamarac,** 8 Wells Rd. (tel. 834327), has biscuits in every room and plenty of novels to peruse (singles from £17.50; doubles from £32). You'll find flowery rooms with TV at **The Bolt Hole,** 32 Chilkwell St. (tel. 832800), opposite the Chalice Well, a 12-minute walk from the town center. Sit at breakfast with Mrs. Eastoe and gaze out over the rolling, misty hills (one twin and two doubles, £32).

FOOD Set up for a picnic on the Tor at **Truckle of Cheese,** 33 High St. (open M-Sa 8:30am-5:30pm), or at **Heritage Fine Foods** across the street (open daily 7am-9pm). **Rainbow's End,** 17a High St. (tel. 833896), serves vegetarian and wholefood specials on earthenware. Changing menu and hours, depending on vegetables in season, and karma (open M and W-F 10am-4pm, Tu 9:30am-4pm, Sa 10am-4:30pm, Su 11:15am-4pm). The age of Aquarius meets the age of technology at **Café Galatea,** 8 High St. (tel. 834284), a wholefood vegetarian-vegan cafe and cyberspace station. *Mmm,* pita with a side of slow 'net access. (£3 per 30min., £5 per hr.; open M-Tu 10:30am-6pm, W-Su 10:30am-9pm.) **Abbey Tea Room,** 16 Magdalene St. (tel. 832852), serves a prim and proper lunch for under £4, and tasty cream teas with scones and jam for £2.75 (open daily 10am-5:30pm).

SIGHTS Behind the archway on Magdalene St. lurk the ruins of **Glastonbury Abbey** (tel. 832267), the oldest Christian foundation and once the most important abbey in England. The building was constructed "so as to entice even the dullest minds to prayer." Let your travel-worn mind marvel at the model of the Abbey as it looked in 1539 when Henry VIII commenced his antics around Glastonbury. *(Open daily June-Aug. 9am-6pm; Sept.-May 9:30am-6pm. £2.50, students £2, children £1.)* Modern religion finds an outlet in the open-air masses which are periodically held among the ruins—inquire at the tourist office.

ENGLAND

Abbey Road

Glastonbury has served as a backdrop to almost two thousand years of Christian history and legend. Joseph of Arimathea supposedly built the original wattle-and-daub church on this site in AD 63; larger churches were successively raised (and razed), until the current abbey was erected in 1184. Its sixth and final abbot, Richard Whiting, refused to obey Henry VIII's order that all Catholic churches dissolve. Displaying his characteristic religious tolerance, Henry had Whiting hanged, drawn, and quartered on Glastonbury Tor.

Two national patron saints, Patrick of Ireland and George of England, have been claimed by the abbey—Patrick is said to be buried here and George to have slain his dragon just around the corner. St. Dunstan hails from Glastonbury, where he served the diocese. King Arthur most captivates the legend-makers—in 1191, his remains were discovered just in time for an abbey rebuilding campaign; the bones were reinterred in 1276.

Present-day pagan pilgrimage site **Glastonbury Tor** towers over Somerset's flatlands. Visible miles away, the Tor was known in its earlier incarnation as St. Michael's Chapel, and is supposedly the site of the mystical Isle of Avalon, where the Messiah is slated to reappear. Once surrounded by water, the Tor at times resumes its island appearance, rising supernaturally from the morning fog. From the top of the hill, you can survey the Wiltshire Downs and the Mendips. To reach the Tor, turn right at the top of High St. and continue up to Chilkwell St., turning left onto Wellhouse Ln.; take the first right up the hill. Magicians get their kicks by burning incense in the remaining tower. In summer, the Glastonbury **Tor Bus** takes weary pilgrims around (50p).

On the way down from the Tor, visit the **Chalice Well,** at the corner of Wellhouse Ln., the supposed resting place of the Holy Grail. Legend once held that the well ran with Christ's blood; in these post-Nietzschean days, rust deposits at the source turn the water red. Water gurgles from the well down through a tiered garden of hollyhocks, climbing vines, and dark, spreading yew trees. Expect guitars, topless women, and people sniffing flowers with disturbing vigor. (*Open daily Easter-Oct. 10am-6pm; Nov.-Feb. 1-4pm. £1.50, children and seniors 75p.*)

Head down Bere Ln. to Hill Head to reach **Wearyall Hill,** where legend has it that Joseph of Arimathea's staff bloomed and became the **Glastonbury Thorn.** The Thorn has grown on Wearyall Hill since Saxon times, and, according to legend, should burst into bloom in the presence of royalty. Horticulturists here and abroad (where offshoots of the thorn are planted) have wasted considerable time making the trees bloom each time the Queen comes to visit.

SOUTHERN MIDLANDS

■ Cheltenham

A spa town second only to Bath, Cheltenham (pop. 86,500) sits elegantly in its room with a view of the Cotswolds. Manicured gardens of bursting red adorn expensive shops while wide tree-lined lanes exude a carefree sophistication. Though Cheltenham's panache does seem superficial at times (some of the Hellenistic statues look like permanent lawn ornaments), budget travelers should not be dismayed by its Laura Ashley-esque quality: walking its streets is like retiring to a velveted parlor between the heavily touristed centers of Bath and Stratford and the gloomy industrial megaliths of Bristol and Birmingham.

GETTING THERE

Cheltenham lies 43 mi. south of Birmingham. Daytrips from Oxford and other locales are possible, and Cheltenham makes an excellent stopover for cyclists and walkers traveling the Cotswolds. **Trains** (tel. (0345) 484950) run regularly to **London** (2½hr.,

1 per hr., £26), **Bath** (1½hr., 1 per hr., £11.40), and **Exeter** (2hr., every 2hr., £25.70). Frequent **buses** pull into the colorful **Royal Well,** behind the tourist office. **National Express** (tel. (0990) 808080) runs to **London** (3hr., 1 per hr., £9.50), **Bristol** (1¼hr., every 2hr., £6), **Exeter** (3½hr., every 2hr., £17), and **Stratford-upon-Avon** (1hr., 2 per day, £6.75). **Swanbrook Coaches** (tel. (01452) 712386) also run to **Oxford** (return £6.50). Pick up the tourist office's free edition of *Getting There* for more detailed information on travel within the area.

ORIENTATION

The majority of attractions in Cheltenham line a compact square formed by **Albion St.** to the north, **Bath Rd.** to the east, **Oriel Rd.** to the south, and **Royal Well Rd.** to the west. The **Promenade** is the main street in town and home to the tourist office. To reach the tourist office from the train station, walk down Queen's Rd. and bear left onto Lansdown Rd. Head left again at the Rotunda onto Montpellier Walk, which leads to The Promenade. Or save yourself the 15-minute walk and jump on one of the frequent F or G buses (70p); a new free city center bus service is available from the Royal Well station walk around the block.

PRACTICAL INFORMATION

Trains: Cheltenham Spa Station (tel. (0345) 484950), on Queen's Rd. at Gloucester Rd. Ticket office open M-F 5:45am-8:15pm, Sa 5:45am-7:15pm, Su 8:15am-8:15pm; if closed buy tickets on board.

Buses: Royal Well, Royal Crescent. **National Express** office (tel. (0990) 808080) open M-Sa 9am-5:30pm. **Luggage lockers** £1-2. Tickets can also be purchased at the tourist office or on board.

Taxis: Central Taxi (tel. 228877). **Associated Taxis** (tel. 523523).

Bike Rental: Crabtrees, 50 Winchcombe St. (tel. 515291). Mountain bikes £8 per day, £35 per week; deposit £50. Open M-Sa 9am-5:30pm, Su 10am-1pm.

Tourist Office: Municipal Offices, 77 The Promenade (tel. 522878), 1 block east of the bus station. Vacancies posted after hours. Sells National Express tickets. Open July-Aug. M-Sa 9:30am-6pm, Su 9:30am-1:30pm, Sept.-June M-Sa 9:30am-5:15pm.

Tours: Guided 1¼hr. walking tours depart July to mid-Sept. M, W, and F from the tourist office at 2:15pm; £2. Call the office for more information.

Financial Services: Lloyds, 130 High St. (tel. 518169). Open M-Tu and Th-F 9am-5pm, W 9:30am-5pm, Sa 9:30am-12:30pm.

Launderette: Soap-n-Suds, 312 High St. Soap and change available. Open daily 7am-7:30pm; last wash 7pm.

Market: On Henrietta St. Thursday mornings.

Emergency: Dial 999; no coins required.

Police: Holland House, Lansdown Rd. (tel. 521321). From the town center follow The Promenade until it becomes Montpellier Walk; Lansdown is on the right.

Hotlines: Samaritans (crisis), 3 Clarence Rd. (tel. 515777). Open 24hr. **Gay and Lesbian Hotline,** Gloucestershire Friend (tel. (01452) 306800).

Hospital: Cheltenham General, Sandford Rd. (tel. 222222). Follow the Bath Rd. southwest from town and turn left onto Sandford; near the college.

Internet Access: Netscafé (tel. 232121), on Bennington St., off High St. Warm beverages and modems. £2.50 per 30min. Open daily 10am-10pm.

Post Office: 227 High St. (tel. 263820). Open M-Sa 9am-5:30pm. **Postal Code:** GL50 1AA.

Telephone Code: 01242.

ACCOMMODATIONS

Standards in Cheltenham's B&Bs tend to be high, but so do their prices. The tourist office publishes a thick accommodations booklet to help plan your stay. A handful of B&Bs can be found in the Montpellier area of town and along Bath Rd.

YMCA (tel. 52402), Vittoria Walk. At Town Hall, turn left off Promenade and walk 3 blocks—it's on the right (look for the "Y"). Men and women accepted. Large and well-located with clean, standard rooms. Booming loudspeaker informs guests of phone calls. Many long-term tenants. Singles £14. Continental breakfast included. Cafeteria sandwiches 60p-£1.10. Office open 24hr. Porter lets in guests after 11pm.

Bentons Guest House, 71 Bath Rd. (tel. 517417). Floral patterns greet you everywhere, with an exuberant garden on the outside and a classical cherrywood interior. Well-kept rooms and fireplaces. No extra charge for private facilities. Platter-sized plates can't hold the Benton Breakfast. £22.

Cross Ways, 57 Bath Rd. (tel. 527683). Large, clean rooms kept by an extremely friendly proprietor who invites guests to use her piano. Be sure to mark your home-town with a pin on the map of the world. TV, coffee- and tea-making facilities in each room. £18-30, depending on facilities.

Hamilton Guest House, 65 Bath Rd. (tel. 527772). High ceilings and comfortable rooms; Mrs. Davies serves an English breakfast, and speaks French, German, and Chinese. Smoking allowed. £20, with bath £22.

Lonsdale House, Montpellier Dr. (tel. 232379). Large home with a bounty of singles, all with TV. The Mallinsons offer vegetarian options as well as shelves full of English classics. £19, with bath £22.

Camping: Longwillows, Station Rd., Woodmancote (tel. 674113), 3½mi. north of Cheltenham. Take the A435 (Evesham Rd.) north toward Evesham and turn off at Bishops Cleeve onto Station Rd.; it's on the left after the railway bridge. 80 sites. £6 per tent for up to 2 adults and 2 children in July and Aug. 1-person tents half-price. Bar and restaurant on grounds. Laundry; hot water; shower facilities free. Open mid-Mar. to Oct.

FOOD

Food in Cheltenham runs the gamut from fast food to haute cuisine. The tourist office serves *What's Cooking in Cheltenham* (free). Fruit stands, butchers, and bakeries dot High St., while down the road, **Tesco** has it all under one roof (open M-Tu and Sa 8am-6:30pm, W-F 8am-8pm). **The Orange Tree,** 317 High St. (tel. 234232), pampers vegetarians with entrees under £5. (Open M 9am-5pm, Tu-Th 9am-9pm, F-Sa 9am-10pm. Reservations recommended on weekends.) For atmosphere as dainty as the delicious food, try **Choirs Restaurant** (tel. 235578), off Well Walk. Lovely French owner serves lunch (£4); prices rise after 7pm. For a sophisticated sandwich (from £2.10), or exquisite baked goods (apricot macaroon bar 75p), head to **Tiffen's,** 4 Montpellier Walk (tel. 22492). To save a few pence, get it to go and head over to the gardens across the street (open M-Sa 8:30am-4:30pm). Combining the atmosphere of an English pub with a trendy Californian cafe, **Pepper's Café Bar** on Regent St. near the Playhouse, offers creative sandwiches from £2.85, and salads for about £5. **Caffè Uno,** 15-17 Clarence St. (tel. 221186), is one link in a Tuscan style chain that dishes up pasta and pizza for £4-7 (open M-Th 10am-11pm, F-Sa 10am-noon, Su 11am-10:30pm). **Moran's Eating House,** 127-9 Bath Rd. (tel. 581411), combines excellent food with a young, lively atmosphere (open M-Sa 10:30am-2pm and 6:30-10:30pm). Crowded **Montpellier Wine Bar** (tel. 527774), at the end of Montpellier St., also offers tasty meals, though the atmosphere has a price tag attached (open M-F noon-2:30pm and 6-10pm, Sa and Su noon-9:30pm).

SIGHTS

Cheltenham proudly possesses the only naturally **alkaline water** in Great Britain. Crazy George III took the waters in 1788; in the 19th century the Duke of Wellington claimed that the spring cured his "disordered liver." You need not have such an ill-ness to enjoy the diuretic and laxative effects of the waters at the **Town Hall.** *(Open M-F 9am-1pm and 2:15-5pm. Free.)* The **Pittville Pump Room** (tel. 523852), in Pittville Park, offer the same magic water. Sip, don't gulp—trust us. **Pittville Park** (reservations tel. 261017) hosts summertime Sunday concerts and brunches in a tent full of goodies. The Pump Room and Town Hall serve as venues for a wide range of entertainment throughout the year, from symphonies and big band concerts to cabarets.

The **Cheltenham Art Gallery and Museum,** Clarence St. (tel. 237431), two blocks from the bus station, houses an impressive collection of pottery, mementos of the Arts and Crafts movement, and curious curios culled from the region since the Bronze Age. It also features a chonological series of typical table settings, including those of Roman nobility, a 1790 aristocratic lady, and an 1880 lawyer. Special exhibits are changed every month. *(Open M-Sa 10am-5:20pm. Free. Wheelchair accessible.)* The **Gustav Holst Birthplace Museum,** 4 Clarence Rd. (not Clarence *Street;* tel. 524846), presents a picture of middle-class family life in the Regency and Victorian periods while portraying the composer's early life. Follow the signs in the direction of the bus station, then walk one block to Clarence Rd. *(Open Tu-Sa 10am-4:20pm. £1.50, students, seniors, and children 50p.)*

A walk down Clarence St. and a left at St. James Sq. will bring you to the house in which **Tennyson** wrote *In Memoriam.* No museum here—the house is in disrepair, with windows thickly crusted, one and all. If you're traveling with a Gold Card, a one-block stroll over from the Promenade immerses you in the city's shopping district. Walk down Regent's Arcade between Regent St. and Rodney Rd. Along **Montpellier Walk,** caryatids (pillars in the shape of female figures) guard everything from banks to tobacconists, and elegant shops and cafes line the neighborhood streets. Devoid of arms, the figures are a nightmare of beauty without agency. Sunbathe with bouffants and bikers at the **Imperial Gardens,** just past the Promenade away from the center of town. Exquisite blooms show why Cheltenham has thrice received the prestigious Britain in Bloom award. *(Summer Sunday concerts 2:30-4:30pm; free. Occasional open-air art exhibits; usually June and July; check with the tourist office.)*

ENTERTAINMENT

The helpful monthly *What's On* poster, displayed on kiosks and at the tourist office, will fill you in on the many concerts, plays, and evening hot-spots. The lush Victorian **Everyman Theatre,** Regent St. (tel. 572573), is a stop for traveling performers and touring productions, ranging from the London City Ballet to pre-London productions. *(Box office open M-Sa 10am-9pm. Tickets £5-16.)* The **Playhouse Theatre,** Bath Rd. (tel. 522852), stages amateur productions. *(Box office open M-Sa 10am-4pm.)*

For a relaxing pint and good conversation, try **Dobell's,** 24 The Promenade. *(Open M-Sa 11am-11pm, Su noon-2:30pm and 7-10:30pm.)* Also try the **Fish and Fiddle;** Imperial Ln. (tel. 238001), for live music on Tuesday and Thursday nights. Hours vary—call and ask. **Club Mondo,** Bath Rd. (tel. 263456), pumps chart hits from 9pm-2:30am on Friday and Saturday, and until 1:30am on weeknights. *(Cover runs £2-4, increasing on the hour.)* **Enigma,** Regent St. (tel. 224085), caters to Cheltenham's students. On Friday and Saturday nights, the club opens its two cavernous levels. *(Cover £1-5. Casual dress. Open 9pm-2am.)* **Axiom Centre for the Arts,** 57-59 Winchcombe St. (tel. 253183), provides a venue for activities as diverse as yoga and juggling; the center also houses an art gallery, a theater, and a bar with frequent live music. *(Cover £1-4.)*

Cheltenham hosts superb cultural events; most notable is the **Cheltenham International Festival of Music** in early to mid-July, which celebrates modern classical works, as well as opera, dance, and theater. The **Fringe** branch of the Festival features jazz, rock, and world premiers; many performances are free. The **Jazz Festival**—now in its third year—is held in early April. Full details on both festivals are available in March from the box office, Town Hall, Imperial Sq., Cheltenham, Glos. GL50 1QA (tel. 227979). *(Tickets first come, first served £1.50-19.)*

The **Cheltenham Cricket Festival,** the oldest and longest in the country, commences in mid-July. *(Tickets can be purchased at the gate. Inquire about game times at the tourist office.)* October heralds the **Cheltenham Festival of Literature,** which runs for a fortnight. Poets, prose writers, and playwrights converge on Cheltenham for readings, lectures, and seminars. Recent writers have included Seamus Heaney, P.D. James, and Stephen Spender. For a full program of events, write to the Town Hall or call the 24-hour **Festival Box Office** (tel. 237277). *(Advance tickets £1.50-4.)*

ENGLAND

■ Near Cheltenham: Tewkesbury

Ten miles northwest of Cheltenham, on the A38 to Worcester and at the confluence of the Rivers Avon and Severn, lies **Tewkesbury.** Consecrated in 1121, stately **Tewkesbury Abbey** (tel. 850959) strikingly captures the beautiful masculinity of Norman (or "English Romanesque") architecture. Heaving forests of stone cross branches at gilded bosses, illuminated by 14th-century stained glass. The abbey stands today only because townsfolk raised £453 to save it from Henry VIII's planned dissolution. During the summer, free Tuesday lunch concerts are given on the grounds. *(Open in summer M-Sa 7:30am-6:30pm, Su 7:30am-7pm; in winter M-Sa 7:30am-6pm, Su 7:30am-7pm. Requested donation £1.50. Abbey services Su at 8, 9:15, 11am, and 6pm. Also maintains an Evensong. Photography permits £1, video permits £3.)* The **Country Park,** Crickley Hill, once an Iron Age fort, offers ethereal views and artifacts of archaeological interest.

Small museums dot the town. The **Tewkesbury Town Museum,** 64 Barton St. (tel. 295027), displays models of the town and the Battle of Tewkesbury. *(Open daily 10am-1pm, 1:30-4pm. 75p, seniors 50p children 25p.)* The **John Moore Countryside Museum,** 42 Church St. (tel. 297174), places environmental exhibits amid stuffed animals. *(Open Apr.-Oct. Tu-Sa 10am-1pm and 2-5pm. £1, students and seniors 75p, children 50p., families £2.50)* The **Little Museum,** Church St. (tel. 297174), is a merchant's cottage built in 1450 and restored five centuries later. *(Open Apr.-Oct. Tu-Sa 10am-5pm. Free.)*

Tewkesbury makes a leisurely day trip from Cheltenham and can be adequately visited in a few hours. Overnighters should go to Mrs. Wells's **Hanbury Guest House,** Barton Rd. (tel. 299911), five minutes from the town center on the left. Comfortable rooms boast quilts to die for; breakfast is in Mrs. Wells's homey quilt shop. Rooms have washbasins and color TV (£16, with bath £18.50; no smoking). Mrs. Warnett's lovely Welsh accent welcomes you to **Crescent Guest House,** 30 Church St. (tel. 293395), next to the Abbey. Rooms include color TV and washbasins (doubles £36).

Cheltenham District bus #41 (tel. (01242) 522021) departs every hour until 7pm (M-F, return £2, Sa 2 per hr.). The town's friendly **tourist office** (tel. 295027), nests in the Town Museum, 64 Barton St. (open Apr.-Oct. M-Sa 9am-5pm, Su 10am-4pm; Nov.-Mar. M-Sa 9am-5pm). Buy a 5p map; a pamphlet outlines walks through Tewkesbury's alleyed streets (20p). **ATMs** and major **banks** line High St. Tewkesbury's **post office** (tel. 293232) is at 99-100 High St. (open M-F 9am-5:30pm, Sa 9am-4pm). The **postal code** is GL20 5PX; the **telephone code** for Tewkesbury is 01684.

▒ The Cotswolds

Stretching across the west of England, these whimsical hills enfold small towns barely touched by modern life—save periodic strings of antique shops and summer tourists. Hewn straight from the famed Cotswold Stone (termed "oolite" after the microscopic sea creatures that comprise it), Saxon villages and Roman settlements link a series of trails accessible to walkers and cyclists. Walls of the same stone delineate rugged fields dotted with sheep and linseed. Rounding a bend in the road, it's easy (and disconcerting) to mistake an expanse of purple linseed for a body of water. Townspeople and tourists traverse the Cotswold terrain in harmony, skirting pastureland and treading near larger cities. Even the towns seem like scenes from a rustic past, and brilliant greens, golds, and purples color the entire area with natural beauty.

GETTING THERE

The Cotswolds lie mostly in Gloucestershire, bounded by Banbury in the northeast, Bradford-on-Avon in the southwest, Cheltenham in the north, and Malmesbury in the south. The range hardly towers: a few areas in the north and west rise above 1000 ft., but the average Cotswold hill reaches only 600 ft. A 52 mi. long unbroken ridge, **The Edge,** dominates the western reaches of the Cotswolds.

Though not readily accessible by public transportation, the glorious Cotswolds demand entry in any itinerary. **Trains** (tel. (0345) 484950) and buses frequent the area's major gateways (Cheltenham, Bath, and Gloucester—Moreton on the Marsh and Charlbury are the only villages with train stations), but buses between the villages themselves are few and far between. The Cheltenham and Gloucester tourist offices offer transportation information to get you started. Decide beforehand which villages you aim to hit, as those in the so-called "Northern" Cotswolds (Stow-on-the-Wold, Bourton-on-the-Water, Moreton-on-the-Marsh) are more easily reached via Cheltenham, while the "Southern" Cotswolds (notably Slimbridge and Painswick) are served more frequently by Gloucester.

Trains zip from **Oxford** to **Moreton** (£6.70) and **Charlbury** (£3.40). Several **bus** companies operating under the auspices of the county government cover the Gloucestershire Cotswolds, comprising most of the range, though many buses run only one or two days a week. Two unusually regular services are **Pulham's Coaches** (tel. (01451) 820369) from **Cheltenham** to **Moreton via Bourton-on-the-Water** and **Stow-on-the-Wold** (50min., M-Sa 7 per day, £1.40) and **Castleton's Coaches** (tel. (01242) 602949) from **Cheltenham** to **Broadway via Winchcombe** (about 1hr., M-Sa 4-5 per day, £1.45). The *Connection* timetable is free, indispensable, and available from all area bus stations and tourist offices. In Cheltenham pick up the tourist office's invaluable *Getting There from Cheltenham* pamphlet and have it bronzed.

Various firms offer **coach tours** of the Cotswolds, departing from **Cheltenham, Cirencester, Gloucester, Stroud,** and **Tewkesbury.** Inquire at the tourist information centers. Cheltenham's tourist office (tel. (01242) 522878) offers less frantic tours of the North and South Cotswolds at a heftier £8.50 (students, seniors, and children £7.50). **Guide Friday** (tel. (01789) 294466) runs coach tours from **Stratford-upon-Avon.** If you prefer to run your own tour, **Country Lanes Cycle Center** (tel. (01608) 650065) hires bikes at the Moreton-on-the-Marsh train station. Phone ahead—wheels are popular in these rolling hills. (£12 per day, plus 2 pieces of ID and refundable deposit. Gear and maps included. Open daily 9:30am-5pm.)

PRACTICAL INFORMATION

Tourist offices in the area, which all book accommodations for a 10% deposit, include the following (listed north to south):

Chipping Campden: Noel Arms Courtyard, High St. GL55 6AT (tel. (01386) 841206). Open daily 10am-6pm.

Broadway: 1 Cotswold Ct. WR12 7AA (tel. (01386) 852937). Open Mar.-Oct. M-Sa 10am-1pm and 2-5pm. Booking service available year-round.

Stow-on-the-Wold: Hollis House, The Square GL54 1AF (tel. (01451) 831082). Open Easter-Oct. M-Sa 9:30am-5:30pm, Su 10:30am-4pm.

Cirencester: Corn Hall, Market Pl. GL7 2NW (tel. (01285) 654180). Open Apr.-Oct. M 9:45am-5:30pm, Tu-Sa 9:30am-5:30pm; Nov.-Mar. daily 9:30am-5pm.

Cheltenham: 77 The Promenade GL50 1PP (tel. (01242) 522878). Open July-Aug. M-Sa 9:30am-6pm, Su 9:30am-1:30pm; Sept.-June M-Sa 9:30am-5:15pm.

Gloucester: 28 Southgate St. GL1 1PD (tel. (01452) 421188). Open M-Sa 10am-5pm.

Bath: Abbey Chambers BA1 1SW (tel. 477101; fax 477787). Open June-Sept. M-Tu and F-Sa 9:30am-6pm, W-Th 9:45am-6pm, Su 10am-4pm; Oct.-May M-Sa 9am-5pm, Su 10am-4pm.

ACCOMMODATIONS AND FOOD

The *Cotswold Way Handbook* (£1.50) lists B&Bs along the Way; they are usually spaced in villages 3 mi. apart and offer friendly lodgings to trekkers, or pick up *The Cotswolds Accommodation Guide* (50p). Call ahead in the morning to reserve same-day lodging. Savvy backpackers stay outside the larger towns to enjoy the silence. **YHA** has a number of **hostels** in the area:

Charlbury: The Laurels, The Slade, Charlbury, Oxford OX7 3SJ (tel. (01608) 810202). On the River Evenlode, 1mi. north of Charlbury, 5mi. northwest of Blenheim Palace, 13mi. northwest of Oxford; off the Oxford-Worcester rail line. From town center, follow road sign-posted *Enstone*. At B4022 crossroads, go straight across; the hostel is 50yd. on left. £7.70, under 18 £5.15. Breakfast £2.85, packed lunch £2.45, evening meal £4.25. Open Apr.-June daily; July-Aug. M-Sa; Feb.-Mar. and Sept.-Oct. W-Su; Jan. F-Su.

Slimbridge: Shepherd's Patch, Slimbridge GL2 7BP (tel. (01453) 890275; fax 890625), across from the Tudor Arms Pub, next to the swing bridge. Off the A38 and the M5, 4mi. from the Cotswold Way and ½mi. from the Wild Fowl Trust Reserve and Wetlands Centre. Easiest approach is by bus from Gloucester. Comes complete with its own ponds and wildfowl. 56 beds, showers, small store. £9.40, under 18 £6.30. Breakfast £3, packed lunch £2.55, evening meal £5. Open Mar.-Aug. daily; Sept.-Nov. M-Sa; Jan.-Feb. M-F.

Stow-on-the-Wold: The Square, Cheltenham GL54 1AF (tel. (01451) 830497). In the center of the village, between the White Hart Hotel and the Old Stocks. On the A424 highway; Pulham's bus passes about 1 per hr. from Cheltenham (17mi.), Bourton-on-the-Water, and Moreton-in-Marsh (4 mi.). 12mi. from Charlbury hostel. Bright rooms with wooden bunks; facilities are older but clean. Lovely, helpful warden. 56 beds; annex with 18 beds. £8.80, students £7.80, under 18 £6. Breakfast £2.85, packed lunch £2.45 or £3.25, and evening meal £4.25. Self-catering kitchen. Lockout 10am-5pm. Open Apr.-Aug. daily; Sept.-Oct. M-Sa; Nov.-Dec. Sa-Su; closed Jan.-Mar. Closed through Dec. 1998 for renovation. Call ahead for reopening date and definite hours.

Campsites congregate close to Cheltenham; the villages Bourton-on-the-Water, Stow-on-the-Wold, and Moreton-on-the-Marsh also provide convenient places to bivouac. When in doubt consult the *Gloucestershire Caravan and Camping Guide* (free and annually updated) at local tourist centers.

You'll never go hungry in the Cotswolds. Supermarkets, fast food establishments, and full-fledged restaurants call larger towns like Cheltenham and Cirencester home; smaller towns have "if-we-don't-have-it-you-don't-need-it" general stores. Country pubs crop up every 3 mi. or so in hamlets and villages along the way.

HIKING THROUGH COTSWOLD VILLAGES

Experience England as the English have for centuries—by treading well-worn footpaths from village to village. Speed-walking will enable you to see several settlements in a day, which proves especially convenient for daytrippers based in Cheltenham. Tourist office shelves strain with the weight of various books orchestrating your walk. Those in search of long-distance hiking routes have a choice among a handful of carefully marked trails. B&Bs and pubs rest conveniently within reach of both the **Cotswold Way** and the **Oxfordshire Way.** Local roads are perfect for biking, and the rolling hills welcome casual and hardy cyclers alike; the closely-spaced, tiny villages make ideal watering holes. Bear in mind that the Northern Cotswolds have a decidedly different feel from the South; many think the former are the more quaint and picturesque, while the latter suffer from less congestion. Check listings for local springtime festivities like cheese rolling or woolsack races, where participants dash up and down hills laden with 60 pounds.

The more extensive of the two, the **Cotswold Way,** spans just over 100 mi. from Bath to Chipping Campden. The way affords glorious vistas of hills and dales, and fortunately tends to be uncrowded. The entire walk can be done in about a week at a pace of about 15 mi. per day. Due to pockmarks and gravel, certain sections of the path are not suitable for biking and horseback riding. What's more, many sections cross pastureland; try not to disturb Cotswold sheep and cattle, two breeds we're told it's fatal to mess with. Consult the **Cotswold Voluntary Warden Service** (tel. (01452) 425674) for details. Tourist information centers sell trail guides specially designed for the cyclist. Also available at the centers, the *Cotswold Way Map* (£5) provides a basic guide to the area, and *Cotswold Way* (£4) has maps and explicit directions. Tourist offices give out *Guided Walks and Events in the Cotswolds,* which tells about free guided walking groups led by informed locals. For additional reference, consult Ordnance Survey Maps 1:50,000: sheets 151 (Stratford), 150 (Worcester and the Malverns), 163 (Cheltenham), 162 (Gloucester), and 172 (Bath and Bristol), each £4.50. In addition, the Cotswolds Voluntary Warden Service provides guided walks through the Cotswolds, some with historical or ecological bents. The free walks last from 1½-7½ hours.

Years back, quiet **Chipping Campden** became the capital of the rampant Cotswold wool trade. Later, the village became a market center ("chipping" means "market"). The town is currently famous for its **Cotswold Olympic Games at Dovers Hill,** highlighted by the obscure sport of shin-kicking. This sadistic activity was prohibited from 1852 to 1952, but has since been enthusiastically revived in late May and early June to the glee of local bone-setters. *(Tickets available day of game.)*

Only 3 mi. west of Chipping Campden, restored Tudor, Jacobean, and Georgian buildings with thatch or Cotswold tile roofs scheme to make **Broadway** a museum. Since it became a stopover on the London-Worcester route in the 16th century, Broadway has bustled with visitors. **Broadway Tower** (tel. (01386) 852390) enchanted the likes of the decorator-designer-poet William Morris and his pre-Raphaelite comrade Dante Gabriel Rossetti. Built in the late 1700s in a superfluous attempt to intensify the beauty of the landscape, the tower affords a view of 12 counties. *(Open early Apr. to late Oct. daily 10am-6pm. £3, children £2.20, families £9.)*

A sleepy village that recently opened its eyes to protest a proposed supermarket, **Stow-on-the-Wold** features fine views of the surrounding countryside. Stow will confirm your suspicion that Cotswold settlers looked no farther than their backyards for building materials. Stick your feet into Stow's authentic stocks and snap a photo (everybody else does it). Stow also boasts one antique shop for every 33 residents. A few yards away from the stocks stands a **YHA Youth Hostel** (see **Accommodations and Food,** p. 255). Replenish glucose at **Cotswold Fruit Store,** the Square, or down a pint at **The King's Arms** across the way.

The **Oxfordshire Way** (65mi.) runs between the popular hyphen-havens of Bourton-on-the-Water and Henley-on-Thames. A comprehensive *Walker's Guide* can be found in tourist offices. Plod over cow paddies to wend your way from Bourton-on-the-Water to Lower and Upper Slaughter along the **Warden's Way** (takes a half day). Parts of the footpaths are hospitable to cyclists, if slightly rut-ridden. Most adventurous souls can continue on to Winchcombe for a total of about 14 mi.

Like the proverbial lamb, travel a few miles southwest to the **Slaughters (Upper and Lower),** a pair of tranquil villages. Fortunately, your visit will be heralded by a host of lively sheep, not an unhinged butcher. Footpaths connect Upper and Lower Slaughter and also lead to **Bourton-on-the-Water.** Rather inexplicably touted as the "Venice of the Cotswolds" (no gondolas, just a picturesque stream and a series of footbridges), Bourton hosts its fair share of tourists, including many polo-shirted English men and women in straw hats with real flowers. Many of the larger trails (Cotswold and Oxfordshire Ways) converge at Bourton. Between the olfactory heaven and hell of rose-laden gates and fields strewn with sheep dung lies **The Cotswold Perfumery** (tel. (01451) 820698), on Victoria St. The Perfumery houses a theater equipped with "Smelly Vision," that releases actual scents into the theater as they're mentioned on screen. *(Open daily 9:30am-5pm, sometimes later in summer. £1.75, students, seniors, and children £1.50. Wheelchair accessible.)*

West of Stow-on-the-Wold and 6 mi. north of Cheltenham on the A46, lies **Sudeley Castle** (tel. (01242) 602308), neighboring the town of **Winchcombe.** Once the manor estate of King Ethelred the Unready, the castle was a prized possession in the Middle Ages, with lush woodland, a royal deer park, and Charles I's gloriously carved four-poster bed. The Queen's Garden is streamlined by a pair of yew-hedge corridors leading to rose and herb beds, while the newly planted Knot Garden was inspired by a pattern on a gown worn by Queen Elizabeth in 1592. **St. Mary's Chapel** contains the tomb of Henry VIII's Queen Katherine Parr. The castle also schedules falconry shows. Present occupants Lord and Lady Ashcombe welcome you and your admission fee into their home. *(Open Apr.-Oct. daily 10:30am-5pm. £5.50, seniors £3.20, children £3; grounds only £4, seniors £3.20, children £1.80, families £15.)*

Prehistoric remains are stowed in the Cotswolds; archaeologists have unearthed some 70 ancient habitation sites. **Belas Knap,** a 4000-year-old burial mound, stands about 1½ mi. southwest of Sudeley Castle, accessible from the Cotswold Way. The **Rollright Stones,** off the A34 between Chipping Norton and Long Compton (a 4½ mi. walk from Chipping Norton), comprise a 100 ft. wide ring of 11 stones. Consult Ordnance Survey Tourist Map 8 (£4.25) for locations of other sites.

The Cotswolds contain some of the best examples of Roman settlements in Britain—most notably **Cirencester** and **Chedworth.** Sometimes regarded as the capital of the region, Cirencester is the site of Corinium, a Roman town founded in AD 49 and second in importance only to Londinium, which has continued to be the more successful sister. Cirencester today largely caters to its older population. The town is small and the pension crowd is large. Stay in Cheltenham or Gloucester and take a daytrip to see the Roman remains. Although only scraps of the amphitheater still exist, the **Corinium Museum,** Park St. (tel. (01285) 655611), has culled a formidable collection of Roman paraphernalia, including a hare mosaic comprised of thousands of *tessarae,* tiny handworked bits of ceramic. *(Open Apr.-Oct. M-Sa 10am-5pm, Su 2-5pm; Nov.-Mar. Tu-Sa 10am-5pm, Su 2-5pm. £2.50, students £1, seniors £2, children 80p, families £5.)* The second longest yew hedge in England bounds Lord Bathwist's mansion in the center of town; the garden is scattered with Roman ruins. On Fridays, the entire town turns into a bedlamic antique marketplace; a smaller craft fair appears every Saturday inside Corn Hall, near the tourist office at the Marketplace. **B&Bs** cluster a few minutes from downtown along Victoria Rd. Prices are steep, but it is possible to bargain successfully. Stop by the **Golden Cross** on Black Jack St. or the **Crown** at W. Market Pl. near the Abbey for a pint.

Tucked away in the Chedworth hills southwest of Cheltenham is the well-preserved **Chedworth Roman Villa** (tel. (01242) 890256), equidistant from Cirencester and Northleach off the A429. The famed Chedworth mosaics were discovered in 1864 when a gamekeeper noticed fragments of tile revealed by clever rabbits. The site now displays a water shrine and two bathhouses just above the River Coln. *(Open Mar.-Nov. Tu-Su and bank holidays 10am-5pm. £3.20, children £1.60, families £8. Partially wheelchair accessible.)*

Fowl deeds occur at **Slimbridge** (tel. (01453) 890065), 12½ mi. southwest of Gloucester off the A38, the largest of the **Wildfowl Trust's** seven centers in Britain. Sir Peter Scott has cached the world's largest collection of wildfowl here, with a total of over 180 different species. All six varieties of flamingos nest here, and white-fronted geese visit from their Siberian homeland. In the tropical house, hummingbirds skim through jungle foliage. The visitor center has exhibits and food—don't ask for duck. *(Open in summer daily 9:30am-5pm; grounds close 6pm; in winter daily 9:30am-4pm. £5, children £3, families £13.)* **YHA Slimbridge** benefits from Sir Peter's aviary efforts as well, hosting its own flocks of birds (see **Accommodations and Food,** p. 255).

Like a Rolling Stone

According to legend, the curious group of stones which comprise the Rollright Stones near Chipping Norton were created when an evil witch told an ambitious king:

> *Seven long strides shalt thou take:*
> *If Long Compton thou canst see, then King of England thou shalt be.*
> *If Long Compton thou cannot see, then King of England thou shalt not be.*

The king bounded up the hill, but found a large stone blocking his view. To ensure the accuracy of her prophecy, the witch turned all the king's party, and the poor king himself, into stone. Today the king stone, an 8 ft. loner, is still surrounded by his circle of men, 77 stones 100 ft. in diameter. The group of stones ¼ mi. west, known as the Whispering Knights, are said to have been a group of knights who were plotting treason. Too bad the beleaguered king couldn't just climb the Broadway Tower!

Just south of Slimbridge on the A38 rises the massive **Berkeley Castle** (BARK-lay; tel. (01453) 810322), ancestral home of the Berkeley family (founders of a university in California). This stone fortress truly deserves the castle moniker, with its impressive towers, dungeon, and timber-vaulted Great Hall, where barons of the West Country met before forcing King John to sign the *Magna Carta*. *(Open July-Aug. M-Sa 11am-5pm, Su 2-5pm; June and Sept. Tu-Sa 11am-5pm, Su 2-5pm; Apr.-May Tu-Su 2-5pm; Oct. Su 2-5pm. £5, students and seniors £4, children £2.60, families £13.50.)*

▓ Worcester

The city of Worcester (WOO-ster) crouches by the Severn River, halfway between Cheltenham and Birmingham, lacking both the gentility of the former and the frenetic pace of the latter. In fact, Worcester's sights are somewhat lackluster; the city hordes such crumbs of fame as the site of the Civil War's final battle and makes great pomp of its circumstantial role as the birthplace of the composer Elgar. Because of its waterway, Worcester (pop. 93,000) has been a center of trade since prehistoric times, and like Severn waters, its citizens' blood mixes streams of Saxon and Celtic, English and Welsh, all flowing more or less seamlessly.

GETTING THERE

Trains (tel. (0345) 484950) connect Worcester to **London** (2½hr., 1 per hr., £22), **Birmingham** (2 per hr. 9am-6pm, £4.30, day return £4.40), **Oxford** (1½hr., 1 per hr., £9.60, return £17), and **Cheltenham** (¼hr., 1 per hr., £4.80, day return £5.60). **Buses** dock at the station on Angel Pl. **National Express** (tel. (0990) 808080) runs to **London** (4hr., 1 per day, £11.50), **Birmingham** (1hr., 1 per hr., £3.10, return £3.90), and **Bristol** (1½hr., 2 per day, £8.10, return £10). A **Midland Red West Day Rover** ticket allows unlimited one-day travel throughout the region (£4, seniors £3.10, children £2.50, families £8.20). **Cambridge Buses** (tel. (01223) 236333) run three a day to Stratford (45min., £4) and Cambridge (3½hr., £15).

ORIENTATION AND PRACTICAL INFORMATION

The city center is bounded by the train station on its northern end and by the cathedral on its southern side. A crowded pedestrian street spans the length between the two; this fickle street switches names along the way from **Barbourne Rd.** to **The Tything** to **Foregate St.** to **The Foregate** to **The Cross** to **High St.** To reach town from the rail station, turn left onto **Foregate St.** From the bus station, turn left onto **Broad St.** and right onto **The Cross.**

Trains: Foregate St. (tel. (0345) 484950), on the edge of the town center, next to the post office. Serves travelers going through Birmingham to destinations including Oxford and London. Ticket window open M-Sa 6am-11:20pm, Su 6:30am-11:05pm. Travel Centre open M-Sa 9am-4pm. Also **Shrub Hill Station** (mainly serving the southwest), just outside town. To get to town from Shrub Hill Station, take a right onto Shrub Hill Rd., then a left onto Tolladine Rd., which becomes Lowesmoor; follow Lowesmoor to St. Nicholas St., which intersects Foregate, the town's main drag (10min. walk). Ticket window open M-Sa 5:30am-7pm, Su 7am-7pm. Travel Centre open M-Sa 9am-4pm.

Buses: Angel Pl. off Broad St. near the Crowngate Shopping Centre. For information call **Midland Red West** (tel. 763888) or **National Express** (tel. (0990) 808080). National Express tickets sold and inquiries answered at the **Worcester Travel Shop** in the Crowngate Shopping Centre. Open M-F 8:45am-5:30pm, Sa 9am-4pm.

Taxis: Queue at The Cross and High St., across from Lloyds, or call **Associated Radio Taxis** (tel. 763939).

Bike Rental: Peddlers, 46-48 Barbourne (tel. 24238). £8 per day, £30 per week; mountain bikes £15 per day, £60 per week; £50 deposit. Open M-Sa 9:30am-6pm, Su 9:30am-4:30pm.

ENGLAND

Tourist Office: The Guildhall, High St. (tel. 726311; fax 722481). Quiet, helpful, and packed with free maps and pamphlets. Books beds for 10% deposit. Open Easter-Oct. M-Sa 10:30am-5:30pm; Nov.-Easter M-Sa 10:30am-4pm. **Tours:** 1½hr., from Guildhall. May-Aug. W 11am and 2:30pm; £3, children £1.50.

Financial Services: Thomas Cook, 26 High St. (tel. 28228; fax 610089), across from the Guildhall. Open M-W and F-Sa 9am-5:30pm, Th 10am-5:30pm. **Lloyds,** 4 The Cross (tel. 722800). Open M-Tu and Th-F 9am-5pm, W 9:30am-5pm, Sa 9:30am-12:30pm. **Barclays,** 54 High St. (tel. 684828). Open M-F same hours as Lloyds, Sa 9:30am-1pm.

Market: Angel Pl., open M-Sa 8:30am-4:30pm (Thursday is a bric-a-brac market).

Launderette: Severn Laun-Dri, 22 Barbourne Rd. Change machine. Open daily 9am-9pm; last wash 8pm.

Space Pod Toilet: Copenhagen St. off High St. Sleek facility automatically sanitizes after each use. This is not the work of human hands. 20p.

Emergency: Dial 999; no coins required.

Police: Deansway (tel. 723888), directly behind the Guildhall, across from St. Andrew's Park.

Hotlines: Samaritans (crisis; tel. 21121). Open 24hr. **AIDS** (tel. 22957). **Gay and Lesbian Switchboard** (tel. 723097).

Hospital: Ronkswood Hospital (tel. 763333), on Newtown Rd. Bus #29D and 31A.

Post Office: 8-10 Foregate St. (tel. 23208), next to the train station. Bureau de change. Open M-Sa 9am-5:30pm. **Postal Code:** WR1 1AA.

Telephone Code: 01905.

ACCOMMODATIONS

B&B prices in Worcester are high, as proprietors cater to Londoners looking for a weekend in the country; the beginning and end of summer tend to be the busiest times. Call ahead or try your luck on Barbourne Rd., the fifth manifestation of High St. about a 15- to 20-minute walk from the city center. The nearest **YHA Youth Hostel** is 7 mi. away in Malvern, 12 min. by train (see **Near Worcester: Malvern,** p. 261). **Osbourne House,** 17 Chestnut Walk (tel./fax 22296), in a convenient and quiet location, offers TVs and electronic, touch-operated showers in every bedroom, three types of cookies on your nightstand, and brilliant marmalade (singles £20; doubles £34; wheelchair access). Monty Python fans will appreciate the B&B's name and everyone else will appreciate Mrs. Law's laying down of supremely comfortable beds in the **Shrubbery Guest House,** 38 Barbourne Rd. (tel. 24871; fax 23620). Rooms have TV and shower (singles £18; doubles £34, with bath £40). Campers may want to try **Ketch Caravan Park,** Bath Rd. (tel. 820430), on the banks of the Severn, with a restaurant, phones, toilets, and showers on-site (£6-7 per tent, £7 per car, electricity hook up £1.75; open Easter-Oct.). Take the A38 2 mi. south of Worcester or take local bus #32 from town (every 10min.).

FOOD

Satisfy your appetite and your fashion mag-deprived mind at **Clockwatchers,** 20 Meal-cheapen St. (tel. 611662). Farm-fresh sandwiches from £1.40 take-away (eat-in £2.50-2.90) and bagels only 60p. Bonus fun with street name puns (open M-Sa 8:30am-5pm). **Natural Break** (tel. 26654), off Foregate St. at The Hopmarket, offers organic respite in the form of sandwiches and pasties from £1.45. Another branch pokes out at 17 Mealcheapen St. (tel. 26417; both stores gyre and gimble M-Sa 9am-5pm). For chic bistro atmosphere and even more chic dishes call on **Café Olive** (tel. 29640), on Angel St. Pastas, seafood, and colorful house salads go for £1.50 (open M-Sa 8am-10pm). For Indian food, try one of the restaurants in **The Tything.** Groceries find their place in the world at **Sainsbury's,** tucked into the Lynchgate Shopping Centre off High St. (open M-Th 8am-6pm, F 8:30am-7pm, Sa 7:30am-6pm). The **Hodson Coffee House and Patisserie,** 99-100 High St. (tel. 21036), has a cafeteria-style interior. Try the regal coronation chicken or "scrambling prawns" (both £5.25; open M-Sa 9:30am-5pm). **The Cardinal's Hat,** 31 Friar St. (tel. 21890), is Worcester's oldest pub;

sit in front of open fires sipping ales brewed on site (open daily 11am-11pm). They'll put another shrimp on the barbie for you at **Bushwacker's,** a gargantuan Australian pub-turned-nightclub at the end of The Avenue off the Cross. Ladies drink free Monday nights (open M-Sa 11am-1am).

SIGHTS

Worcester Cathedral (tel. 28854), founded in AD 680, towers majestically by the river at the southern end of High St., cloaking a frail internal structure—the buttresses supporting the central nave have deteriorated and the central tower is in danger of collapsing. Though steel rods have been set into the tower's base, renovation efforts fail to detract from the awe-inspiring detail of the nave and quire. To the delight of schoolchildren and puerile *Let's Go* researchers, one of the tombs in the south wall is that of Bishop Freake (1516-91). In the quire are lovingly detailed 14th-century misericords and the tomb of King John; copies of the *Magna Carta* stand outside. Steps lead down to Wulston's Crypt, an entire underground level with a chapel. *(Cathedral open daily 7:30am-6:30pm; choral Evensong M-F 5:30pm, Su 4pm. Suggested donation £2. Tower tours £2; free guided tours May-Sept. Touch and Hearing Centre for the visually impaired. Wheelchair access.)*

Retrace the 1651 Battle of Worcester at the **Commandery,** Sidbury Rd. (tel. 355071), occupying the vast buildings of Charles II's former headquarters. Sit in on the trial of Charles I and choose whether to sign the king's death warrant. Your vote counts. *(Open M-Sa 10am-5pm, Su 1:30-5:30pm. £3.25, seniors and children £2.50, families £8.75.)* The **Worcester City Museum and Art Gallery,** Foregate St. (tel. 25371), near the post office, evokes the military past of England in an exhibit that includes Hitler's clock (frozen at 5:51), found hanging in his office when it was captured by the Worcester Regiment in 1945. *(Open M-W and F 9:30am-6pm, Sa 9:30am-5pm. Free.)* Southeast of the cathedral on Severn St., legions of blue-haired women swarm the **Royal Worcester Porcelain Company,** manufacturer of the tremendously famous and incredibly beautiful blue-red-and-gold-patterned bone china, the finest in England. The company has serviced the royal family since George III visited in 1788. A showroom sells high-quality pieces; seconds are available in a shop also on the grounds. Porcelain junkies should visit the adjacent **Worcester Museum of Porcelain** (tel. 23221), which has the largest collection in England. *(Open M-Sa 9am-5:30pm. £2, children £1. Tours M-F every 10min. 10:30-11:10am to 1:15-3:15pm. £4, seniors £3.50, students and children £3. Museum and tours £6, seniors £4, students and children £3.50. Wheelchair accessible.)*

Behind the Guildhall, all that remains of the demolished St. Andrew's Church is a magnificent 245 ft. spire. It is known locally as the **Glover's Needle** because of its comely shape and the area's ties with glove-making. Half-timbered buildings lie on Friar St., as well as the **Museum of Local Life** (tel. 722349), which showcases the Worcester lifestyle during World War II, among other things. *(Open M-W and F-Sa 10:30am-5pm. Free.)* The **Swan Theatre's** (tel. 27322) professional company entertains museum-weary crowds. *(Box office open M-Sa 10:30am-8pm. Wheelchair accessible.)*

Three miles south of town lies **Elgar's Birthplace Museum** (tel. 333224), filled with manuscripts and memorabilia of England's finest composer. **Midland Red West** bus #419/420 makes the journey (10min., return £1.80). From there walk 15 minutes to the museum. Otherwise, cycle 6 mi. along the Elgar trail, based on routes taken by the composer. *(Open May-Sept. Th-Tu 10:30am-6pm; Oct. to mid-Jan. and mid-Feb. to Apr. Th-Tu 1:30-4:30pm. £3, students £1, seniors £2, children 50p.)*

■ Near Worcester: Malvern

The name **Malvern** refers collectively to the contiguous towns of Great Malvern, West Malvern, Malvern Link, Malvern Wells, and Little Malvern, all of which hug the base and the eastern side of the Malvern Hills. As you might expect, Great Malvern, the center of the towns, served as a spa resort during Victorian times. The tops of the Malvern Hills peek over the A4108 southwest of Worcester and offer the hiker 8 mi.

of accessible trails and quasi-divine visions of greenery. The **Worcestershire Way** slips through the Malverns for 36 mi. to Kingsford County Park in the north. The **Countryside Service** (tel. (01905) 766476), in the County Hall in Worcester, will inform you on hiking in the area. The **tourist office,** 21 Church St. (tel. 892289; fax 892872), by the post office, assists in hill-navigation (short distance walk pamphlets 30p; open daily 10am-5pm).

Great Malvern was built around the 11th-century parish church that stands along Abbey Rd. Benedictine monks completely rebuilt the structure in the mid-15th century and added stained glass windows. *(Suggested donation £1.)* On the steep hillside above town, **St. Ann's Well** supplies the famous restorative "Malvern waters" that fueled Great Malvern's halcyon days as a spa town. Beautifully redone **Malvern Theatres,** Grange Rd. (tel. 892277), host plays, including a season of top-quality London theatre by the Almeida Company in August. *(Box office open M-Sa 9:30am-8pm. Wheelchair accessible.)* The **priory** in Little Malvern, noted for its chancel and 15th-century stained glass, also harbors whimsical carvings of three rats attempting to hang a cat. *(Open daily 9:30am-6pm. Free.)*

The **YHA Hatherly** (tel. 569131) sits at 18 Peachfield Rd. in Malvern Wells; take Citibus #42 from Great Malvern or walk 20 minutes from the train station. (£8, under 18 £5.40. Meals available. Lockout 10am-5pm. Curfew 11pm. Open mid-Feb. to Oct. daily; Nov.-Dec. F-Sa.) The Malverns are accessible from Worcester via **British Rail** (25min., 10 per day) and **Midland Red West bus** (M-Sa 2 per hr., less frequently on Su), stopping at Great Malvern.

■ Stratford-upon-Avon

> *The remarkable thing about Shakespeare is that he is really very good—*
> *in spite of all the people who say he is very good.*
> —Robert Graves (1895-1985), British poet and novelist

Shakespeare lived here. This fluke of fate has made Stratford-upon-Avon a town more visited than most. Knick-knack huts hawk "Will Power" T-shirts, while proprietors tout the dozen-odd properties linked, however tenuously, to William Shakespeare and his extended family. But behind the tourist industry, Stratford-besides-Shakespeare lurks as well, concealed in the nooks of the Avon and the crannies of the Teddy Bear Museum. Of course, all the perfumes of Arabia will not sweeten the exhaust from tour buses, but the ghosts are here if you know where to seek them: collecting flowers by the weeping Avon, ducking into groves in the once-Forest of Arden, guzzling sack under the timbers of 16th-century inns, and appearing in the pin-drop silence before a soliloquy in the Royal Shakespeare Theatre.

JOURNEYS END

Thames Trains (tel. 579453) run from London's **Paddington Station** several times a day (2¼hr.). **National Express** (tel. (0990) 808080) runs to and from London's **Victoria Station** (3hr., 3 per day, £17 return, students and seniors 30% discount, under 5 free). The **Slow Coach** stops here on its circuit of England (see **By Bus and Coach,** p. 33) and there are also connections from **Oxford** (Stagecoach; £6 day return, departs from bay 6, Gloucester Green Station) and **Cambridge.** (Cambridge Coach (tel. (01223) 423900). Day return £14, students and seniors £10.50, children £7.)

HERE CEASE MORE QUESTIONS

Transportation
  Train Station: off Alcester Rd. (tel. (0345) 484950).
  Bus Station: The corner of **Waterside** and **Bridge St.,** opposite McDonald's, services **Stagecoach, Cambridge Coach,** and **Midland Red South** buses. Local **Stratford Blue** service also stops on **Wood St. National Express** has withdrawn to

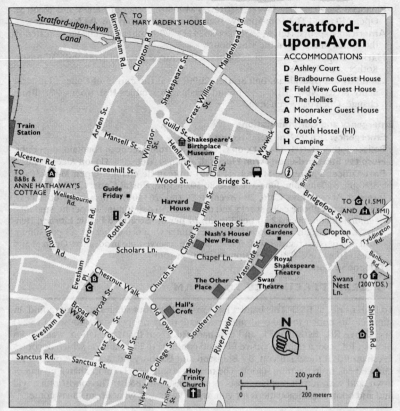

Stratford-upon-Avon

ACCOMMODATIONS

D Ashley Court
E Bradbourne Guest House
F Field View Guest House
C The Hollies
A Moonraker Guest House
B Nando's
G Youth Hostel (HI)
H Camping

Riverside Car Park off Bridgeway Rd. by the Leisure Centre. You can buy tickets for National Express buses at the tourist office.

Local Transportation: Stagecoach operates the major local bus system, **Midland Red.** However, the center of Stratford is small enough that walking will easily get you most everywhere.

Taxi: Main Taxis (tel. 414514) or **007 Taxis** (tel. 414007). Both open 24hr.

Bike Rental: Clarke's Cycle Rental, Guild St. (tel. 205057), at Union St.; look for the Esso sign. £7 per day, £25 per week; deposit £50. Open Tu-Sa 9:15am-5:30pm; in summer Su 10am-1pm as well.

Boat Rental: Stratford Marina, Clopton Bridge. Rowboats £4 per hr.; 6-seater motorboats £10 per hr. **Behind the RST,** rowboats £3 per hr.

Tourist and Financial Services

Tourist Office: Bridgefoot (tel. 293127). Cross Warwick Rd. at Bridge St. toward the waterside park. Their free *Accommodations Guide* lists places to stay in the area. Books accommodations for £3 plus a 10% deposit. Open Apr.-Oct. M-Sa 9am-6pm, Su 11am-5pm; Nov.-Mar. M-Sa 9am-5pm.

Tours: Guide Friday, Civic Hall, 14 Rother St. (tel. 294466). Handles all of Shakespeare's houses. Runs tours departing daily 4 per hr. from shrines around town. £8, students and seniors £6.50, children under 12 £2.50. They also offer tours of the Cotswolds. £16, students and seniors £13.50, children £8.

Royal Shakespeare Theatre Box Office, Waterside (tel. 295623; 24hr. recorded ticket information 412666; fax 261974). Standby tickets for students and seniors (£11-15) available just before the show at the RST, the Swan, and The Other Place. Open M-Sa 9:30am-8pm, closes at 6pm when there's no performance.

Financial Services: Barclays (tel. (01203) 814000), corner of Henley and Wood St. Open M-Tu and Th-F 9am-5pm, W 10am-5pm, Sa 9:30am-noon. **ATMs** outside.

American Express: (tel. 415856; fax 262411). With bureau de change. Located in the tourist office; open the same hours.

Market Day: Friday 8:30am-4:30pm, at the intersection of Greenhill, Windsor, Rother, and Wood St.

Launderette: Sparklean, Bull St. (tel. 269075), at the corner of College Ln. Near many B&Bs. New "HUGE 35 pound washer" resembles HAL from *2001*. Bring change. Open daily 9am-9pm.

Emergency and Communications

Emergency: Dial 999; no coins required.

Police: Rother St. (tel. 414111), up Greenhill St. from American Fountain, turn right.

Hospital: Stratford-upon-Avon Hospital, Arden St. (tel. 205831), off Alcester Rd.

Post Office: 2-3 Henley St. (tel. 414939). Bureau de change. Open M-F 8:30am-5:30pm, Sa 9am-6pm; June-Aug. also Su 10am-3pm. **Postal Code:** CV37 6PU.

Internet Access: Java Café, 28 Greenhill St. (tel. 263400). Offers fast web access, cut-price telephone calls, snacks and drinks. £3.50 per 30min., £5 per hr; students, seniors, unemployed £2.50 per 30min., £4 per hr. **Stratford Public Library,** Henley St. (tel. 292209 and 296904). One computer with dial-up access. £1 per 30min. You will need to register with the library and reserve time in advance. Open M and F 9:30-7pm, Tu-W 9:30am-5:50pm, Sa 9:30am-4pm.

Telephone Code: 01789.

TO SLEEP, PERCHANCE TO DREAM

To B&B or not to B&B? This hamlet has tons of them, but singles are hard to find. In summer, 'tis nobler to make advance reservations by phone. Guest houses (£15-22) line **Grove Rd., Evesham Pl.,** and **Evesham Rd.** From the train station, walk down Alcester Rd., take a right on Grove Rd., and continue to Evesham Pl., which becomes Evesham Rd. If these fail you, try **Shipston** and **Banbury Rd.** across the river, a 15-minute walk from the train station. The nearest youth hostel is more than 2 mi. out of town, and with return bus fare costs as much as some B&Bs. The tourist office will find and book accommodations for you, while you await what dreams may come.

Field View Guest House, 35 Banbury Rd. (tel. 292694). Quiet, peaceful rooms with a welcoming owner. Bathroom scale gives your weight in stones. Vegetarian options at breakfast. Singles £16; doubles £32.

The Hollies, 16 Evesham Pl. (tel. 266857). Warm and attentive proprietors for whom the guest house has become a labor of love. From the mint walls to the ivy scaling the outer wall, green prevails. No singles. Spacious doubles £35, with bath £45.

Ashley Court, 55 Shipston Rd. (tel. 297278). A most luxurious B&B. Spacious rooms in an immaculate guest house. All rooms with private facilities, remote control TV, radio, and private phone. Half-acre garden in back. Only a 5min. walk across a footbridge to all the sights. Singles £38; doubles £40; twins £45.

Nando's, 18 Evesham Pl. (tel./fax 204907). Friendly owners, bright, comfortable rooms—all have TVs and most have private facilities. 5 singles £22-29; doubles £44. Prices lower in the winter.

YHA Youth Hostel, Hemmingford House, Wellesbourne Rd., Alveston (tel. 297093; email YHAStratfordUponAvon@compuserve.com), 2mi. from Stratford. Follow the B4086; take bus #18 or X18 from Bridge St., across from the McDonald's (theoretically 1 per hr., £1.50). Large, attractive grounds and a 200-year-old building with RSC photos on the wall. Friendly staff offers Shakespearian wisdom and full English breakfasts. £13.45, under 18 £10.05. Breakfast included. Packed lunch £3.35. 3-course dinner with vegetarian options is the best deal around (£4.40). 130 beds in rooms of 2-14. Kitchen. Reception open 7am-midnight.

Bradbourne Guest House, 44 Shipston Rd. (tel. 204178). Pleasant family provides oil-painted landscapes and brass in quiet rooms about 8min. from town center. Singles £25; doubles £44-48. Rates lower Oct.-Apr. Breakfast menu with veggie options. Cable TV in every room.

Moonraker House, 40 Alcester Rd. (tel. 267115 or 299346; fax 295504). 5-10min. from town center. Luxurious crimson sitting rooms, canopied beds, and optional champagne service (for a fee). All private facilities; homemade jams. Singles £35-40; doubles or twins £24-35 per person (£35 includes a private garden).

Camping: Riverside Caravan Park, Tiddington Rd. (tel. 292312), 1mi. east of Stratford on the B4086. Sunset views on the Avon, but can get crowded. £6, each additional person £1. Bargain restaurant (70p burger!). Showers. Tent and 2 people Open Apr.-Oct.

DRINK DEEP ERE YOU DEPART

Faux Tudor fast food and pub grub clogs the Bard's hometown. Small grocery stores hover like itinerant minstrels along Greenhill St., boat vendors sell baguettes to passersby, and a **Safeway Supermarket** beckons on Alcester Rd. Take the Avon shuttle from town center, or walk: the store rests just across the bridge past the rail station (open M-Th and Sa 8am-8pm, F 8am-9pm, Su 10am-4pm). A **Marks and Spencer** sits on Bridge St. (open M-F 9am-7pm, Sa 8:30am-6pm, Su 11am-5pm).

ASK Pizza and Pasta, in Old Red Lion Court off Bridge St. Enjoy heaping portions of Italian food in simple surroundings. Many pizza and pasta options; entrees £5-7.

Hussain's Indian Cuisine, 6a Chapel St. (tel. 267506). Probably Stratford's best Indian cuisine, with a slew of tandoori prepared as you like it. A favorite of Ben Kingsley. 3-course lunch £6. Entrees £6 and up; 15% discount for take-away. Open daily 12:30-2:30pm and 5pm-midnight.

Dirty Duck Pub, Waterside (tel. 297312). River view outside, huge bust of Shakespeare within. Theater crowds abound; drink your cider before the barmaid snatches it away. Traditional pub lunch £2-4.50; double for dinners. Open M-Sa 11am-11pm, Su noon-10pm.

Thai Kingdom, 11 Warwick Rd. (tel. 261103). Tropical plants and friendly staff. Vegetarian entrees £6; meat dishes around £8; 20-25% discount on take-away. Open daily noon-2pm and 6-10:45pm.

Stratford Health Foods Cafe, 10 Greenhill St. Serves quiche, flan, and pasta dishes for £4.50. Take-away bakery includes tofu seaweed pasties and vegan sausage rolls. Open M and W-Sa 9am-4:30pm, Tu 9:30am-4:30pm.

Kingfisher, tucked in an alley at 13 Ely St. A take-away that serves chips with everything (fish, chicken, beans). Cheap, greasy, and very popular. Meals £2-3.60. Open M-F 11:30am-1:45pm and 5-10pm, Sa 11:30am-11pm.

THE GUILDED MONUMENTS

Stratford's sights are best seen before 11am (when the herds of daytrippers have not yet arrived) or after 4pm (when the hurlyburly's done). Bardolatry peaks at 2pm. Five official **Shakespeare properties** (tel. 204016) grace the town: Shakespeare's Birthplace, Anne Hathaway's cottage, the so-called Mary Arden's House and Countryside Museum, Hall's Croft, and New Place or Nash's House. Diehard fans should buy the **combination ticket,** a savings of £8 if you make it to every shrine. *(£10, students and seniors £9, children £5.)* If you don't want to visit them all—dark-timbered roof beams and floors begin to look the same no matter who lived between them—buy a **Shakespeare's Town Heritage Trail ticket,** which covers the town sights—the Birthplace, Hall's Croft, and New Place. *(£7, students and seniors £6, children £3.50.)*

The least crowded way to pay homage to the institution himself is to visit his grave, his little, little grave in **Holy Trinity Church,** Trinity St., though the arched door bulges with massive tour groups at peak hours. *(60p, students and children 40p.)* In town, begin your walking tour at **Shakespeare's Birthplace** (tel. 204016), on Henley St.; enter through the adjoining museum (partial wheelchair access). The Birthplace, half period recreation and half Shakespeare life-and-work exhibition, includes an admonishment to Will's father for putting his rubbish in the street. Sign the guestbook and enter the company of such distinguished pilgrims as Dickens.

On High St. sits the **Harvard House** (tel. 204507), another example of humble Elizabethan lodgings. Period pieces and pewter punctuate this authentic Tudor building, vaguely connected with the man who lends his name to the American college that owns it. The "Harvard-Only" guestbook contains the names of such notables as Nick Grandy. Learn about how John Harvard's grandfather, a butcher, spent the 16th century. *(Open late May to Oct. Tu-Sa 10am-4:30pm, Su 10:30am-4:30pm. Free.)* **New Place,** down the road and opposite, was Stratford's hippest home when Shakespeare bought it in 1597 after writing some hits in London. Only the foundation remains; it can be viewed from the street above. Adjacent to the site is **Nash's House,** containing Tudor furnishings and a local history collection. The disappointing red-brick wall of New Place is only accessible through admission to Nash's House. *(Open Mar.-Oct. M-Sa 9:30am-5pm, Su 10am-5pm; Nov.-Feb. M-Sa 10am-4pm, Su 10:30am-4pm. £3, children £1.50.)* Down Chapel Ln. from Nash's House, the **Great Garden of New Place** offers a peaceful retreat from Stratford's streets. *(Open daily dawn-dusk. Free.)*

The violets have not withered in the **Royal Shakespeare Theatre Gardens,** on the pilgrim's progress between the theater and Holy Trinity. *(Free.)* The riverbank between the RST and Clopton Bridge is a sight in itself. Gazing out at the serene rowers, you'd never guess that approximately six million buses are groaning behind you. The **RST Summer House** (tel. 297671) in the gardens contains a **brass-rubbing studio,** an alternative to plastic Shakespeare memorabilia. *(Open daily Apr.-Sept. 10am-6pm; Oct.-Mar. 11am-4pm. Free, but frottage materials cost £1-10, average £3.)* In the afternoons and after performances, the RSC offers **backstage tours** (tel. 412602) that cram camera-happy groups into the wooden "O"s of the RST and the Swan. *(Tours daily at 1:30 and 5:30pm, and following performances. £4, students and seniors £3.)*

Anne Hathaway's Cottage (tel. 292100), the birthplace of Shakespeare's wife, lies about 1 mi. from Stratford in Shottery; take one of the ill-marked footpaths north. This is probably the thatch-roofed cottage you saw on the travel agent's poster. Admission entitles you to sit on a bench Will may or may not have sat on; view from outside if you've already seen the birthplace. *(Open Mar.-Oct. M-Sa 9am-5pm, Su 9:30am-5pm; Nov.-Feb. M-Sa 9:30am-4pm, Su 10am-4pm. £3.50, children £1.50.)* **Mary Arden's House,** a farmhouse restored in the style a 19th-century entrepreneur determined to be precisely that of Shakespeare's mother, stands 4 mi. from Stratford in Wilmcote. A footpath connects it to Anne Hathaway's Cottage. *(Open Mar.-Oct. M-Sa 9:30am-5pm, Su 10am-5pm; Nov.-Feb. M-Sa 10am-4pm, Su 10:30am-4pm. £4, children £2, families £11.)*

Those seeking non-Shakespearian wonders should try the **Stratford-Upon-Avon Butterfly Farm** (tel. 299288), a collection of exotic butterflies and insects located at Tramway Walk, just across the river from the Tourist Information Center. *(Open daily summer 10am-6pm; winter 10am-dusk. £3.25, students and seniors £2.75, children £2.25.)*

THE PLAY'S THE THING

He was born on Henley St., died at New Place, and lives on at the **Royal Shakespeare Theatre,** towering eloquently over the slanting willows. One of the world's most acclaimed repertories, the **Royal Shakespeare Company** boasts such recent sons as Kenneth Branagh and Ralph Fiennes. Call or visit the **box office** (tel. 295623, 24hr. recording 269191; fax 261974) in advance to reserve seats, which range in price from £5 (standing room) to £49 (superseats). Located in the foyer of the RSC Theatre, the box office is open daily 9:30am-6pm (until 8pm on performance days), and a group gathers outside about 20 minutes before opening for same-day sales. Phones open at 9am. Without payment, seats can only be held for three days. **Matinee** seats are usually available on the day of show. A happy few get customer returns and standing-room tickets later in the day for evening shows; line up 1-2 hours before curtain. **Student and senior** standbys exist in principle. *(£11; available just before curtain—be ready to pounce.)* **Disabled travelers** should call in advance to advise box office of their needs. The RSC's newly extended season lasts from November to September. The RSC also offers daily 45-minute **tours** (tel. 412602; £6.90).

The **Swan Theatre,** resembling a model of Shakespeare's Globe made from giant matchsticks, is a thrust stage designed for RSC productions of Renaissance and Restoration plays. House lights stay on to promote audience involvement; at a recent production, theater-goers were served ale and had a food-fight with the actors. The theatre is located down Waterside, behind the Royal Shakespeare Theatre, on the grounds of the old Memorial Theatre. *(Tickets £9-32, standing room £5.)* It's smaller and often more crowded than the RST; line up early for tickets. The Swan also reserves a few same-day sale tickets. *(£12-14.50.)* Standbys are rare. **The Other Place** is the RSC's newest branch, producing modern dramas, avant-garde premieres, and rarely performed plays. *(Tickets £15-19, standbys £11.)*

Astonishingly, the **Stratford Festival** (for 2 weeks in July) celebrates artistic achievement other than Shakespeare's, from music to poetry. Tickets (when required) can be purchased from the Festival box office (tel. 414513), on Rother St. The modern, well-respected **Shakespeare Centre,** Henley St. (tel. 204016) hosts the annual **Poetry Festival** throughout July and August every Sunday evening. Over the past few years, Seamus Heaney, Ted Hughes, and Derek Walcott have put in appearances. *(Tickets £6-7.)* The Centre also has a library and a bookshop (across the street), and opens archives to students and scholars. For library-privilege inquiries, call well in advance. No Twelfth Night revels here—chimes at midnight in Stratford are next to nil; go to the theater or go to bed early, or what you will.

■ Near Stratford: Warwick and Coventry

Within an hour's drive of Stratford gather dozens of stately homes and castles, all children of England's teeming womb of royal kings. Many historians, architects, and P.R. hacks regard **Warwick Castle** (tel. (01926) 406600), between Stratford and Coventry, as England's finest medieval castle. From the towers of Warwick—especially on an otherwise dreary day—the countryside unfolds like a fairytale kingdom of hobbits and elves. But the farther one plunges into the depths of the castle, the less enchanting the sights become. The exhibitions and medieval reenactments are thrilling for marauding school groups, less so for the average visitor. *(Open daily Mar.-Oct. 10am-6pm; Nov.-Feb. 10am-5pm. Admission is a king's ransom at £9, students £6.65, seniors £6.40, children £5.40; limited wheelchair access; lockers £1.)* Stagecoach **Midland Red buses** journey from Stratford to Warwick every hour (bus #X16, 20min.; bus #18, 40min.; £2.50 return). **Trains** run frequently to Warwick (20min., 10 per day, £2.20). **Ragley Hall** (tel. (01789) 762090), 2 mi. southwest of Alcester and 8 mi. from Stratford on the Evesham Rd. (A435), houses the Earl and Countess of Yarmouth. Set in a 400-acre park, the estate boasts a collection of paintings and a captivating **maze.** *(Open July-Aug. daily, grounds 10am-6pm, house 11am-5pm; same hours Apr.-Oct. Th-Su and bank holidays only. £5, children £3.50.)* Take a bus (M-Sa 5 per day) from Stratford to Alcester, then walk 1 mi. to the gates of Ragley Hall and another half-mile up the drive.

Twenty miles northeast of Stratford burgeons the city of **Coventry.** Bombed during World War II, Coventry has rebuilt itself into a modern city and a major transportation hub. The phrase "sent to Coventry" used to mean the silent treatment, which arose from the Royalist/Puritan antagonism during the Civil War. Now Coventry is united around its two **cathedrals**—the destroyed and the resurrected. The shards of the old cathedral are visible through the glass "west wall" of the new (actually the south wall), which was dedicated in 1962 to the strains of Benjamin Britten's *War Requiem.* The organist also fills the walls with occasional bursts of *Star Trek.* A small bell in the cathedral is inscribed "Peace, *Friede*," a theme which resounds throughout the building. *(Open daily 9am-6pm; £2 requested.)*

Besides the cathedral, Coventry boasts a pedestrian-only downtown area which resembles a jumbled suburban shopping mall, littered with fast-food shops and junk stores. Those staying in Coventry can visit the **tourist office,** Bayley Ln. (tel. (01203) 831345), and pick up *Your Where to Stay Guide.* Once home to **Lady Godiva,** the city honors her memory with a (fully clothed) June parade. The **Museum of British Road Transport,** Hales St. (tel. 832425) home to the world's fastest car, pays tribute to the city's other benefactor: the Daimler Company (free until Mar. 1999).

■ Birmingham

Castle-scouring, monument-seeking history buffs, move on—no great battles were fought in Birmingham, and no major landmarks of medieval times are sited here. Instead, Birmingham, industrial heart of the English Midlands and fondly known as "Brum," is resolutely modern in its style and packs its city center with cell phones and three-piece suits. The U.K.'s second-largest city proper (although the full Greater Manchester area is larger), Birmingham has undergone much civic renovation. Witness the elegant statues and fountain of Victoria Sq., or the chi-chi cafes bordering the redeveloped canalsides. But it isn't until night that the city—fueled by world-class entertainers and some of Britain's best clubs—comes alive.

GETTING THERE

Birmingham snares a clutch of train and bus lines between London, central Wales, southwest England, and all points north. **Trains** (tel. (0345) 484950) leave for London **Euston** (2hr., 2 per hr., £30), **Manchester** Piccadilly (1¾hr., 1 per hr., £18.50, return £19.50), **Liverpool** Lime St. (1½hr., 1 per hr., £17.80, return £15.30), **Nottingham** (1¼hr., 1 per hr., £10.80, return £10.90), and **Oxford** (1¼hr., 1 per hr., £14.50, return £17). **National Express** (tel. (0990) 808080) and **Midland Red West** (tel. (01345) 212555) bus services depart **Digbeth Station** on New St. National Express drives to **London** (3¼hr., 1 per hr., return £13), **Manchester** (2½hr., every 2hr., return £11.25), **Liverpool** (2½hr., 6 per day, return £10), and **Cardiff** (2¼hr., 5 per day, return £17.50). Birmingham is surrounded by major highways (M90, M5, M6, M54) on which **hitching** is nearly impossible, dangerous, and illegal to boot.

ORIENTATION AND PRACTICAL INFORMATION

To reach the city center from Digbeth Bus Station, turn left and follow the signs up the hill to the New St. Rail Station. **New St.** culminates in **Victoria Sq.**; **Corporation** and **High St.** cross New St. near the rail station. Streets beyond the central district can be dangerous. As always, take care at night.

Trains: Most trains (tel. (0345) 484950) arrive at **New St. Station,** one of the busiest in the U.K. The remainder pull into **Moor St.** and **Snow Hill Stations.**

Buses: Digbeth Station (tel. 622 4373). **Luggage storage** £1-3. **National Express** office open M-Sa 7:15am-7pm, Su 8:15am-7pm. Also at Colmore Row and Bull Ring. Open 24hr.

Public Transportation: Centro (tel. 200 2700), in the New St. Station. Stocks local transit map and bus schedules. Bus and train day pass £4, children £2.35; bus only £2.40. Passes can also be purchased from bus drivers. Open M-Tu and F 8:30am-5:30pm, W-Th and Sa 9am-5pm.

Tourist Office: 2 City Arcade (tel. 643 2514; fax 616 1038). Books rooms (10% deposit or £2 booking fee) and provides information on the arts scene. Open M-Sa 9:30am-5:30pm. There's also a branch at **Victoria Sq.** (tel. 693 6300). Open M-Sa 9:30am-6pm, Su 10am-4pm.

Budget Travel: Campus Travel, 90-98 Corporation St. (tel. 233 4611), in the YHA Adventure Shop, under the Virgin Megastore. Open M, W, and F 9:30am-5:30pm, Tu 10am-5:30pm, Th 9:30am-6pm, Sa 9am-6pm.

Financial Services: Barclays, 56 New St. (tel. 480 2351). Open M-Tu and Th-F 9:30am-4:30pm, W 10am-4:30pm.

American Express: Bank House, 8 Cherry St. (tel. 644 5533). Open M-F 8:30am-5:30pm, Sa 9am-5pm.

Emergency: Dial 999; no coins required.

Police: Lloyd House, Colmore Circus, Queensway (tel. 626 5000).

Post Office: 1 Pinfold St., Victoria Sq. (tel. 643 5542). Bureau de change. Open M-F 8:30am-5:30pm, Sa 8:30am-6pm. **Postal Code:** B2 4AA.

Internet Access: Input Output Centres, Central Library, Chamberlain Sq. (tel. 233 2230; fax 233 2250), near Colmore Row. Quick access at a low rate. £2 per 30min., £3 per hr. Open M-F 9am-7pm, Sa 10am-5pm.

Telephone Code: 0121.

ACCOMMODATIONS AND FOOD

Despite its size, Birmingham has no YHA Youth Hostel. Hotels in Birmingham cater to convention-goers, and inexpensive B&Bs are rare. Try to book through the tourist office. B&Bs line Hagley Rd.; take bus #9, 109 or 139. Note that Hagley Rd. is a major thoroughfare, so be prepared to sleep to the sounds of passing traffic. Call ahead to reserve a place at the YMCA or YWCA; they are often booked solid.

YMCA: 200 Bunburg Rd. (tel. 475 6218); take bus #61, 62 or 63 to Church Rd., Northfield. **300 Reservoir Rd.** (tel. 373 1937); take bus #104 to Six Ways in Erdington. Both YMCAs cost £15.50, breakfast included; dinner £3.50; weekly £107, breakfast and dinner included. Women over 21 and men accepted.

YWCA: Alexandra Residential Centre, 27 Norfolk Rd. (tel. 454 8134). Take bus #9 or 19 from Broad or Corporation St. Singles £10; weekly £49. Required membership fee 50p. Key deposit £15. **5 Stone Rd.** (tel. 440 2924). Take bus #61, 62, or 63 to the stop after Belgrave Rd. Ask the bus driver to announce the stop if possible; it's not clearly marked. Be wary in the neighborhood, especially after dark. Singles £9.50; weekly £50. Women and men accepted.

Grasmere Guest House, 37 Serpentine Rd., Harborne (tel./fax 427 4546). Take bus #22, 23, or 103 from Colmore Row to the Duke of York pub. Tidy rooms and a lovely back garden. £15 per person, with bath additional £5 per room.

Lyby, 14-16 Barnsley Rd., Edgbaston (tel. 429 4487). Take bus #9 from Corporation St. to Quantum Pub, walk 50m back, and turn left at the New Talbot. Large rooms, TVs; no private baths. Location allows you to grab a late-night kebab. £12.50.

Brum's eateries conjure up expensive delights as well as the requisite cheap cod and kebabs (*Let's Go* does not recommend eating the two together). What Birmingham is proud of, however, is *balti,* a kind of Kashmiri-Pakistani cuisine cooked in a special pan. Brochures at the tourist office map out the city's numerous Balti restaurants. Vegetarians in the area partake of the multicultural variety at the **Warehouse Café,** 54 Allison St. (tel. 633 0261), off Digbeth, sited above the Friends of the Earth office. (Lunch veggie burgers £2, sandwiches £1.60-2. Open M-F noon-2:30pm and 5:30-9pm, Sa noon-9pm, Su noon-2:30pm.) Bakeries and fruit stores surround the markets.

SIGHTS AND ENTERTAINMENT

Twelve minutes south of town by rail lies **Cadbury World** (tel. 451 4180; http://www.cadbury.co.uk/cadworld.htm), an unabashed celebration of the chocolate firm and its enlightened treatment of workers. The smells alone make fending off the hordes of school children worthwhile. Bring back a 1kg chocolate bar (£4.85) and indulge. Take the train from New St. to Bournville Station. *(Open daily 10am-5pm; closed certain days Nov.-Feb. £6.25, students and seniors £5.25, children £4.50, families £18.60; price includes about 3 free bars of chocolate. Wheelchair accessible.)* The more than 100 jewelry shops that line the **Jewellery Quarter** hammer out almost all of Britain's jewelry. A selection is showcased at the **Jewellery Quarter Discovery Centre,** 77-79 Vyse St., Hockley (tel. 554 3598), signposted from the city center. *(Open M-F 10am-4pm, Sa 11am-5pm. 1hr. tours £2, students, seniors, and children £1.50. Wheelchair accessible.)* The **City Museum and Art Gallery** (tel. 235 2834), at Chamberlain Sq. off Colmore Row, boasts **Big Brum,** a northern cousin to London's Big Ben. The museum houses eclectic collections of costumes, pre-Raphaelite paintings, and William Blake illustrations of Dante's *Inferno. (Open M-Th and Sa 10am-5pm, F 10:30am-5pm, Su 12:30-5pm. Free. Wheelchair accessible.)* Further afield, the **Barber Institute of Fine Arts** (tel. 414 7333), at the University of Birmingham, Edgbaston Park Rd., displays works by artists as diverse as Rubens, Gainsborough, and Magritte. *(Open M-Sa 9:30am-5pm, Su 2-5pm. Free. Wheelchair accessible.)* Take bus #61, 62, or 63 from the city center.

The **Hippodrome Theatre,** Hurst St. (box office tel. 622 7486), continues Birmingham's rich theatrical tradition. Originally a variety music hall featuring big-name vaudevillians, the theater now stages musicals transferred from the West End, and is one of Britain's leading opera houses. *(Open M-Sa 10am-8pm. Tickets £8-28; call about the*

ENGLAND

many child, senior, and disabled person discounts.) A less grandiose, but still celebrated, the-ater in Birmingham is the **Birmingham Repertory Theatre,** Centenary Sq. (box office tel. 236 4455), on Broad St. *(Open M-Sa 9:30am-8pm, Su 4-8pm when there's a per-formance. £4.50, student standby tickets available.)*

The world-class **City of Birmingham Symphony Orchestra** (tel. 212 3333), in the superb Symphony Hall at the Convention Centre on Broad St., takes cues from its much-lauded conductor Sir Simon Rattle. *(Box office open M-Sa 10am-8pm, Su 2-5pm. Tickets £4-25; some student, senior, child, and group discounts; students standbys £7.50 after 1pm on concert days. Wheelchair accessible; facilities for hearing-impaired.)* Birmingham has poured money into revitalizing its 32 mi. of canal; take a walk along the canal bank that parallels Gas St. past the hordes of yuppies for a lovely stroll, or cruise in one of the many boats that go down the canals. *(About £5.)* The **Birmingham Jazz Festival** (tel. 454 7020) brings over 200 jazz bands, singers, and instrumentalists to town dur-ing the first two weeks in July; book through the tourist office.

Birmingham's **club** scene is one of the hippest in the U.K.—forget run-of-the-mill "dance floor classics." The name of the night can be more important than the club itself as an indicator of atmosphere. **Bakers,** 192 Broad St. (tel. 633 3839), hosts *Jel-lybaby* (student night) on Tuesday, *Lovesexy* (female DJs) on Friday, and the packed *Republica* on Saturday, as well as brilliant *Decadence,* one of the finest Wednesday nights in the country. *(Cover £5-8.)* **Stoodibakers,** 162 Broad St. (tel. 643 5100), is Bak-ers's sister pre-club bar and draws a lively crowd into its neon interior. Also on Broad St. lies **The Church** (tel. 633 9273), a veritable shrine for weekend clubbing pilgrim-ages. *(Cover £7-12. Our thumbs-up is only tempered by the prices.)* Clubbers on a budget should grab a guide to the Night Network from the Centro office in New St. Station; **night buses** generally run until 4:30am on Friday and Saturday nights (1 per hr.).

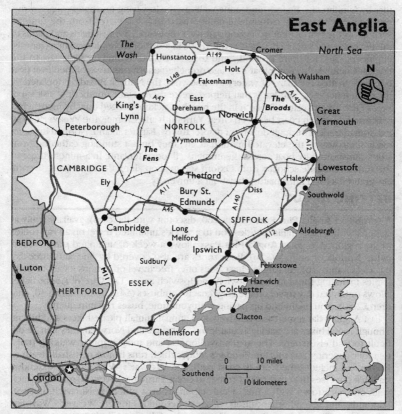

East Anglia

For what is water, children, but a liquid form of Nothing? and what are
Fens, which so imitate in their levelness the natural disposition of water,
but a landscape which, of all landscapes, most approximates Nothing?
—*Graham Swift*, Waterland

The plush green farmlands and delicate watery fens of East Anglia stretch northeast
from London, cloaking the counties of Cambridgeshire, Norfolk, and Suffolk. While
high-tech industry is modernizing the economies of Cambridge and Peterborough,
the college town and cathedral city are still linked by flat fields sliced into irregular

✍ HIGHLIGHTS OF EAST ANGLIA

- Stroll through the colleges (but keep off the grass!) in the university city of **Cambridge** (p. 272), with its oodles of history and bundles of brainpower. Don't miss punting on the Cam, or the exquisite King's College Chapel.
- The cathedral at **Ely** rises out of former fenland like an oasis of civilization, a medieval masterpiece that remains breathtaking to this day (see p. 283).
- The wool-trading town of **Norwich** was the largest city in Anglo-Saxon England. Museums, churches, markets, and festivals maintain the city's link to its past (see p. 285).

tiles by windbreaks, hedges, and stone walls. In the low-lying northwest quarter, rivers course between raised embankments that catch the water from the drained swamps of the Fens. Literally England's newest landscape, the vast fields and plains of the Fenlands were drained as late as the 1820s in a sort of technological neo-Genesis: engineers said "let there be land," and there was land. From Norwich east to the English Channel, the water that long ago drenched enormous areas of medieval peat bogs has created the maze of waterways known as the Norfolk Broads, populated by the continental-style windmills that helped create them. Once numbering 700, survivors of the towery clan still perch in the marshes, acknowledged only by moorhens.

Skirting the north coast between Great Yarmouth and Cromer, the **Weaver's Way** led Roman traders through dozens of market towns. Farther inland, Norman invaders made their way to the elevated mound at Ely; they built a stunning cathedral from stone transported by boat across the immense flooded fenland. In a minor village to the south, renegade scholars from Oxford set up shop along the River Cam. Eventually granted a royal imprimatur, they built a university.

GETTING ABOUT

A **combined Anglia Plus Pass** (about £60, discount with Railcard), available only at stations within East Anglia, entitles you to a week's unlimited travel on all **rail** routes in the region. A **regular Anglia Plus Pass** allows a week of unlimited travel within either Norfolk or Suffolk (£26). Both zones are also covered by one- and three-day passes (£7 and £16). All Anglia Plus passes offer free travel on various local bus companies including those in the Norwich and Ipswich areas. The **Out 'n' About** ticket allows unlimited day travel on the Stagecoach Cambuses (£4.20, students £3.30, children £2.80). You might end up paying with your time; **buses** run infrequently.

East Anglia's flat terrain and relatively low annual rainfall please bikers and hikers. Though rental bikes are readily available in Cambridge and Norwich, they can be difficult to find elsewhere. The area's two longest and most popular walking trails, together covering 200 mi., are **Peddar's Way,** which runs from Knettishall Heath to Holme and includes the Norfolk coast path, and **Weaver's Way,** a newly extended trail that traverses the coast from Cromer to Great Yarmouth. Every 10 mi. or so, each walk crosses a town with a bus or rail station. Tourist offices in Norwich, Bury St. Edmunds, and several other Suffolk villages offer guides for the Weaver's Way. For the Peddar's Way, pick up *Peddar's Way and Norfolk Coast Path* at tourist offices.

CAMBRIDGESHIRE

▓ Cambridge

The winds of change have so often weathered Cambridge that it has grown aslant. This Roman-invaded trading town endured a series of nasty Viking raids before the Normans arrived in the 11th century. The 13th century brought Oxford's refugees, an invasion that would permanently alter the city more than any military conquest. The term-time invaders now come as battalions of bicycling students. In contrast to museum-like Oxford, Cambridge is feistily determined to remain a city under its academic robes. The tourist office will tell you that they manage, not encourage, visitors.

In recent years, Cambridge has ceased to be an exclusive preserve of upper-class sons, although roughly half of its students still come from independent schools and only 40% are women. While tradition mandates that students bedeck themselves with cravat and cane, almost none actually preserve this staid image, except during exams, when they are required to deck themselves out in full regalia. The University itself exists mainly as a bureaucracy that handles the formalities of lectures, degrees, and real estate, leaving to individual colleges the small tutorials and seminars that comprise a Cambridge education. At exams' end, Cambridge explodes with gin-soaked glee, and May Week (in mid-June, naturally) launches a dizzying schedule of cocktail parties; in the middle of the week, students down a health-threatening number of alcoholic beverages on aptly named Suicide Sunday.

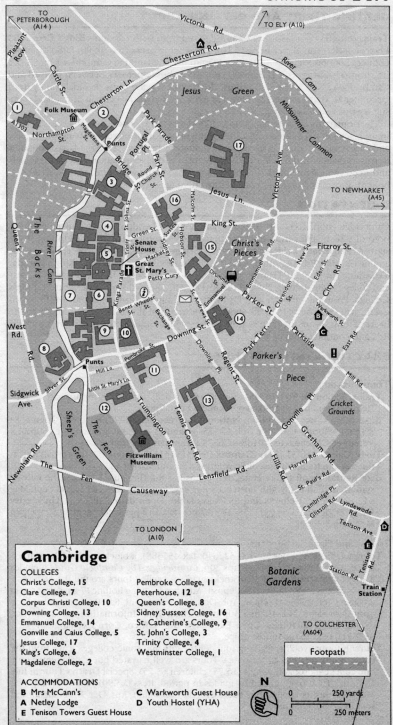

TO PETERBOROUGH (A14)

TO ELY (A10)

Victoria Rd.

Chesterton Rd.

River Cam

Pleasant Row

Castle St.

Chesterton Ln.

Jesus Green

Folk Museum

Magdalene St.

Northampton St.

Punts

Portugal Pl.

Park Parade

Midsummer Common

Victoria Ave.

TO NEWMARKET (A45)

Bridge

Round Church St.

Park St.

Jesus Ln.

Malcolm St.

King St.

Christ's Pieces

The Backs

River Cam

Queen's

St. Johns St.

Trinity St.

Green St.

Senate House

Market St.

Great St. Mary's

Petty Cury

Sidney St.

Hobson St.

Emmanuel Rd.

New St.

Fitzroy St.

Eden St.

City Rd.

King's Parade

Benet St.

Wheeler St.

Corn Exchange St.

St. Andrews St.

Downing St.

Emmanuel St.

Drummer St.

Parker St.

Clarendon St.

Warkworth St.

Parkside

East Rd.

Mill Rd.

West Rd.

Silver St.

Pembroke St.

Mill Ln.

Punts

Little St. Mary's Ln.

Downing Pl.

Regent St.

Park Terr.

Parker's Piece

Gonville Pl.

Cricket Grounds

Sidgwick Ave.

Newnham Rd.

Sheep's Green

The Fen

Trumpington St.

Tennis Court Rd.

Fitzwilliam Museum

Lensfield Rd.

The Fen

Causeway

Hills Rd.

Gresham Rd.

Harvey Rd.

St. Paul's Rd.

Cambridge Pl.

Glisson Rd.

Lyndewode Rd.

Tenison Ave.

Tenison Rd.

TO LONDON (A10)

Botanic Gardens

Station Rd.

Train Station

TO COLCHESTER (A604)

ENGLAND

Cambridge

COLLEGES

Christ's College, 15
Clare College, 7
Corpus Christi College, 10
Downing College, 13
Emmanuel College, 14
Gonville and Caius College, 5
Jesus College, 17
King's College, 6
Magdalene College, 2

Pembroke College, 11
Peterhouse, 12
Queen's College, 8
Sidney Sussex Colege, 16
St. Catherine's College, 9
St. John's College, 3
Trinity College, 4
Westminster College, 1

ACCOMMODATIONS

B Mrs McCann's
A Netley Lodge
E Tenison Towers Guest House

C Warkworth Guest House
D Youth Hostel (YHA)

Footpath

N

0   250 yards
0   250 meters

GETTING THERE AND GETTING ABOUT

Trains (tel. (0345) 484950) to Cambridge run from both London's **King's Cross** and **Liverpool St.** (1hr., 1 per hr., £15.10). **National Express** (tel. (0990) 808080) buses connect London **Victoria Station** and Drummer St. Station in Cambridge (2hr., 1 per hr., from £8). **Stagecoach Express** runs 10-12 buses per day between Oxford and Cambridge (2¾hr., £6.40). **Cambus,** the town's service, runs regional routes from Drummer St. (fares vary). The **Slow Coach** stops here on its circuit of England (consult **By Bus and Coach,** p. 33).

The primary mode of transport in Cambridge is the **bicycle.** This city claims to have more bikes per person than any other in Britain. A confusing series of one-way streets and an armada of teenagers used to riding on the other side of the road make summer transport decidedly difficult. Chaos. If you plan to ride, emphatically use hand signals and heed road signs; most do not. Pedestrians should look both ways—as well as behind, above, and under—twice before crossing.

ORIENTATION

Cambridge (pop. 105,000), about 60 mi. north of London, has two main avenues, both of which suffer from multiple personality disorder. The main shopping street starts at **Magdalene Bridge** and becomes **Bridge, Sidney, St. Andrew's, Regent St.,** and finally **Hills Rd.** The other—alternately **St. John's St., Trinity St., King's Parade, Trumpington St.,** and **Trumpington Rd.**—is the academic thoroughfare, with several colleges lying between it and the River Cam. The two streets merge at **St. John's College.** From the bus station at **Drummer St.,** a hop-skip-and-jump down **Emmanuel St.** will land you right in the shopping district near the tourist office. To get to the heart of things from the train station, go west along **Station Rd.,** turn right onto **Hills Rd.,** and continue straight ahead.

PRACTICAL INFORMATION

Transportation

Trains: Station Rd. (tel. (0345) 484950). Open daily 5am-11pm to purchase tickets. Help desk open M-Sa 8:30am-6:30pm, Su 11am-7pm.

Buses: Drummer St. Station. National Express (tel. (0990) 808080). Open M-Sa 8:15am-5:30pm. **Cambus** (tel. 423554) handles city and area service (60p-£1). **Whippet Coaches** (tel. (01480) 463792) runs daytrips from town.

Taxis: Cabco (tel. 312444). **Camtax** (tel. 313131). Both open 24hr. Or hail one at the bus and train stations, or St. Andrew's St. and Market Sq.

Bike Rental: Geoff's Bike Hike, 65 Devonshire Rd. (tel. 365629), near the railway station, behind the youth hostel. £6 per day; June-Aug. £15 per week, Sept.-May £12 per week. Helmets and locks available. Open daily 9am-6pm. **University Cycle,** 9 Victoria Ave. (tel. 355517). £7 per day, £12 per week; deposit £25. Open M-Sa 9am-5:30pm.

Tourist and Financial Services

Tourist Office: Wheeler St. (tel. 322640; fax 457588), a block south of the marketplace. Mini-guide 40p, town maps 20p. *Cambridge: The Complete Guide* includes a street-indexed map (£1.30). Stocks maps of cycling tours around the area (£4). Books rooms for £3 and a 10% deposit. Advance booking hotline (7 days or more in advance; tel. 457581). Open Apr.-Oct. M-F 10am-6pm, Sa 10am-5pm, Su 11am-4pm; Nov.-Mar. M-F 10am-5:30pm, Sa 10am-5pm. Information on Cambridge events also available at **Corn Exchange Box Office,** Corn Exchange St. (tel. 357851), next to the tourist office.

Tours: Informative 2hr. walking tours of the city and some colleges leave from the main tourist office. Call for times. Tours are well narrated but usually enter only one college—probably King's (£5.75, children £3.75). Special **Drama Tour** in July and Aug. Tu at 6:30pm, led by guides in period dress (£3.90). **Guide Friday** (tel. 362444) runs its familiar **bus tours** every 15 or 30min. Apr.-Oct. £7, students and seniors £5.50, children £2.

Budget Travel: STA Travel, 38 Sidney St. (tel. 366966). Open M-W and F 9am-5:30pm, Th 10am-5:30pm, Sà 10am-4pm. **Campus Travel,** 5 Emmanuel St. (tel. 324283). Open M-Tu and Th-F 9am-5:30pm, W 10am-5:30pm, Sa 10am-5pm. Also on Bridge St. (tel. 360201), with same hours.

Financial Services: Thomas Cook, 18 Market St. (tel. 366141). Open M-Tu and Th-Sa 9am-5:30pm, W 10am-5:30pm. **Lloyds,** 3 Sidney St. (tel. 365141). Open M-Tu and Th-F 9am-5pm, W 9:30am-5pm, Sa 10am-1pm.

American Express: 25 Sidney St. (tel. 351636). Open M-W and F 9am-5:30pm, Th 9:30am-5:30pm, Sa 9am-5pm.

Local Services

Camping: YHA Adventure Shop, 6-7 Bridge St. (tel. 353956). The place for camping, hiking, and backpacking equipment. Open M-Tu and Th-F 9:30am-5:30pm, W 9:30am-6pm, Sa 9am-6pm.

Launderette: Monarch Coin-Op, 161 Mill Rd. (tel. 247599).

Emergency and Communications

Emergency: Dial 999; no coins required.

Police: Parkside (tel. 358966).

Hotlines: Samaritans (crisis; tel. 364455). Open 24hr. **AIDS** (tel. (0800) 697697). **Alcoholics Anonymous** (tel. 833900). **Crime Victims** (tel. 363024). **Rape Crisis** (tel. 358314). **Victim Support** (tel. 329000). **Young People's Counselling and Information Service** (tel. 316488).

Hospital: Addenbrookes, Hills Rd. (tel. 245151). Catch Cambus #95 from Emmanuel St. (95p).

Post Office: 9-11 St. Andrew's St. (tel. 323325). Open M-Tu and Th-F 9am-5:30pm, W 9:30am-5pm, Sa 9am-12:30pm. *Poste Restante* and bureau de change. **Postal Code:** CB2 3AA.

Internet Access: CBI, 32 Mill Rd. (tel. 576306), near the hostel. 10p per min.

Telephone Code: 01223.

ACCOMMODATIONS

The lesson this university town teaches budget travelers is to book ahead, especially in summer. Rooms are scarce, which makes prices high and quality remarkably low. Most B&Bs aren't in the town center; many around **Portugal St.** and **Tenison Rd.** house students during the academic year and are open to visitors in July and August. If a house is full, ask about others in the neighborhood (B&Bs are often not labeled as such). Check the comprehensive list in the tourist office window after they close, or pick up their guide (50p).

YHA Youth Hostel, 97 Tenison Rd. (tel. 354601; fax 312780). Relaxed, welcoming atmosphere. 100 beds, mostly 3-4 beds to a room; a few doubles. Well-equipped kitchen, laundry facilities, TV lounge. Small lockers in some rooms. More showers wouldn't hurt. Bureau de change. Cafeteria could pass as a restaurant in its own right. £10.70, under 18 £7.30. Breakfast £3, packed lunch £2.55-3.35, 3-course evening meal £4. Luggage storage available. No curfew or lockout. Crowded Mar.-Oct.; in the summer, call a week ahead with a credit card.

Home from Home B&B, Liz Fasano, 39 Milton Rd. (tel. 323555). A 20min. walk from the city center. Pricey, but worthwhile. Sparkling, light-filled rooms, wicker chairs, and an exceptionally accommodating hostess. 2 doubles and 1 twin; rooms include TV and showers. Full English breakfast with fresh fruit, cereal, and croissants. Yum. Biscuits and hot chocolate in every room. Yum. Singles £30; doubles £40; discounts for longer stays. Call ahead for reservations. Yum.

Mrs. McCann, 40 Warkworth St. (tel. 314098). A jolly hostess with comfortably lived-in twin rooms in a quiet neighborhood near the bus station. £15 per person; discount after 3 nights. Breakfast included.

Warkworth Guest House, Warkworth Terr. (tel. 363682). 15 sunny, white and fresh rooms near the bus station. TV in every room. Singles £22.50, with bath £30; twins £35, with bath £45. Breakfast included; packed lunch on request.

ENGLAND

Tenison Towers Guest House, 148 Tenison Rd. (tel. 566511). Fresh flowers grace rooms near the train station; Mrs. Tombo keeps añ impeccable house. Singles £15-22; doubles £28-32; triples £42; quads £48-56.

Netley Lodge, Mr. and Mrs. Mikolajczyk, 112 Chesterton Rd. (tel. 363845). Plush red carpets and a conservatory lush with greenery welcome you to sunny rooms in a large Victorian home. Roses inside and out. Mrs. M. is a study in elegance. Singles £22; doubles £37, with bath £45.

The tourist office lists campsites in the Cambridge area (30p). To reach the **Highfield Farm Camping Park,** Long Rd., Comberton (tel. 262308), head west on A603 for 3 mi., then turn right on B1046 to Comberton for 1 mi.; or take Cambus #118 from the Drummer St. bus station (every 45min.). Enjoy flush toilets (whee!), showers, and laundry (call ahead; £4-5 per tent, £8-9 with car). The **Camping and Caravanning Club Site,** 19 Cabbage Moor, Great Shelford (tel. 841185), has toilets, showers, a washing machine, and facilities for travelers with disabilities. Head 3 mi. south on the M11, then left onto the A1301 for three quarters of a mile, or take Cambus #103. (£4.30 per person plus £3.50 pitch fee; call before arrival in July and Aug.; open Mar.-Oct.)

FOOD

Market Square has bright pyramids of fruit and vegetables for the budgetarian. The produce is far superior to that of the supermarkets (open M-Sa usually 8am-5pm). For vegetarian and wholefood groceries, try **Arjuna,** 12 Mill Rd. (tel. 364845; M-F 9:30am-6pm, Sa 9am-5:30pm). Students buy gin and cornflakes at **Sainsbury's,** 44 Sidney St., the only grocery store in the middle of town (open M-F 8am-8pm, Sa 8am-7pm, Su 10am-4pm). Curry and Greek restaurants sate the curious tastebuds of hungry students (make sure that the Christ's College football club has not arrived on their ritual curry night out). South of town, Hills and Mill Rd. brim with good, cheap restaurants.

Rainbow's Vegetarian Bistro, 9a King's Parade (tel 321551). Duck under the rainbow sign on King's Parade. A tiny, creative burrow featuring delicious international vegan and vegetarian fare, all for £5.45. Try the Cypriot-style *moussaka.* Open daily 9am-9pm.

Nadia's, 11 St. John's St. (tel. 460961). An uncommonly good bakery with reasonable prices. Wonderful flapjacks and quiches (65p-£1). You'll get smiles from the chocolate-chocolate-chip cookie. Sandwiches and muffins that are a brunch unto themselves. Take-away only; sit outside Trinity across the street or try the branches on King's Parade and Silver St. Open June-Aug. M-Sa 8am-6pm, Su 8am-5pm; Sept.-May M-Sa 7:30am-5:30pm, Su 7:30am-5pm.

The Little Tea Room, 1 All Saints' Passage, off Trinity St. As hopelessly precious as it sounds; tip-top teas served in a teeny basement room opposite Trinity. "Post-tutorial tea" £5 (pot of tea, scone, cucumber sandwich, jam, and choice of cake). Open M-Sa 9:30am-5:30pm, Su 11:30am-6pm.

Tatties, 26-28 Regent St. Yummy baked potatoes in a roof garden over Downing College. Platters of large vegetable skewers (£4-5). Hot potato with butter (£2), more studly spuds (pineapple or curry potatoes) are £3.25. Freshly squeezed orange juice (£2.25). Open daily 10am-10:30pm.

Hobbs' Pavillion, Parker's Piece (tel. 367480), off Park Terr. Renowned for imaginative, overpowering, rectangular pancakes. The English like their pancakes thin, like French crepes. Mars Bar and cream pancake £4—don't expect to feel like eating again for 2 weeks. Open Tu-Sa noon-2:15pm and 7-9:45pm.

Gallena Restaurant-Café, 33 Bridge St. (tel. 362054). Elegant cafe serves up artistic culinary creations in a lovely setting overlooking the river. Pizza Gauguin (with seafood and herbs) £5. Open daily 11am-11pm.

Clowns Coffee Bar, 54 King St. (tel. 355711). A meeting place for foreigners, bozos, and beautiful people. Clowns line the walls. Practice your Esperanto over a mean cappuccino (£1.10), quiche (£2), or cake (£1.50). Open daily 9am-midnight.

PUBS

Cantabrigian hangouts offer good pub crawling year-round, though they lose some of their character and their best customers in summer. Most pubs stay open from 11am to 11pm, noon to 10:30pm on Sundays. A few close from 3 to 7pm, especially on Sundays. The local brewery, Greene King, supplies many of the pubs with the popular bitters IPA (India Pale Ale) and Abbott. Students drink at the **Anchor,** Silver St. (tel. 353554), pouring their pints onto Silver St. Bridge when the weather permits. The other undergraduate watering hole, the **The Mill,** Mill Ln. (tel. 357026), off Silver St. Bridge, claims the riverside park as its own on spring nights for punt- and people-watching. In the summer, both fill with the odd remaining Cantabrigian and hordes of overdressed international teenagers. The brew becomes even stranger once you add the cows that roam the river banks. Beware the remains of the day. A quieter riverside alternative is **The Rat and Parrot,** Thompsons Ln. (tel. 311701), where a crowd of all ages sips cider overlooking the Cam and Jesus Green.

At 3-4 King St. wobbles the **Cambridge Arms** (tel. 505015), a large renovated brewery that hides a courtyard and a dim beer garden. **The Eagle,** Benet St. (tel. 505020) off King's Parade, was the spot where Watson and Crick first rushed in breathless to announce their discovery of the DNA double helix. The barmaid insisted they settle their four-shilling back-tab before she'd serve them a toast. Farther along rests the **Champion of the Thames,** 68 King St. (tel. 352043), a broom closet of a pub—groups of more than five might not even fit. King St. gets a bit dodgy around closing time on Saturday nights, so take care. A favorite with Magdalene men and Cambridge secretarial college women, the **Pickerel** (tel. 355068), on Bridge St., where it turns into Magdalene St., holds the grand distinction of being Cambridge's oldest pub. **The Maypole** (tel. 352999), on Portugal Pl. between Bridge and New Park St., celebrates a lengthy "happy hour" (5-11pm) and sports a billiards table. Locals and collegiate crew members pack the **Free Press** (tel. 368337), a non-smoking pub on Prospect Row behind the police station; tourists might not feel comfortable walking in alone. The **Burleigh Arms,** 9-11 Newmarket Rd. (tel. 301547), serves up beer and lager to its primarily gay clientele. Amble to the **Bird in Hand** or **The Town and Gown** near the Elizabeth Bridge on New Market St. (tel. 354034), where gay men gather and have a pint in the beer garden. Summer months can be markedly mellow.

SIGHTS

Cambridge is an architect's fantasia, packing some of the most breathtaking monuments to English aesthetics into less than one square mile. The soaring grandeur of King's College Chapel and the postcard-familiar St. John's Bridge of Sighs are sightseeing staples, but if you explore some of the more obscure quads, you'll find delicacies undiscovered by most visitors.

If you're pressed for time, visit at least one chapel (preferably King's College), one garden (try Christ's), one library (Trinity's is the most interesting), and one dining hall (though many are emphatically closed to visitors). Most historic university buildings line the east side of the Cam between Magdalene Bridge and Silver St. On both sides of the river, the gardens, meadows, and cows of the **Backs** bring a pastoral air to Cambridge. If you have time for only a few colleges, **King's, Trinity, Queens', Christ's, St. John's,** and **Jesus** should top your list, though the I-think-I'll-do-Europe-in-a-week traveler could trample through 12 or 14 colleges in a few hours: most cluster around the center of town. Five of the most prestigious and most photographed colleges (King's, Trinity, Queens', St. John's, and Clare) charge admission; some planning can help you allocate those precious pence.

The University of Cambridge has three eight-week terms: Michaelmas (Oct.-Dec.), Lent (Jan.-Mar.), and Easter (Apr.-June). Visitors can gain access to most of the college grounds daily from 9am to 5:30pm, though many close to sightseers during the Easter term, and virtually all are closed during exam period (mid-May to mid-June); your safest bet is to call ahead (tel. 331100) for hours. Plump bowler-bedecked ex-servicemen, called porters, maintain security. Those who look and act like a student (i.e., those who wear no traveler's backpack, no camera, and, for heaven's sake, no Cambridge sweatshirt) are often able to wander freely through most college grounds even after hours (never on the carefully tended lawns). In the summer, a few undergrads stay to work or study, but most skip town, leaving it to mobs of teenage students. Some university buildings shut down during vacations.

King's College

King's College, on King's Parade, is the proud possessor of the university's most famous chapel, a spectacular Gothic monument. In 1441, Henry VI cleared away most of the center of medieval Cambridge for the foundation of King's College, and he intended this chapel to be England's finest. Although Hank wanted the inside to remain unadorned, his successors spent nearly £5000 carving an elaborate interior. If you stand at the southwest corner of the courtyard, you can see where Henry's master mason John Wastell (who also worked on the cathedrals of Peterborough and Canterbury) left off and where work under the Tudors began. The earlier stone is off-white, the later, dark. The interior of the chapel consists of one huge chamber cleft by a carved wooden choir screen, one of the purest examples of the early Renaissance style in England. Crowned by trumpeting angels, the screen's designs were destroyed by their Italian creators, who didn't want their work replicated. The heralding angels flit about against the backdrop of the world's largest fan-vaulted ceiling; Wordsworth described the ceiling as a "branching roof self-poised, and scooped into ten thousand cells where light and shade repose." Stained-glass windows depicting the life of Jesus were preserved from the iconoclasm of the English Civil War, allegedly because John Milton, then Cromwell's secretary, groveled on their behalf. Symbols of Henry VIII's reign abound; look for the Tudor roses.

Behind the altar hangs Rubens' magnificent *Adoration of the Magi* (1639), a gift to the College and the most expensive painting ever auctioned at the time of its purchase. The canvas has been protected by an electronic alarm since a crazed would-be stonemason attacked it with a chisel several years ago. Free musical recitals often play at the chapel—pick up a schedule at the entrance. Enjoy the classic view of the chapel and of the adjacent **Gibbs Building** from the river. As you picnic by the water, think of those who have gone before you: E.M. Forster was an undergraduate at King's, basing *The Longest Journey* and *Maurice* on his Cambridge days; Salman Rushdie walked the King's courts before running from the Court of Allah. *(College open M-F 9:30am-4:30pm, Su 10am-5pm. £3, students and children £2, under 12 free with adults. Guided 45min. tours £1.50, under 12 free. Check notices in the chapel for daily times. Chapel open term-time M-Sa 9:30am-3:30pm, Su 1:15-2:15pm and 5-5:30pm; chapel and exhibitions open college vacations 9:30am-4:30pm. Free.)* In early June the university posts the names and final grades of every student in the Georgian **Senate House** opposite the King's College chapel, designed by Gibbs and built in the 1720s; about a week later, degree ceremonies are held there.

Trinity College

Trinity College, on Trinity St. (tel. 338400), holds the largest purse at the University. The college's status as the wealthiest at Cambridge has become legendary—myth-mongers claim that it was once possible to walk from Cambridge to Oxford without stepping off Trinity land. Founded in 1546 by Henry VIII, Trinity once specialized in literati (alums include George Herbert, John Dryden, Lord Byron, Lord Tennyson, and A.E. Housman), but in this century has spat forth scientists and philosophers (Ernest

---

M.A.? B.S.?

Cambridge graduates are eligible for the world's easiest master's degrees: after spending three and one-third years out in the Real World, a graduate sends £15 to the university. Provided that said graduate is not in the custody of one of Her Majesty's Gaols, the grad receives an M.A. without further ado, making Cambridge the world's easiest correspondence school.

Rutherford, Ludwig Wittgenstein, G.E. Moore, and Bertrand Russell). Inside the courtyard, in a florid fountain built in 1602, Byron used to bathe nude. The eccentric young poet lived in Nevile's Court and shared his rooms with a pet bear, whom he claimed would take his fellowship exams for him. Generations later, Prince Charles was an average anthropology student. The expanse of Trinity's **Great Court**—the largest yard in Cambridge—encompasses an area so large you can almost fail to notice its utter lack of straight lines and symmetry. The courtyard race in *Chariots of Fire* is set here, although Eton College, a university preparatory school, took its place for the filming. What William Wordsworth called the "loquacious clock that speaks with male and female voice" still strikes 24 times each noon. Sir Isaac Newton, who lived on the first floor of E-entry for 30 years, originally measured the speed of sound by stamping his foot in the cloister along the north side of the court. Underneath the courtyards lie the well-hidden, well-stocked Trinity wine cellars. The college recently purchased over £20,000 worth of port that won't be drinkable until 2020.

Amble through the college toward the river to reach the reddish stone walls of the impressive **Wren Library**. Treasures in this naturally lit building include A.A. Milne's handwritten manuscript of *Winnie the Pooh* and less momentous works such as John Milton's *Lycidas*. The collection also contains works by Byron, Tennyson, and Thackeray. German-speakers certain of the existence of books might look for Wittgenstein's journals. His phenomenal *Philosophical Investigations* was conceived here during years of intense discussion with G.E. Moore and students in his top-floor K-entry rooms. *(Library open M-F noon-2pm; Hall open 3-5pm; chapel and courtyard open 10am-6pm. College and library closed during exams. £1.75.)*

St. John's, Queens', St. Catherine's, and Clare Colleges

Established in 1511 by Lady Margaret Beaufort, mother of Henry VIII, **St. John's College** (tel. 338600) is one of seven Cambridge colleges founded by women (but *for* men). The striking brick-and-stone gatehouse bears Lady Margaret's heraldic emblem. St. John's centers around a paved plaza rather than a grassy courtyard, and its two most interesting buildings stand across the river from the other colleges. A copy of Venice's Bridge of Sighs connects the older part of the college to the towering neo-Gothic extravagance of New Court, likened by philistines to a wedding cake in silhouette. *(Chapel open M-Sa 9:30am-6:30pm, Su 10:30am-6:30pm. Evensong at 6:30pm most nights. College open daily during vacation. £1.50, seniors and children 75p, families £3.)* Next door, you can see more adventurous college architecture, the modern **Cripps Building**, with clever bends that create three distinct courts under the shade of a noble willow. The **School of Pythagoras**, a 12th-century pile of wood and stone rumored to be the oldest complete building in Cambridge, hides in St. John's Gardens. *(Courtyard and some buildings open until 5pm.)*

Queens' College (tel. 335511), was founded not once, but twice—by painted Queen Margaret of Anjou in 1448 and again by Elizabeth Woodville in 1465. It has the only unaltered Tudor courtyard in Cambridge, housing the half-timbered President's Gallery. The **Mathematical Bridge**, just past Cloister Court, was built in 1749 without a single bolt or nail, relying only on mathematical principle. A meddling Victorian dismantled the bridge to see how it worked and the inevitable occurred—he couldn't put it back together without using a steel rivet every two inches. *(College open daily 1:45-4:30pm; during summer vacation also 10:30am-12:45pm. Closed during exams. £1.)*

Clare College (tel. 333200), founded in 1326 by the thrice-widowed, 29-year-old Lady Elizabeth de Clare, has preserved an appropriate coat of arms: golden teardrops on a black border. Across Clare Bridge (the most elegant on the river) lie the **Clare Gardens**. *(Open M-F 2-4:45pm; during summer vacation also 10am-4:30pm.)* Walk through Clare's **Old Court** for a view of the University Library, where 82 mi. of shelves hold books arranged according to size rather than subject. George V called it "the greatest erection in Cambridge." *(College open daily 10am-5pm. £1.50, under 10 free. Old Court open during exams after 4:45pm to groups of 3 or fewer.)*

ENGLAND

Christ's, Jesus, Magdalene, Peterhouse, and Robinson Colleges

Christ's College (tel. 334900), founded as "God's-house" in 1448 and renamed in 1505, has won fame for its association with the poet John Milton and for its gardens. *(Open in summer M-F 10:30am-noon; in session M-F 10:30am-12:30pm and 2-4pm.)* To reach the gardens, walk under the lovely Neoclassical Fellows Building dubiously accredited to Inigo Jones. Charles Darwin dilly-dallied through Christ's before informing man he was little more than a clean-shaven ape with a tie. His rooms (unmarked and closed to visitors) were on G staircase in First Court. **New Court,** on King St., is one of the most stunning modern structures in Cambridge; its symmetrical, gray concrete walls and black-curtained windows look like the whelp of an Egyptian pyramid, a Polaroid camera, and a typewriter. Bowing to pressure from aesthetically-offended Cantabrigians, a new wall has been built to block the view of the building from all sides except the inner courtyard of the college. The college closes during exams, save for access to the chapel (inquire at the porter's desk).

Cloistered on a secluded site, **Jesus College** (tel. 339339) has preserved an enormous amount of unaltered medieval work, dating from 1496. Beyond the long, high-walled walk called the "Chimny" lies a three-sided court fringed with colorful gardens. Through the archway on the right sit the remains of a gloomy medieval nunnery. The Pre-Raphaelite stained glass of Burne-Jones and ceiling decorations by William "Wallpaper" Morris festoon the chapel. Sterne made a sentimental journey through Jesus, along with Malthus, Coleridge, and Alistair *"Masterpiece Theatre"* Cooke. *(Courtyard open until 6pm; closed during exams.)*

Inhabiting buildings from a 15th-century Benedictine hostel, **Magdalene College** (MAUD-lin; tel. 332100), founded in 1524, has acquired an aristocratic reputation. Don't forget to take a peek at the **Pepys Library** (ridiculously labeled **Bibliotheca Pepysiana**) in the second court; the library displays the noted statesman and prolific diarist's collection in their original cases. Pepys wrote his diaries in shorthand, which took three years to decipher. *(Library open Easter-Aug. 11:30am-12:30pm and 2:30-3:30pm; Sept.-Easter M-Sa 2:30-5:30pm. Free. Courtyards closed during exams.)*

Thomas Gray wrote his *Elegy in a Country Churchyard* while staying in **Peterhouse,** on Trumpington St., the oldest and smallest college, founded in 1294. In contrast, **Robinson College,** across the river on Grange Rd., distinguishes itself by being the college's newest. Founded in 1977, this mod-medieval brick pastiche sits just behind the university library. Bronze plants writhe about the door of the college chapel, which features some fascinating stained glass. James Stirling's **History Faculty Building,** between West Rd. and Sidgwick Ave., once provoked much debate about its aesthetic merits; of its leaky roof, there were never any doubts.

Corpus Christi, Pembroke, Emmanuel and Downing Colleges

Corpus Christi College (tel. 338000), founded in 1352 by the common people, contains the dreariest and oldest courtyard in Cambridge, forthrightly called Old Court and unaltered since its enclosure. The library maintains the snazziest collection of Anglo-Saxon manuscripts in England, including the Parker Manuscript of the *Anglo-Saxon Chronicle*. Alums include Sir Francis Drake and Christopher Marlowe. The 1347 **Pembroke College** next door harbors the earliest architectural effort of Sir Christopher Wren and counts Edmund Spenser, Ted Hughes, and Eric Idle among its grads. *(Courtyards open until 6pm; closed during exams; call ahead for hours—stone repairs could be delayed and inhibit access.)*

A chapel designed by Sir Christopher Wren dominates the front court of **Emmanuel College** (tel. 334200). Emmanuel, founded in 1584, on St. Andrew's St. at Downing St., and **Downing College** (tel. 334800), founded in 1807, just to the south along Regent St., are both pleasantly isolated (courtyards open until 6pm; chapel open when not in use). Downing's austere Neoclassical buildings flank an immense lawn (open daily until 6pm; dining hall open when not in use; closed during exams). John Harvard, benefactor of a certain New England university, attended Emmanuel; a stained-glass panel depicting Harvard graces the college chapel. Among alumni with more tangible accomplishments is John Cleese.

Museums, Churches, and Gardens

The **Round Church (Holy Sepulchre),** Bridge St. and St. John's St., one of five circular churches surviving in England, was built in 1130 (and later rebuilt) on the pattern of the Church of the Holy Sepulchre in Jerusalem. The pattern merits comparison with **St. Benet's Church,** a rough Saxon church on Benet St. The tower of St. Benet's, built in 1050, is the oldest structure in Cambridge. The tower once had a spire, but spire-building was a technology the Normans lacked, so they spitefully knocked it down: "Saxon freaks! We'll show *you!*" The tower of the **Church of St. Mary the Great,** just off King's Parade, lets you ogle the mind-boggling collection of colleges and 123 steps in a single glance. *(Tower open M-Sa 10am-5pm, Su 12:30-5pm. £1.50, children 50p.)*

You can easily get caught up in the splendor of the colleges, but try also to take in a few museums. The **Fitzwilliam Museum,** Trumpington St. (tel. 332900), a 10-minute walk down the road from King's College, dwells within an immense Roman-style building; the mosaic tile floors alone should be on display. Inside, an opulent marble foyer leads to an impressive collection including paintings by Michelangelo, Cezanne, Picasso, Degas, and Monet. A goulash of Egyptian, Chinese, Japanese and Greek antiquities bides its time downstairs, coupled with an extensive collection of 16th-century German armor. Check out the illuminated manuscripts under protective cloths. The drawing room displays William Blake's books and woodcuts. *(Open Tu-Sa 10am-5pm, Su 2:15-5pm. Free, but suggested donation £3.)* Call to inquire about lunchtime and evening concerts. *(Guided tours Sa 2:30pm. £3.)*

The **Museum of Zoology** (tel. 336650), off Downing St., houses a fine assemblage of wildlife specimens in a modern, well-lit building. *(Open M-F 2:15-4:45pm. Free. Wheelchair accessible.)* Across the road, on Downing St. opposite Corn Exchange St., the **Museum of Archaeology and Anthropology** (tel. 333516) contains an excellent display of prehistoric artifacts from American, African, Pacific, and Asian cultures, as well as exhibits on Cambridge through the ages. Special exhibits change regularly. *(Open mid-June to Aug. M-F 10:30am-5pm, Sa 10am-12:30pm; Sept. to mid-June M-F 2-4pm, Sa 10am-12:30pm. Free. Wheelchair accessible, but call ahead.)* **Kettle's Yard** (tel. 352124), at the corner of Castle and Northampton St., houses early 20th-century art. *(House open Apr.-Sept. Tu-Sa 1:30-4:30pm, Su 2-4:30pm; Oct.-Mar. Tu-Su 2-4pm; gallery open year-round Tu-Sa 12:30-5:30pm, Su 2-5:30pm. Free.)* The **Scott Polar Research Institute,** Lensfield Rd. (tel. 336540), commemorates icy expeditions with photographic and artistic accounts and memorabilia. *(Open M-Sa 2:30-4pm. Free.)*

Cambridge's **Botanic Gardens** (tel. 336265; enter from Hill Rd. or Bateman St.) were ingeniously designed by Henslow, Sir Joseph Hooker's father-in-law (c. 1846). When the wind gets rolling, the scented gardens turn into a perfume factory. *(Open daily 10am-4pm or 6pm, depending on season. £1.50, seniors and under 18 £1.)*

ENTERTAINMENT

Punts (gondola-like boats) are a favored form of entertainment in Cambridge. Punters take two routes—one from Magdalene Bridge to Silver Street, and the other from Silver Street along the River Granta (as the Cam is called when it passes out of town) to Grantchester. On the first route—the shorter, busier, and more interesting of the two—you'll pass the colleges and the Backs. Beware: punt-bombing, in which students jump from bridges into the river next to a punt (thereby tipping its occupants into the Cam) has been raised to an art form. **Tyrell's,** Magdalene Bridge (tel. 363080), has punts and rowboats for £8 an hour, plus a £30 deposit. Student-punted **guided tours** (about £10), are another option for those unwilling to risk a plunge. Inquire at the tourist office.

Those who prefer to drink to **live music** can take their choice of pubs. The newest on the local circuit is **Fresher & Firkin,** 16 Chesterton Rd. (tel. 324325), a link in a London-based chain that mixes music nights with comedy and party specials—Friday is the biggest night. To the east, **The Geldart,** 1 Ainsworth St. (tel. 355983), features jaunty Irish folk every Thursday night. **The Junction,** Clifton Rd. (tel. 412600), off Cherry Hinton Rd. south of town, proves a popular alternative dance venue on Friday and Saturday nights and hosts top local bands. **5th Avenue,** upstairs at Lion Yard (tel. 364222), pumps music every night save Sunday, with Tuesday reserved for students. *(Cover £3-5. Smart casual dress and over 18 only on weekends. Open 9pm-2am.)* **The Chicago Rock Café,** 22 Sidney St. (tel. 324600), has a Wednesday student night with discounted pints. The tourist office can give you a free *Cambridge Nightlife Guide* with a map of the spots, but popular night spots change constantly. Students, bartenders, and the latest issue of *Varsity* will be your best sources of information. Bringing the monthly *What's On Nightlife Guide* can garner occasional discounts.

During the first two weeks of June, students celebrate the end of the term with **May Week** (a May of the mind), crammed with concerts, plays, and elaborate balls that feature everything from hot air balloon rides to sleeping face-down drunk in the street to recuperative breakfasts by the river. Along the Cam, the college boat clubs compete in an eyebrow-raising series of races known as the **bumps.** Crews line up along the river (rather than across it) and attempt to ram the boat in front before being bumped from behind. Visitors may enjoy the annual fireworks from the vantage of one of the city's bridges. May Week's artistic repertoire stars the famous **Footlights Revue,** a collection of comedy skits; its performers have gone on to join such troupes as Beyond the Fringe and Monty Python. John Cleese, Eric Idle, and Graham Chapman all graduated from the Revue.

The third week of June ushers in the **Midsummer Fair,** which dates from the early 16th century and appropriates the Midsummer Common for about five days. The free **Strawberry Fair,** (tel. 350542), Cambridge's answer to Glastonbury granola, offers games and music the first Saturday in June. Address inquiries to the tourist office.

During the rest of the summer, Cambridge caters to tourists more than students. **Summer in the City** and **Camfest** brighten the last two weeks of July with a series of concerts and special exhibits culminating in a huge weekend celebration, the **Cambridge Folk Festival** (tel. 357851). Tickets for the weekend, which cost about £38, should be booked well in advance; camping on the grounds is £5-18 extra. The **Arts Cinema,** Market Passage (tel. 504444), screens comedy classics and undubbed foreign films and holds a film-fest during the Festival. *(Tickets £3.20-4.20, seniors and children £2.30. Box office open daily from 10am until 15min. after start of the last screening.)* The Arts Box Office also handles ticket sales for the newly reopened **Arts Theatre,** which stages traveling productions, and the **ADC Theatre** (Amateur Dramatic Club; tel. 503333), Park St., which offers lively performances of student-produced plays as well as movies during the term and the Festival. The **Cambridge Shakespeare Festival,** in association with the festival at that other university on the Thames, features four plays in open-air repertory throughout July and August. Tickets are available from the Arts Box Office or at the Corn Exchange. *(£9, students, seniors, children £6.)* You can get an earful of concerts at the **Cambridge Corn Exchange** (tel. 357851), at the corner of Wheeler St. and Corn Exchange, next to the tourist office, a venue for band, jazz, and classical concerts. *(£7.50-16; 50% off for student standby on the day of performance for certain concerts. Box office open M-Sa 10am-6pm, on show nights 10am-9pm.)*

■ Near Cambridge

Immortalized by Rupert Brooke in 1912 with his clumsy verse "Stands the Church clock at ten to three? And is there honey still for tea?" **Grantchester** is a mecca for Cambridge literary types. When the clock was stopped for repairs in 1985, its hands were pedantically left frozen at ten to three. You can see the church clock tower next to Brooke's home at the Old Vicarage (closed to the public). To reach Grantchester Meadows from Cambridge, take the path that follows the River Granta (about 45min.; the river is the namesake of Britain's venerable literary journal). Grantchester itself lies about 1 mi. from the meadows; ask the way at one of the neighborhood shops. If you have the energy to pole or paddle your way, rent a punt or canoe from Scudamore's Boatyards (see above). After tying up your craft, follow the signs to the road. Or hop aboard **Stagecoach Cambus** #118 (8 per day). The **Rupert Brooke,** 2 Broadway (open daily 11am-11pm), and the **Green Man,** High St. (open M-Sa 11am-3pm and 6-11pm, Su noon-3pm and 7-10:30pm), will reward the famished and parched for their efforts. Or, wander a bit further down the road to the idyllic **Orchard** (tel. 845788), on Mill Way. The Orchard was the leisurely Sunday afternoon haunt of the "neo-Pagans," a Grantchester offshoot of the famous literary Bloomsbury Group. Outdoor plays are occasionally performed on summer evenings; ask at the Cambridge tourist office. *(Open daily 9:30am-6:30pm.)* The posh town still attracts members of the literati; author and politicking Jeffrey Archer's large and comfortably anonymous red brick house hides just beyond the Orchard. Before returning to Cambridge, stop by the weathered **Parish Church of St. Andrew and St. Mary,** on Millway. Some fragments date to the 14th century.

Wimpole Hall, Cambridgeshire's most spectacular mansion, done in elegant 18th-century style, lies 10 mi. southwest of Cambridge. The hall holds works by Gibbs, Flitcroft, and Joane, and gardens sculpted by Capability Brown. *(Open Aug. daily 1-5pm; Apr.-July and Sept.-Oct. Tu-Su 1-5pm; bank holidays 11am-5pm. £5.20, children £2.25.)* **Wimpole's Home Farm** (tel. 207257) brims with Longhorn and Gloucester cattle, Soay sheep, and Tamworth pigs. *(Open Apr.-Oct. Tu-Su 10:30am-5pm. £4, children £2.50.)*

Northeast of Cambridge, 12th-century **Anglesey Abbey** (tel. 811200) has been remodeled to house the priceless exotica of the first Lord Fairhaven. One of the niftiest clocks in the universe sits inconspicuously on the bookcase beyond the fireplace, but don't worry if you miss it—there are 55 other clocks to enjoy. In the 100-acre gardens, trees punctuate lines of clipped hedges and manicured lawns. *(House and gardens open Easter to mid-Oct. W-Su and bank holidays 11am-5:30pm, last admission 4:30pm. Gardens also open July to early Sept. M-Tu. Admission M-Sa £5.60, Su and bank holidays £6.60; gardens only £3.30. Wheelchair accessible.)* The abbey lies 6 mi. from Cambridge on the B1102 (off the A1303). Bus #111 runs from Drummer St. Station (1 per hr.); ask to be let off at Lode Crossroads.

Dating from the days of the Saxon invasions and possibly the Neolithic and Bronze Ages, the market town of **Saffron Walden** (pop. 15,000), 15 mi. south of Cambridge, was named after the saffron that used to be sold here and from the Anglo-Saxon word for "wooded valley." The town is best known for the "pargetting" (plaster moulding) that adorns many of its Tudor buildings.

The **tourist office,** 1 Market Pl., Market Sq. (tel. (01799) 510444), stocks a fine map and guide (20p; open Apr.-Oct. M-Sa 9:30am-5:30pm; Nov.-Mar. 10am-5pm). The **YHA Youth Hostel,** 1 Myddylton Pl. (tel. (01799) 523117), in the north part of town on the A130, occupies one of the oldest buildings in the village. (£7.70, under 18 £5.15. Meals available. Lockout 10am-5pm. Curfew 11pm. Open May-July M-Sa; Aug. daily; Mar.-Apr. and Oct. Tu-Sa; Feb. F-Sa.)

Trains leave Cambridge semi-hourly for nearby **Audley End** (tel. (01799) 522399), a magnificent Jacobean hall set on grounds designed by Capability Brown. Watch for the Little Drawing Room. Despite Robert Adam's careful design, one lady of the manor altered it to suit her own taste—in clothes, that is: the room had to be modified to fit her voluminous evening dress. *(Open Apr.-Sept. W-Su and bank holidays 11am-6pm, last admission 5pm. £5.50, students £4.10, children £2.80, families £13.80; grounds only £3.30, students £2.50, children £1.70. Wheelchair accessible.)*

■ Ely

The ancient town of Ely (EEL-ee) was an island until the surrounding fens were drained in the 17th century. Legend has it that St. Dunstan saw fit to turn the local monks into eels as punishment for their lack of piety, a transformation that earned Ely its name. A more likely story is that "Elig" (eel island) was named for the eels that lived in the surrounding fens. "Insular" still describes this cathedral city, lovely and lonely in a sea of leafy fields. Here brave Hereward the Wake defended himself against Norman invaders, earning the title "the last of all the English." One of the most spectacular structures in all of England, Ely's Cathedral commands the land. The breathtaking colossus is reason enough for a quick visit.

ORIENTATION AND PRACTICAL INFORMATION Ely's two major streets run parallel to the cathedral; the town's sights and businesses line **High** and **Market St.,** with Cromwell's House and some shops trailing behind on **St. Mary's St.** Ely serves as the junction on the train lines between **London, King's Lynn, Norwich,** and **Peterborough,** with frequent connections to each.

Trains (tel. (0345) 484950) snake between **Cambridge** and Ely (20min., 1 per hr., day return £3) and **Norwich** (1½hr., 1 per hr., £10.80). To reach the cathedral and tourist office from the train station, walk up Station Rd. and continue on Back Hill, which becomes The Gallery. **Cambus** (tel. (01223) 423554) slithers from Market St. to **Cambridge** (#109, 20 min., 1 per hr., £2.90). The **tourist office** (tel. 662062) shares and operates the Cromwell House, 29 St. Mary's St. Its dedicated staff will book rooms for a 10% deposit and provide you with free maps and accommodations lists (open Apr.-Sept. daily 10am-6pm; Oct.-Mar. M-Sa 10am-5:15pm). The office also operates **tours** of the city (about £2), but schedules are irregular; consult the office. The **police** (tel. 662392) are posted on Nutholt Ln. The **post office** (tel. 669946) is in Lloyd's Chemist on High St. Ely's **postal code** is CB7 4HF, its **telephone code** 01353.

ACCOMMODATIONS AND FOOD Cheaper accommodations make Ely a good base for exploring Cambridge. Check the tourist office for accommodations listings. Two options are **The Post House,** 12a Egremont St. (tel. 667184), which offers rooms from £17, and **Mrs. Hull's,** 82 Broad St. (tel. 667609), for £15 per person—close to the train station and the river. Camp among spuds and sugarbeet, with a view of the cathedral, at **Braham Farm,** Cambridge Rd. (tel. 662386), off the A10 past the golf course (£5 per tent; toilets and cold water available; electricity hook-up £1 per night).

Tea houses—and only tea houses—abound in Ely. For a bargain meal, stop at one of the numerous take-away places (be forewarned: many close early). Most shops in the town close down on Tuesday afternoons at about 1pm. On Thursdays (8:30am-4:30pm) stock up on provisions at the **market** in Market Pl. A glorious apparition behind a Georgian wall, **Waitrose Supermarket,** Brays Ln. (tel. 668800), unfolds her splendors to visitors. Pick up a map at the door. (Open M-Tu 8:30am-6pm, W-Th 8:30am-8pm, F 8:30am-9pm, Sa 8:30am-6pm.) Fill up on a lunch of roast beef, Yorkshire Pudding, two vegetables, and potatoes (£4.25) at the crowded, somewhat elegant restaurant above **Bonnet's Bakery,** 13 High St. (lunch only; closes at 5pm). The **Minster Tavern,** Minster Pl., opposite the cathedral, is popular for lunches (£2-5; open M-Sa 11am-11pm, noon-10:30pm). **The Steeplegate,** 16-18 High St., across from the cathedral, serves tea and snacks in two rooms built over a medieval undercroft; fall into a romantic reverie over a pot of Earl Grey (80p) and then visit the medieval exhibition below (open M-Sa 10am-5pm). On the banks of the Great Ouse (OOZE), the pub at the **Maltings,** Ship Ln., a restored brewery, serves bar meals on its patio (£2-7; open daily noon-2pm and 6-9pm).

SIGHTS **Ely Cathedral's** towers (tel. 667735) tack against the low-blown continental clouds. The massive cathedral was founded in 1081 on the spot where St. Etheldreda had formed a religious community four centuries before. It was redecorated in the 19th century, when the elaborate ceiling above the nave and many of the stained-glass windows were completed. The space now greets visitors with a rare, joyful combination of light and color. In 1322, the original Norman tower collapsed and the present **Octagon Altar,** topped by the **lantern tower,** replaced it. The eight-sided cupola appears to burst into mid-air, but is in fact held up by eight stone pillars (total weight: 400 tons). To the north, headless figures in the Lady Chapel and empty grottoes throughout mark visits by Reformation iconoclasts. In the south transept lies the tomb of Dean of Ely, Humphrey Tyndall, an eternal PR boost for the monarchy: heir to the throne of Bohemia, Humphrey refused the kingdom, saying he'd "rather be Queen Elizabeth's subject than a foreign prince." Incongruous, but precisely-rendered stained glass windows depict pilots and planes from World Wars I and II. *(Open Easter-Sept. daily 7am-7pm; Oct.-Easter M-F 7:30am-6:30pm, Su 7:30am-5pm. £3, students and seniors £2.20. Evensong M-Sa 5:30pm, Su 3:45pm. Tours of the Octagon May-Sept. about*

3 per day. Tours of the West Tower July-Aug. 1 per hr., weather permitting. £2, students and seniors £1.40. Wheelchair accessible.) The **Stained Glass Museum** overlooks the nave. *(Open daily 10:30am-4:30pm. £2.50, students, seniors, and children £1.50.)* The **brass-rubbing center** is free, but you pay for the materials you use in your frottage. *(Open July-Aug. daily 10:30am-4pm, Su noon-3pm. Materials £1.70-8.70.)*

The monastic buildings surrounding the cathedral are still in use: the **infirmary** now houses one of the resident canons, and the **bishop's palace** is a home for children with disabilities. The rest of the buildings are used by the **King's School,** one of the older public (read: private) schools in England. For an architectural tour of the town, follow the path outlined by the tourist office's overwhelmingly detailed *Town Trail* pamphlet (35p). The **Ely Museum** (tel. 666655), at the Old Gaol on the corner of Market St. and Lynn Rd., tells the story of a fenland city and its people in a chronological tour. *(Open Tu-Su 10:30am-4pm. £1.80, students, seniors, and children £1.25.)* Perturbing Royalists everywhere, **Oliver Cromwell's House,** 29 St. Mary's St. (tel. 662062), has been refurbished with wax figures, 17th-century decor, and the quintessential haunted bedroom. *(Open Apr.-Sept. daily 10am-6pm; Oct.-Mar. M-Sa 10am-5:15pm. £2.30, students, seniors, and children £1.80, families £5.)* Amble through pedestrian-only **Market Place,** which offers market days every Thursday and Saturday. In early June, Ely hosts a **flower festival.** Admire the palm-leaf crosses adorned with lilies that decorate the cathedral, and adore the grannies selling marmalade.

NORFOLK AND SUFFOLK

A thriving center of wool production and trade in days gone by, Norfolk and Suffolk counties now serve as a testament to the alarming amount of wealth accumulated in the past. Numerous small towns boast imposing houses, halls, and magnificent "wool churches." But despite the obvious impact humans have made on this region, the green hills and waterways maintain the rustic beauty that inspired the landscape paintings of natives Constable and Gainsborough. The frenetic pace of life in southeast East Anglia has slowed in recent years, leaving an air of quiet serenity amongst the hundreds of crooked timber-framed buildings.

■ Norwich

One of England's largest cities before the Norman invasion and its most populous until London became the capital, Norwich (NOR-ridge, like porridge), "England's city in the country," is a medieval town in modern attire. The city's new dress of shopping pavilions and fast food restaurants bursts at the seams to reveal cobblestoned undergarments. An 11th-century cathedral and a 12th-century castle reign over the city's smaller structures, and the weighty remains of the old city's walls girdle the central district. Norwich's puzzling streets wind through a fascinating city which prefers to convert its medieval churches (one for every other Sunday) into puppet theaters and homeless shelters rather than knock them down and start anew. Each day, one of England's oldest markets rouses itself with all the bargaining women and pleading fruitsellers of a medieval fayre: some dresses never go out of style.

GETTING THERE

Regional Railways (tel. (0345) 484950) goes to **Great Yarmouth** (1hr., M-Sa 12 per day, Su 6 per day, £3.20), **Peterborough** (2hr., M-Sa 15 per day, Su 8 per day, £14.30), **Cambridge** (change at Ely, 1½hr., M-Sa 12 per day, £10.20), and **London Liverpool St. Station** (2hr., M-Sa 19 per day, saver fare £27.40). Those under 16 ride at half-price. Regional Railways offers the **Fenland Day Ranger,** for a day of unlimited travel in the Fenland area (£16). **Hitching** is reported to be scarce.

Easily accessible by bus, coach, or train, Norwich makes a decent base for touring both urban and rural East Anglia, particularly the Norfolk Broads. Departing from Surrey St., **National Express** (tel. (0990) 808080) coaches run to **Cambridge** (2½hr., 1

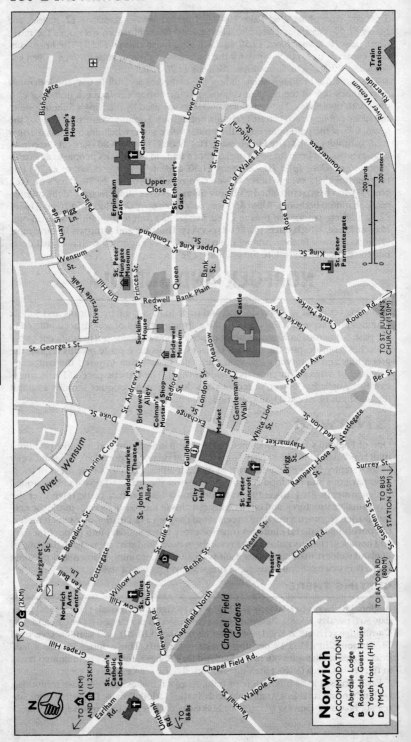

Norwich

ACCOMMODATIONS
A: Aberdale Lodge
B: Rosedale Guest House
C: Youth Hostel (HI)
D: YMCA

per day, £8.75) and **London** (3hr., 5 per day, £14.50), among other destinations. Book tickets at the tourist office. **Cambridge Coach Services** (tel. (01223) 236333) runs a direct service from **Cambridge** (#74, 2hr., 4 per day, £9, students and seniors £6.75, children £4.50). **Explorer tickets** (£5, seniors £4, children £3, families £10) offer a day's worth of unlimited travel on **Eastern Counties** buses, which travel to **King's Lynn, Peterborough,** and other Norfolk villages. For more bus information, consult timetables at the Surrey St. station, call the Eastern Counties information line (tel. 622800), or use the **Norfolk Bus Information Centre (NORBIC),** 4 Guildhall Hill (tel. (0500) 626116), behind the tourist office (open M-Sa 8:30am-5pm).

ORIENTATION AND PRACTICAL INFORMATION

Although the architect of Norwich's old city had a wobbly hand, most sights are fairly close together, and walking is an effective way to see the city. Ask often for directions. The hostel and many B&Bs lie to the west of the city walls in a more modern and navigable part of town. Avoid the center of town and the market area after dark.

Trains: (tel. (0345) 484950), at the corner of Riverside and Thorpe Rd., a 15min. walk uphill to the town center. All buses that stop here go to the city center for 40p. Ticket window open M-Sa 4:45am-8:45pm, Su 6:45am-8:45pm. Information open M-Sa 9am-7pm, Su 10:15am-5:30pm. **Lockers** £1-3.

Buses: Surrey St. (tel. 622800), off St. Stephen St. southwest of the castle. Information center and ticket desk open M-F 8:30am-5:15 pm, Sa 9am-5pm. **Luggage storage** available in the cafeteria £1-3.

Taxi: Express Taxis (tel. 767626). One wheelchair taxi (tel. 300300).

Bike Rental: Anglia Cycles, 72a Gloucester St. (tel. 632467). £5-10 per day, £30-50 per week. Reservations not required, but try to call a day or 2 in advance. Discounts for YHA members. Open M-Sa 9am-6pm.

Tourist Office: Guildhall, Gaol Hill, Norwich NR2 1NF (tel. 666071), on the west continuation of London St. in front of City Hall. Brochures about the region, many free. City guide map 30p. Books rooms for £2.50 and a 10% deposit. **Luggage storage** £2 plus £2 key deposit. Open June-Sept. M-F 9:30am-5pm, Sa 10am-5pm; Oct.-May M-F 9:30am-4:30pm, Sa 9:30am-1pm and 1:30-4:30pm. 1½hr. guided **tours** leave from here Apr.-Oct. £2.25, children £1.

Financial Services: Banks line **London St.,** and, predictably, **Bank Plain,** including **Barclays** (tel. 660255). Scads of **ATMs** in town.

Market: In the square facing City Hall and the tourist office. Open M-Sa 8am-4:30pm. Vendors sell fresh fruits and vegetables, clothing, and greasy chips.

Launderette: Laundromat, 179a Dereham Rd. (tel. 626685). Open M-Sa 8am-8pm, Su 10am-7pm; last wash 1½hr. before closing. Change and soap available.

Emergency: Dial 999; no coins required.

Police: Bethel St. (tel. 768769), around the corner from City Hall.

Hotlines: Samaritans (crisis; tel. 611311). Open 24hr. **AIDS-HIV,** The Fightback Trust (tel. (01502) 501509). **Childline** (tel. (0900) 1111). **Lesbian Line** (tel. 628055). **Rape crisis** (tel. 667687). Open M-F 10am-4:30pm, Th 7-9pm.

Hospital: Norfolk and Norwich Hospital (tel. 286286), corner of Brunswick Rd. and St. Stephen's Rd.

Post Office: Castle Mall, 84-85 Castle Meadow Walk (tel. 761635). Branches at Queen St. (tel. 220278), and 13-17 Bank Plain (tel. 220228), near Anglia Television. Open M-F 9am-5:30pm, Sa 9am-12:30pm. **Postal Code:** NR2 1AA.

Telephone Code: 01603.

ACCOMMODATIONS

Earlham and Unthank Rd. offer many pleasant B&Bs in the £15-18 range, but they are at least a 20-minute westward hike from downtown and even farther from the train station. From the tourist office, follow St. Giles St. to the Ring Rd. rotary and cross the footbridge headed toward the Catholic cathedral. Unthank Rd. branches off to the left, Earlham Rd. to the right. The guesthouses on both streets appear when house numbers reach the 100s. B&Bs may also be found along Dereham Rd.; follow St. Benedict's St., which eventually becomes Dereham. Consult the tourist office for accommodations listings.

288 ■ EAST ANGLIA

YHA Youth Hostel, 112 Turner Rd. (tel. 627647), 1½mi. from the center. From the train station, cross the river and either wait at the shelter in front of the Furniture Store for bus #19 or 20 (85p), take a taxi, or drag your bones along Prince of Wales Rd. until Bank Plain. Take a right and continue as the road becomes Dereham Rd. Upon reaching the Earl of Leicester Pub, turn right onto Turner Rd.; the hostel is the last building on your right (when you think you must have passed it, walk 10min. more). Clean rooms of varying sizes (2-8 bunks per room). £8.80, under 18 £6; family rates available. Breakfast £3, packed lunch £2.45-3.25, dinner £4.25. Luggage storage. Lockout 10am-1pm. Curfew 11pm, but guests can arrange to stay out late. Often full July-Aug.; call ahead. Open Feb.-Oct. daily; Nov.-Dec. F-Sa.

YMCA, 46-52 St. Giles St. (tel. 620269). From the station, cross the bridge and continue up Prince of Wales Rd. until you reach the Anglia Television building on the left; turn right onto the pedestrian London St. and stay on it 4-5 blocks until you reach the marketplace. St. Giles begins behind it. Central location and simple, clean rooms. Local teens socialize on the stairwells. Wings segregated by gender. Laundry facilities, TV lounge. The yogurt and cereal beat the industrial-strength breakfast. Dorms £8.50; singles £12.50. Refundable key deposit £5. No curfew; porter lets you in after midnight.

Rosedale Guest House, Mrs. Curtis, 145 Earlham Rd. (tel. 453743). 8 bedrooms 15min. from the city center; formica furniture and plush headboards. Push-button showers, TVs, breakfast on blue china. Singles £18; doubles £34.

Aberdale Lodge, 211 Earlham Rd. (tel. 502100), 18min. walk from the city center. A relaxed and unpretentious B&B. Alas, 1 shower for 10 guests. TV in each room. Mrs. Gilbert serves up a full English breakfast to early birds (7-8:30am). £15 per person, children sharing parents' room £9.

Camping: Closest is the **Lakenham** campsite, Martineau Ln. (tel. 620060; no calls after 8pm), 1mi. south of the city center. Eastern Counties bus #9, 29, and 32 stop nearby. Gates locked to cars at 11pm, though foot traffic permitted. July-Aug. £3.90, children £1.50; Easter-June £3.55, children £1.50; Sept.-June £2.60, children free. £3.50 pitch fee for non-members; family deals available. Toilets and showers; facilities for disabled travelers. Also near is **Scouts Headquarters,** Eaton Vale, Church Ln., Eaton (tel. 501228). Take bus #1, 2, or 6 from the bus station or Castle Meadow to Cellar House Pub and turn left onto Church Ln. £2 per person. Toilet facilities and showers free. Call ahead in summer.

FOOD AND PUBS

In the heart of the city and just a stone's throw from the castle keep spreads one of England's largest and oldest open-air **markets** (M-Sa roughly 8am-4:30pm). Feast your eyes on it from the steps of the tourist office, then feast your gut on everything from fresh fruits and cheeses to ice cream. Or, if you prefer not to bargain for your bananas, visit the Metro **Tesco** nestling alongside the square on St. Andrew's St. (open M-Sa 8am-8pm, Su 11am-5pm).

The Waffle House, 39 St. Giles St. (tel. 612790), near the Ys. Family restaurant with wicker galore. Astounding Belgian waffles (wholemeal or white) made with organic ingredients. Fillings range from ham, cheese, and mushrooms to tuna and bean sprouts (£1.40-6). Spiced fruit with cinnamon sugar. Strawberry wine and fruity milkshakes to top off your waffle. Live music Tuesday and Sunday nights. 10% student discount. Open M-Th 11am-10pm, F-Sa 11am-11pm, Su 11am-9pm.

The Treehouse, 14 Dove St. (tel. 763258). Fresh vegetarian cuisine on earthenware with stuffed parrots eyeing you hungrily from their perches. Daily menu £4-5.50; bowl of assorted salads and wholebread £3 (take-away £2.50). Store downstairs sells healthy vittles. Open M-W 10am-5pm, Th-Sa 10am-9:30pm.

The Canadian Muffin Co., 4 Opie St. (tel. 766755), off London St. Decadent muffins (banana-chocolate-coconut, eh?), frozen yogurt, and coffees (all £1-2). Mini-muffins for the less decadent (55p). Open M-F 8am-6pm, Sa 8:30am-6pm, Su 10am-6pm.

The Adam and Eve, Bishopgate (tel. 667423), at the Palace St. end of Riverside Walk, behind the cathedral. Older than sin. The first pub in Norwich (est. 1249) and one of its most pleasing watering holes (half-pint of cider £1.10). Cheesy jacket potatoes and other treats served noon-7pm. Bar open daily 11am-11pm.

Pizza One and Pancakes Too, 24 Tombland (tel. 621583), by the cathedral. Creative pizza and crepe dishes. Have the 4-cheese "charity pizza" (£5) and 50p goes to charity; order the banana-dog (£2) and ask questions later. Students get 10% off main course. Open M-Sa noon-11pm, Su noon-10pm.

The Britons Arms Coffee House, 9 Elm Hill (tel. 623367). Location, location, location. A thatch-roofed Tudor cottage near the cathedral on a restored, cobbled street. Morning coffee and lunch served; a pleasant spot for afternoon tea in the garden. Tea £1, cakes from 55p. Open M-Sa 9:30am-5pm.

One of the best spots for an evening drink in town isn't, in fact, a pub. Head to **Take 5,** St. Andrews St. (tel. 763099), in the old Suckling House, an exhibition center including the Cinema City movie theater (see **Entertainment,** p. 290), a bookshop, information desk, and a fantastic 14th-century bar. Scope out biweekly art exhibits in the restaurant (open M-Sa 10am-11pm, Su 6-10:30pm).

SIGHTS

The original **Norwich Castle** was a wooden structure built in 1089 by a Norman monarchy intent on subduing the Saxon city. The stone keep was erected in 1160, but its current exterior dates from the 1830s, when it was refaced and restored to its boxy self. It was here that English nobles forced King John to sign the Magna Carta in 1215, thereby curbing the power of the monarchy (see **The Medieval Period and Tudor Renaissance,** p. 53). The castle was used as a jail from 1345 until 1887. The **Castle Museum** (tel. 223624), which occupies the castle keep, contains an eclectic jumble of art, archaeology, and natural history: everything from bits of armor to a prized chunk of 12,500-year-old mammoth poo. Only a guided **tour** permits entry into the dungeons and onto the battlements. The battlements provide a superb view of Norwich; look for the 36 remaining churches and 385 pubs—a church for every other Sunday and a pub for every day of the year (plus a few extras). *(July-Sept. £3.10, students and seniors £2.10, children £1.50; Oct.-June £2.30, students and seniors £1.50, children £1. Open M-Sa 10am-5pm, Su 2-5pm. Tours 1hr. £1.50, children 50p. M-F 4 per day, Sa and holidays 6 per day, Su 3 per day. Wheelchair accessible.)*

Off St. Andrew's St., in Bridewell Alley, rests the **Bridewell Museum** (tel. 667228). All kinds of rabble-rousers paced this medieval merchant's house when it served as a prison from 1583 to 1828. The prisoners carved dates and initials (still visible) in the far left corner of the courtyard above the bench. Today, the museum displays an array of curiosities that document turn-of-the-century Norwich. *(Open Easter-Sept. Tu-Sa 10am-5pm. £1.20, students and seniors 80p, children 50p. Limited wheelchair access.)* Farther down at 3 Bridewell Alley, **Colman's Mustard Shop** (tel. 627889) chronicles the spicy rise and fall of one of the city's oldest industries. *(Open M-Sa 9:30am-5pm. Free.)* On Princes St., the **St. Peter Hungate Church Museum** holds art, books, and church artifacts. *(Open Apr.-Sept. M-Sa 10am-5pm.)*

The castle and the Norman **Norwich Cathedral** (tel. 764385) dominate the skyline; follow the cathedral's spire to **Tombland.** Though it sounds like a macabre amusement park, Tombland is the burial site of thousands of victims of the Great Plague, and is preserved as the quiet village Norwich might have remained if skipped by the urban juggernaut. The cathedral itself, built by an 11th-century bishop as penance for having bought his episcopacy, features unusual two-story cloisters (the only ones of their kind in England) and flying buttresses that help support the second tallest spire in the country (315ft.; the Salisbury Stake is the tallest). Use the mirror in the nave to examine the overhead bosses carved with Biblical scenes, or check for bad hair. *(Open daily mid-May to mid-Sept. 7:30am-7pm; mid-Sept. to mid-May 7:30am-6pm. Free. Guided tours June-Sept. M-Sa 11am-2:15pm. Evensong M-Sa 5:15pm, Su 3:30pm. Wheelchair accessible.)* In the summer, the cathedral frequently hosts orchestral concerts and small art exhibitions. Call for information, and, as usual, listen for free rehearsals.

Long before Aphra Behn held a pen, a 14th-century nun named Juliana of Norwich took up a cell of her own here and became the first known woman to write a book in English. Her 20-year work, *Revelations of Divine Love,* is based on her mystic experiences as an anchoress at **St. Julian's Church** (tel. 767380), between King St. and Rouen Rd., where you can visit her lonely cell and shrine. (*Open daily May-Sept. 8am-5:30pm; Oct.-Apr. 8am-4pm. Free.*)

At the **University of East Anglia,** 3 mi. west of town on Earlham Rd., is the **Sainsbury Centre for Visual Arts** (tel. 456060). Buses #4, 5, 26, 27, and 35 (evenings and Sundays buses #4, 6, 26, 27) journey from Norwich **City Centre,** Ask for the Constable Terr. stop. Destroyed during the English Reformation, it was restored in the wake of World War II. Sir Robert Sainsbury (of the supermarket chain) donated his superb collection of 20th-century and earlier art to the university in 1973, including works by Picasso, Moore, Degas, and contemporary artists. (*Open Tu-Su 11am-5pm. £2, students, seniors, and children £1. Wheelchair access.*) Stern but beautiful, 19th-century **St. John's Roman Catholic Cathedral** stands just over the footbridge at Earlham Rd.

ENTERTAINMENT

Norwich offers a rich array of cultural activities, especially in summer. Information on all things vaguely entertaining in Norwich is kept by **The Ticket Shop,** Guildhall (tel. 764764), next door to the tourist office. (*Tickets for virtually all venues.*) Located next to the Assembly House on Theatre St., the Art Deco **Theatre Royal** (tel. 630000) houses touring companies of operas and ballets, as well as theater troupes such as the RSC and Royal National. (*Tickets £3-17; some shows have discounts for students and seniors. Box office open M-Sa 9:30am-8pm, until 6pm on non-performance days.*) The home of the Norwich Players, **Maddermarket Theatre,** 1 St. John's Alley (tel. 620917), has revived high-quality amateur drama, performed in an Elizabethan-style theater. Adhering to a bizarre tradition, all actors remain anonymous, adding new meaning to "Who's Who in the Cast." (*Box office open M-Sa 10am-5pm and after 7pm performances; on non-performance Sa open 10am-1:30pm. £3.50-7.50, Tu-Th and Sa matinees £4. Wheelchair accessible.*) The **Norwich Arts Centre** (tel. 660352) provides the city's most versatile venue with folk and world music, ballet, and comedy. (*Box office open M-F 10am-5pm, Sa 11am-4pm. £5-10; discounts for students, seniors, and disabled. Wheelchair accessible.*) The **Norwich Puppet Theatre,** St. James (tel. 629921), comes in handy with shows for all ages. (*Box office open M-F 9:30am-5:30pm, Sa 2hr. prior to show. £5, children £3.75.*) In summer, look for the City Council's free presentations of **Theatre in the Parks** (tel. 212137).

A few pubs and clubs offer live music. **Boswells,** 24 Tombland (tel. 626099), near the cathedral, serves up food, drink, and nightly jazz and blues. (*Tu-Sa cover £1-3 after 9pm. Open M-Sa noon-2am, Su 11:30am-6pm.*) Slide (electrically) to **Hy's** (tel. 621155), next door, where Tuesday nights bring rhythms of salsa. (*Cover £1-4. Open Tu-Sa 9pm-2am.*) Top 40 blares on Thursday and Friday at the **Lamb Inn** (tel. 625365), located in an alleyway off Haymarket and attracting a teenage to twentysomething crowd.

The **Norfolk and Norwich Festival**—featuring theater, dance, music, and visual arts—explodes in mid-October. **Picture this,** at the end of May, offers two weeks of open artists' studio around the county. Pick up leaflets at the tourist office or call 764764 for information and tickets. July welcomes the **LEAP Dance Festival** (mostly contemporary dance). Norwich's several outdoor parks also host a stream of other **festivals** and **folk fairs** in the summer.

■ Near Norwich: Norfolk Broads and Wroxham

The ports along the northeast East Anglian coast, among England's first, yielded to the iron fists of London and other towns to the south, which pirated away much of their trade; despite the loss, folk around here still engage in seafaring adventures. Birds, beasts, and humans alike flock to the **Norfolk Broads,** a watery maze of navigable marsh lands, where traffic in narrow waterways hidden by hedgerows creates the surreal effect of sailboats floating through flowery fields. The broads didn't occur naturally, but were formed in medieval times when peat was dug out to use for fuel. Over the centuries, water levels rose and the shallow lakes or "broads" were born.

The marshes and the hills looming nearby beckon nature enthusiasts traveling by foot, cycle, or boat. Exercise care when walking about the Broads, an Environmentally Sensitive Area; continual abuse by humans has tremendously damaged the area.

Among the many **nature trails** that pass through the Broads, Cockshoot Broad lets you birdwatch, a circular walk around Ranworth points out the Broad's various flora, and Upton Fen is popular (it's true!) for its bugs. Hikers can challenge themselves with the 56 mi. long **Weaver's Way** between Cromer and Great Yarmouth. By collecting stamps along the way, the hearty receive an exclusive woven patch upon completion...girl scouts eat your heart out.

Pleasure boats of all sizes cruise the canals, and it's possible to sail from one pub to the next all the way from Norwich to Great Yarmouth. The tourist offices in Norwich and villages in the area sell helpful mini-guides to the Broads that describe various trails, waterways, and nature reserves. Swat flies and learn cowspeak.

Wroxham, 7 mi. northeast of Norwich, provides a good base for exploring the more remote areas of the Broads. From Norwich, take **Eastern Counties** buses (35min., M-Sa bus #5, 51, 54, 723, or 726, 2 per hr., Su bus #718, 3 per day, £1.85). Procure information from the **Hoveton tourist office,** Station Rd. (tel. (01603) 782281). The office also has lists of boat rentals and of campsites scattered through the area (open Easter-Oct. 9am-1pm and 2-5pm). The sheer number of guesthouses and hotels (which may be booked through the tourist office) within Wroxham proper and just outside attests to the popularity of the waterways and byways. While in the tourist office, pick up a free copy of *The Broadcaster,* which outlines local happenings, or *Explore the Broads by Bike,* which lists cycle rentals—certain areas of the Broads are accessible only by car or by bike.

From Wroxham, **Broads Tours** (tel. (01603) 782207), on the right hand side before the Bridge, runs cruises (1¼-3½hr.) through the Broads. *(Most at 11:30am and 2pm; 7 per day in July and Aug. £4.40-6.75, children £3.40-5.)* Also has departures from Potter Heigham (tel. (01692) 670711). **Southern River Steamers,** 65 Trafford Rd. (tel. (01603) 624051), offers cruises from Norwich to Surlingham Broad May-September, leaving from quays near the cathedral and train station. *(30min.-3¼ hr., excursions leave periodically 11am-5:30pm. £1.30-6.70, children 80p-£4.30. Wheelchair accessible.)* **Strumpshaw** (tel. (01603) 715191) is especially popular among birdwatchers *(Open daily 9am-9pm or dusk. £2.50, students and seniors £1.50, children 50p. Wheelchair accessible trails.)* From Norwich, take bus #30, 31, 32, or 33 (30min., M-Sa 8 per day, return £2.)

To reach the Broads, take a **train** from Norwich, Lowestoft, or Great Yarmouth to the smaller towns of Beccles, Cantley, Lingwood, Oulton Broad, Salhouse, or Wroxham. Check with tourist offices about accommodations. From Norwich, **Eastern Counties buses** leave from St. Stephen's St. and Surrey St. to **Wroxham** (#723-726, 30min., M-Sa 2 per hr., Su 3 per day, return £2), **Horning** (#723 or 726, 45min., 4 per day, £3), **Potter Heigham** (#723-6, 1hr., 4 per day, return £3.10), and other Broads towns (#705, M-F 1 per day in the evening).

■ King's Lynn

King's Lynn (pop. 40,000) meets the earth tones of the flat East Anglian countryside with a somber red-brick facade. Once a member of the Hanseatic League (a 16th-century EU), this dockside city on the banks of the Great Ouse borrows its Germanic look from trading partners such as Hamburg and Bremen. The town slumbers early and heavily, but makes a perfect stopover for cyclists exploring the region.

ORIENTATION AND PRACTICAL INFORMATION The **train station** (tel. (0345) 484950) rests on Blackfriars Rd. Trains steam to London **King's Cross** (1½hr., 19 per day, £23.30), **Cambridge** (1hr., 20 per day, £6.70), and **Peterborough** (change at Ely, 1hr., 6 per day, £6.80). **Eastern Counties** bus #X94 leaves from **Vancouver Centre** (tel. 772343; office open M-F 8:30am-5pm, Sa 8:30am-noon and 1-5pm) for **Norwich** (1½hr., 8 per day, £4.30), and **Peterborough** (1¼hr., 11 per day, £3.80). **National Express** (tel. (0990) 808080) runs once daily to **London** (9am, London to Lynn 4:30pm, £9, students, seniors, and children £6.50). Buy tickets from **West Norfolk Travel,** 2 King St. (tel. 772910). The **tourist office,** Old Gaolhouse, Saturday Market Pl. (tel. 763044), books rooms, provides bus and train information, and houses exhibits (see **Sights**, p. 292). To get to the office from the train station, turn left onto Black-friars Rd., take a right onto St. John's Terr., and a quick left onto St. James Rd. Turn right at St. James St., which becomes Saturday Market Pl.; the tourist office is just past High St. From the bus station, walk out the rear entrance onto Broad St. and turn left. Turn right onto New Conduit St., then left onto High St. (open M-Sa 9:15am-5pm, Su 10am-5pm; free with 10% deposit). Send *Let's Go* a postcard from the **post office** at Baxter's Plain on the corner of Broad and New Conduit St. King's Lynn's **postal code** is PE30 1YB; the **telephone code** is 01553.

ACCOMMODATIONS AND FOOD   A quayside **YHA Youth Hostel** (tel. 772461; fax 764312) occupies part of the 16th-century Thoresby College, on College Ln., opposite the tourist office. The hostel often fills, so call ahead. Keep your eyes peeled; it's easy to miss. (£8.80, under 18 £5.40. Lockout 10am-5pm. Curfew 11pm. Open May-Aug. daily; Apr. and Sept.-Oct. W-Su.) **B&Bs** are a hike from the city center; the less expensive ones span **Gaywood Rd.** and **Tennyson Ave.** Late arrivals should consult the list of guesthouses outside the tourist office. Reasonable accommodations can be found at the **Havana Guest House**, 117 Gaywood Rd. (tel. 772331; £15-16 per person), or the **Fairlight Lodge**, 79 Goodwins Rd. (tel. 762234; £16 per person).

King's Lynn restaurants operate on their own sweet time—closed Sunday (look for a take-away or grocer instead). A **Sainsbury's** supermarket (tel. 772104) is one of several located at St. Dominic's Sq., Vancouver Centre (open M-W 8am-8pm, Th-F 8am-9pm, Sa 7:30am-8pm, Su 10am-4pm). For fresh fruits and vegetables, visit the **markets** (Tu and F roughly 8:30am-4pm), held at the larger Tuesday Market Pl. on the north end of High St., or on Saturday at the Saturday Market Pl. For unlimited trips to the salad bar with your main dish (£4-8), try **Griffin's** in the posh Duke's Head Hotel on Tuesday Market Pl., which boasts an eclectic "international" menu. Try the *hongos*—yummy mushrooms and cheese in tortillas. (Open M-F 10am-4pm and 6-10pm, Sa 10am-5:30pm and 6-10pm, Su noon-3pm and 6-9:30pm.) **Giffords**, Purfleet St. (tel. 769177), serves homemade dishes and teas in a music-filled atmosphere. Dinners are mostly under £4; vegetarian fare is also served (open M-Sa 9am-10pm, Su noon-3pm).

SIGHTS   King's Lynn's most interesting buildings snooze by the River Ouse on the city's western edge. The huge 15th-century **Guildhall of St. George,** 27-29 King St. (tel. 774725), near the Tuesday Market, is said to be the last surviving building in England where Shakespeare appeared in his own play as well as the oldest surviving medieval guildhall in England; it now hosts the **King's Lynn Arts Centre.** *(Open M-F 10am-5pm, Sa 10am-12:30pm and 2-4pm.)*

The tourist office exhibits the **Tales of the Old Gaol House,** including the Regalia Room where the priceless 14th-century "King John Cup" is displayed. Filled with treasures from King's Lynn's past, the Regalia Room merits a quick peek. Next door, a personal stereo guide leads you through the town's old jail, spinning stories of Lynn's murderers, robbers, and witches in gory detail. *(Open Easter-Oct. daily 10am-5pm; Nov.-Easter F-Tu 10am-5pm; last admission 4:15pm. Gaol House £2, seniors and children £1; Gaol House and Town House Museum (see below). £2.90, seniors and children £1.90.)*

Across the street is **St. Margaret's Church** (tel. 772858), bits of which date from the 13th century. **The Town House Museum,** 46 Queen St. (tel. 773450), catalogs the minutia of Lynn life through the ages. *(Open in summer M-Sa 10am-5pm, Su 2-5pm; in winter M-Sa 10am-4pm. £1.10, students and seniors 60p, children 50p.)* Although it looks like a space rocket, the octagonal **Greyfriars Tower,** St. James St., is in fact the final remnant of a 14th-century monastery.

During the last half of July, the guildhall hosts the **King's Lynn Festival,** an orgy of classical and jazz music, along with ballet, puppet shows, and films. Get schedules at the Festival Office, 27 King St., PE30 1HA (tel. 774725). *(Tickets £3-10. Box office open M-F 10am-5pm, Sa 10am-1pm and 2-4pm.)*

■ Near King's Lynn

The stomping grounds of the wealthy, punctuated by sumptuous mansions, give way to wilder country as the road leading north from King's Lynn bends east to flank the Norfolk coast. Ten miles north of King's Lynn lies **Sandringham** (tel. (01553) 772675), a home of the Royal Family since 1862. King George V once described the place as "Dear old Sandringham, the place I love better than anywhere else in the world." Its 600 acres are open to the public when not in use by the royals. It's usually closed during July; ask at the King's Lynn tourist office. The best time to visit, though, is during the **flower show** in the last week of July. *(Open Apr.-Sept. 11am-4:45pm. House, grounds, and museum £4.50, seniors £3.50, children £2.50; museum and grounds £3.50, seniors £3, children £2.)* Eastern Counties bus #411/414 serves Sandringham (25min., M-Sa 8 per day, last return 6pm, Su 5 per day, last return 8:30pm, £1.80).

Closer to King's Lynn, **Castle Rising,** a solid, intimidating keep set atop massive earthworks, was home to Queen Isabella, "She-Wolf of France," after she plotted the murder of her husband, Edward II. *(Open Apr.-Oct. daily 10am-6pm; Nov.-Mar. W-Su 10am-4pm. £2.30, students and seniors £1.70, children £1.20.)* Eastern Counties buses #410 and 411 run from Lynn (15min., M-Sa 16 per day plus a few that don't stop at the castle, last return 8:45pm, service 415 Su 11 per day, £1.40).

Built in the mid-18th century for Sir Robert Walpole, the first prime minister of England, **Houghton Hall** (tel. (01485) 528569) is a magnificent example of Palladian architecture, with paintings, tapestries, and "the most sublime bed ever designed." *(Open Easter to late Sept. Th, Su, and bank holidays 2-5:30pm; gates close 5pm. House and grounds £5.50, children £3.)* Reach the hall (14mi. northwest of King's Lynn) by bus (45min., M-Sa 2 per day). If you plan to visit more than one of these properties in a day, buy an **Explorer ticket** (£5, seniors £4, children £3, families £10).

The northern **Norfolk Coast,** with its expanses of beach, sand dunes, and salt marsh, stretches from **Hunstanton,** 16 mi. north of King's Lynn, to **Wells-next-the-Sea** and beyond. Bird sanctuaries and nature preserves abound; the **Scolt Head Island Reserve** and the **Holme Bird Observatory** are superb. Buses #410 and 411 run from Vancouver Centre in King's Lynn to Hunstanton (2hr., M-Sa 2 per hr., Su every 2hr., £2.40). A **YHA Youth Hostel** (tel. (01485) 532061), 15 Avenue Rd., perches in the center of Hunstanton near the Wash. (£8.80, under 18 £6. Open July-Aug. daily; Easter-June M-Sa.; Sept.-Oct. Tu-Sa; closed Nov.-Easter.) Holme is found 3 mi. to the east; buses run from Hunstanton to Holme's Crossing in the summer only (Tu-Th and Su). To visit Scolt Head Island go via Brancaster Staithe (an Anglo-Saxon word meaning "pier"), 10 mi. east along the A149.

■ Bury St. Edmunds

Bury St. Edmunds' nationally acclaimed flowers bloom at the center of the pastoral county, surrounded by the villages of Lavenham, Long Melford, Woodbridge, and Sudbury. Bury St. Edmunds stands above the site where invaders beheaded Saxon King Edmund in AD 869 after tying him to a tree and using him for target practice. The busy commercial and administrative center that grew up around Edmund's mythical burial place attracts fewer travelers than the milling centers of Cambridge and Norwich. Geraniums and McDonald's cohabitate in Bury, which retains its small town flavor despite a growing number of commercial venues.

GETTING THERE AND GETTING ABOUT

Suffolk enjoys frequent train and coach service. There are actually "commuter buses" between Bury St. Edmunds and London, 2½ hours away. Bury St. Edmunds makes a good daytrip from either Norwich or Cambridge, especially if you include a jaunt to Lavenham, Sudbury, Lona, Melford, or any of the other historic villages scattered throughout Western Suffolk. The region is also explorable by bike, but local laws have made rentals difficult to come by, especially in Bury. Try **Barton's Bicycles,** 5 Marrio's Walk (tel. (01449) 677195), Stowmarket (£8 per day, £30 per week).

> ### One Talking Head
>
> All decent saints have a fantastic story surrounding their birth or death, and Bury's St. Edmund is no exception. According to legend, after Edmund's beheading, a voice crying "Here I am!" led the saint's faithful friends to the spot in the brush where his noggin had rolled. A helpful wolf had taken it upon himself to guard the gory head, nestling it between his paws. When Edmund's followers located the source of the exclamation, they rushed to the wolf, snatched back what was rightfully theirs, and founded the town's abbey in Edmund's honor.

Trains (tel. (0345) 484950) leave **London Liverpool St. Station** for Bury St. Edmunds via **Ipswich** (£20), **Felixstowe** (2 per hr., £5.60), and **Colchester** (1 per hr., £12.70). Trains also run between **Cambridge** (£5.30) and **Norwich** (£11.50) via Bury (M-Sa 1 per hr., Su every 2hr.); some change at **Stowmarket** (1¼hr., £2.70). **National Express** (tel. (0990) 808080) leaves from London **Victoria Station** for Bury St. Edmunds (2hr., 2 per day, £11). **R.W. Chenery** (tel. (01379) 741221) runs an express to Victoria once each day (period return £15). **Cambus** #X11 runs from Drummer St. Station in **Cambridge** to Bury (55min., M-Sa every 2 hr., Su every 3 hr., return £3.80).

ORIENTATION AND PRACTICAL INFORMATION

Laid out according to their original 12th-century plan, Bury's streets are easier to untangle than those of its neighbors. The **tourist office**, 6 Abbeygate St. (tel. 764667; fax 757084), distributes both a free and an indexed map (£1), an accommodations list, and a copy of *What's On* (open Easter-Oct. M-Sa 9:30am-5:30pm; Nov.-Easter M-F 10am-4pm, Sa 10am-1pm). To reach the office from the train station, follow Outnorthgate past the roundabout onto Northgate St.; turn right onto Mustow St. and walk up to Angel Hill. From the bus station, follow St. Andrew's St. past the library to Brentgovel St., turn right at Lower Baxtel St. and then left onto Abbeygate St. The office also runs **guided walking tours** of the city (June-Sept. M-Tu and Th-F 2:30pm, W and Su 11am). Banks in town include **Lloyds** (tel. 767161), on Buttermarket St., half a block from the marketplace (open M-W and F 9am-5pm, Th 9:30am-5pm, Sa 9:30am-12:30pm), **Barclays**, 52 Abbeygate St. (tel. 763241), and a branch of **Thomas Cook**, 43b Cornhill St. (tel. 753372; open M and W-Sa 9am-5:30pm, Tu 10am-5:30pm). **ATMs** munch lemon scones throughout town. The **post office** (tel. 760995) can be found at 17-18 Cornhill St. (open M-F 9am-5:30pm, Sa 9am-12:30pm). The **postal code** is IP33 1AA; the **telephone code** is 01284.

ACCOMMODATIONS AND FOOD

For those staying in Bury, the tourist office books B&Bs in town or on a nearby farm (£16-20). The most central B&B is Mrs. Williams's **The Garden House,** Mustow St. (tel. 703880), a re-faced Tudor cottage across the street from the abbey ruins, with simple, comfortable bedrooms (£15 per person). Or call on **Mrs. Norton,** 16 Cannon St. (tel. 761776), for warm conversation (£15, discounts after first night).

For comestibles, head half a block down Cornhill St. from the post office to **Iceland,** which dispenses a cornucopia of produce from warmer climates than its namesake (open M-W 9am-5:30pm, Th 9am-7pm, F 9am-8pm, Sa 8:30am-5:30pm). Pints go for £1.66 at the pint-sized **Nutshell,** Abbeygate at the Traverse (tel. 764867), the world's smallest pub. The hostess speaks with reverence about her entry in the pages of *Guinness*. The 15 by 17 ft. pub fit 102 people and one dog into its tiny depths…frightening. Take refuge in **The Sanctuary** (tel. 755875), off Hatter St., for tea, coffee, and chocolate, orange, and Grand Marnier cake (open M 11:30am-4pm, Tu-Th 10am-4pm, F 10am-3pm and 7-9pm, Sa 9:30am-4:45pm). Booty comes in many shapes and spices at the multinational **Galleon Restaurant,** Angel Hill (tel. 725475). Enjoy Chinese, curry, or pizza—all under £3 (closed Mondays).

SIGHTS AND ENTERTAINMENT

A few hours of whimsical wandering reveals Bury's modest charms. Along Crown St., across from the tourist office on the soggy banks of the River Lark, lie the beautiful ruins of the **Abbey of St. Edmund,** the 11th-century home to cadres of foraging ducks. The weathered, massive pillars look like stone refugees from Easter Island; it was here that the 25 *Magna Carta* barons met in 1214 to discuss their letter to the king. The formal gardens next to the remains won a special award in the annual Britain in Bloom competition; go in late June when the flowers blossom. Be sure to see the aviary and the Olde English Rose Garden that would set Frances Hodgson Burnett a-twitter. *(Ruins and garden open M-Sa 7:30am-sunset, Su 9am-sunset. Free.)* The **Abbey Visitor Centre,** Samson's Tower (tel. 763110), a block south of the Abbey Gate on Crown St., dwells in the Norman ruins, featuring three plaster-of-paris statues and abbey artifacts strategically placed throughout a gift shop. Don earphones to hear a 12th-century monk named Jocelin tell religious execution stories with slightly too much glee. *(Open Easter-Oct. daily 10am-5pm. Tour £1.50, students, seniors, and children £1.)*

Next door, the delightfully surprising 16th-century **St. Edmundsbury Cathedral** (tel. 754933) sports a recently repainted hammerbeam roof—a cross between a gingerbread house and a cuckoo clock, in green, red, yellow, and other music-box colors—flanked by guardian angels. The cherub overhanging the entrance, allegedly pilfered years before, was serendipitously rediscovered by a Bury businessman in a Belgian antique shop. *(Cathedral open daily June-Aug. 8:30am-8pm; Sept.-May 8:30am-6pm. Suggested donation £2. Choral Evensong Su 3:30pm.)*

The **Manor House Museum** borders the abbey gardens to the south. This elegant Georgian house contains dozens of synchronized timepieces, including a replica of the first rolling-ball clock, as well as an impressive collection of Victorian and 1920s costumes. *(Open Apr.-Oct. Su-Tu 10am-5pm; Nov.-Mar. 10am-4pm. £2.50, students, seniors, and children £1.50, families £7.)* The **Moyses' Hall Museum** (tel. 757488), Corn Hill, in the marketplace, houses a wonderful collection of historical junk, including a violin made out of a horse's skull. The museum also contains artifacts from the 1828 murder of local Maria Marten, such as the convicted murderer's scalp and ear, as well as a book covered with his skin. Afraid that an evil criminal might slip unnoticed into heaven, the people of the time were convinced that skinning the murderer would expose his soul so that no one would mistake him. *(Let's Go* does not recommend covering your guide with human skin.) *(Open M-Sa 10am-5pm, Su 2-5pm. £1.50, students, seniors, and children 95p, families £4.50.)* Bury bustles on **market** days. *(W and Sa 8am-4pm.)* To put some spark into your stay, visit in mid-May, when the festival brings music, plays and street entertainment, all culminating in a firework finale with vibrant colors bursting in the sky like the flowers that cover Bury's ground.

■ Near Bury St. Edmunds

Just 3 mi. southwest of Bury in the village of **Horringer** is **Ickworth** (tel. 735270), the massive home of the Marquis of Bristol, designed by **Capability Brown.** Dominated by a 106 ft. rotunda, the opulent state rooms are filled with 18th-century French furniture and several portraits (some by Reynolds and Gainsborough) of the mansion's founding family, the Herveys. The classical Italian garden is splendid. *(House open Apr.-Oct. Tu-W, F-Su, and bank holidays 1-5pm, last admission 4:30pm; park open year-round daily 7am-7pm; garden open Apr.-Oct. daily 10am-5pm; Nov.-Mar. daily 10am-4pm. £5.20, children £2.20; park and garden only £2, children 50p. Wheelchair accessible.)* Eastern Counties (tel. 766171) buses #141-144 leave Bury's St. Andrew's Station for Horringer and Ickworth (15min., M-Sa 10 per day, last return from Horringer M-Sa 7:20pm, £1.55).

The medieval village of **Lavenham** lies 10 mi. south of Bury on the A1141. **Lavenham Guildhall** (tel. (01787) 247646), in the marketplace, displays an exhibition on 700 years of the wool trade under its 450-year-old timbers, as well as a working loom. *(Open Apr.-Oct. daily 11am-5pm. £2.80, children free.)* H.C. Chambers (tel. (01787) 227233) bus #753 leaves Bury from St. Andrew's Station for Lavenham (25min., M-Sa

11 per day, £1.20). The **tourist office,** Lady St. (tel. (01787) 248207), provides information on sights in and around the village (open Easter-Sept. daily 10am-4:45pm).

Along the bus route 8 mi. farther is the village of **Sudbury** and **Thomas Gainsborough's House,** 46 Gainsborough St. (tel. (01787) 372958), where the artist was born. Feast your eyes on the largest collection of his paintings anywhere in the world. Look for the 15th-century mulberry tree in the town garden. *(Open Easter-Oct. Tu-Sa 10am-5pm, Su 2-5pm; Nov.-Easter Tu-Sa 10am-4pm, Su 2-4pm. £2.80, seniors £2.20, students and children £1.50.)* Sudbury is accessible from Bury by H.C. Chambers bus #753 (M-Sa 11 per day). The elegant Edwardian guest house, **The Orchard** (tel. (01787) 881184), on the Potkilns in Sudbury, welcomes all to its exquisite gardens (£18; doubles £28).

Turrets and moats await those who visit **Long Melford,** a mile-long Suffolk village, graced by two Tudor mansions: Melford Hall (tel. (01787) 880286) and Kentwell Hall (tel. (01787) 310207). **Hitchers** report that Melford is a feasible 12 mi. ride south of Bury on the A134.

In **Alpheton** there is a simple independent **hostel,** Monk's Croft, Bury Rd. (tel. 828297), on the A134 (£5.50, under 16 £3; open Apr.-Oct. daily). The hostel, 3 mi. north of Long Melford, 4 mi. northwest of Lavenham, and 10 mi. south of Bury St. Edmunds, is well situated for cyclers touring the region. There's also a basic **YHA Youth Hostel,** 7 Falcon Sq. (tel. (01787) 460799), in Castle Hedingham, Halstead, near Cambridge and Colchester and south of Bury St. Edmunds on the A604. (£8.80, under 18 £5. Meals available. Open July-Aug. daily; Sept.-Oct. M-Sa; Mar. M-Th; Apr.-June M-Sa; Nov. to mid-Dec. M-Th. Wheelchair accessible.)

■ Harwich and Felixstowe

Continent-bound travelers head south to **Harwich** (HAR-idge), a ferry depot for trips to Holland, Germany, and Scandinavia, and to **Felixstowe,** where boats sail to Belgium (see **By Ferry,** p. 32). Call the **Harwich tourist office** (tel. (01255) 506139) for details about ferries and their new-and-improved location and opening times. The **Felixstowe tourist office** (tel. (01394) 276770) also offers aid. (Open Easter-Sept. M-F 9am-5:30pm, Sa-Su 9:30am-5pm; Oct.-Easter M-Sa 9am-5:30pm, Su 10am-1pm.)

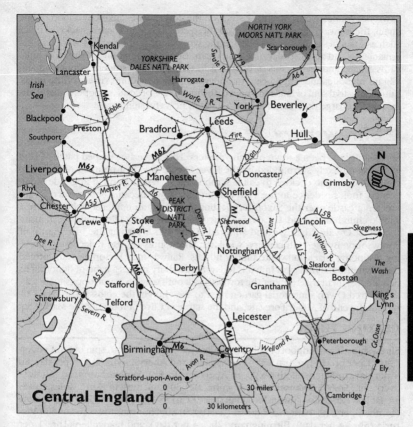

Central England

Central England

The 19th century swept into central England in an industrial sandstorm, revolutionizing quiet village life. By the end of the 1800s, the "dark satanic mills" that William Blake had foreseen overran the Midlands; even now, great cables still criss-cross the land in incomprehensible patterns of Progress. Like monuments to the irreversible transformation, towering smokestacks set winding trails of brown against the expansive blue and grey. Still, much has changed since the time when, according to D.H.

HIGHLIGHTS OF CENTRAL ENGLAND

- **Robin Hood** brought economic justice to the poor in **Sherwood Forest** (p. 302). Today visitors can wander the forest, joust in the annual Robin Hood Festival, and visit the cottage of another Nottinghamshire native: **D.H. Lawrence.**
- City-hopping travelers will revel in **Manchester's** wealth of nightlife options. Begin your evening at one of the trendy **cafe-bars** (p. 321), many of which morph into late-night venues for dancing and drinking.
- Thrillseekers take note: you can ride the highest, fastest, steepest rollercoaster in the world—known as the **Big One**—at **Blackpool's Pleasure Beach** (p. 327).
- **Beatles** fans cannot miss **Liverpool** (p. 329), where each pub, restaurant, and corner claim a connection to the Fab Four.

Lawrence, mines were "like black studs on the countryside, linked by a loop of fine chain, the railway." Prosperity followed these coal mines and smokestacks, as cities such as Manchester and Leeds became the workshops of the world's wool textiles, armaments, and autos. Today, the "fine chain" brings together one of the most innovative music and arts scenes in Britain. Add to that a large student population and vibrant nightlife, and you'll begin to understand the newfound vitality of the undisputed industrial soul of England. Indeed, the region has become so popular that B&Bs frequently charge ridiculous rates for a night of peaceful slumber.

■ Shrewsbury

Shrewsbury has been a town of many masters. This horseshoe-shaped patch of land almost completely surrounded by the River Severn was first peopled with pugnacious Saxons, who decided to call it Scrobbesbyrig. When Norman Roger de Montgomery took residence in the 11th century, the town became Shrewsbury. Roger erected a castle over the Saxon fortifications and built an immense abbey where a simple church had stood. Local rebel Harry "Hotspur" Percy allied with Welsh insurrectionist Owain Glyndŵr, and suffered Henry IV's wrath at the 1403 Battle of Shrewsbury. By the 16th century, wool-rich Shrewsburyites had redecorated, building distinctive black-and-white timber houses. Railway-mad Victorians transformed the town into the transport hub it is today. Shrewsbury makes a habit of honoring its native sons; memorials pepper the town. Check out Darwin's statue opposite the castle, Wilfred Owen's memorial garden next to the church, the colossal Lord Hill Column at the end of Abbey Foregate, and the statue of Clive of India outside Market Sq.

GETTING THERE

Shrewsbury is a whirlpool of rail ties. **Trains** (tel. (0345) 484950) spin out to **London** (3hr., 1 per hr., £34, return £35), **Machynlleth** and **Aberystwyth** (M-Sa 5 per day, Su 4 per day, to Machynlleth £6.90, to Aberystwyth £8), **Wolverhampton** (50min., every 2hr., £4.60), **Swansea** (4hr., 1 per hr., £24.30), and most of North Wales. **Buses** are far less expensive. **Shropshire Link** (tel. (0976) 559909) bus #435 runs to **Ludlow** (1¼hr., 5 per day). **National Express** (tel. (0990) 808080) runs buses to London **Victoria** (5hr., 4 per day), **Birmingham** (2hr., 4 per day), and **Llangollen** (1hr., 1 per day). All bus and train schedules are listed in the bulky *Shrewsbury Public Transport Guide,* available at the bus station and tourist office.

ORIENTATION

The **River Severn** encircles Shrewsbury's town center in a horseshoe shape, with the curve toward the south. Running from the train station in the northeast to the Quarry Park in the southwest is the town's central axis, which undergoes various name changes: starting as **Castle St.** near the station, the road becomes the pedestrian-only **Pride Hill,** and then **Shoplatch. Raven Meadows,** where the bus station is located, runs parallel to this axis, separated by the Darwin Shopping Centre. One end of High St. joins the bottom of Pride Hill at right angles; at its other end, it becomes **Wyle Cop,** then crosses the river via the **English Bridge,** and becomes **Abbey Foregate. Princess St.** runs parallel to High St.; the two streets are connected by **The Square.** Also perpendicular to the axis, but in an opposite direction from High St. is **Mardol,** which heads northwest towards the **Welsh Bridge.** Signposts help travelers navigate.

PRACTICAL INFORMATION

Trains: (tel. (0345) 484950), in a splendid neo-Gothic building at the end of Castle St. Ticket office open M-Sa 5:30am-10pm, Su 7:30am-8:30pm.

Buses: Raven Meadows (tel. 244496), parallel to Pride Hill. Office open M-F 8:30am-5:30pm, Sa 8:30am-4pm.

Taxi: Access Taxis (tel. 360606). Taxis also queue in front of the train station.

Tourist Office: Music Hall, The Square (tel. 350761; fax 355323), across from the Market Bldg. Free town maps and accommodations booking service, oversized town trail leaflets (95p), the beautiful *Shrewsbury Guide* (95p), and piles of literature. Office open Easter-Oct. M-Sa 10am-6pm, Su 10am-4pm; Nov.-Easter M-Sa 10am-5pm.

Tours: Running through Shrewsbury's "shuts" (lanes that could be—what else?—shut), tours give an insight into historic Shrewsbury. Ask about the origins of Grope Lane's name. Start at 2:30pm from the tourist office. 1½hr. Open May-Sept. daily; Oct. M-Sa; Nov.-Apr. Sa only. £2, children £1.

Financial Services: **Barclays,** 44-46 Castle St. (tel. 843800). Open M-Tu and Th-F 9am-5pm, W 10am-5pm, Sa 9:30am-1pm. **ATM** in the lobby.

American Express: 27 Claremont St. (tel. 357204), off Mardol St. Open M-Tu and Th-F 9am-5:30pm, W 9:30am-5:30pm, Sa 9am-5pm.

Launderette: Stidgers Wishy Washy, Monkmoor Rd. (tel. 355151), off Abbey Foregate. Open M-F 7:30am-6:30pm, last wishy washy 5:30pm; Su 7:30am-2:30pm, last wishy washy 1:30pm.

Emergency: Dial 999; no coins required.

Police: Raven Meadows and Clive Rd., Monkmoor (tel. 232888). Open M-Sa 9am-5pm.

Hotlines: Samaritans (crisis; tel. 369696). Open 24hr. **Lesbian and Gay Switchboard** (tel. 232393). Open Tu-W and F 8-10pm. **Victim Support** (tel. 362812).

Hospital: Shrewsbury Hospital, Mytton Oak Rd. (tel. 261138).

Post Office: St. Mary's St. (tel. 362925), just off Pride Hill. Bureau de change. Open M-Sa 9am-5:30pm. **Postal Code:** SY1 1ED.

Telephone Code: 01743.

ACCOMMODATIONS

The **YHA Shrewsbury,** The Woodlands, Abbey Foregate (tel. 360179; fax 357423), lies about 1½ mi. from the city center. From town, cross the English Bridge, pass the abbey, and head straight down Abbey Foregate; the hostel is opposite the Lord Hill monument. Or catch bus #8 or 26 from the town center. The hostel offers laundry facilities, video games, a pool table, and a juke box in a Victorian house (£8, under 18 £5.40; open Feb.-Oct. daily; Nov. to mid-Dec. F-Sa). **B&Bs** in town (£15-18) cluster on Abbey Foregate and Monkmoor Rd. across the English Bridge. TVs watch over pastel rooms at **Glynndene Guest House,** Park Terr. (tel. 352488), a left off Abbey Foregate before the Abbey—look for the elaborate bell pull (£18). **Abbey Lodge,** 68 Abbey Foregate (tel./fax 235832), will put you to sleep (so to speak) in flowery rooms with fresh, scented air (singles £17; doubles with bath £40). The red-carpeted staircase of **Allandale Abbey,** Abbey Foregate (tel. 240173), is lined with baby prints (£16).

FOOD AND PUBS

The **Good Life Wholefood Restaurant,** Barracks Passage (tel. 350455), off Wyle Cop, offers cheap, tasty vegetarian dishes (everything under £2.25) in a restored 14th-century building in an alley between the Lion Hotel and the house where Henry VII stayed in 1485 (open M-Sa 9:30am-4:30pm). Crayon-in the crazy-happy cat logo in the **Blue Cat Café,** 1 Fish St. (tel. 232236), as you munch on sandwiches and bagels (£1.75-2.10; open M-Sa 10am-4pm). **The Little Gourmet,** 21 Castle St., serves up French bread sandwiches from £1.10 (open M-Sa 8am-4pm). **The King's Head** pub, Mardol St., displays a medieval wall painting of the Last Supper uncovered during renovation (open M-Sa noon-3pm and 6-11pm, Su 6-11pm). In a space much larger than its name suggests, the polished wood walls of **The Hole in the Wall,** 1 Shoplatch, shelter a young but sedate crowd (open M-Sa 11:30am-11pm, Su 7-10:30pm).

SIGHTS

The original earth and timber version of **Shrewsbury Castle** (tel. 358516), just up from the train station, was constructed in 1083 by William the Conqueror's buddy Roger de Montgomery, who demolished 50 Saxon houses to make way for the project. Climb up Laura's tower for a grand view of Shrewsbury. *(Castle, grounds, and* *tower open Easter-Sept. daily 9am-5pm; Oct.-Easter M-Sa 9am-5pm. Free. Museum open May-Aug. Tu-Su 10am-4:30pm; Sept.-Apr. Tu-Sa only. £2, students and seniors £1, children 50p.)*

Shrewsbury's biggest attraction is undoubtedly its architecture. Tudoresque houses dot the central shopping district and rally in full force at the **Bear Steps,** which start in the alley on High St. across from the Square. At the end of Castle St., **Quarry Park's** riverside acres explode with bright flowers. According to local law, sheep can graze anywhere; a number even infiltrate the churchyard at **St. Mary's. Rowley's House Museum,** Barker St. (tel. 361196), off Shoplatch, displays Iron Age log boats, Roman funeral stones, and the silver Wroxheter mirror (c. AD 130). *(Open Easter-Sept. Tu-Sa 10am-5pm, Su 10am-4pm; Oct.-Easter Tu-Sa 10am-5pm. £3, students and seniors £1, children 50p.)* Beyond the English Bridge, the red **Shrewsbury Abbey** (tel. 232723) holds a shrine to St. Winefride, a 7th-century princess who was beheaded, then miraculously put back together again to become an abbess. *(Open daily Easter-Oct. 9:30am-5:30pm; Nov.-Easter 10:30am-3pm.)* Just across the road, **Shrewsbury Quest** (tel. 243324) throws you into a medieval time-warp. Shrewsbury Abbey is the home of novelist Ellis Peters's popular fictional medieval sleuth Brother Cadfael, and the "quest" consists of solving "mysteries"; clues are strewn unobtrusively along the way. *(Open daily Apr.-Oct. 10am-6:30pm, last admission 5pm; Nov.-Mar. 10am-5:30pm, last admission 4pm. £4.25, students and seniors £3.60, children £2.95, families £13. Wheelchair accessible.)*

Stewart supporters with cars may want to swing by nearby **Boscobel House** (tel. (01902) 850244) past Telford on a minor road between the A41 and A5, which holds a direct descendant of the famous royal oak, in whose branches the future Charles II hid from pursuing Roundheads. Unfortunately, mere commoners are not allowed to climb the nearly 300-year-old tree. *(House open Apr.-Oct. daily 10am-6pm, last admission 5:30pm; Nov.-Mar. W-Su 10am-4pm. £4, students and seniors £3, children £2.)*

■ Nottingham

Redistribution of wealth continues in modern-day Nottingham, as money-toting visitors make contributions to the native Robin Hood industry. But today you'll see more savvy city youths than rural outlaws; Nottingham's 20,000 university students wear all hair colors and styles, a few of which blend with Lincoln Green. Along with flourishing hair, the nearby *Sons and Lovers* cottage and a vibrant club scene prove that life here continues even without Friar Tuck and Maid Marian.

ORIENTATION

Nottingham is a busy city, unfortunately without the streets to match. Its hub is **Old Market Sq.,** a paved, fountain-filled plaza near the Council House (beware the pigeons). The train and bus stations lie at the extreme south of the city. The trendy neighborhood of Hockley is east of the city center. Walkers and drivers beware: Nottingham was not designed for either of you. Four- and five-way intersections render maps and vocal directions hard to follow, a problem compounded by inconsistent street signs and address numbers, as well as a host of one-way streets.

PRACTICAL INFORMATION

Trains: Carrington St. (tel. (0345) 484950), in the south of the city, across the canal. To **Lincoln** (1hr., M-Sa 32 per day, Su 7 per day, £4.20), **Sheffield** (1 per hr., £6), **London** (2hr., 1 per hr., £21.50), and many other cities.

Buses: Broad Marsh Bus Station (tel. 934 6224), on the south side, between Collin and Canal St. **National Express** (tel. (0990) 808080) runs to **London** (about 6 per day, £12.25), **Sheffield,** and other destinations. Many bus lines service the city, including **Nottinghamshire County Council Buses,** connecting to points throughout the county. For shorter urban journeys, hop on a **Nottingham City Transport** bus (up to 70p). For information on public transit call **Nottinghamshire Buses Hotline** (tel. 924 0000; open daily 7am-8pm).

Tourist Office: City Information Centre, 1-4 Smithy Row (tel. 915 5330), just off Old Market Sq. Many reference guides. Books rooms daily 8:30am-4:30pm for a

10% deposit; ask for the accommodations list. Open M-F 8:30am-5pm, Sa 9am-5pm; Apr.-Oct. also Su 10am-4pm.

Budget Travel: STA Travel, Byron House, Shakespeare St. (tel. 952 8802), near Nottingham Trent University. Open M-F 10am-5pm.

Financial Services: Thomas Cook, 4 Long Row (tel. 9470311). Open M-Sa 9am-5:30pm. Also offers budget travel services. **Barclays,** 2 High St. Open W 10am-5:30pm, Th-Tu 9am-5:30pm.

American Express: 2 Victoria St. (tel. 924 1777). Open M-Th 9am-5:30pm, F-Sa 9am-5pm.

Launderette: Brights, 150 Mansfield Rd. (tel. 948 3670), near the Igloo Hostel. Change available. Open M-F 8:30am-7pm, Sa 8:30am-6pm, Su 9:30am-5pm.

Emergency: Dial 999; no coins required.

Police: N. Church St. (tel. 948 2999).

Hotlines: Samaritans (crisis; tel. 941 1111). Open 24hr. **Rape crisis** (tel. 941 0440). Open M and W-F 10am-1pm, Tu 10am-8pm. **Lesbian and Gay Switchboard,** 33 Mansfield Rd. (tel. 941 1454). Open M-F 7-10pm.

Hospital: Queen's Medical Center, Derby Rd. (tel. 924 9924).

Post Office: Queen St. (tel. 947 4311). Open M-F 9am-5:30pm, Sa 9am-7pm. *Poste Restante,* bureau de change. **Postal Code:** NG1 2BN.

Internet Access: Nottingham Youth Shop, 24 Carlton St. (tel. 958 5111). 2 computers with dialup access in a youth support center. 50p per 10min. Open M-Tu noon-6pm, W-Sa noon-4pm.

Telephone Code: 0115.

ACCOMMODATIONS

B&Bs are scattered throughout the central city and also in neighboring hoods to the north and south. A number of guesthouses cluster along Goldsmith Rd. (near Nottingham Trent University) and generally run £16-20 per person.

Igloo, 110 Mansfield Rd. (tel. 947 5250). Located on the north side of town. From the train station, take bus #90 to Mansfield Rd. From the tourist center, walk right to Clumber St., then take a left and walk straight for 10min. Well-kept, homey hostel operated by an experienced, affable backpacker. Colorful walls, an info-stocked lounge with TV, individual bathrooms, a kitchen, and 2 black cats. £9. Sleepsacks available. Curfew 3am.

Castle Rock Guest House, 79 Castle Blvd. (tel 948 2116). 5min. walk from the train station. Check maps at station. Mid-sized rooms, TV in each room. £17.50.

Adams Castle View Guesthouse, 85 Castle Blvd. (tel 950 0022), 5min. from train station and opposite the castle. Elegant rooms, most with bath. £19.50.

YMCA, 4 Shakespeare St. (tel. 956 7600; fax 956 7601). Large building with bland decor on a busy street. Dorms £10; singles £15; £5 key deposit. Breakfast included.

FOOD

Quick, inexpensive bites are easily found, especially on Milton St. and Mansfield Rd. There's a gaggle of sandwich shops, trendy cafes, and ethnic eateries on Goosegate, and a **Tesco** supermarket in the Victorian Shopping Centre stocks groceries.

Ye Olde Trip to Jerusalem, 1 Brewhouse Yard (tel. 947 3171). With its first drink pulled in 1189, and a "new" section added in the 17th century, this place lays claim to the title "Oldest Inn in England." Soldiers stopped here en route to the Crusades. Locally known as "The Trip," the pub is actually carved into the sandstone base of ye olde Nottingham Castle. Bang your head on the 6ft. stone ceiling and bring a piece of the pub home in your hair. Open M-Sa 11am-11pm, Su noon-10:30pm; food served noon-6pm.

Café Hiziki, 15 Goosegate, 2nd fl. (tel. 948 1115 for cafe, 950 5523 for store). Divine vegetarian and vegan food. Specials £1.50-4. Vegan groceries sold downstairs. Cafe open M-Sa 9:30am-4pm; store open M-Tu and Th-F 9:30am-6pm, W and Sa 9:30am-5:30pm.

Balti House, 35 Heathcote St. (tel. 947 2871). A tandoori treasure trove. Cauliflower or chickpea starter, followed by a sizzling Balti dish with *chapati* and *naan* bread, for £6.35. Open daily 6-10pm.

SIGHTS

Nottingham Castle was originally constructed in 1068 by William the Conqueror and tops a sandstone rise in the south of the city. In 1642, Charles I raised his standard against Parliament here, kicking off the Civil War. For his troubles, the king was beheaded and the castle destroyed. It now houses the **Castle Museum** (tel. 915 3700), which features historical exhibits, a collection of Victorian art, an English silver collection, and the regimental memorabilia of the Sherwood Foresters, as well as temporary exhibits. *(Museum open Mar.-Oct. daily 10am-5pm; Nov.-Feb. Sa-Th 10am-5pm, F 1-5pm. M-F free; Sa-Su £1.50, students, seniors, and children 75p; free for disabled visitors.)*

Nearby, the **Tales of Robin Hood** (tel. 948 3284) cable cars will carry you and your five-year-old through Robin's "Sherwood Forest." *(Open daily 10am-4:30pm. £4.50, students and seniors £4, children £3.50.)* The **Galleries of Justice** (tel. 952 0555), on High Pavement St., provide hands-on access to the 19th-century prison system, including stops behind bars and in front of merciless courts. *(Tourists regularly sentenced to Australia. Open Tu-Su 10am-5pm. Crime and Punishment and Police Galleries £8, students, seniors, and children £7. Police Galleries only £3.95, students, seniors, and children £3.75.)*

ENTERTAINMENT

As is appropriate for a large city with thousands of students, Nottingham offers a wide range of entertainment and nightlife options, from high culture to clubs, drinking, and dancing. The **Theatre Royal** (tel. 948 2626), at Theatre Sq., **Nottingham Playhouse** (tel. 941 9419), at Wellington Circus, and a number of other theatres offer musicals, dramas, and comedies. *(Tickets from £6.)*

Clubs and pubs blanket the city. *Dirty Stop Out's Guide to Nottingham,* published by the tourist office, describes many of the best places and includes a helpful map. Nights, covers, and crowds vary tremendously, but students can be found everywhere. **The Hippo,** 45 Bridlesmith Gate (tel. 950 6667), carries up to 270 loyalists on its royal ship of funk, dance, and garage music. *(Open 10:30pm-2am. Disabled access by arrangement.)* Its upstairs companion, **The Bomb** (tel. 953 6993)—by day a cafe—offers soul, swing, and blues. **Rock City,** 8 Talbot St. (tel. 950 0102), entertains up to 1700 with local bands and mainstream rock. *(Alternative night on Sa. Cover £3-4. Open 8:30pm-2am.)* The **Rig** (tel. 959 9407), next door, features frequent live local music.

■ Near Nottingham: Sherwood Forest

North of Nottingham, in the village of **Linby,** stands **Newstead Abbey** (tel. (01623) 793557), the gorgeous ancestral estate of Romantic poet Lord Byron. Byron took residence as a 10-year-old and remained here until forced to sell. *(House open early Apr. to late Sept. daily noon-5pm; grounds open year-round daily 9am-dusk. House and grounds £4, stu-*

Nottingham's Underground Scene

Beneath Nottingham lie hundreds of ancient caves. As early as the 10th century, Nottingham dwellers dug homes out of the soft and porous "Sherwood sandstones" on which the city rests. Even in medieval times, the caves were often preferred to more conventional housing—they required no building materials and incurred lower taxes. While cave residency dwindled during the Industrial Revolution, Nottingham citizens (and pub owners) continued to use some for storage, and during World War II many caves were converted to air raid shelters. Visitors can tour one cave complex beneath the Broadmarsh Shopping Centre. The 35-minute audio tour of the "Tigguo Cobauc," or "city of caves," includes a trip through Britain's only underground medieval tannery—authentic smells included (tel. 924 1424; M-Sa 10am-5pm, Su 11am-5pm; £2-2.75). Untouristed caves await rediscovery.

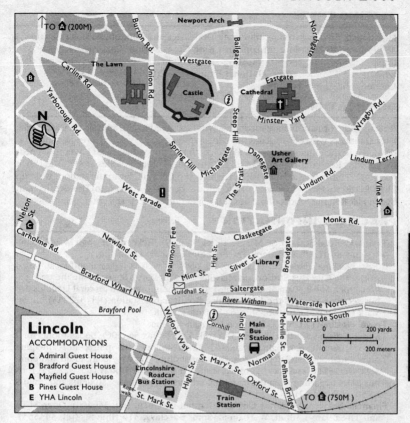

Lincoln

ACCOMMODATIONS

C Admiral Guest House
D Bradford Guest House
A Mayfield Guest House
B Pines Guest House
E YHA Lincoln

dents and seniors £2, under 16 £1.50. Grounds only £2, students, seniors, and children £1.) To the north spreads the famed **Sherwood Forest,** considerably thinned since the 13th century. (Open daily dawn-dusk.) At the **Sherwood Forest Visitor Centre** (tel. (01623) 823202), beware the multitude of children circling with mini-archery sets, heedless of the warning "do not fire at close range." (Open daily Apr.-Oct. 10:30am-5pm; Nov.-Mar. 10:30am-4:30pm. Take bus #33 or 36 from Victoria bus station.) The period **Robin Hood Festival** (tel. 977 4774) centers around a jousting tournament each August. Stay at the new **YHA Sherwood Forest** (tel. (01629) 825850) at Forest Corner, Edwinstowe. Forty beds and laundry facilities grace this convenient abode (£7-10).

Another of Sherwood Forest's merry men, D.H. Lawrence, was a Nottinghamshire native and schoolteacher who went on to write blessedly dirty books of prose and poetry. Once he was banned from the bookshelves; now he's buried in Westminster Abbey. The **D.H. Lawrence Birthplace Museum** (tel. (01773) 717353) awaits at Mansfield Rd., Eastwood. (Open daily Apr.-Oct. 10am-5pm; Nov.-Mar. 10am-4pm. £1.75, students, seniors, and children £1.) The **Sons and Lovers Cottage,** 28 Garden Rd., Eastwood (tel. (0151) 653 8710), where young Lawrence and family lived from 1887-1891, is free and open by appointment.

■ Lincoln

Lincoln's imposing hilltop cathedral dominates the view from the surrounding countryside for miles. Medieval streets climb their cobbled way past half-timbered Tudor houses to the 12th-century cathedral, itself a relative newcomer in a town built for retired Roman legionnaires. Today, the city is known for its annual Christmas Market, which draws natives and tourists alike.

GETTING THERE

Lincoln sits on a rail route connecting Doncaster and London. **Trains** (tel. (0345) 484950) run to Lincoln from London's **King Cross** Station (2hr., M-Sa 1 per hr., Su departs every 2hr., £36.50), **Nottingham** (1-1½hr., M-Sa 2 per hr., Su 7 per day, £4.20), and 42 other cities. **National Express** (tel. (0990) 808080) sends **buses** to **London** (5hr., 2 per day, £18).

ORIENTATION

Roman and Norman military engineers were attracted to the summit of **Castle Hill;** later engineers who constructed the railway preferred its base. As a result, Lincoln is divided into the affluent acropolis to the north and the cottage-filled lower town near the railway. Regrettably for backpackers, the tourist office perches atop Castle Hill; it has also recently opened a booth at High St. and Cornhill. From the station, walk up **High St.** (across the street and to the left a bit), which turns into **The Strait,** then **Steep Hill Rd.;** the tourist office lies at the junction of Steep Hill and Castle Hill.

PRACTICAL INFORMATION

Trains: Central Station, St. Mary's St. (tel. 513269). Ticket office open M-Sa 5:45am-7:30pm, Su 10:30am-9:20pm. Travel Center open M-Sa 9am-5pm.

Buses: National Express (tel. (0990) 808080), as well as regional and local buses, stop at the **City Bus Station,** on Melville St. off St. Mary's St., opposite the train station. Open M-F 8:30am-5pm, Sa 9am-1:45pm. For information on rural Lincolnshire bus services, contact the **Lincolnshire Roadcar** bus station (tel. 522255), on St. Mark St. Open M-F 8:30am-5pm, Sa 8:30am-4:30pm.

Travel Hotline: (tel. 553135). Open M-F 8am-4:45pm.

Tourist Office: 9 Castle Hill, LN1 3AA (tel. 529828; fax 564506). Books rooms for a fee of 10% of the first night. Open M-Th 9am-5:30pm, F 9am-5pm, Sa-Su 10am-5pm.

Tours: One-hour tours depart from the tourist office July-Aug. daily 11am and 2pm; Sept.-Oct. Sa-Su 11am and 2pm. £2, children £1. **Guide Friday** (tel. 522255) runs bus tours departing from the cathedral (at least 1 per hr.; £5, students and seniors £3.50, children £2).

Financial Services: Thomas Cook, 4 Cornhill Pavement (tel. 346400). Open M-Tu and Th-Sa 9am-5:30pm, W 10am-5:30pm. **Barclays,** 316 High St. (tel. 343555). Open M-Tu and Th-F 9am-5pm, W 10am-5pm, Sa 9:30am-noon. Most **ATMs** are located on lower High St.

Launderette: Burton Laundries, 8 Burton Rd. (tel. 543498), at Westgate near the cathedral. Dry cleaning available. Open daily at 8:30am; M-F last wash 7pm, Sa-Su last wash 4pm.

Emergency: Dial 999; no coins required.

Police: West Parade (tel. 529911), near City Hall.

Hotlines: Samaritans (crisis; tel. 528282). Open 24hr. **Lincoln Gay Switchboard** (tel. 513999). Open Tu and Th 7-9pm.

Hospital: Lincoln County Hospital, Greenwell Rd. (tel. 512512).

Post Office: Cornhill (tel. 532288), just off High St. Bureau de change. Open M-F 9am-5:30pm, Sa 9am-12:30pm. **Postal Code:** LN5 7XX.

Internet Access: Central Library, Free School Ln. (tel. 510800). It's busy, so call ahead to reserve a time. Library open M-F 9:30am-7pm, Sa 9:30am-4pm. £3 per hr.

Telephone Code: 01522.

ACCOMMODATIONS

B&Bs line Carline and Yarborough Rd., west of the castle. Most can be had for £16-18 a person. Call ahead in summer, as rooms fill quickly. Also pick up *Where to Stay* free at the tourist office.

YHA Lincoln, 77 S. Park (tel. 522076; fax 567424), opposite S. Common at the end of Canwick Rd. Veer right from station, make a right onto Pelham Bridge (becomes Canwick Rd.), and take the first right after the traffic lights at S. Park Ave. 47-bed

Victorian villa. £8.80, under 18 £6. Breakfast £2.85. Dinner at 7pm £4.25. Reception closed and lockout 10am-5pm. Curfew 11pm. Open July-Aug. daily; Apr.-June M-Sa; mid-Feb. to Mar. and Sept.-Oct. daily; Nov.-Dec. F-Sa.

Mayfield Guest House, 213 Yarborough Rd. (tel./fax 533732), entrance behind house on Mill Rd., a 20min. walk from train station and near the **Ellis Mill,** a working windmill. If you've got a backpack, spare yourself and take bus #7, 8, 17 or 117 (50p). Bright Victorian mansion with large rooms and gigantic fluffy quilts, almost all with bath. Panoramic breakfast view of the countryside. No smoking. £18.

Bradford Guest House, 67 Monks Rd. (tel. 523947), across from North Lincolnshire College. 10min. from High St., 5min. from theater and town center. Private bathrooms with showers. Singles £16; doubles £30; family room £40.

Admiral Guest House, 18 Nelson St. (tel./fax 544467), in the lower part of town. From the railway station, take Wigford Wy. across the canal, then take the immediate steps down to the canal and walk along Brayford Wharf N.; turn left onto Carholme Rd., then right onto Nelson St. Mrs. Robertson's decor is so nautical, you'll think you're at sea! £17.50, all rooms with bath.

Pines Guest House, 104 Yarborough Rd. (tel./fax 532985). Take bus #7, 8, 17 or 117, or a 15min. walk from the station. Large, thickly carpeted B&B. All rooms have TV. Singles £16, with bath £20; twins or doubles £30, with bath £35.

FOOD

The **Market,** at Sincil St. outside Astoria shopping center, sells sundries including fresh produce and clothing (open M-F 9am-4pm, Sa 9am-4:30pm). Wholefood can be found at **Holland and Barrett Health Foods and Natural Remedies,** 319 High St. (tel. 567615; open M-Sa 9am-5:30pm). A variety of restaurants, tearooms, and takeaways grace High St. On Bailgate St. on the other side of the hill, pubs abound.

The Spinning Wheel, 39 Steep Hill Rd. (tel. 522463), 1 block south of tourist office in a leaning, half-timbered building. Tea (£1.50-1.65) and vegetarian dishes (£3.45-5) are nicely priced; others a bit steeper. Open daily 11:30am-10pm.

Lion and Snake, 79 Bailgate St. (tel. 575567), up by the cathedral. An alluring pub setting (picnic tables out back) for a restorative pint and 3-course meal (£5). Open M-Sa 11am-11pm, Su noon-10:30pm. Food served M-F 11:30am-2:30pm, Sa noon-2pm, Su noon-3pm.

Stokes High Bridge Café, 207 High St. (tel. 513825). Busy tearoom in a Tudor-style house-cum-bridge. Displayed on every Lincoln postcard. Sit by a window upstairs and watch swans float by on the green canal. Savory quiche (£4.20) and steak pie (£4.30). 2-course lunches (£4.90) served 11:30am-2pm; tea served 9:30am-5pm. Coffee and tea shop downstairs. Open daily 9am-5pm.

SIGHTS

After a millennium of rumblings and crumblings, in which Roman barricades, bishops' palaces, and conquerors' castles were all erected and destroyed, the undefeated king of the hill is the magnificent **Lincoln Cathedral** (tel. 544544). Although construction began in 1072, the cathedral wasn't completed until three centuries later, when it towered over Europe as the continent's tallest building. The cathedral's many alluring features include the legendary imp in the Angel Choir, who turned to stone while attempting to chat with angels. A treasury room displays ancient sacred silver and a shrine to child martyr Sir Hugh, mentioned in Chaucer's *Prioress's Tale* and Marlowe's *The Jew of Malta*. Other exhibits reside in a library designed by Christopher Wren. You can visit a statue of Lord Tennyson and his dog in the northeast grounds. (*Cathedral open May-Aug. M-Sa 7:15am-8pm, Su 7:15am-6pm; Sept.-Apr. M-Sa 7:15am-6pm, Su 7:15am-5pm. Suggested donation £3, students, seniors, and children £1. Photography permit £1. Free tours depart May-Aug. daily 11am and 2pm; Sept.-Apr. Sa only. W and Sa roof tours £2. Book in advance. Library £1, children free.*)

Home to one of the four surviving copies of the *Magna Carta*, the great-great-great-grandparent of all modern constitutions and civil liberties, **Lincoln Castle** (tel. 511068) was also the house of pain for the inmates of the Victorian Castle Prison. A cheerful tour guide will let you share in "The Prison Experience." The handsome castle also affords a beautiful view of the countryside. *(Open Apr.-Oct. M-Sa 9:30am-5:30pm, Su 11am-5:30pm; Nov.-Mar. M-Sa 9:30am-4pm. Guided tours Apr.-Oct. 11am-2pm. £2.50, seniors £1.50, children £1, families £6.50.)*

Rather than destroy the leftovers of Lincoln's ancient imperial settlers, the pragmatic Lincolnites of the Middle Ages put them to good use. The medieval **Bishop's Palace** (tel. 527468), for example, was originally wedged between the walls of the upper and lower Roman Cities. Thanks to 12th-century cleric Bishop Chesney, a passageway through the upper city wall links the palace remains to Lincoln Cathedral at the top of the hill. The palace itself, in Chesney's time the seat of England's largest diocese, was brought to ruins in the Civil War, but the vineyard, art exhibitions, and the splendid view of Lincolnshire make a visit worthwhile. *(Open Apr.-Oct. daily 10am-6pm; Nov.-Mar. Sa-Su 10am-1pm and 2-6pm. £1.10, students and seniors 80p, children 60p.)*

ENTERTAINMENT

Lincoln offers respectable nightlife. Head for High St., where the nightlife will make itself known; watch for **Yates** and **Barracuda's.** On the corner of Silver St. and Flaxengate, **Mustang Sally's** offers a variety of theme nights including karaoke. Next door, **Ritzy** (tel. 522314) is one of the more popular clubs. For information on less strenuous entertainment, pick up the monthly *What's On In Lincoln* pamphlet at the tourist office, or ask at the Cathedral about choral and organ performances. The **Theatre Royal,** Clasketgate (tel. 525555), between High St. and Broadgate, stages all sorts of dramas, musicals, and comedies year-round. *(Box office open M-Sa 10am-6pm. Tickets £7-16.50; £2 student discounts sometimes available. Wheelchair access.)* The **Lawn Visitor Centre** (tel. 560330), on Union Rd. west of the castle, hosts frequent summer events.

The **Arts Festival** in mid-summer features performances by touring theater companies. You can sample wines from Neustadt, Lincoln's German sister city, at the June **Wine Festival.** Visitors flock to town for the **Christmas Market,** where Lincoln celebrates the holiday season in country style with carolers, roasting chestnuts, and luminous trees galore.

■ Near Lincoln: Grantham and Boston

It was in **Grantham,** about 25 mi. south of Lincoln, that Sir Isaac Newton attended the **King's School** (tel. (01476) 563180), on Brook St., and left a carving of his schoolboy signature in a windowsill. *(Open by appointment only. Free, but donations accepted.)* The **Grantham Museum** (tel. (01476) 568783), on St. Peter's Hill by the tourist office, features exhibits on Newton's life and work, as well as a video exhibit on another Grantham prodigy, Margaret Thatcher. *(Open M-Sa 10am-5pm. Free.)* Seven miles south in **Colsterworth** is **Woolsthorpe Manor** (tel. (01476) 860338), birthplace of Sir Isaac Newton. It was here, under an apple tree, that the scientist conceptualized gravity and dreamt up calculus, the bane of students everywhere. *(Open Apr.-Oct. W-Su 1-5pm. £2.50, children £1.30, families £5.70.)* Reach Grantham from Lincoln by **train** (45min., about 1 per hr., £7.50 return) or by **Lincolnshire Road Car** (tel. (01476) 522255) from St. Mark's Bus Station (1¼hr., 1 per hr.).

East of Grantham, near the mouth of the River Witham, life goes on in tiny **Boston,** despite the departure of a band of Puritans for New England in 1630. Originally chartered for Holland, the crusading Calvinists were betrayed by their captain (leaving the country was a crime) and imprisoned in the **Guildhall** (tel. (01205) 365954), which is now a museum. *(Open M-Sa 10am-5pm; in summer also Su 1:30-5pm. £1.25, students and seniors 80p, children free; free entry for all on Th.)* Holding no grudges, they named their new settlement on Massachusetts Bay after the Lincolnshire town that had held them prisoner. The refreshingly happy folk in the **tourist office** (tel. (01205) 356656), in Market Pl., can give you information about the area. *(Open M-Sa 9am-5pm.)* Boston can be reached by **train** from Lincoln, changing at Sleaford (1hr., roughly 1 per hr., £7).

■ Sheffield

In a flurry of chopping, scooping, carving, and spreading, Sheffield rose to fame on the handles of its cutlery. While Manchester was clothing the world, Sheffield was setting its table, first with hand-crafted flatware, then with mass-produced goods, and eventually with stainless steel, invented here. The city's population soared in the boom years of the mid-19th century, and Sheffield remains England's fourth-largest city. *The Full Monty* fans know the consequence of all that industry, and Sheffield is only slowly transforming itself to face the new millennium. Construction will hopefully alleviate the heartless laceration of the city center by divided highways that make walking tortuous; the sleek super tram system does its part to provide order to the chaos. Still, this last refuge of urbanity before the Peak District to the west is a good connection point and also has a massive nightlife scene; nighttrippers are unfortunately foiled by a dearth of budget city-center accommodations.

GETTING THERE Sheffield lies on the M1 Motorway, about 30 mi. east of Manchester and 25 mi. south of Leeds. **Trains** (tel. (0345) 484950) run to **Manchester** (1½hr., M-Su 1 per hr., £9.30, return £12.60), **Birmingham** (1½hr., 1-2 per hr., £18), and London **St. Pancras** (2-3hr., M-Sa 1-2 per hr., £38-39), as well as **Liverpool, York,** the **Lake District** (via Preston or Stockport), and **Chester** (via Stockport). **National Express** coaches (tel. (0990) 808080) run to **London** (3½hr., 8 per day, £11, return £16), **Birmingham** (2½hr., 6 per day, £14), and **Nottingham** (1¼hr., 1 per hr., £7.75). All buses leave from the **Sheffield Interchange.**

PRACTICAL INFORMATION Buses arrive at the **Sheffield Interchange** (tel. 275 4905), between Pond and Sheaf St. (open M-F 8am-5:30pm; lockers £1-2). The **train station** (tel. (0345) 484950) is a block south on Sheaf St. (lockers £1-3). Sheffield's **tourist office** (tel. 273 4671; fax 272 4225) meekly hides in Peace Gardens, a corner of the massive Town Hall Extension on Union St., and distributes information on the city. It also books rooms for a 10% deposit (open M and F 10:30am-5:15pm, Tu-Th 9:30am-5:15pm, Sa 9:30am-4:15pm). Cash your traveler's checks at **American Express,** 20 Charles St. (tel. 275 1144; open M and W-Sa 9am-5:30pm, Tu 9:30am-5:30pm; client mail held). The **post office** (tel. 733525) blinks at Fitzalan Sq. uphill from the Interchange (open M-Tu and Th-F 8:30am-5:30pm, W 9am-5:30pm, Sa 8:30am-12:30pm). Sheffield's **postal code** is S1 1AB. **Internet access** is available at Havana Bistro (see below). The **telephone code** is 0114.

ACCOMMODATIONS AND FOOD Pick up the thorough *Where to Stay* at the tourist office. The **B&Bs** scattered around town cost at least £16 per night. Unless you opt to stay in a pub, expect a hilly westward hike from the city center. Most places fill up quickly, especially in summer; as always, call in advance. The **YMCA,** 20 Victoria Rd. (tel. 268 4807), between Broomhall and Victoria Rd., offers clean room and a continental breakfast on a quiet street a few blocks from the University. Men and women, 18 and older, are accepted. Take bus #60 to Hallamshire Hospital, bear left on Clarkehouse Rd. to Park Ln., turn left again and then right onto the unmarked Victoria Rd. (£16; weekly £52). The charming, aptly named duo **Mr. and Mrs. Chambers,** 17 Sale Hill (tel. 266 2986) make the hike worthwhile, with their flower garden above the city, large lounge chairs, and TVs. Take bus #60 to the beginning of Manchester Rd., then climb one block to Sale Hill (£15, breakfast not included).

Stimulating nourishment in the city center is hard to come by; instead, head for the student haunts on Ecclesall Rd., or the ubiquitous cafe-bars on Division and Devonshire St., where pre-clubbers prepare for the night ahead. A sprawling **Safeway** supermarket resides at the corner of Hanover Way and Ecclesall Rd. (open M-F 8am-10pm, Sa 8am-8pm, Su 10am-4pm). **Somerfield** offers supermarket options on Pinstone St. (open M-F 7:30am-7pm, Sa 7:30am-6:30pm). **Mamas and Leonies,** 111-115 Norfolk St. (tel. 272 0490), serves up every kind of pizza imaginable, including "a la fruit," topped with bananas, apples, pineapples, and raisins (open M-Sa 9:30am-11:30pm). **Havana Bistro,** 32-34 Division St. (tel. 249 5452; email havana@havana.co.uk), dishes

Peak District National Park

Axe Edge Moor, 25
Birchinlee Pasture, 12
Black Ashop Moor, 13
Blue John Cavern, 19
Broomhead Moor, 9
Derwent Moors, 14
Dick Hill, 4
Edale Head, 17
Edale Moor, 15

Hartington Upper Quarter, 22
Hobson Moss, 10
Hope Woodlands, 11
Jacob's Ladder, 18
Kinder Low (elevation 2077), 16
Longsett Moors, 6
Margery Hill (elevation 1793), 8
Middle Hills, 26
Peak Cavern, 21

Raven's Low, 24
Saddleworth, 3
Shining Clough Mass, 7
Shining Tor (elevation 1854), 23
Thor's Cave, 27
Thurlstone Moor, 5
Treak Cliff Cavern, 20
Wessenden Head Moor, 2
Wessenden Moor, 1

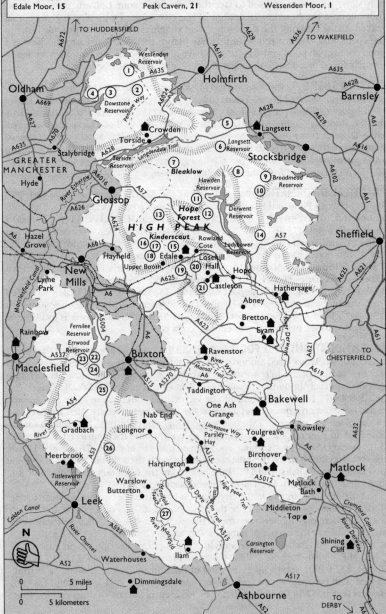

up out-of-the-ordinary cybercafe fare (chicken goujons and melted brie £3.50) to accompany your net surfing (£2 per 30min., £3.50 per hr.; open M-Th 10am-10pm, F-Sa 10am-7pm, Su noon-7pm). **The Showroom Café-Bar,** 7 Paternoster Row (tel. 275 3588), draws sophistes into its minimalist interior. Loll on the couch and watch the large screen, or catch one of the arthouse films showing next door.

SIGHTS AND ENTERTAINMENT The **Kelham Island Industrial Museum,** Alma St. (tel. 272 2106), documents depressing working and living conditions over the past 300 years, and displays hammers, sickles, and other proletarian tools churned out by Sheffield's famed steel industry. It also holds a working 420-ton steam engine and the mother of all pocket knives, with 365 blades. *(Open M-Th 10am-4pm, Su 11am-4:45pm. £3, students, seniors, and children £1.50, families £6, disabled free. Wheelchair accessible.)* Take bus #53 from the Interchange (1 per hr.), alight at Nursery St.; turn left on Corporation St.; take a right on Alma St. and wind 200 yd. through an industrial park to the museum on the right.

In 1875, Victorian critic and artist John Ruskin established a museum to show the working class that "life without industry is guilt, and industry without art is brutality." What emerged was the Guild of St. George Collection: works by Audubon and Turner, illuminated manuscripts, and architectural details. The **Ruskin Gallery,** 101 Norfolk St. (tel. 273 5299), now displays this miscellany. *(Open Tu-Sa 10am-5pm.)* At night, the **Crucible** and **Lyceum Theatres** (tel. 276 9922; both on Tudor Sq., joint box office on Norfolk St.) stage musicals, plays, and dance performances, many of which are West End transfers. *(25% discount for students, seniors, and children; same-day tickets £4.)* Set to open in March is the **National Centre for Popular Music,** Brown St. (tel. 279 8941). Look for the buildings that resemble refugees from a B-movie set. Another of Sheffield's main attractions is the gigantic **Meadowhall** (tel. 256 8800) shopping mall with its own "streets," supertram and bus stations, and over 270 shops. *(Open M-Th 9am-8pm, F 9am-9pm, Sa 9am-7pm, Su 11am-5pm.)*

Most **clubs** are in the southeastern section of the city, around Matilda St. Groove is in the heart of **The Republic,** 112 Arundel St. (tel. 249 2210). Gatecrasher, its Saturday night bash, is *the* party in Sheffield, but the cover is steep. Other nights are healthier to the wallet and body; expect crowds at this superclub. *(Cover M and Th £2-3, F £3-5, Sa £10-12.50. Open M and Th-F 10pm-2am, Sa 10pm-6am.)* The **Roxy,** Arundel Gate (tel. 272 1927), has an otherworldly lighting system and 3000-odd chart-busters.

▨ Peak District National Park

Formed in 1951 as Britain's first national park, the 555 sq. mi. of Peak are devoid of towering peaks; the area in fact derives its name from the Old English *peac,* meaning "hill." In the northern Dark Peak area, deep **groughs** (gullies) gouge the hard peat moorland against a backdrop of gloomy cliffs. Stone walls line fields of grass nibbled by sheep and cattle. In the Northern Peak area, well-marked public footpaths (sometimes turning into small streams) cross mildly rocky hillsides and village clusters. The whisper of a forgotten age can be heard in the abandoned millstones, derelict lead mines, and stately country homes of the southern White Peak.

Wedged between industrial giants like Manchester, Sheffield, Nottingham, and Stoke-on-Trent, the park serves as a playground to its 17 million urban neighbors. Come summer, streams of daytrippers leave a thin but persistent layer of smog. Of the world's national parks, only Mt. Fuji can top the Peak's 26 million visitors, as trampled trails attest. For a more tranquil visit, strike for the bleaker northern moors, beyond the reach of commuter rail lines. Although protected from development by national park status, the land is privately owned, so be respectful and stay on designated paths. Ramblers' guidebooks and the park's invaluable (and free!) newspaper, the *Peakland Post,* are available at National Park Information Centres. Contact Peak District National Park, National Park Office, Aldern House, Barlow Rd., Bakewell DE4 5AE (tel. (01629) 816200), for information and a list of publications.

GETTING THERE AND GETTING ABOUT

A sturdy pair of legs, veteran hikers grumble, are more than sufficient for intervillage journeys. A fairly extensive network of **buses** serves the less-robust majority. Derbyshire County Council's *Peak District Timetable* (60p, available in all Peak tourist offices) is invaluable; it includes all bus and train routes as well as a large map. The Council also staffs a bus information line (tel. (01298) 23098; open daily 7am-8pm). Coverage of many routes actually improves on Sundays, especially in summer. **Trent** (tel. (01298) 23098) bus TP, the "Transpeak," winds for 3½ hours through the park from **Manchester** to **Nottingham,** stopping at **Buxton, Bakewell, Matlock, Bath, Derby,** and towns in between; this mainline service is a counterpart to the north's Hope Valley rail line. (Every 2hr.; morning and evening buses may not cover the whole route, so check the timetable.) Buses also trundle regularly into the Peaks from **Sheffield. PMT** (tel. (01782) 747000) bus #X23 serves **Bakewell** and **Buxton** (1hr. to Buxton, 5 per day), and **Mainline** (tel. (0114) 256 7000) #272 hits **Castleton** (1hr., M-Sa 1 per hr., Su 1 per hr.). **Stagecoach East Midland** (tel. (01246) 250450) bus #65/66 shuttles between **Buxton, Eyam,** and **Sheffield** (40min., M-Sa 5 per day, Su 3 per day), and Stagecoach #173 goes from **Bakewell** to **Castleton** (45min., 3 per day).

   Rail service (tel. (0345) 484950) to the park is limited at best. Two lines start in **Manchester** and enter the park from the northwest: the Buxton line terminates at **Buxton** near the park's western edge, while the Hope Valley line continues across the park to **Sheffield via Edale, Hope** (near Castleton), and **Hathersage.** Both lines enter the park at **New Mills** (1 per hr.)—the Buxton line at Newtown Station and the Hope Valley line at Central Station (a sign-posted 20min. walk separates the stations). A third line leaves **Nottingham** and runs north via **Derby** to **Matlock** on the southeastern edge of the Peak District.

   Those who plan to use public transport frequently should buy a **Derbyshire Wayfarer** (£7.75, seniors and children £3.65), available from Peak tourist offices or train stations. It covers virtually all rail and bus services within the Peak District, and to and from Sheffield, for one day. An even better deal is the **Manchester Wayfarer** (£6.60, seniors and children £3.30), which gives unlimited travel within Greater Manchester and the Peak District as far east as Matlock (including Buxton, Bakewell, Castleton, Edale, and Eyam). Tickets are sold at Manchester rail stations and Peak National Park Information Centres. The **Trent Explorer** ticket (£6, one child free with each adult) gives you one-day access to all Barton and Trent buses (buy tickets on board).

ORIENTATION AND PRACTICAL INFORMATION

Facilities in the Peak District generally stay open through the winter, due to the proximity of large cities. Some B&Bs and youth hostels stay open into December.

Tourist Offices
   Ashbourne: 13 The Market Pl. (tel. (01335) 343666; fax 300638). Open Mar.-Oct. M-Sa 9:15am-5pm; Nov.-Feb. M-Sa 10am-4pm.
   Buxton: The Crescent (tel. (01298) 25106). Open daily Mar.-Oct. 9:30am-5pm; Nov.-Feb. 10am-4pm.
   Matlock Bath: The Pavilion (tel. (01629) 55082), along the main road. Open Mar.-Oct. daily 9:30am-5:15pm; Nov.-Feb. W-M 10am-4pm.

National Park Information Centres
These centers display the park's symbol of a circle resting atop a rectangle. All carry detailed walking guides and other park fun-facts.

   Bakewell: Old Market Hall (tel. (01629) 813227; fax 816201), at Bridge St. From the bus stop, walk past Sandringham Fabrics's right flank. Doubles as tourist office. Along with an accommodations booking service (10% deposit), has a good selection of maps and guides. Open daily Mar.-Oct. 9am-5:30pm, Nov.-Feb. 9:30am-5pm.
   Castleton: Castle St. (tel. (01433) 620679), near the church. From the bus stop, follow the road into town, and turn left at the youth hostel sign. Open daily July-Sept. 9am-6pm, Oct.-June 10am-5:30pm.

Edale: Fieldhead (tel. (01433) 670207; fax 670216), between the rail station and village. Open daily Easter-Oct. 9am-1pm and 2-5:30pm; Nov.-Easter closes at 5pm.

Fairholmes: Upper Derwent Valley (tel. (01433) 650953), near Derwent Dam. Open Apr.-Oct. M-F 9am-5:30pm, Sa-Su 9am-6pm; Nov.-Mar. Sa-Su 9am-4:30pm.

Langsett Barn: (tel./fax (01226) 370770), near Penistone. Open Easter-Sept. Sa-Su 10:30am-5pm, Oct. 10am-5pm.

Torside: in Longdendale Valley (no phone). Open Easter-Sept. F-Sa and bank holidays about 10:30am-5pm; Oct. Su 10:30am-5pm.

ACCOMMODATIONS AND CAMPING

Park information centers and tourist offices distribute free park-wide and regional accommodations guides; a camping guide costs 30p. **B&Bs** are plentiful and cheap (from £14), as are youth hostels (around £8). Most of the hostels are not open every day of the week. Buxton and Matlock Bath are particularly well-stocked with inexpensive B&Bs. Many farmers allow **camping** on their land, sometimes for a small fee; remember to leave the site exactly as you found it.

YHA Youth Hostels

Most hostels lie within a feasible day's hike of one another, and each sells maps that detail routes to neighboring hostels. Unless noted, these hostels have a lockout 10am -5pm and an 11pm curfew. Hostels often fill with rambunctious kiddies on school trips; call or write ahead to reserve, and invest in earplugs.

Bakewell: Fly Hill, Derbyshire DE45 1DN (tel./fax (01629) 812313). A 5min. walk from the town center. Huge meals and a cheerful warden. £7.20, under 18 £5. Open mid-June to Aug. daily; Apr. to mid-June and Sept.-Oct. M-Sa; Nov.-Mar. F-Sa.

Bretton: Snug, self-catering hostel 2mi. from Eyam atop Eyam Edge (1250ft.). £6.50, under 18 £4.45. Open Aug. daily; Sept.-July F-Sa. Send bookings c/o John and Elaine Whittington, 7 New Bailey, Crane Moor, Sheffield S30 7AT (tel. (0114) 288 4541).

Buxton: Sherbrook Lodge, Harpur Hill Rd., Derbyshire SK17 9NB (tel./fax (01298) 22287). The sloped 25min. walk from the train station is rewarded with a charming stone hostel surrounded by trees. £7.20, under 18 £5. Meals available. Open Apr.-Dec. M-Sa; Feb.-Mar. F-Sa.

Castleton: Castleton Hall, Castleton, Hope Valley S33 8WG (tel. (01433) 620235). Pretty country house and attached old vicarage in the heart of town at the base of the menacing Peveril Castle ruins. £9.75, under 18 £6.55. Vicarage with bath and no curfew £11.65, under 18 £8. Open daily Feb. to late Dec. Book *way* in advance.

Crowden-in-Longdendale: Peak National Park Hostel, Crowden, Hadfield, Hyde, Cheshire SK14 7HZ (tel./fax (01457) 852135). £7.20, under 18 £5. Meals available. Open May-Oct. daily; Apr. Th-Tu; Mar. and Nov. F-Sa.

Dimmingsdale: Little Ranger, Dimmingsdale, Oakamoor, Stoke-on-Trent, Staffordshire ST10 3AS (tel. (01538) 702304). £6.50, under 18 £4.45. Open June-Aug. daily; Apr.-May and Sept.-Oct. M-Sa.

Edale: Rowland Cote, Nether Booth, Edale, Hope Valley S33 2ZH (tel. (01433) 670302; fax 670243), 2mi. from Edale. Full-featured hostel caters mostly to groups who come for multi-activity holidays or "adventure trail" courses, but individuals are welcome. Travelers arriving between 4-8pm can arrange to be picked up. £9.75, under 18 £6.55. Meals available. No lockout. Open year-round daily.

Elton: Elton Old Hall, Main St., Elton, Matlock, Derbyshire DE4 2BW (tel. (01629) 650394). £6.50, under 18 £4.45. Open mid-Feb. to Oct. daily.

Eyam: Hawkhill Rd., Eyam, Hope Valley S32 5QX (tel./fax (01433) 630335). Old, castle-like building with 60 beds in clean rooms. £8, under 18 £5.40. Meals available. Open Apr.-Sept. daily; Mar. and Oct. M-Sa; Feb. and Nov. F-Sa.

Gradbach Mill: Gradbach, Quarnford, Buxton, Derbyshire SK17 0SU (tel. (01260) 227625; fax 227334). A former mill 7 mi. from Buxton along the River Dane. £8.80, under 18 £6. Open Feb.-Nov. daily.

Hartington Hall: Hartington, Buxton, Derbyshire SK17 0AT (tel. (01298) 84223; fax 84415). 128 beds in a 17th-century manor house with oak paneling. Bonnie Prince Charlie once slept here, *sans* YHA membership. £8.80, under 18 £6. Open mid-Feb. to late Dec. daily.

Hathersage: Castleton Rd., Hathersage, Hope Valley S32 1EH (tel. (01433) 650493). £8, under 18 £5.40. Open Apr.-Oct. M-Sa; Nov. and Jan.-Mar. F-Sa.

Ilam Hall: Ilam Hall, Ashbourne, Derbyshire DE6 2AZ (tel. (01335) 350212; fax 350350). A stately mansion along the River Manifold. £9.75, under 18 £6.55. No lockout. Open Feb.-Oct. daily; Nov. F-Sa.

Langsett: near Penistone. Send bookings to same address as Bretton Hostel. £6.50, under 18 £4.45. Self-catering only. Open mid-July to Aug. daily; Jan.-July and Sept. to mid-Dec. F-Sa.

Matlock: 40 Bank Rd., Matlock, Derbyshire DE4 3NF (tel. (01629) 582983; fax 583484). £9.75, under 18 £6.55. Lockout 10am-1pm. Open year-round daily.

Meerbrook: Old School, Meerbrook, Leek, Staffordshire ST13 8SJ (tel. (01538) 300148). Book through Mrs. E. Nettle, Cornerhouse, Roache Rd., Upperhulme, near Leek ST13 8UQ. £6.50, under 18 £4.45. Open July to mid-Sept. daily; Apr.-June and mid-Sept. to Oct. F-Sa.

Ravenstor: Millers Dale, Buxton, Derbyshire SK17 8SS (tel. (01298) 871826; fax 871275). £9.75, under 18 £6.55. Open Apr.-Oct. daily; mid-Feb. to Mar. M-Sa; Nov. to mid-Dec. F-Sa.

Shining Cliff: Shining Cliff Woods, near Ambergate, Derbyshire (tel. (01629) 760827). Book through Matlock Hostel. £5.85, under 18 £4. Open late July to Aug. daily; Apr. to late July and Sept.-Oct. Sa only.

Youlgreave: Fountain Sq., Youlgreave, near Bakewell, Derbyshire DE45 1UR (tel./ fax (01629) 636518). £8, under 18 £5.40. Open July-Aug. daily; Apr.-June and Sept.-Oct. M-Sa; Nov.-Dec. F-Sa.

Camping Barns

The 11 park-operated **camping barns** are simple night shelters for hikers and bikers, providing a sleeping platform, water tap, and toilet (£3.25 per person). Bring a sleeping bag and the usual camping equipment. You must book and pay ahead with the **Peak National Park Office,** Aldern House, Baslow Rd., Bakewell, Derbyshire DE451AE (tel. (01629) 816316). The following telephone numbers are to confirm arrival time *only;* direct all booking inquiries to the Peak National Park Office.

Abney: Mr. and Mrs. Chadwick, Ivy House Farm (tel. (01433) 650481), between Eyam and Castleton. Sleeps 8.

Birchover: Mr. Heathcote, Barn Farm, Birchover, near Matlock off the B5056. Sleeps 10.

Butterton: Mr. and Mrs. Renshaw, Fenns Farm, Wetton Rd. (tel. (01538) 304226). 2 barns near the southern end of the park, along the Manifold track. Sleeps 21.

Edale: Mr. and Mrs. Gee, Cotefield Farm, Ollerbrook (tel. (01433) 670273). Close to Edale, one endpoint of the Pennine Way. Sleeps 8.

Losehill: Losehill Hall (tel. (01433) 620373), near Castleton. Sleeps 8.

Middleton-By-Youlgreave: Mr. and Mrs. Butterworth, Castle Farm, Middleton-by-Youlgreave, Bakewell (tel. (01629) 636746). Sleeps 12.

Nab End: Mr. and Mrs. Cox, Nab End Farm, Hollinsclough, Buxton (tel. (01298) 83225). Sleeps 16.

One Ash Grange: Mr. and Mrs. Wells, 1 Ash Grange, Monyash, Bakewell (tel. (01629) 636291). Sleeps 12.

Taddington: Mr. Gillott, The Woodlands, Main Rd., Taddington, Buxton (tel. (01298) 85308 or 85730). Sleeps 10.

Underbank: Mr. Waller, Blaze Farm, Wildboarclough (tel. (01260) 227229). Sleeps 10.

Upper Booth: Mr. and Mrs. Hodgson, Upper Booth Farm (tel. (01433) 670250), near Eyam. Sleeps 12.

HIKING AND BIKING

The central park is marvelous territory for rambling. Settlement is more sparse and buses are fewer north of Edale, in the land of the Kinder Scout plateau, the great Derwent reservoirs, and the gritty cliffs and peat moorlands. From Edale, the **Pennine Way** (see p. 338) runs north to Kirk Yetholm, across the Scottish border. The Peak

District is on the same latitude as Siberia; people have died in the mist on Bleaklow and Kinder Scout, just 30 minutes from two large cities. Be sure to *dress warmly and bring all necessary supplies* (see **Wilderness and Safety Concerns,** p. 47).

The park authority operates the following six **Cycle Hire Centres,** where you can rent bikes. All are open in summer daily 9:30am-6pm; call for opening days and times Oct.-Mar.—they may close for lunch. (£5.70 per 3hr., under 18 £4.60; £8 per day, under 15 £5.80; helmet included. £20 deposit. 10% discount for YHA members, seniors, and Wayfarer ticket holders.)

Ashbourne: Mapleton Ln. (tel. (01335) 343156).
Derwent: (tel. (01433) 651261), near the Fairholmes Information Centre.
Hayfield: (tel. (01663) 746222), near New Mills on Station Rd. in the Sett Valley.
Middleton Top: (tel. (01629) 823204), near Matlock on the High Peak Trail.
Parsley Hay: (tel. (01298) 84493), at the meeting of Tissington and High Peak Trails.
Waterhouses: (tel./fax (01538) 308609), between Ashbourne and Leek on the A523 near the southern end of the Manifold Truck.

■ Edale

The northern Dark Peak area contains some of the wildest, most rugged hill country in England, with vast moorlands like **Kinder Scout** and **Bleaklow** left undisturbed by motor traffic. In these desolate mazes of black peat hags and deep groughs, paths are scarce and weather-worn. Sparse towns and villages huddle in valleys, offering provisions and shelter for bone-weary hikers. Less experienced hikers should stick to Edale and the southern paths.

The deep dale of the River Noe cradles a collection of hamlets known collectively as **Edale.** The area offers little in the way of civilization other than a church, railway stop, cafe, pub, school, and nearby youth hostel. Its environs, however, are arguably the most spectacular in northern England. On summer weekends this tranquil village brims with hikers and campers preparing to tackle the **Pennine Way** (which passes out of the Peak District and into the Yorkshire Dales after a 3-4 day hike, see p. 338), or trek one of the shorter (1½-8½mi.) trails closer to Edale detailed in the National Park Authority's *8 Walks Around Edale* (£1.10). The 3½ mi. path to Castleton affords a breathtaking view of both the Edale Valley (Dark Peak) and the Hope Valley (White Peak) to the south. A new flagstone detour on the ridge between these valleys runs as far as **Mam Tor.** This decaying Iron Age hillside fort receives over 250,000 visitors each year. The hill was known locally as the "shivering mountain" because of the appearance of its shale sides; one such shiver left the road below permanently blocked. Cliffs on three sides beckon fearless hang-gliders from near and far. The trip should take about 6½ hours at an easy pace. Stop at the huge **National Park Information Centres,** near the rail stations (see p. 310), for weather forecasts and training with a map and compass.

Unless you reserve centuries ahead, your tent could be your best friend in this town, where the only accommodations lie within the popular 140-bed **YHA Edale** (tel. (01433) 670302; see p. 311). Ask at the park center about the 30-minute short-cut through the fields to the hostel. **Fieldhead** (tel. (01433) 670386), behind the tourist office, charges £3.20 (£2.20 per child, and £1.10 per car, shower 50p). Near the school, **Cooper's Camp and Caravan Site,** Newfold Far (tel. (01433) 670372), asks £2.50. Edale lies on the Hope Valley **rail** line between Manchester and Sheffield, and is served every two hours (from Sheffield £2.90).

■ Castleton

Two miles southeast of Edale, **Castleton** (pop. 750) is more conscious of tourist-potential than the soporific Edale. Craft shops and tea rooms blink under the small bower-decked houses. Castleton's river-carved limestone engulfs several famous caverns and Blue John, a rich blue-and-brown mineral found nowhere else in the world. In the depths of **Blue John Cavern** (tel. 620642), a spectacular dome arches over a massive crystalline chamber. *(Open year-round 10am-5pm. 50min. tours every 20min. £5, seniors £4, children £3, families £15; YHA members 10% off.)* **Treak Cliff Cavern** (tel. 620571) is known for its impressive spires—the "stork" stalagmite and stalactite pair will form a column in a thousand years. *(£5, students £3, seniors £4, children £2.25. 40min. tours every 12min.)* Both caverns are about 1½ mi. west of town on the A625. Farther along the A625, at **Speedwell Cavern** (tel. 620512), relentless miners carved a flooded route to a huge natural complex of caves and underground streams. Eerie boat trips retrace their journey, stopping at the subterranean lake, Bottomless Pit. Tours leave frequently—call for times. *(Open Easter-Oct. 9:30am-5pm; Nov.-Easter 10am-4:30pm. £5, students, seniors, and YHA members £4, children £3.)* Gigantic **Peak Cavern** (tel. 620285), right in town at the end of a steep-walled gorge cut by a mild stream, features the second-largest aperture in the world (the largest is in New South Wales, Australia). Unfortunately, it is obscured by the entrance structures. Decorously known in the 18th century as the "Devil's Arse," the cavern now features tours by guides pale from spending altogether too much time in Old Harry's sphincter. *(Open daily Easter-Nov. 10am-4pm; Dec.-Easter 10am-4pm. £4.50, students, seniors, and YHA members £3.50, children £2.50, families £12; discount with flyer from tourist office.)*

William Peveril, son of William the Conqueror, chose a visually arresting and defensively ideal setting in which to build **Peveril Castle** (tel. 620613). The 11th- and 12th-century ruins, still dominated by a hollowed keep, crown a dramatic peak overlooking the town. Bounded by a 230 ft. gorge on one side, by the limestone cliffs of Cave Dale on another, and by a stubbornly steep hill facing the town—the ruins make an exhausting climb. Good luck. *(Open Apr.-Oct. daily 10am-6pm; Nov.-Mar. W-Su 10am-4pm. £1.60, students and seniors £1.20, children 80p.)* Hikers looking for a challenge can set off southward from Castleton on the 26 mi. **Limestone Way Trail** to Matlock.

Castleton lies 2 mi. west of the **Hope** rail station (don't ask for Castleton, or you'll end up in a suburb of Manchester), and **buses** arrive from Sheffield, Buxton, and Bakewell (see **Getting There and Getting About**, p. 310) The **National Park Information Centre** on Castle St. (see p. 310), sells *Walking the Limestone Way* (£5.50), distributes free accommodations listings, and offers 90-minute **guided walks** through Castleton (June-Sept. M 2:30pm. £2, children £1). The nearest **bank** and **ATM** lie 6 mi. east in **Hathersage.** Ramblers preparing to assault the moorlands should visit the **Peveril Outdoor Shop** (tel. 620320), off Castle St. by the hostel (open M-F 9:30am-5pm, Sa-Su 9:30am-6pm). The **post office,** How Ln. (tel. 620241), near the bus stop, asks why the **postal code** is S33 8WJ (Open M-Tu and Th-F 9am-1pm and 2-5pm, W and Sa 9am-12:30pm). Meanwhile, the **telephone code,** 01433, is never in doubt.

The super-duper **YHA Castleton** (tel. 620235) lies by the castle entrance (see p. 311). The guest houses nearby include ivy-walled **Cryer House,** Castle St. (tel./fax 620244), where Mr. and Mrs. Skelton keep two lovely rooms (doubles only £36, with bath £40). The tea room downstairs is a superb place for a home-baked scone.

■ Bakewell

With lower, gentler terrain and more highly developed transport links, the southern portion of the Peak District draws significantly more visitors than its northern counterpart. Fifteen miles southwest of Sheffield and 30 mi. southeast of Manchester, Bakewell makes the best spot from which to explore this region and transfer for more elaborate bus trips. Located near several scenic walks through the White Peaks, the town itself is best known as the birthplace of Bakewell pudding, created in the 1860s when a flustered cook of the Rutland Arms Hotel tried, in spite of his town's name, to make a tart by pouring an egg mixture over strawberry jam instead of mixing it into the dough. Some have suggested that Jane Austen stayed in the Rutland Arms, and based the town in *Pride and Prejudice* on Bakewell. Bakewell's stone buildings are huddled around a handful of narrow streets and a central square bursting with flowers, wrapped by a lazy bend in the River Wye. Ducks float under the graceful five arches of the medieval **bridge** (c. 1300). On the hill above town **All Saints Church** lies in a crowded park of Celtic gravestones and carved-cross fragments. In the south transept, three very curious human gargoyles guard the remains of Anglo-Saxon and Norman headstones. Nearby, a 16th-century timber-frame house encased in stone shelters the **Old House Museum** (tel. (01629) 813165), which displays ancient tools, 19th-century dolls, a cluttered Victorian kitchen, and a Tudor plank cupboard found inside the wall during renovation. *(Open daily July-Aug. 11am-4pm; Apr.-June and Sept.-Oct. 1:30-4pm. £2, children £1.)*

Two miles southwest of town (go down Matlock St. as it becomes Haddon Rd. and then the A6), the Duke of Rutland's **Haddon Hall** (tel. 812855) may be recognizable to visitors as the setting for Franco Zefferelli's 1996 *Jane Eyre,* as well as *The Princess Bride.* The house lends itself to cinematic romance and glitz because it has been so little altered since the reign of Henry VIII, preserving its antler-lined great hall and frescoed chapel. *(Open Apr.-Sept. daily 11am-5:45pm, last admission 5pm. £5.50, seniors £4.75, children £3, families £14.75; discounts for YHA members. No wheelchair access.)* Another "great house" near Bakewell is the ornate **Chatsworth House** (tel. (01246) 582204), home of the Duke and Duchess of Devonshire. There's almost too much to absorb in the 26 decorated rooms, but the extensive gardens (100 acres), with cascades and mazes, offer a more manageable spectacle. *(Open daily Mar.-Oct. 11am-4:30pm. House and gardens £6.25, students and seniors £5, children £3.)*

Buses arrive in Rutland Sq. from **Sheffield, Castleton,** and **Buxton** (#X23, 40min., 5 per day; #240, 1hr., 7 per day; see **Getting There and Getting About,** p. 310). Bakewell boasts a **National Park Information Centre** (tel. 813227), at the intersection of Bridge and Market St. (see p. 310). Punch in your PIN at **Midland's ATM,** Rutland Sq. (bank open M-F 9:30am-4:30pm). A modest selection of camping supplies is sold at **Yeoman's,** 1 Royal Oak Pl. (tel. 815371), off Matlock St. (open M-Sa 9am-5:30pm, Su 11am-5pm). Treat clothes to a wash at **Bakewell Launderama,** on the appropriately-named Water St. off Rutland Sq. (open daily 7:30am-7pm, last wash 6pm). The **police** chill on Granby Rd. (open M 8:30am-9pm, Tu-Th 8:30am-5pm, F 8:30am-8:30pm, Sa 10am-2pm, M-F closed for lunch 12:30-1:30pm). The **post office,** Unit 1 Granby Croft (tel. 814427), in the Spar on Granby Rd., waits for postcards (open M-Sa 8:30am-6pm). The **postal code** is DE45 1EF, the **telephone code** 01629.

Bakewell has an intimate and comfy **YHA Youth Hostel** (tel./fax (01629) 812313), on Fly Hill, a short walk from the tourist office (see **YHA Youth Hostels,** p. 311). **B&Bs** here are more costly than in Matlock Bath; many lie on or near Haddon Rd., the continuation of Matlock St. Cafes aim to cash in on Bakewell's confectionery reputation. On Rutland Sq., **The Old Original Bakewell Pudding Shop** (tel. 812193) sells lunches and sinful desserts in a wood-paneled restaurant with a vaulted ceiling. Skip lunch and order the £3.60 cream tea, which includes sandwiches, two fruit scones with jam and cream, a Bakewell pudding, and tea. (Open July-Aug. daily 8:30am-9pm; Sept.-June M-Th 9am-6pm, F-Su 8:30am-6pm.) Take foodstuffs purchased at the **Gateway Foodmarket,** Rutland Sq. (tel. 812686), to the grassy bank of the Wye (open M-Sa 8am-8pm, Su 10am-4pm). Entire villages pour into Bakewell's **market,** held since

---

Not from Nottingham

Robin Hood fans may have thought that Kevin Costner's portrayal of the Prince of Thieves as some sort of American prospector was a unique travesty, but Kevin isn't the only one confused about the origin of Robin and his merry men. The bandits didn't come from Nottingham, as is often supposed, but from the Peak district, the more plebeian base from which they made sporadic and fruitful inroads on the wealth of nearby Nottingham. "Little John" (examinations of his remains have established that he was actually a giant) is buried in Hathersage where a corner pub is now emblazoned with his name. It was also in tiny Hathersage that Charlotte Brontë saw another formidable band of men: the twelve apostles eerily painted on a cupboard at the home of one of her acquaintances, Thomas Eyre. Charlotte's mind bore both cupboard and surname back to Haworth where she recreated them in *Jane Eyre.*

ENGLAND

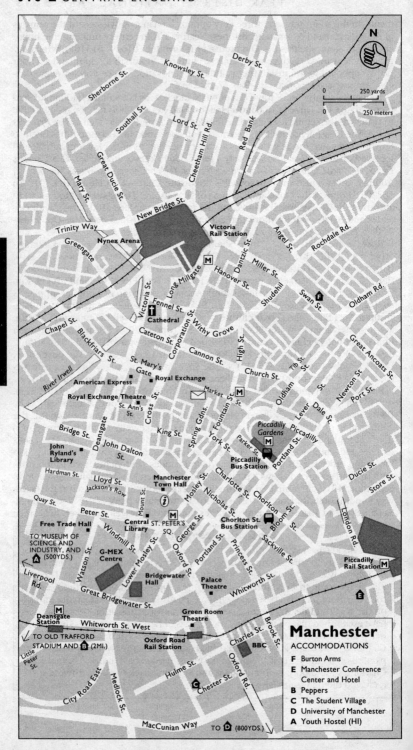

N

0   250 yards
0   250 meters

Knowsley St.
Derby St.
Sherborne St.
Southall St.
Lord St.
Cheetham Hill Rd.
Red Bank
Great Ducie St.
Mary St.
Trinity Way
Greengate
New Bridge St.
Nynex Arena
Victoria Rail Station
Dantzic St.
Miller St.
Angel St.
Rochdale Rd.
Shudehil
Swan St.
F
Oldham Rd.
Long Millgate
Hanover St.
Victoria St.
Fennel St.
Cathedral
Chapel St.
Blackfriars St.
Cateon St.
Corporation St.
Withy Grove
High St.
Great Ancoats St.
River Irwell
St. Mary's Gate
Cannon St.
Church St.
Tib St.
Newton St.
Port St.
American Express
Royal Exchange
Royal Exchange Theatre
St. Ann's St.
Cross St.
Market St.
Oldham St.
Lever St.
Dale St.
Bridge St.
Deansgate
John Dalton St.
King St.
Spring Gdns.
Fountain St.
York St.
Parker St.
Piccadilly Gardens
M
Piccadilly
Ducie St.
Store St.
John Ryland's Library
Hardman St.
Lloyd St.
Jackson's Row
Manchester Town Hall
Mosley St.
Charlotte St.
Chorlton St.
Bloom St.
Piccadilly Bus Station
Quay St.
Peter St.
Mount St.
Central Library
ST. PETER'S SQ.
George St.
Nicholas St.
Oxford St.
Portland St.
Princess St.
Sackville St.
Chorlton St. Bus Station
London Rd.
Free Trade Hall
Windmill St.
G-MEX Centre
Lower Mosley St.
Watson St.
Bridgewater Hall
Palace Theatre
Whitworth St.
Piccadilly Rail Station
M
E
TO MUSEUM OF SCIENCE AND INDUSTRY, AND
A (500YDS.)
Liverpool Rd.
Great Bridgewater St.
Green Room Theatre
Deansgate Station
M
Whitworth St. West
Oxford Road Rail Station
Charles St.
Brook St.
Oxford Rd.
BBC
TO OLD TRAFFORD STADIUM AND B (2MI.)
Little Peter
Hulme St.
City Road East
Medlock St.
C
Chester St.
MacCunian Way
TO D (800YDS.)

Manchester
ACCOMMODATIONS
F   Burton Arms
E   Manchester Conference Center and Hotel
B   Peppers
C   The Student Village
D   University of Manchester
A   Youth Hostel (HI)

1330 (off Bridge St.; follow the doomed mooing of 3000 cows; open M 9am-4pm).
The Outback Bar, Granby Rd. (tel. 814909), off Matlock St., draws a lively, grizzled
crowd and offers Outback Bruce Burgers (£3.75), among other Aussie-themed meals.

■ Eyam

Just 5 mi. north of Bakewell, the hamlet of **Eyam** underwent a self-imposed quarantine when the plague spread here from London in 1665, during which 259 of its 350
residents died a miserable bubonic death. Plaques on old houses tally the numbers
that died in each, and makeshift graves lie in strangely vibrant gardens (victims were
buried quickly to prevent the spread of the disease). The first three victims perished
in the flower-ringed stone of Plaque Cottage, Edgeview Rd. Tiny **Eyam Museum** (tel.
(01433) 631371), on Hawkhill Rd., commemorates all the grisly details; the register of
names of all who died is strangely moving. *(Open Apr.-Oct. Tu-Su 10am-4:30pm. £1.50,
seniors and children £1, families £4.25.)* A hundred yards west of the church on Edgeview
Rd., the main drag, **Eyam Hall** (tel. (01433) 631976) traces the owner's family history
in a 17th-century manor house. The hall boasts a wall-to-wall tapestry room, an eight-
line love stanza carved into the library window, and a 1675 pop-up human anatomy
textbook. *(Open Apr.-Oct. W-Th and Su 11am-4:30pm. £3.50, students and seniors £3, children £2.50, families £10.50; price includes a 50min. guided tour.)*

It's difficult to get from Bakewell to Eyam on any day other than Monday, and no
sights are open in Eyam on Monday. **Stagecoach** East Midland (tel. (01246) 250450)
#65/66 hits Eyam on its route between **Buxton** and **Sheffield** (bus #65 M-Sa 5 per day,
Su 3 per day; bus #66 from **Chesterfield** to **Buxton via Eyam** M-Sa 4 per day). The
YHA Youth Hostel (tel. (01433) 630335; see p. 311) plants its flag 800m above the
town on Hawkhill Rd. Next door to Eyam Hall, the **Buttery's** stone walls, thick
beams, and light-grain tables make for a pleasant lunch spot. Filled baguettes come
light and tasty at £2.50. Sadly, they don't still use the centuries-old family recipes that
adorn the walls (open Mar. to late Dec. Tu-Su 10:30am-5:30pm). The shelves of **Robert Turner's Greengrocers,** Hawkhill and Edgeview Rd. (tel. (01433) 630942), bend
under the weight of fruit and vegetables. (Open M-W 8:30am-12:30pm and 2-5:30pm,
Th-F 8:30am-1pm and 2-5:30pm, Sa 8:30am-1pm.)

■ Manchester

The Industrial Revolution quickly transformed the once unremarkable village of
Manchester into a bustling northern hub. Greater Manchester is now England's second-largest urban area. A vigorous industrial leader, Manchester also developed into a
center of liberal politics (Engels lived here), and now savors its reputation as one of
the hippest spots in England. Derided by Ruskin as a "devil's darkness," the partially
gentrified city is still considered dangerous by England's strict standards. But the city
draws thousands with its pulsing nightlife, and its vibrant arts scene appeals to the
Ruskin in us all. Although the dearth of budget accommodations in the city center
often forces travelers to lodge in the outskirts, Manchester is well worth a stay.

GETTING THERE

Along with Heathrow and Gatwick, **Manchester International Airport** (tel. 489
3000) serves North America (tel. (0839) 888747 for information on international
arrivals, (0839) 888757 for domestic arrivals, both 50p). Trains run to the airport
from Piccadilly Train Station (25min., 4 per hr., 24hr. a day). Buses #44 and 105 connect the airport with Piccadilly Bus Station in the center of town.

Manchester is served by two main **rail stations: Piccadilly** (mostly for trains from
south and east) and **Victoria** (mostly for trains from west and north). They are connected by trams and city buses #185 and 187. **Trains** (tel. (0345) 484950) run to London **Euston** (2½hr., at least 1 per hr., £61), **Liverpool** (50min., 2 per hr., about £6),
Chester (1hr., 1 per hr., £7.20), and **York** (40min., 2 per hr., £13.30, return £17).
Buses stop in the **Chorlton St.** Coach Station. **National Express** (tel. (0990) 808080)

ENGLAND

serves Sheffield (1½hr., 6 per day, £6.50), **Glasgow** (4½-5hr., 5 per day, £21.75), **London** (4hr., 8 per day, £22), as well as other cities. **Metrolink trams** (tel. 205 2000), run every 5-15 minutes, linking Altrincham in the southwest with Bury in the northeast. Manchester proper boasts eight of the 24 stops in between (80p-£4.90).

ORIENTATION AND PRACTICAL INFORMATION

The city center lies mostly within the triangle formed by **Victoria Station** to the north, **Piccadilly Station** to the east, and the **G-Mex** in the west. Although the area is fairly compact, and several pedestrian streets makes it easy to get around on foot, the many by-ways and side streets require a good map. Fortunately, many streets bear adequate, poster-sized maps, and Manchester residents are generally helpful.

Transportation

Trains: Piccadilly Station, on London Rd. Travel Centre open M-Sa 8am-8:30pm, Su 11am-7pm. **Victoria Station,** on Victoria St. Travel Centre open M-Sa 8:30am-6pm. Both stations open 24hr.

Buses: Piccadilly Bus Station consists of about 50 bus stops around Piccadilly Gardens. Pick up a route map (free) at the information desk in the station, or from the tourist office. Bus service until 11:30pm, weekend service until 2:30am. Office open M-Sa 7am-6:30pm, Su 10am-6pm. **National Express** (tel. (0990) 808080) rolls into **Chorlton St.,** 2 blocks south and 1 block east of Piccadilly. Office open M-F 7:15am-7pm, Sa-Su 7:15am-6:15pm. **Luggage storage** 9am-6pm (£2).

Public Transport Hotline: GMPTE information line (tel. 228 7811). Open 8am-8pm.

Taxis: Mantase (tel. 236 5133).

Tourist and Financial Services

Tourist Office: Manchester Visitor Centre, Town Hall Extension, Lloyd St. (tel. 234 3157, 24hr. info (0891) 715533), in St. Peter's Sq. Be sure to grab a free map of the city center. Helpful staff seeks out accommodations (£2.50). The *Manchester Visitor Guide* (£1.50) proves invaluable, listing hours, prices, wheelchair access, and other details on most of the city's sights. *What's On* (free) lists local events. Information about city **tours** also available. Open M-Sa 10am-5:30pm, Su 11am-4pm.

Budget Travel: Campus Travel, YHA Adventure Centre, 166 Deansgate (tel. 834 7119). Hostel memberships, ISICs, Travelsave stamps. Camping supplies. Open M-W and F 9:30am-5:30pm, Th 9:30am-6pm, Sa 9am-6pm, Su 1am-5pm.

Financial Services: Thomas Cook, 2 Oxford St. (tel. 236 8575), off St. Peter's Sq. and 23 Market St. Open M-W and F 9am-5:30pm, Th 10am-5:30pm, Sa 9am-5pm. **Barclays,** 51 Mosley St. (tel. 228 3322). Open M-W and F 9am-5pm, Th 10am-5pm.

American Express: 10-12 St. Mary's Gate (tel. 833 0121), at Deansgate and Blackfriars. Client mail held. Open M-F 9am-5:30pm, Sa 9am-4pm.

Local Services

Launderette: Mr. Bubbles, 246 Wilmslow Rd. (tel. 257 2640), near University and Didsbury. Change and soap available. Open daily 8am-9:30pm; last wash 8:30pm.

Disabled Services: Shopmobility, Old Smith Market (tel. 839 4060), corner of Coop and Swan St. Offers a range of services. Open M-Sa 9am-5pm.

Emergency and Communications

Emergency: Dial 999; no coins required.

Police: Chester House, Bootle St. (tel. 872 5050 or 273 2081).

Hotlines: Samaritans (crisis), 72-74 Oxford St. (tel. 236 8000). **Lifeline** (drug helpline; tel. 839 2054). Open M-F 9am-5pm. **Manchester Lesbian and Gay Switchboard** (tel. 274 3999). Open daily 4-10pm. **Racial Harassment** (tel. 234 3584). **Rape crisis** (tel. 834 8784). Open Tu and F 2-5pm, W-Th and Su 6-9pm.

Pharmacy: Cameolord, 7 Oxford St. (tel. 236 1445), off St. Peter's Sq. Open daily 8am-midnight.

Hospital: Manchester Royal Infirmary, Oxford Rd. (tel. 276 1234). Buses #42-49 run down Oxford Rd.

Post Office: 26 Spring Gdns. (tel. 839 0687), near Market St. Open M-Tu and Th-F 8:30am-6pm, W 9am-6pm, Sa 8:30am-1pm. *Poste Restante* (separate entrance; tel. 834 8605). Open M-F 6am-5:30pm, Sa 6am-12:30pm. **Postal Code:** M2 2AA.
Internet Access: Cyberia, 12 Oxford St. (tel. 661 1106; http://manchester.cyberia-cafe.net). Quite possibly the hippest net access point in the U.K. Open M-Sa 11am-11pm, Su 11am-9pm. £3 per 30min., students and seniors £2.40.
Telephone Code: 0161.

ACCOMMODATIONS

Manchester is only slowly awakening to the demand for budget accommodations, and cheap stays in the city center are still hard to find. Summer offers the possibility of taking up **student housing,** a decently priced option. The highest concentration of budget lodgings is found 2 or 3 mi. south of the city center in the suburbs of **Fallowfield, Withington,** and **Didsbury;** take bus #42 or 45 to reach any of the small hotels, B&Bs, and university residence halls which inhabit in these areas. **B&Bs** are usually spare rooms in people's homes, so be prepared to feel like a visiting relative. The tourist office's *Where to Stay* lists the possibilities, and the staff scour the town for places within your price range. Although they can sometimes get better rates and special prices for lodging, don't forget there's a £2.50 booking fee. They can also direct you to the city's various clubs.

ⓦ**YHA Manchester,** Potato Wharf, Castlefield (tel. 839 9960). Behind the Castlefield Hotel across Liverpool Rd. from the Museum of Science. If a posh hotel were to design a youth hostel, this would be it: cascading water, a sleek rotunda reception area with black leather couches, and a smiling, blazer-attired receptionist with brass nametag. Rooms with bath and large cupboards. They call themselves "England's premier hostel," and we're not surprised. Lounge area, game room, and spacious TV room. From £13, under 18 £9. £1 ISIC discount. Meals available. Laundry room with lockers (£1 deposit) and a *huge* modern kitchen. Reception open 7am-11pm. Open 24hr. Wheelchair access.
Manchester Conference Centre and Hotel, Sackville St. (tel./fax 955 8000). Part of this center is a hotel; budget travelers stay clear. However, the center is owned by the university, and offers student dorms in a convenient location from mid-June to Sept. Book through the tourist office for the reduced rate. £22.50, £19 through the tourist office (includes booking fee).
The Student Village, Lower Chatham St. (tel. 237 6045), has 1039 summer singles available. A 10min. walk from St. Peter's Sq. £17 includes breakfast.
University of Manchester: St. Gabriels Hall, 1-3 Oxford Pl., Victoria Park (tel. 224 7061). Self-catering dorm available during school vacations. Singles £11.75, students £7; twins £20, students £12. Reserve a week or more in advance with deposit. Minimum stay 3 days. If full, try **Woolton Hall,** Whitworth Ln., Fallowfield (tel. 224 7244). £12. Rates subject to additional VAT. For information on these and other residence halls, contact the University Accommodation Office, Precinct Centre, Oxford Rd., Manchester M13 9RS (tel. 275 2888). Open M-F 9:30am-5pm.
Peppers, 17 Great Stone Rd., Stretford (tel./fax 848 9770). Take the Metro to Old Trafford (12min.), walk past the cricket ground and turn left, then take the first right onto Great Stone Rd. Simple hostel accommodations, but it's cheap and close to the Metro as well as the famed football ground. Dorms £7.50; twins £18. £1 optional sheet rental. £3 key deposit.
Mrs. Turner, 13 Lynway Dr., Didsbury (tel. 434 2542). Get off a Didsbury bus (#40, 42, 45, 59) at the Golden Lion Pub (on your left), walk a half-block, and turn left on Ferndene Rd.; Lynway Dr. is first left. Beautiful floral-patterned rooms and a lounge. Singles £18; doubles £36. Continental breakfast included; larger breakfast at extra cost.
Burton Arms, 31 Swan St. (tel./fax 834 3455). Basic rooms above a pub on a busy street. A 15min. walk from both train stations and St. Peter's Sq. £19.50, with bath £25. Full English breakfast included.

FOOD

Downtown Manchester offers numerous fast food places and cheap, charmless cafes. Outwit the pricey Chinatown restaurants by eating the multi-course "Businessman's Lunch" offered by most of them (served M-F noon-2pm; £4-8, with or without the briefcase and masculine gender). Several Middle Eastern and Indian (including *halal* and vegetarian) restaurants and take-out counters line Wilmslow Rd. (take bus #40, 42, or 45 to the University). Hip youths and yuppies wine and dine in the cafe-bars (see p. 322). For nocturnal appetites, kebab/burger/fish and chips joints on Whitworth St. West. are open until 4am. **Tesco** awaits on Market St. (tel. 835 3339; open M-Sa 8am-8pm, Su 11am-5pm).

Cornerhouse Café, 70 Oxford St. (tel. 228 7621). Part of the Cornerhouse Arts Center, it features a bar, 3 galleries, 3 art-house cinemas, and trendy crowds. Salads £2.50, entrees from £3.50, desserts from 70p. Open daily 11am-8:30pm; hot meals served noon-2:30pm and 5-7:30pm; bar open M-Sa noon-11pm, Su noon-10:30pm.

Spice, Whitworth St. West (tel. 237 3949). Fast food and Jetson-inspired decor make for a major student hangout. Add to that a 10% student discount and CRAZY, CRAZY hours, and—presto!—Spice is *the* joint in town. Pizzas (£2.50-3.70), tall burgers (£1.60-3.40), kebabs (£1.50-4.50), noodles (£3.25). Open M-Tu 5pm-2:30am, W-Th 5pm-3am, F-Sa 5pm-4am, Su 5pm-midnight.

Green Room Theatre Café, 54-56 Whitworth St. West (tel. 950 5777). The minimalist metal and wood interiors of this cafe make it as hip as you'd expect from a cafe next to a theatre. Menu includes "leafy herby salad" and no red meat. Snacks £1.50-4.25. Delectable main courses from £5. Open M-Sa noon-7:30pm.

Giovanni's Pantry, 14 Oxford St. (tel. 237 3505), across from the cinema. Good, cheap, and smack dab in the heart of the city. 45 stuffings served in a variety of breads (£1.10-2.50). Open M-F 7am-6pm, Sa 8am-6pm.

Feed the Five Thousand (FT5K), 16 St. Mary's Gate (tel. 819 1200). Fast becoming a city-wide chain, this original branch is still handy with the bread and fish, as well as other funky combinations (£1-2.50).

SIGHTS

Few of Manchester's buildings are notable; an exception is the Neo-Gothic **Manchester Town Hall,** at St. Peter's Sq. behind the tourist office. Behind the Town Hall Extension is the city's real jewel, the **Central Library** (tel. 234 1900). One of the largest municipal libraries in Europe, the domed building has a music and theater library, an excellent language and literature library, and the U.K.'s largest Judaica collection outside London. *(Open M-Th 10am-8pm, F-Sa 10am-5pm.)* The **John Rylands Library,** 150 Deansgate (tel. 834 5343), conceals rare books and nifty exhibits in a Neo-Gothic fortress. *(Open M-F 10am-5:30pm, Sa 10am-1pm. Free. Guided tours W at noon. £1.)*

The **City Art Galleries** (tel. 236 5244) are closed for renovation until 2000. In the **Museum of Science and Industry,** Castlefield (tel. 832 1830 or 832 2244; http://www.msim.org.uk), on Liverpool Rd., working steam engines and looms provide a dramatic vision of the awesome power, danger, and noise of Britain's industrialization. Check out the "Manchester Underground" exhibit, where you can walk through faux sewers and give thanks for modern plumbing. *(Open daily 10am-5pm, last admission 4:30pm. £5, students, seniors, children, and disabled £3; includes entrance to all galleries for 1 day, which may not be enough. Wheelchair accessible.)* The Spanish and Portuguese Synagogue-turned-**Jewish Museum,** 190 Cheetham Hill Rd. (tel. 834 9879), north of Victoria Station, traces the history of the city's sizable Jewish community and offers city tours. *(Open M-Th 10:30am-4pm, Su 10:30am-5pm. £2.75, students, seniors, and children £2, families £7. Wheelchair access to ground floor.)* In equal parts loved and reviled, Manchester United is probably the best-known English football team. At the new **Manchester United Museum and Tour Centre,** Sir Matt Busby Way (tel. 877 4002), at the football ground (follow the signs from the Old Trafford Metrolink stop), you can see memorabilia that commemorates the club's evolution from its inception as Newton Heath in 1878 to its remarkable success in recent years. *(Museum open daily Apr.-Oct. 9:30am-9pm, Nov.-Mar. 9:30am-5pm. Tours run 9:30am-4:40pm. Museum only £4.50, seniors and children £3. Museum and tour £7.50, seniors and children £5.)*

ENTERTAINMENT

Manchester's biggest draw is its artistic community, most notably the energetic theater and music scenes. The **Royal Exchange Theatre** (tel. 833 9833; fax 832 0811) has returned to its home on St. Ann's Sq., two years after an IRA bomb destroyed the original building. *Waiting for Godot* (May 12-June 26), *King Lear* (Sept. 8-Oct. 23), and four world premiers grace the 1999 season. *(Box office open M-Sa 10am-7:30pm. M-Th and Sa £7-23, students, seniors, and children £5 when booked 3 days in advance; separate concession rates apply to W and Sa matinees without advance booking.)* Proving that glass and metal can make stunning architecture, the **Bridgewater Hall** (tel. 907 9000), across from the G-Mex, is the new home for the superb Hallé Orchestra directed by Kent Nagano. Pop, jazz, and classical concerts are frequently held at the **G-Mex** (Greater Manchester Exhibition and Event Centre; tel. 832 9000 or 834 2700), a renovated train station on Lower Mosley St.; the front side closely resembles the head of space villain Darth Vader. Manchester's other major concert area is the **Nynex Arena** (tel. 950 8000), behind Victoria Station.

The **Central Library Theatre** (tel. 236 7110; fax 228648), in the intimate former lecture hall of the Central Library, St. Peter's Sq., houses a professional company that performs plays classical to modern. *(Box office open M-Sa 10am-6pm; July-Aug. until 8pm. £8-15, students and seniors £3 discount. Wheelchair accessible.)* The **Green Room Theatre** (tel. 950 5900) puts on heady works in its 54-56 Whitworth St. West location. *(Box office open M-F 10am-5pm; on performance days also Sa-Su 6-8pm. Some discounts available.)* The **Palace Theatre,** Oxford St. (tel. 242 2503), caters to more bourgeois tastes in theater, opera, and ballet. *(Box office open M-Sa 10am-8pm, Su 2hr. before performance. On non-performance days open M-Sa 10am-6pm. Call for student discounts.)*

Manchester does not lack **festivals** to further entertain the weary traveler. **The Boddington Manchester Festival of the Arts and Television** takes place in September and October—call the Central Library (tel. 234 1944) for information. The Gay Village also hosts a number of festivals, most notably **Mardi Gras** (tel. 237 3237), in late August, which raises money for AIDS relief. The **Independence Festival** (tel. 234 3160) brings in millions of disabled people in a giant early September celebration.

CAFE-BARS

Manchester's *très* chic cafe-bar scene defies categorization. Excellent lunchtime chatting spots with reasonable food prices, the bars morph into perfect pre-club drinking venues—or even become clubs themselves. Classifications are murky: in the **Clubs** section, Generation X and Joop both have good cafe-bars; in the **Food** section, the Cornerhouse and Green Room Cafés both offer stylish locales for the chic to drink, not just eat. Listed below are our picks for the hippest lubricating spots.

Cyberia, 12 Oxford St. (tel. 661 1106; http://www.manchester.cyberiacafe.net). Not your average technogeek locale, it's a cybercafe clothed in chill, metallic decor that perfectly houses the digerati filling it at night. Open M-Sa 11am-11pm, Su 2-9pm.

Atlas Bar, 376 Deansgate (tel. 834 2124). This trendy bar sports small tables that encourage chatting, or allow you to enjoy the abstract art on the walls in solitary peace. 29 beers for true beer connoisseurs. *Let's Go* recommends anything from Belgium. Open M-Sa 11am-11pm, Su noon-10:30pm.

Dry Bar, 28-30 Oldham St. (tel. 236 9840). Famous for its association with British indie music (founded by Factory Records and the band New Order) the sleek super-long bar still draws in the beautiful people. Open M-Sa 11am-11pm, Su 11am-10:30pm; happy hour 4-7pm M-F.

Temple of Convenience, 100 Great Bridgewater St. (tel. 288 9834). A small subterranean location creates an intimate atmosphere that draws a bohemian crowd. The name refers to the place's former life as a public restroom. Open daily 11am-11pm.

The Lass O'Gowrie, 36 Charles St. (tel. 273 6932). Traditional pubs aren't *passé* when the late evening crowd is as lively as this. Try some of their own brews. In the afternoon, BBC celebrities often trickle in from the neighboring studio. Open M-Sa 11am-11pm, Su 11:30am-10:30pm.

CLUBS

Manchester's clubbing and live music scene remains a national trendsetter, although the loss of the Hacienda has left the city without any truly large-scale club. Those in the know hang around Oldham St. during the day to get a whiff of what's on for the evening; don't forget to collect flyers—they often get you a discount. **Afflecks Palace,** 52 Church St. (tel. 834 2039), at Oldham St., supplies groovesters with paraphernalia—from punk to funk—for their exploits; the walls of the stairway are postered with flyers advertising the evening's events. *(Open M-F 10am-5:30pm, Sa 10am-6pm.)* Just up Oldham St., **Fat City** (tel. 237 1181) sells drum 'n' bass and hip hop records and passes to hip and happening events. *(Open M-Sa 10am-5:30pm.)* Nearby **Eastern Bloc Records** (tel. 228 6432) does the same. *(Open M-Sa 10am-5:30pm.)* For a list of everything that's going on, the *City Life* paper (£1.60), at newsstands around the city, lists gay and straight clubs, as well as covers, hours, regular nights, and special events.

Generation X, 11-13 New Wakefield St. (tel. 236 4899), off Oxford St. If you're "mod for it," house and breakbeat plays on the roof terrace; the cafe-bar below plays more conventional music. Our favorite aspect, though, has to be **Regeneration,** its Sunday *après*-clubbing mellow chill-down. Cover £2 after 11pm. Open F-Sa until 2am, Su 3-10:30pm.

Joop, 47 Peter St. (tel. 839 6263). Packed shoulder to shoulder on weekends, Joop attracts an 18-25 crowd. House and garage on weekends, 70s music on Wednesday, anything-goes mix on Thursdays. Just don't wear sneakers. No cover. Open M-Tu noon-11pm, W-Sa noon-2am.

The Boardwalk, Little Peter St. (tel. 228 3555; http://www.boardwalk.co.uk). Take a break from all the cutting-edge club music and indulge in your taste for commercial dance—funk on Fridays, and an eclectic Molotov Pop night on Saturdays, spinning big beat funk-hip-hop-and-other-genre mix. Plastic cups for drinks are a bit of a put-off. Open W-Th 10pm-midnight, F 10pm-2am, Sa 10:30pm-3am.

Velvet Underground, 111 Deansgate (tel. 834 9975). Speed garage and underground house play to the delight of the twentysomething, women-strong crowd. Chill out on the plush red sofas. Cover £8, students £4. Open F-Sa 10pm-3am.

The Northern Quarter

The revitalization of this area continues; however, some of the streets are dimly lit. If you're crossing between Piccadilly and Swan/Great Ancoats St., use Oldham, where the bright lights of late-night clubs (and the presence of their bouncers) provide reassurance. **Sankeys Soap,** Jersey St. (tel. 237 5606), offers mainstream dance and a massively packed Saturday night *(Golden),* though it's slightly out of the way. **Band on the Wall,** 25 Swan St. (tel. 834 1786), has an eclectic mix of live music, including jazz, blues, and pop. *(Open M-Sa 8:30pm-2am.)*

The Gay Village

Gay and lesbian clubbers will want to check out **The Gay Village,** east of Princess St., At its heart, evening crowds fill the bars lining **Canal St. Manto's,** 46 Canal St. (tel. 236 2667), fills its purple interior with all ages, genders, and orientations. *(Saturday night/Sunday morning "Breakfast Club" 2-6am. Cover £2.)* **Paradise Factory,** 114-116 Princess St. (tel. 228 2966), runs two of the biggest nights in Manchester's gay scene—Friday's *Chocolate Factory* and Saturday's *Paramount Paradise*—playing a mix of house, commercial dance, and more from their musical bag of tricks. *(Occasional student promotions. Cover M-Th varies, F £3, Sa £6-8.)* **Ballans of Bloom St.,** 94-98 Bloom St. (tel. 236 6556), spins music from all decades in its two bars. *(Open M-Sa until 2am.)*

■ Chester

With fashionable shops tucked in mock medieval houses, tour guides in full Roman armor, a town crier in full Georgian uniform, and a Barclays bank occupying a wing of the cathedral, Chester at times resembles an American theme park pastiche of Ye

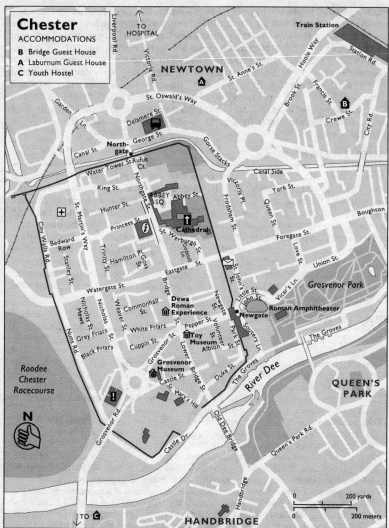

Chester
ACCOMMODATIONS
B Bridge Guest House
A Laburnum Guest House
C Youth Hostel

Liverpool Rd.

TO HOSPITAL

Train Station

NEWTOWN

St. Anne's St.

Hoole Way

Station Rd.

St. Oswald's Way

Brook St.

Francis St.

Crewe St.

City Rd.

Victoria Rd.

Garden Ln.

Delamere St.

George St.

Gorse Stacks

Canal St.

North-gate

Water Tower St. Rufus Ct.

Canal Side

York St.

King St.

Northgate St.

Victoria Pl.

Boughton

Hunter St.

ABBEY SQ.

Abbey St.

Frodsham St.

Queen St.

St. Martin's Way

Princess St.

Cathedral

St. Werburgh St.

Foregate St.

Love St.

Bedward Row

City Walls Rd.

Trinity St.

Hamilton Pl.

St. Werburgh Ln.

Union St.

ENGLAND

Stanley St.

Eastgate St.

St. John's St.

Grosvenor Park

Watergate St.

Bridge St.

Little St. John St.

Vicar's Ln.

Nicholas St. Mews

Commonhall St.

Newgate St.

Roman Amphitheater

Nicholas St.

Weaver St.

Dewa Roman Experience

Newgate

Grey Friars

White Friars

Pepper St.

Volunteer St.

Souters Ln.

The Groves

Black Friars

Cuppin St.

Grosvenor St.

Toy Museum

Park St.

Num Rd.

Albion

River Dee

Roodee Chester Racecourse

Grosvenor Museum

Lower Bridge St.

Duke St.

The Groves

QUEEN'S PARK

Castle St.

Mary's Hill

Queen's Park Rd.

N

Grosvenor Rd.

Castle Dr.

Old Dee Bridge

Handbridge

TO C

HANDBRIDGE

0   200 yards
0   200 meters

Olde English Towne. Sleek Victorian chain stores easily outnumber the smattering of authentic medieval buildings. Originally built by frontier-forging Romans, Chester flourished in the 10th century under Æthelflæd, "Lady of the Mercians," who managed to keep Vikings out by extending the city walls. In subsequent years, Chester became a base for Plantagenet campaigns against the Welsh, and established a web of trading connections throughout continental Europe. As silt blocked the River Dee in the 17th century, Liverpool became a commercial center, and Chester was left to turn its archaism into a selling point. Crowded but lovely, the city now allows foreigners inside its fortified walls, while maintaining a watchful eye on nearby Wales.

GETTING THERE

Chester serves as a **rail** gateway to North Wales through the Northern Coast Line. You can travel by train from Chester **via Shrewsbury** to central and southern Wales as well. **Trains** (tel. (0345) 484950) run to London **Euston** (3hr., 1 per hr., £38.50, return £39.50), **Holyhead** (1 per hr., £13.80, return £16.70), **Manchester Piccadilly** station (1hr., 1 per hr., £7.20, day return £7.30), and **Birmingham** (2hr., 2 per hr., £9.60). Frequent **Merseyrail** service makes Chester an easy daytrip from **Liverpool** (45min., 1 per hr., £2.80). **National Express buses** (tel. (0990) 808080) run to **London** (5½hr., 5 per day, £12), **Birmingham** (2½hr., 5 per day, £7.70, return £9.50), **Manchester** (1hr., 3 per day, £5.75), and **Blackpool** (3½hr., 3 per day, £7.10, return £8.75). **Northwestern** (tel. (0151) 933 1000) runs a service between **Liverpool** and Chester (#X8, 1hr., M-Sa 1 per hr., £2.90). **Huxley Coaches** (tel. (01948) 770661) bus #C56 rattles over the Welsh border to **Wrexham** from Forgate St. (M-F 2 per hr., Sa 1 per hr., £2.15). Pick up the hefty *Chester Public Transport Guide* at the bus station or tourist offices.

ORIENTATION

Chester's center is encircled by a medieval **city wall**, which is breached by seven gates. The train and bus stations both lie 15 minutes to the north, outside the walls. Save your legs the walk and take bus #20 from the rail station to **Foregate St.,** free with a valid rail ticket. From Foregate St., enter the city walls onto **Eastgate St.,** and turn right onto **Northgate St.** to reach the main tourist office. From the bus station, turn left onto **Upper Northgate St.** and head through **Northgate** to the tourist office. The cross of St. Peter Cross is formed by Eastgate St., Northgate St., Watergate St. to the west, and **Bridge St.,** which passes under the wall as it reaches and crosses over the River Dee; **The Groves,** a left just before the bridge, hugs the river for a mile. Buses run from the bus station (6 per hr.) to the Market Square Bus Exchange, near the tourist office.

PRACTICAL INFORMATION

Trains: City Rd. (tel. (0345) 484950). Office open M-Sa 5:30am-12:30am, Su 8am-midnight.

Buses: Delamere St. (tel. 381515), just north of the city wall off Northgate St. Long-distance and county coaches and buses stop here. Office open M-Sa 9am-5pm (tel. 602666; call M-F 8am-6pm, Sa 9am-1pm, for info on all local services). Some intra-city buses stop on Delamere St.; most stop at the **bus exchange** in Market Sq. around the corner from the Town Hall.

Tourist Office: Town Hall, Northgate St. (tel. 402111 or 313126). Open May-Oct. M-Sa 9am-7:30pm, Su 10am-4pm; Nov.-Apr. M-Sa 9am-5:30pm, Su 10am-4pm. Two smaller **branches** are located at the train station (tel. 322220; open daily 10am-8pm), and at the **Chester Visitor Centre,** Vicars Ln. opposite the amphitheater (tel. 351609; fax 403188; open M-Tu and Th-Sa 9am-7:30pm, W 10am-7:30pm, Su 10am-5pm). All 3 book accommodations for free and sell city maps (£1).

Tours: Chester has more tours than intact Roman columns. A legionnaire sweating in full armor leads the **Roman Tour** from Town Hall (June-Sept. Th-Sa 11:30am and 2:30pm; £1.80, students, seniors, children £1). The open-top **Guide Friday** (tel. 347457) buses do their usual schtick (4 per hr.; £5.50, students and seniors £4, children £1.50). Beings ghoulish and ghastly lurk on the **Ghost Hunter Trail** (May-Oct. Th-Sa 7:30pm; £3, children £2). Let us know if you see any. **Boats** (tel. 342694) embark from the tree-lined riverside street The Groves, a left off Lower Bridge St.; a 2½mi. trip down the River Dee lasts 1 hr. and costs £2.50 (children £1.50).

Financial Services: Barclays, in the cathedral's west wing and at 35 Eastgate St. Open M and W-F 9am-4:30pm, Tu 10am-4:30pm. Eastgate branch open M and W-F 9am-5pm, Tu 10am-5pm, Sa 9:30am-3:30pm. Both have **ATMs** too.

American Express: 12 Watergate St. (tel. 311145). Client mail held. Open M-F 9am-5:30pm, Sa 9am-5pm; currency exchange also open June-Sept. Su 11am-4pm.

Launderette: The Launderette, 56 Garden Ln. (tel. 371406), a right off Canal St. (itself a left off Northgate St.). Open daily 9am-6pm, last wash 4:30pm.

Hospitality Service: Chester at Home provides overseas visitors with tea, biscuits, and conversation in an English home 8-10:30pm, free of charge. Phone the Richardsons (tel. 677644 or 678868) daily 5:30-7pm to find a host. Pick-up arranged.

Emergency: Dial 999; no coins required.

Police: Grosvenor Rd. (tel. 350222).
Hotlines: Samaritans (crisis), 36 Upper Northgate (tel. 377999). Open 24hr. **Lesbian and Gay Switchboard** (tel. (01743) 232393). Open Tu-W and F 8-10pm. **Rape Crisis** (tel. 317922). Open W 7-8pm, Sa 11am-noon.
Hospital: Countess of Chester (West Chester) Hospital, Liverpool Rd. (tel. 365000). Take bus #40A from the station or bus #3 from the bus exchange.
Post Office: 2 St. John St. (tel. 348315), off Foregate St. just before the wall. Open M-Sa 9am-5:30pm. Bureau de change and photo booth. **Postal Code:** CH1 1AA.
Telephone Code: 01244.

ACCOMMODATIONS

The highest concentration of decent B&Bs (£13.50 and up) is along **Hoole Rd.,** a 5-minute walk from the train station (turn right from the exit, climb the steps to Hoole Rd., and turn right over the railroad tracks) and **Brook St.** (right from the train station exit, then the first left). Buses #21, C30, and 53 run to the area from the city center.

YHA Youth Hostel, Hough Green House, 40 Hough Green (tel. 680056; fax 681204), 1½mi. from the city center. Cross the river on Grosvenor Rd. and turn right at the roundabout (40min.), or take bus #7 or 16 and ask for the youth hostel. Beautiful, renovated Victorian house on a quiet street. Hostel has left luggage facilities, a laundry room and even a nightlight to read by. Thunderous showers restore lost youth and vitality. £9.75, under 18 £6.55. Reception open 7-10am and 3-11pm. Lockout 10am-noon. Closed late Dec.

Bridge Guest House, 18-20 Crewe St. (tel. 340438). From the train station, the first right off City Rd. The exceptionally thick wood door and sturdy whitewashed walls were erected for railway workers, but now shelter weary train passengers. Comfy TV lounge downstairs. Singles £17; doubles £30.

Laburnum Guest House, 2 St. Anne St. (tel./fax 380313), across the road from the bus station. 4 sparkling rooms, all stocked with TV and bath, lie about as close to the town center as you can get without having to face hordes of marauding shoppers. Singles £19; doubles £36.

FOOD

Beware the rustic restaurants lurking behind faux-Tudor facades along Chester's distinctive "rows"; their prices are decidedly up-to-date. **Tesco** supermarket, hidden at the end of an alley off Frodsham St., offers better bargains (open M-Sa 8am-10pm, Su 11am-5pm). The town's **market,** beside the bus exchange on Princess St. (M-Sa 8am-5pm), numbers fruit, vegetables, and meat among its disparate array of bargains. **Dutton's Health Foods,** 8 Godstall Ln. (tel. 316255), near the cathedral entrance, offers cheap packed lunches (roll with cheese, apple, and Brazil nuts 70p; open M-Sa 8:30am-5:30pm). For a smaller, more chic range of the same, try **Owen Owen,** 44-50 Bridge St. (open M-F 9:30am-5:30pm, Sa 9am-6pm). Picnic in the shade of the lovely **Grosvenor Park;** its sloping, flowered acres contain neither Roman artifacts nor tourists. From Bridge St., take a left onto Pepper St. cross under Newgate, pass the amphitheater, and enter on your right.

The Garden House, 1 Rufus Ct. (tel. 320004), off Northgate St. In a former executioner's home, reputedly haunted, now elegantly restored. Although dinners are pricey, the lunch menu is pleasantly cheap and vegetarian friendly. Choose from filled sandwiches (£3), samosas (£3.10), or creamy peppered mushrooms (£3.50), all served in the spacious lounge. Open M-Sa noon-2pm and 6:30-10pm.

Hattie's Tea Shop, 5 Rufus Ct. (tel. 345173), off Northgate St. Scrumptious homemade cakes and inexpensive lunchtime snacks. The "giant topless" ham salad sandwich turns on porcine fetishists (£4). Open M-F 9am-5pm, Sa 9am-7pm, Su 11am-4pm. Wheelchair access.

The Kalldra Tearooms, 49 Watergate St. (tel. 323003). Serves a filling selection of lunch meals (around £3-3.50). Sandwiches and rolls (£1.40-1.75). Open M-Sa 8:30am-4pm.

326 ■ CENTRAL ENGLAND

SIGHTS

The faux-medieval buildings (constructed by Victorians) effectively mask the fact that the center of Chester is really one vast outdoor shopping mall. On summer Saturdays, the already thick crowds coagulate, and a bizarre variety of street musicians, from cowpoke trios to accordion-wielding matrons, set up shop. The famous **city walls** completely encircle the town, and you can walk on them for free. Also free, unless you give in to the relentless pressures of bourgeois capitalism, are the **rows** of Bridge St., Watergate St., and Eastgate St.; above the street-level shops, a walkway gives access to another tier of storefronts. Some historians theorize that Edward I imported the idea from Constantinople, which he visited while crusading. Chester's streets are credited to the Romans, but their character is strictly medieval.

A number of pathways slither over and under the walls and pass through unimaginatively named gates. **Northgate,** one such gate with a fine-grained view of the Welsh hills, was rebuilt in 1808 to house the city's jail 30 ft. below ground. The bridge outside the gate is dubbed the Bridge of Sighs; it carried soon-to-be executed convicts from the jail to the chapel for their last mass.

Fight your way through the throngs for an awe-inspiring visit to Chester's **cathedral,** just off Northgate St. In 1092, Hugh Lupus, the newly named Earl of Chester, founded a Benedictine Abbey here. The abbey was founded on the site of a church (built AD 907) dedicated to St. Werburgh, a Mercian princess who passed up royal comfort for the religious austerity of a nunnery, and who resurrected geese as a hobby. A gothic facelift in 1250 set off a flurry of decorative makeovers, transforming the Romanesque cathedral into a stunning architectural hodgepodge. Intersecting stone arches named "The Crown of Stone" support the tower, and brilliant stained-glass windows sparkle throughout. The choir showcases an enormous pipe organ and ledges along the back walls, carved with aged, infirm, or fidgety monks. Check out the carvings *under* the choir seats as well. *(Cathedral open daily 7am-6:30pm. Free.)*

Just outside Newgate sits the unimpressive base of the largest **Roman amphitheater** in Britain. Excavated in 1960, it once accommodated the Roman legion at Dewa (Chester) for gladiatorial bouts, but now scarcely elicits a yawn in its utterly ruined state. *(Open daily Apr.-Sept. 10am-6pm; Oct.-Mar. 10am-1pm and 2-4pm. Free.)* Next door, the **Roman Garden and Hypocaust** offers picnic space on a shaded, narrow strip of grass lined with stunted Roman columns.

The **Grosvenor Museum,** 27 Grosvenor St. (tel. 321616), flaunts Chester's archaeological history with an extensive collection of Roman artifacts. The museum spills into the adjoining building, which contains a history of Chester and a natural history section full of stuffed animals shot by Victorians. *(Open M-Sa 10:30am-5pm, Su 2-5pm. Free.)* In a final stop on your whirlwind Roman tour, wander through a half-hearted re-creation of Roman Chester, past the dimly lit hull of a galley and a snoring centurion at the **Dewa Roman Experience,** Pierpoint Ln. (tel. 343407), off Bridge St. The "Experience" sits on the sight of Roman ruins and the archaeological digs can be viewed. *(Open daily 9am-6pm, last admission 5pm. £3.80, seniors £3, under 16 £1.90.)* The **Toy Museum,** 13a Lower Bridge St. Row (tel. 346297), has the largest collection of matchbox cars in the world, as well as the bug-eyed monsters on a 1964 series of "revolting bubble-gum cards." *(Open Easter-Oct. daily 10am-5pm; Nov.-Easter M-Sa 10am-5pm, Su noon-4pm. £2, students, seniors, and children £1, families £4; YHA members 10% off.)*

ENTERTAINMENT

Chester has 30-odd pubs to assuage thirst (and hunger); many parrot Ye Olde English decor. Watering holes group on Lower Bridge and Watergate St. Decidedly non-traditional in decor is **Claverton's Café Bar** (tel. 319760), on Lower Bridge St., whose cozy couches attract a chic, female-strong crowd. *(Open M-Sa noon-11pm, Su noon-10:30pm.)* Traditionalists cross the road into **Ye Olde King's Head,** 48-50 Lower Bridge St. (tel. 324855), where an assortment of steins hangs from beams in a restored 17th-century house. *(Open M-Sa 11am-11pm, Su noon-10:30pm.)* Or have a pint in the tranquil 16th-century upstairs room at **The Falcon,** 6 Lower Bridge St. *(Open M-*

Sa 11am-11pm, Su noon-10:30pm.) The **Boat House** (tel. 328719), at the end of a pleasant walk along the River Dee at the end of The Groves, lets the sun shine in the pub-length glass window facing the Dee; be prepared to fight off couples to get a window seat. *(Open M-Sa 11am-11pm, Su noon-10:30pm.)*

A twentyish crowd lines up to enter the sweaty throng at **Rosie's** nightclub (tel. 327141), which takes up three floors of the Northgate Row. At ground level is a pub littered with Route 66 signs and other bits of Americana. *(Open Tu-Sa 8pm-1am.)* Commercial dance/chart music envelopes the floor above. Funk/soul brothers get down on the top floor. *(Cover £3-5. Open Th-Sa 9:30pm-2am. F-Sa over 21 only and males must wear collars.)* **Alexander's Jazz Bar,** Rufus Ct. (tel. 313400), off Northgate St., hosts jazz or blues bands at least three nights a week. *(Open M-Th 11am-midnight, F-Sa 11am-12:30am, Su noon-10:30pm.)*

On sporadic spring and summer weekends, England's oldest **horse races** are held on the Roodee (tel. 323170), formerly the Roman harbor. Lodgings fill up quickly on these weekends; write or call the tourist office for schedules and advance booking. *(Entrance £2 and up.)* The **Chester Summer Music Festival** (box office tel. 320700 or 341200) draws orchestras and other classical performers from across Britain into the Cathedral during the third and fourth weeks of July. Contact the Chester Festival Office, 8 Abbey Sq., Chester CH1 2HH. *(Open M 9:30am-8pm, Tu-F 9:30am-4pm, Sa 10am-4pm.)* Latin, rock, cajun, folk, and jazz artists perform at the concurrent **Chester Fringe Festival** (box office tel. 340392; open M-Sa 10am-7pm). Actors and story tellers also take part. During the last week in June and the first week of July, Chester hosts a Sports and Leisure Fortnight. Celebrations center around a river carnival and raft race down the winding Dee. Write the tourist office, which also carries the free monthly *What's On in Chester.*

■ Blackpool

At the end of the 18th century, Blackpool was a quiet resort town that catered to a small number of well-to-do holiday-makers. The present era of raucous gaudiness grew from the railways built in 1840, and the introduction of open-air dancing (1870) and electric street lighting (1879). By the end of the 19th century, droves of working class Britons from Lancashire and Yorkshire were pouring in. Today, the resort town's amusements are mind-numbingly numerous—a 7 mi. hyperactive promenade of giant dinosaurs, palm-readers, fruit machines, and fun palaces. Blackpool, for all its unabashed tackiness (or, more likely, because of it), is unrivaled worldwide (*pace* Las Vegas) as a tasteless dispenser of uninhibited fun of the piss drunk, lounge act variety.

GETTING THERE

Most **trains** do the cha-cha-cha at Blackpool North (tel. 620385), though some local locomotives hustle at Blackpool South or Pleasure Beach. Regular service foxtrots to **Manchester** (1¼hr., 2 per hr., £8.20), **Liverpool** (1½hr., 1 per hr., £9.20), **Buxton** (2hr., 1 per hr., £12.60, return £12.70), and London **Euston Station** (change at Preston; 4hr., 1 per hr., £43, return £44). **National Express** (tel. (0990) 808080) waltzes from Talbot Rd. bus station to **Chester** (4hr., 3 per day, return £8.75), **Liverpool** (1½hr., 4 per day, £5.50, return £9), **Manchester** (2hr., 5 per day, return £6.50), and **London** (6½hr., 6 per day, return £26).

ORIENTATION AND PRACTICAL INFORMATION

At the **Blackpool North** train station, one block farther down Talbot Rd., direct inquiries to the travel center (open daily 8am-8pm). The office at the Talbot Rd. **bus station** (tel. 21175) dispenses local and National Express information (open M-Sa 8:15am-midnight, Su 10am-6pm). A one-day **Travelcard** (£4.25, seniors and children £3.75) buys unlimited travel on buses (bus #1 covers the Promenade every 8min.) and the vintage trams; a single ride from the Tower to Pleasure Beach costs 80p. The friendly staff at the main **tourist office,** 1 Clifton St. (tel. 621623; fax. 478210), books beds and hands out street maps. From Talbot Rd., take a left onto Corporation St. (open M-F 9am-5pm, Sa-Su 10am-4pm). A **branch** crouches on the Promenade in the shade of the Tower and shares the same hours. A third office offers wisdom across from Pleasure Beach, 87a Coronation St. (tel. 403223). Summon cash at **Midland Bank,** 1 Victoria St. (tel. 613000), or its **ATM** (bank open M-F 9:30am-4:30pm, Sa 9:30am-3:30pm), behind the tower. Wash the dirt right outta your shirt at the **Albert Rd. Launderette,** corner of Albert and Regent Rd. (open M-F 9am-4pm, Sa 10am-2pm). The crowded **post office** (tel. 622888) sorts at 26-30 Abingdon St. (open M-Sa 9am-5:30pm). The **postal code** is FY1 1AA; the **telephone code** is 01253.

ACCOMMODATIONS AND FOOD

With over 3500 hotel and guest houses, and 120,000 beds—more than in all of Portugal—you won't have trouble finding a room (except on weekends during the Illumination, when advanced bookings are essential, and prices go up). **B&Bs** dominate the blocks behind the Promenade between the North and Central Piers and, thanks to cutthroat competition, are budget-friendly (£10-14). Pick up the free Bible-sized *Blackpool Rock On* at the tourist office for an impressive list. Your chip-heavy, dance-weary body will thank you for the comfortable beds at **Clarron House,** 22 Leopold Grove (tel. 623748), and for the delicious range of breakfast choices. From the bus station or North train station, head toward the sea on Talbot Rd., take a left on Topping St. and turn right on Church St.; Leopold Grove is on the left one block down (TVs in each room; £15). The maternal proprietress at the **Silver Birch Hotel,** 39 Hull Rd. (tel. 622125), has spoiled guests with warm hospitality for 22 years. From the bus and train stations, head down Talbot Rd. toward the ocean, take a left onto Market St., pass the Tower and a bend in the road, and turn left. TVs occupy each room, and a boundless breakfast sizzles in the green dining room (for *Let's Go* users £10, with bath £13; breakfast £3). Bay windows, tall ceilings, and an aristocratic red decor—all redone by the new handy-with-the-toolbox owner—fill **York House,** 30 S. King St. (tel. 624200). Follow the Clarron House directions, but turn left on Church St.; S. King St. is one block down on the right (£16.50, all with TVs and bath).

You know you're in Blackpool when McDonald's begins to look like a classy restaurant. Blackpool's hundreds of plastic-faced eating spots are sickeningly uniform in their oily indulgence. The first glimpse of **Food Giant Supermarket,** 1 Dickson Rd. (tel. 293051), across from the bus station, is like discovering a shaded spring in the Sahara (open M-Th 9am-8pm, F-Sa 8:30am-8pm, Su 10am-4pm). Take along a warm loaf from **Sayers the Baker,** 1 Birley St. (tel. 624913; open M-Sa 8:30am-5pm), to the 256 acres of **Stanley Park,** about 1 mi. east of the tower. The fish and chips at **Harry Ramsden's** (tel. 294386), corner of the Promenade and Church St., unlike many, aren't floating in grease, and the seating area isn't from a school cafeteria (open daily M-Th and Su 11:30am-9pm, F 11:30am-10pm, Sa 11:30am-10:30pm).

ENTERTAINMENT

No fewer than 36 nightclubs, 38,000 nightly theater seats, several circuses, and even more rollercoasters squat along the 7 mi. Promenade, still served by Britain's first electric tram line. Even the three 19th-century **piers** are smothered by amusement centers, ferris wheels, and greasy chip shops. The hedonistic hordes don't come for the ocean; Blackpool South Pier is among the ten most polluted beaches in the U.K. Instead, most careen down the rollercoaster tracks of **Pleasure Beach** (tel. 341033), just across from South Pier. Around 7½ million people visited the sprawling 40-acre amusement park last year, second in Europe only to its more refined, though mousier, competitor outside Paris. Although known for its historic wooden rollercoasters—the twin-track Grand National is something of a mecca for coaster enthusiasts—thousands of thrill-seekers line up for the aptly-named **Big One,** and aren't disappointed (their screams vie with the seagulls' cries as they fleetingly enter orbit); the 235 ft. high steel behemoth rockets down a heartstopping 65° slope at 87 mph—the highest, steepest, and fastest in the world. Although admission to the gritty, theme-

Shall We Dance?

Bodies at the Palace may gyrate to techno, but hundreds of dancers step to a different beat each May. Blackpool's Winter Gardens is home to one of the largest, and undeniably the most prestigious **ballroom dancing** competitions in the world (recently featured in the Japanese film *Shall we Dance?*). Each spring, hundreds of competitors—both professional and amateur—face off in grueling rounds of serious dancing until there are six couples left. In the final round, these couples compete in each of the following: **Latin** competitors dance the cha-cha, the samba, the rumba, the paso doble, and the jive; **Standard** or **Ballroom** competitors dance the waltz, the tango, the foxtrot, and the quickstep. The overall score determines the winning couple. Those not accustomed to the colorful costumes, heavy make-up, and theatrical expressions of ballroom dancing may find the competitors yet another garish spectacle in Blackpool's bright lights, but take a little time to sway to a waltz or hop to a jive, and the allure of the dance just might draw you in.

less park is "free," rides aren't—kiddy rides go for £1, most coasters cost £2.10, while the Big One costs a whopping £4.20. On the good side, the pay-as-you-ride system means queues for rides are shorter than at other theme parks. *(£20 Ride Tickets get you about £25 worth of rides. Park opens daily at 10-11am; closing time varies; call ahead or check the posted time at the entrance.)*

When a London businessman visited the 1890 Paris World Exposition, he returned determined to erect Eiffel imitations throughout Britain. Only Blackpool embraced his enthusiasm, and in 1894 the 560 ft. **Blackpool Tower** graced the city's skyline. **Towerworld** (tel. 622242) at its base is a bizarre, old-fashioned hotel-like building with a daily circus at 2:30 and 7:30pm, and a small aquarium lying off its carpeted staircases. Couples (mostly senior citizens) dance sedately in the astonishingly ornate Victorian ballroom complete with a Wurlitzer organ. *(Open Easter-Oct. daily 2-11pm; tower open Easter-Oct. daily 10am-11pm; Nov.-Easter Sa-Su 10:30am-4pm. £6, children and seniors £5; circus only £2, children and seniors £1.)* Blackpool consummates its crazed love affair with bright lights—it was the first electric town in Britain—in the orgiastic bulbed **Illumination** of 5 mi. of the Promenade. In a colossal waste of energy, 72 mi. of cables light up the tower, the star-encased faces of Hollywood actors, corporate emblems, and bizarre, gaudy placards. *(Sept. 3-Nov. 9 in 1999, Sept. 1-Nov. 5 in 2000.)*

Stretching from North to Central Pier, Blackpool's famous **Golden Mile** hosts scores of sultry theaters, cabaret bars, and bingo halls. Criss-crossed by laser beams, the cavernous, multi-tiered dancefloors of the U.K.'s largest nightclub, **The Palace,** Central Promenade (tel. 26281), pulsate with bodies. Up to 3000 revelers pack it in for 70s night on Thursday. *(Cover £1-9. Open Th-Sa 9pm-2am.)* The more upscale **Main Entrance** (tel. 292335), directly below the Palace, can only hold 1000. *(Frequent theme nights. Cover £2-12. Open M-Tu and Th-Sa 9pm-2am, second Su of the month 9pm-midnight.)* Head to the swanky marble counters at the Blackpool branch of the **Yates Wine Lodge** (tel. 752443), at the corner of Talbot Rd. and Clifton St., for a non-tacky pub with decent grub. *(Open M-Sa 11am-11pm, Su noon-10:30pm.)*

■ Liverpool

On the banks of the Mersey, Liverpool (pop. 450,000) was on its way to becoming an important port as early as 1715, when it opened England's first commercial dock. Unfortunately, much of its early wealth was dependent on the slave trade. But it was the growing Lancashire cotton industry that allowed Liverpool to export more cargo than London by 1900. As a major 19th-century port, Liverpool was also the departure point for many an emigrant to Canada, the U.S., and the Antipodes; its Chinatown shows it was also a popular settling locale. After World War I, both the decline of the Empire and the advent of air travel dealt serious blows to the city's shipping industry. In the 1980s, high unemployment rates and local government scandals inhibited any

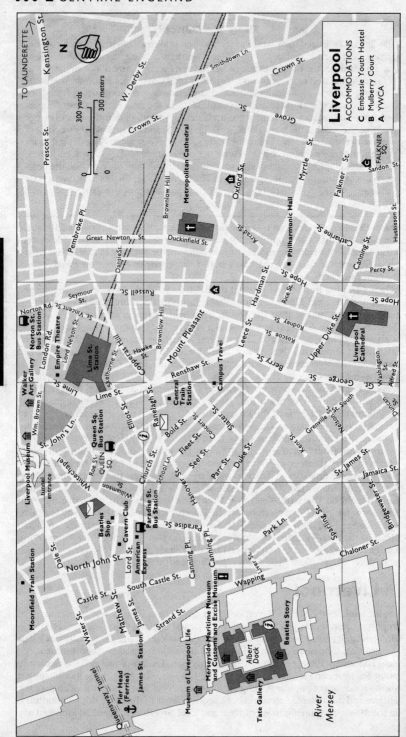

revival of former prosperity. Economic hardship is still evident, and most areas of the city should be explored with a measure of caution. Despite this, Liverpool is a great destination, with a transformed Albert Dock clustered with museums, two enormous cathedrals, two of England's most passionately supported football teams, and friendly locals, who'll be happy to introduce you to their Scouse dialect and unique brand of humor. Oh, yeah—and the Beatles.

THE LONG AND WINDING ROAD

Trains (tel. (0345) 484950) connect Liverpool to most major cities in North and Central England. They run to **Manchester** (1½hr., 2 per hr., £6, day return £6.30, return £9), **Birmingham** (2hr., 1 per hr., £14.80, return £15.30), **Chester** (45min., 2 per hr., £2.90, day return £3.20), and London **Euston** (2hr., 1 per hr., £38.50). Virgin Trains offers Virgin Value single tickets at £19, but tickets must be purchased by 6pm the previous day. **National Express** (tel. (0990) 808080) runs to London **Victoria** (4-5hr., 6 per day, day return £12.50, return £22), **Manchester** (1hr., 1 per hr., £6), and **Birmingham** (2½hr., 6 per day, return £10). The **Isle of Man Steam Packet Company** (tel. (0990) 523523) ferries to the Isle of Man. A **Superseacat** (tel. (0990) 523523) ferry runs twice a day to Dublin (see p. 32 for details). Private bus companies blanket the city and the surrounding Merseyside area; consult the transport mavens at Mersey Travel (see below), or take advantage of the cheap and efficient taxi fleet.

HELP!

Although Liverpool is part of a vast metropolitan area that sprawls across the **River Mersey,** its central district is pedestrian-friendly. Two clusters of museums flank the central shopping district: those on **William Brown St.,** near the main train station at Lime St., and those at **Albert Dock,** on the river. Train and bus stations are both centrally located, and most sites are within a 20-minute walk of either.

Transportation
Trains: Lime St. Station. Address inquiries to Lime St. Travel Centre in the station. Ticket office open M-Sa 5:15am-12:30am, Su 7:15am-12:30pm. **Luggage storage** (tel. 702 2477). £2; open daily 7am-10pm. **Moorfields, James St.** and **Central** train stations serve mainly as transfer points to local **Merseyrail** trains (including service to Chester and Crewe).
Buses: National Express (tel. (0990) 808080) coaches stop at the **Norton St. Coach Station.** Other buses stop at the **Queen Sq.** and **Paradise St.** stations.
Local Transport Information: Mersey Travel (tel. 236 7676), in the tourist office. Open daily 8am-8pm.
Taxis: Mersey Cabs (tel. 298 2222).

Tourist and Financial Services
Tourist Office: Merseyside Welcome Centre (tel. 709 3631; fax. 708 0204), in the Clayton Sq. Shopping Centre. From the train station at Lime St., exit onto Skelhorne St. and turn right; Clayton Sq. is the brick building with horizontal bands of sandstone. From the National Express coach station, turn right and go down North St., take the first right onto London Rd., turn left on Lime St. and right after the train station into the shopping center. Pick up the *Visitor Guide to Liverpool and Merseyside* (£1), which contains lists of sights in the county and a map of the city. Books beds for a 10% deposit. A smaller tourist information **branch** exists at Atlantic Pavilion, Albert Dock (tel. 708 8854). Open daily 10am-5:30pm.
Tours: Beatles **Magical History Tour** (tel. 236 9091) leaves once a day from Albert Dock and the Welcome Centre (2hr., £9; definitely book ahead). **Phil Hughes** (tel. 228 4565 or (0961) 511223) runs an excellent Beatles tour in a smaller, more personal 8-seater bus (call for times; £8 including a 2-for-1 coupon for admission to the Beatles Story). For a tour not overrun by Fab Four fanatics, hop aboard the hop-on-hop-off **Liverpool Heritage Tour** (tel. 293366; 1hr.; £5, students, seniors, and children £3). 20-odd other bus tours (from £3) and thirtysomething walking tours (£1)

rotate throughout the summer; the tourist office has the leaflets if you have the feet. **Fantasia Cruises** operates 30min. boat tours from Albert Dock (1 per hr., £4).

Budget Travel: Campus Travel, YHA Adventure Shop, 25 Bold St. (tel. 709 9200). Open M-Tu and Th-F 9:30am-5:30pm, W 9:30am-6pm, Sa 9am-6pm.

Financial Services: Barclays, 9-11 Whitechapel (tel. 801 3500), has an **ATM.** Open M-Tu and Th-F 9am-5pm, W 10am-5pm, Sa 9:30am-5pm.

American Express: 54 Lord St. (tel. 708 6673). Client mail held. Open M-F 9am-5:30pm, Sa 9am-5pm.

Local Services

Bookstore: News From Nowhere, 96 Bold St. (tel. 708 7270). Feminist bookshop run by a women's cooperative with a wide selection of literature and gay and lesbian periodicals, as well as a bulletin board. Information and tickets are available from the staff. Open M-Sa 10am-5:45pm. Wheelchair access.

Launderette: Fabricare Dry Cleaners, 104 Prescot Rd. (tel. 263 7451; take bus #9 or 10). Change and soap available. Open M-F 8am-8pm, Sa-Su 8am-7pm.

Emergency and Communications

Emergency: Dial 999; no coins required.

Police: Canning Pl. (tel. 709 6010).

Hotlines: Samaritans (crisis; tel. 708 8888). Open 24hr. **Gay/Lesbian Friend** (tel. 708 9552). Open daily 7-10pm. **Rape Crisis** (tel. 666 1392). Open M and Th 7-9pm, W 2-5pm, Su 3-5pm.

Pharmacy: Mass Chemists, London Rd. Open daily 6am-11pm.

Hospital: Royal Liverpool Hospital, Prescot St. (tel. 706 2000), ½mi. from the train station.

Internet Access: Cafe Internet, 28 North John St. (tel. 255 1112; http://www.cafe-liv.com). Sandwiches and hot drinks accompany your surfing. £2.50 per 30min. Open M-Sa 10am-5pm.

Post Office: 33-34 Whitechapel (tel. 708 4165). Bureau de change and photo booth (£2.50). Wheelchair accessible. **Branch** in the splendid Lyceum building on Bold St. Both open M-F 9am-5:30pm, Sa 9am-7pm. **Postal Code:** L1 1AA.

Telephone Code: 0151.

HARD DAY'S NIGHT

Your best bet for cheap accommodations lies east of the city center. **Lord Nelson St.,** adjacent to the train station, is lined with modest hotels, and similar establishments are found along **Mount Pleasant,** one block from Brownlow Hill and the bus stop. The **YHA Hostel** is scheduled to open by the end of 1998 on Chalenor St. near Albert Dock; call (0171) 248 6547 for details. Stay only at places approved by the tourist office. Demand for rooms is highest in early April when jockeys and gamblers gallop into town for the Grand National Race; call ahead for reservations.

Embassie Youth Hostel, 1 Falkner Sq. (tel. 707 1089), in the southeast part of town at the end of Canning St. 15-20min. walk from the bus or train stations or take a taxi (£2). Feels like a laid-back student's flat—laundry, TV lounge, pool table, and kitchen, as well as all the toast and jam you can eat, all day, every day. Ask the energetic staff for pub-crawling tips, or ask Kevin to tell you about the time his band outplaced John Lennon's in a talent competition. One of England's friendliest hostels. £10.50; discounts for extended stays. No lockout or curfew.

YWCA, 1 Rodney St. (tel. 709 7791), just off Mt. Pleasant. For single women only. Renovated rooms are sparkling clean, attractively decorated, and surprisingly spacious, with firm beds. Singles £12; doubles £22; discounted weekly rates. Kitchen, laundry facilities (no soap or change available), and hot showers. Key deposit £15 for stays longer than 5 nights. No lockout or curfew.

University of Liverpool: Mulberry Court, Oxford St. (tel. 794 3298), offers clean but spartan self-catering accommodations for £15. The university-wide conference office (tel. 794 6440) has information on other halls open to travelers (£14.10 including continental breakfast). Open mid-July to mid-Sept.

Camping: Wirral Country Park, Thurstaston (tel. 648 4371). Take Mersey Ferries across the river to Woodside, then take bus #71 (2 per hr.), which passes within 1mi. of the site. £3.20, seniors and ages 5-18 £1.60; no reservations. **Abbey Farm,** Dark Ln., Ormskirk (tel. (01695) 572686), on the northern rail line from Lime St. station. £6.50 for 2-person tent. Enjoy the free showers. Wheelchair access.

SAVOY TRUFFLE

Trendy vegetarian cafes line **Bold St.** while cheap takeouts cluster on Hardnon and Berry St. Many restaurants stay open late. Try **St. John's Market** (sprawled across the top of St. John's shopping mall) for fresh produce and local color. **Matta's,** 51 Bold St. (tel. 709 3031), sells foods from all corners of the earth in two compact spicy rows (open M-Sa 9am-6:30pm, Su 11am-5pm). The **Kwik Save** supermarket sits at 58 Hanover St. (open M-Tu 8:30am-6pm, W-Sa 8:30am-6:30pm).

Café Tabac, 126 Bold St. (tel. 707 3735). Plan your evening by perusing the postered primary-colored walls. Limited but inexpensive, tasty menu (£3 and under) and eclectic international wines. Open M-Sa 9:30am-11pm, Su 10am-5pm.

Metz Café-Bar, Rainford Gdns. (tel. 227 2282), off Mathew St. "Don't discriminate, integrate," they proclaim—this candle-lit underground establishment is gay-friendly, but everyone's welcome to taste their esoteric and tasty lunch sandwich and soup combos (£4.75; between noon-7pm)—try the brie and bacon. Open M-Th noon-11pm, F-Sa noon-midnight, Su noon-10:30pm.

not sushi, 23 fleet St. (tel. 709 8894). main courses £5-6.45. open tu-th noon-10pm, f-sa noon-midnight; no sushi except on first monday of month. poem by daryl sng.

> the fish swim idly
> in underground japanese
> eating place; great staff

Hub Café Bar, Berry St. (tel. 707 9495). Furniture made out of bicycle parts in a cafe that dishes out light veggie and vegan meals (£1.50-3); the cycle store next door rents out bikes to be used as originally intended. Bike rental £2 per hr., £8 per day. Open M 9am-7pm, Tu-Su 9am-midnight.

MAGICAL MYSTERY TOUR

Liverpool has two 20th-century cathedrals, both southeast of the city center. The Anglican **Liverpool Cathedral,** Upper Duke St. (tel. 709 6271), begun in 1904 and completed in 1978, is *vast,* featuring the highest Gothic arches ever built (107ft.), the largest vault and organ (9704 pipes), and the highest and heaviest bells in the world. Climb to the top of the 300 ft. tower for a view stretching to north Wales. *(Cathedral open daily 9am-6pm; tower open daily 11am-4pm, weather permitting. Tower £2, children £1.)* In contrast, the inside of the Roman Catholic **Metropolitan Cathedral of Christ the King,** Mt. Pleasant (tel. 709 9222), dubbed "Paddy's Wigwam" by locals, looks more like a rocket launcher than a house of worship. Inside, long strips of neon blue stained glass cast a warm soothing glow on the circular interior. You half expect big-haired priests to shimmy out in silvery, skin-tight robes. *(Open daily in summer 8am-6pm; in winter M-Sa 8am-6pm, Su 8am-5pm. Wheelchair accessible.)*

Albert Dock, at the western end of Hanover St., is an open rectangle of Victorian warehouses transformed into a modern-day shopping mall replete with offices, restaurants, and museums. The **Tate Gallery** (tel. 709 3223), a branch of the London institution, contains an impressive range of 20th-century artwork. British artists dominate the first floor (Lucian Freud, Damien Hirst, Francis Bacon, etc.), while above, an excellent Cubist exhibition is running until mid-April 1999, alongside most major international artists of the last century. By prior arrangement, the staff will fit the visually impaired with special gloves and allow them to touch some of the art. *(Museum and cafe open Tu-Su 10am-6pm. Free, but some special exhibits £3, students, seniors, and children £1. Wheelchair accessible.)*

Also at Albert Dock is **The Beatles Story** (tel. 709 1963), with recreations of Hamburg, the Cavern Club (complete with the disinfectant "basement smells"), and a shiny Yellow Submarine. Shed a tear on John Lennon's white piano before you leave. *(Open daily Apr.-Oct. 10am-6pm; Nov.-Mar. 10am-5pm. £6.45, students, seniors, and children £4.75, families £16.)* For other Beatles-themed locales, pick up the **Beatles Map** *(£2)* at the tourist office: it takes you down to Strawberry Fields and Penny Lane. Souvenir hunters can raid the **Beatles Shop,** 31 Mathew St. (tel. 236 9091), which is stuffed with memorabilia. *(Open M-Sa 9:30am-5:30pm, Su 11am-4pm.)*

The £3 eight-museum pass (students, seniors, children £1.50), valid for 12 months, is an excellent purchase. On Albert Dock, it gets you into the 6-story **Merseyside Maritime Museum** (tel. 478 4499), which recreates something of the horror of the slave trade and the bomb-induced carnage of the Battle of Britain. Wander through the cramped hull of a slave trader's ship or down a dimly lit dockside street to the voices of desperate immigrants. Fans of a certain movie starring Leonardo DiCaprio can check items recovered from a certain "unsinkable" ship. The pass also includes entry to the attached **H.M. Customs and Excise Museum,** with an intriguing array of confiscated goods from would-be smugglers, including throwing stars and a fountain pen that shoots chili powder. The **Museum of Liverpool Life** (tel. 478 4080), next door, tells the story of Merseyside culture, stormy labor struggles and race relations, and the city's sporting heritage. A TV runs footage of legendary matches between the city's two major football teams, Everton and Liverpool, while a plaque marks out Grand National-winning horses. *(All 3 museums open daily 10am-5pm, last admission 4pm.)*

Near the Lime St. train station on William Brown St. and also included in the eight-museum deal is the stately **Walker Art Gallery** (tel. 478 4199), which houses the famous *And When Did You Last See Your Father,* depicting Cromwell's forces interrogating an innocent-looking child while his royalist mother and sister fret in the background. The museum's huge collection contains works that date from 1300, and includes a variety of impressive post-Impressionist and pre-Raphaelite paintings. The **Liverpool Museum,** William Brown St. (tel. 478 4399), which holds a natural history section with a carved narwhal horn, a vivarium with live animals, including a tarantula and fire-bellied toads, and a planetarium. *(Both open M-Sa 10am-5pm, Su noon-5pm.)*

If you're not here for the Beatles, you're probably here for the football. Both Everton's **Goodison Park** (tel. 330 2266) and Liverpool's **Anfield** (tel. 260 6677) offer tours as well as match tickets. *(Tours £5. Tickets from £14.)*

PLEASE PLEASE ME

Liverpool has a thriving arts and nightlife scene. *In Touch* and *Bigmouth,* available at the tourist office and at newsagents, are useful monthly entertainment guides (£1). For alternative events, check the bulletin board in the **Everyman Bistro,** 9-11 Hope St. (tel. 708 9545), where bohemian happenings often occur in their own **Third Room.** *(Acoustic music every Th 9pm-midnight; see **Savoy Truffle,** p. 333.)* The emporia of **Quiggins,** 12-16 School Ln. (tel. 709 2462), and the **Palace,** 6-10 Sater St., both sell hipster paraphernalia and have flyers detailing nightlife events. Read about special events at gay and lesbian clubs in **News From Nowhere** (see **Help!,** p. 331). The *Liverpool Echo,* an evening newspaper sold by streetcorner vendors, offers the most up-to-date arts information as well as local news (28p).

Pubs are everywhere. Slayter St. brims with £1 pints. **The Jacaranda,** Sayter St. (tel. 708 0233), was the site of the first paid Beatles gig. *(Open M-Th 8pm-2am, F-Sa noon-2am.)* John Lennon once said that the worst thing about being famous was "not being able to get a quiet pint at the Phil." You, however, can at **The Philharmonic,** 36 Hope St. (tel. 709 1163). Howling like a futuristic warehouse, **Baa Bar,** 43-45 Fleet St. (tel. 707 0610), off Bold St., attracts a far-from-sheepish lesbian, gay, trendy crowd for cappuccino during the day and cheap beer at night. *(Open M-Sa 10am-2am, Su 11am-6pm.)* John Lennon finished off lathery pints at **Ye Cracke,** Rice St. (tel. 708 4355). Even Hitler dropped by as a student. *(Closes 11pm.)* **Flanagan's Apple,** Mathew St. (tel. 236 1214), offers live music in an Irish pub setting.

Liverpool's nightclubs prove that the city is far from constrained by the legacy of the Beatles. **Cream** (tel. 709 1693), in Wolstonholme Sq. off Parr St., is—in a word—*brilliant.* Wave your hands in the air like a trashtalking semaphorist at Liverpool's superclub—people travel for miles to come here. **Garland's,** 8-10 Eberle St. (tel. 236

Abbadabba

Many residents of Merseyside region (Liverpool and its suburbs) speak a dialect of English called **Scouse**. Scouse is properly spoken with the intonation of someone who has a cold. It is strewn with double negatives and ignores past tense grammar conventions (hence, *clum* instead of *climbed*). The following is a list of particularly indecipherable (or to a Scouse, abbadabba) Scousisms.

don' cum ther rubber duck: don't be foolish or silly
frilly lips: a general term of abuse
fugginell: denotes surprise, anger, or any other strong reaction
got a neck like a mad giraffe: said of an impudent person
it's sky-blue pink wit' a finny-addy border: describes something particularly luxurious, such as a Rolls Royce or an elaborate mansion.
take 'is kecks down: to put a person in his place (kecks=trousers)

3307), off Dale St., is a lesbian and gay club featuring off-the-wall special events. *(Cover £3-8. Open Th 10pm-3am and Sa 10pm-4am.)* **The Cavern Club,** 10 Mathew St. (tel. 236 9091). On the site where the fab four gained prominence, and with the same decor, the Cavern now plays regular club music *(M and F-Sa 9pm-2am; free admission before 10pm)* and showcases live music *(Sa 2-6pm).* **Aquarium**, 40 Steele St. (tel. 708 6730), enforces a strict dress code—you're there to be looked at—and plays excellent house music. *(Cover £3-8. Open Th-F 10pm-3am, Sa 10pm-4am.)*

The **Royal Liverpool Philharmonic Orchestra** (tel. 709 3789), one of the finest English orchestras, performs at Philharmonic Hall, Hope St. *(Tickets from £7.50; 25% student and disabled persons discount; half-price on day of show for Wednesday and Saturday concerts.)* The Philharmonic Hall also features a random array of concerts, including jazz and funk. *(Box office open M-Sa 10:30am-5:30pm. Wheelchair accessible.)* The **Liverpool Empire Theatre** (tel. 709 1555), on Lime St., hosts drama and comedy, welcoming such famous troupes as the Royal Shakespeare Company. *(Box office open M-Sa 10am-8pm on performance days, M-Sa 10am-6pm on other days. Tickets from £5.50; 50% student discounts sometimes available week of performance. Wheelchair accessible.)* At the end of August, a week-long **Beatles Convention** draws pop fans and bewildered entomologists from around the world.

■ Leeds

As the U.K.'s third-largest metropolitan district, Leeds (and its neighbor Bradford) is home to over 700,000. Its textile prosperity bloomed in the ornate Victorian period (building facades boast a curious cast of stone lions, griffins, and cherubs), but the last 50 years have battered Leeds, sending most textile jobs overseas. Still, the city center remains dedicated to relentless capitalism. This founding city of Marks and Spencer's (or Marks and Sparks, as it's known) now sports block upon block of shops and attendant yuppies, while the desperate poor look on. Most visitors come on business; travelers sampling the exuberant nightlife should dress smart.

ORIENTATION AND PRACTICAL INFORMATION Leeds is about 50 mi. northeast of Manchester and 10 mi. east of Bradford, midway between the South Pennines and the Yorkshire Dales. **Trains** (tel. (0345) 484950) run to Leeds from most major cities, including **Bradford** (20min., 4 per hr., £1.70, day return £1.80), **Manchester** (1½hr., 2 per hr., £8.60), **York** (2hr., 2 per hr., £5), and London **King's Cross** (2½hr., 1 per hr., £48). **National Express** (tel. (0990) 808080) serves most major cities.

The **train station** sits on City Sq. (information office open 24hr.). The **bus station** (tel. 245 7676), which serves National Express, hides behind the Kirkgate Market on York St. (office open M-F 8:30am-5:30pm, Sa 8:30am-4:30pm). Both the train and bus stations glorify the institution of the **luggage locker** for £1-3. The **tourist office,** "Gateway Yorkshire" (tel. 242 5242; fax 246 8246), at the train station, offers shelves of guides and transportation schedules, and books beds for £1.25 and a 10% deposit (open M-Sa 9:30am-6pm, Su 10am-4pm). Every conceivable **bank** and **ATM** lie on Park Row. The **post office** (tel. 372853) shines on City Sq. (open M-Sa 9am-5:30pm). Leeds's **postal code** is LS1 2UH. The **telephone code** is young and sweet at 0113.

ACCOMMODATIONS AND FOOD **Mr. and Mrs. D. Hood,** 17 Cottage Rd., Head-ingly (tel. 275 5575), will charm you with conversation over coffee, and phat ginger-bread, yo (£17; take bus #93 or 96 from City Sq.). **Mrs. Clayton,** 66 Avenue Hill, Harehills (tel. 262 3394), offers self-catering accommodation, large rooms with TV and a crockery-stocked kitchen (£11). From opposite the Corn Exchange, take bus #9, 10, or 21 to the Ford Greene pub, then walk back and turn onto Harehills Ln., which crosses Avenue Hill. At the south end, **Kirkgate Market** conceals an entire block of food stalls (open M-Sa 9am-5:30pm, W 9am-1pm). **La Dolce Vita,** 130-134 Vicar Ln. (tel. 242 0565), serves pasta (£5-6) with *amore*. (Open M-Th noon-2:30pm and 5:30-11pm, F-Sa noon-2:30pm and 5:30-11:30pm, Su 6-11pm.)

SIGHTS AND ENTERTAINMENT Leeds's main museums and galleries cluster conve-niently on the Headrow, across Calverly St. from the massive Victorian **Town Hall.** The **City Art Gallery** (tel. 247 8248) features one of the best permanent collections of 20th-century British art outside London. The adjacent **Henry Moore Centre for the Study of Sculpture** (tel. 234 3158) holds an excellent sculpture collection, including a Robert Morris installation piece. *(Open M-Tu and Th-Sa 10am-5pm, W 10am-8pm, Su 1-5pm. Free.)* In the Central Library building nearby stands the **Leeds City Museum** (tel. 247 8275), which has an amazing natural history collection, including fossils, a huge brain coral, and a 512 lb. clam. *(Open Tu-Sa 10am-5pm. Free.)*

Like other major English cities, Leeds has succumbed to the lure of the cafe-bar. Call Ln., near the Corn Exchange, is particularly saturated: try **Oporto** or **Art's,** but make sure you follow the urban-sophiste dress code. **Club Nato,** 66-69 Boar Ln. (tel. 244 5144), packs 'em in with guest DJs over the weekend, as well as solid resident spinners. *(Cover varies. Open M and Th 10pm-2am, F 10pm-3am, Sa 10pm-6am.)*

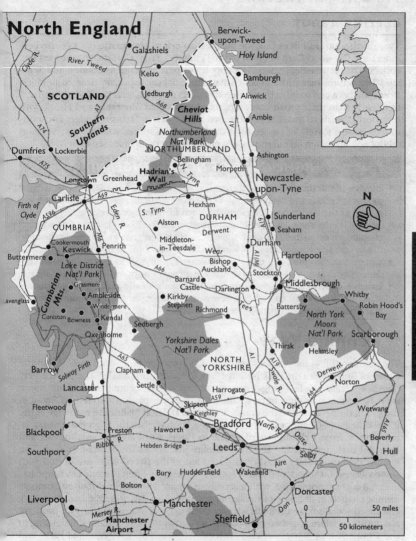

North England

Even before the Victorians invented tourism, travelers were drawn to this quiet area between central England's industrial belt and the rugged wilderness of Scotland. Bisected by the Pennine Mountains, North England's main attractions lie in four national parks and several calm coastal areas. Walkers and ramblers flock here, and no trail tests their stamina more than the Pennine Way, the country's first official long-distance path and still its longest. Extensive systems of shorter paths traverse the grey and purple moors that captured the imagination of the Brontës, the emerald green dales that figure so prominently in the stories of James Herriot, and the stunning crags and lakes that sent the Romantics into pensive meditation. Isolated villages uphold a pastoral tradition that contrasts the polluted din of cities to the south.

GETTING ABOUT

Two north-south **rail lines** link the far north: **York** to **Newcastle** (east of the Pennines) and **Crewe** to **Carlisle** (west of the Pennines). From **Carlisle**, an east-west line connects to **Newcastle**. Express Intercity trains pass en route to **London** and **Scotland**. Day returns may prove cheaper than single tickets, especially near major cities. **Buses** run between some of the scattered hamlets of agricultural England, though less frequently than their urban counterparts; plan detailed itineraries and check with transport officials to avoid being stranded for a week in Hebden Bridge. Local bus offices issue a variety of passes for a day's travel on routes within a given region (about £5), and often on rail routes as well; some bus companies sell their own.

⊛ HIGHLIGHTS OF NORTH ENGLAND

- Explore the dramatic peaks and sparkling waters of the **Lake District** (p. 375), the most famous and definitely one of the most beautiful regions in the country, as well as the landscape which inspired much of Wordsworth's poetry.
- Don't miss the splendid **York Minster,** Britain's largest Gothic cathedral, which contains an estimated half of all the medieval stained glass in England, including the largest single medieval glass window in the world (p. 349).
- Check out the pubs and clubs of **Newcastle,** home of brown ale. Crowded dance floors and lively locals have made this town's nightlife legendary (p. 365).
- Balance upon the remains of Roman **Hadrian's Wall** (p. 373), which once stretched from coast to coast. It now borders sheep-dotted **Northumberland National Park,** near England's northern coast.

■ Pennine Way

The Pennine (PEN-nine) Peaks form England's spine, arching south to north up the center of Britain from the Peak National Park to the Scottish border. The 268 mi. Pennine Way, England's first long-distance trail, crowns the central ridge of the watershed. Beginning at Edale, it traverses the massive, boggy plateau atop **Kinder Scout** in the south, then passes into the craggy **Yorkshire Dales** at Malham to reemerge at the formidable Pen-y-Ghent peak. The northern section crosses the **High Pennines,** a 20 mi. stretch from below Barnard Castle to Hadrian's Wall and Northumberland National Park, terminating at Kirk Yetholm, just across the Scottish border. The heather-clad moorland and arbored slopes left in the rivers' wake are dotted with stone villages and abandoned textile factories. The grim, often desolate landscape has fostered a gritty population with a rebellious strain. They erected modest Nonconformist chapels in defiance of Canterbury, shook their fists at textile barons as they embraced socialism, and relentlessly struggled to break the will of private property absolutists in winning public right-of-way access for these very trails, culminating in the 1932 arrest of 5 "trespassers" on Kinder Scout. The 1949 National Parks and Access to Countryside Act finally paved the way for open access.

HIKING

Hikers (with a capital H) have completed the hike in ten days, but most spend three weeks on the long, often remote trail. The less ambitious can make brief but still rewarding forays into the landscape or well-traveled walkways leading from the major towns. The unusual limestone formations in the Yorkshire Dales and the lonely moor of KinderScout are especially captivating, though any two wayfarers might recommend five different stretches.

The classic Wainwright's *Pennine Way Companion* (£10), a pocket-sized volume available from bookstores, is a worthwhile supplement to Ordnance Survey maps (£6, available from National Park Information Centres and tourist offices). Sudden storms can reduce visibility to under 20 ft., leave low-level paths boggy, and sink you knee-deep (or worse) in peat. At some points (especially in the Yorkshire Dales), and in ominous weather, you should stay on the narrow roads that run nearby. Those in the know recommend staying away from the Pennines in the wintertime unless you are, in truth, a Hiker. Whatever the weather, bring a good map and compass and know how to use them together. Complete rain gear, warm clothing, and extra food are also essential. Consult **Wilderness and Safety Concerns**, p. 47, for more advice.

ACCOMMODATIONS

YHA Youth Hostels are spaced within a day's hike (7-29mi.) of one another; note which ones are closed on certain nights. YHA offers a handy **Pennine Way Package:** you can book a route of 18 or more hostels along the walk (booking 50p per hostel) and obtain useful advice on paths and equipment. Send a self-addressed envelope to YHA Northern Region, P.O. Box 11, Matlock, Derbyshire DE4 2XA (tel. (01629) 825850). Any **National Park Information Centre** or **tourist office** can supply details on trails and alternate accommodations. The *Pennine Way Accommodations Guide* (90p) proves as valuable as moleskin.

The following hostels are arranged alphabetically, with the distance from the nearest southerly hostel listed after the phone number. Lockout is 10am-5pm, curfew is 11pm, and breakfast and evening meals are served, unless otherwise noted.

Alston: The Firs, Alston CA9 3RW (tel./fax (01434) 381509), 22mi. from Dufton. £8, under 18 £5.40. Shop in hostel. Open Apr.-Aug. daily; Sept.-Oct. Tu-Sa.

Baldersdale: Blackton, Baldersdale, Barnard Castle DL12 9UP (tel./fax (01833) 650629), 15mi. from Keld in a converted stone farmhouse overlooking Blackton Reservoir. £7.20, under 18 £5. Open mid-May to Aug. daily; Mar. to mid-May and Sept.-Oct. F-Tu.

Bellingham: (tel. (01434) 220313), 14mi. from Once Brewed in Northumberland. See **Greenhead to Bellingham,** p. 370.

Byrness: (tel. (01830) 520425), 15mi. from Bellingham in Northumberland. See **Kielder to Byrness,** p. 371.

Crowden-in-Longdendale: (tel. (01457) 852135), 15mi. from Edale in Peak National Park. See **YHA Youth Hostels,** p. 311.

Dufton: Redstones, Dufton, Appleby CA16 6DB (tel. (017683) 51236), 12mi. from Langdon Beck. £8, under 18 £5.40. Shop in hostel. Open May-Aug. W-M; mid-Mar. to Apr. and Sept.-Oct. Th-M; Feb. to mid-Mar. F-Su.

Earby: Katharine Bruce Glasier Memorial Hostel, Glen Cottage, 9-11 Birch Hall Ln., Earby, Colne BB8 6JX (tel./fax (01282) 842349), 15mi. from Haworth. £7.20, under 18 £5. Self-catering. Open Apr.-Oct. W-M.

Edale: (tel. (01433) 670302), in Peak National Park. See **YHA Youth Hostels,** p. 311.

Greenhead: Carlisle CA6 7HG (tel./fax (016977) 47401), 17mi. from Alston. Converted chapel 16mi. east of Carlisle and steps away from Hadrian's Wall. £7.20, under 18 £5. Open July-Aug. daily; mid-Apr. to June M-Sa; Sept. to mid-Dec. and mid-Feb. to Mar. F-Tu.

Hawes: (tel. (01969) 667368), 19mi. from Stainforth in Yorkshire Dales National Park. See **Accommodations and Camping,** p. 345.

Haworth: Longlands Hall, Longlands Dr., Lees Ln., Haworth, Keighley BD22 8RT (tel. (01535) 642234; fax (01535) 643023), 12mi. from Mankinholes. 1mi. from the tourist office. 100 beds in a lovely Victorian mansion. £8.80, under 18 £6. Shop in hostel. No lockout. Open mid-Feb. to Oct. daily; Nov. to mid-Dec. M-Sa.

Keld: (tel. (01748) 886259), 9mi. from Hawes in Yorkshire Dales National Park. See **Accommodations and Camping,** p. 345.

Kirk Yetholm (SYHA): (tel. (01573) 420631), 27mi. from Byrness. See **Accommodations,** p. 478.

Langdon Beck: Forest-in-Teesdale, Barnard Castle DL12 0XN (tel. (01833) 622228), 15mi. from Baldersdale. £8.80, under 18 £6. Shop in hostel. Open mid-July to Aug. daily; Mar. to mid-July M-Sa; Sept.-Oct. Tu-Sa; Feb. and Nov. Su-Th.

Malham: (tel. (01729) 830321), 15mi. from Earby in Yorkshire Dales National Park. See **Accommodations and Camping,** p. 345.

Mankinholes: Todmorden OL14 6HR (tel./fax (01706) 812340), 24mi. from Crowden. £7.20, under 18 £5. Shop in hostel. Open mid-Mar. to Aug. M-Sa; Sept.-Oct. Tu-Sa; Feb. to mid-Mar. and Nov. F-Sa.

Once Brewed: Military Rd., Bardon Mill, Hexham NE47 7AN (tel. (01434) 344360; fax 344045), 7mi. east of Greenhead. 3mi. from Househeads Fort, 2½mi. northwest of Bardon Mill's train station, 1mi. from Vindolanda, ½mi. from Hadrian's Wall. Binocular rental after 1pm. £9.75, under 18 £6.55. Check-in after 1pm. Open Apr.-Oct. daily; Feb.-Mar. and Nov. M-Sa. Wheelchair accessible.

Stainforth: (tel. (01729) 823577), 8mi. from Malham in Yorkshire Dales National Park. See **Accommodations and Camping,** p. 345.

In the High Pennines, YHA operates 3 **camping barns,** hollow stone buildings on private farms with wooden sleeping platforms, (very) cold water, and a toilet. To book, send a check to YHA Camping Barns, 16 Shawbridge St., Clitheroe, BB7 1LZ (tel. 01200) 428366). The telephone numbers below are for confirming arrival times *only;* direct all bookings to the address above.

Holwick Barn: Mr. and Mrs. Scott, Low Way Farm, Holwick (tel. (01833) 640506), 3mi. north of Middleton-in-Teesdale. Sleeps 20. £4.50 per person.

Wearhead Barn: Mr. Walton, Blackcleugh Farm, Wearhead (tel. (01388) 537395), 1mi. from Cowshill. No electric lights. Sleeps 12. £3.50 per person.

Witton Barn: Witton Estate, Witton-le-Wear (tel. (01388) 488322), just off the Weardale Way. Sleeps 15. £3.50 per person.

■ South Pennines

Expecting the sense of isolation and bleakness portrayed in *Wuthering Heights,* visitors to the South Pennines may be surprised at the domesticated feel of this landscape where the villages of Haworth and Hebden Bridge have made substantive inroads into the gorse-strewn moorlands. Deserted, heathery slopes unfold themselves quietly between the towns but are patterned into well-cultivated fields.

GETTING THERE AND GETTING ABOUT

Two **rail lines** (tel. (0345) 484950) chug frequently through the region; carry the free pocket-sized *West Yorkshire Train Times.* The Claverdale Line reaches **Hebden Bridge** (45min., 4 per hr.) and **Mytholmroyd** (40min., 3 per hr.) on its way from **Leeds** to **Manchester** or **Blackpool.** The Airedale Line, from Leeds, stops at **Keighley** (30min., 2 per hr.), 5 mi. north of Haworth, en route to **Carlisle** or **Morecambe.**

Keighley and District (tel. (01535) 603284) buses #663, 664, and 665 link **Keighley** and **Haworth** (25min., M-Sa 3 per hr., Su 2 per hr., 70p). The painfully infrequent **Yorkshire Rider** (tel. (01422) 365985) bus #500 shuttles between **Haworth** and **Hebden Bridge** (30min., June-Sept. 5 per day; Oct.-May W and Sa only, 85p.). A family **Metro Day Rover** ticket is available for bus and rail services (£4.40). Day rover tickets on West Yorkshire train services cost £2.80. Local bus questions are helpfully answered by the **Metro Travel Centre** staff (tel. (0113) 245 7676).

The Haworth tourist office boasts a wide selection of trail guides. One of the trails, the **Worth Way,** traces the 5½ mi. from Keighley (KEETH-lee) and Oxenhope; ride the steam-train back to your starting point. The private **Keighley and Worth Valley Railway** (tel. (01535) 645214) issues steam from Oxenhope to Keighley and passes through Haworth (mid-June to Aug. M-F 4 per day, Sa 7 per day, Su 12 per day; Sept. to mid-June Sa-Su 4 per day, return £5, children £2.50). From the Carlisle mainline trains, change at Keighley. From Haworth to Hebden Bridge, choose a trail from the tourist office's *Two Walks Linking Haworth and Hebden Bridge* (30p).

■ Hebden Bridge

A historic gritstone village built on the side of a hill, Hebden Bridge lies in Calderdale, close to the Pennine Way and the circular 50 mi. Calderdale Way. In medieval times, the bridge was made of timber and used by those transporting goods to Halifax. The hamlet, only a three-farm cluster, stitched its way to rapid growth in the booming textile years of the 18th and 19th centuries, wrapping the steep hillsides in Hebden's trademark "double-decker" houses, many still standing. Today, patched with derelict textile mills, Hebden Bridge's lack of sights means most visitors only use it as a starting point for day or longer hikes.

Calder Valley Cruising (tel. 845557) gives horse-drawn boat trips along the recently restored Rochdale Canal. *(Office open M-Sa 10am-5pm, Su 10am-5:30pm; in winter shorter hours. Usually departs Hebden Bridge Marina at 1 and 3pm; times vary; pick up a schedule at the tourist office and call in advance. £6, seniors £5, children £3.)* From Hebden Bridge, you can make day hikes to the villages of **Blackshaw Head, Cragg Vale,** or **Hepstonstall.** Hepstonstall holds the restless remains of Sylvia Plath (husband Ted Hughes lived in nearby Mytholmroyd) and the ruins of a 13th-century church and a 1764 chapel, the oldest Methodist house of worship in the world. Trails also wind to the National Trust's **Harcastle Crags** (tel. 844518), a ravine-crossed wooded valley known locally as Little Switzerland, 1½ mi. northwest along the A6033.

Hebden Bridge lies about half-way down the Manchester-Leeds rail line, with **train** service in both directions every hour. The **Transpennine Express** also serves the town, running between **Newcastle-upon-Tyne, Manchester,** and **Liverpool** (every hr. 7am-9pm, fewer on Su). **Buses** stop at the train station and on New Rd. The **tourist office,** 1 Bridge Gate (tel. 843831; fax 845266), distributes free town maps, indexed maps (25p), walking guides (40p), and leaflets (open Apr.-Oct. M-Sa 10am-5pm, Su 11am-5pm; Nov.-Mar. daily 10am-4pm). The **post office** (tel. 842366) caresses mail at Holme St. (open M-F 9am-5:30pm, Sa 9am-12:30pm). The **postal code** is HX7 8AA, and the **telephone code** 01422.

If you're planning to stay in Hebden Bridge, call the tourist office for **B&B** suggestions; prices start at £15. **Watergate Tea Shop,** 9 Bridge Gate (tel. 842978), near the tourist office, is worth breaking into (meals around £4; open daily 10:30am-5pm). The cobblestoned **St. George's Sq.** brims with inexpensive bakeries and sandwich shops, and pricier pubs. **The White Swan,** Bridge Gate (tel. 844650), offers a good range of pub grub for under £5 and worthwhile daily specials for a bit more. Stock up on groceries at **Spar,** Crown St. (open M-Sa 8:30am-11pm, Su 9am-10:30pm).

■ Haworth

> *I can hardly tell you how the time gets on at Haworth. There is no event whatever to mark its progress. One day resembles another...*
> —Charlotte Brontë

Haworth's (HAH-wuth) *raison d'être* stands at the top of its hill—the parsonage at the pinnacle of Brontë-land. Haworth's cobbled main street shamelessly exploits the town's association with the Brontës; tea rooms and souvenir shops fall over themselves in efforts to solicit the crowds in their ascent to the **Brontë Parsonage** (tel. 642323), which lies behind the Church down a tiny laneway. Here the Brontë Society has created a tasteful, low-key museum whose quiet rooms provide relief from the bustling commerce outside along with informative detail about the family. The rooms are furnished as they would have been when Charlotte, Emily, Anne and Branwell lived here with their father, and artifacts owned by the sisters—few enough to have acquired the aura of relics—occupy glass cases; Charlotte's miniscule boots and mittens are displayed alongside one of her extraordinarily tiny dresses. Branwell's untalented oil paintings are (luckily) confined to one room. Reader, check Branwell's impassioned love letter to his employer's wife, 17 years his senior, as well as the sofa on which valiant Emily died. The exhibition traces the Brontës' humble origins in Ireland (their real name was either Brunty or Prunty but was changed out of veneration for Lord Nelson, the Duke of Brontë). *(Open Apr.-Oct. 10am-5:30pm.)* A footpath behind the church leads up the hill toward the pleasant (if disappointingly untempestuous) Brontë Falls, a 2½ mi. hike over the moor.

The **train station** only runs the private trains of the Keighley and Warth Valley Railway. **Buses** stop at the base of Main St., and also on Mill Hey near the steam rail station. **West Yorkshire** buses #663-5 run every 20 minutes between Haworth and Keighley (70p). The **tourist office,** 2-4 West Ln. (tel. 642329; fax 647721), at the summit of Main St., beckons with maps and guides. Most useful to the daytripper are *Three Walks from the Centre of Haworth* and the town's mini-guide (both 30p). The office also offers a free map, an accommodations list, and booking service (10% deposit; open Easter-Oct. daily 9:30am-5:30pm; Nov.-Easter 9:30am-5pm). The **post office,** 98 Main St. (tel. 644589), is the only place in bankless Haworth to **change money** (open M and W-F 9am-1pm and 2-5:30pm, Tu 9am-1pm, Sa 9am-12:30pm). Haworth's **postal code** is BD22 8DP. The Brontë-sore reenter the world of 20th-century media at **Click-On Computers,** 11 Bridgehouse Ln. (tel. 643133), which offers modem-based **Internet access** (£2.50 per 30min.). The **telephone code** is 01535.

Haworth boasts an elegant **YHA Hostel** (tel. 642234; see **Accommodations,** p. 339). B&Bs for about £15-17 await at Main St., all up the hill from the tourist office. The 1850 **Ebor House,** Lees Ln. (tel. 645869), was built for the owner of the nearby mill. To get to the large TV and radio-laden rooms, walk from the touristy steam railway station down Mill Hey, which becomes Lees Ln. (singles £16; doubles £30). The luxurious **Ashmount,** Mytholmes Ln. (tel. 645726), was built by the doctor who attended Charlotte's death. The elaborate plasterwork, finely furnished rooms with TVs and baths, and sweeping views will please (singles £25; doubles £35; triples £45). Facing each other, **Snowden's,** 98 Main St. (tel. 643214), and **Southams,** 123 Main St. (tel. 643196), combine to form an almost adequate grocery store. Head to Mill Hey for nourishment, as shops on Main St. are mostly overpriced.

■ High Pennines

The area known as the **High Pennines** stretches north to south about 20 mi. west of Durham City, from below Barnard Castle in the south to Hadrian's Wall in the north. This vast landscape straddles the counties of Cumbria, County Durham, and Northumbria and gives rise to the great northern rivers: the Tees, Tyne, Derwent, and Wear, whose sources perch high in the moorlands. Unlike the neighboring Yorkshire Dales and Lake District, access to this region is limited, and it remains largely untouched by the frenetic tourist trade. Open moorland, tree-lined slopes, quiet stone villages, turbulent rivers, and waterfalls greet the visitor in the Derwent Valley and the region's other dales—Teesdale, Weardale, and Allendale. The Pennine Way crosses each dale as it winds up to Hadrian's Wall and the Scottish border.

GETTING THERE AND GETTING ABOUT

Given the livestocky pastures and relatively level roads that greet the explorer here, the area is best suited to **hiking** and **biking.** Cars can successfully navigate the roads, but buses tackle the region with distressing hesitancy. Four motorways bound the region: the A66 in the south, hugs Darlington's latitude; the A6 or M6 from Penrith to Carlisle in the west; the A69 from Carlisle to Newcastle to the north; and in the east the A167 from Newcastle through Durham and Darlington. The B6277 cuts a diagonal through the area, running northwest from Barnard Castle through Middleton-in-Teesdale to Alston. **Arriva** (tel. (0345) 124125) bus #75/76 runs from **Darlington** to **Middleton via Barnard Castle** (2 per hr.). Arriva also runs bus #5/6 from **Durham** to **Bishop Auckland** (40min., 1 per hr., £1.80). From Bishop Auckland, **Go OK's** bus #8 travels to **Barnard Castle.** The **North East Explorer** pass, available on any bus service, gives unlimited bus and Metro travel from **Berwick** and **Newcastle** down to **Whitby,** and from **Barnard Castle** across to Sunderland. (Valid June-Aug. daily all day; Sept.-May M-F after 9am, Sa-Su all day; £5, seniors and children £4, families £10.)

■ Barnard Castle

Twenty miles southwest of Durham along the River Tees, **Barnard Castle,** the name of both a castle and the peaceful market town in which it is found, is the best base for exploring the castles of Teesdale, and the peaks and waterfalls of the North Pennine Hills. The town's calm exterior belies a history of struggle for control by the nearby Prince Bishops of Durham. Along the river, the ruins of the 13th-century Norman **castle** (tel. 638212) sprawl over six acres. *(Open Apr.-Sept. daily 10am-1pm and 2-6pm; Oct.*

daily 10am-1pm and 2-4pm; Nov.-Mar. W-Su 10am-1pm and 2-4pm. £2.20, students £1.70, under 16 £1.10.) Past Newgate stands the magnificent **Bowes Museum** (tel. 690606), which houses a remarkable collection of European art that matches any of London's offerings. Built in the 19th century by John and Josephine Bowes to bring continental culture to England, the gallery houses the couple's huge private collection, including the largest collection of Spanish paintings in Britain. Two works alone make the entry worthwhile—El Greco's *Tears of St. Peter* and a life-size mechanized silver swan, mentioned in Mark Twain's *Innocents Abroad*. *(Open Apr.-Oct. M-Sa 10am-5pm, Su 2-5pm; call to check if it's open Nov.-Mar. £3.90, students, seniors, and children £2.90, families £12. Free tours May-Aug. Tu-Sa 2 per day, Sept.-Oct. Sa-Su 1 per day.)* Dickens fans won't want to miss the chance to follow the master's footsteps by car on **Dickens Drive,** a 25 mi. circular path tracing the route Dickens took in 1838 while researching *Nicholas Nickleby*. The tourist office has pamphlets describing the route. Just northeast of Barnard Castle on the A688 looms **Raby Castle** (RAY-bee; tel. (01833) 660202), an imposing 14th-century fortress with a superb kitchen and gardens. *(Open July-Sept. Su-F; May-June W and Su; castle 1-5pm, park and gardens 11am-5:30pm. £4, seniors £3, children £1.50; park and gardens only £1.50, seniors and children £1.)*

Five gracious and witty women manage the small but well-stocked **tourist office,** Woodleigh, Flatts Rd. (tel. 690909; open daily Apr.-Oct. 10am-6pm; Nov.-Mar. 10am-4pm). **Guided walks** of town leave from here (1½hr.; July-Sept. Th 2:30pm; £1, seniors and children 50p). **Midland** pops out cash at its 19 Market Pl. **ATM** (bank open M-F 9:30am-4:30pm). The **post office** (tel. 638247) licks stamps at 2 Galgate (open M-F 9am-5:30pm, Sa 9am-12:30pm). Barnard Castle's **postal code** is DH128BE; its **telephone code** is 01833.

Barnard Castle has no youth hostel, but is blessed with superb B&Bs, many of which line Galgate. **Mrs. Williamson,** 85 Galgate (tel. 638757), gives comfortable rooms with color TVs and payphones (singles £18, with bath £24; doubles £42, all with bath). **Mrs. Kilgarrif,** 98 Galgate (tel. 637493), offers Sky TV, an exercise room, sauna, and an impressive knick-knack collection in her B&B (£18, with bath £19). Most pubs and restaurants along **The Bank** and **Market Pl.** serve lunch and dinner; try the **Golden Lion** pub.

■ Middleton-in-Teesdale and Bishop Auckland

A pleasant 12 mi. hike northwest along the **Pennine Way** leads to **Middleton-in-Teesdale,** a mining town. In between Middleton and Langdon Beck lies the **High Force Waterfall,** one of England's most spectacular falls; follow Wainwright's advice and "tarry long in the presence of beauty, for so much in life is barren." *(Viewing platform 50p, children 25p.)* **Arriva Bus** #75 runs from Barnard Castle to Middleton (1 per hr.); on Sundays, it runs also to the waterfall. *Where to Stay in Teesdale* lists dozens of B&Bs in town; direct all enquiries to the Barnard Castle tourist office. The **Hudeway Centre hostel** (HEWD-way), Stacks Ln. (tel. (01833) 640012; fax 641044), off the Hude, offers 24 beds and adventure courses (£9, with breakfast £11.50; linen £2).

The town of **Bishop Auckland** is the connection point for buses between Durham and Barnard Castle; while you're waiting to change buses, stroll down to **Auckland Castle,** presently the home of the county's Prince Bishops and of the world's largest private chapel. *(Open July Th-F and Su 2-5pm; Aug. Th-Su 2-5pm; May-June and Sept. F-Su 2-5pm.)* The Bishop Auckland **tourist office** (tel. 604922; fax 604960) stands in the town hall on Market Pl. (open M-F 10am-5pm, Sa 9am-4pm; May-Oct. also Su 1-4pm).

■ Yorkshire Dales National Park

The Yorkshire Dales National Park is a sea of emerald hills and valleys liberally laced with sparkling rivers, subterranean caverns, and uncountable stone walls. In fact, no one seems to know exactly how many dales there are. Each dale is a valley formed by a swift river or a lazy glacial flow. Ancient traces of earlier residents enhance the beauty of the Dales. Bronze and Iron Age tribes blazed winding "green lanes" (foot-

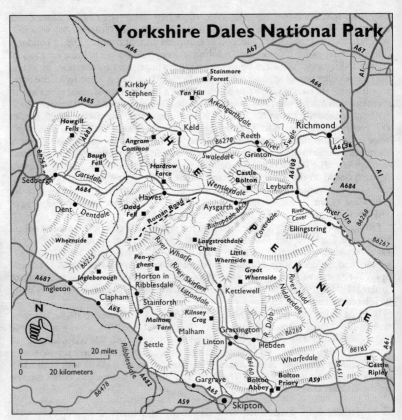

Yorkshire Dales National Park

paths that remain upon the moorland tops), while Romans built straight roads and stout hill-forts, and 18th-century workers pieced together the countless stone walls. Those seeking beautiful English countryside and rolling hills need look no further.

GETTING THERE AND GETTING ABOUT

Sampling the many parts of the Dales requires several days and a pair of sturdy feet (or a sturdy vehicle). In the south of the park, **Skipton** serves as a transportation hub and provides goods and services not available in the smaller villages. **Grassington** and **Linton,** just north, are scenic bases for exploring southern Wharfedale. **Malham** is a sensible starting point for forays into western Wharfedale and Eastern Ribblesdale. To explore Wensleydale and Swaledale in the north, move out from **Hawes** or **Leyburn.**

The most convenient way to enter the park is to take a bus or train from Bradford, Leeds, or Lancaster to Skipton, then switch to a bus that ventures into the smaller villages. **Trains** (tel. (0345) 484950) run from **Bradford** (2 per hr., £2.70), **Leeds** (2 per hr., £4.10), **Carlisle** (2 per hr., £12.10), **Morecambe** (4 per day, £9.50), and **Lancaster** (4 per day, £9.50). Other options include the daily **National Express** (tel. (0990) 808080) bus from **London** to Skipton (£12). **Yorkshire Rider** (tel. (0113) 242 9614) bus #784 goes to Skipton from **Leeds** (1½hr., 1 per hr. until 6:30pm, £2).

Those relying on public transport should procure the *Dales Connection* timetable, free at any tourist office or National Park Information Centre. From Skipton, **Pride of the Dales** (tel. (01756) 753123) buses #71 and 72 connect to **Grassington** (M-Sa about 1 per hr., Su 4 per day, return £3.50) and occasionally to **Kettlewell. Pennine Bus** (tel. (01756) 749215) #580 joins Skipton to **Settle** (M-F 1 per hr., Su every 2hr., return £6). Bus #210 runs from Skipton to **Malham** (M-Sa 2 per day; in summer also Su, return £5.30). Other villages are served less regularly. Inter-village buses tend to be infrequent, often running only on certain days of the week; post buses run once a day to scheduled towns. Note that in winter, buses and their drivers tend to hibernate. **Hitchers** complain that pickups are infrequent and settle for rides that carry them only part way. If you miss your bus, you may be stuck walking.

PRACTICAL INFORMATION

The following **National Park Information Centres** are staffed by well-informed Dales devotees. Many offer guided walks; call for details. Be sure to pick up the invaluable annual park guide, *The Visitor* (free). From April through October, all info centers are open daily 10am-5pm. Centers which remain open in the winter have opening hours noted below. In addition, most towns have **tourist information centers.**

Aysgarth Falls: (tel. (01969) 663424) Wensleydale, less than 1mi. east of the village. Open Nov.-Mar. Sa-Su 10am-5pm.
Clapham: (tel. (015242) 51419), in the village center.
Grassington: Hebden Rd., Wharfedale (tel. (01756) 752774). Off-season hours vary.
Hawes: Station Yard, Wensleydale (tel. (01969) 667450). Open selected winter weekends.
Malham: Malhamdale (tel. (01729) 830363), at the southern end of the village. Open Nov.-Mar. Sa-Su 10am-4pm.
Reeth: (tel. (01748) 884059), in the Green. Open winter weekends with reduced hours.
Sedbergh: 72 Main St. (tel. (015396) 20125). Open Nov.-Easter F-Sa 10am-4pm.

ACCOMMODATIONS AND CAMPING

Hostels, converted barns, tents, and B&Bs are all good options in the Dales. The *Yorkshire Dales Accommodation Guide* (free) is available at National Park Information Centres and at the York tourist office. Ask tourist offices for their lists of area caravan and camping sites. See **Accommodations**, p. 339, for more information.

Twelve **YHA Youth Hostels** play host in the Yorkshire Dales area. Hawes, Keld, and Malham lie on the Pennine Way. Ingleton, on the western edge of the park, is a good jumping-off point to the Lake District. Linton, Stainforth, Kettlewell, Dentdale, Aysgarth Falls, and Grinton Lodge all sit a few miles off the Pennine Way. Ellingstring, near Ripon, and Kirkby Stephen, north of Hawes and served by rail, are set farther away from the trail. Most of the hostels listed serve meals for additional fees (breakfast £3, packed lunch £3.35, evening meal £4.40).

Aysgarth Falls: (tel. (01969) 663260; fax 663110), ½mi. east of Aysgarth on the A684 to Leyburn. £8, under 18 £5.40. Lockout 10am-1pm. Open Apr.-Oct. daily; Nov.-Mar. F-Sa.
Dentdale: Cowgill (tel./fax (015396) 25251), on Dentdale Rd. 6mi. east of Dent, 2mi. from the Hawes-Ingleton Rd. On the River Dee. £8, under 18 £5.40. Open Apr.-Aug. F-W; Sept.-Oct. and Mar. F-Tu; Nov.-Feb. F-Sa.

For Whom the Fell Tolls

Each year, all across northern England and southern Scotland, a few proud parents begin training their young children in the great art of fell running. Fells are hills—sometimes enormous ones—and it requires a particularly well-trained and confident athlete to complete a full race in a respectable time. Few will go on to become professionals, but many will run the fells for life, local fame, personal pride, and family honor being greater rewards than (most) cash prizes. In the past century, fells races have become a familial and clan tradition in these regions, and children racing one another today are driven by a passion inherited, sometimes, from four or five generations of runners.

Ellingstring: Lilac Cottage (tel. (01677) 460216), in the village. No smoking. £5.85, under 18 £4. Self-catering. Lockout 10am-5pm. Open July-Aug. daily; Apr.-June and Sept.-Oct. F-Tu.

Grinton: Grinton Lodge (tel. (01748) 884206; fax 884876), on the "Herriot Way," ¾mi. south of Grinton on the Reeth-Leyburn Rd. £8, under 18 £5.40. Reception opens 5pm. Lockout 10am-1pm. Open Apr.-Sept. daily; Oct. M-Sa; Nov.-Mar. Tu-Sa.

Hawes: Lancaster Terr. (tel. (01969) 667368; fax 667723), west of Hawes on Ingleton Rd. £8.80, under 18 £6. Shop in hostel. Open July-Aug. daily; Apr.-June M-Sa; Mar. F-Tu; Sept.-Dec. W-Su.

Ingleton: Greta Tower (tel. (015242) 41444; fax 41854), down the hill from Market Sq. £7.20, under 18 £5. Reception closed noon-5pm. Open June-Aug. daily; Apr.-May and Sept. M-Sa; Oct.-Dec. Tu-Sa.

Keld: Keld Lodge, Upper Swaledale, Richmond (tel. (01748) 886259; fax 886013), west of Keld village. £7.20, under 18 £5. Shop in hostel. Open June-Aug. daily; Apr.-May Tu-Su; Sept.-Oct. W-Su; Jan.-Mar. and Nov. F-M.

Kettlewell: Whernside House (tel. (01756) 760232; fax 760402), in the village center. No smoking. £8.80, under 18 £6. Open Apr.-Sept. daily; Oct.-Mar. F-Tu.

Kirkby Stephen: Fletcher Hill, Market St. (tel./fax (017683) 71793). Former chapel. Kitchen. Laundry. No smoking. Open July-Aug. daily; Apr.-June and Sept.-Oct. Th-M.

Linton: The Old Rectory, Linton-in-Craven (tel./fax (01756) 752400), next to the village green. Skipton-Grassington buses #71 and 72 pass near the hostel, a 17th-century stone rectory. No smoking. £8.80, under 18 £6. Lockout 10am-5pm. Open July-Aug. daily; Apr.-June and Sept.-Oct. M-Sa; Jan.-Feb. and Nov. to mid-Dec. M-Th.

Malham: John Dower Memorial Hostel, Skipton (tel. (01729) 830321; fax 830551), at Malham Tarn. 2 lounges, a classroom, and storage lockers. £9.75, under 18 £6.55. Open all year. Wheelchair access.

Stainforth: "Taitlands" Stainforth, Settle (tel. (01729) 823577; fax 825404), 2mi. north of Settle, ¼mi. south of Stainforth. Georgian house with walled garden. £8, under 18 £5.40. Shop in hostel. Open Apr.-Oct. daily; Feb.-Mar. and Nov. F-Sa.

Numerous **Dales Barns** offer cheap accommodations: £5-7 per night in dorm rooms in converted barns (up to 30 people per barn, split up hostel-style into smaller bunk rooms; most have showers, kitchens, and drying rooms). For lists of barns, ask at a tourist office. The barns cater to small groups but are also ideal for hikers exploring the Pennine or Dales Way. Book weeks in advance with individual barns: **Airton** (tel. (01729) 830263; £5, under 16 £3), in the village; **Catholes** (tel. (015396) 20334; £5.50, children £4.50); **Dub Cote** (tel. (01729) 860238; £6.75), in Horton Village; **Grange Farm** (tel. (01756) 760259; £6, children £5); **Hill Top Farm** (tel. (01729) 830320; £7) in Malham; and **Skirfare Bridge** (tel. (01756) 752465; £7), Northcote Farm, Kilnsey, north of Grassington on the B6265.

   Campgrounds are difficult to reach on foot, but farmers may let you sleep on their bit of dale if you ask. In **Hawes,** try **Bainbridge Ings** (tel. (01969) 667354), half a mile out of town on the Old Gale back road (£2 per person, £5.70 per 2-person tent and car, showers 20p; open Apr.-Oct.). In **Richmond,** try **Brompton-on-Swale Caravan Park** (tel. (01748) 824629; £5.50 per 2-person tent, with car £7.25; open Apr.-Oct.).

HIKING

> **Warning:** Be aware that all the Dales are filled with **shake holes,** small depressions similar to grassy potholes that indicate underground caverns. *Don't step on them*—they can give way, and kill you if the cavern is large. Ordnance Survey maps and a compass are essential, especially on the smaller, unmarked trails. See **Wilderness and Safety Concerns,** p. 47, for other important tips.

Since buses are few, hitching abysmal, and the scenery breathtaking, hiking remains the best way to see the Dales. The park's seven Information Centres can help you prepare for a trek along one of three long-distance footpaths through the park. The ever-challenging 270 mi. **Pennine Way** curls from Gargrave in the south to Tan Hill in the north, passing Malham, Pen-y-ghent, Hawes, Keld, and most of the major attractions in the Dales. The more manageable **Dales Way** (84mi.) edges from Bradford and Leeds past Ilkley, through Wharfedale via Grassington and Whernside, and by Sedbergh on its way to the Lake District; it crosses the Pennine Way near Dodd Fell. The **Coast-to-Coast Walk** (190mi.) stretches from Richmond to Kirkby Stephen.

Trail guides for sale at the centers detail less crowded routes of varying lengths. The park authority encourages visitors to keep to designated walks to protect grasslands and to avoid falling into hidden mineshafts. They sell leaflets (70p) describing over 30 of these walks, beginning at Ingleton, Longstone Common, Malham, Aysgarth Falls, Grassington's Centre, and Clapham's Centre. YHA produces a series of leaflets detailing day-long walks between hostels (available from hostels for 20p, or write Yorkshire Walking Routes, YHA, P.O. Box 11, Matlock, Derbyshire DE4 2XA). Information centers list cycle rentals and sell route cards plotting the **Yorkshire Dales Cycleway,** a series of six 20 mi. routes connecting the dales (£2). Ordnance Surveys are available for most smaller paths; purchase them at any center or hiking supply store (£4-7).

■ Skipton

Skipton (pop. 13,000) shines as a transfer point; once you've gathered your gear, skip town and head for the Dales. The empty **Skipton Castle** (tel. 792442) is the main sight in town, but unless you're a castle buff, save your gold for a better attraction. *(Open Mar.-Sept. M-Sa 10am-6pm, Su noon-6pm; Oct.-Feb. M-Sa 10am-4pm, Su noon-4pm. £3.60, seniors £2.90, ages 5-18 £1.80.)*

Skipton's **train station** is a quarter mile west of the city center on Broughton Rd. **Buses** stop on Keighly St. between Hirds Yard and Waller Hill, behind Sunwin House. You'll find the **tourist office,** 9 Sheep St. (tel. 792809; fax 797528), in the center of town (open Easter-Oct. M-Sa 10am-5pm, Su 2-5pm; Nov.-Easter M-Sa 10am-4pm, Su 1-4pm). **Midland** and **Barclays,** on the east side of High St., have **ATMs.** For mountain bike rental and repairs, try **Dave Ferguson Cycles,** 1 Brook St. (tel. 795367 or 748030; £12 per day; £40 deposit; open daily 9:30am-5:30pm). Stock up on camping and hiking supplies at **George Fisher** (tel. 794305), at the south end of Coach St. (open M and W-Sa 9am-5:30pm, Tu 10am-5:30pm, Su 10am-4pm). Skipton's **post office** (tel. 792724) resides with a **supermarket** in Sunwin House, 8 Swadford St. (post office open M-Th 9am-5:30pm, F 9am-6pm, Sa 9am-4pm). The **postal code** is B23 1JH; the **telephone code** is 01756.

If you're staying the night, ring up **Ringwood House,** 1 Salisbury St. (tel. 791135). Complete with bathtub and bidet, the mauve W.C. is as luxurious as the gracefully curtained bedrooms (singles £20; doubles £35, with bath £37; no smoking). Load up on fresh produce at the **market,** which floods High St. and the area nearby (open M, W, and F-Sa). **Healthy Life,** 10 High St. (tel. 790619), near the church, peddles revitalizing snacks; the cafe upstairs, **Herbs,** serves peanut butter and apple sandwiches (£1.75) and ten kinds of herbal tea (85p each). (Store open M and W-Sa 8:30am-5:30pm, Tu 10am-5pm; cafe open M and W-Sa 9:30am-4:45pm.)

■ Grassington and Wharfedale

Set amid sheep and stone walls, recently re-cobbled Grassington makes a picturesque base from which to explore the southern part of the Dales region. More pragmatically, it has an information center, loads of trails, and regular bus service to Skipton (Pride of the Dales buses #71, 72, and 272, M-Sa about 1 per hr., Su 4 per day). Spectacular **Kilnsey Crag** lies 3½ mi. from Grassington toward Kettlewell. *Wharfedale Walk #8* guides you there through a deep gorge, Bronze Age burial mounds, and views of Wharfedale. **Stump Cross Caverns** (tel. 752780), adorned with beautiful stalagmite columns and glistening curtains of rock, are 5 mi. east of Grassington toward Pateley Bridge; some travelers choose to hitch on the B6265. Dress warmly; it gets chilly down under. *(Open Mar.-Oct. daily 10am-5pm. £3.90, under 13 £2.)* During the second half of June, soak in the art and music of the annual **Grassington Festival.**

The **National Park Information Centre** (tel. 752774) on Hebden Rd. offers occasional guided walks. (Mar.-Oct., £1.80-2.50, children 70p-£1. Centre open May-Aug. daily 9:30am-5:30pm; call for winter hours.) **Barclays's ATM** is at the corner of Main St. and Hebden Rd. **The Mountaineer,** Pletts Barn Centre (tel. 752266), at the top of Main St., sells camping gear (open daily 10am-5pm). The **telephone code** for both towns is 01756.

Florrie Whitehead, 16 Wood Ln. (tel. 752841), supplies excellent B&B and legendary hospitality for £14. Or try **Burtree** (tel. 752442), a stone cottage with a glorious garden, a few steps from the info center (£16). Pubs and tea shops abound on Main St., including **Picnic's Café** (tel. 753342), which serves sandwiches and hot traditional meals (£1.25-4.45; open in summer daily 10am-5pm; winter daily 10am-3pm).

■ Malhamdale

Malhamdale is renowned for its spectacular limestone scenery. A 4-hour hike will take you past the stunning pavement of **Malham Cove** and "Dry Valley" with its Iron Age caves to **Malham Tarn,** Yorkshire's second-largest natural lake. Two miles from Malham is the equally impressive **Gordale Scar,** cut in the last Ice Age by a rampaging glacier. Catch all of these beauties on the park's *A Walk in Malhamdale* (leaflet #1). Malham contains a **National Park Information Centre** (tel. (01729) 830363) and a superior-grade **YHA Youth Hostel** (tel. (01729) 830321), thronged by Pennine Way groupies (see p. 345). **Townhead Farm** (tel. (01729) 830287), the last farm before Malham Cove, provides tent sites with showers and toilets (£2.50 per person; £1 per tent; £1 per car; showers 50p).

North of Malham, the high peaks and cliffs of **Ingleborough, Pen-y-ghent,** and **Whernside** form the so-called Alpes Penninae. The 24 mi. **Three Peaks Walk** connecting the Alpes begins and ends in **Horton-in-Ribblesdale** at the clock of the **Pen-y-ghent Café,** a hiker's haunt with mammoth mugs of tea. The best place to break your journey is **Ingleton** (pop. 2000), where the local **tourist office** (tel. (015242) 41049) in the community center car park books rooms (open Apr.-Oct. daily 10am-4:30pm). Several small **B&Bs** on Main St. charge around £15, or walk 1 mi. to **Stacksteads Farm,** Butterthorne Rd. (tel. (015242) 41386), which offers B&B (£16) and also a bunk barn with 22 beds (£8, self-catering). **YHA Youth Hostel,** Greta Tower (tel. (015242) 41444; see p. 345), sits in town.

■ Hardrow Force and Aysgarth Falls

The northerly Wensleydale landscape of potholes, caves, clints, and grikes melds into a broad swath of fertile dairyland. Base your forays in **Hawes,** which has a **National Park Information Centre** (tel. (01969) 667450), and a **YHA Youth Hostel** (tel. (01969) 667368; see p. 345). Spit out 20p at the Green Dragon Pub to see the overrated **Hardrow Force,** England's highest above-ground waterfall (1mi. north along the Pennine Way).

More worthwhile are the **Aysgarth Falls** to the east—rolling in successive tiers down the craggy Yoredale Rocks—and the natural terrace of the **Shawl of Leyburn.** A **National Park Information Centre** (tel. (01969) 663424) idles in the car park above Aysgarth Falls; a **tourist office** (tel. (01969) 623069) sits in the center of **Leyburn** (open Easter-Sept. daily 9:30am-5:30pm; Oct.-Easter M-Sa 9:30am-noon and 1-4pm). Both Aysgarth and Leyburn are serviced by United buses #156 and 157 from Hawes to Richmond. Aysgarth has a **YHA Youth Hostel** (tel. (01969) 663260), half a mile east of the village (see p. 345).

The solid, elegant form of **Castle Bolton** (tel. (01969) 623981) graces Wensleydale—explore it from the dungeon to the 100 ft. battlements. The castle makes a nice day-walk from YHA Aysgarth. *(Open Mar.-Nov. daily 10am-5pm. Free.)* Farther north, **Swaledale** is known for picture-perfect barns and meadows.

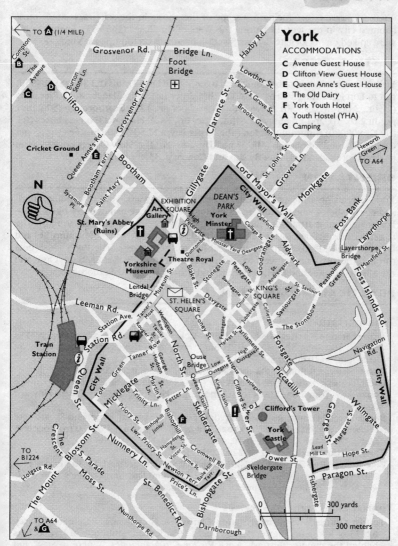

■ York

With a pace suitable for ambling and its tallest building a cathedral, York is as different from nearby Manchester as it is from its new American namesake. Although its well-preserved city walls have foiled many a marauding invader, York fails to impede hordes of tourists, who come to conquer medieval thoroughfares, a Viking legacy, and Britain's largest Gothic cathedral. York has retained so many of its old buildings and streets that structures dating back 600 years seem run of the mill.

In AD 71 the Romans founded "Eboracum" as a military and administrative base for Northern England; the town remained important as Anglo-Saxon "Eoforwic" and Viking "Jorvik" (Norse for "Hey, this town's got some serious tourist potential"). William the Conqueror permitted York's Archbishop to officiate at his consecration. In 1069, York thanked him by joining with the Danes to massacre 3000 men in the Conqueror's garrison, producing just some of the ghosts in the self-proclaimed "most haunted city in the world." During the Wars of the Roses (1455-85), enemy heads were spiked on Micklegate Bar like Swedish meatballs on toothpicks. Yum.

GETTING THERE

York is on the main London-Edinburgh Intercity rail line. **Trains** (tel. (0345) 484950) run to London's **King's Cross** Station (2hr., 2 per hr., £54), Manchester's **Piccadilly** (1½hr., 2 per hr., £13.30), **Newcastle** (1hr., 2 per hr., £22), **Scarborough** (50min., 1 per hr., £8.50), and **Edinburgh** (2-3hr., 1 per hr., £45). **National Express buses** (tel. (0990) 808080) run from **London** (4hr., 6 per day, £17.50), **Manchester** (3hr., 3 per day, £7.50), and **Edinburgh** (5hr., 2 per day, £20.25). The **Slow Coach** stops here on its circuit of England (consult **By Bus and Coach**, p. 33, for details).

ORIENTATION

York's streets now present a greater obstacle than its walls. They're winding, short, and rarely labeled, and the longer, straighter streets change names every block or so. Fortunately, most attractions lie within the city walls, so you can't get too lost. The half-mile thoroughfare formed by **Station Rd.,** the **Lendal Bridge, Museum St.,** and **Duncombe Pl.** leads from the train station to the **Minster.** The River Ouse cuts through the city, curving west to south. The city center lies between the Ouse and the Minster; **Coney** and **Parliament St.,** and **Stonegate** are main thoroughfares.

PRACTICAL INFORMATION

Transportation

Trains: Station Rd. (tel. (0345) 484950). Ticket and information office open M-Sa 5:45am-10:15pm, Su 7:30am-10:10pm. Travel center open M-F 8am-7:45pm, Sa 9am-5pm, Su 10am-4pm.

Buses: Stations at Rougier St., the train station, Exhibition Sq., and on Piccadilly.

Local Transportation: Call **Rider York** (tel. 435609) for information. Ticket office open M-Sa 9am-5pm. Buses to **Scarborough, Harrowgate,** and **Castle Howard** (see p. 355) board at Rougier St.

Boats: Several companies along the River Ouse near Lendal, Ouse, and Skeldergate Bridges offer 1hr. cruises. **Yorkboat,** Lendal Bridge (tel. 623752). 30 trips per day. £5.50. Open Apr.-Oct. daily at 10am.

Taxis: Station Taxis (tel. 623332 or 628197).

Bike Rental: Bob Trotter, 13 Lord Mayor's Walk (tel. 622868). £9.50 per day plus £50 deposit. Open M-Sa 9am-5:30pm, Su 10am-4pm. The tourist office's *York Cycle Route Map* (behind the counter, but free!) is helpful.

Tourist and Financial Services

Tourist Offices: Tourist Information Centre, De Grey Rooms, Exhibition Sq. (tel. 621756). Room-finding service £3 plus a 10% deposit. Multitude of free leaflets behind the counter; just ask. *York Visitor Guide* includes "Where to Stay" and "What to See" sections. *York for Less* booklet (£3.50) offers a collection of discount coupons for tours and sights. The *Disabled Guide to York* (£2.25) and *Snickelways of York* (£5), an off-beat self-tour guide, are also available. Open July-Aug. M-Sa 9am-7pm, Su 9am-6pm; Sept.-June daily 9am-6pm. **Smaller branch** (tel. 640316) awaits in the train station. Open Apr.-Oct. M-Sa 9am-8pm, Su 9:30am-5pm; Nov.-Mar. M-Sa 9am-5pm, Su 10am-5pm. **York Visitor and Conference Bureau,** 20 George St., by the bus station, offers similar services. £3.50 room booking fee. 24hr. information screen. Open M-Sa 9am-6pm.

Tours: Free 2hr. **walking tour,** offered by the Association of Voluntary Guides, emphasizes York's architectural glories and provides a thorough introduction to the city. Meet in front of the **York City Art Gallery,** directly across from the tourist office. Runs daily Apr.-Oct. 10:15am and 2:15pm; July-Aug. also 7pm. Bewildering array of **ghost tours** available, all offering similar experiences. Join the nearest one, or attend **The Ghost Hunt of York** (tel. 608600; daily at 7:30pm; £2-3). **York**

Pullman (tel. 622992) and **YorkTour** (tel. 645157) offer a variety of regional half- and full-day tours of the Yorkshire Dales and Moors (£7-20).
Financial Services: Banks are ubiquitous. Try **Thomas Cook,** 4 Nessgate (tel. 653626). Open M-W and F 9am-5:30pm, Th 10am-5:30pm.
American Express: 6 Stonegate (tel. 670030). Open M-F 9am-5:30pm, Sa 9am-5pm; in summer foreign exchange also open Su 10am–4pm.

Local Services

Luggage Storage: Luggage Storage Office, at the train station. Open M-Sa 8:10am-8:50pm, Su 9:10am-8:50pm. £2-4.
Market: M-Sa 8am-5pm between Shambles and Parliament St. Take Jubbergate to Little Shambles. Stalls and stalls of faux name-brand bras.
Launderette: Haxby Road Washeteria, 124 Haxby Rd. (tel. 623379). Change and soap available. Open M-Sa 8am-4pm, Su 8am-3pm. Last wash 1½hr. before close.

Emergency and Communications

Emergency: Dial 999; no coins required.
Police: Fulford Rd. (tel. 631321).
Hotlines: Samaritans (crisis), 89 Nunnery Ln. (tel. 655888). Open 24hr. **Gay and Lesbian Switchboard** (tel. 612828). Open Tu 8-10pm and Th 9-11pm. **Lesbian Line** (tel. 646812). Open F 7-9pm. **Rape Crisis Centre** (tel. (0171) 837 1600).
Pharmacy: Gillygate Pharmacy, 6 Gillygate (tel. 642557). Open M-F 9am-8pm, Sa 9am-6pm.
Hospital: York District Hospital (tel. 631313), off Wigginton Rd. Take bus #1, 2, 3, or 18 from Exhibition Sq.
Post Office: 22 Lendal (tel. 617285). Bureau de change. Open M-Sa 9am-5:30pm. **Postal Code:** YO1 2DA.
Internet Access: Impressions Gallery, Castlegate (tel. 654724). 2 computers. Open M-Tu and Th-Sa 9:30-5:30pm, W 10am-5:30pm, Su 11am-5pm. £2.50 per 30min.
Telephone Code: 01904.

ACCOMMODATIONS

Competition for inexpensive B&Bs (from £16) can be fierce during the summer. The **York Visitor and Conference Bureau** can be helpful (see p. 350). B&Bs are most concentrated on the sidestreets along **Bootham/Clifton** (Bootham becomes Clifton at Grosvenor Terr.), in the **Mount area** (past the train station and down Blossom St.), and on **Bishopsthorpe Rd.** (due south away from town). Book weeks ahead in the summer, even for hostels and campsites. The Tourist Information Centre offices provide bed-finding services for £3 plus 10% of first night price.

Avenue Guest House, 6 The Avenue (tel. 620575), off Bootham/Clifton on a quiet, residential sidestreet. River footpath from the train station leads to the bottom of the Ave. Enthusiastic hosts provide 7 bright, immaculate rooms with soft, puffy beds. Charming view and plush towels make it a step up without the usual increase in price. Some family rooms with baths available. No smoking. All rooms with TV. Singles £15-17; doubles £28-32, with bath £30-40.
Queen Anne's Guest House, 24 Queen Anne's Rd. (tel. 629389), a short walk out Bootham from Exhibition Sq. Spotless single, double, and family rooms with TV. Large bathrooms and breakfasts. No smoking. Mar.-Oct. £14-16 per person; Nov.-Feb. £13-15 per person. £11 without breakfast.
YHA Youth Hostel, Water End, Clifton (tel. 653147), 1mi. from town center. From Exhibition Sq. tourist office, walk about ¾mi. out Bootham/Clifton, and take a left at Water End; or take a bus to Clifton Green and walk ¼mi. down Water End. Superior-grade hostel with excellent facilities: kitchen, TV room, hot showers, laundry. 156 beds. Dorms £14.40, under 18 £11; singles £17.50; twins £37; family rooms £52 or £78. Breakfast included (served 7:30-9:30am), packed lunch £3.35, dinner £4.40 (served 5:30-7:30pm). Snacks available 11am-10pm. Reception open 7am-11:30pm. Bedroom lockout 10am-1pm. Closed Dec. 5-Jan. 15.

The Old Dairy, 10 Compton St. (tel. 623816). Walk ½mi. up Bootham from Exhibition Sq., and make a left onto Compton, or take a bus to Clifton Green. Look for the doorway with the *Let's Go* sign. Charming doubles with wrought-iron bedsteads. £28, breakfast included. Midnight curfew.

Clifton View Guest House, 118-120 Clifton (tel. 625047), ¾mi. from town. Soft-spoken Mrs. Oxtoby offers 13 comfortable rooms, most of which have private showers, and a hearty breakfast. £12-16 per person. Laundry £1.50 per load. No singles.

York Youth Hotel, 11-15 Bishophill Senior (tel. 625904 or 630613). From the train station, turn right onto Queen St., then left onto Micklegate and right on to Trinity Ln. which becomes Bishophill. The cheapest lodging around with a great location and variety of rooms. But picky travelers beware: the open space shower will take you back to your gym class days, and half the toilets are unisex. Coed 20-bed Room 12 is an excellent place to meet fellow travelers; the rest of the building is often booked by youth groups. Coed and single-sex rooms. Sleeps 140. Dorms £9-11; singles £13; twins £24-33. Continental breakfast £1.50, full breakfast £2.50. Sheets £1. Laundry and snacks available. £2 key deposit. 24hr. reception. Bar open 9pm-1am, after pubs close.

Camping: Riverside Caravan and Camping Park, York Marine Services, Ferry Ln., Bishopthorpe (tel. 705812), 2mi. south of York off the A64. Riverside site. Take bus #23 from the bus station, and ask the driver to let you off at the campsite (every 30min., £1.30 return). July-Aug. £7 for 2 people and a tent; Sept.-June £6.

Poplar Farm (tel. 706548). 3½mi. south of York. Catch bus #13 across from the train station; bus stops at the gates of the park. Reception open 8am-10pm. £8.50 for 2 people and a tent; £1 for each extra person.

FOOD AND PUBS

Expensive tea rooms, medium-range bistros, fudge shops, and cheap eateries rub elbows throughout York. Fruit and vegetable grocers peddle at the **Newgate market** between Parliament St. and the Shambles (open M-Sa 9am-5pm; Apr.-Dec. also Su 9am-4:30pm). **Holland & Barrett,** 28 Coney St. (tel. 627257), shelves ever-reliable wholefoods (open M-Sa 9am-5:30pm). **Jackson's,** 25 Bootham (tel. 623558), is a small supermarket near the city center, which also sells pizza (open daily 7am-11pm).

Oscar's Wine Bar and Bistro, 8 Little Stonegate (tel. 652002), off Stonegate. Hearty dishes in massive amounts keep you going for a week (£5-7). Popular and classy with a swank courtyard, varied menu, and lively mood. Open daily 11am-11pm; happy hour Su-M 4pm-close, Tu-F 5-7pm. Live jazz and blues on Monday nights.

La Romantica, 14 Goodramgate (tel. 636236), at the corner with Aldwark and Ogleforth. Enjoy delicious pastas (£5-7) and pizzas (£5-5.75) in a sensuous candlelit setting with peppy Italian music in the background. Bring your own wine or buy it there. Open daily noon-2:30pm and 5:30-11:30pm.

The Rubicon, 5 Little Stonegate (tel. 676076), off Stonegate. Upscale vegetarian restaurant offers 2-course lunches (£5) and 3-course dinners (£12.50), both with juice and coffee. Vegan and gluten-free options. Open Tu-Sa noon-2pm and 5-10pm, Su-M 5-10pm.

St. William's College Restaurant, 3 College St. (tel. 634830). Tapestry-adorned cafe inside the 15th-century building and cobbled courtyard of St. William's. Small but tasty portions of quiche (£3.25) and soup (£2.50). Luscious desserts £1.60. Open daily 10am-5pm; lunch served noon-2:30pm; bistro Tu-Sa 6:30-9:30pm.

Theatre Royal Café Bar, St. Leonards Pl. (tel. 632596). Enjoy elegant sandwiches (£1.50-1.80), cakes (£1.20), and salads (60p) in an attractive, windowed, theater-side location, or dine outdoors in the courtyard. Open M-Sa 10am-6pm; open for theater-goers until 8pm.

Little Shambles Café, Little Shambles (tel. 627871), off Shambles. Upstairs eatery tucked in a Tudor house overlooking the market. Open for English breakfast (£2), lunch, and afternoon tea. Open M-Sa 7am-5:30pm, Su 9am-5pm.

Waggon and Horse, 48 Gillygate (tel. 654103). Mighty platters at mild prices will set your tongue a waggin'. Soup, veggies, Yorkshire pudding, and half of a sizable roast chicken for £4.75. Open M-Sa noon-2pm and 6-9pm, Su noon-2pm only.

There are more **pubs** in the center of York than gargoyles on the east wall of the Minster. Whether Tudor, Victorian, or in between, most are packed on weekend nights and all serve bar meals during the day. For beer and history, pick up the *Historic Pubs of York* pamphlet at the main tourist office (£1). **Ye Old Starre,** Stonegate (tel. 623063), is the city's oldest pub, with a license that goes back to 1644. It also has the best pub meals, with sumptuous *chili con carne,* bursting Guinness pie, and giant Yorkshire puddings for lunch (meals £4-5; open M-Sa 11am-11pm, Su noon-3pm and 7-10:30pm). The **Roman Bath,** St. Sampson's Sq. (tel. 620455), has an original Roman bath in the basement. Ask the proprietor to let you into the subterranean mini-museum. (Open M-Sa 11am-11pm, Su noon-10:30pm. Bath admission £1, 50p if you eat there.) The carpeted **Black Swan,** Peasholme Green (tel. 686911), where Aldwark meets the Stonebow, is more sedate, though several ghosts allegedly haunt the premises. Free Thursday night folk music starts at 8:30pm (open M-Sa 11am-11pm, Su noon-10:30pm).

SIGHTS

The best introduction to York is a 2½ mi. walk along its medieval walls. Beware the tourist stampede, which weakens only in the early morning and just before the walls and gates close at dusk—the best times for a walk, regardless of crowds. At the tourist office, ask for the useful brochure *Historic Attractions of York,* and then hit the cobbled streets. Everyone and everything in York converges at **York Minster** (tel. 639347), the largest Gothic cathedral in Britain. *(Open in summer daily 7am-8:30pm; off-season 7am-5pm. £2 donation requested.)* The present structure, erected between 1220 and 1470, was preceded by the Roman fortress where Constantine the Great was hailed emperor in 306 and the Saxon church where King Edwin converted to Christianity in 627. Within this Minster, Miles Coverdale translated and published the first complete printed English Bible in 1535. An estimated half of all the medieval stained glass in England glitters as it holds the walls together. The **Great East Window,** constructed from 1405 to 1408 and depicting both the beginning and the end of the world in over a hundred small scenes, is the largest single medieval glass window on Earth. The choral **evensong** is a mind-blowing combination of organ and choir. *(M-F 5pm, Sa-Su 4pm.)* The cathedral is currently undergoing renovations scheduled to be completed in 2000.

It's a mere 275 steps up to the top of the **Central Tower,** from which you can stare down at the red roofs of York. The Tower is open daily from 9:30am to 6:30pm (until dark in winter), but there is only a five-minute period every 30 minutes during which you may ascend, as the stairs don't allow two people to pass. *(£2, children £1.)* Join one of the frequent free **tours** for an informative overview. *(Usually 9:30am-3:30pm.)* **The Foundations and Treasury** tell the incredible story of how the central tower began to crack apart in 1967. You can tour the huge concrete and steel foundations inserted

The Bell's Appeal

Bells. You're standing in a cathedral square, slipping rapidly into madness because the bells have been ringing for hours and hours—and not tunes either, just unmelodious pitches in varying order. Consider yourself privileged, not harassed; you may be listening to a **peal:** 5,040 or more never-repeating **changes,** or orders in which the bells are rung. Peals usually take at least three hours to complete, but the record is an insomniacal 18-plus. We aren't sure why they do it, but we do know how. There's usually one ringer (**campanologist** in elitist terms) per bell. The ringer memorizes various **methods,** or patterns, with fancy names like "Oxford Treble B Flat Minor" or "Cambridge Surprise Royal," and then rings variations on these methods, guided by a conductor. While the bells ring out nearly infinite variations, one fact never changes: the ringers go to a pub to celebrate at the end. Bell enthusiasts can pick up the obscure but interesting pamphlet "20 Questions and 19 Answers about English Bell Ringing" (20p) at St. Mary's Church in Whitby, Yorkshire (see **Whitby,** p. 360).

by engineers, the remnants of the previous buildings they unearthed, and treasured items of the cathedral. *(Open in summer M-Sa 9:30am-6:30pm, Su 1-6:30pm; in winter until 4:30pm. £1.80, students and seniors £1.50, children 70p.)* Also worth a look are the **crypt** and the **chapter house**. *(Both open M-F 9:30am-4:30pm, Sa 9:15am-3:30pm, Su 1-3:30pm. Crypt 60p, children 30p. Chapter house 70p, children 30p.)* The **Minster Library** guards books at the far corner of the grounds. *(Open M-Th 9am-5pm, F 9am-noon. Free.)*

The **Yorkshire Museum** (tel. 629745), hidden within the 10 gorgeous acres of the Museum Gardens (enter from Museum St. or Marygate), presents Roman, Anglo-Saxon, and Viking art galleries, as well as the £2.5 million **Middleham Jewel** (c.1450), a gold amulet engraved with the Trinity and the nativity, and holding an enormous sapphire. *(Open daily 10am-5pm; last admission 4:30pm. £3, students, seniors, and children £2; 2 adults and 2 children £9. Disabled access.)* In the museum gardens, peacocks fan themselves among the haunting ruins of **St. Mary's Abbey,** once the most influential Benedictine monastery in northern England. Visit the basement of the Yorkshire Museum to get the lowdown on what abbey life was like.

Housed in a former debtor's prison, the huge York **Castle Museum** (tel. 613161), Minster Yard, by the river and Skeldergate Bridge, is billed as a museum of extraordinary objects and everyday life—for the last 300 years. The tormented brainchild of eccentric collector Dr. Kirk, the museum contains attractions like Kirkgate, an intricately reconstructed Victorian shopping street, and Half Moon Court, its Edwardian counterpart. *(Open Apr.-Oct. M-Sa 9:30am-5:30pm, Su 10am-5:30pm; Nov.-Mar. M-Sa 9:30am-4pm, Su 10am-4pm. £4.50, students, seniors, and children £3.15.)* Across from the museum squats the haunting **Clifford's Tower** (tel. 646940), one of the last remaining pieces of York Castle, and a reminder of the worst outbreak of anti-Semitic violence in English history. In 1190, Christian merchants tried to erase their debts to Jewish bankers by destroying York's Jewish community. On the last Sabbath before Passover, 150 Jews took refuge in a tower that previously stood on this site and, faced with the prospect of starvation or butchery, committed suicide. *(Tower open daily Apr.-Oct. 10am-6pm; Nov.-Mar. 10am-4pm. £1.70, students and seniors £1.30, children 90p.)*

Nearby, the **York City Art Gallery** (tel. 551861), in Exhibition Sq. across from the tourist office, has a mixed bag of Continental work, a better selection of English painters, and a sprinkling of pottery. *(Open M-Sa 10am-5pm, Su 2:30-5pm; last admission 4:30pm. Free. Wheelchair access.)* The **Jorvik Viking Centre** (tel. 643211), on Coppergate, travels even further back in time, and is one of the busiest places in York; visit early or late to avoid lines. Visitors ride through the York of 948 (with authentic artifacts and painfully accurate smells) to discover Norse truths. No, the Vikings did not wear horns. *(Open daily Apr.-Oct. 9am-5:30pm; Nov.-Mar. 9am-3:30pm. £5, students and seniors £4.59, children £4, families £16.50.)* The morbidly inclined should try **York Dungeon,** 12 Clifford St. (tel. 623599). Stare at sore-ridden bodies in a Plague exhibit—who's ready for lunch? *(Open daily Apr.-Sept. 10am-6:30pm; Oct.-Mar. 10am-5:30pm. £4.50, students and seniors £3.50, children £3.)*

ENTERTAINMENT

For the most current information, pick up the weekly *What's On* and *Artscene* guides from the tourist office. They include listings on live music, theater, cinema, exhibitions, festivals and more.

A **Ghost Tour of York** makes a lively start to the evening (see p. 350). In **King's Sq.** and on **Stonegate,** barbershop quartets and recorder ensembles share the pavement with jugglers, magicians, politicians, and evangelists. In addition, the Minster and local churches host a series of summer concerts. Next to the tourist office on St. Leonards Pl., the **Theatre Royal** (tel. 623568; 24hr. info 610041), stages Broadwayesque productions. *(Box office open June-Feb. M-Sa 10am-8pm; Apr.-May 10am-6pm; closed Mar. Tickets £6-30, student standbys day of show £3. Wheelchair access.)* The **York Arts Centre,** Micklegate (tel. 627129) at Skeldergate, is housed in—what else?—a medieval church, and features musical events several nights a week. When performers aren't doing their thing, the Centre turns into a dance club. On selected Fridays, it's "East Orange," a gay disco. The excellent **Toff's,** 3-5 Toft Green (tel. 620203), offers alternative, indie, and rock. *(Open daily 9:30pm-2am.)* **Fibber's,** Stonebow House, the Stonebow (tel. 651250), doesn't lie about the quality of the live music playing every night at 8pm. Celebrate Purcell and friends July 2-11, 1999 at the **York Early Music Festival** (tel. 658338).

■ Near York: Castle Howard

Castle Howard (tel. (01653) 648333), still inhabited by the Howard family, made its TV debut as the home of Sebastian's family in the BBC version of Evelyn Waugh's *Brideshead Revisited.* The famous hall is a lavish monument to English Baroque, dubbed "one of the greatest treasure houses of England." Grand entrance halls and stairways are festooned with portraits of the Howard ancestors in full regalia and cluttered with ancient busts of a variety of famous Romans. Head to the **Orléans Room** to view the impressive art collection of a former duke or to the **chapel** for the kaleidoscopic stained glass. *(10min. services Sa-Su 5:15pm.)* More stunning than the castle itself are its 999 acres of glorious grounds, including luxurious gardens, fountains, and lakes. Be sure to see the white and gold domed **Temple of the Four Winds,** whose hilltop perch offers views of water and sheep-dotted fields. *(Castle and galleries open daily mid-Mar. to Oct. at 11am, last admission 4:30pm. Grounds open at 10am. Call for winter hours. £7, students and seniors £6, children £4. 10min. chapel services Sa-Su 5:15pm. Wheelchair access.)* **York Pullman** (tel. 622992), in Bootham Tower, Exhibition Sq., offers half-day excursions to the Castle (£3.75). As an extra perk, the driver will alert you to the finer points of Yorkshire law. ("A man born and bred within the walls of York is legally entitled to shoot a Scotsman with a bow and arrow—but only on a Sunday, mind you, between the hours of 8 and 11am.") By showing your bus ticket, you can receive reduced admission at the Castle. *(Office open M-Sa 9am-5pm, Su 9am-4pm.)*

■ North York Moors National Park

Upon Yorkshire's windy moors, Heathcliffe and Dracula require no suspension of disbelief. The moors have changed little since inspiring the Brontë sisters, Bram Stoker, and Sir Arthur Conan Doyle: heathered hills and cliff-lined coasts still lend themselves easily to images of passionate men and bloody immortals. Wayfarers can pace the deserted flagstone "trods" (once used by journeying monks), or guide themselves by the famous stone crosses. **Lilla Cross,** on Fylingdales Moor, stands in tribute to the servant Lilla, who used his own body to shield King Edwin from an assassin's dagger in AD 626. The landscape is also dotted with castles at Helmsley, Pickering, and Scarborough, and the ruins of medieval abbeys and hermitages.

The kidney-shaped park, about 30 mi. north of York, shelters the Vale of Pickering in the south, the Vales of York and Mowbray in the west, the flat Cleveland and Teeside Plains in the north, and the rugged North Sea coastline in the east. Some of the highest cliffs in England line the park's coastal border, interspersed with tiny harbors such as Staithes and Robin Hood's Bay. While most neighboring towns provide amenities to those exploring the park, coastal **Whitby** proves the most hospitable, with **Pickering** to the south a distant second.

GETTING THERE AND GETTING ABOUT

No single town serves as an obvious transport hub—Malton, Helmsley, and Pickering near the southern edge of the park, Whitby and Scarborough in the east, and Middlesbrough to the north, all have adequate connections.

The essential document for transport within the park is the *Moors Connections* pamphlet, a life-saver which covers both bus and rail service in glorious detail (free at information centers). Pick it up early and plan ahead—service varies according by season and is minimal in the winter. **Train** service is limited but efficient; **buses** cover more turf and run more frequently. The **Northern Spirit North East** York-Scarborough route provides convenient access to the Moors from **York** (1hr., up to 16 per day). The **North York Moors Railway** (tel. (01751) 472578) offers north-south trans-

ENGLAND

ENGLAND

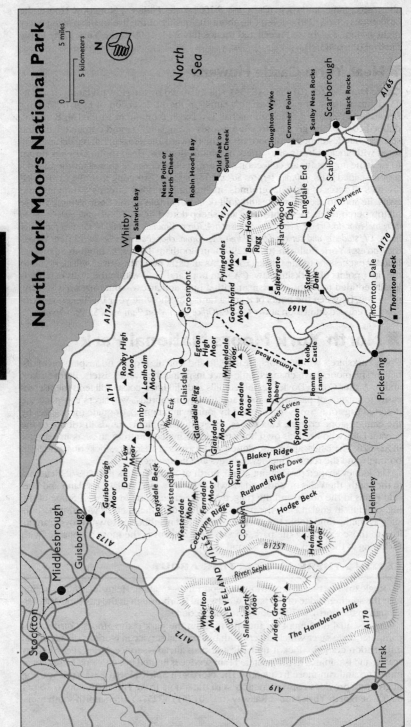

North York Moors National Park

N

North Sea

5 miles

5 kilometers

0

Scarborough

Black Rocks

A165

Scalby Ness Rocks

Cromer Point

Cloughton Wyke

Scalby

A170

Old Peak or
South Cheek

Robin Hood's Bay

Ness Point or
North Cheek

Langdale End

River Derwent

Hardwood
Dale

Saltwick Bay

Whitby

A171

Burn Howe
Rigg

Fylingdales
Moor

Saltergate

Stain
Dale

Thornton Dale

A174

Grosmont

Goathland
Moor

A169

Thornton Beck

Roxby High
Moor

Ledholm
Moor

Egton
High
Moor

Wheeldale
Moor

Roman Road

Kelby
Castle

Pickering

A171

Danby

River Esk

Glaisdale

Glaisdale Rigg

Rosedale
Moor

Rosedale
Abbey

Roman
camp

Glaisdale
Moor

River Seven

Spaunton
Moor

Guisborough
Moor

Danby Low
Moor

Baysdale Beck

Blakey Ridge

River Dove

Church
Houses

Middlesbrough

Guisborough

A173

Westerdale
Moor

Cockayne
Farndale
Ridge

Cockayne

Rudland Rigg

Hodge Beck

Helmsley

A172

Helmsley
Moor

B1257

Stockton

River Seph

CLEVELAND HILLS

Whorlton
Moor

Snilesworth
Moor

Arden Great
Moor

The Hambleton Hills

A170

A19

Thirsk

port in the park, from **Pickering** in the south to **Grosmont** in the north, with three stops in between (1¼hr., 5 per day). By **bus, Yorkshire Coastliner** (tel. (0113) 245 7676) offers a number of useful routes: buses #840, 842, and X40 travel **Leeds-York-Whitby** with many stops at villages along the way (2½hr., up to 16 per day). Bus #843 travels **Leeds-York-Scarborough** (2½hr., up to 16 per day). Journey between **Middlesbrough, Whitby,** and **Scarborough** on **Tees & District** bus #93 or 93A; between **Helmsley** and **Malton** on Yorkshire Coastliner bus #94; or between Malton and **York** on Yorkshire Coastliner bus #81. On Sundays from April to September, watch for additional **Moorsbus** services crawling like ants all over the Moors; these buses go everywhere you could want (£2 for an all-day ticket).

Approaching the Moors on **bicycle** is tough, but on the plateaus the paths are pleasantly level. Tourist information centers offer several guides to cycling in the Moors (£1.80-7). Stores that rent bikes can be found in most of the towns surrounding the park. Biking on footpaths is both destructive and dangerous; cycles should be used on roads and bridleways *only*.

PRACTICAL INFORMATION

Along with the free *Moors Connections,* the *North York Moors Visitor* (50p) is as crucial as sturdy shoes for exploring the park. Available at all information centers, it contains advice, and lists attractions, events, and accommodations throughout the Moors. In general, tourist offices in the area are outstandingly helpful, and they've got the awards to prove it. Visitors should bear in mind that many shops and services are open daily only in the summer; hours can be significantly reduced off-season.

National Park Information Centres

Danby: The Moors Centre, YO21 2NB (tel. (01287) 660654). Largest National Park Information Centre in the area, with a colossal amount of information, a sleek cafe, and a huge garden. 20min. walk from the train station. Turn right as you leave the platform, left after you pass the gate, and right at the crossroads before the Duke of Wellington Pub; the Centre is ½mi. ahead on the right. Northern Spirit North East's Middlesbrough-Whitby connection stops off at Danby. Open Easter-Oct. daily 10am-5pm; Nov.-Easter weekends only 11am-4pm.

Sutton Bank: (tel. (01845) 597426), 6mi. east of Thirsk, on the A170, on top of Sutton Bank. Open Apr.-Oct. daily 10am-5pm; Nov.-Mar. Sa-Su 10am-4pm.

Tourist Offices

Goathland: Moors Outdoor Centre (tel. (01947) 896459). Open Easter-Oct. daily 9:30am-5pm; Nov.-Easter Tu-Su 10am-4pm.

Helmsley: Market Pl. (tel. (01439) 770173). Open Mar.-Oct. daily 9:30am-6pm; Nov.-Feb. F-Su 10am-4pm.

Malton: Old Town Hall, Market Pl. (tel. (01653) 600048). Open Mar.-Oct. M-Sa 9:30am-1pm and 1:30-5:30pm, Su 10am-4:30pm; Nov.-Feb. M-W and F-Su 10am-1pm and 1:30-4:30pm (sometimes open until 5:30pm, depending on the mood of the staff and the position of the stars).

Pickering: Eastgate Car Park, Y018 7DP (tel. (01751) 473791). Accommodations list posted in window at all times. Open mid-Feb. to Oct. M-Sa 9:30am-6pm, Su 9:30am-5:30pm; Nov. to mid-Feb. M-Sa 10am-4:30pm.

Scarborough: Unit 3, Valley Bridge Rd. (tel. (01723) 373333). Open May-Sept. daily 9:30am-6pm; Oct.-Apr. 10am-4:30pm.

Whitby: Langborne Rd. (tel. (01947) 602674). Open daily May-Sept. 9:30am-6pm; Oct.-Apr. 10am-12:30pm and 1-4:30pm.

ACCOMMODATIONS

Local tourist offices will book beds for a small fee plus 10% deposit. The following YHA hostels provide lodging in the Moors; reservations are recommended. Most offer meals at shared, fixed prices (breakfast £2.85, packed lunch £2.50-3.25, evening meal £4.25).

ENGLAND

Boggle Hole: Mill Beck, Fylingthorpe (tel. (01947) 880352; fax 880987). Easy access to Cleveland Way and Coast-to-Coast trails. Renovated 19th-century mill in a wooded ravine on Robin Hood's Bay. £8.80, under 18 £6. Lockout 10am-1pm. Curfew 11pm.

Helmsley: (tel./fax (01439) 770433). From Market Pl. walk along Bondgate Rd., turn left onto Carlton Rd., and left again at Carlton Ln.; hostel is on the left (5min.). New bunks with unyielding mattresses. £8, under 18 £5.40. Open mid-July to Oct. daily; mid-Mar. to mid-July and Sept.-Oct. M-Sa; mid-Jan. to mid-Mar. M-Th; Nov. to mid-Jan. groups only.

Lockton: The Old School (tel. (01751) 460376), just off the Pickering-Whitby Rd. Take the Coastlines bus #840. Fresh, self-catering hostel. £5.85, under 18 £4. Open July-Aug. daily; June and Sept. M-Sa; Oct.-Mar. groups only.

Osmotherley: Cote Ghyll, Northallerton (tel. (01609) 883575; fax 883715). Modernized former mill between Stockton and Thirsk, just north of Osmotherley. £8.80, under 18 £6.

Scarborough: The White House, Burniston Rd. (tel. (01723) 361176; fax 500054), 2mi. from Scarborough. Former mill on a river and 10min. from the sea. Take bus #3 from outside the railway station. £7.20, under 18 £5. Open Mar.-Aug. daily; Sept. to mid-Dec. Tu-Sa; Feb. to mid-Mar. F-Sa; closed mid-Dec.to Jan.

Thixendale: The Village Hall (tel. (01377) 288238). £5.85, under 18 £4. No meals or showers. Open Good Friday to Sept. W-M.

Wheeldale: Wheeldale Lodge, Goathland, Whitby (tel. (01947) 896350). From Goathland take Egton Bridge Rd. and turn left on Hunt House Rd. Rustic former hunting lodge: no showers; flashlights a must. £5.85, under 18 £4. Lockout 10am-5pm. Open July-Aug. daily; Apr.-June and Sept. to mid-Oct. F-Tu.

Whitby: (tel./fax (01947) 602878). Take bus #97 from the bus or train station. 12th-century stone building next to the abbey atop 199 loathsome steps. £7.20, under 18 £5. Lockout 10am-5pm. Curfew 11pm. Moor-bound school groups often fill the place until mid-July, so call ahead. Open Apr.-Oct. daily; Feb.-Mar. and Nov. to mid-Dec. F-Sa; closed mid-Dec. to Jan.

YHA operates five **camping barns** in the Moors. These provide a roof, water, and toilets. A good sleeping bag, flashlight, and cooking equipment are essential. For listings, pick up the *Stay in a Camping Barn* leaflet (free) from information centers or contact the YHA Northern Region, P.O. Box 11, Matlock, Derbyshire DE4 2XA (tel. (01629) 825850). Barns cost £3.25-4.75 per person, are open for arrival at 4pm, and must be vacated by 10am.

HIKING AND BIKING

Hiking is the best way to travel these vast, lonely moors. Ambitious hikers might consider tackling one of the long-distance footpaths in the park: the 93 mi. **Cleveland Way,** the 79 mi. **Wolds Way,** the famous (and hence eroding) **Lyke Wake Walk,** or the shorter and unofficial 37 mi. **White Rose** and **Crosses Walks.** The 35 mi. **Esk Valley Trail** hugs the lowlands near the railway track. Not all of the trails are well marked or even visible, and many cunningly intersect. Hikers should pick up the free *Moorland Safety* pamphlet, available from the Danby or Sutton Bank information centers, and should always carry a detailed map and a compass (see **Wilderness and Safety Concerns,** p. 47).

The amount of literature on the North York Moors is astounding; information centers stock reams of guidebooks. The *Waymark* guides (30-40p), produced by the National Park authority, detail short (up to ½ day) walks starting from villages or points of interest. The Ordnance Survey Tourist Map 2 (£4.25) covers the whole park, but may be too general for hikers. The 1:25,000 *Outdoor Leisure* sheets 26 and 27 (£6) are more precise. Before hitting the trails, purchase a few *Waymark* guides, consult more expensive books (£3-6), and get good advice (£0) from tourist officials. **Disabled travelers** should ask at tourist offices for Forest Enterprise's *Easy Going* guides (free), which note paths most easily accessible for those in wheelchairs or those who have difficulty walking.

Cyclists roll gleefully through the **North Riding Forest Park,** located in the middle of the Moors between Pickering, Scarborough, and Sleights. The park holds mountain-bike paths for riders of all skill levels in addition to short walking trails (some of which are accessible by train). For details visit the **Low Dalby Visitor Centre** (tel. (01751) 460295), off the A169 about 4 mi. north of Pickering and 1 mi. south of Lockton (open Easter-Oct. daily 11am-5pm), or inquire at the **Forest District Office,** Crossgates Ln., Pickering (tel. (01751) 472295; open M-F June-Sept. 10am-5pm; Mar.-May and Oct.-Nov. 11am-4pm). Pick up a list of cycle hire stores from an information center, or check *The Moors Visitor.*

The Moors can be horribly hot or bitterly cold in the summer—sudden changes in weather can make or break a hike. Check the **weather forecast** (tel. (01891) 500418) before setting out, but be aware that it reports on all of northeast England; the weather can vary dramatically even within the park. Bring a rain jacket.

■ The Northern Park: Whitby

Straddling a harbor between two desolate headlands, Whitby has been the Muse for many a struggling oddball. Here **Caedmon** sang the first English hymns, **Bram Stoker** conjured up evil, and **Lewis Carroll** wrote *The Walrus and the Carpenter,* while eating oysters. One of two English ports where the midsummer sun can be seen both rising and setting over the sea, Whitby also inspired **Captain Cook** to set sail for Australia. The commercialized strip of slot-machines, gift shops, and fish and chips huts lends a circus-like atmosphere to Whitby, inexplicably enhancing the dirty grandeur of city and sea.

ORIENTATION AND PRACTICAL INFORMATION Buses and trains deposit their passengers at **Station Sq.** on **Endeavor Wharf** on the west side of town, which is split by the River Esk. The **train station** is a one-track affair with no ticket or information desks. For tickets and timetables, stop by **Getaway Travel,** 11 Baxtergate (tel. 820092; open M-F 9am-5pm, Sa 9am-4pm). The **bus station** (tel. 602146), across the street, stores **luggage,** but retrieval is only possible during open hours (£1 per article; open M-Th 9am-4:30pm, F-Sa 9am-12:25pm and 1-3:30pm). Whitby's **tourist office** (tel. 602674) is also at Station Sq. (see p. 357). **ATMs** are plentiful; check the **Nationwide ATM** next to the **bus station.** On the east side of the river, turn left at either Sandgate or Church St. to find the **market** (Tu and Sa 9am-4pm). The main **post office** (tel. 602327) hides at the back of the **Whitby Northeastern Superstore,** Endeavor Wharf (tel. 600710). (Post office open M-W and Sa 8:30am-5:30pm, Th-F 8:30am-7pm; store open M-Sa 8am-8pm, Su 10am-4pm.) The **postal code** is YO2 1DN; the **telephone code** is 01947.

ACCOMMODATIONS AND FOOD Whitby's hilltop **YHA Youth Hostel** provides incredible views (see **Accommodations,** p. 357). Another hostel, **Harbor Grange** (tel. 600817), is located off Spitel Bridge about seven minutes from Station Sq. Walk south on Church St.; the hostel is on your right just after Green Ln. The 26-bed independent hostel offers a riverside patio, kitchen, quiet atmosphere, and velveteen decor at a great price. (Dorms £7, with sheets £8; singles £8. Curfew 11:30pm.) B&Bs mass on the western cliff, along Bellevue Terr. and adjacent roads; confusingly, each side of those roads has a different name. Try **Jaydee Guest House,** 15 John St. (tel. 605422), where the friendly Nicholsons offer pleasant conversation and a nautically-inclined dining room (£16-19). The **High Tor Guest House** (tel. 602507), on Normandy Terr., opposite Jaydee's, offers color-schemed rooms and fireplaces (£15, with bath £17). Campers should look for the **Northcliffe Caravan Park** (tel. 880477), 3 mi. south of town in High Hawkser. Take bus #93 or 93A from the bus station (£1), or head down the A171 and turn onto the B1447. (July-Aug. £4 per person; Apr.-June and Sept. £3.50 per person; Oct.-Mar. £3 per person. £10 shower deposit. Laundry.)

Cafes and fish and chips stores are abundant. A vegetarian restaurant, **Shepherd's Purse,** 95 Church St. (tel. 820228), cooks up a wealth of tasty morsels. Walk past the aromatic herbs and spices to the cafe and tea garden in back. Homemade soups and baguette sandwiches go for £2.50, and pizzas and pasta start at £5. (Open M 10am-5pm, Tu-Th and Su 10am-5pm and 6:30-9:30pm, F-Sa 10am-5pm and 6:30-10pm.) If you want to sate yourself with superb food in a relaxed, elegant atmosphere, try **The Vintner,** 42a Flowergate (tel. 601166). Specials go for £8-9. Try the leek and Roquefort canneloni. (Open M-Tu 5:30-9:30pm, W-Sa noon-2:30pm and 5:30-9:30pm, Su noon-8:30pm. Hours restricted Nov.-Mar.; call for details.)

SIGHTS AND ENTERTAINMENT Proceeding westward from Station Sq. on Bagdale, visitors arrive at **Pannett Park,** most easily accessible via Union Rd. on the right. The heady smell of roses (in season) provides olfactory stimulation, followed by the visual pleasures of the **Pannett Art Gallery and Whitby Museum.** Fossils—including the elusive *Ichthyosaurus Crassimanus* ("the reptile that was perfectly at home in the sea")—rub flippers with everything from weaponry to taxidermy to Captain Cook regalia. *(Gallery and museum open May-Sept. M-Sa 9:30am-5:30pm, Su 2-5pm; Oct.-Apr. Tu 10am-1pm, W-Sa 10am-4pm, Su 2-4pm. Gallery free. Museum £1.50, children £1.)*

Point yourself uphill and keep walking to reach the top of the cliffs. There, at East Terr., stands **Captain Cook** himself. With charts in his left hand, sextant in his right, he squints at Australia, the continent he charted. You can visit his memorial **museum** (tel. 601900), on Grape Ln. across the river. *(Open daily Apr.-Oct. 9:45am-5pm. £2.30, seniors £1.80, children £1.60.)* Nearby, the self-explanatory "Whalebone Arch" pays tribute to the 17th-century whaling industry. The western cliffs also cradle the **Whitby Pavilion Theatre** (tel. 604855), which hosts everything from tea dances to comedy shows (from £1.80). Go a little farther, look right, and choose your torture: will it be the 199 steps or the nearly vertical, winding church lane? Both lead to the YHA Hostel, as well as the ancient and imposing **St. Mary's Church,** which was built in 1100 and has a cliff-top graveyard full of 6 ft. tombstones.

As you crest the headland, you enter a world of shrieking wind and ancient structures. Glancing over to the brooding, skeletal remains of **Whitby Abbey,** it feels as though Dracula could be lurking nearby. Bram Stoker was a frequent visitor to Whitby, and several scenes in his famous *Dracula* occur in St. Mary's Churchyard, with the haunting Abbey mentioned as background. *(Open daily Apr.-Sept. 10am-6pm; Oct.-Mar. 10am-4pm. £1.70, students and seniors £1.30, children 90p.)*

Like other local towns, Whitby parties occasionally; the **Whitby Festival** (tel. 602674), featuring dancing, singing, exhibitions, and organized walks, enlivens early June. Whitby also hosts a **folk week** (tel. 708424) in August, with 200 hours of dance, concerts, and workshops. The *What's On* seasonal brochure and its weekly supplement at the tourist office describe other events around town.

■ Near Whitby: Danby and Castleton

From Whitby, you can head west or south. To the west, villages like Grosmont, Danby, Castleton, and Kildale are accessible by the Northern Spirit Middlesbrough-Whitby connection. At Danby, pay a visit to the mother of all Park Information Centres (see p. 357). You can also ascend the 1400 ft. **Danby Rigg** (Ridge) to the top of **Danby High Moor,** or stroll to **Danby Castle,** a jumble of roofless 14th-century stones attached to a working farm. Despite the castle's current state of disrepair, the easy hour-long walk across the valley and back will inspire you to romp through the fields and sing "I Feel Pretty" to attentive sheep. In the area, try the walks up **Castleton** and **Glaisdale Riggs,** which are also accessible from the train station at Castleton, Glaisdale, and Lealholme. Farther afield, walk from the Little Ayton rail station (on the Esk Valley line) or from Newton-under-Roseberry to the summit of **Roseberry Topping** (not a dessert, but deserted).

■ The Southern Park: Pickering

Pickering (pop. 6200), beyond the park's southern border, is a popular jumping-off point for jaunts to the park and the nearby coast. It also serves as the southern terminus of the steamy, scenic **North York Moors Railway.** Remnants of a Norman castle still command an inspiring view from the hill in the center of town. **Pickering Castle** was once a vacation home for monarchs who hunted the boar and deer in a nearby royal forest. Commoners now use this lush and grassy spot as a picnic ground. *(Castle open daily Apr.-Sept. 10am-1pm and 2-6pm; Oct.-Mar. W-Su 10am-1pm and 2-4pm. £2, students and seniors £1.50, children £1, under 5 free.)*

Pickering's **tourist office** is located at Eastgate Car Park (see p. 357). An **ATM**-armed **Barclays** is on Market St. The **post office**, 7 Market Pl. (tel. 72256), is inside Morland's Newsagents, and has a bureau de change (open M-F 9am-5:30pm, Sa 9am-1pm). The **postal code** is YO1 87AA, the **telephone code** 01751.

The **tourist office** stocks a free accommodations listing, including **farmhouses**. Stay with **Mrs. Kelleher,** Lingfield, Middleton Rd. (tel. 473456), just cityside of Swansea Ln., for a family setting on a quiet street (£14). **Wayside Caravan Park,** Wrelton (tel. 472608), 2½ mi. down the Pickering-Helmsley Rd., will let you and a friend camp in your tent for £5 (£1.25 for each extra person). On the road up to the castle, enjoy tea and baguette sandwiches (£1.50-2.25) and tasty desserts with tastier names (Kansass Kiss Kake £1.75) in a busy oversized dollhouse called the **Forget-Me-Not Tea Room,** 37 Burgate (open Apr.-Oct. daily 10am-5pm; sporadically thereafter). For a truly gourmet meal, hit **The White Swan,** the best restaurant in town. The restaurant is smart-casual, but if you order from the bar you get the same food for less cash. The roast lamb shank is to die for (entrees £7-10).

■ The Southern Park: Helmsley

PRACTICAL INFORMATION To the south of Pickering lies **Helmsley,** surrounded by excellent walks and sights. The town centers around the **Market Pl.,** where buses stop and shops and eateries abound. The **tourist office** in Helmsley is also at Market Pl. (see p. 357). **Barclays,** at Bondgate and Bridge St., provides an accommodating **ATM.** The **police station** is at Ashdale Rd. and The Crescent (open between 9-10am and 6-7pm; otherwise call (01653) 692424). The **post office** (tel. 770237) loves you at Bridge St., across from Borgate (open M-Tu and Th-F 9am-12:30pm and 1:30-5:30pm, W and Sa 9am-12:30pm). The **postal code** is YO62 5BG; the **telephone code** is 01439.

ACCOMMODATIONS Helmsley is graced by the **youth hostel** (see p. 357), small hotels, and B&Bs. Try **Mrs. Wood's** rooms at Buckingham House, 33 Bridge St. (tel. 770613; £16.50, rooms with basin and TV). The **Tudor Rose,** 1 Bridge St. (tel. 770131), provides shelter and sustenance, with pub and cafe dishes for £4-5.

Those exploring the fern-lined **Newtondale Gorge** and the lush **Newtondale Forest** (via the scenic North Yorkshire Moors Railway from the Newtondale or Levisham stations) can lodge at the **YHA Lockton,** near Levisham (see p. 358). From Pickering or Whitby take York City District bus #840 or 842 (tel. (01904) 624161). Three miles southwest of the Moors Railway at **Goathland** (past **Mallyan Spout,** a beautiful waterfall) is the secluded **YHA Wheeldale** (tel. (01947) 896530; see p. 357).

SIGHTS AND ENTERTAINMENT The main sight in town is **Helmsley Castle** (tel. 770442) first built in the early 1100s and rebuilt in 1190. It was an intimidating fortress until a 1644 Civil War siege blew much of the place to bits. *(Open Apr.-Oct. daily 10am-1pm and 2-6pm; Nov.-Mar. W-Su 10am-1pm and 2-4pm (or dusk). £2.20, students and seniors £1.70, under 16 £1.10, under 5 free.)* The beautiful **Walled Garden** with its "glasshouses" also deserves a visit. *(Open Apr.-Oct. M-Sa 10:30am-4:30pm, Su 11:30am-4:30pm. £1.50, students and seniors £1, children 75p.)* **Duncombe Park** (tel. 771115), near the castle, features an 18th-century estate, a Baroque mansion, and 100 acres of beautifully landscaped gardens and forests. Interestingly enough, it is now mostly a National Nature Reserve due to its rare beetle population. *(Open May-Sept. daily 11am-4:30pm; Apr. and Oct. Sa-M 11am-4:30pm. House and grounds £5, students and seniors £4, children £2.50; grounds only £3, children £1.50.)* A short 3½ mi. hike out of town leads to the stunning 12th-century **Rievaulx Abbey** (REE-vo AA-bee; tel. 798228). Established by St.

Bernard and a host of monks from Burgundy, the abbey was an ascetic masterpiece until Thomas Mannus, first Earl of Rutland, stripped it of everything valuable (including the roof), initiating a swift decay. It is now one of the most spectacular ruins in the country. Grab the Waymark Walk #20 guide at the tourist office (40p) and explore. *(Open daily July-Aug. 9:30am-7pm; Apr.-June and Sept.-Oct. 10am-6pm; Nov.-Mar. 10am-4pm. £2.90, students and seniors £2.20, children £1.50. Wheelchair access.)* In late July and early August, music, drama, and literary talks take center stage in the Helmsley area at **The Ryedale Festival.** Contact the Festival Office (tel. 771518) for more info and bookings.

■ Durham City

The dominating presence of England's greatest Norman cathedral lends grandeur to small-town Durham. For 800 years the Bishops of Durham ruled the region with their own currency, army, and courts. In the 1830s, new rulers, otherwise known as students of Durham University, took over the cliff-top city. The heart of County Durham, Durham City slows down during summer recess, but the town is by no means a sleepy haven—tourists and festival-goers flow steadily into the narrow, winding streets, ensuring a lively atmosphere year-round.

GETTING THERE

Durham lies 20 mi. south of Newcastle on the A167 and an equal distance north of Darlington. **Trains** (tel. (0345) 484950) from Newcastle stop frequently at the main railway station, on a steep hill just north of town, en route to London **King's Cross** (3hr., 1 per hr., £63), **York** (1hr., roughly 2 per hr., £16, return £19.60), and **Newcastle** (20min., at least 2 per hr., £2.40, day return £4). Many **bus** companies serve local routes, stopping at the station on North Rd. **National Express** (tel. (0990) 808080) runs to **Edinburgh** (4½hr., 1 per day) and **London** (5½hr., 6 per day). **Go Northern** and **United** run a joint service #722/723 from the Durham bus station to the **Eldon Sq.** station in Newcastle (1hr., every 10min., £2).

ORIENTATION AND PRACTICAL INFORMATION

The **River Wear** coils around Durham City, creating a partial moat on three sides. Modern marauders need not fret, for plentiful footbridges abound. With its cobble-stoned medieval streets and restricted vehicle access, Durham is generally foot-friendly, if sometimes difficult for disabled persons and those with heavy packs to haul. The **bus station** (tel. 384 3323) squats on North Rd. across Framwellgate Bridge from the city center (office open M-F 9am-5pm, Sa 9am-4pm). The **train station** (tel. 232 6262) also lies west of town. (Ticket office open M-F 6am-9pm, Sa 6am-8pm, Su 7:30am-9pm. Advance ticket sales M-Sa 8:30am-5:45pm, Su 10am-5:45pm.)

To reach the **tourist office,** Market Pl. (tel. 384 3720; fax 386 3015), from the train station, descend the hill on Station Approach and take the set of steps on the left down to the Millburngate Bridge roundabout. Take Millburngate to the right, then turn left and follow Silver St. uphill to Market Pl. (Open July-Aug. M-Sa 9:30am-6pm, Su 2-5pm; June and Sept. M-F 10am-5:30pm, Sa 9:30am-5:30pm; Oct.-May M-Sa 10am-5pm.) **Banks** aplenty in Market Pl. fulfill capitalist urges. The bright yellow **Cycle Force Ltd.,** 29 Claypath (tel. 384 0319), rents road and mountain bikes. (£12 per day; £35 deposit. Open M-W and F 9am-5:30pm, Tu 9am-7pm, Sa 9am-5pm.) The **post office** (tel. 386 4644) can be found at 33 Silver St. (open M-Sa 9am-5:30pm). Durham's **postal code** is DH1 3RE. **Internet access** is available at **Reality-X Durham,** 1 Framwellgate Bridge (tel. 384 5700; £3 per 30min., £5 per hr.; open M-Sa 11am-10pm). Durham's **telephone code** is 0191.

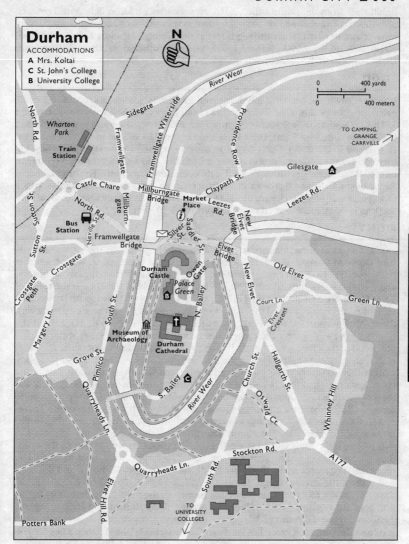

Durham
ACCOMMODATIONS
A Mrs. Koltai
C St. John's College
B University College

ACCOMMODATIONS

The large supply of inexpensive and often beautiful **dormitory rooms** (tel. 374 3454) around the cathedral and south of town is a boon for travelers (available roughly July-Sept., mid-Mar. to mid-Apr., and Dec.-Jan.; breakfast included). Live like the Prince Bishops of old in **University College,** Durham Castle (tel. 374 3863; fax 374 7470). Others tour the castle, but you can pretend to be its lord or lady, as you consume breakfast in the massive dining hall (£20.50, children £12.50). On a quiet cobbled street behind Durham Cathedral, **St. John's College,** 3 South Bailey (tel. 374 3566; fax 374 3573), offers B&B in single and twin rooms—vie for a room in the spacious theology students' section or in riverside Cruddas House (£18, children £9). Or join bilingual **Mrs. Koltai,** 10 Gilesgate (tel./fax 386 2026), and the TVs in her B&B, a steep uphill walk from the tourist office (£16). **Mrs. Fowler's B&B,** 4 Belle Vue Terr. (tel. 386 4800), a five-minute ride from the town center on bus #220, offers small, comfortable rooms (£16). The **camping** is fine at the **Grange,** Meadow Ln., Carrville (tel. 384 4778), on the A690 off the A1, 2½ mi. away (office open daily 8:30am-6pm; £4.20 per person, £2.75 per pitch; showers available).

FOOD

Bakeries crowd the center of town. Eat your fill of rolls, scones, and cakes (under £1 each), or get a healthful sandwich or salad from **Marks and Spencer,** Silver St. (open M-Th 9am-5:30pm, F-Sa 8:30am-5:30pm). Even more vegetables and fruits fill **Market Hall** (open daily 9am-5pm). For a local specialty try Lindisfarne mead, still made on Holy Island to the north. University students congregate in **Vennel's** quiet, 16th-century courtyard to discuss Rimbaud over a fresh brie-and-walnut sandwich (entrance next to Waterstone's in Saddler's Yard; cafe open daily 9am-5pm). The bright, cheery **Almshouses Café and Restaurant,** 10 Palace Green, next to the cathedral, serves a changing menu of light, elegant meals. (£4-6. Open daily in summer 9am-8pm; in winter 9am-5:30pm; meals served noon-2:30pm and 5:30-8pm.)

SIGHTS

Durham's tourist attractions are sparse but spellbinding. Built in 1093, the extraordinary **Durham Cathedral** (tel. 386 4266) stands, in the words of Sir Walter Scott, as "half church of God, half castle 'gainst the Scot." The pamphlet on the layout, history, and architecture of the cathedral (50p) is invaluable. Behind the choir is the **tomb of Saint Cuthbert.** St. Cuthbert died in 687, and was buried on Holy Island; Danish raiders in the 9th century caused the island's monks to flee, carrying the saint's body with them. After wandering to various towns for 120 years, a vision in AD 995 led the monks to Durham, where the cathedral was built to shelter the saints shrine. At the other end of the church lies the tomb of the **Venerable Bede,** author of the *Ecclesiastical History of the English People,* the first history of England. Note the strip of black marble that separates Bede's tomb and the eastern side from the main part of the church; women had to stay behind this strip during the time when the church was used as a monastery. *(Open daily May-Aug. 7:15am-8pm; Sept.-Apr. 7:15am-6pm. Suggested donation £2.50. Wheelchair accessible.)* The spectacular view from the top of the **Tower** is well worth the 325-step climb it takes to get there. *(Open M-Sa 10am-4pm, weather permitting. £2, children 50p.)* The **Monks' Dormitory** off the cloister is an enormous hall that houses elaborately carved stones and stone crosses, as well as part of the cathedral library. *(Open M-Sa 10am-3:30pm, Su 12:30-3:30pm. 80p, children 20p.)* The reopened **Treasures of St. Cuthbert** holds the relics of St. Cuthbert, and the rings and seals of the all-powerful Bishops. *(Open M-Sa 10am-4:30pm, Su 2-4:30pm. £2, children 30p, families £5.)* The entire cathedral is open to the public. **Guided tours** lasting one hour are available between June and August. *(Daily 10:30am and 2:30pm; Aug. also 11:30am. Suggested donation £2.50.)*

Across the cathedral green lies **Durham Castle** (tel. 374 3863). Once a key fortress of the county's Prince Bishops, the castle is today a splendid residence for students at the university (see **Accommodations,** p. 356). *(Tours daily July-Sept. 10am-12:30pm and 2-4:30pm; Oct.-June 2-4:30pm. £3, children £2.)* Those seeking solitude should head below the cathedral for a walk along the wondrously serene riverbank, which offers splendid views of the castle and cathedral. The riverbank also hold the **Museum of Archaeology** (tel. 374 3023), where posters for local nostalgia societies lie cheek by jowl with bits of Roman carving. *(Open Apr.-Oct. daily 11am-4pm; Nov.-Mar. M and Th-F 12:30-3pm, Sa-Su 11:30am-3:30pm. £1, students, seniors, and children 50p, families £2.50.)*

ENTERTAINMENT

Get on the water in a rowboat from **Brown's Boathouse Centres,** Elvet Bridge (tel. 386 3779 or 386 9525), and wind around the horseshoe curve of the River Wear, dodging scullers and ducks. *(£2.50, children £1.25; £5 deposit.)* For a less arduous boat journey, the centre offers a 1hr. cruise on the 150-seat **Prince Bishop River Cruiser.** *(£3, children £1.50.)*

After-hours entertainment in Durham is closely tied to university life; when students depart, most nightlife follows suit. A young crowd fills the popular **Hogshead,** 58 Saddler St. (tel. 386 4134), which has an excellent selection of wines and a wall filled with the theatrical history of Durham. *(Open M-Sa 11am-11pm, Su noon-10:30pm.)* The sporty riverside **Coach and Eight,** Bridge House, Framwellgate Bridge (tel. 386 3284), is gosh-darn enormous and has a giant-screen TV to match. *(Disco Th-Su. Open M-Sa noon-11pm, Su noon-10:30pm.)* The small **Traveller's Rest,** 72 Claypath St. (tel. 386 5370), has an attractive selection of ales. *(Open daily noon-3pm and 6-11pm.)*

Durham holds a **folk festival** in August with singing, clog dancing, musicians, and general frolicking. Many events are free; others cost £2-7. Get a leaflet at the tourist office. **Camping** is free along the river during the festival (F-Su), so pitch your tent early. Other major town events include the **Durham Regatta** in the middle of June held since 1834, and a massive, sodden **beer festival** (the second largest in the country) in early September; call the tourist office for details on all festivals.

■ Newcastle-Upon-Tyne

Hardworking Newcastle (pop. 284,000) bills itself as a city of firsts. Beyond such constructive contributions to civilization as the hydraulic crane and the steam locomotive, this gritty, industrial capital also brought us the world's first beauty contest and first dog show. Not to mention Sting, the first human to invoke Vladimir Nabokov in a pop song. You won't find dreaming spires or evening hush here, but Newcastle has plenty to offer the motivated pleasure-seeker. What looks a bit worn and grimy by day becomes upbeat and scintillating by night. Locals, students, and tourists (many of them British) flock to Newcastle's pubs and clubs, and a good time is had by all. Newcastle Geordies are proud of their accent, very proud of their football club, and usually happy to show you around.

GETTING THERE

Newcastle is the last English stronghold before crossing the Scottish border. The city lies 1½ hours north of York on the A19 and about 1½ hours east of Carlisle on the A69. Edinburgh is a straight run up the coast along the A1, or through pastures and mountains via the A68. **Trains** (tel. (0345) 484950) leave Newcastle's **Central Station** for London **King's Cross** (3hr., 1 per hr., £40.50), **Edinburgh** (1½hr., M-Sa 23 per day, Su 16 per day, £26.40, return £27), and **Carlisle** (1½hr., M-Sa 15 per day, Su 9 per day, £7.80, day return £10.20).

Most **buses** depart from **Gallowgate Coach Station. National Express** (tel. (0990) 808080) runs to **London** (6hr., 6 per day, return £27), and **Edinburgh** (3hr., 3 per day, return £18.50). From the Haymarket Station, local **Northumbrian Line** buses #505, 515, and 525 go to **Berwick-upon-Tweed** (2½hr., M-Sa roughly every 2hr., Su 5 per day, £3.55). **Ferries** float to the continent from **International Ferry Terminal,** Royal Quays. Bus #327 serves all departures, leaving Central Station 2½ hrs. and 1¼ hrs. before each sailing. For complete listings, see **By Ferry,** p. 32.

ORIENTATION AND PRACTICAL INFORMATION

The tourist office's free, full-color map of Newcastle is essential—streets switch direction and name without batting an eye. When in doubt, remember that the waterfront is at the bottom of every hill. The center of town is **Grey's Monument,** an 80 ft. stone pillar in **Monument Mall,** directly opposite **Eldon Sq.** The Monument is dedicated to Charles, Earl of Grey, who nudged the steep 1832 Reform Bill through Parliament and who mixed glorious bergamot into Britain's bleak tea.

Transportation

Trains: Central Station, Neville St. (tel. 232 6262). Travel Centre sells same-day tickets M-Sa 5:40am-9pm, Su 7:10am-8pm. Advance tickets M-F 7am-8pm, Sa 7am-7pm, Su 8:30am-8pm. Offers **luggage storage** £1-3 (open daily 8am-6pm).

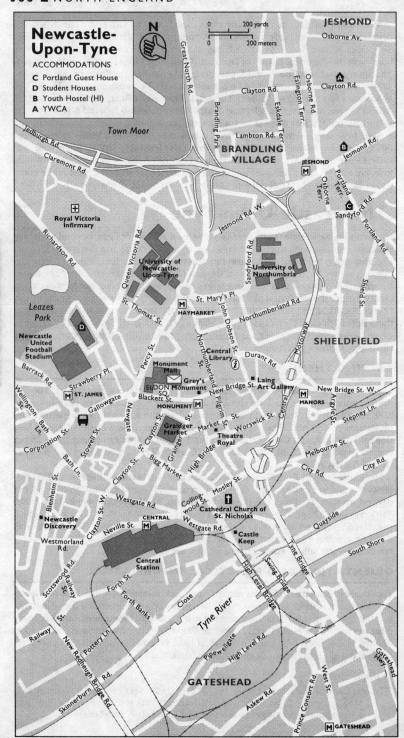

Newcastle-Upon-Tyne

ACCOMMODATIONS

C Portland Guest House
D Student Houses
B Youth Hostel (HI)
A YWCA

Buses: National Express (tel. (0990) 808080) operates from **Gallowgate Coach Station,** off Percy St. **Northumbria** (tel. 232 4211) runs from the bus stand at **Haymarket,** beside the Metro Stop.

Ferries: Ferries leave from **International Ferry Terminal,** Royal Quays. Take bus #327, taxi (£10), or Metro to Percy Main (£1.10) and walk 20min. to the quay.

Travel Information: Travel Line (tel. 232 5325). Open M-Sa 8am-8pm, Su 9am-5pm.

Bike Rental: Newcastle Cycle Centre, 11 Westmorland Rd. (tel. 230 3022). £10 per day, £35 per week; £50 deposit. Open M-F 9am-5:30pm, Sa 9am-5pm.

Tourist and Financial Services

Tourist Office: Central Library (tel. 261 0610; fax 221 0115), off New Bridge St. Leave Monument Metro station through the exit next to the Virgin Megastore in Monument Mall, then walk up the dark bricks of Northumberland Pl. to the library. Open M and Th 9:30am-8pm, Tu-W and F 9:30am-5pm, Sa 9am-5pm. **Central Station** (tel. 230 0030; fax 214 6555). Open June-Sept. M-F 10am-8pm, Sa 9am-5pm, Su 10am-4pm; Oct.-May M-Sa 10am-5pm.

Tours: City tours leave M-Sa from the Central Library. May-Oct. 2pm; £2.

Budget Travel: Campus Travel, Newcastle University Student Union Bldg., Kings Walk (tel. 232 1798). Open M and W-Th 9:30am-5pm, Tu 10am-5pm, F 9:30am-4:30pm; closes 4:30pm when the University is not in session.

Financial Services: Barclays, Grainger St. (tel. 200 2000), at Market St. Open M-Tu and Th-F 9am-5:30pm, W 10am-5:30pm, Sa 9:30am-12:30pm. **Thomas Cook,** 6 Northumberland St. (tel. 261 2163), at New Bridge St. W. Open M-Tu and F-Sa 9am-5:30pm, W 10am-5:30pm, Th 9am-8pm.

Emergency and Communications

Emergency: Dial 999; no coins required.

Police: (tel. 214 6555), on Market St. at Pilgrim St.

Hotlines: Samaritans (crisis; tel. 232 7272). Open 24hr. **Friend to Newcastle** (gay and lesbian; tel. 261 8555). Open M-F 7-10pm. **Rape Crisis Line** (tel. 261 5317). Open M 10:30am-1pm and Th 2:30-5pm.

Hospital: Royal Victorian Infirmary, Queen Victoria Rd. (tel. 232 5131).

Post Office: 24-26 Sidgate (tel. 261 7787), in the Eldon Sq. Shopping Centre. Open M-Sa 9am-5:30pm. **Postal Code:** NE1 7AB.

Internet Access: McNulty's Internet Café, 26-30 Market St. (tel. 232 0922; http://www.mcnultynet.co.uk), offers pricey but swift connections (£7 per hr., £4 per 30min.) "Cyberbreakfast" weekday mornings: full English breakfast, bottomless cup of tea or coffee, and internet access for £4.50 (9-11:30am). Open M-W 9am-8:30pm, Th-F 9am-9pm, Sa 9am-7:30pm, Su 11am-5pm.

Telephone Code: 0191.

ACCOMMODATIONS

Many costlier lodgings neighbor the Youth Hostel and YWCA in residential **Jesmond,** just northeast of town via a 50p Metro ride (3min.). Slightly less expensive alternatives are scattered a few blocks to the north of Jesmond on Osborne Rd. The cheapest B&Bs run about £15, more for singles; call in advance to secure a room.

YHA Youth Hostel, 107 Jesmond Rd. (tel. 281 2570; fax 281 8779). From Jesmond Metro station, turn left onto Jesmond Rd., and walk past the traffic lights—it's on the left. A good sightseer's base, this funky townhouse attracts backpackers. £9.15, under 18 £6.20. Breakfast £2.80, packed lunch £2.45, and evening meal £4.40. Linen free. Lockout 10am-5pm. Curfew 11pm; ask for the late entry code. Overrun by ferry traffic, so call several days in advance. Closed Dec.-Jan.

Newcastle University, Leazes Terrace Student Houses, 10 Leazes Terr. (tel. 222 8150). Near city center; steps from St. James Metro stop and 2 blocks north of Gallowgate Bus Station, directly across from the massive soccer stadium. Commonplace dorms within converted townhouses retain their grandeur despite the departure of the bourgeoisie. Singles £14, with breakfast £16.50; doubles £23, with breakfast £28; students £40 per week, room only. Open July-Sept.

Portland Guest House, 134 Sandyford Rd. (tel. 232 7868). From Jesmond Metro stop, turn left onto Jesmond Rd., then right onto Portland Terr.—it's at the end. Clean, basic rooms with parking and bike storage. Singles £17; doubles £34.

YWCA, Jesmond House (tel. 281 1233), on Clayton Rd. From Jesmond Metro station turn left onto Jesmond Rd., then left onto Osborne Rd., and right onto Clayton Rd. at the hospital—it's on the left. Basic accommodations. Men and women over 18 accepted; supports many longer-term working-class men. B&B £15.50; weekly £90, dinner included. Call a day ahead.

FOOD

Every other restaurant offers inexpensive pasta and pizza, and those in between serve everything from tandoori specialties to enchiladas, veggie burgers, and peanut butter casserole; prices are generally £2-5. Chinese eateries line Stowell St. near Gallowgate; many offer all-you-can-eat specials for £4-6. **Don Vito's,** 82 Pilgrim St. (tel. 232 8923), stands out among the many Italian eateries. The don offers generous pastas and pizzas with glorious toppings and inventive sauces for just £3. Try the *gnocchi* (open M-F 11am-2pm and 5-10pm, Sa 11am-11pm). Opposite the Guild hall, the **Bob Trollop** pub, 35 Sandhill, Quayside, proffers tasty vegetarian dishes for £2.50-5 (open daily 11am-11pm; food served M-Sa 11am-7pm, Su noon-7pm). Expect cheap food and paranormal activity at the **Supernatural Vegetarian Restaurant,** 2 Princess Sq. (tel. 261 2730). Facing the Central Library main entrance, take a left and go up the ramp; it's on your left. They offer entrees for £2.30-3.75 (10% student discount; open M and Sa 10:30am-7pm, Tu-F 10:30am-7:30pm). The earth tones and folded sheet metal artwork of the **Fox Talbot,** 46 Dean St. (tel. 230 2229), house some of the best lunch deals in town. Try the lamb in orange (£4.70) or the feta-spinach-strawberry salad (£4). Or go for the lunch special: two courses *and* a glass of wine for £5 (open M-Sa noon-11pm; lunch served noon-5pm, dinner 5-11pm).

SIGHTS

Newcastle's monuments rear their hoary heads smack dab in the middle of modern chain stores and rushing traffic. Between Central Station and the architectural masterpiece that is **Tyne Bridge** lingers the **Castle Keep.** The keep is all that is left of the **New Castle** built in 1080 by Robert Curthose, bastard son of William the Conqueror. *(Museums open Apr.-Sept. Tu-Su 9:30am-5:30pm; Oct.-Mar. daily 9:30am-4:30pm. £1.50, students, seniors, and children 50p.)* **Grey's Monument** imposes its 80 ft. structure in the center of town; it is occasionally open for climbing. The most elegant tower in Newcastle crowns the **Cathedral Church of St. Nicholas.** This set of small towers around a double arch, called "The Lantern," is meant to resemble Jesus' crown of thorns. *(Open M-F 7am-6pm, Sa 8am-4pm, Su 9am-noon and 4-7pm. Free.)* **Newcastle Discovery,** Blanford House, Blanford Sq. (tel. 232 6789), houses a science museum and displays on Newcastle's history. The often-interactive displays are child-friendly and indeed child-oriented: "You are Mathilda," reads a placard on a giant, Roman-era loom, "Most

---

I Looked over Geordie, and What Did I See?

What exactly is a Geordie (JOR-die)? Anyone born in Northumberland, Durham, or Tyne and Wear can claim Geordie status; but possessive as these sturdy Northerners are of their nickname, its origins are debatable. Try one of these:

1. During the Jacobite Rebellion of 1745, Newcastle's denizens supported George I, the reigning king, and were deemed "for George" by the Jacobites.
2. In 1815, George Stephenson invented the miner's lamp, which quickly gained favor among Northumberland miners. The lamp, and eventually the miners, became known as Geordies.
3. In 1826, good ol' George Stephenson spoke before the Parliamentary Commission of Railways, and his dialect amused the snooty Southrons, who began to call all keelmen carrying coal to the Thames "Geordies."

of your time is spent weaving." The **Laing Art Gallery,** New Bridge St. (tel. 232 7734), showcases an excellent collection of local art. *(Both open M-Sa 10am-5pm, Su 2-5pm. Free. Wheelchair accessible.)*

ENTERTAINMENT

Home of the nectar known as brown ale, Newcastle's pub and club scene is legendary throughout England. Nightlife is divided into two distinct areas: **Bigg Market,** a rowdy Geordie haven, and **Quayside** (KEY-side; Metro: Central Station), which is slightly more relaxed and attracts local students. Be cautious at Bigg Market—this is where stocky footballer Paul "Gazza" Gascoigne got beaten up *twice* for deserting Newcastle, and underdressed student-types are frowned upon. Most pubs offer happy hours from 4 to 8pm (Su 7-8pm). You're less likely to stand out if you dress up a bit, although northward-bound hikers may have to settle for slicking their hair back and hoping for the best. Milder pubs include **Blackie Boy** and **Macey's.** Down at the Quayside visit **The Red House,** 32 Sandhill, opposite the Guild hall, and **The Cooperage,** a 16th-century-style pub, on The Close as you walk past the swing bridge. Under the Tyne Bridge floats the **Tuxedo Royale** (tel. 477 8899). As if dancing on a boat weren't disorienting enough, one of this huge club's two dance floors actually rotates. The gay and lesbian crowd flocks to the corner of Waterloo and Sunderland St. in the southwest part of the city center, where you can find **The Village** (a pub), as well as **Powerhouse** (a nightclub). Finish the evening in true Newcastle style with a kebab (with extra chili sauce) at one of Newcastle's late-night eateries.

If you fancy entertainment on the more refined side, treat yourself to some Shakespeare or Tchaikovsky at the lush red, velvet, and gold **Theatre Royal,** 100 Grey St. (tel. 232 2061). *(Box office open M-Sa 10am-8pm. Tickets from £4; occasional discounts—call for details.)* The **Royal Shakespeare Company** makes a month-long stop in Newcastle around October. Call the tourist office for more information.

■ Northumberland

Northumberland is perched at the edge of the English frontier, forever battered by sea and, until recent times, by Scots. The region is ancient and rugged, freckled with forts from a passionate past. The 400 sq. mi. **Northumberland National Park** stretches south from the grassy Cheviot Hills near the Scottish border through the Simonside Hills to the dolomitic crags of Whin Sill, where it engulfs part of Hadrian's Wall. When Romans ruled, this line marked the northern limit of the empire; later, the Anglo-Saxon kingdom of Northumberland extended northward over the valleys and woodlands from the river Humber to the present-day Borders. No longer the site of hurled spears and clashing swords, the park today hosts an equally lively (and less deadly) array of activities, including rock climbing and horseback riding.

GETTING THERE AND GETTING ABOUT

If you don't have a car or bicycle, staying overnight in Berwick-upon-Tweed, with its train and bus service, is your best bet. From there buses depart to most coastal hotspots. If you plan to village-hop, obtain the essential 256-page tome *Northumberland Public Transport Guide* (£1), available at any tourist office or bus station, or by sending £1.75 to Public Transport Officer, County Hall, Morpeth, Northumberland NE61 2EF (tel. (0191) 212 3000; open M-F 8am-5:15pm, Sa 8:30am-3pm).

Trains (tel. (0345) 484950) run from **York** and **Newcastle** to Berwick (M-F and Su 13 per day, Sa 16 per day, £9; York 2hr., £28.40; Newcastle 1hr., £9.70). **Edinburgh** is 45 minutes north (M-F 23 per day, Sa 27 per day, Su 18 per day, £10.80). **Buses** are cheaper, if less comfortable. Bus #505 goes from **Newcastle** to Berwick via **Alnwick** (2hr., every 2hr.). From Alnwick, #501 leaves for Craster, going up the coast to Dunstanburgh Castle, Seahouses, and Bamburgh Castle (every 2hr.). Smart ramblers will invest in a **Northeast Explorer** ticket (£5, seniors and under 14 £3.85, families £10), good for unlimited one-day use on most local buses.

ENGLAND

As buses run more frequently up the coast than between national park towns and villages, **Newcastle, Alnwick,** and **Berwick** make the best bases for park exploration. On the park's border, **Rothbury** (southwest of Alnwick) and **Wooler** (northwest of Alnwick) enjoy the most frequent connections, halfway between "slightly accessible" and "left for dead" on Ye Olde Access Meter. Postbuses creep like snails on somewhat erratic schedules; contact a post office for schedules. You may find it easier to stick with the **Northumbria** line. Bus #464 connects **Wooler** and **Berwick** (3-4 per day); #470 and 473 connect **Wooler** to **Alnwick** (M-F 9 per day, Sa 4 per day), where buses connect for Newcastle. Bus #416 runs from Newcastle to Morpeth and Rothbury (M-Sa 8 per day, Su 2 per day). The main **National Park Information Centre** is in **Hexham,** at the south end of town (tel. (01434) 605225).

■ Berwick-upon-Tweed

Just south of the Scottish border is **Berwick-upon-Tweed** (BARE-ick), which has nationalized and denationalized more often than just about any town in Britain—14 times between 1100 and 1500 alone. Most of Berwick's castle is now buried beneath the present **railway station** (open M-Sa 6:30am-7:50pm, Su 10:15am-7:30pm), although the 13th-century Breakneck Stairs still absorb sun rays. For a sense of Berwick and its turbulent history on the border, walk along the **Elizabethan Walls,** which encircle the Old Town; the astounding view of Berwick and the River Tweed from **Meg's Mount** is even better now that the arrows have stopped flying. Berwick also makes a good base for exploration of the Scottish Borders; many of the fine houses and abbeys are a short bus ride away. Berwick is also the end of **St. Cuthbert's Way,** a long-distance hike that begins in Melrose (see p. 478).

The **Bus Information Shop** (tel. 307283) is at the uphill end of Marygate, providing timetables and selling National Express tickets (open M-F 9am-5pm, Sa 9am-4pm). Buses stop at either the train station or across from the bus shop; check the schedule to be sure. Berwick's **tourist office** (tel. 330733) is in the Maltings Art Theatre, on Eastern Ln.; it's sign-posted from Marygate, the main street. (Open July-Aug. M-W 10am-6pm, Th-Sa 10am-8pm, Su 10am-4pm; Apr.-June and Sept.-Oct. M-W 10am-6pm, Th-Sa 10am-8pm, Su 11am-3pm.) Rest up at **Mirando's Guest House,** 43 Church St. (tel. 306483). From the train station, walk into town on Castlegate; once you've passed the clock tower, turn left. It's two blocks ahead on the left (£15.50-16.50). Stock up at the **Coop,** 15 Marygate (tel. 302596; open M-Sa 9am-5:30pm).

Just off the coast—halfway between Bamburgh Castle and Berwick-upon-Tweed—lies romantically lonely and wind-swept **Holy Island.** Seven years after Northumberland's King Edwin converted, the missionary Aidan came here from the Scottish island of Iona to found England's first Christian monastery, **Lindisfarne Priory** (tel. (01289) 389200), the ruins of which still stand. *(Open daily Apr.-Oct. 10am-6pm; Nov.-Mar. 10am-4pm. £2.70, students and seniors £2, children £1.40.)* Check tide tables at a tourist office before you go. You can cross the 2¾ mi. causeway only at low tide; otherwise you'll have to swim (which would be dumb). Bus #477 runs from Berwick to Holy Island (tel. (0191) 212 3000; Feb.-Aug.; schedules vary day-to-day due to tides).

PARK ACCOMMODATIONS AND SIGHTS

Greenhead to Bellingham

The northernmost section of the Pennine Way penetrates the park at **Greenhead,** a meek village on Hadrian's Wall 25 mi. east of Carlisle and 40 mi. west of Newcastle, which possesses a **YHA Youth Hostel** (tel. (016977) 47401; see **Accommodations,** p. 339). The path winds 7 mi. east to **Once Brewed,** home of the **YHA Once Brewed** (tel. (01434) 344360; see **Accommodations,** p. 339). From there, the path continues 14 mi. northeast to **Bellingham** (BELL-in-um), due west of Morpeth. In town rests the **YHA Bellingham,** Woodburn Rd., Bellingham (tel. (01434) 220313; no smoking; £6.50, under 18 £4.45; open mid-July to Aug. daily; Mar. to mid-July and Sept.-Oct. M-Sa). The Bellingham **tourist office,** Fountain Cottage (tel. (01434) 220616), on Main

St., details nearby walks, including a 1 mi. stroll through a woodland ravine to the **Hareshaw Linn Waterfall.** (Office open Apr.-Oct. M-Sa 10am-1pm and 2-6pm, Su 1-5pm; Nov.-Mar. M-F 2-5pm.)

Kielder to Byrness

From Bellingham, bus #814 and post bus #815 run west to **Kielder** (30min., M-F 3-5 per day, Sa 2 per day), on the northern tip of **Kielder Water,** the largest man-made lake in Europe. **Water Cruises** (tel. (01434) 240436) depart from five docks on the lake. *(4 per day. July-Aug. 10am-6pm; Easter-June and Sept.-Oct. 10am-5pm. £4, seniors £3.20, children £2.45, families £11.50.)* Built in 1775 by the Earl Percy, Duke of Northumberland, **Kielder Castle** now houses the **Kielder Forest Visitor Centre** (tel. (01434) 250209) which glorifies the park's flora and fauna. *(Open Aug. daily 10am-6pm; Apr.-July and Sept.-Oct. daily 10am-5pm; Nov.-Dec. Sa-Su 11am-4pm.)* The **tourist office** (tel. (01434) 240398) at Tower Knowe, near the village of **Falstone** on the lake's south-eastern shore, knows all about the lay of the lake. (Open daily July-Aug. 10am-6pm; May-June and Sept.-Oct. 10am-5pm; Nov.-Apr. 10am-4pm.)

High hills to the east and dense forests to the west accompany the 15 mi. Pennine stretch from Bellingham northwest to **Byrness,** home to a **YHA Youth Hostel,** 7 Otterburn Green (tel. (01830) 520425), with a god-given drying room and a cafe and shop nearby. (£6.50, under 18 £4.45. Open July-Aug. daily; Apr.-June and Sept. W-M.) Bus #915 runs from **Bellingham** and **Byrness** (45min., M-F 2 per day). From Byrness, the Pennine finishes with an uneven, boggy 27 mi. through the Cheviots, bereft of hostels until it ends at **Kirk Yetholm,** Scotland (tel. (01573) 420631; see p. 479).

Wooler

At the northern boundary of the park, **Wooler,** miles from the Pennine Way and decent bus service, provides access to less strenuous daytrips into the **Cheviots,** especially around the Glendale and Kyloe areas. Barring possession of a cycle or car, serious hikers can speed to trailheads at Dunsdale, Mounthooly, and Hethpool—each over 8 mi. away—by taxi. Inquire at the tourist office about taxis. A wonder-warden runs the revamped **YHA Wooler,** 30 Cheviot St. (tel. (01668) 281365), with full wheelchair access, enviable bathrooms, and comfortable dormitories 300 yd. uphill from the bus station. (£8, under 18 £5.40. Open Apr.-Aug. daily; Sept.-Oct. M-Sa; Feb. to mid-Mar. and Nov. F-Sa.) Camp at **Highburn House** (tel. (01668) 281344; £3 per adult, 50p per child, £1.50 electricity; showers 20p.) The **tourist office,** 11 Market Pl. (tel. (01668) 282123), offers details on hilly climbs in the Cheviots and gentler, low-level walks through the Happy and College Valleys. (Open daily July-Aug. 10am-1pm and 2-6pm; Apr.-May and Sept. 10am-1pm and 2-5pm; Oct. 10am-1pm and 2-4pm.)

The nearest **National Park Visitor Centre** is 7 mi. south in **Ingram** (tel. (01665) 567248; open daily July-Aug. 10am-6pm; Apr.-June and Sept. 10am-5pm). A **Gold Leaf Travel bus** runs between Wooler and Ingram every 1½ hours. Twenty-five miles farther south of Wooler off the A697 on the B6341, the village of **Rothbury** sits in a densely wooded valley carved by the River Coquet. There's another **National Park Visitor Centre** (tel. (01669) 620887), networked with a **tourist office** on Church St. (open daily July-Aug. 10am-6pm; Apr.-June and Sept.-Oct. 10am-5pm).

COASTAL ACCOMMODATIONS AND SIGHTS

Twenty miles north of Newcastle (linked by bus #X18), the evocative ruins of the 12th-century **Warkworth Castle** (tel. (01665) 711423) guard the mouth of the River Coquet. Best viewed from the river, the magnificent 15th-century keep, foundation rubble, and largely intact curtain wall come to life in an excellent, self-guided audio tour. *(Tours £1.50, children 75p. Castle open daily Apr.-Oct. 10am-6pm; Nov.-Mar. 10am-1pm and 2-4pm. £2.20, students and seniors £2, children £1.40.)* Almost 200 years after the castle was built, Shakespeare set much of *Henry IV Part I* here; the 14th-century **hermitage** carved from the Coquet cliffs is the reputed site of Harry Hotspur's baptism. For the price of admission to the hermitage, the staff at the castle will row you there. *(Apr.-Sept. W and Su 11am-5pm. £1.50, students and seniors £1.10, children 80p.)*

ENGLAND

About 7 mi. northwest of Warkworth off the A1, the tiny town of **Alnwick** (AHN-ick) oozes charm beside the magnificently preserved **Alnwick Castle** (tel. (01665) 510777), another former Percy family stronghold. This rugged Norman fortification gives way to an ornate Italian Renaissance interior, with Titians, Van Dycks, and numerous likenesses of the Duke and Duchess of Northumberland. Over the years an eccentric series of duchesses swamped the castle with items such as Cromwell's nightcap and sash, a scrap of the bedsheet in which he died, King Charles II's night-cap, and, (man!) yet another cap made entirely of hair plucked from Mary, Queen of Scots. *(Open Easter-Sept. Sa-Th 11am-5pm, last admission 4:30pm. £6, students and seniors £5.45, children £3.50, families £15.)* Alnwick's well-supplied **tourist office,** 2 The Sham-bles Market Pl. (tel. 510665), rests at the town's vortex. (Open July-Aug. M-Sa 9am-6:30pm, Su 9am-5pm; Mar.-June and Sept.-Oct. M-Sa 9am-5pm and Su 10am-4pm.) Across from the **bus station office** (tel. 602182; open M-F 9am-5pm and Sa 9am-4pm) is a **launderette,** 5 Clayport St. (tel. 604398; open M-F 8am-7pm, Sa-Su 9am-5pm; bring change). Alnwick's **telephone code** is 01665.

Stay with Mrs. Givens and her affectionate mutt at **The Tea Pot,** 8 Bondgate With-out, and yes, that's a street name (tel. 604473). Mind the low door frames in the 300-year-old building (£16-18; £1 off if you mention *Let's Go*). Munch at the **Plough Hotel,** 20 Bondgate Without (tel. 602395; open M-Sa noon-2pm and 6-9:30pm, Su noon-3pm; game pie £5). Pick up food supplies at the large **Safeway** next to the bus station (open M-Th 8:30am-8pm, F-Sa 8am-8pm, Su 10am-4pm).

■ Carlisle

Ages ago, in the absence of urban planners, Carlisle became Britain's largest city, spreading over 398 sq. mi. Nicknamed "The Key of England," Carlisle has endured a turbulent history as a strategic point in the conflicts between England and Scotland. In addition to unofficial raids on Carlisle over the years, Robert the Bruce besieged the city in 1315 and Bonnie Prince Charlie captured it in 1745. Carlisle today best serves civilians as a base for visits to Hadrian's Wall.

GETTING THERE Carlisle is a hub for trains and buses throughout North England and Scotland. **Trains** (tel. (0345) 484950) depart from London's **Euston Station** for Carlisle (4½hr., M-Sa 12 per day, Su 9 per day, £58). From Carlisle, trains run to **New-castle** (1½hr., M-Sa 1 per hr., Su 9 per day, £7.80), **Leeds** (2¾hr., M-Sa 7 per day, Su 5 per day, £16.40), **Settle** (1½hr., M-Sa 6 per day, Su 5 per day, £12.10), **Glasgow** (2½hr., M-Sa 18 per day, Su 12 per day, £20.50), and **Edinburgh** (2hr., 1 per hr., £20.50). **National Express buses** (tel. (0990) 808080) leave London's **Victoria Sta-tion** three times daily (£17). **Cumberland** (tel. (01946) 63222) drives to **Keswick** in the Lake District (#555, 1¼hr., M-Sa 4 per day, Su 2 per day, £3.55; #104, connects with the #X5 at Penrith, M-Sa 13 per day, Su 8 per day, £3.55). Cumberland also offers **bus excursions** to the **Lake District, Northumberland, and Scotland.**

ORIENTATION AND PRACTICAL INFORMATION Carlisle's **train station** lies on Botchergate, diagonally across from the citadel (ticket office open M-Sa 5am-11:30pm, Su 9:15am-11:30pm). At the **bus station,** on the corner of Lowther and Lonsdale St., book **National Express** or local tickets (open M-Sa 8:30am-6:30pm, Su 10:45am-6:30pm). Cyclists should consider the **Cumbria Cycle Way,** which runs along the outskirts of the Lake District from Carlisle (see **Hiking, Biking, and Climb-ing,** p. 377). The closest **bike** rental to Carlisle dwells 10 mi. east of the city center—but still in the city!—in **Brampton.** Call the Brampton tourist office for more informa-tion (tel. (016977) 3433).

The **tourist office,** Old Town Hall, Green Market (tel. 625600; fax 625604), lies in the pedestrianized city center, formed by **English, Scotch,** and **Bank St.** From the train station, turn left and walk about three blocks—Botchergate becomes English St., which meets the office. From the bus station, cross Lowther St., walk through the shopping center, and look right. The museum-like tourist office offers day-long **lug-**

gage storage for 75p a bag. The office also reserves rooms, exchanges currency, and books **National Express** trips. The £3 Discovery Pass offers excellent discounts on sights. (Open July-Aug. M-Sa 9:30am-6pm, Su 10:30am-4pm; May-June and Sept. M-Sa 9:30am-5pm, Su 10:30am-4pm; Mar.-Apr. and Oct. M-Sa 9:30am-5pm; Nov.-Feb. M-Sa 10am-4pm.) **ATMs** are on English and Bank St. The **post office**, 20-34 Warwick Rd. (tel. 512410), has a bureau de change (open M-F 9am-5:30pm, Sa 9am-7pm). **Internet access** is available at Carlisle Library, 11 Globe Ln. (tel. 607310; £3 per 30min., £5 per hr.; open M-F 9:30am-7pm, Sa 9:30am-4pm). Carlisle's **postal code** is CA1 1AB; its **telephone code** is 01228.

ACCOMMODATIONS AND FOOD

Warwick Rd., running east out of the city, is the primary site for Carlisle's many B&Bs. **Cornerways Guest House,** 107 Warwick Rd. (tel. 521733), sports a graceful, sky-lit staircase and three floors of big rooms with TVs and profanely high ceilings (£13-14, with bath £16). Nearby **Calreena Guest House,** 123 Warwick Rd. (tel. 525020), supplies excellent breakfasts and crimson carpets (singles £16; doubles £28). The **Market Hall,** off Scotch St., built in 1889 to house Carlisle's market, offers fresh produce and other goods in a pastel fairground interior (open M-Sa 8am-5pm). **La Petite Française,** Scotch St. (tel. 599145), just outside the Market Hall, offers sandwiches on hot-from-the-oven baguettes for £1.40 (open M-F 10am-4:30pm, Sa 9am-3pm).

SIGHTS

Built in 1092 by William II with stones from Hadrian's Wall, **Carlisle Castle** (tel. 591922) stands at the northwest corner of the city. Mary, Queen of Scots was imprisoned here until Elizabeth I wanted her a wee bit farther from the border. Hundreds incarcerated after the 1745 Jacobite rebellion stayed alive by slurping water that collected in the narrow trenches carved into "licking stones." *(Open daily Apr.-Oct. 9:30am-6pm; Nov.-Mar. 10am-4pm. £2.90, students and seniors £2.20, children £1.50. Guided tours May-Oct. once daily; £1.20, children 70p.)*

Carlisle's **cathedral** (tel. 548151), founded in 1122, houses some fine 14th-century stained glass and the Brougham Triptych, a carved Flemish altarpiece, in a peculiarly reddish exterior. Sir Walter Scott married his French sweetheart on Christmas Eve, 1797, in what is now called the Border Regiment Chapel. *(Open M-Sa 7:30am-6:15pm, Su 7:30am-5pm. Suggested donation £2. Evensong during school year M-F 5:30pm.)*

■ Hadrian's Wall

In AD 122 when Roman Emperor Hadrian ordered his magnificent wall to be built, the official word was that he wanted to mark his boundaries, but everyone knows he was just scared of the barbarians (see **Celts, Romans, Angles, and Saxons,** p. 52). Over time, Hadrian's anxieties created a permanent monument to the Roman frontier—first a 27 ft. wide V-shaped ditch, then a stone barrier 15 ft. high and 8-9 ft. across. Eight years, 17 milecastles (forts), 5500 cavalrymen, and 13,000 infantrymen later, Hadrian's Wall stretched unbroken from modern-day Carlisle to Newcastle. Today, most of the wall is destroyed and the portions that remain stand at only half their original height. The highest concentration of remains scatter along the western part, at the southern edge of Northumberland National Park (see p. 369).

GETTING THERE AND GETTING ABOUT

The wall is best accessed by car; failing that, bus services are most convenient. **Stagecoach Cumberland** (tel. (01946) 63222) sends bus #682 (a.k.a. **The Hadrian's Wall Bus**) from English St. in **Carlisle** to **Hexham,** stopping at all the major sights on the wall (2hr., 4 per day). A day-long **Rover ticket,** available from tourist information centers or from the driver, costs about as much as a return ticket (£5, under 14 £3, families £10).

Trains (tel. (0345) 484950) run frequently between **Carlisle** and **Newcastle,** but stations all lie 1½ to 4 mi. from the wall, so be prepared to hike to the nearest stones. From **Carlisle,** trains stop at **Brampton,** 2 mi. from **Lanercost** and 5 mi. from **Birdoswald** (20min., M-Sa 6 per day, Su 5 per day, £1.90), and **Bardon Mill,** 2 mi. from **Vindolanda** and 4½ mi. from **Housesteads** (40min., M-Sa 6 per day, Su 5 per day,

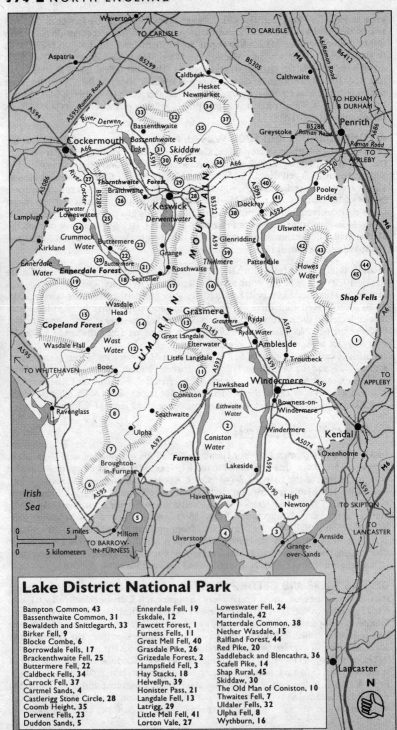

Lake District National Park

Bampton Common, 43
Bassenthwaite Common, 31
Bewaldeth and Snittlegarth, 33
Birker Fell, 9
Blocke Combe, 6
Borrowdale Fells, 17
Brackenthwaite Fell, 25
Buttermere Fell, 22
Caldbeck Fells, 34
Carrock Fell, 37
Cartmel Sands, 4
Castlerigg Stone Circle, 28
Coomb Height, 35
Derwent Fells, 23
Duddon Sands, 5

Ennerdale Fell, 19
Eskdale, 12
Fawcett Forest, 1
Furness Fells, 11
Great Mell Fell, 40
Grasdale Pike, 26
Grizedale Forest, 2
Hampsfield Fell, 3
Hay Stacks, 18
Helvellyn, 39
Honister Pass, 21
Langdale Fell, 13
Latrigg, 29
Little Mell Fell, 41
Lorton Vale, 27

Loweswater Fell, 24
Martindale, 42
Matterdale Common, 38
Nether Wasdale, 15
Ralfland Forest, 44
Red Pike, 20
Saddleback and Blencathra, 36
Scafell Pike, 14
Shap Rural, 45
Skiddaw, 30
The Old Man of Coniston, 10
Thwaites Fell, 7
Uldaler Fells, 32
Ulpha Fell, 8
Wythburn, 16

£3.50). Trains depart more frequently for **Haltwhistle**, 2 mi. from **Cawfields** (35min., M-Sa 12 per day, Su 7 per day, £3.10). Call **Northumberland Transport Enquiries** (tel. (01670) 533128) or **Cumbria Journey Planner** (tel. (01228) 606000) for help.

ACCOMMODATIONS Both **Carlisle** and **Hexham** make good bases for day journeys to the wall. The **Greenhead** and **Once Brewed Youth Hostels** lie close to the wall and surround seven well-preserved miles. The **Hadrian Lodge** (tel. (01434) 688688) is a convenient hostel for serious walkers; take a train to Hayden Bridge, then follow the main road uphill for 2½ mi. (dorms £8; singles £18.50; doubles £37; breakfast £3.50). See **Accommodations**, p. 339, for more details.

SIGHTS Pick up the free *Visitors' Guide to Hadrian's Wall* from the tourist information center. The most popular sight is Housesteads (tel. (01434) 344363), a fort with most of its foundations and some of its walls still intact. There is a good length of unbroken wall stretching west from Housesteads, offering good scenery and fewer crowds. Sheep ignore the "Please keep off the walls" signs. *(Housesteads open daily Apr.-Oct. 10am-6pm; Nov.-Mar. 10am-4pm. £2.70, students and seniors £2, under 16 £1.40.)*

The **Roman Army Museum** (tel. (016977) 47485) at **Carvoan**, a half mile north of Greenhead hostel, stockpiles artifacts and interactive stations. *(Open daily July-Aug. 10am-6:30pm; May-June 10am-6pm; Apr. and Sept. 10am-5:30pm; Mar. and Oct. 10am-5pm; late Feb. and early Nov. 10am-4pm. £2.80, students and seniors £2.40, children £1.90. Wheelchair accessible.)* Several well-preserved milecastles and bridges lie between Greenhead and **Birdoswald Roman Fort** (tel. (016977) 47602). The fort, 15 mi. east of Carlisle, is the site of recent excavations. *(Open mid-Mar. to Nov. daily 10am-5:30pm. Museum and walls £2.50, students and seniors £1.50, children £1; ruins only "honesty box" £1, children 50p.)*

Seven miles east of the Army Museum lies **Vindolanda** (tel. (01434) 344277), a fort and civilian settlement which predates the wall. Extensive excavations have revealed hundreds of inscribed wooden tablets that give insight into Roman life. Examples include "I have sent you socks and two pairs of underpants" and "June 24th AD 100: Wine 15 liters, Celtic beer 25 liters, Fish sauce ½ liter, Pork fat 8 liters." *(Open daily July-Aug. 10am-6:30pm; May-June 10am-6pm; Apr. and Sept. 10am-5:30pm; Mar. and Oct. 10am-5pm; late Feb. and early Nov. 10am-4pm.)* **Supersaver tickets** are good for admission to Vindolanda and the Roman Army Museum. *(£5.25, students and seniors £4.30, children £3.65, families £17.50.)*

■ Lake District National Park

Although rugged hills make up much of England's landscape, only in the northwest do sparkling waterholes fill the spaces in between. Dramatic peaks tower above small flower-filled towns; water wends its merry way in every direction, from glistening hillside waterfalls to gurgling peat-filled rivers and into the tranquil, stately lakes. The jagged peaks and windswept fells are often isolated; the shores are packed. The major lakes diverge like spokes of a wheel from Wordsworth's village of **Grasmere,** south of Keswick and north of Ambleside on the A591. **Lake Derwentwater** is perhaps the most beautiful of the lakes; **Wastwater** is the most bewitchingly wild; **Windermere** remains supremely popular, if partially bludgeoned by condos and marinas.

Windermere, Ambleside, Grasmere, and **Keswick** all make convenient bases for touring the Lake District. To enjoy the best of the region, though, ascend into the hills and wander through smaller towns, especially those in the more remote north and west. The farther west you go from the busy bus route along the A591, the more countryside you'll have to yourself. In summer, hikers, bikers, and boaters almost equal sheep and cattle in number. The ratio is particularly disastrous in July and August, when tour buses spew their contents onto the lakeshores.

GETTING THERE

Trains (tel. (0345) 484950) run to **Oxenholme** from London's **Euston Station** (4-5hr., M-Sa 16 per day, Su 11 per day, £50), **Manchester** (3hr., M-Sa 15 per day, Su 5 per day, £14.20), and **Edinburgh** (2½-3hr., M-Sa 6 per day, Su 5 per day, £26.50). Two

ENGLAND

rail lines flank the park: the **Preston-Lancaster-Carlisle** line (trains connect with **Leeds** at Lancaster) runs south to north along the eastern edge of the park, while the **Barrow-Carlisle** line serves the western coast. If your first destination is the remote western or southern area, hiking from one of the stations along the Barrow-Carlisle line might be your best bet. Otherwise, catch the Preston-Carlisle line to either **Oxenholme** or **Penrith.** From Oxenholme, a short branch line covers the 10 mi. to **Windermere** (20min., 1 per hr., £2.65).

Twice daily, **National Express** (tel. (0990) 505050) arrives at Windermere from **Manchester** (4hr., £13), **Birmingham** (5½hr., £21), and **London** (8hr., £21). Contact the Windermere tourist office (tel. (015394) 46499) for more info. The **Slow Coach** also stops in the Lake District on its circuit of England (consult **By Bus and Coach,** p. 33). **Stagecoach Cumberland** "Lakeslink" shuttles frequently between Lancaster and **Carlisle,** stopping at many points within the Lake District; #555 travels the area from Kendal to Keswick most often, stopping at Windermere (30min.), Ambleside (45min.), and Grasmere (to Keswick 1½hr., M-Sa 12 per day, Su 5 per day).

GETTING ABOUT

Stagecoach Cumberland buses (tel. (01946) 63222) serve over 25 towns and villages. The essential *Lakeland Explorer* magazine presents wonderful up-to-date timetables, maps, and walking routes and is free from tourist offices. For wider-ranging transport, consult *Getting Around Cumbria and the Lake District* (free from tourist offices). An **Explorer** ticket offers unlimited all-day travel on all area Stagecoach buses. (Exceptional value at £5.50, seniors and children £4, families £12; 4-day pass £13.60, seniors and children £9.50; passport photo required for 4-day pass.) The YHA offers a convenient **minibus service** (tel. (015394) 32304) between hostels. For £2 you can travel between any of the following hostels: Windermere, Ambleside, Hawkshead, Coniston Holly How, Elterwater, Langdale, and both Grasmere hostels (1 per day; get a schedule from a hostel). Or send your backpack ahead so you can enjoy the inter-hostel walk burden-free. The minibus also offers free transport from every train at Windermere station to the Windermere and Ambleside hostels.

Two trains make scenic trips through the Lakes. The **Lakeside and Haverthwaite Railway** (tel. (015395) 31594) steam locomotive travels through the scenic River Leven Valley (18min., Apr.-Oct. 6-7 per day, return £3.40, children £1.70). The trip runs between Lakeside, which connects from the southwest shore of Lake Windermere to Bowness Pier, and Haverthwaite via Newby Bridge. The **Ravenglass and Eskdale Railway** (tel. (01229) 717171) is England's oldest and narrowest (15in.) narrow-gauge railway, affectionately known as "La'al Ratty." (Mar.-Nov. 2-15 per day, return £6.30, children £3.30, families £14.90; disabled travelers should call ahead.) La'al Ratty meets British Rail's Barrow-Carlisle line, but is primarily for sightseeing.

For those who wish to explore the park with minimal effort, **Mountain Goat** (tel. (015394) 45161), located downhill from the tourist office in Windermere, does the climbing for you in a series of friendly, off-the-beaten-track, themed minibus and bus tours, including "Literary" and "Goat and Boat" (£13-23). **Lakes Supertours,** 1 High St., Windermere (tel. (015394) 42751; fax 46026), offers similar half- and full-day minibus tours, as does **Falcon Budget Tours,** 1 High St., Windermere (tel. (015394) 88133; free pickup in Bowness-Ambleside area). Prices range £10-14.50 per half-day, £18.50-23 per full day; call for more information.

PRACTICAL INFORMATION

For an introduction to the Lake District, including exhibits, talks, films, and special events, visit the beautifully landscaped grounds and newly renovated house of the **National Park Visitor Centre** (tel. (015394) 46601) in **Brockhole,** halfway between Windermere and Ambleside (open Apr.-Nov. 10am-5pm). Most buses will drop you off at the site. The following **National Park Information Centres** dispense free information on the camping-barn network, sell a camping guide (£1), and book accommodations (10% deposit; non-local services additional £2.80). They also supply free town maps, as well as the thrilling *Enjoy the Fells in Safety*. *Lake District Holidays '99* lists accommodations, sights, and entertainment; pick up the quarterly newspaper *Park Life* for regional headlines (both free). Veggie-lovers can collect the *Viva! Vegetarian and Vegan Guide to the Lake District* (75p).

Ambleside (Waterhead): (tel. (015394) 32729; fax 33592). Walk south on Lake or Borrans Rd. from town to reach Waterhead Pier. Open mid-July to Aug. daily 9:30am-6pm; Easter to mid-July and Sept.-Oct. daily 9:30am-5:30pm; Nov.-Easter F-Su 10am-3:30pm.

Bowness Bay: Glebe Rd. LA23 3HJ (tel. (015394) 42895). Open July-Aug. M-Th 9:30am-6pm, F-Su 9:30am-6:30pm; Apr.-June and Sept.-Oct. daily 9am-5:30pm; Nov.-Mar. 10am-4:30pm.

Coniston: Ruskin Ave. LA12 8DU (tel. (015394) 41533), behind the bus stop at Tilberthwaite Ave. Open Easter to early Nov. daily 9:30am-5:30pm; early Nov. to Easter F-Su 10am-3:30pm.

Grasmere: Red Bank Rd. LA22 9SW (tel. (015394) 35057). Open Easter-Oct. daily 9:30am-5:30pm; Nov.-Easter F-Su 9:30am-4pm.

Hawkshead: Main Car Park LA22 0NT (tel. (015394) 36525). Open mid-July to Aug. daily 9:30am-6pm; Easter to mid-July and Sept.-Oct. daily 9:30am-5:30pm; Nov.-Easter F-Su 10am-3:30pm.

Keswick: Moot Hall, Market Sq. CA12 5JR (tel. (017687) 72645). Open July-Aug. daily 9:30am-6pm; Sept.-June 9:30am-5pm.

Pooley Bridge: The Square CA10 2NP (tel. (017684) 86530). Open Easter-Oct. daily 10am-5pm.

Seatoller Barn: Borrowdale CA12 5XN (tel. (017687) 77294), at the foot of Honister Pass. Open Easter-Oct. daily 10am-5pm.

Ullswater: Main Car Park, Glenridding, Penrith CA11 0PA (tel. (017684) 82414), on the main road through town. Open Apr.-Oct. daily 9am-6pm; Nov.-Mar. F-Su 10:30am-4pm.

HIKING, BIKING, AND CLIMBING

Outdoor enthusiasts outnumber water molecules in the Lake District. Information centers have guidebooks for all occasions—mountain bike trails, pleasant family walks, tough climbs, and hikes ending at pubs. Among the many available pamphlets is *Countryside Access for People with Limited Mobility* (70p). Hostels are also an excellent source of information, with large maps and posters on the walls and free advice from experienced staff.

If you plan to go on a long or difficult outing, check first with the Park Service, call **weather information** (24hr. tel. (017687) 75757; YHAs also post daily forecasts), and leave a route plan with your B&B proprietor or hostel warden before setting out. Steep slopes and reliably unreliable weather can quickly reduce visibility to 5 ft. A good map, compass, and the ability to use them are necessities. The Ordnance Survey Outdoor Leisure Maps 4, 5, 6, and 7 provide good detail of the four quadrants of the Lake District (£7). A public right-of-way does not always mean a path, and vice versa.

Any cyclist planning an extensive stay in the Lake District should consider investing in the gripping *Ordnance Survey Cycle Tours* (£10), which provides detailed maps of on- and off-trail routes. A selection of cycleshops is listed alphabetically by town below, but any tourist office will provide listings. Consider touring some of Cumbria's less-traveled areas via the circular **Cumbria Cycle Way**. The 259 mi. route runs from Carlisle in the north around the outskirts of the Lake District. Pick up *The Cumbria Cycle Way* (£6) from the tourist offices for detailed information.

Ambleside: Ghyllside Cycles, The Slack, (tel. (015394) 33592). £12.50 per day, about £60 per week; ID deposit; return by 5pm. Discounts for rentals longer than 3 days if you smile. Open Apr.-Oct. daily 9am-5:30pm; Nov.-Apr. F-W 9am-5:30pm.

Coniston: Summitreks, 14 Yewdale Rd. (tel. (015394) 41212). £10 per half-day, £13 per day; deposit £20. Open May-Oct. daily 9am-5:30pm; Nov.-Apr. F-W 9am-5pm.

ENGLAND

Grizedale: Grizedale Mountain Bike Hire Centre, Old Hall Carpark (tel. (01229) 860369), at the Forest Park Centre. Call ahead. £3 per hr., £9 per half-day, £14 per day. Open Feb.-Oct. daily 9am-5pm.

Keswick: Keswick Mountain Bikes, Southey Hill Industrial Estate (tel. (017687) 75202). £13 per day, £10 per half-day. Open daily 9am-5:30pm.

Windermere: Country Lanes Cycle Hire, (tel. (015394) 44544), at the train station. Nice new bikes £9 per half-day, £14 per day; £2 off if you traveled there by train (show train ticket). Open Easter-Oct. daily 9am-5:30pm.

Every town has stores that can describe the best climbs, advise on the necessary precautions, and give current weather reports; a few establishments also rent boots and backpacks. In Ambleside, **The Climber's Shop** (tel. (015394) 32297), on the corner of Rydal and Compston Rd., rents boots (£2 per day, £10 per week; deposit £20; open daily 9am-5:30pm). **Stuart's Sports,** 32 Lake Rd. (tel. (015394) 43001), between North and South Terr., awaits in Bowness (open daily mid-July to Aug. 9am-9pm; Sept. to mid-July 9am-5:30pm). Try **Keswick Mountain Sports,** 73 Main St. (tel. (017687) 73843), for boots (£5 per day, £10 per week; open daily 9am-5:30pm). In Grasmere, try **Outdoor World,** Red Lion Sq. (tel. (015394) 35614; open Easter-Oct. M-Sa 9am-6pm, Su 9:30am-5:30pm; Nov.-Easter M-Sa 9am-5:30pm, Su 9:30am-5pm).

ACCOMMODATIONS AND CAMPING

Despite the fact that **B&Bs** line every street in every town (£13-18) and that the Lakes have the highest concentration of youth hostels in the world, lodgings in the Lake District do fill up in July and August; book far ahead. Tourist offices and National Park Centres will book local rooms for a 10% deposit. **Campers** should pick up the National Park Authority's *Caravan and Tent Guide* (£1) and the YHA's *Camping Barns in England* (free), and call ahead to reserve space at **camping barns** (tel. (017687) 72645). The following **YHA Youth Hostels** provide accommodations in the park. Reception is usually closed 10am-5pm, but public areas and restrooms are usually accessible through the day. All serve meals (breakfast £3, dinner £4.40, packed lunch varies), except Skiddow House. Use the YHA **minibus** to get between the bigger hostels (see **Getting Around**). Ambleside Hostel provides a free Lake District-wide booking service (tel. (015394) 31117); you can find out which places have beds left (open daily 9am-6pm; requires credit card to reserve a bed).

Ambleside: Waterhead, Ambleside LA22 0EU (tel. (015394) 32304; fax 34408), 1mi. south of Ambleside on Windermere Rd. (the A591), 3mi. north of Windermere on the Lake's shores. Bus #555 and the Slow Coach stop in front. The mother of all hostels. 245 beds in a superbly refurbished old hotel. Distinctive country club feel—you can even swim off the pier. All the luxuries—lovely lake views, stupendous common rooms, glass-walled cafeteria. Books tours, rents mountain bikes, and operates the YHA shuttle. £10.70, under 18 £7.30. Open year-round.

Arnside: Oakfield Lodge, Redhills Rd., Arnside, Carnforth LA5 0AT (tel. (01524) 761781; fax 762589), 1mi. south of Arnside on the region's southern tip. 72-bed stone house above Kent estuary. £8.50, under 18 £6. Laundry facilities. Open Apr.-Oct. daily; Feb.-Mar. M-Sa; Nov. F-Sa.

Black Sail: Black Sail Hut, Ennerdale, Cleator CA23 3AY (no phone). Splendidly set in the hills between Grasmere and the coast. Take CMS bus #79 from Keswick to Seatoller and walk 3½mi. from there. 18 beds. Chilly outdoor showers. No smoking, car access, or electricity. £6.50, under 18 £4.45. Open July-Aug. daily; June and Sept.-Oct. Tu-Su; Apr.-May Tu-Sa.

Borrowdale: Longthwaite, Borrowdale, Keswick CA12 5XE (tel. (017687) 77257; fax 77393). Cedar-timbered dwelling on the River Derwent's shores. 1mi. south of Rothswaite village. Bus #79 from Keswick drops you nearby. 94 beds. £8.80, under 18 £6. Open mid-Feb. to Dec. daily.

Buttermere: King George VI Memorial Hostel, Buttermere, Cockermouth CA13 9XA (tel. (017687) 70245; fax 70231). Overlooking Lake Buttermere, ¼mi. south of the village on the B5289. 71 beds. £8.80, under 18 £6. Open Apr.-Sept. daily; Oct. Tu-Su; Jan.-Mar. Tu-Sa.

Carrock Fell: High Row Cottage, Haltcliffe, Hesket Newmarket, Wigton CA7 8JT (tel./fax (016974) 78325). Between Caldbeck and Mosedale in the northern area of the park. 20-bed farmhouse with fireplace affords views of the Carrock Fell. £7.20, under 18 £5. Open July-Aug. daily; Apr.-June and Sept.-Oct. W-Su.

Cockermouth: Double Mills, Cockermouth CA13 0DS (tel./fax (01900) 822561), in the town center off Fern Bank at Parkside Ave. Converted 17th-century water mill. 28 beds. £7.20, under 18 £5. Open July-Aug. daily; Apr.-June and Sept.-Oct. Th-M.

Coniston (Holly How): Far End LA21 8DD (tel. (015394) 41323; fax 41261), just north of Coniston village at the junction of Hawkshead and Ambleside Rd. A modernized country house with rickety beds and a dank common room. 70 beds. £8, under 18 £5.40. Curfew 11pm. Open Apr. and July-Sept. daily; May-June and Oct.-Nov. and mid-Jan. to Mar. F-Su.

Coniston Coppermines: Coppermines House LA21 8HP (tel. (015394) 41261), northwest along the Churchbeck River, 1¼mi. from Coniston. No need to venture into the hills; the rugged journey to the mines is itself a scenic challenge. 28-bed hostel overlooking the water. £7.20, under 18 £5. Open June-Aug. M-Sa; Apr.-May and Sept.-Oct. Tu-Sa

Derwentwater: Barrow House, Borrowdale, Keswick CA12 5UR (tel. (017687) 77246; fax 77396), 2mi. south of Keswick on the B5289. Take Borrowdale bus #79 to Seatoller (1 per hr.), or take the Keswick-bound ferry to arrive by boat. It's worth the inconvenience to stay in this 89-bed, 200-year-old house with a splendid view of Derwentwater, extensive grounds and trails, home-cooked meals, and its own 108ft. waterfall. £9.75, under 18 £6.55. Open Jan.-Oct. daily.

Elterwater: Ambleside LA22 9HX (tel. (015394) 37245), 1mi. west of High Close near lots o' falls and fells. CMS bus #516 from Ambleside passes about 1mi. from the 46-bed hostel. £8, under 18 £5.40. Open Apr.-Sept. daily; Oct. Tu-Su; Nov. to mid-Dec. Tu-Sa; mid-Feb. to Mar. F-Sa.

Ennerdale: Cat Crag, Ennerdale, Cleator CA23 3AX (tel. (01946) 861237), 1¼mi. west of Ennerdale. Difficult to reach—May-Oct. take bus #77 from Keswick to Buttermere and hike 3mi.; otherwise, hike 7mi. from Seatoller (bus #79 from Keswick). 24 beds, no electricity. £6.50, under 18 £4.45. Open July-Aug. daily; Apr.-June and Sept.-Oct. Th-M.

Eskdale: Boot, Holmrook CA19 1TH (tel. (019467) 23219; fax 23163). In a quiet valley 1½mi. east of Boot on the Ravenglass-Eskdale railway. Pool and ping-pong tables. 54 beds. £8.80, under 18 £6. Laundry, kitchen, showers. Open July-Aug. daily; Apr.-June M-Sa; mid-Feb. to Mar. and Sept. to mid-Dec. Tu-Sa.

Grasmere: Butterlip How, Ambleside LA22 9QG (tel. (015394) 35316; fax 35798). 96-bed Victorian house north of Grasmere village; follow road to Easedale 150yd. and turn right down sign-posted drive. £8.80, under 18 £6. Open Apr.-Oct. daily; Jan.-Mar. Tu-Su.

Grasmere: Thorney How, Ambleside LA22 9QW (tel. (015394) 35591; fax 35866). Follow Easedale Rd. ½mi. and turn right at the fork; hostel is ¼mi. down on the left. 48-bed farmhouse with a kindly staff. £8.80, under 18 £6. Open Apr.-Sept. daily; mid-Feb. to Mar. and Oct.-Dec. Th-M.

Hawkshead: Esthwaite Lodge, Ambleside LA22 0QD (tel. (015394) 36293; fax 36720). Bus #505 from Ambleside drops off at Hawkshead, 1mi. north. Overlooking Lake Esthwaite, this was the home of novelist Francis Brett Young; his library makes good bedtime reading. 115 beds. £9.75, under 18 £6.55. Open Apr.-Oct. daily; mid-Feb. to Mar. Tu-Sa; Nov. to mid-Dec. F-Sa.

Helvellyn: Greenside, Glenridding, Penrith CA11 0QR (tel./fax (017684) 82269). A mere 1½mi. from Glenridding village, 3mi. from Ullswater Lake. Bus #555 from Keswick and Windermere will stop at Glenridding. 64 beds. £8, under 18 £5.40. Open July-Aug. daily; Apr.-June M-Sa; Sept.-Oct. W-Su; Jan.-Mar. F-Sa.

High Close: Langdale, Loughrigg, Ambleside LA22 9HJ (tel. (015394) 37313; fax 37101), 4mi. north of Loughrigg. Semi-accessible by bus #516 from Ambleside; go ¾mi. south of Elterwater; the hostel is another ¾mi. to the west. 96-bed Victorian mansion is comfortable and seldom full. Pool table, ping-pong. £8.80, under 18 £6. Open Apr.-Oct. daily; mid-Feb. to Mar. M-Sa; mid-Jan. to mid-Feb. F-Sa.

Honister Hause: Seatoller, Keswick CA12 5XN (tel. (017687) 77267). A grey building at the summit of imposing **Honister Pass,** 9mi. north of Keswick. May-Oct. bus #77 takes you there from Keswick; #79 stops within 1½mi. 30 beds. £6.50, under 18 £4.45. Open June-Aug. daily; Apr.-May and Sept.-Oct. F-Tu.

Kendal: 118 Highgate, Kendal LA9 4HE (tel. (01539) 724006), in town, convenient to both the bus and train stations on Highgate St. near Gillingate. £8.80, under 18 £6. Open Apr.-Aug. daily; mid-Feb. to Mar. and Sept. to mid-Dec. Tu-Sa.

Keswick: Station Rd., Keswick CA12 5LH (tel. (017687) 72484; fax 74129). From the tourist office, bear left down Station Rd.; look for the YHA sign on the left. 91 beds in a former hotel with balconies over a river, spanking new rooms, and a decent kitchen. 6 showers, laundry facilities, TV, and game room. £9.75, under 18 £6.55. Curfew 11:30pm. Open daily mid-Feb. to late Dec.

Patterdale: Goldrill House, Patterdale, Penrith CA11 0NW (tel. (017684) 82394; fax 82034), 1mi. south of Ullswater and off the A592, ¼mi. south of the village. 82 beds. £9.40, under 18 £6.30. Open Apr.-Aug. daily; Sept.-Oct. F-W; mid-Feb. to Mar. and Nov. to mid-Dec. F-Tu.

Skiddaw House: Bassenthwaite, Keswick CA12 4QX (call Carrock Fell hostel at (016974) 78325). A pair of shepherd's cottages 1550ft. above sea level, the highest hostel in the U.K. Basic and isolated. No one loony enough to trek this far will be turned away. No car access—4½mi. from Threlkeld and 5mi. from Bassenthwaite on foot. £5.85, under 18 £4. Self-catering only. Open Apr.-Oct. daily.

Tebay: The Old School, Penrith CA10 3TP (tel./fax (015396) 24286), in Tebay village on the A685. No kitchen in this 46-bed former schoolhouse, but they've got a dryer. No smoking. £8, under 18 £5.40. Open mid-June to mid-Sept. F-W; Feb. to mid-June and mid-Sept. to Nov. Tu-W and F-Su.

Thirlmere: The Old School, Stanah Cross, Keswick CA12 4TQ (tel. (017687) 73224), 5mi. south of Keswick off the A591 in the hamlet of Legburthwaite. Bus #555 drives by. 33 beds. No central heating for those who like to chill. No smoking. £5.85, under 18 £4. Meals must be ordered in advance. Open July-Aug. Tu-Su; Apr. to June and Sept.-Oct. W-Su.

Wastwater: Wasdale Hall, Wasdale, Seascale CA20 1ET (tel. (019467) 26222; fax 26056), ½mi. east of Nether Wasdale. 50-bed house on the water. Climber's paradise. Bus #6 from Whitehaven to Seascale stops 5mi. away in Gosforth. £8.80, under 18 £6. Open Apr.-Aug. daily; mid-Jan. to Mar. and Sept.-Oct. Th-M.

Windermere: High Cross, Bridge Ln., Troutbeck, Windermere LA23 1LA (tel. (015394) 43543; fax 47165), 1mi. north of Windermere off the A591. Ambleside bus stops in Troutbeck Bridge; walk ¾mi. uphill to hostel, or catch the YHA shuttle from the train station. Spacious, 73-bed house with lovely grounds and panoramic views, but few showers. £8.80, under 18 £6. Open mid-Feb. to Dec. daily.

■ Windermere and Bowness

Windermere and Bowness (pop. 8500) fill to the gills with vacationers in July and August when sailboats, rowboats, and water-skiers swarm over Lake Windermere. Stay only long enough to find transportation to a more remote spot. The only major destination in the towns is **Bowness Pier,** overpopulated with people and belligerent swans (1½mi. to the south). The downhill walk from Windermere's station is easy; turn left onto High St., then right on Main St.; walk through downtown to New Rd., which becomes Lake Rd., leading pierward. Or catch **Lakeland Experience** bus #599 to Bowness from the rail station (3 per hr.). For quieter strolls, grab a local walk map from the tourist office (20-30p).

PRACTICAL INFORMATION Windermere's **train station** (tel. (01539) 720397) also serves as the town's primary **bus depot.** For information and advice, visit the **Windermere tourist office** (tel. 46499), next door to the rail station (open daily Easter-Oct. 9am-6pm; Nov.-Easter 9am-5pm; disabled access), or the **National Park Information Centre** beside Bowness Pier (see **Practical Information,** p. 376). The Windermere office stocks a guide to lake walks (25-30p), books **National Express** buses, and exchanges currency (£2.50 commission). Fast funds flow from **ATMs** in Windermere and Bowness—stock up before departing for a more rustic town. Try Windermere's

Midland Bank, on the west side of Crescent Rd. between Beech and Birch St.; in Bowness, head to **Barclays,** at the top of town opposite the tourist office. Let your socks regain their pre-manure luster at **Windermere Laundry,** 19 Main Rd. (tel. 42326; open M-F 9am-6pm, Sa 9am-5pm; change and soap available). Windermere's **post office** (tel. 43245) resides at 21 Crescent Rd. (open M-F 9am-5:30pm, Sa 9am-12:30pm). The **telephone code** for both towns is 015394.

ACCOMMODATIONS Bowness has more **B&Bs** than the hills have sheep. Nevertheless, those who neglect to book ahead (singles especially!) risk joining the livestock in cold, lonely fields amid cowpies and wool tufts. Stay at the social **Lake District Backpackers Hostel** (tel. 46374), on High St., a 2-minute walk from the train station. Look for the sign on the right as you descend the hill (£9.50; reception 9am-1pm and 5-9pm; free pickup from train station available). **Brendan Chase,** 1-3 College Rd. (tel. 45638), offers attractive rooms in two converted Victorian townhouses with an efficient, lively proprietress. Sinks in the rooms and sewing kits in the halls promise a pleasant stay (£10, with breakfast £12.50-15). Other fine B&Bs include **The Haven,** 10 Birch St. (tel. 44017; £16-17.50), **Dalecote,** 13 Upper Oak St. (tel. 45121; £13.50-16.50), and **Greenriggs,** 8 Upper Oak St. (tel. 42265; singles £16-18; doubles £36-50). The nearest **campground, Limefitt Park** (tel. 32300), lies 4½ mi. north of Bowness on the A592 just below the Kirkstone path, and has the necessary amenities, except for public transport (£3 per person; 2-person tent and car £12).

FOOD All groceries great and small can easily be found in the area. **Booths Supermarket** (tel. 46114) is housed in Windermere's "The Old Station" at the end of Cross St., by the new train station (open M-W 9am-6pm, Th 9am-7pm, F 9am-8pm, Sa 8:30am-6pm, Su 10am-4pm). **The Village Store** (tel. 44105), on the west side of Crag Brow just north of Helm Rd., offers the best selection of goods in Bowness (open M-Sa 8am-9pm, Su 9am-6pm), but its competition across the street, **Booker's** (tel. 88798), is more interesting, with a selection fit for a Bacchanalian revel—bountiful fresh fruit and loads of liquor (open daily 8am-10pm). In Windermere, pink decor brightens the simple offerings at espresso-sized **Coffee Pot,** 15 Main Rd. (tel. 88738), where your hosts put inventive sandwiches in a pita or potato pocket for £1.75-2.60 (open M-W and F-Sa 10am-5:30pm, Su 1-5pm). Try the **Hedgerow Teashop** (tel. 45002), on Lake Rd. above Cumbria Books, which feels like the rustic cottage of a rich lord—teas (75p) and ploughman's lunch (£4; open W-M 10:30am-5pm).

SIGHTS A number of boating companies offer their services at Bowness Pier. **Windermere Lake Cruises** runs its own **Lake Information Centre** (tel. 43360 or (015395) 31188) at the north end of the pier that vends maps and accommodation guides, and rents rowboats or motorboats. The center also books passage on two popular cruises. From Easter to October, boats sail north to Waterhead Pier in Ambleside (*30min., about 2 per hr. 9am-6pm; return £5.50, ages 5-15 £2.75*) and south to Lakeside (*40min., 1 per hr. 9am-5pm; return £5.70, ages 5-15 £2.85*). All-day passes are available. (*£9, children £4.50.*)

In town, **The World of Beatrix Potter** (tel. 88444), in the Old Laundry Theatre complex, Crag Bow, solicits with fresh scents and smarmy-cutesy displays. Unless you are five, feel as if you're five, or are inextricably bound to a five-year-old, explore other sights in the Lakes. (*£3, children £2. Open daily Easter-Sept. 10am-5:30pm; Oct.-Easter 10am-4:30pm.*) The accompanying **Tailor of Gloucester Tea Room,** however, serves yummy rabbit (oops! rarebit £2.50-2.75).

■ Ambleside

Just under a mile north of Lake Windermere, Ambleside has adapted to the tourist influx without selling its soul to the industry. Oft-times dubbed "anorak capital of England" in recognition of the numerous outdoors stores (14 at last count), Ambleside is geared towards helping you enjoy the Lake District (with some wicked bargains) rather than milking your last pound for a rustic hat.

PRACTICAL INFORMATION Buses (tel. 32231) stop on Kelsick Rd. (open M-W and F 10am-7pm, Sa 10am-6pm). **Lakeslink** bus #555 runs to Grasmere, Windermere, and Keswick (1 per hr.). Buses #505 and 506 join Hawkshead and Coniston (M-Sa 10 per day, Su 3 per day). The **tourist office** (tel. 32582) sits on Church St. (open Easter-Oct. daily 9am-5pm; Nov.-Easter Tu-Th 10am-1pm and 2-5pm, F-Sa 9am-1pm and 2-5pm). The **National Park Information Centre** at Waterhead offers both advice and **currency exchange.** (£3 per transaction. Open daily mid-July to Aug. 9:30am-6pm; Easter to mid.-July and Sept.-Oct. 9:30am-5:30pm.) **Barclays,** on Market Pl., has an **ATM** (bank open M-W and F 9:30am-4:30pm, Th 10am-4:30pm). The **launderette** winks at the bus station across the street on Kelsick Rd. The **post office,** Market Pl. (tel. 32267), can **exchange money** for £2.50. (Open July-Sept. M-F 9am-5:30pm, Sa 9am-12:30pm; Oct.-June M-Tu and Th-F 9am-12:30pm, W 1:30-5:30pm, Sa 9am-12:30pm.) Ambleside's **postal code** is LA22 9AA, the **telephone code** 015394.

ACCOMMODATIONS There are almost as many **B&Bs** and guesthouses here as private residences. Most B&Bs cost £14.50-16 and fill up quickly in summer; call ahead in July and August, or at least arrive early in the day to hunt down a room. Some B&Bs cluster on Church St. and Compston Rd.; others line the busier Lake Rd. leading in from Windermere. Ambleside's **YHA** resides near the steamer pier, a pleasant 1 mi. walk from the town center (see **Accommodations and Camping,** p. 378). Closer to town, the **YWCA,** Iving Cottage, Old Lake Rd. (tel. 32304), is open to both women and men. Though they cater predominantly to school groups, the wardens take the bunks down in July and August to create a B&B. (Closed for school groups Easter to early July—call ahead. £13.50, discount after 2 nights.) **Shirland, Linda's B&B** (tel. 32999), on Compston Rd., has four rooms (doubles, triples, and quads) with TV, cramped attic space for three, and a private, hostel-style bunkhouse (£10-13, without breakfast £7). The five-minute hike up the hill is outweighed by the privilege of staying in **Raasebeck** (tel. 33844), on aptly named Fair View Rd., a fascinating ancient cottage—cherish the warped floor boards—they're 350 years old (£16). Ask the proprietress why mill workers are short. Hospitable Mr. and Mrs. Richardson run **3 Cambridge Villas** (tel. 32307), on Church St. next to the tourist office, and will make vegetarian breakfasts on request (£16.50, with bath £20). Across the street from the tourist office, the Irelands offer crisp, clean rooms with TV at **Melrose Hotel,** Church St. (tel. 32500; £15-17). Camp at **Hawkshead Hall Farm** (tel. 36221), 5 mi. south of Ambleside off the B5286 (£1 per person, £1 per tent, £1 per car; open Mar.-Oct.). Toilets and drinking water available.

FOOD Ambleside specializes in trail food, from the omni-present **mint cakes** to gourmet sandwiches. On Compton Rd., **Scoffs** (tel. 34558) serves a huge selection of sandwiches on yummy baguettes (from £1.40; open daily 9am-3pm). Assemble your own picnic at the **Co-op Village Store,** Compston Rd. (tel. 33124; open M-Sa 8:30am-6pm, Su 10am-4pm), or visit the Wednesday **market** on King St. The **Golden Rule** (tel. 33363), on Smithy Brow, does unto residents with good local beer, while young people hunt down pizza and disco at the **Sportsman** (tel. 32535), on Compston Rd. (both open M-Sa 11am-11pm, Su noon-10:30pm). A local band plays Sunday evenings at **Unicorn** (tel. 33216), on North Rd. (food served daily noon-2pm and 7-9pm).

SIGHTS Ambleside's only noteworthy sight (aside from the surrounding nature) is the tiny **House on the Bridge** (tel. 32617), off Rydal Rd.; actually, house and bridge are one and the same. About four paces long and one pace wide, it was once inhabited by a basket weaver, his wife, and six children; it now houses one lone representative of the National Trust, and even he looks cramped. *(Open Apr.-Oct. daily 10am-5pm. Free.)* You can view the surrounding landscape most vividly from the middle of the lake; rent a rowboat at the Waterhead pier (£3 per hr., £1.50 for each additional person), and drift under the splendor of the **Horseshoe Falls.**

Although you can't go wrong hiking in any direction out from Ambleside, hidden trail markings, steep slopes, and reliably unpredictable weather that can quickly limit visibility, all make a good map, a compass, and the ability to use them a necessity (ask at the tourist or National Park Information Centres for the best maps). The mountain rescue service averages two to three crises a day in this area; don't let yourself be one. For an introduction to the area, you might try one of the excellent warden-guided walks which leave from Ambleside's and Grasmere's National Park and tourist information offices. Bring a sweater, rain gear—*it will rain!*—sturdy walking shoes or boots, a lunch, and water to fuel you for the four- to six-hour rambles of varying degrees of difficulty.

From the oft-trodden top of **Loughrigg,** you can lift your eyes up to the other, higher surrounding fells—it's only a 2½ mi. hike from Ambleside, with a 3½ mi. circuit descent. For gentler, shorter hikes, buy the *Ambleside Walks in the Countryside* (20p), which lists three easy walks from the town's center.

■ Coniston

With fells to the north and a lake to the south, Coniston makes a phenomenal base for hikers and cyclists. On rainy days, admire the sketches, photographs, and geological hammers of the writer-philosopher-art-critic John Ruskin at the aptly named **John Ruskin Museum** (tel. 41164), on Yewdale Rd. *(Closed for refurbishment until Easter 1999; call for hours.)* Ruskin might nod approvingly at the labor and craftsmanship that went into the carving of his **gravestone** in St. Andrew's Churchyard. **Brantwood** (tel. 41396), Ruskin's manor from 1872, looks across the lake at Coniston and the Old Man; it holds Ruskin's art, as well as works by Tolstoy, Proust, and Gandhi. *(Open mid-Mar. to mid-Nov. daily 11am-5:30pm; mid-Nov. to mid-Mar. W-Su 11am-4pm. £3.90, students £2.10, under 18 £1; gardens only £1.75.)* The easiest way to reach Brantwood is by water: the **Coniston Launch** (tel./fax 36216) travels to and from Brantwood (Apr.-Oct. 6-8 per day; return £3; combined £6.80 ticket for ferry and admission).

Coniston is accessible by **bus** #505 or 506 (the "Coniston Rambler"), which begins in Kendal and turns, twists, stops, and starts between Windermere, Bowness Pier, Ambleside, and sometimes Hawkshead on its way to Coniston and the lake (from Ambleside 45min., M-Sa 10 per day, Su 3-6 per day). Buses stop at the corner of Tilberthwaite and Ruskin Ave. Coniston's **tourist office** (tel. 41533), on Ruskin Ave. behind the bus stop, also poses as a **National Park Information Centre** (open Easter-Oct. daily 9:30am-5:30pm; Nov.-Easter F-Su 10am-3:30pm). A **Barclays** (tel. 41249) bereft of ATM sits at Bridge End (open M-F 9:30am-3:30pm). Rent bikes from **Coniston Mountain Bikes,** 14 Yewdale Rd. (tel. 41212; £13 per day, £10 per half-day). The **post office** (tel. 41259) is on Yewdale Rd. (Open M-Tu and Th-F 9am-12:30pm and 1:30-5:30pm, W closes at 5pm, Sa 9am-noon.) The **telephone code** is 015394.

Accommodations are available at **YHA Holly How** (tel. 41323) or the delightful **YHA Coniston Coppermines** (tel. 41261; see **Accommodations and Camping,** p. 378). Hikers and climbers will find their ideal hosts in the ice-, rock-and mineshaft-climbing proprietors of **Holmthwaite** (tel. 41231), on Tilberthwaite Ave. near the tourist office. Large rooms and lots of advice make for excellent resting and hiking (£17-18; discounts for stays over 2 nights). For **groceries,** head to the **Coop** on Yewdale St. (open M-Sa 9am-9pm, Su 10am-8pm).

Coniston serves as the base for a variety of outdoor activities. Ambitious hikers tackle the steep **Old Man** (5mi. round-trip) or the less lofty but equally vertical **Yewdale Fells.** For a more moderate hike, explore the Coppermines area and search for the "American's stope"—an old copper mine shaft named in honor of an American who leapt over it twice successfully and survived a 160 ft. fall the third time (*Let's Go* does not recommend 160 ft. falls). Cyclists roll down the 40 mi. of forest tracks criss-crossing though **Grizedale Forest,** while climbers tackle **Dow Crag.**

■ Near Coniston: Hawkshead

The harmless hamlet of **Hawkshead,** 4 mi. east of Coniston, proffers an assortment of tenuously historic attractions amidst "country wear" shops. Imagine pulling Wordsworth's hair and passing him notes at the **Hawkshead Grammar School,** across Main St. from the information center, where the poet studied from 1779 to 1787. (Open Easter-Oct. M-Sa 10am-12:30pm and 1:30-5pm, Su 1-5pm. £2, children 50p.) A walk north up Main St. leads to the Tiggy-Winkle-sized white building with green trim that once was **Mr. Beatrix Potter's** office (tel. 36355). It now houses a gallery, displaying the artwork of his better-known wife. (Open Apr.-Oct. Su-Th 10:30am-4:30pm; last admission 4pm. £2.80, children £1.40.)

More points of interest lie south of town. Esthwaite Lodge, the **YHA Hawkshead** (tel. 36293; see **Accommodations and Camping,** p. 378), sits on the shores of Lake Esthwaite, 1 mi. south of Hawkshead on the Rusland road. Over 2 mi. to the southwest, the hamlet of **Grizedale,** sponsors **Theatre in the Forest** (tel. (01229) 860291), which hosts folk and classical music and drama. (Box office open M-Sa 10am-4pm.) Two miles southeast of Hawkshead, in the hamlet of **Near Sawrey,** Beatrix Potter's 17th-century home, **Hilltop** (tel. 36269), contains her furniture, china, and art collection. The lovely gardens may look remarkably familiar, but as you round the end of a cucumber frame, you probably won't meet Mr. McGregor waving a rake and calling out "Stop, thief!" (Open Apr.-Oct. Sa-W 11am-4:30pm. £3.80, children £1.80.) Take the ferry from Bowness and walk 1½ mi., or take bus #505 from Ambleside, Coniston, or Hawkshead directly to Hilltop.

■ Grasmere

The attractive village of Grasmere, with a lake and a poet all to itself, suffers its fair share of camera-clicking tourists. The sightseers crowd in at midday to visit the Wordsworth home, grave, and museum, but in the quiet mornings and evenings the peace that the poet so enjoyed returns for a brief appearance. The early 17th-century **Dove Cottage** (tel. 35544), where Wordsworth lived with his wife, his sister Dorothy, Samuel Taylor Coleridge, Thomas de Quincey, and up to a dozen assorted children, opium-eaters, and literati from 1799 to 1808, is almost exactly as Wordsworth left it. A multitude of guides provide 20-minute tours. Browse the hot stories of 1802 on the newspapers which plaster the walls of the nursery room. Next door the excellent **Wordsworth Museum** includes pages of his handwritten poetry and info on his Romantic contemporaries. (Open mid-Feb. to mid-Jan. daily 9:30am-5:30pm, last admission 5pm. Cottage and museum £4.40, students £3.75, seniors £4.20, children £2.20; museum alone £2.20, children £1.10.) The cottage is 10 minutes from the center of Grasmere. Bus #555 stops here hourly en route to Ambleside or Keswick. A 40-minute hike up the **Old Coffin Trail** towards Ambleside (or one bus stop nearer to Ambleside on bus #555) leads to **Rydal Mount** (tel. 33002), the poet's home from 1813 until his death in 1850. A stroll across the garden terrace (designed by Wordsworth himself) leads to the small hut where he frequently composed verses. (Open Mar.-Oct. daily 9:30am-5pm; Nov.-Feb. W-M 10am-4pm. £3.50, students and seniors £3, children £1.) Hydrophiles can walk down Grasmere's Red Bank Rd. and hire a boat to row on the deep green lake. (Open in summer daily 10am-5pm. £2-4 per person depending on number of people; deposit £10.) Or you can purchase a pot of tea (80p) at the same port and direct a Romantic gaze across the water at the fells.

The combined **tourist office** and **National Park Information Centre** (tel. 35245; fax 35057) lies in town on Red Bank Rd. The staff of experienced hikers frequently hosts free guided walks on summer Sundays; details are in the *Events 1999* magazine. (Also exchanges foreign currency £3 per transaction. Open Easter-Oct. daily 9:30-5:30pm; Nov.-Easter F-Su 9:30am-4pm.) Grasmere's **telephone code** is 015394.

There are two **YHA Youth Hostels** within eight minutes' walk. **Butterlip How** (tel. (015394) 35316) and **Thorney How** (tel. (015394) 35591; see **Accommodations and Camping,** p. 378). All B&Bs in town cost at least £17 and fill up quickly, so pray that the **Glenthorne Quaker Guest House** (tel. 35389), a quarter mile up Easedale Rd. and past the Butterlip How Hostel, has a place for thee. The communal lounge and dining area feel like a hostel, but most rooms are clean, spacious singles with sinks. (B&B£18.50, full board£35, long-term deals available. Optional 15min. Quaker meeting each morning. Wheelchair access.) **Langman's,** Red Lion Sq. (tel. 35248), can pack up superb sandwiches and pastries (from £1.25), or let you enjoy lunch in the back room (open M-Sa 9am-5:30pm, Su 9:30am-5:30pm). Sarah Nelson's famous Grasmere Gingerbread (a staple since 1854), somewhere in between ginger snaps and ordinary gingerbread, is a bargain at 22p in **Church Cottage** (tel. 35428), outside St. Oswald's Church. Follow your nose from Wordsworth's grave. (Open Mar.-Nov. M-Sa 9:30am-5:30pm, Su 12:30-5:30pm; Dec.-Feb. M-Sa 9:30am-5pm, Su 2-4:30pm).

■ Near Grasmere

As Wordsworth well knew, Grasmere is a good base for walkers. A steep two-hour scramble (up Easedale Rd. until it ends, then follow the signs) leads to the top of **Helm Cragg,** dubbed by locals "the lion and the lamb." Can you find that magic angle? Hint: the lion is lying beside the lamb. Walk to the other side and it's supposed to look like a woman playing an organ. The 6 mi. **Wordsworth Walk** circumnavigates the two lakes of the Rothay River, passing the poet's grave, Dove Cottage, and Rydal Mount (hence the name of the walk) along the way. Star-seeking fell-climbers can tackle the path from Rydal to Legburthwaite (near Keswick) in an athletic day, passing the towering Great Rigg and Helvellyn on the way. Bus #555 will bring you back to Ambleside—hiking back is not advised—or you can stay at the basic **Thirlmere** hostel (see **Accommodations and Camping,** p. 378).

■ Keswick

Sandwiched between towering Skiddaw peak and the northern edge of Lake Derwentwater, Keswick (KEZ-ick) rivals Windermere as the Lake District's tourist capital, but far surpasses it in charm. The **National Park Info Centre** *cum* tourist office, Moot Hall (tel. 72645), behind the clock tower in Market Sq., sells a lodgings booklet (£1) and a town map (20p), and will find you B&B for a 10% deposit. They'll **exchange currency** for £3. (Open daily July-Aug. 8:30am-6pm, Sept.-June 9:30am-5pm.) A variety of **guided walks** leave from the tourist office, including the popular "Keswick Ramble" which leaves daily at 10:15am and lasts about seven hours (bring a lunch and rain gear; £4, children £2). Serious climbers should ask about taking a trip with one of Lakeland's finest, Ray McHaffie. Book a tour of the area at the **Mountain Goat Office** (tel. 73962), in the car park (open Apr.-Oct. M-F 9am-5pm, Sa-Su 9am-2pm; Nov.-Mar. M-F 9am-4pm). The **ATM** at **Barclays** (tel. 864221), on Market Sq. shall extrude cash (open M-Tu and Th-F 9:30am-4:30pm, W 10am-4:30pm). Reserve **National Express** and **Cumberland** tickets that link the Lakes at the **post office,** 48 Main St. (tel. 74269), at Bank St. and Market Pl. (open June-Oct. M-F 8:30am-5:30pm, Sa 8:30am-7:30pm, Su 10:30am-5pm). The **postal code** goes bonkers at CA12 5GAGA; the **telephone code** is 017687.

The **Keswick** and **Derwentwater hostels** (tel. 72484 and 77246) grace this small town (see **Accommodations and Camping,** p. 378). Vast quantities of **B&Bs** nestle between Station St., St. John St.-Ambleside Rd., and Penrith Rd. Many also line Station Rd. across the River Greta. The tidy rooms and central location of **Bridgedale's,** 101 Main St. (tel. 73914), at the mini-roundabout, compensate for the noisy buses outside (£14, with continental breakfast £15, with full breakfast £16, with bath £19.50). The B&B will also provide **luggage storage** for non-guests (£2-3 depending on size and duration). No-frills **Elmtree Lodge,** 16 Leonard St. (tel. 74710), at Church St., promises quieter slumber (£17; bed only £12). **Century House,** 17 Church St. (tel. 72843), has bright peaches-and-cream bedrooms in a Victorian-style house (£16.50-18.50). **Dorchester Guest House,** 17 Southey St. (tel. 73256) has lacy curtains and a floral decor (£16, with bath £19; Nov.-Easter weekends only). **Campers** can pitch a tent at

Castlerigg Hall (tel. 72437), 1 mi. southeast of Keswick (£2.70-3.20 per person, children £2, £1 per car; open Apr.-Nov.). The site has phones, toilets, showers (50p), and is on the Windermere bus route. **The Camping and Caravan Club Site** (tel. 72392), on Crow Park Rd., rests right by the lake, a 7-minute walk from the bus station (open Feb.-Nov; an extravagant £14 for two adults with a tent).

Sundance Wholefoods, 33 Main St. (tel. 74712), sells nature-friendly groceries at Market Pl. (open daily in summer 9am-9pm; in winter 9am-5pm, give or take). For meatless treats, dine at the **Lakeland Pedlar** (tel. 74492) in an alley off Main St.: excellent sandwiches (£3), pizzas (from £4.45), and desserts (open daily May-Aug. 9am-8pm; Sept.-Apr. 9am-5:30pm). When the thirst for pub-crawling hits you, duck into a little alley and join the Lost Generation at **Ye Olde Queen's Head** (tel. 73333), behind the Queen's Hotel on Main St. (open M-Sa 11am-11pm, Su 11am-10:30pm).

■ Near Keswick

One of the best ridge hikes in the Lake District begins only 1 mi. from Keswick. Ascend the **Cat Bells** from the west shore of Derwent Water at Hawes End and stroll a gentle 3 mi. atop the ridge, passing **Maiden Moor** and **Eel Crags** on the way to **Dale Head,** one of the highest peaks in the area. Descend via the saddle-shaped Honister Pass to reach Seatoller (total distance 10-12mi.). For another excellent daytrip, walk southwest through the village of **Portinscale** ("harlot's hut"), over the rugged Derwent Fells, and eventually descend into **Buttermere.** Intrepid hikers can attempt Skiddaw (3054ft.), possibly staying a night at the Skiddaw House YHA (see **Accommodations and Camping,** p. 378)—bring your own food. The easy **Castlehead Walk** from Keswick's Lake Rd. leads to spellbinding **Friar's Crag,** praised by Ruskin, Wordsworth, and *Let's Go* (3mi.). For another gentle amble, visit the **Castlerigg Stone Circle,** in a sheep-laden field a half-hour walk east of Keswick (take Penrith Rd.). Cyclists can purchase the stirring *6 Cycle Routes Around Keswick* (£1) from the information center or bike the easy 11 mi. circuit around Derwentwater. Very serious hikers can defy death on **Blencathra,** 4 mi. to the east above Threlkeld. The ascent takes you along **Sharp Edge,** which is just that—a ridiculously narrow solid rock ridge with 60° slopes on either side. Take bus #X5 to Threlkeld and look up.

■ Western Lake District

With comparatively few visitors and spectacular scenery, the Western Lake District is delightful. Getting there is not, unless you have a car or like to climb steep hills while carrying a heavy pack. Approach the remote southern villages of Eskdale and Wasdale from Ravenglass (or less easily from Coniston). Noses grow a little every third Thursday in November at **Santon Bridge,** a village near Eskdale, which hosts its "Biggest Liar in the World" competition. The Ravenglass-Eskdale railway (tel. (01229) 717171) stops in Boot, 1½ mi. from **YHA Eskdale** (tel. (019467) 23219; see **Accommodations and Camping,** p. 378). B&Bs cluster at Wasdale Head. Try **Mrs. K. Naylor,** Row Mead Farm (tel. (019467) 26244), who rents rooms for £16. Facing the famous and forbidding Wastwater Screes is the standard grade **YHA Wastwater** (tel. (019467) 26222; see p. 378). Climb the nearby **Whin Rigg** or venture over to the many waterfalls of **Greendale Valley.**

While the fell blockade across the Western Lake District can be attacked from the south, the best approach is from the north. From Keswick, take bus #79 8 mi. south to Seatoller, or bus #79 1½ mi. farther to the harrowing **Honister Pass** where the **YHA Honister Hause** nestles on its summit (tel. (017687) 77267; see p. 378). From Seatoller, hike 1¼ mi. south to **Seathwaite** and pick your mountain. To climb craggy **Great Gable** (2949ft.) and its sidekick **Green Gable** (2628ft.; no pig-tailed red-heads in sight) follow the trail on your left, which climbs steeply along the side of a waterfall (2¼mi. up from Seathwaite to the summit). Glory-seekers can try the 8 mi. round-trip hike from Seathwaite up **Seafell Pike** (3162ft.); it's the highest peak in England.

Set in a splendid valley between two icy mountain lakes on the other side of Honister Pass, **Buttermere** is a ripping town and a remote fishing hole, reachable by bus #77 from Keswick (2 per day). Nearby, **Sour Milk Gill Falls** curdles from the slopes of Red Pike. The hike up **Haystacks** is tough, but the summit delivers bone-chilling views of surrounding mountains. **Red Pike** (2479ft.), **High Stile** (2644ft.), and **High Cragg** are the three main challenges for ambitious hikers in the area. Those more sensible might take a constitutional up **Ranndale Knotts**. The **YHA Buttermere** grants a hiker's reprieve (tel. (017687) 70245; see p. 378). Find B&B or camping at **Sike Farm** (tel. (017687) 70222) in the village (£17; discount for longer stays; camping £4.50 per person; showers 20p). Spend the night at **Crag Foot Cottage** (tel. (017687) 70220), a wonderfully friendly B&B (£18; discount for longer stays). Just south of Buttermere, **Ennerdale Forest** shades the **YHA Ennerdale** (tel. (01946) 861237) and—at its southeastern edge, about 1½ mi. from Great Gable—the amazingly remote **YHA Black Sail** (tel. (0411) 108450; see **Accommodations and Camping,** p. 378).

ENGLAND

WALES (CYMRU)

*This nation, O King, may now as in former times, be harassed, and in a
great measure weakened and destroyed by your and other Powers…but it
can never be totally subdued through the wrath of man, unless the wrath
of God shall concur. Nor do I think that any other nation than this of
Wales, or any other language, whatever may hereafter come to pass,
shall, on the day of severe examination before the Supreme Judge, answer
for this corner of the earth.*
—*an Old Man of Pencader to Henry II, quoted by Giraldus Cambrensis*

Wales borders England, but if many Welsh had their way, it would be floating miles
away. Since England solidified its control over the country with the murder of Prince
Llewelyn ap Gruffydd (Llewelyn the Last) in 1282, relations between the two have
been marked by a powerful unease. Until late in the 19th century, schoolchildren
were forbidden to speak Welsh in the classroom. Those who did were made to wear
a "Welsh Knot" around their necks, which was passed around to the next child who
dared speak Welsh; whoever was wearing the knot at the end of the day would get
some form of punishment. Despite this dominating presence, Wales clings steadfastly
to its Celtic heritage, continuing a centuries-old struggle for independence. Especially
in the North, Welsh endures in conversations, commerce, and literature, both oral
and written. As churning coal, steel, and slate mines have fallen victim to Britain's fal-
tering economy, the unemployment rate has risen, and Wales has turned its economic eye from heavy industry to tourism. Travelers from near and far come for the
miles of sandy beaches, grassy cliffs, and dramatic mountains that typify the rich landscape of this corner of Britain. Against this backdrop, Welsh nationalists have
expressed their dissatisfaction mostly in the peace of the voting booths and in a celebration of the distinctive Welsh culture and language at events like the Royal National
Eisteddfod. When in Wales, enjoy the differences that make this land unique and,
please, do not refer to the Welsh as "English."

■ Getting There and Getting About

BUSES

Pronouncing your destination properly will probably be the least of your problems as
you navigate the overlapping routes of Wales's 65 different bus operators. Most of
these are small local services; almost every region is dominated by one or two companies. Life-saving regional public transport guides exist for most places (available free
in tourist offices), but for some areas you'll have to consult an array of small brochures. The free *Wales Bus, Rail, and Tourist Map and Guide* provides bus information, but routes are often mislabeled. Also, remember that many local buses don't run
on Sunday.

In the south, take all bus schedules with a grain of salt—buses are usually late.
Cardiff Bus (tel. (01222) 396521) blankets the area around Cardiff. **Stagecoach Red
and White** (tel. (01633) 266336) buses serve the routes from Gloucester and Hereford in England west through the Wye Valley, past Abergavenny and Brecon. **South
Wales Transport (First Cymru)** (tel. (01792) 580580) covers the Gower Peninsula
and the rest of southwest Wales, while **Edwards Bros.** (tel (01437) 890230) visits the
Pembrokeshire Coast National Park. **TrawsCambria** (tel. (01443) 682673) is the
north-south bus line. On it, you can travel easily from Cardiff or Swansea north to
Machynlleth, and Bangor.

Passes vastly simplify the bus fare system in the south. Cardiff Bus offers the **Capital
Ticket** day pass (£3.30, children £2.10) and one-week **Multiride** passes (£9.50, chil-

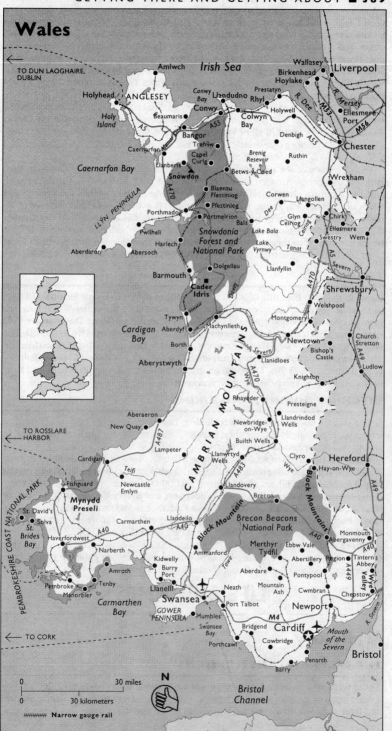

Wales

TO DUN LAOGHAIRE, DUBLIN

Irish Sea

Amlwch

Holyhead

ANGLESEY

Holy Island

Beaumaris

Conwy Bay

Llandudno

Rhyl

Prestatyn

Wallasey

Birkenhead

Hoylake

Liverpool

R. Mersey

Ellesmere Port

M53

M56

Conwy

Colwyn Bay

Holywell

Denbigh

Chester

Bangor

Trefriw

Caernarfon

Capel Curig

Llanberis

Snowdon

Betws-y-Coed

Ruthin

A55

Wrexham

Caernarfon Bay

A5

A470

Blaenau Ffestiniog

Ffestiniog

Corwen

Llangollen

Chirk

Porthmadog

Portmeirion

Bala

Dee

Glyn Ceiriog

Ellesmere

Wem

Pwllheli

LLŶN PENINSULA

Lake Bala

Lake Vyrnwy

Tanat

Swestry

A5

Harlech

Abersoch

Snowdonia Forest and National Park

Llanfyllin

Severn

Aberdaron

Barmouth

Dolgellau

Cader Idris

Shrewsbury

Welshpool

Montgomery

A470

Tywyn

Aberdyfi

Machynlleth

Newtown

Bishop's Castle

Church Stretton

A49

Cardigan Bay

Borth

CAMBRIAN MOUNTAINS

Severn

Llanidloes

Ludlow

Aberystwyth

A470

Wye

Rhayader

Knighton

Aberaeron

New Quay

A487

Presteigne

Llandrindod Wells

Lampeter

Newbridge-on-Wye

Builth Wells

Hereford

Cardigan

Teifi

Llanwrtyd Wells

Llanwrtyd Wells

Clyro

Hay-on-Wye

A49

Fishguard

Newcastle Emlyn

A483

Llandovery

Wye

Black Mountains

Mynydd Preseli

St. David's

Solva

St. Brides Bay

PEMBROKESHIRE COAST NATIONAL PARK

Haverfordwest

Narberth

A40

Carmarthen

Llandeilo

A40

Black Mountain

Brecon

Brecon Beacons National Park

Monmouth

Abergavenny

A40

A449

Tintern Abbey

Wye Valley

Chepstow

R. Severn

Pembroke

Amroth

Tenby

Manorbier

Kidwelly

Burry Port

Ammanford

Towe

Merthyr Tydfil

Ebbw Vale

Abertillery

Region

Pontypool

Cwmbran

Newport

Carmarthen Bay

Llanelli

Swansea

GOWER PENINSULA

Neath

Port Talbot

Aberdare

Mountain Ash

M4

Cardiff

Mumbles

Swansea Bay

Bridgend

Cowbridge

Penarth

Mouth of the Severn

Bristol

Porthcawl

Barry

Bristol Channel

TO ROSSLARE HARBOR

TO CORK

| 0 | | 30 miles |
| 0 | | 30 kilometers |

N

++++++++ Narrow gauge rail

WALES

dren £4.75; available at their office near the bus station). From Hereford south to Swansea and as far west as Carmarthen, one-day **Roverbus** tickets (£5) cover all bus travel, and are sold by bus drivers on Stagecoach Red and White, South Wales Transport (First Cymru), Silverline or Rhondda (passes honored by all four companies). South Wales Transport (First Cymru) also sells a week-long **Master Rider** ticket (£14), which can be purchased at the Swansea South Wales Transport office (bring a passport-sized photo).

Because of a pre-existing regional governmental pass, South Wales Transport buses west of Carmarthen will not honor Rover bus tickets; instead purchase the **Dyfed Rover** for a day's travel in all of Pembrokeshire, as far north as Cardigan (day rover about £5). Remember that shuttle services like National Express, TrawsCambria, and SWT Shuttles do not honor any rover tickets.

The efficiency of the **northern Wales** bus service will amaze you; **Crosville Bus,** Park Ave., Aberystwyth, Ceredigion SY23 1PG (tel. (01970) 617951), provides excellent service throughout most of the area. Buy one of their special packages, valid north of Aberystwyth and as far east as Chester. Buy the **Five Day Wanderer** (£14, under 16 £9, under 4 free) and the **One Day Explorer** (£4.80, £3.20). **Arriva Cymru** (tel. 01492) 596969), operating extensively in the north, offers similar deals. If your travel is confined to the Gwynedd area, extending from Machynlleth north to Holyhead and Llandudno, instead buy a Gwynedd **Red Rover** (£4.40, children £2.20).

TRAINS

Passes help lessen the costs of travel. The **Freedom of Wales Rover Flexipass** (8 days in 15; June 5-Sept. 27 £69, Sept. 28-June 4 £59) is good on the entire Welsh network plus Chester to Abergavenny via Crewe. The **Cambrian Coast Day Ranger** (£6) earns a day's rail travel from Aberystwyth north to Pwllheli on the Llŷn Peninsula. The **North and Mid-Wales Ranger** covers a week's bus and rail travel within the Aberystwyth-Shrewsbury-Crewe area, including free travel on the Ffestiniog Railway (£40; 3 days in 7 £25.70). These passes are available for sale only in Britain; call **British Rail** (tel. (0345) 484950) for more information.

HITCHING, HIKING, AND BIKING

Let's Go does not recommend **hitchhiking,** but many people choose this form of transport, especially in the summer. Cars stop most readily for hitchers who stand in lay-by (pull-off) areas along narrow roads.

Wales has hundreds of well-marked footpaths. *Walking in Wales,* available at tourist offices, highlights interesting walks with sights and accommodations along the way. Long-distance **hikers** should buy 1:50,000 Ordnance Survey maps and bring along proper equipment. Please see **Wilderness and Safety Concerns,** p. 47, before heading out into the wild. The **Offa's Dyke Path** (see p. 403) and the **Pembrokeshire Coast Path** (see p. 419) are popular long-distance walks. For more information, write to the **Countryside Council Wales,** 43 The Parade, Roth, Cardiff DF2 3UH.

Bikers cycling in northern Wales should obtain a copy of the indispensable *Cyclists' Guide to North Wales* at tourist offices. Bicycles can easily be rented from dealers, especially in Betws-y-Coed, Llanberis, and Shrewsbury.

LIFE AND TIMES

■ History

THE CELTS AND THE NORMANS

As the western terminus of many waves of emigration, Wales has been influenced by a wide array of peoples since prehistoric times. Inhabitants from the Stone, Bronze, and Iron Ages left their mark on the Welsh landscape in the form of stone villages, forts covered in earth, *cromlechs* (standing stones also known as menhirs and dolmens), and partially subterranean burial chambers. It is the early **Celts** about whom we know the most, however, and who made Wales most distinct from her neighbors. In the 4th and 3rd centuries BC, Wales witnessed two waves of immigration, the first from Celtic northern Europe and the second from the then-Celtic Iberian peninsula. By the time the **Romans** arrived in AD 50, the Welsh Celts had consolidated into four main tribes with links to each other and the Celts of western Scotland, Ireland, and Brittany. By AD 59, the Romans had reached the Menai Straits, across the water from Ynys Môn (Anglesey), the center of druidic, bardic, and warrior life in northern Wales. Crossing the water, the Romans were faced with the bedlam of a Celtic attack; undaunted, they proceeded to kill or capture all the residents of the isle. Though the Romans symbolically conquered the Welsh, their domination was never fully consolidated, and Welsh resistance compelled them to station two of their four legions in Britain along the Welsh border.

> When the Romans finally departed in the early 5th century AD, they left their language and the first seeds of Christianity

The Romans left a legacy of complete towns, amphitheaters, roads, and mines. When the Romans finally departed in the early 5th century AD, they also left their language—**Latin**—and the first seeds of Christianity, both of which heavily influenced further development of Welsh scholarship and society. For 700 years the Welsh ruled themselves. Welsh princes and the Christian religion firmly established their power, and the Welsh bravely held at bay invading Saxons, Irish, and Vikings, their efforts perhaps spearheaded by the legendary figure **King Arthur.** Yet they were not entirely successful, for in the 8th century King Offa of Mercia and his troops pushed the Welsh into the corner of Britain they inhabit today and built **Offa's Dyke,** a 150 mi. earthwork, to keep them there. The newly contained Wales consisted of many kingdoms united by a single language, a uniform system of customary law, a shared social system based on kinship ties, and a ruling aristocracy linked by common ancestry and marriage. These kingdoms did not achieve political unity until Gruffydd ap Llywelyn united them in the 11th century.

Within 50 years of William the Conqueror's invasion of Britain, one-quarter of Wales had been subjugated. The newcomers built a series of castles and market towns, introduced the feudal social system, and brought a variety of Continental monastic orders. Though the Welsh greeted the rule of the Christian Norman barons with less resistance than they had directed toward previous pagan invaders, conflict never subsided, and the Normans were unable to enter the heart of North Wales.

THE ENGLISH CONQUEST

The kings of the English House of **Plantagenet** invaded Wales throughout the 12th century, but it was not until 1282, when a soldier of **Edward I** (the Longshanks, of *Braveheart* fame) killed Prince **Llywelyn ap Gruffydd,** that the independence of the Welsh symbolically ended. Llywelyn's head was taken to London, paraded through the streets wearing a crown of ivy, and displayed at the Tower of London, lest anyone imagine the Welsh still had a leader. Edward then appointed his son Prince of Wales, and in 1284 dubbed the Welsh English subjects. He would go on to use Welsh expertise with the longbow in his campaigns in Scotland and France. To keep the perennially unruly Welsh in check, Edward constructed a series of massive castles—the fortresses of Rhuddlan, Flint, Aberystwyth, Conwy, Caernarfon, Harlech, and Beaumaris—at strategic spots throughout Wales.

In the early 15th century, the bold insurgent warfare of Owain Glyndŵr (Owen Glendower in English) temporarily freed Wales from English rule. Reigniting Welsh nationalism and rousing his compatriots to arms, Glyndŵr and his followers captured the castle at Conwy, threatened the strongholds of Caenarfon and Harlech, and convened a national parliament in Wales. While poverty, the plague, and warfare ravaged the country, Glyndŵr created the ideal of a "unified" Wales that has captured the imagination of the Welsh ever since. But despite support from Ireland, Scotland and

WALES

France, by 1409 the rebellion had been reduced to a series of guerrilla raids. By 1417 Glyndŵr had disappeared into the mountains a fugitive, leaving only legend to guide his people. Though Wales had placed her hope in the Welsh-born **Henry VII** of the Welsh House of Tudor, who ascended to the English throne in 1485, alliance with the Tudors did not bring independence.

Full integration with England came during Henry VIII's reign with the **Act of Union** (1536), which granted the Welsh the same rights as English citizens and returned the administration of Wales to the local gentry. However, the price of power was assimilation and the act banished the distinctive Welsh legal and administrative system, officially "united and annexed" Wales, and sought to "extirpate all and singular the sinister usages and customs differing." Thus began the rise of the English language in Wales, which quickly became the language of the courts and government as well as the courtly language of the gentry.

METHODISM AND THE INDUSTRIAL REVOLUTION

In the 18th and 19th centuries, religious shifts in Wales changed the nature of society and culture. As the Anglican church in Wales became more (surprise!) anglicized, and church tithes grew increasingly burdensome, the Welsh were ripe for the appeal of new Protestant sects. Nonconformists, Baptists, and Quakers all gained a foothold in Wales as early as the 17th century. The 18th-century Methodist revolution was most influential, with its fiery preachers and austere lifestyle. Life in Wales centered on the chapel, not the church, where people created tight local communities through shared religion, heritage, and language. Chapel life remains one of the most distinctive features of Welsh society; strict Sabbath closure of stores in parts of Wales is but one of the lasting effects.

The 19th century brought the Industrial Revolution to Wales, as industrialists from within and without sought to exploit coal veins in the south and iron and slate deposits in the north. New roads, canals, and—most important—steam railways were built throughout Wales to transport these raw materials. Especially in the south, pastoral landscapes were transformed into grim mining wastelands, and the workers who braved these dangerous workplaces faced lives of taxing work, poverty, and despair. Industrial tycoons in Wales grew conspicuously rich, and workers found life increasingly harsh. Early attempts at unionism failed and workers turned to violence to improve conditions. In the 1830s Welsh discontent was channeled into the **Chartist Movement.** Welsh society became characterized by two forces: a strongly leftist political consciousness—aided by the rise in organized labor—and large-scale emigration. Welsh miners and religious outgroups emigrated to America (founding particularly vibrant settlements in Pennsylvania) and in 1865 a group of Welsh men and women founded **Y Wladfa** (The Colony) in the Patagonia region of Argentina.

The strength of the Liberal Party in Wales bolstered the career of **David Lloyd George,** who rose from being a rabble-rousing Welshman to Britain's Prime Minister (1916-1922). The Great War sent 280,000 Welshmen to fight on the Continent; over 35,000 never returned. This loss of a generation, combined with Prime Minister Winston Churchill's violent smothering of a Welsh **coal-miners' strike** and the economic depression of the 1930s (from which Welsh industry has never truly recovered), led to growing dissatisfaction.

MODERN POLITICS

The late 20th century has been especially characterized by Welsh political nationalism and a vigorous campaign to retain Europe's oldest living modern language. The establishment of Welsh language classes, Welsh publications, Welsh radio, the Welsh-language television channel S4C, and Welsh societies like *Cymdeithas yr Iaith Cymraeg* (The Welsh Language Society), clearly indicates the energy invested in the Welsh language, the binding feature of the Welsh people today. In 1967 the **Welsh Language Act** established the right to use Welsh in the courts, and the 1988 **Education Reform Act** ensured that all children aged 5 to 16 in Wales would be introduced to the Welsh language in school. Welsh nationalism has typically found its expression in the political realm: The **Welsh Nationalist Party,** *Plaid Cymru,* has performed increasingly well since its founding, consistently garnering seats in Parliament.

Welsh citizens today possess a fierce pride in their history, language, and culture. As the Labour Party, which claimed an overwhelming majority of seats in Wales in the 1997 elections, begins to institute long-promised plans for Scottish and Welsh devolution, Wales may at long last begin to feel a greater independence.

■ Lliterature and Music

> The Welsh prefer philosophy to philology; music and poetry to both.
> —T. Charles Williams

In Wales, as in other Celtic countries, much of the national literature stems from a vibrant bardic tradition. The earliest extant poetry in Welsh comes to us from 6th-century northern England, where the **cynfeirdd** (early poets), including the influential poet **Taliesin,** orally composed verse of praise for their patron lords. The *Gododdin,* a series of heroic lays totalling over 1000 lines and attributed to the poet **Aneirin,** is the most noted celebration of valor and heroism from this period. The 9th through 11th centuries brought emotional and often melancholy poetic sagas focusing on pseudo-historical figures such as the poet **Llywarch Hen, King Arthur,** and **Myrddin** (Merlin). Ushering in the most prolific period in Welsh literature, 12th-century monastic scribes compiled manuscripts in the Middle Welsh language. Most notable from this period is the collection of prose tales known as the **Mabinogion** (after a later translation by Lady Charlotte Guest). Under this title are the *Four Branches of the Mabinogi,* four loosely connected and highly dramatic tales of legendary Welsh figures, as well as seven other tales, including one of the earliest Arthurian stories in European literature, *Culwch ac Olwen.*

In the 14th century, Wales saw the development of the flexible poetic form, *Cywydd,* and the writing of **Dafydd ap Gwilym,** often called the greatest Welsh poet. He combined playfulness, irony, and emotional depth in his verse. His poetry continued to influence the works of later poets such as **Dafydd Nanmor** and **Iolo Goch** well through the 17th century. Yet a growing anglicizing of the Welsh gentry and the influence of the bourgeois ethic in the 18th century led to a decline in the tradition of courtly bards. Active composers of verse found their venue mainly at eisteddfodau, local poetic competitions, and the Royal National Eisteddfod (see **Ffestivals,** p. 395).

Modern Welsh literature has been influenced heavily in its use of language by Bishop William Morgan's 1588 Welsh translation of the Bible, which helped standardize Welsh and provided the foundation for literacy throughout Wales. A circle of Welsh romantic poets, **Y Beridd Newydd** (the New Poets), developed in the 19th century, included T. Gwynn Jones and W.J. Gruffydd. The horrors of World War I touched Wales as much as England and produced an anti-romantic poetic voice typified in the work of **Hedd Wyn,** who won the chief prize at the 1917 National Eisteddfod but was killed on the fields of France before accepting the honor.

Twentieth-century Welsh prose (in Welsh and English) features a compelling self-consciousness in addressing problematic questions of identity and national ideals. **R.S. Thomas's** incisive poetry treads a fine line between a fierce defense of his proud heritage and a bitter rant against its claustrophobic provincialism. **Kate Roberts's** short stories and novels, such as *The Chains Around My Feet,* dramatize Welsh fortitude in the face of dire poverty. The best-known Welsh writer is, of course, **Dylan Thomas,** who has become something of a national industry. His sonorous poetry, as well as popular works like *A Child's Christmas in Wales,* and the radio play *Under Milk Wood* (a microcosm of Wales told through a day in the life of a seaside town), describe his homeland with nostalgia, humor, and a tinge of bitterness.

Music in Wales—sometimes referred to as "the land of song"—has, like literature, occupied an important place in the life of people. Little is known about early Welsh music, but the fact that the Welsh word **canu** (to sing) is also used for reciting poetry suggests an intimate historical connection between the spoken and the sung word. There is little extant Welsh music dating prior to the 17th century; nonetheless, historians know of three traditional instruments in medieval Wales: the harp, the pipe (hornpipe or bagpipe), and the **crwth,** a six-stringed oblong instrument played with a bow. Wales began to "lose" its indigenous music tradition when Welsh harpists were incorporated into England's 16th-century Tudor court; traditional playing died out by the 17th century. In the 18th century, the rise of chapels led to an energetic hymn-writing and singing culture, as Welsh folk tunes were adapted to sacred songs of praise to God. Hymn-writers like **Ann Griffiths** made their mark in this period. Their works, sung in unison in the 18th century, became the basis for the harmony **choral singing** of the 19th and 20th centuries that is now Wales's best-known musical tradition. With the choir (both single-sex and mixed) as an integral part of Welsh social life, singing festivals like the **cymanfa ganu** developed throughout Wales.

Today Welsh musical life includes much more than the chorus; Cardiff's **St. David's Hall** (opened in 1983 and regarded as one of the finest venues in Britain) regularly hosts both Welsh and international orchestras, and the Welsh National Opera has established a worldwide reputation. Modern Welsh composers of orchestral and vocal works such as **Alun Hoddinott** and **William Mathias** have won respect in the classical genre; Mathias composed an anthem for the wedding of Prince Charles and the late Lady Diana. Rock music in English and Welsh has gained strength in this century—singer **Tom "What's New Pussycat" Jones** and **John Cale** (one of the founding members of the Velvet Underground) hail from Wales and, most recently, a variety of Welsh-language rock bands have gained national prominence. Popular Brit-pop bands from Wales include Catatonia, Stereophonics and Super Furry Animals.

■ Ffood

Traditional Welsh cooking relies heavily on potatoes, onions, leeks, dairy products, lamb (considered some of the best in the world), pork, fish, and seaweed. Soups and stews are ubiquitous and often quite good. **Cawl** is a complex broth, generally accompanied by bread; most soups brim with leeks and generous helpings of lamb or beef. The pub dish **Welsh rabbit** (also called "Welsh rare-bit") is buttered toast topped with a thick, cheesy mustard-beer sauce. But it is the baked goods of Wales that tempt most. **Crempogen** (griddle cakes), resembling miniature pancakes, are made with sour cream, studded with currants, and topped with butter. Wales abounds with unique, tasty **breads**—the adventurous should sample **laverbread,** not really bread at all but a cake-like slab made of seaweed. Those with a sweet tooth will love **bara brith,** a fruit and nut bread served with butter, or **teisennau hufen** (cream cakes), fluffy doughnut-like cakes filled with freshly whipped cream. Not surprisingly, **cwrw** (beer), is a staple.

■ Llanguage

The word "Welsh" comes from the Old English *wealh,* or "foreigner," and the language does seem alien to most English speakers. Though modern Welsh borrows significantly from English for vocabulary, as a member of the Celtic family of languages, *Cymraeg* is based on a grammatical system related to Irish, Cornish and Breton. Out of a total population of three million, more than 500,000 people in Wales speak Welsh, and just over half are native speakers. Increasingly, Welsh is becoming the language of the shops, streets, and buses, especially north of Aberystwyth.

Though English suffices nearly everywhere in Wales, it's a good idea to familiarize yourself with the language. Mastering Welsh grammar takes time, especially given the many dialectical variations; try at least to learn the mechanics of pronunciation. Welsh shares with German the sound ch, the deep, guttural "kh" heard in "Bach" or "loch." Ll—the oddest of Welsh consonants—is produced by placing your tongue against the top of your mouth, as if you were going to say "l," and blowing. If this technique proves baffling, try saying "hl" (Hlan-GO-hlen for "Llangollen"). Also

unique to Welsh is dd, said like the "th" in "there." C and g are always h.
erally used as a vowel and sounds either like the "oo" in "drool," or "goo
nounced like the "e" in "he." Y trickily changes its sound with its placen
word, sounding either like the "u" in "ugly" or the "i" in "ignoramus." F is s
"v," as in "vertigo," and ff sounds exactly like the English "f." Emphasis nearl
falls on the next to last syllable, and there are (fortunately) no silent letters in

Most Welsh place names are naturally derived from prominent features of the landscape. *Afon* means river, *bedd* grave, *betws* or *llan* church or enclosure, *bryn* hill,
caer fort, *ffordd* road, *glyn* glen or valley, *llyn* lake, *môr* sea, *mynydd* mountain, *pen*
top or end, *pont* bridge, *tref* or *tre* town, and *ynys* island. *Mawr* is big, *bach* is little.
The Welsh call their land **Cymru** (KIM-ree) and themselves *Cymry* ("compatriots").
Because of the Welsh system of letter mutation, many of these words will appear in
usage with different initial consonants. **Welsh Words and Phrases,** p. 693, provides
more information to aid you in your travels.

▓ Ffestivals

Every July (July 6-1 in 1999), Wales turns its attention to the **Llangollen International
Eisteddfod,** held in the small town of Llangollen in North Wales. The International
Eisteddfod, not to be confused with the Royal National Eisteddfod (below), draws
folk dancers, singers, and choirs from around the world for performance and competition. Though not focused on all things Welsh as is the Royal National Eisteddfod, the
festival equally epitomizes both Welsh hospitality and the Welsh love of music.

The Royal National Eisteddfod

The most significant of Welsh festivals is the *eisteddfod*, which literally means a
sitting together or session. In practice, an *eisteddfod* is a competition of Welsh literature (chiefly poetry), music, and arts and crafts. Hundreds of local *eistedd-
dfodau* (the plural) are held in Wales each year, generally lasting one to three
days. Chief of these is the *Eisteddfod Genedlaethol Frenhinol Cymru*, the **Royal
National Eisteddfod of Wales,** established in 1568 by Queen Elizabeth to address
her concern over the "intolerable multitude of vagrant and idle persons calling
themselves minstrels, rhymers, and bards." Today the National Eisteddfod is a
grand festival held the first week of August, alternating each year between a different location in North and South Wales. Its present incarnation owes much to the
fancy of Iolo Morgannwg, poet and writer, who "invented" a tradition reaching
back into the Druidic past of Wales. He created the *Gorsedd Beirdd*—a honorary
group of great poets—who parade in white, green, and blue robes at two ceremonies, officiated by the "Archdruid," at which the winners of the crown and the
chair (the two main poetry prizes) are introduced to the crowd amid much
pomp. In recent years Eisteddfod events, which are conducted in Welsh, have
made headsets available with translations for non-Welsh speakers.

South Wales

Distinctions between Wales and England are less vivid in the South, where there is a larger English population and a smaller number of Welsh speakers. Dotted with market towns and graced by gritty harbors, the landscape itself is reminiscent of its neighbor to the east. Though unemployment remains high, national pride has a potent presence, and the South boasts its own share of Welsh natural beauty. The Wye Valley forms a rich, tranquil shelter shared by England and Wales, while rugged hills, forests, limestone caves, and moorlands stud the Brecon Beacons National Park. Both the Gower Peninsula and the far larger Pembrokeshire Peninsula to the west flaunt unmatched coastal scenery and fine beaches.

HIGHLIGHTS OF SOUTH WALES

- Peruse the books in literary wonderland, **Hay-on-Wye,** which boasts the largest second-hand bookstore in the world (p. 407).
- Sunbathe on the white beaches of **Tenby,** known as the "Welsh Riviera," home to picturesque houses, soft cliffs, and seagulls (p. 417).
- **Swansea** is home to Wales's most famous literary son, **Dylan Thomas.** Walk among his haunts and confront his statue in Wales's second-largest city (p. 414).
- Recall Wordsworth's lines on **Tintern Abbey** as you stand before it (p. 405).
- Once the richest diocese in Wales, now the smallest city in Britain, **St. David's** stands perched on a 500-million-year-old peninsula, guarded by the purple walls of its cathedral (p. 423).

◼ Cardiff (Caerdydd)

Cardiff's 2000-year lineage stretches back to a Roman settlement at Cardiff Castle's present site, though the city wasn't named capital of Wales until 1955. Little more than a sleepy provincial seat until the rise of the coal industry, Cardiff exploded into prominence in the late 19th century when it served as the main port for Welsh coal. Now home to the Welsh regional government (gaining power since the 1997 vote for devolution) and the University of Wales at Cardiff, the city (pop. 300,000) is a vibrant mix of youthful flair and traditional culture. Its hot music scene contrasts with the artifacts at the National Museum of Wales. Host to the 1998 EU Summit and 1999 Rugby World Cup, Cardiff is gaining prominence at the dawn of the new millenium.

GETTING THERE

British Rail (tel. (0345) 484950) trains leave from London's **Paddington Station** and stop in Cardiff before heading westward (2hr., 1 per hr., 2 per hr. after 4:30pm, £35). Trains also speed from **Bath via Bristol** (1-1½hr., 2 per hour, £11.80), **Glasgow** and **Edinburgh** (7hr., 7 per day, £77), **Birmingham** (2½hr., 14 per day, £20.60), and **Swansea** (1hr., 4 per hr., £7.60). **National Express** (tel. (0990) 808080) careens between Cardiff and London's **Victoria Station** (3hr., 8 per day, £23), **Heathrow** (3 hr., 11 per day, £27), **Gatwick Airport** (4hr., 11 per day, £29), and **Glasgow** (8½hr., 3 per day, £22), and many other English cities. Check the invaluable *Wales Bus, Rail and Tourist Map and Guide* for further information. An array of day and week passes is offered by competing regional bus lines, and British Rail sells a seven-day **Freedom of Wales Rover** (see **Getting There and Getting About,** p. 388).

ORIENTATION AND PRACTICAL INFORMATION

Cardiff Castle stands triumphantly in the city center, with massive **Bute Park** stretching out behind it and shopping arcades before it. To the east, along Park Pl., are the Civic Centre, university buildings, and the National Museum. Shops, pedestrian walks, and indoor arcades cluster between **St. Mary** and **Queen St.,** southeast of the castle. The bus and train stations lie south of the city center, by the River Taff.

Cardiff (Caerdydd)

ACCOMMODATIONS
A Annedd Lon
B Bon Maison
D Cardiff International Backpackers
E Mrs. Bracken
C Ty Gwyn
F Youth Hostel (YHA)

TO E (1 MILE) & F (1.5 MILES)

TO ROYAL INFIRMARY (100YDS.)

West Grove
Newport Rd.
Fitzalan Place
Queen Street Station
Adam St.
Herbert St.
Bute Terr.
Customhouse St.

Dumfries Pl.
Churchill Way
Charles St.
Queen St.
QUEEN'S ARCADE
St. David's Hall
Bridge St.
The Hayes
Mill La.
Crockherbtown La.

Cathays Station
Park Pl.
Cardiff University College
National Museum of Wales
City Hall
Blvd. De Nantes
Greyfriars Rd.
The Friary
American Express
Working St.
Trinity St.
Duke St.
Queen St.

Welsh Office
Corbett Rd.
College Rd.
Museum Ave.
Cathays Park
King Edward VII Ave.
War Memorial
City Hall Rd.
North Rd.

Cardiff Castle
Castle St.
High St.
Womanby St.
Westgate St.
St. Mary St.
Wood St.
Central Sq.
Central Square
Central Station

Bute Park

Cardiff Arms Park

Fitzhamon Embankment

Sophia Gardens

Neville St.
Clare St.
Lower Cathedral Rd.
Launderama & Gallery
Tudor St.

Pontcanna Fields

Cathedral Rd.
Plasturton Rd.
Plasturton Ave.
Plasturton Gardens
King's Rd.
Talbot St.
Hamilton St.
Wyndham St.
Craddock St.
Cowbridge Rd. East
Wellington St.
Ninian Park Rd.

Dyfrig St.

Pontcanna St.
Severn Rd.
Severn Grove

300 yards
300 meters

N

WALES

Transportation

Trains: Central Station, Central Sq. (tel. (0345) 484950), south of the city center, behind the bus station. Ticket office open M-Sa 5:40am-9:30pm, Su 6:30am-9:30pm. Travel center open M-Sa 9am-6pm, Su noon-4:20pm.

Buses: National Express (tel. (0990) 808080) operates a booking office and travel center from Wood St. Show up at least 15min. before closing to book a ticket. Open M-Sa 7am-5:45pm, Su 9am-5:45pm.

Local Transportation: Cardiff Bus, or **Bws Caerdydd** (tel. 396521), in St. David's House on Wood St., runs an extensive 5-zone network of orange buses in Cardiff and environs. If you're far from the city center, show up 5min. early at the bus stop; schedules can be unreliable. Bus service in general ends early (M-Sa 11:20pm, Su 11pm). Fares 50p-£1.35; reduced fares for seniors and children; lower fares M-F 9:15am-3:45pm (40p-£1). Have exact fare ready; local buses sometimes cannot make change. Week-long **Multiride Passes** are available here (£9, children £4.50); **Capital Tickets** can be purchased from drivers (£3.20 per day for up to 3 days, children £2 per day).

Taxi: Metro Cabs (tel. 464646), open 24hr. **Supatax** (tel. 226644), open 24hr. Taxi stands in front of the train station and on Wood St. in front of the bus station.

Tourist and Financial Services

Tourist Office: Cardiff Central Railway Station (tel. 227281). Free accommodations list. Booking service costs £1 plus 10% deposit. Pick up a free, detailed map at the desk showing all the sights. Buy a **Cardiff Card** (£11 for 1 day, £18.50 for 2 days, £24 for 3 days) which pays bus fare and admission costs to various sights, such as the castle, and includes discounts at certain shops and restaurants. Open Apr.-Sept. M, W-Sa 9am-6:30pm, Tu 10am-6:30pm, Su 10am-4pm; Oct.-Mar. M, W-Sa 9am-5:30pm, Tu 10am-5:30pm, Su 10am-4pm.

Tours: Leisurelink (tel. 522202) runs a 1hr. bus tour visiting 19 sites. Starts from the main gate of Cardiff Castle every 30min. Open daily 10am-4pm. £6, students and seniors £5, children £4.

Budget Travel: Campus Travel, 13 Castle St. (tel. 220744; fax 344229), inside the YHA Adventure Shop. Student airfares, train discounts, ISIC cards. Open M, W, and F 9:30am-5:30pm, Tu 10:30am-5:30pm, Th and Sa 9:30am-6pm.

Financial Services: Barclays, 114-116 St. Mary St. (tel. 239055; fax 828381). Disabled access available (ring doorbell for service). Open M-Tu and Th-F 9am-5pm, W 10am-5pm. **Thomas Cook,** 16 Queen St. (tel. 224886). Open M-Th and Sa 9am-5:30pm, F 10am-5:30pm. **ATMs** abound.

American Express: 3 Queen St. (tel. 668858; fax 666931). Holds mail for members only; full address should include "Cardiff CF1 4AF, Wales." 1% commission for other traveler's checks, £3 for currency. Open M and W-F 9am-5:30pm, Tu 9:30am-5:30pm, Sa 9am-5pm.

Local Services

Camping Equipment: YHA Adventure Shop, 13 Castle St. (tel. 399178). Wide selection and 10% discount for YHA members and Brits in the National Union of Students. Open M-W and F 9:30am-5:30pm, Th 9am-6pm, Sa 9:30am-6pm, Su 10am-4pm. Other outdoor equipment stores lie along Castle and Duke St.

Launderette: Launderama, 60 Lower Cathedral Rd. (tel. 228326). Open Th-Tu 9:30am-5:30pm.

Emergency and Communications

Emergency: Dial 999; no coins required.

Police: Civic Centre (tel. 222111), opposite Cathay's Park.

Hotlines: Samaritans (crisis), 75 Cowbridge Rd. East (tel. 344022), opposite St. David's Hospital. Drop-in daily 8am-10pm; open 24hr. **AIDS Line** (tel. 223443), M-F 10am-10pm. **Cardiff Friends** (Lesbian and Gay Switchboard; tel. 340101), W-F 8-10pm, youth help Su 8:30-9:30pm. **Rape and Sexual Abuse Hotline** (tel. 373181), M and Th 7-10pm. **Women's Aid** (tel. 460566), open 24hr.

Hospital: Royal Infirmary, 50 Newport Rd. at Glossop Rd. (tel. 492233).

Post Office: 2-4 Hill's St. (tel. 227305), off The Hayes. Open M-F 9am-5:30pm, Sa 9am-4:30pm. Bureau de change. Money Gram wiring service. **Postal Code:** CF1 2ST.

Internet Access: Cardiff **Cybercafé,** 9 Duke St. (tel. 235757; email info@cardiffcy-bercafe.co.uk), first staircase on the left in Crown Court alley. £2.50 per 30min., £4.50 per hr.; printing 10p per page. 10 terminals. Open daily 10am-10pm. See also **Havabyte Cafe** (p. 400).

Telephone Code: 01222.

ACCOMMODATIONS

Few budget accommodations lie in the center of Cardiff, but the tourist office lists reasonably priced B&Bs (£16-18) on the outskirts and books rooms for £1. Many of the B&Bs along **Cathedral Rd.** are expensive (£20-25). Bargains are more plentiful in the smaller neighborhoods around Cathedral Rd. (a short ride on bus #32 or a 15min. walk from the castle). Ask for student discounts—some B&Bs may provide them upon request.

YHA Cardiff Youth Hostel, 2 Wedal Rd., Roath Park (tel. 462303), 2mi. from city center; take bus #78, 80, or 82 from Central Station. Helpful staff with bountiful tips on deciphering bus timetables. £9.75, under 18 £6.55. Meals available (£3-5). Open 24hr., security code required after 11pm. Check-in 10am-10:30pm. Checkout 10am. Open daily Jan.-Nov.

Annedd Lon, 157-159 Cathedral Rd. (tel. 223349). Proprietress Maria Tucker recently expanded these Victorian-era houses to cater to budget travelers. Ring the bell and wait to be let into the elegantly furnished interiors. £15, with bath and breakfast £20. No smoking. All rooms have color TV.

Cardiff International Backpacker, 98 Neville St. (tel. 345577; fax 230404), down Wood St. and across the river from the city center, turn right onto Fitzham Embankment. Turn left at the end of the road onto Neville St. Sion (pronounced "Shawn") Llewelyn, the hostel's owner, was a backpacker himself and provides all the amenities a traveler could want. Close to the city center, this colorful new hostel has a kitchen, cable TV, and (best of all) a 24hr. liquor license! After dark, take a cab or call for pickup from the station. 4- to 8-bed single-sex dorms £12.50, weekly £75; doubles £29; triples £35. Breakfast included. Locker deposit £2.

Ty Gwyn, 5-7 Dyfrig St. (tel. 239785; fax 390810), off Cathedral Rd. A fascinating house filled with Victorian furniture and formidable cast-iron fireplaces. Rooms are enormous and well-sunned, and some have showers and TV. A gate at the end of nearby Dyfrig St. leads onto the gorgeous Taff Trail, where you can stroll along the beautiful River Taff on your way to the castle. £12, with breakfast £15.

Bon Maison, 39 Plasturton Gdns. (tel. 383660), off Cathedral Rd. Turn left onto Plasturton Pl., right onto Plasturton Gdns. If it's warm, enjoy the large breakfast on the garden patio. Singles and doubles are budgetbreakers (singles £23; doubles £32, with bath £35; £1 discount for *Let's Go* users), but 3 or 4 traveling together can share the 4-person bedroom for £14-15 each. All rooms have TV. No credit cards.

Mrs. Bracken, 302 Whitchurch Rd. (tel. 621557), take bus #35 from the central station and ask to be let off at McJohn's (an auto shop). The Irish proprietress offers a generous breakfast in her family home. £14.

Camping: Acorn Camping and Caravanning, Rosedew Farm, Ham Ln. South, Llantwit Major (tel. (01446) 794024). Take a 1hr. ride on bus #92 from the central station; it's a 15min. walk from the stop at Ham Ln. South. June-Aug. £2 per pitch and £2.50 per person, £1.50 per child; Sept.-May £2 per pitch and £2 per person, £1 per child; electricity £2. No extra charge for cars. Showers and laundry.

FOOD

Though traditional Welsh cooking is generally a more stoic version of England's meat-and-two-veggies, Cardiff offers a reasonable variety of tasty comestibles. Budget travelers gleefully scour the many stalls of the Victorian **Central Market,** in an arcade between **St. Mary** and **Trinity St.,** where you can purchase anything from peaches to octopi (open M-Sa 8am-5:30pm). Also try the open-air **fruit market** on **Caroline St.**

(open M-Sa 9am-5pm). **The Firkin Brewery,** 39-41 Salisbury Rd. (tel. 239388), close to the University, offers £1 dishes on Monday nights. To get some quick fish and chips, head to **Tony's Fish Bar** (open daily 11am-3am), or a host of similar shops on Caroline St. The stretch of **Whitchurch Rd.** closest to the university has a number of inexpensive ethnic restaurants. To get there, take bus #35 to St. Joseph's School. As elsewhere, pub grub is a good option for travelers on a budget; check out the "two for a fiver" deals.

Crumbs, 33 David Morgan Arcade (tel. 395007). Tucked away between St. Mary St. and The Hayes, this vegetarian restaurant has great salads (£2-3) and deliciously healthy curry and brown rice (£3.45). Open M-F 10am-3pm, Sa 10am-4pm.

⊛**Celtic Cauldron Wholefoods,** 47-49 Castle Arcade (tel. 387185), across from the castle on Castle St. Traditional Welsh food, including faggots (unfortunately named and misshapen meatballs dunked in gravy), rarebit and laver-bread (£4-5), and a good selection of vegetarian fare (£3.50-4.50 or attempt the £8.10 Mighty Vegetarian For Two by yourself and earn the title). The spicy fruit punch is just the thing for a rainy Welsh day (£1.10). Open June-Aug. M-Sa 8:30am-9pm, Su 11am-4pm; Sept.-May M-Sa 8:30am-6pm, Su 11am-4pm.

Havabyte Cafe, 101 Woodville Rd. (tel./fax 388815). Walk north down Senghennydd Rd.; Woodville Rd. is to the right of Woodville pub. Deep in a student grotto, the Havabyte offers internet access (£2.50 per 30min.; £4 per hr.) and cheap tasty sandwiches, each named after an Italian city (£2.50-4). Check out the Spanish courtyard and the Arabic works on the bookshelf. Open daily 9:30am-10pm.

Top of the Shop Restaurant, 23 and 24 The Hayes, 3rd floor of David Morgan. Brave your way through the department store and be rewarded with a rooftop view of Cardiff. More a cafeteria than a restaurant, this place serves various forms of caffeine, chicken curry (£4), large salads (£2.45), and filled baguettes (£2.20). Open M-W and F 9am-5:15pm, Th 4-8pm, Sa 9am-6pm; hot food served until 3pm.

SIGHTS

The interior of **Cardiff Castle** (tel. 878100) is no less flamboyant than the peacocks and peahens which mewl inside the gates. *(Open daily Mar.-Oct. 9:30am-6pm, last entry 5pm; Nov.-Feb. 9:30am-4:30pm, last entry 3:30pm. Tours Mar.-Oct. every 20min. 10am-1pm and 2-5pm; Nov.-Feb. 5 tours daily. £4.80, students £3.60, seniors and children £2.40.)* The third Marquess of Bute employed William Burges, most lavish of Victorian architect-designers, to restore the castle in a mock-medieval style. Each room is done in a different theme, from the Victorian nursery to the Arab room. At the back, the Norman keep presides over the grounds; climb the stairs and you'll be rewarded with a sweeping view of Cardiff. The castle (second largest in Britain after Windsor) also contains the museums of the **1st Queen's Dragon Guards** and the **Welsh Regiment** *(museum and grounds only £2.40, students £1.80, seniors and children £1.20).*

Across North Rd. stands Cardiff's **Civic Centre,** the grassy lawns of Cathay's Park and stately white buildings combine to give Cardiff a heart of beauty. The giant asparagus stalk in the sky is the belfry of Cardiff's **City Hall,** which contains a "Hall of Welsh Heroes," marble statues of Welsh historical figures with St. David at center stage. Walk into the **National Museum and Gallery of Wales** (tel. 397951; fax 373219; http://www.cf.ac.uk/ngw) and experience the startling audio-visual display of "The Evolution of Wales," which speeds you through millennia of geological transformation. *(Open Tu-Su 10am-5pm. £3.25, students, seniors, and disabled £2, children £1.50.)* The museum also has a large collection of European art, especially Impressionist works.

Corporate promotion is alive and well on the high-tech landscape of **Cardiff Bay,** (bus #8 from Central Station) where a massive waterfront development is nearing completion. For its submarine-like shape, the view offered through its giant oval window, and the free advice contained therein, the **Visitor Centre** (tel. 463833; fax 486650) is worth a look *(open M-F 9:30am-7:30pm, Sa-Su 10:30am-7:30pm).* Nearby, the **Welsh Industrial and Maritime Museum** (tel. 481919) preserves the oily smell of the Industrial Revolution. *(Open Tu-Su 10am-5pm. £2.75, students, seniors and children £1.25.)*

Fight off rambunctious children at **Techniquest** (tel. 475475; fax 482517; email ge@tquest.org.uk), Britain's largest hands-on science discovery museum. *(Open M-F 9:30am-4:30pm, Sa-Su 10:30am-5pm. £4.75, students, seniors, and children £3.50.)*

ENTERTAINMENT

Cardiff's signature odor emanates from **Brains Brewery** (tel. 399022) on the corner of St. Mary and Caroline St. Its specialty is Brains S.A. (Special Ale), known to locals as "Brains Skull Attack" and served proudly by many pubs in the city center. Tours of the brewery can be arranged in advance; call and ask for the marketing department. Around the corner at 49 St. Mary St., **The Old Brewery Shop** (tel. 395828) hawks a fine range of Brains souvenirs, including inevitable punning T-shirts such as "Brains Storm." *(Open M-Sa 9:30am-5:45pm.)*

Cardiff's clubbing scene has the advantage of density—if you don't like a club, move on (or just move on anyway, whether you like it or not). The clubs rotate the music played, so check out *Buzz!*, the free listing guide, to help you plan ahead. "Student night" often means good deals with hordes taking advantage of cheap cover and £1 drinks. After dark, avoid the docks and wharf, and don't hesitate to hail a cab.

Clwb Ifor Bach (a.k.a. the **Welsh Club**), 11 Womanby St. (tel. 232199). This manic, 3-tiered club hosts live bands on Mondays and Sundays, a "rock inferno" on Tuesdays, pop/Britpop on Wednesdays, and acid jazz on Thursdays. Saturday is reserved for Welsh-fluent members and their guests; the rest of the week English speakers predominate. Cover £2-3 plus £1 "associate membership." Open M-Th until 2am, F varies, Sa until 4am, Su until 10:30pm.

Zeus (tel. 377014), on Greyfriars Rd. Beautiful people congregate in this cavernous club. Dress smart casual, emphasis on the smart. Weeknights see alcohol cheaper than soft drinks! Cover £2.50-6. Tu 8:30pm-2am, W-Th 9pm-2am, F-Sa 9pm-3am.

Sam's Bar (tel. 345189), on the corner of St. Mary and Mill St. Occasional live performances and a nightly DJ until 2am. Cover F-Sa £3-4. Open Sa until 4am, Su until 10:30pm.

Club CF1 (tel. 224754), on Womanby St. "No nonsense boogie and beer." Cover F-Sa after 9pm £3-4. Open M-W 7pm-11pm, Th 9pm-2am, F 6pm-2am, Sa 6pm-2am.

Po NaNa, 3-5 St. Mary's St. (tel. 303233), in the basement. Plays great music and makes a virtue of its small size by placing couches everywhere—*voila!* Intimacy! Cover £2.50-5. M-Sa 8:30pm-2am.

Philharmonic, 76-77 St. Mary St. (tel. 230678). Wood panels and subdued pictures of Old Cardiff blend with the whistles and beeps of game machines. Cover £1-4. Open M-Sa 11am-2am, Su 11am-10:30pm.

Exit Bar, 48 Charles St. Cardiff's "out" crowd dances and drinks the night away. Open M-Tu 6pm-2am, no entry after midnight, W-Sa 6pm-midnight, Su 7pm-midnight.

More sedate, but equally enjoyable, is Cardiff's art scene. The elegant **Chapter Arts Centre** (tel. 399666), Market Rd. in Canton, features an eclectic program of dance, drama, gallery exhibitions, and film. *(Open M-Th 10am-11pm, F 10am-midnight, Su 10am-10:30pm. Cinema prices £3.70, students and seniors £2.60. Discounts on early evening shows.)* Take bus #17, 18, or 19 from Castle St. up Cowbridge Rd. and get off opposite the Canton police station. All types of music and dancing, including the **BBC National Orchestra of Wales**, are found in the modern **St. David's Hall**, The Hayes (tel. 878444), considered one of Britain's finest concert venues. *(Prices vary, students, seniors and children £3.)* Contemporary plays and dance are featured at the **Sherman Theatre** (tel. 230451), on Senghennydd Rd., which also serves as the home for one of Britain's finest Young People's Theatre groups. **The New Theatre**, Park Pl. (tel. 878889), off Queen St., hosts the **Welsh National Opera** and a variety of musical performances and plays.

Adornments on the **John Bachelor Statue**, corner of Hill's St. and The Hayes, are a good gauge of the festive atmosphere in Cardiff. Scarves and hats signify rugby or football matches, and a clumsily held can of Brains S.A. is often a sign of sport-induced bacchanalia. Rugby games are played at the **National Rugby Stadium** (tel. 390111), Westgate St., which is due to re-open in June 1999 for the Rugby World Cup (regular season Sept.-Apr.). Tickets for international games sell (out) for £8-26. Try your luck at the club games next door at the **Cardiff Rugby and Football Club** (tel. 383546; £8-12, students and children £5, seniors £8).

■ Near Cardiff

Give it half a chance (and half a day) and be astounded by the **Museum of Welsh Life** (Amgueddfa Werin Cymru; tel. 569441), 4 mi. west of Cardiff, spread across **St. Fagan's Park.** Nearly 30 buildings transported from all across Wales have been reassembled here from a primitive Celtic Village and a 16th-century farmhouse to a turn-of-the-century schoolhouse. Many of the sites feature craft demonstrations, such as leather-tanning and blacksmithing. *(Open daily July-Sept. 10am-6pm; Oct.-June 10am-5pm. £5.25, students and seniors £3.75, children 5-16 £3, families £13.50; in winter £4, students, seniors, and children £3.)* While in the park, be sure to see **St. Fagan's Castle,** a grand home built on the site of a medieval Norman castle and now furnished as a 19th-century Welsh mansion. Down through the castle garden and across the mossy ponds is an exhibition center with displays on agriculture and "Welsh fashion through the ages." The hourly bus #32A or 32B runs from Central Station, and the hourly bus #56 leaves from Castle St.

Two miles northwest of the city center near the River Taff is **Llandaff Cathedral** (tel. 564554). Built by the Normans, used by Cromwell as an alehouse, restored by the Victorians, and gutted by a German land mine in 1941, the Cathedral is now an architectural mince pie—a stern and solid Norman arch behind the altar is overshadowed by an intrusive reinforced-concrete arch from 1957, surmounted by a strangely aquatic-looking Christ. Worth a longer gaze is the Rosetti triptych (to the left as you step into the Cathedral). Enter without making a peep if you're lucky enough to come upon one of the two choirs in performance. *(Open M-Sa 7am-7pm, Su 7am-8pm.)* Nearby, the ivy-covered, ruined arches of the **Castle of the Bishops of Llandaff** loom over a small, quiet garden. Take bus #25 from Castle St. or bus #33, 62C, 65C, or 133 from Cardiff Central or walk down Cathedral Rd. and through Llandaff Fields; turn left onto Western Ave., right onto Cardiff Rd., and right onto Llandaff High St. For those seeking pastoral diversion, the 55mi. **Taff Trail** winds from Cardiff Bay, through the Taff Valley to the heart of the Brecon Beacons National Park (see p. 409). The Cardiff tourist office provides a free pamphlet detailing the route.

Bute and Burges, the same dastardly duo that renovated Cardiff Castle, struck again at **Castell Coch** (tel. 810101). Reputedly the richest man in the world in the late 19th century, Lord Bute's money allowed him free rein to remake the castle in faux medieval style, with birds turning to butterflies to stars on the ceiling and scenes from *Aesop's Fables.* Check out the lascivious monkeys on Lady Bute's ceiling—*très risqué. (Open Apr.-Sept. daily 9:30am-6:30pm; Oct.-Mar. M-Sa 9:30am-4pm, Su 11am-4pm. £2.50, students, seniors, and children £2, families £7, audio tour 50p extra.)* Take bus #26 (1 per hr.) up the A470 to the village of **Tongwynlais,** where a brisk 15-minute walk up the hill brings you to the castle. Bus #126 (M-F 5 per day) unloads at the castle gate.

Eight miles north of Cardiff, sprawling **Caerphilly Castle** (tel. 883143) dwarfs everything around it. The 30 acres of man-made lakes and walls were built by the 13th-century Norman warlord Gilbert de Clare. The castle's famous leaning tower edges 3 degrees closer to the ground than its Pisan counterpart, but the impressive moat prevented invaders from exploiting that weakness. *(Open late Mar. to late Oct. daily 9:30am-6:30pm; late Oct. to late Mar. M-Sa 9:30am-4pm, Su 11am-4pm. £2.40, students, seniors, and children £1.90, families £6.70.)* Take the hourly bus #26 from Cardiff Central and get off in the shadow of the endless curtain wall, or save time by train (20min., M-Sa 2 per hr., £2.30).

Cardiff Bus whisks travelers to nearby **Barry Island** to visit the fairgrounds and bask on sandy beaches 11 mi. outside of the city (bus #354, 30min., 1per hr, £2 return).

■ Wye Valley

Wordsworth once came to the Wye Valley to escape the "fever of the world." Though its tranquility has since been disturbed by a feverish tourist trade, much of the region remains unsullied and pleasing to hikers and castle-lovers. The River Wye (Afon Gwy) powers its way from the hills of central Wales to its confluence with the broad and muddy river Severn just south of Chepstow. Moving past Wordsworth's "steep cliffs," "orchard tufts," and "pastoral farms," the river brings green to the door of even the larger towns. Signposts point in every direction to walkways which allow escape from the motorway network that links the Valley to Gloucester and England's major cities.

GETTING THERE AND GETTING ABOUT

The valley is best entered from the south, at Chepstow, which connects to both Cardiff and **Newport**, 20mi. east of Cardiff. **Trains** chug from **Cardiff** or **Newport** to both Chepstow (40min., M-Sa 12 per day, Su 7 per day, £4.80) and **Hereford**, north of Chepstow in England (1hr., 1 per hr., £12.20). **Stagecoach Red and White** (tel. (01633) 266336) bus #X14 leaves the **Cardiff** station (1hr., 9 per day, £3.15), while buses #64 and 74 go from Newport to Chepstow (1 per hr., fewer in the evenings). **National Express** (tel. (0990) 808080) buses also ride to Chepstow from **Cardiff** (50min., 5 per day, £3.15), **Newport** (30min., 5 per day, £2.25), **London** (2¼hr., M-Sa 6 per day, Su 5 per day, £16.50), and **Heathrow** (2hr., 5 per day, £23).

Be aware that there is almost no Sunday **bus** service in the Wye Valley. See the indispensable *Wales Bus, Rail and Tourist Map and Guide* in any tourist office. **Stagecoach Red and White** loops through Chepstow, Tintern, and Monmouth (bus #69, M-F 7 per day, Sa 8 per day, no Su service). From Monmouth take **H&H Coaches** (tel. (01989) 566444) to Hereford (bus #416, 5 per day, no Su service). To get to Hay-on-Wye from Hereford, take the **Stagecoach** (bus #39, M-Sa 5 per day, Su take Yeoman's bus #40, 2 per day, £3.20). **Phil Anslow Travel** careens between Monmouth and Abergavenny (bus #83, 6 per day, 40min.). One-day **Roverbus** passes (£4.50, children £3) and week-long **Primerider** passes (£17, children £11.35), available from Stagecoach drivers will save you money if you plan to take more than one bus in a given day (see **Getting There and Getting About,** p. 388). **Hitching** is said to be good on the A466 in the summer; some stand near the entrance to Tintern Abbey or by the Wye Bridge in Monmouth.

Hiking

The valley yields walks of varying difficulties and lengths. The **Wye Valley Walk** starts at Chepstow and passes along cliffs, wooded hills, and farmland. The abbey at Tintern and the cathedral at Hereford each provide an hour's diversion. From the breathtaking vista at Symonds Yat, the walk continues northward to Hay-on-Wye and ends at Prestatyn in the far north. Across the river, **Offa's Dyke Path** runs the entire length of the English-Welsh border, offering 177 mi. of hiking trails (Chepstow-Tintern 5mi., Tintern-Monmouth 11mi., Monmouth-Symonds Yat 6mi.). The Wye Valley Path accommodates bikes; Offa's Dyke Path does not. East of Symonds Yat lies the 20,000-acre **Royal Forest of Dean**, once the happy hunting ground of Edward the Confessor and Williams I and II. For information on the forest, contact **Forest Enterprise** (tel. (01594) 833057) on Bank St. in Coleford, England, across the river from Monmouth (open M-Th 8:30am-5pm, F 8:30am-4pm). Or try the **Coleford tourist office,** High St. (tel. (01594) 812388; open M-Sa 10am-5pm). Several trails lead to the Wye Valley Walk and Offa's Dyke Path. Tourist offices sell pamphlets; pick up the beautifully bound (and free) *Walking Wales* guide for an idea of which path to take. A 1:25,000 Ordnance Survey map (£6) shows every path, pit, and remarkable rock in the lower Wye Valley and the Forest of Dean. For information on Offa's Dyke Path, write to the **Offa's Dyke Association,** West St., Knighton, Powys, Wales LD7 1EN (tel. (01547) 528753). If you're hiking between towns, some B&B owners will send your luggage to the next B&B—ask nicely.

■ Chepstow (Cas-Gwent)

Chepstow's strategic position at the mouth of the River Wye and the base of the English-Welsh border made it an important fortification and commercial center in Norman times and a frontier town during the English Civil War. Chepstow's **train station** lies on Station Rd. while **buses** stop above the town gate in front of the Somerfield supermarket. Both stations are unstaffed, but you can ask about National Express tickets at **Fowlers Travel,** 9 Moor St. (tel. 623031; open M-F 9am-5:30pm, Sa 9am-3:30pm). Chepstow's **tourist office** (tel. 623772) confronts the castle from the car park and books rooms for a 10% deposit (open daily Apr.-Sept. 10am-5:45pm; Oct.-Mar. 10am-4pm). **Barclays Bank** is located in Beaufort Sq. (open M-Tu and Th-F 9am-4:30pm, W 10am-4:30pm. ATM outside). The **post office** (tel. 622607) resides in Albion Sq. (open M-F 9am-5:30pm, Sa 9am-12:30pm). Chepstow's **postal code** is NP6 5DA, its **telephone code** 01291.

The **YHA Youth Hostel** at **St. Briavel's Castle** (tel. (01594) 530272; fax 530849), 4 mi. northeast of Tintern, occupies a 12th-century castle complete with a dungeon accessible through a trapdoor in the floor and offers tours for residents (65p). One stone bedroom holds poignant inscriptions carved in the walls by prisoners from as early as 1674. From the A466 (bus #69 from Chepstow) or Offa's Dyke, follow signs for 2 mi. from Bigsweir Bridge to St. Briavel's. (£9.40, under 18 £6.30. Kitchen and meals £6.55. No laundry. Lockout 10am-5pm. Curfew 11:30pm. Open daily Feb.-Dec.) In Chepstow, **Lower Hardwick House** (tel. 622162) on Mt. Pleasant, 300 yd. up the hill from the bus station, is a 200-year-old Georgian mansion run by the delightful and wonderfully solicitous Eileen Grassby. The proprietress fills her home with handsome and mysterious furniture collected during her years in Asia (singles £15-18; doubles £30-35). The vast garden accommodates **campers** as well as sculptures by Eileen's son—look for the tree ringed with disembodied heads (£5 per tent, with continental breakfast £7). Or try **Langcroft,** 71 St. Kingsmark Ave. (tel./fax 625569), by the Castle Dell, where you can relax in the conservatory and peer at lurking fish or your own TV (£15). For more **camping** options, try **Beeches Farm,** Tidenham Chase (tel. 689257), 5 mi. north of Chepstow and just east of Offa's Dyke Path, convenient for walkers (£1.50 per person; no showers).

Britain's oldest stone castle, **Chepstow Castle** (tel. 624065), was built by Earl William, a Norman companion of William the Conqueror who undoubtedly had too much pocket money. Look over the castle walls for an enthralling view of the Avon Wye. The newly formed Chepstow Garrison stages Civil War reenactments (tel. 623316—ask for Keith; every last Su of the month; 11:30am-4pm). The old **town wall,** in some places as thick as 7 ft. and as high as 15 ft., was designed as an extension of the castle. (Open Apr. to late Oct. daily 9:30am-6:30pm; late Oct. to Mar. M-Sa 9:30am-4pm, Su 11am-4pm. Last admission 30min. before closing. £3, students, seniors and children £2, families £18.) The **Chepstow Festival,** held throughout July in even-numbered years, features open-air Shakespeare and musical events punctu-

---

Let Them Eat Cheese

Don't be alarmed if you wake from an afternoon nap at St. Briavel's youth hostel to a rhythmic chant. The villagers gathered across the street leaping at flying chunks of cheese aren't preparing to storm the castle, but rather engaging in a somewhat mysterious ceremony unique to this tiny village. Every Whitsunday since the 17th century, bread and cheese have been distributed outside the Roman church to this chant:

> *St. Briavel's water and Whyrl's wheat*
> *Are the best bread and water King John ever eat.*

Centuries ago, the English Earl of Hereford withdrew local villagers' right to gather wood, but when his compassionate wife protested, the Earl backed down. As a gesture of thanks, his wife suggested that each villager contribute a penny to feed the poor. The ritual has since evolved from its charitable roots, and now residents from all social strata feast on the hurled cheese.

ated by fully armored battles in the castle. The 2000 festival is expected to be quite an event. On Bridge St., the **Chepstow Museum** (tel. 625981; fax 625983), on the site of a former hospital, details the history of Chepstow. (Open July-Sept. M-Sa 10:30am-1pm and 2-5pm, Su 2-5pm; Oct.-June M-Sa 11am-1pm and 2-5pm, Su 2-5pm. £1, students, seniors 75p, children free.) For a stunning view, walk down Bridge St. to the **Wye Bridge**, once the highest bridge in Britain. On the river bank lies the **Wye Knot,** where Welsh emigrants set off (or were shipped off, in some cases) for Australia and America.

■ Tintern

Five miles north of Chepstow on the A466, dense trees fill the gaps in the delicate arches of **Tintern Abbey** (tel. 689251; fax 628000). Immortalized by Wordsworth in a very long poem, the abbey was built by Cistercian monks in the 12th and 13th centuries as a center for religious austerity; this did not prevent it from becoming the richest abbey in Wales, until Henry VIII dissolved it. Arrive in the morning and beat the hordes of tourists. *(Open mid-Mar. to mid-Oct. daily 9:30am-6:30pm; mid-Oct. to mid-Mar. M-Sa 9:30am-4pm, Su 11am-4pm. £2.20, students, seniors, and children £1.70, families £6.10.)* If crowds overwhelm, cross the iron footbridge and head for the hills. Marked paths lead to **Offa's Dyke** (45min.) and **Devil's Pulpit** (1hr.), a huge stone from which Satan is said to have tempted the monks as they worked in the fields.

A mile north of the abbey on the A466 lies Tintern's **Old Station.** Once a stop on the Wye Valley Line, the now unused train station holds a series of train carriages within which is the **information service** (tel./fax 689566; open Apr.-Oct. daily 10:30am-5:30pm). The 400-year-old **Wye Barn Bed and Breakfast** (tel. 689456) offers a view of the Wye in every room (£20; doubles with bath £44). Off the A466 at the village, next to the Moon and Sixpence Pub, **The Old Rectory** (tel. 689519; fax (0374) 570395) has a magnificent brick fireplace and water from its own natural spring (singles £17, with bath £19; special rates for longer stays). Campers can use the field opposite the train station (£1.50 per person; toilets and water available). Tintern's **postal code** is NP6 6SB; it shares Chepstow's **telephone code** of 01291.

■ Monmouth (Trefynwy)

The market town of Monmouth is nestled between the Rivers Wye, Monnow, and Trothy, 8 mi. north of Tintern. The town is the birthplace of Geoffrey of Monmouth, who gave a shred of historical credibility to King Arthur and Merlin in his *History of the Kings of Britain.* The history of the town blends with its present on Monnow St., where an archaeological dig takes place amidst a row of shops. The famous 13th-century **toll bridge,** still intact, glowers at visitors crossing the Monnow, but time has so ruthlessly ruined the Norman castle on Castle Hill (where Henry V was born in 1387) that it barely rises above its parking lot and is overshadowed by the **Regimental Museum** building next to it.

Buses stop on a sidestreet off Monnow St. near the fortified bridge. Monmouth is the last stop for bus #69 from Chepstow and Tintern; bus #60 goes to Newport. A **tourist office** (tel. 713899; fax 772794) hides in Shire Hall, the 1724 courthouse on Agincourt Sq. where the leaders of the Chartist movement were tried (open Apr.-Oct. daily 10am-6pm). **Barclays Bank** and its **ATM** stand across from the tourist office on Priory St. (open M-Tu and Th-F 9am-5:30pm, W 10am-5:30pm). Farther up the hill on Priory St. sits the **post office,** Market Hall (open M-Th 9am-5:30pm, F 9:30am-5:30pm, Sa 9am-12:30pm). The **postal code** is NP5 3TA; the **telephone code** is 01600.

Monmouth's **YHA Youth Hostel** (tel. 715116) by St. Mary's Church, near the town center, occupies the 15th-century Priory St. School where Geoffrey of Monmouth is thought to have studied; admire the grand, gargoyle-studded Geoffrey's Window facing Priory St. (£7.20, students £6.20, children £5. Kitchen. Lockout 10am-5pm. Curfew 11pm. Open Mar.-Oct. daily. Light chores expected.) In Monmouth proper, B&Bs lie along Hereford Rd. and in St. James' Square. **Wye Avon** (tel. 713322), Dixton Rd., about ¼ mi. from the city center, provides rooms in a beautiful house apparently built from the stone of the old town wall (£16).

Near Monmouth

About halfway between Monmouth and Abergavenny on the A40 lies **Raglan Castle** (tel. (01291) 690228). Raglan was designed more for residential living than actual defense, as the absence of arrow slits suggests. Heavily bombarded in the Civil War, the castle lies mostly in ruin. Take Phil Anslow bus #416 (6 per day). (Open Apr. to late Oct. daily 9:30am-6:30pm; late Oct. to Mar. M-Sa 9:30am-4pm, Su 11am-4pm. £2.40, students, seniors, children £1.90, families £6.70.)

■ Hereford, England

Although Hereford (HAIR-uh-fuhd) is English, its bus and rail connections make it an excellent springboard for a trip to Wales. This small border town has recently grown to a population some 60,000 strong, extending beyond the ruins of the old city walls.

GETTING THERE The train and bus **stations** are both located on Commercial Rd. Facing the tourist office along Broad St. is the **bus stop** for local services. **Trains** from London's **Paddington Station** arrive every hour (3hr., £31). They also run to **Abergavenny** (25min., 2 per hr., £5.50), **Shrewsbury** (1hr., 1 per hr., £10.90), **Cardiff** (1hr., 1 per hr., £11.40), and **Chepstow via Newport** (14 per day, £17.80). For bus info, pick up the free *Hereford and Worcester County Public Transport Map and Guide* at the tourist office. **Stagecoach Red and White** (tel. (01633) 266336) connects Hereford to **Newport** (#20, M-Sa, 4 per day), among other Wye Valley towns; there is no Sunday service. Bus #39 runs to **Brecon via Hay-on-Wye** (1¾hr., M-Sa 5 per day, £4); on Sundays, **Yeoman's** bus #40 takes over (2 per day).

PRACTICAL INFORMATION The helpful staff at the **tourist office,** 1 King St. (tel. 268430; fax 342662), in front of the cathedral, books beds for a 10% deposit (open May-Sept. M-Sa 9am-5pm, Su 9am-1pm and 2-5pm; Oct.-Apr. M-Sa 9am-5pm). **Walking tours** leave from the tourist office. (Runs mid-May to mid-Sept. M-Sa 10:30am, Su 2:30pm. 1½hr. £2, seniors and children over 12 £1, under 12 free.) On Broad St., the **Barclays ATM** spits out crisp pound notes (bank open M and W-F 9am-5pm, Tu 10am-5pm, Sa 9:30am-noon). Laundry can be done at the **Coin-op Launder Centre,** 136 Eign St. (tel. 269610; open daily 6am-7:15pm). The **County Hospital** sits on Union Walk (call the operator); any **Hopper** bus will take you there. Next to the bus stop on 20 Broad St. is the **post office** (tel. 273611). The **postal code** is HR4 9HQ. The **telephone code** is 01432.

ACCOMMODATIONS Luxurious accommodations near the bus and rail stations are available at **Somerville,** Bodenham Rd. (tel. 273991), with TV and radio in each room (singles £18, with bath £25; doubles £30, with bath £40).

SIGHTS AND ENTERTAINMENT Rising above surrounding greens and the River Wye is the 11th-century **Hereford Cathedral** (tel. 359880). Most visitors flock to catch a glimpse of the **Mappa Mundi,** a map of the world drawn on animal skin in 1290. Sodom and Gomorrah lie drowned in the Dead Sea, mandrakes lurk in Egypt, and mythical beasts roam far and wide. Peer into the **Chained Library,** where 1500 rare books are linked to their shelves by slender chains. *(Cathedral open daily until Evensong. Free. Mappa Mundi and Chained Library shown M-F 10am-4:15pm, Sa 10am-5:15pm, Su noon-3:15pm. £4, students, seniors, and children £3, families £10.)* The steeples of St. Peter's Church and All Saints' Church act as bookends on either end of the pedestrianized **High Town,** which occupies the triangular site of the medieval market and features shopping and summer street performers. High Town was once completely lined with half-timber Tudor buildings, but only one—the early 17th-century **Old House** (tel. 364598)—remains fully intact. *(Open Apr.-Sept. Tu-Sa 10am-5pm, Su 10am-4pm; Oct.-Mar. Tu-Sa 10am-5pm. Free.)* A former butcher's shop, the Old House's creaky wooden floors now support loads of 17th- and 18th-century furniture. "Cheers!" *(iechyd da!),* written in several languages, greets visitors to the **Cider Museum,** Pomona Pl. (tel. 354207) where you can learn about traditional cider-making. *(Open Apr.-Oct. daily 10am-5:30pm; Nov.-Mar. Tu-Sa 1-5pm. £2.20, students, seniors and children £1.70.)* Art and music create a carnival atmosphere during the two-week **festival** in mid-July.

Those looking for a night out on the town will find that Hereford offers decent, if unspectacular, options. **Booth Hall** (tel. 344487), on East St., where St. Peter's St. meets High Town, is large, loud and jumping. *(Open M-Sa 11am-11pm, Su noon-3pm and 7:30-10:30pm.)* Prescribe your own music at **Doc's the Nightclub** (tel. 355350), on Aubrey St. off West St. Ignore the cheesy DJ and party with the game-for-anything crowd. *(Open F-Sa 9pm-2am.)*

■ Hay-On-Wye (Y Gelli)

With 35 secondhand and antiquarian bookstores, Hay-on-Wye certainly is "the town of books." After weathering eight centuries of wars, fires, and neglect, its Norman castle has finally been conquered by mobs of unruly first editions. To remind outsiders that they *really like books,* the townspeople throw a 10-day **literary festival** each year at the end of May, during which luminaries like Harold Pinter, Toni Morrison, and P.D. James give readings while Salman Rushdie darts nervously about. Be forewarned: festival crowds strain the plentiful accommodations, and many readings charge admission (£4-10).

PRACTICAL INFORMATION The closest **train station** is in Hereford. **Stagecoach Red and White** bus #39 runs between Hay, **Hereford,** and **Brecon** (M-Sa 5 per day, £2.50-3.15). On Sundays, **Yeoman's** buses (tel. (01432) 356201) runs twice between Brecon, Hay, and Hereford (#40, £1.50-2.65). The **tourist office** (tel. 820144; fax 820015), on Oxford Rd. next to the bus stop, offers information on booksellers, antique stores, and outdoor activities. (Books beds for £2-3. Open daily Apr.-Oct. 10am-1pm and 2-5pm; Nov.-Mar. 11am-1pm and 2-4pm.) Next to The Granary is a **Barclays** bank with an **ATM** (open M-Tu and Th-F 9:30am-4:30pm, W 10am-4:30pm). Rent bikes at **Paddles and Pedals Canoe and Cycle Hire,** 15 Castle St. (tel. 820604; £7.50 per ½day, £12.50 per day). The **post office** is 3 High Town (open M and W-F 9am-1pm and 2-5:30pm, Tu 9am-1pm, Sa 9am-12:30pm; **postal code** HR3 5AE). Hay-on-Wye's **telephone code** is 01497.

ACCOMMODATIONS AND FOOD The **YHA Youth Hostel** nearest to Hay-on-Wye lies 8 mi. out of town at **Capel-y-Ffin** (tel. (01873) 890650; see **Accommodations,** p. 411). One hundred yards from the tourist office down Oxford Rd., **I Garibaldi Terrace** (tel. 820351) offers rooms with views of the surrounding hills (doubles £28). Or try sleeping under the solid beams of 16th-century **Brookfield**, Brook St. (tel. 820518), where each room gets its own Welsh name (singles £18; doubles £30). If you're willing to walk, head straight for the beautifully restored **Old Post Office** (tel. 820008), 2 mi. away in the sleepy village of **Llanigon.** Take Brecon Rd. (B4350) out of Hay, turn left after 1½ mi. at the Llanigon sign, follow the road for a half-mile, and turn left just before you reach the primary school; the former Royal Mail outpost is opposite the church. You'll be rewarded with rustic Welsh furniture and delicious breakfasts (doubles only; £15 per person, with bath £20). It's easy to camp near Hay along the **Wye Valley Walk** or **Offa's Dyke** (see **Hiking,** p. 403). **Radnor's End Campsite** (tel. 820780), on a tiny plateau in the valley, is the closest to town; cross Bridge St. and go 300 yd. to the left towards Clyro (£3 per person).

Hay's Day

Hay-on-Wye stands on the England-Wales border. This indeterminate status, and the compelling logic that the independent city-states of Ancient Greece and Renaissance Italy were the greatest world civilizations ever seen, led to Richard Booth's grand April Fool's joke: a declaration of independence on April 1, 1977. Booth, owner of the largest second-hand bookstore in the world (Booth's Books brings in more books than every university and public library in Wales combined), made his proclamation as an attack on bureaucracy and big government and managed to draw national notice. Now Booth and his wife reign as King and Queen of Hay Castle. Turn up in Hay around April 1 and join in their Independence Day celebrations.

At **The Granary,** Broad St. (tel. 820790), you can sit outside and enjoy home-cooked food (£4.50-7; special veggie menu; open daily 10am-5:30pm). Hay's oldest pub, the dimly lit 16th-century **Three Tuns** on Broad St., has one bench, one table, and a horse-mounting block outside (open from 8pm). Shoot pool as you wait for your food (£2.20-6.25) at the **Wheatsheaf Inn,** Lion St. (tel. 820186).

■ Abergavenny (Y Fenni)

The market town of Abergavenny styles itself as the "traditional gateway to Wales." Many visitors take this literally and dash right through the gateway on their way to the hills; the Black Mountains in the eastern third of Brecon Beacons National Park and the Seven Hills of Abergavenny invite hikers to romp.

Trains run north from Abergavenny to **Hereford** (30min., 1 per hr., £5.50), **Shrewsbury** (1½hr., 1 per hr., £15.20), **Newport** (25min., 22 per day; £4.70), **Cardiff** (40min., 19 per day, £7.10), **Chepstow** (30min., departs every 2hr., £8.10), **Bristol** (1¼hr., departs every 2hr., £7.40), and **London** (2½hr., departs every 2hr., £31). The **bus station** bows at the foot of Monmouth Rd., across from the tourist office. Get **National Express** information at **Gwent Travel,** 55a Frogmore St. (tel. 857666; open M-F 9am-5pm, Sa 9am-4pm). **Stagecoach Red and White buses** (tel. (01633) 266336) rolls to **Hereford** (bus #20, 1hr., M-Sa 4 per day, £3), **Brecon** (bus #21, 1hr., 6 per day, £2.50), **Newport** (bus #20, 1hr., 12 per day, £2.60), and **Cardiff via Merthyr** (bus #X4, 2¼hr., 11 per day, £3.50).

The **tourist office** (tel. 857588; fax 850217) shares space with the **National Park Information Centre** (tel. 853254) on Monmouth Rd. by the bus station. (Tourist office open daily Apr.-Oct. 9:30am-6pm; Nov.-Mar. 9:30am-4pm. National Park Office open Mar.-Oct. daily 9:30am-5:30pm.) **Banks** line High St. and Frogmore St. including **Barclays,** at 57 Frogmore St., with a 24-hour **ATM** (open M-Tu and Th-F 9am-5pm, W 10am-5pm, Sa 10am-12:30pm). Piles of camping supplies may be purchased at **Crickhowell Adventure Gear,** 14 High St. (tel. 856581; open M-Sa 9am-5:30pm). From the train station take a right at the end of Station Rd. to get into town, and expect a 15-minute walk. The **post office,** with a bureau de change and a photobooth, sits at St. John's Sq. where Tudor St. abuts Castle St. (open M-F 9am-5:30pm; Sa 9am-12:30pm). The **postal code** is a grinning NP7 5EB. For £4 an hour, **internet access** is available from **Celtic Computer Systems,** 20 Monk St. (tel./fax 858111; email celtic.systems@virgin.net; open M-F 9am-5:30pm, Sa 9am-5pm). The **telephone code** is a toothy 01873.

Budget-busting B&Bs (£15-20) lie in wait on Monmouth Rd., and the tourist office lists several others in a similarly bleeding price range (£15-22). Unfortunately, no youth hostels lie near Abergavenny. A better bet is the **Ivy Villa Guest House,** 43 Hereford Rd. (tel. 852473), a 10-minute walk from town (up from the tourist office and right at the Great George pub, continue to Monk St, and keep walking) which provides coziness and full English breakfast (£14). **Mrs. Bradley,** 10 Merthyr Rd. (tel. 852206) at the end of Frogmore St., keeps a flowery house with a TV in every room (with continental breakfast £10, with cooked breakfast £12). On Tuesdays, the bustling indoor and outdoor **market** up Market St. offers produce, cheese, baked goods, and live sheep. If you'd like your sheep (or perhaps something else) on a modestly priced toasted sandwich, head to **Focus,** 53 Frogmore St. (open M-Sa 9:30am-4:45pm). At **Pinch the Baker's,** 16 Frogmore St., sit in the cafe and enjoy jelly doughnuts so sugary they crunch (open M-Sa 8am-5pm). For a traditional pub with surprisingly good grub, drop by **The Greyhound Vaults** on Market St. (tel. 858549; food served noon-2pm and 7-9pm). If you don't mind eating take-away, the **Peking Chef Restaurant,** 59 Cross St. (tel. 857457), offers quality food at a 20% discount between 5:30-6:45pm (open daily noon-2:30pm and 5:30-11pm).

In 1175, the Norman knight William de Breos invited the Welsh lords to his table at **Abergavenny Castle,** and then killed them while they were well-sated and unarmed. Dining out in Abergavenny hasn't been the same since. (Open daily 8am-dusk. Castle Museum open M-Sa 11am-1pm and 2-5pm, Sun 2-5pm.) William's castle is now an inscrutable ruin, with stairs leading nowhere and views of the valley and of the mountains looming up in the gaps between its fragmented walls.

WALES

Near Abergavenny

The real attractions of Abergavenny lie in the hills around it, conveniently accessible from the **YHA Capel-y-Ffin Youth Hostel** (see **Accommodations, p. 411**). **Blorenge** (1833ft.), 2½ mi. southwest of town, is by far the most massive of the hills. A path begins off the B4246, traversing valley woodlands to the upland area; it climbs the remaining 1500 ft. in 4½ mi. Climbers adore **Sugar Loaf** (1955ft.) 2½ mi. north; the trailhead to the top starts about 1 mi. west of town on the A40. Many report that hitching a ride to the car park and starting the hike from there is the best way to save up for the difficult hike to the summit. The path to **Skirrid Fawr** (or the Holy Mountain; 1595ft.) lies northeast of town and starts about 2 mi. down the B4521. *Walks From Abergavenny* (£1.80), available from the park office, details mountain climbs and valley walks. The tourist office provides information about **pony trekking,** popular around Abergavenny, in the comprehensive *Activity Wales* guide. Reputable local establishments include **Grange Trekking Centre** (tel. 890215; £15 per ½ day for beginners, includes instruction), **Werr Riding Center** (tel. 810899), and **Llanthony Pony Trekking** (tel. 890359; £10 per ½ day, no experience necessary).

All the megaliths in the Black Mountains are believed to point toward the ruined 12th-century **Llanthony Priory,** perhaps to help errant friars find their way home. The founder of the priory, William de Lacy, was a nobleman who, while hunting, found the natural beauty humbling enough to give up the comfortable life of an aristocrat for one of religious contemplation. Take Stagecoach Red and White bus #20 or the A465 to Llanfihangel Crucorney, where the B4423 begins. Most walk and some hitch the last 6 mi. to the priory. The **YHA Capel-y-Ffin** is an additional 4 mi. (see **Accommodations,** p. 411). At the **Big Pit Mining Museum** (tel. (01495) 790311) in Blaenavon, 5 mi. southwest of Abergavenny, ride a 300 ft. shaft to the subterranean workshops of a 19th-century colliery which was operative until 1980. (Open daily Mar.-Nov. 9:30am-5pm. Last guided tour at 3:30pm. £5.50, seniors £5.25, children £3.75, under 5 admitted free to surface facilities, not admitted underground.) Dress warmly and wear sensible shoes. Ex-miners guide you through with stories as grim as the mine. Take #X4 to Bryn Mawr then #30 to Blaenavon.

■ Brecon Beacons National Park

Brecon Beacons National Park (Bannau Brycheiniog) encompasses 519 sq. mi. of barren peaks, well-watered forests, and windswept wastelands. The park divides into four regions: the rugged country around the remote western Black Mountain; Fforest Fawr, containing the spectacular waterfalls of Ystradfellte; the Black Mountains to the east; and the impressive Beacon peaks where King Arthur's mountain fortress was once thought to have stood. The market towns on the fringe of the park, especially Brecon and Abergavenny, make pleasant touring bases. Since the park's beauty isn't as well-known as that of northern Snowdonia, the crowds are less dense—and the buses much more scarce.

GETTING THERE AND GETTING ABOUT

The **train** line (tel. (0345) 484950) from London's **Paddington Station** to South Wales runs via Cardiff to Abergavenny at the park's southeastern corner and to Merthyr Tydfil on the south edge. The **Heart of Wales** rail line passes through the towns of **Llandeilo** and **Llandovery** in the more remote Black Mountain region. The indispensable *Powys Travel Guides,* free at area tourist offices, details the sometimes sketchy bus coverage. **Stagecoach Red and White** (tel. (01633) 266336) regularly crosses the park en route from **Brecon,** on the northern side of the park, to **Cardiff via Merthyr Tydfil** (bus #43 changing to #X4, 1½hr., M-Sa 6 per day, £3-4), to **Swansea** (bus #63, 1½hr., M-Sa 2 per day, £2-3), or to **Abergavenny** or **Hay-on-Wye.** If you plan to travel on more than one bus route in a day, buy a **South Wales Rover-bus** day pass, honored by all regional providers except Yeomans (£4.50, children £3.50). Rent from **Brecon Bikes and Hikes,** 10 The Struet (tel. (01874) 610071), in

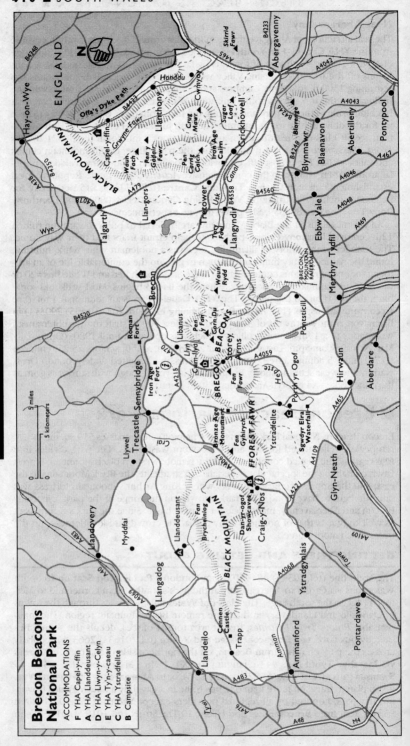

W A L E S

Brecon Beacons National Park

ACCOMMODATIONS
F YHA Capel-y-ffin
A YHA Llanddeusant
D YHA Llwyn-y-Celyn
E YHA Ty'n-y-caeau
C YHA Ystradfellte
B Campsite

5 miles

5 kilometers

the Y Lwyfen house (£9 per ½day, £13 per day, £75 per week). Tours are available for all levels; prices depend on group size. **Hitchers** say the going is tougher on the A470 than on minor roads, where drivers often stop just to enjoy the view.

SAFETY

The mountains are unprotected and in places difficult to scale. Cloud banks slam down over the Beacons, breeding storms within minutes. In violent weather, do not shelter in caves or under isolated trees, as they tend to draw lightning. A **compass** is essential: much of the park is trackless waste, and landmarks get lost in sudden mists. Never hike alone. If you're in trouble and can reach a telephone, dial **999**. Otherwise, the standard six blasts on your whistle should summon help (three are the reply). See **Wilderness and Safety Concerns,** p. 47, for advice on safety in the wilds.

PRACTICAL INFORMATION

Stop at a **National Park Information Centre** (listed below) before venturing forth. While tourist offices are helpful in planning a route by car or bus, the Park Centres provide pamphlets and advice on hiking as well as updated weather reports. Free maps of the park are available, but the 1:25,000 scale Ordnance Survey Maps 12 and 13 (£6) are indispensable both for serious exploring and for reaching safety in bad weather. The National Park staff offers guided walks of varying difficulties (Apr.-Nov.). Consider registering with the police before setting out. Centres also stock leaflets detailing several activities from lovespoon carving (see **Love Your Cutlery,** p. 432) to sheepdog demonstrations.

National Park Information Centres

Abergavenny: Monmouth Rd. (tel. (01873) 853254), in the tourist office opposite the bus station. Open Easter-Oct. daily 9:30am-5:30pm.

Brecon: Cattle Market Car Park (tel. (01874) 623156), off Lion St. next to the tourist information office. Open Apr.-Oct. daily 9:30am-5:30pm. Main Park office around the corner on Glamorgan St.

Craig-y-nos: Pen-y-cae (tel. (01639) 730395). Open daily late June to Aug. 10am-7pm; ring the doorbell for assistance Sept.-June.

Libanus National Mountain Park Visitor Centre (Mountain Centre), Brecon Beacons (tel. (01874) 623366; fax. 624515). Catch the Stagecoach Red and White Brecon-Merthyr bus #43 to Libanus, 5mi. southwest of Brecon (8min., M-Sa 6 per day), and walk the remaining 1½mi. uphill. Disabled access. Open daily July-Aug. 9:30am-6pm; Mar.-June and Sept.-Oct. 9:30am-5pm; Nov.-Feb. 9:30am-4:30pm.

Llandovery: Kings Rd. (tel. (01550) 720693). Open Easter-Sept. M-Sa 10am-5:30pm, Su 2-5:30pm; Oct.-Easter daily 10am-1pm and 1:45-4pm. Take either the Heart of Wales train or bus #279/280 from Carmathen in the west.

ACCOMMODATIONS AND CAMPING

B&Bs are sparse in the park; the Brecon tourist office's free *Where to Stay in Brecknockshire and Brecon Beacons National Park* lists a few. Scattered about the park are five **YHA Youth Hostels,** including Brecon's (see p. 409).

YHA Capel-y-ffin (kap-EL-uh-fin; tel. (01873) 890650), near the River Honddu at the eastern edge of the Black Mountains along Offa's Dyke Path; 8mi. from Hay-on-Wye. Take Stagecoach Red and White bus #39 from Hereford to Brecon, stop before Hay and walk uphill; or take a taxi from Hay (tel. 821266; £9). Ideal for hikers and bikers of the Path or of the Brecons, the road to the hostel climbs up Gospel Pass. No smoking. Horseback riding trips, in conjunction with Black Mountain Holidays, leave from here. £6.50, under 18 £4.45. Breakfast £2.85, dinner £4.25. Lockout 10am-5pm. Open July-Sept. daily; Apr.-June and Sept.-Oct. Th-M; Feb. and Nov. F-Sa; closed Dec.-Jan. **Camping** allowed on grounds.

YHA Llanddeusant (HLAN-thew-sont; tel. (01550) 740619; fax 740225), take the Trecastle-Llangadog Rd. In the isolated Black Mountain area near Llangadog village. Adjacent to a 14th-century church. £6.50, under 18 £4.45. Reservations recommended. Open Apr.-Aug. daily; year-round with advance booking.

YHA Llwyn-y-Celyn (HLEWN-uh-kel-in; tel. (01874) 624261; fax 625916), 7mi. south of Brecon, 2mi. south of Libanus, and 2mi. north of the Storey Arms car park on the A470. Take Stagecoach Red and White bus #43 from Brecon or Merthyr Tydfil (M-Sa 7 per day, Su 2 per day). Close to Pen-y-Fan and the rest of the Beacons range. Traditional Welsh farmhouse. Wooded nature trail, brooks and grazing sheep. £7.20, under 18 £5. Excellent breakfast (£2.85) and dinner (£4.25). Lockout 10am-5pm, but a rain shed keeps you dry. Open July-Aug. daily; Apr.-June M-Sa; Sept.-Oct. Tu-Sa; mid-Feb. to Mar. F-Tu; Nov. F-Sa; closed Dec. to mid-Feb.

YHA Ystradfellte (uh-strahd-FELTH-tuh; tel. (01639) 720301), south of the woods and waterfall district, 3mi. from the A4059 along a paved road; 4mi. from the village of Penderyn; 5min. walk from the Porth-yr-Ogof cave. £6.50, under 18 £4.45. Two small 17th-century cottages. Self-catering kitchen. Open Apr. to mid-July and Sept.-Oct. F-W; mid-July to Aug. daily; Feb.-Mar. and Nov. F-Sa; closed Dec.-Jan.

Commercial **campsites** are plentiful and fairly evenly dispersed, but often difficult to reach without a car. *Where to Stay in Brecknockshire and Brecon Beacons National Park* details 14 sites in the park. Many offer laundry and shopping facilities, and all have parking and showers (£2-5.50 per tent). Farmers may let you camp on their land if you ask first and promise to leave the site as you found it; be prepared to make a donation toward feeding the sheep.

■ Brecon (Aberhonddu)

Although not actually in the mountains, Brecon (pop. 8000) is the best base for hiking through the craggy Brecon Beacons to the south. This quiet market town takes on temporary vibrance with an exceptional **jazz festival** during the second weekend in August, attracting such luminaries as Branford Marsalis, Keb' Mo.', and Van Morrison.

ORIENTATION AND PRACTICAL INFORMATION Brecon has no bus or train station, but **buses** arrive regularly from spots in the area. Ask for bus schedules at the tourist office. **Stagecoach Red and White** (tel. (01633) 266336) connects Brecon with Swansea (#63, M-Sa 2 per day). Service #43 goes to **Merthyr Tydfil** (35min., M-Sa 6 per day) while the #X4 goes from Merthyr Tydfil to **Cardiff** every 30 minutes. Bus #21 runs to **Abergavenny** and **Newport** (M-Sa 6 per day). Bus #39 runs to **Hereford via Hay-on-Wye** (M-Sa 5 per day); on Sundays, **Yeomans** (tel. (01432) 356201) follows the same route (bus #40, 2 per day). Along the A40 from Abergavenny or the A470 from Merthyr Tydfil, **hitchers** stay near intersections.

The **tourist office**, located in the Cattle Market Car Park (tel. 622485; fax 625256; walk through Bethel Sq. off Lion St. to the car park), has an abundance of pamphlets (open daily 10am-6pm). The supremely competent **Brecon Beacons National Park Information Centre** (tel./fax 623156), in the same building, can help plan your foray into the wilds (open Apr.-Oct. daily 9:30am-5:30pm). A **Midland** bank with **ATM** stands on 5 High St. (open M-F 9am-5pm). **Millitts**, 31-32 High St. (tel. 623252), has all the camping supplies you'll need (open M-Sa 9am-5:30pm). The **police** prowl their territory at Lion St. (tel. 622331). The **post office** (tel. 611113) posts at 6 Church Ln., off St. Mary St. (open M-F 8:30am-5:30pm, Sa 9:30am-12:30pm). Brecon's **postal code** is LD3 7AS. **Internet access** is available at Berkeley Computers, 4 Berkeley Pl. (tel. 625625; £2.50 per 30min.; open M-Sa 9am-5pm). The **telephone code** is 01874.

ACCOMMODATIONS AND FOOD Only a three-minute walk from town, the Watton is ripe with B&Bs (£14-17). If you plan to visit during mid-August, book far in advance—the Jazz Festival claims every pillow in town. The nearest hostel is **YHA Ty'n-y-Caeau** (tin-uh-KAY-uh; tel. 665270), 3 mi. from Brecon. From the town center, walk down the Watton and continue until you reach the A40-A470 roundabout. Follow the branch leading to Abergavenny on the A40. Just after the roundabout you'll see a footpath tucked away to the left. Follow the path until you reach the hamlet of **Groesffordd;** then turn left onto the main road. Continue for 10-15 minutes, bearing left at the fork; the hostel is the second house on the right. The Brecon-Abergavenny bus will stop at a footpath that leads to Groesffordd *if you ask the driver.*

(£8, under 18 £5.40. Open July-Aug. daily; Apr.-June and mid-Sept. to Oct. M-Sa; Nov. F-Sa; Feb. W-Sa; Mar. Tu-Sa; closed Dec.-Jan.) Itinerants can seek respite in the spacious interiors of **Walker's Rest,** 18 Bridge St. (tel. 625993). Warm yourself by the fireplace in the bathroom (£14; closed Wednesdays). **Mrs. J. Thomas's** signless B&B, 13 Alexandra Rd. (tel. 624551), rests behind the tourist office. The warm proprietress has traveled in 27 countries, lived in 18, and collected exotic memorabilia from each (singles £15.50; doubles £31). For **camping** try **Brynich Caravan Park** (tel. 623325), 1½ mi. east of town on the A40, signposted from the A40-A470 roundabout (£3.50-4 per person, £1 per car; showers and laundry; open Apr.-Oct.).

Fill your pack at the **Top Drawer** on High St. Superior (open M-Tu and Th-Sa 9:30am-5pm, W 9am-1pm) or at the **Cooperative Pioneer,** Lion St. (tel. 625257; open M-Sa 8am-8pm, Su 10am-4pm). **St. Mary's Bakery,** 4 St. Mary St., offers enormous puffy breads, custards, and slammin' veggie pasties (open M-F 7:30am-5pm, Sa 7:30am-2pm). Meanwhile, **Ye Olde Cognac** (tel. 622725), on High St., kicks up a mean Shepherd's Pie (£3.85).

SIGHTS AND ENTERTAINMENT Brecon Cathedral (tel. 625222) squats in a grove on a hill by the River Honddu, thought to be a former site of Celtic worship. *(Open daily 9am-Evensong.)* The 13th-century church gracefully wears 900 years of redesign. The nearby 16th-century tithebarn houses the **Heritage Centre** (tel. 625222), which uses multimedia to describe the cathedral's history. *(Open May-Sept. Tu-Sa 10:30am-4:30pm; Apr. and Oct. Tu-Sa 10:30am-2:30pm. £1.)* The **Brecon Jazz Gallery,** the Watton (tel. 625557), traces the history of jazz from its roots in the African slave trade to the annual Brecon frenzy. *(Open daily summer 11am-7pm, winter 2-5pm.)* Brecon draws crowds to its **antique fairs** (last Sa of the month Feb.-Nov.), and craftspeople from all over southern Wales congregate in Market Hall on High St. for the **craft fairs** (third Sa of the month Mar.-Dec.). The **Jazz Festival,** held in mid-August, dubs itself "the only festival in Britain bigger than the town itself." Additional campsites are open on farms during the festival. For information, contact the Festival Office, Watton Chambers, Brecon, Powys, Wales LD3 7EF (tel. 625557; fax 622387).

■ The Brecon Beacons

At the center of the park, the Brecon Beacons lure hikers with pastoral slopes and barren peaks. A splendid view of the range complements an exhibit on its history at the **Mountain Centre** outside Libanus (see **National Park Information Centres,** p. 411). From the Mountain Centre, a one-hour stroll among daredevil sheep and extraordinary views leads to the scant remains of an **Iron Age fort.** The most convenient route to the top of **Pen-y-Fan** (pen-uh-van), the highest mountain in southern Wales at 2907 ft., begins at **Storey Arms,** a large parking lot and bus stop 5 mi. south of Libanus on the A470. Unfortunately, the paths to the peak are so popular that they have been eroded; scree (loose rocks) often shakes underfoot.

A far more pleasant hiking route starts in nearby **Llanfaes,** a western suburb of Brecon, and follows leafy roads past streams and waterfalls. Walk or drive the first 3 mi. from Llanfaes down Ffrwdgrech Rd. to the parking lot (take the middle fork after the first bridge). From the car park a trail to the peak passes **Llyn Cwm Llwch,** a 2000 ft. glacial pool in the shadow of **Corn Ddu** peak. An arduous ridge path leads from Pen-y-Fan to other peaks in the Beacons.

The touristy **Brecon Mountain Railway,** Pant Station, Merthyr Tydfil (tel. (01685) 722988), allows a glimpse of the southern side of the Beacons. Take the narrow-gauge steam train north to Pontsticill, where the station provides information on walks in the area. *(Train runs 10:45am-3:45pm; June-Aug. daily; Apr.-May and Sept. Tu-Th and Sa-Su; Oct. Tu-Th and Su. £5.90, accompanied children £1.60.)*

■ The Waterfall District (Fforest Fawr)

Forest rivers tumble through rapids, gorges, and spectacular falls near **Ystradfellte,** about 7 mi. southwest of the Beacons. At **Porth-yr-Ogof** ("mouth of the cave"), less than 1 mi. from the **YHA Ystradfellte** (see p. 411), the River Mellte ducks into a cave at the base of the cliff and emerges as an icy pool. Swimming is decidedly *not* recom-

WALES

mended: the stones are slippery, the pool deepens alarmingly in the middle, and dipping here has proved fatal in the past. Porth-yr-Ogof provides no solitude, and litter crowds the banks. Remote but worth the sweat is the **Sgwdyr Eira** waterfall (on the River Hepste one-third of a mile from its confluence with the Mellte); you can stand behind the thundering water in a hollow in the cliff-face and keep dry. Follow the marked paths to the falls from Gwann Hepste.

Hikers can reach the waterfall district from the Beacons by crossing the A470 near the Llwyn-y-Celyn hostel, climbing Craig Cerrig-gleisaid cliff and Fan Frynych peak, and descending by way of a rocky Roman road. The route crosses a nature reserve as well as some of the park's most trackless heath. Just north of the falls the village of Ystradfellte is rumored to have a pub that will renew your vigor.

Near **Abercrave,** midway between Swansea and Brecon off the A4067, the **Dan-yr-Ogof Showcaves** (tel. (01639) 730284) are huge and impressive, with enormous stalagmites. From YHA Ystradfellte, 10 mi. of trails pass Fforest Fawr (the headlands of the Waterfall District) on their way to the caves. Walk along the cemented pathways inside the caves or slalom down the dry ski-slope outside. *(Self-guided tours every 20min. Open Apr.-Oct. 10am-3:30pm, slightly later in summer. £6.50, children £4, under 5 free.)* A large **campsite** near the caves has full facilities (£3, children £2). Relax from your adventures at the **Craig-y-nos Country Park** (tel. (01639) 730395; ½mi. away). *(Park open daily June-Aug. 10am-6pm; Sept.-Oct. and Mar.-Apr. 10am-5pm; Nov.-Feb. 10am-4pm; May 10am-6pm, with extended hours on the weekend. Free.)* **Stagecoach Red and White** buses pause at the hostel, caves, and country park en route from Brecon.

■ The Black Mountains

Located in the easternmost section of the park, the Black Mountains are a group of long, lofty ridges offering 80 sq. mi. of solitude. Summits like **Waun Fach,** the Black Mountains' highest point (2660ft.), may seem dull and boggy, but the ridge-walks are unsurpassed. The 1:25,000 Ordnance Survey Map 13 (£6) is essential.

Crickhowell, on the A40 and the bus route between Brecon and Abergavenny (Stagecoach Red and White bus #21 M-Sa every 2-3hr.), is the best starting point for forays into the area. You can also explore by bus: the route linking Brecon and Hay-on-Wye (Stagecoach Red and White bus #39 from Brecon to Hereford) descends the north side of the Black Mountains. **Gospel Pass,** the highest mountain pass in the park, often reveals sunshine above the cloud cover. Nearby, **Offa's Dyke Path** (see **Hiking,** p. 403) sprints down the park's eastern boundary. The ridge valleys are dotted with a handful of impressive churches, castles, and other ruins. There is almost no public transportation along valley routes.

■ Swansea (Abertawe)

Native son Dylan Thomas may have called Swansea "this ugly lovely town," but after Wales's second-largest city was blitzed by the Germans, even his assessment seemed generous. The first sight greeting travelers are the box houses that creep up the hills and the shopping avenues; Swansea is a haven for consumers and night-owls, but serves best as a transit point. Peek down Wind St. or into the Maritime Quarter, and you'll sense the wave of renewal in the city. Better yet, take a walk along the bracing seafront of Swansea Bay.

PRACTICAL INFORMATION Swansea has direct connections to most major cities in Britain. **Trains** (tel. (0345) 484950) leave the station on 35 High St. for **Cardiff** (1hr., 1-2 per hr., £7.60), **Birmingham** (4hr., 1 per hr., £30.60), and **London** (3hr., 1 per hr., £37, on Friday £46.20). **National Express buses** (tel. (0990) 808080) depart for **Cardiff** (1¼hr., 11 per day, £6.25 day return), **Birmingham** (4hr., 3 per day, £21.50), and **London** (4hr., departs every 2hr., £27). **South Wales Transport** (tel. 580580) covers the Gower Peninsula and the rest of southwest Wales; Monday to Friday a shuttle runs every hour to **Cardiff** (1hr., £6). Buses #4 and 4A run between the train station and the Quadrant Bus Station (tel. 475511; 5min., departs every 10min., 30p). **Cork-Swansea ferries** (tel. 456116) leave for **Cork, Ireland** (see **Wales to Ireland,** p. 32). **Cruises** (tel. (01446) 720656) leave from Swansea to **Ilfracombe** (£18) and other spots on the Bristol Channel from July to September.

The **tourist office,** Singleton St. (tel. 468321; fax 464602), one block from the bus station, supplies the free *Swansea Bay* booklet as well as 20p maps of the city (open M-Sa 9:30am-5:30pm). Find a **Barclays** and **ATM** on the Kingsway beside the Tesco (bank open M-Tu and Th-F 9am-5pm, W 10am-5pm, Sa 10am-12:30pm). An **American Express** (tel. 455006) can be found at 28 The Kingsway (open M-F 9am-5pm, Sa 9am-4pm). The **police** (tel. 456999) are at the corner of Orchard St. and Alexandra Rd. The **post office** is at 35 The Kingsway (open M-F 9am-5:30pm, Sa 9am-7pm). The **postal code** is SA1 5LF; the **telephone code** is 01792.

ACCOMMODATIONS AND FOOD
Finding quality accommodations can be quite a challenge. The tourist office books rooms for a 10% deposit, but you may be able to find cheaper prices at non-registered B&Bs. You may want to dash over to the **Harlton Guest House,** 89 King Edward's Rd. (tel. 466938; take bus #16, 2 per hr.). The Harlton's clean TV-stocked rooms are a bargain at £10. The **YMCA,** 1 The Kingsway (tel. 652032), also offers cheap—if spartan—rooms (£10 plus £6 key deposit; open July-Sept.). The closest youth hostels are the popular **YHA Port Eynon Hostel** and **YHA Stouthall,** both about an hour out of town by bus (see **Accommodations and Food,** p. 416). In high season, many travelers **camp** along the peninsula.

Budget travelers can check out the various ethnic take-aways along **St. Helen's Rd.,** or the pubs along **Wind St.** Many offer all-you-can-eat options. Low ceilings and better-than-average pub fare await at **Eli Jenkins,** 24 Oxford St. Try their special two meals for £6 (offered M-Th 5-7:30pm; open M-Th noon-7:30pm, F noon-7pm, Sa noon-6pm). The city waxes agricultural in the **Swansea Market,** on the other side of the Quadrant Shopping Centre from the bus station. Forage for fresh fruit or try a tub of laver bread (80p) to prove your immortality (market open M-Sa 8:15am-5:30pm).

SIGHTS AND ENTERTAINMENT
Rebuilders have transformed the **maritime quarter,** a block down Bathwurst St. from Oystermouth Rd., accessible by footbridge from the St. David Sq. Shopping Area. A derelict dock only a few years ago, the area now houses the **Maritime and Industrial Museum** (tel. 650351) amidst colorful apartment blocks, tiny shops, and touristy cafes. *(Open Tu-Su 10am-5pm. Free.)* In front of the museum, climb aboard the lightship **Helwick** and admire the plush, stained-wood bunks. *(Open Apr.-Sept.)* A diminutive and surprised-looking **Dylan Thomas** sits at the end of the marina, in the square bearing his name. A full page of the *Swansea Bay* guide is devoted to guiding poetry junkies along the **Dylan Thomas Uplands Trail** past the poet's favorite haunts. Swansea's **castle,** reduced to humble ruins by Welsh rebel Owain Glyndŵr, lies between Wind St. and The Strand, overshadowed by brash young office buildings. Near the castle in the Parc Tawe complex off The Strand, the jutting glass-and-steel pyramid **Plantasia** (tel. 474555) incubates 5000 varieties of plants, and some animals. Sleepy piranhas guard the gift shop. *(Open Tu-Su 10am-5pm. £2, students, seniors, and children £1.25. Wheelchair access.)*

Nightlife in Swansea centers around the Kingsway and the Mumbles. The enormous joint **Icon** and **Ritzy's** clubs, 72 The Kingsway (tel. 653142), have taken over the former Odeon Cinema, creating an enormous space that's quite popular. *(Cover M and Th-F £1-3, Sa £5-6. Open M and Th-Sa 8pm-2am.)* The monthly *What's On,* free at the tourist office, lists arts performances around Swansea. The mural-covered **Dylan Thomas Theatre** (tel. 473238), along the marina, stages dramas and musicals. *(Tickets £4-5.)* Close by is the **Dylan Thomas Centre** (tel. 463892), home to dramatic, cinematic, and literary performances. *(Open daily 10:30am-5:30pm.)* The **Grand Theatre** (tel. 475715), on Singleton St. next to the tourist office, puts on operas, ballets, and concerts. *(Tickets £6-40, student discounts sometimes available on day of show.)* The **Taliesin Arts Centre,** University College (tel. 296883), hosts films, dramatics, visual arts, and dances (Sept.-July). For the entire month of October, the **Swansea Festival** (tel. 205318, bookings 475715) presents a variety of classical concerts. In mid-August, the village of Pontardawe, 8 mi. north of Swansea (take bus #120 or 125), is deluged by folk and rock musicians from all over the world attending the **Pontardawe International Music Festival** (tel. 830200).

■ Gower Peninsula

The 18 mi. Gower Peninsula clings to the southwest of Swansea. Split by the Cefn Bryn hills, the Gower stretches to the sea with its limestone cliffs, headlands, and numerous beaches. Crumbling castles and ancient burial sites lurk among the greenery; the peninsula is rife with unexpected finds. Best of all, its proximity to Swansea means you'll be spared a leg-breaking hike to get there.

GETTING ABOUT Buses overrun the peninsula from Swansea's Quadrant Station. **First Cymru/South Wales Transport** (tel. 580580) departs for Oystermouth Sq. in **Mumbles** (buses #2, 2A, and 3, 20min., 20 per hr., £2.25 return). Bus #18 runs to **Oxwich** (40min., every 2hr.), while #18A lurches through the hills to **Rhossili via Port Eynon** (1hr., every 2hr., £3.10 return). Bus #14 makes its way to **Pennard** hourly. Regular services cease on Sunday, but between May and September a bus runs through the peninsula with unlimited hop-on/hop-off service (£3.10, seniors and children £2.30). A **Swansea Bay Day Out** ticket (£3.10, children £2.30) allows unlimited travel for a day in the Swansea area (including the Gower Peninsula). **Hitchhiking** is reported to be quicker than public transport and allows hikers to see more of the coast, since most buses follow inland routes. *Let's Go* urges you to consider the risks if you do choose to hitchhike. The 4½ mi. **Swansea Bikepath** leads directly to Mumbles pier.

PRACTICAL INFORMATION Most useful services can be found in **Mumbles**. The **tourist office** (tel. 361302) temporarily stands in the car park near the bus station (open Apr.-Sept. M-Sa 9:30am-5:30pm, Su 10am-4pm). Mumbles and the Gower are colorfully plotted in the *Swansea Bay* guide and in the tourist office map of Mumbles town center. **Barclays** sits on Newton Rd. (open M-Tu and Th-F 9am-4:30pm, W 10am-4:30pm). **Clyne Valley Cycles,** Dunvant Village Green, Dunvant (tel. 208889), lies on the main cycle path and rents bikes (£3.50 per 2hr., £7 per day). The **police station** (tel. 456999) guards Newton Rd. near Castle St. The **post office,** 522 Mumbles Rd. (tel. 366821), adores its **postal code,** SA3 4HH. The **phone code** is a loving 01792.

ACCOMMODATIONS AND FOOD The farther west you go on Gower, the more likely you are to find campsites free of tents and caravans. B&Bs in Mumbles charge upwards of £16 and cluster on Mumbles Rd. and in the South End area; singles can be hard to find. You may want to consider taking bus #14 to nearby **Bishopston**. Walk down the lush pink halls of **Rock Villa,** 1 George Bank (tel. 366794; 10min. down Mumbles Rd.), to rooms with TVs and views of the sea (singles £17; doubles £34-36). **Three Cliffs Bay Caravan Park,** North Hills Farm, Penmaen (tel. 371218), has showers and overlooks the Bay (bus #18 or 18C from Swansea; £3.50 per person). Port Eynon, west of Mumbles, hosts the no-frills but busy **YHA Port Eynon** (tel./fax 390706), a former lifeboat house on the beach; take bus #18A. (£7.20, under 18 £5. Lockout 10am-5pm. Curfew 11pm. Open mid-July to Aug. daily; Apr. to mid-July and Sept.-Oct. M-Sa.) Beachside **camping** is also possible in Port Eynon.

Stuff your pack at the **Cooperative Local** supermarket, 512 Mumbles Rd. (open M-F 8am-10pm, Sa 8am-8pm, Su 10am-4pm). Various bakeries also dot the streets. Try **T. and G. Davies Bakeries'** filled baps (£1), baguettes (£1.55), and other brown buns. For a complete meal, try the £6.25 all-you-can-eat special (children £4.25) at **Seaview Tandoori Restaurant,** 728 Mumbles Rd. (open daily 6-10pm). **Hightide Cafe,** 61 Newton Rd. (tel. 363462), serves fusion cuisine (bagels with Welsh smoked salmon £3.20) and daily lunch specials (open Tu-F 9am-6pm, Sa-Su 9am-10:30pm).

SIGHTS AND ENTERTAINMENT Situated in the southeast corner of the Gower Peninsula, **Mumbles** is a quiet fishing village by day and a raving Gomorrah of student indulgence by night. The short stretch of Mumbles Rd. at Mumbles Head is lined with pubs, some of them former haunts of the area's most famous dipsomaniac, Dylan Thomas. To hang out on Mumbles Rd. is, in University of Swansea parlance, to "go mumbling"; to start at one end and have a pint at each pub is to "do the Mumbles Mile." Flower's, Usher's, Buckley's, and Felin Foel are the local real ales.

Birds lurk in the serene 13th-century **Oystermouth Castle,** Castel Ave. off Newton Rd., where tiny pink flowers have overrun the battlements. *(Open Apr.-Sept. daily 11am-5pm. £1, students, seniors, and children 80p.)* Picnickers should attempt the heart-stopping ascent to the 56-acre **Mumbles Hill Nature Reserve,** an urban oasis of scrub woodland, wildflowers, and rocky crags overlooking Mumbles and the sea. The endless staircase begins by the George Hotel, a 15-minute walk from the bus station on Mumbles Rd. The people at the **Lovespoon Gallery,** 492 Mumbles Rd. (tel. 360132), will give you advice on what it means when a wild-eyed Welshman comes lurching after you with a big wooden spoon in his fist (see **Love Your Cutlery,** p. 432). Lovespoons cost £5-50. *(Open M-Sa 10am-5:30pm.)*

If you're searching for a serene spot to plant yourself and your towel, **Three Cliffs Bay** and **Southgate-on-Pennard** on the south coast are quiet beach areas between Swansea and Port Eynon. From Pennard, a half-hour walk along the Coast Path brings you to Three Cliffs, a secluded, cave-ridden, and stupefyingly beautiful beach. **Caswell Bay** and **Oxwich Bay** are also popular. **Llangannith Beach** north of Rhossili draws surfers from all over Wales with its wild waves. On the peninsula's western tip, green cliffs clutch the sexy curve of **Rhossili Beach,** whose expanse makes overcrowding unlikely. At low tide, a causeway of tortured rock gives foot-breaking access to **Worms Head,** which actually resembles a snail.

The **Gower Festival** (tel. 468321; box office 475715) fills the peninsula with the sounds of string quartets and Bach chorales during the last two weeks of July. Check the *What's On* guide (free at the tourist office) for locations.

■ Tenby (Dinbych-y-pysgod)

Nicknamed the "Welsh Riviera," Tenby lacks only a decent *Beaujolais,* sexy nude bathers, and *provençale* cuisine. The promotional literature touting "fair and fashionable" Tenby isn't all that misleading; its walled, narrow streets crouch along a rugged peninsula softened by cliffside gardens, pastel houses, and seagulls overhead. Once a medieval stronghold, Tenby and its arched gates now fortify young and old alike, each racing for that perfect patch of sand.

GETTING THERE

Trains (tel. (0345) 484950) chug into Tenby (M-F 8 per day, Sa 10 per day, Su 5 per day) from **Cardiff** (2½hr., £13.60), **Swansea** (1½hr., £80), **Pembroke** (30min., £2.90), and **Carmarthen** (45min., £5.10). **Bus** routes in Pembrokeshire are slightly easier to untangle than those further east. The *Public Transport Timetables for South Pembrokeshire,* available at tourist offices, lists bus, rail and ferry schedules for the area, including Tenby, Pembroke, Saundersfoot, and Manorbier. **South Wales Transport** (SWT; tel. (01792) 580580) bus #358/359 arrives hourly from **Haverfordwest via Pembroke** (M-Sa until 5:30pm). The SWT Shuttle #302 bolts between Swansea and Tenby (1½hr., M-Sa 2 per day, in summer also Su 2 per day, £5.25). Or take the hourly #X11 or X30 from Swansea to **Carmarthen** (M-Sa) and transfer to the **Silcox Coaches** (tel. (01834) 842189) bus #333 (2½hr., M-Sa 4 per day). A separate **Bws Dyfed Rover** ticket must be purchased for unlimited travel west of Carmarthen (£4.40); Rover tickets are not accepted on SWT shuttle service.

ORIENTATION AND PRACTICAL INFORMATION

The old town, encircled by the stone wall, hugs the cliffs above the bay. **High St., Upper Frog St.,** and **South Parade** run parallel to the waterfront and the wall. The main passage through the wall is **Five Arches,** at the corner of **St. Georges St.** and S. Parade. From the rail station, walk up **Warren St.** and along **White Lion St.** until you see the beach; the tourist information center is on The Croft, to the left.

Trains: At the bottom of Warren St. Unstaffed. **Tenby Travel** (tel. 843214), in the Tenby Indoor Market between High St. and Upper Frog St., does bookings. Travel office open M-Tu and Th-F 9am-5pm, W and Sa 9am-4pm.

Buses: Buses leave from an island across from the car park at Upper Park Rd. off S. Parade. Get info from posted schedules or Silcox Coaches (tel. 842189) in the arcade between S. Parade and Upper Frog St., across from the market hall.

Taxi: Tenby Taxis (tel. 843678) operates 24hr. Taxis also flirt by the bus station.

Tourist Office: The Croft (tel. 842402; fax 845439), overlooking North Beach. Free accommodations list; booking service (10% deposit plus £1 fee). Open daily July-Aug. 10am-9pm, Apr.-June and Sept.-Oct. 10am-5pm, Nov.-Apr. 10am-4pm.

Financial Services: Barclays, 18 High St. (tel. 765521). Open M-W and F 9am-4:30pm, Th 10am-4:30pm.

Launderette: Washeteria, Lower Frog St. (tel. 842484). Change machine. Open daily June-Aug. 8:30am-9pm, last wash 8:30pm; Sept.-May 10am-6pm, last wash 5:30pm.

Emergency: Dial 999; no coins required.

Police: Warren St. (tel. 842303), near the church off White Lion St.

Hospital: Tenby Cottage Hospital, Church Park (tel. 842040).

Post Office: Warren St. at South Parade (tel. 843213). Open M-F 9am-5:30pm, Sa 9am-12:30pm. **Postal Code:** SA70 7JR.

Internet Access: Cyber Centre, Nelson's Walk (tel. 844700), off Upper Frog St. £2.50 per 30min., £4.50 per hr. Open M-Sa 9:30am-6pm.

Telephone Code: 01834.

ACCOMMODATIONS AND FOOD

Warren St., just outside the town wall near the train station, has loads of B&Bs for £12-16; the sidestreets of **Greenhill Ave.,** as well as the streets off Esplanade and Trafalgar Rd., are almost as well endowed. The nearest hostel is **YHA Pentlepoir** (tel. 812333; see **Accommodations and Camping,** p. 421). For the world's funkiest carpeting and huge windows, head to **Somerville,** 12 Warren St. (tel. 843158; singles with cooked breakfast £13, with continental breakfast £12; doubles £25; *Let's Go* readers get 50p off). Those traveling in pairs can try **Langdon Guest House,** Warren St., with TV (doubles £25). **Camp** at **Meadow Farm** (tel. 844829) at the top of The Croft overlooking North Beach (£3; showers). Should these areas fail you, take a short bus ride to **Saundersfoot.**

Tenby has plenty of restaurants, but many are so expensive you'll be tempted to drink the ketchup just to get your money's worth. Lunch specials can soften the blow. Buy meat, veggies, and bread for a picnic at the **Tenby Market Hall** between High St. and Upper Frog St. (open M-Sa 9am-5pm). **Somerfield,** across from the bus station on Upper Park Rd., will fill your pack (open M-Th and Sa 8am-8pm, F 8am-9pm, Su 10am-4pm). Hidden in an alley connecting Bridge and St. Julians St., the **Plantagenet,** Quay Hill (tel. 842350), serves excellent Welsh and continental cuisine in a house with a towering 800-year-old stone chimney. (Entrees £10-15, lunch sandwiches £3.50-4.50. Open Apr.-Oct. daily 10am-12:30am; Nov.-Mar. F-Su.) **Candy,** High St. and Crackwell St. (tel. 842052), feels like a ship cabin hanging precariously over the sea—go for salads and omelettes, or brave the traditional steak and kidney pie (£3.60-7; open Apr.-Oct. daily 9am-8:30pm). **Pam Pam,** 2 Tudor Sq. (tel. 842946), serves up hearty portions (£5-12; open daily 10:30am-10pm).

SIGHTS

On a sunny day, pick your way through pensioners and naked toddlers on sandy **North Beach** by The Croft or **South Beach,** beyond the Esplanade. If you're feeling lithe, try the cliffs and caves of **Castle Beach** at the eastern tip of Tenby. Or channel your aggression into parasailing, water-skiing, and scuba-diving offered by **Dragonfly Water Sports** (tel. 843553), Castle Slipway on Castle Beach. *(Open daily Easter to late Sept. 9am-late.)* Just off Castle Hill sits the craggy spur of **St. Catherine's Island,** which bears an abandoned fort once used as a warning outpost. A variety of trips leave from the harbor (check the kiosk at Castle Beach). **Coastal and Island Cruises** (tel. 843545) does boat trips. *(Apr.-Oct. £5, students and seniors £4.50, children £3.)*

Low, timbered ceilings, leaning floors, and a cavernous fireplace betray Tenby's medieval past at the 500-year-old weathered-stone **Tudor Merchant's House** (tel. 842279), Quay Hill off Bridge St. *(Open Apr.-Sept. M-Tu and Th-Sa 10am-5pm, Su 1-5pm. £1.80, children 90p.)* The tired ruins of Tenby's castle—no more than patches of crumbled, mossy stone—rest atop the wildflower-ringed summit of **Castle Hill,** almost completely surrounded by ocean.

■ Near Tenby

The strange, handsome **Carew Castle** (tel. (01646) 651782) rests 5 mi. northwest of Tenby. Nearby, a **tidal mill** dating from 1558 (one of three in Britain) turns quietly alongside a medieval bridge and an 11th-century, 13 ft. Celtic cross. *(Open Easter-Oct. daily 10am-5pm. Mill and castle £2.50, seniors and children £1.60; castle only £1.70, seniors and children £1.20.)* Take Silcox bus #360 from Tenby (M-Sa every hr.).

Halfway between Tenby and Pembroke stands the superbly preserved **Manorbier Castle** (tel. 871394), a 13th-century Norman baron's palace with a garden in the keep and a beach below the ramparts. *(Open Easter-Sept. daily 10:30am-5:30pm. £2, seniors and children £1.)* Trains run from Tenby and Pembroke to the staffed train station (10 per day). Bus #358/359 shuttles between Tenby, Manorbier, and Pembroke (M-Sa 1 per hr.; in summer also Su 4 per day). **Manorbier** also offers a **YHA Youth Hostel** (tel. 871803; see **Accommodations and Camping,** p. 421). **B&Bs** and **camping** sites line the roads between Tenby and Pembroke. The national park organizes guided walks in the area, which are outlined in their free seasonal publication *Coast to Coast.*

Dylan Thomas spent his last 16 years in the **Boat House** (tel. (01994) 427420) in Laugharne (LAHN) at the mouth of the River Taff, about 15 mi. northeast of Tenby. The boat house, now fairly commercialized, displays Thomas's photographs, art, and books. *(Open daily Easter-Oct. 10am-5pm; Nov.-Easter 10:30am-3pm. £2.50, children and seniors £1.50.)* Take Silcox bus #333 to St. Clear's (5 per day), then switch to South Wales Transport bus #222 from St. Clear's to Laugharne.

Three perfume-drenched miles to the south lies **Caldey Island,** site of an active **monastery** founded in the 6th century, sacked by the Vikings, refounded around 1100, sacked by Henry VIII, and refounded again early this century. The land now hosts a community of 20 Cistercian monks who produce perfume, dairy products, and chocolate, sold at **The Caldey Shop** (tel. 842296), on Quay Hill. The island's **post office (postal code** SA70 5UH) dispenses information and fake stamps. **Caldey Boats** (tel. 842296) sail from Tenby harbor to the island. *(Runs Easter-Oct. M-F 9:30am-5pm; mid-May to mid-Sept. also Sa 11am-4pm. 20min. 4 per hr. £6 return, £3 children.)*

▨ Pembrokeshire Coast National Park

The 225 sq. mi. Pembrokeshire Coast Park, best known for craggy, peninsular coasts, also boasts islands full of wildlife, the wooded Gwaun Valley, and prehistoric Celtic remnants buried in the Preseli Hills. The landscape tells of dramatic contrasts: rows of potatoes planted up to the crashing Atlantic; the silhouette of the weathered stone chapel at St. Govar's Head against towering St. David's cathedral. Drawn by the cliffs and inlets of the popular 186 mi. Coastal Path, hikers share the park with island-hopping bird watchers and pilgrims to Stonehenge's 4000-year-old quarry.

GETTING THERE AND GETTING ABOUT

The best place to enter the region is centrally located **Haverfordwest,** on the main **rail** line (tel. (0345) 484950) from **London** (£42-54) and **Cardiff** (7 per day, £13.60). Another line also runs to **Fishguard** on the north coast (change at Clarbeston Rd.) and to **Tenby** and **Pembroke Dock,** both on the south coast (change at Whitland). **Buses** offer more frequent, wide-ranging service than trains in this area. Find schedules in *Public Transport Timetables for Pembrokeshire.* From Haverfordwest, **Richards**

Froggie's Fumble

In yet another ringing tribute to French military prowess, three frigates garrisoned by men of unflappable mettle landed on the shores just outside Fishguard in 1797. In what was to be Britain's last invasion, this dashing band of 1500 Frenchmen (all convicts), led by the Irish-American General Tate, gallantly risked life and limb to recapture the glory days of 1066. Or that, at least, was the plan. But when Tate and his warriors landed, they set up headquarters in a farmhouse that was, in a stroke of bad luck, stocked for a wedding—and thus more than quenched the hapless soldiers' thirst. Tate's force, now a drunken mob, couldn't hold out long enough to recover from the hangover. Just two days after reaching British soil, the French sued for peace, their morale drained by the battlefield heroics of Welsh women: Jemima Nicholas, a 47-year-old cobbler, captured 14 Frenchmen single-handedly, when Tate's keen eyes mistook red-cloaked females for British soldiers. *La gloire,* indeed.

Brothers (tel. (01239) 613756) run to **St. David's** every hour (bus #411, 45min.), with some buses going on to **Fishguard** (1½hr., 4 per day). **South Wales Transport** (tel. (01792) 580580) blankets the rest of the region, from Haverfordwest to **Tenby via Pembroke** (bus #358/359, 50min. to Pembroke, 1½hr. to Tenby, M-Sa 1 per hr., summer also Su 1 per day), to **Broad Haven** (bus #311, 15min., M-Sa 6 per day), and to **Milford Haven** (bus #302, 20min., M-Sa 2 per hr., Su 1 per hr.).

The Dale Peninsula, southwest of Haverfordwest, is poorly serviced by public transport. **Edwards Brothers** (tel. (01437) 890230) bus #315/316 visits the peninsula twice on Tuesdays and Fridays (35min., return £3.40). While *Let's Go* does not recommend hitching, **hitchers** rave about this area.

PRACTICAL INFORMATION

The **National Park Information Centres** listed below sell 10 annotated maps covering the coastal path (25p). Brian John's *The Pembrokeshire Coast Path* (£11) is a methodically thorough option. Helpful National Park officers will aid your planning for free; ask them about the guided walks offered by the park. Write for brochures to National Park Information Services, Pembrokeshire Coast National Park Head Office, Winch Ln., Haverfordwest, Pembrokeshire, Wales SA61 1PY (tel. (01437) 764636). For **weather info,** call any park office; dialing 999 connects you to **rescue rangers.**

National Park Information Centres

Haverfordwest: 40 High St. (tel. (01437) 760136; fax 775140). Open Easter-Sept. M-Sa 10am-1pm and 1:45-5:30pm.

Newport: Bank Cottages, Long St. (tel./fax (01239) 820912). Open Easter-Oct. M-Sa 10am-5:30pm.

St. David's: High St. (tel./fax (01437) 720392). Open Easter-Oct. daily 9:30am-5:30pm; Nov.-Easter M-Sa 10am-4pm.

Tourist Information Centres

Fishguard: Town Hall (tel. (01348) 873484; fax 875246). Open daily 9am-6pm.

Haverfordwest: 19 Old Bridge (tel. (01437) 763110; fax 767738). Open 9am-6pm.

Milford Haven: 94 Charles St. (tel. (01646) 690866; fax 690655). Open Easter-Oct. M-Sa 10am-5pm.

Saundersfoot: The Barbecue, Harbour Car Park, Saundersfoot (tel. (01834) 813672; fax 813673). Open June-Aug. daily 10am-5:30pm; Easter-May and Sept. M-Sa 10am-5pm.

Tenby: The Croft (tel. (01834) 842402). Open Easter-Oct. daily 10am-5pm; July-Aug. 10am-9pm.

The park is also aflutter with **Outdoor Activity Centres,** which rent canoes, kayaks, ponies, bicycles, and other archaic means of transport (£10-20 per day). Check the *Coast to Coast* pamphlet available at Park Information Centres. Mountain bikes are excellent for the park's one-lane roads, many of which lead to secluded beaches. Do not, however, ride on the coastal path itself; it is illegal and extraordinarily dangerous. **Mr. Codd,** Cross Inn Garage, Broadmoor, Saundersfoot (tel. (01834) 813266), rents bikes (£6 per day plus £30 deposit; open M-Sa 8am-6pm; July-Aug. book ahead). Aspiring conquerors of the Welsh terrain can try **Preseli Venture** (tel. (01348) 837709), on the coast between Fishguard and St. David's. Preseli's offers bikes (£10 per ½day, £16 per day), kayaks (£25 per ½day, £40 per day; call in advance), or the whole shebang: kayaking, coasteering, and mountain biking for 2 days and nights (£139, food and accommodations included; book ahead).

ACCOMMODATIONS AND CAMPING

Book ahead for hostels in July and August. If you plan your route in advance, you can book at all of the hostels at least 14 days in advance through the **West Wales Booking Bureau,** Anna Davis, YHA Llaethedy, St. David's, Pembrokeshire SA62 6PR (tel. (01437) 720345; booking £2.50). The **Poppit Sands hostel** (tel./fax (01239) 612936), not on the Coastal Path, is 30 mi. past Pwll Deri near Cardigan and offers rooms with views of the sea and the occasional dolphin. (£7.20, under 18 £5. Open Apr.-June and Sept.-Oct Tu-Sa; mid-July to Aug. daily.) The roads between Tenby, Pembroke, and St. David's teem with **B&Bs** (£14-23). Despite the quantity, B&Bs can be hard to secure in Pembrokeshire, especially in the summer. The coast is lined with **campsites,** as many farmers convert fallow fields into summer sites (about £3 per tent). Always ask first. The youth hostels at Manorbier, Poppit Sands, and Pwll Deri also allow camping.

YHA Youth Hostels are conveniently spaced along the coastal path. The following are all within a reasonable day's walk of one another.

Broad Haven: (tel. (01437) 781688; fax 781100), on St. Bride's Bay off the B4341. 75 beds and some of the best facilities on the Walk. £9.75, under 18 £6.55. Laundry facilities. Lockout 10am-5pm. Curfew 11pm. Wheelchair access. Open mid-Feb. to Oct. daily. Easily accessible; take the #311 from Haverfordwest.

Manorbier: Skrinkle Haven (tel. (01834) 871803; fax 871101), near Manorbier Castle. From the Manorbier train station, walk up past the A4139 to the castle, make a left onto the B4585 and then a right up to the army camp and follow the hostel signs, or take bus #358/359 from Tenby to Haverfordwest, which stops at the castle. £9.75, under 18 £6.55, camping £5. Vigorously hot showers and spotless laundry facilities. Wheelchair access. Open mid-Feb. to Oct. daily.

Marloes Sands: (tel./fax (01646) 636667), near the Dale Peninsula. A cluster of farm buildings on National Trust Property. £6.50, under 18 £4.45. No laundry. Lockout 10am-5pm. Open Apr.-Oct. daily.

Pentlepoir: The Old School, Pentlepoir (tel. (01834) 812333), 4mi. north of Tenby near Saundersfoot. Take one of many buses to Saundersfoot from Tenby and ask the driver to let you off at this cheery, spartan hostel. £6.50, under 18 £4.45. Meals available on request; self-catering kitchen. Lockout 10am-5pm. Curfew 11pm. Open July-Aug. daily; Apr.-May and Sept.-Oct. Tu-Sa.

Pwll Deri: (tel. (01348) 891233), on breath-taking cliffs just around Strumble Head from Fishguard. £7.20, under 18 £5, camping £3.60. Lockout 10am-5pm. Curfew 11pm. Open July-Aug. daily; Apr.-June and Sept.-Oct. W-Su.

St. David's: (tel. (01437) 720345), near St. David's Head at the foot of a mountain. Take the path past the bishop's palace and follow signs to the hostel, or call Tony's Taxis (tel. 720931; £3-4). Beds in a converted stable. £6.50, under 18 £4.45. Lockout 10am-5pm, access to dining hall. Curfew 11pm. Open mid-July to Aug. daily; Apr. to mid-July and Sept.-Oct. F-W.

Trevine: (tel. (01348) 831414), between St. David's and Fishguard. Ask and bus #411 will stop at the hostel. £7.20, under 18 £5. Lockout 10am-5pm. Open July-Aug. daily; Apr.-June and Sept.-Oct. Tu-Sa.

Those wishing to base themselves in a larger town can try the comfortable wooden bunk beds of **Hamilton Backpacker's Lodge,** 21-23 Hamilton St. (tel. (01348) 874797), in Fishguard town center. (Dorms £9, £50 per week; singles £12; doubles £22. Continental breakfast included. No lockout. No curfew.)

HIKING

For short hikes, stick to the more accessible St. David's Peninsula, in the northwest. Otherwise, set out on the coastal path, which is marked with acorn symbols and covers mostly manageable terrain. The path begins in the southeast at Amroth and continues westward through Tenby to St. Govan's Head. Steep, worn steps down a cliffside lead to the diminutive **St. Govan's Chapel,** possibly from the 6th century. Clinging to a tiny patch of rock surrounded by cliff and ocean, the church and its well were reputed to heal and grant wishes; legend has it that the steps cannot be counted. From here to Elegug Stacks, birds cling to the rocks. The path passes natural sea arches, mile-wide lily pools at Bosherton, and limestone stacks. Unfortunately, the 6 mi. stretch from St. Govan's Head past the Stacks to Freshwater West is sometimes used as an artillery range; it is usually closed to hikers. Call Pembroke National Park Office (tel. (01646) 682148) for open times.

From Freshwater West to Angle Bay, the coastline is relatively easy to walk and exceptionally pretty. There is a small break in the path at Milford Haven at the mouth of the extensive waterway, a channel which runs for over 25 mi. inland. Geologists call it a "ria" (a drowned river valley). From the Dale Peninsula, the path passes by the long, clean beaches of St. Bride's Bay, turns up to Newgale, and arrives at the ancient **St. David's Head,** the site of pre-Cambrian formations and the oldest named feature on the coast of Wales. The ocean has carved away caves and secluded inlets; the surrounding jagged terrain is awe-inspiring.

A number of islands freckle the coast. On **Grassholm,** farthest from the shore, 35,000 pairs of gannets nest and raise their young. **Dale Sailing Company** (tel. (01646) 601636) runs trips around (not to) the island from Martin's Haven on the Dale Peninsula. *(May-Sept. M and F at 10am and noon. Guided trips Th 5pm. £20. Reservations required.)* They also sail to the island of **Skomer,** a marine reserve and breeding ground for auks, seals, and puffins. *(Apr.-Oct. Tu-Su. £6, children £4; landing fee £6, students £3, seniors £5, children under 16 free.)*

Serious bird enthusiasts sing the praises of **Skokholm Island,** accessible on Mondays via cruises run by the National Park, June to mid-August. Contact any National Park Information Centre or the Wildlife Trust (tel. (01437) 765462); reservations are required. *(Departs 10am. £6.50, children £4; landing fee £6, children free.)* Seals and rare seabirds live on **Ramsey Island,** farther up the coast. On the east side of the island lurk the **Bitches,** a chain of offshore rocks where sailors have come to grief. A **Thousand Islands Expeditions** (tel. (01437) 721686 or (800) 163621) craft leaves Whitesands Bay or St. Justinians for a two-hour tour around Ramsey Island. *(Easter-Nov. daily, weather permitting. £18, children £10.)* Landing trips to Ramsey Island leave St. Justinians. *(Runs W-M. £10, children £5.)* The adventurous will brave the frothy passages between the Bitches on a one-hour white-water jet boat trip *(£15, adults only).*

■ Pembroke (Penfro) and Pembroke Dock

Bounded by a towering Norman castle and 14th-century walls, Pembroke today is not the military stronghold it once was. A former bastion of anti-Cromwell resistance now invites visitors to stroll down Main St., above the surrounding houses and countryside. Nearby Pembroke Dock lacks the ancestry of its neighbor—the ferry to **Rosslare, Ireland,** is its greatest attraction today. Both towns are stepping stones to Pembrokeshire National Park, but Pembroke is the more popular place to stay.

ORIENTATION AND PRACTICAL INFORMATION Pembroke Castle lies up the hill on the western end of Main St.; the street's other end fans into five streets from a roundabout. On one of these, Lower Lamphey Rd., sits the unstaffed **train station. Trains** (tel. (0345) 484950) run daily from Pembroke Dock to Swansea and further east, passing through Pembroke and Tenby (Su-F 5 per day, Sa 9 per day). **South Wales Transport/Silcox Coaches** #358/359 (tel. (01646) 683143) leave from Pembroke for Albion Sq. in Pembroke Dock on their way to **Haverfordwest** (M-Sa 1 per hr.). Buses stop in Pembroke at the castle (going toward Haverfordwest) and outside

Somerfield (going toward Tenby), and in Pembroke Dock at the **Silcox Garage** (tel. 683143; M-F 9am-5pm). Be sure to walk to the front of the bus to signal the bus driver for your stop. **Irish Ferries** (tel. (0990) 171717) and **Stena Sealink** (tel. (0990) 707070) send **ferries** and **catamarans** from Pembroke Dock and nearby **Fishguard** to **Rosslare, Ireland** (see **Wales to Ireland,** p. 32).

The **tourist office** (tel. 622388; fax 621396) occupies a former slaughterhouse on Commons Rd. below the elevated heights of the town center. The staff books ferries and accommodations. (Open May-Oct. daily 10am-5:30pm; Mar.-Apr. Tu, Th, and Sa 10am-4pm; office may not be open Nov.-Feb.) An **ATM** yields its bounty from **Barclays**, 35 Main St. (tel. 684996; open M-W and F 9am-4:30pm, Tu 10am-4:30pm). The nearest **police station** (tel. 682121) is on Water St. in Pembroke Dock. Pembroke's **post office** sorts at 49 Main St. (tel. 682737; open M-F 9am-5:30pm, Sa 9am-1pm). Its **postal code** is SA71 4JT, its **telephone code** 01646.

ACCOMMODATIONS AND FOOD The few B&Bs in Pembroke are scattered about. Originally a Victorian merchant's house, **Merton Place House,** 3 East Back off Main St. (tel. 684796), boasts a walled rose garden (£15). Spacious **Beech House,** 76-78 Main St. (tel. 683740), has an inviting pool table (£14). **YHA Manorbier** is on the bus line between Tenby and Pembroke (see **Accommodations and Camping,** p. 421).

Restaurants in Pembroke know well that hungry tourists will gobble up anything within reach. Gather a bargain feast at **Somerfield** on Main St. (open M-W and Sa 8:30am-6pm, Th-F 8:30am-8pm, Su 10am-4pm). **Mallard's,** 16 Main St. (tel. 686860), sells sandwiches and baguettes (£1.75-3), and selections of fudge and truffles (open M-Sa 10am-5pm). Across the Northgate St. Bridge on your right is **Watermans Arms,** which offers seating by Mill Pond with a view of swans and the occasional carousing otter (veggie menu available; open M-Sa 11am-3pm and 6-11pm, Su 7-10:30pm).

SIGHTS Pembroke Castle (tel. 684585), at the head of Main St., the birthplace of Henry VII, is among the most impressive fortresses in South Wales. The mill pond, directly beneath the castle walls, amuses coots and cormorants. (Castle open daily Apr.-Sept. 9:30am-6pm; Mar. and Oct. 10am-5pm; Nov.-Feb. 10am-4pm. £3, seniors and children £2, families £8. Tours June-Aug. 4 per day. 50p, children free.) Pembroke swells with churches: have a look at the 12th-century **St. Daniel's Church,** St. Daniel Hill by the train station; **St. Mary's Church,** Main St., with its 13th-century windows; or **Monkton Priory Church,** Church Terrace, which has a hagioscope—a wall-slit that enabled leprous monks to watch the service at the altar. In the **Museum of the Home,** 7 Westgate Hill (tel. 681200), opposite the castle, masses of household gadgets trace the history of the common home from the 16th century to the present. Items include an ivory and tortoise-shell tongue-scraper "for removing excesses of poor claret" and what is reputed to be, at 27 in., the longest Welsh lovespoon. (Open May-Sept. M-Th 11am-5pm. £1.20, seniors and children 90p.)

▪ St. David's (Tyddewi)

St. David's (pop. 1700) was once the largest and richest diocese in medieval Wales; now it proudly stands as Britain's smallest city, nearly out of reach on the western extremity of the coastal path, clinging to a narrow peninsula often shrouded in mist and worn by heavy winds. While you may have to plan ahead vigilantly with bus schedules in hand to avoid being stranded, it's well worth the time and effort. **St. David's Cathedral,** perhaps the finest in Wales, stands majestically along a sloping, grassy graveyard below the village. Its squat, rounded arches and massive crumbled buttresses give an impression of age. The contents of its reliquary betray the cathedral's importance as a religious site: a chest holds the bones of St. David and his comrade St. Justinian, who was killed on nearby Ramsey Island but managed to carry his own head back to the mainland for burial. (Suggested donation £2, children £1.) The **Bishop's Palace** (tel. 720517), a few yards away across a bridged brook, eschews frugality and proclaims the wealth of the medieval bishop. (Open Apr.-Oct. daily 9:30am-6:30pm; Nov.-Mar. M-Sa 9:30am-4pm, Su 2-4pm. £1.70, students, seniors, and children £1.20,

---

Gotta Love the Leek

The leek has more than culinary significance for the Welsh. Long associated with St. David, the patron saint of Wales, the leek is also one of the nation's emblems (along with the dragon and the daffodil). The story holds that David was one day leading his Christian Welsh followers in battle against a host of pagan English soldiers. The battlefield was covered with leeks, so David wisely commanded his troops to wear them as a means of discerning friend from foe. Today, as they have since the 16th century, Welsh men and women continue to adorn themselves with the vegetable on March 1 in celebration of St. David's Day.

---

families £4.60.) A half-mile south of town, the ruined seaside walls of **St. Non's Chapel** mark the site of St. David's birth around AD 500. According to *Historia o Uuched Dewi (The Life of St. David)*, at the moment of his birth, the saint split a rock poised to fall on his mother, saving them both. Water from the nearby well supposedly cures all ills; take Goat St. downhill from the town and follow signs to health and happiness.

Blue and white **Richards Bros. buses** (tel. (01239) 613756) hug the coast from Haverfordwest to Fishguard, via St. David's (#411, 50min., M-Sa 5 per day with many other buses going only to St. David's). The **National Park Information Centre** (tel. 720392), in the City Hall on High St., will book you a bed (open Easter-Oct. daily 9:30am-5:30pm; Nov.-Easter M-Sa 10am-4pm). The **telephone code** is 01437.

The **YHA Youth Hostel** in St. David's lies 2 mi. northwest of town at the foot of a rocky outcrop near the 500 million-year-old St. David's Head (see **Accommodations and Camping,** p. 421). B&Bs in the village charge £14-20. **Pen Albro Bed and Breakfast,** 18 Goat St. (tel. 721865), has TVs and stereos in every room; the doubles have art deco fireplaces and wedding-cake canopies on the beds (£13.50).

North Wales

North Wales is more fiercely nationalistic and linguistically independent than South Wales. Monolinguists will struggle to get their tongues around the markedly un-Anglicized town names, and to make sense of streets whose names appear in Welsh on their maps but in English on the signs (or vice versa.) Even the topography of the region seems to pronounce its distinctiveness. Jagged, uneven Welsh hills contrast sharply with the placid English flatlands to the east. The northern coastline is peppered with famous castles. If you want to escape the crowds that invariably flock to these edifices, head inland to the mountain footpaths and hamlets of **Snowdonia National Park,** which covers the larger part of northern Wales. Mount Snowdon itself, at 3560 ft., is the highest, barest, and most precipitous peak in England and Wales. Other ranges, such as the Glyders or **Cader Idris,** challenge blissfully smaller numbers of serious hikers. To the west of Snowdonia, the largely unspoiled **Llŷn Peninsula** invites visitors to its sandy beaches; to the northwest, the **Isle of Anglesey** sends ferries to Ireland and beckons with prehistoric remains. The lush **Vale of Conwy** languishes to the east. Near the English border, Llangolen hosts the International Musical Eisteddfod in July, a festival attended by singers and dancers from around the world (see **Ffestivals,** p. 395).

HIGHLIGHTS OF NORTH WALES

- Hikers will want to dash up **Mount Snowdonia,** the highest peak in England and Wales, and the center of Snowdonia National Park (p. 436).
- Only travelers with a nimble tongue should dare to visit **Llanfairpwllgwyngyllgogerychwyrndrobwllllantysiliogogogoch** (p. 446), which holds the world record for the village with a longest name. Llanfair P.G.—as it's otherwise known—lies near the Celtic prehistoric ruins on the **Isle of Anglesey.**
- Don't miss one of Wales's largest festivals, the **International Music Eisteddfod,** a competition held annually in **Llangollen,** and part of the grand tradition of Welsh hospitality and music (see p. 395 and p. 453).

■ Aberystwyth

Ever since a bevy of academics moved in—the University College of Wales was established here in 1874, and the National Library of Wales in 1909—the crowded streets of Aberystwyth (Abber-RIST-with) have been packed with students. Though salt-stained buildings, a hotel-lined quay, and the inevitable camera-toting tourists betray Aberystwyth's hybrid role as a resort town, it's the backpacking scholars who fill seaside flats, raucous pubs, and veggie cafes. Visitors fresh from the somewhat anglicized south will be surprised to hear the guttural inflections of Welsh in everyday conversation: as in the rest of North Wales, the ll's and dd's evince a robust, independent spirit.

GETTING THERE

Aberystwyth is a travel hub for all of Wales. The city rests at the western end of the Heart of Wales **rail line** that cuts across to **Shrewsbury** in England (2hr., M-Sa 9 per day, Su 5 per day, £7.90). To rail destinations along the northern coast, change at **Machynlleth** (30min., M-Sa 11 per day, Su 6 per day, £3.80). The £6 **Cambrian Coaster Day Ranger** (tel. (01766) 512340) covers coastal rail travel up to **Pwllheli. Arriva Cymru Buses** (tel. 617951; jointly operated with Richard Bros.) sends its green and white buses south to **Cardigan,** changing at Synod Inn (#550, 1½hr., M-Sa 1 per hr., Su 4 per day, £3.50) and north to **Machynlleth** (#2, M-Sa 6 per day, Su 5 per day, £2.80). A single **TrawsCambria** bus runs daily to **Cardiff** (4hr., £5.90). **Day Rover** tickets (£6; one dog rides free!) can be purchased on Arriva buses, and are valid on all their buses, from Cardigan to virtually all of northern Wales. The **North and Mid-Wales Rail Rover,** available for a day, three days, or a week, is valid on both buses and trains north of the imaginary Aberystwyth-Shrewsbury line (see **Getting There and Getting About,** p. 388).

ORIENTATION AND PRACTICAL INFORMATION

Alexandra Rd. houses the train station and bus stops. **Terrace Rd.** bisects Alexandra Rd. and also cuts through **North Parade, Portland St.,** and the oceanside **Marine Terr.** on its way north to the sea front. Terrace Rd. marks the separation point of North Parade and Great Darkgate St., roughly the center of the town. At the top of Great Darkgate St., parallel to Terrace Rd., is **Pier St.,** which becomes **Bridge St.** as it heads toward Aberystwyth bridge. To the east, North Parade Rd. extends into North-gate St. and then **Penglais Rd.,** which climbs a hill to the university and the white stone National Library.

Trains: Alexandra Rd. (tel. (0345) 484950). Office open M-F 6:20am-5:25pm, Sa 6:20am-3:20pm. The touristy **Vale of Rheidol Railway** (tel. 625819 or 615993) runs from the station. Open Sept. to late July daily 10am-2:30pm; late July to Aug. M-Th 10am-4pm, F-Su 10am-2:30pm.

Buses: Buses stop on Alexandra Rd. in front of the train station. Dodge buses to reach the information desk inside the **Crosville Cymru** garage, Park Ave. (tel. 617951). Open M-F 10am-12:30pm and 1:30-4pm.

Taxi: Express (tel. 612319). Open 24hr.

Tourist Office: Lisburne House, Terrace Rd. (tel. 612125; fax 626566), on the corner of Bath St. Chipper, helpful staff doles out dossiers of B&B photos and rates. Open daily July-Aug. 10am-6pm; Sept.-June M-Sa 10am-5pm.

Financial Services: Barclays, 26 Terrace Rd. (tel. 612731). Open M and W-F 9:30am-4:30pm, Tu 10am-4:30pm. **ATM** on Terrace Rd.

Launderette: Wash 'n' Spin 'n' Dry, 16 Bridge St. Bring change. Open daily 8am-7pm, last wash 6:30pm.

Market: Market Hall, St. James Sq. Open M-Sa 8am-5pm.

Emergency: Dial 999; no coins required.

Police: Blvd. St. Breiuc (tel. 612791), at the end of Park Ave.

Hotlines: Samaritans (crisis), 5 Trinity Rd. (tel. 624535). Open 24hr. **Women's Aid** (tel. 625585). **Rape Crisis,** Manchester (tel. (0161) 272 7005).

Hospital: Bronglais General Hospital, Caradog Rd. (tel. 623131), 5min. walk up Penglais Rd. 24hr. switchboard.

Post Office: 8 Great Darkgate St. (tel. 632630) with a bureau de change. Open M-F 9am-5:30pm, Sa 9am-12:30pm. **Postal Code:** SY23 1DE.

Telephone Code: 01970.

ACCOMMODATIONS

Expensive B&Bs (£16-30) snuggle up with student housing on the waterfront. Bridge St. has a small B&B community, and a few cheap establishments are scattered on South Rd. and Rheidol Terr.

YHA Youth Hostel (tel. 871498), 9mi. north in Borth. Beautifully set among beaches, the hostel is often full. Take the train to Borth Station (10min., M-Sa 12 per day, Su 8 per day) or Crosville bus #511 or 512 from Aberystwyth. From the train station, turn right onto the main road and walk 5min. £8.80, under 18 £6. Self-catering kitchen. Meals available. Breakfast £3, dinner £4. Open Apr.-Aug. daily; Sept. M-Sa; Oct. and Mar. Tu-Sa; closed Nov.-Feb.

Mrs. E. V. Williams, 28 Bridge St. (tel. 612550). Large rooms with staggeringly comfortable beds. Kind proprietress bakes heavenly Welsh cakes. £12.50.

Mrs. P. E. Thomas, 8 New St. (tel. 617329), off Pier St. Digest the mammoth breakfast amid Chinese paintings and a giant harp. All rooms have TV. £12.50.

Bryn-y-don, 36 Bridge St. (tel. 612011). Large rooms with TV. £15.

Linda Davis, 28 South Rd. (tel. 612115), off Bridge St. TV and washbasins share space with retro furniture and floral designs. £14.

Camping: Midfield Caravan Park (tel. 612542), 1½mi. from town center on the A4120, 200yd. uphill from the junction with the A487. Ask for any bus going to Southgate from the bus stop on Alexandra Rd. One of the most pleasant campsites in the area, with a view of town and the hills. £4.50 per camper, £8.50 for two.

FOOD AND PUBS

On Pier St., take-away spots are cheap and open on Sundays; try the two Chinese restaurants. **Spar,** 32 Terrace Rd. (open daily 8am-11pm), and the larger **Somerfield** (open M-Th and Sa 8am-8pm, F 8am-9pm, Su 10am-4pm), behind the railway station, sell sundries. Soy milk, herbal elixirs, and adzuki beans await consumption at the **Health Food Centre,** 42 Terrace Rd. (open M-Sa 9:30am-5:30pm).

◉**Gannet's Bistro,** St. James Sq. (tel. 617164). The former head of British Airways' catering department runs the place; we only wish airlines served food half as good. Entrees may stretch the budget (£6.50-10), but a satisfying meal can be made of three or so starters (£1.50-3); check out the grilled sardines (£1.50). Veggie options abound. Open M and W-Sa noon-2pm and 6-9pm, last orders 1:30pm and 8:30pm.

The Treehouse Café, 2 Pier St. (tel. 615791). Checkered tablecloths and wood floors atop the Treehouse Organic Shop. Offers organic dishes, including beefburger (£4.50), hummus with pita (£2.10), and a selection of cakes and ice cream. Open M-W 9:30am-5:30pm, Th-Sa 9:30am-5:30pm and 6:30-9pm.

Y Graig Wholefood Café, 34 Pier St. (tel. 611606). Berkeley radicalism meets Welsh nationalism as tie-dyed t-shirts, political slogans and ads for meditation retreats compete for space on the walls. Wholefood for vegans, vegetarians, and carnivores for under £4. Savory pies and chili (£1.50-2.10). CYMRU DDI NIWCLIAR (Nuclear Free Wales)! Open daily 9:15am-6pm, though hours may vary.

Sunclouds, 25 North Parade (tel. 617750). Sit at the wooden counters of this cafe and watch the world go by as you bite into a tasty baguette (£1.75-2.25, take-away £1-1.50). Open M-Sa 10am-4pm.

The Ancient Ruin Vegetarian Café, 13 Cambrian Pl. (tel. 612363), arrayed in bright blue and yellow, serves amazing pancakes (around £2.50) and dinners from £4.35. Open for lunch and snacks M-Sa 10am-5pm, dinner Sa only 7-9pm.

The Cabin Coffee Bar, 11 Pier St. (tel. 617398), at Eastgate. The walls read like a history of Hollywood machismo—Bogie and Cagney stare intently into your coffee. Sandwiches, including a good chicken *tikka,* for £1-2. Open daily 9am-5:30pm.

There are over 50 **pubs** in Aberystwyth. A vine-covered beer garden and reveling students make **Rummer's,** Trefecher Bridge (at the end of Bridge St.), the choicest spot to enjoy a pint (open M-W and Sa 7pm-midnight, Th-F 7pm-1am, Su 7-10:30pm). After you swig some ale, the creaky floors of the oldest pub in town, the **Angel,** 57-59 Upper Great Darkgate St., beg for a dance. Smashed mirrors quake in the **Pier Pressure** nightclub, The Royal Pier, Marine Terr. (tel. 617000; open M-Sa 9pm-1am; cover £1-4). A signpost points the way in the center of **K2,** at the corner of Great Darkgate and Pier St. (tel. 623479; open Th 7pm-1am, F-Sa 5:30pm-1am; cover £1-3).

SIGHTS

Aberystwyth's charming *fin-de-siècle* pier has been battered by the tourist trade. The beachfront and promenade remain much as they were in Victorian times, and pastel townhouses still lend the town a tamed, aristocratic air. At the south end of the promenade stands the university's **Old College,** a neo-Gothic patchwork structure opened in 1877 as a hotel and restored in 1885 as Wales's first university. Prince Charles was drilled in Welsh here before being crowned Prince of Wales in 1969.

Just south of the Old College on a hilly peninsula, **Aberystwyth Castle** has witnessed centuries of Welsh rebellion and English repression. Before Edward I built the present castle in 1277, previous forts had burned down nearly half a dozen times, the fifth at the hands of the last Welsh Prince of Gwynedd, Llewelyn ap Gruffydd. Antisocial Oliver Cromwell made quick work of the diamond-shaped fortress in 1649; when night falls, the crumbling walls are illuminated against the shimmering Atlantic. Wheelchair access to most of the castle is available.

At the other end of the promenade, the **Electric Cliff Railway** (tel. 617642) creaks up an angle one normally associates with roller coasters to the top of **Constitution Hiil.** At the top lies the wide lens of the *camera obscura,* a popular Victorian amusement which acts as a giant pinhole camera onto the whole city. *(Open daily July-Aug. 10am-6pm; mid-Mar. to June and Sept.-Oct. 10am-5pm. Camera obscura free. 6 trains per hr. £2 return, students and seniors £1.75, children £1, under 5 free.)* You can also walk across the small series of wooden bridges to the *camera.* Check at the pier for fishing trips, or call **Sunshine Boat Trips** (tel. 828844).

An imposing classical structure sitting on a bluff overlooking the bay, the **National Library of Wales** (tel. 632837), off Penglais Rd. past the hospital, houses almost every book or manuscript written in, or pertaining to, Wales. *(Open M-Sa 10am-5pm. Free.)* The well-designed **Gregynog Gallery** displays the first Welsh written text (c. 800), the first Welsh printed book (1546), the first Welsh dictionary (1547), the first Welsh map (1573), the first Welsh "Beibl" (1588), and the first Welsh magazine (1735), which managed one issue before it folded. In another corner, scalded toutes and lusty bachelors rise from the pages of the earliest surviving manuscript of the *Canterbury Tales,* dating to the early 15th century. Further up Penglais Rd., in the University of Wales at Aberystwyth campus, stands the **Aberystwyth Arts Centre** (tel. 623232), which sponsors fine Welsh drama and film in Welsh and English. *(Box office open daily 10am-5pm.)*

■ Near Aberystwyth: Devil's Bridge

The **Vale of Rheidol Railway** (tel. 625819) chugs and twists its way on tracks less than 2 ft. apart from Aberystwyth to the waterfalls and gorges of **Devil's Bridge.** *(Mid-July to Aug. 4 per day; Apr. to mid-Jul. and Sept.-Oct. 2 per day. £10.50, accompanied children £1, dogs £1. Woof woof.)* The three bridges were inexplicably built on top of one another; the lower bridge, attributed to the Architect of Evil, was probably built by Cistercian monks from the nearby **Strata Florida Abbey** in the 12th century. The paths are turnstile-operated, so take some change. The rungs of **Jacob's Ladder** (£1) descend into the depth of the **Devil's Punchbowl** gorge, cross the torrent on an arched footbridge, and climb back beside the waterfall to the road. The hostel closest to the gorge is the **YHA Ystumtuen** (tel. 890693), near the end of the railway off the A44 in Ponterwyd, with simple accommodations (£5.85, under 18 £4; open Apr.-Aug. daily). Take bus #501 from Aberystwyth (M-Sa 7 per day, last bus 5:40pm) and ask to be dropped off near the hostel, a 1½ mi. walk (signposted "Ystumuen") from the A44.

▓ Cardigan (Aberteifi)

Cardigan introduces itself discreetly at the tiny bridge fronting its castle, fanning uphill from this nodal point. In the 19th century, the quiet town was a major port along with London, Bristol, and Liverpool. Today, the once bustling port has all but disappeared. Cardigan draws visitors for the Pembrokeshire Coast National Park's haunting Preseli Hills, which hide a swath of shrines (see **Pembrokeshire Coast National Park,** p. 419). To the north, the Caredigon Heritage Coast offers miles of scenic walks and sandy resort towns.

No railroads lead to Cardigan. Find **bus** information in the *Guide to Local Services Book 2,* free at the tourist office. Buses stop in Finch Sq.; from the Guild Hall on High St., head down Priory St. for **Richards Bros.** (tel. 613756) buses. Bus #412 connects Cardigan with **Haverfordwest** (1½hr., M-Sa 1 per hr., £2.85); #411 runs from **St. David's** every two hours to connect with #412 at **Fishguard** (1hr., M-Sa, £2.15). Bus #550, operated by Richards and **Arriva Cymru** (tel. (01970) 617951), runs to and from **Aberystwyth** (2hr., M-Sa 2 per hr., £3.60). Cardigan is reportedly a **hitcher's** paradise: thumbers stand near the roundabout connecting A487 and A485.

The **tourist office**, Bath House Rd. (tel. 613230; fax 613600), lies in the Theatr Mwldon off Pendre Rd. (open July-Aug. daily 10am-6pm; Sept.-June M-Sa 10am-5pm). Cash flows at **Lloyd's**, 14 High St. (open M-Tu and Th-F 9am-5pm, W 9:30am-5pm). The **post office**, 26 High St., contemplates its **postal code**, SA43 1JH (open M-F 9am-5:30pm, Sa 9am-12:30pm). The **telephone code** is a reflective 01239.

The nearest youth hostel is 4 mi. northwest of Cardigan at **Poppit Sands** (see **Accommodations and Camping**, p. 421). Try Pendre Rd. for a smattering of B&Bs. Built on the site of the 1793 gaol designed by John Nash, the **Highbury House**, Pendre Rd. (tel. 613403) allows guests liberty—though not before they finish breakfast in the sun-washed conservatory (£12.50). At **Llys Peris**, 28 Pendre Rd. (tel. 615205), rooms have tiled fireplaces (£14).

For groceries, head to the busy **market**, housed under the multi-colored brick arches of the 1858 Guild Hall, at the corner of High and Priory St. (open M-Tu and Th-Sa 9:30am-4:30pm; produce sold Th and Su 8am-2pm). Cream-filled pastries float at the **Queen's Bakery**, 48 Pendre Rd. (tel. 612110; open M-Sa 8am-5:30pm). **Branney's Restaurant and Café** (tel. 615167), upstairs at Priory St., serves garlic mushrooms (£4.60) and delectable seafood specials (£7; open daily noon-8:30pm). The oldest inn in Wales, established in 1105, the **Black Lion Hotel**, 30 High St. (tel. 612532), contains a timber-ceilinged **pub** (entrees £4.50-8, lunch sandwiches £1.70-3).

The High St.-Pendre Rd. stretch forms the main spine of this town. Cardigan's 13th-century **castle**, overlooking the river and town off High St., exposes only the exterior of its crumbling, iron-girded battlements; the octogenarian owner won't allow visitors. In its early years, the castle changed hands from Welsh prince to Norman lord, and in 1176 Lord Rhys ap Gruffydd held the first National Eisteddfod here (see **Ffestivals**, p. 395). Cardigan has permanently established its own Eisteddfod, the **Gwyl Fawr Aberteifi**, a 6-week exuberant festival held annually in mid-July. An eclectic array of films, concerts, dance, and dramatic productions fills the **Theatr Mwldan** (tel. 621200), on Bath House Rd. off Pendre Rd., which also hosts a European film festival in November.

■ Near Cardigan

The 12th-century ruins of **St. Dogmael's Abbey**, 1 mi. northwest on the B4546, lie along the Teifi estuary. The romantic ruins sit atop the site of a previous Celtic monastery; the nearby parish church contains the 6th-century Sagranus stone, whose Latin and Ogham inscriptions provided the key for interpreting the Ogham alphabet. Richards Bros. bus #407 heads to the Abbey (10min., M-Sa 2 per hr.).

Perched on a crag above the Teifi Gorge, the ruins of **Cilgerran Castle** (tel. 615007) were the site of the 1109 abduction of Nest, the Welsh Helen of Troy, by the lovelorn Prince of Powys. The present structure, with two heavyset round towers, was built in the 1220s and withstood multiple sieges before Owain Glyndŵr captured it in 1405. (Open Apr.-Oct. daily 9:30am-6:30pm; Nov.-Mar. M-Sa 9:30am-4pm, Su 11am-4pm. £1.70, students, seniors, and children £1.20, families £4.60.) Midway Motors bus #430 departs from Cardigan (10min., 5 per day).

■ Machynlleth

At Machynlleth (mach-HUN-hleth) Owain Glyndŵr, the great Welsh leader of the early 15th century, summoned four men from every commote in the territory to a vast open-air parliament. (A commote is an old Welsh administrative unit that corresponds roughly to 50 hamlets, each typically containing 9 houses, 1 plow, 1 oven, 1 churn, 1 cat, 1 cock, and 1 herdsman. We do not jest.) When the delegates departed, the rebellion quickly unraveled, and Machynlleth collapsed into the slumber from which it has not yet awakened. However, the town still revels in its Welsh character, with bilingual street names and the thriving celebration of Celtic life.

WALES

GETTING THERE British Rail (tel. (0345) 484950) chugs to Machynlleth from **Birmingham** (2½hr., M-Sa 9 per day, Su 4 per day, £10.90), **Shrewsbury** (1½hr., M-Sa 9 per day, Su 4 per day, £7), **Aberystwyth** (30min., M-Sa 14 per day, Su 6 per day, £4.50), and **Harlech** (1½hr., M-Sa 11 per day, Su 3 per day, £8.70), but the **Cambrian Coast Day Rover** will also suffice and is only £5.80. **Arriva Cymru** (tel. (01970) 617951) bus #2 winds from **Aberystwyth** on its way to **Dolgellau** (40min., M-Sa 7 per day, Su 1 per day, £3); the scenic ride along the A487 is worth the extra minutes. Bus #32A swerves inland from Dolgellau on a even lovelier route (6 per day, in summer only Su 1 per day, £2). A **Traws-Cambria** bus rolls in twice daily from **Cardiff** (£14).

ORIENTATION AND PRACTICAL INFORMATION The unmistakable heart of town is the **clock tower,** standing Eiffel-like where Pentrerhedryn, Penrallt, and Maengwyn St. form a T. **Buses** stop by the tower. From the **rail station** (tel. 702311), turn left onto Doll St., veer right at the church onto Penrallt St., and continue until you see the clock tower; Maengwyn St. is on the left. The **tourist office** (tel. 702401; fax 703675) lies in the Owain Glyndŵr Centre on Maengwyn St. (open Easter-Oct. daily 10am-6pm; Nov.-Easter M-F 9am-5pm). **Barclays** and its **ATM** await under the shadow of the tall timepiece (open M-W and F 9am-4:30pm, Th 10am-4:30pm). Mountain **bikes** can be rented at **Greenstiles,** 7 Penrallt St. (tel. 703543), next to the clock tower (£8 per ½ day, £12 per day, £60 per week; open M-Sa 9:30am-5:30pm; Apr.-Sept. also Su 10am-4pm). The weekly **market** on the town's two main streets offers food, crafts, underwear, and much, much more (open W 9am-4pm). The **police** (tel. 702215) keep watch from Doll St. **Chest Hospital** (tel. 702341) busts out on Newton Rd. Send and shop at the **post office,** 51-53 Maengwyn St. (tel. 702323), inside Spar (open M-Sa 8:30am-6pm). Machynlleth's **postal code** is SY20 8AE; its **telephone code** is 01654.

ACCOMMODATIONS AND FOOD Machynlleth lacks a hostel, but the **YHA Corris** (tel./fax 761686), in the old school on Corris Rd. in Corris, is just 15 minutes away on buses #30, 32 or 34. Reminders of nature abound, from the hostel's position on the southern side of Cader Idris to its conservation motif. Laundry facilities and meals are available (£8, under 18 £5.40; lockout 10am-5pm; open Mar.-Oct. daily; Nov.-Feb. Th-Sa). Machynlleth has a fair number of **B&Bs,** but you'd be hard pressed to find a budget-friendly location. **Haulfryn** (tel. 702206), on Aberystwyth Rd. near Celtica, blooms with large, flowery rooms and does full veggie breakfasts if asked (£15). Turn off Maengwyn St. at New St., and take the first left onto Heol Powys. Noah's Ark aspirants can go two by two to the doubles-only **Melin-y-Wig** (tel. 703933), next door to Haulfryn on Aberystwyth Rd., with TVs in each room (doubles £30). **Campers** can seek out **Llwyngwern Farm** (tel. 702492), off the A487 next to the Centre for Alternative Technology (£4 per person, £6.50 per 2 people; open Easter-Oct.). Machynlleth pubs offer nothing spectacular in the way of affordable gluttony, although inventive dishes are served alongside the massive stone hearth at the **Skinners Arms,** 10 Penrallt St. (tel. 702354), near the clock tower. Come nightfall, it's the liveliest pub in town. (Open M-Sa 11am-11pm, Su noon-10:30pm; food served M-Sa noon-2pm and 6-9pm.) Cheap healthy feasts can be had at the pine tables of the **Quarry Shop Café and Wholefoods,** 13 Maengwyn St. (tel. 702624; open M-W and F-Sa 9am-4:30pm, Th 9am-2pm). Craft your own menu at **Spar,** 51-53 Maengwyn St. (open M-Sa 7am-11pm, Su 7am-10:30pm).

SIGHTS From the gargoyled clock tower, a two-minute downhill walk along Aberystwyth Rd. (A487) will bring you to **Celtica** (tel. 702702), in Y Plas on Aberystwyth Rd. The exhibit uses advanced high-tech wizardry to trace the millennia-old story of the Celtic peoples. Darkened chambers shrouded in mist feature rising cauldrons, rotating stone masks, and startling flashes of light, all to the thundering echo of a narrator's voice. In a bizarre but entertaining denouement, a druid atop a gnarled tree whisks you on a video tour of Celtic history through time, bringing you back to the present. *(Open daily 10am-6pm. £4.65, students, seniors, and children £3.50, families £12.75. Wheelchair accessible.)* For a more robustly informative walk through history, visit the **Owain Glyndŵr Interpretive Centre,** Maengwyn St. (tel. 702827), which occupies a primitive stone building on the site of Glyndŵr's parliament house; placards place the rebel's career in the context of Welsh mythology. *(Open Easter-Sept. M-Sa 10am-5pm; winter by appointment. Free.)*

High on a hill 3 mi. north of town along the A487, the **Centre for Alternative Technology** (tel. 702400) is like a giant summer camp whose counselors never leave. A railway, powered by nifty water counter-balancing, draws visitors (including those in wheelchairs) up a 200 ft. cliff into a green village of lily ponds, wind turbines, and energy-efficient houses (including the best-insulated house in Britain). Glimpse into the life-styles of those living communally here, or climb into the Mole Hole with giant insect replicas. *(Open daily Easter-Oct. 10am-5pm; Oct.-Easter 10am-dusk. £5.70, students and seniors £4, children £2.80, families £15.50, under 5 free. YHA members and bus riders get a 10% discount. Visitors arriving by bike or foot get a 50% discount. Joint admission and train ticket with a 50% discount can be purchased in staffed railway stations.)* Take Crosville bus #34 (M-Sa 2 per hr.).

■ Harlech

About 50 mi. north of Machynlleth along the Cambrian Coast, the tiny town of Harlech halts just shy of the Llŷn Peninsula. Hunched on a steep rocky hillside overlooking wave-beaten sand dunes, the town's weathered buildings long ago determined that the streets would remain narrow and sidewalk-free. Refugees from busy Barmouth (to the south) find solitude and sea breezes amid the grassy dunes at Harlech beach, a 20-minute walk from town. Harlech's chief attraction, however, is not its low-lying sands, but its dominating castle, perched 200 ft. above the sea on part of the world's oldest known geological rock formation. It affords a haunting view of the misty, craggy mountains of Snowdonia and the towns of the Llŷn to the north. The Rock of Harlech was the favorite resting spot of the legendary King Bendigeidfran, whose fair sister's troubled marriage to an Irish king provoked a storied battle. Modern travelers often stop and rest in Harlech on their way to Snowdonia and the Llŷn.

PRACTICAL INFORMATION Harlech lies midway on the Cambrian Coast line. It's a trying uphill walk to town from the unstaffed **train station** (tel. (0345) 484950), or try a tempting route through the castle. Trains arrive from **Machynlleth** (1½hr., M-Sa 7 per day, Su 3 per day, £8), connecting to **Pwllheli** and other spots on the **Llŷn Peninsula** (M-Sa every 2hr., Su 3 per day). The **Cambrian Coast Day Ranger** (£6, Evening Ranger £3.25) is cheaper than the single fare from **Machynlleth** or **Aberystwyth.** **Arriva Cymru** (tel. (01970) 617951) bus #38 links Harlech to southerly **Barmouth** and northerly **Blaenau Ffestiniog,** stopping at the station and at the car park, just past the tourist office on Stryd Fawr (to Harlech M-Sa 8 per day; to Blaenau Ffestiniog M-Sa 4 per day).

The castle opens out onto Twtil; slightly uphill is the town's major street, Stryd Fawr (High St.). The **tourist office,** Gwyddfor House, Stryd Fawr (tel./fax 780658), doubles as a **National Park Information Centre.** The helpful staff provides guides to walks and maps while you stock up on Ordnance Survey maps and pamphlets detailing walks around Snowdonia (open daily Apr.-Oct. 10am-1pm and 2-6pm). The erratic **Midland** bank sports its dependable **ATM** on Stryd Fawr (open M, W, and F 9:30-11:30am, Tu and Th 12:45-3pm). The little **post office** (tel. 780231) that could lies on Stryd Fawr (open M-Tu and Th-F 9am-12:30pm and 1:30-5:30pm, W and Sa 9am-12:30pm). Harlech's **postal code** is LL46 2YA; its **telephone code** is 01766.

ACCOMMODATIONS AND FOOD The **YHA Llanbedr** (tel. (01341) 241287), 4 mi. south of town, is the closest hostel to Harlech; take the 10-minute train ride to the Llanbedr stop or ride bus #38 and ask to be let off at the hostel. (£7.70, under 18 £5.15. Open May-Aug. daily; mid-Feb. to Apr. and Sept.-Oct. Th-M; Jan. to mid-Feb. F-Su.) Those wishing to sample Barmouth's overly commercial beaches can stay at **Just Beds,** King Edward St., Barmouth (tel. (01341) 281165), just before the Catholic Church, a 20-minute train ride away from Harlech (£9, no lockout or curfew). Good

B&Bs in and around Harlech can save you the trip, though the price is a stiff £14. Forgive the lifeless architecture and revel in what may be the best view in Harlech (spanning the castle, Mt. Snowdon and the Llŷn Peninsula) at **Arundel,** Stryd Fawr (tel. 780637). From Barclays Bank head down High St. and take a right before the Bistro. The Scottish proprietress's son built those intimidating guns hanging on the wall. If the climb from the train station does not appeal, call and ask to be picked up (doubles only, £29). The **Byrdir Hotel** (tel./fax 780316), on Stryd Fawr near the tourist office, has comfortable rooms with TV and washbasins, and a nearby water trough for your thirsty horse (£16, with bath £20). **Camp** at **Min-y-Don Park,** Beach Rd. (tel. 780286), with showers and laundry (£2 per person, children £1; open Mar.-Oct.).

Yr **Ogof Bistro** (tel. 780888), left from the castle on Stryd Fawr, offers some of the best cuisine in town, with a wide range of creative vegetarian dishes (£6.10) and Welsh specialties (open daily 10am-3pm and 6-10:30pm). The ocean view from the grassy patio of the **Plas Café,** Stryd Fawr (tel. 780204), demands a long afternoon tea with gorgeous desserts (£1.50-3) or a sunset dinner (£6; open daily Mar.-Oct. 10am-8:30pm; Nov.-Dec. 10am-5pm). Harlech's sole grocery, **Spar,** greets travelers next to the Plas Café on Stryd Fawr (open M-Sa 8am-11pm, Su 10am-10:30pm). The **Lion Hotel's** bar offers cheap, simple food (£4-5) and reigns as the top beer joint in this publess town (open M-F noon-11pm, Sa 11am-11pm, Su noon-10:30pm).

SIGHTS **Harlech Castle** (tel. 780552), Edward I's fortress, crowns a 200 ft. rock with sweeping views of prefabs, caravan parks, the Snowdonian mountains, and the sea. From the outer bailey, 151 steps descend the cliff to the train station, where the sea once reached. *(Open Apr.-Oct. daily 9:30am-6:30pm; Nov.-Mar. M-Sa 9:30am-4pm, Su 11am-4pm. £3, students, seniors, and children £2.)* Public **footpaths** snake in and around Harlech, running from the grassy dunes to the forested hilltops above the town; pick up brochures at the tourist office. **Theatr Ardudwy,** Coleg Harlech (tel. 780667; fax 780778), is the town's cultural axis, hosting films, plays, concerts, and exhibitions. *(Some concerts are free; other performances £2.50-6; students, seniors, and children £1-2 discount. Wheelchair accessible.)*

Love Your Cutlery

Some suitors bring flowers, others serenade with a guitar and a ballad, but in Wales, wooing often involved a large wooden spoon. Making and giving a lovespoon to one's beloved is a centuries-old Welsh custom. The oldest known lovespoon dates from the 17th century, but lovespoons have been around for much longer. The romantic eating utensils, extremely popular during the 18th and 19th centuries, were often carved as a pastime on long winter evenings. Gentlemen wooers tried to convey the extent of their love through fancy designs, which made for some ridiculously enlarged, elaborate spoons. Acceptance of the spoon meant courting could begin, and the term "spooning" has found its way into the English language, implying what might follow. Although the custom has languished, lovespoons can still be found in homes and tourist traps across Wales.

■ Llŷn Peninsula (Penrhyn Llŷn)

The Llŷn has been a tourist hotspot since the Middle Ages, when religious pilgrims tramped through on their way to Bardsey Island. Endless sandy beaches lining the 25 mi. southern coast now draw different sorts of pilgrims—sun worshippers coddled by the towns between Pwllheli and Abersoch. A hilly region of simple beauty, the Llŷn boasts green fields spreading down to the coast, bounded by hedges filled with bright *blodau wylltion* (wildflowers). The farther west you venture, the more unsullied the Llŷn becomes and the more scarce certain conveniences grow—make sure you stock up on cash from the ATMs in Porthmadog, Pwllheli, and Criccieth.

GETTING THERE AND GETTING ABOUT

The northern end of **British Rail's** (tel. (0345) 484950) Cambrian Coast line reaches through Porthmadog and Criccieth (KRIK-key-ith) to Pwllheli (pwih-HEL-lee), stopping at smaller towns in between. The line begins in mid-Wales at **Aberystwyth** and changes at **Machynlleth** for northern destinations (M-F 5 per day, Sa 6 per day, Su 3 per day, Aberystwyth-Porthmadog £11.50, Aberystwyth-Pwllheli £14.30). The **Cambrian Coast Day Rover** is often the best deal, offering unlimited travel on many stops along the line (£6 per day). The Conwy Valley line's western end is at **Blaenau Ffestiniog** and continues via **Betws-y-Coed** to **Llandudno** on the northern coast; this line in turn connects to **Chester** and **Bangor** (M-Sa 6 per day, Su 2 per day).

A daily **National Express** coach (tel. (0990) 808080) from **London** arrives in **Pwllheli** at 7:40pm and departs Pwllheli for London at 9:45 the next morning, passing through **Porthmadog, Caernarfon, Bangor,** and **Birmingham** on the way (Porthmadog-London £16). **TrawsCambria** bus #701 connects Porthmadog once a day with **Aberystwyth, Carmarthen, Swansea,** and **Cardiff** (Porthmadog-Cardiff 6½hr.). A smattering of bus companies, most prominently **Arriva Cymru** (tel. (01248) 351879), serves most spots on the peninsula with reassuring haste for £1-2. **Express Motors** (tel. (01286) 674570) bus #1 winds from **Blaenau Ffestiniog** to **Porthmadog** on its way to **Caernarfon** (30min., M-Sa 1 per hr. until 9:40pm, in summer also Su 4 per day, £2). Arriva and **Caelloi** (tel. (01758) 612719) share the running of bus #3, which is often open-top in the summer, from **Porthmadog** to **Pwllheli via Criccieth** (M-Sa 1 per hr. until 10:10pm, Su 6 per day). **Berwyn** (tel. (01286) 660315) and **Clynnog & Trefor** (tel. (01286) 660208) run bus #12 between **Pwllheli** and **Caernarfon** (1hr., M-Sa 1 per hr., Su 3 per day, £1.80). Arriva buses #17, 17B, and 18 all leave Pwllheli to weave around the western tip of the peninsula; only #18 runs on Sunday. A **Gwynedd Red Rover,** bought from the driver, is good for a day of travel throughout the peninsula and the rest of Gwynedd County (£4.40, children £2.20).

■ Porthmadog

Don't pass judgment on the rest of the Llŷn on account of Porthmadog's nondescript line of shops; sun-drenched sand is only a bus connection away. This travel hub's principal attraction is the **Ffestiniog Railway** (tel. 512340), whose terminus is on High St. at the opposite end of the tourist office. This justly famous narrow-gauge railway runs northeast through the Ffestiniog Valley into the hills of Snowdonia, terminating in **Blaenau Ffestiniog.** *(1hr., Mar. to mid-Nov. 2-10 per day. £12.80, seniors £9.60, one child with adult free, additional children £6.40, families £25.60, dogs and bikes £3.)* At the other end of Porthmadog, across from the British Rail station, rests Ffestiniog's humble cousin, the **Welsh Highland Railway** (tel. 513402). Once the longest narrow-gauge railway in Wales, the track is now being laid for a reconnection to **Caernarfon,** though as of yet the engines only crawl to **Pen-y-mount** (¾mi.) and back. *(Mid-May to Sept. 5 per day, also runs some days in Apr. and Oct. £2, children £1.25, seniors £1.75, families £6.)* Narrow-gauge railway buffs can purchase a **Great Little Trains of Wales Wanderer** ticket, which gives unlimited travel on both lines above, as well as the Bala Lake, Brecon Mountain, Talyllyn, Llanberis Lake, and Vale of Rheidol lines. *(4-day pass £28, children £14; 8-day pass £38, children £19.)* You also can splatter paint or torture clay behind the largest mural in Wales at **Porthmadog Pottery** (tel. 510910), five minutes down Snowdon St. which crosses High St. near the bus stop. *(Open July-Aug. daily 9am-5pm; Sept.-June M-F 9am-5pm. Free; £2.75 to throw a pot or paint a plate.)*

From the **train station,** a right-hand turn onto Stryd Fawr will bring you into town; further up the street are Bank Pl. and Snowdon St. **Buses** stop at various points along Stryd Fawr, most commonly outside the **Australia Inn** (see below) or across the street in front of the park; check posted schedules. The well-stocked **tourist office** (tel. 512981) is on Stryd Fawr next to the railway station (open Easter-Oct. daily 10am-6pm; Nov.-Easter Tu-Su 9:30am-5pm). Stock up on cash at the **Barclays ATM,** 79 Stryd Fawr (open M and W-F 9am-4:30m, Tu 10am-4:30pm). Clothes find redemption at the **launderette,** 34 Snowdon St. (open daily 7:30am-5pm). The **police** patrol

WALES

begins on Stryd Fawr opposite the Sportsman Hotel. Porthmadog's **post office** (tel. 512010) is at the corner of Stryd Fawr and Bank Pl. (open M-F 9am-5:30pm, Sa 9am-12:30pm). The **postal code** is LL49 9AD; the **telephone code** is 01766.

Watch for small **B&B** signs in windows along Madoc and Snowdon St., although you may not always be allowed to look before you commit. **Vro Gain,** Bank Pl. (tel. 513125), provides a full breakfast and orange curtains that give the bedrooms a twilight glow in the morning (£14, students £12.50). **Llys Caradog,** 12 Snowdon St. (tel. 512635), boasts well-kept rooms, TV, dressing gowns, and much-celebrated breakfasts (in summer £16; in winter £15). **Mrs. Skellern,** 35 Madoc St. (tel. 512843), offers rooms at £14. Scatter sandwich crumbs along the stool-lined counter at **Jessie's,** 75 Stryd Fawr (tel. 512814; open M-Sa 9am-5pm). The **Australia Inn,** 31-33 Stryd Fawr, features good pub grub and a wide-screen TV.

■ Near Porthmadog: Portmeirion

An eccentric landmark of Italy-fixation, the private village of **Portmeirion** stands 2 mi. east of Porthmadog (tel. (01766) 770000). Mediterranean courtyards, buildings layered in pastels, and the occasional palm tree provide an otherworldly diversion from the standard castles and cottages. The village was built between 1925 and 1972 by Sir Clough Williams-Ellis, whose sole concern was beauty, "that strange necessity." Through the statued, softly colored gates rise a sun-baked assortment of buildings transported from distant locales and cobblestone lanes bordered by pooled gardens. Dogs can't enter the village, but they go the way of all flesh at the **dog cemetery** in the nearby woods, where Pepys (1965-76, "a brave and much loved cavalier") and Dearest Darling Woofy (1977-94, "a very exceptional dog and mother of Softy") slumber peacefully. *(Open daily 9:30am-5:30pm. £3.70, students and seniors £3.20, children £1.90; reduced admission Nov.-Mar.)* Bus #98 leaves **Porthmadog** for Portmeirion (M-Sa 6 per day, Su 2 per day). Follow signs to the village, an easy and scenic 20-minute walk.

■ Criccieth and Llanystumdwy

Above the coastal town of **Criccieth,** 5 mi. west of Porthmadog, stand the remains of **Criccieth Castle** (tel. 522227), built by Llewelyn the Great in 1230, taken by the Normans in 1283, and destroyed by Owain Glyndŵr in 1404. The castle still puzzles architectural historians, who debate which portion was English and which was Welsh. Its gatehouse, silhouetted against the skyline, glowers over Tremadog Bay, with views of Snowdonia to the northeast and Harlech across the water. *(Castle open daily Apr.-Sept. 10am-6pm; Oct.-Mar. 9:30am-4pm, access to grounds only. Castle and grounds £2.20, students, seniors, and children £1.70; grounds only free.)* The hourly **Crosville** bus #3, which connects Criccieth to Porthmadog and Pwllheli (M-Sa), also stops at **Llanystumdwy,** a tiny town 1½ mi. north of Criccieth that was the boyhood home of **David Lloyd George** (prime minister 1916-1922). The town preserves his boyhood home, the school where he first made mischief, and his simple grave along the banks of the Dwyfor. The **Lloyd George Museum** (tel. 522071), on the village's only street, displays relics from his career, including his working copy of the Treaty of Versailles and the pen he used to sign it. *(Open July-Sept. daily 10:30am-5pm; June M-Sa 10:30am-5pm; Apr.-May M-F 10:30am-5pm; Oct. M-F 11am-4pm. £2.50, students, seniors, and children £1.50, families £6.)*

Trains (tel. (0345) 484950) stop in town on their way to and from **Pwllheli.** From the station, turn right onto High St. to reach the town center. Criccieth runs its own **tourist office** (tel. 523633), separate from the Welsh Tourist Board, in a caravan on the green near the bus stop; they book beds for a 10% deposit (open May-Sept. M-F 10:30am-1pm and 1:30-6:30pm, Sa-Su 2-6pm). **Midland** and its **ATM** sit on 51 High St. (open M-F 10:30am-1pm). Near the bus stop on High St. lies the **post office,** which responds to its LL52 OBV **postal code** (open M-Tu and Th-F 9am-5:30pm). Criccieth and Llanystumdwy share the **telephone code** 01766.

B&Bs (£15-25) are scattered on Tan-y-Grisiau Terr., just across the rail track from the bus stop. Marine Terr. and Marine Crescent, by the beach near the castle, also have a smattering of B&Bs. Dinner-seekers head to **Poachers Restaurant,** 66 High St. (tel. 522512), downhill from the bus stop (entrees £6.50-8; open M-Sa 6-9pm, Su book ahead). Two doors down, **Spar** somehow stocks shelves of groceries in a closet-sized store (open M-Sa 8am-10pm, Su 9am-10pm). The beer garden of **The Bryn Hir Arms** (tel. 522493), along High St. in the opposite direction, provides the ideal setting for a quiet pint (open M-Sa 11:30am-11pm, Su noon-10:30pm). Branches of **Cadwalader's** ice cream store dot the Llŷn, but the original lies on Castle St. Grab a cone (65-90p) to complement a beach walk (open M-F 10:30am-8pm, Sa-Su 10am-9:30pm).

■ Pwllheli

Pwllheli (poohl-HEL-ly), 8 mi. west of Criccieth, has little to attract the traveler besides the station that spews buses to every corner of the peninsula and beyond. The town has two **beaches:** sandy Abererch Beach to the east, and pebbly South Beach. The **tourist office**, Station Sq. (tel. 613000), offers information and books B&Bs (open Apr.-Oct. daily 10am-6pm; Nov.-Mar. Tu-Sa 10:30am-4:30pm). **Midland** and its **ATM** take the corner of High St. and Penlong St. (open M-F 9am-5pm). Squeeze past frenzied shoppers to reach fresh Welsh cakes and a wealth of fruit and vegetables at the sprawling open-air **market** in front of the bus station (open W 9am-5pm). The **Spar** and **Iceland** supermarkets nearby pick up the slack the rest of the week. The **Bodawen Cafe**, on Y Maes near the bus station, offers tasty sandwiches (£1.50-2). Look sweet on the seat of a bicycle-built-for-two at the **Llŷn Cycle Centre** (tel. 612414), on lower Ala Rd. (£10 per day, £45 per week; deposit £25; open M-W and F-Sa 10am-5pm). The **post office** sits opposite the station (open M-F 9am-5pm, Sa 9am-1pm). The **postal code** is LL53 5HL; the **telephone code** is 01758.

Mrs. Jones, 26 High St. (tel. 613172), lets out comfortable rooms (£12). From the tourist office, cross the street and follow Penlon St. until it meets High St., where a right will take you to her door. Across the street, **Bank Place Guest House**, 29 High St. (tel. 612103), safeguards spacious rooms and huge breakfasts (£11). **Camping** options abound in the area. **Hendre** (tel. 613416), on the road to Nefyn at Efailnewidd, offers camping near Pwllheli (£8 per tent; launderette and showers available; open Mar.-Oct.). **Cae Bach Site** (tel. 612536) lies three-quarters of a mile from Pwllheli (£3-6; open July-Aug.; Sept.-June in good weather).

■ Aberdaron and Tre'r Ceiri

Tucked in a sandy cove close to the peninsula's western tip, the peaceful village of **Aberdaron** has nothing crass to distract visitors from the wind and the gray-blue sea. Sheep and white houses cling to scattered hilltops. By the beach, the plain stone **Church of Saint Hywyn** surrounds the oldest doorway in northern Wales and two 5th-century gravestones carved in Latin. Water in the **wishing well**, 1½ mi. west of town, stays fresh even when the tide crashes over it. Follow road signs from Aberdaron 2 mi. to what may be the finest sands in the Llŷn, **Por Oer**. If conditions are right, the sands live up to their nickname, the "Whistling Sands." *(£1.50.)* Off the southwest corner of the peninsula, 20,000 saints somehow find the space to sleep beneath **Bardsey Island,** one of the last Welsh Druid strongholds and a seaswept haven for migratory birds. For details on trips from Criccieth call (01766) 522239. Bus #17 runs from **Pwllheli** (40min., M-Sa 6 per day), and #17B follows a scenic coastal route from **Pwllheli** to Aberdaron and **Port Oer** (2 per day). Rest in elegant rooms with sea views (and TV) at **Bryn Mor** (tel. (01758) 760344), which crowns a hill above the village (£16). Since 1300, pilgrims to Bardsey have fended off hunger between the uneven walls and low ceilings of **Y Gegin Fawr** cafe (tel. 01758) 760359). Tear into the large salads (£4-5), or the tasty Welsh rarebit (£3; open daily July-Aug. 9:30am-7pm; Easter-June and Sept.-Oct. noon-5pm).

Tre'r Ceiri (trair-KAY-ree: "town of the giants"), on the peninsula's north shore, is Britain's oldest fortress, dating back some 4000 years. Take the **Pwllheli-Caernarfon** bus #12 to **Llanaelhaearn,** 7 mi. from Pwllheli (M-Sa 1 per hr., Su 4 per day), then look for the public footpath signpost 1 mi. southwest of town on the B4417. At its upper reaches, keep to the stony track, which is more or less a direct uphill route (elevation 1600ft.). The remains of 150 circular stone huts are clustered within a dou-ble defensive wall. It's windy; wear warm clothing.

■ Snowdonia National Park

The 840 sheep-dotted sq. mi. of Snowdonia National Park, stretching from Machyn-lleth in the south to Bangor and Conwy in the north, embrace narrow-cut valleys, ele-vated moorhead, and the sun-pierced coves of Harlech and the Llŷn peninsula. The varied landscape is dominated by the rough, scree-strewn countenance of its ancient mountains, the highest in England and Wales. Nineteenth-century traveler and writer George Borrow was moved to speculate that it was the most "picturesquely beauti-ful" region in the world.

Since the last ice sheets receded 10,000 years ago, Snowdonia's misty crags have sheltered Celtic hillforts, Roman camps, and, in recent centuries, stone hamlets where the Welsh language remains dominant. Most of the park is in private hands, but tilled hillsides do not deter droves of visitors, who scale Mount Snowdon and eagerly descend into dormant slate mines. Even in peak season, the park's broad expanse provides untrammeled corners for those in search of a quiet hike.

GETTING THERE AND GETTING ABOUT

Narrow-gauge railway lines running through Snowdonia let you enjoy the country-side without enduring a hike. The immensely popular **Snowdon Mountain Railway** (tel. (01286) 870223) offers an easy way to lose yourself in the clouds on the summit of Snowdon. The locomotives, some still steam-operated, set off from Llanberis. The two-hour round-trip stops at the peak for 30 minutes. Weather conditions and passen-ger demand dictate the schedule from July to early September; on a clear day the first train leaves Llanberis at 9am (if there are at least 25 passengers), with subsequent trains about every half-hour until 5pm. Line up early to ensure a ticket (runs mid-Mar. to Oct. return £14.80, children £10.70, standby for trips back down £10.70). The **Ffestiniog Railway** (tel. (01766) 512340) romps through the mountains from Porth-madog to Blaenau Ffestiniog, where the mountains of discarded slate rival those of Snowdonia. You can travel part of its route to Minffordd, Penrhyndeudraeth, Tan-y-bwlch, or Tanygrisiau. At Porthmadog, the narrow-gauge rail meets the Cambrian Coast service from Pwllheli to Aberystwyth; at Blaenau Ffestiniog, it connects with the Conwy Valley Line to Llandudno via Betws-y-Coed (2-10 per day, return £8.20-12.40). The **Llanberis Lake Railway** (tel. (01286) 870549) takes a short, scenic route from Gilfach Ddu station at Llanberis through the woods. (40min., Apr.-Oct. 4-11 per day, £4.10; Nov.-Mar. 4 per day, £3, children £1.50. Wheelchair accessible.)

Snowdon Sherpa buses maneuver between the park's towns and trailheads with somewhat irregular service, but will stop at any safe point in the park on request. A **Red Rover ticket** (£4.40, children £2.20) buys unlimited travel on the Sherpa buses and any other bus in Gwynedd; individual trips cost about £1.50. Most routes are ser-viced by a bus every two hours, but not always on Sundays. Tell the driver if you plan to switch buses; connections sometimes fail due to late or impatient buses. Buses run to the interior from many towns near the edge of the park; consult the *Gwynedd Public Transport Guide* available in tourist offices.

PRACTICAL INFORMATION

Tourist offices and National Park Information Centres stock leaflets on walks, drives, and accommodations, as well as Ordnance Survey maps. Contact the **Snowdonia National Park Information Headquarters,** Penrhyndeudraeth (pen-rin-DAY-dryth), Gwynedd, Wales LL48 6LF (tel. (01766) 770274), for details. The annual *Snowdonia,* stacked to the roof at tourist offices across North Wales, has fistfuls of information on the park, accommodations, and overly enthusiastic writeups of selected attractions.

National Park Information Centres

Aberdyfi: Wharf Gdns. (tel./fax (01654) 767321). Open Apr.-Oct. daily 10am-1pm and 2-6pm.

Betws-y-Coed: The Old Stables (tel. (01690) 710665 or 710426). The busiest and best-stocked. Open daily Apr.-Oct. 10am-6pm; Nov.-Mar. 9:30am-4:30pm. See p. 451.

Blaenau Ffestiniog: Isallt Church St. (tel. (01776) 830360). In the shadow of Ffestiniog Railway's slate heaps and smoke clouds. Open Easter-Sept. daily 10am-6pm.

Dolgellau: Eldon Sq. (tel. (01341) 422888), by the bus stop. Crowded with sedentary tourists in cars, as well as climbers assaulting Cader Idris. Open Easter-Sept. daily 10am-6pm; Oct.-Easter Th-M 10am-1pm and 2-5pm.

Harlech: Gwyddfor House, High St. (tel./fax (01766) 780658). Located in an untrampled region of the park. Open daily Apr.-Oct. 10am-1pm and 2-6pm. See p. 431.

ACCOMMODATIONS AND CAMPING

The eight **YHA Youth Hostels** in the mountain area are some of the best in Wales. They are marked clearly on Gwynedd bus schedules and on the general Wales transport map. Summer school excursions can make getting into the hostels a challenge. Except where noted, **breakfast** (£3) and **dinner** (£4-4.40) are available.

Bryn Gwynant: (tel. (01766) 890251; fax 890479), a mansion ¾mi. from the Watkin path to Snowdon, above Llyn Gwynant and along the road from Penygwryd to Beddgelert (4mi. from Beddgelert). Take Sherpa bus #95 from Caernarfon or Llanberis (M-Sa 5 per day, Su 3 per day). £8.80, under 18 £6. Lockout 10am-1pm. Curfew 11pm. Open Mar.-Oct. daily; Jan.-Feb. Th-Sa; closed Nov.-Dec.

Capel Curig: (tel. (01690) 720225; fax 720270), 5mi. from Betws-y-Coed on the A5. Sherpa buses #19 and 54 from Betws-y-Coed and Llanberis stop nearby. Located at the crossroads of many mountain paths; a favorite with climbers and rowdy school kids. £8.80, under 18 £6; doubles £20. Lockout 10am-5pm. Curfew 11pm. Open mid-Feb. to mid-Dec. daily.

Idwal Cottage: (tel. (01248) 600225; fax 602952), just off the A5 at the foot of Llyn Ogwen in northern Snowdonia. Within hiking distance of Pen-y-Pass, Llanberis, and Capel Curig. Buses come here less frequently than the other hostels—take Sherpa bus #65/66 from Bangor changing at Bethesda (M-Sa 7 per day) or #7 on Su (2 per day). £7.20, under 18 £5. Self-catering only. Lockout 10am-5pm. Curfew 11pm. Open Apr.-Aug. daily; Mar. and Sept. F-M.

Kings (Dolgellau): (tel. (01341) 422392; fax 422477), Penmaenpool, 4mi. from Dolgellau. Take Arriva bus #28 from Dolgellau (M-Sa 6 per day). Endure the walk uphill from the large house in the Vale of Ffestiniog. £7.20, under 18 £5. Lockout 10am-5pm. Curfew 11pm. Open Apr.-Aug. daily; mid-Feb. to Mar. and Sept. to mid-Nov. W-Su.

Llanberis: (tel. (01286) 870280; fax 870936). ½mi. from town up Capel Coch Rd. Plenty of sheep and cows keep hostelers company as they take in the views of Llyn Peris and Llyn Padarn below and Mt. Snowdon above. £8, under 18 £5.40. Open Apr.-Aug. daily; Sept.-Oct. and Jan.-Mar. Tu-Sa; closed Nov.-Dec.

Lledr Valley: (tel. (01690) 750202; fax 750410), on a bluff 5mi. west of Betws-y-Coed, ¾mi. past Pont-y-Pant train station, 2mi. from the majestic square tower of Dolwyddelan Castle. No washers. £8, under 18 £5.40. Lockout 10am-5pm. Curfew 11pm. Open mid-Apr. to Aug. daily; Sept.-Oct. M-F; mid-Feb. to Mar. F-Sa.

Pen-y-Pass: (tel. (01286) 870428; fax 872434), 6mi. from Llanberis and 4mi. from Nant Peris. Commands the most unusual and splendid position of any hostel in Wales: 1170ft. above sea level at the head of Llanberis Pass between the Snowdon and Glyders peaks. Open the door to the Pyg track, or the Llyn Llydaw miner's track to the Snowdon summit. Rent hiking boots, waterproofs, and ice axes. Take Sherpa bus #19 (3 per day) from Llanberis or Llandudno, or bus #95 from Caernarfon (M-Sa 4 per day, Su 3 per day). £8.80, under 18 £6. Lockout 10am-1pm. Open Jan.-Oct. daily.

Snowdon Ranger: Llyn Cwellyn (tel. (01286) 650391; fax 650093). The base for the grandest Snowdon ascent, the **Ranger Path.** Take bus #95. No washers. £8.80, under 18 £6. Lockout 10am-5pm. Curfew 11pm. Open Apr.-Aug. daily; Sept.-Oct. W-Su; mid-Feb. to Mar. and Nov.-Dec. F-Su.

WALES

The land in Snowdonia is privately owned—stick to public pathways and **campsites** or ask the owner's consent. In the high mountains, camping is permitted as long as you leave no mess, but the Park Service discourages it because of recent and disastrous erosion. In the valleys, owner's consent is required to camp. Public camping sites dot the roads in peak seasons; check listings below for sites in specific towns.

HIKING

Weather on the exposed mountains shifts quickly, unpredictably, and wrathfully. No matter how beautiful the weather is below, *it will be cold and wet in the high mountains*. Dress as if preparing for armed confrontation with the Abominable Snowman: bring a waterproof jacket and pants, gloves, a hat, and wool sweater. You can peel off the layers as you descend. Look at **Wilderness and Safety Concerns,** p. 47, and pick up the Ordnance Survey Maps Landranger 115: *Snowdon and Surrounding Area* (£5), and Outdoor Leisure 17: *Snowdonia, Snowdon, and Conwy Valley Areas* (£6), as well as individual path guides (40p each). Maps are available at Park Centres and most bookstores. Call **Mountaincall Snowdonia** (tel. (01839) 505330) for the local forecast, ground conditions, and a three- to five-day forecast (36-48p per min.). Weather forecasts are tacked outside the National Park Information Centres. Park rangers lead day walks; ask at the Park Information Centres.

OTHER OUTDOOR PURSUITS

Snowdonia National Park Study Centre, Plas Tan-y-Bwlch, Maentwrog, Blaenau Ffestiniog, Gwynedd LL41 3YU (tel. (01766) 590324), offers courses on naturalist favorites such as wildlife painting and geology. **YHA Pen-y-Pass,** Nant Gwynant, Caernarfon, Gwynedd LL55 4NY (tel. (01286) 870428; fax 872434) can put groups in touch with mountaineering, climbing, canoeing, and sailing guides (see **Accommodations and Camping,** p. 437).

Guided horse and pony rides canter from the **Snowdonia Riding Stables** (tel. (01286) 650342), 3 mi. from Caernarfon just off the A4085 near Waunfawr (£10 per hr., £40 per day). Take Sherpa bus #95 and ask to be let off at the turn-off road (M-Sa 4 per day, Su 3 per day). Guided cycle tours leave from Caernarfon for multinight forays in the park, thanks to **Beics Eryri Cycle Tours** (tel. (01286) 676637; from £40 per night including bike and accommodations). Brave lunatics can paraglide off the peaks of Snowdonia with the help of **Enigma: The Snowdonia School of Paragliding** (tel. (01248) 602103; call for prices) in Llanberis. Myriad aquatic, equestrian, and artistic adventures are detailed in the *The Snowdon Peninsula: North Wales Activities* brochure, available in tourist offices and information centers.

■ Mount Snowdon and Vicinity

By far the most popular destination in the park, **Mount Snowdon** (*Yr Wyddfa,* "the burial place") is the highest peak in England and Wales, measuring in at 3560 ft. Over half a million hikers and their dogs ramble around the mountain each year. Because multiple trails make the mountain accessible to enthusiasts of all strengths, Mt. Snowdon has become eroded and its ecosystem disrupted. Park officers request that all hikers stick to the well-marked trails to avoid further damage. Also, as Snowdonia is sheep country, *dogs must be kept on a leash at all times.* Six principal paths of varying degrees of difficulty wend their way up Snowdon; tourist offices and information centers stock guides on these ascents (40p each).

Though Mt. Snowdon is the main attraction in the northern part of the park, experienced climbers cart pick-axes and ropes to the **Ogwen Valley,** where climbs to **Devil's Kitchen** *(Twll Du),* the **Glyders** (*Glyder Fawr* and *Glyder Fach*) and **Tryfan** all begin from **Llyn Ogwen.** Those attempting the climbs should pick up both the appropriate Ordnance Survey maps and the card-sized *Walk About Guides* (35p), which give directions, map references, and severity ratings for the climbs.

■ Llanberis

One of the few small Welsh villages to be lively even on Sundays, Llanberis owes its bustle to the popularity of the mountain which looms over it. Most of the town's attractions lie near the fork where the A4086 meets High St.

PRACTICAL INFORMATION Situated on the western edge of the park, Llanberis is a short ride from Caernarfon on the A4086. Catch **KMP** (tel. 870880) bus #88 from **Caernarfon** (25min., M-Sa 2 per hr., Su 1 per hr., return £1.20), or the hourly **Williams Deinioien** (tel. 870484) bus #77 from **Bangor** (40min., M-Sa 8 per day). **Sherpa** buses #19 and 54, operated by Arriva, wind past Capel Curig and Pen-y-Pas on their way from **Betws-y-Coed** (1½hr., 4 per day), while Sherpa bus #95, operated by KMP, stops at the Bryn Gwynant and Pen-y-Pas **YHAs** on its way from **Beddgelert** (M-Sa 5 per day, Su 4 per day). The **tourist office,** 41b High St. (tel. 870765), doles out tips on hikes and books accommodations (open Apr.-Oct. daily 10am-6pm; Nov.-Mar. W and F-Su 10:30am-4:30pm). You can't have it all—either you get the ATM-less **Midland** bank, 29 High St. (open M-F 9:30am-3pm), or the bank-less **ATM** of **Barclay's,** at the entrance to the Electric Mountain Railway on the A4086, near its fork with High St. Pick up gear at **Joe Brown's Store,** Menai Hall, High St. (tel. 870327), owned by one of the world's greatest pioneer climbers. (Open July-Aug. daily 9am-6pm; Sept.-June M-F 9am-5:30pm, Sa 9am-6pm, Su 9am-5pm; closed daily 1-2pm for lunch). Address the **post office,** 36 High St. (open M-Sa 9am-1pm and 2-5:30pm), with **postal code** LL55 4EU. Llanberis's **telephone code** is 01286.

ACCOMMODATIONS AND FOOD Those looking for a group experience have two choices in Llanberis. Besides the **YHA Llanberis,** half a mile up Capel Goch Rd. (see **Accommodations and Camping,** p. 437), the **Heights Hotel,** 74 High St. (tel. 871179; fax 872507), has 24 bunk beds packed into big rooms (£9, with breakfast £12.50). Half the town crowds into the **bar** on weekends. (Bar open May-Sept. daily breakfast-10pm; Oct.-Apr. Su-Th 6-10pm, F-Sa breakfast-10pm.) The town also has flocks of **B&Bs** starting at £14. A 19th-century temperance house, **Snowdon Cottage,** Pentre Castell (tel. 872015), sits behind a mossy rock-filled hillside and the shadow of Dolbadarn Castle. Follow High St. and its extension, A4086, toward the park and past the Victoria Hotel for 10 minutes. Tired climbers can seek relief from the proprietors: one is a sports therapist, the other an aromatherapist (£15). **Gellhirbart,** York Terr. (tel. 870967), offers modern luxury, satellite TV, and a lovely sun-lit lounge. Turn right past the Snowdon Mountain Railway terminus onto Victoria Terr. and left at York Terr.; the house is at the end of the road (£15). Head 2 mi. north to find camping at the **Snowdon View Caravan Park** (tel. 870349), which has excellent facilities, including a heated swimming pool (£5-6 per tent).

Llanberis's restaurants have adapted their fare to the healthy demands (and appetites) of hikers. Though cooked breakfasts are high in demand at **Pete's Eats,** 40 High St. (tel. 870358), opposite the tourist office, you can also go for a vegetarian mixed grill (£4.60) or awe-inspiring chili. (Open Easter-Oct. M-F 9am-8pm, Sa-Su 8am-8pm; Nov.-Easter M-F 9am-6:30pm, Sa-Su 8am-8pm.) At **Poptyr Bakery,** on High St. near Pete's, try one of the tempting pastries (delectable shortbread 45p; open M-F 9am-5pm, Sa 9am-noon). **Spar,** on the corner of High St. and Capel Goch Rd., is generally overrun by hungry hikers who leave the shelves, particularly those stocking fruit, bare (open M-Sa 7am-11pm, Su 7am-10:30pm).

SIGHTS The **Snowdon Mountain Railway** (tel. 870223) whisks you up Mt. Snowdon from its terminus on the A4086. *(Return £14.50.)* The paths of **Parc Padarn** weave past

W A L E S

two lakes, forested hills, waterfalls, and a 13th-century castle, all set against a moun-

---

Never Cry Dog

Not only did Llewelyn the Great imprison his brother (see Dolbadarn Castle), but he also did his dog a great wrong. According to legend, Llewelyn left his infant son in the custody of his trusty dog, Gelert, while he went out hunting. A hungry wolf, sensing tasty baby nearby, entered Llewelyn's tent, only to be slaughtered by the canine babysitter. On returning home, however, Llewelyn saw the blood, and immediately speared Gelert, only to hear his baby's healthy cry. He saw the mangled wolf and the untouched child and immediately realized his mistake; Gelert—faithful to the end—licked his master's hand as he died.

---

tain disturbingly carved away for its slate. The **Llanberis Lake Railway** (tel. 870549) begins its 2 mi. slide into the woods at the park entrance. Also near the entrance is the **Welsh Slate Museum,** which houses live demonstrations and exhibits on the importance of slate to Welsh history. Within the park lies **Llŷn Padarn,** a needle-shaped lake whose banks bear a plaque honoring Thomas Jefferson, whose ancestors hail from the area. Follow the road into the park until it crosses the footbridge and brings you to the ruins of nearby **Dolbadarn Castle,** where Prince Llewelyn imprisoned his brother for 23 years. Only a single tower of the castle remains. To reach **Ceunant Mawr,** one of Wales's most impressive waterfalls, take the footpath on Victoria Terr. by the Victoria Hotel, then the first right and first left (about 1mi.). For more information on the railways, see **Getting There and Getting About,** p. 436.

■ Cader Idris

The origin of the mountain name **Cader Idris** ("Chair of Idris") remains a mystery. One story has it that in AD 630, a national hero named Idris was killed in battle here by a host of marauding Saxons, while another maintains that Idris was a giant who kept house here. Mystic legends abound in this region: the Cwn Annwn, "Hounds of the Underworld," are said to fly around the peaks of the Idris range. The town of Dolgellau (see below) forms the best base for exploring the mountain, although the village of Corris near Machynlleth is another good base. This portion of Snowdonia National Park offers scenic walks less crowded than those of Mt. Snowdon to the north. A number of paths catering to all levels of experience cover Cader Idris (all cross privately owned farm and grazing land). The pony track from **Llanfihangel y Pennant** is the easiest, but also the longest, way to the summit (over 5mi.). A rather complicated route, the path climbs steadily after a relatively level initial one-third. The **pony track** from **Tŷ Nant** begins at Tŷ Nant farm, 3 mi. from Dolgellau. While the trail is eroded in spots, it is also not particularly strenuous, and offers the most striking views of the surrounding countryside. The **Minffordd Path** (about 3mi.) is the shortest but steepest ascent, not to be taken lightly. On its way to the summit, the path traverses an 8000-year-old oak wood and rises above the lake of **Llyn Cau,** the "Bearded Lake." An 18th-century story holds that a young man swimming in the lake was ingested by a grotesque monster and was never seen again. Another legend claims that anyone who sleeps by the lake for one night will awaken either a poet or a madman. (*Let's Go* does not recommend sleeping by haunted lakes.) Booklets charting these walks are available at the National Park Information Centre in Dolgellau (40p). For longer treks, the Ordinance Survey Outdoor Leisure 23 or Landranger 124 maps are essential.

The 6000 hectares of the **Coed-Y-Brenin Forest Park** crawl with world-renowned biking trails, in addition to miles of trails reserved exclusively for hikers. Covering the peaks and valleys around the Mawddach and Eden Rivers, the forest is best entered 7 mi. north of Dolgellau off the A470, near the **visitor center** (tel. (01341) 440666; open Apr.-Oct. daily 10am-5pm; Nov.-Mar. Sa-Su 10am-4pm).

■ Dolgellau

Deep in the conifers of the Idris mountain range, the imposing, dark stone buildings of **Dolgellau** (dol-GETH-lee) resemble Margaret Thatcher: grim and roughly cut, they glare with calloused severity at the wildness around them. **Buses** stop in Eldon Sq. near the tourist office. **Crosville** (tel. (01970) 617951) bus #94 shuttles between **Barmouth** to the west and **Llangollen** to the east, stopping en route in Dolgellau (M-Sa 6 per day, Su 2 per day). Crosville bus #2 follows a winding, scenic route through the mountains to Dolgellau from **Machynlleth** on its way to **Porthmadog** (2½hr., M-Sa 6 per day; in summer also Su 3 per day). A lone **TrawsCambria** bus (tel. (01792) 580580) also stops in daily on its way to Cardiff (6½hr.).

The **tourist office** (tel. 422888; fax 422576), at Eldon Sq. in Ty Meirion by the bus stop, doubles as a **Snowdonia National Park Information Centre** (open Easter-Oct. daily 10am-6pm; Nov.-Easter Th-M 10am-1pm and 2-5pm). Money mavens raid the **ATM** at Midland Bank, Eldon Sq. (open M-F 9am-5pm). Equip yourself with warm and waterproof clothing from **Cader Idris Outdoor Gear** (tel. 422195), at Eldon Sq., which also stocks Ordnance Survey maps and compasses (open M-Sa daily 9am-5:30pm). Mail that postcard from the **post office** which shares space with the **Spar** at Plas yn Dre St. (open M-F 9am-5:30pm, Sa 9am-12:30pm). Dolgellau's **postal code** is LL40 1AD; the **telephone code** is 01341.

Four miles away at Kings is a **YHA Youth Hostel** (tel. 422392; see **Accommodations and Camping,** p. 437). Lodging is scarce and expensive in Dolgellau; expect to pay at least £15. Two **B&Bs** with spectacular views of the Idris range cling to the heights just north of town. **Arosfyr,** Pen-y-Cefn St. (tel. 422355), an old farmhouse, harbors plush furniture and gleaming brass candlesticks over its fireplace. From the bus stop, walk with the Midland Bank on your right, down over the bridge, turn left, then turn right at the school, and follow the steep road until a sign directs you past some tractors (singles £16; doubles £27-28). **Dwy Olwyn,** Coed-y-Fronallt (tel. 422822), also has candlesticks, as well as a conservatory. We're still waiting for Colonel Mustard to show up. Cross the Bont Fawr bridge, turn right, then left after you pass the Kwik Save; it's five minutes uphill (singles £20; doubles £30-32). **Camping** is available at the hostel and at the deluxe **Tanyfron Caravan and Camping Park** (tel./fax 422638), a 10-minute walk south on Arron Rd. onto the A470 (£5 per tent, £1 per person, £1 per car; open year-round).

Groceries can be found at **Spar,** Plas yn Dre St. (open daily 8am-10pm). Duck under the low portal at the **Y Sospan,** Queen Sq. (tel. 423174), behind the tourist office, for sandwiches (£2) or savory quiche with a salad. A sign on the side proclaims the escape of a prisoner from the local jail in 1808—one hopes he's not still lurking (open in summer M-Sa 9am-5pm; in winter M-Th 9am-4pm, F-Sa 9am-4pm and 6-9pm). A heavenly aroma greets those who descend into the **Popty'r Dref** bakery (tel. 422507), on Smithfield St., just off Eldon Sq., where crowded shelves host homemade jams, large filled rolls (85p-£2), and a delectable butter cream sponge (£1.70; open M-Sa 8am-5pm).

In town the **Quaker Interpretive Centre,** on the 2nd floor of the tourist office, details the history of this hotbed of anticonformity and the circumstances which fueled Quaker emigration to the United States. *(Open same times as tourist office. Free.)* Huddled in the shadow of **Cader Idris** (see above), Dolgellau's main function for travellers is the easy access it offers to the mountain and local walks. The famous 3 mi. **Precipice Walk** rewards with views of the Mawddach Estuary and Cader Idris, while the 2½ mi. **Torrent Walk** circles past waterfalls and through mossy woodlands. Pamphlets for area treks are available at the tourist office (30p).

■ Caernarfon

The world-famous castle and walled city of Caernarfon (car-NAR-von) seem to float on the waters of the Menai Strait and Seiont River. Situated across the estuary from the Isle of Anglesey, the town once served as the center of English government in northern Wales. Occupied since pre-Roman times, Caernarfon has been the center of struggle for political control; during a tax revolt in 1294 the Welsh managed to break in, sack the town, and massacre the English settlers. Vestiges of English domination remain (Prince Charles was invested as Prince of Wales at the castle in 1969), but Caernarfon is thoroughly Welsh in character—visitors can hear the town's own dialect of Welsh on the streets and in the pubs. But for all the romance associated with castles and town walls, Caernarfon owes its current size to a mundane trade in slate export.

GETTING THERE

Caernarfon is the well-greased pivot for **buses** from mid-Wales and the **Llŷn Peninsula,** swinging northeast to Bangor and Anglesey. **Arriva** (tel. (01248) 351879) buses #5 and 5B flit between Caernarfon and **Bangor** every 20 minutes and continue on to **Conwy** every 30 minutes (Su 1 per hr., Caernarfon-Bangor £2.70, return £3.80; Caernarfon-Conwy £1.40, £1.75). **Express Motors** (tel. 674570) bus #1 runs to **Porthmadog** (45min., M-Sa 1 per hr., £2.20, return £2.50). On Sundays, both bus #1 and Arriva's #2 run the same route (5 per day). **Clynnog & Trefor** (tel. 660208) and **Berwyn** (tel. 660315) run bus #12 down narrow B-roads to **Pwllheli** (45min., M-Sa 1 per hr., Su 3 per day, £1.80). **KMP** (tel. 870880) bus #88 zooms to **Llanberis** (25min., 2 per hr., £1.20), while its Sherpa bus #95 takes a passing route through **Beddgelert** and by many **YHA** hostels to **Llanberis** (1½hr., M-Sa 5 per day, Su 3 per day). A lone **TrawsCambria** bus #701 strikes off daily for **Cardiff** (7½hr.). Caernarfon has no train station, but **trains** leave nearby **Bangor** for **Holyhead, Chester,** and beyond. A Gwynedd **Red Rover** ticket earns unlimited bus travel in the county (£4.40, children £2.20); the *Gwynedd Public Transport Guide* offers timetables and handy maps of the major towns of Gwynedd.

ORIENTATION

The heart of Caernarfon is the area within the town walls, and just outside. Buses arrive on **Penllyn,** which runs perpendicular to **Bridge St.** To the right, Bridge St. becomes **Bangor St.,** while a left onto Bridge St. reveals the wide expanse of Castle Sq. A right from the square's entrance leads to **Castle Ditch,** which holds the castle entrance and the tourist office. **Eastgate St.** is perpendicular to the point where Bridge St. meets Bangor St. and continues on to **High St.**

PRACTICAL INFORMATION

Tourist Office: Castle St., Oriel Pendeitsh (tel. 672232), opposite the castle gate. Pick up the helpfully illustrated, grid street map within the free *Visitor's Guide to Caernarfon.* Huge lists of accommodations available; the staff can also book you a bed. Open Apr.-Oct. daily 10am-6pm; Nov.-Mar. Th-Tu 9:30am-4:30pm.

Financial Services: Barclays, 5-7 Bangor St., loves its **ATM.** Open M-Tu and Th-F 9am-4:30pm, W 10am-4:30pm.

Camping Supplies: 14th Peak, 9 Palace St. (tel. 675124). Excellent discounts. Open M-W and F-Sa 9am-5:30pm, Th 9am-5pm, Su 1-4pm.

Market: Castle Sq. Open all day Sa.

Laundrette: Pete's Laundrette, Skinner St. (tel. 678395), off Bridge St. Open daily 9am-6pm; last wash 5:30pm. Full service wash available.

Emergency: Dial 999; no coins required.

Police: Maes Incla Ln. (tel. 673333, ext. 5242).

Hotline: Samaritans (crisis; tel. (01248) 354646). Open 24hr.

Hospital: Bangor General Hospital, Ysbyty Gwynedd (tel, (01248) 384384). Take Crosville bus #5 or 5B to Bangor.

Post Office: Castle Sq. (tel. 672116). Open M-F 9am-5:30pm, Sa 9am-12:30pm. **Postal Code:** LL55 2ND.

Internet Access: Dimensiwn 4, 4 Bangor St. (http://www.dimensiwn4.co.uk). £2 per 30min., £4 per hr. Open M-Sa 10am-6pm.

Telephone Code: 01286

ACCOMMODATIONS

The privately run **Totter's Hostel,** 2 High St. (tel. 672963), at the end of High St. toward the strait, should be the first stop for budget travelers. Tucked inside the walls at the Plas-Porth-Yr-Aur (Grand House of the Golden Gate), the rooms boast polished wood bunks for £30. A massive stone hearth and breakfast essentials surround a 600-year-old arch in the cellar (£9.50; no curfew or lockout). Budget-busting **B&Bs** line Church St. inside the old town wall; instead, walk 5 minutes from the castle to St. David's Rd., off the Bangor St. roundabout. The welcoming proprietress of **Bryn Hyfryd,** St. David's Rd. (tel 673840), cares for guests in style, offering spacious, well-furnished rooms, TVs, and a boundless breakfast. Dote over the friendly pair of tiny dogs and a duo of Persian cats (July to mid-Sept. £16; mid-Sept. to June £14-15). Or try **Marianfa,** St. David's Rd. (tel. 675589), with its collection of statues. Spacious rooms contain TVs and chairs for lounging (singles £17; doubles £32, with bath £40). **Camp** half a mile from town at **Cadnant Valley,** Llanberis Rd. (tel. 673196); expect caravans in the summer (£4-8 per person).

FOOD AND PUBS

Cafes and pubs crowd the area within the town walls. Vast culinary options fan out at **Safeway,** the Promenade (open M-F 8am-10pm, Sa 8am-8pm, Su 8am-4pm). **Crempogau** (tel. 672552), at the corner of Palace and High St., cooks up sweet and savory dinner pancakes: the chicken supreme is £2.20, the Bavarian apple goes for £1.60 (open daily Apr.-Oct. 10:30am-6pm). **Stones Bistro,** 4 Hole-in-the-Wall St. (tel. 671152), near Eastgate, is candlelit and crowded. Welsh lamb costs £10 and is worth it—you get a vast limb, sweet and tender; vegetarian entrees go for £8 (open Tu-Sa 6-11pm). **Bechdan Bach,** on Castle Sq., offers tasty toasties (£1.50-2.50; open M-Sa 9am-5pm). The stout wooden doors of the **Anglesey Arms** open onto the Promenade; watch the sunset with pint in hand (open M-Sa 11am-11pm, Su noon-10:30pm).

SIGHTS

In a nod to Caernarfon's Roman past (and, no doubt, to his own ego), Edward I built **Caernarfon Castle** (tel. 677617), featuring eagle-crowned turrets and polygonal towers in imitation of the capital at Constantinople. Starting in 1283, Edward spent the equivalent of £25 million—far more than on any of his other Welsh castles—to construct what one Welshman called "this magnificent badge of our subjection." Despite its swagger, the fortress was left unfinished (note the masonry jutting out at points in the castle); Eddie ran out of money. In the summer, choirs, musicians, and *Mabinogi* actors often perform here. The "tradition" of the investiture of the Prince of Wales is actually a 20th-century creation, which has led to the castle's restoration and growing prominence in the town. Entertaining and cynical tours run about once an hour for £1. *(Open Apr.-Oct. daily 9:30am-6:30pm; Nov.-Mar. M-Sa 9:30am-4pm, Su 11am-4pm. £4, students, seniors, and children £3, families £11.)* The castle also contains the regimental museum of the **Royal Welsh Fusiliers.**

Most of Caernarfon's 13th-century **town wall** survives, and a short stretch between Church St. and Northgate St. is open for climbing during the same hours as the castle. Those curious to see what today's youth hostels will look like in 2000 years should inspect the ruined barrack blocks at the **Segoritium Roman Fort** (tel. 675625). Cross under the A487 at the end of Pool St., and walk five minutes up the A4085 toward Beddgelert. *(Open May-Sept. M-Sa 9:30am-6pm, Su 2-6pm; Apr. and Oct. M-Sa 9:30am-4pm, Su 2-4pm. £1.25, students, seniors, and children 75p.)*

Atop **Twt Hill,** alongside the Bangor St. roundabout, lie the scattered remains of a Celtic settlement; the jutting peak also offers sweeping vistas of the town and castle. Across the Aber bridge near the castle, **Parc Coed Helen** is a peaceful, green spot to picnic. Check at Slate Quay opposite the Castle Gift Shop for 40-minute **cruises** (tel. 672902, evening tel. 672772) to the southwest entrance of the Menai Strait and back. *(£3.50, seniors £3, under 16 £2.)*

WALES

■ Bangor

After spending time in Snowdonia or the Llŷn, travelers may find Bangor's more urban nature both reviving and disappointing. Crowded into a valley by the Menai Strait, Bangor draws travelers by virtue of its status as a rail and bus hub. The city also forms a convenient (and cheap) base for exploring the nearby Isle of Anglesey (see p. 446). Perched gracefully over the city, the stately Top College of the University of North Wales reminds visitors of Bangor's role as a university town, and of the students who fill the pubs on High St.

GETTING THERE

Bangor is the transportation depot for the Isle of Anglesey to the north, the Llŷn Peninsula to the southwest, and Snowdonia to the southeast. **Arriva Cymru** (tel. 351879) buses #4 and 44 travel north to **Holyhead via Llangefni** and **Llanfair P.G.** (1¼hr., M-Sa 2 per hr., Su 6 per day), while buses #53, 57, and 58 head to **Beaumaris** and its castle (30min., M-Sa 2 per hr., Su 6 per day). Arriva buses #5 and 5B leave **Caernarfon** for Bangor on their way east to **Conwy** (30min. to Bangor, 1½hr. total, M-Sa 2 per hr., Su 1 per hr.). Transfer at **Caernarfon** for the **Llŷn Peninsula,** where buses shuttle to **Pwllheli** and **Porthmadog** (see **Getting There,** p. 442). Mt. Snowdon and the rest of the park surround Llanberis; from Bangor, take Arriva bus #77 (50min., M-Sa 1 per hr., Su 4 per day) and connect to various **Sherpa** buses. A solitary **TrawsCambria** bus #701, run by Arriva, follows the coast all the way to **Cardiff** (7¾hr.).

ORIENTATION AND PRACTICAL INFORMATION

A centuries-old street plan and roads that often do not advertise their names at all might leave you scratching your head. Bangor sprawls over its hills, but most visitors will stay in the lower portion near High St. Bangor's two main streets—**Deiniol Rd.** and **High St.**—run parallel to each other and sandwich the city. **Garth Rd.** starts from the town clock on High St., and winds past the bus station, where it meets and takes over from Deiniol Rd. **Holyhead Rd.** begins its ascent at the rail station, also the starting point for Deiniol Rd. The University College of North Wales sits on both sides of **College St.,** a right off Holyhead Rd. as it reaches the summit. The **train station** (tel. (01492) 585151) is on Holyhead Rd., at the end of Deiniol Rd. (ticket office open daily in summer 5:30am-6:30pm; in winter 11:30am-6:30pm). The **bus station** is on Garth Rd., down the hill from the town clock. The **National Express** agent is **Brian Kellett Travel,** 364 High St. (tel. 351056; open M-F 9am-5pm, Sa 9am-4pm). The **tourist office** (tel. 352786) is in the Town Hall on Deiniol Rd., opposite Theatre Gwynedd. The staff provides a free booklet with an essential town map and books beds as well. They also keep an index of local bus fares (open Easter-Sept. daily 10am-1pm and 2-6pm; Oct.-Easter F-Sa 10am-1pm and 2-6pm). **Midland,** 274 High St., proffers its **ATM** (open M-F 9am-5pm, Sa 9:30am-12:30pm). Find **camping equipment** at **The Great Arete,** 2 College Rd. (tel. 352710), just off Holyhead Rd. (open M-Sa 9am-5:30pm). Bangor's **post office** (tel. 373329) sits at 60 Deiniol Rd. with a bureau de change (open M-F 9am-5:30pm, Sa 9am-12:30pm). **Bangor Computer and Internet Centre,** 17-19 High St. (tel. 352459), satisfies computer cravings. The **postal code** is LL57 1AA; the **telephone code** is 01248.

ACCOMMODATIONS AND FOOD

Finding a room in Bangor during the University College of North Wales's graduation (the second week of July) is a nightmarish prospect unless you book many months ahead. The most agreeable B&Bs occupy the Victorian townhouses on Garth Rd. and its extensions. **YHA Bangor,** Tan-y-Bryn (tel. 353516), lies half a mile from town center. Follow High St. to the water and turn right at the end, turning right again at the hard-to-spot Youth Hostel sign. The rich wood paneling of the entrance hall and vaulted wide-beam ceilings betray its former role as country estate, though the packed bunks are probably not original furnishings. Vivien Leigh and Sir Laurence

Olivier always chose Room 6. (£8.80, under 18 £5.70. Meals, laundry facilities, and map rentals available. Reception open 7am-11pm. Open Jan.-Nov.) TV and tea-making facilities are the creature comforts provided by **Mrs. Jones** (tel. 355242), who resides in Bro Dawel near the end of Garth Rd. (£14). **Mrs. S. Roberts,** 32 Glynne Rd.

A Woman's Christmas in Wales

In certain areas of Wales, it was the women, and not the halls, that were once decked with holly. A bizarre tradition made female domestics the targets of "holly-beating" on St. Stephen's Day, December 26. Men and boys assembled large branches of prickly holly and whacked the arms of women. Two traditional but troubling explanations for the origin of the cruel and unusual custom include the bleeding of martyr St. Stephen and the practice of bleeding animals on St. Stephen's Day. Holly-beating continued in various Welsh towns through the 19th century, but was eventually outlawed as sick and wrong. Merry Christmas!

(tel. 352113), between Garth Rd. and High St., has TVs and 13 choices for breakfast, including omelette options (£13). **Dinas Farm,** on the banks of the River Ogwan, offers camping and showers. Follow the A5 past Penrhyn Castle and then turn left off the A5122 leading out of Bangor.

High St. holds a wide array of fruit shops and cafes, as well as a **Kwik Save** supermarket (open M-W and Sa 8:30am-5:30pm, Th-F 8:30am-7pm, Su 10am-4pm). The green couch at **Herbs,** 307-309 High St. (tel. 351249), creates a relaxed setting for consuming veggie feasts (around £7, lunch £2.25-4; open M-Sa 9am-9pm). The sidewalk tables of the **Penguin Café,** 260 High St. (tel. 362036), are an ideal spot to people-watch (sandwiches £1.50-2; open M-Sa 8am-5:30pm).

SIGHTS AND ENTERTAINMENT

The short but venerable **Bangor Cathedral** (tel. 353983), on Fford Gwynedd just off High St., with its humble, steepleless stature, has been the ecclesiastical center of this corner of Wales for 1400 years; its Bible Garden provides a haven for weary shoppers. *(Cathedral open daily about 8am-6pm.)* Nearby, the **Museum of Welsh Antiquities and Art Gallery** (tel. 353368), on Ffordd Gwynedd, houses an authentic man-trap, used as an anti-poaching device. *(Open Tu-F 12:30-4:30pm, Sa 10:30am-4:30pm. Free.)* Watch tides ebb and flow at the onion-domed Victorian **pier** at the end of Garth St. *(Open daily until sunset. Admission 20p; fishing rod rental £1.)*

The grey bleakness of **Penrhyn Castle** (tel. 353084), George Hay Dawkins-Pennant's 19th-century neo-Norman grotesquerie, squats over two acres just outside of Bangor. Its chiseled square towers glare across a 40,000 acre estate, testament to the staggering wealth accumulated by the owners of Gwynedd's slate mines. Picnickers will find the grounds a brilliant location. The castle's luxury contrasts starkly with the poverty and toil known to the residents of nearby mining towns, a point not overly stressed on the audio tour. Inside, Penrhyn's opulence makes Versailles seem tastefully understated; the intricately carved stone staircase took 10 years to complete, and even the servants' version manages to seem pretentious. A fine collection of Old Masters and some historical artifacts are also housed inside. The cafe of the castle goes far above quality one associates with tourist attractions, conjuring up a delectable array of Welsh dishes (£4-5), including a Cottage Pie with Leeky Roof, and full Welsh teas (tea, scones, and Welsh cheese; £3). Walk up High St. toward the pier, then turn right onto the A5122 and go north for 1 mi., or catch bus # 5/5B from the town center; the castle is an additional mile from the gate. *(Open July-Aug. W-M 11am-5pm; Apr.-June and Sept.-Oct. W-M noon-5pm. Castle and grounds £4.50, children £2.25.)*

The modern **Theatr Gwynedd** (tel. 351708), Deiniol Rd. at the base of the hill, houses a thriving troupe that performs in both Welsh and English and hosts visiting companies. *(Box office open M-Sa 9:30am-5pm; on performance days M-Sa 9:30am-8:30pm, Su 6-8:30pm. Films £3.60, students and seniors £3, children £1.80; plays £5-15. Tickets also available at most tourist offices on the north coast.)* Bangor's nightlife scene isn't particularly notable, especially since closing times never go beyond 1am. For the determined, **Barrels** (tel. 372040) rolls with it on High St., offering a packed bar and dance floor. *(Open W 7-11pm, Th-Sa 7pm-12:30am (last admission 10:30pm), Su 7-10:30pm.)*

■ Isle of Anglesey (Ynys Môn)

The Isle of Anglesey, connected by the massive Menai and Brittania Bridges, feels more like a parallel landscape than an island. Once a center of Celtic druidic culture, the vast, flat, arable land of Anglesey has provided both spiritual and physical sustenance for the entire region: the isle's old name is *Mona mam Cymru* (Mona the mother of Wales). While Beaumaris Castle and Ireland-bound ferries sailing into the mists off Holyhead are what attract most visitors, the well-preserved prehistoric sites and molded cliff coastline should not be neglected.

GETTING THERE AND GETTING ABOUT

Arriva Cymru (tel. (01248) 351879) spins a web around most of the island, with a handful of smaller operators filling in the gaps. Buses #4 and 44 travel north from **Bangor** to **Holyhead via Llanfair P.G.** and **Llangefni** (1¼hr., M-Sa 2 per hr., Su 6 per day, £4), while #53, 57, and 58 hug the southeast coast in a scenic run from **Bangor** to **Beaumaris** (30min., M-Sa 2 per hr., Su 6 per day, return £2.30). Bus #62 sputters from **Bangor** to **Amlwch,** on the northern coast (50min., M-Sa 1 per hr., Su 3 per day), while #42 curves along the southwest coast up to **Abe-ffraw,** before cutting north to Llangefri (1hr., M-Sa 8 per day, Su 2 per day). From Amlwch, **Lewis y Llan** (tel. (01407) 832181) bus #61 cruises into **Holyhead** (50min., M-Sa 8 per day). **Gwynfors** (tel. (01248) 722694) #32 shuttles north from **Llangefni** to **Amlwch** (40min., M-Sa 5 per day). Pick up the *Isle of Anglesey Public Transport Guide* in tourist offices; the Gwynedd **Red Rover** ticket (£4.40, children £2.20) covers a day's bus travel in Gwynedd, including Bangor. **BritRail** (tel. (0345) 484950) runs from **Bangor** to **Holyhead** (30min., express 1-3 per hr., £5.20); some of these trains stop at **Llanfair P.G.**

SOMEWHAT PRACTICAL INFORMATION

Llanfairpwllgwyngyllgogerychwyrndrobwllllantysiliogogogoch (hlan-vire-poohl-gwin-gihl—ah, screw it), the longest-named village in the world, is linked to Bangor by the Brittania Bridge. Devised by a 19th century humorist to attract attention, the name translates roughly as "Saint Mary's Church in the hollow of white hazel near the rapid whirlpool and the Church of Saint Tysillio near the red cave" (or, alternatively, "we-couldn't-find-a-compelling-reason-to-get-you-to-come-here-so-we-just-created-a-ridiculous-name-and-gave-our-tourist-official-a-sore-tongue"). Sensibly, the town's war memorial reads "Llanfair P.G." so as not to overwhelm the roll call of the dead; the spot is also known locally as "Llanfairpwll." It boasts the superior of Anglesey's two **tourist offices** (tel. (01248) 713177). (Open Apr.-Oct. M-Sa 9:30am-5:30pm, Su 10am-5pm; Nov.-Mar. M-F 9:30am-1pm and 1:30-5pm, Su 10am-5pm.) The other office is at Holyhead. Llanfair P.G. also houses James Pringle woolens factory, mobbed by tourists taking photos under the sign with the town's name. Puts antiecclesiodisestablishmentarianism in the lexicographical dustbin.

■ Beaumaris

Four miles northeast of the Menai Bridge on the A545, the main street of **Beaumaris** (bew-MAR-is; don't you dare say it the French way) runs quietly along the coastline. Yachts dot the harbor, surveying the mountains of Snowdonia. In town, savor the magnificent symmetry of **Beaumaris Castle** (tel. 810361), the last and largest of Edward I's Welsh fortresses. Begun in 1295 and built on a marsh, the moat-ringed castle couldn't depend on rugged geography to discourage would-be invaders. Edward's architect relied instead on a concentric design, with an inner gate off-center from the outer one to force would-be attackers to turn and expose their left flanks. Trouble in Scotland (see *Braveheart*) forced Edward to divert resources, leaving the fortress unfinished. *(Open Apr.-Oct. daily 9:30am-6:30pm; Nov.-Mar. M-Sa 9:30am-4pm, Su 11am-4pm. £2.70, students, seniors, and children £1.70, families £6.10.)*

On Bunkers Hill, off Steeple Ln., stands the former Beaumaris Gaol (tel. 810921), whose cells now show what it meant to be a prisoner in Victorian times, including the treadwheel used during "hard labor," and the chilling walk down Death Row. *(Open June-Sept. daily 10:30am-5pm. £2.75, students, seniors, and children £1.75.)* For something completely different, the **Museum of Childhood Memories,** 1 Castle St. (tel. 712498), offers trains, yo-yos, and other pre-*Teletubbies* diversions. *(Open Easter-Oct. M-Sa 10:30am-5:30pm, Su noon-5pm. £3, students and seniors £2.50, children £1.75, families £8.50.)* Beaumaris hosts a week-long **Gŵyl Beaumaris Music Festival** at May's end, which includes concerts, opera, theater, jazz, and street performances. A catamaran **cruise** (tel. 810379) down the Menai Strait to Puffin Island (1hr., £4, seniors £3.50, children £3), as well as longer trips and fishing trips, leaves from the Starida booth on the pier.

Buses stop on Castle St. An independently run **tourist office,** Town Hall (tel. 810040), on Castle St., provides brochures and accommodation info (open Easter-Oct. daily 10am-5:45pm). Financial puzzles are solved at **Lloyd's,** Castle St., without the help of an ATM (open M-F 9:30am-3pm). A **post office** guards its **postal code** LL58 8AB, but shares its **telephone code** 01248 with the whole town and with Bangor (open M-Tu and Th-F 9am-12:30pm and 1:30-5:30pm, W and Sa 9am-12:30pm).

The closest **youth hostel** to Beaumaris is in Bangor (tel. 353516; see **Accommodations and Food,** p. 444). Only three **B&Bs** reside in Beaumaris; accommodations are mostly provided by pubs, and beds come at high prices; budget travelers should sleep across the strait at Bangor. **Swn-y-Don,** 7 Bulkeley Terr. (tel. 811362), down Castle St., offers elegant rooms, some overlooking the strait, all with TV and private bathrooms (singles £25; doubles £38; off-season £20 and £34-36). Institutionalized **camping** is best at **Kingsbridge Caravan Park** (tel. 490636), 2 mi. out of town toward Llangoed. At the end of Beaumaris's main street, follow the coastal road 2 mi. past the castle until you come to the crossroads. Turn left for Llanfaes; Kingsbridge is 400 yd. on the right (£2.90 per person; showers available). Gratify gluttony at the stocked shelves of **Spar,** 11 Castle St. (open M-Sa 8am-11pm, Su 8am-10pm).

ISLAND SIGHTS

From prehistory, people fancied living on Anglesey. Burial chambers, cairns, settlement remains, and more recent constructions are scattered on Holyhead and both the eastern and western coasts. Explore with Ordnance Survey Map 114, available at most tourist offices (1:50,000; £5). Most ancient monuments sit quietly in farmers' fields; a map detailing exactly how to reach them (without walking through a herd of bulls) is your best bet. *Anglesey: A Guide to Ancient and Historic Sites on the Isle of Anglesey* (£2.25), produced by Cadw, gives good directions to 22 sites.

The late medieval priory of **Penmon** is perhaps the most readily accessible of Anglesey's sites; Arriva Cymru (tel. (01248) 351879) bus #57 travels from Beaumaris to Penmon (20min., M-Sa 1 per hr., Su 3 per day); from there it's a short walk to Penmon Pt., where the priory lies. **St. Seiriol's Well,** found here, is reputed to have healing qualities; some take advantage of it by downing a draught or plunging in. After curing yourself of that pesky rheumatism, scamper like a sprite into the church itself, where an elaborately carved cross stands.

Three sets of remains cluster near the town of **Llanallgo.** Getting to them requires a bit of effort; Crosville bus #62 (M-Sa 1 per hr., Su 3 per day) passes between Benllech and Moelfre, hitting Llanallgo en route. Ask the driver to stop at the roundabout heading to Moelfre. Follow the minor road (to the left of the Moelfre road) to the ancient **Ligwy Burial Chamber.** Between 15 and 30 people were entombed in this squat enclosure, covered with a 25-ton capstone. Farther on stands the 12th-century chapel **Hen Capel Ligwy,** and the remains of the Roman **Din Ligwy Hut Group.**

Bryn Celli Ddu, "The Mound in the Dark Grove," a burial chamber built in the middle of a henge, is the most famous of Anglesey's remains, dating from the late Neolithic period. Bring a flashlight to admire the fascinating designs carved on the inside. Try bus #4 from Bangor to Holyhead, which sometimes goes via Llandaniel (M-Sa 9 per day); ask the driver. You can also walk from Llanfair P.G.; get directions at the tourist office. If you're walking you'll pass **Plas Newydd,** the country home of the Marquess of Anglesey, dates "only" to the 19th century; still, it's worth going to see the 58 ft. Rex Whistler painting that covers an inside room. *(Open daily Apr.-Oct. noon-5pm. £4.20, children £2.10, families £10.50.)*

■ Holyhead (Caergybi)

A narrow strip of land attached to the Isle of Anglesey by a causeway and a bridge, Holyhead has only one lure for the traveler: **ferries to Ireland.** The harbor has a grim collection of houses rotting beneath tin bandages. If you have time, explore the many paths of **Holyhead Mountain.** Its **North** and **South Stacks** are good for birdwatching, and the lighthouse looks longingly out to sea. **Irish Ferries** and **Stena Sealink** operate ferries and catamarans to **Dublin** and its suburb, **Dun Laoghaire,** respectively. Only car-ferry parties leave from the docks; foot passengers embark at the rail station. Arrive 30 minutes early and remember your passport. See **Wales to Ireland,** p. 32, for more information.

Holyhead can be reached from land by **Arriva Cymru** bus #4 or 44 from **Bangor via Llanfair P.G.** and **Llangefni** (1¼hr., M-Sa 2 per hr., Su 7 per day, return £3.70). **National Express** (tel. (0990) 808080) hits Holyhead from most major cities. Hourly **trains** run to **Bangor** (30min., £5.40, day return £5.50), **Chester** (1½hr., £13.70, day return £14.10), and **London** (6hr., £44). **Lockers** (£1-2), if open, are located on Platform 1 of the rail station, monitored by closed-circuit TV. Holyhead's **tourist office** (tel./fax 762622), really more of a booth, rests inside the ferry departure terminal, connected to the rail station, and books rooms (open daily Apr.-Oct. 10am-6pm; Nov.-Mar. 10am-5pm). The **Midland ATM** sits at William and Market St. (bank open M-F 9am-5pm, Sa 9:30am-12:30pm). The **post office** ebbs, flows, and changes money at 13a Stryd Boston, off Market St. (open M-F 9am-5:30am, Sa 9am-12:30pm). Holyhead's **postal code** is LL65 1BP, its **telephone code** 01407.

As in most ferry ports, Holyhead **B&Bs** are accommodating to passengers arriving and departing at the beck and call of boat schedules. Information is available from the tourist office (see below); the ferry staff at the car dock and railway station also have a B&B list. If you call ahead, B&B owners can usually arrange to greet you in the middle of the night, but don't go ringing doorbells unannounced in the wee hours. Some will provide B&PL (packed lunches for ferry riders). **Roselea,** 26 Holborn Rd. (tel./fax 764391), extremely near the station, will pack you a lunch for the day after you sleep in their orthopedic beds and watch their TVs (£14). **Orotovia,** 66 Walthew Ave. (tel. 760259), has TV, and a dining room with woodcraft for sale, as well as every possible cereal (£15 with *Let's Go*). Go up Thomas St., which becomes Porth-y-Felin Rd. as it passes the school, and turn right onto Walthew Ave. Just down the road, the proprietress of **Witchingham,** 20 Walthew Ave. (tel. 762426), is hardly the broom-riding-pointy-hat-wearing type. Despite her residence's name, her magic is focused only on the comfortable beds and TVs in the rooms. Just think before you book for St. David's Day, when a ghost has been known to drop by (£15).

There are sights aplenty on Holyhead, but it takes some effort to reach them. **Caer Gybi,** the Roman walls which surround St. Cybi's church, are in the middle of the city, between Stanley St. and Victoria Rd. West of Holyhead lies **South Stack Island. Caer y Twr** and **Holyhead Mountain Hut Group** sit at the mountain's base. The former is an Iron Age hillfort, the latter a settlement inhabited from about 500 BC until Roman times. **Jones** (tel. 730204) bus #22 runs from Holyhead to the South Stack (15min., M-Sa 3 per day). On Sundays, Arriva bus #44 runs the route (3 per day).

■ Conwy

Conwy has a rough, ossified beauty, born under English subjugation and preserved admirably through its tiring role as a modern tourist mecca. Edward I's 13th-century castle solemnly guards Conwy and reminds camera-crazed tourists that it was Edward who squashed a revolt by the brothers Llywelyn. Below the castle stands a worn but intact wall, a bundle of narrow lanes, and a gaggle of eclectic attractions.

GETTING THERE

Arriva Cymru (tel. 596969) buses #5 and 5B stop in Conwy as they climb the northern coast between **Caernarfon** and **Bangor** to Llandudno (Caernarfon-Conwy 1¼hr.; M-Sa 2 per hr., Su 1 per hr.). Bus #19 makes a journey down the vale of Conwy from **Llandudno** to **Llanrwst**, taking in Conwy on the way (M-Sa 2 per hr.); **Alpine Travel** runs bus #19S on the same route on Sundays (7 per day). **National Express** coaches (tel. (0990) 808080) leave for **London** (7hr.) and **Birmingham** (4hr.).

Arriva's **One-Day Explorer** pass offers unlimited travel (£4.80, children £3.20). If you're moving on west on bus #5 and plan to explore the area around Bangor, try the Gwynedd **Red Rover** (£4.40, children £2.20). The **North & Mid Wales Rover** offers limited bus or rail travel throughout much of Wales above the imaginary Aberystwyth-Shrewsbury line (£16.90 per day; £25.70 for 3 days; £39.90 per week). Pick up information on bus and train schedules, as well as maps, in the comprehensive *Conwy Public Transport Information* booklet.

Although Conwy lies on the North Coast Rail Line, **trains** only stop at the station by request. Tell the conductor you intend to stop or disembark across the Conwy River at the Llandudno Junction Station, a 15-minute walk after crossing the bridge, or take Arriva bus #22 from the bus stop down the ramp from the station (M-Sa 1 per hr., Su 4 per day).

ORIENTATION

The town wall squeezes Old Conwy into a roughly triangular shape. The castle lies in one corner, by the Conwy and Gyffin Rivers; **Castle St.**, which becomes **Berry St.**, runs from the foot of the fortress parallel to the Quay on the other side of the wall. **High St.** stretches from the Quay's edge to **Lancaster Sq.**, crossing Castle St. en route. From Lancaster Sq., **Rosehill St.** circles back to the castle, while in the opposite direction **Bangor Rd.** scrunches through a small arch in the wall.

PRACTICAL INFORMATION

Trains: The station in Conwy is off Rosehill St., but trains generally opt to stop instead at the nearby, fully staffed Llandudno Junction train station. **Lockers** £1-2. Booking office open M-Sa 5:30am-6:30pm, Su 11:25am-6:30pm.

Buses: Buses stop at various points on the major streets; check posted schedules or the tourist office for timetables.

Tourist Office: Tourist Information Centre, Castle Entrance (tel. 592248). Clear street maps available, as well as a booking service for £1 and a 10% deposit. Open Easter-Oct. daily 9:30am-6:30pm; Nov.-Easter M-Sa 9:30am-4pm, Su 11am-4pm.

Financial Services: Barclays, 23 High St. (tel. 616616). Open M-Tu and Th-F 9am-4:30pm, W 9:30am-4:30pm; **ATM** outside.

Camping Supplies: Conwy Outdoor Shop, 9 Castle St. (tel. 593390). Extensive selection, slightly overpriced. Open daily in summer 9am-7pm; in winter 9am-6pm.

Market: In the train carpark. Open Sa 8:30am-5pm; Apr.-Aug. also Tu.

Emergency: Dial 999; no coins required.

Police: Lancaster Sq. (tel. 592222).

Hospital: Llandudno Hospital, Maesdu Rd. (tel. 860066). Take Crosville bus #19.

Post Office: Lancaster Sq. (tel. 573990), at High St., sharing The Wine Shop's pints. Open M-F 8:30am-6pm, Sa 9am-5:30pm. **Postal Code:** LL32 8DA.

Telephone Code: 01492.

WALES

ACCOMMODATIONS

B&Bs crowd the **Cadnant Park** area, a 10-minute walk from the castle. Head from the castle down Rosehill St., past Lancaster Sq., through the arch down Bangor Rd., then turn left into a sea of well-tended gardens.

◉YHA Conwy (tel. 593571; fax 593580). From Lancaster Sq., head down Bangor Rd., turn left up Mt. Pleasant, and right at the top of the hill. The hostel is on the left after 150yd. All-singing, all-dancing YHA has absolutely everything a budget traveler could wish for: a huge self-catering kitchen, laundry facilities, TV room, and luggage lockers for daytime arrivals. £9.75, under 18 £6.55. Open mid-Feb. to Dec.

Cadwern, 5 Cadnant Park (tel. 593240). The delightfully jolly proprietress offers sunny ground floor TV-adorned rooms braced by huge, veggie-breeding gardens. Includes a mammoth purple room with a bay window for 3-4 people. £15.

Glan Heulog, Llanrwst Rd., Woodlands (tel. 593845). Go under the arch before the Visitor Centre on Rosehill St., down the steps, and across the carpark. Turn right and walk 5min. down Llanrwst Rd. Huge house on a hill with TVs and a "healthy option" breakfast available. £13-17.

Llwyn Guest House, 15 Cadnant Park (tel. 592319). Lose yourself in the fluffy expanse of the comforters while vegging in front of your personal TV, or absorb UVs in the carefully cultivated garden. £15.

Camping: Conwy Touring Park, Llanrwst Rd. (tel. 592856). A steep mile or so out of town. Follow Llanrwst Rd. and posted signs. Launderette and showers. 2-person tent £4.85-7. Families and couples only; no large groups. Open Easter-Oct.

FOOD

Most Conwy restaurants cater to the tourist crowds; they serve ordinary grub at extraordinary prices. High St. is *the* place to unload your wallet. The ever-reliable **Spar** grocery store stands here next to Barclays (open daily 8am-10pm). Herds of broccoli gazelles graze on vegetarian meals (£2-7) at **The Wall Place,** Chapel St. off Berry St. (tel. 596326). Some evenings traditional Celtic music wafts across the light grain wood floor; on winter afternoons, the cafe hosts creative workshops. (Open July-Aug. daily noon-3pm and 7-10pm; Jan.-June and Sept.-Nov. Sa-Th noon-3pm, F-Sa noon-3pm and 7-10pm.) Sip tea under the beams of the 420-year-old **Pen-y-Bryn Tearooms** (tel. 569445), on High St. at Lancaster Sq. Light fare runs £2.50-4 (open M-Sa 10:30am-5pm, Su 11am-5pm; Nov.-Easter closed M).

SIGHTS AND ENTERTAINMENT

Though the compact battlements of **Conwy Castle** (tel. 592358) are dwarfed by Edward I's colossal fortresses at Caernarfon and Beaumaris, its menacing stone stance is challenge enough for would-be attackers. *(Open Apr.-Oct. daily 9:30am-6:30pm; Nov.-Mar. M-Sa 9:30am-4pm, Su 11am-4pm. £3.50, students, seniors, and children £2.50, families £9.50. Tours £1.)* Invaders would need to scale the slippery rock promontory, shielded by water on three sides, and then somehow breach one of two massive barbicans, amidst a shower of crossbow bolts. And that's just to get to the grim walls and turreted towers of the inner curtain. Ruins romanticists will enjoy the vertigo-inducing turrets, the lengthy corridors of wall-walks, and the nooks that occasionally bear seagull's nests. The prison tower saw many prominent Normans and English rot beneath its false bottom, and the castle chapel witnessed Henry "Hotspur" Percy's betrayal of Richard II in 1399; two years later Welsh rebel Owain Glyndŵr and his band of armed nationalists seized the ramparts. Telford's elegant 1826 **suspension bridge** (tel. 573282) stretches across the Conwy River from the foot of the castle's grassy east barbican; at the end stands the tollmaster's house, carefully recreated. *(Bridge and house open July-Aug. daily 10am-5pm; Apr.-June and Sept.-Oct. W-M 10am-5pm. £1, children 50p.)* Both bridge and castle can be seen by boat; vigorous bellowing heralds the departure of the **Queen Victoria** from the quay at the end of High St. *(30min., £2.50, children £1.80.)* The **town wall,** almost a mile long, was built at the same time as the castle and shielded burghers with its 21 towers and 480 arrow slits—the twelve latrine shoots may have proved useful too. Many sections are open for climbing; the steep section bordering Mt. Pleasant rewards the fit with a magnificent view.

Two impeccably restored houses form part of Conwy's tourist trail. **Plas Mawr** (tel. 580167), on High St., is the best-preserved European townhouse in Britain. Lovingly restored, Plas Mawr sports exquisite plasterwork and a pantry with (faux) rabbit and deer hanging from the walls. *(Open Tu-Su Apr.-Sept. 9:30am-6pm; Oct. 9:30am-4pm. £4, students, seniors, and children £3, families £11.)* Walk along tilted floors past displays of armor and period furnishings in the 14th-century **Aberconwy House,** Castle St. (tel. 592246), the oldest house in Conwy. *(Open Apr.-Oct. W-M 10am-5pm. £2, children £1.)* Most of the tranquility in Conwy has migrated to **St. Mary's Church.** Just outside the South Porch rests the grave that inspired Wordsworth's poem "We are seven."

Conwy has more than its share of oddities. Head down High St. and onto the quay to bang your head in the **Smallest House** (tel. 593484), billed as the world's smallest house. With a frontage of 72 in., the 380-year-old two-story cell first housed an elderly couple and then one 6-foot 3-inch fisherman. *(Open daily July-Aug. 10:30am-9pm; Easter-June and Sept.-Oct. 10:30am-6pm. 50p, students, seniors, and children 30p, payable to friendly, Quaintly Dressed Lady out front.)* Two grand British traditions—tea and eccentricity—meet at the **Teapot Museum** (tel./fax 593429), on Castle St., which displays 300 years of teapots—some short, some stout, and some shaped like Gladstone, Reagan, and Donald Duck. Glimpses of *risqué* teapots reward the diligent museum-goer. *(Open Easter-Oct. M-Sa 10am-5:30pm, Su 11am-5:30pm. £1.50, students, seniors, and children £1.)* The **Conwy Butterfly Jungle** (tel. 593149), in Bodlandeb Park outside the town wall, is a swarming greenhouse. Some frightening specimens, including a "giant armored jungle nymph," measuring a spiky 8 in., are locked in cages for safety. Your safety. *(Open daily Apr.-Sept. 10am-5:30pm; Oct. 10am-4pm. £3, students £1.85, seniors £2.60, 50p discount for YHA members.)* In September, the **Conwy Festival** draws local musicians, dancers, and medieval performers into the streets and castle courtyard.

■ Vale of Conwy and Betws-y-Coed

The lazy, undulating hills that hug the Conwy River descend from the lofty mountains and sharp rocks of Snowdonia to the west. Well-watered by river and rain, the Conwy Valley casts a spear of chlorophyll from northern Llandudno into the wooded mountains around Betws-y-Coed in the south. Cyclists take advantage of the scenery and terrain here, where views are glorious and gear-changes infrequent.

GETTING ABOUT

The **Conwy Valley Line** (tel. (0345) 484950) offers unparalleled views as its trains hug the river banks between **Llandudno** and **Bleaunau Ffestiniog,** stopping at Llandudno Junction (near **Conwy**) and **Betws-y-Coed** on the way (6 per day). The **British Rail North and Mid Wales Day Rover** ticket (£16) gives a day of unlimited bus and rail travel as far south as **Aberystwyth,** but you'll have to scurry like a squirrel on a hotplate to make it pay off. Most **buses** elect to stop at Betws-y-Coed and Llandudno; the rest of the valley is untouched by coaches. The main bus along the Conwy is **Arriva Cymru's** (tel. (01492) 641847) bus #19/19A, which winds from Llandudno and Conwy down to Llanrwst (M-Sa 1 per hr., Su 7 per day). Some of those services continue as **Sherpa** bus #19 from Llanberis via Betws-y-Coed (4 per day). Arriva sells a one-day **Explorer** pass good for unlimited travel on any of its buses (£4.80, children £3.20; longer options available).

■ Betws-y-Coed

Situated at the southern tip of the Vale of Conwy and the eastern edge of the Snowdonia Mountains, the crowded but picturesque village of Betws-y-Coed (bet-TOOS uh COYD, often just Betws) exudes vibes of the great outdoors; *everyone* seems to be embarking on or returning from an adventure. Crouched between forested mountains along the A5, the line of navy blue hillstone houses shades the foamy beds of the Conwy and Llugwy rivers.

ORIENTATION AND PRACTICAL INFORMATION Trains (tel. (0345) 484950) pass through Betws-y-Coed, halfway down the Conwy Valley line between **Llandudno** and **Blaenau Ffestiniog** (M-Sa 6 per day; peak season also Su 2 per day). **Sherpa** bus #19/ 54, operated by Arriva, connects Betws-y-Coed with **Llanrwst** and **Llanberis**, stopping at most of the area hostels (4 per day). On Sundays, **Sherpa** bus #96 runs between Betws and **Llanberis** (5 per day). Some of the Sherpa services continue to Conwy. Rent **bikes** from the laid-back cyclists at **Beics Betws** (tel. 710766), behind the post office. (Mountain bikes £4 per hr., £12 per ½ day, £16 per day; helmet included. Open M-F 9am-5:30pm, Su 10am-5:30pm.)

The spirited and tireless staff at the self-proclaimed busiest **tourist office** in northern Wales (tel. 710426 or 710665) is also a **National Park Information Centre** and is located at the Old Stables along Holyhead Rd., provides information on sights, bus and train timetables, and a well-stocked bookshop (open daily Apr.-Oct. 10am-6pm; Nov.-Mar. 9:30am-4:30pm). **Midland Bank** and its **ATM** hide at the southern edge of town on Holyhead Rd. (open M-Tu and Th-F 9:30am-3:30pm, W 10am-3:30pm). Two giant emporia on Holyhead Rd. sell mountaineering supplies and canoe equipment: **Climber and Rambler** (tel. 710555; open M-Th 9am-6pm, F-Su 9am-7pm) and **Cotswold** (tel. 710234; open M-W 9am-6pm, Th 10am-6pm, F-Su 9am-7pm). The friendly staff at the **post office,** Holyhead Rd. next to St. Mary's Church, can simultaneously **exchange currencies** and pleasantries (open M-F 9am-1pm and 2-5:30pm, Sa 9am-12:30pm). The **postal code** is LL24 0AA, the **telephone code** 01690.

ACCOMMODATIONS AND FOOD Most B&Bs in town charge £13.50 and up, and cluster in two bundles, both along Holyhead Rd. (the A5), south of St. Mary's Church. **Riverside,** Holyhead Rd. (tel. 710650), just past the Climber and Rambler camping store, offers comfortable beds and TVs; in the restaurant below, miniature jazz figures jam atop the mantle (£12-15; full breakfast £4; July-Aug. no singles). Or try **Glan Llugwy,** Holyhead Rd. (tel. 710592), on the western edge of town, whose subdued, TV-endowed rooms gaze upon lambs by the river (£16). Two hostels rest conveniently near town: **YHA Lledr Valley** (tel. 750202) and **YHA Capel Curig** (tel. 720225); see **Accommodations and Camping,** p. 437, for directions, opening times, and prices. **Riverside Caravan Park** (tel. 710310) suns itself beside a cemetery in the back of Betws rail station (tents or caravans £4.50 per person; families and couples only; open Mar.-Oct.). The **Dol Gam Campsite** (tel. 710228), midway between Betws-y-Coed and Capel Curig on the A5, charges £2.50 per person.

Most of the restaurants in Betws-y-Coed cater to unsuspecting tourists—and are priced accordingly. Luckily, there are a few exceptions. The homey staff at **Dil's Diner,** Station Rd. (tel. 710346), in front of the train station, cheerfully dishes out greasy platters of eggs and sausages (£3-6). Young backpackers and local revelers saddle up on the picnic tables in front of **Royal Oak Stables,** Holyhead Rd. (tel. 710219), across from the tourist office (open M-Sa 11am-11pm, Su noon-10:30pm).

SIGHTS Betws is famous for its eight bridges, especially Telford's 1815 cast-iron **Waterloo Bridge** at the village's southern end, built the year the famous battle ensured Napoleon's political demise. Near St. Michael's Church, the miniature **suspension footbridge,** which sways when trod upon, crosses the Conwy. **Pont-y-Pair Bridge,** "the bridge of the cauldron," Betws's most serene, bounds the River Llugwy to the north. The first bridge was built in 1475; Inigo Jones may have contributed to building the second, which consists of eleven stone arches hopping from rock to rock. Behind the train station, weathered gravestones surround the humble, ivied 14th-century **St. Michael's Church,** whose sobriety is tempered by the fragments of stained glass which remain in the east and west windows.

Two miles west, signposted off the A5, the swift waters of the River Llugwy crash furiously over descending plateaus of rocks at the poorly translated **Swallow Falls** (the original Welsh name, *Rhaeadr Ewyrnol,* meant "foaming falls"). Bring a 50p piece to operate the turnstile. **Sherpa** bus #19 between Betws and Llanberis stops at the falls. Further along the A5 lies "the Ugly House," **Tŷ Hyll** (tel. 720287), whose uncarved stone facade is due to its hasty construction. At the time it was built, a house constructed in a day and night (with smoke wafting out of the chimney in the morning) earned the builder the surrounding common land. *(Open Apr.-Sept. daily 9:30am-5:30pm; call for winter hours.)* **Guided walks** around Betws leave from the Information Centre. All walks are 6-8 mi. *(5-6hr. Apr.-Sept. Th-Su 10am. £3.50, children 50p.)*

■ Valley Villages

The Conwy valley is still largely untouched by coach-bound tourists, leaving walkers, cyclists and *Let's Go* loyalists to explore its gorgeous scenery and small towns. At the 80-acre **Bodnant Gardens** (tel. (01492) 650460), 8 mi. south of Llandudno off the A470, Chilean Fire Bush flirts shamelessly with eurcypheas and hydrangea. The entrance is by the Eglwysbach Rd. *(Open mid-Mar. to Oct. daily 10am-5pm. £4.60, children £2.30.)* Take **Crosville** bus #25 from Llandudno (M-Sa 7 per day) or the **Conwy Valley train** line to Tal-y-Cafn Station (request the stop; M-Sa 5 per day, Su 3 per day).

A bit farther south, the town of **Trefriw** sleeps along the River Crafnant. **Lake Crafnant,** 3 mi. uphill from town (along the road opposite the Fairy Hotel), is surrounded by some of the highest peaks in Snowdonia. A 1½ mi. walk from town north along the main road, a rust grotto offers up the world's only fully licensed spa water medicine at the **Trefriw Wells Spa** (tel. (01492) 640057). *(Open Easter-Oct. daily 10am-5:30pm; Nov.-Easter M-Sa 10am-dusk, Su noon-dusk. £2.65, seniors £2.40, children £1.50, under 10 free.)* Originally used to treat rheumatism and eczema, today the spa water eases iron deficiency as well. A month's supply goes for £6.50 and tastes like rancid chicken broth. Yum. B&Bs (£15-18) line Trefriw's long main street. To reach Trefriw, take **Arriva** bus #19 from Conwy, Llandudno, or Llandudno Junction.

A useful transit town, **Llanrwst** has an **ATM,** more than one bank, and a **market day** on Tuesdays. Cramped beside the Conwy River, just across the 1636 Old Bridge built by Inigo Jones, the 15th-century stone **Tu-Hwnt-i'r-Bont** hides a tea room beneath a roof that is level to the road. Before banging your head, check the timbers for graffiti in all languages (tea with scone and *bara brith* £3.60; open Easter-Oct. Tu-Su 10am-5:30pm). A 10-minute walk past the tea house deposits you at **Gwydir Castle** (tel. (01492) 641687), the 16th-century manor house of Sir John Wynne. The grounds shelter peacocks and a selflessly named yew tree. *(Open daily 10am-4:30pm. £3, children £1.50.)* The rustic **YHA Youth Hostel** in **Rowen** (tel. (01492) 650089), half-way between Trefriw and Conwy, is a superb place to rest your weary bones (£6.50, under 18 £4.45; lockout 10am-5pm; open May-Aug. daily). **Arriva** bus #19 stops in Rowen village (1 per hr.); the hostel is 1 mi. up a steep hill.

■ Llangollen

Near the English border and once a refuge for English Romantics, Llangollen (hlan-GO-hlen) has become a drab patch of red brick and white stucco in a hollow in the hills. With the notable exception of the annual International Music Eisteddfod, all of the town's current attractions spawn from Nature. Walkers gently tread the surrounding hills on their way to Horseshoe Pass, and weekends bring whitewater canoeists slashing through neighboring streams. Tucked beneath a 14th-century bridge, the River Dee rolls on peacefully, blissfully unaware of the bad architecture nearby.

PRACTICAL INFORMATION For such a booming tourist town, Llangollen is difficult to reach for the carless and coachless. Most public transport from outside Wales comes as far as Wrexham, 30 minutes from Llangollen. **Trains** (tel. (0345) 484950) connect **Wrexham** with **Chester, Shrewsbury, Birmingham,** and **London.** A closer train station to Llangollen, though less well-served, is **Ruabon,** from which B&B may owners transport weary backpackers. **National Express** (tel. (0990) 808080) Coach #521 leaves London daily, stopping at Llangollen on its way to **Wrexham. Arriva**

Cymru (tel. (01745) 343721) bus #94 connects Llangollen to Wales's west coast at **Barmouth via Dolgellau** (M-Sa 6 per day, Su 2 per day); **Bryn Melyn** (tel. 860701) bus #5/X5 rumbles to Wrexham and back (M-Sa 1 per hr.). On Sundays, **Arriva Midland** (tel. (01691) 652402) runs a winding version of bus #5 (50min., 6 per day).

The **tourist office,** Town Hall, Castle St. (tel. 860828; open June-Sept. Th-Tu 10am-6pm; Oct.-May 9:30am-5pm), and the Eisteddfod office keep an emergency list of accommodations, although some are as far as 15 mi. away. The **post office,** 41 Castle St., sorts mail and **exchanges currency** (open M-F 9am-5:30pm, Sa 9am-1pm). The town's **postal code** is LL20 8RW; its **telephone code** is 01978.

ACCOMMODATIONS AND FOOD

The **YHA Hostel,** Tyndwr Hall, Tyndwr Rd. (tel. 860330; fax 861709), lies 1½ mi. out of town. Expect to share this 124-bed activity center with a group of some sort. From town, follow the A5 towards Shrewsbury, bear right up Birch Hill, and after ½ mi. take a right at a Y junction (£8.80, under 18 £5.95; no lockout or curfew; open mid-Feb. to Oct.). **B&Bs** (£15-20) are numerous in Llangollen, especially along Regent St. Expect a warm greeting from the proprietress of **Bryant Rose,** 31 Regent St. (tel. 860389). TV and flowers glow in large rooms (£15, student discounts available). In the peach rooms of **Bryn y Coed,** 66 Berwyn St. (tel. 860339), TVs drown out the noise of passing lorries (£13.50). **Campsites** abound; investigate **Tower Farm,** Tower Rd. (tel. 860798), at the far end of Eisteddfod campgrounds (£2.50 per person, £10 per caravan).

The most exciting of Llangollen's many restaurants is **Robbin's Nest,** Market St. (tel. 861425), which serves healthy portions for £4 or less (open Mar.-Dec. Tu-Sa 10am-2pm; W-Sa also 6:30-9:30pm). At **Café and Books,** 17 Castle St. (tel. 861963), you can thumb hundreds of used volumes upstairs while they fry your fish and chips downstairs (open daily Apr.-Sept. 9am-7pm; Oct.-May 9am-5pm). Nearby **Spar** sells produce and refreshments (open daily 8am-11pm).

SIGHTS AND ENTERTAINMENT

Every summer, the town's population of 3,000 swells to 80,000 during the **International Music Eisteddfod** (ice-TETH-vod), not to be confused with the roaming Royal National Eisteddfod (see **Festivals,** p. 395). From July 6-11 in 1999, competitors from 50 countries will sing and dance until the fields and hills seem truly alive—to the chagrin of groggy livestock. Book tickets and rooms *far in advance* through the **Eisteddfod Box Office,** Llangollen International Music Eisteddfod Office, Llangollen, Denbighshire, Wales LL20 8NG (tel. 861501; fax 861300; email lime@celtic.co.uk). *(Phone bookings M-F 9am-5pm. Box office open M-Th 9am-4pm, F 9am-3pm. Unreserved seat and admission to grounds on day of show £4, seniors and children £2, families £9; concert tickets £9-12.)*

Up Hill St. from the town center stands **Plas Newydd** (tel. 861314), former home of two women of noble birth who fled unalluring fates in Ireland in 1778. Charmed by Llangollen, they settled into village life, dividing their time between charitable works and the elaborate decoration of this house, including the carved wooden walls. Wellington and Walter Scott visited, as did Wordsworth, who was moved to pen a little poem in their honor. *(Open Apr.-Oct. daily 10am-5pm. £2, children £1, families £5.)*

A 30-minute walk from Llangollen along Abbey Rd., the ruins of 13th-century **Valle Crucis Abbey** (tel. 860326) grace a leafy valley. With its serene, empty arches framing trees and sky, the abbey would be entirely beautiful were it not for the giant caravan park that surrounds it and slithers up to the cloister. *(Open daily Apr.-Sept. 10am-5pm; Oct.-Mar. 9:30am-dusk. £1.70, students, seniors, and children £1.20; free in winter.)* Perched on a hill overlooking the town are the lyrical ruins of **Dinas Brân** (Crow's Castle). The footpath up the hill begins behind the canal museum, and the walk takes about an hour each way. The exquisite view from the castle stretches from the mountains near Snowdonia to the flat English Midlands.

SCOTLAND

Scotland at its best is a world apart, a defiantly distinct nation within the United Kingdom. Its cities revel in a culture and worldview all their own, from the rampant nightlife of Glasgow to the Festival activities of Edinburgh. A little over half the size of England but with a tenth of its population, Scotland possesses open spaces and natural splendor its southern neighbor cannot rival—the Scottish highlands contain some of the last great wilderness in Europe. The craggy, heather-sloped mountains and silver beaches of the west coast and the luminescent mists of the Hebrides demand any traveler's awe, while the farmlands to the south and the peaceful fishing villages of the east coast display a gentler beauty.

A native of Scotland is a Scot; a Scot may be British, but *never* English. Most Scottish folk will welcome you with geniality and pride; as in the other few unharried corners of the world, hospitality and conversation are valued highly. Before reluctantly joining with England in 1707, the Scots defended their independence with the claymore for over 400 years. Since the union, they have nurtured a separate identity, retaining control over a number of social and political institutions, such as schools, churches, and the judicial system. While the kilts, bagpipes, and find-your-own-clan kits of Glasgow, Edinburgh, and Aberdeen may grow cloying, a visit to the less touristed regions of Scotland will allow you to encounter the inheritors of the ancient traditions: a B&B proprietor talking to her grandchildren in soft Gaelic cadences, a crofter cutting peat, or a fisherman setting out in his skiff at dawn.

■ Getting There

The cheapest way to Scotland from outside Britain is usually through London. Although the **bus** trip from London's **Victoria** Station takes more than seven hours, it is significantly cheaper than train travel. **National Express** (tel. (0990) 808080) services connect England and Scotland via **Glasgow** and **Edinburgh** (4 per day; single £17, return £27). Buses depart London before 1pm (day service) and after 9pm (overnight). Overnight trips are usually a few pounds more expensive. Contact National Express for prices and be sure to book in advance. National Express offers student and youth (25 and under) discount cards for £8 for 1 year, which reduce all fares except APEX.

From London, **Scottish Rail trains** (tel. (0141) 343180, inquiries (0345) 484950) to Scotland take only six hours, but fares are steep—trains to Edinburgh and Glasgow Central cost about £50 return. Overnight trains offer sleeper berths for an extra £30.

Air travel is predictably expensive. **British Airways** (tel. (0345) 222111) sells a limited number of APEX return tickets starting at £70. **British Midland** (tel. (0345) 554554) offers a Saver fare from **London** to **Glasgow** (from £58 return). Book as far in advance as you can (2 weeks if possible) for the cheapest fare.

Scotland is also linked by **ferry** to **Northern Ireland** (see **By Boat,** p. 30) and to the Isle of Man (see **To the Isle of Man,** p. 32).

Before you leave London, visit the **Scottish Tourist Board** office, 19 Cockspur St., London SW1 Y5BL (tel. (0171) 930 8661; Tube: Charing Cross or Piccadilly Circus). They stock gads of books and free brochures and can book train, bus, and plane tickets (open M-W and F 9am-6pm, Th 9am-6:30pm, Sa noon-4pm).

■ Getting About

The *Touring Map of Scotland* (about £3.50) and the *Touring Guide of Scotland* (£5), available at tourist offices, provide a good overall view for planning any sojourn in Scotland. Train or bus travel in the Lowlands (south of Stirling and north of the Borders) is facilitated by frequent rail and bus connections. In the Highlands trains snake slowly north on a few restricted routes, bypassing almost the entire Northwest

Scotland

Shetland Islands
Fetlar
Unst
Yell
Mainland
Lerwick

TO FAROES, HANSTHOLM, DENMARK

NORTH ATLANTIC OCEAN

ORKNEY ISLANDS
Stromness
Hoy
Kirkwall

North Sea

Cape Wrath
Kyle of Tongue
Durness
Scrabster
Thurso
John O'Groats
Wick

OUTER HEBRIDES
Stornoway
Lewis
North Minch
Eddrachillis Bay
Achiltibul
Ullapool
Helmsdale
HIGHLANDS
Carbisdale Castle
Tarbert
Stockinish
North Uist
Raasay Island
Gairloch
Torridon
Moray Firth
Elgin
Banff
Forres
GRAMPIAN
Lochmaddy
Uig
Portree
Inverness
Skye
Loch Ness
Spey River
Don River
South Uist
Broadford
Kyle of Lochalsh
Aviemore
Cairngorm Mtns.
Dee River
Aberdeen
Lochboisdale
Armadale
Braemar
Barra
Canna
Castlebay
Rum
Muck
Eigg
Mallaig
Fort William
Ben Nevis
Ballater
Stonehaven

INNER HEBRIDES
Coll
Glencoe
Loch Etive
GRAMPIAN MTS.
Pitlochry
Tobermory
Craignure
Staffa
Mull
Iona
Oban
Loch Tay
Dunkeld
Birnam
Dundee
Killin
Perth
St. Andrews
Tiree
Ben More
TAYSIDE
Anstruther
Loch Long
Trossachs
Firth of Tay
Argyll
Loch Lomond
Stirling
FIFE
Kirkcaldy
Inveraray
CENTRAL
Firth of Forth
Jura
Clonalsay
STRATHCLYDE
Glasgow Airport
Edinburgh Airport
LOTHIAN
Edinburgh
Islay
Tarbert
Glasgow
Pentland Hills
Moorfoot Hills
Melrose
Bowmore
Androssan
Peebles
Tweed River
Saltcoats
Galashiels
Kelso
Port Ellen
Lochranza
Prestwick Airport
Jedburgh
Brodick
Arran
Firth of Clyde
Nith River
Ayr
Cheviot Hills
Culzean Castle
ENGLAND
Galloway Forest Park
Newton Stewart
Dumfries
Castle Douglas
Glencaple
Carlisle
Hexham
NORTHERN IRELAND
Stranraer
Portpatrick
Kirkcudbright
Larne
Luce Bay
Isle of Whithor
Whithorn
Solway Firth
Keswick
Penrith

N

region. Bus service declines in the Northwest Highlands and grinds to a standstill on Sundays. Many stations are unstaffed or non-existent (purchase tickets on board).

In general, **buses** are your best bet for travel. They're usually more frequent and far-reaching than trains and always cheaper, although non-smokers may find smoggy buses less hospitable than non-smoking train cars. **Citylink** (tel. (0990) 505050) provides much of the inter-city service in Scotland. In most rail stations **Scottish Rail (ScotRail)** offers free timetables to services in particular regions. If you plan to do most of your sightseeing by train, a possible money-saver is the **Freedom of Scotland Travelpass** (£64 for 4 within 8 days, £93 for any 8 within 15 days, £122 for 15 days), which allows unlimited travel on ScotRail trains and transportation on Caledonian Macbrayne and Strathclyde ferries to the islands. Purchase the pass at almost any train station or order through Rail Europe (see **Getting About: By Train,** p. 32).

Two **minibus** services provide a variety of cheap and flexible ways for hostelers to see Scotland. The **Haggis Backpackers** minibus (tel. (0131) 557 9393) provides an excellent **hop-on, hop-off** service from Edinburgh through Perth, Pitlochry, Aviemore, Inverness, and Loch Ness to Skye, and from Skye through Glen Nevis, Fort William, Glencoe, Oban, Invernaray, Loch Lomond, Glasgow, and (finally) back to Edinburgh (unlimited travel £85). Their six-day tours take in Edinburgh, Stirling, Oban, Glencoe, Fort William, Glenfinnan, Skye, Ullapool, and Achininver, including points of interest along the way (£139). They also offer two three-day tours for £75 each. **Go Blue Banana** minibus, 12 High St. (tel. (0131) 556 2000), near the Edinburgh tourist office, offers similar services: two three-day tours for £75, a six-day tour for £139, and a nine-day tour for £199. Although they don't offer hop-on, hop-off service, they do have "mad Scottish driver/guides" who will be your best friend for three to nine days.

Air travel is naturally expensive between major cities, but British Airways offers a decent deal for reaching the far-flung Shetlands—their 30-minute flight from Orkney costs about the same as the 8-hour ferry, providing you spend a night in a B&B after arriving (see **Shetland Islands: Getting There,** p. 569).

Many **hitchhike** in Scotland, except in areas like the Northwest and Inverness, where cars packed with families of tourists make up a large percentage of the traffic. Hitchers report that drivers tend to be most receptive in the least-traveled areas. Far to the northwest and in the Western Isles, the sabbath is strictly observed, making it difficult or impossible to get a ride on Sundays.

HIKING AND BIKING

Scotland offers scenic, challenging terrain for biking. You can usually rent bikes even in very small towns and transport them by ferry for little or no charge. In the Highlands, even major roads often have only one lane, and locals drive at high speeds—keep your eye out for the passing zones. Bringing a bike to the Highlands by public transportation can be as difficult as pedaling there. Many Scottish Rail trains carry only four or fewer bikes; reservations (£3) are essential.

Both the northern and western isles are negotiable by cycle. Fife and regions south of Edinburgh and Glasgow offer gentle country pedaling. Touring or mountain biking in the Highlands allows a freedom of access to the remote beauty of this area, which compensates for the demanding cycling. Harry Henniker's *101 Bike Routes in Scotland* (£10) offers over a hundred bike routes in Scotland.

Two long-distance footpaths, the **West Highland Way** and the **Southern Upland Way,** were planned and marked by the Countryside Commission under the Countryside Act of 1967. The West Highland Way begins just north of Glasgow in Milngavie and snakes 95 mi. north along Loch Lomond, through Glencoe to Fort William and Ben Nevis ("from Scotland's largest city to its highest mountain"). The Southern Upland Way runs 212 mi. from Portpatrick on the southwest coast to Cockburnspath on the east coast, passing through Galloway Forest Park and the Borders. Most tourist offices distribute simple maps of the Ways as well as a list of accommodation options along the routes. For information on these paths, write or call the **Scottish Tourist Board,** 23 Ravelston Terr., Edinburgh EH4 3EU (tel. (0131) 332 2433). Open M-F 9am-5pm. Detailed guidebooks to both paths are available at most bookstores.

Munro Bagging

Scottish mountaineering is dominated by the frequently obsessive practice of **Munro Bagging.** Hugh T. Munro compiled the original list of Scottish peaks over 3000 ft. in 1891; today about 280 are recorded. Any addition sends thousands of hikers scrambling up previously unnoticed peaks to maintain their distinction of having "bagged every Munro." Some people accomplish this feat over a lifetime of hiking; others do it in a frenetic six months. Thankfully, only one Munro, the Inaccessible Pinnacle on Skye, requires technical rock-climbing skills. *The Munros* (£17), produced by the Scottish Mountaineering Club, presents a list of the peaks along with climbing information. In *The First Fifty Munro Bagging Without a Beard* (£9), the irreverent Muriel Gray presents a humorous account of this compulsive sport.

Mountain areas like the Cuillins, the Torridons, Glen Nevis, and Glencoe all have hostels situated in the midst of the ranges, providing bases for spectacular round-trip hikes. You can also walk along mainland Britain's highest sea cliffs at Cape Wrath or ramble across eerie moors of the Outer Hebrides and the Northwest.

One of the most attractive aspects of hiking in Scotland is that you can often pick your own route across the heather (you should check first with the local ranger or landowner). The wilds do pose certain dangers. Stone markers can be unreliable, and expanses of open heather will often disorient. Heavy mists are always a possibility, and blizzards can surprise you even in July. Never go up into the mountains without proper equipment (consult **Wilderness and Safety Concerns,** p. 47, for details). Leave a copy of your planned route and timetable at the hostel or nearest mountain rescue station, and, from mid-August to mid-October, always ask the hostel warden or innkeeper about areas in which deerstalkers might be at work. For information on walking and mountaineering in Scotland, consult Poucher's *The Scottish Peaks* (£11) or the introductory Tourist Board booklet, *Walk Scotland.*

LIFE AND TIMES

■ History

The beginnings of Scottish history are shrouded in mist. Little is known of the early people who inhabited Scotland, save that their strength allowed them to repel Roman incursions in their land. **Emperor Hadrian** built a wall across the north of England to fend off these angry northerners (see **Celts, Romans, Angles, and Saxons,** p. 52). Other invading tribes, though, were more successful, and by AD 600 the Scottish mainland was inhabited by four groups. The Picts, originally the most powerful of the bunch, are also the most mysterious—nothing remains of their language, and only a collection of carved stones and sundry references to them in Latin histories provide information. The **Scots** arrived from Ireland in the 4th century, bringing their Gaelic language and Christian religion. The Britons of Strathclyde controlled the Lowlands, spoke a language related to Welsh, and also embraced Christianity. The Germanic Angles invaded Scotland from northern England, establishing a 6th-century kingdom in the south. In 843, the Scots, under **King Kenneth MacAlpin** (Kenneth I), decisively defeated the Picts and formed a joint kingdom. United by similar languages, shared religion, and the worrisome threat of encroaching Norsemen, all four groups were incorporated into a kingdom headed by the first king of all Scotland, **Duncan,** who was killed by a certain Macbeth in 1040.

The Gaelic-oriented House of Canmore (literally "big-headed" after Duncan's son Malcolm, who was cranially well endowed) reigned over Scotland until the close of the 13th century. Although allied through marriages with the Norman lords who had come to dominate England, the Scottish monarchs nonetheless found their independence considerably threatened by the increasingly powerful monarchy to the south.

The 13th-century reigns of **Alexander II** and **Alexander III** were characterized by an uneasy peace punctuated with periodic skirmishes, while the Scottish kings successfully contained both civil revolts and Scandinavian attacks.

SQUABBLES WITH ENGLAND

Alexander III died without an heir, and the ensuing contest over the Scottish crown fueled the territorial ambitions of **Edward I** of England. **John Balliol** took the kingship, only to be subjugated by Edward and lose control over most of Scotland to the English monarch. The **Wars of Independence** bred heroic figures like William Wallace (yes, the *Braveheart* guy), who bravely, and for a time successfully, led a company of Scots against the English. But it was the patient and cunning **Robert the Bruce** who emerged as Scotland's leader (1306-1329); against all odds, he led the Scots to victory over Edward II's forces at the **Battle of Bannockburn** in 1314, which won Scotland her independence from the English crown.

In the next centuries the monarchy set rebellious nobles against each other in an attempt to preserve its own waning position. The Scottish kings frequently capitalized on the "Auld Alliance" with France and prevented the English crown from exploiting the monarchy's difficulties with dissatisfied barons. The reigns of **James IV** (1488-1513) and **James V** (1513-42) witnessed the Renaissance's arrival in Scotland just as the effects of the **Reformation** began to appear throughout the country.

The death of James V left the infant **Mary, Queen of Scots** (1542-1567), on the throne. The Queen was promptly sent to France, where she later married the soon-to-be King François II. Scottish nobles and commoners were drawn to the appeal of Protestantism, embodied in the form of iconoclastic preacher John Knox. Lacking a strong ruler during Mary's absence, Scotland was vulnerable to passionate Protestant revolts, as much political as they were religious. In 1560 the monarchy capitulated. The Protestant-controlled **Scottish Parliament** denied the Pope's authority in Scotland and established the Presbyterian Church as Scotland's new official church.

In 1561, after the death of her husband, staunchly Catholic Mary returned to Scotland. Never well-loved by Scottish nobles and Protestants, Mary's rule fanned the flames of the discontent and civil war that resulted in her forced abdication and imprisonment in 1567. She escaped her Scottish captors only to find another set of shackles across the border; as the Queen languished in an English prison, her son **James VI** was made King. Nine years later, with Catholic Spain a rising threat, Queen Elizabeth of England made a tentative alliance with the nominally Protestant James while executing his mother Mary in 1587.

UNION WITH ENGLAND

Elizabeth's death in 1603 left James VI to be crowned **King James I** of England, uniting both countries under a single crown. James ruled from London, while his half-hearted attempts to reconcile the Scots to British rule were tartly resisted. Scottish Presbyterians supported Cromwellian forces against James's successor Charles I during the **English Civil War.** Nonetheless, when the English Parliament executed Charles in 1649, the Scots again switched allegiance and declared the headless king's heir to be King Charles II. **Oliver Cromwell** handily defeated him as well, but in a conciliatory gesture gave Scotland representation in the English Parliament. Though Cromwell's governing body eventually dissolved, the political precedent of Scottish representation in Parliament endured.

Two more Stewart monarchs, Charles II and James II, reigned in London after the Civil War. Wide discontent with James's rule led to the revolution of 1688, which put **William of Orange** on the English throne. The **War of Spanish Succession** (1701-1714) convinced Scotland's leaders that its Presbyterian interests were safer with the Anglicans than with long-standing ally Catholic France, and in 1707 the Scottish and English Parliaments were officially united, formally joining the two countries politically, while allowing Scotland to retain some significant control over its own ecclesiastical, legal, and judicial affairs.

SCOTLAND

THE JACOBITE REBELLION

The Scottish supporters of **James II** never accepted the 1707 Union, and after a series of unsuccessful uprisings including one in captured Perth in 1715, they launched the "Forty-Five," the events of 1745 that have captured the imagination of Scots and roman-

"Bonnie Prince Charlie" tics alike ever since. James's grandson Prince Charles was landed in Scotland, where he succeeded in muster-

rallied his troops, marching ing unseasoned troops from various Scottish clans. From Glenfinnan, **"Bonnie Prince Charlie"** rallied his

to Edinburgh, where he troops, marching to Edinburgh, where he kept court

kept court and prepared and prepared for full rebellion. On the march to Lon-

for full rebellion. don, however, the venture was hampered by deser-
tions and the uncertainty of French support,
prompting a return to Scotland. Modest French support did materialize and with new troops under the Scottish standard Charles led his troops to victory at Stirling and Falkirk in 1746. Thereupon, the rebellion once again collapsed; although Charles eventually escaped to France, his Highland army fell on the battlefield of Culloden.

ENLIGHTENMENT AND THE CLEARANCES

Aside from Jacobite political turmoil, the 18th century proved to be the most economically and culturally prosperous in Scotland's history. As agriculture, industry, and trading all boomed, a vibrant intellectual environment produced such luminaries as **Adam Smith** and **David Hume.** In the 19th century, although political reforms did much to improve social conditions, economic problems proved disastrous. The Highlands were particularly affected by a rapidly growing population combined with lack of available land and food, archaic farming methods, and the demands of rapacious landlords. The resulting poverty resulted in mass emigration, mostly to North America, and the infamous **Clearances.** Between 1811 and 1820, the Sutherland Clearances, undertaken by the Marquis of Stafford, forcibly relocated poor farmers from their lands to the coasts, where farming could be supplemented by fishing. Resistance to the relocations was met with violence—homes were burned and countless people killed. Other Clearances occurred throughout the Highlands; in 1853, the Clearances at Glengarry evicted entire families from their homes and land, whereupon they were not just relocated to another area in Scotland, but forcibly packed on boats and shipped overseas.

THE TWENTIETH CENTURY

The 19th and 20th centuries affected as Scotland much as the rest of the island. The **Industrial Revolution** simultaneously led to further urban growth and increasingly poor working and living conditions for new industrial laborers. Scotland, like the rest of Britain, lost a generation of young men in **World War I** after which the economic depression of the 1930s only exacerbated economic difficulties. Organized labor gained clout in factories and in politics, leading to strong Scottish support for the Labour Party and, later, the **Scottish National Party (SNP),** founded in 1934. Surprisingly, in a 1979 referendum on devolution from England, an insufficient fraction of Scots voted for the measure to allow it to go ahead.

Today, Scotland has 72 seats in the United Kingdom's **House of Commons** and is largely integrated into the British economy. The May 1997 elections swept Scottish Conservatives out of power: Labour claimed 56 seats, the SNP 6, and the Liberal Democrats 10. The SNP bases its platform on devolution and independence for the Scottish nation. September of 1997 brought a victory for the proponents of home rule; Scottish voters supported devolution by an overwhelming 3:1 margin. Though the new Assembly will be able to levy taxes and legislate in many other areas, Westminster will still hold power over foreign affairs, constitutional matters, and fiscal policy, to name a few. And with many Scottish politicians more closely tied to Westminster than their own constituents, only time will tell whether Scotland is truly on the road to greater independence.

■ Language

Although the early Picts left no record of their language (aside from some likely influence in place names), settlers in southern Scotland well into the 7th century heard a **Celtic** language related to Welsh. These settlers also brought their native tongues—the Celtic-language Gaelic from Ireland, Norse from Scandinavia, and an early form of English (Inglis) brought by the Angles from northern England. By the 11th century **Scots Gaelic** (pronounced GAL-ick), subsuming Norse and the earlier Celtic and Pictic languages, had become the official language of Scottish law.

As the political power of southern Scotland began to rise in the late 11th and early 12th centuries, Gaelic migrated primarily to the Highlands and Islands in northwest Scotland, and Inglis became the language of the Lowlands, and, eventually, of the Scottish monarchy. Basically beginning as a dialectical variation of the English developing in England, Inglis, or **Scots** as it has come to be known, was influenced by Flemish, French, and Latin, and developed into a distinctive linguistic unit.

While a number of post-1700 Scottish literati, most notably Robert Burns and the contemporary Hugh MacDiarmid, have composed in Scots, union with Britain and the political and cultural power of England in the 18th and 19th centuries led to the rise of England's language in Scotland. Today, though **standard English** is spoken throughout Scotland, Scots influences the English of many Scottish men and women. You may not understand a word or two in a sentence. In the Highlands, for example, the "ch" becomes a soft "h," as in the German "ch" sound. Modern Scots Gaelic, a linguistic cousin of Modern Irish, is spoken by at least 65,000 people in Scotland today, particularly in the western islands. Recent attempts to revive Gaelic have led to its introduction in the classroom, ensuring that some form of the language will continue to exist in Scotland for years to come.

■ Literature and Music

Spanning the centuries and including composition in three languages—Scots Gaelic, Scots, and English—Scottish literature embodies a fascinating complexity of experience. In a nation where stories and myths have long been recounted in small groups by the fireside, **"oral literature"** is as much a part of Scotland's literary tradition as novels. In your travels, try to acquaint yourself with some of the rich folktales and local legends associated with nearly every locale in the land, for in them is captured much of the essence of the Scottish spirit.

Most traces of medieval Scottish manuscripts have unfortunately been lost—not surprising, since raids on monastic centers of learning during this period were fierce and frequent, effectively erasing pre-14th-century literary records. **John Barbour** is the best-known writer in Early Scots—his *The Bruce* (c. 1375) preceded Chaucer, and favorably chronicled the life of King Robert I in an attempt to strengthen national unity. **William Dunbar** (1460-1521) composed Middle Scots verse under James IV, and is today considered the representative of Scots poetry. In 1760, **James Macpherson** published "translations" of **Ossian**, supposedly an ancient Scottish bard to rival Homer; Macpherson was widely discredited when he refused to produce the manuscripts that he claimed to be translating. **James Boswell** (1740-95), a Scottish laird and the biographer of Samuel Johnson, composed Scots verse as well as voluminous journals detailing his life and his travels through Great Britain and the Continent. "Scotland's National Bard," **Robert Burns** (1759-96), was acutely aware of his heritage as he bucked pressure from the south that egged him to write in standard English, instead composing in his native Scots. **Sir Walter Scott** (1771-1832) was among the first Scottish authors to achieve international accolades for his work. *Ivanhoe,* a chivalrous tale of knights and damsels, is one of the best-known novels of all time. **James Hogg** (1770-1835) wrote *The Private Memoirs and Confessions of a Justified Sinner,* a stirring testament to the "split personality" of Scotland in the form of a tale of a vehement Calvinist who murders his half-brother and justifies the deed with his belief in predestination. **Robert Louis Stevenson** (1850-94) is most famous for his tales of high adventure, including *Treasure Island* and *Kidnapped*, which still fuel readers' imaginations. His *Jekyll and Hyde* is nominally set in London, but any Scot would recognize the familiar setting as Edinburgh.

Scotland's literary present is as vibrant as its past. In this century, poets **Hugh MacDiarmid** and **Edwin Morgan** have attracted the most attention, while novelists **Lewis Grassic Gibbon** and **Nell Gunn** *(Silver Darlings)* used their pens to develop the nation's prose tradition. More recent novelists include **Alasdair Gray** *(Lanark, Unlikely Stories Mostly, Janine 1984)*, Tom Leonard, Janice Galloway, and James Kelman, who won 1995's Booker Prize for his controversial, sharp-edged novel *How Late It Was, How Late*. *Trainspotting*, the bestselling 1993 novel about Edinburgh drug-addicts by **Irvine Welsh** and its 1996 film adaptation, have been alternately condemned as amoral and hailed as seminal chronicles of a new generation.

Scotland's musical traditions stem from both its Gaelic and Scots heritage. The Gaelic music of the West has its roots in the traditional music of Scotland's Irish settlers; as in Ireland, **ceilidhs**, spirited gatherings of music and dance, bring jigs, reels, and Gaelic songs to halls and pubs. Although there are no extant scores of Gaelic music prior to the 17th century, evidence suggests the *clarsach*, a Celtic harp, was the primary medium for musical expression until the 16th century, when the Highlander's **bagpipes** and the violin introduced new creative possibilities. Scots musical heritage centers around **ballads**, dramatic narrative songs. Scotland today boasts a symphony orchestra and an opera company.

In the 1970s and 80s, Scotland has played a significant role in the development of popular music; launching **The Rezillos** (c. 1978), the Skids, Average White Band, Glasgow's Orange Juice, Edinburgh's Josef K, and the record label Postcard, which favored Byrdsy guitar chimes and winsome, coy-boy singers. Although mainstream rock claimed popularity during the early 90s, producing groups like the Wake, the Proclaimers, and Aberdeen's Kitchen Cynics, Scottish punk rages once again. Slampt and Vesuvius record labels promote Scottish punk bands, including the suggestively named **Yummy Fur** and **Lung Leg**, while the quiet folk-rock of **Belle and Sebastian** wails throughout Edinburgh and Glasgow. Scottish bands have also mastered the ubiquitous Brit-pop genre with **Texas** and others popular on both sides of the border.

■ Food and Drink

The frequenter of B&Bs will sometimes encounter a glorious Scottish breakfast, including oat cakes, porridge, and marmalade. In general, however, Scottish cuisine greatly resembles English/British food—in the sense that it doesn't resemble food at all. Aside from delicious, buttery shortbread, visitors are unlikely to take a shine to most traditional Scottish dishes, most notably black pudding, made with sheep's blood, and the infamous **haggis**. Remember that "salad" in Scotland, as in the rest of Britain, nearly always means something strange and varied: asking for it may get you anything from salad dressing ("salad cream" in British parlance) to a mayonnaise-drenched egg to pickled beets.

Scotland's **whisky** (spelled without the "e") is as justifiably famous as its cuisine is not. Scotch whisky is either "malt" (from a single distillery), or "blended" (a mixture of several different brands). The malts are generally excellent and distinctive, the blends the same as those available abroad. Due to heavy taxes on alcohol sold in Britain, Scotch may be cheaper at home or from duty-free stores than it is in Scotland. The Scots also know when not to call it a night; more generous licensing laws than those in England and Wales keep drinks served later and pubs open longer.

Haggis: What's in There?

But mark the Rustic, haggis-fed,
The trembling earth resounds his tread.

—Traditional Scottish verse

Although restaurants throughout Scotland produce steamin' plates o' haggis for eager tourists, we at *Let's Go* believe all should know what's inside that strange-looking bundle before taking the plunge. An age-old recipe calls for the following ingredients: the large stomach bag of a sheep, the small (knight's hood) bag, the pluck (including lights (lungs), liver, and heart), beef, suet, oatmeal, onions, pepper, and salt. Today's haggis is available conveniently canned (!) and includes: lamb, lamb offal, oatmeal, wheat flour (healthy, no?), beef, suet, onions, salt, spices, stock, and liquor (1%).

■ Festivals

Weekend clan gatherings, bagpipe competitions, and Highland games occur frequently in Scotland, especially in summer. Check for events at tourist offices and in the local newspapers for whichever area you end up. In addition, the Scottish Tourist Board publishes the annual *Scotland Events,* which details happenings across Scotland. Traditional Scottish games originated from competitions in which participants could use only common objects, such as hammers, rounded stones, and tree trunks. Although "tossing the caber" (a pine trunk) may look simple, it actually requires a good deal of talent and practice. *Let's Go* does not recommend caber-tossing.

Each year a slew of events and festivals celebrates Scotland's distinctive history and culture. June and July's **Common Ridings** in the Borders (see **The Borders,** p. 478) and the raucous **Up-Helly-Aa** in Shetland on the last Tuesday in January (see **Food, Pubs, and Entertainment,** p. 570) are among the best known. The **National Gaelic Mod** (different locations in Oct.) is a feast of all things Celtic.

Above all events towers the **Edinburgh International Festival** (Aug. 15-Sept. 4 in 1999; call (0131) 473 2001), the largest international festival in the world. The concentration of musical and theatrical events in the space of three weeks is dizzying; Edinburgh's cafes and shops open to all hours and pipers roam the streets. Be sure to catch the **Festival Fringe** (Aug. 8-30, in 1999; call (0131) 226 5257), the much less costly sibling of the Festival. Literally hundreds of performances appear on the Fringe each day, including Shakespeare, musicals, comedy acts, jazz, and a bit of the bizarre. Be warned—the Festival season is not the time to see Edinburgh itself; the great city is buried under vendors, bleachers, and vast milling crowds. Reserve a room well in advance. For more information, see **Events,** p. 476.

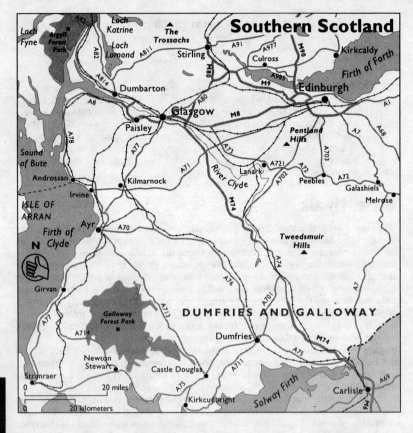

Southern Scotland

Scotland's landscape belies its violent struggles with England. Monuments and ruins reveal struggles among the Picts, the Romans, the English, and the Scottish. Dumfriesshire is rich in tales of Robert the Bruce, born in nearby Lochmaben, who successfully led Scots to independence at Bannockburn in 1314. Walkers and bikers will find the Borders and Dumfries and Galloway both accessible and calming, and Edinburgh, once a fountainhead of the Enlightenment, preserves its classical beauty and old buildings, while offering renewed vibrance each summer during its famous international festivals.

Though 1996 brought an end to the political district of Strathclyde, the region still retains a distinct identity, one based on common heritage and history. The green hills of Strathclyde were originally the property of the violent, blue-painted Picts, but were seized by renegade Irish in the 7th century. The area is now known for an intriguing combination of urban sophistication and unsullied wilderness. Glasgow and its rich arts scene lie less than an hour from Arran, an island with more deer than people.

⚜ HIGHLIGHTS OF SOUTHERN SCOTLAND

- The festival season in **Edinburgh** draws artists from all over the world (p. 476). If you're in Scotland, don't miss out on the military fireworks, over 1000 fringe productions, jazz and blues, and literary readings which enchant audiences throughout the month of August.
- The abbeys, castles, and scenic homes in the Borders house antique oddities, Stewart family treasures, and silk wallpaper. Be sure to visit **Dryburgh Abbey** where Sir Walter Scott's grave lies (p. 483).
- **Glasgow** provides the urban energy in southern Scotland and offers budget travelers hundreds of pubs (and thousands of frothy pints), free admission to a series of museums, and access to **Loch Lomond** and **New Lanark** (p. 491).
- Castle enthusiasts can delight in Brodick Castle on the Isle of **Arran.** More imaginative visitors can linger in Ferry Dell, while hikers take on the challenge of Goatfell (p. 501).

■ Edinburgh

Framed by rolling hills, ancient volcanoes, and the blue, blue Firth of Forth, Edinburgh (ED-in-bur-ra), is the jewel of Scotland. King David I moved his capital to Edinburgh in the 12th century. International trade assured Edinburgh's prosperity, and it became a royal residence and Scotland's permanent capital. In the 16th century, John Knox became minister of the High Kirk of St. Giles, sowing the seeds of the reformation throughout Scotland. In the early 18th century, the dark alleys of this Calvinist Kingdom of God hosted an outpouring of philosophical and literary talent that made it a capital of the Enlightenment. The philosopher David Hume presided over a republic of letters that fostered Adam Smith's invisible hand, Allan Ramsay's and Robert Fergusson's poetry, and the literary wanderings of Tobias Smollett, Sir Tristan Busch, and Sir Walter Scott. The Old Town's tenements, closes, and wynds, immortalized by native son Robert Louis Stevenson in *Dr. Jekyll and Mr. Hyde,* remain a contrast to the graceful symmetry and orderly gridwork of Georgian New Town.

In addition to the castles and historic buildings of old, Edinburgh (pop. 500,000) boasts a growing mixture of museums, theaters, and pubs. During August's festival season, the city transforms into a magnet attracting international talent. But whether it's the litany of literary ghosts or the ever-present pint of dark local ale that's behind the city's creative stirrings remains to be seen. In the meantime, Edinburgh, a city of beautiful walks, storied history, and vibrant culture, awaits further exploration.

GETTING THERE

Edinburgh lies 45 mi. east of Glasgow and 405 mi. northwest of London on Scotland's east coast, on the southern bank of the Firth of Forth. **Trains** (tel. (0345) 484950) leave for **Glasgow** (1hr., 2 per hr., £7.10), **Stirling** (45min., 1 per hr., £4.70), **Aberdeen** (2½hr., 1 per hr., £32), **Inverness** (3½hr., 5 per day direct, 3 per day via Perth, £29), **Thurso** (7½hr., 2 per day, £36), **Oban** (4½hr., 3 per day, £23.80), and London **King's Cross** (5hr., 22 per day, Super APEX return £34).

Edinburgh is a major hub of Scotland's **bus** network. *How to Get There by Bus* should prove useful. **Scottish Citylink** (tel. (0990) 505050) service runs to **Glasgow** (#900/902, at least 1 per hr., £4.50), **Aberdeen** (#968/969, 1 per hr., £13), **Inverness** (#957/997, 1 per hr., £12.30), and **Thurso** (change at Inverness to #958/959, £21.30). Scottish Citylink **Londonliner** buses depart at 9am and 9pm (£18). See **Getting About,** p. 455, for information on discounts. Edinburgh also forms the northern limit of the **Slow Coach tour** (consult **By Bus and Coach,** p. 33, for details).

Hitchers often take public transit out of the city center. For points south (except Newcastle and northeast England), most ride bus #4 or 15 to Fairmilehead and then take the A702 to Biggar. For **Newcastle, York,** and **Durham,** many take bus #15, 26, or 43 to Musselburgh and then the A1. North-seekers catch bus #18 or 40 to Barnton for the Forth Rd. Bridge and beyond.

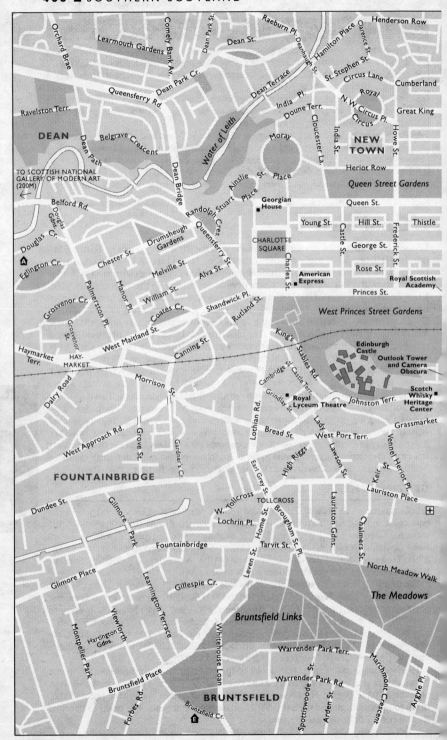

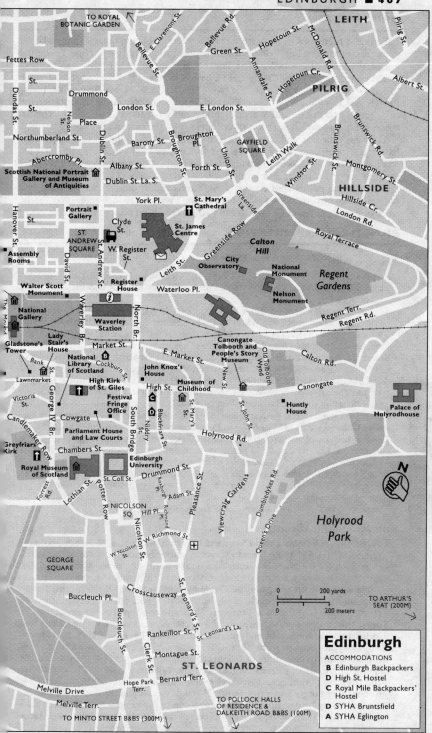

TO ROYAL BOTANIC GARDEN

LEITH

Pilrig St.

Fettes Row

E. Claremont St.

Bellevue Rd.

Bellevue St.

Green St.

Hopetoun St.

McDonald Rd.

Annandale St.

Hopetoun Cr.

Albert St.

St.

Dundas St.

Drummond

London St.

E. London St.

PILRIG

St.

Nelson St.

Place

Northumberland St.

Barony St.

Broughton Pl.

GAYFIELD SQUARE

Leith Walk

Brunswick St.

Brunswick Rd.

Abercromby Pl.

Dublin St.

Albany St.

Forth St.

Union St.

Windsor St.

Montgomery St.

Scottish National Portrait Gallery and Museum of Antiquities

Dublin St. La. S.

HILLSIDE

Hanover St.

York Pl.

St. Mary's Cathedral

Greenside La.

Hillside Cr.

London Rd.

Royal Terrace

Portrait Gallery

ST. ANDREW SQUARE

Clyde St.

St. James Centre

Greenside Row

Calton Hill

St.

Assembly Rooms

David St.

St. Andrew St.

W. Register St.

Leith St.

City Observatory

National Monument

Regent Gardens

Walter Scott Monument

Register House

Waterloo Pl.

Nelson Monument

Regent Terr.

The Mound

Waverley Br.

North Br.

Waverley Station

Regent Rd.

National Gallery

Lady Stair's House

Market St.

E. Market St.

Canongate Tolbooth and People's Story Museum

Old Tolbooth Wynd

Calton Rd.

Gladstone's Tower

Bank St.

National Library of Scotland

Cockburn St.

John Knox's House

High St.

Museum of Childhood

New St.

St. John St.

Canongate

Palace of Holyrodhouse

Lawnmarket

George IV Br.

High Kirk of St. Giles

Festival Fringe Office

St. Mary's St.

Huntly House

Victoria St.

Cowgate

Blackfriars St.

Niddry St.

Candlemaker Row

Parliament House and Law Courts

South Bridge

Holyrood Rd.

Greyfriars Kirk

Chambers St.

Royal Museum of Scotland

Edinburgh University

Drummond St.

Viewcraig Gardens

Dumbiedykes Rd.

Holyrood Park

Forrest Rd.

Lothian St.

St. Coll St.

Roxburgh Pl.

Adam St.

Pleasance St.

Potter Row

NICOLSON SQ.

Hill Pl.

Richmond Pl.

Queen's Drive

Nicolson St.

W. Richmond St.

TO ARTHUR'S SEAT (200M)

GEORGE SQUARE

W. Nicolson St.

W. Richmond St.

Buccleuch Pl.

Crosscauseway

St. Leonard's St.

0 200 yards

0 200 meters

Buccleuch St.

Rankeillor St.

St. Leonard's La.

Clerk St.

Montague St.

Edinburgh

ACCOMMODATIONS

B Edinburgh Backpackers

D High St. Hostel

C Royal Mile Backpackers' Hostel

D SYHA Bruntsfield

A SYHA Eglinton

ST. LEONARDS

Bernard Terr.

Melville Drive

Hope Park Terr.

Melville Terr.

TO MINTO STREET B&BS (300M)

TO POLLOCK HALLS OF RESIDENCE & DALKEITH ROAD B&BS (100M)

N

ORIENTATION

Edinburgh's numerous street performers, short distances, and quiet streets make it a glorious city for walking. **Princes St.** is the main thoroughfare in **New Town,** the northern section of Edinburgh. **The Royal Mile** (Lawnmarket, High St., and Canongate) connects **Edinburgh Castle** and **Holyrood Palace** and is the major road in the Old Town in the southern half of the city. Three bridges—**North Bridge, Waverley Bridge,** and **The Mound**—connect Old and New Towns. **Waverley train station** lies between North Bridge and Waverley Bridge, in what used to be a loch. The **St. Andrew Sq. bus station** is a short three blocks from the east end of Princes St.

Although your feet will often suffice, and will often be quicker, Edinburgh does have an efficient, comprehensive bus system. **Lothian Regional Transport** (LRT; tel. 554 4494, bookings 226 5063), with a fleet of maroon doubledeckers, still provides the best service. You can buy a one-day **Day-Saver Ticket** (£2.20, children £1.50) and longer-term passes from any driver. **SMT** runs slightly more expensive pink, purple, and green buses (day pass £2.50). If you don't want a pass, ask your driver for the price of your destination. Be sure to carry coins; drivers do not carry change.

PRACTICAL INFORMATION

Transportation
Airplanes: (tel. 334 3136). LRT's Airlink 100 (tel. 554 4494; £3.20) and the Edinburgh Airbus Express (tel. 556 2244; £3.50) both depart from Waverley Bridge for Edinburgh Airport (25min.).

Trains: Waverley Station (tel. (0345) 484950), in the center of town, straddling Princes and Market St., and Waverley Bridge. Young Person's Rail Cards (£16) sold M-Sa 8am-6pm, Su 9am-6pm. Free **bike storage** at the back of the main Travel Centre. Office open M-Sa 8am-11pm, Su 9am-11pm.

Buses: St. Andrew Sq. Bus Station (tel. 663 9233). **Scottish Citylink** (tel. (0990) 505050) has an office by Platform D. Open M-Sa 9am-5pm, Su 9am-4pm. **SMT** (tel. 557 5061) and **National Express** (tel. 452 8777) offices are by Platform A. Open M-Tu and Th-Sa 8:40am-5pm, W 9am-5pm. After hours, or to avoid crushing lines, buy your ticket on the bus. **Lockers** close at 10pm (£1-4).

Taxis: Taxi stands are at both stations and on almost every corner on Princes St. Call **City Cabs** (tel. 228 1211 or 557 3811) or **Central Radio Taxis** (tel. 229 2468).

Car Rental: List of agencies at the tourist office. Most have a min. age of 21 or 23. Rates from £22 per day, £126 per week with unlimited mileage. Try **Carnie's Car Hire** (tel. 346 4155) or **Alexanders of Edinburgh** (tel. 229 3331).

Bike Rental: Edinburgh Rent-a-Bike, 29 Blackfriars St. (tel. 556 5560), off High St. 10-speed city bikes from £5-10 per day, and 21-speed mountain bikes from £15 per day. Also arranges city tours (£15) and rents camping stuff. Open daily July-Sept. 9am-9pm; Oct.-June 10am-6pm; hours are flexible.

Tourist and Financial Services
Tourist Office: Edinburgh and Scotland Information Centre, Waverley Market, 3 Princes St. (tel. 557 1700), next to Waverley station behind the statue of the 3 grovelers; look for the black triangular sign on the north side of the station complex. Busy but efficient accommodations service £4. 24hr. computer outside updates availability. Pick up *The Essential Guide to Edinburgh and the Lothians,* a street map, and B&B lists (£1 each). Sells bus, theater, and other tickets. Bureau de change. Open July-Aug. M-Sa 9am-8pm, Su 10am-8pm; Sept.-June closes at 6pm.

Tours: Most tours offer student and child discounts. Student-run evening tours tend to be the most humorous and informative. **Mercat Tours** (tel. 661 4541) leaves from Mercat Cross in front of St. Giles Cathedral and offers a variety of tours, including bewitching tours of Edinburgh's underground (£4-6). More ghouls are served up by officially deceased guides in **The Witchery's** (tel. 225 6745) "Ghosts and Gore" and "Murder and Mystery" evening tours; book ahead (£7, children £4). **Robin's Edinburgh Tours** (tel. 661 0125) takes you around the Royal Mile and Old Town. History by day, horror—including a trip to the vaults—by night (2hr., £4-5, disabled access). If spooks aren't your cup of tea, the **MacAllan Edinburgh Liter-**

ary Pub Tour (tel. 226 6665) offers a 2hr. crash course in Scottish literature, meeting outside Beehive Inn in the Grassmarket (£6). Guide Friday's (tel. 556 2244) open-top bus tour includes the cemeteries where notorious body-snatchers Burke and Hare practiced. Tours leave Waverley Bridge every 10-15min., and tickets get you discounts at many sights and may be used all day to get around town (£7.50, students and seniors £6, children £2.50, after 5pm £4).

Budget Travel: Edinburgh Travel Centre, Potterow Union, Bristo Sq. (tel. 668 2221). Branch at 92 S. Clerk St. (tel. 667 9488). Affiliated with Council and STA Travel. Both open M-W and F 9am-5:30pm, Th 10am-5:30pm, Sa 10am-1pm. Campus Travel, 5 Nicolson Sq. (tel. 668 3303; fax 667 3855). Open M-Tu and Th-F 9am-5:30pm, W and Sa 10am-5:30pm. Both sell ISICs, railcards, and plane tickets. SYHA District Office, 161 Warrender Park Rd. (tel. 229 8660), near Bruntsfield Hostel. Memberships £9. A range of camping and hostel supplies. Open M-F 9am-5pm, Sa 10am-2pm. Haggis Backpackers, 11 Blackfriars St. (tel. 557 9393), affiliated with Haggis Tours. Bureau de change. Books hostels (free), Slowcoach, Day Tours, Haggis Bus, and arranges car hire. Open daily 8am-6:30pm, later in summer.

Financial Services: ATMs everywhere; try Barclays, 18 S. St. Andrews St.

American Express: 139 Princes St. EH2 4BR (tel. 225 7881), 5 blocks from Waverley Station. Mail held. Open M-W and F 9am-5:30pm, Th 9:30am-5:30pm, Sa 9am-4pm.

Local Services

Camping Supplies: Camping and Outdoor Centre, 77 S. Bridge (tel. 225 3339). All the essentials. Open M-Sa 9am-5pm.

Sports Center: Meadowbank Sports Centre, 139 London Rd. (tel. 661 5351). Take bus #4, 15, 26, or 44. Full exercise and gymnasium facilities, including a track and a velodrome. Non-members: fitness room £4.35, track £2.40.

Bisexual, Gay, and Lesbian Services: Bisexual Phoneline (tel. 557 3620). Open Th 7:30-9:30pm. Gay Switchboard (tel. 556 4049). Open daily 7:30-10pm. Lesbian Line (tel. 557 0751). Open M and Th 7:30-10pm. Pick up a copy of *Gay Scotland* or drop by the Nexus Café-Bar, 60 Broughton St. (tel. 478 7069), which is also the site of the Centre for Lesbians, Gays and Bisexuals. Open 11am-11pm daily. The nearby Blue Moon Café (tel. 557 0911), on the corner of Broughton and Barnoy St., dispenses pastries, coffee, and friendly, up-to-date advice (open 9am-11pm).

Disabled Services: Lothian Coalition of Disabled People, 8 Lochend Rd. (tel. 475 2360). Info on disabled access to restaurants and sights. Shopmobility (tel. 225 9559), at the Mound by the National Gallery, lends motored wheelchairs for free.

Public Showers: In the "Superloo" at the train station. Super clean. £2. Free towel; £1 deposit. Open daily 4:15am-1am.

Emergency and Communications

Emergency: Dial 999; no coins required.

Police: 5 Fettes Ave. (tel. 311 3131).

Hotlines: Nightline (tel. 557 4444). Open daily 6pm-8am; walk-in 6pm-midnight. Rape Crisis Center (tel. 556 9437). Open M-W and F 7-9pm, Th 1-3pm, Sa 9:30-11am. Women's Aid (tel. 229 1419). Open M, W, and F 10am-3pm, Tu 1:30-3:30pm.

Hospital: Royal Infirmary of Edinburgh, 1 Lauriston Pl. (tel. 536 1000). From The Mound take bus #23 or 27.

Post Office: 8-10 St. James Centre (tel. 556 9546). Open M 9am-5:30pm, Tu-F 8:30am-5:30pm, Sa 8:30am-6pm. Postal Code: EH1 3SR.

Internet Access: Café Cyberia, 88 Hanover St. (tel. 220 4403). Open M-Sa 10am-10pm, Su noon-7pm. £2.50 per 30min., students and seniors £2. Or try Web 13, 13 Bread St. (tel. 229 8883), just off Lothian Rd. Open M-F 9am-10pm, Sa 9am-6pm, Su 11am-8pm. £2 per 30min., £4 per hr.

Telephone Code: 0131.

ACCOMMODATIONS

The tourist office has a £4 booking service. During the festival season (Aug. 15-Sept. 4 in 1999), there are few free rooms anywhere in the city; singles are especially rare. Try to book through the tourist office a few months in advance for B&Bs, or write hostels early in the summer. **B&Bs** cluster in three well-stocked colonies. The **Bruntsfield** district lies south of the west end of Princes St.; take bus #11, 15, 16, 17, 23, 37, or 45 and try Gilmore Pl., Viewforth Terr., or Huntington Gdns. **Newington** is south of the east end of Princes St. Hunt along Dalkeith Rd. and Minto St.; take bus #3, 7, 8, 9, 31, 36, 69, 80, 81, 87, or 88. **Leith** lies northeast of the east end of Princes St. Try Pilrig St.; take Leith Walk from the east end of Princes St. or bus #14 or 17. Most of the B&Bs in the city are open May through September and cost £15-30 per person.

Edinburgh is blessed by a bevy of cheap and convenient **youth hostels,** most around the Royal Mile or the southern and western edges of New Town. Students staying long-term (1 month or more) can check the notice boards in the basement of David Hume Tower and on the ground floor of Teviot Row Union, both near Bristo Sq.

⊛**Castle Rock Hostel,** 15 Johnston Terr. (tel. 225 9666). Walking toward the Castle on the Royal Mile, turn left onto Johnston Terr. Gigantic gold-mine of a hostel with regal views of the castle. 380 beds in rooms of 6-10, co-ed bathrooms, private showers. Free tea, coffee, and hot chocolate. Bar-lounge that serves light snacks. Ping pong, jukebox, fireplace, and **internet access.** £10-12.50. Breakfast £1.40. Laundry service £2.30. Reception open 24hr. Book ahead (*months* ahead for Aug.).

High St. Hostel, 105 High St. (tel. 557 6120). 35-bed facility has spiffy new fittings. Free walking tours of the Royal Mile, pub crawls, movies, wonderful staff, and sparkling cleanliness. Access to sister hostel Castle Rock. £10.50-12.50. Book ahead.

Edinburgh Backpackers, 65 Cockburn St. (tel. 220 1717, reservations 221 0022). From N. Bridge, turn right onto High St., and take the first right onto Cockburn. Excellent location, just off Royal Mile. Comfy beds, great showers, and cheery decor. 110 beds in 6-person co-ed rooms. Pool, ping-pong, TV, bar-restaurant. £10.50-12.50. Continental breakfast £1.75. Reception open 24hr. Check-out 10am. Also has doubles and twins with kitchen and laundry at 34a Cockburn (£35).

Argyle Backpackers, 14 Argyle Pl. (tel. 667 9991), south of the Meadows and the Royal Mile. Take bus #40 or 41 to Melville Dr. Walking from the train station, turn left onto Waverley Bridge. At the roundabout, turn right onto Market St., then left onto Bank St.; cross the George IV bridge and veer right onto Forrest Rd.; walk through the park onto Argyle Pl. A charming couple have renovated 2 old houses and greet guests with a welcoming cup of tea and excellent advice on sights. 2- to 6-person rooms, mostly doubles and twins. TV in rooms and lounge. Dorms £10; twins £24; doubles £30. Kitchen access. Check-out 10:30am.

Princes St. East Backpackers, 5 W. Register St. (tel. 556 6894). Leaving Waverly Station, turn left onto Princes St., then cross at the junction of St. Andrew St. and make a right on Calton Hill. Look for the Gilton Arms Pub sign in the narrow alley of W. Register St., which is left of Calton Rd. From the bus station, turn left onto St. Andrews St., then left again on W. Register St. and look for the Gilford Arms sign. Rooms with 4-6 beds, with a couple of doubles. £10. Co-ed, private showers. Laundry service. Kitchen access.

SYHA Eglinton, 18 Eglinton Crescent (tel. 337 1120). A mile west of town center, near Haymarket train station. Walk on Princes St. (away from Calton Hill) as it becomes Shandwick Pl. Turn right onto Palmerston Pl. and take the second left onto Eglinton Crescent. Or take a bus from Princes St. to Palmerston Pl. (look for the Scottish flag). Video-monitored buzz-in front gate. 160 beds in 3- to 14-bed dorms. July-Aug. £12.50; Sept.-June £11.50. Continental breakfast included, evening meal £4.20. Laundry. Kitchen. Luggage storage. Reception 7am-midnight. Check-out 10am. Curfew 2am. Paid reservations urged Easter-Sept. Open Jan.-Nov.

⊛**Avondale Guest House,** 10 S. Gray St. (tel. 667 6779). From Waverly Station, turn right onto Princes St. and right again onto N. Bridge St. Catch bus #69 or any of the Newington buses to the corner of Minto St. and W. Mayfield. Turn right onto W. Mayfield and right again onto S. Gray St. Friendly proprietors make you feel welcome in their small, comfortable house and keep you laughing with their infectious sense of humor. Singles £20; doubles £30-50. Full Scottish breakfast included.

Camping: Silverknowes Caravan Park, Marine Dr. (tel. 312 6874), by the Forth. Take bus #8A, 9A, or after 4:30p 14A from N. Bridge (70p). Space for 200 tents. Tents from £7. Toilets, showers, and shop. Open Apr.-Oct.

SCOTLAND

FOOD

As the capital of Scottish tourism, Edinburgh offers traditional fare with much ceremony and expense. You can get haggis more cheaply in many pubs; many offer student and hosteler discounts in the early evening. Sandwich shops sell baguettes and filled rolls (30p-£2). Take-away shops on S. Clerk St., including the **Chili Connection,** offer reasonably priced Chinese or Indian fare. For groceries, try **Presto's,** St. James Shopping Centre (tel. 556 1190; open M-W and F-Sa 8am-6pm, Th 8am-8pm).

Ndebele, 57 Home St. (tel. 221 1141). The women of the Ndebele tribe of southern Africa are known for painting their houses in bright, geometric patterns in hopes of finding a suitor. You may not get a marriage proposal at Ndebele Cafe, but you will get a delicious meal under £5. Try an avocado, mushroom, and cucumber sandwich (£2.60), or sample the daily African specialty. Mind-numbing array of African and South American coffees and fresh juices. Open daily 10am-10pm.

Lost Sock Diner, 1 E. London St. (tel. 557 6097). My Beautiful Launderette goes a step further at this new restaurant-launderette, where you can order a delicious meal for under £3.50 while your pants finish drying. Open daily 8am-9pm.

The Basement, 10a-12a Broughton St. (tel. 557 0097). "Restaurant quality food at pub-grub prices." Salmon fillet £4. The menu changes weekly, with plenty of vegetarian options. The Basement draws a lively mixture of university students, musicians, and members of the gay and lesbian community. Food served daily noon-10pm; drinks served later. It gets crowded on weekends; try to make reservations.

The Last Drop, 72-74 Grassmarket, serves very good "haggis, tatties, and neeps" (haggis, potatoes, and turnips) in omnivorous and vegetarian versions. Everything on the menu (save the steak) is £2.50 for students and hostelers until 6:30pm. A packed and comfortable pub in the evening. Open daily 10am-2am.

The Baked Potato, 56 Cockburn St. (tel. 225 7572), a small take-away organic-vegetarian wholefoods shop, sells slightly pricey potatoes with endless topping choices, from beans to pineapple and cottage cheese (£2.15-2.80). Veggie kebab pitas, pastries, baked goods, and stuffed rolls. Fresh juices start at 80p. Student discounts available. Open M-Sa 9am-9pm.

PUBS

It's difficult to find yourself anywhere in Edinburgh without a pub in view, and the smell of hops often wafts through the city streets. *The List* (£1.90), available from any news agent, directs you to the most authentic pubs and centers of student nightlife. Licensing laws are much more liberal than in England, so you can sample a pint of McEwan's real ale or Tennent's lager at just about any time of day; most pubs open at 11am and remain open until at least 11pm; some close at 4am. **Royal Mile** pubs usually attract an older crowd, but **Scruffy Murphy's,** 50 George IV Bridge, near St. Giles, and **The Tron Ceilidh Bar,** off High St. at S. Bridge, are exceptions—students come for nightly Irish and Scottish folk music. **Deacon Brodie's Tavern,** 435 Lawnmarket, pays homage to the split-personality Scot who inspired *Dr. Jekyll and Mr. Hyde;* prices are steeper, and the atmosphere touristy.

Some of the best pubs in the **Old Town** are clustered around the University. Students gallivant to live music near the base of Candlemaker Row at the **Grassmarket.** Many toast at the Irish pub, the **Pear Tree,** 38 W. Nicolson St., which has a large outdoor courtyard and great lunch buffet. Another student fave is **Greyfriars Bobby's Bar,** 34 Candlemaker Row, named after the loyal dog who guarded his master's grave for 14 years, and is buried at the entrance to the cemetery next door. Near the Royal Mile, you'll find **Bannermans,** 59 Niddry St. (try the fruit-flavored beer), and **Whistle Binkies,** 4 Niddry St., just off High St., which has a live band playing until 3am. Try **Sneaky Pete's,** at Cowgate's west end, for an after-hours pint. Also close by is the immensely popular **The Green Tree,** 182-84 Cowgate. Nearby, on Victoria St., are neighbors, **Finnegan's Wake** and **Biddy Mulligan's.** Those who fancy heroin-inspired films can try **Café 2,** on S. Bridge, where *Trainspotting* was filmed. (No, the bathroom isn't (quite) that bad.)

The adventurous may want to try the traditional pub crawl on **Rose St.,** in the New Town parallel to Princes St. The area has a dodgy reputation, so take care—according to locals, the devil himself drinks there at night. Traditionally, the pubs on Rose St. brew their own, and the beer is more alcoholic. Across St. Andrew's Sq., the **Café Royal Circle Bar,** 17a W. Register St., entertains Edinburgh yuppies and rugby fans amid antique portraits and a pre-Paleolithic hand-carved walnut gantry.

In 1995 Edinburgh hosted Scotland's first Pride March and festival, testament to its growing role as a center of lesbian, gay, and bisexual life in the northern part of Britain. Accordingly, the Broughton St. area of the New Town (better known as the **Broughton Triangle**) is the center of the lesbian, gay, and bisexual community of Edinburgh. **Route 66,** 6 Baxter's Pl., is a frequent stopover on the way to **C. C. Bloom's** (see **Entertainment,** p. 475). The **Nexus Bar and Café,** also in the Broughton Triangle, is another local favorite (open daily 10am-11pm).

SIGHTS

The Royal Mile

The **Royal Mile** (Lawnmarket, High St., Canongate) defines the length of Old Town, the medieval center of Edinburgh. Defended by Edinburgh Castle at the top of the hill and later by Holyrood Palace at the bottom, the Old Town once packed thousands of inhabitants into a scant few square miles. City planners built down, resulting in tenements both above and below the Royal Mile. When anxiety over invaders waned, the elegant New Town was built. Today, this classical Georgian area north of the city center houses much of the municipal, professional, and financial life of the city.

At the top of the Royal Mile, **Edinburgh Castle** (tel. 668 8600) overlooks the city from the peak of an extinct volcano. Those willing to pay royally at the gate will find the 15th-century Scottish Crown Jewels within, as well as a view north all the way to Fife. **Tour** guides revel in recounting how many Englishmen fell in various attempts to take the stronghold. *(Tours every 15min. from just inside the walls.)* A comprehensive audio guide of the castle's history is also provided. Inside the castle stands **St. Margaret's Chapel,** a Norman church that dates back to the 12th century and is believed to be the oldest structure in Edinburgh. Also on display are the royal scepter, sword and crown, as well as the storied, but unimpressive, Stone of Scone. The state apartments include Queen Mary's bedroom and the French prison where Napoleon's armies scratched *graffiti français* on the ancient walls. *(Castle open daily Apr.-Sept. 9:30am-6pm; Oct.-Mar. 9:30am-5pm; last admission 45min. before closing. £6, seniors £4.50, children £1.50, under 5 free.)* If you're low on funds, the view is also available at other spots, such as the **Nelson monument,** without the admission fee and the hour-long wait common on summer afternoons. The view from the path on the embankment below the castle isn't bad either.

The walk along the **Royal Mile** from the castle to the palace passes some of Edinburgh's classic old houses and attractions. Because space on the Royal Mile was limited, shopfronts are narrow and buildings rise to five or six stories. The tenement **Gladstone's Land** (tel. 226 5856), behind the sprawling pig at 483 Lawnmarket, built in 1617, is the oldest surviving house on the route and well worth a visit; inside, everything remains as it was almost 400 years ago, right down to the wooden baby walker and ceilings painted with bouncing citrus fruits. Charming and informative guides lurk in each room. *(Open Apr.-Oct. M-Sa 10am-5pm, Su 2-5pm; last admission 4:30pm. £3, students £1.90.)* Through the passage at 477 Lawnmarket is **Lady Stair's House,** a 17th-century townhouse. It is now the home not of Lady Stair but of **The Writer's Museum** (tel. 529 4901), a reliquary of memorabilia and manuscripts belonging to three of Scotland's greatest literary figures—Robert Burns, Sir Walter Scott, and Robert Louis Stevenson. Die-hard fans will not want to miss the plaster cast of Bobbie Burns's skull. *(Open M-Sa 10am-5pm; during Festival also Su 2-5pm. Free.)* Walking down George IV Bridge you'll come to the 1620 **Greyfriars Kirk** (tel. 225 1900), in a beautiful churchyard beyond the gates atop Candlemaker Row; linguistics mavens can listen to Gaelic services. *(Su 12:30pm. Disabled access.)* Look for the grave of that loyal pooch Greyfriars Bobby in front of the Church.

Where Lawnmarket becomes High St., the Mile is dominated by the principal church of Scotland, **St. Giles Cathedral** (tel. 225 4363, shop tel. 226 2998), properly called the **High Kirk of St. Giles.** For two brief spells in Scotland's turbulent religious history, this church was pressed into service as an Episcopal cathedral, against the will of some locals. From the pulpit of St. Giles, John Knox delivered the fiery Presbyterian sermons that drove Mary, Queen of Scots into exile. Spectacular stained-glass windows illuminate the structure; its crown spire is one of Edinburgh's hallmarks. *(Open Easter to mid-Sept. M-F 9am-7pm, Sa 9am-5pm, Su 1-5pm; mid-Sept. to Easter M-Sa 9am-5pm, Su 1-5pm. £1 donation requested, both in the Thistle Chapel and for a guided tour.)*

Canongate, the steep hill that constitutes the last segment of the Royal Mile, was once a separate burgh and part of the Augustinian abbey that gave the royal palace its ecclesiastical name. Each of its three free museums merits at least a walk-through. The **Museum of Childhood,** 42 High St. (tel. 529 4142)—"the noisiest museum in the world"—displays games, marionettes, and dolls, including a 19th-century teething doll complete with a rather adult-looking molar. **Canongate Tolbooth** (c. 1591), with its beautiful clockface and hangman's hook projecting over the Royal Mile, houses **The People's Story Museum** (tel. 529 4057), which honors the builders of Edinburgh with reconstructions of settings from everyday life in the past, including a pub and a prison cell. The mannequins are barely distinguishable from the tourists. Sixteenth-century **Huntly House** (tel. 529 4143), a nobleman's mansion, contains a hodge-podge of Edinburgh artifacts, including the key to the Canongate Tolbooth. *(All Canongate museums open M-Sa 10am-5pm; during Festival also Su 2-5pm. All free.)*

The **Palace of Holyroodhouse** (tel. 556 7371), at the eastern end of the Royal Mile, abuts Holyrood Park and the peak of Arthur's Seat (see **Gardens and Parks,** p. 475). This Stewart palace dates from the 16th and 17th centuries and was home to Mary, Queen of Scots, whose antechamber bears the bloodstain of her murdered secretary. Behind the palace and grounds lies a 12th-century abbey ransacked during the Reformation. The palace remains Queen Elizabeth II's official Scotland residence. *(Open Apr.-Oct. daily 9:30am-5:15pm; Nov.-Mar. M-Sa 9:30am-3:45pm; closed during official residences in late May and late June to early July. £5.30, seniors £3.70, under 17 £2.60, families £13.)* When in residence, royalty attend services at **Canongate Kirk,** a 17th-century chapel up the Mile and opposite Huntly House. The economist Adam Smith and Robert Burns' beloved Clarinda, though unlikely bedfellows, lie together in the kirkyard, while Greyfriar's Bobby joins his master and is immortalized by a tail-wagging statue.

South of the Mile on Chambers St. is the Old College of **Edinburgh University,** with numerous exhibits and events year-round. Nearby, the **Royal Museum of Scotland** (tel. 225 7534), also on Chambers St., provides free gallery talks about its large collection of decorative art and exhibits on archaeology and natural history. *(Open M and W-Sa 10am-5pm, Tu 10am-8pm, Su noon-5pm. £3, seniors £1.50, students and children free.)*

The New Town

Edinburgh's **New Town** is a masterpiece of Georgian planning. James Craig, a 23-year-old architect, won the city-planning contest in 1767 with his rectangular, symmetrical gridiron of three main parallel streets (Queen, George, and Princes) linking two large squares (Charlotte and St. Andrew). Queen and Princes, the outer streets, were built up only on one side to allow views of the Firth of Forth and the Old Town, respectively. The **New Town Conservation Centre,** 13a Dundas St. (tel. 557 5222), provides a number of thoroughly-researched booklets, including the well-conceived *4 Walks in Edinburgh New Town* (free) and *New Town Guide* (£2), and answers questions about the area. *(Open M-F 9am-1pm and 2-5pm.)*

A stroll through the New Town ought to include a stop at the discreetly labeled **Georgian House,** 7 Charlotte Sq. (226 3318). From Princes St., take a right onto Charlotte St. and then your second left. The House is in the middle of the road. A guide staffs each room in this elegantly restored townhouse—ask one of them about the

SCOTLAND

The World's Most Fun Janitorial Work

What golf is to St. Andrews, curling is to Edinburgh. Conceived by Flemish immigrants in the 15th century, curling quickly became a Scottish favorite, appearing in native prose and verse and surfacing in the paintings of Bruegel. Modern curling involves a heavy granite stone, several small brooms, and a long sheet of ice. Curlers compete in teams of four; one member of each team, "the Skip," tells a second curler to hurl the stone down the ice; the other two curlers hop in front of the stone, using their brooms to smooth the surface of the ice, guiding the stone to a spot chosen by the Skip. The winner is the team that gets more of its stones close to the designated spots. Sadly, Scotland has all but abandoned its brooms to Canada. Well over one million of today's curlers hail from the Commonwealth nation; the rest of the world boasts fewer than a quarter million mad sweepers.

---

speaking tubes that connect the upstairs hall to the kitchen. *(Open Apr.-Oct. M-Sa 10am-5pm, Su 2-5pm; last admission 4:30pm. £4.20, students, seniors, and children £2.80.)*

The chandeliered **Assembly Rooms** (tel. 220 4348, box office tel. 220 4349), near the corner of Frederick and George St., embody classical Edinburgh. They host all kinds of performances in the Festival and during summer. *(Open M-Sa 9am-5pm. Box office open M-Sa 10am-8pm, Su 11am-6pm.)* On Princes St. between The Mound and Waverley Bridge sits the **Walter Scott Monument,** a grotesque Gothic "steeple without a church." Statues of Scott and his dog preside inside the spire. Climb the winding 287-step staircase and get an eagle's-eye view of Princes St. Gardens, the castle, and Old Town's Market St. *(Open Apr.-Sept. M-Sa 9am-6pm; Oct.-Mar. M-Sa 9am-3pm. £2.)*

At the eastern end of the New Town is **Calton Hill,** from which the 143-step **Nelson Monument** (tel. 556 2716) provides as fine a view of the city and the Firth of Forth as that of Edinburgh Castle. *(Open Apr.-Sept. M 1-6pm, Tu-Sa 10am-6pm; Oct.-Mar. M-Sa 10am-3pm. £2.)* Calton Hill also supports an *ersatz* Parthenon built, oddly enough, to commemorate those killed in the Napoleonic Wars, and the **City Observatory** (tel. 556 4365), where you can see a 20-minute slide show on Edinburgh's history. *(Open Apr.-Oct. daily 10:30am-5pm. £2, students, seniors, and children £1.20, families £6.)*

Galleries

The *Edinburgh Gallery Guide* at the tourist office will lead you through the marble halls of Edinburgh's vast and varied collections. On The Mound between the two halves of Princes St. Gardens, the **National Gallery of Scotland** (tel. 624 6516) stashes a superb collection of works by Renaissance, Romantic, and Impressionist masters, including three Raphaels, several Titians, and a remarkable collection of Italian and French icons. The basement houses a fine spread of Scottish art. *(Open M-Sa 10am-5pm, Su 2-5pm; during Festival M-Sa 10am-6pm, Su 11am-6pm. Free.)* Draped in yellow gorsebushes, Queen Victoria is perched atop the **Royal Scottish Academy** (tel. 225 6671), next door at Princes St. and The Mound, which shows temporary exhibits of contemporary Scottish art. *(Open same hours as National Gallery. £4, students and children £2.)* Beneath The Mound down Market St. are galleries of a similarly newish bent. The **Fruitmarket Gallery** (tel. 225 2383) flaunts cheeky modern artwork. *(Open M-Sa 10am-6pm, Su noon-5pm. Free.)* Explore material and space at **The City Art Centre,** 2 Market St. (tel. 529 3993), where exhibits of Scottish modern artwork slip away faster than Dalí's clocks. *(Open M-Sa 10am-5pm, Su noon-5pm. £3, students £2.)* Don't miss **i2 art and design,** 66 Cumberland St. (tel. 557 1020), a remarkable venue whose past shows have included Picasso, Miró, and Brit David Hockney.

The **Scottish National Portrait Gallery,** 1 Queen St. (tel. 556 8921), north of St. Andrew Sq., mounts the mugs of famous Scots, including a sensuous portrait of the young and corpulent Queen Anne. *(Open M-Sa 10am-5pm, Su 2-5pm. Free.)* Next door, the **Museum of Antiquities** (tel. 225 7534), contains Pictish stones and bagpipes old and new. The exhibits are still growing. *(Same hours as the National Portrait Gallery. Free.)* West of New Town, Palmerston Pl. leads down the hill past Douglas Gardens to the medieval village of **Dean,** on the banks of Leith Water. Several picturesque paths lead along the water to Belford Rd. to reach the Scottish **National Gallery of Modern Art,** 75 Belford Rd. (tel. 556 8921), an excellent rotating collection that includes works by Braque, Matisse, and Picasso, as well as a disturbingly lifelike statue of two American tourists. Take bus #13, or walk a mile from Princes St. to Belford Rd. *(Same hours as National Portrait Gallery. Free.)*

Gardens and Parks

Just off the eastern end of the Royal Mile, you can wink at the Highlands with a stroll through **Holyrood Park,** or by a manageable 45-minute climb up **Arthur's Seat** (823ft.)—the exposed volcanic summit offers a stunning view. The hill was considered to be a holy place by the Picts because it appeared and disappeared in the frequent fogs. **Radical Rd.,** named for the politically extreme, unemployed weavers who built it, allows a shorter walk up to the steep Salisbury Crags on the cityward side of Arthur's Seat. The best access to the park is from Holyrood Rd., by the Palace, where a small tourist center displays information on the variegated history, geology, and wildlife of the park. Call **Scottish Wildlife Trust** (tel. 312 7765) for information on guided tours of the park.

Hidden away from the city, the sleepy village of **Duddingston,** at the foot of Arthur's Seat, makes a great grazing stop—try the **Sheep's Heid Inn** (tel. 661 1020; bus #42 from The Mound), Scotland's oldest licensed drinking establishment, with an ancient outdoor garden. *(Open M-Sa 11am-11pm, Su 12:30-11pm.)* A smaller refuge, located directly in the city center, is **Princes St. Gardens,** a lush green park where the castle's moat once intimidated marauders. Now, visitors can rest on the grass and listen to the Scottish bands that perform on summer afternoons. **The Flower Clock,** composed of 30,000 varieties of dwarf plants and surely one of the few floral displays to have its own security camera, symbolically ticks in a well-fenced corner opposite the Royal Scottish Academy. The Scottish equivalent of miniature golf—minus the dinosaurs and windmills—is available below the Scott Monument at **Princes St. Putting.** (tel. 225 6844). Rent clubs at the tiny shack in the southwest corner of the main green. *(Open mid-Apr. to mid-Sept. Su and W-F 11:30am-7:30pm, Sa noon-6pm. 18 holes £1.50, seniors and children 65p.)* Those fond of hitting small objects with long sticks can also head to the **Meadows,** an enormous grassy park in southern Edinburgh containing an impromptu golf course as well as public football fields and tennis courts.

Edinburgh's requisite romantic oasis is the **Royal Botanic Gardens** (tel. 552 7171), on Inverleith Row. Take bus #23 or 27 from Hanover St. and stroll around the splendid rock garden and plant houses. *(Open daily May-Aug. 9:30am-7pm; Mar.-Apr. and Sept. 9:30am-6pm; Feb. and Oct. 9:30am-5pm; Nov.-Jan. 9:30am-4pm.)* The **Edinburgh Zoo,** 134 Corstorphine Rd. (tel. 334 9171), lies just outside the city to the west. Penguins (including the world's largest) parade daily in the summer at 2pm. *(Open Apr.-Sept. M-Sa 9am-6pm, Su 9:30am-6pm; Mar. and Oct. M-Sa 9am-5pm, Su 9:30am-5pm; Nov.-Feb. daily 9:30am-4:30pm. £6.50, students and seniors £4.50, children £3.50.)* Take red bus #2, 12, 26, 31, 36, 69, 85, or 86; green bus # 16, 18, 80, 86, or 274.

ENTERTAINMENT

The summer season sees a joyful round of events—music in the gardens, plays and films, and *ceilidhs* (KAY-lees; country dances accompanied by much singing and drinking)—and that's all *before* the Edinburgh International Festival comes to town. In winter, shorter days and the crush of students promote a flourishing nightlife. For details, no one does it better than *The List* (£1.90), a bi-weekly comprehensive guide to events in Glasgow and Edinburgh, available at any local bookstore, newsstand, or record shop. Also useful is *Day by Day,* free from the tourist office.

King's Theatre, 2 Leven St. (tel. 529 6000), offers serious and comedic fare, musicals, opera, and pantomime. The **Royal Lyceum Theatre,** 30 Grindlay St. (tel. 229 9697), presents Scots, U.K., and international theater. The **Playhouse Theatre,** 18-22 Greenside Pl. (tel. 557 2590), often hosts musicals and popular singers. The **Netherbow Theatre,** 43-45 High St. (tel. 556 9579), stages more informal but equally delightful productions each week. Edinburgh University's **Bedlam Theatre,** 11b Bristo Pl.

(tel. 225 9893), presents excellent student productions of both straight-laced and experimental drama in a converted church with a bedlam-red door. The **Traverse Theatre,** 10 Cambridge St. (tel. 228 1404), performs innovative, sometimes controversial drama, while Edinburgh's **Festival Theatre,** 13-29 Nicholson St. (tel. 529 6000), offers ballet and opera.

Thanks to an overabundance of university students who never let books get in the way of a good night out, Edinburgh's music scene is alive and well. Excellent impromptu and professional folk sessions abound at pubs. Jazz can be found at **L'attache,** Rutland St., **Navaar House Hotel,** Mayfield Gdns., and the **Cellar Bar,** Chambers St. For a complete run-down of Edinburgh's jazz scene, pick up the *Jazz News* at the International Jazz Festival Office, 116 Canongate (tel. 225 2202). For rock and progressive shows, try **The Venue** (tel. 557 3073) and **Calton Studios** (tel. 556 7066), both on Calton Rd. One Saturday per month, the Calton comes out as **Joy,** Scotland's largest gay club. *(Cover £3 before midnight, £5 after. Open 11pm-late.)* **Ripping Records,** 91 S. Bridge (tel. 226 7010), lists and sells tickets to rock, reggae, and popular performances in Edinburgh. Many of the university houses also sponsor live shows; look for flyers near Bristo Sq. **Negociant's,** 45-47 Lothian St. (not Lothian Rd.; tel. 225 6313), is a pub with a wide range of Continental beers upstairs and frequent live shows downstairs, not to mention the best cappuccino in Edinburgh. *(Open daily 9am-3am.)* **Whistle Binkies,** 4-6 S. Bridge (tel. 557 5114), bills itself as Edinburgh's Original Unplugged Cellar Bar, with nightly live music. *(Open daily 5pm-3am.)* **C.C. Blooms,** 23 Greenside Pl., is a hot spot with a restaurant, disco bar, and lounge bar.

"Scottish Evenings" sponsored by many of the larger hotels are about as authentic as vegan haggis. Instead, try Scottish folk sessions which heat up nightly at the **Tron Ceilidh Bar** (see **Pubs,** p. 471). You'll also find Scottish bands and country dancing at the **Ross Open-Air Theatre** (tel. 529 4147), under the tent in Princes St. Gardens (usually begins about 7pm), and at a number of smaller local pubs. Edinburgh's **Folk Festival** will begin April 3; for more information, contact the tourist office.

EVENTS

For a few weeks in August, Edinburgh is *the* place to be in Europe. Prices go up, pubs and restaurants stay open late, and viewing stands are erected in the streets. No, it's not a royal visit (though you might just see that as well), it's the **Edinburgh International Festival** (Aug. 15-Sept. 4 in 1999), with a kaleidoscopic program of music, drama, dance, and art. For tickets and a full schedule of events, contact the **Festival Box Office,** 21 Market St. EH1 1BW (inquiries tel. 473 2001, bookings tel. 473 2000; fax 473 2003). Tickets (£4-44) are sold by phone and over the counter starting the third week of April, and by post or fax from the second week of April. You can also purchase tickets at the door for most events. Inquire about half-price tickets after 1pm on the day of the performance.

Around the established festival has grown a less formal **Fringe Festival** (Aug. 8-30 in 1999), which now includes over 500 amateur and professional companies presenting theater, comedy, children's shows, folk and classical music, poetry, dance, mime, opera, revue, and various exhibits. Budget travelers may find the Fringe better suited to their wallets than official offerings. Reviews of a few of the 1000-odd Fringe productions appear in most papers, including *The List.* Or get the scoop on the best shows at some main haunts: the Fringe Club at the Teviot Row Union, the Pleasance Theatre on Pleasance St., the Gilded Balloon on Cowgate, the Assembly Rooms, the Theatre Workshop, and the Traverse Theatre. The *Fringe Programme* (available from mid-June) and the *Daily Diary* list performances; get brochures and tickets by mail from the **Fringe Festival Office,** 180 High St., Edinburgh EH1 1QS (tel. 226 5257, bookings 226 5138). For programs, include £1.50 (from the U.K. and EU countries) or £3.50 (all others) for postage; cash, stamps, and foreign currency are accepted. Bookings can be made by post starting in mid-June, by phone (with a credit card) from late June, and in person from July 28. *(Box office open M-Sa 10am-6pm; Aug. and during the Festival daily 9am-9pm.)* You can sometimes get free tickets from actors who give them away outside the Fringe Festival Office. Tickets range in price £3-16.

Roughly concurrent with the Edinburgh International Festival are several other festivals. Tickets for other performances (£5-17) are available at the **Ticket Centre** on Waverley Bridge from five days before the festival, by phone (tel. 557 1642; credit card required), and by post from the **Festival Office,** 116 Canongate EH8 8DD (tel. 225 2202; fax 225 3321). The office stocks complete listings of events and venues. For information, call 467 5200.

Military Tattoo: Tattoo Ticket Sale Office, 33-34 Market St. (tel. 225 1188; fax 225 8627). A spectacle of military bands, bagpipes, and drums performed M-Sa nights in the Esplanade. Saturday performances are followed by fireworks. Tickets £7.50-16. Phone and mail bookings from early January. Open M-F 10am-4:30pm; on performance days, open until the show.

Edinburgh International Film Festival: Film Festival, The Cameo, 38 Home St., EH3 9LZ (tel. 229 2550, bookings 623 8030). Box office sells tickets starting in late July.

Edinburgh International Jazz and Blues Festival: July 31-Aug. 9 in 1999. Opens with a day of free jazz at the Princes St. Gardens.

Edinburgh Book Festival: Scottish Book Centre, 137 Dundee St., EH11 1BG (tel. 228 5444). Concentrated in Charlotte Sq., the largest book celebration in Europe. Runs mid- to late Aug.

The **Edinburgh International Highland Games** (tel. 473 3838) toss cabers into the artsy mix of mid-July to August. Bagpipes, dancing, and craft displays make less of an impact on the overloaded festival-goer. *(Tickets around £5.)* Edinburgh is worth visiting at New Year's for **Hogmanay** (tel. 473 3800), which (surprise) emphasizes drinking. Just show up and follow the noise. May Day sparks the **Beltane Fires.** This pagan event begins with coal jumping around Calton Hill and then moves to Arthur's Seat at sunrise where, legend has it, those who wash their face with the morning dew will receive eternal youth (no office, no tickets, no towels, no guarantees).

■ Near Edinburgh

Edinburgh's extensive bus service allows for a host of daytrips. South of the city, enjoy the Lowland countryside at **The Braids,** where a trail cuts through the woods around Braid Burn. From Braid Burn you can head up to **Blackford Hill** for a piquant view of the city. The **Braid Hermitage Nature Trail** is accessible from Braid Rd.; take bus #40 or 41 from The Mound. The **Royal Observatory** (tel. 668 8405) on Blackford Hill has Scotland's biggest telescope; you can reach it by bus #40 or 41. *(Open Apr.-Sept. M-Sa 10am-5pm, Su noon-5pm; Oct.-Mar. M-F by arrangement, Sa 10am-5pm, Su noon-5pm. £2, children £1.25.)*

Bus #41 from Frederick St. runs to the placid fishing village of **Cramond. Lauriston Castle,** 2a Cramond Rd. S. (tel. 336 2060), a mansion with a 16th-century tower house and 19th-century additions, exudes Edwardian privilege. Its gardens offer a view of the Firth of Forth. *(Guided tours only. Open Apr.-Oct. Sa-Th 11am-5pm; Nov.-Mar. Sa-Su 2-4pm. £4, students, seniors, and children £3.)*

In **South Queensferry,** about 10 mi. west of the city center, stand two grandiose homes. **Hopetoun House** (tel. 331 2451) is the more spectacular, considered by most to be Scotland's stateliest "Adam" mansion, designed by 18th-century Scottish architect William Adam and his sons Robert and John. The house has a rooftop viewing platform which provides a panoramic vista of the Firth of Forth and its bridges. *(Open Apr.-Sept. daily 10am-5pm, last admission 4:30pm. £4.70, students and seniors £4.20, children and disabled £2.60, families £14.50; grounds £2.60, students and seniors £1.60, families £17.50.)* **Dalmeny House** (tel. 331 1888), the first Tudor Gothic building in Scotland, boasts a grand hammer-beamed hall. Its Napoleon Room holds furniture that propped up the great emperor at the height of his glory and later in the despair of his exile on St. Helena. The **Rothschild Collection,** acquired through a strategic marriage, includes remarkable 18th-century French furniture, tapestries, and porcelain. *(Open July-Aug. M-Tu noon-5:30pm, Su 1-5:30pm. £3.60, students £2.80, seniors £3.20, under*

16 £2, under 10 free.) Take a bus from St. Andrew Sq. to Chapel Gate in the center of South Queensferry, then walk 1 mi. up the drive.

In **Penicuik,** 7 mi. south of Edinburgh, you can watch glass being blown and cut at the **Edinburgh Crystal Visitors Centre** (tel. (01968) 675128); take bus #81 or 87 from North Bridge or call to ask about the free bus (Apr.-Sept.) from Waverley Bridge. *(Open M-Sa 9am-5pm, Su 11am-5pm. £3, seniors and ages 8-18 £2, children under 8 deemed too clumsy to enter.)* East of Penicuik in **Roslin** is the **Rosslyn Chapel** (tel. 440 2159). Its exotic stone carvings raised eyebrows in late medieval Scotland. The most famous part of the church is the pier known as Prentice Pillar, supposedly the work of an apprentice who was later killed by the jealous master mason. *(Chapel open M-Sa 10am-5pm, Su noon-4:45pm. £2.50, students and seniors £2, children £1.)* Roslin lies by the **Pentland Hills,** a superb hiking area and haunt of the stripling Robert Louis Stevenson.

■ The Borders

From the time that Hadrian and his legions were repelled in the 2nd century until 200 years ago, this 1800 sq. mi. region was continually caught in a tug-of-war between Scotland and England. Signs of strife remain: fortified houses and castles brace the region, and spectacular abbeys at Dryburgh, Jedburgh, Kelso, and Melrose lie in ruins. These grim relics stand in contrast to a landscape of gentle rivers and rolling sheep-ish hills. The River Tweed runs eastward through the center of the Borders, providing the setting for many towns and stately homes. As in most of southern Scotland, winding roads and spectacular hill paths reward walkers and cyclists.

GETTING THERE AND GETTING ABOUT

Ask the local tourist office for the utterly essential *Scottish Borders Travel Guide* (free), which summarizes all bus information. There are seven "areas" in the Borders, and each has a more detailed *Travel Guide* of its own. There is no **rail service** in the Borders, but **bus service** is frequent. From Edinburgh, take **Lowland** bus #62 to **Peebles, Galashiels,** or **Melrose** (2½hr., 1 per hr.); #95 to **Galashiels** or **Hawick** (2hr., 9 per day); or #29 and 30 to **Jedburgh** and **Kelso** (1½hr., 6 per day). **National Express** (tel. (0990) 808080) #383 travels once a day between **Newcastle** and **Edinburgh via Jedburgh** and **Melrose;** #394 also hits **Galashiels** and **Glasgow. McEwan's** bus #195 runs from the **Carlisle** train station to **Galashiels** (2hr., M-Sa 7 per day, Su 3 per day). No routes lead directly from **Dumfries** and **Galloway** in the west; either come through Carlisle or change buses at **Biggar** or **Lanark.**

Intra-Borders buses run frequently, if not always promptly. Several **taxi services** operate in the Borders, and will pick you up and drop you off wherever you want. Three or four people can share a cab for the same price as bus fare; ask at the tourist information center for more information.

Hitchers report the lethargy of Border hitching is least painful along the main roads; the A699 runs east-west between Selkirk and Kelso, the A68 connects Edinburgh to Newcastle via Jedburgh, and the A7 runs south through Galashiels and Hawick en route to Carlisle. The labyrinth of B roads is less traveled.

HIKING AND BIKING

The Borders region welcomes hikers of all levels; take a late afternoon stroll in the hills or wander the wilds for days at a time. Be sure to pick up the superb *Walking in the Scottish Borders,* provided free by the Tourist Board, which details many half-day scenic walks based around towns. The same series includes booklets on cycling and fishing. Trails weave through the **Tweedsmuirs** (all over 2500ft.) to the west along the A708 towards Moffat, as well as the **Cheviot Hills** to the southeast. Closer to Edinburgh, the **Moorfoots** and **Lammermuirs** offer gentler day walks. Eighty-two miles of the 212 mi. **Southern Upland Way,** Scotland's longest footpath, wind through the Borders. The Way is clearly marked (with a thistle in a hexagon), and the Countryside Commission for Scotland annually publishes a free pamphlet with route and accommodations information. (Also see **Western Galloway,** p. 489.) **St. Cuthbert's Way** rambles for 62 mi. from Melrose to Lindisfarne on the English coast. Retrace ancient footsteps along **Dere St.** (an old Roman road), **Girthgate** (a pilgrimage from Edinburgh to Melrose Abbey), or **Minchmoore.** Track these trails with the helpful booklet *Scottish Hill Tracks—Southern Scotland.*

The annual regional **Walking Festival** is held in early September; for more information, contact Roger Smith, Walking Development Officer (tel. (01896) 758991). Local tourist offices provide plenty of trail guides, leaflets on walks (45p), and Ordnance Survey Map Sheets 1:50,000 (£5). Consult the **Scottish Borders Tourist Board** office in Jedburgh at Murrays Green (see **Jedburgh,** p. 482).

Both on-trail and off-trail **bikers** can enjoy the Borders. The *Tweed Cycleway* pamphlet, free from any tourist office, describes an 89 mi. route which hugs the Tweed River from **Biggar** to **Berwick** and lists bike shops in the Borders. The new **Four Abbeys Cycle Route** connects the abbeys at Melrose, Dryburgh, Jedburgh, and Kelso, and is detailed in a free pamphlet from tourist information centers. The following cycle shops rent a range of bikes and give advice on routes:

Gala Cycles, 58 High St., Galashiels (tel. (01896) 757587). £10 per day, £50 per week. Open M-Tu and Th-F 10am-5pm, W 10am-noon, Sa 10am-4:30pm.

Crossburn Caravan Park, Edinburgh Rd., Peebles (tel. (01721) 720501). £11 per day; helmets £1; £50 deposit. Open daily 9am-5pm.

Hawick Cycle Centre, 45 N. Bridge St., Hawick (tel. (01450) 373352). £5 per 8hr., £10 per day, £50 per week; £20 deposit. ID required. Open M and W-F 9am-8pm, Tu and Sa 9am-5pm, Su noon-4pm.

Melrose Cycles, Buccleuch St., Melrose (tel. (01896) 823782). £10 per day, £16 per weekend. Open M-W and F-Sa 10am-1:30pm and 2:30-5pm, Th 10am-1:30pm.

ACCOMMODATIONS

The *Scottish Borders Holiday Guide,* dispersed free at tourist offices, lists a wide range of Borders accommodations by town, including campsites. All tourist offices can help you find a bed, usually for a 10% deposit on the first night's stay. The four **SYHA Youth Hostels** of the Borders are strategically dispersed. Opened in 1931 as the first SYHA hostel and providing footholds for an ascent into the Tweedsmuir Hills, **Broadmeadows** (tel./fax (01750) 76262), lies west of Selkirk off the A708 and is 1¼ mi. south of the Southern Upland Way. (£4.65, under 18 £3.85. Reception closed 10:30am-5pm. Curfew 10:45pm. Open late Mar. to Sept.). The hostel at St. Abbs Head, just outside of **Coldingham** (tel./fax (018907) 71298), near the ocean, surveys the entire east coast and the eastern end of the Southern Upland Way. (£6.10, under 18 £5. Lockout 10:30am-5pm. Curfew 11:30pm. Open late Mar. to Oct.) Watch hikers collapse at the **Kirk Yetholm Youth Hostel** (tel. (01573) 420631), located at the northern terminus of the Pennine Way, at the junction of the B6352 and B6401 (£6.10, under 18 £5; curfew 11:30pm; open late Mar. to Oct.). Buses run to Kirk Yetholm from **Kelso** (30min., M-Sa 5-7 per day, Su 3 per day, £2.65 day return). The fourth hostel is in **Melrose** (see below).

■ Melrose

PRACTICAL INFORMATION Buses stop at Market Sq. The **tourist office,** Abbey House (tel. 822555), next to a small park and across from the abbey on Abbey St., books rooms for a deposit. (Open July-Aug. M-Sa 9:30am-6:30pm, Su 10am-6pm; June and Sept. M-Sa 10am-5:30pm, Su 10am-2pm; Apr.-May M-Sa 10am-5pm, Su 10am-1pm; Oct. M-Sa 10am-4:30pm, Su 10am-1pm; closed Nov.-Mar.) A **Bank of Scotland ATM** adorns Market Sq. The **post office** (tel. 822040) is on Buccleuch St. (open M-F 9am-1pm and 2-5:30pm, Sa 9am-12:30pm). The **postal code** is TD6 9LE. The **telephone code** is 01896.

ACCOMMODATIONS AND FOOD The comfortable **SYHA Youth Hostel** (tel. 822521), off High Rd., is a superb base for exploring the Borders. One minute from the center of town, it features 86 beds, an excellent kitchen, laundry facilities, and a relaxing picnic-tabled yard. Grab a trashy romance novel from the shelves and gaze at the abbey's Gothic ruins out the window. (£7.75, under 18 £6.50. Continental breakfast £2, dinner £4.40. 9 showers. Reception 7am-midnight. Bedroom lockout 10am-1:30pm. Curfew 11:30pm. Open year-round.) If you prefer roomier accommodations, stop by **Mrs. Aitken's Orchard House,** 17 High St. (tel. 822005; £16-18; closed Nov.-Mar. and sometimes Oct.). Or try **Birch House** (tel. 822391), down High St., which offers homey, pine-furnished rooms (from £17). Camp at the super-deluxe **Gibson Park Caravan Club Park,** St. Dunstan's Park (tel. 822969; off-season tel. (01342) 329644), off High St. Renovated in April '98, it features the cleanest bathrooms you'll ever see at a campsite. (£3.25 per person, children £1.50; £3 per tent. Excellent facilities for the disabled. Open Apr.-Oct.)

Though not known for its budget fare, Melrose does offer farm-fresh food, including gourmet cheeses and wholefoods, at **The Country Kitchen,** Market Sq. (tel. 822586), at Palma Pl. The store also serves vegetarian haggis at £2 per lb.—now you have no excuse (open M-Sa 9am-5pm). Also try the cafeteria-style **Abbey Mill Coffee Shop** (tel. 822138), above the Abbey Mill Woolen Shop on Annay Rd. The food is good, and the coffee fabulous (open Apr.-Oct. daily 9am-5pm; Nov.-Mar. M-Sa 10am-4pm, Su noon-4pm). The award-winning **Melrose Station Restaurant,** Palma Pl. (tel. 822546), in a renovated railway station, serves wholemeal sandwiches (£2.35-3.25), homemade soups (£1.60), and exquisite entrees for excruciating prices. (Lunch entrees around £6, 2-course dinner £15.50. Lunch served W-Su noon-2pm; dinner served Th-Sa from 6:45pm.)

SIGHTS Among the loveliest of the region's towns, Melrose is also within convenient reach of the area's sights. Centerpiece of the town, Cistercian **Melrose Abbey** (tel. 822562) was begun in 1136, destroyed by the English, rebuilt in an ornate and Gothic style, then destroyed again by the English. Some walls remain remarkably intact while others provide good ventilation. Search the extensive grounds for the tombstone of Robert the Bruce's embalmed heart (see **Squabbles with England,** p. 459). Bruce's dying wish was to go on a crusade against the Moors; his knight obliged by sealing his heart in a lead casket and journeying with it to the Holy Land. After the knight's death, the casket was returned and buried here. *(Open Apr.-Sept. daily 9:30am-6:30pm; Oct.-Mar. M-Sa 9:30am-4pm, Su 2-4:30pm; last admission 30min. before closing. £2.80, seniors £2.10, under 16 £1.)* Admission to the Abbey includes the **Abbey Museum,** displaying objects unearthed from the Abbey and regional Roman forts. The museum also details Sir Walter Scott's life, death, and poetic dishonesty. Come, see, and briskly conquer the **Trimontium Exhibition** (tel. 822651), in Market Sq., which jams information about the ancient Roman fort upon the three Eildon Hills into one small room. *(Open Apr.-Oct. 10:30am-4:30pm. £1.30, students, seniors, and children 80p, families £3.60.)*

Bike routes fan out from town, and the **Eildon Hills,** an easy 5 mi. hike, supply sweeping views from three volcanic summits. Legend has it that Arthur and his knights lie in an enchanted sleep (fully armed, of course) within a cavern deep beneath the Hills. To reach the Hills, walk 200 yd. south of Market Sq. on the Dingleton Rd.; after passing Newlyn Rd. on the right, look for the footpath on the left.

■ Galashiels

Birthplace of tartan and tweed and center of the woolen-weaving industry since the 13th century, welcoming "Gala" is to be thanked for the garb of tweed-bound professors and plaid-clad preppies who congregate in certain corners of the globe. The town is a great transportation hub; start (and end) your exploration of Galashiels with a visit to **Lochcarron's Scottish Cashmere and Wool Centre,** Huddersfield St. (tel. 752091). The tour of the working mill will quench any curiosity you might have had about the history of Galashiels's famous fabrics. *(40min. tours—the only way to see the mill—M-F 10:30am, 11:30am, 1:30pm and 2:30pm, or by appointment. £2, children free.)*

Tremendously helpful folks await at the **bus station** (tel. 752237), across Gala Water, where you can buy National Express and CityLink tickets to just about anywhere in the Borders (open M-F 9am-5pm, Sa 9am-noon). The seasonal **tourist office,** 3 St. John's St. (tel. 755551), off Bank St., will help with beds, buses, and the like. (Open July-Aug. M-Sa 10am-6pm, Su 1-5pm; Apr.-June and Sept. M-Sa 10am-5pm, Su 2-4pm; Oct. M-Sa 10am-4pm.) **ATMs** abound on Bank and Channel St. Galashiels's **post office** is at 1 Channel St. (tel. 754731; open M-F 9am-5:30pm, Sa 9am-12:30pm). The **postal code** is TD1 1AA; the **telephone code** is 01896. Hospitable **Morven Guest House,** 12 Sine Pl. (tel. 756255), around the corner from Poundstretcher on High St., boasts goldenrod decor; don't be dissuaded by the permanent "no vacancy" sign (£16.50 with bath, children £8.25). Tasty sandwiches (brie-and-apple £1.30) await at the grocery-deli **Supa-Fresh,** 7 Overhaugh St. (tel. 757307; open M-Sa 9am-5pm).

■ Peebles

Eighteen miles west of Galashiels, **Peebles** nurtures the River Tweed with gentle grass and restful benches along its banks. The **tourist office,** 23 High St. (tel. 720138), sells a slew of local maps and books accommodations for a deposit. (Open July-Aug. M-F 9am-8:30pm, Sa 9am-7pm, Su 10am-6pm; June and Sept. M-Sa 9:30am-5:30pm, Su 10am-4pm; Apr.-May M-Sa 9:30am-5pm, Su 10am-2pm; Oct. M-Sa 9:30am-4:30pm, Su 10am-2pm; Nov.-Mar. M-Sa 9:30am-12:30pm and 1:30-4:30pm.) The **Royal Bank of Scotland ATM** gapes at the intersection of Eastgate and Northgate. The Peebles **post office** (tel. 720119) is at 14 Eastgate, as is the **bus stand** (open M-F 9am-5:30pm, Sa 9am-12:30pm). **Internet access** is available at the library, the Chambers Institute (tel. 720123; £2.50 per 30min.; open M, W, and F 9:30am-5pm, Tu and Th 9:30am-7pm, Sa 9am-12:30pm). The **postal code** is EH45 8AA; Peebles's **telephone code** is 01721.

Stay with **Mrs. Mitchell,** Viewfield, 1 Rosetta Rd. (tel. 721232), for fresh, clean rooms above a wonderful front garden (singles £17; twins £33). Rest up, for tomorrow is another day, in huge-windowed rooms at **Mrs. O'Hara's,** Rowanbrae, 103 Northgate (tel. 721360), down the road from the Somerfield supermarket (£16.50, with bath £19; open Mar.-Nov.). Campers find comfort at the **Rosetta Camping and Caravan Park,** Rosetta Rd. (tel. 720770), a 15-minute walk from town center on the wooded grounds of the Rosetta House. The former owner of the house accompanied Abercrombie to Egypt to secure the Rosetta Stone for England. (£3.50-4 per person, under 17 50p, one night free with each week's stay. Laundry facilities and amenity complex with 2 bars. Open Apr.-Oct.) For dried fruits, specialty breads, and treats, duck into **The Olive Tree Delicatessen,** 7 High St. (tel. 723461; open M-Sa 9am-5:30pm). At **Big Eb's,** just out of the town center at 14-16 Northgate (tel. 721497), the friendly proprietor ladles out a healthy dollop of travel experience with his tasty fish and chips (£2.55 take-away, £3.50 sit-down with tea and bread included) and pizza (£1.80; open M-Sa 11:45am-11pm, Su noon-8pm).

A 20-minute sally upstream yields **Neidpath Castle** (tel. 720333), a small but sturdy fortress with something for everyone—crumbling rooms, river views, batik art depicting the life of Mary, Queen of Scots, and a tartan display. *(Open Easter-Sept. M-Sa 11am-5pm, Su 1-5pm. £2.50, students and seniors £2, children £1, families £6.50.)* The **Chambers Institute** (tel. 720123) houses a modest museum, a contemporary art gallery, and the Secret Room (containing Greek friezes placed here in 1859 to "ennoble and enlighten" the viewer). The room's secret remains, appropriately, a secret. *(Open M-F 10am-noon and 2-5pm, Easter-Oct. also Sa 10am-1pm.)* On Cross Rd. in a small wooded park, ruins of **Cross Kirk**—supposedly founded in 1262 when Alexander III and his pals discovered a fourth-century cross here—represent one of the two remaining Trinitarian monasteries in Scotland. Across town in the Cemetery stands **St. Andrew's Tower,** the ruins of which were used as stables by Cromwell's troops. On the main drag, High St., Peebles has a **Beltane Festival** the third Saturday in June. Formerly a pagan holiday of random sexual encounters, the ceremonies now focus on elementary school children, not fertility. Near Peebles, the forests of the Tweed Valley—such as **Glentross** and **Cardrona**—have hiking and cycling paths. For information, pick up a copy of *Forests of the River Tweed,* free from the tourist office.

SCOTLAND

■ Jedburgh

Thirteen miles south of Melrose bustles the town of Jedburgh (JED-burra), known to locals as "Jethart," complete with abbey, castle jail, and town trail. Founded in 1138 by King David I and located smack in the middle of town, **Jedburgh Abbey** (tel. 863925) suffered repeated attacks from 1237 until 1546, when the Earl of Hertford reduced it to rubble. *(Open Apr.-Oct. M-Sa 9:30am-6:30pm, Su 2-6:30pm; Nov.-Mar. M-Sa 9:30am-4:30pm, Su 2-4:30pm; last admission 30min. before closing. £2.80, seniors £2.10, under 16 £1.)* Of course, one of the advantages of demolition is that you can see almost everything from the outside for free. Down Smiths Wynd on Queen St., the **home of Mary, Queen of Scots** (tel. 863331) survives as one of the few remaining examples of a 16th-century fortified house. Mary spent six weeks here recovering from a near-deadly fall from a horse. Long after, facing death after years of imprisonment, she is said to have wished aloud, "Would that I had died at Jedworth." On her gruesome death mask, look for signs of the bandaging used to hold her head together after it was messily hacked off. *(Open mid-Mar. to mid-Nov. M-Sa 10am-5pm, Su 10am-4:30pm. £2, students, seniors, disabled, and children £1.)* The **Castle Jail** (tel. 863254) stands atop a hill on Castlegate over the original Jethart Castle, which was destroyed by its owners in 1409 to prevent the English from taking it. Enter boldly between two cannons to learn about local history and prison conditions. *(Open Easter-Oct. M-Sa 10am-4:30pm, Su 1-4pm. £1.25, students, seniors, and children £1.)*

The **bus stance** on Canongate does not have an office, but is located behind the helpful **tourist office,** Murrays Green (tel. 863435; fax 864099), opposite the abbey, which dispenses information, books **National Express** tickets, reserves rooms for a deposit, and exchanges currency for free. Pick up *Jedburgh Town Trail* (50p), *What's On: Scottish Borders* (free), or your favorite Scottish romance novel. (Open July-Aug. M-F 9am-8pm, Sa 9am-7pm, Su 10am-7pm; June M-Sa 9am-6pm, Su 10am-6pm; Sept. M-Sa 9:30am-6pm, Su noon-6pm; Apr.-May and Oct. M-Sa 10am-5pm, Su noon-5pm; Nov.-Mar. M-Sa 10am-4pm.) An **ATM** at the **Royal Bank of Scotland,** on the corner of Jeweller's Wynd and High St., accepts Cirrus cards. The **post office** rests at 37 High St. (tel. 862268; open M-F 9am-5:30pm, Sa 9am-12:30pm). The **postal code** is TD8 6DG; the **telephone code** 01835.

B&Bs pepper the town; look for the ubiquitous Scottish Tourist Board B&B signs. At 7 Queen St., near the house of Mary, Queen of Scots, **Mrs. Elliott** (tel. 862482) offers fresh fruit salad with peaches and cherries for those weary of bacon and eggs (singles £14; twins £25). Star-gazers can camp at the **Jedwater Caravan Park** (tel. 840219), 4 mi. south of the town center off the A68; watch for the signs and a side road (tent and two people £7, extra adult £1, children 50p; open Easter-Oct.). Self-caterers should visit the **Co-op Superstore,** 38 High St. (tel. 862944), at Jeweller's Wynd (open M-Sa 8am-8pm, Su 10am-5pm). Try the sweet **Brown Sugar Coffee Shop and Bakery** at 12 Canongate. Quick snacks include burgers (£1.50-3), teacakes (95p), and toasted sandwiches (£1.25-2; open M-Sa 9am-5pm).

The Secret Life of Mary, Queen of Scots

Mary Stewart (1542-1587) endured a flurry of spicy rumors during her lifetime. Her first husband, King François II of France, reportedly had a shriveled male organ. Wits at the French court speculated on the King's ability to have inter-course, and remarked that if the Queen were to become pregnant, the child could not be the King's. In any case, Mary experienced a "hysterical" (false) pregnancy during her year as Queen of France before François died. Mary's later marriage to the wicked Lord Darnley did bear fruit. During the long and agonizing birth, Mary's companion Lady Reres moaned and thrashed in empathy beside Mary, as a lady-in-waiting supposedly drew Mary's pains into the Lady Reres through witch-craft. Rumor has it that Mary's son was stillborn, and that the future King James I was actually another infant smuggled in to replace the dead child—a story made more tantalizing by the discovery years later of an infant's skeleton hidden between the walls of Mary's apartments.

■ Kelso

The busy town of Kelso is one of the larger in the region and provides access to the north and east of the Borders. It is home to palatial **Floors Castle** (tel. (01573) 223333), the home of the Duke of Roxburghe, which endures tourist masses. Nearly 400 windows offer spectacular views of the Tweed. A holly in the gardens memorializes the site where James II was killed while inspecting a cannon. Try not to make the same mistake. Scores of turrets and vast grounds make this the most impressive sight in the area. (*Open Easter-Sept. daily 10am-4:30pm; Oct. Su and W 10:30am-4pm. £4.50, seniors £3.75, children £2.50; grounds only £2.*) The ruins of yet another King David-raised, Earl of Hertford-razed **abbey** linger near the Market Sq. in Kelso. (*Open Apr.-Sept. M-Sa 9:30am-6pm, Su noon-6pm; Oct.-Mar. M-Sa 9:30am-4pm, Su noon-4pm. Free.*)

The **bus station** (tel. 224141) is off Roxburgh St. near Market Sq. and offers **luggage services** for 50p per bag (open M-F 8:45am-1pm and 2-5pm, Sa 8:45-11am). Kelso's **tourist office** (tel. 223464) is in the old town hall in Market Sq., and books rooms for a deposit. (Open July-Aug. M-Sa 9:30am-6:30pm, Su 10am-5pm; Sept. M-Sa 10am-5:30pm, Su 10am-5pm; Apr.-May M-Sa 10am-5pm, Su 10am-1pm; June M-Sa 10am-5:30pm, Su 10am-1pm; Oct. M-Sa 10am-4:30pm, Su 10am-1pm.) The **post office** (tel. 224795) is on Woodmarket, off the square (open M-F 9am-5:30pm, Sa 9am-12:30pm). The **postal code** is TD5 7AT. The **telephone code** is 01573.

Stay with **Mr. Watson,** Clashdale, 26 Inchmead Dr. (tel. 223405), for simple, spacious rooms (£15). **Mrs. Robertson,** Duncen House, Chalkheugh Terr. (tel. 225682), offers a huge 5-person room with a view of the river and Floors Castle (£15.50). Munch away at **The Home Bakery** (tel. 226782), on Horsemarket, which offers pies and sandwiches (around £1.50). Restock your supplies at the **Safeway** on Roxburgh St. (open M-W and F 8am-8pm, Th 8am-9pm, Sa 8am-6pm, Su 9am-6pm).

■ Majestic Homes of the Borders

The Borders are replete with stately homes and abbeys scattered among the towns, including the Floors Castle (Kelso), Neidpath Castle (Peebles) and the house of Mary, Queen of Scots (Jedburgh). Of the four abbeys, Melrose and Jedburgh are impressive and easily accessible, but more touristy. There's not much left at Kelso, but for those with time and the willingness to walk, the real treasure is **Dryburgh Abbey** (tel. (01835) 822381), which has extensive ruins, including a cloister, Sir Walter Scott's grave, and serene grounds. Climb the dangerously narrow spiral staircase at the southeast corner for a 50 ft. view and slight vertigo. The Abbey is 5 mi. southeast of Melrose; take a bus that goes through St. Boswell's and ask the driver to drop you off. Follow the marked road, cross the footbridge, then turn right—about a 20-minute walk. (*Open Apr.-Sept. M-Sa 9:30am-6:30pm, Su 2-6:30pm; Oct.-Mar. M-Sa 9:30am-4:30pm, Su 2-4:30pm; last admission 30min. before closing. £2.30, seniors £1.75, children £1.*) A 22 ft. statue of William Wallace and the spectacular **Scott's Point** vista are nearby.

Sir Walter Scott settled into his mock-Gothic **Abbotsford** estate (tel. (01896) 752043), 3 mi. west of Melrose, to write most of his Waverley novels, and died here by the river in 1832. Scott was an avid collector, and the house is stuffed with books, armor, and knick-knacks, including a lock of Bonnie Prince Charlie's hair and a piece of the gown worn by Mary, Queen of Scots at her execution. (*Open mid-Mar. to Oct. M-Sa 10am-5pm, Su 2-5pm. £3.50, children £1.80.*) Buses traveling between Galashiels and Melrose via Tweedbank stop nearby. Ask the driver to drop you at the bus stop on the east side of the River Tweed bridge; from the Galashiels side of the road, a dirt path dips down a hill, then climbs uphill to the entrance.

Twelfth-century **Traquair House** (tel. (01896) 830323), the most ancient inhabited house in Scotland, stands 12 mi. west of Galashiels off the A72 and then 1½ mi. from Innerleithen on the B709. The family treasures of the Stewarts of Traquair, including embroideries and letters of the better-known Stewarts of Scotland, are displayed upstairs. The main gates are permanently closed; legend has it that the Earl of Stair swore after Prince Charlie's defeat at Culloden in 1745 that they would not be reopened until another Stewart took the throne. Catherine Stewart, the present resident, brews ale in the 200-year-old brewery below the chapel. *(Open June-Aug. daily 10:30am-5:30pm; mid-Apr. to May and Sept. daily 12:30-5:30pm; Oct. F-Su 2-5pm; last admission 30min. before closing. £4.50, seniors £4, children £2.25. Beer tasting June-Sept. F 2-4pm.)*

Ten miles north of Melrose on the A68 near Lauder stands **Thirlestane Castle** (tel. (01578) 722430), easily accessible by bus. One of the most beautifully restored castles in Scotland, Thirlestane is worth a visit if only to relive its bloody history. Jealous nobles hanged a host of King James III's low-born supporters here in 1482. *(Castle open July-Aug. Su-F noon-5pm; May-June and Sept. Su-M and W-Th 2-5pm; last admission 4:30pm. £4, children £3. Grounds open May-Sept. same days as castle noon-6pm. £1.50.)*

Near Kelso on the A6089 is the Georgian **Mellerstain House** (tel. (01573) 410225), begun in 1725 by William Adam and completed by his son Robert. *(Open May-Sept. Su-F 12:30-4:30pm. £4.50, students and seniors £3.50, children £2.)* Most buses from Galashiels to Kelso drive by the turnoff to Mellerstain; ask the driver to stop, then walk the mile to the house. You haven't really experienced ornate until you've walked the sumptuous halls of **Manderston House** (tel. (01361) 883450), 2 mi. east of the town of Duns on the A6105. The doors reveal a silver staircase, silk wallpaper, and a marble dairy and tower. *(Open mid-May to Sept. Th and Su 2-5:30pm. £5, children £1; grounds only £2.50, children 50p.)* The 18th-century, Neopalladian **Paxton House** (tel. (01289) 386291) lies 5 mi. west of Berwick-upon-Tweed. *(Open mid-Apr. to Oct. daily 11am-5pm; last admission 4:15pm; grounds open daily 10am-sunset. £4, seniors £3.50, children £2.)*

■ Dumfries and Galloway

Galloway, the southernmost region of Scotland, derives its name from medieval Welsh neighbors who dubbed the area *Galwyddel* ("Land of the stranger Gaels"). The area today is stranger-free; there are few tourists, and local officials proclaim the region "undiscovered." Through the centuries, the region has passed into the hands of Romans, Vikings, and English feudal lords; each of these owners has left behind at least a few sights to visit. The local hero is Dumfriesshire native Robert the Bruce, who finally won independence for Scotland in 1314.

Although the region is known as Scotland's "quiet country," locals know how to celebrate as well as any bunch of Scots. Dumfries's **Guid Nychburris Festival** (pronounced "good neighbors"), starting on the third Saturday in June, is a week-long celebration with performances and riding reenactments. The **Dumfries and Galloway Arts Festival,** held at the end of May throughout the region, offers a variety of music and dance performances, craft shows, painting exhibits, poetry recitations, and plays.

GETTING ABOUT

Buses run frequently, but it's hard to know when. The tourist offices provide a **Public Transport Map** and several regional **Public Transport Guides,** including the useful Wigtownshire (Western Galloway) and Stewartry (between Kirkcudbright and Dumfries). Several bus companies crisscross the area; call **Western Buses** (tel. (01387) 253496), **MacEwan's Service** (tel. (01387) 710357), **McCulloch's Coaches** (tel. (01776) 830236), or the **Travel Information Line** (tel. (0345) 090510; M-F 9am-5pm) for schedule information. A **Day Discoverer Ticket,** purchased from the driver, allows unlimited travel in the Dumfries and Galloway region, as well as Stagecoach travel in Cumbria (£5, children £2, families £10).

HIKING AND BIKING

Dumfries and Galloway stock a magnificent stretch of coastline, with a reserve supply of fields, forests, and hills. Two peninsulas—the **Machars** and the **Rhins of Galloway**—jut southward; hikers can follow the 30 mi. **Pilgrim's Way** down the Machars from the Glenluce Abbey to the Isle of Whithorn at the southern tip, where St. Ninian founded a church in the 4th century. For those with leisure and ambition, the **South Upland Way** begins at Portpatrick, then snakes its way in a northeasterly direction, passing **SYHA hostels** in **Kendoon, Wanlockhead, Broadmeadows,** and **Melrose.** For shorter walks, ask a tourist office for the free *Walking in Dumfries and Galloway* guide, which describes over 30 possible walks. Also pick up *Ranger Led Walks and Events* (free). If you're planning a strenuous hike, check the weather (tel. (0891) 500420) and bring the necessary survival supplies, maps, and compass.

Cyclists will find *Cycling in Dumfries and Galloway* (£1 at tourist offices) equally useful. The Forest Enterprise also puts out smaller leaflets describing on- and off-trail routes in some of the area's forests—ask at the tourist office. For bike rental, try **Ace Cycles,** Church St., Castle Douglas (tel. (01556) 504542; £10 per day, £50 per week; open Apr.-Dec. M-Sa 9am-5pm; Jan. and Mar. M-W and F-Sa 9am-5pm; closed Feb.), or **Belgrano Bike Hire,** 6 Church Ln., Newton Stewart (tel. (01671) 403307; open daily 9:30am-5pm). You can also pick up and drop off bikes at the owner's **B&B,** 81 Main St., Glenluce, by prior arrangement (£6 per 6hr., £10 per day, £25 per week).

■ Dumfries

Dumfriesshire hangs its tam upon tales of two famous Roberts. Robert the Bruce proclaimed himself King of Scotland in Dumfries after stabbing throne-contender Red Comyn at Greyfriars. Robert Burns lived and wrote in Dumfries from 1791 until his death in 1796. Along with its historical claims, Dumfries's central location and transportation connections make it the unofficial capital of southwest Scotland. Even so, Dumfries fails to catch—let alone hold—one's interest; hurry through the town to reach the charm of the countryside.

PRACTICAL INFORMATION Dumfries is easily reached by public transport. **Trains** (tel. (0345) 484950) run from **Newcastle via Carlisle** to Dumfries, continuing to **Glasgow** (Carlisle to Dumfries 35min., M-Sa 7 per day, Su 3 per day, £6.20; Glasgow's Central Station to Dumfries 1¾hr., M-Sa 7 per day, Su 2 per day, £15.90). **London** can be reached by rail, with a train change in **Carlisle** or **Glasgow. Stagecoach Western Scottish** (tel. 253496) bus #X2 runs directly to Dumfries from **Glasgow's** Buchanan Station (2hr., M-F 5 per day, Sa-Su 1 per day, £6.30); bus #100 sets out for Dumfries from **Edinburgh's** St. Andrew's Sq. (2-3hr., M-Sa 3 per day, Su 1 per day, £5.50).

The Dumfries **tourist office,** 64 Whitesands Rd. (tel. 253862; fax 250462), houses a host of helpful pamphlets and other literature, including a shelf of (no, really?) Burns books. Pick up the free, info-laden *Dumfries and Galloway Visitors Guide, What's On,* and *Fascinating Facts about Dumfries and Galloway.* (Open daily June-Sept. 9:30am-6pm; Oct. 10am-5pm; Nov.-May 10am-5pm.) The **Royal Bank of Scotland ATM** resides at Queensberry Sq. off High St. Dumfries's **post office** is at 7 Great King St. (tel. 256690; open M-F 9am-5:30pm, Sa 9am-12:30pm); its **postal code** is DG1 1AA. The superb **Cybercentre,** Ewart Library, Catherine St. (tel. 253820), provides **Internet access** (£3 per 30min., £5 per hr.; open M-W and F 10am-7:30pm, Th and Sa 10am-5pm). The **telephone code** is 01387.

ACCOMMODATIONS AND FOOD B&Bs are easy to find with the help of the *Accommodations Guide* from the tourist office; a number of reasonably priced abodes lie along Lockerbie Rd., at the north of the city and across the train tracks. Try **Selmar House,** 41 Cardoness St. (tel. 250126), for simple, clean, and refreshing rooms with TV in a family environment (£15 per person). The friendly proprietors of the **Knock Guest House,** 1 Lockerbie Rd. (tel. 253487), more than make up for the noisy street outside (£15 per person). Cafes line the pedestrian zones of High St. and its offshoots between English St. and the statue of Bobby Burns, while fish and chips can be caught along Whitesands Rd. Politically correct munchies are distributed at **Dumfries Health and Wholefoods,** 29-31 English St. (tel. 261065; open M-Sa 9am-5:30pm).

SIGHTS The **Dumfries Museum,** Church St. (tel. 253374), is a restored windmill housing artifacts of local history, some dating back to the Stone Age. For a bird's-eye view of town, take a peek from the top of the windmill at the oldest *camera obscura* built for stargazing in the world (c. 1836). *(Open Apr.-Sept. M-Sa 10am-5pm, Su 2-5pm.*

Oct.-Mar. Tu-Sa 10am-1pm and 2-5pm. Free. Camera obscura £1.20, students, seniors, and children 60p.) Lest its auld acquaintance be forgot, Dumfries has devoted many a site to Burns. The wee **Burns House,** Burns St. (tel. 255297), contains many of the poet's original manuscripts and editions. Burns died here after aggravating an illness by bathing—on a doctor's advice—in a nearby well. The well's water, which looks like rusty cola, can be seen in all its glory in the short film at the Burns Centre. *(House hours same as Dumfries Museum. Free.)* Nearby, in an ornate **mausoleum** (tel. 255297), in St. Michael's Kirkyard, St. Michael St., the poet rests in peace; an immaculate, white marble Burns leans on a plow and seems surprised to see an attractive muse inspiring him overhead. Across the river, the **Robert Burns Centre,** Mill Rd. (tel. 264808), contains a bookshop, a scale model of 18th-century Dumfries Town, and, of course, Robert Burns paraphernalia, including a cast of his skull. A 20-minute film runs through a sentimental version of Burns's life; the 10 million Burns songs make it worth the small entry fee. *(Open Apr.-Sept. M-Sa 10am-8pm, Su 2-5pm; Oct.-Mar. Tu-Sa 10am-1pm and 2-5pm. Film £1.20, students, seniors, disabled, and children 60p.)* In the evenings, the audio-visual room becomes the **Robert Burns Centre Film Theatre,** which screens award-winners and cult classics. Pick up a schedule at the tourist office or the Centre, or check local papers for listings. *(Shows Tu-Sa 8pm. £4, students, seniors, disabled, and children £2.45, families £10.45. Buy tickets in advance.)* The **Old Bridge House Museum,** Mill Rd. (tel. 256904), at the end of the bridge, packs many a gruesome tale in its eclectic period paraphernalia and four tiny rooms. Attractions include a chair once sat upon by Grierson of Lag, who had women tied to stakes on the beach while the tide came in because they wouldn't become Episcopalians. The fake teeth in the dentistry collection, juxtaposed with nightmarishly primitive equipment, conjure up scenes of gore. *(Open Apr.-Sept. M-Sa 10am-5pm, Su 2-5pm. Free.)*

■ Near Dumfries

Seven miles south of Dumfries on the B725 just beyond Glencaple, is moated triangular **Caerlaverock Castle** (car-LAV-rick; tel. (01387) 770244), one of the finest medieval ruins in Scotland. No one is sure whether this strategic marvel was built for Scottish defense or English offense; it was seized by England's Edward I in 1300 and passed around like a hot kipper thereafter. *(Open Apr.-Sept. daily 9:30am-6:30pm; Oct.-Mar. M-Sa 9:30am-4:30pm, Su 2-4:30pm. £2.30, seniors £1.75, children £1.)* **Western Bus** #371 runs to the castle from the Loreburn Shopping Centre, off Irish St. (not Loreburn Rd.), in Dumfries (M-Sa 11 per day, Su 2 per day, return £2). Many thumb along the B725 (Bankend Rd.). To get there from Whitesands at the center of Dumfries, turn left onto St. Michael's St., right onto Nithbank Ave., and left onto Bankend Rd.

Also within easy reach of Dumfries is **Sweetheart Abbey** (tel. (01387) 850395), 7 mi. southwest along the A710. The abbey was founded by Lady Devorguilla Balliol in memory of her husband John. She was later buried in the abbey with her husband's embalmed-and-probably-no-longer-sweet heart clutched to her breast—how romantic. One of the three Cistercian abbeys of Galloway, the rose-tinted limestone church dates from the late 13th century. *(Open Apr.-Sept. daily 9:30am-6:30pm; Oct.-Mar. M-W and Sa 9:30am-4:30pm, Th 9:30am-1pm, Su 2-4:30pm. £1.20, seniors 90p, children 50p.)* Take **MacEwan's** bus #372 to New Abbey from Dumfries's Whitesands depot stance 5 (M-Sa 7 per day, Su 4 per day; £1.10 return).

Nine miles southeast of Dumfries, **Ruthwell's** church contains the magnificent 7th-century **Ruthwell Cross,** which bears dense carvings of vine scrolls, beasts of Celtic art, and everyone's favorite Anglo-Saxon poem, *The Dream of the Rood,* in the margins. Get the key to the church from Mrs. Coulthard (tel. (01387) 870249). **Western Buses** connect Dumfries and Ruthwell. Take the bus to Annan via Clarence Field, and get off at Ruthwell. (30min., M-Sa 1 per hr., Su every 2hr., return £2.80).

Nearby **Wanlockhead** is Scotland's highest village, complete with nosebleeds and a **SYHA Youth Hostel** (tel./fax (01659) 74252; 28 beds; £6.10, under 18 £5; open Apr.-Oct. daily). You can reach Wanlockhead by walking along the Southern Upland Way; there is an **Information Shelter** here. Some opt to hitch the B797, which branches off the A76 2 mi. south of Sanquhar, miles downhill from Wanlockhead.

Eighteen miles north of Dumfries off the A76 is **Drumlanrig Castle** (tel. (01848) 330248), home of the Duke of Buccleuch. See the impressive grounds and birds of prey exhibitions. *(Castle open by guided tour daily May to mid-Aug. noon-4pm. Reserved for pre-booked groups 11am-noon. Grounds open May-Aug. daily 11am-5pm; exhibitions everyday except Th; call for times. £6, students and seniors £4, children £2, families £14.)*

■ Kirkcudbright

In the center of Dumfries and Galloway lies the dignified old coastal town of Kirkcudbright (Car-COO-bree), also known as "the artists' town." Its angular High St. holds some lovely examples of old Scottish buildings and Georgian homes.

PRACTICAL INFORMATION Buses #500, 501, and 505 travel to **Dumfries** (1 per hr.), while #431 connects to **Newton Stewart.** (1hr., M-Sa 7-8 per day, Su 2 per day, £3.05; many continue also to **Stranraer**). The **tourist office,** Harbour Sq. (tel. 330494), can direct you to galleries and workshops; the staff also books rooms for a deposit and exchanges currency (open daily July-Aug. 9:30am-6pm, Sept.-Oct. 10am-5pm, Apr.-June 10am-5pm). A **Royal Bank of Scotland ATM,** St. Cuthbert and St. Mary's St., accepts Cirrus cards. The small **post office** preens at 5 St. Cuthbert's Pl. (tel. 330578; open M-F 9am-12:30pm and 1:30-5:30pm, Sa 9am-12:30pm). Kirkcudbright's **postal code** is DG6 4DH. **Internet access** (tel. 31240) is available at the library, Sheriff Court House, High St. (£3 per 30min., £5 per hr.; open M and W 2:30-7:30pm, Tu and F 10am-12:30pm and 2:30-7:30pm, Th and Sa 10am-12:30pm and 2-5pm.) The **telephone code** is 01557.

ACCOMMODATIONS AND FOOD For B&B above a fountained garden, contact fabulous **Mrs. McIlwraith,** 22 Millburn St. (tel. 330056), in her bright blue house with oh-so-comfortable beds (singles £16; twins £30). Pick up groceries at the **Safeway** on St. Cuthbert's St., at Millburn St. (open M-W and Sa 8am-7pm, Th and F 8am-8pm, Su 10am-4pm). The **Royal Hotel** offers an all-you-can-eat lunch buffet for £5 (M-Sa noon-2:30pm), and an almost all-you-can-eat dinner buffet for £6.50 (F-Sa 6:30-9pm, Su noon-3pm). A live band entertains here on Sunday nights.

SIGHTS Attracted by the town's colorful harbor and miles of surrounding idyllic countryside, a circle of prominent Scottish painters and designers took residence in Kirkcudbright in the 1890s and transformed it into a hotbed of artistic creativity. Today, some aspiring and established artists still frequent the town. An excellent gallery and audio-visual show detail the town's history at the **Tolbooth Art Centre,** High St. (tel. 331556). The exhibit is housed in the oldest surviving tolbooth in Scotland (c. 1629-1762), which once imprisoned mariner John Paul Jones. *(Open July-Aug. M-Sa 10am-6pm, Su 2-5pm; Mar.-Apr. and Sept.-Oct. M-Sa 11am-4pm; Nov.-Feb. Sa 11am-4pm. £1.50, students and children 75p.)* **Broughton House,** 12 High St. (tel. 330437), displays the artwork (mostly carefree girls cavorting amidst wildflowers) of E.A. Hornel, leader of the turn-of-the-century group of artists. The garden is everything a British garden could ever hope to be; bright green lawns, thick hedges, lily ponds, sundials, greenhouses, rose beds, and harbor views await. Though not vast like some country estates, this garden has plenty of charm. *(Open daily Apr.-Oct. 1-5:30pm, last admission 4:45pm. £2.40, students, seniors and children £1.60, families £6.40.)* **MacLellan's Castle,** a 16th-century tower house, dominates the town from Castle St. near Harbour Sq. You can sneak into the "Laird's Lug," a secret chamber behind a fireplace from which the Laird could eavesdrop on conversations in the Great Hall. Not a bad ruin, but it'll take 20 minutes tops. *(Castle open Apr.-Sept. daily 9:30am-6:30pm, Su 2-6:30pm; Oct.-Nov. M-W and Sa 9:30am-4:30pm, Th 9:30am-12:30pm, Su 2-4:30pm, closed Dec.-Mar.; last admission 30min. before closing. £1.20, students and seniors 90p, children 50p.)* The **Kirkcudbright Summer Festivities** include everything from treasure hunts to fishing contests; ask for a schedule at the tourist office. *(Mid-July to Aug.)*

■ Near Kirkcudbright

Gatehouse of Fleet lies northwest of Kirkcudbright in the 300-year-old **Murray Arms,** where Robert Burns penned the words to "Scots Wha Hae," a popular native ditty. The banks of sleepy **Water of Fleet,** about 3 mi. north of Gatehouse of Fleet, turn a rich gold in autumn. About a mile west on the A75 is **Cardoness Castle** (tel. (0131) 668 8800), a rocky stronghold of the McCullochs for five centuries. This is the only castle in Scotland with a two-seat toilet; if you ask nicely, the castle curator may let you try it out with a friend. *(Castle open Apr.-Sept. daily 9:30am-6:30pm; Oct.-Mar. Sa 9:30am-4:40pm and Su 2-4:30pm. £1.80, seniors £1.30, children 75p. Toilet free.)* **Mossyard Beach,** a pleasant sandy strip, is sign-posted off the A75, 2 mi. from Gatehouse of Fleet. The **tourist office** in the carpark (tel. (01557) 814212) can direct you to these and other area attractions. (Open daily July-Aug. 10am-6pm; May-June and Sept. 10am-5pm; Apr. and Oct. 10am-4:30pm.) **Bus** #500 runs between Stranraer and Dumfries via Gatehouse (M-Sa 4 per day, Su 2 per day).

■ Castle Douglas

Northeast of Kirkcudbright on the A75 lies **Castle Douglas,** an attractive town with a cattle auction and market every Tuesday. One mile west, the wonderful 60-acre **Threave Garden** bursts with blooms gingerly pruned by students of the School of Gardening. *(Garden open daily 9:30am-sunset, walled garden and glasshouses open daily 9:30am-5pm; visitor's center open Apr.-Oct. daily 9:30am-5:30pm. £3.70, children £2.50.)* Buses between Kirkcudbright and Castle Douglas pass the Garden turnoff; ask the driver to stop, and walk 10 minutes. A mile or two further west, **Threave Castle** commands an island on the **River Dee.** Built by Archibald the Grim—a reference to his hideous countenance in battle—Threave was the last stronghold of the Earls of Douglas to surrender to James II in 1453; it was taken again and ravaged in 1640 by Covenanters. The Kirkcudbright-Castle Douglas bus can drop you off at the roundabout on the A75; follow signs for Threave Castle on the road that ends at Kelton Mains Farm. Follow the well-marked path until you see the roofless keep; when you ring the ship's bell nearby, a boatperson should arrive to ferry you across the River Dee (included in the entrance fee). The castle lies in glorious ruin, with excellent views through holes in the walls and lots of nesting swallows. *(Open Apr.-Sept. daily 9:30am-6:30pm; last boat 6pm. £1.80, seniors £1.30, children 75p.)*

    MacEwan's buses #500 and 501 zip from **Kirkcudbright** to Castle Douglas (12 per day, £1.30). For beds nearby, ask the staff at the **tourist office,** Market Hill (tel. (01556) 502611), to help you find a room for a deposit. (Open daily July-Aug. 10am-6pm; May-June and Sept. 10am-5pm; Apr. and Oct. 10am-4:30pm.) Castle Douglas has an **ATM** at the **Royal Bank of Scotland** on King St. To reach the simple but charming **SYHA Kendoon Hostel** (tel. (01644) 460680), take the A713 north to Dalry, turn off and follow the A702 towards Moniaive for less than a quarter mile, then make a left onto the B700 north towards Carsphairn; the hostel is 3 mi. ahead on your left. (£4.65, under 18 £3.85. No showers. Open mid-Mar. to Sept.) Castle Douglas brims with **B&Bs;** for pastoral delights, try the spacious accommodations at **Chapmonton Farm** (tel. (01556) 503029), where Mrs. Bothwell has rooms that overlook miles of pleasant pasture (£15, children 4-12 £7.50). Head northwest out of town on Abercromby Rd., continue under the overpass, and a sign on the right will direct you to the farm. Head southeast from Castle Douglas (southwest from Dumfries) through the town of **Dalbeattie** to the beaches at **Sandyhill** and **Rockcliffe.**

■ Stranraer

On the westernmost peninsula of Dumfries and Galloway, Stranraer (stran-RAHR) is the place to get a ferry to Northern Ireland and a good base for exploring the sights of Western Galloway. In town, the only sight is the looming form of **Castle of St. John** (tel. 705088), on George St., built in 1510 by the Adairs of Kihilt. Today, the walls defend exhibits on law and order. *(Open Apr.-Sept. M-Sa 10am-1pm and 2-5pm. £1, chil-*

dren 50p.) Four miles east of Stranraer on the A75, the ivy-clad ruins of **Castle Kennedy** (tel. 702024) sit beside splendid gardens. **Lochinich Castle,** seat of the Earl of Stair, is visible across the lake. *(Open Apr.-Sept. daily 10am-5pm. £2, seniors £1.50, children £1. Wheelchair access.)* Frequent buses run from Stranraer past the castle; it's about a mile off the main road.

Trains (tel. (0345) 484950) connect **Glasgow** to Stranraer (MacEwan; 2½hr., M-Sa 7 per day, Su 2 per day, £18.50). From Stranraer, **buses** run to **Dumfries** (#500, 3hr., M-Sa 4-5 per day, Su 3 per day) and to **Ayr** and **Glasgow** (Citylink #923, 1½ hr., to Ayr, 2½hr. to Glasgow, 2 per day). **National Express** (tel. (0990) 808080) lumbers to **London** (9hr., 1 per day) **via Carlisle** (3hr.), **Manchester** (6½hr., 1 per day), and **Birmingham** (7½hr., 2 per day). **Seacat** (tel. (0990) 523523) skims the water to **Belfast** in 1½hr. (5 per day, £24, students and seniors £16, children £14). **Stena Line** (tel. (0990) 707070) also sends ferries to **Belfast** (1¾hr., 10 per day, £23, students and seniors £17, children £12). Five miles up the coast at **Cairnyan,** P&O Ferries (tel. (0990) 980777) depart for **Larne** (1-2¼hr., 8 per day, £22, students, seniors and children £11). See **By Ferry,** p. 32, for more information. The **tourist office,** 1 Bridge St. (tel. 702595; fax 889156), posts a list of B&Bs and books rooms for a deposit. Pick up the handy *What's On* guide as well. (Open June-Sept. M-Sa 9:30am-6pm, Su 10am-6pm; Apr.-May and Oct. M-Sa 9:30am-5pm, Su 10am-4pm; Nov.-Mar. M-Sa 10am-4pm.) If you need money to placate the pirates, visit the **ATM** on Hanover St. The Tesco on Charlotte St. houses Stranraer's **post office** (tel. 702587; open M-W 8:30am-6pm, Th-F 8:30am-8pm, Sa 8am-6pm, Su 11am-4pm). Stranraer's **postal code** is DG9 74F; the **telephone code** is 01776.

If you're marooned, check B&Bs on the A75 towards the castles (London Rd.), or try the **Jan Da Mar Guest House,** 1 Ivy Pl. (tel. 706194), on London Rd, whose owners supply superb rooms and conversation (singles £18; twins £32). Should you fancy munchies, the **Tesco** supermarket, on Charlotte St. at Port Rodie near the ferry terminal, burgeons with goods (open M-F 8:30am-8pm, Sa 8am-6pm, Su 10am-5pm). **Romano's,** 36-38 Charlotte St., serves good, quick food (hot rolls 85p-£1.20; toasted sandwiches £1-1.20; take-away haggis—carry it with pride!—95p; open daily in summer 9am-10pm; about 9am-8pm in winter).

■ Western Galloway

Western Galloway splits time between two peninsulas. The western one, a north-south hammerhead, lies just 25 mi. from Ireland across the North Channel. Eight miles southwest of Stranraer on the A77 is the quiet family vacation village of **Portpatrick,** one end of the **South Upland Way** (see p. 478). On weekends, wealthy yacht owners sail here from Northern Ireland for Sunday lunch—you can stroll by the harbor with your crusty bread and overladen pack and yearn for the good life. Bus #367 makes the 20-minute jaunt from Stranraer to Portpatrick (M-F 5-8 per day, Sa 7 per day; on Tu and Th also #411; £2.10 return).

Sixteenth-century **Dunskey Castle** lies on a spectacular cliff overlooking the ocean, a 20-minute walk from Portpatrick harbor. On the left side of the harbor as you face the water, a long flight of steps leads up to the path to the castle. As the castle ruins are neither publicly nor privately owned (and as they are ruins), they are free and open to the public 24 hours a day. Dunskey might be the most secluded, romantic castle you'll visit; beautiful wildflowers and stunning sea views await. Several caravan parks back onto the castle and cliffs; to reach them from the front, take the first left after the war memorial on the A77 from Stranraer. Sleep on a breathtaking stretch of lawn at the **Castle Bay Caravan Park** (tel. (01776) 810462), the furthest down the road. The park has excellent facilities, including showers, bathrooms, and a "giant-screen cinema" (£5 per tent; open Mar.-Oct.).

At **Sandhead,** on the eastern shore of peninsula and south of Stranraer, the eerie **Kirkmadrine Stones,** three of the earliest Christian monuments in Britain, stand on a windswept hill. The *chi-rho* symbol and other inscriptions date from the 5th or 6th century. Bus #407 on the Stranraer-Stoneykirk-Drummore line stops at Sandhead (4

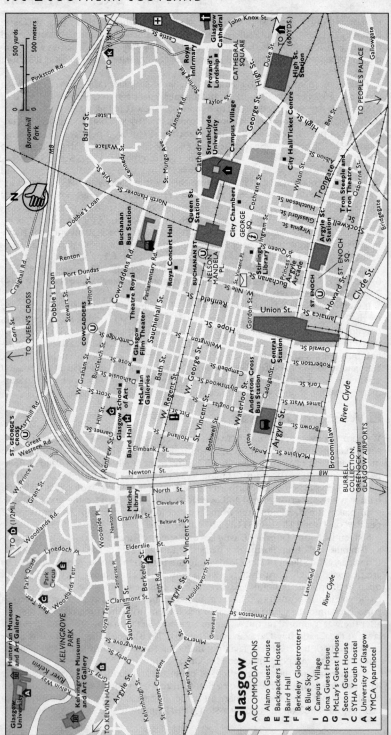

SCOTLAND

500 yards
500 meters

Pinkston Rd.

Broomhill Park

TO QUEEN'S CROSS

Corn St.

Dobbie's Loan

Craigball Rd.

Baird St.

Lister

St. Mungo Ave.

Kennedy St.

Kyle St.

North Hanover St.

Dobbie's Loan

Renton

Port Dundas

Stewart St.

Milton St.

Cowcaddens Rd.

Parliamentary Rd.

Castle St.

Stirling Rd.

St. James's Rd.

Wallace St.

Taylor St.

✚ Royal Infirmary

Glasgow Cathedral

Provand's Lordship

CATHEDRAL SQUARE

John Knox St.

George St.

High St.

Duke St.

High St. Station

TO PEOPLE'S PALACE

Gallowgate

(6807DS.)

Campus Village

Strathclyde University

Cathedral St.

City Hall/Ticket Centre

Queen St. Station

Cochrane St.

City Chambers

GEORGE SQ.

ℹ

Ingram St.

Glassford St.

Hutcheson St.

Wilson St.

Albion St.

Bell St.

Osborne St.

Trongate

Tron Steeple and Tron Theatre

Stockwell St.

Bridgegate

Clyde St.

St. ENOCH SQ.

St. ENOCH

Argyle St. Station

Howard St.

Jamaica St.

Union St.

Gordon St.

Central Station

Oswald St.

Robertson St.

York St.

James Watt St.

Brown St.

McAlpine St.

Broomielaw

BURRELL COLLECTION, GREENOCK and GLASGOW AIRPORTS

M8

River Clyde

Lancefield Quay

River Clyde

Finnieston St.

Minerva Way

Minerva St.

Houldsworth St.

Greenhill Pl.

Kent Rd.

Berkeley St.

St. Vincent St.

Claremont St.

Royal Terr.

Sauchiehall St.

Kelvingrove St.

Derby St.

Gray St.

Argyle St.

Kelvinhaugh St.

St. Vincent Crescent

TO KELVIN HALL

Kelvin Way

River Kelvin

Glasgow University

Kelvingrove Museum and Art Gallery

Hunterian Museum and Art Gallery

KELVINGROVE PARK

Park Terr.

Park Quad.

Park Circus

Woodlands Terr.

Lynedoch Pl.

Woodlands Rd.

Woodside Pl.

Newton St.

Granville St.

Cleveland St.

North St.

Mitchell Library

Elderslie St.

Berkeley St.

St. Vincent St.

Somerset Pl.

Lynedoch St.

Great Western Rd.

W. Prince's St.

Grant St.

Woodlands Rd.

ST. GEORGE'S CROSS

Maryhill Rd.

Garnethill St.

Renfrew St.

Garnet St.

Hill St.

Buccleuch St.

Rose St.

Scott St.

Dalhousie St.

Cambridge St.

COWCADDENS

Sauchiehall St.

Bath St.

Baird Hall

Glasgow School of Art

McLellan Galleries

Glasgow Film Theater

Theatre Royal

Buchanan Bus Station

Renfield St.

Hope St.

W. Regent St.

Holland St.

Pitt St.

Bothwell St.

Douglas St.

Wellington St.

W. George St.

St. Vincent St.

Blythswood St.

Waterloo St.

Cadogan St.

Campbell St.

Anderston Cross Bus Station

Argyle St.

Anderston

Newton St.

Elmbank St.

Bath St.

Royal Concert Hall

BUCHANAN ST.

NELSON MANDELA PL.

Nile St.

Buchanan St.

Princes Sq.

Argyle Arcade

Stirling's Library

Queen St.

Virginia St.

Vincent Pl.

West Nile St.

TO D (1/2MI.)

TO QUEEN'S CROSS

N

Glasgow

ACCOMMODATIONS

B Alamo Guest House
E Backpackers Hostel
H Baird Hall
F Berkeley Globetrotters & Blue Sky
I Campus Village
D Iona Guest Hosue
G McLay's Guest House
J Seton Guest House
C SYHA Youth Hostel
A University of Glasgow
K YMCA Aparthotel

per day, return £1.60); from Sandhead follow the signposts for about 2 mi. off the A716. Four miles from Drummore at the end of the peninsula—Scotland's southern-most point—a lighthouse stands on a cliff 200 ft. above the sea. Seven miles south of Sandhead, near Port Logan, lie the tropical-esque Logan Gardens (tel. (01776) 860231). The Gulf Stream's warming effect allows visitors to enjoy such exotic flora as eucalyptus and chusan palms. Watch the pheasants wander among the flower-beds. *(Open Mar.-Oct. daily 9:30am-6pm. £3, students and seniors £2.50, children £1. Group discounts available. Limited disabled access.)*

The town of **Newton Stewart** lies just north of Galloway's other peninsula. **The Museum** (tel. (01671) 402472) on York Rd. has an intriguing bouquet of local arti-'facts, from coal scuttles to ball gowns. *(Open daily May-June and Sept.-Oct. 2-5pm; July-Aug. 10am-12:30pm and 2-5pm; call for off-season visits. £1, children 20p.)* The friendly **tourist office,** Dashwood Sq. (tel. (01671) 402431), by the bus stop, books lodgings in the region for £1 and a 10% deposit. (Open daily July-Aug. daily 10am-6pm; May-June and Sept. 10am-5pm; Apr. and Oct. 10am-4:30pm.) **Mrs. Wallace,** Kiloran, 6 Auchendoon Rd. (tel. (01671) 402818), has a beautiful garden and comfortable rooms (£15 per person). The **SYHA Minnigaff** (tel. (01671) 402211), adjacent to Newton Stewart in the town of **Minnigaff,** is rarely full and has well-kept facilities. From Newton Stewart, cross the Cree Bridge at the end of town and make the first left on Cree Bridge Rd.; the hostel is about one-half mile on the left. (£6.10, under 18 £5. Self-catering kitchen. Showers. Bedroom lockout 10:30am-5pm. Curfew 11:30pm. Open late Mar. to Oct. Disabled access.)

From Newton Stewart, you can wander north to **Galloway Forest Park,** which sur-rounds **Glen Trool.** A 240 sq. mi. inland reserve with peaks over 2000 ft., the park offers superb day hikes and camping. Contact the Newton Stewart Forest District, Creebridge, Newton Stewart DG8 6AJ (tel. (01671) 402420).

In AD 397, St. Ninian founded the first Christian church in Scotland at **Whithorn Priory,** 45-47 George St., about 18 mi. south of Newton Stewart (tel. (01988) 500508). The present priory, currently under excavation, dates from the 12th cen-tury. A wealth of early Christian crosses resides in the museum next door. Fee includes guided tour, admission to Priory, a slide show, and the privilege of visiting an authentic 20th-century gift shop. *(Priory and dig open Apr.-Oct. daily 10:30am-5pm; last tour 4:30pm. £2.70, students, seniors, disabled, and children £1.50, families £7.50.)* Bus #415 runs from Newton Stewart (1hr., M-Sa 6 per day, Su 3 per day, return £2.90). Three miles south of Whithorn are 8th-century carvings in **St. Ninian's Cave,** the saint's rocky hermitage. Follow the A746 south from Whithorn, turn left onto the A747 toward Isle of Whithorn, and take a right at the signpost for Physgill Lodge; a beautiful ¾ mi. walk leads from the car park to the cave.

Farther south, the **Isle of Whithorn** is an old port creaking with fishing boats. The 13th-century chapel on the headland to the south is supposedly situated on the site of St. Ninian's original chapel. It also marks the end of the **Pilgrim's Way** (see **Hiking and Biking,** p. 484), which begins at **Glenluce** (tel. (0131) 668 8800), just north and west of the peninsula. The abbey has deteriorated since its founding in 1192 by Roland, Earl of Galloway; only Chapterhouse has retained a roof (and some killer acoustics). Legend has it that a wizard lured the black plague into the cellar of the abbey and starved it to death. *(Open Apr.-Sept. daily 9:30am-6:30pm; Oct.-Mar. Sa 9:30am-4:30pm, Su 2-4:30pm. £1.50, seniors £1, children 75p.)* Take bus #500 to Glenluce and walk 1½ mi. north along the road to New Luce.

■ Glasgow

Glasgow is a city of cultural opportunity. A gaggle of museums and galleries, all free, compete for the attention of locals as well as tourists. The city center's vital grid of Victorian buildings thrives with reawakened energy and urban commerce; Glasgow, which has suffered a reputation of industrial lackluster, is back on track.

A small town until Scotland's union with England in 1707, Glasgow grew as it exploited new markets, especially the tobacco trade, in the North American colonies.

In the 19th century, the tobacco lords turned their attention to heavy industry, and Glasgow became the greatest center of shipbuilding and steel production in the world, and a Victorian city second in importance only to London took root above the ruins of the medieval city. Glasgow suffered a long depression in the post-war period, which began to lift only in the 1980s. The watershed came in 1990, when Glasgow was proclaimed European City of Culture. The city pours millions of pounds into the arts, including public displays and exhibitions. A mile northwest of the gridded, frenetic downtown, the West End seethes with trendy creativity and artistic energy. Though not as heavily touristed as Edinburgh, Glasgow, Scotland's largest city and the 1999 European City of Architecture, is unique and unforgettable.

GETTING THERE

Glasgow lies in central Scotland on the Firth of Clyde, 45 minutes due west of Edinburgh. The M8 motorway links east and west coasts and Scotland's two largest cities. Glasgow's **Queen St. Station** serves **train** routes to the north and east: to **Edinburgh** (50min., 2 per hr., £7.10), **Aberdeen** (2½hr., M-Sa 1 per hr., Su 11 per day, £34), **Inverness** (3¼hr., 5 per day, £29), **Fort William** (3¾hr., M-Sa 3 per day, Su 2 per day, £22.70). **Central Station** serves southern Scotland, England, and Wales. Trains also run to **Stranraer** (2½hr., M-Sa 8 per day, Su 3 per day, £19.50), **Ardrossan** (connections to Brodick on the Isle of **Arran,** 1hr., 30 per day, £4.10), and **Dumfries** (1¾hr., M-Sa 7 per day, Su 2 per day, £16.40). The most frequent trains from **London** to Glasgow's Central Station leave from **King's Cross** Station and run via **York** and **Newcastle** (5-6hr., M-F up to 16 per day, Sa 20 per day, Su 5 per day, about £65).

All intercity **buses** leave **Buchanan Station. Scottish Citylink/National Express** goes to **Perth** (1½hr., 1 per hr., £6.80), **Aberdeen** (4hr., M-Sa 1 per hr., Su 12 per day, £13.30), **Edinburgh** (50min., M-Sa 4 per hr., Su 2 per hr., £4.50), **Oban** (3hr., M-Sa 3 per day, Su 2 per day, £10), and **Inverness** (3½-4½hr., 1 per hr., £11.50). National Express buses also depart daily from **London** to Glasgow (8hr., 4 per day from Victoria Station, £16). Many trains to Stranraer connect with the **ferries** to **Larne** in Northern Ireland or to **Dublin.** Sea passage for adults is discounted with a rail ticket. Students should check with the student travel offices at Glasgow University for cheap fares to Dublin via Stranraer. See **By Ferry,** p. 32, for route information.

GETTING ABOUT

Glasgow's transportation system includes suburban rail, a confusing variety of private local bus services, and the circular **Underground (U)** subway line, a.k.a. the "Clockwork Orange." (U trains run M-Sa 6:30am-11pm, Su 11am-6pm; 65p, children 30p.) Wave your hand to ensure that buses stop for you, and carry exact change (fares usually 55-80p, depending on destination). Strathclyde Transport Authority runs an immensely useful **Travel Centre,** St. Enoch's Sq. (tel. 226 4826; U: St. Enoch), two blocks from Central Station (open M-Sa 8:30am-5:30pm), dishing out advice on the best means of transportation and passes. **Underground Season Tickets** are a good deal at £5.40 for seven days (children £2.70), or £19 for 28 days (children £9.50; bring a photo and ID to the Underground office at St. Enoch station). The **Underground Heritage Trail** ticket (£2) provides unlimited underground transport for a day and an information leaflet. For a whirlwind tour, see if you can travel fast and far enough to get your money's worth from a **Roundabout Glasgow ticket,** which covers one day of unlimited Underground and train travel (£3.40, children £1.70). A **Roundabout Glasgow Plus** includes unlimited use of a city bus tour service (£6.50, children £3.25; £13 for 3 days, children £6.50).

ORIENTATION

George Sq. is the physical center of town; the train and bus stations, tourist office, and cathedral are all within a few blocks. Areas such as **Sauchiehall St.** (SAW-kee-hall), **Argyle,** and **Buchanan St.** have been pedestrianized and form busy shopping districts in the city center. **Charing Cross,** in the northwest where Bath St. crosses the M8 Motorway, is used as a general locator. The vibrant **West End** revolves around **Byres Rd.** and **Glasgow University,** one mile northwest of the city center.

To reach the tourist office from Central Station, exit on **Union St.,** turn left and walk two blocks (ignoring the alleys), then take a right on **St. Vincent St.;** the tourist office is 3½ blocks up on your right. From Buchanan Station, exit onto **N. Hanover** at the opposite end of the station from the information booth, and with your back to the station, take a right and walk two blocks after **Killermont St.** to George Sq. and look across it. From Queen St. Station, exit onto **George St.,** and cross George Sq.

PRACTICAL INFORMATION

Transportation

Airplanes: Glasgow Airport (tel. 887 1111), 10mi. west in Abbotsinch. Served by Air Canada, Air France, Aer Lingus, Air UK, American, British Airways, British Midland, Lufthansa, Northwest, and others. Citylink buses run to Glasgow's Buchanan station (20min., 2 per hr., £2); and to **Edinburgh** (1¾hr., 2 per hr., £6.50).

Trains: Central Station, Gordon St. U: St. Enoch. Open daily 5:30am-midnight. **Travel Centre** open M-Sa 5:30am-10pm, Su 8am-10pm. Bathrooms 20p; shower with soap and towel £2. **Lockers** £2-4, for up to a day (all luggage is searched; open daily 6am-midnight). **Queen St. Station,** beside Copthorne Hotel, George Sq. U: Buchanan St. Bathrooms 20p. Open M-Sa 5am-12:30am, Su 7am-12:30am. **Travel Centre** open M-Sa 5:15am-11:15pm, Su 7am-11pm. Lockers available M-Sa 7:30am-9:15pm, Su 11:15am-7pm; £2-4; all luggage is searched. Bus #398 runs between the stations (4 per hr., 40p, children 20p); it's an 8-10min. walk. Credit card purchases (tel. (0800) 450450).

Buses: Buchanan Station (tel. 332 7133), 2 blocks north of Queen St. Station on N. Hanover St. The station houses **National Express** (tel. (0990) 808080 or 332 4100) and **Scottish Citylink** (tel. (0990) 505050). Bathrooms 20p. **Luggage storage** £1-2.50 per item (lockers open daily 6:30am-10:30pm). Ticket office open M-Sa 6:30am-10:30pm, Su 7am-10:30pm.

Taxi: Wide TOA Taxis (tel. 332 6666). **Dennistown Belvidere Private Hire Ltd.** (tel. 556 3111 or 554 4469).

Tourist and Financial Services

Tourist Office: 11 George Sq. (tel. 204 4400; fax 221 3524), off George Sq. south of Buchanan and Queen St. Stations, northeast of Central Station. U: Buchanan St. Travel bookshop; accommodations bookings £2; theater tickets; bureau de change; exhibition and 10min. film on the history of Glasgow. Pick up the *The Essential Guide to Glasgow, City Live!* (an entertainment guide, free), and *Where to Stay* (free). Open July-Aug. M-Sa 9am-8pm, Su 10am-6pm; June and Sept. M-Sa 9am-7pm, Su 10am-6pm; Oct.-May M-Sa 9am-6pm.

Tours: The Heart of Glasgow Walking Tour M-F 6pm, Su 10:30am. **The Cathedral Walk** W-Su 2:15pm. Both tours depart from the James Watt statue opposite the tourist office in George Sq. (tel. 204 4400; 1½hr.; May-Sept. £4, students, seniors, and children £3).

Bus Tours: Discovering Glasgow (tel. 204 0444) buses leave from George Sq. (9:30am-4pm, 3 per hr.; £6.50, students, seniors, and children £5, families £15). Or hop on **Guide Friday's** green-and-cream buses, also leaving from George Sq. (9:30am-5pm, 2 per hr.; £6.50, students and seniors £5, children £2, families £15).

Banks: Most are open M-F 9:30am-4:30pm; some also open Sa. **Thomas Cook,** 15-17 Gordon St. (tel. 204 4484), rests inside Central Station. Open daily 9:30am-9:30pm.

American Express: 115 Hope St. (tel. 221 4366; fax 204 2685). Client mail held. Open M-F 8:30am-5:30pm, Sa 9am-noon.

Local Services

Luggage Storage: Central, Queen, and **Buchanan Stations.** Subject to security search.

Launderette: Coin-Op Laundromat, 39-41 Bank St. (tel. 339 8953). U: Kelvin bridge. Soap and change available. Open M-F 9am-7:30pm, Sa-Su 9am-5pm.

Emergency and Communications

Emergency: Dial 999; no coins required.

Police: Stewart St. (tel. 532 3000).

Hotlines: Samaritans (crisis; tel. 248 4488). Open 24hr. **AIDS, HIV, and STD Helpline** (tel. (01324) 613944). **Gay and Lesbian Switchboard** (tel. 332 8372). Open daily 7-10pm. **Rape Crisis** (tel. 331 1990). Hours vary.

Pharmacy: Boots, 200 Sauchiehall St. (tel. 332 0774 or 332 1925). Open M-W and F-Sa 8:30am-6pm, Th 8:30am-7pm, Su 11am-5pm. Smaller branches, including ones at 400 Sauchiehall St., St. Enoch Sq., and Central Station.

Hospital: Glasgow Royal Infirmary, 84-106 Castle St. (tel. 211 4000).

Post Office: Post offices are sprinkled about the city center on Bothwell, Sauchiehall, Hope, and Renfrew St. near George Sq. Try 47 St. Vincent St. (tel. 204 3688). Open M-F 8:30am-5:45pm, Sa 9am-5:30pm. **Postal Code:** G2 5QX.

Internet Access: The Internet Café, 569 Sauchiehall St. (tel. 564 1052; fax 564 1054). £2.50 per 30min., students, seniors, and children £2. Open M-Th 9am-11pm, F 9am-9pm, Sa 10am-9pm, Su 10am-11pm. **Java Internet Cafe,** 152 Park Rd. (tel. 337 6814). £1.75 per 30min., students £1.50. Open daily 9am-11pm.

Telephone Code: 0141.

ACCOMMODATIONS

Glasgow undergoes a perennial bed shortage in the hot months. Book guesthouses, B&Bs, and hostels at least a month in advance, especially in August. Last-minute planners may wish to stay on the outskirts, particularly at the accessible and elegant **SYHA Loch Lomond** (see **Loch Lomond**, p. 509), or the **SYHA New Lanark** (see p. 499). If you enjoy paying £15-18 for mediocre urban B&Bs, the tourist office can often find you a room. If you'd rather wander, come early; most of Glasgow's B&Bs scatter to either side of the **Great Western Rd.** in the University area or east of the Necropolis near **Westercraigs Rd.**

SYHA Youth Hostel, 7-8 Park Terr. (tel. 332 3004; fax 331 5007), in a lovely residential area overlooking Kelvingrove Park. U: St. George's Cross. From Central Station, take bus #44 or 59 and ask for the *first stop* on Woodlands Rd. (at Lynedoch St.), then follow the sign. From Queen St. Station or Buchanan Station take bus #11. Once the residence of an English nobleman and later an upscale hotel, this hostel maintains an air of luxury. All rooms with bath. TV and game rooms, bike shed, laundry facilities, and in-house discotheque. July-Aug. £12.50, under 18 £11; Sept.-June £11.50, under 18 £10. Includes breakfast.

Alamo Guest House, 46 Gray St. (tel. 339 2395). No Texas flags here, just congenial proprietors and serene lodgings. Remember the spacious, quiet rooms with plenty of bathrooms! Singles £19; doubles £36.

Glasgow Backpackers Hostel, Kelvin Lodge, 8 Park Circus (tel. 332 9099). U: St. George's Cross. Beautiful Georgian terrace house with an experienced, friendly staff. £9.50; twins £22. Open July-Sept.

Blue Sky Hostel and **Berkeley Globetrotters Hostel,** 63-65 Berkeley St. (tel. 221 7880). 2 adjoining hostels with the same management, which can be separated to accommodate large groups. 4 lounges and 3 kitchens give the hostels a more homey, less institutional feel. £9.50, minimum stay 3 nights. Breakfast included.

University of Glasgow, 52 Hillhead St. (tel. 330 5385). Summer housing at several dorms. Open M-F 9am-5pm. **Queen Margaret Hall,** 55 Bellshaugh Rd. (tel. 334 2192), near Byres Rd., offers mostly singles. Tea and coffee, soap, towels, linen, and free laundry facilities available. £20.50, students £14.75. Breakfast included.

University of Strathclyde, Office of Sales and Marketing, 50 Richmond St. (tel. 553 4148), offers B&B in summer at a number of campus dorms. **Baird Hall,** 460 Sauchiehall St. (tel. 332 6415). Small kitchen on each floor, nicely furnished rooms, laundry facilities, and towels. Singles £18; twins £15.50 per person. No lockout or curfew. Available mid-June to Sept. Also 11 **guest rooms** usually filled by visiting professors. Singles £23.50; otherwise £19 per person. Available year-round. Wheelchair access. Accommodation also available at the 5 **Campus Village** dorms (tel. 552 0626), off Cathedral St. "Backpacker" bed (no sheets, towels, or breakfast) £9.50; bed with sheets, towels, tea, and coffee £11.50; B&B singles £17.50, with shower £22.50; doubles with shower £37.

MCI Spoken Here

Worldwide Calling Made Simple

For more information or to apply for a Card call: **1-800-955-0925**

Outside the U.S., call MCI collect (reverse charge) at: **1-916-567-5151**

International Calling As Easy As Possible.

Calling Card

MCI

123 456 7890 1234
J.D. SMITH

WorldPhone

The MCI Card with WorldPhone Service is designed specifically to keep you in touch with the people that matter the most to you.

The MCI Card with WorldPhone Service....

- Provides access to the US and other countries worldwide.

- Gives you customer service 24 hours a day

- Connects you to operators who speak your language

- Provides you with MCI's low rates and no sign-up fees

For more information or to apply for a Card call:
1-800-955-0925

Outside the U.S., call MCI collect (reverse charge) at:
1-916-567-5151

Pick Up the Phone, Pick Up the Miles.

You earn frequent flyer miles when you travel internationally, why not when you call internationally? Callers can earn frequent flyer miles if they sign up with one of MCI's airline partners:

- American Airlines
- Continental Airlines
- Delta Airlines
- Hawaiian Airlines
- Midwest Express Airlines
- Northwest Airlines
- Southwest Airlines
- United Airlines
- USAirways

Please cut out and save this reference guide for convenient U.S. and worldwide calling with the MCI Card with WorldPhone Service.

Your MCI Worldphone Access Numbers

COUNTRY	WORLDPHONE TOLL-FREE ACCESS #
# Singapore	8000-112-112
# Slovak Republic (CC)	00421-00112
# Slovenia	080-8808
# South Africa (CC)	0800-99-0011
# Spain (CC)	900-99-0014
# Sri Lanka	440100
# Sri Lanka (Outside of Colombo, dial 01 first)	
# St. Lucia ÷	1-800-888-8000
# St. Vincent	1-800-888-8000
# Sweden (CC) ♦	020-795-922
# Switzerland (CC) ♦	0800-89-0222
# Syria	0800
# Taiwan (CC) ♦	0080-13-4567
# Thailand ★	001-999-1-2001
# Trinidad & Tobago ÷	1-800-888-8000
# Turkey (CC) ♦	00-8001-1177
# Turks and Caicos ÷	1-800-888-8000
# Ukraine (CC) ÷	8▼10-013
# United Arab Emirates ♦	800-111
# United Kingdom (CC) To call using BT ■	0800-89-0222
To call using C&W ■	0500-89-0222
# United States (CC)	1-800-888-8000
# Uruguay	000-412
# U.S. Virgin Islands (CC)	1-800-888-8000
# Vatican City (CC)	172-1022
# Venezuela (CC) ÷ ♦	800-1114-0
Vietnam ●	1201-1022
Yemen	008-00-102

#	Automation available from most locations.
(CC)	Country-to-country calling available to/from most international locations.
÷	Limited availability.
★	Wait for second dial tone.
▼	When calling from public phones, use phones marked LADATEL
◆	International communications carrier.
■ ★ ♦	Not available from public pay phones.
●	Public phones may require deposit of coin or phone card for dial tone.
● ▲ ÷	Local service fee in U.S. currency required to complete call. Regulation does not permit intra-Japan calls. Available from most major cities

And, it's simple to call home.

1. Dial the WorldPhone toll-free access number of the country you're calling from (listed inside).

2. Follow the voice instructions in your language of choice and hold for a WorldPhone operator.
   - Enter or give the operator your MCI Card number or call collect.

3. Enter or give the WorldPhone operator your home number.

4. Share your adventures with your family!

MCI

The MCI Card with WorldPhone Service... The easy way to call when traveling worldwide.

MCI — Calling Card
123 456 7890 1234
J.D. SMITH
WorldPhone

For more information or to apply for a Card call:
1-800-955-0925

Outside the U.S., call MCI collect (reverse charge) at:
1-916-567-5151

Please cut out and save this reference guide for convenient U.S. and worldwide calling with the MCI Card with WorldPhone Service.

COUNTRY	WORLDPHONE TOLL-FREE ACCESS #
#American Samoa	633-2MCI (633-2624)
#Antigua (available from public card phones only)	#2
Argentina (CC)	0800-5-1002
#Aruba ÷	800-888-8
#Australia (CC) ◆ To call using OPTUS ■	1-800-551-111
To call using TELSTRA ■	1-800-881-100
#Austria (CC) ◆	022-903-012
#Bahamas	1-800-888-8000
#Bahrain	800-003
#Barbados	1-800-888-8000
#Belarus (CC) From Brest, Vitebsk, Grodno, Minsk	8-800-103
From Gomel and Mogilev	8-10-800-103
#Belgium (CC) ◆	0800-10012
#Belize From Hotels	557
From Payphones	815
#Bermuda ÷	1-800-888-8000
#Bolivia (CC) ◆	0-800-2222
#Brazil (CC)	000-8012
#British Virgin Islands ÷	1-800-888-8000
#Brunei	800-0011
#Bulgaria	00800-0001
#Canada (CC)	1-800-888-8000
#Cayman Islands	1-800-888-8000
#Chile (CC) To call using CTC ■	800-207-300
To call using ENTEL ■	800-360-180
#China ✦	108-12
For a Mandarin-speaking Operator	108-17
#Colombia (CC) ◆	980-16-0001
Collect Access in Spanish	980-16-1000
#Costa Rica ◆	0800-012-2222
#Cote D'Ivoire	0800-22-0111
#Croatia (CC) ★	0800-22000
#Cyprus ◆	080-90000
#Czech Republic (CC) ◆	00-42-000112
#Denmark (CC) ◆	8001-0022
#Dominica	1-800-888-8000
#Dominican Republic Collect Access	1-800-888-8000
Collect Access in Spanish	1121
#Ecuador (CC) ÷	999-170
#Egypt (CC) ◆ (Outside of Cairo, dial 02 first)	355-5770
El Salvador	800-1767

--- FOLD ---

COUNTRY	WORLDPHONE TOLL-FREE ACCESS #
#Federated States of Micronesia	624
#Fiji	004-890-1002
#Finland (CC) ◆	08001-102-80
#France (CC) ◆	0800-99-0019
#French Antilles (CC) (includes Martinique, Guadeloupe)	0800-99-0019
French Guiana (CC)	0-800-99-0011
#Gabon	00-1-195
#Gambia ÷	00-1-99
#Germany (CC) ◆	0-800-888-8000
#Greece (CC) ◆	00-800-1211
#Grenada ÷	1-800-888-8000
#Guam (CC) ◆	1-800-888-8000
Guatemala ◆	99-99-189
Guyana	177
#Haiti ÷	193
Collect Access in French/Creole	190
Honduras ÷	8000-122
#Hong Kong (CC)	800-96-1121
#Hungary (CC) ◆	00 ✦800-01411
#Iceland (CC) ◆	800-9001
#India (CC) Collect Access	000-127
	000-126
#Indonesia (CC) ◆	001-801-11
Iran ✦	(SPECIAL PHONES ONLY)
#Ireland (CC)	1-800-55-1001
#Israel (CC)	1-800-940-2727
#Italy (CC) ◆	172-1022
#Jamaica ÷	1-800-888-8000
Collect Access	873
#Japan (CC) ◆ (from Special Hotels only)	0039-121▼
(from public phones)	✱2
To call using KDD ■	0066-55-121
To call using IDC ■	0044-11-121
To call using ITJ ■	0044-11-121
#Jordan	18-800-001
#Kazakhstan (CC)	8-800-131-4321
#Kenya ÷	080011
#Korea (CC) To call using KT ■	00939-14
To call using DACOM ■	00309-12
To call using ONSE	00369-14
Phone Booths ÷	Press red button, 03, then ✱
Military Bases	550-2255
#Kuwait	800-MCI (800-624)

--- FOLD ---

COUNTRY	WORLDPHONE TOLL-FREE ACCESS #
Lebanon Collect Access	600-MCI (600-624)
#Liechtenstein (CC) ◆	0800-89-0222
#Luxembourg (CC)	0800-0112
#Macao	0800-131
#Macedonia (CC)	99800-4288
#Malaysia (CC) ◆	1-800-80-0012
#Malta	0800-89-0120
#Marshall Islands	1-800-888-8000
#Mexico (CC) Avantel	01-800-021-8000
Telmex ▲	001-800-674-7000
Collect Access in Spanish	01-800-021-1000
#Monaco (CC) ◆	800-90-019
#Montserrat	1-800-888-8000
#Morocco	00-211-0012
#Netherlands (CC) ◆	0800-022-9122
#Netherlands Antilles (CC) ÷	001-800-888-8000
#New Zealand (CC)	000-912
Nicaragua (CC) Collect Access in Spanish	166
(Outside of Managua, dial 02 first) From any public payphone	
#Norway (CC) ◆	800-19912
Pakistan	✱2
#Panama	00-800-12-001
#Papua New Guinea (CC)	108
Military Bases	2810-108
#Paraguay ÷	05-07-19140
#Peru	0-812-800
#Philippines (CC) ◆	0-800-500-10
To call using PLDT ■	105-14
To call using PHILCOM ■	1026-14
Collect Access via PLDT in Filipino	105-15
Collect Access via ICC in Filipino	1237-77
#Poland (CC) ÷	00-800-111-21-22
#Portugal (CC) ÷	05-017-1234
#Puerto Rico (CC)	1-800-888-8000
#Qatar ✱	0800-012-77
#Romania (CC) ÷	01-800-1800
#Russia (CC) ÷ ◆ To call using ROSTELCOM ■	747-3322
(For Russian speaking operator)	747-3320
To call using SOVINTEL ■	960-2222
#Saipan (CC) ÷	950-1022
#San Marino (CC) ◆	172-1022
#Saudi Arabia (CC) ÷	1-800-11

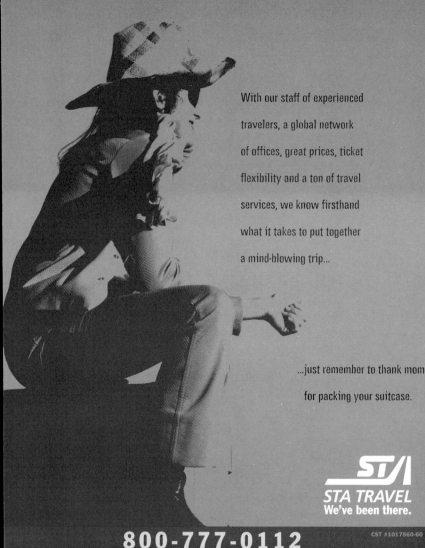

If you're stuck for cash on your travels, don't panic. Millions of people trust Western Union to transfer money in minutes to 153 countries and over 45,000 locations worldwide. Our record of safety and reliability is second to none. So when you need money in a hurry, call Western Union.

YMCA Aparthotel, David Naismith Ct., 33 Petershill Rd. (tel. 558 6166; fax 558 2036). Take bus #12A or 16 from Queen St. Station. Comfortable rooms in a 30-story monstrosity. TV lounge, game room, and evening activities. Restaurant and lounge bar. B&B singles £17; doubles £28. Breakfast included. Reception open 24hr. Kitchen flats available.

Iona Guest House, 39 Hillhead St. (tel. 334 2346), near Glasgow University, on a street lined with B&Bs. U: Hillhead. Convenient to reach Byres Rd. Stunning front hall, subterranean breakfast nook, and floral rooms. Haggis available for breakfast. Singles £22; doubles £36.

Seton Guest House, 6 Seton Terr. (tel. 556 7654), 20min. east of George Sq. Kindly hosts keep immaculate large rooms with ornate chandeliers. Out of the way, but all the quieter. Singles £17; twins £30.

McLay's Guest House, 268 Renfrew St. (tel. 332 4796; fax 353 0422), near the Glasgow School of Art and Sauchiehall St. With satellite TV in each of the 64 rooms and 3 dining rooms, it looks and feels more like a hotel than a B&B. Singles £21, with bath £25; doubles £38, with bath £44; family room (sleeps 4) £52, with bath £60.

FOOD

Universities in Glasgow have bred a number of cheap hole-in-the-wall restaurants with excellent food. **Byres Rd.** and **Ashton Ln.,** a tiny hard-to-find cobblestone alley parallel to Byres Rd., thrive with cheap, trendy cafes and bistros. Bakeries along High St. below the cathedral serve scones for as little as 15p. Glasgow is often called "the curry capital of Scotland," and for good reason. The area bordered by Otago St. in the west, St. George's Rd. in the east, and along Great Western, Woodlands Rd., and Eldon St. brims with cheap kebab 'n' curry joints. Ask around for the best deals. Try the **Safeway,** 373 Byres Rd. (tel. 339 6721; open M-Sa 8am-8pm, Su 9am-7pm), or **Grassroots,** 20 Woodlands Rd. (tel. 353 3278), near the hostels, which offers a delicious selection of wholefood, including sandwiches and pasties (from 85p), and fresh salads and breads (open M-W and F 8:45am-6pm, Th 8:45am-7pm, Sa 9am-6pm, Su 11am-3pm). If you're in town for a while you might want to invest in the *Eating & Drinking Guide* (£2.50 from news agents or the tourist office).

✺**Insomnia Cafe,** 38-40 Woodlands Rd. (tel. 564 1700), near the hostels. The place to gorge throughout the day and night. Dine on the soup of the day (£1.55) and pasta with Italian sausage (£4.25) or satisfy a 3am craving for samosas with riata and onion (£2.45)—all amidst energetic students and a bathtub-and-fishtank. Open 24hr. The adjoining deli, **Crispins,** is also open. Always.

Cafe Antipasti, 337 Byres Rd. (tel. 337 2737) and 305 Sauchiehall St. (tel. 332 9002). Excellent Italian food in a bustling but intimate atmosphere. The "Fusilli baked with Tuscan Bolgnoise and cream" is delicious and filling (£5.25). Pizzas, pastas, and fancy caesar salads (with swordfish) are all £4.45-6.25. Breakfast and lunch also available. Open daily 8am-midnight, if it's busy enough.

Grosvenor Café, 31-35 Ashton Ln. (tel. 339 1848). Stuff yourself silly from the endless menu, but beware of the long lines. Stuffed rolls 70-90p, bigger dishes £3-4. A more elaborate dinner menu (entrees £4.75-6.50) is available Tu-Sa 7-11pm. Open M 9am-7pm, Tu-Sa 9am-11pm, Su 11am-5:30pm and 7-11pm.

Pierre Victoire, 167 Hope St. (tel. 221 9130) and 91 Miller St. (tel. 221 7565). French, reasonably priced, and delicious. Bump elbows with others in the know, as you settle down to a pre-theater 2-course meal and coffee (£7; 5-6:30pm). Ample vegetarian options. Open M-Sa noon-3pm and 5-11pm, Su 5-9pm.

The Willow Tea Room, 217 Sauchiehall St. (tel. 332 0521), upstairs from Henderson the Jewellers. A Glasgow landmark, designed by Glaswegian Charles Rennie Mackintosh; everything in the building matches, down to the antiquated bathroom which they're not allowed to modernize. Select from over 28 kinds of tea (£1.30 per pot), then sit and admire silver and purple elegance of the well-preserved Mackintosh room. Marvelous sweets—try the meringue with strawberries and cream (£2). 3-course afternoon tea runs £7.25. Open M-Sa 9:30am-4:30pm, Su noon-4:15pm.

The Bay Tree Vegetarian Café, 403 Great Western Rd. (tel. 334 5898), at Park Rd. Near the hostels (cut through Kelvingrove Park) and very popular, this cramped cafe serves up delicious vegan dishes in mid-sized portions. Hummus-type dip, salad, and pita break £3.65-4.25. Don't be fooled by the desserts' attractive appearances; their taste doesn't measure up. 10% student discount, 15% senior discount. Open M-Sa 9am-9pm, Su 10am-8pm.

PUBS

There are hundreds of pubs in Glasgow, and you'll never find yourself much more than half a block from a frothy pint. The infamous **Byers Rd.** pub crawl slithers past the Glasgow University area, beginning at **Tennant's Bar** and proceeding toward the River Clyde. Drinks are cheap to start, but watch for happy hours; many pubs reduce drinks to a joyous £1.

Cul de Sac Bar, 46 Ashton Ln. (tel. 334 4749). *The* artsy hangout—chic, young clientele. Ground-floor restaurant serves magnificent crepes (£6.45; half-price 5-7pm). The main crowd gathers on the second floor; the upscale top-floor "Attic" allows the pretentious to escape students. Open Su-Th noon-11pm, F-Sa noon-midnight.

Horseshoe Bar, 17-21 Drury St. (tel. 204 4056), one block north of Gordon St. This fabulous Victorian horseshoe-shaped bar, with etched mirrors and carved wooden walls, is a Glasgow institution. Longest continuous bar in the U.K.; 25 bartenders staff it when the mostly older male crowd begins to swell by mid-afternoon. Head upstairs for a hearty 3-course pub lunch (£2.40; served M-Sa noon-2:30pm). Karaoke in the lounge daily 8pm-midnight. Open M-Sa 11am-midnight, Su 12:30pm-midnight.

Halt Bar, 160 Woodlands Rd. (tel. 564 1527), 2 blocks from the youth hostel. One side is dark and deafening, the other hot and humid. Attracts all sorts. Live music. Quiz night Monday; Wednesday unplugged; Thursday "loud" music; Friday reggae; Saturday more unplugged. Open M-Th 11am-11pm, F-Sa 11am-midnight.

Uisge Beatha (oos-ga BAH), 232 Woodlands Rd. (tel. 332 0473). With its blackened wood furnishings, old paintings, red velveteen seats, and kilt-clad bartenders, this place is worth a peek. "Uisge Beatha" is Gaelic for "water of life" (read: whisky). Sip up the national drink as you listen to Gaelic tunes. Open M-Th 11am-10:45pm, F-Sa 11am-midnight, Su 6:30-10:45pm.

Blackfriars, 36 Bell St. (tel. 552 5924), at Albion St. U: St. Enoch. Popular with young locals. Live jazz F and Sa, comedy Su nights. Tasty, cheap food £1.10-4.25. Look for the beer- and whisky-of-the-month specials. Open daily noon-midnight.

Variety Bar, 401 Sauchiehall St. (tel. 332 4449). Older men's pub by day, art students' hangout by night. No frills, just a quality pub. Reggae on Tu; DJ on Th (house); Su jazz. Happy hour daily 11am-5pm—pints of lagers and heavies £1.35, Guinness £1.45, spirits 25p. Open M-Sa 11am-11:45pm, Su 12:30-11:45pm.

SIGHTS

Glasgow is a budget sightseer's paradise. There are grand museums, funky modern art galleries, splendid Georgian and Victorian constructions, and more. Many of the best sights are part of the **Glasgow Museums** group, whose museums are scattered across the city and are all free. Pick up a free guide at the tourist office. **The List** reviews current exhibitions and lists galleries (£1.90 from newsagents).

The City Center

Begin your exploration of Glasgow at **George Square,** a grassy but busy respite in the busier city. Named for George III, the square's 80 ft. column was originally designed to support a statue of His Royal Highness. But, in the ultimate snub, Glaswegians replaced George with a statue of Sir Walter Scott. The author wears his plaid (as he always did) over the wrong shoulder (the right).

The **City Chambers** (tel. 287 4017), on the east side of George Sq., conceal an ornate marble interior in Italian Renaissance style. Pop into the lobby for 30 seconds, or take a free tour which starts at the main entrance. *(Open M-F 10:30am and 2:30pm.)*

The Gothic **Glasgow Cathedral** (tel. 552 6891), near the center of town on Castle St., was the only full-scale cathedral spared the fury of the mid-16th-century Scottish Reformation. Its blackened exterior brings to mind the city's industrial past, but the interior, especially the Quire (choir), is quite pretty. The stained glass is mostly post-war; look for the graphic purple Adam and Eve in the Western window, rendered in almost scary detail (the ancients would not have been pleased). The downstairs Laigh Kirk, sole remnant of the original 12th-century building, shelters the tomb of St. Mungo (Kentigern), patron saint of Glasgow. To reach the cathedral, walk to the eastern end of Cathedral St., which runs behind Queen St. Station. *(Open Apr.-Sept. M-Sa 9:30am-6pm, Su 2-5pm; Oct.-Mar. M-Sa 9:30am-4pm, Su 2-4pm. Free.)* Around the corner is the entrance to the giant **Necropolis,** a spectacular and terrifying hilltop cemetery. Tombstones, statues, and obelisks lie aslant, broken and flat on the ground. A 50-ft. high statue of John Knox, leader of the Scottish Reformation, tops the hill where good (but spooky) views await. Wander amid the 20 ft. tall tombs of most of the city's 19th-century industrialists and remember where all paths of glory lead. *Let's Go* recommends only daytime visits to the Necropolis. *(Free.)*

Near the cathedral is the **St. Mungo Museum of Religious Life and Art,** 2 Castle St. (tel. 553 2557), which surveys every religion you can think of, from Hindu to Native American faiths to Yoruba. The museum holds an impressive collection of sacred objects and artwork, including works by Dalí and Dürer, complemented, appropriately, by views of the cemetery. *(Open M-Sa 10am-5pm, Su 11am-5pm. Free.)* Just across the street at 3-7 Castle St. sits **Provand's Lordship** (tel. 553 2557), the oldest house in Glasgow. Built in 1471, the house preserves a collection of heavy old furniture in musky air; the garden features some of Glasgow's finest healing herbs. *(Closed until April '99 for renovation; thereafter open M-Sa 10am-5pm, Su 11am-5pm. Free.)* Just south of George Sq. rests the **Gallery of Modern Art,** Queens St. (tel. 229 1996), housed in a beautiful classical structure, once the Royal Exchange. *(Open M-Sa 10am-5pm, Su 11am-5pm. Free. Wheelchair access.)* In their eagerness to join the Industrial Revolution, Glaswegians destroyed most remnants of their medieval past, only to recreate it later on the ground floor of the **People's Palace** (tel. 554 0223), on Glasgow Green by the river. The museum and greenhouse tell the story of Glasgow. *(Open M-Sa 10am-5pm, Su 11am-5pm. Free.)*

The West End

Starting one block west of Park Circus is **Kelvingrove Park,** a large wooded expanse on the banks of the River Kelvin, where locals tan on the grassy slopes and university students make out behind the trees. In the southwest corner of the park, just off the intersection of Argyle and Sauchiehall St., sits the magnificent, spired **Kelvingrove Art Gallery and Museum** (tel. 287 2000; U: Kelvin Hall). The excellent art collection includes Rembrandt and Van Gogh. The museum includes a display on arms and armor (from medieval knights to imperial stormtroopers), as well as silver, clothing, and natural history exhibits. *(Open M-Sa 10am-5pm, Su 11am-5pm. Free.)*

Across Argyle St. from the Kelvingrove museum, the **Museum of Transport** (tel. 221 9600), houses a collection of full-scale original trains, trams, and automobiles including a Karl Benz automobile of the pre-Mercedes variety. *(Open M-Sa 10am-5pm, Su 11am-5pm. Free. Wheelchair access off Old Dunbarton Rd.)* At the north edge of Kelvingrove Park is **Glasgow University;** the central spire, a Gothic revival devised by Gilbert Scott, is visible from afar. The main building is on University Ave. (U: Hillhead), which runs into Byres Rd., a busy thoroughfare of the West End. While you're walking the campus that has churned out 57 Nobel laureates, briefly visit the **Hunterian Museum** (tel. 330 4221). The oldest museum in Scotland includes a death mask of no-longer-so-Bonnie Prince Charlie. *(Open M-Sa 9:30-5pm. Free.)* The **Hunterian Art Gallery** (tel. 330 5431), across the street, displays 19th-century Scottish art, a sizeable Whistler collection, and reconstructed rooms from the house of Charles Mackintosh. *(Open M-Sa 9:30am-5pm. Free.)* At the end of Byres Rd. lie the beautiful, serene **Botanic Gardens,** Great Western Rd. (tel. 334 2422). The drab, glorified greenhouse **Kibble Palace** houses a fish pond and some exotic but unimpressive plants. **Main Range,** another greenhouse, contains hot and humid rooms with gorgeous (and impressive) orchids, ferns, palms, and cacti. *(Gardens open daily 7am-10pm. Kibble Palace open daily Apr. to late Oct. 10am-4:45pm; late Oct. to Mar. 10am-4:15pm. Main Range open Apr. to late Oct. M-F 10am-4:45pm, Sa 1-4:45pm, Su noon-4:45pm; late Oct. to Mar. closes daily at 4:15pm. All free.)* **Princes Sq.** (tel. 221 0324) to the west of George Sq. at 48 Buchanan St., is a gorgeous high-end shopping mall—the classiest place to shop outside of London. **Sauchiehall St.,** another pedestrianized shopping area, is home to several art galleries. *(Open M-Sa 9am-7pm.)* Check out the **Center for Contemporary Arts,** 350 Sauchiehall St., (tel. 332 0522), which houses temporary original exhibitions. *(Open M-Sa 10am-6pm, Su noon-5pm.)* The **McLellan Galleries,** 270 Sauchiehall St. (tel. 353 0480), play host to temporary exhibits of anything and everything, from Impressionist paintings to original film props and costumes. *(Open M-Sa 10am-5:30pm, Su 11am-5:30pm. £3.50, students and seniors £13, children £2.50.)*

Several buildings designed by Charles Rennie Mackintosh, Scotland's most famous architect, are open to the public. Pick up the free leaflet *Charles Rennie Mackintosh: Buildings & Tours Guide* at the tourist office or any Mackintosh sight and plan your route. The best place to start is probably the **Glasgow School of Art,** 167 Renfrew St. (tel. 353 4526), completed in 1898. Mackintosh fused wrought iron Art Nouveau with Scottish Baronial styles to obtain a proto-Modernist salad. *(Interior tours M-F 11am and 2pm, Sa 10:30am. £3.50, students £2.)* The Charles Rennie Mackintosh Society is based at the stark **Willow Tea Rooms;** stop by to imbibe in Mackintosh surroundings (see **Food,** p. 495). In the large **Pollok Country Park,** 3½ mi. south of town but worth the trek, sits **Pollok House** (tel. 616 6410), a lovely 18th-century mansion with a fine array of Spanish paintings. Take bus #45, 48, or 57 from Jamaica St. (£1). The **Burrell Collection** (tel. 649 7151), Sir William Burrell's personal collection of 19th-century French paintings and sculpture (including a Rodin *The Thinker*), Chinese ceramics, and Persian tapestries, is housed in an award-winning patchwork building. *(Both museums open M-Sa 10am-5pm, Su 11am-5pm. Free.)*

ENTERTAINMENT

Glaswegians play more and party harder than most urban Scots. Three universities and the highest student/resident ratio in Britain ensure constant film, theater, music, and party offerings, including 44 nightclubs. The **Ticket Centre** (tel. 287 5511), City Hall, Candleriggs, will tell you what's playing at the city's dozen-odd theaters. Pick up a free copy of the *City Live!* events calendar here. *(Phone answered M-Sa 9am-9pm, Su noon-5pm. Office open M-Sa 9:30am-6:30pm, Su noon-5pm.)* *The List,* an excellent resource for the entertainment seeker, details not only the museum scene, but also film, theater, music, comedy, and art in both Glasgow and Edinburgh. *(£1.90 from newsagents and the tourist office.)* Glasgow's many theaters include the **Theatre Royal,** Hope St. (tel. 332 9000), and the **Tron Theatre,** 63 Trongate (tel. 552 4267). The **Cottier Theatre,** 935 Hyndland St. (tel. 357 3868), and **Cottier's Restaurant** (tel. 357 5825) host a wide variety of musical and theatrical events, from avant-garde plays to opera. *(Tickets £3-9.50.)* Or swig a pint in the restaurant's courtyard beer garden while contemplating the Leiper stained glass. *(Beer garden open Su-Th 11am-11pm, F-Sa 11am-midnight.)* The **Glasgow Film Theatre,** 12 Rose St. (tel. 332 8128), screens sleepers and cult classics (snatch a schedule at the theater) and also features a bar with food, and regular art exhibitions. *(£4.25, matinees £3.25; students, seniors, and children £3, matinees £2. No discounts on Sa evenings. Call for wheelchair access.)* The **Royal Concert Hall,** Sauchiehall St. (tel. 287 5511), is host to frequent concerts by the Royal Scottish National Orchestra.

Glasgow's sizable student population guarantees a lively nightlife scene. Most clubs are open from 11pm to 3am, but the bacchanalia reaches a fevered pitch after the pubs close at midnight. Head to **Nice 'n' Sleazy,** 421 Sauchiehall St. (tel. 333 9637), for 15 flavors of Absolut (mmm…shrimp!), and special Absolut nights, when £1 equals one mixed drink. Eclectic, live music is free Saturday through Wednesday. *(Occasional cover Th-F. Open daily 11:30am-midnight.)* Look for two skeletons just outside the second floor windows of **Archaos,** 25 Queen St. (tel. 204 3189). With frequent student discounts, musical variety, and several floors, no wonder it's packed. Thursdays and Sundays attract the most students; dress well on Saturday. *(Cover £2.50-8.)* Across the street, the **Garage,** 490 Sauciehall St. (tel. 332 1120), beckons with Mad Hatter decor. *(Dance, alternative, club classics. Tu and Th vodka 50p. Cover £2-5, student discounts usually available. Look for the yellow truck sitting out over the sidewalk.)* At the sweating **Sub Club,** 22 Jamaica St. (tel. 248 4600), all types grind to techno in the purple basement. "Sub-culture Saturdays" run to the shocking hour of 5am. *(Cover £3-6, Sa £8.)* Grunge and indie please mostly student crowds in the **Cathouse,** 15 Union St. (tel. 248 6606). *(Cover £2-5, frequent student discounts; often free before 11:30pm.)*

Mayfest, a festival in May, offers a fine program of Scottish and international theater and music. For info, write 18 Albion St., Glasgow, G1 1LH (tel. 552 8444). The annual **Glasgow International Jazz Festival,** in late June through early July, draws such greats as Betty Carter, B.B. King, and Herbie Hancock (same address as Mayfest; tel. 552 3552). In early August, Glasgow hosts the largest **International Early Music Festival** in the U.K. (2 Port Dundas Pl.). During the annual **World Pipe Band Championships,** in mid-August, the skirl of bagpipes can be heard for miles

■ Near Glasgow: New Lanark

Thirty miles southwest of Glasgow, in the peaceful Clyde River valley, the stunning village of **New Lanark** (tel. (01555) 661345) recalls the early industrial revolution and 19th century utopian dreams. It was founded in 1785 on a steep and rapid stretch of the Clyde River, and for much of the 19th century was the most productive and well-known manufacturing site in Scotland. This was partially due to the socialistic tendencies of the cotton mill owner; instead of sending eight-year-olds to work twelve-hour days, Robert Owen sent them to school, paid workers decent wages, founded an Institute for the Formulation of Character, and spawned the first semi-cooperative village store. For a single ticket visitors can walk through the restored village store, a millworker's house, and Owen's own abode (which, despite his socialism, was somewhat nicer). *(£3.75, students, seniors, and children £2.50, families £9.95.)* Price also includes a trip on the 10-minute **Annie McLeod Experience,** an evocative ride past scenes of village and mill life narrated by 10-year-old Annie herself: "And then me granddad died, and he's to be buried tomorrow, and Mr. Owen likes it if we keep on learning…" *(Open daily 11am-5pm.)* The visitor center also educates on the cloth production process (carding, spinning, weaving) and lets you try it out yourself. The river valley also supplies some lovely hikes free of charge, especially the mile-long walk upriver (past the hydro-power plant) to the **Falls of Clyde.**

To get to New Lanark, you'll need to go through **Lanark,** where the **tourist office** (tel. (01555) 661661) is located next to the train station (open Apr.-Sept. M-Sa 10am-6pm, Su noon-5pm; Oct.-Mar. M-Sa 10am-5pm). Pick up the superb, glossy, and free **Lanark Heritage Trail** guidebook, which will guide you to sights including **Old St. Kentigern's Church**—the ruins where, legend has it, William Wallace married Marion Braidfute. Trains run to Lanark from Glasgow's Central Station (45 min., 1 per hr., return £5). **Stuart's Coaches** (tel. 01555) 773533) run to New Lanark Monday to Sat-

---

The Plaid Fad

The desperate tourist's quest for his or her ancestral tartan has brought lots of business—and lots of amusement—to modern Scots. In fact, tartans originally had no clan affiliation, indicating only the geographic base of the weaver. It wasn't until the 19th century's mounting romanticization of the Scottish medieval past that the kilt craze really began. King George IV, who was fat, kicked it all off by buying £1354 worth of the Regal Stuart tartan and wearing most of it during his 1822 visit to Edinburgh. Very few clans actually had any defining plaid, but the shortage was solved by the happy 1842 publication of *Vestiarium Scotium* (a fraudulent "discovery" of an ancient manuscript revealing all). Today, tartans are mostly used for ceremonial occasions—and for milking tourists.

urday from the tourist office (6 per day, 65p), and from Easter to October on Sundays a bus runs every hour from the train station (65p), or endure the 20 minute walk. Stay at the **New Lanark Youth Hostel,** Wee Row (tel. (01555) 666710; fax 666719), a restored mill workers' dwelling with modern luxuries only dreamed of by previous occupants. (£9.75, under 18 £8.50, rooms with bath. Continental breakfast. Laundry facilities, river views, and Paddy the dog to socialize with.)

■ Ayr

The city of Ayr (as in fresh AIR; pop. 50,000) makes a good base from which to explore the rolling hills and seaside cliffs of Ayrshire, home to Robert Burns' birth-place and a host of other sights glorifying the poet. Lovely, but unexciting, country-side and Burns, Burns, Burns, await. The city is set against 3 mi. of sand beach and a vast green lawn (the Esplanade). For horseracing fans, the **Ayr Racecourse** (tel. 264179), host of the **Scottish Grand National** (Apr.) and the **Ayr Gold Cup** (Sept.), promises untold horsey thrills (tickets £8-22; call for race dates, or pick up a schedule at the tourist office).

From the **train station,** at the crossroads of Station, Holmston, and Castle Hill Rd., trains travel to and from **Glasgow** (1hr., about 2 per hr., £4.80) and **Stranraer** (M-Sa 6 per day, Su 2 per day, £13.70). For local transport details, call the **bus station,** 23 Sandgate (tel. 613500), near Wellington Sq. (office open M-Sa 8am-5pm). Catch buses here for **Dumfries** (£4.30), **Stranraer** (£5.75), or **Glasgow** (£3).

The sleek Ayr **tourist office,** Burns House, Burns Statue Sq. (tel. 288688), near the rail station, provides free guides to history, heritage, cycling, and water sports. Pick up the trademark infringement named *Let's Go,* a guide to events in Ayrshire and Arran. (Open July-Aug. M-Sa 9am-6pm, Su 10am-5pm; Apr.-June and Sept. to mid-Oct. M-Sa 9:15am-5pm, Su 11am-5pm; mid-Oct. to Mar. M-Sa 9:15am-5pm.) **Banks** reside across from the Robert Burns statue on High St. A **post office,** 29 Burns Statue Sq. (tel. 262689), stands near the tourist office (open M-Sa 9am-5:30pm). The **postal code** is KA7 1AB. There is **Internet access** at Carnegie Library, 12 Main St. (tel. 618492; £3 per hr.; open M-Tu and Th-F 10am-7:30pm, W and Sa 10am-5pm). Ayr's **telephone code** is 01292.

The **SYHA Ayr,** Cragweil House (tel./fax 262322), in a prime location at the corner of the Esplanade, offers breathtaking, second-story views. The hostel is 15 minutes by foot from the town center; take a right off Racecourse Rd. onto Blackburn and then a right onto Cragweil Rd. (£7.75, under 18 £6.50. Laundry facilities. Self-catering kitchen. Curfew 11:45pm. Open Mar.-Oct.). A gargantuan **Safeway** (tel. 283906) rests on Castlehill Rd. across the street from the train station (open M-Th 8am-8pm, F 8am-9pm, Sa 8am-6pm, Su 9am-5pm). For cheap sandwiches on heavenly bread, head for **Café Ginger,** 57 Fort St. (tel. 264108), near the bus station (open M-Sa 7:30am-5pm, Su 10am-5pm). Drink at the most popular pub in town, the proud-to-be-Scottish **Chapman Billie's** (tel. 618161), near the town center on Dallair Rd. at Barnes St.

■ Near Ayr

Two miles south of Ayr, the village **Alloway** blazes with Burnsian sites. Visit the **Burns Cottage and Museum** (tel. (01292) 441215), built by you-know-whose dad, where guess-who was born. The museum's excellent collection of Burnsian material redeems the too-touching tableaux of family life and realistic barnyard smells. *(Open Apr.-Oct. daily 9am-6pm; Nov.-Mar. M-Sa 10am-4pm, Su noon-4pm; last entry 30min. before closing. £2.50, seniors and children £1.25, families £6.)* The **Tam o' Shanter Experience** (tel. (01292) 443700) supplies an audio-visual presentation on the life of the poet as well as a multi-media enactment of its namesake poem. *(Open daily Apr.-Oct. 9am-6pm, Nov.-Mar. 9am-5pm; first show at 9:30am, then every 30min. until last show at 4:30pm. £1.75, seniors and children £1.25, families £6; joint ticket with the Cottage and Museum £4.25, seniors and children £2.)* The nearby **Burns Monument and Gardens** are superb and free, though much better on a sunny summer day than at the end of winter. Climb up the monument for a view of the **Brig o' Doon,** a bridge which features in the "Tam o'

Shanter" poem. Also stop by the ruined Alloway Kirk, where, according to Burns, the devil played the bagpipes. Take **Western** bus #57 to Alloway from Ayr's bus station (10min., 1 per hr., £1.45).

Twelve miles south of Ayr, **Culzean Castle** (cul-LANE; tel. (01655) 760274) perches on a coastal cliff. According to legend, one of these caves shelters the Phantom Piper who plays to his lost flock when the moon is full. The castle was redesigned in the late 18th century by master architect Robert Adam. The famed oval staircase, unfortunately, looks more impressive in brochures than in real life, but there is a stunning armory. The castle's top floor was given to Dwight Eisenhower for use during his lifetime, and lesser persons are not allowed up. *(Castle and park open Apr.-Oct. daily 10:30am-5:30pm, last admission 5pm. Free tours daily July-Aug. 11am and 3:30pm. Castle and park £6.50, seniors and children £4.40, families £17. Park only £3.50, seniors and children £2.40, families £9. However, the park can be accessed for free by walking north along the beach from the nearby town of Maidens and climbing an unguarded stairway to the grounds.)* To reach Culzean, take the **Western bus** #60 (30min., M-Sa 6 per day, day return £3.40) from Ayr's Sandgate bus station. Tell the driver where you're going and follow the signs from the main road for about 1 mi. The **Electric Brae,** a stretch of the coastal drive down the A719 from Ayr to the castle, is an optical illusion: although it looks like a downhill ride, it's actually an uphill climb.

■ Arran

The glorious Isle of Arran (AH-ren) justifiably bills itself as "Scotland in Miniature." Gentle lowland hills and majestic Highland peaks co-exist on an island less than 20 mi. long. In the north, the gray, craggy peaks of Goatfell and the Caisteal range surge above their foothills' pines. Amid the bog-grass near the western coast, prehistoric stone circles and lone standing stones rise suddenly out of the mist. The eastern coastline winds south from Brodick Castle past the conical hump of Holy Island into meadows and white beaches. On sunny days, the waters turn crystalline, providing an enchanting view of the marine life below.

GETTING THERE AND GETTING ABOUT

Trains and Buses

To reach Arran, take a **train** (tel. (0345) 484950) from **Glasgow's** Central Station west to Ardrossan on the Firth of Clyde (45min., M-Sa 5 per day, Su 4 per day, £4). From **Ardrossan,** the **Caledonian-MacIntyre** ferry (tel. 302166) makes the crossing to **Brodick** on Arran in sync with the train schedule (1hr., M-Sa 5-6 per day, Su 3-4 per day, £4). There's also ferry service from **Claonaig** on the Kintyre Peninsula to Lochranza on Arran (30min., usually mid-Apr. to mid-Oct. 9-11 per day, £3.50). When returning to Claonaig, be sure of your connection. On Mondays, Wednesdays, and Fridays, a ferry runs from Rothesay on the Isle of Bute to Brodick (2hr., May-Sept. 1 per day, £4.15). On all ferries, bikes ride for £1. **Cal-Mac** (tel. 302166) is at Brodick Pier (open M-Sa 7:40am-5pm and 6:30-7:20pm, Su 10am-5pm and 6:30-7:20pm).

Bus transportation is convenient; buses run frequently, and for every ferry there is a connection to and from every part of the island. There are bus stops, but drivers will pick you up anywhere; just be sure to flag them down. The best pass is the **Rural Day Card** granting a full day of travel on Arran's buses (available on the bus; £3, children £1.50). Pick up a bus timetable (includes ferry times) at a tourist office or on a bus. **Stagecoach Western Buses** (tel. 302000) offer half-and full-day tours of the island, as well as an all-day open-top bus ticket between Brodick and Whiting Bay (12 per day, tours £4-6). The **Stagecoach** (tel. 302000) office is at Brodick pier (open M-F 9am-5pm, Sa-Su 10am-5pm). **Hitchhikers** report that getting rides out of Brodick isn't hard; otherwise, locals are friendly, but pass infrequently.

Biking and Hiking

Biking on the hilly island is a rewarding challenge; the full circuit takes about 9 hours. Pick up a free copy of the SYHA's *Cycling on Arran*. In Brodick, **Mini-Golf Cycles** (tel. 302272), behind the miniature golf course on Shore St., rents mountain and touring bikes. (State-of-the-art hillmonsters £8.50 per day, their lesser cousins £4-7.50 per day; helmets included; deposit £20 plus ID; open Easter-Oct. daily 9am-6pm; call ahead for winter bike hire.) **Brodick Cycles** (tel./fax 302460), farther down Shore Rd., opposite Village Hall and just past the post office, rents all kinds of bikes (£2-5 per 2hr., £4.50-9 per day, £17-36 per week; deposit £5-25; open mid-Mar. to early Oct. M-Sa 9am-1pm and 2-6pm, Su 10am-1pm and 2-6pm). In **Lochranza**, you can rent 3-speed bikes from Mrs. Kerr (tel. 830676), just up the road from the hostel next to a ruined stone house (£1 per hr., £4.50 per day; open Easter-Oct. daily 9am-8pm). In **Blackwaterfoot,** rent wheels at Sandycroft (tel. 860385), next to the post office (£1 per hr., £2.50 per day; open Easter-Oct. daily 9am-5pm). In **Whiting Bay,** rent from Whiting Bay Hires (tel. 700382), who deposit a rental van on the shore on pleasant days. (£8 per day).

Despite Arran's proximity and excellent connections to Glasgow, large swaths of wilderness in the northwest and southeast remain untouched and some of the villages in these areas are quiet and untouristed. The best walks on the island are well-marked, but more demanding hikes are detailed in *Seventy Walks in Arran* (£2.50) and *My Walks of Arran* (£2.25), both available at the tourist office. The Forestry Commission arranges various **guided walks** on the island (2-5hr.; £2-4, children free) as does the National Trust for Scotland (tel. 302462); schedules are at the Brodick tourist office.

■ Brodick

Arran's main town (pop. 1000) offers important services and transport connections to the rest of the island. Shops stretch along the shoreline, and ferries leave for Ardrossan.

ORIENTATION AND PRACTICAL INFORMATION The center of Brodick is along Shore Rd., which is to the right as you disembark from the ferry. Arran's only **tourist office** (tel. 302140; fax 302395) answers questions at the base of the pier. The staff distributes free maps and books local B&Bs for a £1.50 fee, plus deposit. (Open May-Sept. M-Sa 9am-7:30pm, Su 10am-5pm; Apr. and Oct. M-Th 9am-5pm, F 9am-7:30pm, Sa 10am-5pm; mid-Feb to Mar. and Nov.-Dec. M-F 9am-5pm, Sa 10am-5pm; Jan. to mid-Feb. M-F 9am-5pm, Sa 10am-noon.) **Bank of Scotland** (tel. 302144), is on Shore Rd. (open M-Tu and Th-F 9am-5pm, W 10am-5pm). The **launderette** (tel. 302427) is in town next door to Collins' Good Food Shop at the western end of Shore Rd. (soap available; open M-Sa 9am-5pm; last wash 4:15pm) The **post office** (tel. 302245) is set back from Shore Rd. on Mayish Rd. (open M-F 9am-5:30pm, Sa 9am-12:45pm). The **postal code** is KA27 8AA. Brodick's **telephone code,** 01770, covers the entire island.

ACCOMMODATIONS AND FOOD Brodick B&Bs fill quickly, so call ahead. **Mrs. Wilkie** (tel. 302828) offers comfortable rooms at Cala Sona, at the top of Alma Pk. From the tourist office, turn left just before the Co-op; after the road curves to the right, take a left onto the well-marked Alma Pk.; look for the "Cala Sona" house a few blocks up on your left (£14). To reach **Mrs. Macmillan,** Glenard House, Manse Rd. (tel. 302318), head away from the pier on Shore Rd.; turn left just after the Heathfield Hotel, and it's the fourth house on the left (singles £15; doubles £34; open Apr.-Oct.). Mrs. Rayburn's **Crovie** (tel. 302193) promises a great view and a pleasant (if challenging) hike. Take a left from the pier, and walk away from town on the main road; turn onto Crovie Rd. after 1 mi., and follow it for half a mile; Crovie is on your right (£16). The **Glen Rosa Farm** (tel. 302380), 2 mi. north of Brodick on the coastal road to Corrie (the B880), lets campers pitch tents (£2 per person; toilets and cold water available). You can also look for grassy spots by the beach, but the golf course is off-limits.

Stock up at the **Co-op** (tel. 302515), across from the ferry terminal (open M-Sa 8am-8pm, Su 9am-6pm). **Collins' Good Food Shop,** at the western end of Shore Rd. just past the bridge on your left, boasts streamside outdoor seating and mouth-watering items like quiche (£2) and vegetarian haggis-filled rolls (£1.50); the shop also vends health food (open M-Sa 9am-5pm). Cheap, traditional fare will find you at the obsessively just-like-home **Stalkers Restaurant** (tel. 302579), on Shore Rd., complete with a dozen screaming toddlers (most dishes £2-6; open daily Apr.-Oct. 9am-9pm; Nov.-Mar. 9am-5pm).

SIGHTS AND ENTERTAINMENT Shore Rd. becomes Low Glencloy Rd., leading past shops and eateries, finally arriving at the **Arran Heritage Museum** (tel. 302636), which features a working forge (the beloved "Smiddy"), and a cottage stuffed with 19th-century household implements, a display on Arran's geology, and more. On selected summer Sundays, the museum explodes into a flurry of activity: blacksmiths fire up the forge for a demonstration of horseshoeing while woolly sheep are shorn. *(Open June-Aug. M-Sa 10am-5pm, Su 11am-4pm; Apr.-May and Sept.-Oct. daily 11am-4pm. £2, seniors £1.25, children £1, families £5.)* Another well-signposted mile down the road, splendid **Brodick Castle** (tel. 302202) surveys the harbor above fantastic wild and walled gardens. Ancient seat of the Dukes of Hamilton, the castle contains a fine porcelain collection, paintings, and scores of dead beasties—including 87 stags' heads in the entrance hall alone. That's 174 baleful eyes waiting to greet you. If you can't visit the castle, look on the back of a Royal Bank of Scotland £20 note. *(Castle open Apr.-Oct. daily 11:30am-5pm, last admission 4:30pm; gardens open daily 9:30am-dusk. Castle and gardens £4.50, students, seniors, and children £3.20; gardens only £2.40, students, seniors, and children £1.60.)* Stagecoach runs a Vintage Coach service to the castle from Brodick Pier (June-Sept. 9 per day, return £2). The wooded **country park** surrounding the castle offers marked trails for self-guided walks. **Guided ranger walks** (tel. 302462) run from April to September (3½-7hr.; £2-5, children £2; call to book ahead).

Popular **Goatfell** (2866ft.), Arran's highest peak, begins on the road between the castle and the heritage museum. The well-marked path averages 4-5 hours. The view from the cold and windy peak is well worth the hike; on a clear day, it includes jagged Castail range to the north and Holy Island to the southeast. The **Arran Highland Games,** replete with weird sports and bagpipe parades, arrives in Brodick in early August. The **Isle of Arran Folk Festival** spreads merriment in early June.

Eight miles south of Brodick, the shores of **Whiting Bay** harbor a stone **SYHA Hostel** (tel./fax 700339; £6.10, under 18 £5; lockout 10:30am-5pm, curfew 11:45pm). Take the easy 1 mi. path to **Glen Ashdale Falls.** Between Brodick and Whiting Bay lies **Lamlash,** Arran's largest town and one of the best natural harbors in Europe. The bay is protected by the steep form of Holy Island, to which ferries run frequently.

■ Lochranza and Blackwaterfoot

Idyllic **Lochranza,** 14 mi. from Brodick at the island's northern tip, shelters a serene harbor ringed by high hills and guarded by a 13th century castle. In town, you can visit the castle and several craft workshops. *(Castle key available from the Post Office. Open Apr.-Sept. Free.)* Head to the Lochranza Golf Course, a 5 min. walk on the main road towards Brodick, to see antlered red deer graze amidst golfers. An excellent half-day walk is the 7 mi. Cock of Arran route, which circles the northern tip of the island. The beach section takes you past **Fairy Dell** (a small lushly ferned sandstone ravine), the bard **Ossian's Cave** (a hole-in-the-cliff with no historical importance), and the now-headless **Cock of Arran** (features are hard to spot unless you bring along a magic spyglass, a local, or your own stone rooster). Alternatively, you can head south up **Glen Catacol** to **Loch Tanna,** passing several waterfalls on your way (4mi. each way). Before setting out, buy the waterproof *Walker's Map: Arran North* (£6.45) or the Ordnance Survey *Isle of Arran* (£5.40), both available at the Brodick tourist office or SYHA hostels. The third weekend in July brings the **Lochranza Gala Weekend** to town when boats with silly themes compete in a down-and-dirty race.

Three minutes inland of the castle, a **SYHA Youth Hostel** (tel./fax 830631) graces the town on the main road. This peaceful white mansion has 68 beds, 5 showers, 2 friendly and helpful wardens, and a chlorophyllic common room (£7.75, under 18 £6.50; no lockout; curfew 11:30pm; open Mar.-Oct.). Housed in the former town church across from the castle, **Castlekirk** (tel. 830202) offers gracious B&B amid high, arched ceilings, an atmospheric stone stained-glass-windowed lounge, and enchanting quietude. The ground floor is an art gallery for local artists (£18). Campers can pitch at the **Lochranza Golf Caravan Camping Site** (tel. 830273; fax 830600), half a mile inland of town on the main road: laundry, hot water, disabled facilities, and much more (£3 per person, £2 per tent; golfing £10; open Easter-Oct.).

One mile down the coast from Lochranza, the village of **Catacol Bay** harbors the **12 apostles:** 12 connected white houses that differ only in the shapes of their windows. The fisherfolk residents would turn on a light at night so that their returning comrades could tell who was still out at sea. The **Machrie Stones,** various bronze-age arrangements of upright stones and boulders, are 10 mi. down the road. Ask the bus driver on the Lochranza-Blackwaterfoot to drop you off. A mile down the main road brings you to a car park and footpath signposted to **King's Cave,** where Robert the Bruce allegedly killed some hiding time watching the spiders. Now fenced off, this cave contains ancient carvings as well as modern graffiti. The small gap betwixt fence and stone on the left may look tempting, but be warned: getting out is tougher than getting in. The cave is open for tours on selected summer days; ask at the tourist office. A rocky, coastal jaunt 2 mi. south brings you to **Blackwaterfoot,** a small town dominated by the fancy-schmancy but bland Kinloch Hotel. You may want to make use of its sauna (£2.50 per 30min.) or pool (£2.25). The **Morvern Guest House** (tel. 860254) offers spacious rooms with a family atmosphere (£17, with bath £19). On the ground floor of the same building, Blackwaterfoot's only **grocery store** (tel. 860220) sells all the basics. (Open Easter-Oct. M-Sa 9am-6pm, Su 12:30-5:30pm; Nov.-Easter M-Tu and Th-Sa 9am-1pm and 2-5:30pm, W 9am-1pm). The **post office** (tel. 830641) is located in the town's only **grocery store,** overlooking the castle ruins. The town's **post office** keeps essentially the same hours. The **postal code** is KA27 8EU.

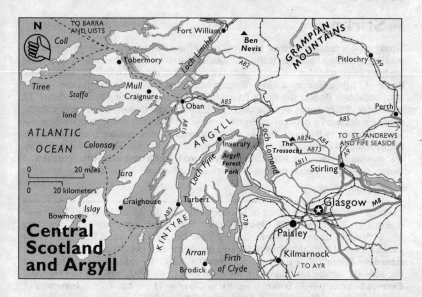

Central Scotland and Argyll

Less dramatic than the lofty, barren Highlands to the north and more subdued than Glasgow and Edinburgh to the south, central Scotland is less touristed but equally worthwhile. Scotland's eastern shoulder extends from historic Tayside and Fife in the south to the endless Grampian summits and chilly curve of the North Sea. Descending from snow-covered mountains, the countryside flattens into coastal plains strewn with castles of all vintages and sizes. Further off, the oil boomtown of Aberdeen punctuates the valley, rising grimly from the stark shore. To the west, the hills and islands of Argyll embody a remote, natural splendor usually associated with the Hebrides and Northern Isles. Transportation in Argyll is good, but less dependable to the east. The A82 from Loch Lomond to Glen Coe has some of the best views in Scotland.

🖐 HIGHLIGHTS OF CENTRAL SCOTLAND

- Visitors to central Scotland will not want to give up a hike along the shores of **Loch Lomond** (p. 509), one of the most popular and most beautiful of Scotland's inland lochs, and inspiration for the haunting ballad of the same name.
- *Braveheart* fans can admire the 66 in. sword of William Wallace, displayed in **Stirling,** where Mary, Queen of Scots, was crowned. Pay homage at nearby **Bannockburn,** where Robert the Bruce defeated the English (p. 507).
- The golf capital of the world, **St. Andrews** (p. 511) has played host to the British Open a number of times. Here you'll find the immaculate **Old Course,** with manicured lawns awaiting your polished swing.
- The misty Isle of **Iona** (p. 526) has been a center of Christianity since St. Columba landed in AD 563 and remains a spiritual stronghold. Journey here for a retreat of any kind.

SCOTLAND

■ Stirling

Sitting atop a triangle formed by Glasgow to the southwest and Edinburgh to the southeast; Stirling has historically controlled north-south movement in central Scotland; it's been said that he who controlled Stirling controlled Scotland. At the 1297 Battle of Stirling Bridge, William Wallace outwitted and overpowered the English army, enabling Robert the Bruce to lead Scotland to longlasting independence 17 years later. When James VI took the English throne and dissolved the Stirling Parliament, he declared a new capital to the south—with its *own* castle atop a volcano— leaving Stirling to languish. Despite its development into a bustling (peaceful) settlement, Scotland's former capital has not forgotten its heroes. The city's rich history and stirring architecture have been rediscovered, and it abounds with tourists and *Braveheart* fans set on capturing the glorious Scotland of old.

GETTING THERE

Stirling's central location, west of Edinburgh and on the A9 to Perth and Inverness, makes it a hub for **trains** (tel. (0345) 484950). Both **Edinburgh** (50min., at least 2 per hr., £4.50) and **Glasgow** (30min., M-Sa 2-3 per hr., Su 9 per day, £5.60) are a short journey away. Trains also chug to **Inverness** (3hr., M-Sa 8 per day, Su 4 per day, £27), **Aberdeen** (2½hr., M-Sa 1 per hr., Su 7 per day, £28.10), and **London** (5½hr., 1 per hr., £66-70). Stirling also enjoys frequent **Citylink** (tel. (0990) 505050) and **National Express bus** (tel. (0990) 808080) service to **Glasgow** (1 per hr., £2.90), **Inverness** (1 per hr., £9.80), and **London** (5-6 per day and 2 overnight, £13).

PRACTICAL INFORMATION

The **train station** is on Goosecroft Rd. (Travel Centre open M-F 6am-9pm, Sa 6am-8pm, Su 8:30am-10pm. **Luggage storage** available M-Sa 10am-6pm.) Down the street, the **bus station** (tel. 446474) is under the Thistle Marches Shopping Centre. (Ticket office open M-F 8:30am-6pm, Sa 8:30am-5pm. Free **luggage storage** is available M-Sa 7am-9pm, Su 12:30-7:30pm.) The **Stirling Visitor Centre** (tel. 479901; fax 451881), next to the castle, is Stirling's high-altitude, high-tech version of a tourist office, featuring informative exhibits and a 12-minute movie. The upstairs staff exchanges currency (£3 commission) and vends the *Stirling Heritage Trail* guide (75p). (Open daily July-Aug. 9am-6:30pm; Apr.-June and Sept.-Oct. 9:30am-6pm; Nov.-Mar. 9:30am-5pm.) The less thrilling **tourist office** (tel. 475019) nonetheless greets visitors warmly at 41 Dumbarton Rd. (Open July-Aug. M-Sa 9am-7:30pm, Su 9:30am-6:30pm; June and Sept. M-Sa 9am-6pm, Su 10am-4pm; Apr.-May M-Sa 9am-5pm; Oct. M-Sa 9:30am-5pm; Nov.-Mar. M-F 10am-5pm, Sa 10am-4pm. Or something.) Both offices provide the free *What's On* and *Royal Stirling Events* calendars, as well as National Express and Citylink timetables. If you balk at walking up Stirling's hills, **Guide Friday** (tel. (0131) 556 2244) operates one-hour open-top bus tours which begin at the castle esplanade, and offer pick-up/drop-off throughout the city (tours 10am-5pm; £5.50, students and seniors £4, children £2, families £11). An **ATM** graces the corner of Port St., Upper Craigs, and Dumbarton Rd. and shells out sterling. Mail Mom and Dad postcards of Wallace's tortured body or exchange currency at the **post office**, 84-86 Murray Pl. (tel. 465392; open M-F 9am-5:30pm, Sa 9am-12:30pm). The office's **postal code** is FK8 2BP; the **telephone code** is 01786.

ACCOMMODATIONS AND FOOD

B&Bs abound near the train station and the university; the tourist offices will help you find a room. **SYHA Stirling** (tel. 473442; fax 445715), on St. John St., halfway up the hill to the castle, occupies the shell of the first Separatist Church in Stirling. Each of the two- to five-bed rooms has its own shower and toilet. (July-Aug. £12.50, under 18 £11; Sept.-June £11.50, under 18 £10. Continental breakfast included. Reception open 7:30am-11pm. Bedroom lockout 10am-2pm. Curfew 2am.) In July and August, don't despair if the hostel is full. Overflow guests receive their own room (within a

SCOTLAND

suite) in the Union St. **Annexe,** known in cooler months as University of Stirling campus housing. Two spotless singles—one with a view of the Wallace Monument—and a breakfast that will hold you until dinner await at **Mrs. Helen Miller's,** 16 Riverside Dr. (tel. 461105). Turn right from the train station, cross the bridge, go down Seaforth Pl. and Abbey Rd. until the road ends, and turn left onto Riverside Dr. (£11).

The **Stirling Health Food Stores,** 29 Dumbarton Rd. (tel. 464903), is a vegster's paradise (open M-Tu and Th-Sa 9am-5:15pm, W 9am-4:30pm). **The Greengrocer,** 81 Port St. (tel. 479159), offers some of the freshest fruits and veggies in town (open M-Sa 9am-5:30pm). For sit-down, the friendly staff at **Qismat Tandoori,** 37 Friar St. (tel. 463075), serves a filling three-course lunch for £4 (M-Sa noon-2:30pm) and an all-you-can-eat dinner buffet for £9 (daily 5:30-10pm). Or choose from the 195 entrees (10% take-away discount; open M-Sa noon-midnight, Su 3pm-midnight).

SIGHTS

Planted atop a defunct volcano, and embraced on all sides by the scenic Ochil Hills, **Stirling Castle** (tel. 450000) possesses prim gardens and superb views of the Forth Valley that belie its militant and occasionally murderous past. Robert the Bruce determined the castle was the cause of too much bloodshed and had it destroyed. It was rebuilt nonetheless in the 1380s, and Robert's statue ironically stands guard in front of the present structure. The castle's hideous gargoyles glowered over the 14th-century Wars of Independence, a 15th-century royal murder, and the 16th-century coronation of the infant Mary, Queen of Scots; its final military engagement came in 1746, when Bonnie Prince Charlie besieged it while retreating from England (then gave up and kept retreating). After years of use as an army barracks (a practice begun when King James I housed his new "British Army" in the Great Hall), the castle is now being restored to its original splendor. The scaffolding will disappear in the year 2000. Beneath the cannons pointed at Stirling Bridge lie the 16th-century **great kitchens;** visitors can walk among the recreated chaos of cooks, dogs, bakers, and large slabs of meat in the recently unearthed kitchens. Free half-hour **guided tours,** leaving on the hour and on the half, give a background for further exploration. *(Castle open daily Apr.-Oct. 9:30am-6pm; Nov.-Mar. 9:30am-5pm; last admission 45min. before closing. £4.50, seniors £3.50, under 16 £1.20.)* The castle also contains the **Regimental Museum of the Argyll and Sutherland Highlanders,** a fascinating military museum. *(Open Easter-Sept. M-Sa 10am-5:45pm, Su 11am-4:45pm; Oct.-Easter daily 10am-4:45pm. Free.)*

Down Castle Hill Wynd, the high walls and timbered roof of the **Church of the Holy Rude** witnessed the coronation of James VI, and shook under the fire and brimstone of John Knox. *(Open daily May-Sept. 10am-5pm; Su service July-Dec. 10am, Jan.-June 11:30am. Frequent organ recitals. Donations requested.)* **Ladies Rock,** a lookout point in the large **Valley Cemetery** behind the Church, provides free views nearly as impressive as those from the castle battlements. Next to the Rude lies the 17th-century **Guildhall,** or "Cowane's Hospital." Legend has it that at the stroke of midnight each New Year, the statue of Guildhall founder John Cowane descends from its niche over the front door and dances a jig in the courtyard. *(Open M-Sa 9am-5pm, Su 1-5pm. Free.)*

Donnie, We Hardly Knew Ye

Alcohol was omnipresent at the traditional Scottish funeral. Lowlanders considered it their responsibility to keep watch over the dead prior to burial, and wiled away the hours imbibing drinks in solitude beside the corpse. On the day of the funeral, mourners were advised to show up at noon—and expected to arrive several hours later. Friends and neighbors watched the body being lowered into the coffin, and then gathered nearby to sip tea together and chase down the afternoon with two glasses of wine and one of rum or whisky. Highland funerals were generally more festive, and the music, dancing, and bacchanalia following those of some chieftains put their descendants into the dustbin of debt. According to E.J. Guthrie, a 19th century observer, the relatives of the deceased were granted the high honor of opening a grand ball and were expected to dispense a few pence to beggars stopping by their home.

SCOTLAND

On the east side of town, cross the Abbey Rd. footbridge over the River Forth to find the ruins of the 12th-century **Cambuskenneth Abbey** (tel. 450000). The occasional black-faced sheep may eyeball you across the graves of James III and his wife Margaret. *(Open Apr.-Sept. M-Sa 9:30am-6pm, Su 2-6pm, grounds open all year. Free.)* From the Abbey, walk half a mile north on Ladysneuk Rd., turn left on Alloa Rd., continue through the playground on your right, go up the steep stairs at the back, and head uphill to the 200 ft. **Wallace Monument** (tel. 472140), which houses the 66 in. sword William Wallace wielded against King Edward I of England. When finally captured by the English, Wallace was hanged until semi-conscious, then disemboweled, castrated, beheaded, and quartered, his entrails burnt, and parts of his body dispersed to the corners of Scotland. The 19th-century Gothic-esque tower offers incredible views to those bravehearted enough to climb the 246-step, wind-whipped spiral staircase to the top. *(Open daily July-Aug. 9:30am-6:30pm; June and Sept. 10am-6pm; Mar., May, and Oct. 10am-5pm; Nov.-Feb. Sa-Su only 10am-4pm. £2.50, seniors and children £1.50.)* Back at sea-level (or closer to it, anyway), buses leave from the parking lot at the base of Abbey Craig for Stirling's train and bus stations (5 per hr., £1).

Two miles south of Stirling, at **Bannockburn** (tel. 812644), a statue of a battle-ready Robert the Bruce overlooks the field where his men decisively defeated the English in 1314. After the victory, Scotland kept its independence for 400 years. *(Heritage Centre open daily Apr.-Oct. 10am-5:30pm; Mar. and Nov.-Dec. 11am-3pm; grounds open all year.)*

■ Inveraray

Comely and unpretentious, whitewashed Inveraray (rhymes with contrary, somewhat), has been home to the powerful Campbells since the early 15th century. Situated within the wooded glens of mid-Argyll, Inveraray merits a visit as much for its splendid lochside setting as for its strategic position on one of the few bus routes providing access to the region. The captivating **Inveraray Jail** (tel. 302381) is easily the most interesting sight in town. Visitors are greeted by the "Torture, Death, and Damnation" exhibit (did you know the 17th-century punishment for impersonation was having a hole burnt through your tongue?). Listen to trials in the real-life 19th-century courtroom. Tour the Old Prison (1820) and New Prison (1849), stuffed with superb specimens of prison fun. Lookin' for more? Interactive exhibits abound; try the thumbscrews, whipping table, and the "Crank Machine," on which prisoners cranked out 14,400 revolutions a day as a form of useless hard labor. *(Open daily Apr.-Oct. 9:30am-6pm; Nov.-Mar. 10am-5pm; last admission 1hr. before closing. £4.30, students £2.65, seniors £2.75, children £2.10, families £11.75.)*

Home of the Duke and Duchess of Argyll, carefully cultivated **Inveraray Castle** (tel. 302203) contrasts strikingly with the rugged mountains that enclose it. Inside the castle, find Rob Roy's dirk handle, sporran, and belt, portraits of all the earls and dukes of Argyll, as well as enough weapons and armor to defend all of Scotland. *(Open July-Aug. M-Sa 10am-5:45pm, Su 1-5:45pm; Apr.-June and Sept.-Oct. closed M-Sa 1-2pm; last admission 5pm. £4.50, students and seniors £3.50, under 16 £2.50, families £12; grounds free.)* Also on castle grounds is the one-room **Combined Operations Museum** (tel. 500218), which details the town's function as a major WWII training site; troops practiced D-Day shore landings here. *(Open Apr. to mid-Oct. M-Th and Sa 11am-6pm, Su 1-6pm; last admission 5:30pm. £2, students, seniors, and children £1.50, families £6.50)* Look up to find the 126 ft. **Bell Tower.** The free bellringing exhibit (see **The Bell's Appeal**, p. 353) does not include the view from the rooftop. *(Open daily May-Sept. 10am-1pm and 2-5pm. Tower £1.50, students, seniors, and children 75p.)* The fun-packed **Fortnight Festival** parties away the last week in July and the first week in August.

Buses #976 and 926 run to Inveraray from **Glasgow** (1¾hr., M-Sa 9 per day, Su 4 per day, £5.50). The town has a small **tourist office** (tel. 302063) on Front St. *(Open July to mid-Sept. daily 9am-6pm; May-June M-Sa 9am-5pm, Su 11am-5pm; Apr. and mid-Sept. to late Oct. M-Sa 9am-5pm, Su noon-5pm; Nov.-Mar. M-F 10am-4pm, Sa-Su noon-4pm.)* The **Bank of Scotland** kneels at Church Sq. The **post office** (tel. 302062) is on Black's Land (open M-Tu and Th-F 9am-1pm and 2-5:30pm, W 9am-1pm, Sa 9am-12:30pm). Its **postal code** is PA32 8UD. Inveraray's **telephone code** is 01499.

The small **SYHA Inveraray** (tel./fax 302454) is just north of town; take a left through the arch next to the Inveraray Woolen Mill onto Oban Rd. and walk past the gas station. This compact, no-nonsense hostel is blessed with an omniscient warden. (£6.10, under 18 £5. Self-catering. 38 beds, 2 showers—you do the math. Lockout 10:30am-5pm. Curfew 11:30pm. Open mid-Mar. to Oct.) Inveraray hides a stash of **B&Bs** up the road past the post office; among the best is **Mrs. Campbell** (tel. 302258), Lorona, Main St. S., by the gas station/Renault dealer, where the six rooms soothe and the lounge has a great view of the loch (£15; open Easter-Oct.). The **Old Rectory,** Main St. S. (tel. 302280), farther down the road, is home to nine large rooms with fluffy beds (singles £19; doubles £34). **Spar supermarket** lies on Main St. (tel. 302107; open M-Sa 8:30am-8pm, Su 10am-4pm).

■ Loch Lomond

Scotland's upland region lies north of the Highlands Boundary Fault, which stretches southwest across the land from Aberdeen to Arran Island. The hills begin to swell 30 mi. north of Glasgow and 10 mi. west of Stirling and grow into majestic peaks as they undulate northward. Less than an hour's drive north of Glasgow along the scenic A82, **Loch Lomond** is, unfortunately, the closest most visitors to Scotland get to the Highlands. Meandering through lush bays, dotted with thickly wooded islands in the south and ringed by bare hills to the north, Loch Lomond is captivating. A number of small, rough beaches dot the shores and make fine spots for lazy picnics and paddles. Hikers adore the **West Highland Way,** which snakes along the entire eastern side of the Loch, and in full measure stretches 95 mi. from Milngavie north to Fort William. One of the best introductions to the area is Sweeney's Cruises **boat tours** of Loch Lomond; one-hour tours start on the tourist office's side of the River Leven. *(Run subject to demand. £4.50, children £2.)* Avert your eyes (or don't) from the nudist colony on one of the islands in the lake's center (brrr!). Ruins of the **Lomond Castle Hotel** are also visible on shore; the hotel's owner burnt it down in an attempted insurance scam. Even the lochside towns that shamelessly commercialize "The Bonnie Bonnie Banks" are largely unpolluted by tourists and overdevelopment. Visitors who undertake challenging hikes in such roadless areas as the northeastern edge of Loch Lomond or most of Loch Katrine are rewarded with stunning views and the quiet splendor of untrampled swaths of space which inspired the sweet ballad.

■ Balloch

At the southern tip of Loch Lomond, Balloch is the major town in the area, the word "major" being used loosely: with the exception of the youth hostel, everything you need to survive in Balloch is within a casual 1½-minute walk from the tourist office. Across the River Leven, the **Balloch Castle Country Park** provides 200 acres of gorgeous beach lawn, woods, and gardens, as well as a 19th-century castle which houses a **Visitor's Centre.** If the weather is good, don't miss the opportunity to walk around and look for the pixies in **Fairy Glen.** *(Gardens open daily dawn-dusk. Free. Visitor's Centre, doubling as a Loch Lomond Park Ranger Station, open Easter-Oct. daily 10am-6pm.)*

The Balloch **train station** is across the street from the tourist office on Balloch Rd. **Trains** (tel. (0345) 484950) serve Balloch from **Glasgow's** Queen Station, lower level (45min., at least 2 per hr., £3). The bus stance is a few minutes down Balloch Rd., across the bridge to the left of the tourist office, but buses bypassing the town center (including **Citylink** buses) pick up passengers on the A82 near the roundabout. **Citylink** buses #926, #975, and #976 also make the trek (M-Sa 5 per day, Su 3 per day). To reach the eastern side, take bus #309 from Balloch to **Balmaha** (40min., M-F 3 per day, Sa-Su 6 per day). Bus #305 and #307 bounce to the conservation village of Luss (6 per day). Get local bus schedules from the tourist office. The town's **tourist office,** Old Station Building, Balloch Rd. (tel. (01389) 753533), books rooms (£1) and shows a 7-minute introductory film on Loch Lomond. Pick up the useful *In and Around Loch Lomond* and the *Glasgow-Loch Lomond Cycleway,* detailing the 21 mi. route between the two. (Open daily July-Aug. 9:30am-7:30pm; June 9:30am-6pm; Sept. 9:30am-7pm; Apr.-May and Oct. 10am-5pm.) Conveniently close to the tourist office, **B&Bs** congregate on Balloch Rd. The **SYHA Loch Lomond** (tel. (01389) 850226) is one of Scotland's largest hostels, a stunning 19th-century castle-like building 2 mi. north of Balloch. Unlike many hostels, much of this mansion remains in its original splendor—the double-height common room is astounding. Other amenities include the ghost of the damsel Veronica, who, pregnant with the child of a stable boy, took a steep dive from the window of the tower in which her family had locked her. You can now sleep soundly (or not) in said tower. With nine entrances, 53 chimneys, and 180 beds, it gets crazy in mid-summer; call ahead to book a room. (July-Aug. £9.60, under 18 £8.10; Sept.-Oct. and early Mar. to June £8.60, under 18 £7.10).

The **Tullichewan Caravan and Camping Site** (tel. (01389) 759475; fax 755563), the Club Med of campsites, is located on Old Luss Rd. up Balloch Rd. from the tourist office on the right. The site offers an opportunity to sleep under the stars, luxuriate in a sauna, spa bath, or sunbed (£4), or rent mountain bikes (£7 per 4hr., £10 per 8hr.; £100 deposit required if you aren't staying at the site). The friendly staff is on call at all hours; reception is ordinarily open 8:30am-10pm, but may be open later for *quiet* campers. (Tent and 2 people £6.50-9, with car £8-12; additional guests free in winter, otherwise £1.50; extra children 10p; closed Nov.)

To reach the other SYHA hostel on the loch, take the Inverberg ferry (tel. (01301) 702356) across the Loch to Rowardennan (Apr.-Sept. daily; leaves Rowardennan at 10am, 2pm, 6pm; leaves Inverberg 30min. later; £4, children £1.50). The **SYHA Rowardennan** (tel. (01360) 870259) is the first hostel along the West Highland Way. Huge windows put the loch in your lap (£7.75, under 18 £6.50; curfew 11:30pm; open Mar.-Oct.).

■ Loch Long

Loch Long stretches like a salty finger northeast toward Loch Lomond. The **Ardgartan Forest Park** on the northern side of the Loch has excellent cycling potential. This Forest Park lies beneath the "Arrochar Alps," a series of rugged mountains including five Munros and **The Cuckolded Cobbler** (2891ft.). Also known as Ben Arthur, The Cobbler is unmistakable for its unusual, jagged rock formations—the peak appears to have sprouted horns befitting a cuckold. A leisurely trail with some rocky parts near the tip begins in the town of Arrochar, halfway between Tarbet and Ardgartan (inquire in town or at the hostel about the exact location of the trailhead). Once at the top, look for the Eye of the Needle, an opening in one of the horny rock-stacks, where you can sit and enjoy the view over the rest of the mountains. To tackle this hike knowledgeably, pick up the Pathfinder Ordnance Survey Map 368 (£4.25) or the Landranger Map 56 (£5), available at area tourist offices. The easiest way to enter the area of Loch Long is by **train** via the Arrochar-Tarbet station. Trains run from **Glasgow** (1¼hr., M-Sa 4 per day, Su 3 per day, £7). Pick up the *Cycling In The Forest* pamphlet (30p) in the Ardgartan **Tourist Centre** (tel. (01301) 702432), off the A83 at the northern end of the Loch (open daily July-Aug. 10am-6pm, Apr.-June and Sept.-Oct. 10am-5pm). Half a mile away, the **SYHA Ardgartan** (tel./fax (01301) 702362) has glorious loch views (£7.75, under 18 £6.50; curfew 11:45pm; closed Jan.). Citylink bus #976 passes the hostel. Spend long enough here and you may reach the top of the steep **Rest and be thankful.** Really.

■ The Trossachs

The gentle mountains and lochs of the **Trossachs** form the southern boundary of the Highlands. Sir Walter Scott and Queen Victoria lavished praise on the region, the only easily accessible Scottish wilderness prior to the 20th century. Ironically, the Trossachs today are less accessible than much of the northern wilds; only a few buses each day link Glasgow and Stirling to **Aberfoyle** and **Callander,** the area's two main towns. The A821 winds through the heart of the Trossachs between Aberfoyle and Callander, passing near beautiful **Loch Katrine,** the Trossachs' original lure and the setting of Scott's "The Lady of the Lake." A road for walkers and cyclists traces the Loch's shoreline. Unfit tourists drop like flies after a half mile, leaving the Loch's joys to more hardy travelers. The **Steamship Sir Walter Scott** (tel. (0141) 955 0128) steams between Loch Katrine's Trossachs Pier and Stronachlachar. The scenery is arresting, but in July and August, the crush of passengers may make the trip a hassle. *(Cruises depart from Trossachs Pier. Apr.-Oct. Su-F 11am, noon, 1:45 and 3:15pm, Sa 1:45 and 3:15pm. £3.80-5, under 16 and over 60 £2.40-2.75.)* Nearby, **Ben A'an'** (1207 ft.) hulks over the Trossachs; the rocky one-hour hike up begins a mile from the pier, along the A821.

Getting to this area is tough: **Citylink** bus #974, running through Edinburgh and Stirling to Fort William, stops in **Callander** (1 per day). Or try **The Trossachs Trundler**, a 1950s-style bus that creaks to **Callander, Aberfoyle,** and **Trossachs Pier** at the tip of Loch Katrine in time for the sailing of the *Sir Walter Scott* (buses run July-Sept. Su-F 4 per day, Day Rover £5.40, seniors and children £3.60). Service #59 leaving from Stirling bus station connects with the Trundler in **Callander** (Stirling-Trossachs Rover £8.10, seniors and children £5.40). You can also make use of post buses, which slowly wind their way through selected towns every day. Grab all the timetables at tourist offices, or call the **Stirling Council Public Transport Helpline** (tel. (01786) 442707). **Trossachs Cycle Hire** (tel. (01877) 382614), on the pier, rents high-quality bikes (£3 per hr., £7.50 per half-day, £12 per day; open Apr.-Sept. daily 10am-5:30pm).

■ St. Andrews

> Would you like to see a city given over,
> Soul and body to a tyrannising game?
> If you would, there's little need to be a rover,
> For St. Andrews is the abject city's name.
>
> —Robert F. Murray (1863-1894)

In St. Andrews, "the tyrannising game" is golf—the windows of the Royal and Ancient Golf Club look out over the Old Course, the sport's world headquarters and frequent site of the British Open. Golf tourism, and multitudes of students from England and America, have diluted the "Scottishness" of the town and raised prices sky-high. But a few steps away, one can glimpse the town's other glories, including the gray stone buildings of Scotland's oldest university and the ruins of the seat of pre-Reformation Christianity. Restored medieval streets lead to castle ruins overlooking the North Sea and the magnificent West Sands, giving St. Andrews a unique beauty which transcends even golf itself. Nonetheless, the university students depart in the summer, only to be replaced by at least as many golf-seekers.

GETTING THERE

ScotRail (tel. (0345) 550033) keeps a respectful distance from St. Andrews, stopping 5 mi. away at **Leuchars** (LU-cars) on its London-Edinburgh-Dundee-Aberdeen line (from Edinburgh 1hr., 1 per hr., £7; from London 3-4 per day including 1 overnight). From Leuchars, buses go to St. Andrews (5 per hr., 7am-6pm, £1).

It's easier, cheaper, and quicker to take **Fife Scottish buses** (tel. 474238) along the scenic coastal route from **Edinburgh** to St. Andrews, located on the other side of the Fife Peninsula from the capital (#X58, 2hr., M-Sa 1 per hr., fewer on Su, £5.50, students £3.60). Twelve buses (fewer on Su) make the trip between St. Andrews and **Glasgow** (#X24, change to #X58, X59, or X60 at Dunfermlane, 2hr., £5.50). From **Aberdeen, Perth,** and **Inverness,** first take Citylink to **Dundee** (1 per hr., £6.50), and then Scottish Fife #59, 60, or 95 to St. Andrews (£2.15).

Hitchers often approach from Leuchars in the north on the A919 to the A91. Hitchers report the route from Edinburgh or Glasgow is tricky because of the manic crisscrossing of roads outside these cities; once reaching the A91 or A915, they usually hitch straight to town. **Drivers** beware of limited parking; parking vouchers are available from stores (30p per 30min., 2hr. limit).

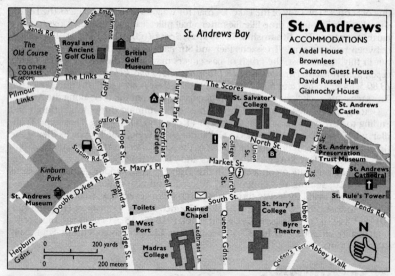

ORIENTATION AND PRACTICAL INFORMATION

St. Andrews's three main streets—**North, Market,** and **South St.**—run nearly parallel east to west, culminating near the cathedral at the town's east end. Most buses stop at the **St. Andrews Bus Station,** City Rd. (tel. 474238). Manicured golf greens and shops dedicated to the "game of gentlemen" rule the northwest part of town.

The marvelous **tourist office** (tel. 472021; fax 478422) swings at 70 Market St. From the bus station, slice right on City Rd. and then take the first left onto Market St. and continue for 300 yd. (Open July-Aug. M-Sa 9:30am-8pm; Su 11am-6pm; Sept.-June M-Sa 9:30am-6pm, Su 11am-4pm.) The office provides the free guide, *The Kingdom of Fife,* which includes an extensive list of local B&Bs and their prices. Makes bookings in St. Andrews' very limited accommodations for £1.50 (outside St. Andrews £3) plus a refundable 10% deposit. The **Royal Bank of Scotland,** South St. (tel. 472181), changes currency and has an **ATM** (open M-Tu and Th-F 9:15am-5pm, W 10am-5pm). A **launderette** (tel. 475150) is at 14b Woodburn Terr. (open M-Sa 9am-7pm, Su 9am-5pm; last wash 1½hr. before closing). The **post office** (tel. 472321) tees off at 127 South St. (open M-F 9am-5:30pm, Sa 9am-12:30pm). The **postal code** is KY16 9UL, while the **telephone code** for St. Andrews proper is 01334.

ACCOMMODATIONS

High local taxes and golfers with chubby wallets have made St. Andrews unbearably expensive. Near the golf links, Murray Park and Murray Pl. greet the backpacker with astronomically priced B&Bs. Summer housing at the university and B&Bs farther away are your best bet, or make St. Andrews a daytrip from Glasgow or Edinburgh.

Gannochy House, North St. (tel. 464870), next to Younger Hall. Over 80 dorms, including 40 singles, in a cinderblock building. Great location. £10. Sheets included. No kitchen. Reception open 2-6pm. Check-out 9:30am. Open June-Aug.

Cadzow Guest House, 58 North St. (tel. 476933). 10min. walk from the bus station; turn right on City Rd., left on Market St., left on College St., and right on North St. Well located near cathedral and castle ruins. Vivacious owner. TV and coffeemakers. Phone and mail reservations accepted. Singles with bath £23; doubles £32, with bath £42. 5% discount for stays longer than a week.

David Russell Hall, 79 North St. (tel. 462000), at the University. Offers slightly more posh summer dorm housing. Singles £22; doubles £31. Open June-Aug.

Aedel House, 12 Murray Pl. (tel. 472315). Offers attractive golfer-ready doubles and one single with bath. Book ahead. Singles £15; doubles £24. Open Feb.-Nov.

Brownlees, 7 Murray Pl. (tel. 473868). Elegant housing only a few blocks from the Old Course and hours of golfing satisfaction. £20-25. Check-out 10:30am. Phone or mail reservations accepted. Subtract £1 for stays longer than 3 days.

FOOD AND DRINK

Housing may be pricey, but inexpensive eats abound in this college town. Find the cheapest at the **Tesco** supermarket, 130 Market St. (tel. 472448; open M-W 8:30am-7pm, Th-F 8:30am-8pm, Sa 8am-7pm, Su 10am-6pm). For light snacks in view of the castle ruins, **Ma Brown's,** near the St. Andrews Preservation Trust Museum on North St., featured in 1997's *The Winter Guest,* steeps tea in bone china (75p per pot), bakes gingerbread (80p), and offers the best carrot cake known to man (open daily summer 10am-5pm, closes at 4:30pm in winter).

Kinness Fry Bar, 79 Bridge St. (tel. 473802), down the road from the 2 gas stations just outside the West Port on South St. Classic fish and chips and good pizza (£2-7). No sitting area. Open daily 4:30pm-1am.

Brambles, 5 College St. (tel. 475380), between North and Market St. Anything but prickly. Long lines of locals and vegetarian-friendly menus await. Lasagna with salad £4.70, omelettes £3.35. Open M-Sa 9am-5pm, Su noon-5pm.

B. Jannetta, 31 South St. (tel. 473285). 52 flavors (!) of award-winning, homemade ice cream. Overrun by sticky-chinned children when school gets out. 55p per scoop. Open daily Apr.-Aug. 9am-6pm; Sept.-Mar. 9am-5:30pm.

PM's Diner, 1 Union St. (tel. 476425), at Market St. All sorts of inexpensive take-away, including fish and chips (£2.10) and steak and kidney pie (£1.30). Open daily 9am-11:30pm.

St. Andrews's student **pubs** are worth a peek. **The Central** (tel. 478296), stereotyped as a Yah hangout ("yes" to the commoner; "yah" mocks the English public school accent), attracts a broad student clientele to its digs on Market and College St. Inexpensive pub meals go for £2-4 (open M-Sa 11am-11:45pm, Su 12:30-11:45pm). **The Victoria,** 1 St. Mary's Pl. (tel. 476964), is the lovechild of a Scottish pub and a Western saloon. Sip whisky at either of the two adjoining bars. Daily happy hour 8-9pm, karaoke on Thursdays during term-time, occasional live bands (open Sa-W 11am-midnight, Th-F 11am-1am). The **Lizard Lounge,** 127 North St. (tel. 473378), in the basement of the Argyle House Hotel, has great atmosphere and drink specials (£1 shots, £1.30 lager pints) from 8:30-9:30pm (open M-W noon-midnight, Th-F noon-1am, Sa-Su 12:30pm-midnight).

SIGHTS AND ENTERTAINMENT

St. Andrews's non-golf sights arise from the foams of the North Sea at the east end of town. In the Middle Ages, thousands of pilgrims journeyed to **St. Andrews Cathedral** (tel. 472563) to pray at the Saint's Shrine. During the Reformation, iconoclast Protestants defaced the interior of the Church, which was later pillaged by locals. Only a few piles of rubble remain of what was once Scotland's largest building, but according to legend, the cathedral's stones make up the foundation of many of St. Andrews's houses. **St. Rule's Tower** (157 steps), a square building that was part of the original 12th-century church, provides incredible views. (*Open daily Apr.-Sept. 9:30am-6:30pm; Oct.-Mar. 9:30am-4:30pm. Cathedral free; museum and tower £1.80, seniors £1.30, children 75p.*) The high stone walls of **St. Andrews Castle** (tel. 477196) now tumble down to the North Sea. Once the local bishop's residence, the castle maintains explorable secret tunnels, bottle-shaped dungeons, and high stone walls to keep out (or in) rebellious heretics. (*Same hours as cathedral. £2.30, seniors £1.75, children £1; joint ticket with cathedral £3.50, seniors £2.70, children £1.25.*) Mid-July through August, admission includes short historical dramas.

Scotland's oldest university, **St. Andrews University,** founded in the 15th century, stretches just west of the castle between North St. and The Scores. The university's well-heeled student population participates in a strong performing arts program and takes red-gowned walks by the pier after chapel on Sundays. For a one-hour **official tour** (tel. 462245) buy a ticket from the Admissions Reception, Butts Wynd, beside St. Salvator's Chapel Tower on North St. *(June-Aug. M-Sa 11am and 2:30pm. £3.60, students, seniors, and children £2.50, under 6 free.)* The tour is your key to the interiors of most university buildings; it is possible, however, to meander into placid quads through the parking entrances on North St.

St. Andrews's main industry is golf, which was here so avidly practiced that Scotland's rulers thrice outlawed the sport fearing for the national defense ("The men neglected their archery for golf!"). At the northwest edge of town, St. Andrews's **Old Course** (tel. 466666; fax 477036), the golf pilgrim's Canterbury, stretches regally to a gorgeous beach as manicured as the greens (you may recognize it from *Chariots of Fire*). According to the 1568 Book of Articles, Mary, Queen of Scots, played here just days after her husband was murdered. Nonmembers must present a handicap certificate or a letter of introduction from a golf club to play the Old Course. The few starting times not reserved months in advance are distributed by lottery. Call ahead to enter the lottery or reserve a time at the Old, New, Jubilee, Eden, or Strethtyrum courses. *(Old Course May-Oct. £72 per round; Nov.-Apr. £51. All other courses May-Oct. £16-31; Nov.-Apr. £14-25.)*

If you happened to leave your clubs at home, you can still learn about the ancient origins of golf next door at the **British Golf Museum** (tel. 478880). Papier-maché mannequins whittle putters and stitch balls into eternity. Try your knowledge at the interactive video quiz. *(Open Easter-Oct. daily 9:30am-5:30pm; Nov.-Easter Th-M 11am-3pm. £4, students and seniors £2.75, under 15 £1.50. Wheelchair accessible.)* A wax chemist distills elixirs among the reproductions of early 20th-century shops at the tiny **St. Andrews Preservation Trust Museum** (tel. 477629), down North St. from the cathedral. *(Open early June to Sept. daily 2-5pm. Donations welcome.)* The small **St. Andrews Museum** (tel. 412690), at Kinburn Park down Double Dykes Rd. from the bus station, travels back to the arrival of St. Regulus and points out that golf is but "a small dot" (a tee, perhaps?) in the town's history. *(Open Apr.-Sept. daily 10am-5pm; Oct.-Mar. M-F 10:30am-4pm, Sa-Su 12:30-5pm. Free.)* The **Byre Theatre** on Abbey St. is set to reopen in 2000. Call the tourist office for information and tickets.

■ Fife Seaside

The Kingdom of Fife fills the fields faring from the Firth of Forth and the Firth of Tay. **The East Neuk,** a series of sun-warmed coastal fishing villages south of St. Andrews concentrates on Fife's main "f": fish. Near the point of Fife (Fife Ness) sleeps the village of **Crail,** just like St. Andrews—but without the golf, university, and tourists. It's the perfect place to do nothing but relax and gnaw on freshly caught crab claws sold at a little stall by the harbor. From St. Andrews, take the A917 to the coast, or catch bus #95 (hourly) from St. Andrews or Anstruther. Crail's **tourist office,** 62-64 Marketgate (tel. (01333) 450869), is also home to a small local history museum. (Office and museum open Apr.-May Sa-Su 2-5pm and June-Sept. M-Sa 10am-1pm and 2-5pm, Su 2-5pm.) **Guided walks** of town leave from the museum (1½-2hr., every Su June-Aug. 2:30pm, £1).

About 5 mi. west of Crail along the A917 (or 9mi. southeast of St. Andrews along the direct connecting road) lies **Anstruther,** home to a quiet harbor, 13 pubs, great fish and chips, and **Mr. Pennington's Bunkhouse** (tel. (01333) 310768). Mr. Pennington, a diving expert and historian, and his family provide rustic, quiet living in a 700-year-old fortified farmhouse. A while back, a *Let's Go* researcher stopped in for one night and spent 11 months here. (Bunkhouse sleeps 15 in 3 walk-through rooms £6.50; twin room £8.50. Sheets 50p. No curfew.) The fastest, cheapest way to Anstruther is by Minibus #61, 61A, or 61B from Blackfriars Chapel on South St. (20min., M-Sa 7-8 per day, £2). Fife Scottish bus #95 also makes 17 runs daily to Anstruther and

Elie (£1.80). Near Anstruther, the **Isle of May** rises from the Firth of Forth, and is home to Scotland's first lighthouse, built in 1636. A nature reserve, the Isle is home to puffins, ducks, grey seals, and the 2000-year-old remains of human inhabitants. In summer, **Jim Raeper** (tel. (01333) 310103) sails from Anstruther to the Isle (July-Aug. daily; May-June and Sept. W-M; £15, students £12, children £6) and offers 3 hr. charter fishing trips (£10 per person, bait and lines supplied). All trips are highly contingent on the weather and tides; call ahead for times or check with the **Anstruther Tourist Office,** St. Ayles Head (tel. (01333) 311073; open Easter-Oct. M and F-Sa 10am-5pm, Tu-Th 10am-1pm and 2-5pm, Su noon-5pm; closed Nov.-Easter). Halfway between Anstruther and St. Andrews, the **Secret Bunker** crouches hidden below a farmhouse. This subterranean shelter would have been home for British leaders during a nuclear war. *(Open Apr.-Oct. 10am-5pm. £6, students and seniors £5, children £3.25.)* Land-lubbers can rent bikes at **East Neuk Cycles,** 63 James St. (tel. (01333) 312179; £4 per day).

Five miles west of Anstruther, along the A917 and near the village of **Elie** (EEL-y), lies beautiful **Ruby Bay,** named for the garnets seldom found on its sands. While Fife boasts excellent bathing waters (among the purest in Great Britain), you can command a better, quieter view of sporting seals, tidal-pool marine life, and slippery yellow rocks from the headland by the lighthouse. Down the coast lies the **Lady's Tower,** built in the 18th century as a bathing box for Lady Jane Anstruther, who reportedly sent a bell-ringing servant through the streets to warn the village of her presence to prevent (or promote?) anyone seeing her scantily clad. Deciding among 12 delicious varieties of scones at the **Elie Coffee House,** 41 High St. may prove no easier than garnet-searching.

North of St. Andrews, in Fife's northeastern nook, stretches the **Tentsmuir Point Nature Reserve,** a young forest park hemmed in from the sea by a 10 mi. beach. Gain access to the park from **Leuchars,** on the St. Andrews-Dundee road and on Scotrail's Edinburgh-Dundee line (see **Getting There,** p. 511). The only **SHYA Youth Hostel,** Back Wynd (tel. (01337) 857710; £4.65, under 18 £3.85) in the area is 20 mi. inland in **Falkland,** one of the most complete "auld toons" in Fife. The nearby **Falkland Palace and Gardens** (tel. (01337) 857397), once the hunting lodge of the Stewarts, epitomizes outstanding early Renaissance architecture and features a 1539 tennis court, still in use. *(Open Easter-Oct. M-Sa 11am-4:30pm, Su 1:30-4:30pm; grounds open until 5:30pm. £4.80, seniors and children £3.20.)* Falkland is most easily accessible from the town of **Kirkcaldy,** due south on the coast (tel. (01592) 642394; #36, 1hr., M-Sa 8 per day, return £3.10). Kirkcaldy is on the Edinburgh-St. Andrews bus route (#X59 or #X60, 2 per hr.). Many **hitch** from St. Andrews to Falkland along the busy A91.

■ Perth

A large, metallic sculpture in Perth's pedestrian city center depicts two figures: a man relaxing and enjoying the vista, and another leaning forward, blindfolded. Follow the example of the former and open your eyes to the city's well-tended riverbank, jack-of-all-trades museum, and aura of comfortable prosperity. Untrampled by university students (a proposal to move St. Andrews here was squashed in 1691), placid Perth caters primarily to residents and mild-mannered guests. Once voted the best place to live in Britain, Perth is well worth a brief visit.

GETTING THERE Trains (tel. (0345) 484950) depart for **Inverness** (2½hr., 8-9 per day, £14.50), **Edinburgh** (1½hr., 2 per hr., £8.40), **Glasgow** (1hr., 1 per hr., £11), and **Aberdeen** (1½hr., 2 per hr., £19.20). **Buses** run to most major towns in **Scotland,** including **Inverness** (2½hr., 1 per hr., £9), **Edinburgh** (1½hr., 16 per day, £4.50), **Glasgow** (1½hr., 1 per hr., £6.80), **Dundee** (45min., 16 per day, £3), **Pitlochry** (45min., 1 per hr., £4.50), and **Aberdeen** (2½hr., 1 per hr., £9).

ORIENTATION AND PRACTICAL INFORMATION The **train station** (tel. (0345) 484950), on Leonard St., faces the **bus station** (tel. (0990) 505050; open M 7:45am-5pm, Tu-F 8am-5pm, Sa 8am-4:30pm). The **tourist office,** 45 High St. (tel. 638353; fax

444863), several blocks away from the train and bus stations, offers an unparalleled selection of maps. From the bus station, turn right on Leonard St., continue along S. Methven St., and turn right on High St., which becomes a pedestrian precinct. (Open July-Aug. M-Sa 9am-8pm, Su 11am-6pm; Apr.-June and Sept.-Oct. M-Sa 9am-6pm, Su 11am-4pm; Nov.-Mar. M-Sa 9am-5pm.) The **Royal Bank of Scotland,** next to the post office, has an **ATM** which gobbles Visa and Cirrus. The **post office** (tel. 624413) sits at 109 South St. (open M-F 9am-5:30pm, Sa 9am-7pm). The **postal code** is PH1 3AA; the **telephone code** 01738.

ACCOMMODATIONS AND FOOD A musical warden presides over Perth's **SYHA Youth Hostel** (tel. 623658), off Glasgow Rd. Take Hillend bus #7 from the South St. post office, or walk 15 minutes up South St. as it becomes County Pl., York Pl., and Glasgow Rd. Near the crest of the hill, turn right on Rosebank. This 64-bed hostel also has one five-bed cottage for families with young children. Lockers are available; bring your own padlock. (£7.75, under 18 £6.50. Laundry. Reception open 7am-11:30pm. Check-out 9:30am. Lockout 9:30am-1:30pm. Curfew 11:30pm. Open Mar.-Oct.) **B&Bs** line Glasgow Rd. below the hostel (£14-20).

Perth has a measure of reasonably priced food. A spicy three-course lunch (with giant *naan*) costs £4 at **Shezan Restaurant,** 21 Princes St. (tel. 620415; open M-Th noon-2pm and 5pm-midnight, F-Sa noon-2pm and 5pm-1am, Su 5pm-midnight). **The Lemon Tree,** 29-41 Skinner Gate (tel. 626412), provides savory wholefood and a selection of vegetarian dishes (£3-4; open M-Sa 9:30am-5pm). Pick up more veggies (or steaks!) at the enormous **Safeway** on Caledonian Rd. (open M-Tu and Sa 8am-8pm, W-Th 8am-9pm, F 8am-10pm, Su 9am-6pm).

SIGHTS A stroll along the swiftly flowing River Tay lets you peek under the arches of the **Perth Bridge.** Some of the small, cypress-laden islands in the Tay are explorable when the water is low—look for designated bridges. Across the bridge, a nature trail leads up to a panoramic view from **Kinnoull Hill Park.** In 1559, John Knox delivered an incendiary sermon from the pulpit of Perth's oldest church, **St. John's Kirk,** south of the tourist office on St. John's Pl. The result was the Reformation's destruction of churches and monasteries. *(Open M-F 10am-noon and 2-4pm. Guided tours available.)*

In the **Perth Museum and Art Gallery,** at the intersection of Tay St. and Perth Bridge, an intriguing display on the excavations of medieval Perth rubs shoulders with a hodgepodge collection of antique clocks, fine silverware, and an effigy of a 64 lb. salmon caught in 1922. *(Open M-Sa 10am-5pm. Free.)* The **Fergusson Gallery** (tel. 441944), housed in the Old Perth Water Works on Marshall Pl., houses an excellent collection of watercolors by the Scottish artist J.D. Fergusson, who was heavily influenced by his life companion, the dancer Margaret Morris. *(Open M-Sa 10am-5pm. Free.)*

Balhousie Castle (tel. 621281), off Hay St., the 16th-century home of the Earls of Kinnoull, now accommodates the **Black Watch Regimental Museum,** which includes hundreds of documents, weapons, and medals of the Black Watch from the 18th century, among them the key to the back door of Spandau prison in Berlin. *(Open May-Sept. M-Sa 10am-4:30pm; Oct.-Apr. M-F 10am-3:30pm. Free.)* **North Inch** spans a lush 100-acre park next to the castle on the beaches of the Tay.

The **Dewar's Rink** (tel. 624188), on Glasgow Rd., stays open all summer and on alternate weekends in winter. Skate or watch a game of curling—a Scottish sport fusing bowling, darts, the custodial sciences, and ice. To the west, **Bell's Cherrybank Gardens** (tel. 627330) has the largest collection of heather in the U.K. *(Open daily Apr.-Oct. 9am-5pm. £2, seniors and children 50p.)*

■ Near Perth

Less than 3 mi. northeast of Perth on the A93, sumptuous **Scone Palace** (SKOON; tel. (01738) 552300) witnessed the coronation of many a Scottish monarch on the famous Stone of Scone. The English stole the Stone in the 13th century (perhaps they mistook it for a typical English breakfast), but returned it some 700 years later on St. Andrew's Day in 1996. Many Scots believe this Stone is a fake (see **Stoned,** p. 98).

Pre-Modern Prenuptials

In an early experiment with family structure, Scottish men and women gathered at the River Esk to choose a potential mate for life. In a custom known as "hand-fasting" or "hand-in-fist," each participant in the festival chose one member of the opposite sex to live with. Exactly one year later, the couple had the option of marrying or parting in search of a better prize. Allegedly, both parties had equal "hand" in determining the fate of the relationship, but any children born during the year were considered the property of the father if the couple chose not to marry. Handfasting ceased throughout most of Scotland when the Reformation deemed it an abomination.

The present palace is the lavish Georgian/Neogothic home of the Earls of Mansfield, surrounded by peacock-strewn gardens. *(Open Apr.-Oct. daily 9:30am-5pm. £5, seniors £4.20, children £2.80; grounds only £2.50, children £1.40.)* During the school year, take bus #41 (1 per day), or ride **Guide Friday** out of Perth any time of year. *(£4.50, students and seniors £3, children £1.)* **Glamis Castle** (GLOMZ; tel. (01307) 840393; fax 840733), Macbeth's purported home and childhood playground of the Queen Mum, pokes its dozen storybook turrets into the sky 35 mi. northeast of Perth on the A94 toward Dundee. The castle houses collections of armor, paintings, and furniture. *(Open Apr.-Oct. daily 10am-5:30pm. £5, students and seniors £3.80, children £2.60.)*

■ Dunkeld and Birnam

Huddled on either side of the River Tay, amid the forested hills of Perthshire, the wee twin towns of Dunkeld (dun-KELD) and Birnam (a 15min. walk apart) provide easy access to one of Scotland's most blessedly isolated regions. The region welcomes walkers and hikers to its snow-capped mountains. The scintillating waters of Loch Tay reflect hilltop forts, 16th-century castles, and immaculate gardens in their depths.

Dunkeld's painstakingly restored 18th-century houses line the way to a partially charred 13th-century **Dunkeld Cathedral,** whose choir is now a restored parish church, and whose nave is pleasantly roofless. Alexander Stewart, the illegitimate son of English King Robert II, sought revenge for his excommunication by razing several Tayside villages and pilfering the gold chalices from the cathedral. *(Open Apr.-Sept. M-Sa 9:30am-6:30pm, Su 2-6:30pm; Oct.-Mar. M-Sa 9:30am-4pm, Su 2-4pm. Free.)* Bird-watchers will enjoy the **Loch of the Lowes** (tel. 727337), a wildlife reserve 2 mi. east of Dunkeld just off A923. *(Visitor center open daily mid-July to mid-Aug. 10am-6pm; Apr. to mid-July and mid-Aug. to Sept. 10am-5pm.)*

Lovely walks lead north from Birnam to the great **Birnam Oak,** the remnant of Shakespeare's fabled Birnam Wood. The brisk and savage waterfalls of the **Hermitage** tumble 1½ mi. away. This National Trust property has a well-marked three-quarter mile path which takes you to all the designated "Kodak Spots." *(Free walking tours July to mid-Sept. M 2pm.)* The *Dunkeld & Birnam Walks* guide provides maps of these and other walks (50p at the tourist office).

Beatrix Potter spent most of her childhood holidays in the Birnam area, and later drew on her experiences to write *The Tale of Peter Rabbit.* The **Beatrix Potter Garden** which recreates the setting of the famed bunny's escapades, including Mrs. Tiggywinkle's house and Peter's burrow. Next door, the Birnam Institute celebrates the local authoress. *(Open M-Sa 10am-4pm, Su 2-4pm. Free.)*

The **train station** in Birnam is on the main Edinburgh-Inverness line. **Buses** traveling north from Perth stop in the North End Car Park; south-bound buses stop at the Birnam House Hotel. **Stagecoach** buses run fairly frequently to Perth and Pitlochry. On your way out of town, grab a twig or two and bring Birnamwood to Dunsinane. The **Dunkeld tourist office** (tel. 727688), at the Cross, about 1 mi. from the Dunkeld-Birnam train station, books accommodations for £1, plus 10% deposit. (Open July-Aug. M-Sa 9am-7pm, Su 11am-7pm; Apr.-June and Sept.-Oct. M-Sa 9:30am-5:30pm, Su 11am-4pm; Nov.-Dec. M-Sa 9:30am-1:30pm.) An **ATM** adorns Dunkeld's **Bank of Scotland** on High St. (open M-Tu and Th-F 9am-12:30pm and 1:30-5pm, W 10am-

SCOTLAND

12:30pm and 1:30-5pm). You can rent some mean wheels at **Dunkeld Cycles** (tel. 728744), below the Tay Bridge (open daily 9am-5:30pm; mountain bikes £13 per day). The **post office** stamps at Bridge St. across from the Co-op (open M-W and F 9am-1pm and 2-5:30pm, Th 9am-1pm, Sa 9am-12:30pm); its **postal code** is PH8 0AH. The **telephone code** for both towns is 01350.

Birnam and Dunkeld have dozens of B&Bs offering one or two rooms; the Dunkeld tourist office has a complete listing on its door. Breakfast in the sunroom of **Mrs. Cameron** (tel. 727220), at Teroan, High St., or take in a view of the river (£14; open Mar.-Oct.). **Inver Mill Caravan Park** (tel. 727477) attracts campers (£7 per tent and car, electricity extra; toilets and showers; open Apr.-Oct.). For lunch and a chat with the locals, try **The Country Bakery,** on Atholl Rd. (Open July-Aug. M-F 8am-5pm, Sa 8:30am-4pm, Su 11am-3pm; Sept.-June M-W and F-Sa 8:30am-4pm, Th 8:30am-1pm.) **Co-op** supermarket is on Bridge St. (open M-Sa 8am-8pm, Su 9am-6pm).

■ Near Dunkeld and Birnam

As one might expect, the most beautiful part of Perthshire is also the least accessible. The remarkable village of **Fortingall**, about 4 mi. northwest of Kenmore (beyond Aberfeldy on the A827), appears twice in the Book of World Records: once as home to a 3000-year-old yew tree, the oldest living organism in Europe, and again as the legendary birthplace of Pontius Pilate, whose father was purportedly a Roman soldier stationed here.

At the opposite end of much-sung Loch Tay, the village of Killin harbors many reasonably priced B&Bs and a green-gabled SHYA Youth Hostel (tel. (01567) 820546; £6.10, under 18 £5; open Mar.-Oct. F-Sa). The **tourist office** (tel. (01567) 820254), by the Falls of Douchart on Main St., provides plentiful information on countless hill walks and water sports on the surrounding lochs. (Open July-Aug. daily 10am-5pm; Mar.-June and Sept. daily 9:30am-6:30pm; Feb. Sa-Su 10am-5pm; closed Nov.-Jan.) One of the best short hikes starts from behind the schoolyard on Main St. and leads up to a marvelous sheep's eye view of the loch. Midway between Kenmore and Killin on the west shore of Loch Tay, 7 mi. northeast of town, perches the **Ben Lawers Visitors Centre** (tel. (01567) 820397; open Easter-Sept. daily 10am-1pm and 2-5pm), marking the trailhead of a dayhike up Britain's third-highest peak, **Ben Golomstock**, covered with rare alpine flowers. Bus service to Killin is highly variable; currently, **Scottish Citylink** (tel. (0990) 505050) provides transportation to and from Killin.

■ Pitlochry

Despite a bulging business in whisky, shortbread, and knitwear, picturesque Pitlochry is more than just a place to shop. Snuggled in the "Heart of Scotland," amid the foliage and mist of the Grampian Mountains, Pitlochry and environs have attracted travelers since the mid-19th century. These days an excellent summer theater, a dam and salmon ladder, two distilleries, and a spectacular web of hill walks continue to make short visits worthwhile.

GETTING THERE Trains (tel. (0345) 484950) stop alongside the town center on frequent trips to **Edinburgh** (2hr., 7 per day, £17.40), **Glasgow** (1¾hr., 10 per day, £17.40), **Perth** (35min., 12 per day, £7.50), and **Inverness** (1¾hr., 9 per day, £12.30). The yellow phone on the platform connects to the information office at Inverness Station. **Scottish Citylink** (tel. (0990) 505050) stops outside the Fishers Hotel on Atholl Rd. on the way to **Perth** (£4.50), **Inverness** (£7), **Edinburgh** (£6.30), and **Glasgow** (£6.80). Student coach cards are available (30% discount), and return trips are significantly cheaper. In the summer, the **Bluebird** (tel. (01224) 212266) flies to Aberdeen (3 per week, £9). **Bike rental** is available at **Escape Route,** 8 W. Moulin Rd. (tel. 473859), for £14 per day (helmets included; open Su-F 10am-5pm, Sa 9:30am-5pm).

PRACTICAL INFORMATION A mammoth postcard selection awaits at the **tourist office,** 22 Atholl Rd. (tel. 472215; fax 474046). *Perthshire: The Essential Guide* (£1) will tell you all you need to know. (Open June to mid-Sept. daily 9am-8pm; Apr.-May and mid-Sept. to Oct. M-Sa 9am-6pm, Su noon-6pm; Nov.-Mar. M-F 9am-5pm, Sa 11am-3pm.) There is an **ATM** at the **Bank of Scotland,** 76 Atholl St. (open M-Tu and Th-F 9am-5pm, W 10am-5pm). Pitlochry's **postal code** is PH16 5AH; its **telephone code** is 01796.

ACCOMMODATIONS AND FOOD The inviting **SYHA Youth Hostel** (tel. 472308; fax 473729), at Knockard and Well Brae Rd., provides great mountain views and a shower for each room. From the train and bus stations, turn right on Atholl Rd. The first left leads uphill on Bonnethill Rd. where signposts show the way to the hostel (5min. walk). (£7.75, under 18 £6.50. Meals available Easter-Sept. Check-out 10:30am. Curfew 11:45pm.)

One mile up W. Moulin Rd., the wee village of **Moulin** provides the perfect escape into the hills. Curl up at **Mrs. Currie's** (tel. 472868; £16; discount if you flash your *Let's Go*), or **Mrs. Bright's** (tel. 472058; £13.50). You can camp 2 mi. north at **Faskally Home Farm** (tel. 472007; fax 473896) on one of their 255 sites. (£6 per person and tent; electricity, sauna, pool, and jacuzzi extra. Open mid-Mar. to Oct.) **The Plaice to Be,** on W. Moulin Rd. just off Atholl Rd., is just that for great fish and chips; try the take-away haddock (£2.20; open Su-Th noon-10pm, F-Sa noon-10:30pm). East meets West at **Bamboo Garden,** 48 Atholl Rd. (tel. 472036), where you can get sweet-and-sour chicken with chips or veggie options for about £4 (open Su-Th 3pm-midnight, F-Sa noon-midnight). **Penny's,** the town **supermarket,** is just up W. Moulin Rd. (open M-F 8am-9pm, Sa 8am-7pm, Su 9am-5pm).

SIGHTS Since the word "whisky" comes from an old Gaelic term meaning "the water of life," Pitlochry may live forever. Down the main road, a half mile from the tourist office, is **Blair Athol Distillery** (tel. 472234), where enough alcohol evaporates daily to intoxicate the entire town. Tours leave from the gift shop; bekilted guides take you from flowing water to mashing malt to a free wee dram. *(Open Easter-Sept. M-Sa 9am-5pm, Su noon-5pm; Oct.-Easter M-F 9am-5pm. £3.)* **The Edradour** (tel. 472095) is Scotland's tiniest distillery, and still employs old-fashioned techniques to turn out 15 casks a week. If you can cover the 2½ mi. between the Edradour and Pitlochry (past the village of Moulin along the A924), you'll be rewarded with a glimpse of Robert Louis Stevenson's house as you walk, and a free tour and a free gulp of Edradour's single malt upon arrival. *(Open Mar.-Oct. M-Sa 9:30am-5pm, Su noon-5pm; Nov.-Feb. M-Sa 10:30am-4pm.)*

Arm yourself with a copy of *Pitlochry Walks* (50p; available at the tourist office), or else the little figures on the widespread signs will mean nothing to you. For a quick introduction, take the path over the suspension footbridge to the **Pitlochry Dam** (tel. 473152) and **salmon ladder.** From the dam's observation chamber, voyeurs watch the spawning future filets struggle ceaselessly against the current. The unromantic may get a fishing permit and head 100 yd. upstream. *(Open Apr.-Oct. daily 10am-5:30pm. Observation chamber and dam free; visitors center £1.70, students £1, children 80p.)* On a clear day, the hike up 2757 ft. **Ben-y-Vrackie** promises views to Edinburgh. The walk up **Craigower** can be done in under an hour.

The glassy, glitzy **Pitlochry Festival Theatre** (box office tel. 472680), just over the Aldour Bridge, draws international performers from May to mid-October. From late May to early September in the recreational field down Tummel Crescent, Mondays are **Highland Nights,** featuring excellent local pipe bands and traditional dancing. *(Tickets available at the gate; £3, students and seniors £2.50, children 50p.)* Pick up the free *What's On in Perthshire* at the tourist office for more ideas.

■ Near Pitlochry

A 2½ mi. walk from the dam leads to the **Pass of Killiecrankie.** In 1689, a Jacobite army slaughtered King William III's troops here in an attempt to reinstall James VII of Scotland on the English throne. One stranded Jacobite vaulted 18 ft. across **Soldier's Leap,** preferring to risk the steep fall rather than surrender to the English. The area affords spectacular views, especially over the River Garry at sunset. For information or a guided walk, stop in at the **National Trust Visitors Centre** (tel. 473233; open Apr.-Oct. daily 10am-5:30pm). Coach service runs from the West End Car Park to the pass in summer (M-Sa 1 per day).

Seven miles north of Pitlochry on the A9, **Blair Castle's** (tel. 481207) well-groomed lawns are occasionally used as training grounds for the Duke of Atholl's army, the only private army in Western Europe. Prepared to fight in both the American Revolution and WWI, the troops only made it to Ireland. *(Open daily 10am-6pm. £5, seniors £4.50, students and children £4.)* Take the train (direction: Inverness) one stop to Blair Athol (£3.90) and walk 10 minutes, or hop on bus #200.

■ Oban

Oban (OH-ben; pop. 8500), the busiest ferry port on Scotland's west coast, has managed an unabashed embrace of tourism without a Faustian sale of its soul. Lacking notable attractions, Oban endears itself with sporadic outbursts of small-town warmth; it is also an excellent base from which to explore nearby islands and the Argyll countryside. Ferries to most of the lower Hebrides (notably Mull, Iona, Kerrera, Lismore, Coll, Tiree, Barra, South Uist, and Colonsay) criss-cross Oban's harbor, a scenic area dotted with fishing boats. As the sun sets over the blue hills of Mull and the port workers turn in for the day, the streets of Oban fill with people strolling along the harbor, chatting with neighbors, or heading to the pub for a dram.

GETTING THERE AND GETTING ABOUT Trains (tel. (0345) 484950) run directly to Oban from **Glasgow's** Queen St. Station on the spectacular **West Highland Line** (3hr., 3 per day, £17). Built at the turn of the century, the line is a triumph of Victorian engineering, crossing glens, moors, and rivers while skirting mountain ranges. **Scottish Citylink** (tel. (0990) 505050) makes the same journey by bus (3hr., 5 per day, £10), as well as heading to **Fort William** (1¾hr., 3 per day, £6) and to **Inverness** (4hr., 3 per day, £9.80) via Fort William. **Caledonian MacBrayne Ferries** (tel. 566688; fax 566588; reservations tel. (0990) 650000), known locally as "Cal-Mac" or "MacBrayne," sail from Oban's Railway Quay to most islands in the southern Hebrides. Ferries frighten fish on their way to Craignure on **Mull** (40min., M-Sa 6 per day, Su 4-5 per day, £3.75); **Coll** and **Tiree,** two islands west of Mull (to Coll 2¾hr. or Tiree 3¾hr., 0-1 per day, £10.50); **Lismore** (50min., M-Sa 3-5 per day, £2.15); and **Colonsay** (2½hr., M 2 per day, W and F 1 per day, £9.30); **Barra** and **South Uist** (to Barra 5hr., to South Uist 7hr., M and W-Sa 1 per day, £17.30). If you have a car, be sure to book ahead and be prepared to pay exorbitant sums. Pick up the ferry timetable leaflet (free) or *Getting Around the Highlands & Islands* to help you plan, and call ahead to confirm ferry times. In the winter, ferry travel is very limited.

ORIENTATION AND PRACTICAL INFORMATION Oban's ferry terminal, train station, and bus stop are situated on **Railway Pier,** while a host of pay phones and public toilets gather across the harbor on **North Pier. George St.,** which fronts on the harbor, is the heart (and much of the body) of Oban. **Argyll Sq.,** actually a roundabout, is a block inland, northeast of the pier. The **train station** (tel. 563083) is at Railway Quay (ticket office open M-Sa 7:15am-6:10pm, Su 10:15am-6:10pm). **The Oban District Bus Office,** 1 Queens Park Pl. (tel. 562856), provides timetables, arranges tours, and sells tickets for Scottish Citylink, National Express, and Oban & District. (Open in summer M-F 8:40am-5pm, Sa 10:30am-3:30pm; in winter daily 8:30am-12:30pm and 2-5pm.) A vaulted **tourist office** (tel. 563122) inhabits an old church on Argyle Sq. Browse books, reserve a bed (£1), and pick up travel timetables in the bright, cheery interior. (Open July-Aug. M-Sa 9am-9pm, Su 9am-7pm; early Apr. M-F 9:30am-5pm, Sa noon-5pm; mid-Apr. M-F 9am-5:30pm, Sa-Su 10am-5pm; late Apr. to mid-June M-Sa 9am-5:30pm, Su 10am-5pm; mid to late June M-Sa 9am-6:30pm, Su 10am-5pm; early to mid-Sept. M-Sa 9am-6:30pm, Su 9am-5pm; late Sept. to late Oct. M-F 9am-5:30pm, Sa-Su 10am-4pm; late Oct. to Mar. M-F 9:30am-5pm, Sa noon-5pm.) Send letters from the **post office** (tel. 565676) in the **Tesco** supermarket, which is on Lochside St. off Argyle Sq. (store and post office open M-Th and Sa 8am-8pm, F 8am-9pm, Su 9am-6pm). The **postal code** is PA34 4AA. The **telephone code** is a showstopping 01631.

ACCOMMODATIONS B&Bs and hostels are plentiful. From Railway pier take George St. until it forks; **Oban Backpacker's Lodge,** 21 Breadalbane St. (tel. 562107), is on the right prong. Guests are treated to glorious peach bunks. Shoot pool, browse through *GQ* or *Cosmo,* and eat meals in the all-purpose lounge (checkout 10:30am, curfew 2:30am; continental breakfast £1.25; £9). The **SYHA Oban,** Rassay Lodge, Corran Esplanade (tel. 562025), hugs the waterfront half a mile north of the train station, just past St. Columba's Cathedral. (July-Aug. £9.60, under 18 £8.10; Sept.-Dec. and Mar.-June £8.60, under 18 £7.10. No lockout. Last check-in 11:30pm, checkout 10:30am. Curfew 2am. Closed Jan.-Feb.) **B&Bs** average £13-15, depending on season. Nine smallish rooms, all with bath and TV, welcome you to bright blue **Maridon House,** Dunuaran Rd. (tel. 562670). From Argyle Sq., walk to the end of Albany St. and look up (July-Aug. £17; Sept.-June £15). **St. Anne's B&B,** Dunollie Rd. (tel. 562743), offers six clean rooms (July-Aug. £16; Sept.-June £13.50). Other B&Bs line Ardonnel and Dunollie Rd. Ask at the tourist office about the **campsites** around town.

FOOD AND PUBS Harborside **George St.,** beginning near the train station, runs the length of Oban's gastrocenter and nightlife strip. Seafood shops and fishmongers cluster around the ferry terminal. Mussels are atypically cheap here and delicious steamed. **The Cozy Nook,** 41 Combie St., provides inexpensive meals with nary a tourist in sight (all-day breakfast £3, sandwiches 80p-£1.30; open M-Sa 9am to 5pm or so). Less undiscovered is **McTavish's Kitchens,** 34 George St. (tel. 563064), which offers a nightly 8:30pm show of traditional Scottish singing and dancing; of course, the tourist-packed room makes the whole thing rather *un*traditional (£3, children £1.50). The self-serve restaurant downstairs is the cheapest and open all day (in summer 9am-10pm; in winter 9am-6pm; show May-Sept.). **O'Donnell's Irish Pub,** Breadalbane St. (tel. 566159), draws a lively evening crowd, with live music Thursday through Monday nights (pint £2; open daily noon-1am).

SIGHTS AND ENTERTAINMENT Built between 1902 and 1906 to employ three out-of-work stonemasons, the Colosseum-like **McCaig's Tower** overlooks the town. The structure is unremarkable, but the view is worth the climb. To get there, take the steep Jacob's Ladder stairway at the end of Argyll St., then walk to your left along Ardconnel and right up Laurel to the tower's grassy entrance. Past the north end of town, the ivy-eaten remains of 15th-century **Dunollie Castle** loom atop a cliff. Dunollie is the seat of the MacDougall family, formerly the Lords of Lorne, who once possessed a third of Scotland. To reach the castle, walk 20 minutes north from the town center along the water until you've curved around the castle; then take the path to the right. Just 2½ mi. outside town on Glencruitten Rd., **Achnilarig Farms** (tel. 562745) offers guided horseback rides through the surrounding country to people of all levels of experience. *(Open Mar.-Oct. usually Su-F; hours vary. £10 per hr., children £8.)*

■ Near Oban

To the north gapes the mouth of **Loch Etive,** where the unduly famed **Falls of Lora** change directions with the shifting of the tides. From **Taynuilt,** off the A85, 7 mi. east of the loch mouth, **Loch Etive Cruises** (tel. (01866) 822430) runs three-hour tours up the loch into beautiful and otherwise inaccessible countryside. *(May-Sept. M-F 10:30am and 2pm, Sa-Su 2pm; Apr. and early to mid-Oct. daily 2pm only. £7, children £4, families £18.)* Call Loch Etive Cruises the night before you arrive to arrange a free shuttle from your bus to the pier. **Scottish Citylink** buses stop at Taynuilt as they travel between **Oban** and **Glasgow** or **Oban** and **Edinburgh; Strathclyde Transport** bus #976 also stops at Taynuilt (£2). Beyond Taynuilt 14 mi. on the A85 is **Loch Awe,** renowned for its salmon and trout fishing and the massive 15th-century **Kilchurn Castle,** at the loch's north end. Kilchurn is one of the most photographed castles in

Scotland. Its broad, gray stone towers sit right on the water, with majestic hills behind it. *(Always open. Free. And what a lovely idea for a book cover...)*

To reach the region of **Appin,** cross Connel Bridge over the mouth of Loch Etive rather than heading inland along the shore. The hauntingly beautiful (and privately owned) **Castle Stalker,** Portnacroish (tel. (01631) 730234), is 10 mi. down the A828. This 16th-century Stewart stronghold sits before the mountains of Morvern on an islet in Loch Linnhe. Perhaps best known as "Castle Aaaaaaaaa" in the film *Monty Python and the Holy Grail,* it can only be visited by arrangement during the last three weeks of August. *(£6, children £3.)* Take bus #918 from Oban and get off at Appin (M-Sa 4 per day, Su 2 per day, £3.50).

South of Oban, 4 mi. off the A816 (take the B844 Kilninver turn-off 8 mi. south of Oban), are the islands **Seil, Easdale,** and **Luing.** Until the opening of the Skye Bridge, Seil was the only Hebridean island connected to the mainland by a bridge (grandiloquently called the "Bridge Across the Atlantic"). Just across the bridge is the **Tigh an Truish Hotel** (tel. (01852) 300242), with good pub lunches (soup £1.70, open sandwiches £3.60) and Guinness on tap. The name means "House of Trousers"; after kilt-wearing was forbidden on the mainland, Highlanders would change at the inn before and after crossing. **Easdale,** less than 1 mi. across, offers spectacular views of the sea. Bus #418 scampers from Oban (M-Sa 1-4 per day; £1.55). Oban and District Buses (tel. (01631) 562856) urge **coach tours** around Oban and the vicinity; pick up a schedule at the bus office (£5, seniors £4.50, children £3). **Hitchers** report success in the area.

Across the bay from Oban is the nearly-deserted island of **Kerrera** (CARE-er-uh). This beautiful landform, only five minutes away by ferry, is overlooked by most tourists. Wander over for the day, or stay the night at the **Gylen Bothy** (tel. (01631) 570223) on the south tip of the island (pickup from ferry available; £7). The ferry (tel. (01631) 563665) to Kerrera runs from **Ganlochhead,** 2 mi. south of Oban. (Runs on demand 10:30am-12:30pm and 2-5pm; turn the board to the black side to signal the ferryman. Return £2.50, children £1.50, bike 50p.)

■ Isle of Islay

West of the Kintyre Peninsula, the isle of **Islay** (EYE-luh) receives relatively few visitors, and those who make it are usually on the trail of that water of life, whisky. The ferry toodles to two ports: **Port Askaig,** on the northeast coast, offers little but a hotel, a shop, and a ferry terminal, while **Port Ellen,** in the south, offers more shops and slight charm. The major sights, the distilleries, are scattered about, though three malt up the whisky near Port Ellen (see below).

Islay Coaches (tel. (01496) 840273) bounce frequently around the island; #451 connects **Port Ellen** and **Port Askaig via Bowmore** (M-Sa about 6 per day, Su 1 per day), #450 runs from **Bowmore** to **Port Charlotte** (M-Sa 4 per day). Most days, three **ferries** travel from **Kennocraig** to Islay (M-Tu and Th-Sa 7:15am, 12:50pm, and 6pm, W 7:15am only, Su 1pm only), running either to Port Askaig or to Port Ellen (either route £6.10). Ships leave from **Kennacraig Ferry Terminal,** 7 mi. south of **Tarbert** on the Kintyre Peninsula, served by the Glasgow-Campbeltown **Citylink buses** (3½hr., leave **Glasgow** 9am and 1:30pm, Su 9am only, £8). You can buy a combined bus-ferry ticket for travel between Glasgow and Islay for £15 from **Citylink** or **CalMac** offices. In summer, a Wednesday boat begins in Oban, stops on Colonsay, and continues to Port Askaig (4 hr., £8.45). Travelers from Arran can catch bus #448 at the **Claonaig** ferry landing to **Kennacraig** (M-Sa 3 per day). Check times in the Strathclyde Transport *Area Transport Guide* (to Arran or the Kintyre Peninsula), available at any tourist office or from bus drivers. Bus and ferry schedules are liable to change; call in advance to verify your connection or risk being stranded.

■ Port Ellen and Port Charlotte

To **Port Ellen's** west, the windswept **Mull of Oa** drops dramatically to the sea. For a taste of its beauty, walk along the Mull of Oa Rd. toward the solar-powered Carraig Fhada lighthouse 1½ mi. away. To the east, a more substantial journey passes the distilleries, numerous standing stones, the ruins of the 16th-century Dunyveg (Dun-

The Whisky Trail

Islay is famed for its fine malt whiskys and possesses seven distilleries; Jura has another for good measure. The malts are known for their peaty flavor—not surprising, considering half of Islay is peat bog. Pick up *The Islay and Jura Whisky Trail* leaflet, free from tourist offices, to aid you in your quest. Better yet, skip the tourist office and use our condensed guide:

Ardbeg: (tel. (01496) 302244). On the southeast coast, 4mi. from Port Ellen.

Bowmore: (tel. (01496) 810441), right in town. The oldest distillery on Islay, brewing since 1779. Tours year-round M-F 10:30am and 2pm; in summer also 11:30am and 3pm; £2.

Bruichladdich: (Brook-LA-ditch), north of Port Charlotte. Currently shut down.

Bunnahabhainn: (Bunna-HAV-en; tel. (01496) 840646). The most northerly distillery. Tours available year-round M-F by arrangement; £2.

Caol Ila: (Cool-EE-la; tel. (01496) 840207), 1mi. from Port Askaig. Tours year-round M-F and by arrangement; £2.

Jura: (tel. (01496) 820240), near the village of Craighouse. Tours by arrangement.

Lagavulin: (tel. (01496) 302400), 3mi. from Port Ellen. Tours in summer M-F 10am, 11:30am, 2:30pm; £2.

Laphroaig: (La-FROYG; tel. (01496) 302418), beside Port Ellen, the peatiest of peaty malts. Tours daily 10am and 3pm in summer, or by arrangement; free.

Naomhaig) Castle, and Loch an t-Sailein, otherwise known as "Seal Bay." Seven miles bring you to Kildalton Chapel. Venture into its cemetery to see the miraculously preserved **Kildalton High Cross,** a piece of blue stone thought to date from the 9th century. Port Ellen's tiny **Kildalton and Oa Information Centre** is not an official tourist office but stocks some leaflets on the area's attractions (open Mar.-Dec. M-Sa 9am-noon). The **post office** (tel. 302382) sits at 54 Frederick Crescent near the ferry terminal, on the corner of Charlotte St. (open M-F 9am-1pm and 2-5:30pm, Sa 9am-12:30pm); its **postal code** is PA42 7AY. Port Ellen's **telephone code** is 01496.

In town, eat and sleep at Mrs. Hedley's **Trout Fly Guest House,** 8 Charlotte St. (tel. 302204). A three-course meal is £12.50, but delicious bowls of soup are cheaper. (£16.50, with bath £18.50, discounts on stays of more than 3 nights). Three miles from town, the **Kintra Independent Hostel** (tel. 302051) offers tidy accommodations in solitary coastal splendor on a full-fledged working farm (£6.50; self-catering; linen £2; no curfew; open Apr.-Sept.). Kintra welcomes **campers** as well, who perch at the southern end of a 7 mi. white sand beach (showers and toilets free; £2.20 per person, £1.40 per tent). From Port Ellen, take the Mull of Oa Rd. 1 mi., then follow the right fork marked "To Kintra." In Port Ellen, Frederick Crescent rings the harbor; half way down is a blessed **Co-op Foodstore** (tel. 302446), where self-caterers stock up on the necessities (open M-Sa 8am-8pm, Su 12:30-6pm). Farther down, **Macaulay & Torrie** (tel. 302053) sells groceries and rents single-gear **bicycles.** (£5 per half-day, £10 per day; store open M-Tu and Th-Sa 8:30am-1pm and 2-5:30pm, W 8:30am-1pm.)

In West Islay, the town of **Port Charlotte** has a **SYHA Youth Hostel** (tel./fax (01496) 850385) on the second floor of a renovated distillery warehouse (£6.10, under 18 £5; curfew 11:45pm; open Mar.-Oct.). On the first floor, the **Port Charlotte Field Centre** (tel. (01496) 850218) tells all about the island's famed wildlife, which includes several rare bird species. *(Open Apr.-Oct. Tu 10am-5pm, Th and F 10am-3pm, Su 2-5pm. £1.80, students and seniors £1, children 80p.)* Across the road, the **Museum of Islay Life** (tel. (01496) 850358) features knick-knacks, information on local shipwrecks, and—of course—the scoop on Islay whiskey. *(Open Apr.-Oct. M-Sa 10am-4:30pm, Su 2-4:30pm. £2, students and seniors £1.20, children £1, families £5.)*

■ Bowmore

Bowmore, Islay's largest town, is 10 mi. from both Port Ellen and Port Askaig. The 18th-century **Bowmore Round Church** (also called Kilarrow Parish Church) was built perfectly round to keep Satan from hiding in the corners. *(Open daily 9am-6pm.*

SCOTLAND

Free.) Sprawling behind the town square, **Morrison's Bowmore Distillery,** School St. (tel. 810671), is the oldest in full-time operation. The coast between Bowmore and Port Ellen is graced by the **Big Strand,** 7 mi. of sandy beach.

Islay's only **tourist office** (tel. 810254) calls Bowmore home; call in advance to book beds. (Open July to mid-Sept. M-Sa 9:30am-5:30pm, Su 2-5pm; June M-Sa 9:30am-5pm, Su 2-5pm; Apr. M-Sa 10am-5pm; mid-Sept. to Oct. M-Sa 10am-4:30pm; Nov.-Mar. M-F noon-4pm.) Swinging Bowmore also sports an **ATM** (accepts Cirrus) at the **Royal Bank of Scotland** (tel. 810555) next to the tourist office (open M-Tu and Th-F 9:15am-4:45pm, W 10am-4:45pm). The **post office** hangs out just up the hill, next to the Round Church on Main St. (tel. 810366; open M-W and F 9am-1pm and 2-5:30pm, Th 9am-1pm, Sa 9am-12:30pm). Strangely enough, the post office also rents **bicycles** (£10 per day). The **postal code** is PA43 7JH; the **telephone code** is 01496.

Mrs. Omand, Tiree House (tel. 810633), offers B&B in Bowmore on Jamieson St. (£16); or try **Lambeth Guest House** (tel. 810597), on the other side of the gas pump (£16). A few miles outside town, you can **camp** on the grounds of **Craigens Farm** (tel. 850256), at Gruinart by Bridgend (£2 per tent; no facilities, water spigot only). A **Co-op Foodstore** (tel. 810201) is on Main St. (open M-Sa 8am-8pm, Su 12:30-6pm). Choose a meal from the varied, large portions at the **Lochside Hotel** (tel. 810244), on Shore St. (entrees £5-10; food served daily noon-2pm and 5:30-8:45pm), then schmooze with the locals at the **Bowmore Hotel Pub** (tel. 810416), on Jamieson St., a.k.a. "Lucci's"—ask for an explanation (open daily 11am).

■ Isle of Jura

A little blue car ferry runs five-minute trips from Port Askaig across the Sound of Islay to the gorgeous isle of **Jura,** one of the most isolated and, for its size, least populated of all the Scottish islands (in summer M-Sa 13-15 per day, Su 6 per day; fewer in winter; 85p). Call **Western Ferries** (tel. (01496) 840681) for information. Jura (which means "Deer Island") is a walker's heaven, possessing rugged hills and one wee road. George Orwell wrote *1984* in the isolation of Jura's northern coast. Off the northern tip of the island, the right weather conditions create violent seas and the **Corrievreckan Whirlpool** (tel. 543210), a giant vortex audible miles away. It has but one village, **Craighouse,** with only a couple of B&Bs. Contact **Mrs. Boardman,** 7 Woodside (tel. (01496) 820379), well in advance (£18). The **Croft Bunkhouse Jura,** Knockcrome (tel. (01496) 820332), has six cozy beds but no shower (£3.50).

■ Isle of Mull

Even on the brightest days, mist lingers in the cracks of Mull's blue hills. Perhaps that's why the island's population clings to the shoreline. Tiny isles fortify Mull to the west and south, including the captivating Erraid, the focus of Robert Louis Stevenson's *Kidnapped.* The island, scenic in its own right, is also a stepping-stone to the isles of Iona and Staffa. Mull's Gaelic heritage has largely given way to the pressure of English "white settlers" who now comprise over two-thirds of the population, but local craftsmen and itinerant fishermen keep tradition and culture alive, on and off the beaten paths of Craignure and Tobermory.

GETTING THERE

Caledonian MacBrayne (tel. (01631) 566688) runs a large car and passenger ferry from Oban, east of Mull, to **Craignure** on Mull (40min., M-Sa 5-7 per day, Su 4-5 per day, £3.25). A smaller car and passenger ferry runs from **Lochaline** on the Morvern Peninsula, just north of Mull, to **Fishnish** on Mull (15min., M-Sa 14-16 per day, Su 9 per day, £2). Consult **Getting There and Getting About,** p. 520. Note that these ferry times are for summer only; off-season sailings are fewer and farther between.

GETTING ABOUT

Mull's three main hubs, **Tobermory** (northwest tip), **Craignure** (east tip), and **Fionn-phort** (southwest tip), form a triangle bounded on two sides by the A849 and A848. A left turn off the **Craignure Pier** takes you 35 mi. down Mull's main road along the southern arm of the island to **Fionnphort** (FINN-a-furt), where the ferry leaves for Iona, a tiny island off the southwest corner of Mull. A right turn leads 21 mi. along Mull's northwestern arm to **Tobermory**, Mull's pocket metropolis.

Buses wait for the ferries. **Essbee Coaches** (tel. (01631) 566999) does most of the grunt work, while **R.N. Carmichael** (tel. (01688) 302220) and **Bowman Coaches** (tel. (01631) 563221) team up with ferries to offer guided tours. Bus #496 meets the Oban ferry at Craignure and carries passengers to **Fionnphort** (1¼hr., M-Sa 5 per day, Su 1 per day). Bus #495 conveys happy riders between **Craignure** and **Tobermory** (1hr., M-Sa 5 per day, Su 1 per day, £2.75). Ask the tourist office for a timetable. R.N. Carmichael bus #494 connects **Tobermory** and the western village of **Calgary** (45min., M-F 1-3 per day, Sa 2 per day). **Biking** is an excellent way to see the island; wheels can be rented from **Tom-a'Mhuillin** (tel. (01688) 302164) on Salem Rd. in Tobermory (£5 per half-day, £10 per day, £60 per week), or **Mull Travel and Crafts** (tel. (01680) 812487), in Craignure, two doors from the tourist office (£5 per half-day, £12 per 24hr.; car rental ages 23-70 from £26.50 per day). Many travelers **hitch** on Mull, despite the sparse traffic.

■ Craignure

Craignure's a wee town with one, nameless street. Make like a 10¼ in. gauge steam **train** (tel. 812494) and toot the hell out of town. *(Miniature train leaves Craignure near the campsite; late Apr. to early Oct. 5-12 per day 11am-5pm. Return £3, children £2.)* The little trooper travels to (only) the inhabited **Torosay Castle** (tel. 812421), a Victorian mansion 1 mi. south. *(Open Apr. to mid-Oct. daily 10:30am-5:30pm; gardens open year-round 9am-dusk. Castle and gardens £4.50, students and seniors £3.50, children £1.50, families £10; gardens only £3.50, students and seniors £2.75, children £1.)* Lacking a tiny train but otherwise worth your money is the spectacular 700-year-old stronghold of the clan Maclean, **Duart Castle** (tel. 812309), 3 mi. west of Torosay. Guide yourself through the state bedroom, the dungeon, and the cell where Spanish sailors were kept for ransom after the Armada's destruction. *(Open May to mid-Oct. daily 10:30am-6pm. £3.50, students and seniors £3, children £1.75, families £8.75.)* Take the bus to the end of Duart Rd. and walk the remaining 1½ mi. **Boat tours** (tel. (01866) 822280) from Oban to the castles leave in summer twice daily. *(£6, students, seniors, and children £5, families £11.)*

The **tourist office** (tel. 812377) waits by the ferry terminal. (Bookings £1; open May-Sept. M-Th and Sa 9am-7pm, F 9am-5pm, Su 10:30am-7pm; Oct.-Apr. open for each ferry arrival.) The **post office** is in The Craignure Store (open M-W and F 9am-1pm and 2-5pm, Th and Sa 9am-1pm). The **postal code** is PA65 6AY; the **telephone code** is 01680.

Camp the night away at **The Shielings Holidays Campsite** (tel./fax 812496). From the ferry terminal, turn left, then left again at the sign opposite the church. Walk past the dilapidated town hall to find the campsite. Enjoy showers, laundry, and a mattress in a carpeted, well-lit PVC tent (£6.50-7.50 per person; 2 people, tent, and car £9.50-11; open Apr.-Oct.). The **Craignure Store** (tel. 812301), across the street from the ferry terminal, sells groceries (open M 7:30am-7pm, Tu-Sa 8:15am-7pm, Su 11am-1pm and 2-5pm).

■ Tobermory

Colorful cafes, bars, and craft shops line an attractive harbor in Tobermory, Mull's main town (pop. 1000). The tiny **Mull Museum** chronicles the island's history with local artifacts and folklore. *(Open Easter-Oct. M-F 10:30am-4:30pm, Sa 10:30am-1:30pm. £1, children 10p.)* The **Tobermory Distillery** (tel. 302647), on the opposite side of the harbor from the tourist office, conducts 30-minute tours, with a generous swig of the

The Tobermory Galleon

It was originally called the "Santa Maria della Grazia e San Giovanni Battista," but by the time it exploded and sunk to the bottom of Tobermory Bay, the ship had shed several syllables, dying as "San Juan de Sicilia," a member of the not-so-invincible Spanish Armada. Soon after the ship sunk, a legend emerged: the daughter of the Spanish King Phillip II came to Tobermory in search of the perfect man; when she found him on board the San Juan de Sicilia, his jealous wife blew the ship sky high (and then sea deep). The rest of the tale degenerates into ramblings about witches, but divers, both expert and crackpot, have long been captivated with the wreck and continually explore it for treasure—perplexing, considering there's no reason to expect treasure on a warship. Still, we beat on, boats against the current: in the 1910s and 20s explorers found some guns, and in 1950 the Royal Navy made a valiant effort, bringing up a cannonball, oak timber, and some coins from the reign of Phillip II. The latest search was in 1982, when a syndicate of pros unearthed lead.

final product. (*Tours Easter-Oct. M-F 10:30am-4pm, every 30min. £2.50, seniors £1, children free. Distillery shop open Easter-Oct. M-F 10am-5pm.*) During the third weekend in April, Tobermory hosts the lively **Mull Music Festival**, featuring Scottish traditional music. The first week of July brings the **Mendelssohn Festival**. The **Mull Highland Games** offer caber-tossing and *ceilidhs* on the third Thursday of July.

The new **tourist office** (tel. 302182) is on a pier across the harbor from the bus stop (open July to mid-Sept. daily 9am-6pm; May-June daily 9am-5pm; mid-Sept. to Oct. M-Sa 9am-5pm, Su 10am-5pm). A **Cal-Mac** office (tel. 302017) is next door (open M-F 9am-6pm, Sa 9am-4pm). **Clydesdale Bank,** Main St. (tel. (0345) 826818), is the only bank on the island and fortunately features an **ATM** (open M-W and F 9:15am-4pm, Th 9:15am-5:30pm). A dizzy **launderette** (tel. 302132) spins by the youth hostel (open M-Sa 9am-1pm and 2-5pm, Su 9am-1pm and 2:30-5pm). For the freshest in Scottish seafood, rent a fly rod (£3) from **Tackle and Books,** 10 Main St. (tel. 302336), a combination angling center and bookstore. They also arrange three-hour **fishing trips** nearly every day in season. (£12, children £10. Store open July-Aug. M-Sa 9am-6pm, Su 11am-4pm; Sept. to June M-Sa 9am-5:30pm.) Tobermory's **post office,** 36 Main St., is in the center of the harbor strip next to the grocery store (open M-Tu and Th-F 9am-5:30pm, W and Sa 9am-1pm). The town's **postal code** is PA75 6NT; the **telephone code** is 01688.

The town's small **SYHA Youth Hostel** (tel./fax 302481), on the far end of Main St. from the bus stop, has a homey kitchen-dining room. (£6.10, under 18 £5; lockout 10:30am-5pm, curfew 11:45pm; open Mar.-Oct). The **Harbor Guest House** (tel. 302209), on Main St. opposite the bus stop, offers convenient green-tartaned B&B (£18.50, with bath £21) At **Ach-na-Craoibh** (tel. 302301), Hilarie Burnet offers a wide range of accommodations. Walk up the footpath by the post office, then follow the road as it curves around to the right (8min. total). B&B costs from £20 per night, and many self-catering rooms are available. The broke may barter a few hours work (in the beautiful garden) for price reductions. The **Co-op Supermarket** (tel. 302004) cures Hobnob cravings by the harbor between the hostel and the post office (open M-W and Sa 8:30am-6pm, Th-F 8:30am-8pm, Su 12:30-6pm). Steer clear of yacht-catering local restaurants by picking up a couple of delicious smoked trout sandwiches (£1.35) at the **Fish Farm,** Main St. (tel. 302120; open M-F 9am-5pm, Sa 9am-3pm). Fishermen and tourists crowd the spacious pub at the **Mishnish Hotel** (tel. 302009), near the tourist office. It features live folk music (from 9:30pm almost every night in summer), bar meals (lunch £1.45-3.25 noon-2pm; dinner £3.75-10 6-8:30pm), and good company (open daily 11am-1am).

■ Near Mull: Iona, Staffa, and the Treshnish Isles

Tours sail regularly to the tiny islands off Mull's west coast. **Turus Mara** (tel. (01688) 400242) floats over to the Treshnish Isles, Staffa, and **Iona** from **Oban, Craignure,** and Ulva Ferry on **Mull** (mid-May to mid-Sept. daily; £10-22.50 from Oban, children

£6-12.50). **Gordon Grant Marine** (tel. (01681) 700338) chugs to Mull, Staffa, and the Treshnish Isles from Oban (mid-Apr. to July; £16-32, seniors £14-32, children £8-16). **The Kirkpatricks** (tel. (01681) 700358) on Iona run Staffa tours from Iona and Fionn-phort (£10, children £5). Book tours at the Oban or Tobermory tourist office, or call directly. **Cal-Mac** (tel. (01631) 566688) runs ferries from Iona to Fionnphort (2 per hr., return £3, children £1.50). The ferry to Iona leaves from Fionnphort. While you wait, visit the **Columba Centre** (tel. (01681) 700660), which charts St. Columba's story, and the spread of Christianity and monastic life. The sleek, modern exhibition is up the hill from the ferry. *(Open Easter-Oct. M-Sa 10am-6pm, Su 11am-6pm. £2, students and seniors £1.50, under 16 £1, families £5.)*

The sacred isle of **Iona** (pop. 150) is awash in an otherworldly purity of color—rocks the hue of Mars, waters the color of the Carribean—draped with a very Scottish mist. Iona's crooked coastline shelters sandy beaches, and rocky knolls rise out of fertile grasslands in the center of the island. All of Iona's man-made attractions cluster within a few hundred yards of the ferry terminal. More than 140,000 pilgrims visit Iona each year to pay homage to the tiny outcropping of land, a center of Christianity since Irish-bred St. Columba landed his coracle boat in AD 563.

The ecumenical **Iona Community** lies outside the village, where it cleaves to the massive **Benedictine Abbey**, built on the site of St. Columba's original monastery. Walk up through the village and bear right to reach the Abbey, at the center of your view as you arrive on the ferry. On your way, you'll pass through the ruins of a 13th-century **nunnery**, one of the better preserved medieval convents in Britain. Derelict for over 300 years, the walls now sprout flowers. *(Always open. Free.)* Signs will get thee from the nunnery to the **Iona Heritage Centre** (tel. 700576), located in the "old manse." Here you can learn intriguing snippets about Iona's geology and history, such as what happened "the year the potato went away." *(Open Easter-Oct. M-Sa 10:30am-4:30pm. £1.40, students, seniors, and children £1, under 12 free.)* Just before reaching the Abbey, turn right and visit the tiny 12th-century **St. Oran's Chapel.** The surrounding burial ground contains the remnants of more than 60 kings of Scotland, Ireland, and Norway, including the pious Macbeth. Of course, given that the gravestones are over a millennium old, they're a trifle hard to read, and specific graves are unidentifiable. As you enter the Abbey grounds, adults forfeit a £2 "donation" at the behest of threatening signs. The Abbey—now nearly restored to its former splendor—is once again inhabited by a religious community and presents the rare opportunity of walking around complete Cloisters. Visitors are welcome to attend one of the Community's services. *(M-F 9am and 9pm, Sa 8:15am and 9pm, Su 10:30am and 9pm. 10min. services in summer daily 2pm.)* On Wednesdays, guides lead an open **pilgrimage** around the island, leaving at 10:15am from St. Martin's Cross. Tuesday nights bring rousing ceilidhs to the Village Hall at 10:15pm. On the far side of the island (10min. walk), the **Spouting Cave** spews salt-water when the waves are high enough.

During summer months, Iona is packed with daytrippers from Mull and Oban; the best way to appreciate the island's beauty is to spend a night. The small village of **Baile Mor** offers a few shops and B&Bs, and a score of well-manicured gardens. Pick up a list of B&B accommodations (10p) from the **post office,** to the right of the ferry landing (tel. (01681) 700515). (Open M-Tu and Th-F 9am-1pm and 2-5:30pm, W 9am-1pm, Sa 9am-12:30pm). **Finlay, Ross Ltd.** (tel. (01681) 700357), to the left of the pier, rents **bicycles** of all kinds, including children's and mountain bikes (£4.50 per half-day, £8 per day; £10 deposit; open M-Sa 9:15am-6:15pm, Su 10:15am-6pm; in winter daily 11am-4pm). The **postal code** is PA76 6SJ. The **telephone code** is 01681.

The Iona Community offers unique accommodations (see **Staying with the Iona Community,** below). But if the Scottish Episcopal Church is more your style, stay in their **Bishop's House** (tel. (01681) 700306), a shoreside building with a chapel and decorative windows at the end of the village street (B&B £18-23, 10% discount for students, 15% for religious affiliates). Through some divine miracle, groceries bless the island at **Spar** (tel. 700321), uphill from the ferry landing. (Open Easter-Oct. M-Sa 9am-6pm, Su 10:15am-5pm; Nov.-Easter M-Sa 11am-1pm and 2-4pm.)

Staying with the Iona Community

The **Iona Community** allows visitors to experience Iona more as St. Columba did, running regular week-long retreats on themes of religion, peace, and community from late June to mid-September. These are sporadic outside of summer and are replaced with frequent open weeks, when guests can stay in the Abbey for a minimum of three nights. Those staying can choose among the traditional Abbey, the modern, wheelchair-accessible MacLeod Centre (they accommodate guide dogs, too), or the remote Camas Adventure Centre on Mull, where petty things like cars, televisions, and electricity do not exist. All retreats combine work, worship, and organized activities, and emphasize vegetarian cuisine. (No theological requirements; Abbey £170 per week, students £108, youths £95, children £84, under 5 £23; MacLeod £160 per week, students £98, youths £88, children £78, under 5 £21.50; Camas focuses on young guests, prices vary; insurance required.) For schedules or bookings contact The Iona Community, Iona, Argyll PA76 6SN (tel. (01681) 700404; fax 700460).

The incredible island of **Staffa**, composed of hexagonal basalt columns and rimmed with tidal caves, lies 8 mi. north of Iona. At a weak point in the earth's crust, liquid rock spewed upward and was cooled by ocean water to form columns. Surrounded by treacherous cliffs (particularly slippery in the rain; use of the guardrails is essential along the base), Staffa is ruled by an imperial council of six sheep and four cows. Puffins nest on the cliff edge and allow the curious to examine their personal space. When the tide is low, you can walk far inside **Fingal's Cave** to be surrounded by water and basalt. When rough seas roar into the cave, the sound reverberates around the island; the pounding of wave against rock inspired the surging strings in Mendelssohn's *Hebrides Overture*. The nearby **Treshnish Isles** offer sanctuary to seals, seabirds, and ferrets. Legend holds that monks from the Iona Abbey buried their library on one of the isles to save it from the pillages of the Reformation. Many have tried digging under the third ferret from the left, as yet without luck.

Highlands and Islands

Long live the weeds and the wilderness yet.
　　　　　　　　　　—Gerard Manley Hopkins, S.J.

Sheep have a habit of dying when they tip over, so if you come across one on its back and struggling in vain to get to its feet, do it and the Highland economy a favor and turn it right again. Scotland's sheep-filled northwestern coast, sliced by narrow sea lochs and girded by innumerable islands, remains the most beautiful region in Scotland and one of the last stretches of true wilderness in Europe. The Hebrides arch to the west of the mainland, while the Orkney and Shetland Islands stretch in a northeasterly direction off Scotland's horn at John O'Groats. The mainland towns of Inverness, Fort William, Glencoe, Ullapool, and Thurso are access points to the islands and good bases for exploring the famous but balding Highland mountains.

The northwest has not always been so vacant. Two centuries ago, almost one-third of the Scottish lived north of the Great Glen, but overpopulation made tenant farming unprofitable for absent landlords, who turned to sheep farming and evicted entire Highland communities in the infamous Highland Clearances of the early 19th century. The Clearances dealt a fatal blow to clan-based, Gaelic-speaking Highland society, scattering and dispossessing the population. Many Scots, forcibly evicted or burned out of their homes, emigrated to Canada, Australia, and the United States.

Today, the region's staple is tourism—English, Scottish, and otherwise. Few Highlanders work at a single occupation, and most make ends meet through self-employment, typically by crofting (independent farming), fishing, or running B&Bs. Only in the Outer Hebrides is Gaelic widely spoken (Gaelic rhymes with "Alec," unlike the Irish version, "GALE-ick"). To reinvigorate the language, Gaelic is taught in schools to children, who can turn to their grandparents, if not their parents, for assistance.

GETTING ABOUT

Travel in the Highlands requires a great deal of planning. You can't count on making more than one or two journeys a day on any form of transportation, even in high season. Transport services are, as a rule, drastically reduced on Sundays and during the winter. Most ferries on the west coast are run by **Caledonian MacBrayne** (head office tel. (01475) 650100; fax 650262), which publishes a widely available, free timetable. Special 8- to 15-day tickets provide discounts on ferry trips, but require substantial travel on consecutive days and are not valid on specific sailings during peak times. **Island Hopscotch** tickets can provide modest savings for certain routes. Bikes can cross without reservation for a fee (free-£2), but advance booking for cars is strongly recommended. Borrow your hostel's copy of the priceless *Getting Around the Highlands and Islands* for extra help.

🔊 HIGHLIGHTS OF THE HIGHLANDS AND ISLANDS

- Visitors young and old should try to catch a glimpse of Nessie, the creature that once rose from the mysterious depths of **Loch Ness** and has not yet returned, despite the curiosity of travelers from around the world (p. 541). Cheap accommodations and transportation connections can be found at nearby **Inverness** (p. 537).
- The highest peak in the British Isles, **Ben Nevis** (p. 543) often hides its height (4406ft.) in a layer of clouds. Intrepid hikers take part in the **Ben Nevis Race,** dashing up and down the mountain. Travelers with more leisure can—on a clear day—hike to the top and see all the way to Ireland.
- Surrounded by mountains and water, lovely **Skye** (p. 548) is the most accessible of all the Hebridean Islands.
- Travelers seeking the long summers of northern reaches and the company of sheep, sky, and ocean, should journey to the far-flung **Shetland Islands** (p. 568).

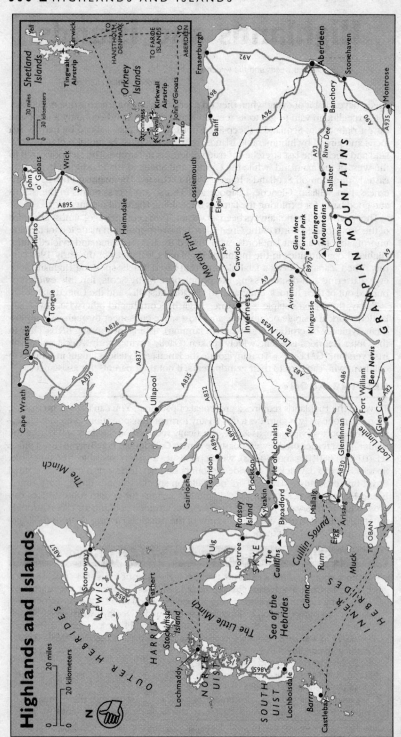

Highlands and Islands

SCOTLAND

■ Aberdeen

Aberdeen deserves to be called "The Granite City." On a standard Scottish day, the greyness of the city's buildings flows seamlessly into the greyness of the skies; underneath it all swishes the black blood of Britain's North Sea oil industry. Offsetting all the dirt and smog are flowered parks, a vibrant university, and an array of marvelous pubs and museums. If all that granite becomes oppressive, the nearby strongholds of Brodie, Crathes, Fraser, Drum, and Fyvie make unforgettable daytrips.

GETTING THERE

Scotrail runs trains to **Edinburgh** (M-Sa 9 per day, Su 10 per day, £31), **Glasgow** (M-Sa 18 per day, Su 6 per day, £34), **Inverness** (M-Sa 10 per day, Su 5 per day, £18.50), and **London** (3 per day direct; 7 or more days in advance £23, otherwise £78).

Scottish Citylink (tel. (0990) 505050) visits Aberdeen from **Edinburgh** (at least 1 per hr., £13) and **Glasgow** (at least 1 per hr., £13.30). **National Express** (tel. (0990) 808080) comes from **London** (3 per day, £27) and the local **Bluebird** buses make the trip from **Inverness** (1 per hr., £9).

The **Aberdeen Ferry Terminal,** Jamieson's Quay (tel. 572615), is the only place on mainland Britain where you can catch a ferry to the Shetlands, though you may prefer the **British Airways** flight from Orkney. Ferries also run to Stromness on Orkney (see **Getting There,** p. 564). To reach the terminal, turn left at the traffic light off Market St. past **P&O Scottish Ferries** (tel. 572615; office open M-F 9am-6pm, Sa 9am-noon).

PRACTICAL INFORMATION

Airplanes: Aberdeen Airport (tel. 722331). **British Airways** (tel. (0345) 222111) makes 5-7 flights daily to London. **Air UK** (tel. (0345) 666777) flies to Heathrow and Stansted.

Trains: Next to the bus station on Guild St. (tel. (0345) 484950). Ticket office open M-Sa 6:15am-8pm, Su 8:45am-7:15pm. **Lockers** £2-3.50; open M-Sa 7:30am-9pm, Su 9am-9pm.

Buses: Guild St. (tel. 212266). Ticket office open M-F 8:15am-6pm, Sa 8:30am-5pm. **Luggage storage:** M-F 8:15am-5pm; £1.50.

Tourist Office: St. Nicholas House, Broad St. AB10 1DE (tel. 632727; fax 620415), a 5min. walk from train and bus stations. Turn right on Guild St., left onto Market St., right onto Union St., and left again at Broad St. The staff is poised to book rooms; £1.25 plus 10% deposit. Bureau de change. Open July-Aug. M-F 9am-7pm, Sa 9am-5pm, Su 10am-4pm; Sept.-June M-Sa 9am-5pm, Su 10am-2pm.)

Financial Services: Banks line Union St. **Thomas Cook,** 335-337 Union St. (tel. 212270). Open M-W and F-Sa 9am-5:30pm, Th 10am-5:30pm.

American Express: 3-5 St. Nicholas St., 2nd fl. (tel. 633119). Housed in Lunn Poly Holiday and Flight Shop. Client mail held. Open M-F 9am-5:30pm, Sa 9am-5pm.

Launderette: 555 George St. (tel. 621211). Open M-F 10am-6pm, Sa 9am-5pm, Su 10am-5pm.

Counseling Services: Women's Centre, Shoe Ln. (tel. 625010). Offers advice on women's issues. Drop-in M noon-4pm, W 10am-4pm. **Rape Crisis Line** (tel. 620772). Open M and Th 7-9pm.

Gay and Lesbian Services: Aberdeen Lesbian Group (tel. 625010), meets in the Women's Centre. Open to the general public. Women's Centre also provides further info on current gay and lesbian group activities. **Gay Switchboard** (tel. 633500). Open W and F 7-10pm.

Emergency: Dial 999; no coins required.

Police: Queen St. (tel. 639111).

Hospital: Aberdeen Royal Infirmary, Forresterhill Rd. (tel. 681818).

Post Office: St. Nicholas Centre, Upperkirkgate (tel. 633065). The Crown St. office, off Union St., accepts *Poste Restante.* Both open M-Sa 9am-5:30pm. **Postal Code:** AB10 1HW.

Telephone Code: 01224.

ACCOMMODATIONS

Great Western Rd., 20 minutes from the train and bus stations and accessible by bus #17, 18, or 19, bursts with B&Bs (£15-23). Close to the downtown area, **Crown St.** also has numerous lodgings. A long walk on Union St. and Albyn Pl., or a short ride on bus #14, 15, or 27 to Queen's Rd., will bring you to the **SYHA King George VI Memorial Hostel,** 8 Queen's Rd. (tel. 646988). The tidy hostel has spacious dorms and a large backyard. Lights-out (11:30pm), curfew (2am), lockout (9:30am-1:30pm), and check-out (9:30am) are all enforced with a friendly yet firm hand. Kitchen and laundry. (June-Sept. £9.60, under 18 £8.10; Oct.-May £8.60, under 18 £7.10. Continental breakfast only available June-Sept. (£2). Kitchen and laundry.) For **camping,** try **Hazlehead Park** (tel. 321268), on Groats Rd. (£4.30-8.50 per tent; open Apr.-Sept.). Take bus #14 or 15.

FOOD AND DRINK

Tins and boxes lure the thrifty to **Tesco,** in the court in front of the St. Nicholas Centre on Union St. (open M-W and Sa 7:30am-7pm, Th 7:30am-9pm, F 7:30am-8pm, Su 10am-5pm), while **Safeway** struts at Union and Huntly St. (open M-F 8am-8pm, Sa 8am-7pm). For vitamins and wholefood snacks, try **Holland & Barrett,** 49 Netherkirkgate, across from Marks & Spencer's (open M 9am-5pm, Tu-W and F-Sa 9am-5:30pm, Th 9am-6pm). Pubs abound with low priced, greasy grub.

> **The New Dolphin** (tel. 639766), at Chapel and Union St., serves meal sized fried haddock (£5-6) and lunch specials, including prawns and chips (£3.50). Next door, the take-away half of the restaurant sells the same, only much cheaper. Open Su-W 11:30am-midnight, Th-Sa 11:30am-2:30am.
>
> **Lucky Boat,** 12-16 Guild St. (tel. 213392), across from the bus station, serves Chinese entrees at lunch prices until 3pm (£3.60-4.20); eat in or take-away. Evening specialities run £4-5.60. Open M-Sa 11:45am-10:30pm, Su 2-10:30pm.
>
> **The Grill,** 213 Union St. Pints £1.50; mince pie 70p; pub grub under £1.75. Open M-Th 11am-11pm, F-Sa 11am-midnight, Su 7:30-11pm.

SIGHTS AND ENTERTAINMENT

Old Aberdeen and **Aberdeen University** are a short bus ride (#1, 2, 3, 4, or 15) from the city center, or a long walk through commercial and residential districts along King St. Peaceful **King's College Chapel** (tel. 272137) dates from the 16th century and features intricately carved "misery seats"—each has its own subtly distinctive pattern. *(Open daily 9am-4:30pm. Guided tours July-Aug. Su 2-5pm.)* The twin-spired **St. Machar's Cathedral,** with a heraldic ceiling and stained glass, was built in the 14th century. *(Open daily 9am-5pm. Sunday services 11am and 6pm.)*

Aberdeen's fine sandy **beach** stretches north for about 2 mi. from the old fishing community of Footdee (fi-TEE, foot of the River Dee) to the Don estuary. Two **amusement parks** rear over the southern end, while the northern sands are cleaner and often quieter. Take bus #14. Good for bicycling, **Duthie Park,** by the River Dee at Polmuir Rd. and Riverside Dr., includes playgrounds, gardens, and the oxymoronic **Winter Gardens Hothouse.** *(Hothouse open daily 9:30am-dusk. Free.)* Aberdeen's largest park, **Hazlehead,** off Queen's Rd., on the western edge of the city, has an aviary and extensive woodlands. Take bus #14 or 15 to Queen's Rd. and walk 1 mi. on Hazlehead Ave. **Victoria Park,** west of the city center on Westburn Rd., has a garden for the visually impaired—strong-scented flowers are identified by Braille plaques.

The **Aberdeen Art Gallery,** Schoolhill (tel. 646333), houses a wide range of English, French, and Scottish paintings; its 20th-century British collection is particularly worthwhile. The gallery also hosts drama, dance, and music performances in the summer—check the *Aberdeen Art Gallery and Museums* for details. *(Open M-Sa 10am-5pm, Su 2-5pm. Free.)* The **Aberdeen Arts Centre,** 33 King St. (tel. 641122), at West North St. offers fine avant-garde and traditional theater performances. *(Tickets £4.50.)* **The Lemon Tree Café Theatre,** Shoe Ln. (tel. 642230), near the corner of

West North St. and Queen St., presents folk, jazz, rock, and drama in its two theaters. Snag the tourist office's *What's On in Aberdeen*, or the bimonthly Lemon Tree programme, available at the tourist office and the art gallery. *(Tickets free-£8.50.)*

■ East Grampian Coast and Mountains

The Grampian coast is dotted with some of the most dramatic castles in Scotland, from well-preserved residences to crumbling ruins. The splendidly decrepit **Dunnotar Castle** (tel. (01569) 762173), stands a romantic half-hour walk from seaside Stonehaven (15mi. south of Aberdeen), along cliffs dotted with sheep and pocked with rabbit holes. Built in the 12th century by the Earl Marischal's family, the castle commands a gut-wrenching view of the crashing sea. *(Open Easter-Oct. M-Sa 9am-6pm, Su 2-5pm; Nov.-Mar. M-F 9am-sunset. £3, children £1.)* Trains (20min., 17-25 per day, £2.70) and Scottish Citylink and Bluebird Northern buses connect Stonehaven to Aberdeen (30min., 2 per hr., return £3.65).

Easily accessible from Aberdeen by bus (Bluebird #201, 45min., 2 per hr.), 16th-century **Crathes Castle** took forty years to complete. The castle houses the ancient ivory Horn to Leys given to the family patriarch, Alexander Burnett, as a "horn of tenure" by Robert the Bruce in 1323. It's a good thing the castle was never attacked— the fierce cannons projecting from the towers shoot only water. A "Green Lady" allegedly haunts the castle, perhaps contributing her thumb to the spectacular gardens. *(Castle open Apr.-Oct. daily 11am-5:30pm, last admission 4:45pm; gardens open year-round daily 9:30am-sunset. Castle and grounds £4.80, students, seniors, and children £3.20.)*

Northwest 25 mi. from Aberdeen on inland A947, the amazingly intact 13th-century **Fyvie Castle** (tel. (01651) 891266) endures a brace of curses: a disgruntled medieval seer by the name of Thammas the Rhymer declared that the castle would never pass to the first son of the family until three stones were retrieved from its structure and returned to the stream from which they were taken. There is also a sealed chamber in one of the towers which, if opened, causes the laird to die and his wife to go blind (it's happened…twice!). *(Open July-Aug. daily 11am-5:30pm; Apr.-June and Sept. daily 1:30-5:30pm; Oct. Sa-Su only 1:30-5:30pm; last admission 4:45pm; grounds open daily 9:30am-sunset. £4.20, seniors and children £3.20.)* Grab a dossier of schedules from the Elgin or Aberdeen tourist office to guide you through the bus service.

West of Aberdeen, the River Dee meanders to the tiny town of **Braemar**. This area offers excellent hillwalking in the summer (pick up *Hillwalking in the Grampian Highlands* for £1 at any regional tourist office), and in winter hosts some of Britain's best alpine and cross-country skiing. The fully furnished 17th-century **Braemar Castle** (tel. (013397) 41219) was once a stronghold of the Farquharson clan. *(Open Apr.-Oct. Sa-Th 10am-6pm. £2.50, seniors £1.50, children £1.)* A 20-minute bus ride away (bus #201 to Crathie) lies **Balmoral Castle** (tel. (013397) 42334), the royal family's holiday residence. *(Open May-July M-Sa 10am-5pm. £3.50, seniors £2.50, under 16 £1.)* On the first Saturday in September, Braemar's population swells from 410 to 20,000 for the annual highland games of the **Braemar Gathering.** The Queen almost always attends; advance bookings are essential (tel. (01330) 825917). Write The Bookings Secretary, Coilacrich, Ballater AB35 5UH (tel. (013397) 55377) for information.

The **regional tourist office,** Mar. Rd. (tel. (013397) 41600), is in Braemar, at the Mews (open daily July-Sept. 9am-7pm; June 10am-6pm; Nov.-May 10am-1pm and 2-5pm). The 64-bed **SYHA Youth Hostel** (tel. (013397) 41659) in Braemar lies just south of town in an old stone house on Glenshee Rd., surrounded by a thicket of Scotland's oldest pine trees (£7.75, under 18 £6.50). The Glenshee ski area is nearby; contact the **SYHA,** 161 Warrender Park Rd., Edinburgh EH9 1EQ (tel. (0131) 229 8660), to find out if any package ski tours for hostelers will be arranged this winter season. If the hostel is full, the **Rucksacks Outdoor Centre,** 15 Mar Rd. (tel. (013397) 41242), has room for 26, with showers, kitchen facilities, and central heating (£8, bunkhouse £7; sleeping bag required for 10 bed spaces). The center also rents cross-country skis (£12.50 per day) and mountain bikes (£15 per day, £9 per half-day). Braemar is a 5 mi. walk from the **SYHA Inverey** (no tel., book ahead through Braemar hostel), where there are usually more deer than guests. The hostel is a favorite stopping point for hikers doing the classic 23 mi. trek from Loch Morlich, up the **Lairig Ghru,** and over the pass to Bracmar (£4.65, under 18 £3.85; open June-Sept.). The **SYHA Glendoll** (tel. (01575) 550236) is a difficult 13 mi. hike from Braemar. Follow the A93 2 mi. south to the Glen Callater turn-off, then take the Jock's Rd. footpath. Be sure to take an Ordnance Survey map and compass and notify the Braemar police of your plans (£6.10, under 18 £5; open late Mar. to Oct.). Glendoll can also be reached from Dundee by taking the bus to Kirriemuir (1 per hr.) and either walking from there or hopping on the Kirriemuir-Glendoll post bus (M-Sa 1 per day).

■ Elgin

Elgin (pronounced with a hard "g"—like Guinness, not gin) is a quiet but growing town halfway between Aberdeen and Inverness; minority travelers may note that Elgin can still be provincial at times. The town's spectacular **Elgin Cathedral,** regarded in the 14th century as the most beautiful of Scottish cathedrals, was looted and burned by the Wolf of Badenoch just as that century ended. Subsequently, the cathedral was further tormented by fire, Edward III, the Reformation, and Cromwell's bullets. Thanks to careful restoration and repair, the grand church is still a breathtaking sight. *(Open Apr.-Sept. M-Sa 9:30am-6:30pm, Su 2-6:30pm; Oct.-Mar. M-W and Sa 9:30am-4:30pm, Th 9:30am-noon, Su 2-4:30pm; last admission 30min. before closing. £1.80, students and seniors £1.20, children 75p.)* The **Elgin Museum** (tel. 543675) displays spoils collected by local notables in the Age of Empire, including a shrunken head from Ecuador and a mummy from Peru. Elgin's other claims to fame include Alexander Graham Bell, who taught at a local school (now appropriately the site of an electronics store) before emigrating to America. *(Open Easter-Oct. M-F 10am-5pm, Sa 11am-4pm, Su 2-5pm; in winter for groups only. £1.50, students and seniors 75p, children 50p.)*

Frequent **Northern Bluebird** buses and trains serve Elgin from **Inverness** (buses 19 per day, £5; trains 11 per day, £6.70) and **Aberdeen** (buses 13 per day, £6.50; trains 10 per day, £12.20). **Buses** stop at the new bus station behind High St. and the St. Giles Centre; the train station lounges five minutes from town along South Guildry St. Ask at the **tourist office,** 17 High St. (tel. 542666; fax 552982), for accommodations listings and bookings. (Open July-Aug. M-Sa 9:30am-6:30pm, Su 1-6:30pm; June and Sept. M-Sa 10am-6pm, Su 1-6pm; Apr.-May and Oct. M-Sa 10am-1pm and 2-5pm, Su 1-5pm; Nov.-Mar. M-F 10am-4pm, Sa 10am-2pm.) The **telephone code** is 01343.

Elgin's only hostel, **The Saltire Bunkhouse,** Pluscarden Rd. (tel. 550624), is about a 30-minute walk west of town. Check out the gardens and the World War II bunker before sleeping in a building flanked with horse and sheep and cows (oh my!)—not to mention countless birds (£7.50-11.50; sauna, kitchen, bikes; open Easter to mid-Sept.). Elgin is chock-full of B&Bs; friendly Mr. Ross (tel. 542035) will set you up with an English breakfast and a room with TV at **The Bungalow,** 7 New Elgin Rd., 5 minutes from the train station, and a 15 minute walk along New Elgin Rd. from the town center (£15). **The Park Café,** 7 N. College St. (tel. 543291), will take you back in time: the decor is vintage 50s and a 3-course lunch with tea costs £7; vegetarian and healthy options are also available (open M-Sa 9am-6:30pm, Su 10am-6:30pm).

Cromwell's Stolen Laundry

Much like the Scottish sun, the Scottish Crown Jewels have been hidden for extended periods of time. The regalia owe their continuing existence to two brave Scotswomen who lived in the 17th century. As Oliver Cromwell stormed his way to Stirling, Catherine, the wife of the minister of Moneydie, covertly transported the items to Dunnator Castle. Dressed as a peasant woman, she crossed through Cromwell's lines with the jewels in sacks of wool. Later, when Dunnotar Castle itself was under siege, a second woman, Christian Fletcher, smuggled them out again, trotting them through the castle on horseback. If only Cromwell had decided to rummage through bags of dirty pillows, the crown, scepter, sword, and scabbard would have been his.

■ Near Elgin

Stay too long in Elgin and you'll miss the marvelous hills surrounding it. The 62 mi. **Malt Whisky Trail** staggers past eight famous distilleries, all of which offer free booze (all open at least M-F 10am-4pm in summer). The best tour is at the **Glenfiddich** distillery (tel. (01340) 820373) in Dufftown. Seventeen miles south of Elgin, Glenfiddich is the only distillery in the highlands where you can see whisky bottled on the premises. Note the black fungus on the trees—when brewing was illegal, it was a dead giveaway to police. *(Open Easter to mid-Oct. M-Sa 9:30am-4:30pm, Su noon-4:30pm; mid-Oct. to Easter M-F 9:30am-4:30pm. Free.)* Take Bluebird bus #335 or 336 to Dufftown.

The bus to the Glenfiddich distillery stops at **The Speyside Cooperage** (tel. (01340) 871108), where casks are still handmade. The Cooperage is located a quarter of a mile south of Craigellachie on the A941. *(Open Easter-Sept. M-Sa 9:30am-4:30pm; Oct.-Easter M-F 9:30am-4:30pm. £2.25, seniors and children £1.60.)* Walkers enjoy the **Speyside Way,** a trail by the river from Spey Bay to the town of Tomintoul, the southernmost village in Moray. Grab a trail map at the Elgin tourist office.

The village of **Forres,** a perennial winner in the cutthroat Britain in Bloom competition, blossoms 30 minutes from Elgin by bus (#10, 2 per hr., £2.60) or 15 minutes by train (4-5 per day, £2.20). Tea rooms and bakeries flower every few doors along High St., as do florists. On a nearby heath, Shakespeare's sisters three revealed Macbeth's destiny. The **tourist office,** 17 High St., lists area B&Bs (open July-Aug. daily 10am-1pm and 2-6pm; Apr.-June and Sept.-Oct. M-Sa 10am-1pm and 2-5pm, Su 1-5pm).

Located 6 mi. north of Elgin on the A941, the barren seaside village of **Lossiemouth** is linked to Elgin by frequent bus service. Two sandy, windswept beaches are nearby: **East Beach** is connected to the mainland by a narrow footbridge and has grassy dunes; **West Beach** is cleaner, less crowded, and leads to a lighthouse. Campers pitch their tents at **Silver Sands Leisure Park** (tel. 813262) for £11.25-13 (open Apr.-Oct.), and the weary find a haven at **Mrs. Stephen's,** 54 Queen St. (tel. 813482; £15).

■ Cairngorm Mountains and Aviemore

The towering Cairngorms, 120 mi. north of Edinburgh, bear witness to the gradual deforestation which nearly stripped Scotland of its native pine and birch forests. The peaks are bare, covered only with heather, reindeer, and, for much of the year, the snow which attracts skiers and dogsledders to the region. Strathspey, however, contains Britain's largest expanse of nature preserves. Careful reforestation is not only blanketing the slopes of the Cairngorms with pine and juniper, but is also increasing the pine marten, capercaillie (a rooster-like bird), wildcat, and red squirrel populations. The hiking, mountain-biking, and skiing are superb—if a little cold and dangerous. Once you've breathed the bracing Cairngorm air, you may never want to leave.

GETTING THERE AND GETTING ABOUT

Aviemore is the largest town in the Cairngorms, conveniently located on the main Inverness-Edinburgh rail and bus lines. This concrete roadside strip has no beauty; get out of town and into the mountains right away. **Trains** (tel. (0345) 484950) leave the station on Grampian Rd., just north of the tourist office, for **Inverness** (45min., 9 per day, £8.80) and **Glasgow** and **Edinburgh** (3½hr., 5-7 per day, £27). **Buses** run nearly every hour to **Inverness** (40min., £4), **Glasgow,** and **Edinburgh** (3½hr., £9.80 to Glasgow, £11.30 to Edinburgh). Heatherhopper jumps between **Elgin** and Aviemore (#402, July to late Sept. 4 per day). Southbound buses stop at the shopping center just north of the train station; northbound buses brake before the Cairngorm Hotel.

The area's prettiest roadtrip is a 10 mi. jaunt along B970 and A951 through the heather moors of the **Ski Rd.** The principal path into the **Glen More Forest Park,** the Ski Rd. begins just south of Aviemore (on the B970) and jogs eastward, continuing north towards Loch Garten. Follow the eastern branch, which merges into the A951. The road passes the sandy beaches of **Loch Morlich,** before continuing into Glenmore and ending at the Cairngorm chairlift. The Cairngorm Chairlift Bus (tel. (01479)

861261) shuttles to the ski lifts frequently in winter (in summer 3-6 per day). Try to rent a bike; travelers find **hitching** slow. **Bophy Bikes** (tel. 810111) and **Inverdruie Bikes** (tel. 810787) both offer bike rental.

PRACTICAL INFORMATION

The **Aviemore and Spey Valley tourist office** (tel. 810363 or 810454), on Grampian Rd., the town's main artery, books local B&Bs (£15-25), sells bus tickets, and exchanges currency for a £2.50 commission during peak season. (Open July to mid-Sept. M-Sa 9am-7pm, Su 10am-6pm; mid-Sept. to June daily 9am-5pm.) The **Rothie-murchus Estate Visitors Centre** (tel. 810858) lies nearly 1 mi. down the Ski Rd. from Aviemore toward the Cairngorms (open daily 8:30am-5:30pm). The Bank of Scotland **ATM** is keepin' it real at the shopping center in Aviemore. The **Cairngorm Service Station** (tel. 810596), on Main St., offers **rental cars** (£34-42 per day; £185-235 per week). Aviemore's **telephone code** is a hearty 01479.

Six miles from Aviemore, **Kincraig Stores** (tel. (01540) 651331) sells postcards, and also serves as the Kincraig **post office** and **tourist office.** (Post office open M-Tu and Th-F 9am-1pm. Store open Apr.-Oct. M-Tu and Th-Sa 9am-1pm and 2-5:30pm, W and Su 9am-1pm; Nov.-Mar. M-Tu and Th-F 9am-1pm and 2-5:30pm, W and Sa-Su 9am-1pm.) **Highland Wildlife Park** (tel. (01540) 651270) is dedicated to preserving local beasties. (Open daily June-Aug. 10am-7pm, last admission 5pm; Apr.-May and Sept.-Oct. 10am-6pm, last admission 4pm; Nov.-Mar. 10am-4pm, last admission 2pm.)

ACCOMMODATIONS AND FOOD

Check the tourist board's *Aviemore and Spey Valley* publication for a complete listing of seasonal hostels and year-round B&Bs.

SYHA Loch Morlich, Glenmore (tel. (01479) 861238). Superb accommodations on Loch Morlich. Sublime views of the mountains. The Cairngorm Chairlift Bus (£1.40) departs from the Aviemore train station and stops in front of the hostel, but runs infrequently in the summer. £7.75, under 18 £6.50. Breakfast £2, cooked breakfast £3.25, dinner £4.40. Curfew 11:30pm.

SYHA Aviemore (tel. (01479) 810345). This spiffy hostel 100yd. south of the tourist office has scorching showers and sinks in every suite—hot and cold in a single tap! 115 beds with 4-8 beds to a room. July-Aug. £9.60, under 18 £8.10; Sept.-June £8.60, under 18 £7.10. No lockout. Curfew 2am.

Glen Feshie Hostel (tel. (01540) 651323), 11mi. south of Aviemore, 5mi. from Kincraig. Call ahead and you might get picked up. Close to numerous walks and hikes. From £8; linen and free porridge breakfast included. Showers, kitchen, and free porridge breakfast. No curfew.

Insh Hall Ski Lodge (tel. (01540) 651272), 1mi. downhill from Kincraig; Scottish Citylink buses run to Kincraig from the hostel. Year-round accommodations (with bath) on Loch Inshfor for skiers and hikers. Sauna and gym. Guests get free use of watersports equipment. From £16.50; B&B plus lunch and dinner £31.25.

Camping: Glenmore Forest Camping and Caravan Park (tel. 861271), across from the Loch Morlich Youth Hostel. Ample space and good facilities, though it may be crowded in the summer. £7.50-8.60 per tent. Open Dec.-Oct. **Coylumbridge Campgrounds of Scotland** (tel. 831652), 1½mi. south of Aviemore on the Ski Rd. £3.50-5.50 per person per tent. Laundry.

Tesco Supermarket, lies just north of the Aviemore train station (open M-W and Sa 8:30am-8pm, Th-F 8:30am-9pm, Su 9am-6pm). **Aviemore Tandoori** (tel. 811118) offers spicy food, near the tourist office (£5-8; open daily 5-11:30pm). **The Glenmore Shop and Café** (tel. 861253), near the Loch Morlich Youth Hostel, has all the essentials. The adjoining store rents bikes, as well as skis and mountain boards. (Bikes £12 per day, £8 per half-day, £3 per hr. Open daily mid-Apr. to Sept. 8:30am-7:30pm; Sept. to mid-Apr. 8:30am-5:30pm.)

HIKING, SKIING, AND OTHER REINDEER GAMES

The Cairngorm region has Scotland's highest concentration of ski resorts. In winter, Alpine skiers from throughout Britain converge at the **Cairngorm Ski Area,** featuring a network of five chairlifts and 17 tows. In summer, the double-legged chairlift becomes a blessing for armchair hikers. *(Bottom to top and back £6, seniors and children £3.60, middle to top and back £4.20, £2.50.)* The first ride ascends a quite walkable 368 ft.; the second lift covers the remaining 1056 ft. to a summit near the peak of Cairngorm Mt. (4084ft.). Arrive early (the first chairlift runs at 9am in summer, the last at 3:55pm) or your view of the surrounding snow-capped peaks and silver lochs may be obstructed by hordes of Teutonic prepubescents. To enjoy the mountains in peace, descend The Saddle into Glen Avon or traverse the southern ridge of Cairngorm to **Ben Macdui,** the second-highest peak in Britain (4296ft.). On a clear day, you can see the first 100 mi. of infinity. With any luck, you may run into the Lapland reindeer. On a rainy day, you won't see much. Contact **Cairngorm Chairlift** (tel. 861261).

The Cairngorm Chairlift bus company no longer runs public transport to the chairlift during the summer. A taxi ride should cost you £17 each way; if you're up for it, you can bike the 10 mi. back and forth. Once at the base of the mountains, the **Cairngorm Rangers** offer guided walks for both experienced and novice hikers (walks vary in length). Several local companies run ski schools and rent equipment; pick up a copy of *Skiing Information* at the Aviemore tourist office for details. Down the hill 3 mi. from the chairlift, the **Cairngorm Reindeer Centre** (tel. 861228) is home to 150 velvet-horned creatures. For a fee, visitors are entitled to a 1½ hour frolic amid the herd. *(Visits daily at 11am; Easter-Oct. also at 2:30pm. Call ahead to confirm availability of afternoon visit. £4, students and children £3.)* Next door, the **Glenmore Forest Park Visitors Centre** (tel. 861220) disburses information on great walks. *(Open daily 9am-5pm.)*

> **Safety Precautions:** Although the Cairngorms rise only 4000 ft., the weather patterns of an **Arctic tundra** characterize the region. Explorers may be at the mercy of bitter winds and unpredictable mists **any day of the year.** Furthermore, many trails are not posted and trekkers must be able to rely on their own proficiency with a map and compass. Make sure to use an Ordnance Survey map, preferably the yellow Outdoor Leisure Sheet covering the Cairngorms (available at the tourist office). **Be prepared to spend a night in sub-freezing temperatures** no matter what the temperature is when you set out. Leave a description of your intended route with the police or at the mountain station, and learn the locations of the shelters *(bothies)* along your trail. See **Wilderness and Safety Concerns,** p. 47.

■ Inverness

To reach just about anything in the Highlands, you'll have to pass through the transportation hub of Inverness. The city's charms are somewhat elusive, but the traveler who hunts them down won't be disappointed. Inverness is comfortably, quietly cosmopolitan, with fine shops, pubs, all the amenities—and street signs in Gaelic, to remind you that you really are in the Highlands. But before venturing north, no trip would be complete without taking in nearby Loch Ness and its associated merchandise. If you don't actually glimpse the monster yourself, thoughtful local vendors can offer you a cute stuffed one instead.

GETTING THERE

One **train** (tel. (0345) 484950) a day runs directly to **London** (£78), and both **Scottish Citylink** (tel. (0990) 505050) and **National Express** (tel. (0990) 808080) make the same trip by **bus** (£41). **Trains** also run to **Aberdeen** (2¼hr., M-Sa 10 per day, Su 5 per day, £18), **Kyle of Lochalsh** (2½hr., M-Sa 3 per day, Su 2 per day, £13.80), **Thurso** and **Wick** (3¾hr., M-Sa 3 per day, Su 2 per day, £11.80), and **Edinburgh** and **Glasgow** (3½-4hr., M-Sa 7 per day, Su 2-3 per day, £28). **Buses** cover the same routes less

SCOTLAND

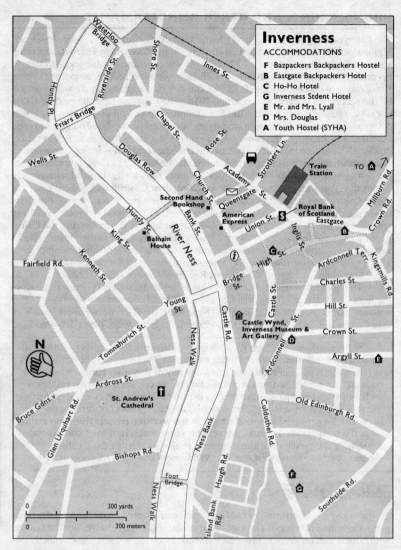

Inverness

ACCOMMODATIONS

- **F** Bazpackers Backpackers Hostel
- **B** Eastgate Backpackers Hotel
- **C** Ho-Ho Hotel
- **G** Inverness Stdent Hotel
- **E** Mr. and Mrs. Lyall
- **D** Mrs. Douglas
- **A** Youth Hostel (SYHA)

expensively and sometimes more quickly. **Scottish Citylink** (tel. (0990) 505050) provides frequent service to most places, including **Edinburgh** (3½-4hr., 8-10 per day, £12.30), **Glasgow** (3½-4¼hr., 11-13 per day, £11.50), **Ullapool** (1½hr., 1-2 per day, on Su take Inverness Traction, £7), **Thurso** and **Wick** (3½hr., 4-5 per day, £9), and **Kyle of Lochalsh** (2hr., £8). Travel to **Oban** requires changing at Fort William.

ORIENTATION AND PRACTICAL INFORMATION

The traveler's Inverness is divided into two; a river runs through it, and most of what you need is on the east side. A huge suspension bridge crosses the River Ness, linking the two sides and bouncing its users up and down.

Trains: (tel. (0345) 84950), down Academy St. in Station Sq. Travel Centre open M-Sa 6:25am-8:30pm, Su 9:15am-8:30pm. Showers £1.50.

Buses: Farraline Park, just off Academy St. **Skye-Ways** (tel. (01599) 534328) has an office in a trailer around the corner from **Highland Bus and Coach** (tel. (0990) 505050) which sells tickets for all other companies and stores luggage (£1).

Taxis: Central Taxis (tel. 222222).

Car rental: Budget Rent-A-Car, Railway Terr. (tel. 713333). Open M-F 8am-5:30pm, Sa 9am-noon.

Bike Rental: Wilder Ness, 4 Culduthel Rd. (tel. 717663), at the Bazpackers Hostel. £10 per day, £7.50 per half-day.

Tourist Office: Castle Wynd (tel. 234353; fax 710609). From the bus and train stations take a left onto Academy St., a right onto Union St., and a left onto Church St. The tourist office is visible from the end of Church St. Bureau de change. The staff can tell you how to track the monster by bus, boat, or brochure, and can book beds. Open July to mid-Sept. M-Sa 9am-8:30pm, Su 9:30am-6pm; mid-May to June M-Sa 9am-6pm, Su 9:30am-5:30pm; mid- to late Sept. M-Sa 9am-6pm, Su 10am-5pm; Oct. to mid-May M-F 9am-5pm, Sa 10am-4pm.

Tours: Guide Friday gives open bus tours of Inverness and Culloden. Buses leave from Bridge St. and the bus station. £6.50, students and seniors £5, children £2.50.

Financial Services: ATMs are as common as Adidas tracksuits. Try the **Royal Bank of Scotland** on 38 Academy St. and on Union St. Takes Plus, Visa, and Mastercard.

American Express: 43 Church St. (tel. 718008). Open M-F 9am-5:30pm, Sa 9am-1pm.

Launderette: 17 Young St. (tel. 242507). Open M-Sa 8am-8pm, last wash 7pm; Su 10am-4pm, last wash 3pm.

Gay and Lesbian Services: Gay Switchboard (tel. (0131) 556 4049) and **Lesbian Line** (tel. (0131) 557 0751).

Emergency: Dial 999; no coins required.

Police: 10 Queensgate (tel. 715555).

Hotline: Rape and Abuse Line, Dingwall (tel. (01349) 865316 or 862686).

Hospital: Raigmore Hospital, Perth Rd. (tel. 704000). Its **Family Planning Clinic** (ext. 3269) doles out condoms for free.

Post Office: 14-16 Queensgate (tel. (0345) 223344). Open M-F 9am-5:30pm, Sa 9am-7pm. **Postal Code:** IV1 1AA.

Internet Access: Invernet Coffee Bar, 13 Bridge St. (tel. 729154). £2.50 per 30min. Open M-Sa 8:30am-10pm, Su noon-6pm.

Telephone Code: 01463.

ACCOMMODATIONS

Inverness is infested with budget accommodations. New hostels have recently opened, adding to the extraordinary range of cheap places to stay. If those listed below are full, the **tourist office** will help you find others. **Thomas Cook** offers a similar service from a booth in the train station, but their commission is higher (£3 versus the tourist board's £1.50).

Inverness Student Hotel, 8 Culduthel Rd. (tel. 236556). Face the tourist office and saunter left along Bridge St., turn right onto Castle St. (not Castle Wynd), which leads to Culduthel Rd. The outgoing, helpful staff operates a travelers' resource center and will take you out to the local pubs. 57 beds in rooms of 6-10. Free coffee and tea all day, small kitchen, powerful showers. Great views. Apr.-Sept. £8.90; Oct.-Mar. £8.50. Breakfast £1.40. Laundry £2.50. Desk open 6:30am-2:30am. Check-out 10:30am. Make reservations with credit card or from Castle Rock in Edinburgh, Backpacker's Guest House in Kyleakin (Skye), Fort William Backpackers, or Oban Backpackers.

Ho-Ho Hostel, 23a High St. (tel. 221225). From the bus and train stations, walk left along Academy St., turn right onto Union, and then left on pedestrian Drummond St. Look for the yellow sign that directs you down an alley. 76 beds in rooms of 8-12, some with bath. Large Victorian lounge and large, fully equipped kitchen. Co-ed rooms optional. £8.50; doubles and twins £9.50. Continental breakfast £1.40. Laundry. Check-out 10am. No curfew.

SYHA Inverness Millburn, Victoria Dr. (tel. 231771). Turn left out of the train station and walk 10-15min. up Millburn Rd.; Victoria Dr. is on your right. A bit of a trek, but worth it. Brand-new, state-of-the-art hostel, boasting 166 beds in rooms of 2-6. Lockers, laundry (£1), kitchen, lounge, and TV room. July-Aug. £12.50, under 18 £11; Sept.-June £11.50, under 18 £10. Continental breakfast included. Check-out 10:30am. Curfew 2am. Disabled facilities.

Bazpackers Backpackers Hotel, 4 Culduthel Rd. (tel. 717663). A down-home smoke-free atmosphere complete with a replica of a wood-burning stove. 30 beds in rooms of 4-8 (2 doubles also available). Kitchen, co-ed rooms and bathrooms. £8.50-9; doubles £24. Desk open 7:30am-midnight. Check-out 10:30am. No curfew. Credit card reservations accepted.

Eastgate Backpackers Hostel, 38 Eastgate (tel. 718756). From the bus and train stations, walk left along Academy St.; at its end, veer right onto Inglis St. and then left onto the wide High St. It's on your right, above a Chinese restaurant. A friendly staff dispenses travel advice like Pez does sugar wafers. 38 beds in rooms of 6-8, but avoid the cramped quarters if they pull out more beds. 2 twins; one family room (4 beds). £8.90; less in winter. Continental breakfast £1.50.

Mr. and Mrs. Lyall, 20 Argyll St. (tel. 710267). Handsome rooms with TV, tea, and coffee. Don't miss the antics of the Lyall's latest parrot. Bed and shower deluxe, an amazing value at £9. Continental breakfast included.

Mrs. Douglas, 32 Ardconnell St. (tel 239909). Bright, airy rooms, all with TV, in a restored Victorian house. A relaxed atmosphere for backpackers. No smoking; no breakfast. Bed and shower £9.

Camping: Most grounds fill with caravans in summer. The closest one to town is the **Bught Caravan and Camping Park** (tel. 236920), in the southern part of town near the Ness Islands. About 90 pitches. £4, additional charge for cars.

FOOD AND PUBS

Inverness boasts a range of fairly unexceptional restaurants. High St. is packed with fast food, including the inevitable McDonald's. **The Castle Restaurant,** 41 Castle St. (tel. 230925), is the local favorite for big portions under £5 (open M-Sa 8am-8:30pm). **Peking House,** 31 Castle St. (tel. 224467), serves a three-course lunch for £4. **Charlie Chan's,** 3 Tomnahurich St. (tel. 232884), across the river, is a bit cheaper (both open daily until midnight). Across from the bus station, buy groceries in **Safeway** (open M-F 8am-10pm, Sa 8am-8pm, Su 9am-6pm).

Most restaurants are in pubs, and a wide array of pubs (over 40) invigorates Inverness. Irish pubs are popular throughout Scotland, and Inverness is no exception. Try **Lafferty's,** 96 Academy St. (tel. 712270), for loud and lively Irish music (open M-Sa noon-11pm, W-Sa usually later). Next door, the **Phoenix** (tel. 220050) also has live music Fridays and Saturdays (open M-W 11am-11pm, Th 11am-midnight, F 11am-12:30am, Sa 11am-11:30pm, Su 12:30-11pm). For a slightly trendier option, try **Chili Palmer's European Cafe Bar,** 73 Queensgate (tel. 715075). Younger clientele buy expensive drinks to pounding music. Across the River Ness on Young St., play pool or darts at **Glenalbyn** (tel. 231637), which features live music, usually rhythm and blues bands, on Monday and Wednesday nights (open M-W 11am-1am, Th-F 11am-11pm, Sa 11am-11:45pm).

SIGHTS AND ENTERTAINMENT

Disillusion awaits those who remember Inverness as the home of Shakespeare's *Macbeth*. Nothing of the "Auld Castlehill" remains; the present reconstructed castle, home to the sheriff's courts, looks like it was made out of pink Legos this very morning. You'll have to commit a crime to get in. Instead, visit the **Inverness Museum and Art Gallery** (tel. 237114), in Castle Wynd, which displays a variety of exhibits about local history and archaeology. *(Open M-Sa 9am-5pm. Free.)* If you have an ear for Highland music, visit the **Balnain House,** 40 Huntley St. (tel. 715757). In addition to various listening booths, visitors can try their hand at the bagpipe, fiddle, or *clarsach*. Live music every day and jam sessions on Thursdays. Ask about *ceilidhs*. *(Open July-Aug. M-F 10am-8pm, Sa-Su 10am-6pm; June Tu-Su 10am-5pm; Sept.-May Tu-Sa 10am-5pm.*

£2, students and seniors £1.50, children 50p.) **Leakey's Secondhand Bookshop** (tel. 239947) deals with more cerebral matters. Located at the end of Church St. in atmosphere Greyfriar's Hall, it claims to be Scotland's largest second-hand bookshop. *(Open M-Sa 10am-5:30pm.)* The **Eden Court Theatre,** Bishop's Rd. (tel. 234234), is the center of cultural life in Inverness and offers an exciting range of plays, dance, and music, as well as cinema.

Like all Scottish cities, Inverness has its share of summertime fêtes. In mid-July, local strongmen hurl telephone poles during the **Inverness Highland Games.** Pipe-and-drum bands and daredevil display teams dominate the **Inverness Tattoo Festival** in mid-July. The **Marymas Fair,** in mid-August, recreates 19th-century street life with crafts stalls, concerts, and proletarian strife. The **Northern Meeting,** the world's premier piping competition, comes to Eden Court Theatre in early September. Five to ten minutes from the town center, the shallow, swiftly flowing River Ness forks and forks again, forming the **Ness Islands**—narrow islets connected to both banks by small footbridges and blanketed with virgin forest.

■ Near Inverness

Unfathomably deep, mysterious, and unbelievably famous, **Loch Ness** guards its secrets 5 mi. south of town. In AD 565, St. Columba repelled a savage sea beast as it attacked a monk; whether a prehistoric leftover, giant seasnake, or cosmic wanderer, the Loch Ness monster has captivated the imagination of the world ever since. Seven hundred feet deep just 70 feet from its edge, the Loch is shaped like a wedge, with caverns at the floor extending down so far that no one has definitively determined how vast it really is, or what life exists at its bottom. One of the easiest ways to see the loch is by tour. Try the one run by **Inverness Traction,** leaving from the tourist office. *(10:30am, 11:15am, and 2:30pm. £7.50, students, seniors, and children £6.)* You can also bike down the eastern side of the loch, where the narrow B582 runs close to the water. Eighteen miles down this road, the River Foyers empties into the loch in a series of idyllic waterfalls.

Sixteen miles down the western shore road (the A82) a lone bagpiper drones from the ruined ramparts of lovely **Urquhart Castle** (URK-hart; tel. (01456) 450551), one of the largest in Scotland before it was blown up in 1692 to prevent Jacobite occupation. A number of photos of Nessie have been fabricated at this spot. Most tours from Inverness stop at these ruins. *(Open daily Apr.-Sept. 9:30am-5:45pm; Oct.-Mar. 9:30am-3:45pm. £3.50, students and seniors £2.80, children £1.)* In nearby Drumnadrochit, not one, but two visitor centers expound on the legend that is Nessie. The better of the two, the **Official Loch Ness Centre** (tel. (01456) 450218) leads you through exhibition rooms on a 40-minute audio-visual display. If you ever sat through an episode of *That's Incredible!,* the exhibition may be redundant. *(Open daily July-Aug. 9am-7:30pm; June and Sept. 9:30am-6:30pm; Oct.-May 10am-4pm. £4.50, students and seniors £3.50, children £2.50.)* The **Loch Ness Backpackers Lodge,** Coiltie Farm House, East Lewiston (tel. (01456) 450807), served by several buses from Inverness (ask for Lewiston) and within walking distance of Loch Ness, has cozy cabin-like rooms and sponsors boat trips (£3.50). The rooms in the annex are larger, but you have to step outside for all facilities (£8.50; doubles £22; continental breakfast with scone! £1.50). The **SYHA Loch Ness** (tel. (01320) 351274) stands on the western shore of the loch, 7½ mi. south of the castle (£6.10, under 18 £5; July-Aug. call ahead; open mid-Mar. to Oct.).

East of Inverness unfold the moors of **Culloden Battlefield.** In 1746 the Jacobite cause died here as Bonnie Prince Charlie, charismatic but no genius in battle, lost 1200 men to the King's army in a 40-minute bloodbath—so ended the last battle on British soil. Check out the Visitor's Centre (tel. 790607). *(Centre open daily Apr.-Oct. 10am-6pm; Feb.-Mar. and Nov.-Dec. 10am-4pm. Battlefield free. Visitor's Centre £2.90, students, seniors, children, and hostelers £2.)*

A picturesque 1½ mi. south of Culloden, the stone circles and chambered cairns (mounds of rough stones) of the **Cairns of Clava** recall civilizations of the Bronze Age. Built in 1580 as the home of the Frasers, **Moniack Castle** (tel. 831283) still houses the family and their wine-making business. Located 7 mi. west of Inverness, the castle offers guided tours of the winery every 20 minutes. *(Open Mar.-Oct. M-Sa 10am-5pm; Nov.-Feb. M-Sa 11am-4pm. £2, children free.)* **Cawdor Castle** (tel. (01667) 404615) has been the residence of the Thane's descendants since the 15th century and is still inhabited for much of the year. The late Lord Cawdor IV detailed his home's priceless items in a series of humorous and witty signs. Don't miss the garden maze and nature walks. *(Open May to mid-Oct. daily 10am-5:30pm. £5.20, students and seniors £4.20, children £2.80.)* Those planning to visit numerous spots should invest in the money-saving **Tourist Trail Day Rover** (July-Aug. £6, students, seniors, and children £4) to travel by bus from Inverness to Culloden Battlefield, Cawdor Castle, Nairn, Fort George, Castle Stuart, and then back to Inverness, in either direction.

■ Glen Coe

Stunning in any weather, Glen Coe is perhaps best seen in the rain, when a slowly drifting web of mist over the valley laces the innumerable rifts and crags of the steep slopes, and silvery waterfalls cascade into the River Coe. Only on rare days is such a view marred by shining sun; Glen Coe records over 100 in. of rain a year. The valley is infamous as the site of the 1692 Massacre of Glencoe, when the Clan MacDonald welcomed a company of Campbell soldiers, henchmen of King William III, into their chieftain's home. After being regaled with music, feasting, and card-playing for two weeks, the Campbells murdered their host and many of his followers as a demonstration to other Scottish clans of the English king's power (MacDonald had been a few days late in signing a loyalty pledge to the crown). Some MacDonalds fled into the hills, a fairy piper allegedly leading their pursuers astray. A sign near Claichaig indicates the site of the massacre. Glen Coe is still known as "the Weeping Glen."

PRACTICAL INFORMATION **Citylink** (tel. (0990) 505050) buses traveling **Glasgow-Fort William** (#914-916, 5 per day) and **Edinburgh-Fort William** (#974, 1 per day) stop in Glencoe. The **Oban-Fort William** service stops at nearby **Ballachulish** (#918, M-Sa 4 per day, Su 1 per day). Another way to see the Glencoe region is by the **Oban & District's coach tour** (tel. (01631) 562856), which starts in Oban, running only if there is interest (4¼hr., F 2-6pm, £7.50, seniors £6.50, children £4.50). Post buses putt daily around the area; get the schedule from the tourist office or hostel.

Glencoe village, essentially one street, rests at the edge of Loch Leven, at the mouth of the River Coe and the western end of Glen Coe. The A82 runs the length of the valley. **Glencoe Visitors Centre** (tel. 811307), operated by the Scottish National Trust, 3 mi. southeast of Glencoe Village on the A82, gives hiking advice, sells maps, and shows a film on the Massacre of Glencoe. (Open daily mid-May to Aug. 9:30am-5:30pm; Apr. to mid-May and Sept.-Oct. 10am-5pm. 50p, students, seniors, and children 30p.) The **tourist office** (tel. 811296), in Ballachulish, 1 mi. west of the village, books accommodations for £1.50 and stores **luggage** for free. (Open Apr.-June M-Sa 9am-5pm, Su 10am-5pm; July-Oct. M-Sa 9am-6pm, Su 10am-5pm.) For bike rental, try **Mountain Bike Hire** (tel. 811252), at the Clachaig Inn, across the river from the Visitors Center (£12.50 per day, £8.50 per half-day). On the A82 on the Ballachulish side of Glencoe, **Glencoe Guides and Gear** (tel. 811402) rents rock- and ice-climbing gear (open M-Sa 9am-6pm, Su 10am-6pm). The **post office** (tel. 811367) sleeps in Glencoe Village at the Scotsman (open M-F 9am-12:30pm and 1:30-5:30pm, W 9am-12:30pm, Sa 9am-12:30pm). The **telephone code** for the entire region is 01855.

ACCOMMODATIONS AND FOOD The agreeable, brown clapboard **SYHA Glencoe** (tel. 811219; fax 811284) rests 2 mi. southeast of Glencoe Village on the east side of the river. (£7.75, under 18 £6.50. Laundry facilities. Check-in 7am-midnight. Curfew midnight. Book 2 days ahead July-Aug. Wheelchair access.) If you hike to the hostel and find it full, you can backtrack 500 yd. to the white-walled **Leacantium Farm Bunkhouse** (tel. 811256). The farm includes three bunkhouses, ranging from basic, (Alpine Barn) to the super-cozy Ben End suite (£6.50-7.50, discounts for week-long stays). The farm's riverside **Red Squirrel Camp Site** (tel. 811256) pitches tents next door (£3.50 per person; under 12 50p; hot showers 50p). The **Clachaig Inn** (tel. 811252), 1 mi. southeast of the hostel and a five-minute walk across a footbridge from the Visitor Centre, serves the best food in the area (£5-9, some vegetarian options, food served noon-4pm and 5-9pm). The public bar is a lively gathering point, especially for the nearby campers and hostelers. (Bar open F 11am-midnight, Sa 11am-11:30pm.) Small but sufficient markets in the Glencoe region include: **The Scotsman** (tel. 811367) in Glencoe Village (open M-Sa 8am-7pm, Su 9am-4pm), and the **Co-op** (tel. 811253) in Ballachulish (open M-W and Sa 8:30am-6pm, Th-F 8:30am-7pm). The SYHA hostel sells very limited groceries.

SIGHTS Glen Coe provides a range of challenges. Walkers stroll the floor of the magnificent cup-shaped valley, rockclimbers head for the cliffs and winter ice-climbers hack their way up frozen waterfalls. Well-equipped and sure-footed hikers, prepared to use hands, knees, and hindquarters, can scramble up **Bidean nam Bian** (3766 ft.) or try the 4 mi. traverse of the **Aonach Eagach** ridge on the north side of the glen. Saner walkers can find the **Lost Valley,** once called the Coire Gubhail—Corrie of Plunder—because the MacDonalds hid their pilfered castle there. The trail follows the stream on the south side of the glen, just west of the Coe Gorge (3hr. round-trip). View-seekers can avoid the 1000 ft. climb on the **Glen Coe Ski Centre Chairlift** (tel. 851226), located off the A82 in the middle of Glen Coe. *(Open July-Aug. daily 9am-5pm; June-Sept. M-F 9am-5pm. £3.75, seniors £3, children £2.50, families £10.)* On a rainy day (year-round, daily), head for the thatch-roofed **Glencoe Folk Museum** in Glencoe Village, which shelters a hodgepodge of old dresses, stuffed birds, puzzle jugs, and a Plunkett Roller Slimming Aid. *(Open Easter-Oct. M-Sa 10am-5:30pm. £1, children 50p.)*

▓ Fort William and Ben Nevis

In 1654, General Monck built Fort William amid Britain's highest peaks to keep out "savage clans and roving barbarians." These days, the town has let down its guard and the surrounding mountains induce, rather than deter, seasonal tidal waves of skiers and hikers. Packed with equipment outfitters, Fort William makes an excellent base camp for mountain excursions. Indeed, thousands each year pass through Fort William on their way to **Ben Nevis** (4406 ft.), the highest peak in Britain. Many tackle Ben Nevis in the morning, then massage their sorry feet in the green grass of the town park, all in time to head to a local pub or *ceilidh* in the evening.

GETTING THERE Fort William shares the magnificent **West Highland Railway** with Oban. Though every West Highland train connects to Edinburgh, the line officially starts at **Glasgow's** Queen St. Station and ends at **Mallaig** on the coast to the west of Fort William (M-Sa 4 per day, Su 2 per day, to Glasgow £30.60, to Mallaig £7). An overnight sleeper train to London's **Euston Station** departs daily (12hr., £129). **Skye-Ways** (tel. (01463) 710119) runs to **Glasgow** (3hr., 4 per day, £9.50), and **Scottish Citylink** (tel. (0990) 505050) ducks to **Kyle of Lochalsh** (1¾hr., 3 per day, £8), **Inverness** (2hr., 5-6 per day, £6), and **Oban** (1¾hr., 2-3 per day, £5.70). **Buses** also run to **Mallaig** (1¾hr., M-Sa 2 per day, £4.50). Pick up complete schedules at the tourist office. Heavy tourist traffic makes Fort William less than a **hitcher's** paradise. To get to the Road to the Isles (see p. 545), hitchers usually walk north and try the intersection of the Fort William road (A82) and the Mallaig road (A830).

ORIENTATION AND PRACTICAL INFORMATION The **train station** (tel. (0345) 484950) seems stuck in the middle of nowhere, but streets full of tourists indicate otherwise. Through a single underpass lies the north end of **High St.,** Fort William's main street. Local **buses** leave from High St. or from the stand opposite the Safeway to the right of the train station. The friendly **tourist office** (tel. 703781), stronger on displays than leaflets, **changes money,** dispenses information on the West Highlands, and dishes the local dirt. (Open May-Sept. M-Sa 9am-8:30pm, Su 9am-6pm; Oct.-Dec.

M-Th 10am-4pm, F 10am-5pm; Jan.-Apr. Sa-Su 10am-1pm.) **ATMs** expectorate cash at the **Bank of Scotland** and **Royal Bank of Scotland,** both on High St.

For mountaineering equipment, good advice, and weather reports from the summits, head to **Nevisport** (tel. 704921), a cathedral of the outdoors at the north end of High St. (open June-Sept. daily 9am-7:30pm; Oct.-May M-Sa 9am-5:30pm, Su 9:30am-5pm), which rents hiking boots (£3.50 per day plus deposit), and a host of maps and literature. **West Coast Outdoor Leisure Centre,** 102 High St. (tel. 705777), rents plastic boots for £5 (open M-Sa 9am-5:30pm, Su 10am-5pm). Across the street, **Off-beat Bikes,** 117 High St. (tel. 704008), rents mountain bikes (£12.50 per day, £8.50 per half-day). To have those wool socks washed, head to the riverside **launderette,** 111 High St. (tel. 705381; open M-F 9am-5pm, Sa 9am-2pm; from £5.70). The **mountain rescue post** (tel. 702361 or 702360), in the **police station** at the south end of High St., has forms to be filled out before climbing Ben Nevis. The **post office** is at 5 High St. (open M-F 9am-5:30pm, Sa 9am-12:30pm). Fort William's **postal code** is PH33 6AA; its **telephone code** is 01397.

ACCOMMODATIONS AND FOOD The **SYHA Glen Nevis** (tel. 702336) stands 3 mi. east of town on the Glen Nevis Rd. (right across from the trail up Ben Nevis). Book well in advance in July and August. (July-Aug. £9.60, under 18 £8.10; Sept.-Oct. and Dec.-June £8.60, under 18 £7.10; open Dec.-Oct.) **Highland Bus and Coach** and **West Highland Motor Service** run from Fort William to the youth hostel and back (M-Sa 14 per day, Su 7 per day; £1). Just five minutes from train, bus, and town, the snug and fun-loving 30-bed **Ft. William Backpackers Guesthouse,** Alma Rd. (tel. 700711), welcomes you with a hot cup of tea and a cozy bed. Elvis has been sighted here, well within the 2am curfew (£10; breakfast £1.40). The **Ben Nevis Bunkhouse** (tel. 702240), at Achintee Farm, sleeps 24 in a 200-year-old wood-paneled granite barn with full kitchen and bathing facilities. The bunkhouse is on the opposite side of the River Nevis from the SYHA hostel, a 2 mi. walk along the Achintee Rd. Though less likely to fill than the official hostel, the bunkhouse still merits reservations in July and August (£8). If all the hostels along the River Nevis are booked, head 4 mi. out of town on the A830 to the **Smiddy Bunkhouse** (tel. 772467) in Corpach. The bunkhouse is immaculately clad in Swedish wood paneling (£8.50, electricity extra). Buses run to Corpach from High St. an amazing 25 times each day (Su 10 per day, 60p, last run 10:25pm); Corpach is also two train stops north.

An early morning walk down Fassifern Rd., behind the Alexandra Hotel, will overpower you with the smell of Scottish breakfasts drifting from the many **B&Bs.** Other B&Bs roost farther up the hill on Alma Rd. and Argyll Rd. At 22 Douglas Pl. off Kennedy Rd. (or up the footpath from Alma Rd.), **Mrs. McKay** (tel. 702473) offers comfortable B&B (£14; less for students in the off-season). The **Glen Nevis Caravan & Camping Park** (tel. 702191) stretches canvas on the Glen Nevis Rd., half a mile before the SYHA hostel (tents £4.60-5.70 plus £1.30 per person; less in off-season; open mid-Mar. to Oct.).

Get provisions from the **Tesco** supermarket at the north end of High St. (open M-W and Sa 8:30am-6:30pm, Th-F 8:30am-7pm, Su 10am-5pm), or aim for the majestic **Safeway** near the train station (open M-W and Sa 8am-8pm, Th-F 8am-9pm, Su 9am-6pm). Before striking out for the hills, grab a packed lunch (juice, 2 filled rolls, cake, fruit, and chocolate for £2.80) at the **Nevis Bakery,** 49 High St. Those eschewing the wilderness can make for the **Garrison,** also at the northern end of High St., which offers daily specials, veggie burgers for £3, and cold, filled rolls from £1.50 (open daily 9am-8pm). Head for the justifiably popular **Ben Nevis Bar and Restaurant,** 103-109 High St. (tel. 702295), for live music at least once a week.

SIGHTS AND ENTERTAINMENT Slickly tourist-oriented as Fort William is, its **West Highland Museum** (tel. 702169), next to the tourist office, is a rustic treasure, with a room full of taxidermy, displays on mountaineering of yore, a stirring Bonnie Prince Charlie exhibit including the famous "Secret Portrait," and an ancient pull-chain toilet (not, strictly speaking, an exhibit). *(Open M-Sa 10am-5pm; shorter off-season hours. £2,* *students and seniors £1.50, children 50p.)* Rock jocks should visit **Treasures of the Earth** (tel. 772283), in Corpach, a fine collection of minerals and gemstones. *(Open daily July-Sept. 9:30am-7pm; Feb.-June and Oct.-Dec. 10am-5pm. £3, seniors £2.75, children £1.50.)*

For the rock-weary, **Marco's An Aird** (tel. 700707), behind Safeway, offers facilities including a 10-pin bowling alley, pool tables, badminton courts, and a bar. *(Open daily 10am-10pm.)* Past Smiddy Alpine Lodge in Corpach sits **Kilmallie Hall,** host of occasional folk-singing and weekly Scottish country dances. *(Mid-June to Aug. M 8-10pm. 75p.)* Buses run frequently from High St.

A few miles up the road past the hostel splash the falls where, on the first Sunday in August, hundreds of businessmen who base their virility on being daredevils rocket down the rapids on tiny air-bed mats during the **Glen Nevis River Race.** On the first Saturday in September, the area hosts the **Ben Nevis Race,** a punishing event in which runners sprint up and down the mountain (you, too, can pick up an entry form at the tourist office). The record time is an incredible 80 minutes. Fort William dons kilts and tosses cabers at the **Lochaber Highland Games** on the last Saturday in July. *Ceilidhs* follow at Marco's An Aird for £3.

HIKING, BIKING, AND CLIMBING On one of the 65 days a year when **Ben Nevis** deigns to lift the veil of cloud from its peak, the unobstructed view spans from Scotland's western coast all the way to Ireland. The interminable switchbacks of the well-beaten tourist trail ascend from the Fort William town park to Ben Nevis's summit; go north a half-mile along the A82 and follow signs for the footpath to Ben Nevis. The hike up takes 3 to 4 hours. A much more arduous ridge walk deviates from the tourist trail when that trail makes a sharp turn to the right near Lochan Meall an t-Suidhe; the experienced can walk parallel to the loch, following a small path by the stream. Leave the path where it descends to Coire Leis and clamber up the steep grass slopes to Carn Dearg Meadhonach; continue to the summit of Carn Mór Dearg. Along the ridge, a trail veers right towards the southeastern slopes of Ben Nevis by a lovely mountain lake; scramble the final 1000 ft. up steep terrain and claim the top of the world. Leave a full 8½ hours for the 9½ mi. round-trip, and don't dare set foot on the trail without weather information, an Ordnance Survey map, a hat, gloves, and warm clothes, a windbreaker, proper footwear, a tank, and plenty of food and drink. See **Wilderness and Safety Concerns,** p. 47, for more info. Okay, maybe not the tank.

Four miles north of Fort William along the A82, the slopes of Aonach Mor (4006ft.) cushion the **Nevis Range** ski area (tel. 705825). Though smaller than the Cairngorm facility, Nevis Range boasts Scotland's longest ski runs and a state-of-the-art **gondola.** *(Open 10am-5pm; longer in summer. Return £6.25, children £4.)* The cable car lifts you 2150 ft. to a restaurant and bar at the base of the trails. Both the gondola and marked hiking trails stay open all year. Buses run year-round from Fort William to the slopes (5 per day, return £2.75-3). **Glen Nevis Rd.,** past the youth hostel, offers glorious biking.

■ Road to the Isles and Mallaig

The scenic **Road to the Isles** ("Rathad Iarainn nan Eilean," now the A830) traverses lochside and mountain valley on its breathtaking journey from Fort William west to Mallaig, on the Sound of Sleet. The **train** ride offers sublime panoramas at a fast clip, while less-frequent **steam locomotives** restore the romance of the grand old days. For the best views, sit on the left side of the train. *(Modern trains run June-Sept. M-Sa 4 per day, Su 3 per day; Oct.-May M-Sa 2 per day, Su 1 per day. £7. Steam locomotives run June-Sept. Su-F. £14.50, return £19.25. BritRail passes not valid; book ahead at any BritRail station. Check in train stations for departure times.)* Two **buses** from Mallaig make the same trip (£4.50). **Hitchers** report sore thumbs on the Road to the Isles.

The road sets off westward from Fort William along Loch Eil, arriving after 12 mi. at **Glenfinnan** (tel. (01397) 722250), on the head of Loch Shiel. A monument recalls August 19, 1745, the day Bonnie Prince Charlie rowed up Loch Shiel and rallied the clans around the Stewart standard in an ill-fated bid to put himself on the British throne. Trains often stop on a nearby bridge for a sentimental gaze and a quick snapshot. After you climb the narrow spiral staircase and squeeze through the hatch at the top, a knee-high railing is all that lies between you and a very short trip to the company of Prince Charlie in the nether region. *Be careful! (£1.50, students, seniors, and children £1. Open daily Apr.-Oct. 9:30am-6pm.)*

At **Lochailort** (Lay-HAY-lort), another 10 mi. west, hikers can step off the train and wander for weeks without encountering another person. The **Lochailort Inn** is literally the only public building and food source for miles. One morning and one afternoon bus (M-F, Sa afternoon only) run south into the desolate districts of Moidart, Ardnamurchan, and Morvern. By planning in advance, you can catch the seasonal ferry to Mull from Kilchoan (Apr. to mid-Oct. M-Sa 7 per day; July-Aug. also Su 5 per day; £3). Connect with the Ardnamurchan-bound bus in Acharacle, 19 mi. south of Lochailort. Between Lochailort and Kilchoan, buses pass **Loch Moidart,** a 1 mi. walk from the nearest bus stop, which opens onto one of western Scotland's most beautiful bays, studded with islets and graced with sandy beaches. The abandoned 13th-century **Castle Tioram** (1mi. walk from the nearest bus stop) was destroyed in 1715 by its owner in an ill-conceived plan to stop his neighbors from moving in while he was off at war. **Kentra Bay,** to the south, welcomes bathers, but there are no lodgings here, and not much of anything else.

From town, head south and then west, *not* west then south, to explore the largely deserted area beneath the Road to the Isles. Drive or take the bus from Fort William along the west side of Loch Linnhe (2hr.), then veer down Gleann Geal to Lochaline. A car ferry from Lochaline skims over to Fishnish on Mull (M-Sa 14-16 per day; Su 9 per day; £1.80). After Lochailort, the Road to the Isles passes **Loch Nan Uamh,** or the Loch of the Caves, the point from which shattered Prince Charlie fled in September 1746, after his brave bid for the crown ended in a whimper.

The road finally meets the west coast at the sandy beaches of **Arisaig.** Murdo Grant (tel. (01687) 450224) operates ferries and day cruises from Arisaig to Rum, Eigg and Muck and does Skye and Canna by charter (£13-17). A 3 mi. walk along the A830 from Arisaig or Morar Station will bring you to a **campsite** near the beach. Dr. Ian Pragnell (tel. (01687) 450272) rents **bikes** (£10 per day) and willingly shares his keen knowledge of local cycling routes.

Across the road and down a short footpath from the campsite, brilliantly white beaches afford arresting views of the Inner Hebrides. Rocky outcrops cut across the sand, creating secluded beach coves accessible only on foot. Don't let nasty stinging jellyfish catch you skinnydipping. Another fine walk follows the banks of **Loch Morar,** Britain's deepest freshwater loch (1017ft.), complete with its own monster, Morag, cousin to Nessie. Cutting over the hills brings you to Tarbert on Loch Nevis.

■ Mallaig

Past Morar looms the relative megalopolis of **Mallaig** (MAL-ig), the small fishing village where cruises and ferries leave for the Inner Hebrides. **Bruce Watt** (tel. 462320) runs ferries and day cruises from Maillaig to **Tarbert** and **Inverie,** both on lovely Loch Nevis (M, W, and F, £7-11), **Rum** and **Canna** (Tu, £15), and Loch Scavaig on the Isle of **Skye** (Th, £15). Book ahead for all cruises. **Cal-Mac** (tel. 462403) skips along from Mallaig to Armadale on **Skye** (see **Getting There,** p. 548) and to the **Small Isles** (see below). The **tourist office** (tel. 462170) sits around the block from the rail station. (Open July-Aug. M-Sa 9am-8pm, Su 10am-5pm; Easter-June and Sept. M-Sa 9am-6:30pm, Su 10am-5pm; mid-Mar. to Easter and late Sept. to mid-Oct. M-Sa 10am-6:30pm.) The **Bank of Scotland** near the station has an **ATM.** The **post office** (tel. 462419) is in a shop up the road from Sheena's (see below; open M-F 9am-5pm, Sa 9am-1pm). Mallaig's **postal code** is PH41 4PU; its **telephone code** is 01687.

Sheena's Backpackers Lodge (tel. 462764), fills fast after early train and ferry arrivals in the summer; book ahead. To find it, turn right from the train station—the lodge is past the bank, above a restaurant Sheena runs. The beds here are roomy enough to sleep two (singles £8.50; doubles £22). **Nevis Stores,** across from the hostel, sells groceries (open M-F 9am-9pm, Sa 9am-5:30pm). The **Fisherman's Mission Café** (tel.

462086), across from the train station, whips up cheap, filling grub. (Pizza £3, lasagne with chips and peas or beans £3.75. Open M-F 8:30am-10pm, Sa 8:30am-noon; hot meals served M-F 8:30am-1:45pm and 5:30-10pm.) Pet the rays at **Mallaig Marine World** (tel. 462292), the town's stellar attraction. Their record-smashing 6½ in. diameter oyster Olive-Ollie changes sex now and then. *(Open July-Aug. M-Sa 9am-7pm, Su 10am-6pm; Sept. to mid-Jan. and early Feb. to June M-Sa 9am-5:30pm, Su noon-5:30pm. Hours may vary. £2.75, students and seniors £2, children £1.50, families £7.50.)*

■ The Small Isles

From the water, they form silent gray-green silhouettes—remote, rugged, and seemingly uninhabited. Lacking roll-on vehicle landing facilities and almost untouched by the hand of tourism, Canna, Muck, Rum, and Eigg often require visitors to jump from their ferry to a small dinghy. Those who make the trip are rewarded with a true taste of island life—jalopies cruise the roads instead of tourist caravans, electricity is provided by generator, seabirds jostle the cattle, and coastline stretches everywhere the eye can see. **Caledonian MacBrayne ferries** (tel. 462403; fax 462281) sail from Mallaig to Rum, Eigg, and Canna and back. There are both non-landing cruises (M 10:30am, Sa 12:30pm, £11.70), and cruises that allow time on the isles (Eigg or Muck: Tu and Th 10:30am, Eigg £7.55, Muck £11.80; Rum or Canna W 10:30am, Rum £11.30, Canna £12.65). **Bruce Watt** (tel. 462320) cruises from Mallaig to Rum and Canna on Tuesday at 10:30am (return £15). **Murdo Grant** (tel. 450224) sails from **Arisaig** (2 train stops from Mallaig) at 11am to **Rum** (Tu and Th year-round, June-Aug. also Sa-Su, return £17), **Eigg** (M-W and F; Easter-Sept. also Sa-Su; return £13), and **Muck** (M, W, and F, return £13). Schedules also vary, so call for information and book ahead. The **telephone code** for all three islands is 01687.

　Rum (also spelled Rhum), the largest island, is owned by National Trust of Scotland and carefully managed by Scottish Natural Heritage. Deer, highland cattle, golden eagles, and rarer creatures are the main residents; the entire human population of Rum emigrated to North America in 1826 during the Highland Clearances, when the laird of the island decided that they presented a threat to his more profitable sheep and sporting deer (today the grand total of full-time residents has risen to about 20). With clearly marked trails and paths, Rum is an excellent place to spend an afternoon (or a week) hiking. A wealthy Lancashire mill owner built **Kinloch Castle** (tel. 462037) on Rum in 1901. An excellent tour of the lavish castle (£3) is offered on Mondays and usually along with Murdo Grant's Tuesday and Thursday cruises to Rum (see above). There is a **hostel** located in back of the castle. *(Advance booking essential. £11.)* To camp on Rum, obtain prior permission from the Chief Warden, Scottish Natural Heritage, Isle of Rum, Scotland PH43 4RR (tel. 462026).

Where Were You When We Were Getting Drunk?

An old Highland saying proclaims that "there are two things a Highlander likes naked, and one is malt whisky." Whisky producers fawn over their ancient distilleries (sometimes refusing to clean them, for fear of losing mysterious but tasty bacteria) and speak dreamily of the Scotch water which feeds them. One malt whisky, Laphroaig's, is said to taste like iodine and is so powerful that some natives violate all propriety and mix it in with oatmeal. The founder of Laphroaig loved the whisky so much that he fell into a vat of it and died.

　With only three ingredients, the whisky-making process seems simple, but the barley, water, and yeast actually undergo an elaborate transformation. **Malting:** The barley is soaked in water until it begins to grow, and then is smoked dry. **Mashing:** Just what you think. The barley is ground into grist and then turned into liquid wort. **Fermentation:** The fun part; here's where the mixture becomes alcoholic. **Distillation:** The low-alcohol liquid passes through large stills to be refined into the strong stuff. Whiskies develop individual qualities at this stage. **Maturation:** The whisky is poured into large oak casks and left alone for a number of years. **Bottling:** From oak to glass, from warehouse to bar.

SCOTLAND

The isle of **Eigg** (pop. about 65) shelters the largest community of the Small Isles. There's a school and Saturday night *ceilidhs,* and everyone knows everyone else's name. Stay a week and they may adopt you. Vertical cliffs overshadow sandy beaches, and black columnar pitchstone juts from lush green hills. There are two places to stay on Eigg: **Kildonan Guesthouse** (tel. 482446; B&B with dinner and lunch £30) and **Laig Farm Guest House** (tel. 482437; self-catering kitchen; B&B £30). Both have comfortable rooms, sea views, and relaxed proprietors. You can camp by the **Singing Sands** on the Bay of Laig (the sands creak underfoot when dry). The only store, in Cleadale, is open irregularly, so bring supplies.

Muck, the tiny (1½mi. by 5mi.) southernmost isle, is an experiment in communal living. The entire island is a single farm owned by the MacEwens, who handle farming, transport along the Muck 1 road, and shopping on the mainland. You can ask to **camp** somewhere near the sandy beach on the island's Atlantic side. Stay with **Mrs. Harper** (tel. 462371; dinner and B&B £22, packed lunch extra), or at **Port Mor Guesthouse** (tel. 462365; dinner and B&B £33). If you intend to muck about outside, bring food, as places to eat or shop are open very sporadically. Miniature **Canna** (which means "porpoise" in Gaelic) offers a few miles of trails for hikers and seabird enthusiasts, but no shops or budget accommodations.

■ Isle of Skye

Skye is often raining, but also fine: hardly embodied; semi-transparent; like living in a jellyfish lit up with green light. Remote as Samoa; deserted, prehistoric. No room for more.

—*postcard from Virginia Woolf*

Often described as the shining jewel in the Hebridean crown, Skye radiates unparalleled splendor from the serrated peaks of the Cuillin Hills to the rugged northern tip of the Trotternish Peninsula. As elsewhere in the Highlands, the 19th-century Clearances saw entire glens emptied of their ancient settlements. Today, as "white settlers" push the English population of the island toward 40%, Skye's traditional Gaelic culture survives mostly in museums and local music events.

The island's natural beauty is by no means a secret; an endless cortège of family-filled Ford Fiestas line Skye's newly completed bridge. But most visitors keep to the main roads, and vast swaths of terrain remain unscarred. Skye's large landmass and spotty, overpriced transportation system will likely force you to concentrate your travels in certain areas of the island. Take the extra time to study the geology of the unusual rock pinnacles on the Trotternish Peninsula, learn the local legends surrounding one of the Cuillins. Whatever you do, save a week for this lovely savage isle.

GETTING THERE With the controversial **Skye Bridge** firmly in place, the tradition of ferries carrying passengers "over the sea to Skye" has come to an end. Pedestrians may now traverse the 1½ mi. footpath, or take the shuttle bus (2 per hr., 55p). Cars no longer need wait in ferry lines, but the one-way bridge toll is a weighty £5.60. A passenger **ferry** (tel. (01599) 534474) still runs between Kyle and Kyleakin (every 15min. M-Sa 9am-6pm, return £1.50, children 75p). **Skye-Ways** (tel. (01599) 534328) and **Scottish Citylink** (tel. (0990) 505050) bus services connect the island to **Glasgow, Fort William,** and **Inverness,** though very infrequently on Sundays. **Trains** (tel. (0345) 484950) from **Inverness** arrive at the Kyle of Lochalsh terminus (tel. (01599) 534205), near the pier (2½hr., M-Sa 4 per day, Su 2 per day). The **MacBackpackers, Haggis Backpackers,** and **Go Blue Banana** minibuses end their northbound route and begin their southbound route at Kyle of Lochalsh (see **Getting About,** p. 455).

From the Outer Hebrides, **Cal-Mac ferries** sail from **Tarbert** on Harris or **Lochmaddy** on North Uist to Uig on Skye (1¾hr., M-Sa 1-2 per day, 5-day return £13.40, children £6.70, return £15.70, children £7.85). Ferries also run from **Mallaig** on the mainland to Armadale in southwestern Skye. For reservations and schedules, call the offices in Uig (tel. (01470) 542219) or Tarbert (tel. (01859) 502444).

GETTING ABOUT Touring Skye without a car takes either effort or cash. **Buses** are infrequent and ruinously expensive (Kyleakin-Broadford £4; Kyleakin-Armadale £5.60). The only decent service hugs the coast from Kyleakin to Broadford to Portree on the A87. On Sundays, nothing runs except **Citylink-Skye Ways, Caledonian Express** long-distance buses, and four buses that meet sailings of the Armadale ferry. Buses on Skye are run by different operators; ask at the tourist office for a complete sheaf of schedules, and be careful not to pay twice when making connections.

Biking is an option, provided you have plenty of rain wear and enjoy miles of steep hills with nearly nonexistent shoulders. Note that buses will not carry bikes. In Kyle of Lochalsh, try **Holiday Hires** (tel. (01599) 534707; £7.50 per day). In Kyleakin **Skye Backpackers** (tel. (01599) 534510; £10 per day) and the **Dun Caan Hostel** (tel. (01599) 534087; £7 per day) offer quality bikes. In Broadford, pedaling options await at **Fairwinds Cycle Hire** (tel. (01471) 822270; £6 per day; £5 deposit), and at the **SYHA** (tel. (01471) 822442; £6 per day). In Portree, try **Island Cycles** (tel. (01478) 613121). In Uig, call **Uig Cycle Hire** (tel. (01470) 542311; £8-10 per day). **Hitching** is fairly easy, and many report that it is the most efficient way to see Skye.

Sutherland's Garage, Broadford (tel. (01471) 822225), rents cars to those 21-70 for a £250 refundable deposit (free collection at Kyleakin; from £30 per day plus 20p per mi. after the first 50). **Ewan MacRae, Ltd.,** Portree (tel. (01478) 612554), rents cars to EU residents over 25 (from £29 per day plus 10p per mi.) In **Kyleakin,** rent cars (tel. (01599) 534431 or 534087) for only £3 per hour or £40 per day.

To see some of Skye's highlights, consider taking a minibus tour: **Nick's Tour** (tel. 534087) leaves from Kyleakin daily at 10:30am (7hr., £12). **Skye Experience** (tel. (01478) 613737 or 612584) offers a similar service from Portree, leaving daily at 10am from the tourist office; pick up from Broadford can be arranged (£15, plus a 50p booking fee). Free guided **walking tours** are offered by Scottish National Heritage and the Highland Council Ranger Service (tel. (01599) 524270).

FESTIVALS In an effort to evade the midges, Skye has developed a vigorous indoor nightlife. Lively traditional music in English and Gaelic is abundant if you know where to look. Snag a copy of the weekly *What, Where and When* leaflet or *The Visitor* newspaper for a list of special events and dances, and look for signs posted in tourist offices and around town. There are frequent local dances—half folk, half rock—at the village halls, usually starting after 11pm (hostelers should note curfews). The **Highland Games,** a mirthful day of bagpipes, foot races, and boozing in Portree on the first Wednesday of August, and the **Skye Folk Festival,** featuring *ceilidhs* in Portree, Broadford, and Dunvegan, during the second week of August, liven up an already lively crowd. Contact tourist offices in Kyle of Lochalsh, Portree, Broadford, and Dunvegan for more information.

■ Kyle of Lochalsh and Kyleakin

Centuries of ferries crossing the strait between Kyle of Lochalsh, on the mainland, and Kyleakin (Kyle-ACK-in), on Skye's southeastern tail fin, have made the twin villages effectively one community. Now permanently connected by the Skye Bridge, the two tiny towns provide plenty of hostels and a gateway to Skye.

The most captivating sights around these two towns lie on the mainland near **Kyle of Lochalsh.** Eight miles east along the A87 on an islet in Loch Duich perches **Eilean Donan Castle** (EL-len DOE-nin or "that KA-sil in HI-lan-der"; tel. (01599) 555202), the restored 13th-century seat of the MacKenzies. Photographs of this castle, connected by a bridge to the mainland, adorn more shortbread boxes and souvenir ashtrays than any other Scottish monument. *(Open daily Apr.-Oct. 10am-6pm. £3, students and seniors £1.75, under 5 free, families £7.)* The view from the hillside behind the castle is more memorable than its restored interior. To reach the castle, take the bus from Kyle of Lochalsh to Inverness, stopping at Dornie, in front of the castle (return £2.50).

Six miles, or two rail stops, north of Kyle of Lochalsh is the lovely village of **Plockton,** with palm trees, a rocky beach, and access to the nearby **Balmacara Estate & Lochalsh Woodland Garden** (tel. (01599) 566325). *(Open 9am-sunset.)* The quiet

Kyleakin harbor is best seen at sunset. Climb to the memorial on the hill behind Castle Moil Restaurant for the best views. A more slippery scramble takes you to the ruins of **Castle Moil** itself. (Cross the little bridge behind the SYHA hostel, turn left, follow the road to the pier, and take the gravel path.) Legend relates that the original castle on this site was built by "Saucy Mary," a Norwegian princess who stretched a stout chain across the Kyle and charged ships a fee to come through the narrows.

The **tourist office** (tel. 534276) overlooking the pier, provides lots of info on B&Bs and books beds on either side of the channel for £1.50-3. (Open June to early Sept. M-Sa 9:15am-7pm, Su 11am-4pm; Apr.-May and mid-Sept. to Oct. M-Sa 9:15am-5:30pm.) Grab groceries at the **Co-op,** beside the post office (open M-Sa 8am-8pm). The last **ATM** for miles stands at the **Bank of Scotland,** Main St. The **post office** is next door (open M-F 9am-5:30pm, Sa 9am-12:30pm). The **postal code** is IV40 8AA; the **telephone code** for both villages is 01599.

Kyle of Lochalsh has only one tiny hostel, **Cu'chulainnsis Backpackers Hostel** (tel. 534492), but the town is full of **B&Bs.** However, the most affordable lodgings cluster in Kyleakin, alongside the park a few hundred yards from the pier. To the right of the pier, the comfy and relaxed **Skye Backpackers** (tel. 534510) offers 78 beds, a natural stone fireplace, and kitchen facilities (£10; breakfast £1.40; laundry service £2.50; curfew 2am). On the pier, the **Dun Caan Independent Hostel** (tel. 534087; fax 534795) provides cozy accommodation for 54 backpackers in co-ed or single-sex rooms of 4-8 bunks, as well as two kitchens and laundry machines (June-Sept. £9.50; Oct.-May £8.50; breakfast £1.50). A Scrabble-whiz warden presides over the large, comfortable, modern **SYHA Youth Hostel** (tel. 534585). The hostel fills *extremely* quickly in the summer, so book weeks ahead. (July-Aug. £9.60, under 18 £8.10; Sept.-May £8.60, under £7.10. Breakfast £2, dinner £4.40. Laundry.) Ask to borrow the hostel's canoe (£5)—a half-hour paddle across the bay and under the bridge takes you to seal territory. The merry mammals may even approach you. Obtain nourishment at the **Pier Coffee Shop** (tel. 534641) in Kyleakin, which serves hearty toasties (£1.75), soup of the day (£1.50), haggis in batter (£3), and "orgasmic" chocolate cake (£1.25; open M-Sa 9:30am-8pm).

■ Southern Skye

The unremarkable town of **Broadford,** located on a silent rocky bay 8 mi. west of Kyleakin, is the hub for all bus transport throughout the southern half of Skye. Two hostels grace the Broadford area: the **SYHA Broadford** (tel. 822442), which lies half a mile from the bus stop along a signposted side road, has soothing harbor views (£7.75, under 18 £6.50; reception 7am-11pm; check-out 9:30am; curfew midnight; open Apr.-Dec.) and tiny **Fossil Bothy** (tel. 822644 or 822297), a renovated stone bunkhouse with room for eight which lies 3 mi. east of Broadford in Lewes, on the coast. The prehistoric creatures trapped in the walls inspired the bothy's name. Book ahead, and bring a sleeping bag (in a pinch they have extras; £7). For food in town, stock up at the **Co-op** (open M-Sa 8am-10pm), or **The Fig Tree** (tel. 822616), near the post office, with a wide selection of filled baguettes (£2), fish and chips (£3.50), and chicken curries (£5.50; open M-Sa 11am-8pm). The **tourist office** (tel. 822361; fax 822141) sits in a parking lot along the bay south of the bus stop. (Open July to mid-Aug. M-Sa 9:30am-7pm, Su 10am-4pm; late Aug. M-Sa 9:30am-5:30pm, Su 10am-4pm; Apr.-June and Sept.-Oct. M-Sa 9:30am-5:30pm.) Five minutes up the road is a blessed **ATM** (accepts Visa, Mastercard, and Cirrus) at the **Royal Bank of Scotland.** The **24-hour convenience store** is open on Sundays; look for the hairy Highland cow model out front. A **launderette** is in the same complex. The **post office** cares for its **postal code,** IV49 9AB (open M-Tu and Th-F 9am-1pm and 2-5:30pm, W and Sa 9am-1pm). Southern Skye's **telephone code** is 01471.

Two miles south of Broadford, the single-lane A851 veers southwest through the thick foliage of the **Sleat Peninsula,** also called "The Garden of Skye." Keep watch for the delicious wild raspberries that grow by the roadside. Seventeen miles of hills bring you to **Armadale,** from which the Mallaig ferries depart, and the 300-year-old

Armadale Castle. *(Open Apr.-Oct. daily 9:30am-5:30pm, last admission 5pm. £3.40, students and seniors £2.20, children 50p.)* The **SYHA Armadale** (tel. 844260), 10 minutes around the bay from the pier, overlooks the water. (£6.10, under 18 £5. Lockout 10:30am-5pm. Curfew 11:30pm. Open mid-Mar. to Oct.) Alternatively, Peter MacDonald, crofter and owner of the **Sleat Independent Hostel** (tel. 844272 or 844440) will pick you up from the ferry and eagerly tell you his clan's history (kitchen, TV; £7; no curfew). Slightly north of Armadale at Ostaig is a Gaelic college, **Sabhal Mor Ostaig** (tel. 844373), which distributes literature on Celtic heritage and offers one-week courses in piping, Gaelic, dance, and fiddling.

■ The Cuillins

The **Cuillin Hills** dominate central Skye from the latitude of Broadford to that of Portree. The smooth, conical Red Cuillins and the rough, craggy Black Cuillins meet in **Sligachan.** The Kyleakin-Portree road wends its way through the Red Cuillins, which rise at dramatic angles from the road and present a bleak and forbidding face to the aspiring hill walker. The highest peaks in the Hebrides, the Cuillin Hills are renowned for hiking paths and fantastic formations of cloud and mist. Legend says the warrior Cuillin was the lover of the Amazon ruler of Skye, who named the hills for him when the ill-fated Cuillin returned to Ireland to die. The booklet *Walks from Sligachan and Glen Brittle* (£2), published by the Skye Mountain Rescue Team and available at tourist offices, offers hiking suggestions. Don't even try hiking without warm, waterproof clothing and an Ordnance Survey map. The best is the 1:25,000 map on the Cuillin and Torridon Hills (£5.75). Consult **Wilderness and Safety Concerns,** p. 47. Expect sopping wet feet; the peat is always drenched and treacherously pitted.

If you have several days, stay at the **SYHA Glenbrittle** (tel. (01478) 640278) in Glenbrittle near the southwest coast, where expert mountaineers can give you advice on exploring the area (£6.10, under 18 £5; open mid-Mar. to Oct.). Campers should head to one of the 200 sites dotting the **Glenbrittle Campsite** (tel. (01470) 521206; £6-7.50 per pitch; open Apr.-Sept.).

Ten miles west of the Cuillins in **Portnalong,** you can stay at the **Croft Bunkhouse** (tel. (01478) 640254). The converted cowshed sleeps 14, and the adjoining section sports a ping-pong table and a Californian dart board (£6). A footpath from Sligachan over the pass to the hostel skirts the 7 mi. walk on the main road. Also in Portnalong is the **Skyewalker Independent Hostel** (tel. (01478) 640250), on Fikavaig Rd., with 34 beds and occasional Jedi Knight training (£7). Below the mountains at the junction of the A863 to Portree and the A850 to Dunvegan is the **Sligachan Campsite** (tel. (01478) 650303), with 80 pitches and showers in an open field across from the hotel in Sligachan (£4 per person; open Easter-Oct.). Across the street, **Seumas' Bar** has a big game room with snooker and serves lovely meals (£3-5; open daily noon-11pm).

A short but scenic path follows the small stream flowing from Sligachan near the campsite to the head of **Loch Sligachan.** After crossing the old bridge, fork left off the main path and walk along the right-hand bank as you go upstream. The narrow and often boggy path leads past pools and miniature waterfalls (3mi. round-trip). In 1899, a fit (and barefoot!) Gurkha soldier ascended and descended **Glamaig,** the arresting 775 yd. oversized anthill to the left, in just 55 minutes. Give yourself 3½ hours, and then only if you feel at ease on steep slopes with unsure footing. Branch off the main trail after about 15 minutes onto the smaller trail which leads up the ridge between the higher peaks, granting views of the ocean and offshore isles.

Experienced climbers might try the ascent into the **Sgurr nan Gillean Corrie,** to the southwest of Glamaig, where the peak rises 3167 ft. above a tiny mountain lake. For more level terrain, take the 8 mi. walk down Glen Sligachan through the heart of the Cuillins to the beach of **Camasunary,** with views of the isles of Rum and Muck.

A less intimate view of the Cuillins unfolds 14 mi. southwest on the A881 from Broadford (a difficult cycle ride) to **Elgol.** You can sail from Elgol to **Loch Coriusk** with **Bella Jane Boat Trips** (tel. (01471) 866244). The trip includes an extraordinary panorama of mountains and water. (Apr.-Oct. daily; call off-season. Return £12.50. Reservations strongly recommended.)

■ Northern Skye

With its busy shops, tree-lined outskirts, and attractive harbor, Skye's capital at **Portree** (pop. 2500) contrasts agreeably with the surrounding rugged wilderness. Bonnie Prince Charlie took shelter with Flora MacDonald here in 1746, Samuel Johnson and James Boswell paid a visit to the divine Miss M. several years later, and tourists have been flocking to Portree ever since, hoping for similar hospitality. Indeed, Portree brims with accommodations, food, and services.

Buses stop at Somerled Sq. The busy **tourist office** (tel. 612137), in the old jail on Bank St. above the harbor, directs wayward tourists to appropriate buses and books accommodations. (£1.50 on Skye, £3 elsewhere, plus 10% deposit. Open July-Aug. M-Sa 9am-8pm, Su 10am-4pm; Sept.-June M-Sa 9am-5:30pm.) Grab some money at the **Bank of Scotland ATM,** Somerled Sq. Portree's **telephone code** is 01478.

An enthusiastic staff and comfy beds await at **Portree Backpackers Hostel,** 6 Woodpark, Dunvegan Rd. (tel. 613641), across from the Co-Op, a 10-minute walk from the center of town along Viewfield Rd. Call and they may pick you up (£8.50; laundry; no curfew). Same name, different **Portree Backpackers** (tel. 613332), rests along the harbor at 2 Douglas Row. It's tiny, laid-back, and has only 10 beds, so book well in advance or come early to save a room (£7.50; sheets £1). The **Portree Independent Hostel,** The Green (tel. 613737), located in the former post office, enjoys a prime location and a spacious kitchen (£8.50; twins £9.50; breakfast £1.50).

The **Safeway** on Bank St. (open M-W and Sa 8am-7pm, Th-F 8am-8pm), **The Bakery** on Somerled Sq. (open M-F 9am-5pm, Sa 9am-4:45pm), and the tiny but well-stocked **Jackson's Wholefoods** (tel. 613326), on Parklane at the end of Wentworth St. (open M-Sa 9am-5pm) should satisfy your portable culinary needs. You can dine in town at the **Café Ice Cream Parlour and Restaurant,** Wentworth St., which offers good pizza and veggie burgers (£2; open M-Sa 9am-5:30pm). Scrumptious culinary concoctions made with organic local produce are created at the **Café Innean** (Anvil Cafe; tel. 613306), located in the An Tuireann Arts Centre; walk up Bridge Rd. and take a left past the Co-Op (about 15min.). Well worth the walk, not least for sinful desserts. (Open daily 10am-5pm, possibly later after special events; call for exact hours.) Seafood restaurants line the harbor: "Janet the Piranha" guards the door to the **fish and chips shop** (tel. 613611), on Quay St., which fries up haddock and chips (£3), Scotch pie (£1.10), and haggis (£1.20; open daily 11am-10:30pm; take-away only).

Thanks to two scenic circular roads and miles of quiet shoreline, the northern part of Skye is able to support more tourists than the rest of the island. The northwestern circuit follows the A850 from Portree to Dunvegan Castle, then down the A863 along the gorgeous west coast; the northeastern circuit hugs the A855 and A856 around the **Trotternish Peninsula** through Uig and Staffin and back to Portree. **Dunvegan Castle** (tel. (01470) 521206), the seat of the clan MacLeod, is well worth a visit. The **Fairy Flag,** more than 1300 years old and looking rather tattered of late, is swathed in clan legend; several stories of its origin persist. Samuel Johnson and James Boswell paid a visit in 1773 on their tour of the Hebrides. Johnson sent a nice thank-you note: "the kind treatment which I have found wherever I go makes me leave with some heaviness of heart an island which I am not likely to see again." *(Castle open daily late Mar. to Oct. 10am-5:30pm; Nov.-Mar. 11am-4pm. £4.80, students and seniors £4.20, children £2.60; gardens only £3.50, children £1.80; buses run from Portree.)*

Northeast of Portree, the A855 snakes along the east coast of the Trotternish Peninsula, past the **Old Man of Storr,** a finger of black rock visible for miles around, and the **Quirang,** a group of spectacular rock pinnacles readily accessible by foot. Nearby **Staffin Bay** offers remarkable views of Skye and the mainland, while **Kilt Rock** bears lava columns similar to those on the isle of Staffa. Strong, well-shod walkers might hike the **Trotternish Ridge,** which runs the length of the peninsula from the Old Man of Storr to Staffin; the challenging and rewarding 12 mi. hike takes about a day.

The ruins of **Duntulm Castle** guard the tip of the peninsula. The castle was the MacDonalds' formidable stronghold until a nurse dropped the chief's baby boy from the window to the rocks below, thereby drawing a curse onto the house. Near Duntulm at Kilmuir, the **Skye Museum** (tel. (01470) 522206), in a village of tiny, 200-year-old black houses, recreates old crofter life. *(Open Easter-Oct. M-Sa 9:30am-5:30pm. £1.75, students £1.50, seniors £1.25, children 75p.)* Nearby, **Flora MacDonald's Monument** pays tribute to the Scottish folk hero who sheltered Bonnie Prince Charlie. Get some R&R in the woods at the **Dun Flodigarry Backpackers Hostel** (tel./fax (01470) 552212), 5 mi. north of Staffin (£7.50).

The town of **Uig** (OO-ig) flanks a windswept bay on the peninsula's west coast, the terminus for ferries to the Outer Hebrides and the final resting place for most long-distance buses from Glasgow and Inverness. The **SYHA Uig** (tel. (01470) 542211) is a tough 45-minute walk on the A586 from the ferry. From the kitchen, gaze at the stunning views of the bay as a dozen fellow hostelers crash into you, trying to use the sink (£6.10, under 18 £5; lockout 9:30am-5pm; open mid-Mar. to Oct.).

■ Outer Hebrides

The landscape of the Outer Hebrides is astoundingly ancient. Much of the exposed rock here has been around for about three billion years, more than half as long as the planet itself. The island's distant past has deposited a rich sediment of ruined tombs and standing stones, including the remarkable stone circle at Callanish on Lewis. The culture and customs of the Hebridean people have also resisted change: the roads are still one-lane, and scattered family crofts remain the norm on the Uists. Although television and tourism have diluted traditional Hebridean speech and ways of life, most islanders speak Gaelic among themselves, and learning the language has become mandatory in schools. In recent years, the area has suffered from emigration, as more and more young people seek work on the mainland.

The strongly Calvinist islands of Lewis, Harris, and North Uist observe the Sabbath strictly. On Sundays, all shops, pubs, and restaurants close, and public transportation grinds to a halt; even the playground swings are chained. Throughout Benbecula, South Uist, and Barra, tight-shuttered Protestant sabbatarianism gives way to Catholic chapels and commemorative plates of the Pope on living room walls. Religion is a source of contention and sometimes hostility among the islanders.

According to a local legend, Bafinn, a Norwegian princess, rests in a 3000-year slumber under a knoll 3 mi. from Lochmaddy on North Uist. When she wakes, the weather on the Outer Isles will improve. Until then, expect a regular riot of high winds and rain. In summer, the weather is usually milder, and the late-evening sunsets huge and enveloping.

GETTING THERE AND GETTING ABOUT

Three major **Caledonian MacBrayne** services ferry travelers out, and ferries and infrequent buses connect the islands lengthwise. **Cycling** is excellent provided you like the challenge of the hills in the wind and don't melt in the rain. Though traffic is light, **hitchers** report frequent rides. You can rent a **car** inexpensively (from £20 per day) at **Mackinnon Self Drive,** 18 Inaclete Rd. (tel. (01851) 702984), in Stornoway, or **Peter Brown Car Hire** (tel. (01871) 810243), in Barra, but they'll probably prohibit you from taking it on ferries. Except in bilingual Stornoway and Benbecula, all **road signs** are now in Gaelic only. Tourist offices often carry translation keys, and *Let's Go* lists Gaelic equivalents after English place names. For more insight into the islands, snag a copy of *The Outer Hebrides Handbook and Guide* (£8 at all tourist offices). For up to date transport information, consult the *Skye and Western Isles Public Transport Travel Guide* (£1 at tourist offices).

ACCOMMODATIONS

Since ferries arrive at odd hours, try to arrange a bed ahead. In addition to two **SYHA hostels,** the Outer Hebrides are home to the unique **Gatliff Hebridean Trust Hostels** (Urras Osdailean Nan Innse Gall Gatliff), four 19th-century thatched croft houses turned into simple year-round hostels whose authenticity and atmosphere more than compensate for the basic facilities (bring a sleeping bag, knife, and fork). These hostels (all £4.65, under 18 £3.85) are affiliated with SYHA and are located at the tip of North Uist in **Berneray,** in **Howmore** on South Uist, in **Garenin** on Lewis, and in **Rhenigidale** on Harris. No advance bookings are accepted, but they never turn travelers away. Refer to the SYHA handbook for details. A tourist office will book you **B&B** for £1. **Camping** is allowed on public land in the Hebrides, but freezing winds and sodden ground often make it miserable.

■ Lewis (Leodhas)

Relentlessly remote and desolate, the landscape of Lewis is flat, treeless, and speckled with quiet lochs among long rectangles of crofters' plots. This island is famous for its atmosphere—photographs fail to convey the strange aura of the place. Pure light and drifting mists off the Atlantic shroud untouched miles of moorland and the right angles of half-cut fields of peat. The unearthly setting is a fitting one for exploring Lewis's many archaeological sites, most notably the Callanish Stones.

■ Stornoway

Stornoway (Steornobhaigh) is unlike anything else in the Outer Hebrides. Its artificially forested bay and small industrial and fishing centers contrast vividly with the rolling tracts of countryside around it. With a population of 8000, it's the largest town in northwestern Scotland, with a post office and some shops.

Though most of Lewis's sights huddle in the outlying countryside, Stornoway has a few attractions of its own. The **An Lanntair Gallery** (tel. 703307), in the Town Hall on South Beach St., hosts art exhibits and events including musical and historical evenings. *(Open M-Sa 10am-5:30pm. Free.)* Lewis has appropriated the Harris Tweed industry from its southern neighbor; although mill shops are no longer open to visitors, crofters often vend from their homes. If Stornoway brings too much human companionship, meander through **Lews Castle,** northwest of town (entrance on Cromwell St.). Built in the 19th century by a merchant and opium smuggler, the castle now sequesters a college. Admire it from across the water at the end of North Beach St. or get to a clearing by turning left after the footbridge from New St.

The Stornoway **tourist office,** 26 Cromwell St. (tel. 703088), offers the usual; turn left from the ferry terminal, then right onto Cromwell (open Mar.-Sept. M-Sa 9am-6pm and 8-9pm; Oct.-Feb. M-Sa 9am-5pm). The office also books **coach tours** of Lewis. A **Westside Rover** bus ticket (£4.50) is a convenient way to see most of the major sights. **Stornoway Trust** (tel. 704733) organizes outstanding, informative, and free **walks** of Stornoway and the countryside, as well as private vehicle tours (Apr.-Oct.; depart from the tourist office). An **ATM** welcomes customers next to the post office at **TSB Bank,** and next to the **Co-op** at the Bank of Scotland. **Erica's Laundrette,** 46 Macaulay Rd. (tel. 704508), is the only one in Harris and Lewis, and a bit of a walk (open M-Tu and Th-Sa 9am-3pm). *Everything* is closed on Sunday. The **post office** sorts at 16 Francis St. (open M-F 9am-5:30pm, Sa 9am-12:30pm). The **postal code** is HS1 2AD, the **telephone code** 01851.

The **Stornoway Backpackers Hostel,** 47 Keith St. (tel. 703628), welcomes travelers just 5 minutes from the pier; turn left onto Shell, which becomes South Beach, then turn right on Kenneth St.; take the second right on Church and the first left on Keith St. Managed by windsurfing wonder-wardens, this relaxed 18-bed hostel includes free tea, coffee, and cereal and is always open (£8). **Mr. and Mrs. Hill** (tel. 706553) offer comfortable B&B at "Kerry Croy" on Robertson Rd.; from the tourist office head up Church St. and turn left onto Matheson Rd. Robertson Rd. is on the right (£18). For those departing on early ferries, many **B&Bs** oblige with a crack-of-dawn breakfast.

Cheap food is easy to come by in Stornoway. **Bodyline Shop** (Nature's Store), 5 Cromwell St. (tel. 702255), sells desirable wholefoods. (Magnesium-rich chocolates! Open M-Tu and Th-Sa 9am-1pm and 2-5:45pm.) Grab groceries at **Safeway,** on Shell St. (open M-Tu and Sa 8am-8pm, W-F 8am-9pm). More central, but slightly smaller is the **Co-op,** on Cromwell St. (open M-Sa 8am-7pm). The An Lanntair Gallery (above) also houses the town's best **cafe** (smoked salmon roll £2, jacket potatoes from £2; closes 30min. before gallery). **The Crown Inn,** on the corner of N. Beach and Castle St., offers reasonably priced food and drink, and has a pool table (open M-W 11am-11pm, Th-F 11am-midnight, Sa 11am-11:30pm). Try **Peking Cuisine,** 30 Church St. (tel. 705548), for Chinese take-away. (Open M-W noon-2pm and 5-11:30pm, Th noon-2pm and 5pm-midnight, F noon-1am, Sa noon-11:30pm.)

SIGHTS

Lewis is home to the impressive **Callanish Stones** (Calanais), 14 mi. west of Stornoway on the A858. Second only to Stonehenge in grandeur and a thousand times less overrun, the speckled greenish-white stones were hewn from Lewisian gneiss, the three-billion-year-old rock hidden beneath the island's peat bogs. Local archaeologists believe that prehistoric peoples used the stones to track the movements of the moon, employing complex trigonometry and displaying a level of technical knowledge still unavailable to the Greeks 2000 years later. Others are skeptical, but admit that the circle may have been designed by primitive astronomers. The Visitor Centre (tel. 621422; fax 621446) has a comprehensive exhibit. *(Open M-Sa Apr.-Sept. 10am-7pm; Oct.-Mar. 10am-4pm.)* Local writer Gerald Ponting has published thorough guides to Callanish and 20 neighboring sites with explicit directions (40p-£4; available in the tourist office and local stores). Take the Carloway bus (4-6 per day, £1.35) from the Stornoway bus station and ask the driver to let you off by the stones. One mile before Callanish, post buses snake off along the B8011 across the bridge to **Great Bernera** (Bearnaraigh), flanked by dozens of deserted islets, and 20 mi. farther west to the surprisingly lush **Glen Valtos** and the expansive sands at **Timsgarry.**

On the A858 five miles north of Callanish is **Carloway** (Carlabhaigh), a crofting town dominated by the imposing 2000-year-old **Dún Carloway Broch,** an Iron Age tower with a partially intact staircase and a breathtaking view of the surrounding hills and lochs. Once it would have protected farmers and their cattle from Viking raiders—now it shelters tourists from high winds. Watch your footing on the broch; a sudden gust of wind may bring you closer to the surrounding landscape than you'd like (free; always open). The Gatliff Trust-SYHA thatched-roof 14-bed **Garenin Youth Hostel** (Na Gearranan), a converted black house, rests 1½ mi. from Carloway. The hostel has a kitchen and hot shower and overflows with atmosphere. A free taxi service meets some buses and will deliver you to the door (£4.65, under 18 £3.85).

North of Carloway in **Shawbost,** visit the **Shawbost School Museum.** Most of the museum's contents, including remarkable paintings and narratives of island life, have been created over the years by the children of Lewis. *(Open M-Sa roughly 9am-6pm. Free.)* Beyond Shawbost on the A858, the **Arnol Black House** (tel. (01851) 710395) is a restored thatched-roof crofter's cottage. A chimney was intentionally left out, as smoke from the peat fire was supposed to conserve heat and improve the thatch by seeping through the roof—hence the name. Inhale a hearty lungful of peat smoke and get a watery-eyed glimpse of the dim interior. *(Open Apr.-Sept. M-Sa 9:30am-1pm and 2-6:30pm; Oct.-Mar. M-Sa 9:30am-1pm and 2-4:30pm. £1.80, seniors £1, children 75p.)*

Too Much Whisky in That Water

In 1831, an otherwise brave man was walking along the dunes of West Lewis, bracing himself against a heavy wind. Suddenly a hard gale tripped him up and, as he regained balance, he witnessed a tribe of small, grim figures rising menacingly from the sand at his feet. Dashing off in fright, he returned to tell his family and friends about his perilous encounter in the Kingdom of Fairies. Actually, he had witnessed nature's form of an archaeological dig: the "tribe" was a set of walrus-tooth gamepieces left behind by ancient Vikings, who also weren't from the Kingdom of Fairies. Today the **"Lewis Chessmen"** can be seen at the Museum of Antiquities in Edinburgh. A native exhibit on the subject is on Francis St. at the Museum nan Eilean (tel. 703773). *(Open Apr.-Sept. M-Sa 10am-5:30pm; Oct.-Mar. Tu-F 10am-5pm, Sa 10am-1pm.)*

SCOTLAND

Farther north, across splashes of grassy moor and scattered villages, lies the **Butt of Lewis** (Rubha Robhanais), the island's northernmost point. A lighthouse on the disintegrating cliffs overlooks beaches below. It is a bleak but beautiful butt, and at night you can hear the growl of the corncrake, a rare and elusive bird.

Buses from Stornoway run frequently around Lewis; the bus station has schedule info. Destinations include **Tarbert** (An Tairbeart) on Harris (M-Sa 3-4 per day, £2.40), and **Ness** (Nis), **Callanish** (Calanais), and **Carloway** (Carlabhaigh) on Lewis. Routes cover all of Lewis's major sights. The island's relatively flat roads are good for **biking**—Pentland Rd. from Stornoway to Carloway earns raves. Check the weather forecasts; on a gusty day you may even have to pedal hard downhill. Rent bikes in Stornoway at **Alex Dan's Cycle Centre,** 67 Kenneth St. (tel. 704025; open M-Sa 9am-6pm; £2 per hr., £5 per day, £25 per week). **Caledonian MacBrayne ferries** from Ullapool on the northwest coast of the mainland serve Stornoway (M-Sa 2-3 per day, £12, return £21).

■ Harris (Na Hearadh)

Although Harris is technically part of the same island as Lewis, it might as well be on Pluto. Lewis is mainly flat and watery, while Harris, formed by volcanic gneiss, has an unkempt ruggedness unique to Scotland. Behind the barricade of the treeless **Forest of Harris** (actually a mountain range), the island's steely-grey mountains, splotched with grass, boulders, and heather, descend on the west coast to brilliant crescents of yellow beaches bordered by indigo waters and *machair*—sea meadows of soft green grass and brilliant flowers in summer. In the 19th century, these idyllic shores were cleared for sheep grazing and the islanders moved to the boulder-strewn waste of the east coast. They responded to the area's complete lack of arable land by developing still-visible "lazybeds," furrowed masses of seaweed and peat compost laid on bare rock. The island's main road, the A859, bumps through the mountains from Tarbert to Stornoway. The **Golden Road** (so named because of the king's ransom spent in blasting it from the rock) twists from Tarbert to Harris's southern tip via the desolate east coast and makes a harrowing bus trip or grueling bike ride. From Tarbert, small roads branch east and west toward the small fishing community on the island of **Scalpay** (Scalpaigh) and the deserted Isle of Scarp, where a mad German scientist launched an ill-fated rocket-powered postal service to the Western Isles in 1934.

The largest peaks on Harris lie within the Forest of Harris. The main entrances to the Forest are off the B887 to Huisinish Point, at **Glen Meavaig** and farther west at **Amhuinnsuidhe Castle,** a Victorian building erected in 1863 (about 15mi. from Tarbert). If you don't have time for exhaustive exploration, hop any fence just outside Tarbert and hike up **Gillaval Glas** (1554ft.), which overlooks the town and harbor islands. The view from the top is stupendous, if you survive the climb. Bring appropriate clothing and give yourself a full afternoon. The hills of South Harris are smaller, but just as rugged. An enjoyable daytrip might involve wandering down the coast-to-coast path that begins on the east coast at the crofts of Ardvey (the tip of Loch Stockinish) and passes 1 mi. north of the Stockinish Youth Hostel. After exploring the mountains, head down to **Rodel** (Roghadal), at Harris's southern tip, site of **St. Clement's Church.** Peek at the three MacLeod tombs; the principal one, built in 1528, is hewn from local black gneiss. Up the road is **Leverburgh,** with a few houses, a tea shop, and the ferry to Otternish on North Uist (M-Sa 3-4 per day, £4.30, return £7.30).

■ Tarbert

Tarbert (An Tairbeart) straddles a narrow isthmus that divides the island into North Harris and South Harris. As the population center of Harris, the town offers the greatest concentration of amenities, including a supply of B&Bs. **Ferries** serve Tarbert from Uig on Skye (1-2 per day, £7.85, return £13.40). Check with **Caledonian MacBrayne Ferries** (tel. 502444), in Tarbert at the pier, for schedule information. A ferry runs from Otternish on North Uist to Leverburgh (An T-ob) at Harris's southern end (M-Sa 2-4 per day, £4.30, return £7.30). From Otternish, you can also reach Berneray (Bearnaraigh), a small island off North Uist (M-Sa 8-11 per day, 90p, return £1.55). Call Lochmaddy (tel. (01876) 500337) for details. Cal-Mac also runs a ferry service between Kyles Scalpay (Caolas Scalpaigh) and the nearby island of Scalpay (M-Sa 12 per day, £1.65).

From Tarbert, **buses** (tel. 502441) run to both Stornoway and Leverburgh (M-Sa 2-3 per day, £1.50) and to Stockinish and Flodabay (M-Sa 1 per day). The beguiling nothingness of the Harris landscape is best seen by **bike** (mountain bike £6 per day, £25 per week; touring bike £5 per day, £20 per week; rent from **D.M. Mackenzie** (tel. 502271) across from the tourist office in Tarbert. Car traffic is sparse, although **hitchhikers** report luck with the few cars that rumble by. **Hiking** is agreeable; the treeless landscape presents little risk of getting lost. Marked trails are scarce, though; be sure to bring a compass, sturdy boots, and an Ordnance Survey map.

A cheerful **tourist office** (tel. 502011) sits on Pier Rd. (open early Apr. to mid-Oct. M-Sa 9am-5pm and for late ferry arrivals). The Bank of Scotland sits uphill from the pier, sadly without ATM (open M-F 9am-12:30pm and 1:30-5pm, W opens at 10am). The **post office** also rents movies (but no TVs or VCRs, ha ha...*ha ha*) at Main St. (Open M-Tu and Th-F 9am-1pm and 2-5:30pm, W 9am-1pm, Sa 9am-12:30pm. *Ha ha ha ha ha!*) The **phone code** is 01859.

Effie MacKinnon's huge rooms rest in **Waterstein House** (tel. 502358) across from the tourist office (£14, with meals £20). The nearest **SYHA Youth Hostel** (tel. 530373) is 7 mi. south along the east coast in **Stockinish** (Stocinis). It's an old school overlooking the dramatic east coast of Harris (£4.65, under 18 £3.85; open mid-Mar. to Sept.). A substantial hike from Tarbert in North Harris, the **Gatliff Trust-SYHA Hostel** at **Rhenigidale** (Reinigeadal) can be reached by road: follow the turnoff to Maaruig (Maraig) from the A859 (13mi. from Tarbert; see **Accommodations**, p. 553). The foot trip from Tarbert is shorter (6mi.) but arduous—take the road towards Kyles Scalpay for 2 mi., then follow the signposted path to Rhenigidale. The path takes you up 850 ft. for stunning views and a sore back before zig-zagging down very steeply (£4.65, under 18 £3.85). **A.D. Munro**, just up from the tourist office, serves Tarbert as grocer, butcher, and baker (open M-Sa 7:30am-6pm). The **Firstfruits Tearoom** (tel. 502439), next door to the tourist office, ladles out tasty soups of the day. (£1.65; open June-Aug. M-Sa 10:30am-6:30pm; Apr.-May and Sept. 10:30am-4:30pm; Oct.-Mar. M-Sa 11:30am-3:30pm.) The **Harris Hotel** (tel. 502154), which serves lunches (£5) and pints (£1.80) in its bar across the road from the main building, has average food and service slower than the speed of light, but come Sunday, it's all you've got (meals served daily noon-8:30pm).

■ The Uists (Uibhist)

The Uists (YOO-ists) take Lewis's flatness to an extreme. Save for a thin strip of land along the east coast, these islands are almost completely level, packed with so many lochs that it's difficult to distinguish where the islands end and the ocean begins. A rare shard of sunlight reveals a strange world of thin-lipped beaches, crumbling black houses, wild jonquils, and quiet streams. The survival of the crofting system has led to a tiny, decentralized population. The main villages of **Lochmaddy** (Loch nam Madadh) on **North Uist** (Uibhist a Tuath) and **Lochboisdale** (Loch Baghasdail) on **South Uist** (Uibhist a Deas) are but glorified ferry points. Small **Benbecula** (Beinn na Faoghla) lies between its two larger neighbors, and possesses the Uists' sole airport. Crossing from North Uist to South Uist, strict Calvinism gives way to celebratory Roman Catholicism. Although Sunday remains a day of church-going, secular public activity is much more acceptable here than in the north.

PRACTICAL INFORMATION Caledonian MacBrayne **ferries** float from **Uig** on Skye to **Lochmaddy** (1¾hr., 1-2 per day, £7.85). The Uig-Lochmaddy ferry also connects with **Tarbert** on Harris (see **Harris**, p. 556, for details). A ferry drifts from **Otternish** to **Leverburh** on Harris (M-Sa 2-4 per day, £4.30). Ferries run from **Oban** to **Lochboisdale** (M-Sa 1 per day; £17.30), some stopping at **Castlebay** on **Barra** on the way.

All modes of transportation are scarce. For car rental, call **Maclennan's Self Drive Hire,** Balivanich, Benbecula (tel. (01870) 602191; from £22.50 plus tax and gas). **Post buses** inch between Lochmaddy and Otternish, Balivanich Airport, Locheport, and other communities (1 per day M-Sa). **Hebridean Coaches** (tel. (01870) 620345) cross between Lochmaddy and Lochboisdale and between Lochboisdale and Ludag (M-Sa). They also connect with the post bus at Balivanich Airport for Lochboisdale. Pick up a schedule in either tourist office. Many buses offer student discounts if you ask. Access to the moorland is free, but there are few well-marked footpaths. The Uists' few drivers are often friendly to **hitchers,** but not on Sundays, when it's rude to ask.

Tourist offices on the piers at Lochmaddy (tel. (01876) 500321) and Lochboisdale (tel. (01878) 700286) book accommodations (both open Apr. to mid-Oct. about 9am-5pm). Lochboisdale has a **Royal Bank of Scotland** (open M and Th-F 9:30am-4:30pm, W 10:30am-4:30pm) and Lochmaddy a **Bank of Scotland** (open M-Tu and Th-F 9:30am-4:30pm, W 10:30am-4:30pm; closed 12:30-1:30pm). The closest **ATM** (tel. (01870) 602044) is at the bank in Benbecula. **Uist Laundry** (tel. (01870) 602876) is by Balivanich Airport, Benbecula (open M-F 8:30am-5pm, Sa 9am-1pm).

ACCOMMODATIONS AND FOOD

The **SYHA Lochmaddy** (tel. (01876) 500368), half a mile from the pier along the main road, overlooks a garden and a small bay. (£6.10, under 18 £5. Lockout 10:30am-5pm. Curfew 11:30pm. Open mid-May to Sept.) About a quarter mile behind the youth hostel is the **Uist Outdoor Centre** (tel. (01876) 500480), which offers cheap accommodations at night and water sports during the day. Bring a sleeping bag, stay for £6 (linen £2), and enjoy the miraculous showers. Both the Hostel and the Outdoor Centre are popular with large groups in the summer, so book ahead. The Uists' other hostel is the very basic **Gatliff Hebridean Trust-SYHA** croft house at **Howmore** (Tobha Mòr), South Uist. Follow the signpost 1 mi. west from the A865. The hostel has thatched roofs, cold-water taps, and coin-operated electricity (£4.65, under 18 £3.85; see **Accommodations,** p. 553).

B&Bs are often tiny and difficult to reach. In Lochboisdale, **Mrs. MacLellan,** Bay View (tel. (01878) 700329; £16-18) and **Mrs. MacDonald,** Kilchoan Bay (tel. (01878) 700517; £15 per person), are close to the pier. You can camp almost anywhere, but, as always, ask the crofters. The cheapest **food stores** on the islands are the Co-ops in Sollas (Solas) on North Uist, Creagorry (Creag Ghoraidh) on Benbecula, and Daliburgh (Dalabrog) on South Uist. The bar at **Lochmaddy Hotel** (tel. (01876) 500331) serves up tasty pub grub (£4-8.50; food served noon-2pm and 6-9pm). Across the street from the hotel, the small **Café Taigh Chearsabhagh** (tel. (01876) 500293) sells baked goods and sandwiches (£2-3; open M-Sa 10am-5pm).

SIGHTS

The A865 runs all along the Uists past a number of historical sites visually indistinguishable from the surrounding landscape. South Uist has paltry attractions, centered around the birthplace of Flora MacDonald at **Kildonan.** Benbecula holds the scanty remains of the 14th-century **Borve Castle,** which was burned down in the 18th century by clansmen in a show of support for George II. Farther north on the B892, the road passes splendid beaches to the west, arriving at **Nunton,** former spiritual home to nuns massacred during the Reformation. In Culla Bay, where the nuns were tied and left to drown, the seaweed grows on the rocks in the shape of hands.

On the southern tip of North Uist at **Carinish** lie the ruins of 13th-century **Trinity Temple,** probably the islands' most noteworthy building. It once housed a medieval college where the great scholar Duns Scotus is said to have pondered the eternal questions. Two miles past the Locheport Rd. on the A867 is the chambered cairn, **Bharpa Langass,** which dates back 3000 years to the Neolithic Age. Bird-watchers head for the **Balranald Reserve** on the western part of North Uist, north of Bayhead (signposted "RSPB"). May and June are the best months for observation, but you'll almost always see lapwings, oyster-catchers, and rare red-necked phalaropes.

For vistas of loch and moor, hop over the roadside fence and climb **Blashaval Hill,** a short walk west of Lochmaddy on the A865. The road continues in a circle around

SCOTLAND

North Uist, passing **Sollas's** wide sandy beaches, **Scolpaig's** sea-carved arches, and **Tigharry,** site of Sloc a'Choire, a spouting cave and hollow arch. It is said that a young lass once hid in the arch rather than marry the man to whom her parents had betrothed her; you can still hear her cries echoing inside.

■ Near the Uists: Berneray and Eriskay

The diminutive island of **Berneray** (Beàrnaraigh), off the north coast of North Uist, is a favorite rustic retreat of Prince Charles and home to the best-equipped of the **Gatliff Trust hostels,** a beautifully thatched and whitewashed affair set on the windswept eastern tip of the island (£4.65, under 18 £3.85; see **Accommodations,** p. 553). Chuck drops in now and again. You can easily walk the 8 mi. circumference. A bridge connecting North Uist and Berneray is scheduled to be completed by 1999.

On February 4, 1941, with strict wartime alcohol rationing in effect all over Scotland, *S.S. Politician* foundered on a reef off the isle of **Eriskay** (Eiriosgaigh), between South Uist and Barra, while carrying 207,000 cases of whisky to America. The concerned islanders mounted a prompt salvage, and Eriskay hasn't been the same since. There are several daily sailings (M-Sa) between Ludag on South Uist and Eriskay. The local pub, the **S.S. Politician,** displays some of the original bottles.

■ Barra (Barraigh)

Little Barra, the southern outpost of the outer isles, is unspeakably beautiful, a composite of moor, *machair,* and beach. On a sunny day, the island's colors are unforgettable; sand dunes and beaches crown waters flecked shades of light-dazzled blue, wreathed below by dimly visible red, brown, and green kelp. The best times to visit are May and early June, when the primroses bloom, and gardens and hills explode in pink and yellow. Believed to be named after St. Findbar of Cork, the island is also the ancient stronghold of descendants of the Irish O'Neils. As late as the 16th century, the Catholic islanders sailed to Ireland for religious festivals.

Kisimul Castle, bastion of the old Clan MacNeil, inhabits an islet in Castlebay Harbor. It lay in ruins for two centuries until Robert Lister MacNeil, an American architect who was the 45th chief of the MacNeils, restored it. The castle's most interesting features are a dungeon, guard chamber (including the first "self-flushing" toilet in Scotland, courtesy of waves dashing the rocks below), and superb views of Stornoway and Vatersay through the battlements. *(Boat trips out M, W, and Sa 2-5pm. £3 includes castle admission.)* To the west of Castlebay, near **Borve** (Borgh), one squat **standing stone** remains visible. Locals say the standing stones were erected in memory of a Viking galley captain who lost a bet with a Barra man; Scandinavian archaeologists who excavated the site did indeed find a skeleton and Nordic armor. A chambered cairn, **Dún Cuier,** north of **Allasdale** (Allathasdal), is opposite a roadside cemetery. **Seal Bay,** opposite Allasdale, is an excellent spot for a picnic. Bring some herring and make a friend.

On the north coast, the huge beach of **Traigh Mhor** provides a spectacular landing spot for daily Loganair flights to Glasgow. Farther north in **Eoligarry** is **Cille Bharra Cemetery.** Still in use, it contains "crusader" headstones engraved with weapons, a galley, and animals thought to have served as ballast in the warship of a clan chief. Inside the neighboring low-ceilinged **St. Barr's Church,** step through shrines, Celtic crosses, and Norman stones, as pilgrim candles flicker through the dust.

A causeway connects Barra to the small island of **Vatersay** (Bhatarsaigh), the southernmost inhabited island in the Outer Hebrides. Check out its scenic beaches and the monument to the *Annie Jane,* a ship that sunk off Vatersay in 1853 while carrying 400 would-be emigrants to Canada. Bird-watchers should visit the deserted island of **Mingulay;** at the Isle of Barra Hotel, **George MacLeod** (tel. (01871) 810223) makes two trips each week in good weather in summer.

A **Cal-Mac ferry** (tel. (01878) 700288) stops at Castlebay (Bagh A Chaisteil) on Barra, on its way between **Oban** or **Mallaig** on the mainland and **Lochboisdale** on South Uist (5-6hr. to Oban, Tu, Th-F, Su 1 per day, £17; 1¾hr. to Lochboisdale, M, W-

Th, and Sa 1 per day, £5). The tiny 12-passenger ferry (tel. (01878) 720265) from **Ludag** on South Uist also runs to **Eoligarry** (Eolaigearraidh) on Barra (times change daily; £4.50, children £2.25, bicycle £2). Phone the **tourist office** (tel. (01878) 720233) for more information. **Hebridean Coaches** (tel. (01870) 620345) run from the **airport** on Benbecula and **Lochboisdale** to **Ludag** (M.-Sa, usually 1 per day).

You can see almost all of Barra in a day. Those without cars can take the **post bus** around the island (departs Castlebay for Eoligarry M-Sa; inquire at tourist office for times; £2), ride with **H. MacNeil's minibus** (tel. (01871) 810262; 4 per day; £2.75), or rent a bike from **Castlebay Cycle Hire** (tel. (01871) 810284; £8-15, discounts for 3-5 day rentals). To see the whole island, follow the single-laned A888, which makes a 14 mi. circle around the rather steep slopes of **Ben Heavel.** An excellent road for biking, this route follows the coast past stunning beaches and mountain views; a detour north to Eoligarry winds by duckponds and dunes.

Castlebay is Barra's primary town, offering a helpful **tourist office** around the bend and to the right from the pier (tel. (01871) 810336; open roughly mid-Mar. to mid-Oct. M-Sa 9am-5pm, Su 11:30am-12:30pm, and for late ferry arrivals). They'll find you a B&B, but book ahead—a wedding or festival can fill every bed for miles. The cheapest B&Bs around Castlebay are **Mrs. MacKechnie** in Nask (tel. (01871) 810574; twins and doubles £30; open Mar.-Nov.). Ask the tourist office where to **camp.**

■ The Northwest

If you can tolerate two hours crammed in among letters and packages in the back of a tiny postal bus, a trip to the Northwest Highlands will deliver you to a place of priceless pristine beauty. Peopled only by rare villagers, the region is dominated by mountains—some black and jagged, others heather-covered and sloping—threaded with lochs and waterfalls and lapped by ocean waves. Great expanses of mountain and moor stretch along the coast, from the imposing Torridon Hills to the eerie gneiss formations of Inverpolly and finally to Cape Wrath, where waves crash against the highest cliffs in mainland Britain.

GETTING ABOUT

Without a **car,** a quick traipse around the northern coast is nearly impossible. Bus service in this area is sparse and post buses from Ullapool do not accept passengers. Those who **hitch** dance with fate. The few locals drive like devils on the area's narrow, winding roads, but will usually pick up hikers if they don't run them over first. Transport is organized on a spoke system with the hub at Inverness. Four daily **trains** (tel. (0345) 484950) run from **Inverness** to **Kyle of Lochalsh** (for ferries to Skye; £13.80), and **Citylink** (tel. (0990) 505050) buses travel the same route (3 per day, £8.50). Citylink also serves **Thurso** (for ferries to **Orkney**) from **Inverness** (M-Sa 4-5 per day, Su 3 per day, £9); trains follow this route three times daily. Buses also serve **Ullapool** on the northwest coast (in summer M-Sa 4 per day, Apr.-May and Sept. to mid-Oct. 2 per day), where ferries leave for the Outer Hebrides. From these main lines, infrequent post and school buses serve more remote towns, though they rarely link with other services. For specific routes in outlying regions, call a local hostel warden, who will probably be well versed in directing lost travelers.

■ Inverness to Kyle of Lochalsh and Applecross

Kyle of Lochalsh is little more than a center for traffic to and from Skye, but the countryside between it and Inverness is lovely. The **Achnashellach Independent Hostel** (tel. (01520) 766232) is in good hill-walking territory (£8; linen £1 linen). Three weekly buses travel from Inverness to Achnasheen. From there, a train also makes a request stop at Achnashellach (M-Sa 3 per day; May-Sept. also Su 2 per day). The hostel is 2 mi. from the same rail stop. The **SYHA Ratagan** (tel. (01599) 511243) is on the Glasgow-Kyle bus route (get off at Shiel Bridge), 1½ mi. west of Shiel Bridge on Loch Duich in the treeless, Munro-laden **Glenshiel** (£7.75, under 18 £6.50). From here, experienced climbers can scale the **Five Sisters of Kintail** (3505ft.) or tackle the 1½ hour hike up Glen Elchaig to see the 370 ft. **Falls of Glomach.**

The adventurous should try the trip from Kishorn up **Bealach-na-Bo Pass,** leading 13 mi. west to the remote coastal village of **Applecross.** The single-lane road winds steeply to an altitude of 2054 ft. On a clear day, one point near the peak offers truly awesome views of Skye and the Small Isles. Once in Applecross, picnic on the small, sheltered beach or celebrate at the diminutive pub. Directly above town lies a **campsite** (with cafe!) where you can watch the sun drop slowly into the water (£4-7.50 per tent). Applecross was one of the first seats of Christianity in Scotland, and the old churchyard just outside the hamlet dates from the days of St. Maelrubha. Much of the west coast is now Free Church country. On Saturday evenings the bull is separated from the cows, and the cockerel from the hens, in preparation for Sabbath.

■ Torridon

Just to the north of Applecross Peninsula, the tiny village of Torridon crouches beneath the Torridon Hills, second in cragginess only to the Cuillins of Skye. The highest and closest peak is **Liathach** (3456ft.), considered by some to be the most bullying mountain in Britain. From Inverness, **trains** run to Achnasheen (M-Sa 3 per day, Su 2 per day), where **postal buses** connect to Torridon. The buses do not meet every train; call the Ranger Station ahead to confirm times. The **Ranger Station and Countryside Centre** (tel. (01445) 791221) at the crossroads into Torridon, 200 yd. from the Torridon hostel, stocks maps and books detailing area walks. In July and August, the Torridon Ranger Service offers guided walks (ask at the station for details). There is a real range of hiking in the immediate area, and off-trail nordic skiing in the winter. You can stay at the large **SYHA Torridon** (tel. (01445) 791284), which crouches at the base of the daunting Liathach (£7.75, under 18 £6.50; open Feb.-Oct.), or venture 13 mi. west of Torridon along the B8021 to the remote, coastal **SYHA Craig** in Diabaig (no phone or bedding—bring a sleeping bag; £4.65, under 18 £3.85; open mid-May to Sept.). Between the hostel and the ranger office is the **Torridon Campsite** (tel. (01445) 791313; £3 per tent; showers 50p).

■ Gairloch

Flanked by magnificent coastal scenery and inland mountains, **Gairloch** is the next town north, providentially served by direct buses from Inverness (M-Sa 5:05pm, £7). Though Gairloch draws most of the area's tourists, it has remained a peaceful village. Gairloch itself offers little to the visitor, save an impressive but cluttered **museum** in town (tel. 712287), and a gorgeous sandy **beach** out toward the pier. Six miles north along the coast road from Gairloch grow the **Inverewe Gardens** (tel. 781229), a glorious profusion of well-tended flowers and shrubs from all over the world. *(Gardens open daily 9:30am-5:30pm; visitor center open Apr.-Oct. daily 9:30am-5:30pm. £4.80, students, seniors, and children £3.20.)* For a quiet, lochside bed, the **SYHA Carn Dearg** (tel. 712219) welcomes visitors 2 mi. northwest of town (£6.10, under 18 £5; open mid-May to Sept.). **B&Bs** abound in Gairloch and Dundonnell, just east of the Ardessie Gorge; inquire at the Gairloch tourist office for specific details. Campers can pitch tents near the gardens at the **Inverewe Campsite** (tel. (01445) 781249; £9, National Trust members £4), at the beachside **Sands Holiday Centre** (tel. 712152; £7-12), or at the **Gairloch Holiday Park** (tel. 712373; £4-8). Gairloch offers a helpful **tourist office.** (tel. 712130. Open July-Aug. M-Sa 9am-7pm, Su 1-6pm; June and Sept. M-F 9am-6pm, Sa 10am-6pm, Su 1-6pm; May M-F 9am-6pm, Sa 10am-5pm, Su 1-5pm; Oct. M-F 9am-5:30pm, Sa 10am-1pm and 2-5pm; Nov.-Mar. M-F 9am-1pm and 2-5pm.) The **telephone code** is 01445.

■ Ullapool

Ullapool draws visitors mostly for its ferries to the Outer Hebrides, but the mountain-ringed fishing port merits a visit for its strategic position in some of Scotland's most arresting countryside. Though the town is generally dull, it houses one of the tiniest, strangest museums in Western Europe. Every shelf within the **Ullapool Bookshop**

and Museum (tel. 612356) bears unexpected joys, from the pointy-heeled slippers of Mary, Queen of Scots to an effigy of Charles I reconstructed from hair, ruff, and ribbons ripped from his body after the execution at Whitehall. The truly morbid can take a gander at the lozenge box pinched from his coat pocket just before the burial. Find the museum at the back of the bookshop across from the Seaforth Inn. *(Open Easter to Christmas Eve M-Sa 9am-10pm, Su 10am-6pm. Free.)* Offering more typical pleasures, the **Ullapool Museum** (tel. 612987) is housed in an old church on W. Argyle St. Sit in the pews and watch a well-done eight-minute audio-visual display on the history of Ullapool and the surrounding region. *(Open July-Aug. 9:30am-8pm; Apr.-June and Sept.-Oct. M-Sa 9:30am-5:30pm; Nov.-Mar. M-Sa noon-4pm. £2, students and seniors £1.50.)*

Except for the 1am arrivals, **ferries** from Stornoway on Lewis (M-Sa 2-3 per day, £12, return £20.55) are met by express **coaches** to and from Inverness (2hr., £7.20). Ullapool's **tourist office,** Argyll St. (tel. 612135; fax 613031), books rooms for £1. (Open May-Sept. M-F 9am-6pm, Sa 10am-5pm, Su noon-5pm; Oct.-Apr. M-F 9am-5pm, Sa-Su 11am-5pm; closed Su in Oct.) Several boats run daily bird- and wildlife-watching **tours** to the nearby **Summer Isles;** inquire at the booths by the pier (around £8). Ullapool's **post office** (tel. 612228) knits socks at W. Argyle St. (open M-Tu and Th-F 9am-1pm and 2-5:30pm, W and Sa 9am-1pm). The **postal code** is a sea-soaked IV26 2TY. The **telephone code** is 01854.

The well-situated **SYHA Youth Hostel,** Shore St. (tel. 612254), lies 100 yd. right of the pier and features splendid views of mist rolling in over the harbor. Book ahead, as large school groups often overrun the town (£7.75, under 18 £6.50; laundry facilities; open Feb.-Dec.). Grab groceries galore at **Mace,** W. Argyle St. (open M-Sa 9am-9pm, Su 9am-6pm). The **Quay Plaice Restaurant,** across from the pier, fries up super-fresh fish and assorted types of filled rolls; it's a bit pricey (£4; open daily 10am-9pm). For a cheaper option, head to the take-away shop around the corner. **The Ceilidh Place,** W. Argyle St. (tel. 612103), is a hotel, cafe, bar, bookstore, and gallery; it serves coffee until 9pm, a rarity in the highlands. As if that weren't enough, it stomps to traditional Celtic music several nights a week in summer; pick up a copy of the program.

■ Near Ullapool

Twelve miles south of Ullapool on the A835, the falls of Measach cascade down 150 ft. through the lush, mossy forest of **Corrieshalloch Gorge.** Northwest of Ullapool washes the secluded beauty of **Achiltibuie.** Buses leave from Ullapool (M-F 2 per day, Sa 1 per day, £2). If driving, take the A835 north for 10 mi., then make a left at the well-marked, one-lane road and follow it west for 15 mi. The small village is flanked by two alluring nature reserves and a trio of sandy beaches. The **SYHA Achininver** (tel. 622254) occupies an old cottage a quarter mile from a sandy beach and 3 mi. from Achiltibuie (£4.65, under 18 £3.85; open mid-May to Sept.). It is also accessible via a difficult 14 mi. walk along Rock Path from Ullapool (allow at least 7hr., and ask for the 60p leaflet from the Ullapool hostel before setting out).

■ Durness, Smoo, and Tongue

Durness, a quiet village on Scotland's north coast, sits not far from gloriously named **Smoo** (ISH-mool). **Iris MacKay** (tel. (01971) 511343) runs a **minibus** to nearby **Cape Wrath,** home of Britain's highest cliffs. *(Daily 9:30am. Return £6; ferry £2.20.)* The nearby Smoo Caves are said to be inhabited by a small crime-solving blob. Traveling along the north coast is difficult; inquire about possible bus service from Thurso in advance. The **tourist office** (tel. (01971) 511259) sniffs out B&Bs. (Open early Aug. to mid-Aug. M-Sa 9am-6pm, Su 10am-5pm; June-July and mid-Aug. to mid-Sept. M-Sa 9:30am-5:30pm, Su 11am-5pm; Apr.-May and mid-Sept. to Oct. M-Sa 10am-5pm, Su noon-4pm.) **SYHA Durness** (tel. (01971) 511244), at Smoo, rests 1 mi. from Durness along the A838 (£4.65, under 18 £3.85; open mid-Mar. to Sept.).

The town of **Tongue** twists east of Durness on the Kyle bearing the same name. A **SYHA Youth Hostel** (tel. (01847) 611301) perches at Tongue's tip, three-quarters of a mile toward the causeway of Loch Eriboll (£6.10, under 18 £5; open mid-Mar. to

Oct.). Gorgeous ridges and mountains rise from the south end of the loch, and the 14th-century ruins of **Castle Varrish** stand precariously above the water. When classes are on, **school buses** from Thurso press into Tongue (M-F). The town is joined to civilization by the divine intervention of the **post bus** from **Lairg** (M-Sa), accessible by **train** on the Inverness-Wick-Thurso line (M-Sa 3 per day, Su 2 per day).

■ Inverness to the Ferry Ports

Across Caithness and Sutherland, the moors and mountains mellow to rolling farm-lands before the lonely Pentland Firth to the north. The most popular stop from Inverness to Caithness is the legendary **SYHA Carbisdale Castle** (tel. (01549) 421232), located in a 20th-century castle not far from the A836. Walk half a mile uphill from the train whistle-stop at **Culrain** to stay in the building's fading grandeur. In 1945, Captain Salvesen donated this castle—great hall, marble statuary, and rich oil paint-ings included—to the SYHA. Consider booking ahead, especially for Carbisdale's Highland Nights (roughly every week in summer), which feature rollicking, Scottish fun. (July-Aug. £12.50, under 18 £11; Sept.-Oct. and late Feb. to June £11.50, under 18 £10. Continental breakfast included, dinner £4.40. Open late Feb. to Oct.).

Two other sites, both on the main rail and bus routes, merit a stopover. Located 5 mi. south of the **Ord of Caithness,** a hilly area that jumps sharply from the ocean and supports a sizable herd of red deer, the **SYHA Helmsdale** (tel. (01431) 821577) makes a good base for fossil-hunting and gold-panning (£4.65, under 18 £3.85; open mid-May to Sept.). The nearby **Timespan Heritage Centre** (tel. (01431) 821327), portrays historical Highland scenes with convincing audio-visual effects, realistic wax figures, and life-size sets. (Open Easter to mid-Oct. M-Sa 9:30am-5pm, Su 2-5pm; July-Aug. until 6pm; last admission 1hr. before closing. £3, students and seniors £2.40, children £1.75.) Trains drop passengers at the gates of **Dunrobin Castle** (tel. (01408) 633177), the spectacular seat of the Dukes of Sutherland. Though sections of the house date back to the 1300s, most of the architecture is ecstatically Victorian: ambitious, gaudy, and lavish. The earl's former summer house has been transformed into a museum, and its grounds are magnificent. (Castle open July-Aug. daily 10:30am-5:30pm; June and Sept. M-Sa 10:30am-5:30pm, Su noon-5:30pm; Easter-May and Oct. M-Sa 10:30am-4:30pm, Su 1-4:30pm. Gardens open all year; free when castle is closed. Castle and gardens £5, students £4, children £3.50.) On the castle grounds, birds of prey fly to gloved hands at the **Falconry Display.** (£2.80, seniors £2, children £1.50.)

■ Northeastern Ferry Ports

Thurso, Scrabster, and John O'Groats—the principal ports sending ferries to Orkney and the Faroe Islands—huddle in the northeastern corner of Scotland. There are sev-eral trips daily from Inverness to the ports. **Buses** glide frequently between Inverness and Thurso (3½hr., £12); call the tourist office to confirm, as stops may vary. **ScotRail** also strikes Thurso along the Highland line from Inverness (3¾hr., M-Sa 3 per day, Su 2 per day, £12.20). A free bus from the Thurso rail station connects with ferry depar-tures at **John O'Groats,** although returns go to Wick train station (£2.10). Orkney fer-ries originate from the ferry ports; see **Getting There,** p. 564, for details. If you're a student, ask about **student prices** on any ferry you take.

If you need to spend the night in one of the ports before catching a ferry, **Thurso** is probably your best bet. Unfortunately, there are no monuments or museums to allevi-ate the tedium. Head to the waterfront and gaze across at the misty blue Orkneys or work off aggression at the riverbank obstacle course. The independent **Thurso Youth Club Hostel** (tel. (01847) 892964), stashed in a converted mill, is open only in July and August (£8, breakfast and linen included). From the train station, walk down Lover's Lane, steam up the car windows, turn left on Janet St., cross the footbridge over the river, and follow the footpath to the right. If it doesn't happen to be July or August, Jean and Bill Brown can provide you with a soft bed, hearty breakfast, and romance novel at **Borlum,** 26 Sinclair St. (tel. (01847) 895830; £15-16). The **Thurso**

tourist office (tel. (01847) 892371) is to the right on Riverside Rd. (Open July-Aug. M-F 9am-6pm, Sa 9am-6pm, Su 10am-6pm; May-June M-Sa 9am-6pm, Su 10am-6pm; Apr. and Sept. M-Sa 10am-6pm; Oct. M-F 10am-4pm.) The **John O'Groats tourist office** (tel. (01955) 611373) is right by the pier. (Open July-Aug. M-F 9am-7pm, Sa 9am-6pm, Su 10am-6pm; June and Sept. M-Sa 9am-6pm, Su 10am-6pm; May M-F 9am-6pm, Sa 10am-6pm; Oct.-Apr. M-Sa 10am-5pm.)

Dunnet Head, about halfway between Thurso and John O'Groats, is the northernmost point of the island of Britain, but **Duncansby Head,** about 2 mi. outside John O'Groats, has a more impressive view overlooking the Pentland Firth.

■ Orkney Islands

Björn was here.

—ancient rune carved into Orcadian standing stone

Across the broad and occasionally rough Pentland Firth, the emerald villages, eroding red sandstone cliffs, and iris-studded farmlands of Orkney are treasures. The landscape between villages is a timeless assemblage of paddocks, beaches, and gardens, trod by Orcadians for millennia. Traces of the ancients are everywhere; Orkney has some of the best-preserved Stone Age, Pictish, and Viking villages, monuments, and burial chambers in Western Europe. The small capital city of Kirkwall encases a dramatic 12th-century cathedral, still in use, and a fine medieval and Renaissance palace. The sea holds secrets as well—at low tide, broken prows and sterns of sunken blockships rear up from the sea foam along the WWII Churchill Barriers.

While a careful walk along the cliffs of the West Mainland displays elderducks, fulmar petrels, and even the occasional puffin in summer, the islands of Westray, Papa Westray, Copinsay, and the Pentland Skerries are sacred to ornithology pilgrims—337 species of birds alight on or inhabit Orkney (birds outnumber people 100 to 1). With rare artifacts preserved by isolation and fine Orkney sand, the islands sing a siren song to their visitors—many become born-again Orcadians themselves.

GETTING THERE

Three ferries connect Orkney to mainland Scotland. The most convenient route may be the **Orkney Bus,** which departs daily (May to early Sept.) from **Inverness** bus station's Platform 10 for **John O'Groats** (2:20pm), where a ferry sails for **Burwick,** Orkney. From Burwick, a local bus travels up the Churchill Barriers to **Kirkwall.** The £37 return fare (buy on the bus) includes all connections (Thurso-Kirkwall-John O'Groats round-trip £25). For more info, call **John O'Groats Ferries** at (tel. (01955) 611353). **P&O Scottish Ferries** (tel./fax (01224) 572615) depart Scrabster near Thurso for Stromness; pick up a schedule at a tourist office. (Apr.-Oct. M and F usually 6am, noon, and 5:45pm, Tu-Th 6am and noon, Sa noon and 5:45pm; Apr.-Oct. also Su noon; return £21-30; 10% discount for students and seniors.) A bus departs Thurso rail station for Scrabster before each crossing (85p). A **P&O Scottish Ferry** from Aberdeen usually stops in Stromness en route to Lerwick, Shetland (June-Aug. Su and Tu noon; May and Sept. Sa noon; Oct.-Dec. Sa 6pm; Jan.-Apr. times vary). Ferries also return to Aberdeen (2 per week) and Scrabster (2-3 per day).

GETTING ABOUT

Peace's buses (tel. (01856) 872866) run between Kirkwall and Stromness, ferry port to the island of Hoy and the northern Shetland Islands (30min., M-Sa 8-10 per day, £2.20). Bus schedules can be picked up in either tourist office; buses do not run on Sunday. The **Orkney Islands Shipping Co.** (tel. (01856) 872044) shuttles passengers to the islets of Eday, Stronsay, Shapinsay, Sanday, Westray, and Papa Westray from the Kirkwall pier. Contact the Orkney Ferries, Shore Street, Kirkwall, Orkney KW15 1LG (tel. (01426) 977170), or pick up their *Timetables & Tariffs* booklet at the tourist office in Kirkwall. **Biking** is an excellent way to see the islands. Bikes can be rented in

Stromness at **Orkney Cycle Hire,** 54 Dundas St. (tel. (01856) 850255; open daily 8:30am-9pm; £5.50-6.50 per day) and in Kirkwall from **Bobby Cycle Centre,** Tankerness Ln. (tel. (01856) 873097), off Broad St. (open M-F 9am-5pm, Sa 9:30am-5pm; £8-10 per day).

■ Kirkwall

Established in the 11th century, the city of Kirkwall (pop. 7000) has expanded through the centuries as the sea receded from its shores to become the administrative and social center of the Orkney Islands. A few ancient structures at the town center testify to its age. South of the tourist office on Broad St., the impressive red and yellow sandstone **St. Magnus Cathedral,** begun in 1137, houses the bones of its founder's saintly and prematurely expired uncle, St. Magnus himself. Grave markers dating from the 16th and 17th centuries line the aisles, their grim *memento mori* and halting poetry poignant reminders of Kirkwall's heritage. *(Open Apr.-Sept. M-Sa 9am-6pm, Su 2-6pm; Oct.-Mar. M-Sa 9am-1pm and 2-5pm.)* Across Palace Rd. from the cathedral, the **Bishop's and Earl's Palaces** once housed the Bishop of Orkney and his enemy, the wicked Earl Patrick Stewart, who was later executed for treason. Though now roofless in parts, the Earl's Palace boasts brightly illustrated plaques in most of its rooms, yielding a good impression of how a 17th-century earl conducted his domestic affairs. *(Open Apr.-Sept. M-Sa 9:30am-6:30pm, Su 2-6:30pm. £1.70, students and seniors £1.20, children £1.)* Under the watchful gaze of the earl, the bishop set about fortifying his palace in order to defend himself from his unpredictable next-door neighbor. *(Same hours as Earl's Palace; admission to both buildings included in ticket. A £7.50 combination ticket allows entry into both palaces as well as Skara Brae, Maes Howe, and the Broch of Guinness.)* Opposite St. Magnus Cathedral, the **Tankerness House Museum** (tel. 873191) introduces visitors to the island's remote and recent past, displaying both finds from the chief archaeological sites in Orkney and paintings by native son Stanley Cursiter. *(Open May-Sept. M-Sa 10:30am-5pm, Su 2-5pm; Oct.-Apr. M-Sa 10:30am-12:30pm and 1:30-5pm. £2, students, seniors, and children free.)*

The **tourist office,** 6 Broad St. (tel. 872856), books B&Bs. (Open Apr.-Sept. M-Sa 8:30am-8pm, Su 8:30am-noon and 4-8pm; Oct.-Apr. M-Sa 9:30am-5pm.) Pick up a guide to each Orcadian island. The **Royal Bank of Scotland,** 56 Albert St., has an **ATM** (open M-Tu and Th-F 9am-5pm, W 10am-5pm). The **telephone code** is 01856.

Kirkwall boasts a **SYHA Youth Hostel,** located on Old Skapa Rd. in a former British Telecom building (tel. 872243). To reach it, turn left and follow the main road from the tourist office for half a mile as it evolves from Broad St. into Victoria St. Cross over Union, Main, and then High St., where SYHA signs will carry you home. Located behind blackened old buildings and machinery, the hostel has all the standards, including conventional laundry and a water-zapping drying room (£7.75, under 18 £6.50; open Mar.-Oct.). For quiet rooms and an occasional harbor view, try the B&B provided by Mrs. Hume at **Vanglee** (tel. 873013), on Weyland Park off Cromwell Rd. (£13-15). **Camping** is available in Kirkwall on Pickaquoy Rd. off the A965 at the **Pickaquoy Caravan & Camping Site** (tel. 873535; £3.50-4.65). You can pitch a tent almost anywhere on the islands, but ask the landowner first.

Safeway (tel. 228876) stands on Broad St. and on Great Western Rd. (open M-W 8am-8pm, Th-Sa 8am-9pm, Su 9am-6pm). Buy extra for Sunday, as only a few hotel restaurants serve breakfast on the Sabbath—everything else in Kirkwall closes. The **Kirkwall & St. Ola Community Centre** (tel. 873354), across from the cathedral on Broad, serves the cheapest food in town. (Open July-Aug. M-Sa 9:30am-4pm and 7-10pm, Su 12:30-5:30pm; Sept.-June M-Sa 9:30am-4pm and 7-10pm.) **Buster's Diner,** 1 Mounthoolie Ln. (tel. 876717), cooks up North American cuisine for under £4.50 (open M-F 11:30am-2pm and 5-10pm, Sa 11:30am-11pm, Su 5-10pm).

■ Stromness

Founded in the 16th century as a fishing and whaling port, Stromness (pop. 2000) is a town of narrow, cobblestone streets and beautiful, open vistas. The **P&O Ferry** floats here from Scrabster; almost everything you need is along the harbor on Victoria

St. The **Stromness Museum,** 52 Alfred St. (tel. 850025), tackles the history of the sea with artifacts from the whaling and fishing industries, relics of explorer John Rae (including his cloth boat), and a photo exhibit on the scuttling (and subsequent recovery) of the German High Seas Fleet in Scapa Flow during World War II. It may be closed part of the year, so call ahead. *(Open May-Sept. daily 10am-5pm; Oct.-Apr. M-Sa 10:30am-12:30pm and 1:30-5pm. £2, children 50p.)* The helpful **tourist office** (tel. 850716) resides in an 18th-century warehouse on the pier. (Office open Apr.-Oct. M-W and F-Sa 8am-8pm, Th 8am-6pm, Su 9am-4pm; Nov.-Mar. M-F 9am-5pm; also open to meet most late ferry arrivals.) The **telephone code** is 01856.

Fewer than five minutes from the tourist office, 14-bed **Brown's Hostel,** 45-7 Victoria St. (tel. 850661), is as warm and toasty as the night is cold and damp (£7.50-8). A half mile from the tourist office (make a right onto Hellihole Rd.) rests the **SYHA Hostel** (tel. 850589), well-kept and hospitable, despite its infernal address (£6.10, under 18£5; lockout 10:30am-5pm; open mid-Mar. to Oct.). The **Ness Point Caravan and Camping Site** (tel. 851235), is a five-minute walk from Stromness (£5.50; open mid-May to Sept.). On the pier, **The Ferry Inn Bar** (tel. 850280) dishes up meal-size appetizers for £2.50-4.50 and main courses (including vegetarian options) for £5-6 (open daily noon-2pm and 5:30-10pm). **The Café,** 22 Victoria St. (tel. 850368), serves up harbor views along with cheap meals (£3-6; open M-Sa 9am-9pm, Su 10am-9pm). The bars at The Ferry Inn and **The Stromness Hotel** on the main street are popular nightspots for locals and tourists; the latter hosts occasional live music.

ORKNEY SIGHTS

While Stromness and Kirkwall certainly merit an afternoon's exploration, Orkney is also endowed with an astonishing wealth of Stone Age and Viking remains—not to mention the billowing mist, rocky promontories, and expanses of buttercups, clover, thrift, and primroses that cover the islands. Excellent walks abound, but getting to many of them without a car or superhuman stamina can be tricky. Public transportation runs almost exclusively between Stromness and Kirkwall. Ferries to the smaller islands are infrequent; at best they run once or twice a day. Despite endless uphills and winds that can make downhills take forever, cycling may be the best and cheapest way to do Orkney justice (see **Getting About,** p. 564, for rental shops).

Ranger Naturalist Michael Hartley of **Wildabout Tours** (tel. 851011) squires visitors around mainland Orkney and Hoy in his minibus. With a vigorous imagination and encyclopedic knowledge of Orkney, Michael asks visitors to envision the Orkney of over 5000 years ago; his tour of Skara Brae will raise the hairs on your neck as you hear, in the surf, the sounds of Stone Age hammers and women at work with mortar and pestle. Michael's dog knows better than to fool with ghosts and refuses to set foot on the site. *(From £14, student and hosteler discounts.)* Orkney native John Grieve leads **Discover Orkney Tours** (tel. 872865), which crafts tour to meet your interests. *(From £12.)* Both tour guides leave from the tourist offices in Kirkwall and Stromness.

Skara Brae

A number of important archaeological sites cluster around Stromness and Kirkwall. Dating back 5100 years, **Skara Brae** was once a bustling Stone Age village miles from the coast. As the ocean crept farther in, waves gradually consumed the village houses; after approximately 600 years of continuous habitation, the villagers abandoned the settlement. Preserved in sand, the village slept quietly until 1850, when a violent storm ripped out the side of the cliff and revealed nine houses, a workshop, and covered town roads. Excavated at least six times, the houses still carry Stone Age luxuries such as brine basins and fire-stained hearths. While the visitor center is open only during the day, the site remains accessible until nightfall—a trip at dusk evades the tourists and the admission fee. The **Skaill House** (tel. 841501) is the 17th-century home of the Lairds of Breckness. The first laird, Bishop Graham, obtained the land when Earl Patrick Stewart was executed. *(Admission to Skara Brae and Skaill House £3, seniors £1.80, children £1. Visitor center open Apr.-Sept. M-Sa 9:30am-8pm, Su 9:30am-4:30pm; Oct.-Mar. M-Sa 10am-8:30pm, Su 2-4:30pm.)*

Ring of Brogdar, the Stones of Stenness, and Maeshowe

Nearby on the A965, the sedimentary sandstones of the **Ring of Brogdar** once witnessed gatherings about which no two archaeologists can agree. Some believe the upright ring marked a meeting place for local chieftains; others propose that the site witnessed the disposal of the dead by leaving the bodies to the elements and the birds. Now filled in for the safety of visitors, a deep ditch around the circle would have warded off dogs and wild predators. Of the original 60, only 36 stones remain.

Close by on the A965, the **Standing Stones of Stenness** once numbered 12, but by 1760 only four remained—it's not known what became of the other eight, but it has been suggested that they were knocked down by locals angered at the monument's pagan origins. Recently, possible evidence of a priests' settlement has been found near the site. Accessible from the A965, the **Maeshowe** (tel. 761606) tomb may have held the bones of the earliest settlers in the area from approximately 2700 BC. According to runic graffiti, Viking raiders broke through the roof and spent three glorious days hauling treasure out of the chamber. The runes are almost more of an attraction than the tomb itself—the largest collection of runic inscriptions in the world, they enabled linguists to crack the runic alphabet and read things like "This was carved by the greatest rune carver" and "Ingeborg is the most exquisite of women." *(Open Apr.-Sept. M-Sa 9:30am-6:30pm, Su 2-6:30pm; Oct.-Mar. M-Sa 9:30am-4:30pm, Su 2-4:30pm. £2.30, seniors £1.50, children £1.)*

The Brough of Birsay and the Churchill Barriers

In the northwest off the A967, the **Brough of Birsay** shows evidence of early Christian and Viking habitation. Once the administrative and religious center of Orkney, the tidal island's kirkyard holds a Pictish stone engraving of a royal figure with a crown, suggesting that Orcadian kings once ruled from Birsay. The island is only accessible one hour before and after low tide. Bird-watching from the cliffs may be absorbing, but linger too long and the puffins may become your bedfellows.

After the sinking of *HMS Royal Oak* in October 1939 by a German submarine, Churchill erected the famous barriers of **Scapa Flow.** Today, the **Churchill Barriers** allow motorists access to the smaller southeast islands of **Lamb Holm, Glimps Holm, Burray,** and **South Ronaldsay.** In the same waters, plucky Rear Admiral Ludwig von Reuter ordered his 74-ship German fleet to be scuttled during World War II, earning him a *Guinness Book of World Records* mention for most ships sunk at one time. Much to the delight of scuba divers, seven German war vessels remain. On tiny Lamb Holm rests the **Italian Chapel,** one of the few buildings remaining from the World War II prison camps on Orkney. The exquisitely decorated chapel was created from two metal Nissen huts. The Italian prisoners of war who designed and decorated it made do with such materials as bathroom tiles, stair rails, and wood from a wrecked ship. *(Open daily Apr.-Sept. 9am-10pm; Oct.-Mar. 9am-4:30pm. Free.)* On **Burray,** archaeoichthyophiles will enjoy the Devonian room at the **Fossil & Vintage Centre** (tel. 731255). The museum also has a closet of glow-in-the-dark rocks and a second floor exhibition that is essentially an antique shop with a few machine guns. *(Open Apr.-Sept. daily 10am-6pm; Oct. to Christmas W-Su 10:30am-6pm. £2, seniors and children £1.)*

South Ronaldsay and Hoy

On the southern tip of South Ronaldsay, 35 mi. from Stromness, perches **The Tomb of the Eagles,** from which a 5000-year-old skull, the remains of over 300 people, and a group of sea eagle talons were unearthed. Knowledgeable Mr. Simison, who accidently discovered the relics, leads tours with members of his family. Visitors are allowed to handle most of the Stone Age tools and skulls. Call ahead (tel. 831339). *(£2.50, students £1, seniors £2, under 13 50p.)*

The landscape of **Hoy** ("High Island"), the second largest island in Orkney, is surprisingly rocky and mountainous. All visitors to Orkney should glimpse the **Old Man of Hoy,** a famous 450 ft. sea stack off the West Coast of the island. On a clear day, the P&O ferry from Scrabster to Stromness gives an excellent view of the landmark; a careful walk along the coast of Hoy affords the hiker a look down on the Old Man

> ### Ba', Ba'... It's not about Sheep
> Amid all the puffin sightings and archeological sites is a more obscure Orkney tra-
> dition—the Ba'. Best described as a large football game with no rules and no limit
> on player numbers, the Ba' takes place on Christmas and New Year's Day. Two
> teams take to the streets of Kirkwall, the Uppies (from the upper part of town)
> and the Doonies (you figure it out). The ranks of the competitors have been
> known to swell to 400. The action begins in front of St. Magnus Cathedral and can
> continue for hours, ending at nightfall. There are no time-outs or penalties and,
> oddly, serious injuries seldom occur. It's just a fierce quest for the ball: the hardy
> soul deemed most valuable player gets to keep it.

himself. A steep marked footpath leads from Rackwick 2 mi. away; allow for a three-
hour round-trip. The hefty North Hoy **bird reserve** offers respite for guillemots and a
host of other species. The dedicated puffin-scout should see several here during
breeding season (late June to early July). The rest of the year the pudgy birds rough it
on the seas. On Hoy, the **SYHA Hoy** near the pier and the **SYHA Rackwick** farther
south, 2 mi. from the Old Man of Hoy, offer accommodations for £6.10 (under 18 £5)
and share a telephone number (tel. 873535; Hoy open May to mid-Sept.; Rackwick
open mid-Mar. to mid-Sept.). No sleeping bags are available on the island—don't
leave home without one. Food and supplies are difficult to procure; on Sundays, getting them is nearly impossible.

Papa Westray and Eday
Papa Westray, "isle of the priests," once supported an early Christian Pictish settlement. Most pilgrims to the island now content themselves with bird-watching and
archaeology. The rare Scottish primrose, thought to grow only in Orkney and isolated
spots in the Scottish highlands, may be found in fields and farmyards. On the West
Coast, **St. Boniface's Church** dates from the 12th century, although 18th-century restoration is responsible for much of the edifice today. South along the coast, the **Knap
of Howar** is the quiet location of the earliest standing houses in northern Europe, dating to 3500 BC. Two miles from the pier, **SYHA Papa Westray**, Beltane House (tel.
(01857) 644267), offers year-round accommodation (£7.75, under 18 £6.50).

   The peat-covered hills of **Eday** island hide Stone Age field walls, chambered tombs,
dykes, and even, on the Calf of Eday, the remnants of an Iron Age roundhouse. As on
all the Orkney Islands, bird-watchers will preen with satisfaction, though the cliffs
can be treacherous and should be avoided in bad weather. **SYHA Eday** (tel. (01857)
622206), along the main north-south road 4 mi. from the pier, also welcomes **campers** (£4.65, under 18 £3.85, £2 for campers; open Apr.-Sept.).

■ Shetland Islands

Local poet Hugh MacDiarmid aptly describes the difference between Orkney and
Shetland: "The Orcadian is a farmer with a boat, the Shetlander is a fisherman with a
croft." The vast expanse of water separating Shetland from Britain is omnipresent;
nowhere can you be more than 3 mi. from the sea. The same isolation that makes
Shetland beautiful exposes it to whimsically unpredictable natural disasters—
recently, the entire island briefly lost electricity when a crow's nest composed of
fencing wire caused a short-circuit. The hardy crops and animals that can survive
here—peat, Shetland ponies, and sheep, sheep, sheep—support Shetland agriculture, while North Sea oil drilling has brought new prosperity. The Shetlands and
Orkneys only became part of Scotland in the 15th century when King Christian I of
Denmark and Norway mortgaged them in order to pay for his daughter's dowry. Shetlanders still look proudly to their Viking heritage, rather than to Scotland or Britain,
for their identity and inspiration. This influence lingers in their Nordic craftmanship,
Scandanavian architecture, and in festivals such as the longship-burning Up-Helly-A'.
Watch your pence—after London, Shetland is the priciest place in Britain.

GETTING THERE

The fastest way to Shetland providing the weather cooperates is the **British Airways/ BABA special** from **Kirkwall**, Orkney. You're eligible for the £83 return fare only if you book ahead at any Shetland B&B, hotel, or guest house *from Orkney*. The same offer holds for the return to Kirkwall if you book ahead in Shetland. A Saturday night stay you can save up to £40 on the flight, and accommodations bookings are not required. The tourist offices and travel agencies in Stromness, Kirkwall, or Lerwick will handle the bookings and distribute further info. **British Airways** (tel. (0345) 222111) also flies from **Aberdeen** (£99), **Edinburgh** (£168), and **Glasgow** (£168). Flights are met by buses to Lerwick (45min., M-Sa 4-6 per day, Su 2 per day, £1.80).

P&O Scottish Ferries leave from **Aberdeen** for Lerwick (14hr., M-F 6pm, June-Aug. also Tu noon; £49-54, berth from £66). P&O also runs from Stromness on **Orkney** to Lerwick (8hr., June-Aug. Tu 10pm and Su noon, Apr.-May and Sept.-Dec. Su noon, Jan.-Mar. variable, £37). P&O leaves Scotland behind with runs from Lerwick to **Bergen, Norway** (June-Aug. Sa 10am, £57, berth from £63). Students get 10% off these fares, which are lower in early June and late August. Contact P&O Scottish Ferries, P.O. Box 5, Jamieson's Quay, Aberdeen AB11 5NP (tel. (01224) 572615).

GETTING ABOUT

Shetland's main bus lines are **John Leask & Son** (tel. 693162) and **Shalder Coaches** (tel. 880217). The tourist office stocks the vital *Inter-Shetland Transport Timetable* (70p) with bus, ferry, and plane schedules. To reach remote areas on Shetland's excellent road system, try **Bolts Car Hire** (tel. (01595) 693636) or **Grantfield Garage** (tel. 692709), both on North Rd. Bolts also has a branch at Samburgh airport (tel. (01950) 460777). **Eric Brown's Cycle Hire,** Grantfield Garage Ltd., North Rd. (tel. 692709), 500 yd. past the P&O ferry terminal, rents fully equipped touring bikes (£6 per day, £35 per week; open daily 8am-5pm). Remember that the strong winds can make biking difficult. **Ferries** within the archipelago are heavily subsidized; the longest trips cost about £2. All except those to Fair Isle transport bikes for free. **Hitchers** report rides on the A970 without thumbing, but sparse traffic makes it less reliable where the road forks north of Voe.

ORIENTATION AND PRACTICAL INFORMATION

Lerwick lies on the eastern coast of the main island (called "Mainland") and is served by the A970 running the length of the island. Ferries arrive at **Holmsgarth Terminal,** a 20-minute walk northwest of the city center, and the smaller **Victoria Pier,** across from the tourist office downtown. **Shetland Islands Tourism** (tel. 693434; fax 695807), at Market Cross, will book you a bed anywhere in the islands for £3. (Open May-Sept. M-F 8am-6pm, Sa 8am-4pm, Su 10am-1pm; July-Aug. also Su 2-5pm; Oct.-Apr. M-F 9am-5pm.) The **Royal Bank of Scotland ATM** and the **post office** (tel. 693372; open M-F 9am-5pm, Sa 9am-12:30pm) are on Commercial St. The **telephone code** for Lerwick is 01595.

ACCOMMODATIONS

The **SYHA Youth Hostel** (tel. 692114), Islesburgh House at King Harald and Union St., has fabulous facilities like electric range-tops, hot and cold water in one tap, elegant window curtains, strong showers, and an on-site **cafe!** (£7.75, under 18 £6.50. Sheets £1.20. Reception open 9-9:30am, 4-4:30pm and 9:45-10:15pm. Open Apr.-Sept.) Harbor views are yours at **Mrs. Nicholson's,** 133 North Rd. (tel. 693362; £16-18). There are three **campgrounds** on Mainland, but you can camp almost anywhere with the landowner's permission. **Clickimin Caravan and Camp Site** (tel. 741000) is closest to the Lerwick ferry terminal; turn left on the A970, then right on the A969 (tents £6-7; open Apr.-Sept.).

Camping **böds** (Nordic for barns) are a unique Shetland accommodations alternative. There are four böds on Mainland: **Betty Movat's** near the airport, **The Sail Loft** next to the pier in Voe, the **Voe House** in Walls, and **Johnnie Notions** at Hamnavoe,

Eshaness in far northeast Mainland. The **Windhouse Lodge,** on Yell, is the best-equipped. All böds cost £3 per night (£15-55 for exclusive use, although not June-Aug.; open Apr.-Oct.) and must be booked in advance through the tourist office. Bring sleeping bags, a camping stove, and 50p coins for electricity (when available); the roof, green grass, and blue, blue sky are already there. For a hot shower (60p), quick swim (£1.25-2), or a sauna and steam room, try one of the **Shetland's Leisure Centres,** funded by oil revenues (tel. 741000).

FOOD, PUBS, AND WOOL

Inexpensive eats cluster in the center of Lerwick. The **Co-op** on Commercial Rd. should satisfy all those in search of golden digestive biscuits and other groceries. Gorge on a cooked breakfast until 11:30am (£1.25) or fish and chips all day long (£3) (open M-W and F 8am-8pm, Th 8am-9pm, Sa 8am-7pm, Su 9am-6pm). Lerwick's cheapest food awaits at the **Islesburgh Community Centre Café** (tel. 692114), on King Harald St. next to the hostel. After a bannock and a biscuit, pool sharks can play a game at the tables in the recreation room (open M-Sa 10am-5pm and 6:30-10:30pm, Su 7:30-10:30pm). On Unst, you can simultaneously shop for knitware and enjoy apple pie at **Nornova** in Muness (open daily 9am-5pm).

The **Lounge,** 4 Mounthooly St., is the town's liveliest pub (open M-F 11am-2pm and 5-11pm, Sa 11am-11pm). Musicians congregate here Saturday afternoons and some Wednesday nights. Shetland songs are distinctive—more melodic and melancholy than the foot-tapping reels of Ireland and Scotland. The **Shetland Fiddlers**—all 40 of them—play at the Islesburgh Community Centre (by the hostel), June through August, Wednesdays and Fridays at 7pm (£2, children £1).

Shetland is, naturally, one of the best places in the world to buy woolens. To avoid paying relatively high prices in Lerwick's tourist shops, get bargains at **Shetland Knit-wear** (tel. 695631) on Commercial St. *(Open M-F 9am-5pm.)* In Scalloway, cuddle up at the **Shetland Woollen Company** (tel. 880243), on Castle Rd. *(Open May-Sept. M-Sa 9am-5pm; Oct.-Apr. M-F 9am-5pm; also branches in Lerwick, Sandwick, and Yell.)*

SIGHTS

Not much of a sight in itself, the giant, pentagonal **Fort Charlotte,** a relic of the Cromwellian era, supplies the best views of Lerwick and its harbor. *(Open daily 9am-10pm. Free.)* Only 1 mi. west of the city center on Clickimin Rd., the ruins of **Clickimin Broch,** a stronghold from the 4th century BC, still look tough enough to repel invaders. *(Always open. Free.)* More modern (by Shetland standards) is the **Town Hall** on Hillhead (tel. 693535), built in 1882. The clock tower is closed, but the main hall contains a lovely series of stained-glass windows depicting scenes from Shetland's Viking past. *(Open M-Th 9-5, F 9am-4pm. Free.)*

The **Shetland Folk Festival** in early May lures fiddlers from around the world (contact the festival office, 5 Burns Ln., or the tourist office). The **Shetland Fiddle and Accordion Festival** takes place in Lerwick in mid-October. The famous **Up-Helly-A' Festival** is a Viking extravaganza with outlandish costumes, a torchlight procession through the streets, and a ship-burning in the town park (last Tues. in Jan.). Shetlanders plan months in advance for this impressive light-bearing event—after the bonfire dies out blackness settles in again (with only short reprieves of daylight) until late spring.

If you miss the real McCoy, visit the permanent **Up-Helly-A' Exhibition** in the Galley Shed, St. Sunniva St. *(Open mid-May to Sept. Tu 2-4pm and 7-9pm, F 7-9pm, Sa 2-4pm. £2, students, seniors and children free.)* Weather permitting, take a cruise around the bay on the **Dim Riv** (tel. 693434), a full-scale replica of a Viking longship which launches every Wednesday evening at 7 and 7:45pm in summer. Riders may be asked to row. Advance booking at the tourist office is essential. *(£5, children £2.)*

Bressay, Noss, and Scalloway

Hourly ferries (£1) sail from Lerwick to the isle of Bressay. Hike to the summit of conical **Ward of Bressay** (743ft.) for a sweeping view of the sea. From Bressay's east coast (3mi. from Lerwick ferry on the west coast; follow the "To Noss" signs), dinghies go to the tiny isle of **Noss;** just stand at the "Wait Here" sign and wave (mid-May to Aug. Tu-W and F-Su 10am-4pm, return £2.50, seniors and children £1). Great Skuas (Bonxies), large primeval birds, enjoy swooping over your head at this spectacular bird sanctuary; carry a stick of driftwood or keep a hand over your head to ward them off, and try not to wear bright red. Overnight stays are forbidden on Noss.

Scalloway, Shetland's ancient capital, lies 7 mi. west of Lerwick. The 17th-century **Scalloway Castle,** once home to the villainous Earl Patrick Stewart, can now be yours. Get the key from the Shetland Woolen Company (next door) or the Scalloway Hotel. From the bus, head to the water and turn left; it's the castle. *(Open M-Sa 9:30am-5pm, Su by appt. only. Free.)* Buses to Scalloway leave from the Thule Bar on the Esplanade in Lerwick (M-Sa 5-6 per day, return £2).

St. Ninian's Isle, Mousa, Jarlshof, and Mavis Grind

An unusual *tombolo*—a sandbar washed by waves on both sides—links **St. Ninian's Isle,** site of an early monastery, to the west coast of the mainland. The tiny, uninhabited island **Mousa,** just off the east coast, holds the world's best preserved Iron Age *broch,* a 50 ft. drystone fortress that has endured 1000 years of Arctic storms, sunning seals in the sheltered West Pool, and Great Skuas. Catch a bus at the Viking Bus Station in Lerwick and ask the driver to let you off at the Setter Junction for Sandsayre; it's a 15-minute walk from there to the ferry. On Sundays, when buses and ferries are rare, **Leask Coach Tours** offers three different tours of the mainland. *(Tours leave at 2:15pm. £6.50.)* On most Mondays at 9am and 1:30pm, Leask leads tours of Mousa, leaving from the Esplanade. *(£8, including ferry.)*

At the southern tip of Mainland, next to Sumburgh Airport, lies **Jarlshof,** one of the most remarkable archaeological sites in Europe. Stacked here are the remains of layers of human settlement from Neolithic times to the Renaissance, discovered in 1896 when a storm uncovered the site. *(Open Apr.-Sept. M-Sa 9:30am-6:30pm, Su 2-6:30pm. £2.50, seniors £1.80, children £1.20.)* On nearby **Sumburgh Head,** thousands of gulls, guillemots, and puffins rear their young each year.

The north Mainland has the wildest and most deserted coastal scenery, much of which is accessible only by car. At **Mavis Grind,** just northwest of Brae, the Mainland is almost bisected; this 100 yd. wide isthmus is flanked by both the Atlantic and the North Sea. Farther northwest, explore the jagged volcanic forms on **Esha Ness.**

Yell and Unst

Shetland's northern islands, **Yell** and **Unst,** are starkly remote. If you tire of bird- and seal-watching on Yell, head for the north end of the main road at Gloup; a 3 mi. hike from here takes you to the desolate eastern coast. The remains of an Iron Age fort on the Burgi Geos promontory have held tenaciously to a perfect defensive position— jagged outcroppings face the sea and a 3 ft. ridge leads between cliffs to the mainland. Killer whales are occasionally spotted in the sound between Yell and Unst.

Unst is home to the most northerly everything in Britain. **Muness Castle** was built in the late 16th century; the key-keeper at the white cottage will give you a flashlight to illumine the spooky darkness of Britain's northernmost castle. At **Harold's Quick Beach,** gannets crash the ocean near the crumbling concrete of abandoned air-raid shelters. The celebrated bird reserve at Hermaness is graced by a pair of blackbrowed albatross, and water, water everywhere.

The cheapest rooms are at **Gardiesfauld Hostel,** in Uyeasound on Unst—the northernmost hostel in Britain (tel. (01957) 755298 or 755311; £7). One bus a day leaves Lerwick and connects with ferries to Haroldwick on Unst, stopping by the hostel on the way (£8, including ferries). Ferries from Belmont on Unst and Gutcher on Yell make routine diversions to the island of **Fetlar** (£1.05), where bird-watchers view the crimson-tailed finch. Camp at **Garths Campsite,** and stock up on food at the **Harold-swick Shop.** Experience Britain's most northerly **postal code** (ZE2 9ED) at **Harold-swick post office** (open M-W and F 9am-1pm and 2-5:30pm, Th and Sa 9am-1pm).

■ The Smaller Islands

Shetland's outermost islands are the most remote in Britain. Rooms and transport are hard to come by, and booking several weeks in advance is a must. Bring supplies to last at least a week, as the ferries often do not operate in inclement weather.

Whalsay, a relatively huge fishing community (pop. 1000), is accessible by bus and ferry from Lerwick. Camp at **The Grieve House.** The **Out Skerries** support 85 hardy fishermen. Planes (5 per week from Tingwall) and ferries (4-8 per week) converge upon them from Lerwick (2 per week) and Vidlin (10 per week). Little **Papa Stour** (pop. 35) boasts a frothy coastline with abundant bird-life and sea-flooded cliff arches. The only place to stay is **Mrs. Holt-Brook's** (tel. (01595) 873238). Planes fly Tuesdays (£15), and boats float from West Burrafirth (4-7 per week; £1.90; call (01595) 810460 to book 24hr. in advance).

Fair Isle, midway between Shetland and Orkney and home of the famous Fair Isle knit patterns, is billed as the most remote island in Britain; one false move and say goodbye to earth. In summer, a **cargo ferry** (tel. (01595) 760222) runs every other Thursday from Lerwick and two to three times a week from Sumburgh (May-Sept., £2); **planes** (tel. 840246) depart Tingwall (6-7 per week, £35) and Samburgh (May-Oct. Sa, £35). Book everything ahead. Lodging is available at the **Fair Isle Bird Observatory Lodge** (tel. (01595) 760258; room and full board £25-40; open Apr.-Oct.).

ISLE OF MAN

The Isle of Man (Mann) is a speck of a country in the middle of the frothy Irish Sea. The 70,000 Manx swear allegiance to Queen Elizabeth, but they aren't part of the U.K. Man has its own parliament, flag, and independent currency, and its language and much of its fauna are unique. Manx home rule created the lax tax laws that have lured hundreds of British tycoons, their presence supplemented by the island's daily population is the crowd of bikers who arrive en masse for the island's famous races.

Farming settlements on the Isle date back to at least 4000 BC. The Vikings landed on Man in the 9th century and established the **Tynwald Court** parliament. When the last Viking king died in 1266, Scottish and English lords fought one another for control and ruled alongside a weakened Tynwald Court. In 1405, home rule ended altogether; the island's tax status both enriched and nearly ruined it, as smugglers imported goods to the Isle and then snuck them to England and Ireland. England responded with the **Isle of Man Purchase Act** (1765), which forced the Isle of Man into its custom union. Deprived of tax revenue, the island fell into poverty. Man's rejuvenation began in 1863; today Man controls its own internal affairs and finances, although its continuing customs union with the U.K. remains a bone of contention.

Ringed by cliffs, sliced by valleys, and criss-crossed by antique trains, the island is small enough to be thoroughly explored in five days. The **Manx language,** a close cousin to Irish and Scots Gaelic, died out at the beginning of the century but is experiencing a revival. It is still heard when the Manx legislature's laws are proclaimed on July 5. **Manx cats** are still bred on the island, as are the terrifying four- to six-horned Manx Loghtan sheep. Man's most famous delicacy is its **kippers,** herring smoked over oak chips. The three-legs-of-Man **emblem** appears on every available surface, asserting Manx identity. Manx **currency** is equivalent to British tender from England, Scotland, or Northern Ireland but not accepted outside the Isle. Coins are reissued each year with different bizarre designs. **Manx stamps** are also unusual, depicting everything from motorcycles to half-naked men. U.K. stamps won't do you much good here. British or Northern Ireland BT cards do not work on Isle of Man **pay phones;** instead, use the common Manx Telecom cardphones. The Isle of Man shares Britain's **international dialing code,** 44. The **phone code** for the entire island is 01624.

What a difference a tail makes

In *A Room of One's Own*, Virginia Woolf writes, "If things had been a little different from what they were, one would not have seen, presumably, a cat without a tail. Certainly, as I watched the Manx cat pause in the middle of the lawn as if it too questioned the universe, something seemed lacking, something seemed different. The tailless cat, though some are said to exist in the Isle of Man, is rarer than one thinks. It is a queer animal, quaint rather than beautiful. It is strange what a difference a tail makes." The people of the Isle of Man embrace the unique tailless Manx cat as a symbol of the Manx identity. "Rumpies," completely tailless cats, are considerably more valuable than their teeny-tailed "stumpie" cousins, which might explain the infamous "Cat of Nine Tails," the whipping device that Manx sailors employed in past times of legal corporal punishment.

GETTING THERE

The **Isle of Man Steam Packet Company** (tel. (01624) 661661; fax 661065; toll-free from Northern Ireland tel. (0990) 523523; email res@steam-packet.com) runs the only ferries to the island (open M-Sa 7am-9pm, Su 9am-9pm). Ferries sail to and from **Belfast** (May-Sept. 1-3 per week, usually Tu-W and Sa), **Dublin** (May-Sept. 1-3 per week, usually M-Tu and Th), **Heysham** (3¾hr., June-Sept. 1-2 per day, Oct.-Jan. and Apr.-May M-F 1 per day), **Liverpool** (2½-4hr., July-Sept. 1-3 per day, Oct.-Jan. and Apr.-

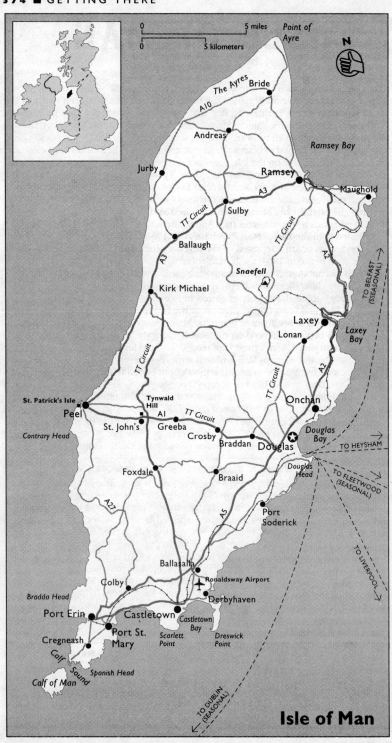

Isle of Man

May 3 per week), and **Fleetwood** (2-3½hr., June-Sept. 1 per week). Many ferries travel in the wee hours of the morning. **Fares** are highest on summer weekends and lowest in winter (£23-33, students and seniors £17-33, ages 5-15 £11-16; bikes free). Book more than four weeks in advance for a discount. It's nearly as cheap to go from England to the Isle of Man to Ireland as to do a roundtrip. Bookings can be made by contacting the offices, travel agents, or at a ferry terminal. If you're returning to the same city, the combination **Sail & Rail** and **Sail & Coach** tickets, available from any British Rail, National Express Coach, or Seacat station, will save you money. The Isle has its own airline, **Manx Airlines** (tel. 824313, U.K. tel. (0345) 256256, Dublin tel. (01) 260 1588), which flies from Ireland, Northern Ireland, and Great Britain to **Ronaldsway Airport** (tel. 821600) in the south of the island. **Jersey European** (U.K. tel. (0990) 676676; Northern Ireland tel. (01232) 457200) and **Emerald Airways** (toll free tel. (0500) 600748) also serve the island.

GETTING ABOUT

The Isle of Man has an extensive system of public transportation managed by **Isle of Man Transport** (train info tel. 663 3666, bus info tel. 662525) in Douglas, which takes you to every sight (often in style). Their **Travel Shop,** on Lord St. next to the Douglas bus station, has information on all of the government-run transportation (train schedule free, 4 regional bus maps 10p) and discount tickets. (Open July-Aug. M-Sa 8am-5:40pm, Su 9:35am-1pm and 2-5:45pm; Sept.-June M-Sa 8am-5:40pm.)

The unique **Isle of Man Railways** (tel. 663366) run along the east coast from Port Erin in the south to Ramsey in the north (operates Easter-Oct.). The **Steam Railway,** dating from 1873, runs from Douglas to Port Erin via Castletown. The **Electric Railway,** dating from 1893, runs north from Douglas to Ramsey. The #1 and 2 trains of the MER (Manx Electric Railway) are the two oldest trains in the world. A separate line heads to **Snaefell,** the island's highest peak. Trains are used mainly by tourists; the stations are museum-like in their restored state. The 2 mi. between the Steam and Electric Railway Stations is covered by bus or **horse-drawn trams** ("toasties").

Frequent buses connect every tiny hamlet on the island. The **Seven Day Rover** is probably the best bet for visitors wishing to see a lot of the island, providing unlimited passage on any public transport—buses, railways, and horse trams—for £28 (children £14). A **one-day Bus Rover** discount ticket allows unlimited bus travel (£4.90, children £2.45); the **three-day Bus Rover** can be used for unlimited travel on three days out of seven (£11.30, children £5.65). Both are available at the Travel Shop or the outlet off Harris Promenade. The privately owned **Tours (Isle of Man Bus Tour) Company,** Central Promenade (tel. 674301 or 676105), provides tours, including the popular "Round the Island" tour (departs Douglas 10:15am, returns 5pm). Other tours change weekly (full-day tours £8, half-day and evening tours £1.50-5).

Since distances between towns and sights are so short, **walking** is a feasible means of transport. Three long-distance **hiking trails** are maintained by the government. **Raad ny Foillan** ("Road of the Gull") is a 90 mi. path around the island marked with seagull signs. **Bayr ny Skeddan** ("The Herring Road") covers the less spectacular 14 mi. between Peel in the west and Castletown in the east. It overlaps the **Millennium Way,** which goes from Castletown to Ramsey along the course of the 14th-century Royal Highway for 28 mi., ending a mile from Ramsey's Parliament Sq. The tourist office in Douglas has information and maps. The island's small size makes it easy to get around by **bike.** The southern three-quarters of the island are covered in challenging rolling hills—manageable, but difficult enough that the island is a venue for professional bicycle races. **Hitching** is a legal alternative to public transport. Locals claim that the Isle of Man is one of the safer places for hitching, although *Let's Go* does not recommend it anywhere.

ISLE OF MAN

EVENTS

The island's economy relies heavily on the tourist trade, so there are always festivals, ranging from jazz celebrations to an angling week. By far the most popular are motor races. A detailed calendar of events is available in the tourist office; ask for the bimonthly *What's on the Isle of Man* or the monthly edition of *Events 1999*. **IOM International Cycling Week** follows the T.T. Race Weeks (see below) and its tracks. Established in 1936, it is now the most respected cycling race on the British Isles. **Manx Heritage Festival** is held the week of July 5. **Tynwald Fair** sees the pronouncement of new laws on July 5, the Isle of Man Bank Holiday and Manx National Day. Representatives don British wigs and robes to read the new laws but do so in the Manx tongue upon a remote hill of ancient significance in the middle of the island. **Southern "100" Motorcycle Races** (tel. 822546) takes place over three days in mid-July: more bikers, more fun, this time based in Castletown.

Each year during the first two weeks of June, peaceful Man is transformed into a merry leather-clad beast. The population doubles, the Steam Packet Co. schedules extra ferries and stocks up on beer, and Manx Radio is replaced by its evil twin, "Radio T.T." The **T.T. (Tourist Trophy) Races** originated in 1904 when the tourist-hungry Manx government passed **Road Closure Act,** under which roads could be closed and speed limits lifted for a motor race. Automobile clubs gravitated to Man, and in 1907, motorcycle racing emerged. Today there are 600 racers and 40,000 fans. The unusual T.T. circuit consists of 38 mi. of hairpin turns and mountain climbs. The winner gets his (no "her," yet) name and make of motorcycle engraved on the same silver "tourist trophy" that has been in use since 1907. The T.T. season is a non-stop two-week party, embraced by locals as part of their national identity.

■ Douglas

Recent capital of an ancient island, Douglas has leveled the natural Manx landscape under a square mile of concrete promenades and tall, narrow Victorian townhouses. In the last century, Douglas bloomed as a Victorian seaside resort; today, it sells still-shiny Victorian relics to a nostalgic, family-oriented pod of tourists. Douglas's economy profits most from the savvy, tax-evading businessmen who hurry down the promenade from nine to five.

ORIENTATION

Douglas proper stretches for 2 mi. along the seafront, from **Douglas Head** in the south to the **Electric Railway** terminal in the north. Douglas Head is separated from the rest of town by the River Douglas, which flows into the harbor. The ferry terminal lies just north of the river, as does the bus terminal. **The Promenade,** which changes names frequently, bends from the ferry terminal to the Electric Railway terminal along the crescent of beach; it is lined on one side with grand though sometimes tattered Victorian terrace houses. The shopping district spreads out around **Victoria St. Nobles Park** is site of recreation facilities and the start of the T.T. course.

PRACTICAL INFORMATION

Airplanes: Ronaldsway Airport, 8mi. southwest of Douglas on the coast road. Port St. Mary-Douglas **bus** M-Sa 6:20am-10:50pm, Su 8:40am-10:50pm (25min., M-Sa 27 per day, Su 12 per day, £1.25). The **steam train** will stop if you notify the guard first.

Trains and Buses: Isle of Man Transport, Strathallan Crescent (trains tel. 663366, buses tel. 662525). See **Getting About,** p. 575.

Ferries: Victoria Pier, at the southern end of town near the bus station.

Local Transportation: Slow but inexpensive horse-drawn **trams** (tel. 675522) run down the Promenade between the bus and Electric Railway station in summer. Stops are posted every 200yd. or so. Continuous service daily June-Aug. 9:10am-8:50pm; May-Sept. 9:10am-6:30pm. £1.40 for unlimited rides in a day, seniors and ages 16 and under 80p. **Buses** also run along the Promenade every few minutes, connecting the bus and Steam Railway stations with the Electric Railway and Onchan (bus station to Electric Railway 70p).

Taxis: A-1 Taxis (tel. 674488). 24hr. service to the whole island.

Car Rental: St. Bernard's Car Rental, Castle Mona (tel. 613878; fax 613879), off the Central Promenade.

Bike Rental: Eurocycles, 8a Victoria Rd. (tel. 624909), off Broadway. Call ahead in summer. Open M-Sa 9am-6pm.

Tourist Office: Sea Terminal Bldg. (tel. 686766). Helpful leaflets on the country and a free map of Douglas. Open Easter-Sept. daily 9am-7:30pm; Oct. M-Th 9am-5:30pm, F 9am-5pm, Sa 10am-4:30pm, Su 10am-4pm; Nov.-Easter M-Th 9am-5:30pm, F 9am-5pm. Open Easter-Oct. for early evening ferry.

Banks: A.T. Mays Travel Agents, 1 Regent St. (tel. 623330). Bureau de change convenient to the ferry terminal. Open M-F 9am-5:30pm, Sa 9am-5pm. **TSB,** 78 Strand St. (tel. 673755), has an **ATM.**

Emergency: Dial 999; no coins required.

Police: (tel. 631212).

Hotlines: Samaritans, 5 Victoria Pl. (tel. 663399), near Broadway. Drop-ins daily 10am-10pm; 24hr. hotline.

Pharmacy: G.J. Maley's Chemists, 15 Strand St. (tel. 626833). Open M-Sa 9am-5:30pm.

Hospital: Nobles Isle of Man Hospital, Westmoreland Rd. (tel. 642642).

Post Office: Regent St. (tel. 686141). Open M and W-F 9am-5:30pm, Tu 9:30am-5:30pm, Sa 9am-12:30pm. **Postal code:** IM1 2EA.

Internet Access: Cyberia Internet Café, 31 North Quay (tel. 440 1624). £2.50-4 per hr. Open M-Sa 10am-10pm, Su 10am-6pm.

Telephone Code: 01624 for the entire island.

ACCOMMODATIONS AND FOOD

With nearly every house along The Promenade providing B&B, it should be possible to find a cheap place to stay except during the race weeks (see **T.T. Race Weeks,** above), when B&Bs raise their rates and still fill up a year in advance. Another option is **camping,** which must be done at a campsite or on the "common land" near the northern tip of the island; consult the tourist office. **Glen Villa,** 5 Broadway (tel. 673394), is near the grassy lawns of the Villa Marina Gardens and has a private bar (£15, with bath £17). **Seaside Hotel,** 9 Empress Dr. (tel. 674765; fax 615041), sports hand-stenciled walls just a minute's walk from the Promenade (£14; open Apr.-Oct.). Pretty, clean **Melrose Guest House,** 18 Christian Ln., is closer to the business district than to the ocean (£13, with bath £16). **Nobles Park Grandstand Campsite** (tel. 621132; open M-F 9am-5pm), behind the grandstand on the site of the T.T. races' start and finish line, is the only campground in Douglas, although others open for T.T. week (£5 per site; showers £1; laundry £2; open mid-June to mid-Aug. and Sept.).

Cheap grill and chip shops proliferate along The Promenade, Duke St., Strand St., and Castle St. The antics of the boss at **Victoria's,** Castle St. (tel. 626003), have Victorian enthusiasts blushing gleefully behind their menus (sandwiches and hoagies £2-3.75; main dishes £3.50-5; open M-Sa 10am-5pm). **Saagar Tandoori,** 1 South View, Summerhill (tel. 674939), has a bay view (entrees £3-6; open daily noon-2:30pm and 6pm-midnight). **Green's,** Steam Railway Station, North Quay (tel. 629129), serves enormous platters of food and sinful desserts (£2-5; open daily 9am-5pm). **Brendann O'Donnell's,** 16-18 Strand St. (tel. 621566), looks like a traditional chipper, but feels like a traditional Irish pub inside. **Cul-de-Sac Bar and Pizzeria,** 3 Market Hill (tel. 623737), by North Quay, has the largest selection of beer on the island. (Lunch served M-F noon-2pm, Sa noon-6pm; dinner M-Sa 5:30pm-late. Free live music F-Su.)

SIGHTS AND ENTERTAINMENT

From the shopping district, signs lead to the Chester St. parking garage, where an elevator leads to the fascinating **Manx Museum** (tel. 648000). The museum chronicles the history of the island from the Ice Age to the present with geological, taxidermic,

ISLE OF MAN

and historical displays. *(Open M-Sa 10am-5pm. Free.)* Just past the Villa Marina Gardens on Harris Promenade, north of the Manx Museum, sits the **Gaiety Theatre** (tel. 625001). The theater, designed in 1900, was lush in Douglas's Victorian seaside resort days. Recently restored, it will be in full splendor on its 100th birthday. To see the fascinating antique machinery you'll have to take a guided **tour.** *(1½hr. Sa 10:30am; July-Aug. also Th 2:30pm. Donation encouraged. Performances Mar.-Dec. Box office open M-Sa 10am-4:30pm and 1hr. before performances. Tickets £12.50-14; discounts for seniors and children.)* The thing that looks like a sand castle sitting in Douglas Bay is the **Tower of Refuge** (not open to public). The southern end of Douglas is marked by **Douglas Head,** with lovely views of the town.

Most of the late-night **clubs** in Douglas are 21+ and free until 10 or 11pm, with a £2-5 cover if you arrive later. **Paramount City,** Queens Promenade (tel. 622447), houses two nightclubs. *(Cover £3-4. Open W, F, and Sa. 21+. No jeans, t-shirts, or sportswear.)*

■ Port Erin

Near the southern tip of the island, small, quiet Port Erin is perhaps the prettiest town on Man. The **Railway Museum** in the railway station is free and contains two antique trains. *(Open Easter-Oct. daily 9:30am-5:30pm. Free.)* Take advantage of cruises to the **Calf of Man** (tel. 832339), the small island and bird sanctuary off the southern tip of Man. Visitors can choose between a ferry ride or a 1¼-hour cruise around the Calf, with views of the cliffs, seals, and the odd basking shark. *(Cruises leave Apr.-Sept. daily 10:15, 11:30am, and 1:30pm, depending on the weather; return £8. No toilets.)*

Steam trains chug to **Douglas** (1hr., Easter-Oct. 6 per day, £3.40). **Buses** zoom to **Douglas** (55min., 21 per day, £1.75) and **Peel** (50min., 2 per day, £1.80). The Commissioners Office, Station Rd. (tel. 832298), dishes basic **tourist information** (open May to late Sept. M-Th 9am-5pm, F 9am-4:30pm, Sa 9am-noon).

The Anchorage, Athol Park (tel. 832355), off Strand Rd. and next to teeny Athol Glen, warmly welcomes you to its sunny rooms (£18, with bath £21). **Balmoral Hotel,** the Promenade (tel. 833126), looks like a hotel but sure tastes like a B&B in the morning (£18.50, with bath £21.50). If you're up for a picnic, try the **Shoprite Supermarket,** Orchard Rd., behind the bus stop (open M-F 8am-8pm, Sa 8am-6:30pm, Su 10am-4pm). **Cozy Nook Cafe,** Lower Promenade (tel. 835020), may have been the inspiration for the Admiral's Inn in Stevenson's *Treasure Island* (sandwiches £1.60-2; open daily Apr.-Sept. 10:30am-5pm; Oct.-Mar. F-Su 10am-5pm).

■ Peel

The "most Manx of all towns" and headquarters of the Manx kipper industry, Peel is a beautiful fishing town on the west coast of Man. Narrow streets and small stone buildings have hardly changed since the days fishers sailed from here to the Hebrides. Romantic **Peel Castle,** located on **St. Patrick's Isle,** is now connected to the mainland by a causeway. *(Open Easter-Oct. daily 10am-5pm. £2.50, children £1.50; includes audioguide.)* Damp, eerie **Bishop's Dungeon** was used for hundreds of years to punish sinners for such terrible offenses as missing church. **Moore's Traditional Curers,** Mill Rd. (tel. 843622), one of Peel's two **kipper factories,** gives tours. *(June to mid-Sept. at 2, 3, and 4pm. £1.50, children 50p.)*

Buses from the station on Atholl St. next to the IOM bank go to **Douglas** (30min., 9-21 per day, £1.45) and **Port Erin** (55min., 2-3 per day). The **tourist office,** Town Hall, Derby Rd. (tel. 842341), has free pamphlets and maps (open M-Th 8:45am-5pm, F 8:45am-4:30pm). **Haven Guest House,** 10 Peveril Ave. (tel. 842585), off Peveril Rd., has delightful mountain views (£18.50-20), while nearby **Seabourne House,** Mt. Morrison (tel. 842571), offers stupendous views of the Irish sea (May-Sept. £16.50; Oct.-Apr. £15). **Peel Camping Park,** Derby Rd. (tel. 842341), has laundry and a wheelchair-accessible bathroom (£3.50 per person; open May-Sept.). The town has two **Shoprite** grocery stores: one on Derby Rd. and the other in the center of town. Have a whoppily big hearty Manx meal at the dainty little **Harbour Lights Cafe and Tearoom,** Shore Rd. (entrees £3-5; open M-Sa 9am-5pm).

Northern Ireland

NORTHERN IRELAND

The strife that makes the North infamous can often hide the land's beauty and appeal from international travelers. What they're missing includes the string of seaside villages on the Ards Peninsula, the pockets of green collectively called the Glens of Antrim, the Giant's Causeway, one of the world's strangest geological sights, and the beautiful Fermanagh Lake District. A major industrial center, Belfast has recently become a hip destination for a range of travelers and students. Pub culture and urban neighborhoods show everyday life in a divided but generally peaceful society.

▓ Essentials

MONEY

Legal tender in Northern Ireland is the British pound. Northern Ireland has its own bank notes, which are identical in value to English, Scottish, or Manx notes of the same denominations but are not accepted outside Northern Ireland. All of these notes, however, are accepted here. Usual weekday bank hours in Northern Ireland are Monday to Friday 9:30am to 3:30pm.

SAFETY AND SECURITY

Although sectarian violence is dramatically less common than in the height of the Troubles, some neighborhoods and towns still experience turmoil during sensitive political times. It's best to avoid traveling in Northern Ireland during **Marching Season,** from July 4 to July 12 (**Orange Day;** see p. 581). The most common form of violence is property damage, and tourists are not generally targets, but transportation and services may shut down if there are problems—you don't want to be stranded. Vacation areas like the Glens and the Causeway Coast are less affected by the parades. Overall, Northern Ireland has one of the lowest crime rates in the world. **Border checkpoints** have been removed and it is rare to see armed soldiers and vehicles in Belfast or Derry; however, it is still generally unsafe to hitch in Northern Ireland. Never take **photographs** of soldiers, military installations, or vehicles; if you do, your film will be confiscated and you may be detained for questioning. Taking pictures of political murals is not a crime, although some people feel uncomfortable doing so.

■ History and Politics

There's a place called "Northern Ireland," but there are no "Northern Irish." The citizens still identify themselves along religious rather than geographic lines—as Catholics or Protestants. The 950,000 Protestants are generally Unionists, who want the six counties of Northern Ireland to remain in the U.K.; the 650,000 Catholics tend to identify with the Republic of Ireland, not Britain, and many are Nationalists, who want the six counties to be part of the Republic. The conflict between them seems to be intractable. A tentative optimism has descended upon the North since the monumental Peace Agreement of 1998, but challenges remain (see p. 583).

The 17th century's **Ulster Plantation** systematically set up English and Scottish settlers on what had been Gaelic-Irish land and gave Derry to the City of London—hence the name "Londonderry." Over the following two centuries, merchants and working-class immigrants from nearby Scotland settled in northeast Ulster. Their ties to Scotland and proximity to England meant that Cos. Antrim and Down developed an Industrial Revolution economy while the rest of the island remained agricultural. Ulster Plantation and Scottish settlement, over the course of 300 years, created a working- and middle-class population in northeast Ulster who identified with the British Empire and didn't support Irish Home Rule. By 1830, the **Orange Order,** named after William of Orange, who had won victories over Catholic James II in the 1690s, organized the Ulster Protestants and held parades to celebrate their heritage.

Edward Carson and his ally **James Craig** translated Ulster Unionism into terms the British elite understood. When Home Rule looked likely in 1911, Carson held a mass meeting, and Unionists signed a covenant promising to resist. When Home Rule appeared imminent in 1914, the Unionist **Ulster Volunteer Force (UVF)** armed itself with smuggled guns. World War I gave Unionists more time to organize and British leaders time to see that the imposition of Home Rule on all of Ulster would mean havoc as the UVF fought the **Irish Republican Army (IRA),** who in turn fought the police. The 1920 **Government of Ireland Act** created one parliament for the North and one for South. The Act went nowhere in the south, but the measure—intended to be temporary—became the basis of the North's government until 1973. The new Parliament met at **Stormont,** near Belfast, and included only six of the nine counties in the province of Ulster. Carson and Craig had approved these odd borders in order to create the largest possible area that would have a permanent Protestant majority. Anti-Catholic discrimination was widespread. The **Royal Ulster Constabulary (RUC),** the new and Protestant police force in the North, filled its ranks with part-time policemen called **B-Specials,** who caused Catholic casualties and rage. The IRA continued sporadic campaigns in the North through the 20s and 30s with little result.

World War II gave Unionists a chance to show their loyalty while the Republic remained pointedly neutral. Bombed by the Luftwaffe, Belfast was one of the U.K.'s most damaged cities. A grateful British Parliament then poured money into the North, where the standard of living stayed higher than the Republic's. But discrimination and joblessness persisted; large towns were segregated by religion. After a brief try at school desegregation, Stormont ended up granting subsidies to Catholic schools. Violence had receded tremendously, and the IRA was seen as finished by 1962.

The American civil rights movement inspired the 1967 founding of the **Northern Ireland Civil Rights Association (NICRA),** which tried to end anti-Catholic discrimination in public housing. Protestant extremists included the forceful **Dr. Ian Paisley,** whose **Ulster Protestant Volunteers (UPV)** overlapped in membership with the illegal, paramilitary, resurrected UVF. The first NICRA march was raucous but nonviolent. The second, in Derry in May 1968, was a bloody mess disrupted by Unionists and then by the RUC's water cannons. This incident is considered the culmination of the **Troubles.**

The IRA was seen as finished by 1962.

Catholic **John Hume** and Protestant **Ivan Cooper** formed a new civil rights committee in Derry but were overshadowed by Bernadette Devlin's student-led, radical **People's Democracy (PD).** The PD encouraged, and NICRA opposed, a four-day march from Belfast to Derry starting on New Year's Day, 1969. The RUC launched an assault on Derry's Catholic Bogside once the marchers arrived. Derry authorities at last agreed to keep the RUC out of Bogside—it became **Free Derry.** When Catholics based in Free Derry threw rocks at the 1969 Orange parade, the RUC attacked the Catholics and a two-day siege ensued. The violence showed everyone that the RUC couldn't maintain order. The British Army arrived—and hasn't left yet.

The rejuvenated IRA split in two, with the Marxist "Official" faction fading as the new **Provisional IRA** (or **Provos**) took aim at the Protestants. More hopefully, the **Social Democratic and Labor Party (SDLP)** was founded in 1970; by 1973 it had become the moderate political voice of Northern Catholics. The British troops became the IRA's main target; British policies of internment without trial outraged Catholics and led the SDLP to withdraw from government. The pattern was clear: any concessions to the Catholics might provoke Protestant violence, while showing favor to the Union risked an explosive IRA response.

On January 30, 1972, British troops fired into a crowd of protesters in Derry, killing 31 Catholics. The famous event, called **Bloody Sunday,** and the reluctance of the ensuing British investigation increased Catholic outrage. Only now is the incident being officially re-examined, with hearings scheduled for February 1999. Stormont was dissolved, and a policy of **direct British rule** from Westminster began. In 1978, 300 Nationalist prisoners in the Maze Prison in Northern Ireland began a campaign to have their special category as political prisoners restored. The campaign's climax was the H-Block **hunger strike** of 1981—10 prisoners fasted to death. Their leader, Bobby Sands, was the first to go on hunger strike; he was elected to Parliament even as he starved to death. Sands died after 66 days and became a prominent martyr; his face is still seen on murals in the Falls section of Belfast.

The hunger strikes galvanized Nationalists, and support for **Sinn Féin,** the political arm of the IRA, surged in the early 80s. British Prime Minister Margaret Thatcher and Taoiseach Garret FitzGerald signed the **Anglo-Irish Agreement** in November 1985. The Agreement grants the Republic of Ireland a "consultative role" but no legal authority in the governance of Northern Ireland. It improved relations between London and Dublin but infuriated extremists on both sides. Protestant paramilitaries began to attack the British Army, while the IRA continued its bombing campaigns in England. In 1991-92, the Brooke Initiative led to the first multi-party talks in the North in over a decade, but they did not include Sinn Féin. In December 1993, the **Downing Street Declaration,** issued by John Major and Taoiseach Albert Reynolds, invited the IRA to participate in talks if they refrained from violence for three months.

On August 31, 1994, the IRA announced a complete cessation of violence. Wanting a permanent end to terrorism, Unionist leaders bickered over the meaning of this statement. Nonetheless, Sinn Féin leader **Gerry Adams** defended the statement and called for direct talks with the British government. Although talks met with some success, progress was slow. The IRA ended their cease-fire on February 9, 1996, with the bombing of a building in London's Docklands. Despite this setback, peace talks, chaired by former U.S. Senator George Mitchell, were finally slated for June 1996. Ian Paisley objected to Mitchell's appointment, calling it a "dastardly deed," but did not boycott the talks. Sinn Féin did not participate in these talks because it did not agree to the **Mitchell principles,** which included the total disarmament of all paramilitary organizations. A June 15, 1996, blast in a busy Manchester shopping district injured more than 200 people and further tarnished the IRA's and Sinn Féin's image.

Violence flared surrounding **Orange Day, 1996,** when the Parades Commission banned an Orange Order march through a Catholic section of Portadown. Protestants reacted by throwing petrol bombs, bricks, and bottles at police, who answered with plastic bullets. After four days of violence, police allowed the marchers to go through, but this time Catholics responded with a hail of debris. Nightly rioting by both sides also took place in Belfast. On October 7, the IRA bombed British army headquarters in Belfast, killing one soldier and injuring 30, in the first bombing in Northern Ireland in two years. In early 1997, the IRA issued bomb threats in Great Britain in an attempt to make Northern Ireland an issue in the upcoming elections.

In May, the Labour party swept the British elections and **Tony Blair** became Prime Minister, bringing hope for peaceful change. Sinn Féin made an impressive showing: Gerry Adams and member Martin McGuinness won seats in Parliament but were barred from taking their seats by their refusal to swear allegiance to the Queen. Despite this refusal, the government ended its ban on talks with Sinn Féin. Sinn Féin, however, refused to join the talks. Hopes for a cease-fire were dashed when the car of a prominent Irish republican was bombed; in retaliation, the IRA shot RUC members.

The British government's Northern Ireland Secretary **Mo Mowlam** had a rough introduction to her new job: **marching season** in 1997 was the most violent since before the cease-fire. The Orange Order held a large march through the town of Portadown a week before Orange Day. More than 80 people were hurt in the ensuing rioting and looting, and Mowlam came under scrutiny for allowing the parade to go on without considering the consequences. On July 10, the Orange Order called off and re-routed a number of contentious parades, offering hope for peace. The marches that were held were mostly peaceful; police fired plastic bullets at rioters in Derry and Belfast, but there were no casualties. On July 19, the IRA announced an "unequivocal" **cease-fire** to start the following day.

> *The Agreement emphasized that change in the North could come only with the consent of the majority of its people.*

In September 1997, Sinn Féin joined the peace talks. Members of the **Ulster Unionist Party (UUP),** the voice of moderate Protestants, joined shortly thereafter and were attacked by Ian Paisley and the DUP for sitting with terrorists. David Trimble, leader of the UUP, assured Protestants that he wouldn't negotiate directly with Sinn Féin. Some groups still opposed the peace process. In January 1998, another 12 people were killed by sectarian violence, mostly committed by extremist Loyalists against Catholic civilians. After two Protestants were killed by Catholic extremists in early February, Unionist leaders charged Sinn Féin with breaking its pledge to support only peaceful actions toward political change and tried to oust party leaders from the talks. Mitchell, Mowlam, Blair, and Irish Prime Minister Bertie Ahern continued to push for progress, holding the group to a strict deadline in April.

After an interminable week of late-night negotiations, the delegates approved a draft of the **1998 Northern Ireland Peace Agreement** in the early morning after April 10, Good Friday. The Agreement above all emphasized that change in Northern Ireland could come only with the consent of the majority of its people. It declared that the "birthright" of the people is the right to choose whether to personally identify as Irish, British, or both; even as the status of Northern Ireland changes, the Agreement says, residents retain the right to hold Irish or British citizenship.

On Friday, May 22, in the first island-wide vote since 1918, residents of both the North and the Republic voted the Agreement into law. A resounding 71% of the North voted yes, and the Agreement won 94% of the vote in the Republic. Overall,

85% of the island voted yes, meaning that a majority of Protestants voted in favor of the Peace Agreement, which divided governing responsibilities of Northern Ireland into three strands. The main body, a new 108-member **Northern Ireland Assembly,** assigns committee posts and chairs proportionately to the parties' representation. Catholics see this body as an opportunity for reclaiming the political power they were long denied. The second strand, a **North-South Ministerial Council,** serves as the cross-border authority. At least 12 possible areas of focus were under consideration by them in 1998, including such social welfare issues as education, transportation and urban planning, environmental protection, tourism, and EU programs. The final strand, the **British-Irish Council,** approaches similar issues as the North-South Council but operates on a broader scale, concerning itself with the entire British Isles.

The Agreement included two other major provisions: the decommissioning of all paramilitary and terrorist groups' arms and the early release of political prisoners. Political parties whose military wings did not disarm themselves by the time of the June elections would not be able to assume their seats in the Assembly. Tensions rose out of the **Northern Ireland (Sentences) Bill,** voted against by members of the UUP, the DUP, and the British Conservative Party, splitting the U.K. Parliament for the first time during the talks. The bill will release all political prisoners, including those convicted of murder, by 2000. Dissenters fear that the bill did not sufficiently link the release of any prisoner to his organization's full disarmament.

The Agreement included the decommissioning of all paramilitary and terrorist groups' arms.

While most felt that Northern Ireland was finally on the verge of lasting peace, a few controversial issues remained unresolved. Sinn Féin called for disbanding the still very largely Protestant RUC, which was cited in an April 1998 United Nations report for its systematic intimidation and harassment of lawyers representing those accused of paramilitary crimes. Blair declared that the RUC will continue to exist, but in June appointed Chris Patten, the former governor of Hong Kong, to head a small one-year commission to review the RUC's recruiting, hiring, and training practices as well as its culture and symbols.

The 1998 marching season brought challenges and tragedy to the newly arrived peace. In the end of May, just a week after the Agreement was voted in, a march by the Junior Orange Order provoked violence on Garvaghy Rd., the Catholic zone in the largely Protestant Portadown where violence had erupted at a 1996 parade. In light of this disturbance, the Parades Commission hesitated in granting the Orange Day marching permits. Aside from two short stand-offs with the RUC, the parade proceeded without conflict. The day after the assembly elections, however, violence broke out between Nationalists and policemen at a parade in West Belfast. The beginning of July saw a wave of violence that included hundreds of bombings and attacks on security forces as well as a slew of arson attacks on Catholic churches.

Other parades passed peacefully, but a stand-off began over the fate of the **Drumcree** parade. This Orange parade, which occurs July 4, was not given permission to march down the Catholic section of Garvaghy Rd. in Portadown. Thousands of people participated in a week-long standoff with the RUC that affected the whole country. Rioting occurred there and elsewhere, and Protestant marchers were angered by what they saw as the disloyalty of their own police force. Neither the Orangemen nor the Parade Commission would budge, and the country looked with anxiety toward Orange Day, July 12, which would be the climax of the tense situation. On July 11, however, a Catholic home in almost entirely Protestant **Ballymoney** was firebombed in the middle of the night by local hooligans, and three boys, Richard, Mark, and Jason Quinn, were killed. The Church of Ireland publicly called for the end of the Drumcree protest. The seemingly intractable stand-off, though never officially ended by extreme Protestant leaders, faded away. Although some tried to distance the attack from the events going on at Drumcree, the murders led both to a reassessment of the Orange Order and to a new sobriety about the peace process.

Peter's Hill

Westlink
Brown St.
Gardiner St.
Boyd St.
Samuel St.
Brown St.
Gresham St.
Millfield
Francis St.

North St.

Royal Ave.

Donegall St.

St. Anne's Cathedral

Talbot St.

Gordon St.

Dunbar St.

Tomb St.

Albert Sq.

Custom House

Queen's Sq.

Tourist Board

North St. Arcade

Garfield

Waring St.

Hill St.

First Presbyterian Church

Rosemary St.

Berry St.

Royal Ave.

Bank St.

Lombard St.

Bridge St.

High St.

Church St.

Ann St.

Divis St.

Hamill St.

Marquis St.

Castle St.

King St.

College Ct.

College Square E.

Queen St.

Fountain St.

Castle Place

Castle Lane

Cornmarket

Callender St.

Arthur St.

Pottinger's Entry

Ann St.

RUC Station

NO-CAR ZONE

Oxford St.

Durham St.

Old Museum

College Square N.

College St.

Linenhall Library

Donegall Place

Chinchester St.

Victoria Square

Town Hall

Athol St.

Wellington Place

Donegall Sq. N.

City Hall

Donegall Sq. E.

Montgomery St.

Gloucester St.

Grosvenor Rd.

Howard St.

Donegall Sq. W.

Donegall Sq. S.

May St.

Little May St.

E. Bridge St.

Opera House

Glengall St.

Europa Bus Station

Europa Hotel

Crown Liquor Saloon

Great Victoria St. Rail Station

James St.

Bedford St.

Franklin St.

Linen Hall St.

Clarence St.

Adelaide St.

Alfred St.

Joy St.

Russell St.

Hamilton St.

Grace St.

Cromac St.

McAuley St.

Sandy Row

Bruce St.

Linfield Rd.

Ormeau Ave.

Bankmore St.

Wellwood St.

Dublin Rd.

Maryville St.

Apsley St.

Lindsay St.

Howard St. South

Charlotte St.

Ormeau Rd.

Albion St.

Blythe St.

SHAFTESBURY SQ.

Donegall Pass

Elm St.

Donegall Rd.

City Hospital Rail Station

Bradbury Pl.

Botanic Ave.

Botanic Rail Station

Vernon St.

Cooke St.

Shaftesbury Ave.

Lower Crescent

McClure St.

Lisburn Rd.

Claremont St.

Camden St.

Fitzwilliam St.

Upper Crescent

Mount Charles

University Rd.

Wolseley St.

Cromwell Rd.

University St.

University Square

College Park

Rugby Rd.

Fitzroy Ave.

University Ave.

College Park Ave.

Rugby Ave.

Elmwood Ave.

Visitor's Center

Queen's University

College Gdn.

Botanic Gardens

River Logan

N

Central Belfast

ACCOMMODATIONS
C Arnie's Hostel
B The Ark
A EYHANI
D YWCA

0   100 yards
0   100 meters

On August 15, 1998, the 29th anniversary of the deployment of British troops in Northern Ireland, a bombing in the religiously mixed town of **Omagh,** County Tyrone, left dozens dead and hundreds injured. Initial analysis blamed a group calling itself the "Real IRA," a splinter group of former IRA fanatics. The obvious motive for the attack, the worst atrocity of the Trouble, was to undermine the Agreement. However, the terrible act could only underline the fact that most people in Northern Ireland, both Catholic and Protestant, had voted for the agreement, and Sinn Féin's Gerry Adams unreservedly condemned the attack. At the time of this printing, it remains to be seen whether the acts of extremists will defeat the will of the people of Northern Ireland.

🅰 HIGHLIGHTS OF NORTHERN IRELAND

- The brightly pigmented **murals** of Belfast (p. 591)—some moving, some frightening—show the history of Northern Ireland through the eyes of its inhabitants.
- The **Glens of Antrim** (p. 598) provide glimpses of traditional life as well as biking opportunities through lush countryside pierced by mountains and waterfalls.
- The tremendous, bizarre honeycomb rock formations of **Giant's Causeway** (p. 600) are Northern Ireland's most famous sight.
- The history of Derry, a religious, cultural, and political center for millennia, is never more intriguing than when viewed from atop its **old city walls** (p. 605).

BELFAST

The second-largest city on the island, Belfast (pop. 330,000) is the center of the North's cultural, commercial, and political activity. The surrounding hills appear suddenly at the end of streets filled with a century's worth of industry. Victorian architecture, acclaimed theater, and the annual arts festival in November maintain Belfast's reputation as a thriving artistic center. West Belfast's political graffiti art and famous murals are both informative and truly moving. The burgeoning bar scene—a mix of British pub culture, Irish pub culture, and less traditional international trends—entertains locals, foreigners, and the lively student population. The past few years have brought a chic cosmopolitan edge to this growing city, which, despite a significant visitor presence, seems unlikely to succumb to tourist culture.

GETTING THERE AND GETTING ABOUT

If arriving by **ferry,** you have two options to reach the city center. A taxi might be your best bet after dark; the docks can be somewhat unsafe at night. If on foot, take a left when you exit the terminal onto Donegall Quay. Turn right onto Albert Sq. about two blocks down at the Customs House. After two short blocks, turn left on Victoria St. (not Great Victoria St.). Turn right again at the clock tower onto High St., which runs into Donegall Pl. Here, a left will lead you to City Hall and Donegall Sq. (at the end of the street), where you can catch a Centrelink bus (see below). For information on ferries and hovercraft to Belfast from **England** and **Scotland,** see **By Ferry,** p. 30.

Trains roll in from **Derry** (2½hr., M-F 7 per day, Sa 6 per day, Su 4 per day, £5.50) and **Dublin** (2½hr., M-F 8 per day, Sa 7 per day, Su 3 per day, £15) to Central Station. To get to Donegall Sq. from Central Station, turn left and walk down E. Bridge St. Turn right on Victoria St. then left after two blocks onto May St., which runs into Donegall Sq. South. Another option is the Centrelink bus service, free with rail tickets. Buses to **Dublin** (M-Sa 7 per day, Su 3 per day, £10.50) and **Derry** (M-Sa 15 per day, Su 6 per day, £6.50). **Hitching** is notoriously hard in and out of Belfast—most people take the bus out as far as Bangor or Larne before they stick out a thumb.

Public transportation within the city is provided by the red **Citybus Network** (24hr. recorded info tel. 246485), and **Ulsterbus** covers the suburbs. Citybuses going south and west leave from Donegall Sq. East; those going north and east leave from Donegall Sq. West (80p). Money-saving 4-journey tickets cost £2.70. Seven-day **gold** cards allow unlimited travel in the city (£10.50); seven-day **silver cards** permit unlimited travel in either North Belfast, West/South Belfast, or East Belfast (£11). All transport cards and tickets can be bought from kiosks in Donegall Sq. and around the city (open M-Sa 8am-6pm). The **Centrelink** green bus connects all of the major areas of Belfast in the course of its cloverleaf-shaped route (Donegall Sq., Castlecourt Shopping Centre, Europa and Langanside Bus Stations, Northern Ireland Rail Station, and Shaftesbury Sq.). The buses can be caught at any of 12 designated stops (4 per hr., M-F 7:15am-8:30pm, Sa 8:35am-8:30pm, 50p, free with bus or rail ticket). Late **Nightline** buses cover five extensive routes from Shaftesbury Sq. to various parts of the city. Tickets must be bought in advance from ticket units in Shaftesbury Sq. (open F-Sa until 1 or 2am, £2).

ORIENTATION

Buses arrive at the Europa bus station on **Great Victoria St.** To the northeast is the City Hall in **Donegall Sq.** A busy pedestrian shopping district extends north four blocks. South of the bus station, Great Victoria St. meets Dublin Rd. at **Shaftesbury Sq.** The stretch of Great Victoria St. running between the bus station and Shaftesbury Sq. is known as the **Golden Mile** for its highbrow establishments and Victorian architecture. Botanic Ave. and Bradbury Pl. (which becomes University Rd.) extend south from Shaftesbury Sq. into the **Queen's University area,** where many cafes, student pubs, and budget accommodations await. The city center, Golden Mile, and university area are quite safe for tourists. Divided from the rest of Belfast by the Westlink Motorway, working class **West Belfast** is more politically volatile than the city center. There remains a sharp division between sectarian neighborhoods. The Protestant neighborhood stretches along Shankill Rd., just north of the Catholic neighborhood, centered around Falls Rd. The two are separated by the **peace line.** The River Lagan divides industrial **East Belfast** from the rest of the city.

PRACTICAL INFORMATION

Transportation

Airports: Belfast International Airport (tel. (01232) 422888) in Aldergrove. **Airbus** (tel. 333000) runs to Belfast's Europa/Glengall St. bus station in the city center (M-Sa 2 per hr. 6:30am-9:30pm, Su about 1 per hr. 7am-8:45pm, £4.50, £7.50 return). **Belfast City Airport,** at the harbor, receives flights by **Manx Airlines** (tel. (0345) 256256) and **Jersey European. Trains** run from the airport to Central Station (M-F 31 per day, Sa 26 per day, Su 2 per day, 60p).

Trains: All trains arrive at Belfast's **Central Station,** E. Bridge St. (tel. 899400). Some also stop at **Botanic Station** (tel. 899400), on Botanic Ave. in the center of the University area, or the **Great Victoria Station** (tel. 434424), next to the Europa Hotel.

Buses: There are 2 main stations in Belfast. Buses traveling to and from the west and the Republic operate out of the **Europa (Glengall St.) Station** (tel. 333000). Open for inquiries M-Sa 7:30am-8:30pm, Su 9am-7:30pm. Buses to and from Northern Ireland's east coast operate out of **Laganside Station** (same tel. and hours as Europa). The **Leaping Leprechaun** bus service (tel. (015047) 42655) takes hostelers to and from IHH hostels on the Antrim coast. Return £18.

Ferries: Ferries arrive at the **Belfast SeaCat terminal** (tel. (01345) 523523). **Larne ferry terminals** are easily accessible by bus or train from the Belfast city center (buses 1hr., M-F 17 per day, Sa 15 per day, Su 3 per day, £2.60).

Taxis: Huge **black cabs** run set routes to West and North Belfast, collecting and discharging passengers along the way (standard 60p charge). Cabs heading to Catholic neighborhoods are marked with a Falls Rd., Andersontown, or Irish-language sign; those going to Protestant neighborhoods have a Shankill sign or a red poppy. Yellow-plated black cabs are official City Hall-registered vehicles. Ordinary 24hr. metered cabs abound: **City Cab** (tel. 242000; wheelchair accessible), **Diamond Taxi Service** (tel. 646666), **Fon a Cab** (tel. 233333), and **Jet Taxi** (tel. 323278).

Car Rental: McCausland's, 21-31 Grosvenor Rd. (tel. 333777), is Northern Ireland's largest car rental company. £39 per day, £170 per week; £10 surcharge to drive in the Republic. Ages 21-70. Open M-Th 8:30am-6:30pm, F 8:30am-7:30pm, Sa 8:30am-5pm, Su 8:30am-1pm. 24hr. car return at all offices. Other offices at **Belfast International Airport** (tel. (01849) 422022) and **Belfast City Airport** (tel. 454141). **Budget,** 96-102 Great Victoria St. (tel. 230700). £40-60 per day, £200-400 per week. Drop-off charge for Dublin £50, Galway £75. Ages 23 and over. Open M-F 9am-5:30pm, Sa 9am-1:30pm. **Belfast International Airport Office** (tel. (01849) 23332). Open daily 7:30am-11:30pm. **Belfast City Airport Office** (tel. 541111). Open daily 8am-9:30pm.

Bike Rental: McConvey Cycles, 10 Pottingers Entry (tel. 330322), or 467 Ormeau Rd. (tel. 491163). £7 per day, £40 per week; deposit £30; panniers £5 per week; locks supplied. Open M-Sa 9am-5:30pm. **ReCycle Bicycle Hire,** 1-5 Albert Sq. (tel. 313113), will pick up cycles M-F from Belfast hostels. F-M £11 per day, Tu-Th £9 per day; £30 per week; deposit £50 or passport. Open M-Sa 9am-5pm.

Tourist and Financial Services

Tourist Office: St. Anne's Court, 59 North St. (tel. 246609). Supplies a great booklet on Belfast, the usual info on the surrounding areas, and an excellent map of the city with bus schedules (free). Staff will get you where you need to go and find you a place to stay (in summer, call until 7:30pm for accommodations), but doesn't have the resources for much more. 24hr. computerized info bank outside. Open July-Aug. M-F 9am-7pm, Sa 9am-5:15pm, Su noon-4pm; Sept.-June M-Sa 9am-5:15pm.

Travel Agency: USIT, 13b The Fountain Centre, College St. (tel. 324073), near Royal Ave. Sells ISICs, European Youth Cards, **TravelSave** stamps (£5.50), and virtually every kind of bus or rail pass imaginable. Books ferries and planes, and compiles round-the-world itineraries. Open M and W-F 9:30am-5pm, Tu 10am-5pm, Sa 10am-1pm. **Branch** (tel. 241830) at Queen's University Student Union. Open M-Tu and Th-F 9:30am-5:30pm, W 10am-5pm.

Youth Hostel Association of Northern Ireland (YHANI): 22 Donegall Rd. (tel. 324733). Books YHANI hostels free, international hostels for £2.80. Sells HI membership cards (£7, under 18 £3). Open M-F 9am-5pm.

Banks: Banks and ATMs are a dime a dozen in Belfast; there is at least 1 on every corner. The major offices are **Ulster Bank,** 47 Donegall Pl. (tel. 244744); **First Trust,** 8 Donegall Sq. South. (tel. 324463); **Bank of Ireland,** 54 Donegal Pl. (tel. 244901); and **Northern Bank,** Donegall Sq. West. (tel. 245277). **Belfast International Airport office** (tel. (01849) 422536). Open May-Oct. M 5:30am-11pm, Tu-Th 5am-10pm, F-Su 5:30am-midnight; Nov.-Apr. M-F 7am-8pm, Sa-Su 7am-10pm.

American Express: Royal Ave. (tel. 242341). Most banks, the YHANI on Donegall Rd., and the post offices also provide bureau de change and traveler's check cashing services for a minimal fee.

Local Services

Luggage Storage: For security reasons there is no luggage storage at airports, bus stations, or train stations. All 3 **hostels** will hold bags during the day for those staying there, and the **Ark** will also hold bags during extended trips if you've stayed there (see **Accommodations,** below).

Laundry: Student's Union, Queen's University, University Rd. Wash £1, dry 20p per 5min. Open M-F 9am-9pm, Sa 10am-9pm, Su 2-9pm. Students only. **Duds & Suds,** Botanic Ave. (tel. 243956). Popcorn and TV while you wait. Wash £1.80, dry £1.80. 15% discount for students and seniors. Open M-F 8am-9pm, Sa 8am-6pm, Su noon-6pm; last wash 1½hr. before closing.

Women's Resources: Ardoyne Women's Centre, Butler St. (tel. 743536).

Bisexual, Gay, and Lesbian Information: Rainbow Project N.I. (tel. 319030). **Lesbian Line** (tel. 238668). Open Th 7:30-10pm. **Belfast Queer Space** (tel. 323419).

Emergency and Communications

Emergency: Dial 999; no coins required.

Police: 65 Knock Rd. (tel. 650222).

Hotlines: Samaritans (crisis; tel. 664422). 24hr. line for depression. **Rape Crisis Centre,** 29 Donegall St. (tel. 321830). Open M-F 10am-6pm, Sa 11am-5pm. **Contact Youth,** 2A Ribble St., offers a hotline M-F 10am-10pm (tel. 456654 to talk) and one-on-one counseling appointments (tel. 457848) 24hr.

Pharmacy: Boot's, 35-47 Donegall Pl. (tel. 242332). Open M-W and F-Sa 8:30am-6pm, Th 8:30am-9pm, Su 1-5pm.

Hospitals: Belfast City Hospital, 9 Lisburn Rd. (tel. 329241). From Shaftesbury Sq. follow Bradbury Pl. and take a right at the fork. **Royal Victoria Hospital,** 12 Grosvenor Rd. (tel. 240503). From Donegall Sq., take Howard St. west to Grosvenor Rd.

Post Office: Central Post Office, 25 Castle Pl. (tel. 323740). Open M-Sa 9am-5:30pm. *Poste Restante* mail comes here. **Postal code:** BT1 1NB. Dozens of **branches: Botanic Garden,** 95 University Rd. (tel. 381309), across from the university. **Postal code:** BT7 1NG. **Shaftesbury Sq.,** 7-9 Shaftesbury Sq. (tel. 326177). Open M-F 8:45am-5:30pm, Sa 10am-12:30pm. **Postal code:** BT2 7DA.

Internet Access: Revelations Internet Café, 27 Shaftesbury Sq. £5 per hr. Open M-F 10am-10pm, Sa 10am-8pm, Su noon-10pm.

Telephone code: 01232.

ACCOMMODATIONS

Nearly all of Belfast's budget accommodations are located near Queen's University. Convenient to pubs and restaurants, this area is by far the best place to stay in the city. Catch the **Centrelink** bus to Shaftesbury Sq., or bus #59, 69, 70, 71, 84, or 85 from Donegall Sq. East to areas farther south; the walk takes 10-20 minutes from the bus or train station. B&Bs multiply like rabbits between Malone and Lisburn Rd.

Arnie's Backpackers (IHH), 63 Fitzwilliam St. (tel. 242867). 10min. walk from Europa bus station on Great Victoria St. Take a right to head away from the Grand Opera House; at Shaftesbury Sq., take the right fork on Bradbury Pl. then fork left on University Rd. Fitzwilliam St. is on your right across from the university. Relaxed, friendly atmosphere provides a real respite from tiring travels. 4- to 6-bed dorms £7.50. Luggage storage during the day.

The Ark, 18 University St. (tel. 329626). Follow the directions to University Rd. given above; University St. is the third left off University Rd. The Ark is the hostel in which guests become resident staff members. Wanted: conversationalists and musicians. 6-bed dorms £7.50; 4-bed dorms £9.50; doubles £28. Kitchen always open, self-service breakfast included. Will keep luggage during weekend trips.

YHANI Belfast, 22 Donegall Rd. (tel. 324733). Clean, airy, modern rooms of 2-6 beds, some with bath. This hostel is located near Sandy Row, a Loyalist area that has seen violence during marching season (July 4-12). Dorms £8-10. Breakfast £1. No kitchen. Lockers 50p. Linen 50p. Laundry £3. 4-day max. stay. 24hr. reception. Book ahead for weekends. Wheelchair accessible.

Queen's University Accommodations, 78 Malone Rd. (tel. 381608). Bus #71 from Donegall Sq. East or a 25min. walk from Europa. University Rd. runs into Malone Rd.; the residence halls are on your left. An undecorated, institutional dorm: spacious singles or twin rooms with sinks and desks. Singles £8.80 for U.K. students, £10.36 for international students, £14 for others; doubles £22. Open mid-June to mid-Sept. and Christmas and Easter vacations.

Mrs. Davidson's East-Sheen Guest House, 81 Eglantine Ave. (tel. 667149). The best deal in Belfast, if you can get a room. Rooms are bright and clean. £19.50.

The George, 9 Eglantine Ave. (tel. 683212). Spic 'n' span rooms, all with shower and TV. Singles £20; doubles £36, with bath £38. 3% Visa/MC surcharge.

Marine House, 30 Eglantine Ave. (tel. 381922). This mansion overcomes the alienating hotel-like implications of its size. Singles £19; doubles £40, with bath £42.

FOOD

Belfast assumes a cosmopolitan character in its eateries, where you can sample flavors from almost any area of the world. Dublin Rd., Botanic Rd., and the Golden Mile have the highest concentration of restaurants, but nearly all close by 5:30pm. The **Mace Supermarket,** on the corner of Castle and Queen St., sells cheap groceries (open M-W and F-Sa 9am-6pm, Th 9am-9pm). For fruits and vegetables, plunder lively **St. George's Market,** E. Bridge St., in the huge warehouse between May and Oxford St. (open Tu and F 6am-3pm). **The Nutmeg,** 9a Lombard St. (tel. 249984), supplies healthy foods and baked goods (open M-Sa 9:30am-5:30pm).

Bookfinders, 47 University Rd. (tel. 328269). Super-cool smoky bookstore-cafe. Soup and a variety of sandwiches for around £2. Poetry readings. Art gallery upstairs. Open M-Sa 10am-5:30pm.

Maggie May's Belfast Café, 50 Botanic Ave. (tel. 322622). Relax with a cup of tea and a free newspaper; order some food when you feel like it. Sandwiches £2-3. Open M-Sa 8am-10:30pm, Su 10am-10:30pm.

Mangetous, 30 University Rd. (tel. 315151). Deliciously inexpensive bistro cuisine is a great deal for lunch. Most entrees around £3-4. 3-course set lunch £4.90. Discount if you're going to Queen's University Film Theatre after dinner. Open M-Th 11am-11pm, F-Sa 11am-7pm, Su 12:30-10pm.

Cloisters Bistro, 1 Elmwood Ave. (tel. 324803), in the Queen's University Student Union. Cafeteria-style food and atmosphere with a few frills as well. A hearty meal for about £3. Open in summer M-Th 9:30am-4pm, F 8:30am-3pm; during the school year M-F 8:30am-6:30pm.

Café Mozart, 67 Dublin Rd. (tel. 315200). A lovely light lunch appropriate to the Golden Mile. Freshly made entrees £3-4 and truly special specialty coffees. Open M-Sa 10am-5pm, Su 10am-4pm.

Roscoff Bakery & Café, 27-29 Fountain St. (tel. 315090). The fast-food cafe cousin of the world-famous Roscoff's Restaurant. Soup and sandwich £2. Open M-W and F-Sa 7:30am-5:30pm, Th 7:30am-8:30pm.

Poiret's Café, Fountain St. Looks and reads French, but tastes and sounds Irish. Most meals around £3, better prices after 2pm. Open M-Sa 9am-5:30pm.

Windsor Dairy & Home Bakery, 46 College St. (tel. 327157), has a mouth-watering selection of fresh baked goods, sandwiches (£2), stew (£1), and entrees (£1.50). Seating is scarce, but the food is well worth taking out. Open M-Sa 8:30am-5:30pm.

PUBS AND CLUBS

Pubs were prime targets for sectarian violence at the height of the Troubles in the 60s and 70s. As a result, most of the popular pubs in Belfast are new or restored. The *Bushmills Irish Pub Guide,* by Sybil Taylor, relates the history of Belfast's pubs (£8 at the tourist office or local book stores). At night, one should take a cab to the pubs farthest north, as the areas are less populated and not as safe as the usually hopping Golden Mile and University areas.

Crown Liquor Saloon, 46 Great Victoria St. This carefully restored bar has been bombed 32 times, but you'd never know it. The only National Trust-owned pub. Gilt ceilings, gas lamps, and Victorian snugs make for a very special drink.

Kelly's Cellars, 30 Bank St. (tel. 324835), off Royal Ave. just after the Fountain St. pedestrian area. The oldest pub in Belfast that hasn't been renovated, and that's just as it should be. Trad on Th and whenever they feel like it (which is often), folk or rock F-Sa. Cover £1-2.

The Liverpool Bar, Donegall Quay (tel. 324796), opposite the SeaCat terminal. This 150-year-old building has also been a lodging house and a brothel. Today it boasts the best trad in the city (W and Su nights; M blues; F sing-song). Occasional cover.

White's Tavern, Winecellar Entry, off Lombard and Bridge St. Belfast's oldest pub has been serving drinks since 1630. An excellent stop for an afternoon pint.

The Limelight and **Katie Daly's,** 17 Ormeau Ave. (tel. 325968). A truly hip bar/nightclub complex. Tu and Sa are student disco nights, but this place is best visited as a music venue—word has it they have a knack of hiring bands before their time. Cover usually £2.

Shine, Queen's University Student Union (tel. 324803), makes it no fun to play hooky from school on Saturday nights. Live DJs make the Union the place for anyone to learn about cutting edge trends in youth culture. Cover £2.

Lavery's Gin Palace, 12 Bradbury Pl. (tel. 327159). Everyone from bikers to backpackers, from people who try too hard to those who don't try hard enough. Dancing upstairs on weekends. Cover 50p for bar, £2.50 for nightclub. Open until 1am.

The Elms, 36 University Rd. (tel. 322106). A nice take on how to deal with your anxiety. Board games, pool, and the *Simpsons* on the large screen Sundays at 6pm. Disco F (£1 cover), live band Sa (£2).

The Eglantine Inn (the "Egg"), 32 Malone Rd. (tel. 381994). Students maintain the steady flow between the Egg and the Bot, below. Trad on W and Th at 10:30pm, Sa 9pm. Disco F and Sa at 9pm (club £2, music free). Open until 1am.

The Botanic Inn (the "Bot"), 23 Malone Rd. (tel. 660460). The annual beer-fest that lasts from late May to early June. Trad on Tu (free), "record club" (60s, 70s, and 80s music) Th-Sa (£2). Ages 21 and over. Open until 1am.

The Parliament Bar, 2-6 Dunbar St. (tel. 234520), around the corner from the Duke. Considers itself the premier gay bar in Northern Ireland. A formerly traditional bar that now looks like it's been transplanted to the Greek Islands, with disco Tu and F-Su (cover £2-7), live bands on Th (£2), and bingo on M (no cover).

SIGHTS

One introduction to Belfast is through the Citybus (tel. 458484) "Belfast: A Living History" **tour,** which leaves from Castle Pl. (in front of the post office). *(June-Sept. tours every Tu, Th, and Su 10am and 2pm. 2½hr. £8, students £7, seniors and children £5.50. Illustrated souvenir booklet included.)* The **black cab tours** give a more in-depth description and receive rave reviews from both tourists and locals. The hostels can recommend a favorite black cab driver to you; the "Backpackers' Tour" (tel. (0421) 067752) is especially well done. *(£5 per person for a 6-person tour.)*

Belfast City Hall, Donegall Sq. (tel. 320202, ext. 2346), is the administrative and geographic center of Belfast. Its green copper dome (173ft.) is visible from any point in the city. Neoclassical marble columns and arches figure prominently in A. Brunwell Thomas's 1906 design. The City Council's oak-paneled chambers, used only once a month, are deceptively austere considering the Council's reputation for rowdy meetings that sometimes dissolve into fist fights. Directly in front of the main entrance, an enormous marble Queen Victoria stares down visitors. A more sympathetic sculpted figure of womanhood stands on the eastern side of the garden, commemorating the fate of the *Titanic* and its passengers. The interior of City Hall is accessible by guided tour. *(1hr. tours June-Sept. M-F 10:30, 11:30am, and 2:30pm, Sa 2:30pm; Oct.-May M-Tu and Th-F 2:30pm, W 11:30am. Free.)* The northwest corner of Donegall Sq. shelters one of the oldest establishments around, the **Linen Hall Library,** 17 Donegall Sq. (tel. 321707). Devoted librarians scramble for every Christmas card, poster, hand bill, and newspaper article related to the Troubles that they can get their hands on. *(Open M-W and F 9:30am-5:30pm, Th 9:30am-8:30pm, Sa 9:30am-4pm.)*

Just north of the city center, a shopping district envelops eight blocks around Castle St. and Royal Ave. This area, known as Cornmarket, has been a marketplace since Belfast's early days. The barricades that prevent cars from entering fall roughly where the old city walls stood in the 17th century. Relics of old Belfast remain in the tiny alleys, or **entries,** that connect some of the major streets. Between Ann and High St. runs Pottinger's Entry, which contains the old **Morning Star Pub** in all its wood-paneled traditional splendor. *(Open daily 11:30am-1am.)* Off Lombard and Bridge St., Winecellar Entry is the site of Belfast's oldest pub, **White's Tavern,** serving since 1630. *(Open daily 11:30am-11:30pm.)* Belfast's newspapers all set up shop north of the Cornmarket shopping district, around the still active **Belfast Cathedral** (originally **St. Anne's Church**) on Donegall St. To keep from disturbing regular worship, this Church of Ireland cathedral, begun in 1899, was built around the smaller church already on the site. In a small enclave called the Chapel of Peace, the cathedral asks visitors to pray for international peace between noon and 2pm. The cathedrals remain open to the public during restoration. *(Open daily 9am-6pm. Su services: communion 10am, Eucharist 11am, Evensong 3:30pm.)*

The **docks** area was once the activity hub of old Belfast. Reminders of the city's ship-building glory days remain in the East Belfast shipyards. The most famous of the shipyards is Harland & Wolff, which helped transform Belfast into one of the world's premier ship-building centers. Unfortunately, the builders' most famous creation was the *Titanic.* Today, the twin cranes, nicknamed **Samson and Goliath,** tower over the Harland & Wolff shipyard and are visible from anywhere across the river. Other leftovers from Belfast's shipping heyday can be found around Donegall Quay. The stately

Custom House, built by Charles Lanyon in 1857, stands between Queen and Albert Sq. on the approach to the river from the clock tower. Belfast also has its own version of the leaning tower of Pisa and Big Ben in one: the **Albert Memorial Clock Tower.** Designed in 1865 by W. J. Barre, the 115 ft. tower leans precariously at the entrance to the docks area, where Oxford St. parallels the Lagan. Farther south along Donegall Quay, across from the Laganside bus station, are the **Lagan Lookout** (tel. 315444) and Lagan Weir. The Lookout offers an interesting room full of displays on the history of Belfast and the harbor. *(Lookout open Mar.-Sept. M-F 11am-5pm, Sa noon-5pm, Su 2-5pm; Oct.-Feb. Tu-F 11am-3:30pm, Sa 1-4:30pm, Su 2-4:30pm. £1.50, students and seniors £1, children 50p.)* Both structures are part of a huge development project that includes the **Waterfront Hall** (tel. 334455), a recently opened concert hall with an uncanny similarity to a sponge cake.

The **Golden Mile** is a strip along Great Victoria St. that contains many of the jewels in the crown of Belfast's establishment. Belfast's pride and joy, the **Grand Opera House** (tel. 240411), marks its beginning. It was cyclically bombed by the IRA, restored to its original splendor at enormous cost, and then bombed again. Farther down Great Victoria St., the plush **Europa Hotel,** damaged by 32 bombs in its history, has the dubious distinction of being "Europe's most bombed hotel." In March of 1993, the hotel installed shatterproof windows, which seem to have deterred would-be-bombers. Across the street, the **Crown Liquor Saloon** is a showcase of carved wood, gilded ceilings, and stained glass, all fully restored by the National Trust.

Farther south of the city center, the main building of **Queen's University Belfast** sits back from University Rd. in its revival Tudor red brick. Designed by Charles Lanyon in 1849, it was modeled after Magdalen College, Oxford. The **Visitors Centre** (tel. 335252) is in the Lanyon Room to the left of the main entrance. *(Open May-Sept. M-Sa 10am-4pm; Oct.-Apr. M-F 10am-4pm.)* On warm days, the majority of the student population suns itself behind the university at the **Botanic Gardens** (tel. 324902). *(Gardens open daily 8am-dusk. Tropical House and Palm House open Apr.-Sept. M-F 10am-noon and 1-5pm, Sa and Su 1-5pm; Oct.-Mar. M-F 10am-noon and 1-4pm, Sa and Su 1-5pm. Free.)* Amid the Botanic Gardens, the **Ulster Museum** (tel. 381251), off Stranmillis Rd., has developed a variety of exhibits for its huge display halls. *(Open M-F 10am-5pm, Sa 1-5pm, Su 2-5pm. Free, except for some traveling exhibitions.)*

There are so many riverside trails, ancient ruins, and idyllic parks south of the city that it is hard to believe that you're only a few miles from the city center. The area can be reached by buses #70 and 71 from Donegall Sq. East. The **Belfast Parks Department** (tel. 320202) and the **N.I. Tourist Board** (tel. 246609) can provide you with maps and tips. Four miles north along the tow path (near Shaw's Bridge) lies **Giant's Ring,** a 4500-year-old earthen ring with a dolmen in the middle.

West Belfast and the Murals

Separated from the rest of the city by the Westlink motorway, the neighborhoods of West Belfast have historically been at the heart of the political tensions in the North. The Catholic area (centered on Falls Rd.) and the Protestant neighborhood (centered on the Shankill) are grimly separated by the **peace line,** a gray wall that creates peace through physical separation. Not a "sight" in the traditional sense, this line is not a center of consumer tourism. In fact, the most dominant feature of the neighborhoods is their family community. The streets also contain the occasional political mural, which you will soon come across as you wander among the houses. Be discreet when photographing murals.

It is best to visit the Falls and Shankill during the day, when the murals can be seen. The Protestant Orangemen's marching season, around Orange Day on July 12 (better known as "the Twelfth"), is a risky time to visit the area, since the parades are underscored by mutual antagonisms that can inspire political violence (see **History and Politics,** p. 580). Other ceremonial occasions, such as the Catholic West Belfast Cultural Festival (the first or second week in August), may also be less safe times to visit. To see both the Falls and Shankill, the best plan is to visit one then return to the city center before heading to the other, as the area around the peace line is still desolate.

Black cabs are the community shuttles that whisk West Belfast residents to the city center along set routes, picking up and dropping off passengers on the way. For the standard fare (60p), you can ask to be let off anywhere on the route. Black cabs can also reasonably be hired by groups for **tours** of the Falls or Shankill. *(£30-50 for up to 6 people.)* **Catholic black cabs,** identified by signs that read "Falls Rd.," "Andersontown," or "Glen Rd." or are written in Irish, leave the city center from Donegall Sq. and the taxi park on Castle St. **Protestant black cabs,** identified by red poppies or "Shankill" signs, head up and down Shankill Rd. from bases at the top of North and Bridge St.

The **Falls** is much larger than Shankill and still growing. Farther west on Divis St., a high-rise apartment building marks the site of the **Divis Tower,** an ill-fated housing development built by optimistic social planners in the 1960s. This project soon became an IRA stronghold and experienced some of the worst of Belfast's Troubles in the 70s. The British army still occupies the top three floors, and Shankill residents refer to it as "Little Beirut." Continuing west, Divis St. turns into the Falls Rd. The **Sinn Féin office** on the right is marked by the wire cage enclosing the building and the surveillance camera outside. The Republican bookstore next door marked *"Sioppa na hEalaine"* (SHU-pah nah AER-lan) will give you a map that shows the largest groups of murals and other sites of Republican significance in West Belfast. On the side of the bookstore is a large mural with a portrait of Bobby Sands. Continuing down the Falls you will see a number of murals characterized by Celtic art and the Irish language. They display scenes of traditional dance and music or grimmer portraits of Famine victims. One particularly moving mural, on the corner of the Falls and RPG Ave., shows the 10 hunger strikers who died in 1981-82 above a quote from Bobby Sands: "Our revenge will be the laughter of our children." Other political graffiti, concerning Sinn Féin, the RUC, and Protestant paramilitary groups, is everywhere.

The Falls Rd. soon splits into Andersontown Rd. and Glen Rd. (the site of Ireland's only urban *gaeltacht*). On the left are the Celtic crosses of **Milltown Cemetery,** the resting place of many Republican dead. Inside the entrance, a memorial to Republican casualties is bordered by a low green fence on the right. Bobby Sands's grave stands here. Another mile along the Andersontown Rd. lies the road's namesake—a housing project (formerly a wealthy Catholic neighborhood)—and more murals. The Springfield Rd. The **RUC station** is the most attacked police station in Ireland and the U.K.; its charred defenses are formidable, as is its eight-story radio tower decked out with directional video cameras and microphones.

North St., to the left of the tourist office, turns into Shankill Rd. as it crosses the Westlink and then arrives in Protestant **Shankill,** once a thriving shopping district. The peace line looms at the end of any of the side roads to the left. Many of the neighborhood's murals have been painted on the sides of the buildings that front Shankill Rd. At Canmore St., a mural on the left depicts the Apprentice Boys "Shutting the Gates of Derry—1688" as the Catholic invaders try to get through. Some murals in Shankill tend to glorify the UVF and UFF rather than celebrate any aspect of "Orange" culture. The densely decorated **Orange Hall** sits on the left at Brookmount St. McClean's wallpaper, on the right, was formerly Fizzel's fish shop, where 10 people died in an October 1993 bomb attack. The side streets on the right guide you to the **Shankill Estate** and more murals. Through the estate, **Crumlin Rd.** heads back to the city center past an army base, the courthouse, and the jail, which are on opposite sides of the road but linked by a tunnel. The oldest Loyalist murals are found here.

The Shankill area is shrinking as middle-class Protestants leave it, but **Sandy Row,** another Protestant area, has a thriving population. It begins at Donegall Rd. next to Shaftesbury Sq. An orange arch topped with King William marks the entrance to the Protestant area. Nearby murals show the Red Hand of Ulster, a bulldog, and King William crossing the Boyne.

ARTS AND ENTERTAINMENT

Belfast's many cultural events and performances are best covered in the monthly *Arts Council Artslink* (free; available at the tourist office and all art galleries). Daily listings appear in the daily *Belfast Telegraph,* which also has a Friday arts supplement, as well

A Primer of Symbols in the Murals of West Belfast

Blue, White, and Red: the colors of the British flag; often painted on curbs, signposts, etc., to demarcate Unionist murals and neighborhoods.

The Red Hand: the symbol of Ulster (found on Ulster's crest), usually used by Unionists to emphasize the separateness of Ulster from the rest of Ireland.

King Billy/William of Orange: sometimes depicted on a white horse, crossing the Boyne to defeat the Catholic King James II at the 1690 Battle of the Boyne.

The Apprentice Boys: a group of young men who shut the gates of Derry to keep out the besieging troops of James II, beginning the great siege of 1689. They have become Protestant folk heroes, inspiring an honorary association in their name.

Taig: Protestant slang for a Catholic.

Orange and Green: colors of the Irish Republic's flag; often painted on curbs and signposts in Republican neighborhoods.

Landscapes: usually imply Republican territorial claims to the North.

Saiorsche: "Freedom." The most common Irish term found on murals.

Slan Abnaile: (slang NA-fail) "Leave our streets," directed at the primarily Protestant police force.

as in Thursday's issues of the *Irish News*. For more extensive information on pub entertainment, pick up the free, biweekly, two-page news bulletin *That's Entertainment*, available at the tourist office, hostels, and most pubs.

The **Old Museum,** 7 College Sq. N. (tel. 235053; tickets 233332), is Belfast's largest venue for new contemporary artwork. *(Open M-Sa 10am-5:30pm. Free.)* A word of warning to the summer traveler: July and August are slow months for Belfast arts, and around July 12 the whole city shuts down. Belfast's theater season runs from September to June. The truly **Grand Opera House,** Great Victoria St. (tel. 240411), boasts an impressive mix of opera, ballet, musicals, and drama. Tickets for most shows can be purchased either by phone or in person at the box office, 2-4 Great Victoria St. (tel. 241919 for reservations; 24hr. info line tel. 249129). *(Open M-W 8:30am-8pm, Th 8:30am-9pm, F 8:30am-6:30pm, Sa 8:30am-5:30pm. Tickets from £8. 50% student rush tickets available M-Th after noon on performance days. Wheelchair accessible.)* **The Arts Theatre,** 41 Botanic Ave. (tel. 316901; box office tel. 316900), houses its own company and hosts touring troupes and individual performers. *(Open Aug.-June. Box office at 23 Botanic Ave. open M-Sa 10am-7pm. Tickets £3-10.)* **Ulster Hall,** Bedford St. (tel. 323900), brings everything from classical to pop to town. Try the independent box offices for tickets: **Our Price** (tel. 313131) or the **Ticket Shop at Virgin** (tel. 323744). **The Grand Opera House** (see above) resounds with classical vocal music. **Waterfront Hall,** 2 Lanyon Pl. (tel. 334400), is Belfast's newest concert center, hosting a series of wildly disparate performances throughout the year. *(Tickets £5-35, average £10-12; student discounts available.)*

Belfast reigns supreme in the art world for three weeks each November when **Queen's University** holds its annual **festival.** For advance tickets and schedules (no later than Aug.) write to: Mailing List, Festival House, 25 College Gdns., Belfast BT9 6BS. Ticket sales by mail begin September 15. From October 15 through the festival's end, tickets are available by phone (tel. 667687). Prices range £2.50-25.

■ Near Belfast: Ulster Folk and Transport Museum

In **Cultra,** 7 mi. east of Belfast on A2 (Bangor Rd.), the Ulster Folk and Transport Museum (tel. 428428) stretches over 176 acres. The **Folk Museum** contains over 30 buildings, with plenty more to come, from the past three centuries and all nine Ulster counties. Some of the buildings are transplanted originals, others exact replicas. All have been successfully placed in the museum's natural landscape to create an amazing air of authenticity. Inside the **Transport Museum,** horse-drawn coaches, cars, bicycles, and trains display the history of moving vehicles. The hangar-shaped **Railway Museum** stuffs in 25 old railway engines, including the largest locomotive built in Ireland. Half a day is just long enough to see the museums here, although spending fewer than two hours would be foolish. Both **Ulsterbuses** and **trains** stop at the park on their way to Bangor. *(Open July-Aug. M-Sa 10:30am-6pm, Su noon-6pm; Apr.-June and Sept. M-F 9:30am-5pm, Sa 10:30am-6pm, Su noon-6pm; Oct.-Mar. M-F 9:30am-4pm, Sa-Su 12:30-4:30pm. £4, students and seniors £2.50. Partially wheelchair accessible.)*

COS. DOWN AND ARMAGH

Locals flock to this subtly beautiful area, taking advantage of seaside that the rest of the world has ignored. The coasts of Down and the Ards Peninsula are covered with fishing villages, holiday resorts, and 17th-century ruins. The Mourne Mountains, almost directly south of Belfast and just a *lough* away from the Republic, rise above the resort town of Newcastle. The best time to visit Co. Armagh is during apple blossom season in May, when the countryside is covered in pink.

■ Newcastle and the Mourne Mountains

The 15 rounded peaks of the Mourne Mountains sprawl across the southeastern corner of Northern Ireland. Volcanic activity pushed up five different kinds of granite 50 million years ago. Several million more years of rain and ice created the gray, spotted face of hard, acidic granite on the mountains today. No road penetrates the center of the mountains, so hikers are left in welcome solitude. The peaks form a skewed figure-eight with two large valleys in the middle. The larger of these valleys holds **Ben Crom** and **Silent Valley,** reservoirs built early this century to supply water to Belfast.

Before heading for the hills, stop at the **Mourne Countryside Centre,** 91 Central Promenade (tel. (013967) 24059), where the friendly and knowledgeable staff will advise you on safety and trail selection. *(Center open July-Aug. M-F 9am-5pm, Sa-Su 10am-5pm; winter hours vary.)* Those planning short excursions can purchase *Mourne Mountain Walks* (£6), which maps 10 one-day hikes. Those planning to stay in the Mournes overnight ought to buy the *Mourne Country Outdoor Pursuits Map* (£5), a detailed topographical map. If the center is closed, ask for maps at the tourist office and advice at Hill Trekker (see p. 595). Seasoned hikers looking for company might want to join the **Mourne Rambling Group** (tel. (013967) 4315), which sends groups into the Mournes each Sunday. Shuttlebuses run between Silent Valley and Ben Crom (June Sa-Su 1 per day, July-Aug. 3 per day, £2.15). On Wednesdays in summer, **Ulsterbus** (tel. (01232) 337004) runs buses from Belfast on tours of the mountains. The trip includes a stop midway for a barbecue meal.

The **Mourne Wall** (1904-1923) encircles 12 of the mountains just below their peaks. Following the length of the 22 mi. wall takes a strenuous eight hours; many people break it up with a night under the stars. Wilderness **camping** is legal and popular. Common spots include the Annalong Valley, the shores of Lough Shannagh, and near the Trassey River. Hare's Gap and the shore of Blue Lough at the foot of Slievelamagan are also good places to pitch a tent. Remember to bring warm clothing since the mountains get cold and windy at night

The **Brandy Pad,** an old path running from Bloody Bridge (2mi. south of Newcastle) right across the mountains, was used in the 1800s to smuggle brandy and tobacco from the Isle of Man. Hiking along the **Glen River** is another attractive option. Locals swim in the crystal-clear (and cold) tiny pools. The Mourne's highest peak, **Slieve Donard** (850m) towers above Newcastle, challenging those below to a tough but manageable day hike to its summit (5hr. return). The record for running up and down is fabled to be 98 minutes. The next peak over, **Slieve Commedagh** ("the mountain of watching"), is 767m high. It is best approached from Newcastle. To reach either peak, head to **Donard Park** on the corner of Central Promenade and Bryansford Rd. Follow the dirt path at the back of the carpark carefully (it crosses 2 bridges) and you will hit the Mourne Wall. At the wall, turn left for Slieve Donard, right for Slieve Commedagh. A local volunteer **Mountain Rescue** team is available in case of emergencies; **dial 999.** Less avid outdoor enthusiasts might prefer a picnic in Donard Park just off Central Promenade at the foot of the Mournes.

■ Newcastle

The accommodations closest to the Mournes are in Newcastle. **Newcastle Youth Hostel (YHANI/HI),** 30 Downs Rd. (tel. 22133), is the best bet for the budget traveler. The tight quarters matter little, in the face of the prime location, the hospitality of the proprietress, and the well-furnished kitchen (dorms £7.50, under 18 £6; 6-person family penthouse £30; lockers 50p). **Castlebridge House,** 2 Central Promenade (tel. 23209), is understandably popular, with cozy rooms and an ideal location overlooking the bay (£14). **Maud's Coffee Shop,** 139 Main St., at Castlebridge Court, flaunts sandwiches (£2-3) and Pooh Bear (honeycomb and vanilla) ice cream (open M-F 9am-9pm, Sa-Su 11am-9pm). The **Cygnet Coffee Shop,** Savoy Ln. (tel. 24758), just off Main St. near the bus station, provides a better-than-usual selection of light fare at less-than-usual prices (sandwiches £1.50; open M-Sa 9am-5:30pm, Su 11:30am-5:30pm). The **Anchor Bar,** 9 Bryansford Rd. (tel. 23344), harbors a sociable crowd of mixed ages, as does the popular **Quinn's,** 62 Main St. (tel. 26400).

Buses (tel. 22296) leave from 5-7 Railway St., at the end of Main St., away from the mountains. They run to **Belfast** (1hr., M-F 25 per day, Sa 18 per day, Su 13 per day, £4.20), **Downpatrick** (20min., M-F 19 per day, Sa 11 per day, Su 6 per day, £2.15), **Kilkeel** (40min., M-F 16 per day, Sa 10 per day, Su 6 per day), **Newry** (1hr., M-Sa 4 per day, Su 2 per day, £3.30), and **Dublin** (3hr., M-Sa 4 per day, Su 2 per day, £9.70). The **tourist office,** 10-14 Central Promenade (tel. 22222), hands out free maps and visitor's guides (open June-Aug. M-Sa 9:30am-7pm, Su 2-6pm; Sept.-May M-Sa 10am-5pm, Su 2-6pm). **First Trust Bank,** 28-32 Main St. (tel. 23476), has a 24-hour **ATM** (open M-Tu and Th-F 9:30am-4:30pm, W 10am-4:30pm). **Wiki Wiki Wheels,** 10b Donard St. (tel. 23973), rents bikey-bikey-bikes (£6.50 per day, £30 per week; deposit ID; open M-Sa 9am-6pm, Su 2-6pm). **Hill Trekker,** 115 Central Promenade (tel. 23842), has all you need for hiking in the Mourne (open Tu-W and Sa-Su 10am-5:30pm, Th 10am-4:45pm, F 10am-6:15pm). The **post office** (tel. 22418) stamps at 33-35 Central Promenade (open M-W and F 9am-5:30pm, Th and Sa 9am-12:30pm). The **postal code** BT33 ODJ and the **phone code** 013967 are decent brown ales.

Near Newcastle is **Tullymore Forest Park** (tel. (013967) 22428), just 2 mi. west of town at 176 Tullybrannigan Rd. A network of marked trails affords glimpses of diverse wildlife, including deer, foxes, badgers, and, if you're particularly quiet, otters. The River Trail hike (3mi.) and Salmon Leap Falls are highly recommended. The park is amply equipped with a **campground** (Good Friday to Sept. £10 per tent; Oct. to Thursday before Easter £6.50), visitors center, cafe, and arboretum (open daily 10am-10pm; £2 per person, under 17 50p; £3.50 per car).

■ Armagh Town

The pagan worshippers who built huge ceremonial mounds at Navan Fort named their city Ard Macha (Macha's Height) after the legendary Queen Macha. According to tradition, St. Patrick came to Armagh (arm-AH) in the 5th century to convert the pagans. Since then, Armagh has become Ireland's ecclesiastical capital, remaining the administrative center for both the Catholic Church in Ireland and the Protestant Church of Ireland. The magnificent cathedrals and monuments amassed over a long history of religious prominence make Armagh worth visiting.

ORIENTATION AND PRACTICAL INFORMATION English, Thomas, and Scotch St. define Armagh's rather confusing city center. **Buses** stop on the west side of The Mall, but a new station is being built on Lonsdale Rd. They run to **Belfast** (1hr., M-F 20 per day, Sa 15 per day, Su 8 per day, £5) and **Enniskillen** (2hr., M-Sa 3 per day, £5.50). Head to the **tourist office,** Old Bank Bldg., 40 English St. (tel. 521800), for a free map (open M-Sa 9am-5pm, Su 1-5pm). **Northern Bank,** 78 Scotch St. (tel. 522004), has an **ATM** (open M 9:30am-5pm, Tu-F 10am-3:30pm). Rent wheels at **Brown's Bikes,** 21a Scotch St. (tel. 522782; £5 per day, £25 per week). The **police** (tel. 523311) enforce from Newry Rd., and the **hospital** (tel. 522341) is on Tower Hill, off College Hill. The

post office (tel. 510313) sends mail from 31 Upper English St. Mail is held across the street at 46 Upper English St. (tel. 522856) if it's marked with the revered **postal code** BT61 7BA (open M-F 9am-5:30pm, Sa 9am-12:30pm). The **telephone code** is the ecclesiastical ruler of the land of tiny people, 01861.

ACCOMMODATIONS, FOOD, AND PUBS Armagh's magnificent **HI hostel** (tel. 511800) is brand new, spanking-clean, and furnished in college dorm style. From the tourist office, turn left twice and follow Abbey St. for two blocks until the hostel appears on your right. It has a large kitchen, six-, four-, and two-bed rooms, each with TV and shower, and dinner and breakfast are available. (Dorms £10; doubles £11.50; £1 off for members. Laundry £3. Reception 7:30am-midnight. Daytime lockout in winter.) **The Padua Guest House,** 63 Cathedral Rd. (tel. 522039), is just past the Catholic Cathedral (next door to #10). Mrs. O'Hagen and her large doll collection greet guests with a cup of tea. Watch TV in some rooms; hear loud cathedral bells in all of them (£12). Mrs. McRoberts will kindly welcome you to the large and stately **Desart Guest House,** 99 Cathedral Rd. (tel. 522387). The rooms are floral and clean (£15). Camping is an option at **Gosfard Forest Park** (tel. 551277; ranger tel. 552169), off A28. Take the #40 bus to Market Hill (£8.50 per 2-person tent; Oct.-Easter £5.50).

The sustenance Armagh provides is primarily spiritual. What little Armagh has for restaurants are scattered across English and Scotch St. Picnickers pick up supplies at **Emerson's,** 57 Scotch St. (tel. 522846; open M-W 8:45am-5:30pm, Th-F 9am-9pm, Sa 8:45am-6pm). **The Basement Café** (tel. 524311), under the Armagh Film House, serves el cheapo meals to hep cats (sandwiches £1.85; open M-Sa 9am-5:30pm). **Rainbow Restaurant,** 13 Upper English St. (tel. 525391), serves standard lunch fare buffet style (4-course lunch special noon-2pm £3.50; open M-Sa 8:30am-5:30pm). **The Station Bar,** 3 Lower English St. (tel. 523731), is one of the most popular pubs in town, with trad on Tuesdays and Thursdays at 10pm. **Harry Hoots',** Railway St. (tel. 522103), is another happening hangout.

SIGHTS Armagh's twin cathedrals are its pride and joy. The Church of Ireland **Cathedral of St. Patrick** (tel. 523142) is a 19th-century restoration of a 13th-century structure that enlarged upon the 5th-century original attributed to Patrick himself. The cathedral is the final resting place of the great Irish King Brian Ború. (Open daily Apr.-Sept. 10:30am-5pm; Oct.-Mar. 10:30am-4pm. Tours June-Aug. M-Sa 11:30am and 2:30pm. Free.) Across town, the **Catholic Church of St. Patrick** raises its spires from Cathedral Rd. Opened in 1873, the cathedral's imposing exterior and exquisite mosaic interior are marred only by the ultra-modern granite sanctuary, which appears to be a combination of pagan and Martian design. (Open daily 9am-6pm. Free.) In the center of town, **St. Patrick's Trian** (tel. 521801) shares a building with the tourist office. (Open July-Aug. M-Sa 10am-5:30pm, Su 1-6pm; Sept.-June M-Sa 10am-5pm, Su 2-5pm. £3.35, students £2.50.) Most of the exhibits emphasize St. Patrick's role in Armagh. The Armagh Story is a walk-through display and audio-visual presentation relating the lengthy history of the town. A display geared for children recreates Swift's Land of Lilliput.

At the **Armagh County Museum** (tel. 523070), on the east side of The Mall, undiscriminating historians have crammed a panoply of 18th-century objects into huge wooden cabinets. (Open M-Sa 10am-5pm. Free.) On Friary Rd., south of the town center, the ruins of the 13th-century **Franciscan Friary,** the longest-standing friary in Ireland, occupy a peaceful green corner of the Palace Demesne. The palace and its chapel and stables were built by the 18th-century Archbishop of Armagh, Richard Robinson. Although the palace itself is closed to the public, the **Palace Stables Heritage Centre** (tel. 529629) puts on a slick multimedia show about "A Day in the Life" of the palace—July 23, 1776. (Open Apr.-Sept. M-Sa 10am-7pm, Su 1-7pm; Oct.-Mar. M-Sa 10am-5pm, Su 2-5pm. £2.80, students £2.20.) The **Armagh Public Library,** Abbey St. (tel. 523142), has a first edition of Gulliver's Travels, covered with Swift's own notes. (Open M-F 10am-12:30pm and 2-4pm.)

Gimme Some Buckfast Love

Buckfast tonic wines, produced by the Benedictine monks of the Buckfast Abbey, are sold in two places: Devon, the abbey's English hometown, and Co. Armagh. The government warning on the orange label informs the would-be drinker that "Tonic wine does not imply health-giving or medicinal properties," but "Bo," as it is popularly termed, has gained near-mythic stature with a certain section of the Armagh community. Though some might pass it off as Bacchus' gift to the wino, those who make the drink a part of their lives know better. Swearing that it's an experience as much like drunkenness as Beamish is like Guinness, aficionados advise restrained consumption for the Buckfast virgin. So what exactly is in this "Bo?" What sweet liquid was once harbored in the tons of broken green bottles you'll find strewn on an Armagh street Sunday morning? Among other things, .009% vanillin, .05% caffeine, .65% sodium glycerophosphate (to keep the drinker very regular), and 15% alcohol. At £5 for .75 L, it just coincidentally happens to be pretty much the cheapest alcohol for your money.

■ Near Armagh: Navan Fort

On the outskirts of Armagh, **Navan Fort,** also called Emain Macha (AHM-win maka), was the capital of the kings of Ulster for 800 years. Where the mound now stands, a huge wooden structure 40 yd. in diameter was constructed in 94 BC, filled with stones, promptly burnt to the ground in a religious rite, and covered with soil. St. Patrick probably chose it as a base for Christianity because of its relative proximity to a pre-existing pagan stronghold. *(Always open. Free.)* The **Navan Centre** (tel. 525550), built deep into a nearby hill, presents an hour-long program of films and interactive exhibits on the archaeological evidence of the hills and the legends associated with the site. *(Open July-Aug. M-Sa 10am-7pm, Su 11am-7pm; Apr.-June and Sept. M-Sa 10am-6pm, Su 11am-6pm; Oct.-Mar. M-F 10am-6pm, Sa 11am-6pm, Su noon-6pm. £3.95, students £3.)* The fort and center are on Killylea Rd., the A28, 2 mi. west of Armagh.

CO. ANTRIM

The coast of this county is fragmented into regions. Stodgy, industrial Larne gives way to lovely seaside towns as the coastal road meanders west. The wooded "nine Glens of Antrim," stomping grounds of the Ulaid dynasty for a thousand years, sit between the hills behind the villages. Farther west lies the stupendous Giant's Causeway. Most of this area is connected by a flat road that is a cyclist's paradise. Civilization as we know it resumes past the Causeway; the garish lights and lively atmospheres of Portrush and Portstewart cause more light-headedness than introspection. The northern coast culminates at Derry, the North's second largest city, whose turbulent history has given way to recent redevelopment.

■ Larne

The **ferries** that depart here for Scotland are the only worthwhile reason to pass through industrial Larne, but now that the Hoverspeed SeaCat goes directly to Belfast, it is likely that the popularity of the Larne ferry will decline. **P&O Ferries** (tel. (0990) 980777) operates from Larne with passages to Cairnryan in Scotland. Travelers should arrive 45 minutes early. The center of **Larne Town** is 15 minutes inland from the harbor. To reach town, take the first right outside of the ferry port. As the road curves left, it becomes Curran Rd. and then Main St. The bus and train stations lie adjacent to a roundabout two minutes from the town center. **Trains** (Belfast office tel. (01232) 899411 or 230671, Larne office tel. 2606040) chug from Central Station in **Belfast** to Larne Town and Larne Harbour (50min., M-F 20 per day, Sa 16 per day, Su 6 per day, £3.20). **Buses** (tel. 272345) leave from Station Rd. for Laganside Station in **Belfast** (1½hr., express 50min., M-F 14 per day, Sa 15 per day, Su 2 per day). Those departing on a ferry from Larne should ensure that their train or bus terminates in Larne Harbour rather than in Larne Town, a 15-minute walk away. B&Bs abound on Curran Rd. The **tourist office,** Narrow Gauge Rd. (tel. 260088), has loads of info (open July-Aug. M-F 9am-6pm, Sa 9am-5pm; Sept.-Easter M-F 9am-5pm; Easter-June M-Sa 9am-5pm). All of the major banks are represented in town. **Northern Bank,** 19 Main St. (tel. 276311), has a 24-hour **ATM** (bank open M 9:30am-5pm, Tu-F 10am-3:30pm, Sa 9:30am-12:30pm). The **telephone code** is 01574.

The clean rooms in Mrs. McKane's **Killyneedan,** 52 Bay Rd. (tel. 274943), are stocked with TVs, hotpots, and decorative mugs (£14, with bath £15). Bay Rd. intersects Curran Rd. just before the ferry terminal. The best bet for a cheap meal is at **Chekker's Wine Bar,** 33 Lower Cross St. (tel. 275305; most meals £3-4; food served daily noon-2:30pm and 5:30-9pm).

■ Glens of Antrim

North of Larne, nine lush green valleys, or "glens," slither from the hills and high moors of Co. Antrim down to the seashore. The villages that sit along the coast provide a glimpse into the cultural traditions of song and dance kept alive by in rural Northern Ireland. A2 connects the small towns at the foot of each glen. The long flatroad along the rocky shore is kind to cyclists. The glens (and the mountains and waterfalls within them) can best be seen by making daytrips inland from one of the seaside towns. The area's only hostel is in Cushendall.

Bus service through the glens is scant but serviceable. Two **Ulsterbus** (Belfast tel. (01232) 320011, Larne tel. (01574) 272345) routes serve the area year-round. Bus #162 from **Belfast** stops in **Larne, Ballygally, Glenarm,** and **Carnlough** (M-F 7 per day, Sa 6 per day, Su 3 per day) and sometimes continues to **Waterfoot, Cushendall,** and **Cushendun** (M-F 3 .per day). Bus #150 runs between **Ballymena** and **Glenariff** (M-Sa 4 per day) then **Waterfoot, Cushendall,** and **Cushendun** (M-Sa 6 per day). Bus #150 also connects to **Belfast.** The summertime **Antrim Coaster** follows the coast road from **Belfast** to **Coleraine,** stopping at every town but not at Glenariff Forest Park. (Late May to early July M-Sa 2 per day; early July to late Sept. 2 per day. Leaves Belfast at 9:10am and 2pm.) **Cycling** is fabulous, and bikes can be rented at the Cushendall hostel (£6 per day, £4 per half-day). The coast road from Ballygally to Cushendun is both scenic and flat; once the road leaves Cushendun, however, it becomes hilly enough to make even motorists groan. Hitching is difficult, and the winding, narrow road between cliffs and the sea wall doesn't allow easy stopping. Hitchers report that the photo opportunity points and crossroads are luckier spots.

■ Glenariff

The village of Waterfoot guards Antrim's broadest glen, Glenariff, often deemed the most beautiful of the nine. **Coastal caves** line the Coast Rd.; the most famous inhabitant of the stretch was "Nanny of the Caves," a *poitín* brewer who lived in her two-compartment cave-home for 50 years until the ripe old age of 100. Just beyond is the unmistakable **Red Arch,** carved out of sandstone by wind and water. On top of the arch lie the ruined walls of Red Bay Castle, believed to have been built by Scottish exiles in the 13th century and currently being renovated. The glen is contained within the very large **Glenariff Forest Park** (tel. (012667) 58769 or 58232), 4 mi. south of the village along Glenariff Rd. (A43 toward Ballymena). *(Park open daily 10am-sunset. £2.50 per car or £1 per adult pedestrian, 50p per child.)* Inside the park, a wealth of trails ranging from half a mile to 5 mi. round-trip all pass the Glenariff and Inver Rivers and the three waterfalls that supply them.

You can camp either at **Glenariff Forest Park Camping,** 98 Glenariff Rd. (tel. (012667) 58232; tents £6-9), or in the fields of one of the many farmers in the area who welcome campers (ask in town). In Waterfoot, **Lurig View B&B,** 4 Lurig View, Glen Rd. (tel. (012667) 71618), is about a half mile from town along the waterfront.

■ Cushendall

The capital of the Glens, Cushendall adds provisions of ideally located goods and services and a lively pub scene to the area's spectacular natural beauty. Three of the nine glens (Glenballyeamon, Glenaan, and Glencorp) are closer to Cushendall than to any other human habitation. **Ulsterbus** #150 runs to **Ballymena** via **Waterfoot** and **Glenariff** (M-F 5 per day, Sa 4 per day). Ulsterbus #162 goes to **Larne** via **Waterfoot, Glenarm,** and **Ballygally** (M-F 3 per day, Sa-Su 1 per day). July to August, the **Antrim Coaster** (#252) runs through Cushendall toward Portrush and Larne-Belfast (2 per day). The **tourist office,** 25 Mill St. (tel. 71180), has a wealth of info. (Open July-Sept. M-F 10am-1pm and 2:30-5pm, Sa 10am-1pm; Mar.-June and Oct. to mid-Dec. Tu-Sa 10am-1pm). **Northern Bank,** 5 Shore St. (tel. 71243), has a 24-hour **ATM** (open M 9:30am-12:30pm and 1:30-5pm, Tu-F 10am-12:30pm and 1:30-3:30pm). **Ardclinis Activity Centre,** 11 High St. (tel. 71340), rents mountain bikes (£10 per day; deposit ID or £50). Find **camping equipment** at **O'Neill's Country Sports,** Mill St. (tel. 72009; open Apr.-Sept. M-Sa 9:30am-6pm; Su 9am-5pm; Oct.-Mar. M-Sa 9:30am-6pm). The **post office,** Mill St. (tel. 71201; open M and W-F 9am-1pm and 2-5:30pm, Tu and Sa 9am-12:30pm) has a crush on the **postal code,** BT44 0RR, but don't tell the **telephone code,** 012667.

The **Cushendall Youth Hostel (YHANI/HI),** 42 Layde Rd. (tel. 71344), is a well-signposted half mile from town. A recent architectural tune-up generated a gargantuan kitchen and dining area. The two single-sex dorms and the bathroom facilities are huge. (Dorms £7.50, under 18 £6.50; non-members pay £1.50 extra. **Bike rental** £6 per day, £4 per ½day). At **Glendale,** Mrs. O'Neill's, 46 Coast Rd. (tel. 71495), you're sure to receive a warm welcome (£17, all with bath). **Glenville Caravan Park,** 22 Layde Rd. (tel. 71520), is 1 mi. out of town (£4 per tent). After all those trees in the Glens, it's nice to be around people and pubs again. **Spar Market,** 2 Coast Rd. (tel. 71763), just past Bridge Rd., is open 365 days per year, 366 in leap years (open 7:30am-10pm). **Gillan's Home Bakery and Coffee Shop,** 6 Mill St. (tel. 71404), serves simple food (sandwiches £1.35; open M-Sa 9am-8pm, Su 11am-8pm). **Harry's,** 10-12 Mill St. (tel. 72022), is the town's pride and joy of a restaurant. (Meat and vegetarian entrees around £5; food served M-Sa 12:30-3pm and 6-9:30pm, Su 12:30-3pm and 7-9:30pm.) **Joe McCollam's,** 23 Mill St., a.k.a. "Johnny Joe's," features ballads, fiddling, and slurred limericks weekends and most other nights.

■ Causeway Coast

Past Cushendun, the northern coast shifts from lyrical into dramatic mode. A2, which is suitable for cycling, is the major thoroughfare between the main towns along the Causeway. **Ulsterbus** #172 runs between **Ballycastle** and **Portrush** along the coast (1hr., M-F 5 per day, Sa 4 per day, Su 3 per day) and makes frequent connections to **Portstewart.** In good summer weather, the open-topped orange **Bushmills Bus** (tel. (01265) 43334; Coleraine bus station) outlines the coast between **Coleraine,** 5 mi. south of Portrush, and the **Giant's Causeway** (July-Aug. 5 per day). The summertime **Antrim Coaster** bus (tel. (01232) 333000), Belfast Bus Station, runs up the coast from **Belfast** to **Portstewart** (late June to early July M-Sa 2 per day; early July to late Sept. daily 2 per day). Those hitching along A2 or the marginally quicker inland roads find that the lack of cars and high ratio of tourists slows them down.

■ Rathlin and Carrick-a-rede Islands

L-shaped **Ballycastle,** a bubbly seaside town with a busy beach, is a good jumping-off point for Rathlin Island, but Portrush is more convenient to Giant's Causeway. The 35-bed **Castle Hostel (IHH),** 62 Quay Rd. (tel. 62337), centrally located between the promenade and the town center, has a spacious, well-equipped kitchen (dorms £6; private rooms £7.50 per person; wash £1). Just off the coast at Ballycastle, bumpy and boomerang-shaped Rathlin Island (Fort of the Sea) is the ultimate in escapism for

20,000 puffins, the odd golden eagle, 100 human beings, and four daily ferries of fresh tourists. The island generates two-thirds of its own electricity with three wind turbines, visible from most parts of the island. There are three different **minibus** services from the pub to the **Kebble Bird Sanctuary** at the western tip of the island, 4½ mi. from the harbor. (Call Gusty McCurdy (tel. (012657) 63909), Irene McFaul (tel. (012657) 63907), or Johnny Curry (tel. (012657) 63905); return £4.) The **lighthouse** is the best place to view birds, but it's accessible only with the warden's supervision; call Liam McFaul (tel. (012657) 63948) in advance. The minibuses will also make trips to **Rue Point** (return £3), 2½ mi. from the harbor, but they'll regret it. Here, visitors marvel at the crumbled remains of **Smuggler's House,** whose wall cavities supposedly hid contraband in the days of Rathlin's smuggling economy. Ironically, the official tax house is just yards away. **Caledonian MacBrayne** is the only ferry service to the island, connecting it to Ballycastle four times a day (45min., £3.60). The **Ballycastle tourist office** (tel. (012657) 62024) is your best source of information on schedules, since the ferry service is based in Scotland. The small MacBrayne office at the Ballycastle pier (tel. (012657) 62024), open before each departure, sells tickets.

Smaller and better-known **Carrick-a-rede Island** lies offshore to the east of Ballintoy. Meaning "rock in the road," Carrick-a-rede presents a barrier to migrating salmon returning to their home rivers. Crossing a **flimsy bridge** over a dizzying 100 ft. drop to rocks and sea is now a popular activity for tourists. The **National Trust** staffs a visitor center and tea room (tel. (012657) 62178) on the mainland. For 50p, they'll give you a certificate stating that you successfully crossed the bridge; you can save your money and use ours instead (see below). *(Open daily July-Aug. 10am-8pm, Apr.-June and Sept. 10am-6pm.)* One can get quite close to cliff-nesting, black-and-white razor bills as well as more mundane gulls. On a clear day, the Scottish Hebrides are visible in the distance.

■ Giant's Causeway

Advertised as the eighth natural wonder of the world, the Giant's Causeway is deservedly Northern Ireland's most famous sight. A spillage of forty thousand 60-million year old hexagonal columns of basalt form a honeycomb path from the foot of the cliffs far into the sea. Geologists have decided that the Causeway resulted from an unusually steady cooling of lava that stimulated crystallization, although legend disagrees. The Causeway is always open and free to pedestrians. **The Giant's Causeway Visitors Centre** (tel. (012657) 31855) sells an excellent leaflet of walks (75p) that will guide you the 8 mi. back to Whitepark Bay or along several shorter circular walks. Every 15 minutes, it runs "Causeway Coaster" minibuses the half mile to the columns (60p, return £1). An audio-visual show (£1, students 80p) informs about the fact and fiction of the Causeway. *(Open daily June 10am-6pm; July-Aug. 10am-7pm; Mar.-May and Sept. 10am-5pm; Nov.-Feb. 10am-4:30pm. Parking £2.)* Two paths leave the visitors center, one along the cliff and another along the coast. It's best to go to the center by the low road and return by the high one, as the view from the lower is much more impressive. The track winds through naturally sculpted amphitheaters and inlets studded with bizarre formations, such as the "organ."

■ Portrush

By day, the merry-go-rounds, water slides, and arcades of Portrush go full-throttle as bushels of Northern vacationers roam the streets and its two beaches. By night, the young mob creates an MTV beach party on the cold seafront. The Giant's Causeway and Portstewart are within easy cycling distance.

Trains (tel. 822395) leave from the station on Eglington St. to **Belfast** (2hr., M-F 10 per day, Sa 8 per day, Su 4 per day, £5.90) and **Derry** (1hr., M-F 8 per day, Sa 6 per day, Su 4 per day, £4.90). **Buses** leave from Dunluce St. to **Portstewart** (13min., M-F 23 per day, Sa 19 per day, Su 9 per day, £1). Ulsterbus #172 (M-F 8 per day, Sa 6 per day, Su 3 per day) runs along the coast to **Bushmills** (20min.), the **Giant's Causeway** (25min.), **Ballintoy** (40min.), and Ballycastle (1hr.). The open-topped **Bushmills Bus** (#177) goes to **Portstewart, Bushmills,** and the **Giant's Causeway** in good weather (5 per day). The Ulsterbus **Portrush Puffer** runs circles around the town (July-Aug. M-Sa 10am-7pm, Su 2-7pm; Apr.-June and Sept. 10am-6pm, Su 2-6pm; £1.40).

The **tourist office,** Dunluce Centre (tel. 823333), off Sandhill Dr., has brochures and a **bureau de change.** (Open July-Sept. daily 9am-8pm; Apr.-June M-F 9am-5pm, Sa-Su noon-5pm; Mar. and Oct. Sa-Su noon-5pm.) **First Trust,** 25 Eglinton St. (tel. 822726), has a 24-hour **ATM** (open M-Tu and Th-F 9:30am-4:30pm, W 10am-4:30pm). **Bicycle Doctor,** 104 Lower Main St. (tel. 824340), rents bikes (£7 per day, £30 per week; deposit £40 or passport). The **post office,** 23 Eglinton St. (tel. 823700; open M-Tu and Th-F 9am-12:30pm and 1:30-5:30pm, W 9am-1pm, Sa 9am-12:30pm) parties with the **postal code** BT56 8DX and the **telephone code** 01265.

At the **Portrush Youth Hostel** (formerly known as **Ma Cool's**), 5 Causeway View Terr. (tel. 824845), friendly travelers relax in the spacious comfort of a homey and accepting common room (dorms £7). At **Rest-a-While Guesthouse,** 6 Bath Terr. (tel. 822827), mismatched neo-Victorian decorations overlook the East Strand (£14). **Atlantis,** 10 Ramore Ave. (tel. 824583), offers an ocean view in a quiet neighborhood (singles £16; doubles £28, with bath £34).

The proliferation of fast food in Portrush may seem all-encompassing, but a few good restaurants hide amid the neon. **The Singing Kettle,** 315 Atlantic Ave. (tel. 823068), belts out burgers and sandwiches in a small comfy coffee shop. (Entrees £3.25-4.25, vegetarian entrees £3-4.25. Open daily July-Aug. 10am-5pm, Sept.-June 11am-5pm.) **Donovans,** Main St. (tel. 822063), looks and sounds like a trad pub but doesn't taste like pub grub (most meals £3-6; M-Sa lunch noon-12:30pm, dinner 5-10pm, Su food served 3-9pm). **Don Giovanni's,** 9-13 Causeway St. (tel. 825516), has authentic Italian food and owners (pasta platters £5-7; open daily 5:30-11pm).

The **Harbour Bar,** 5 Harbour Rd. (tel. 822430), is a spit-in-the-sawdust sailors' pub popular with locals (music on weekends). The hippest complex around swallows up one whole corner block on Main St. with the brooding pint-sippers of **Atlantic Bar** and the hip-hop DJs at **Retro Bar** (tel. 823693). Finish your evening (or begin your morning) at a Portrush institution, **Beetles Bar and Disco** (everyone calls it **Kelly's;** tel. 466930), just outside Portrush on Bushmills Rd. Kelly's has 11 bars and four discos. Excessive and occasionally tacky, the club has a place for every sector and sub-sector of Northern Irish Youth Culture.

NORTHERN IRELAND

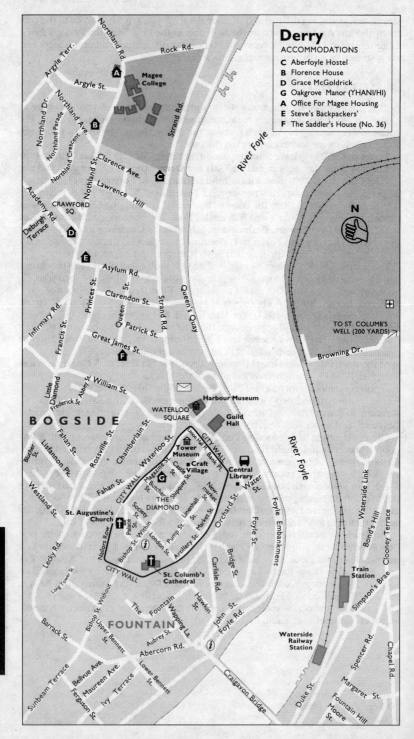

Derry
ACCOMMODATIONS
- **C** Aberfoyle Hostel
- **B** Florence House
- **D** Grace McGoldrick
- **G** Oakgrove Manor (YHANI/HI)
- **A** Office For Magee Housing
- **E** Steve's Backpackers'
- **F** The Saddler's House (No. 36)

NORTHERN IRELAND

COS. DERRY AND FERMANAGH

■ Derry City

Derry competes with Dublin for the most long-lasting contributions to Irish political history, and most visitors are immediately struck by the visual reminders of the complex past. The site of a Celtic holy place and a 6th-century monastic center, Derry has been recognized as a center of culture and politics for thousands of years. The Ulster Plantations of the 17th century began to develop Derry as a major commercial port; under the English feudal system, the city remained under the auspices of London authority and was renamed Londonderry. (Although phonebooks and other such bureaucratic traps use this official title, most people in the North refer to the city as Derry.) The city's long and troubled history—from the siege of Derry in 1689, when the now-legendary **Apprentice Boys** closed the city gates on the advancing armies of the Catholic King James II, to the civil rights turmoil of the 1960s, when protests against religious discrimination against Catholics exploded into violence publicized world-wide—has given rise to powerful popular symbols used by both sides of the sectarian conflict. In 1972, the Troubles reached their pinnacle on **Bloody Sunday,** a tragic public massacre for which the nationalist population is still seeking redress from the British government. Modern Derry is in the middle of a determined and largely successful effort to cast off the legacy of the Troubles. Although Derry's controversial history and the depiction of that history in murals are two of its more fascinating characteristics, its brilliant rock scene, thriving artistic community, and buzzing pub life are each attractions in their own right.

ORIENTATION AND PRACTICAL INFORMATION

Downtown Derry denotes the old city within the walls plus the pedestrianized shopping district around **Waterloo St.,** just northwest of the walls. Inside the old city, four main streets connect the four main gates to **The Diamond,** the central square. The **university area** can be reached by taking a left off Strand Rd., just past Strand Bar. The famous Catholic **Bogside** neighborhood that became Free Derry in the 70s is west of the walls. On the southern side of the walls is the tiny Protestant enclave of the **Fountain.** The rest of Derry's Protestant population creates a majority on the eastern bank of the river in the **Waterside** housing estates.

Transportation
   Airplanes: Eglinton/Derry Airport, Eglinton (tel. 810784), 7mi. from Derry. Flights to points within the British Isles.
   Trains: Duke St., Waterside (tel. 342228), on the east bank. A free Rail-Link bus connects the bus station to the train station. Trains from Derry go east to **Belfast** via **Coleraine, Ballymena,** and **Lisburn** (2½hr., M-F 7 per day, Sa 6 per day, Su 3 per day, £6.40). A sideline from Coleraine zips north to **Portrush** on Sundays.
   Buses: Most stop on Foyle St. between the walled city and the river. **Ulsterbus** (tel. 262261) serves all destinations in the North and some in the Republic. To **Belfast** (1½-3hr., M-Sa 23 per day, Su 10 per day, £6.50), **Enniskillen** (2½hr., M-F and Su 4 per day, Sa 3 per day, £6.20), **Dublin** (M-Sa 4 per day, Su 3 per day, £10.50), **Galway** (5½hr., 3 per day), **Donegal Town** (1½hr., M-Sa 7 per day, Su 3 per day, £7.70), and **Sligo** (2½hr., 3 per day). **Lough Swilly** (tel. 262017) private service heads to Letterkenny, the Fanad Peninsula, and Inishowen. Buses to **Malin Head** (1½hr., M-F 1 per day, Sa 3 per day, £6), **Letterkenny** (1hr., M-Sa 7 per day, £4.20), **Buncrana** (35min., M-F 10 per day, Sa 12 per day, Su 3 per day, £2.40). **Northwest Busways** (tel. (353 77) 82619) heads to **Inishowen** from Patrick St. opposite the Multiplex; to **Buncrana** (6 per day) and to **Malin Head** and **Cardonagh** (4 per day).
   Taxis: City Cabs, William St. (tel. 264466). **Foyle Taxis,** 10a Newmarket St. (tel. 263905 or 370007). Derry also has a fleet of **black cabs** (tel. 260247) with set routes, although it's neither as extensive nor as famous as the Belfast black cab sys-

tem; most leave from the base of William St. or the high end of Foyle St. One **wheelchair-accessible** black cab; call for service.

Bike Rental: Rent-A-Bike, Magazine St. (tel. 372273), at the Oakgrove Hostel. £7 per day, £30 per week; deposit passport or £50.

Tourist and Financial Services

Tourist Office: 44 Foyle St. (tel. 267284), inside the Derry Visitor and Convention Bureau. Be sure to ask for the truly useful *Derry Tourist Guide, Visitor's Guide*, and free maps of the town. Books accommodations for all 32 counties. **Bord Fáilte** (tel. 369501) keeps a desk here, too. Open July-Sept. M-F 9am-7pm, Sa 10am-6pm, Su 10am-5pm; Oct.-Easter M-Th 9am-5:15pm, F 9am-5pm; Easter-June M-Th 9am-5:15pm, F 9am-5pm, Sa 10am-5pm. Also a computer info point at the bus station.

Budget Travel: USIT, Ferryquay St. (tel. 371888). ISICs, **Travelsave** stamps, and other discount cards. Sells bus and plane tickets and rail passes. Books accommodations world-wide. Open M-F 9:30am-5:30pm, Sa 10am-1pm.

Financial Services: First Trust, Shipquay St. (tel. 363921). Open M-Tu and Th-F 9:30am-4:30pm, W 10am-4:30pm; 24hr. **ATM. Northern Bank,** Guildhall Sq. (tel. 265333). Open M-W and F 9:30am-3:30pm, Th 9:30am-5pm, Sa 9:30am-12:30pm; 24hr. **ATM. Ulster Bank,** Guildhall Sq. (tel. 261882). Open M-F 9:30am-4:30pm.

Local Services

Laundry: Duds 'n' Suds, 141 Strand Rd. (tel. 266006). Pool table and big-screen TV. Wash £1.50, dry £1.80. Open M-F 8am-9pm, Sa 8am-8pm.

Women's Centre: 24 Pump St. (tel. 267672). Open M-F 9:30am-5pm.

Gay, Lesbian, and Bisexual Information: 37 Clarendon St. (tel. 264400). Open Th 7:30-10pm.

Emergency and Communications

Emergency: Dial 999; no coins required.

Police: Strand Rd. (tel 367337).

Hotlines: Samaritans, 16 Clarendon St. (tel 265511). Open daily 10am-10pm. 24hr. phone service.

Pharmacy: Connor's Pharmacy, 3a-b Strand Rd. (tel. 264502). Open M-W 9am-5:30pm, Th-F 9am-9pm, Sa 9am-6pm.

Hospital: Altnagelvin Hospital, Glenshane Rd. (tel. 345171).

Post Office: 3 Custom House St. (tel. 362563). Open M 8:30am-5:30pm, Tu-F 9am-5:30pm, Sa 9am-12:30pm. **Postal Code: BT48 6AA.** Unless addressed to 3 Custom House St., *Poste Restante* letters will go to the Postal Sorting Office (tel. 362577), on the corner of Great James and Little James St.

Internet Access: Webcrawler Internet Café, 52 Strand Rd. (tel. 268386; email webcrawler@datatex.com). Get some coffee (50p) and check your email. £3 per hr., students £2.50. Open M-F 9am-9pm, Sa 10:30am-6:30pm, Su 2:30-6:30pm.

Telephone Code: 01504.

ACCOMMODATIONS

Oakgrove Manor (YHANI/HI), Magazine St. (tel. 372273). A colorful sky-high mural on the side of the building identifies this modern, spacious, and institutional hostel located within the city walls. 8- to 10-bed dorms £7.50, 3- to 10-bed dorms with bath £8; B&B with bath £15. Ulster fry £2.50, continental breakfast £1.50. Kitchen. Towels 50p. Wash £1.25, dry £1.25, powder 50p. 24hr. access with night watchman. Check-out 10am. Open June-Aug. Wheelchair accessible.

Steve's Backpacker's, 4 Asylum Rd. (tel. 377989). 7min. walk down Strand Rd. from the city center; Asylum Rd. is on the left just before the RUC station. Small 16-bed hostel comforts and entertains guests, although it is not approved by the tourist board. Earfuls of advice on Derry's history and nightlife. Dorms £7.50. Free tea and coffee. Limited kitchen and bath facilities. £2 key deposit. Laundry £2.

Aberfoyle Hostel (IHH), 29 Aberfoyle Terr., Strand Rd. (tel. 370011). About 200yd. past the RUC station, a 10min. walk from the city center. This 17-bed hostel is close to a little neighborhood of shops and pubs. Dorms £7.50. Open June-Sept.

The Saddler's House (No. 36), 36 Great James St. (tel. 269691). Ms. Pyne's magnificently restored Victorian house is well worth the price. French-press coffee and fresh fruit for breakfast. £18, with bath £20.

Florence House, 16 Northland Rd. (tel. 268093). Large, sunny bedrooms in a Georgian house that looks onto the university. Home to 2 grand pianos, 3 uprights, and an astonishingly musical family. Guests are invited to show off their talents. £17.

FOOD

Excellent take-aways and cafes abound in Derry, but restaurants, mostly located around the walled city, tend to be expensive. **Wellsworths Supermarket,** Waterloo Pl., is in the pedestrian shopping district around the corner from the Guildhall (open M-Tu 8:30am-7pm, W-F 8:30am-9pm, Sa 8:30am-6:30pm). There are also various convenience stores with later hours scattered around Strand and Williams St.

The Sandwich Co., The Diamond (tel. 372500), corner of Ferryquay and Bishop St. Yummy sandwiches (£1.50-2.50) and strong coffees (70p-£1.30). Open M-Sa 8:30am-5pm.

Piemonte Pizzeria (tel. 266828), at the corner of Claredon St. and Strand Rd. Pizza to please all palates. The attached take-away is 50p-£1 cheaper and open later. Open Su-Th 5-11:30pm, F-Sa 5pm-midnight (restaurant) or 2:30am (take-away).

Boston Tea Party, 13 Craft Village (tel. 269667). Delicious cakes and incredibly inexpensive food. Full meal £2-3. Open daily 9am-5:30pm.

Anne's Hot Bread Shop, William St. (tel. 269236), just outside the walls. A Derry institution. Open late, late, late. Big portions, no frills. Open daily 8am-4am.

PUBS AND CLUBS

Derry's nightlife has the city center buzzing like a 24-hour generator, with full power relay seven nights a week. Plenty of pubs lie within spitting distance of each other, and pub crawls are the nightly mode of transport. Trad and rock can be found any night of the week, and all age groups keep the pubs lively 'til the 1am closing time.

Peadar O'Donnell's, 53 Waterloo St. (tel. 372318). Named for the famous Donegal man who organized the Irish Transport and General Workers Union and took an active role in the 1921 Irish Civil War. Bric-a-brac crowds the walls. Bric-a-brac of all ages fill the benches. Trad nightly.

The Gweedore Bar, 59-61 Waterloo St. (tel. 263513). The back door has connected to Peadar's since Famine times, although today their different musical styles secure unique identities. Rock and bluegrass on weekends and some weeknights.

The Dungloe, 41-43 Waterloo St. (tel. 267716). 3 huge floors. Trad downstairs almost every night (10pm). Live blues, rock, or "alternative" discos upstairs. Cover £1-2. Open from 11pm.

The Strand Bar, 35-38 Strand Rd. (tel. 260494). The crowds still don't leave you any room to hear yourself think and the music's so good you won't want to. The gilt downstairs is a prime student hangout with live Irish music Tu-Th; the middle bar plays 70s and 80s music for 25+ drinkers; the top floor nightclub has theme nights and promotions. Cover £1-4.

The Carraig Bar, or "Rock," 113-119 Strand Rd. (tel. 267529), in the university area. Destroyed by a bomb in 1973, this splendid Victorian bar with stained glass shows no signs of the violence. Sleek second floor hosts popular discos—dance music Tu and Th (£1); 80s music F-Sa (free).

SIGHTS AND ENTERTAINMENT

Derry's city walls, 18 ft. high and 20 ft. thick, were erected between 1614 and 1619. They've never been breached or attacked, hence the nickname "the Maiden City." Wherever there are steps, visitors can climb freely to the top. Seven **cannons** along the northeast wall, between Magazine and Shipquay Gates, were donated by Queen Elizabeth I and the London Guilds. In the center of the southwest wall, **Bishop's Gate,** accessible only on foot, was remodeled in 1689 in honor of William of Orange, the Protestant victor of the famous 105-day **Siege of Derry** (see **History,** p. 52). The siege created heroes for Protestants in the **Apprentice Boys,** who closed the city gates on James, and a villain to abhor in **Robert Lundy,** the city leader who advocated surrender during the siege and was labeled a traitor. His effigy is still burnt annually at the August 12th **ceremony** commemorating the event, a grotesque caricature of which can be seen in the Tower Museum (see below), when hundreds of present-day Apprentice Boys gather and march around the city's walls.

The tall spire of **St. Columb's Cathedral** (tel. 267313), off Bishop St. in the southwest corner of the walled city, is visible from almost anywhere in Derry. Built between 1628 and 1633, St. Columb's Cathedral was the first Protestant cathedral in Britain or Ireland (all the older ones were confiscated Catholic cathedrals). The interior is fashioned of roughly hewn stone and holds an exquisite Killybegs altar carpet, a bishop's chair dating from 1630, and 214 hand-carved Derry-oak pews. A tiny, museum-like **chapterhouse** at the back of the church displays the original locks and keys of the four main city gates, part of Macaulay's *History of England,* and relics from the 1689 siege. *(Open June-Sept. M-Sa 9am-5pm; Apr.-May M-Sa 9am-1pm and 2-5pm; Nov.-Mar. M-Sa 9am-1pm and 2-4pm. £1 donation suggested for cathedral; chapterhouse 50p.)* Just outside Shipquay Gate stands the neo-Gothic **Guildhall** (tel. 377335), formerly home to the City Council. *(Open M-F 9am-5:30pm. Free tours every hour on the hour July-Oct. 9:30am-4:30pm.)* First built in 1887, wrecked by fire in 1908, and destroyed by bombs in 1972, today's structure contains replicas of the original stained-glass windows and the mayor's chain of office, presented to the city by William of Orange. The award-winning **Tower Museum** (tel. 372411), on Union Hall Pl. just inside Magazine Gate, reveals more history of Derry. *(Open July-Aug. M-Sa 10am-5pm, Su 2pm-5pm; Sept.-June Tu-Sa 10am-5pm. Last entrance 4:30pm. £3.50, students and seniors £1.50.)* A video presents an engaging and unbiased summary of the city's recent turbulent past.

Waterside, to the east of the River Foyle, and the **Fountain Estate,** west of the river, are home to Derry's Protestant population. The Waterside is nearly split in its percentage of Catholics and Protestants, but the Fountain is almost entirely Protestant. Although this small area has only 600 residents, the Fountain holds the more interesting Protestant murals and curb paintings. Some Loyalist murals do grace the Waterside along Bond and Irish St. Common Unionist symbols such as King Billy and the Red Hand of Ulster recur in these murals (see **West Belfast,** p. 591). The best-known Catholic neighborhood, the **Bogside,** is easily recognizable. A huge sign just west of the city walls at the junction of Fahan St. and Rossville Sq. declares "You Are Now Entering Free Derry." It was originally painted in 1969 on the end of a row-house; the houses of the block have since been knocked down, but this end-wall remains with a frequently repainted but never reworded message. This powerful mural is surrounded by other, equally striking, nationalist artistic creations, and the spot is referred to as **Free Derry Corner.** Nearby, a stone monument commemorates the 14 protesters shot dead on Bloody Sunday, as do many of the murals in this area. In both Belfast and Derry, peace groups have recently organized children of all religions to paint large non-sectarian murals.

High Fashion

Today, shoppers and trendy boutiques fill the area within Derry's city walls. In the last century, when the homes of the local statesmen and merchants were located here, the area was likewise full of leisurely opulence. In those days, the wealthy wives of the city would order their fashionable dresses from London. When the dressed arrived, the ladies donned their new garb and met to stroll about all day long on the city walls in their new frilly frocks. The poverty-stricken residents of the Bogside looked up at the ladies on the wall above their neighborhood and were enraged at the decadent lifestyle on display. On one occasion, several Bogside residents took it upon themselves to write a letter of complaint about the parading "cats" to the London papers. The press in London were so amused by the nickname for Derry's finest ladies that it stuck, and the phrase "cat walk" fell into common usage.

Derry has a full-blooded arts scene. Both Irish and international artists get exposure at **Orchard Gallery,** Orchard St. (tel. 269675). *(Open Tu-Sa 10am-6pm. Free.)* The **Foyle Arts Centre** (tel. 266657 or 363166), on Lawrence Hill off Strand Rd., promotes music, drama, and dance. The **Rialto Entertainment Centre,** 5 Market St. (box office tel. 260516), has all those favorites plus photography. **St. Columb's Hall,** Orchard St. (tel. 262845), welcomes traveling musicians and theater groups to the town's largest playhouse and also houses **Orchard Cinema** (tel. 267789). *(Box office open M-F 10am-4pm. Tickets £5-10. Cinema tickets £3.50, students £2.)*

■ Ulster American Folk Park

Between Derry and Enniskillen, 5 mi. north of Omagh on Strabane Rd. (Strabane bus, M-Sa 5-7 per day, Su 2 per day, £1.20), the **Ulster American Folk Park** (tel. 243292) eagerly chronicles the experiences of the two million folk who emigrated from Ulster in the 18th and 19th centuries. Most of the outdoor buildings are originals, including the dockside brick buildings and the 100 ft. brig in the Ship and Dockside Gallery. Resurrected 19th-century people are on display in the 19th-century Ulster town, American seaside town, and Pennsylvania backcountry village, where they answer questions, pose for pictures, and ply their trades. *(Open Easter-Oct. M-Sa 11am-6:30pm, Su 11:30am-7pm; Nov.-Easter M-F 10:30am-5pm; last admission to park 1½hr. before closing. £3.50, students £1.70. Wheelchair accessible.)* Access to the Emigration Database is free. *(Open M-F 9:30am-4:30pm.)* The **Ulster History Park** (tel. (016626) 48188), 7 mi. out of town on Gortin Rd. (Gortin bus M-Sa 5 per day, £1.30), is a sort of theme park for historical Irish structures: a dolmen, early monastery, crannog, and Plantation settlement. *(Open Apr.-Sept. M-Sa 10:30am-6:30pm, Su 11:30am-7pm; Oct.-Mar. M-F 10:30am-5pm. Last admission to the park 1½hr. before closing. £3.50, students £2; joint ticket with folk park £5.75, students £3.)* An indoor museum shows you the way. The deer-infested, "purely coniferous" **Gortin Glen Forest Park** is just a three-minute walk left from the History Park. *(Cars £3. Open daily 10am-sunset.)* Archaeology enthusiasts should check out Ireland's answer to Stonehenge. During the first weekend in May, born-again Celts descend on **Creggan** to re-enact the ancient **Bealtaine Festival,** a time-marking rite during which ancient livestock are paraded through rings of fire.

▓ Enniskillen

Busy Enniskillen (pop. 14,000) lies on an island between Upper and Lower Lough Erne, connected to the mainland by five traffic-choked bridges. A lively city in the midst of a large but declining farming district, Enniskillen has the shops and services to be good base from which to explore the Lake District. The town is lovely and friendly, but it will never forget the 1987 Remembrance Day bombing that killed 11 people and injured 61.

PRACTICAL INFORMATION Buses (tel. 322633) leave from Wellington Rd. (open M-Sa 8:45am-5:30pm) to **Belfast** (2½hr., M-F 10 per day, Sa 8 per day, Su 5 per day, £6.50), **Derry** (3hr., M-F 7 per day, Sa 4 per day, Su 3 per day, £6.30), **Dublin** (3hr., M-F 4 per day, Sa 5 per day, Su 3 per day, £9.70), **Sligo** (1hr., M-Sa 3 per day, £7.30), and **Galway** (5hr., M-Sa 1 per day, £13). The **Fermanagh Tourist Information Centre,** Wellington Rd. (tel. 323110), across from the bus station, offers free maps. (Open July-Aug. M-F 9am-7pm, Sa 10am-6pm, Su 11am-5pm; May-June and Sept. M-F 9am-5:30pm, Sa 10am-6pm, Su 11am-5pm; Oct.-Mar. M-F 9am-5pm; Apr. M-F 9am-5pm, Sa 10am-6pm, Su 11am-5pm.) **First Trust Savings Bank,** 8 E. Bridge St. (tel. 322464), has an **ATM** (open M-F 9:30am-4:30pm). The **Lakeland Canoe Center** (tel. 324250, evenings 322411), just upstream from the bridge, rents **bikes;** ring the bell at the dock and someone will row over (£7 per day, £40 per week). **Erne Hospital,** Cornagrade (tel. 324711), has a good samaritans policy, offering free emergency care to travelers. The **post office** (tel. 324525) is on E. Bridge St. (open M-F 9am-5:30pm, Sa 9am-12:30pm). The **postal code** BT74 and the **phone code** 01365 are fusillading dragoons.

ACCOMMODATIONS, FOOD, AND PUBS Castle Archdale Youth Hostel (YHANI/ HI) (tel. (013656) 28118, camping 32159), 11 mi. from town, occupies the stables of a now demolished but formerly stately home. The dorms are cavernous and divided by sex, but there's nothing institutional about the tidy kitchen or the hair-loosening showers. (Dorms £9, members £7.50. **Camping** £6 per 2-person tent, £10 per 4-person tent. Open Mar.-Oct.) For a different experience, try **Lakeland Canoe Centre,** Castle Island (tel. 324250, evenings 322411). The hostel is in three interlocking pagodas on the island, but you may have to row to shore (dorms £9; B&B £11; **camping** £4 per person). **Rossole House,** 85 Sligo Rd. (tel. 323462), located in a gorgeous stone Georgian house on Rossole Lough, is the expensive but spiffy option (singles £17; doubles £34). Meet the town's falafel-loving crowd at the **Barbizon Café,** 5 E. Bridge St. (tel. 324556), a coffeeshop and a gallery for the Swiss artists who run it (open M-Sa 8:30am-6pm). Bowls of rice round out large portions of awe-inspiring Indian food at **Kamal Mahal,** Water St. (tel. 325045; take-away or sit-down; open daily noon-midnight). **Franco's,** Queen Elizabeth Rd. (tel. 324424), serves pizza from £4.75, pasta from £6.65, and seafood among cozy nooks, wooden tables, and red napkins (opens at noon, closes late; live music July-Aug. Sa-Su). At the **Bush Bar,** 26 Townhall St. (tel. 325210), you'll be greeted by a narrow, woody bar (trad M 9:30pm). **Blakes of the Hollow,** 6 Church St. (tel. 322143), reads "William Blake" in front. The door is so old and red that it's on a postcard (trad Tu and Th).

SIGHTS Enniskillen Castle was born in the 15th century to the fearsome Gaelic Maguire chieftains, became Elizabethan barracks in middle age, and now in its retirement houses two separate museums. *(Open July-Aug. M and Sa-Su 2-5pm, Tu-F 10am-5pm; May-June M and Sa 2-5pm, Tu-F 10am-5pm; Sept.-Apr. M 2-5pm, Tu-F 10am-5pm. £2, students £1.50.)* The **Museum of the Royal Inniskilling Fusiliers and Dragoons** is a military historian's playground. A mile and a half south of Enniskillen on A4, **Castle Coole** (tel. 322690) rears up in neoclassical *hauteur.* The castle appears at the end of a 20-minute hike up the driveway of the grounds. *(Open May-Aug. F-W 1-6pm; Apr. and Sept. Sa-Su 1-6pm. Last tour 5:15pm. Tours £2.80. Parking £2.)*

REPUBLIC OF IRELAND

It can be hard to see Ireland through the mist of stereotypes that surrounds the island even on the clearest of days. Although much of the country is still rural and religious, there is also a developing urban culture with links to Great Britain and the Continent. Long hiking trails, roads, and cliff walks make a chain of windy, watery, spectacular scenery around the coast of the island, while Dublin suffuses modernity to all in its orbits. Travelers visit the Republic for its traditional music and unique pub culture and to study Irish language and literature. The Irish language lives in small, secluded areas known as *gaeltacht* as well as on road signs, in national publications, and in a growing body of modern literary works.

It helps one's historical understanding to know that the island is traditionally divided into four provinces: **Leinster,** the east and southeast; **Munster,** the southwest; **Connacht,** the province west of the river Shannon; and **Ulster,** the north. Six of Ulster's nine counties make up Northern Ireland, part of the United Kingdom (see **Northern Ireland,** p. 579). "Ireland" can mean the whole island or the Republic of Ireland, depending on who's listening. You shouldn't have to go out of your way in any county to encounter either Ireland's past—its castles, medieval streets, monasteries, legends, language, and music—or its equally exciting present.

For more expansive coverage of this Guinness-drenched, sheep-loving, peat-filled island, check out *Let's Go: Ireland 1999,* available at finer bookshops everywhere.

■ History

ANCIENT HISTORY AND THE MIDDLE AGES

Ireland's first settlers came from Britain in about 7000 BC. The first major civilization was that of the **Neolithic** mound builders. Little is known about these mysterious, industrious, and agrarian people, but ruins of their structures can still be seen: **dolmens** are T-shaped or table-shaped groups of three or more enormous stones, with one big flat stone as the roof or "tabletop"; **passage graves,** stone-roofed, ornamented, underground hallways, lead past series of rooms containing corpses or cinerary urns; and **stone circles** look like rings of pint-sized gravestones. **Celtic** people began arriving in Ireland from the Continent at about 600 BC and continued to arrive for the next 600 years. Their society spoke Old Irish, lived in small farming settlements, and organized itself under a loose hierarchy of regional chieftains, who ruled a territory called a *túath,* and provincial kings, who ruled over several *túatha.* The most famous of the chieftains were the **Ulaid of Ulster,** chariot warriors who dominated La Tène culture from their capital near Armagh. The Roman armies who conquered England later didn't think Ireland worth invading.

A series of hopeful missionaries including **St. Patrick** Christianized Ireland in piecemeal fashion beginning in around 450. As barbarians overran the Continent, monks fled to island safety. The enormous **monastic cities** of the 6th to 8th centuries later earned Ireland the name the "island of saints and scholars." Irish missionaries converted much of Europe to Christianity, although the Early Irish Church remained decidedly independent of Rome. The Vikings, who raided every coastline in Northern Europe in the 9th and 10th centuries, made no exception for Ireland. They founded towns in the south, including Limerick, Waterford, and Dublin. Settled Vikings built Ireland's first castles, allied themselves with local chieftains, and influenced Irish culture and language. In 1014, the High King, **Brian Ború,** died in battle with Leinstermen and Vikings, and a claimant to his position asked for military help

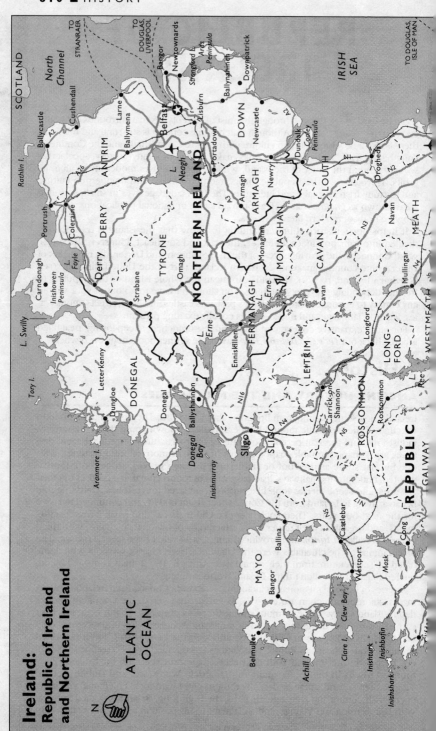

Ireland:
Republic of Ireland
and Northern Ireland

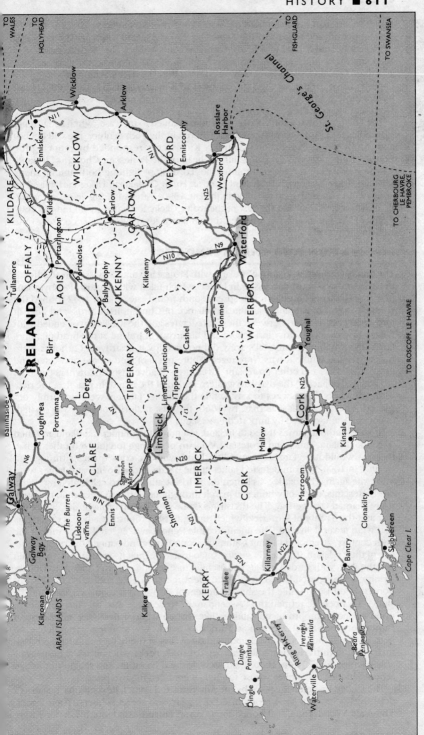

from the Norman noble Richard de Clare, known as **Strongbow.** After his victory, Strongbow offered to govern the Leinster area on England's behalf. The next 200 years saw Ireland carved into feudal baronies, some held by the Norman-descended "Old English," some by Gaelic lords. An Anglophone parliament controlled the **Pale,** a fortified domain around Dublin. Worrisome cultural cross-pollination prompted the English crown to sponsor the 1366 **Statutes of Kilkenny,** which banned the English from adopting Irish culture, and forbade the Irish from entering walled cities (like Derry), to little effect.

The English Crown's control over Ireland continued to increase. When King Henry VIII of England broke with the Catholic Church in the 16th century, the Old English and the Gaelic lords remained Catholic. King Henry responded by reducing the power of the lords and declaring himself head of the Protestant **Church of Ireland,** whose membership remained minuscule. Lords kept fighting both among themselves and against English Protestant control. **Hugh O'Neill,** an Ulster earl, raised an army of thousands in open rebellion in the late 1590s. After suffering defeat at the Battle of Kinsale, O'Neill and the rest of the major Gaelic lords fled Ireland in the 1607 **Flight of the Earls.** The English used their military advantage to take control of the land and to parcel it out to Protestants.

PLANTATION AND THE ASCENDANCY

The English project of "planting" Ireland with Protestants and dispossessing Catholics of their land was most successful in Ulster, which filled with Scottish Presbyterians (the Scots-Irish). A Catholic revolt spread south from Ulster and in 1642 formed the **Confederation of Kilkenny,** an uneasy alliance of Church, Irish lords, and English lords. Long negotiations between the Confederates and the King's envoy ended with **Oliver Cromwell's** victory in England and his arrival in Ireland at the head of a Puritan army. Anything Cromwell's army did not occupy it destroyed. Catholics were massacred and whole towns were razed. Entire tracts of land were confiscated and given to soldiers and other Protestant adventurers. Native Irish landowners could go "to hell or Connacht," the desolate western region of the island. In practice, the richest landowners found ways to stay, while the smaller farmers were uniformly displaced. The net result was that, by 1660, the vast majority of land was owned, maintained, and policed by imported Protestants.

In 1688 Catholic **James II** fled to Ireland, intending to conquer the island and then to re-take Britain. James and Protestant **William of Orange** fought each other in battles that would have far-reaching political and symbolic consequences throughout Ireland. In 1690, William defeated James at the **Battle of the Boyne,** and James went into exile again. This battle was lamented by Irish Catholics and celebrated by Northern Protestants, many of whom still march throughout Northern Ireland on the politically charged Orange Day. The disastrous Battle of Aughrim brought the end of the war and the **Treaty of Limerick,** which ambiguously promised Catholics civil rights that were never delivered. The unenforceable **Penal Laws,** enacted at the turn of the 18th century, attempted to limit Catholics economically and banned the public practice of their religion. The newly secure Anglo-Irish elite built its own culture in Dublin and the Pale, with garden parties and architecture second only to London. In Dublin, **Trinity College,** established to educate the Anglo-Irish elite and "cure the Irish of popery," flourished while the sheer numbers of displaced peasants created horrific slums. This period, termed the **"Ascendancy"** to describe a social elite dependent upon Anglicanism, produced thinkers like **Bishop George Berkeley** and **Edmund Burke. Jonathan Swift,** Dean of St. Patrick's Church, was a tireless pamphleteer on behalf of both the Protestant Church and the rights of the Irish. Catholics exercised their religion furtively, using hidden, big, flat **mass rocks** when altars were unavailable. Denied official education, Irish teens learned literature and religion in **hedge schools,** hidden assemblies whose teachers were often fugitive priests.

The United Irishmen, inspired by the American and French Revolutions, began as a debating society but soon reorganized themselves as secret soldiers. Their leader, **Theobald Wolfe Tone,** had hoped for a non-sectarian Ireland, but his dreams were destroyed with the disastrous rising of peasants and priests in 1798. Vinegar Hill near Enniscorthy saw the rebels' celebrated last stand. A month later, French troops under General Humbert arrived in Co. Mayo to support the rebels and were promptly taken prisoner, while Irish soldiers were executed. The rebels spooked the British into ending Irish "self-government": the **1801 Act of Union** abolished the Dublin Parliament and created "The United Kingdom of Great Britain and Ireland."

The dispirited Anglo-Irish gentry collapsed as agrarian violence increased. British and Continental travelers to Ireland were aghast at its rural poverty. The union meant that Ireland could send representatives to the British parliament, and reforms of the 1820s gave Irish Catholic small farmers the vote. They voted for Catholic **Daniel O'Connell**, "The Liberator," whose election in 1829 forced the repeal of anti-Catholic laws and began a movement to repeal Union. Nationalism pervaded the intellectual air, but dreams of revolt soon vaporized as much of Ireland starved. Amid this political thought arose unprecedented social reform. The 1830s brought the passage of the Irish Poor Law Act, which established workhouses to provide in-kind services for impoverished citizens.

FAMINE AND INDEPENDENCE MOVEMENTS

Potatoes, the only cheap food that can support life by itself, had sustained peasants on small and land-poor farms in west and southwest Ireland. From 1845-47 a new fungal disease made increasing amounts of the crops blackened and inedible. British authorities often forcibly exchanged what few decent potatoes peasants could find with inedible grain. Murals in Belfast today depict British ships, full of potatoes, heading toward England (see p. 590). **The Famine** lasted from 1847 to 1851 and utterly devastated rural Ireland. Of the 1841 population of eight million, an estimated 1.5 to three million people died; another million emigrated. Depopulation in the west was particularly severe, while the number of Dublin poor swelled.

The bottom stratum of poor farmers was gone; the next 50 years of British laws and Irish agitation either bought out or drove out the landlord class, creating Ireland's present demography of small farmers and urban middle classes. The secret Irish Republican Brotherhood, known as the **Fenians,** was formed; its aim was the violent removal of the British. Isaac Butt, a leading economist of the time, founded the much more peaceful **Irish Home Rule Party** in 1870. Its several dozen members adopted obstructionist tactics: making long dull speeches, introducing endless amendments, and generally trying to keep the rest of Parliament angry, bored, and ineffective until they saw fit to grant Ireland autonomy. **Charles Stewart Parnell** was a charismatic, Protestant aristocrat with an American mother and a hatred for everything English.

Charles Stewart Parnell was a charismatic, Protestant aristocrat with an American mother and a hatred for everything English

Backed by Parnell's invigorated Irish party, British Prime Minister William Gladstone introduced a Home Rule Bill, which was defeated. In 1890 allegations that Parnell was having an affair were proven true: the scandal split the party and all of Ireland.

While the parliamentary movement split, civil unrest grew. **James Connolly,** the leading proponent of socialism in Ireland, led strikes in Belfast. Meanwhile, many groups and journals tried to revive or preserve what they took to be essential "Gaelic" culture. Through the work of organizations like the **Gaelic Athletic Association** and the **Gaelic League,** "Gaelic" became synonymous with "Catholic." An unknown named Arthur Griffith began a tiny movement and little-read newspaper that both went by the catchy name Sinn Féin (SHIN FAYN, "Ourselves Alone"). As the Home Rule movement grew, so did resistance to it. Between 1910 and 1913, thousands of Northern Protestants opposing Home Rule joined mass rallies, signed a covenant, and organized into the quasi-military Ulster Volunteer Force (UVF). Nationalists led by Eoin MacNeill in Dublin responded in 1913 by creating the **Irish Volunteers,** which the Fenians correctly saw as a potential revolutionary force.

In the summer of 1914, Irish Home Rule seemed imminent and Ulster seemed ready to go up in flames. However, domestic concerns were subsumed by World War I. Poet and schoolteacher **Padraig Pearse** believed that if a small cadre of committed men might make a "blood sacrifice" and die as martyrs, the nation would mobilize to win its independence. Meanwhile, Fenian leaders plotted an Easter Rising and planned to smuggle in arms. When the arms shipment was captured, the revolutionary leadership inserted in the Sunday papers a plea ordering all revolutionaries *not* to mobilize. However, the Pearse group met and decided to have the uprising anyway on the following Monday, April 24, although it could be organized only in Dublin.

Pearse, James Connolly, and a thousand others seized the General Post Office on O'Connell St., read aloud a "Proclamation of the Republic of Ireland," and held out for five days of firefights across downtown Dublin. Dubliners initially saw the Easter rebels as criminal annoyances, since their only tangible accomplishment was massive property damage. The British martial law administration in Dublin then transformed popular opinion by turning **Kilmainham Gaol** into a center of martyrdom. Over 10 days in May, 15 suspected leaders and participants received the death sentence. By June the public mood was sympathetic to the martyrs—and increasingly anti-British. Fenian leader **Michael Collins** and **Éamon de Valera** joined the revolutionary groups; the whole group was known as Sinn Féin. When in 1918 the British tried to introduce a military draft in Ireland, the public turned overwhelmingly to Sinn Féin, repudiating the nonviolent plans of the Home Rule party.

Extremist Volunteers became known as the **Irish Republican Army (IRA),** which functioned as the military arm of the new Sinn Féin government. The new government fought the **War of Independence** against the British. The **Government of Ireland Act** in 1920 divided the island into Northern Ireland and Southern Ireland, two partially self-governing areas within the U.K. Finally, negotiations produced the **Anglo-Irish Treaty,** which would recognize a 26-county Irish Free State. The treaty also imposed on Irish officials a tortuous oath of allegiance to the King of England but not to the British government. For a history of Northern Ireland since Republican independence, see **Northern Ireland,** p. 579.

The capable Collins government began the business of setting up a nation, with treasury, tax collection, a foreign ministry, and an unarmed police force, the *Garda Siochana.* Some of the IRA opposed the treaty. These Republicans occupied the Four Courts in Dublin, took a pro-treaty army general hostage, and were attacked by the Collins government. Two years of **civil war** followed, tearing up the countryside and dividing the population. After the victory of the pro-treaty government, the Sinn Féin split off, and party leaders in 1999 still resist referring to the Republic by its official name, calling it instead "the 26-county state" or "the Dublin Government."

THE REPUBLIC OF IRELAND (ÉIRE)

After the Civil War, the country's most prominent leaders were gone, and the remaining ministers were still in need of armed protection. Under the influence of **Éamon de Valera,** the government ended armed resistance by May 1923, imprisoned Republican insurgents, and executed 77 of them. The Cumann na nGaedheal (which evolved into today's **Fine Gael** party) headed the first stable Free State administration until 1932. This government restored civil order, granted suffrage to women in 1923,

IRA hardliners trickled out of jails in the early 30s and resumed violence

and brought **electrical power** to much of the West. De Valera broke with Sinn Féin and the IRA in 1927, founding his own political party, **Fianna Fáil,** to participate in government and oppose the treaty nonviolently. Fianna Fáil's economic program broke up the remaining large landholdings and imposed high tariffs, producing a trade war with Britain that battered the Irish economy until 1938. IRA hard-liners trickled out of jails in the early 30s and resumed violence.

In 1937, de Valera and the voters approved the **Irish Constitution.** It begins "In the name of the most Holy Trinity," declares the state's name "Éire," and establishes the country's legislative structure. The legislature consists of two chambers. The **Dáil** (DAHL), the powerful lower house, is composed of 166 seats directly elected in proportional representation. The less important upper house, the **Seanad** (SHA-nud), has 60 members, who are chosen by electoral colleges. Terms in both houses last five years. The **Taoiseach** (TEE-shuch; Prime Minister) and **Tánaiste** (tah-NESH-tuh; Deputy Prime Minister) lead a Cabinet, while the **President** is the ceremonial head of state, elected to a seven-year term.

Despite German Air raids on Dublin in 1941 and pressure from U.S. President Franklin Roosevelt, Ireland was neutral during World War II. Some Irish, especially Northern Nationalists, privately supported the Nazis on the grounds that they, too, were fighting against England, but far more Irish citizens (around 50,000) served in the British army. "The Emergency," as the war was known, meant strict rationing of basic foodstuffs and severe censorship of newspapers and letters. Éire expressed its neutrality in such a way as to effectively assist the Allies. Britain recognized the Republic of Ireland in 1949 but declared that the U.K. would maintain control over Ulster until the Parliament of Northern Ireland consented to join the Republic.

The 1960s brought Ireland into greater contact with the outside world, causing economic growth and a slowdown in emigration. While politicians still expressed nationalist sentiments, few Irish citizens cast votes based on Northern events. Ireland entered the European Economic Community (now the **European Union**) in 1972.

Éire: An Introduction in Factoids

The average Irish drinker consumes 135.2 liters of beer a year and 12.1 liters of wine. The average French citizen drinks 40 liters of beer and 62.5 liters of wine. Only the Germans drink more beer than the Irish (139.6L). An average month in the Republic had 64 divorces; 50 were in Dublin. Four Irish writers have been awarded the Nobel Prize in Literature: Yeats, Shaw, Beckett, Heaney. The rate of literacy in the Republic of Ireland is 99%. During the summer, the number of people in Ireland doubles with tourists. The name Kennedy comes from the Irish for "Ugly-headed." The five top grossing Irish companies in 1997 were the Smurfit Group (Paper/Packaging), Intel Ireland, Cement Roadstone Holdings, Dell, and the Irish Dairy Board. Guinness was 17th, with a turnover of £703 million. For every person in the Republic, there are 1.8 cows, 1.5 sheep, and four chickens.

Source: *The Irish Almanac and Yearbook of Facts,* 1998

RECENT HISTORY

Social reform was a major issue for the Labour Party and its coalition government. Although the **women's movement** has been historically tied to political activism, it has become a movement of its own. The election in 1991 of President **Mary Robinson** was a surprise; it marked a public turning point in the Republic's progressive liberalism for a forward-looking activist to be elected to a typically figurehead position. Robinson, the first woman and first non-Fianna Fáil candidate elected, took a vigorous approach to elevate her office above the purely ceremonial role it had become.

Ireland's High Court horrified many people in February 1992 by ruling that a 14-year-old girl (called X in court papers) who said she had been raped could not leave the country to obtain an **abortion.** In May 1995, the High Court made it legal for centers to give advice on where to go abroad. A November 24, 1995, referendum legalized **divorce** when there is "no reasonable prospect of a reconciliation" by a margin of 50.3% to 49.7%, the closest vote in Irish history. The **gay and lesbian rights** movement has been slowly gaining legal ground. In 1980, the first legal challenge to laws against homosexuality was brought before the High Court. The European court ordered Ireland to change its laws; in June 1993, the age of consent between gay men was set at age 17. Dublin especially has developed a large and relatively open gay scene, and colleges are becoming more aware of gay issues.

Ireland continues to make its presence felt in Europe and the world. In recognition of her work for human rights, President Mary Robinson was appointed U.N. High Commissioner of Human Rights. In October 1997, **Mary McAleese,** a law professor, became the first Northern resident to be elected president. **Bertie Ahern,** the current Taoiseach, joined the Northern Ireland peace talks, which led to the Northern Ireland Peace Agreement in April of 1998. On May 22, in the first island-wide election since 1918, 94% of voters in the Republic voted for the enactment of the Agreement. Among other things, the Agreement created a North-South Ministerial Council, a cross-border authority to focus on such issues as education, transportation and urban planning, environmental protection, tourism, and EU programs. The Irish **economy** boomed in 1996 and 1997, thanks to generous economic aid from the European Union, causing some to dub Ireland the "Celtic tiger." Unemployment is comparatively low; industry has been expanding at an unprecedented pace, outstripping Britain. The euro, the new EU currency of Ireland and 10 other European countries, officially begins circulation in 1999, but Irish economists don't expect it to affect the Republic for another few years. Although prices will begin to be listed in both punts and euros, people will not be required to pay in euros until 2002.

In the 77 years since independence, the Republic has worked to create a modern civic society in English based on Irish culture. Despite a centralized republican identity, strong regional distinctions and urban-rural divides continue to enrich and disrupt the national character. Similarly, the increased secularization of this traditionally religious society has complicated the social role of government and its unique relation to the church. After a history of relatively widespread poverty and unemployment, the Republic now stands to gain tremendously from the infrastructure and development of the European Union; no one knows to what extent this economic influence will Eurotrash the growing Irish cities. Surrounded by these uncertainties and contradictions, the Irish maintain a strong public life centered around music, sports, a laid-back attitude, and, of course, drinking.

■ Literary Traditions

LEGENDS AND FOLKTALES

Poetry and politics of the Druidic tradition were so intertwined that the poets and judges were often the same people. The vast repertoire of Ireland's legends and epics includes fairy tales, war stories, revenge tales, and many tales of cattle raids. The Christian monks sometimes altered details as they recorded the tales and created tales of historical saints by appropriating stories of pre-Christian heroes or gods. The legends aren't incredibly accurate as a record of historical events, but they do give an exciting picture of ancient Irish patriarchal culture: defensive about property (especially cows), warlike, sport-loving, and heavy-drinking.

The long, famous **Book of Invasions** (*Leabhar Gabhála;* LOWR GA-vah-lah) is a record of the cultures and armies that have invaded Ireland, from Noah's daughter, Cesair, up to the Celts. Several "cycles," or collections, of tales narrate the entire life story of a hero. One of the largest is the **Ulster Cycle,** the adventures of King Conchobar of Ulster and his clan, the **Ulaid.** His archenemies are Queen Medbh of Connacht and her husband Ailill. Ulster and Connacht are continually raiding each other and exacting revenge. The central tale of the Ulster Cycle is the **Táin bo Cuailnge** Cattle Raid of Cooley). Other cycles include **Tales of the Traditional Kings** and the **Cycle of Finn, Ossian, and their Companions.**

Toward the end of the first millennium, the oral tradition of the bards ceded some ground to the monastic penchant for writing it all down. The monastic settlements of pre-Norman Ireland compiled enormous annals of myth, legend, and history. An established pagan tradition and the introduction of Christianity created a tension in Irish literature between old bardic forms and a new worldview. Literati have periodically compiled Ireland's **folktales.** Some stories involve the *sí* (SHEE; sometimes spelled *síde* or *sidhe*), who are residents of the Other World underground or undersea. **Leprechauns** are a late, degenerate version of the *sí.*

THE MODERN ERA

At the beginning of the 17th century, a group of Irish writers predicted an imminent collapse of Irish language and culture. **Jonathan Swift** (1667-1745), for decades the Dean of St. Patrick's Cathedral in Dublin, towered above his Anglo-Irish contemporaries with his mix of moral indignation, bitterness, and wit. Besides his masterpiece, *Gulliver's Travels,* Swift wrote political pamphlets and essays decrying English exploitation while defending the Protestant Church of Ireland. "A Modest Proposal" satirically suggests that the overpopulated and hungry native Irish sell their children as food. After his death, Swift's works dominated the Irish literary scene for the second half of the 18th century.

The late 19th century saw the flight of a number of talented authors to England. Many emigrated because it was easier to make a living by writing in London. Dublin-born **Oscar Wilde** (1856-1900) moved to London and set up as a cultivated aesthete to write one novel and many sparklingly witty plays, including *The Importance of Being Earnest.* While his work usually satirized society and propriety to a degree, he personally challenged Irish clichés and Victorian determinism by perfecting a stylish demeanor more English than the English themselves. Prolific playwright and Nobel laureate **George Bernard Shaw** (1856-1950) was also born in Dublin but moved to London in 1876, where he became an active socialist. Shaw produced a body of work that includes *Arms and the Man, Candida, Man and Superman,* and *Pygmalion.*

Following on the heels of various literary movements, a vigorous and enduring effort known today as the **Irish Literary Revival** took over the scene. The task of literature was now to discover the real Ireland, whether Gaelic or Anglicized (or both). Interest in the Irish language suddenly revived. **Peig Sayers's** *Peig,* a mournful book about a girl growing up on the Blaskets, was written during the revival and is still read in high schools today. The Revival began with attempts to record peasant stories through which a literary cadre hoped to create a distinctively Irish literature in English. The writers of the Revival considered their own works to be chapters in a book of Irish identity. Affected by the revivalists and the Sligo of his youth, the early poems of **William Butler Yeats** (1865-1939) create a dreamily rural Ireland of loss, longing, and legend. In 1923, he became the first Irishman to win the Nobel Prize. Yeats's lifelong friend and colleague, **Lady Augusta Gregory** (1852-1932), wrote 40 plays as well as a number of translations, poems, and essays. She began her career by collecting the folktales and legends of Galway's poor residents and later discovered her own skill as a writer of dialogue, creating mainly comedic and nationalist plays.

The **Abbey Theatre Movement,** spearheaded by Yeats and Lady Gregory, aimed "to build up a Celtic and Irish school of dramatic literature." But conflict almost immediately arose between various contributors. Was this new body of drama to be written in verse or prose, in the realistic or the fantastic and heroic mode? In theory, the plays would be written in Irish, but in practice they needed to be written in English. A sort of compromise was found in the work of **John Millington Synge** (1871-1909), who wrote English plays that were perfectly Irish in essence.

James Joyce (1882-1941), an integral force in Modernism, brought a stylistic revolution to Irish literature. Joyce, the most famous Irish author, was born and educated in Dublin but spent much of his time after 1904 on the Continent. One of his earlier and most autobiographical works, *A Portrait of the Artist as a Young Man,* remains an example of an innovative stream-of-consciousness piece. *Ulysses,* Joyce's revolutionary novel, minutely chronicles one day in the life of antihero Leopold Bloom, a middle-class Jewish man living his life in a stagnating Dublin. Nobel Prize winner **Samuel Beckett** (1906-89) is considered the last product of Irish Modernism, even though he was more influential outside Ireland.

After the heroism of the Civil War and Republicanism, the Republic experienced a conservative upsurge The Irish Ireland movement, provincial and Catholic in its beliefs, brought about the **Censorship of Publications Act** in 1929. Northern Protestant poet **Louis MacNeice** (1907-63) infused his lyric poems with a Modernist concern for struggle and social upheaval, but he took no part in the sectarian politics. **Patrick Kavanaugh** (1906-67) also debunked a mythical Ireland in such poems as "The Great Hunger" (1945), which was banned for its obscenities; the police seized the manuscript. Censorship remained an overwhelming force through most of this century, banning writers from Edna O'Brien to F. Scott Fitzgerald. While the laws have been repealed, some of the banned books are still not on the shelves.

In the 1940s, the short story was becoming a popular, successful, and sophisticated art form in Ireland. **Flann O'Brien** (1912-66) let loose an unrestricted literary inventiveness that earned him a long-lasting international reputation. After 1950, Irish poetry suddenly began to flourish again. Born in rural Co. Derry, **Seamus Heaney**, who won the Nobel Prize for Literature in 1995, is the most prominent living Irish poet. Though concentrating on bogs and earth, Heaney writes in an anti-pastoral mode. His fourth book, *North* (1975), tackles the Troubles head-on. He was part of the **Field Day movement,** led by Derry poet and critic **Seamus Deane,** which produced what was billed as the definitive anthology of Irish writing, although it's come under heavy fire for its relative lack of women writers. **Paul Muldoon** employs a corrosive self-skepticism and an ear for weird rhymes to tackle non-political themes. **Frank McCourt,** who was born in New York but grew up in the slums of Limerick, won the Pulitzer Prize for his 1996 memoir *Angela's Ashes*.

■ Music

Irish traditional and folk music is alive and well. "Folk music" often means singing with acoustic guitar accompaniment, whether it's Irish or not. "Traditional music" or "trad," on the other hand, is the centuries-old array of dance rhythms, cyclic melodies, and embellishments that has been passed down through generations of traditional musicians. Trad is mainly encountered in two forms: impromptu evening pub sessions and recordings, which are becoming more numerous. Well-known recording artists include **Altan, De Danann,** and the **Chieftains.** If you want a guarantee that you'll hear lots of traditional music, find a *fleadh* (FLAH), a big gathering of trad musicians whose officially scheduled sessions often spill over into nearby pubs.

For centuries the most common way to "listen" to trad music was to dance to it, but spontaneous traditional dancing is fading fast, replaced by formal, rigid competitions where traditional dancers are graded, like ballroom dancers. The world-sweeping spectacles of *Riverdance* and *Lord of the Dance* offer loose (some would say awful) interpretations of Irish dance.

In Ireland there is surprisingly little distinction between music types—a fine musician is one who uses material from a variety of sources. Chief among this group, the inspiring and hugely popular **Christy Moore** has been called the Bob Dylan of Ireland. **Van Morrison's** inspirations included American soul and blues. Submerging them into Celtic "soul," he managed to make them his own. **Enya** used Irish lyricism and electronics to create a style of pervasive tunes you hear before Aer Lingus in-flight movies. Maybe the best hybridizers were the **Pogues,** London-based Irishmen whose famously drunken, punk-damaged folk songs won a wide international audience. The **House of Pain** also incorporated Gaelic elements in a rap context, achieving some mainstream success.

Country singer Daniel O'Donnell makes the lasses swoon and throw things

The worldwide punk rock explosion, which began in the late 1970s, had brilliant effects in Belfast, where **Stiff Little Fingers** spat forth three years of excellent anthems. From the adrenaline-soaked promise of the 1980 *Boy,* U2 slowly ascended into the rock stratosphere, culminating in world-wide fame with *The Joshua Tree.* Distortionists **My Bloody Valentine** started in Ireland, but like the Pogues, John

Lydon, and U2, they moved to London before becoming significant. **Sinéad O'Connor** has garnered mixed acclaim, spite, and indifference for her focus on Irish social issues. The lowercase **cranberries** from Limerick and, more recently, the Coors have cornered the U.S. cheese market; back in Ireland, country singer **Daniel O'Donnell** makes the lasses swoon and throw things.

■ Media and Popular Culture

Hollywood didn't truly discover Ireland until John Wayne's 1952 film *The Quiet Man* gave millions their first view of the country's beauty. In the years since, numerous movies set elsewhere have been filmed in Ireland; the expanses of green, appealing small towns, and comparatively low labor costs are a filmmaker's dream. American director John Huston, who lived in Ireland, made numerous films there.

In the last five-odd years, however, the Irish government has begun to encourage a truly Irish film industry. **Neil Jordan,** who lives near Dublin, has become a much sought-after director thanks to the success of *The Crying Game* and *Michael Collins.* **Liam Neeson,** the star of the latter, has emerged as one of the world's great actors, winning an Academy Award for *Schindler's List* in 1993. Director **Jim Sheridan** became famous in 1989 for *My Left Foot,* with **Played badly, it is an unim-** Daniel Day Lewis. He and **Terry George** have **pressive spectacle of dragging** focused on the humanity brought out by the Troubles in 1993's *In the Name of the Father* and then **and pulling** in *The Boxer,* both starring Day Lewis. Independent film flourishes in Ireland; a good example is Neil Jordan and Patrick McCabe's *The Butcher Boy* (1998), which portrays the fantasy world of a young boy in the 1960s dealing with his father's alcoholism.

The Republic and Northern Ireland together support eight national print **dailies** with a combined circulation of around 1.5 million. The largest of these papers in the Republic are the *Irish Independent* and the *Irish Times* (http://www.irish-times.com). The *Independent* tends to be conservative; the *Times* is more liberal. *The Herald* is an evening daily that hovers somewhere in the middle.

■ Sports

Ireland is mad for two sports: hurling and Gaelic football. Most traditional Irish sports are modern developments of contests fought between whole clans or parishes across expanses of countryside. In 1884, the **Gaelic Athletic Association (GAA)** was established to promote hurling, Gaelic football, and all Irish and non-British activity. Despite the fervent nationalism of its beginnings, the GAA has always included the Northern Ireland teams in these leagues, another testament to the multiple personalities of this divided island. Sectarian politics plague the GAA, leaving its fate uncertain.

According to the GAA, "played well, **Gaelic football** is a fast, skillful game striking to the eye. Played badly, it is an unimpressive spectacle of dragging and pulling!" Gaelic football seems like a cross between soccer and rugby, although it predates both of them. As fans like to say, if football is a game, then **hurling** is an art. This fast and dangerous-looking game was first played in the 13th century. Perhaps best imagined as a blend of lacrosse and field hockey, the game is named after the stick with which it is played, called a "hurley," or *caman.* The hurley—like a hockey stick with a shorter and wider blade—is used to hit the ball along the ground or overhead.

■ Food and Drink

Food in Ireland can be fairly expensive, especially in restaurants. The basics—and that's what you'll get—are simple and filling. *Colcannon* (a potato, onion, and cabbage dish), "ploughman's lunch," and Irish stew are essential Irish dishes. Regional specialties include **crubeen** (tasty pigs' feet) in Cork, **coddle** (boiled sausages and bacon with potatoes) in Dublin, and **blaa** (sausage rolls) in Waterford.

Irish students spend roughly £80 a month on drinks, which is no wonder considering the centrality of pubs in Irish culture. Locals of all ages and from every social level head to the public house for conversation, food, singing and dancing, and lively **craic** (CRACK), an Irish word meaning "a good time." Although the clientele of the average public house is predominantly male, women still feel comfortable in pubs, especially on the weekends in urban areas when students swarm the town. You might have your ears talked off, however, especially by amateur *seanachaí* (SHAN-ukh-ee), traveling storytellers. In the evening, some pubs host traditional music. Local and traveling musicians toting fiddles, guitars, *bodhráns* (a shallow, one-sided drum), and whistle, drop in around 9:30pm to start impromptu trad sessions.

Pubs in the Republic are generally open Monday to Saturday from 10:30am to 11:30pm (11pm in winter) and Sunday from 12:30 to 2pm and 4 to 11pm (closed for the Holy hour). Some pubs have been granted special "early" licenses, which allow them to open at 7:30am and require an act of Parliament to revoke. Pubs almost never charge a cover price or require a drink minimum. Some pubs, particularly in rural areas, close for a few hours on weekday afternoons as well. Pub lunches are usually served from Monday to Saturday, 12:30 to 2:30pm, while soup, soda bread, and sandwiches are served all day. Children are often not allowed in pubs after 7pm. The legal drinking age in Ireland is 18.

Beer is the default drink in Irish pubs. Beer comes in two basic varieties, **lagers** (blond, fizzy brews served cold, a bit weaker than ales or stouts) and **ales** (slightly darker, more bitter, and sometimes served a bit warmer than lagers). **Stout,** a type of ale, is thick, dark-ruby colored, and made from roasted barley to impart an almost chocolatey flavor. **Guinness** stout inspires a reverence otherwise reserved for the Holy Trinity. Known variously as "the dark stuff," "the blonde in the black skirt," or simply "I'll have a pint, please," it's a rich, dark brew with a head thick enough to stand a match in. It's also far better in Ireland than anywhere else. For a sweeter taste, try it with blackcurrant or cider. **Murphy's** is a similar, slightly sweeter stout brewed in Cork, as is **Beamish,** a tasty "economy" stout. Stout takes a while to pour properly (usually 3-4min.), so quit drumming the bar and be patient. **Kilkenny ale** (called Smithwicks abroad), a hoppy, English-style bitter, and **Harp** lager, made by Guinness, are both popular domestic brews. You might be surprised by the many pubs serving Budweiser or Heineken here and by the number of young people quaffing such imported lagers. In general, the indigenous brews are far worthier. Beer is served in imperial **pint glasses** (about 20oz.) or half-pints (called a "glass"). If you ask for a beer you'll get a full pint, so be loud and clear if you can only stay (or stand) for a half (or just take the pint and drink faster). A pint of Guinness costs anywhere from IR£1.90 to 2.30, and remember never to tip the barman.

> *Guinness stout inspires a reverence otherwise reserved for the Holy Trinity*

Irish whiskey—which Queen Elizabeth I once declared her only true Irish friend—is sweeter than its Scotch counterpart. Irish whiskey is also served in larger measures than you might be used to. **Jameson** is popular everywhere. Dubliners are partial to **Powers and Sons, Bushmills,** distilled in Portstewart, is the favorite in the North, and drinkers in Cork enjoy **Paddy. Irish coffee** is sweetened with brown sugar and whipped cream and laced with whiskey—allegedly invented at Shannon Airport by a desperate bartender looking to appease cranky travelers on a layover, although others place the drink's origin in San Francisco. **Hot whiskey** (spiced up with lemon, cloves, and brown sugar) can provide a cozy buzz, as will the Irish version of **eggnog** (brandy, beaten egg, milk, and a touch of lemon juice). In the west, you may hear some locals praise "mountain dew," a euphemism for **poitín** (po-CHEEN), an illegal distillation sometimes given to cows in labor that ranges in strength from 115 to 140 proof. Bad *poitín* can be very dangerous.

⟨♨⟩ HIGHLIGHTS OF THE REPUBLIC OF IRELAND

- The passage tombs of **Brú na Bóinne** (p. 642) are older than the Pyramids or Stonehenge and as mysterious as either.
- **Kilkenny** (p. 649) is the best-preserved medieval city in Ireland and a hopping tourist destination.
- Hundreds of years of architecture are crammed on the **Rock of Cashel** (p. 651).
- Packed Killarney is fun and sight-filled in its own right, but its best draw is the fantastic **Killarney National Park** (p. 659).
- Visitors to **Dingle** (p. 662) are charmed by its genuine craic and neighborhood dolphin—some even forget to leave.
- Young people flock from all over to the dazzling pub scene of **Galway** (p. 670).
- The quiet **Aran Islands** (p. 675) are dotted with prehistoric structures, traditional villages, and sheer cliff drops.
- The **Cliffs of Moher** (p. 669), possibly the highest seacliffs in Europe, are one of Ireland's most famous sights.
- The desolate white beaches, inland forests, and tiny villages of the **Inishowen Peninsula** (p. 688) comprise some of Ireland's most spectacular scenery.

CO. DUBLIN

Dublin and its suburbs form one economic and commercial unit, most of which can be reached by DART (Dublin Area Rapid Transit), suburban rail, or Dublin buses. On weekends, Dublin's city center teems with suburbanites looking for a good time. Despite the homogenizing effects of a booming economy and suburban sprawl, Dublin's suburbs offer no less excitement for visitors than do Ireland's rural villages.

GETTING ABOUT THE TRANSPORTATION HUBLIN

Rail lines, bus lines (both state-run and private), and the national highway system radiate from Ireland's capital. Major highways N5 and N6 lead to N4. N8, N9, and N10 all feed into N7, pumping buses and cars into Dublin's vehicular sphere. Since intercity transport is so Dublin-centric, you may find it more convenient in the long run to arrange your travel in other parts of the Republic while you're in the capital. Students may wish to get a **TravelSave** stamp for bus and rail discounts (see **Practical Information**, p. 625); for more information on national and international transportation, see **Getting There**, p. 25.

The electric **DART** trains run frequently up and down the coast to serve the suburbs from Connolly, Pearse, and Tara St. Stations in the city center; within a year or two, its range will be even greater. DART trains are faster and more predictable than comparable bus rides and suburban rail. The DART runs every 15 minutes from 6:30am to midnight (75p-£2). Tickets are sold in the station and theoretically must be presented at the end of the trip. The orange trains of the **suburban rail** network continue north to **Malahide** and **Drogheda** south to **Wicklow** and west to **Maynooth**. These trains leave from Connolly Station, although the southern line also stops at Tara St. and Pearse Stations. Trains to **Kildare** leave from Heuston Station. Trains are frequent on weekdays (30 per day), less so on Sundays.

The lime-green **Dublin Buses**, *Bus Átha Cliath* (ATH-ah CLEE-ath), sport "db" logos, run from 6am to 11:30pm, and comprehensively cover the city of Dublin and its suburbs. Buses are cheap (55p-£1.50), but some routes run infrequently (generally every 20min. 8am-6pm, every 30-45min. other times). Most end or begin at the city center, defined by Christ Church, the Trinity facade, St. Stephen's Green, and the top of O'Connell St. It's easiest to figure out bus routes by using the *Map of Greater Dublin* (£4.10) in conjunction with the accurate **Dublin Bus Timetable** (£1.20). Both are available from newsagents and the Dublin Bus office, which also has free route pamphlets (see **Transportation**, p. 625). The **NiteLink** service runs express routes to the suburbs (Th-Sa midnight, 1, 2, and 3am, £2.50, no passes valid). Tickets for the

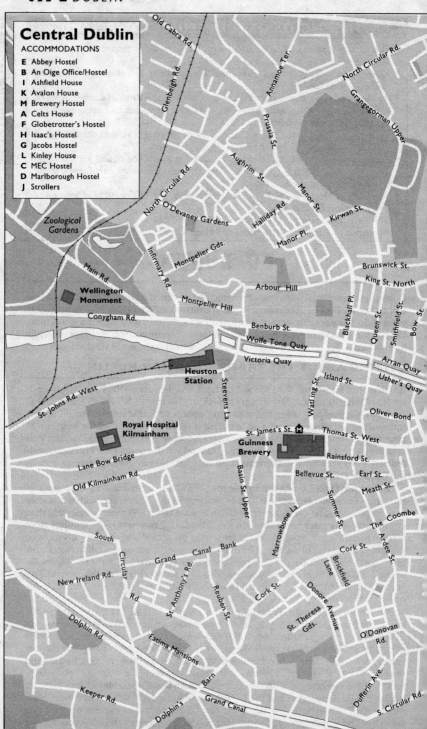

Central Dublin

ACCOMMODATIONS

E Abbey Hostel
B An Oige Office/Hostel
I Ashfield House
K Avalon House
M Brewery Hostel
A Celts House
F Globetrotter's Hostel
H Isaac's Hostel
G Jacobs Hostel
L Kinley House
C MEC Hostel
D Marlborough Hostel
J Strollers

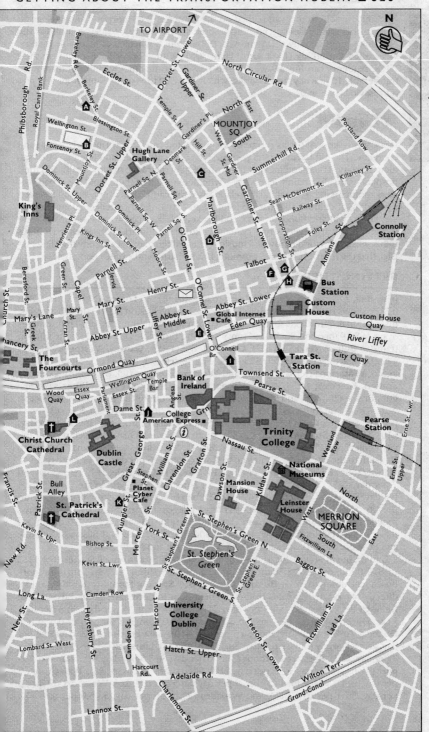

N

TO AIRPORT

North Circular Rd.

Philbsborough Rd.

Royal Canal Bank

Berkeley Rd.
Eccles St.
Berkeley St.
Wellington St.
Blessington St.
Fontenoy St.
Dorset St. Upper

Dorset St. Lower
Gardiner St. Upper
Temple St. N
Gardiner's Pl.
Hill St.
North East. W ess

MOUNTJOY SQ. South

Summerhill Rd.
Portland Row

Killarney St.

A

B

Hugh Lane Gallery

Parnell Sq. N.
Denmark St.
Parnell Sq. E.

C

Marlborough St.
Gardiner St. Mid.

Sean McDermott St.
Railway St.
Foley St.
Corporation St.

King's Inns

Dominick St. Upper
Dominick St. Lower
Dominick Pl.
Parnell Sq. W.
Parnell Sq.
O'Connell St.

Gardiner St. Lower

Amiens St.
Connolly Station

Henrietta Pl.
Kings Inn St.
Green St.
Parnell St.
Jervis
Moore St.

D

Henry St.
O'Connell St.

Talbot St.

F

G

H

Bus Station

Custom House

Church St.
Beresford St.
Capel St.
Mary St.
Mary's Lane
Mary's Greek St.
Arran St.
Liffey St.
Abbey St. Middle
Abbey St. Upper

Abbey St. Lower
Global Internet Cafe
Eden Quay

Custom House Quay

River Liffey

Chancery St.

The Fourcourts

Ormond Quay
Wellington Quay
Essex Quay
Wood Quay
Essex Quay
Parliament St.
Essex St.
Temple Bar

E

O'Connell Br.

Bank of Ireland

Townsend St.

Tara St. Station

City Quay

Pearse Station

Erne St. Lwr.
Erne St. Upper

L

Christ Church Cathedral

Dublin Castle

Dame St.
George St.
Anglesa

American Express
College Grn.

Pearse St.

Trinity College

Nassau St.

Westland Row

Francis St.
Patrick St.
Bull Alley

St. Patrick's Cathedral

K

Planet Cyber Cafe
Stephen St.
William St.
Clarendon St.
Grafton St.

Dawson St.

Mansion House

National Museums

Kildare St.

Leinster House

MERRION SQUARE
North
South
East

New Rd.
Kevin St. Upr.
Bishop St.
Kevin St. Lwr.

Mercer St.
Aungier St.
Great George St.
York St.

St. Stephen's Green N
St. Stephen's Green W
St. Stephen's Green E
St. Stephen's Green S

St. Stephen's Green

Fitzwilliam La.
Baggot St.

Long La.
New St.
Camden Row
Camden St.
Heytesbury St.
Harcourt St.

University College Dublin

Hatch St. Upper.

Leeson St. Lower

Fitzwilliam St.
Lad La.

Lombard St. West
Harcourt Rd.
Adelaide Rd.
Charlemont St.

Wilton Terr.

Grand Canal

Lennox St.

NiteLink are sold from a van parked on the corner of Westmoreland and College St. next to the Trinity College entrance. Some shops also carry tickets; look for the NiteLink sign in windows. Downtown, Dublin runs a wheelchair-accessible bus service called **OmniLink** (M-Sa 8am-11pm, 30p). With a **TravelSave** stamp on their ISICs, **students** can buy £9 weekly bus passes. Groups may want to consider the transferable **10 Journey ticket books,** which allow 10 trips of the same price and produce savings of 50p-£2.

Dublin

In a country known for its relaxed pace of life and rural quiet, Dublin is stylish and energetic. The old Ireland is still present in castles, cathedrals, and fine pubs that saturate the city. The friendliness of the Irish people, their love of good craic, and their hospitality are all certainly legendary—whether you'll find them amid the urban bustle is another issue. The capital of Ireland since the late 17th century, Dublin has seen a blending of cultures that has occasioned an extraordinary intellectual and literary life. From Swift and Burke to Joyce and Beckett, Dublin has produced so many great writers that nearly every street contains a literary landmark. Pubs shelter Dublin's public life and a world-renowned music scene. Dublin may not embody the "Emerald Isle" that the tourist brochures promote, but it charms and excites nonetheless.

GETTING THERE

Irish Rail, *Iarnród Éireann* (EER-ann-road AIR-ann), 35 Lower Abbey St. (tel. 836 6222), spews data on its own InterCity services as well as on DART, suburban trains, international train tickets, and ferries. (Open M-F 9am-5pm, Sa 9am-1pm; phones open M-Sa 9am-6pm, Su 10am-6pm.) "Talking timetables" recite 24-hour info on trains to **Belfast** (tel. 855 4477), **Cork** (tel. 855 4400), **Galway/Westport** (tel. 855 4422), **Killarney/Tralee** (tel. 855 4466), **Limerick** (tel. 855 4411), **Sligo** (tel. 855 4455), **Waterford** (tel. 855 4433), and **Wexford/Rosslare** (tel. 855 4488). **Connolly Station,** Amiens St. (tel. 836 3333), is north of the Liffey and close to Busáras Bus Station. Buses #20, 20A, and 90 at the station head south of the river, but it's faster to walk. Trains run to **Belfast** (2½hr., 10 per day, Su 7 per day, £16.50), **Sligo** (3¼hr., 4 per day, Su 3 per day, £12), and **Wexford via Rosslare** (3hr., 5 per day, Su 2 per day, £10). **Heuston Station** (tel. 703 2132), south of Victoria Quay and well west of the city center, is a 25-minute walk from Trinity College. Buses #26, 51, and 79 go from Heuston to the city center. Trains go to **Cork** (3¼hr., 16 per day, Su 11 per day, £32), **Galway** (3hr., 6 per day, Su 3 per day, £14, F-Sa £24), **Limerick** (2¾hr., 9 per day, Su 7 per day, £25), **Tralee** (4hr., 3 per day, Su 2 per day, £34), and **Waterford** (3hr., 4 per day, Su 3 per day, £11.50). Any of the Dublin buses heading east will take you into the city. **Pearse Station,** just east of Trinity College on Pearse St. and Westland Row, receives southbound trains from Connolly Station. Bus #90 (every 10min., 80p) makes the circuit of Connolly, Heuston, and Pearse Stations and Busáras. Connolly and Pearse are also DART stations serving the north and south coasts.

Info on **buses** is available at the Dublin Bus Office, 59 O'Connell St. (tel. 873 4222 or 872 0000; open M 8:30am-5:30pm, Tu-F 9am-5:30pm, Sa 9am-1pm). Intercity buses to Dublin arrive at **Busáras Central Bus Station,** Store St. (tel. 836 6111), directly behind the Customs House and next door to Connolly Station. Buses run to **Belfast** (3hr., 7 per day, Su 3 per day, £11), **Cork** (4½hr., 4 per day, Su 3 per day, £12), **Derry** (4½hr., 4 per day, Su 3 per day, £10), **Dingle** (7hr., 1 per day, £16), **Donegal Town** (4hr., 4 per day, Su 3 per day, £10), **Galway** (4hr., 8 per day, Su 4 per day, £8), **Killarney** (6hr., 5 per day, Su 3 per day, £14), **Limerick** (3¼hr., 5 per day, Su 7 per day, £10), **Rosslare Harbour** (3hr., 6 per day, Su 5-6 per day, £8), **Shannon Airport** (4½hr., 6 per day, Su 5 per day, £10), **Sligo** (4hr., 3 per day, Su 3 per day, £8), **Tralee** (6hr., 5 per day, £14), **Waterford** (2¾hr., 8 per day, Su 5 per day, £6), **Westport** (5½hr., 3 per day, Su 1 per day, £11), and **Wexford** (2¾hr., 6 per day, Su 5-6 per day, £7).

PAMBO (Private Association of Motor Bus Owners), 32 Lower Abbey St. (tel. 878 8422), can provide the names and numbers of private bus companies serving particular destinations (open M-F 10am-5pm).

Book **ferries** in the Irish Rail office (above). **B&I** docks at the mouth of the River Liffey, just outside central Dublin. From there, buses #53 and 53A run past Alexandra Rd. and arrive near the Custom House (80p). **Stena-Sealink** ferries arrive in Dún Laoghaire (p. 639), from which the DART shuttles passengers to Connolly Station, Pearse Station, or Tara St. Station in the city center (£1.30). Buses #7, 7A, and 8 go from Georges St. in Dún Laoghaire to Eden Quay (£1.30).

ORIENTATION

The **River Liffey** cuts central Dublin in half from west to east. Better food and more famous sights are on the **South Side,** although plenty of hostels and the bus station sprout up on the North Side. Several main streets in Dublin undergo a name change every few blocks. The streets running alongside the Liffey are called quays (KEYS); their names change every block. The "Lower" part of the street is always closer to the mouth of the Liffey. **O'Connell St.,** three blocks west of the central bus station, links north and south Dublin. **Temple Bar** is a street, but the term usually refers to an area. Dublin's version of Soho, this is the city's liveliest nightspot, with tons of students, visitors, and excellent pubs. **Trinity College Dublin** functions as the nerve center of cultural activity, drawing legions of bookshops and student pubs into its orbit. At the base of **Grafton St.,** you'll find more expensive, tourist-oriented shops. Merchandise and services on the north side of the Liffey are more affordable than their southern counterparts. The **North Side** has the reputation of being a rougher area. This reputation may not be wholly deserved, but you should avoid walking in unfamiliar areas on *either* side of the Liffey at night, especially if you're alone. Phoenix Park is extremely shady at night and should definitely be avoided.

PRACTICAL INFORMATION

Transportation

Local Transportation: Dublin Bus, 59 O'Connell St. (tel 873 4222 or 872 0000). Open M 8:30am-5:30pm, Tu-F 9am-5:30pm, Sa 9am-1pm.

Taxis: National Radio Cabs, 40 James St. (tel. 677 2222). **Co-op Taxi** (tel. 677 7777 or 676 6666). **Central Cabs** (tel. 836 5555) and **City Group Taxi** (tel. 872 7272) have wheelchair-accessible taxis (call in advance). All 24hr. £1.80 plus 80p per mi.; £1.20 call-in charge. Taxi stands are in front of Trinity and on Lower Abbey St.

Car Rental: Thrifty, 14 Duke St. (tel. 679 9420). Another office at the airport. **Budget,** 151 Lower Drumcondra Rd. (tel. 837 9611), and at the airport. **Argus,** 59 Terenure Rd. East (tel. 490 4444; fax 490 6328). Offices also in the tourist office on O'Connell St. and the airport.

Bike Rental: Raleigh Rent-A-Bike, Kylemore Rd. (tel. 626 1333). Limited one-way rental system (£12 surcharge; credit card deposit) includes C. Harding (below). Bikes £8 per day, £35 per week; deposit £40. In Dublin, the best selection and advice comes from **C. Harding for Bikes,** 30 Bachelor's Walk (tel. 873 2455; fax 873 3622). Open M-Sa 8:30am-6pm. Other Raleigh dealers include **McDonald's Cycles,** 38 Wexford St. (tel. 475 2586), and **Little Sport,** 3 Merville Ave. (tel. 833 2405), off Fairview Rd. Another company, **Rent-A-Bike,** 58 Lower Gardiner St. (tel. 872 5931 or 872 5399; fax 836 4763), offers cycling holidays in hostels for £82 per week, in B&Bs for £135 per week. Cross-country and mountain bikes £7 per day, £30 per week; deposit £35. Sells bikes for about £100 and buys them back for half-price within 6 months. Open M-Sa 9am-6pm.

Hitchhiking: Since Co. Dublin is well served by bus and rail, there is no good reason to hitch. Hitchers coming to Dublin generally ask drivers to drop them off at one of the myriad bus and DART stops outside the city. Those leaving Dublin ride a bus to the city outskirts where the motorways begin. Buses #25, 25A, 66, 66A, 67, and 67A from Middle Abbey St. travel to Lucan Rd., which turns into N4 (for Galway and the West). To find a ride to Cork, Waterford, and Limerick (N7), hitchers usually take bus #51, 51B, or 69 from Fleet St. to Naas (NACE) Rd. N11 (to Wicklow, Wexford, and Rosslare) can be reached by buses #46 and 84 from Eden Quay or #46A from Fleet St. toward Stillorgan Rd. N3 (to Donegal and Sligo) can be reached on buses #38 from Lower Abbey St. or #39 from Middle Abbey St. to Navan Rd. Buses #33, 41, and 41A from Eden Quay toward Swords send hitchers on their way to N1 (Belfast and Dundalk).

Tourist and Financial Services

Tourist Information: Main Office, Dublin Tourist Centre, Suffolk St. (tel. (1850) 230330 in Ireland; 666 1258 outside Ireland). From Connolly Train Station, walk left down Amiens St. and right on Lower Abbey St. past Busáras until you come to O'Connell St. Turn left, cross the bridge, and walk past Trinity College; Suffolk St. will be on your right (office signposted). The Centre is in a converted church. Accommodation service with £1 booking fee and 10% deposit; £2 charge to book outside Dublin. Bookings by phone (tel. (1800) 668668 in Ireland; 669 2082 outside Ireland). Look for the *Map of Greater Dublin* (£3.90) and the *Handy Map of Dublin* (£4). **American Express** maintains a branch office with currency exchange here (tel. 605 7701). **Bus Éireann** and **Stenalink** have representatives on hand to provide info and tickets. A free list of car rental agencies is available. Open mid-June to mid-Sept. M-Sa 8:30am-7:30pm, Su 9am-5:30pm; mid-Sept. to mid-June M and W-Sa 9am-5:30pm, Tu 9:30am-5:30pm. **Branch Offices: Dublin Airport,** open daily 8am-10pm. **Dún Laoghaire Harbour,** Ferry Terminal Building, open daily 8am-10:30pm (subject to ferry arrivals). **Tallaght,** The Square Towncentre, open daily 8am-10:30pm. **Baggot St.,** open daily 8am-10:30pm. All telephone calls handled by the central office.

Northern Ireland Tourist Board: 16 Nassau St. (tel. 679 1977 or (1800) 230230). Books accommodations. Open M-F 9am-5:30pm, Sa 10am-5pm.

Temple Bar Information Centre: 18 Eustace St. (tel. 671 5717) near Great Georges St. off Temple Bar. Info on the arts. The center has the useful, bimonthly *Temple Bar Guide* and *Gay Community News* (both free). Open June-Sept. M-F 9am-6pm, Sa 11am-4pm, Su noon-4pm; Oct.-May M-F 9am-6pm, Sa noon-6pm.

An Óige Head Office (Irish Youth Hostel Association/HI): 61 Mountjoy St. (tel. 830 4555), at Wellington St. About 20min. north of the river on O'Connell St. through all its name changes. Book and pay for HI hostels here. The *An Óige Handbook* (£1.50) lists all HI hostels on the island. Membership £10; under 18 £4. Open Apr.-Sept. M-F 9:30am-5:30pm, Sa 10am-12:30pm; Oct.-Mar. M-F 9:30am-5:30pm.

Budget Travel: USIT (Irish Student Travel Agency), 19-21 Aston Quay (tel. 679 8833), near O'Connell Bridge. **TravelSave** stamps £8. £3 photo booths. Big discounts, especially for travelers under 26. Open M-F 9am-6pm, Sa 10am-5:30pm.

Financial Services: Bank of Ireland, AIB (Allied Irish Bank), and **TSB (Trustees' Savings Bank)** branches with bureaux de change and **ATMs** cluster south of the river. Most branches open M-F 10am-4pm. **Bureaux de change** also found in the General Post Office and in the tourist office main branch.

American Express: 116 Grafton St. (tel. 677 2874). Traveler's Cheque refunds (tel. (1800) 626000). Client mail held; non-members can change currency. Open June-Sept. M-Sa 9am-5pm, Su 11am-4pm; Oct.-May M-Sa 9am-5pm.

Local Services

Luggage Storage: Connolly Station, Heuston Station, and Busáras.

Women's Resources: Dublin Well Woman Centre, 73 Lower Leeson St. (tel. 661 0083 or 661 0086), a professional health center for women. **Women's Aid** (tel. (1800) 341 900 or 860 0033). Open M-F 10am-10pm, Sa 10am-6pm.

Gay, Lesbian, and Bisexual Information: See p. 637.

Launderette: The Laundry Shop, 191 Parnell St. (tel. 872 3541). Closest to Busáras and North Side hostels. Wash £2.40, dry £1.30, soap 60p. Open M-Sa 8am-7pm.

Emergency and Communications

Emergency: Dial 999; no coins required.

Police/Garda: Dublin Metro Headquarters, Harcourt Sq. (tel. 732 2222). **Garda Confidential Report Line:** (tel. (1800) 666111).

Hotlines: Samaritans, 112 Marlborough St. (tel. (1850) 609090 or 872 7700), for the depressed, lonely, or suicidal. 24hr. **Tourist Victim Support:** Parliament St. (tel. 679 8673). Help for robbed travelers.

Pharmacy: O'Connell's, 55 Lower O'Connell St. (tel. 873 0427). Close to city bus routes. Open M-Sa 8:30am-10pm, Su 10am-10pm.

Hospitals: Meath Hospital, Heytesbury St. (24hr. tel. 453 6555, 453 6000, or 453 6694). Served by buses #16, 16A, 19, 19A, 22, 22A, and 55. **Mater Misericordiae Hospital,** Eccles St. (tel. 830 1122), off Lower Dorset St. Served by buses #10, 22, 38, and 120. **Beaumont Hospital,** Beaumont Rd. (tel. 837 7755). Served by buses #27A, 51A, 101, and 103. **St. James Hospital,** James St. (tel. 453 7941). Served by buses #17, 19, 19A, 21A, 78A, and 123. **Post Office: General Post Office (GPO),** O'Connell St. (tel. 705 7000), on the left from the Liffey. *Poste Restante* pick-up at the bureau de change window, which closes 15min. early. Open M-Sa 8am-8pm, Su 10am-6:30pm. **Postal Code:** Dublin 1.

Internet Access: Global Internet Café, 8 Lower O'Connell St. (tel./fax 878 0295), a block north of the Liffey and on the right. £1.25 per 15min., students £1. Open M-Sa 10am-11pm, Su noon-10pm.

Telephones: Telecom Éireann (inquiries and phonecard refunds, tel. 671 4444). **Directory Inquiries:** tel. 1190 for all of Ireland. No charge. **Telephone Code:** Dear, dirty 01.

ACCOMMODATIONS

Dublin has a host of marvelous accommodations, but the ever-flowing glut of visitors ensures that real dumps stay open as well. Reserve as early as possible to be sure that you've got a bed. The tourist offices only deal in Bord Fáilte-approved B&Bs and hostels, which aren't necessarily better than unapproved ones. Phoenix Park may tempt the desperate, but camping there is a really, really bad idea. If the Garda or park rangers don't get you to leave, the threat of thieves and drug dealers should. If these places are full, consult Dublin Tourism's annually updated *Dublin Accommodation Guide* (£3) or ask hostel and B&B staff for referrals.

Hostels

Hostels on the south side are closest to sights and nightlife. Always **reserve ahead,** especially in summer and on weekends. All listed hostels have 24-hour reception.

Avalon House (IHH), 55 Aungier St. (tel. 475 0001; fax 475 0303; email info@avalon.ie). Turn off Dame St. onto Great Georges St.; the hostel is a 10min. walk down on your right. A new kitchen, email access, and top-notch security. Co-ed showers, toilets, and dorms (all non-smoking). Bike rack. In-house cafe (all meals under £5; open noon-10pm). June-Sept. large dorms £11; 4-bed dorms £13.50; doubles £32. Oct. and Mar.-May £9; £12.50; £30. Nov.-Feb. £8; £11.50; £28. Singles available. Continental breakfast included. Towels £1 with £5 deposit. Wheelchair accessible.

Abbey Hostel, 29 Bachelor's Walk, O'Connell Bridge (tel. 878 0700 or 878 0719; email info@abbey-hostel.ie). From O'Connell Bridge, turn left to face this emphatic yellow addition to Dublin's hostel scene. Clean, comfy, and well kept. Great location. June-Sept. big dorms £12; 6-bed dorms £15; 4-bed dorms £17. Oct. and Mar.-May £10; £13; £15. Nov.-Feb. £8; £11; £13.

Barnacle's Temple Bar House (tel. 671 6277; fax 671 6591; email templeba@barnacles.iol.ie). On the corner of Cecilia St. and Temple Ln. A brand new, well-kept hostel right in Temple Bar. All rooms with bath. June-Sept. 10-bed dorms £11; 6-bed dorms £13; 4-bed dorms £15; doubles and twins £19; Mar.-May and Oct. about £1 cheaper, Nov-Feb. about £2-3 cheaper.

Isaac's Hostel, 2-5 Frenchman's Ln. (tel. 855 6215 or 855 6574; email isaacs@indigo.ie), off the lower end of Gardiner St. behind the Customs House. Cafe. Apr.-Oct. big dorms £8; small dorms £9.25; singles £19; doubles £32; triples £43.50. Nov.-Mar. £1 cheaper per person. Laundry £5.

Jacobs Inn, 21-28 Talbot Pl. (tel. 855 5660; fax 855 5664; email jacob@indigo.ie). On a narrow north-south street 2 blocks north of the Customs House and down the street to the right of the Garda Station. Reception area with cafe; rooms, though all with bath, are standard hostel issue. Apr.-Oct. 6- to 8-bed dorms £11; 4-bed dorms £15.50; 3-bed dorms £16.50; doubles £39. Nov.-Mar. £2 cheaper per person. Towels £1. Bed lockout 11am-3pm. Wheelchair accessible.

Abraham House, 82 Gardiner St. Lower (tel. 855 0600; fax 855 0598; email abraham@indigo.ie). Bright whitewashed cinderblocks give a slightly antiseptic feel to this well-kept hostel. Bureau de change. July-Sept. 12-bed dorms £8.50; 6-bed dorms £11; 4-bed dorms £12.50; singles £18; doubles £32. Oct.-June £1-2 cheaper per person. Light breakfast and towels included. Laundry £5.

Celts House, 32 Blessington St. (tel. 830 0657; email res@celtshouse.iol.ie). 38 comfy, solid wooden bunk beds in a brightly painted, friendly atmosphere. A bit secluded from the city center. Dorms £8-11; doubles £32. Sheets £1.50.

M.E.C., 42 North Great Georges St. (tel. 878 0071; meccles@iol.ie). Walk up O'Connell to Parnell St., turn right, then take the first left. The hostel is ¾ block down on the right. Worn but serviceable. Kitchen and 24hr. TV lounge. Dorms £7.50-12; doubles £24-£32; quads £34-53. Free luggage storage and car park.

Marlborough Hostel (IHH), 81-82 Marlborough St. (tel. 874 7629; fax 874 5172; email marlboro@internet-ireland.ie), up the street from the Protestant cathedral, just 2 quick turns off a main drag. Large rooms, mediocre showers, and exciting barbecue area. Bike shed. 4- to 10-bed dorms £7.50; doubles £26. Continental breakfast included. Sheets 50p. Check-out 10:30am.

Dublin International Youth Hostel (An Óige/HI), 61 Mountjoy St. (tel. 830 1766; fax 830 1600; email anoige@iol.ie). O'Connell St. changes names 3 times before reaching the turn left onto Mountjoy St. A convent converted into an institutional, 420-bed hostel. Guard possessions closely and keep the door to your room shut; security might be an issue. Bureau de change. Secure parking. 24hr. kitchen. Cafe has cheap meals (£3.50) and packed lunches (£2). Big dorms £10, non-members £10.50; 4- to 6-bed dorms £11; doubles £25. Oct.-May £2 cheaper. Breakfast included. Luggage storage 50p. Sheets £1.50. Self-service laundry £5.

Globetrotter's Tourist Hostel (IHH), 46 Gardiner St. Lower (tel. 873 5893). Smoking room, TV room, civilized kitchen. Excellent bathrooms and superb showers. Free luggage storage. July to mid-Sept. dorms £15. Mid-Sept. to June £11, £25 for 3 nights. Great breakfast included. Safety deposit boxes £1.50. Towels 50p.

Strollers, 58 Dame St. (tel. 677 5614 or 677 5422; fax 839 0474). In the middle of Temple Bar action, a short walk from Trinity. Super location, although cars whiz by at all hours. Dorms £12-14.50; doubles £34. Breakfast and discounts at the attached cafe (dinners £5; open daily 9am-11pm). Wheelchair accessible.

Morehampton House Tourist Hostel, 78 Morehampton Rd., Donnybrook (tel. 668 8866; fax 668 8794). On buses #10, 46A, and 46B. Comfortable accommodations. Bike park and rental. 10-bed dorms £9; 6- to 8-bed dorms £12; doubles £32. Oct.-May £1-2 cheaper. Add £2 for rooms with bath.

Ashfield House, 19-20 D'Olier St. (tel. 679 7734; email ashfield@indigo.ie). Steps away from Trinity, Grafton St., and Temple Bar. New beds with thick mattresses and bright, airy rooms. The traffic can get noisy, so you might want to request a quiet room. Bureau de change. Dorm beds around £10; doubles £32; triples £48. Discounts in winter. All rooms with bath. Breakfast included. Free luggage storage. Serviced laundry £4. Wheelchair accessible.

Kinlay House (IHH), 2-12 Lord Edward St. (tel. 679 6644; fax 679 7437), the continuation of Dame St. Bureau de change. Wake-up calls. 10-bed dorms £9.50; 4- to 6-bed dorms £13; singles £18; doubles £28, with bath £32. Oct.-June £1 cheaper. Breakfast and towel included. Lockers. Free luggage storage. Laundry £5.

Bed and Breakfasts

B&Bs with a green shamrock sign out front are registered, occasionally checked, and approved by Bord Fáilte, although the uninspected may be cheaper and better located. Inexpensive B&Bs cluster along Upper and Lower Gardiner St., on Sheriff St., and near the Parnell Sq. area. Exercise caution in this area. Clonliffe Rd., Sandymount, and Clontarf are a 15-minute bus ride from Eden Quay; they offer calm and quality.

Glen Court, 67 Gardiner St. Lower (tel. 836 4022), 1 block west of Busáras, 2 blocks east of O'Connell. Clean, cheap, and well located. Singles £18; doubles £30; triples £42; quads £50.

Parkway Guest House, 5 Gardiner Pl. (tel. 874 0469). Plain but comfortable rooms, and excellent location, just off Gardiner St. Friendly, young proprietor offers discerning advice on food and pubs. Singles £21; doubles £35, with bath £42.

Kingfisher B&B, 166 Parnell St. (tel. 872 8732 or 825 9277), 2 blocks west of the top of O'Connell St. Self-contained, clean, sunny apartments with TV, full kitchen, and bath. Singles £25; doubles £40. Weekly discounts.

Mona B&B, Mrs. Kathleen Greville, 148 Clonliffe Rd. (tel. 837 6723). Firm beds and clean rooms kept tidy by a warm proprietor who is also an avid sports fan. Singles £16; doubles £30. Open May-Oct.

Mrs. R. Casey, Villa Jude, 2 Church Ave. (tel. 668 4982), off Beach Rd. Bus #3 or DART (Lansdowne Rd. stop). Mrs. Casey has nourished 7 children and countless others with her homemade bread and strapping Irish breakfasts. Every room is immaculate and TV-equipped. Singles £14; doubles £26.

Ferryview Guest House, 96 Clontarf Rd. (tel. 833 5893). Thick carpets and fluffy comforters in cheerful, non-smoking rooms. Singles £20; doubles £34.

Camping

Most campsites are far from the city center, but camping equipment is available at **The Great Outdoors,** Chatham St. (tel. 679 4293), off the top of Grafton St. (open M-W and F-Sa 9:30am-5:30pm, Th 9:30am-8pm).

Comac Valley Caravan & Camping Park, Corkagh Park, Naas Rd., Clondalkin (tel. 462 0000; fax 462 0111). Accessible by buses #77, 77A, 49, and 65 (30min. from city center). Food shop, laundry, and kitchen facilities; electricity included. Lounge with cable TV. Tents £3.50-4.50 plus £1 per adult, 50p per child. Caravans £9.

Shankill Caravan and Camping Park (tel. 282 0011). The DART and buses #45, 45A, 46, and 84 from Eden Quay all run to Shankill. Not the ideal accommodation for seeing Dublin. The views of the hills and 20min. walk to the beach are much more convenient. £4.50-5 per tent plus £1 per adult, 50p per child. Showers 50p.

FOOD

Dublin's **open-air markets** sell fresh and cheap fixings. Head to **Moore St. Market** to try to perfect a Dublin Northsider's accent and get fresh veggies to boot (open M-Sa 9am-5pm). Moore St. runs between Henry and Parnell St. The **Thomas St. Market,** along the continuation of Dame St., is a calmer alternative for fruit and vegetable shopping (open F-Sa 9am-5pm). The cheapest **supermarkets** around Dublin are the **Dunnes Stores,** which are at St. Stephen's Green Shopping Centre, ILAC Centre off Henry St., and on North Earl St. off O'Connell St. (all open M-W and F-Sa 9am-6pm, Th 9am-8pm). The **Runner Bean,** 4 Nassau St. (tel. 679 4833), vends wholefoods, homemade breads, veggies, fruits, and nuts (open M-F 8am-6pm, Sa 9am-6pm).

Leo Burdock's, 2 Werburgh St. (tel. 454 0306), uphill from Christ Church Cathedral. Take-out only. Dubliners' pick for best fish and chips in the universe. Haddock or cod £3; large chips 95p. Open M-F 11am-11pm, Sa 2-11pm.

La Mezza Luna, 1 Temple Ln. (tel. 671 2840), corner of Dame St. Stars and half-moons twinkle from a midnight-blue ceiling. The food is celestial, too. Daily £5 lunch specials noon-4pm. Desserts £2-5. Open M-Sa 12:30-11pm, Su 4-10:30pm.

The Stag's Head, 1 Dame Ct. (tel. 679 3701), via an alleyway off Dame St. at Stanley Racing #28. Marked by the logo in tile on the sidewalk. A great pub with even better grub. Food served M-F 12:30-3:30pm and 5:30-7:30pm, Sa 12:30-2:30pm.

The Well Fed Café, 6 Crow St. (tel. 677 2234), off Dame St. Inventive vegetarian dishes served by a worker's cooperative in a stripped-down, bohemian atmosphere. Popular with the gay community. Main courses £2.50-3.50. Open M-Sa noon-8pm. Wheelchair accessible.

Marks Bros., 7 South Great Georges St. (tel. 667 1085), off Dame St. Next door to the George. Thick sandwiches (£1.30-1.70) and high salads for starving artists and punks. Cinnamon buns 40p; herbal teas 50p; salads 95p. Open daily 11am "til late."

Bad Ass Café, Crown Alley (tel. 671 2596), off Temple Bar. Touristy cafe atmosphere. Sinéad O'Connor once worked here, so you can't go wrong. Lunch £3-5. Medium pizza £5.15-7.75. Student menu: coleslaw, scone and butter, "magic mushrooms," medium pizza, and beverage £5.75. Open daily 9am until past midnight.

Bewley's Cafés (tel. 677 6761). A Dublin institution, with plain, inexpensive meals. 4 branches: 78 Grafton St., the largest (open Su-Th 7:30am-1am, F-Sa 7:30am-2am); 12 Westmoreland St., once frequented by James Joyce (open M-Sa 7:30am-9pm, Su 9:30am-8pm); 13 South Great Georges St. (open M-Sa 7:45am-6pm); and Mary St., past Henry St. (open M-W 7am-9pm, Th-Sa 7am-2am, Su 10am-10pm).

PUBLIN

"Good puzzle would be cross Dublin without passing a pub," wrote James Joyce. A local radio station once offered £100 to the first person to solve the puzzle. The winner explained that you could take any route—you'd just have to visit them all on the way! The behemoth **Guinness Hop Store** (p. 635) shares its best-Guinness-in-Dublin prize with **Mulligan's** (p. 632). Honorable mention goes to **The Stag's Head** (p. 632). The **Dublin Literary Pub Crawl** (tel. 454 0228) traces Dublin's liquid history in reference to literary history, spewing bits of info and entrancing monologues. (Meet at The Duke, 2 Duke St. June-Aug. M-Sa 3 and 7:30pm, Su noon and 3pm; May and Sept. daily 7:30pm; Oct.-Apr. F-Sa 7:30pm, Su noon. £6, students £5.) Those yearning for guidance in the matters of *céilí* and Guinness should try the **Traditional Music Pub Crawl,** which meets at Oliver St. John Gogarty's on the corner of Fleet and Anglesea St. *(May-Oct. daily 7:30pm; Nov.-Apr. F-Sa 7:30pm. £6, students £5.)*

The **Let's Go Dublin Pub Crawl Map** aids in discovering the city and researching the best pint of Guinness. We recommend that you begin your crawl at the Trinity gates, then stroll up Grafton St., teeter to Camden St., stumble to South Great Georges St., and triumphantly drag your soused self to Temple Bar. Start early (say, noon).

Grafton Street and Vicinity

1. **The Buttery,** Trinity College, in the front arch on the left. Dark, smoky, no-frills, and crammed with students. Renovations are coming; who knows what the future may bring. Open M-F noon-11pm.

2. **M. J. O'Neills,** Suffolk St. Quiet by day, but a fun, crowded meeting spot by night.

3. **The International Bar,** 23 Wicklow St. (tel. 677 9250), off Grafton St. on the corner of South William St. Improv comedy Mondays, stand-up Wednesdays. All other nights blues at 9pm (cover £3.50). Ballads and trad Sundays 12:30pm.

4. **Davy Byrne's,** 21 Duke St. (tel. 677 5217), off Grafton St. A lively, middle-aged crowd gathers in the comfortable seats that Joyce once wrote about, although the velvet backdrop behind the bar indicates some redecorating since Joyce's time.

5. **McDaid's,** 3 Harry St. (tel. 679 4395), off Grafton St. across from Anne St. The center of Ireland's literary scene in the 50s. Wednesdays feature contemporary ballads; Sundays blues and jazzier tunes.

6. **Café en Seine,** 40 Dawson St. (tel. 677 4151). Built to impress. A large crowd of mixed ages packs into the chic cafe in front and long bar in back, apparently indifferent to the fact that the Seine is not at all nearby.

7. **Sinnott's,** South King St. (tel. 478 4698). Classy 20-somethings gather in this basement pub. Music and beer churned out daily noon-2am.

8. **Major Tom's,** South King St. (tel. 478 3266). Screw Ground Control; this pub with a club feel wants to rock. A DJ keeps it rolling Th-Sa nights.

Harcourt and Camden St.

9. **The Chocolate Bar,** Hatch St. (tel. 478 0225), at Harcourt St. Hugely popular. Young, lively group of clubbers drink here until **The Pod** opens (see p. 633).

10. **The Bleeding Horse,** 24 Camden St. Upper (tel. 475 2705). Wood-paneled hive. Bring cell phone or other phallus substitute. Open Su-W until 11:30pm, Th-F 1:30am, Sa 12:30am.

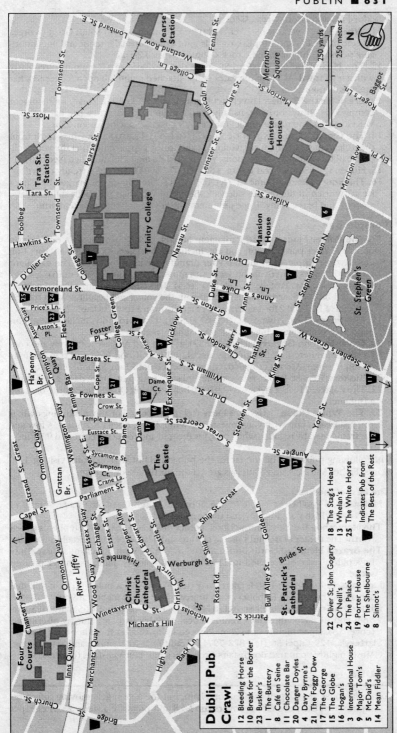

Dublin Pub Crawl

12 Bleeding Horse
10 Break for the Border
23 Busker's
1 The Buttery
8 Café en Seine
11 Chocolate Bar
20 Danger Doyles
4 Davy Byrne's
21 The Foggy Dew
17 The George
15 The Globe
16 Hogan's
3 International House
9 Major Tom's
5 McDaid's
14 Mean Fiddler
22 Oliver St. John Gogarty
2 O'Neill's
24 The Palace
19 Porter House
6 The Shelbourne
8 Sinnot's
18 The Stag's Head
13 Whelan's
25 The White Horse

▼ Indicates Pub from The Best of the Rest

Wexford St. and South Great Georges

11. Whelan's, 25 Wexford St. (tel. 478 0766). Continue down South Great Georges St. One of the hot spots for live rock despite a dark, dismal interior and uncomfortable pews. Nightly Irish indie rock or blues (cover £2-4).

12. The Mean Fiddler, Wexford St., next door to Whelan's. Live music regularly with a hip crowd. At 11pm the gates of the attached nightclub open (cover £5). Bar open daily noon-2am.

13. Break for the Border, Lower Stephen's St. (tel. 478 0300). This "entertainment complex" is always buzzing, usually with an older crowd. Su-Tu late bar and DJs, W-Sa live rock and dance music. Dance club cover £5-8. Open noon-2am.

14. The Globe, 11 South Great Georges St. (tel. 671 1220). Music issues forth from the Roman busts on the walls. Guinness and frothy cappuccinos fuel the young clientele of this cafe-pub. Pretentious, yet cool. **Rí Rá** nightclub attached (see p. 633).

15. Hogan's, 35 South Great Georges St. (tel. 677 5904). Attracts a trendy crowd.

16. The Stag's Head, 1 Dame Ct. (tel. 679 3701). The entrance is marked by "Stag's Head" written in tile on the sidewalk. Beautiful Victorian pub with stained glass, mirrors, and brass. Shiny. Huge mounted whiskey kegs. Truly excellent grub.

Temple Bar

17. The Porter House, 16-18 Parliament St. (tel. 679 8850). Dublin's only microbrewery brews porter, stout, and ale, including Wrasslers 4X Stout, "Michael Collins' favorite tipple—a stout like your grandfather used to drink." The excellent sampler includes a sip of ale brewed with mussels and other oddities (£6).

18. Danger Doyles, Eustace St. (tel. 670 7655). This large pub with celestial painted walls and blaring dance music is packed with the young and beautiful. M-Th from 5-7pm pints £1.75 and 2-for-1 cocktails. Open daily from 11pm "'til late" (2am or so).

19. The Foggy Dew, Fownes St. (tel. 677 9328). Like a friendly, mellow neighborhood pub, but twice as big. Classic rock Sunday nights.

20. Oliver St. John Gogarty (tel. 671 1822), at Fleet and Anglesea St. Lively and convivial atmosphere in a traditionally decorated pub. Good food and trad sessions nightly 7:30pm. Always crowded. Open Th and F until 1am, Sa until midnight.

21. Buskers, Fleet St. Bop to music while you swill your pint. Open daily 11pm-2am.

22. The Palace, 21 Fleet St. (tel. 677 9290), behind Aston Quay. The favorite of many a Dubliner.

23. The White Horse, 1 Georges Quay (tel. 679 3068). For those mornings when you just *need* a pint with your muesli, the White Horse opens at 7:30am. A low-key bar frequented by regulars who come for the trad and rock (starts around 9:30pm).

The following pubs are a bit too far for the pub crawl but are still worth visiting. Lanigan's, Fibber MaGee's, and Slattery's are on the north side of the river.

The Best of the Rest

Mulligan's, 8 Poolbeg St. (tel. 677 5582), behind Burgh Quay off Tara St. A taste of the typical Irish pub: low-key and nothing fancy.

The Horseshoe Bar, Shelbourne Hotel, corner of Kildare St. and St. Stephen's Green North. The center of Ireland's media culture and best place for cocktails in Dublin.

The Brazen Head, 20 North Bridge St. (tel. 679 5816), off Merchant's Quay. Dublin's oldest pub, established in 1198. The courtyard is quite a summer pick-up scene.

Lanigans, Clifton Court Hotel, Eden Quay (tel. 874 3535). A pub with Irish folk that actually attracts more Dubliners than tourists. Live music nightly at 9pm.

Fibber MaGee's, 80 Parnell St. (tel. 874 5253). Pints for only £1.65 daily 10:30am-5pm and £1.80 Wednesday evening. Local rock bands play Saturday afternoons (cover £3). Open nightly until 2am. Pints go up to £2 after the other pubs close.

Slattery's, 129 Capel St. (tel. 872 7971). Traditional Irish music and set dancing. Music nightly 9pm: trad downstairs (free), rock and blues upstairs (cover £4).

CLUBS

As a rule, these spots open at 10:30 or 11pm, but the action gets moving only after 11:30pm when the pubs close. Covers run £4-8 and pints are a steep £3. A cheaper option than clubbing is to go to a pub with late closing, like **Major Tom's, The Bleeding Horse,** or **Fibber MaGees** (see **Pubs,** above). There are also a number of small clubs on Harcourt and Leeson St. that can be fun, if austere. Most clubs close at 2 or 3am, although a few have been known to last until daybreak. To get home after 11:30pm when Dublin Bus stops running, dancing fiends take the **NiteLink bus** (1 per hour Th-Sa midnight-3am, £3), which runs designated routes from the corner of Westmoreland and College St. to Dublin's outer city and its suburbs. **Taxi** stands are in front of Trinity, the top of Grafton St. by St. Stephen's Green, and on Abbey St. Lower. Be prepared to wait 30-45 minutes Friday and Saturday nights. Those hoping to catch the gay/lesbian scene should also check out **Gay and Lesbian Dublin,** p. 637.

The Kitchen, The Clarence Hotel, Wellington Quay, Temple Bar (tel. 662 3066). With 2 bars and a dance floor, this U2-owned club is the coolest spot in town. Half of it is impossible to get into on Fridays and Saturdays because it's filled with "VIPs." Dress to fit in with the rocker/model crowd. Cover £8, students £3 on Tu.

Rí-Rá, 1 Exchequer St. (tel. 677 0485), in the Central Hotel, pumps Top 40 music with old and new favorites. Cover £6. Open daily 11pm-2:30am.

Club M, Blooms Hotel, Anglesea St., Temple Bar (tel. 679 0277). A crowd of diverse ages and styles goes up and down the charts all night. Cover around £6.

Pod, 35 Harcourt St. (tel. 478 0225). A trendy club where people go to press flesh and be seen. The truly brave venture upstairs to the **Red Box,** with warehouse caché, brain-crushing music, and an 8-person-deep crowd at the bar. Cover £8.

SIGHTS

Tours

Most major sights lie within a mile of O'Connell Bridge. The tourist office sells *Visitor Attractions in Dublin,* which lists the main sights (£2.25), as well as a **Ulysses map of Dublin** (£1) that details some of Leopold Bloom's haunts. The entire walk takes 18 hours (including drinking and debauching). **Guided tours** generally last about two hours, but entertaining anecdotes and continuous movement preclude boredom. The **Historical Walking Tour** (tel. 845 0241) is a two-hour crash course in Dublin's history. *(June-Sept. M-Sa at 11am, noon, and 3pm, Su also at 2pm; Oct.-May Sa-Su at noon. Meet at Trinity's front gate. £5, students £4.)* The witty and irreverent **Trinity College Walking Tour** also touches on Dublin's history, concentrating on University lore. *(30min. Leaves every 15min. from the Info Booth inside the front gate. £5, students £4, includes admission to the Old Library and the Book of Kells.)* **Dublin Bike Tours** (tel. 679 0899) offers an alternative to the walking tours. Book ahead. *(July-Oct. daily 10am, 2, and 6pm. Meet 15min. early at Darkey Kelly's Bar, Fishamble St., beside Christ Church. £12 includes bike and insurance.)* The more automotive **Dublin City Sightseeing Tour** (tel. 873 4222) stops at the major sights and lets you get on or off all day. *(1¾hr. Departs Apr.-Sept. daily every 30min. 9:30am-5pm. £6.)* The **hop-on/hop-off tourist buses** offer easy access to sights.

Trinity College and Nearby

Trinity College (tel. 677 2941) sprawls within its ancient walls between Westmoreland and Grafton St., fronting the block-long traffic circle now called College Green. The British built Trinity in 1592 as a Protestant religious seminary that would "civilize the Irish and cure them of Popery." Jonathan Swift, Robert Emmett, Thomas Moore, Edmund Burke, Oscar Wilde, and Samuel Beckett are just a few of the famous Irish Protestants who studied here. The 1712 **Old Library** holds Ireland's finest collection of Egyptian, Greek, Latin, and Irish manuscripts, including the **Book of Kells.** Each page holds a dizzyingly intricate lattice of Celtic knotwork and scrollwork into which animals and Latin text are interwoven. Upstairs, in the Library's Long Room, are "Ireland's oldest harp"—the Brian Ború harp (the design model for Irish coins)—and one of the few remaining 1916 proclamations of the Republic of Ireland. *(Open M-Sa 9:30am-5pm, Su noon-4:30pm. £3.50, students £3.)* Staring down Trinity from across College Green is a monolithic, Roman-looking building, the **Bank of Ireland** (tel. 677 6801). Built in 1729, the building originally housed the Irish Parliament, a body that represented the Anglo-Irish landowning class. The enormous curved walls and pillars were erected *around* the original structure; the bank inside is actually much smaller. *(Open M-W and F 10am-4pm, Th 10am-5pm. 45min. guided tours Tu 10:30, 11:30am, and 1:45pm. Free.)* South of College Green run the three or so blocks of **Grafton Street,** off-limits to cars and ground zero for shopping tourists and residents alike.

Merrion Square and St. Stephen's Green

Leinster House, south of Trinity College, off Leinster St. between Kildare St. and Merrion Sq., was once the house of the Duke of Leinster. Now it provides chambers for the Irish parliament, holding both the Dáil (DAHL), which does most of the government work, and the Seanad (SHA-nud), the less powerful upper house. Together, these two houses make up the parliament, called An tOireachtas (on tir-OCH-tas). The Captain's office conducts some **tours** of the Dáil's galleries. *(Tours Sa 10:30am-12:45pm and 1:30-4:50pm.)*

The **National Museum** (tel. 677 7444), now next to Leinster House, looks as though it may be bidding the square adieu. By the summer of '99, curators hope to move most of the collection to the Gallery's new location across from the train station. The museum focuses on legendary ancient Ireland and the equally epic Easter Rising. *(Open Tu-Sa 10am-5pm, Su 2-5pm. Free.)* Connected to the National Museum, the **Natural History Museum** is a tightly packed proliferation of dead animals in menacing poses. *(Same hours and number as the National Museum. Free.)* On the other side of Leinster House, the **National Library** (tel. 661 2523) chronicles Irish history and exhibits literary objects in its entrance room. *(Open M-W 10am-9pm, Th-F 10am-5pm, Sa 10am-1pm. Free, but open only to those doing academic research.)*

The British influence on Dublin appears throughout the city. **Merrion Square** and **Fitzwilliam Street** near the National Museum are full of Georgian buildings and elaborate rows of colored doorways. The prim Georgian townhouses continue up **Dawson Street,** which connects St. Stephen's Green to Trinity College. A few small, endearing churches line this street, along with **Mansion House,** home of the Lord Mayors of Dublin since 1715. Kildare, Dawson, and Grafton St. all lead south from Trinity to **St. Stephen's Green.** The 22-acre park was a private estate until the Guinness clan bequeathed it to the city. Today the park is a center for activity, crowded with arched bridges, an artificial lake, flowerbeds, fountains, gazebos, pensioners, punks, trees, couples, strollers, swans, ducks, a waterfall, and summer theatrical productions near the old bandstand. *(Gates open M-Sa 8am-dusk, Su 10am-dusk.)* The **Irish Jewish Museum,** 3-4 Walworth Rd. (tel. 676 0737), off Victoria St., is signposted from Victoria St., reachable on South Circular Rd. The most famous Dublin Jew is Joyce's Leopold Bloom. *(Open May-Sept. Tu, Th, and Su 11am-3pm; Oct.-Apr. Su 10:30am-2:30pm.)*

Temple Bar, Dame Street, and Cathedrals

West of Trinity between Dame St. and the Liffey, the **Temple Bar** neighborhood wriggles with activity. Narrow cobblestone streets link cheap cafes, hole-in-the-wall theaters, rock venues, and used clothing and record stores. South of Temple Bar across Dame St. awaits a shopping district. At the west end of Dame St., where it meets Parliament and Castle St., sits **Dublin Castle** (tel. 677 7129), the seat of British rule for 700 years. Since 1938 the presidents of Ireland have been inaugurated here. Next door, the **Dublin City Hall,** designed as the Royal Exchange in 1779, boasts an intricate inner dome and statues of national heroes like Daniel O'Connell.

Dublin's ecclesiastical beauties stand west of the castle. All are owned by the Protestant Church of Ireland, none by the Catholic Church. As Ireland is overwhelmingly Catholic and the Anglo-Irish aristocracy no longer exists, the cathedrals and churches are now considered works of art more than centers of worship. **Christ Church Cathedral** (tel. 677 8099) looms at the end of Dame St., uphill and across from the castle. *(Open daily 10am-5pm except during services. Choral evensong Sept.-May Th 6pm. £1; free with Dublinia, below.)* Christ Church also hosts **Dublinia** (tel. 679 4611), a charming recreation of medieval Dublin with life-size reconstructions of a merchant's house and of Wood Quay circa 1200. Less charming is the buboe-covered mannequin in the

Black Death display. Take buses #50 from Eden Quay or #78A from Aston Quay. *(Open Apr.-Oct. daily 10am-5pm; Sept.-Mar. 11am-4pm. £4, students and children £3, includes admission to Christ Church.)* From Christ Church, Nicholas St. runs south and downhill, becoming Patrick St. and passing **St. Patrick's Cathedral** (tel. 475 4817). Jonathan Swift's crypt rises above the south nave. Take bus #50, 54A, or 56A from Eden Quay. *(Open M-F 9am-6pm, Sa 9am-5pm, Su 10-11am and 12:45-4:30pm. £1.20.)*

Guinness Brewery and Kilmainham

From Christ Church Cathedral, follow High St. west, away from downtown, through its name changes—Cornmarket, Thomas, then James—to reach the giant **Guinness Brewery,** St. James Gate (tel. 453 6700; fax 408 4965). Take bus #68A or 78A from Aston Quay or bus #123 from O'Connell St. Farsighted Arthur Guinness signed a 9000-year lease at the original 1759 brewery nearby. Best of all is the bar, where visitors get two complimentary glasses of the dark and creamy goodness. Don't even ask if it's "good for you." Drink, silly tourist. *(Open Apr.-Sept. M-Sa 9:30am-5pm, Su 10:30am-4:30; Oct.-Mar. M-Sa 9:30am-4pm, Su noon-4pm. £3, students £2, children £1.)*

The Royal Hospital and Kilmainham Gaol lie farther to the west, a 20-minute walk from the city center. The rebels who fought in Ireland's struggle for independence from 1792 to 1921 were imprisoned at **Kilmainham Gaol** (tel. 453 5984). Take bus #51 or #79 from Aston Quay, or #51A from Lower Abbey St. The jail's last occupant was Éamon de Valera, the future Éire leader who had been imprisoned by his own countrymen. Today the former prison is a museum that traces the history of penal practices over the last two centuries. *(Open Apr.-Sept. daily 9:30am-4:45pm; Oct.-Mar. M-F 9:30am-4pm, Su 10am-4:45pm. £2, students and children £1.)* The **Royal Hospital Kilmainham** began in 1679; it wasn't a "hospital" in the modern sense but a hospice for retired or disabled soldiers. *(Tours Su noon-4:30pm and by request. £1.)* Since 1991 the hospital has held the **Irish Museum of Modern Art** (tel. 671 8666). *(Call for changing exhibits, artist talks, or concerts. Museum and building open Tu-Sa 10am-5:30pm, Su noon-5:30pm. Free. Guided tours W and F 2:30pm, Sa 11:30am.)*

North of the River

Rising from the river to Parnell Square, **O'Connell Street** is the commercial center of Dublin, at least for those who can't afford to shop on Grafton St. The center traffic islands are monuments to Irish leaders Parnell, O'Connell, and James Larkin, who organized the heroic Dublin general strike of 1913. Farther up the street, the statue of a woman lounging in water is officially named the Spirit of the Liffey or "Anna Livia," unofficially and scathingly called "the floozy in the jacuzzi," or "the whore in the sewer"—in Dublin, that rhymes. The even newer statue of Molly Malone, of ballad fame, on Grafton St. gets called "the tart with the cart." One monument you won't see is **Nelson's Pillar,** a tall freestanding column that remembered Trafalgar outside the General Post Office for 150 years. The IRA blew it up in 1966 in commemoration of the 50th anniversary of the Easter Rising. The **General Post Office** presides over O'Connell St. Not just a fine place to send a letter, the Post Office was the nerve center of the 1916 Rising. Turn right on Cathedral St., a few blocks up O'Connell St., to find the inconspicuous **Dublin Pro-Cathedral,** the city's center of Catholic worship, where tens of thousands once gathered for Daniel O'Connell's memorial service. "Pro" means "provisional"—Dublin Catholics want Christ Church Cathedral returned (see p. 634).

The **Hugh Lane Municipal Gallery,** Parnell Sq. N. (tel. 874 1903), holds modern art within the Georgian walls of Charlemont House. Lane's death aboard *Lusitania*, which sunk off the Irish coast in 1915, raised decades of disputes over his will, resolved by a plan to share the collection between the gallery in Dublin and the Tate Gallery in London. *(Open Tu-F 9:30am-6pm, Sa 9:30am-5pm, Su 11am-5pm. Free.)* Next door, the **Dublin Writers' Museum,** 18 Parnell Sq. N. (tel. 872207), introduces visitors to the city's rich literary heritage. *(Open June-Aug. M-F 10am-6pm, Sa 10am-5pm, Su 11am-5pm; Sept.-May M-Sa 10am-5pm, Su 11am-5pm. £2.95, students £2.50. Combined ticket with either Shaw birthplace or James Joyce Centre £5, student £3.80.)* One block east of

Parnell Sq. East lies the new **James Joyce Centre,** 35 N. Great Georges St. (tel. 873 1984), up Marlborough St. across Parnell St. This restored 18th-century Georgian house is the best of Dublin's many Joycean institutions. *(Open Apr.-Oct. M-Sa 9:30am-5pm, Su noon-5pm; Nov.-Mar. Tu-Sa 10am-4:30pm, Su 12:30-4:30pm. £2.50, students £1.75, children 70p.)* East of O'Connell St. at Custom House Quay, where Gardiner St. meets the river, is one of Dublin's architectural triumphs, the **Custom House.** It was designed and built in the 1780s by James Gandon, who gave up the chance to be St. Petersburg's state architect to settle in Dublin.

Mummies! Just up Church St., the dry atmosphere has preserved the corpses in the vaults of **St. Michan's Church,** which inspired Bram Stoker's *Dracula. (Open mid-Mar. to Nov. M-F 10am-12:45pm and 2-4:45pm, Sa 10am-1pm; Dec. to mid-Mar. Sa 10am-1pm. £1.20, under 16 50p. Church of Ireland services Su 10am.)* The **Irish Whiskey Corner,** Bow St. (tel. 872 5566), is located in a whiskey warehouse off Mary St. From O'Connell St., turn onto Henry St. and continue straight as the street becomes Mary St., then Mary Ln., then May Ln.; the warehouse is on a cobblestone street on the left. Take bus #10 from O'Connell St. Learn how science, grain, and tradition come together to create the golden fluid with "the coveted appellation, whiskey." *(Tours May-Oct. M-F 11am, 2:30, and 3:30pm, Sa 3:30pm; Nov.-Apr. M-F 3:30pm. £3.50, students £2.)* The **Dublin Zoo** (tel. 677 1425) is one of the world's oldest zoos and Europe's largest. *(Open June-Aug. M-Sa 9:30am-6pm, Su 10:30am-6pm; Sept.-May M-F 9:30am-4pm, Sa 9:30am-5pm, Su 10:30am-5pm. £5.50, students £4, children £3, families £15.)*

ENTERTAINMENT

Be it Seamus Heaney or the Pogues you fancy, Dublin is equipped to entertain you. The *Dublin Event Guide* (free), available at the tourist office, Temple Bar restaurants, and the Temple Bar info center, comes out every other Friday with ads in the back, fawning reviews in the front, and reasonably complete listings of museums and literary, musical, and theatrical events in between. *In Dublin* (£1.50) comes out every two weeks with feature articles and listings for music, theater, art exhibitions, comedy shows, clubs, and movie theaters.

Music

Dublin's music world attracts performers from all over the country. Cover charges run £3-4 on better-known acts. *Hot Press* (£1.50) has the most up-to-date music listings, particularly for rock. Tower Records on Wicklow St. has reams of leaflets. Bills posted all over the city also inform of coming attractions. Scheduled concerts tend to start at 9pm, impromptu ones later. Traditional music **(trad)** is not a tourist gimmick but a vibrant and important element of the Irish culture. Some pubs in the city center have trad sessions nightly, others nearly so (see **Pubs,** p. 630). Big deal bands frequent the **Baggot Inn,** 143 Baggot St. (tel. 676 1430). Big, big acts play to huge crowds at **Tivoli Theatre,** Francis St. (tel. 454 4472), and will be not only well publicized but also quite often sold out. Customers mellow at **Rudyard's Wine Bar,** 15 Crown Alley (tel. 671 0846), to the sound of live jazz sessions. The **National Concert Hall,** Earl's Fort Terr. (tel. 671 1533), provides a venue for classical concerts and performances. July and August bring nightly shows (8pm; tickets £8-15, students half-price). A summer lunchtime series makes a nice break from work on occasional Tuesdays and Fridays (tickets £2.50-3). The biggest names in rock and pop play at **Croke Park,** Clonliffe Rd. (tel. 836 3152), and the R.D.S. in Ballsbridge.

Theater and Film

Dublin's curtains rise on a full range of mainstream productions, classic shows, and experimental theater. Showtime is generally 8pm. **Abbey Theatre,** 26 Lower Abbey St. (tel. 878 7222), was founded by Yeats and his collaborator Lady Gregory in 1904 to promote Irish cultural revival and Modernist theater, which turned out to be a bit like promoting corned beef and soy burgers—most people wanted one or the other. *(Box office open M-Sa 10:30am-7pm. Tickets £10-25; student standby M and Th 1hr. before show, £8.)* The **Peacock Theatre,** 26 Lower Abbey St. (tel. 878 7222), downstairs from the Abbey and more experimental, hosts the usual evening shows plus occasional lunchtime plays, concerts, and poetry. *(Box office open M-Sa at 7:30pm for that night's performance only; advance booking at the Abbey Theatre box office. £8, students £5.)* **An Béal Bocht,** 58 Charlemont St. (tel. 475 5614), hosts Irish-language theater. *(W 9pm. £4.)*

The **Irish Film Centre,** Eustace St. (tel. 679 3477), Temple Bar, mounts a variety of classic and European arthouse films throughout the year, plus a French film festival in October and a gay and lesbian film festival in August. You must be a "member" to buy tickets. *(Weekly membership £1; yearly membership £10, students £7.50. Membership must be purchased at least 20min. before start of show. Each member can buy only 4 tickets per screening. Matinees £2; 5pm showing £2.50; after 7pm £4, students £3.)* Other artsy cinemas are the **Light House Cinema,** Middle Abbey St. (tel. 873 0438; £3 before 5pm, £5 after), and **The Screen,** D'Olier St. (tel. 671 4988 or 872 3922). First-run movie houses cluster on O'Connell St., the quays, and Middle Abbey St.

Sports

Though Dubliners aren't as sports-centered as their country cousins, sports are still a serious business, as witnessed by the frequency of matches and events and the amount of money spent on them. The seasons for **Gaelic football** and **hurling** (the national sports of Ireland) run from mid-February to November (see **Sports,** p. 619). Games are played in **Croke Park** and **Phibsborough Rd.** *(Tickets available at the turnstiles. All-Ireland Finals tickets sell out quickly.)* Home games of the Irish **rugby** team are played in **Lansdowne Rd. Stadium** (Oct.-Mar.). **Camogie** (women's hurling) finals also take place in September. For sports information, check the Friday papers or contact the Gaelic Athletic Association (tel. 836 3232).

Festivals and Events

Dublin returns to 1904 each year on **Bloomsday,** June 16, the day on which the action of Joyce's *Ulysses* takes place. Festivities are held all week long. Check out the June issue of *In Dublin* and the *Dublin Event Guide* for year-to-year details. The tourist office's *Calendar of Events* (£1; info on events throughout Ireland) and bimonthly *Dublin Events Guide* (free; biweekly) describe Dublin's many festivals, provincial parades, mayor's balls, concerts, dances, and art shows. Ask about *fleadhs* (FLAHS), traditional day-long musical festivals. The **Temple Bar Blues Festival** is a three-day blues extravaganza in mid-July. Past guests have included Robert Cray and B.B. King. *(Contact Temple Bar Information Centre (tel. 671 5717) for information. Most acts free. Program guides available in July.)* **St. Patrick's Day** (Mar. 17) occasions enormous parades, drunken carousing, and closed banks.

GAY, LESBIAN, AND BISEXUAL DUBLIN

Gay Community News offers the most comprehensive and up-to-date information on gay life and nightlife in Dublin (free; available at Books Upstairs Bookstore, Temple Bar Information Centre, and the Well Fed Café). *In Dublin*'s gay page lists pubs, dance clubs, saunas, gay-friendly restaurants, bookshops, hotlines, and organizations. Visit **Books Upstairs,** 36 College Green (tel. 679 6687), for your copy of the pricey *Irish Scene Gay Guide* (£7), which lists gay hotlines and venues throughout Ireland. **Gay Switchboard Dublin** (tel. 872 1055) is a good resource for events and updates and sponsors a hotline (open Su-F 8-10pm, Sa 3:30-6pm). **Lesbian Line** offers similar services (tel. 661 3777; open Th 7-9pm). The lesbian community meets at **LOT** (Lesbians Organizing Together), 5 Capel St. (tel. 872 7770). The drop-in resource center and library is open Tuesdays and Thursdays from 10am to 5pm. **Outhouse,** 65 William St. (tel. 6706377), is a gay community and research center. Tune into local radio FM103.8 for the gay talk show **Out in the Open** (Tu 8-10pm).

The George, 89 S. Great Georges St. (tel. 478 2983), is a throbbing, purple man o' war and Dublin's first gay bar. A mixed-age crowd gathers throughout the day to chat, sip, and admire the art. Look spiffy—no effort, no entry. Lesbian night is generally Wednesdays. *(Gay men Th-Su. Cover £4-7. Periodic theme nights.)* At **Out on the Liffey,** 27 Upper Ormond Quay (tel. 872 2480), lesbians are welcome but rarely appear. A small disco on the weekend offers bump and grind opportunities. **Stonewall,** Griffith College, South Circular Rd. (bus #19, 19A, or 22), is large and lively. Dancing, a video screen, and pool tables make this club worth the trip. Some nights are male or female only—check *In Dublin* for details. *(Cover £5.)* **The Mean Fiddler,** Wexford St., hosts **Heaven,** a gay night on Sundays. **The Candy Club,** at the Kitchen, Essex St., draws in an artsy crowd of gays and lesbians. *(Cover £4. Open M 11pm-2:30am.)* **Gosh,** at Rí Rá, 1 Exchequer St., hosts serious, well-dressed gays and lesbians. *(Cover £6, students, seniors, and children £4. Open M 11pm-2:30am.)*

■ Howth

Only 9 mi. from Dublin and quite DARTable, hilly Howth (rhymes with "both") gives a quick look at Ireland's highlights: scenery, pubs, history, literature, a castle, an abbey, and fresh fish all in one town. A one-hour **cliff walk** rings the peninsula and trails through heather and past the nests of thousands of seabirds. To get to the trailhead from Howth, turn left at the DART and bus station and follow Harbour Rd. around the corner and up the hill (about 20min.). The footpath begins where the cul-de-sac ends, at the top of the long, long ascent. The trail is not only unmarked but also uncleared in places. Bus #31B cruises from Lower Abbey St. in Dublin to the cliffs' summit. **Howth Harbour** bustles with fishermen. A strip of fresh-fish shops lines West Pier. Fishing boats come in on Thursday. Just offshore, **Ireland's Eye** once provided both religious sanctuary and strategic advantage for monks, as attested to by the ruins of **St. Nessan's Church** and one of the coast's many Martello towers.

Howth has its own castle on the outskirts of town. To reach **Howth Castle,** take a right on Harbour Rd. as you leave the DART station. The castle turn-off, a quarter mile down the road, is marked by signs for the Deer Park Hotel and the National Transport Museum. The castle itself, not open to the public, is a patchwork of different architectural styles, which gives its exterior an awkward charm. An uncertain path leads around the Deer Park Hotel to the fabulous **Rhododendron Gardens,** in which Molly remembers romance at the end of Joyce's *Ulysses. (Open 24hr. Free.)*

The easiest way to reach Howth is by **DART.** Take a northbound train to the end of the line (30min., 6 per hr., £1.10). **Buses** bound for Howth leave from Dublin's Lower Abbey South. Bus #31 runs every hour to the center of Howth, near the DART station, and #31B climbs Howth Summit. The *Guide to Howth Peninsula,* a hand-drawn map with sights and walking trails clearly labeled, is posted at the harbor entrance across from the St. Lawrence Hotel. There is an ATM at **Bank of Ireland,** 1 Main St. (tel. 839 0271; open M-F 10am-4pm, Th 10am-5pm). The **post office,** 27 Abbey St. (tel. 831 8210), exchanges currency. The **telephone code** is 01.

Howth's B&Bs are all located on or near Thormanby Rd., which runs parallel to the beach one block from the coast. **Gleann na Smól** (tel. 832 2936), on the left at the end of Nashville Rd. off Thormanby Rd., is the most convenient in Howth. Mrs. Rickard's satellite dish pulls in MTV and CNN for the benefit of the post-literate, while a generous supply of books suits wormier guests. (£20, all rooms with bath. Ask about student discounts.) Beautiful, floral **Highfield** (tel. 832 3936) is a 20-minute walk up Thormanby Rd. The sign is obscured by its hedges, but it's on the left as you go up the hill. (£19.50, all rooms with bath.) **Hazelwood** (tel. 839 1391), in the Thormanby Woods estate off Thormanby Rd., provides peace and quiet in an already demure town. (£19.50, all rooms with bath.)

Quash your monstrous traveler's appetite with fabulous pizza and sundaes at **Porto Fino's** (tel. 839 3054), Harbour Rd. (open M-F 6-10:45pm, Sa-Su 1pm-midnight). **Caffè Caira,** Harbour Rd. (tel. 839 3823), is a better-than-average chipper, and its tables soothe the Howth youth (burgers or fish £3, chips £1). Hungry shoppers run to **Spar Supermarket** on St. Laurence Rd. off Abbey St. (open M-Sa 8am-11:30pm). Book a seat in advance to hear trad at **Ye Olde Abbey Tavern,** Abbey St. (tel. 832 2006 or 839 0282), or stand and regret it (cover £4). If you're not up for battling the crowd at ye tavern, the **Lighthouse,** Church St. (tel. 832 2827), offers a mellower atmosphere and has trad Wednesday, Thursday, and Sunday at 9pm.

■ Malahide

Eight miles north of Dublin, rows of prim and proper shops smugly line the main street in Malahide. Left off Main St. (a 10min. walk heading north, past the railroad tracks), **Malahide Castle** (tel. 846 2184) is the town's main attraction. *(Open Apr.-Oct. M-F 10am-5pm, Sa-Su 11am-6pm; Nov.-Mar. M-F 10am-5pm, Sa-Su 2-5pm. No tours 12:45-2pm. £3, students £2.45.)* The Malahide Demesne also surrounds a church, a playground, and stunning botanical gardens. *(Demesne/park open daily June 10am-9pm; July-Aug. 10am-8pm; Oct. 10am-7pm; Nov.-Jan. 10am-5pm; Feb.-Mar. 10am-6pm. Free.)* Between Malahide and **Portmarnock** (2mi. down the coastal road toward Dublin) lies the **Velvet Strand**. This stretch of soft beach makes a fantastic stop on a sunny day.

Turn left from the rail station onto Coast Rd. to reach Malahide's center and all its facilities at the intersection of Church Rd. and New St., called The Diamond. Bus #42, which leaves from behind the Custom House (Beresford Place) in Dublin, drives right up to the Malahide Demesne entrance. You can also take the DART to Sutton Station (a stop before Howth) then take bus #102 to Malahide (M-Sa, 3 per hr.). Malahide distributes brochures and maps at the **Citizens Information Centre** (tel. 845 0627), behind the library on Main St. A number of inexpensive B&Bs huddle along Coast Rd. and its tributaries, particularly Biscayne St. (20min. walk from The Diamond).

■ Dún Laoghaire

As Dublin's major out-of-city ferry port, Dún Laoghaire (dun-LEER-ee) is the first peek at Ireland for many tourists. Fortunately, it is a pleasant, well-developed town and a good spot to begin a ramble along the coast south of Dublin. The **harbor** itself is a sight, filled with yachts, boat tours, car ferries chugging to Wales, and fishermen on the west pier. Boat races Tuesday and Thursday evenings in summer draw most of the town. The sights of dandy **Sandycove**, at the end of Upper George's St., are also accessible from Dún Laoghaire via DART. Sandycove is pretty enough in a Victorian way, but its real allure is the **James Joyce Tower**, Sandycove Ave. West. From the Sandycove DART station, go left at the green house down Islington Ave. and then right along the coast to Sandycove Point; or take bus #8 from Burgh Quay in Dublin. Part I of *Ulysses* is set in and near the tower, with Gogarty transformed into Buck Mulligan and Joyce into Stephen Daedalus, who meditates on the wine-dark sea from the gun platform at the top of the tower. Another scene takes place at the Forty Foot Men's Bathing Place at the foot of the tower. Sylvia Beach, Joyce's publisher, opened the tower as a **museum** (tel. 280 9265) in 1962. The two-room museum contains Joyce's death mask, his bookshelves, some of his correspondence, clippings of Ezra Pound's rave reviews, and lots of editions of *Ulysses,* including one illustrated by Henri Matisse. One letter to Italo Svevo mentions a briefcase "the color of a nun's belly." Genius! *(Open Apr.-Oct. M-Sa 10:30am-1pm and 2-5pm, Su 2-6pm; Nov.-Mar. by appointment. £2.40, students and seniors £2, children £1.15.)*

From the tourist office, Royal Marine Rd. climbs up to the center of town. George's St., at the top of Marine Rd., holds most of Dún Laoghaire's shops, many in the **Dún Laoghaire Shopping Centre** at the intersection (open M-W and Sa 9am-6pm, Th-F 9am-9pm). Patrick St., which continues Marine Rd.'s path uphill on the other side of George's St., offers cheap eateries. Reach Dún Laoghaire on the **DART** south from Dublin (£1.10) or on **bus** #7, 7A, 8, or 46A from Eden Quay. The **tourist office** (tel. 280 6600) in the ferry terminal is accustomed to dealing with delirious travelers and equipped with copious maps and pamphlets on all of Dublin and the Borough of Dún Laoghaire (open in summer daily 9am-5pm; in winter M-F 9am-5pm). Ferry travelers can change money at the **bureau de change** in the ferry terminal, or they can wait for the **Bank of Ireland** on Upper George's St. (Bank open M-W and F 10am-4pm, Th 10am-5pm, and at ferry arrival times. 24hr. ATM.)

As the port for the Stena-Sealink ferries and convenient DART stop from Dublin, Dún Laoghaire is prime breeding ground for B&Bs, some more predatory than others. The **Old School House Hostel (IHH),** Elbana Ave. (tel. 280 8777), right off Royal Marine Rd., sports a TV lounge, an eager, 24-hour staff, and a friendly atmosphere. A cafe enhances hostel life. (6-bed dorms £6 per person; doubles £24; quads £40. Add 50p for rooms with bath. Towels £1. Laundry £3. Wheelchair accessible.) Fall off the DART or ferry, and you'll be at **Marleen's,** 9 Marine Rd. (tel. 280 2456), a venerable Dún Laoghaire institution (£17). A crimson carpet leads honored guests to pampering rooms with high ceilings and big beds in **Avondale,** 3 Northumberland Ave. (tel. 280 9628), next to Dunnes Stores (singles £25; doubles £38). Fast-food restaurants and inexpensive coffee shops line George's St. **The Coffee Bean,** 88b Upper George's St. (tel. 280 9522), virtually rolls customers out, filled to the brim with quiche (£4), soup and brown bread (£1.20), and scrumptious desserts (£1-1.50). A full Irish breakfast is served until noon (£2.45; open M-Sa 8am-6pm). **Smyth's Pub,** Callaghan's Ln. (tel. 280 1139), at the corner of George's St., is a pleasant old pub with tasty entrees (hot open sandwiches £2.50) and some cozy snugs. Live music (contemporary or trad) plays Thursday through Sunday nights.

COS. WICKLOW, MEATH, AND LOUTH

■ Wicklow Town

Wicklow Town is touted both for its coastal pleasures and for its usefulness as a departure point into the Wicklow Mountains. Long, skinny Main St. snakes past the Grand Hotel and the grassy triangular plot by the tourist office to its terminus in Market Square. At the Billy Byrne monument, Main St. becomes Summer Hill, the coastal road, from which beaches extend south to Arklow. From Wicklow, the closest strips of sun and sand are **Silver Strand** and **Jack's Hole.** The most popular is **Brittas Bay,** midway between Wicklow and Arklow, where you can buy ultra-cheap crabs in summer. **Trains** run to **Dublin's** Connolly Station (1hr., £4). The station is a 15-minute walk east of town on Church St. **Bus Éireann** leaves for Dublin from the street uphill from the Billy Byrne monument and from the Grand Hotel at the other end of Main St. (M-Sa 9 per day, Su 7 per day). **Bikes** can be rented from **Wicklow Hire** (tel. 68149), on Abbey St., the continuation of Main St. (£7 per day, £30 per week; deposit £30; open M-Sa 8:30am-5:30pm). The **tourist office,** Main St., Fitzwilliam Sq. (tel. 69117; fax 69118), can fill you in on the Wicklow Way and other county attractions (open June-Aug. M-Sa 9am-6pm; Sept.-May M-F 9:30am-1pm and 2-5:30pm). An **AIB,** with a 24-hour **ATM,** conducts business on Main St. The **telephone code** is 0404.

The **Wicklow Bay Hostel,** The Murrough (tel. 69213), in a big building called "Marine House," offers amazing sea views and a wonderful place to stay. From Fitzwilliam Sq., walk toward the river, cross the bridge, and head left (dorms £8; doubles £20; open Mar.-Oct.). Travelers will be content in almost any of the many B&Bs on Patrick Rd., uphill from Main St. and past the church. Main St. is lined with greasy take-aways and fruit stands, while a number of pubs offer musical evenings for the delectation of Wicklow's residents. The **Bridge Tavern,** Bridge St. (tel. 67718), resounds with traditional music (Th-Su in summer, Th only in winter) and is known to have informal concertina sessions on summer nights to complement the snooker.

■ The Wicklow Way

The lonely mountain heights reach westward and upward along established trails negotiable by foot or horse. The 70 mi. Wicklow Way, Ireland's best-known long-distance path, starts a few miles south of Dublin and heads south along the crests all the way to Co. Carlow. Parts of it are well graded and even paved. Although the path is well marked with yellow arrows, hikers should get the *Wicklow Way Map Guide* (£5). Since the path is mostly out of sight- and hearing-range of the lowlands, traveling alone can be dangerous. Drinking stream water is also not a good idea, and lighting fires within a mile of the forest is illegal (see **Wilderness and Safety Concerns,** p. 47).

The most popular northern 45 mi. of the path (from Dublin to Aghavannagh) have the best scenery and offer better access to hostels. To reach the northern end of the path, take bus #47B from Hawkins St. in Dublin's city center to its terminus at Marlay Park in Rathfarnham, a Dublin suburb. Bus #47 also stops nearby. If you hike seven to eight hours a day, the northern section will take about three days, and the entire trail will take about six. Bikers cover virtually the same mileage by sticking to roads—it is not advisable to take a bike on the Way itself. Bus Éireann serves the southern section of the Wicklow Way at Aughrim, Tinahely, Shillelagh, and Hackettstown.

An Óige prints a list of suggested stages for a six-day walk along the Way, with mileage and expected walking time, available at their main office or any of their nearby hostels. Walking times between the hostels are: Tiglin to Glendalough, five hours; Rathdrum to Aghavannagh, four hours; Aghavannagh to Glenmalure, five hours; Aghavannagh to Glendalough, seven hours. Other trails with other accommodations meander every which way through the Wicklovian wilderness.

ACCOMMODATIONS

Several hostels lie within 5 mi. of the Wicklow Way; these places fill up in July and August. Book An Óige hostels ahead through the An Óige Head Office, 61 Mountjoy St., Dublin (tel. (01) 830 4555).

Knockree (An Óige/HI), Lacklan House, Enniskerry (tel. (01) 286 4036), on the Way. From Enniskerry, take the left fork road leading from the village green, take a left at Buttercups Newsagent, and begin a steep walk, following signs for Glencree Dr. Alternatively, take the DART to Bray and bus #85 to Enniskerry, which drops you off 2mi. from Knockree. Spacious kitchen area with fireplace. Simple, single-sex dorms £5.50, Oct.-May £4.50. Lockout 10:30am-5:30pm (unless it's raining).

Tiglin (An Óige/HI), a.k.a. **Devil's Glen,** Ashford (tel. (0404) 40259), 5mi. from the Way near the Tiglin Adventure Centre. From Ashford, follow Roundwood Rd. for 3mi., then follow the signs for the Tiglin turn-off on the right, a hilly 8mi. from Powerscourt. 50 beds in a basic accommodation. Dorms £7; Oct.-May £6.

Wicklow Way Hostel (tel. (0404) 45398), on the Way. Relatively new, with sturdy beds with warm comforters. The kitchen has a microwave and is open from 7am to 10pm, and there's a TV in the lounge. Dorms £8. Sheets £1.

Old Mill Hostel (tel. 45156). Signposted 10min. down the road from the Wicklow Way Hostel. Older and more cramped, but fine facilities. Dorms £6.50, private rooms £14. Sheets 75p. **Camping** £4.50 per person.

Glendalough (An Óige/HI) (tel. (0404) 45342), 1½mi. from the Way. From Dublin, take bus #65 from Eden Quay, which brings you to Donard, 3mi. to Ballinclea Youth Hostel and 7mi. by mountain track to Glenmalure. West of Glenmalure is an army range, the Glen of Imaal, where military exercises are conducted. The hostel was under reconstruction in 1998 but may be one of the more modern places to stay. Dorms £6.50, Oct.-May £5.50. Open July-Aug. daily; Sept.-June Sa-Su.

▓ Boyne Valley

The thinly populated Boyne Valley safeguards Ireland's greatest historical treasures. The massive passage tombs of Newgrange, Knowth, and Dowth predate the pyramids, and even after so long, archaeologists have failed to unpuzzle the strange symbols carved on their faces or even guess the purpose of their existence. Once upon a time, he who possessed ownership of the Celtic **Hill of Tara** was granted Kingship of Ireland. Every so often, farmers plow up artifacts from the 1690 Battle of the Boyne (see p. 612). Some backpackers report that the several N-roads criss-crossing the valley make it easy to **hitch,** but the grand tour requires a fair degree of hiking. Bikers will find the terrain between the sights welcoming. Several tours herd visitors through the circuit of sights. **Celtic Twilight** (tel. (088) 54787) offers a full sight-seeing "Tour of the Royal Meath" on Sundays in the summer (£14). The coach leaves the Nassau St. entrance to Trinity College Dublin at 10am and returns to Dublin at 5:30pm. **Sightseeing Tours** (tel. (01) 283 9973) visits Newgrange and Knowth on its Boyne Valley tour. The bus leaves from the Dublin Tourist Office (June-Sept. daily at 1:20pm, return at 6pm; £14).

■ Drogheda

Most sights in Co. Meath are bike-able from Drogheda (DRA-hed-a), perched on steep slopes astride the Boyne river. The waterfront's drab industrialness bursts into crowded streets and cheerful pubs on the streets north of and parallel to the Boyne. Encounter a blackened, shriveled head in the imposing, neo-Gothic **St. Peter's Church** on West St. *(Open daily 8:30am-8:30pm.)* Most of the town's medieval churches were sacked or burned, some with people taking refuge inside, by Cromwell, a deeply religious man.

Trains (tel. 38749) depart east of town on Dublin Rd. (follow John St. south of the river) to **Dublin** (1hr., express 30min., M-Sa 26 per day, Su 4 per day, £8, return £12) and **Belfast** (2hr., M-Sa 9 per day, Su 4 per day, £12). The **bus station** (tel. 35023) is on John St. (inquiries desk open M-F 9am-6:30pm, Sa 8:30am-1:30pm). Buses run to **Athlone** (2½hr., M-Sa 3 per day, Su 1 per day, £9), **Belfast** (2hr., M-Sa 6 per day, Su 3 per day, £8), **Dublin** (50min., M-Sa 18 per day, Su 7 per day, £4.80), and **Galway** (4hr., M-Sa 2 per day, Su 1 per day, £12). **Bridge Cycles,** North Quay (tel. 34526), is the best place to rent bikes. (£7 per day, £30 per week; deposit £30. Student and *Let's Go* discounts. Open M-Sa 9am-1pm and 2-6pm.) The **tourist office,** Donore Rd. (tel. 37070), in the bus station off Dublin Rd., offers the *Drogheda Town Map* (£1; open June-Sept. M-Sa 10am-1pm and 2-5:30pm). The **telephone code** is 041.

Drogheda's accommodations, like most things in the town, are north of the River Boyne. **Harpur House,** William St. (tel. 32736), is a small hostel plus simple B&B in a big townhouse. Follow Shop St. up the hill, continue up Peter St., and take a right onto William St.; the hostel is on the right. (9-bed dorms £7, with full breakfast £10. B&B £15. Kitchen available.) Buses from Harpur House do half-day sightseeing tours of the Boyne Valley (£13). Well kept and backpacker-friendly, **Abbey View House,** Mill Lane (tel. 31470), defines B&B courtesy. Head west on West St. and take the first left after it crosses over to Trinity St. (£15). The very popular **Pizzeria,** Peter St. (tel. 34208), cooks all kinds of Italian food (pasta £7) and 13 types of pizza (£5.40; open M-Tu and Th-Su 6-11pm). You can grab a light meal for about £2 at **The Copper Kettle,** 1 Peter St. (tel. 37397), a hole-in-the-wall cafe just up from the junction with West St. (open M-Sa 9:30am-5:30pm). The largest town in the area, Drogheda has a pretty active nightlife. Dark wood engulfs **Peter Matthews,** 9 Laurence St. (tel. 37371), also known as McPhail's, a very old, likable pub (live rock and blues Th-Su nights). **The Earth,** Stockwell Ln. (tel. 30969), is a Flintstones-meet-techno sort of place, with fossils embedded in the walls and bar and rock-themed bathrooms. Dancers come from all around. (Techno F-Sa, 70s disco Th and Su. Cover £5, £3 with concession Su and before midnight Th-Sa. Open Th-Su 11pm-3:30am.)

■ Brú na Bóinne

Brú na Bóinne (brew na BO-in-yeh, "Palace of the Boyne") is saturated not with palaces but with prehistoric tombs older than the pyramids or Stonehenge, made by an indigenous pre-Celtic neolithic culture with mind-boggling engineering talents. Brú na Bóinne is well signposted: all three of the passage-tombs are reached from the turn-off on N51, 7 mi. from Drogheda. Follow the turnoff road for about a half mile, then take a left for Newgrange. Bikers should follow the road to Dowth on their way to the tombs and take Slane Rd. back to Drogheda. **Newgrange** (tel. 24488; fax 24798), the most spectacular, most well restored, and most visited of the sites, is the prime example of a passage-tomb. Built by a highly organized religious society over 5000 years ago, using stones believed to have been carted from Wicklow 40 mi. away, Newgrange is covered with elaborate patterns and symbols that mystify archaeologists. The inner chamber's roof was cobbled together without the use of mortar and has stood since about 3200 BC. The 30-minute **tour** is one part information and nine parts wild speculation, but it's the only way to see the inside of the one-acre tomb. The highlight of the tour is the re-creation of a moment that actually occurs five days each year around the winter solstice, when the sun's rays enter at just the right

Know Your Whiskey

Anyone who drinks his whiskey as it's meant to be drunk—"neat," or straight—can tell you that there's a huge difference between Irish whiskeys (Bushmills, Jameson, Power and Son, and the like), Scotch whiskys (spelled without an e), and American whiskeys. But what makes an Irish whiskey *Irish?* The basic ingredients in whiskey—water, barley malt, and heat—are always the same. It's the quality of these ingredients, the way in which they're combined, and the method of storage that gives each product its distinct flavor. American whiskey is distilled once and is often stored in oak, bourbon is made only in Kentucky, scotch uses peat-smoked barley, and Irish whiskey is triple distilled. We could get more technical, but at *Let's Go* we realize that the best way to understand the distinctions between brands is to taste the various labels in close succession to one another. Line up those shot glasses, sniff and then taste each one (roll the whiskey in your mouth like a real pro), and have a sip of water between each brand. **"But I don't have the money to buy a shot of each brand,"** our budget-traveling readers murmur. Well, then, get thee to a distillery tour. If you're lucky, you'll be selected to be an "Irish Whiskey Taster," trying no less than five kinds of Irish, two scotch, and one bourbon whiskey under the supervision of your highly trained guide. Sure, the certificate is nice, but the haze is even better (up to a point, of course).

angle to illuminate the inner chamber. Bring a coat or sweater; it gets chilly inside even in summer. *(Tours begin every 30min. daily June-Sept. 9:30am-7pm; Mar.-Apr. and Oct. 10am-5pm; Nov.-Feb. 10am-4:30pm; May 9:30am-6pm. £3, students £1.25, seniors £2.)* The **tourist office** (tel. 24274) is just before the entry to the site, near the parking lot (open Apr.-Oct. daily 9am-7pm). The **telephone code** is 041.

■ Athlone

Plopped down in the pastures of Roscommon and Westmeath, Athlone is the center of everything in the middle of nowhere. The city is sort of a transportation hub, but the dearth of any other cities nearby or famous attractions has relegated Athlone to backwater status. Athlone is divided by the Shannon; the bus and train station and the hostel are on the right bank, while the left bank teems with restaurants. Athlone's **train and bus depot** (tel. 73322) is on Southern Station Rd., which runs parallel to Church St. **Trains** leave for **Dublin** (2hr., 8 per day, M-Th and Sa £9, F and Su £12.50) and **Galway** (1hr., 4 per day, M-Th and Sa £7, F and Su £11). **Buses** shuttle off to **Dublin** (9 per day, £7), **Galway** (M-Sa 9 per day, Su 8 per day, £7), and **Cork** (1 per day, £13). The **tourist office** (tel. 94630), in the castle, has free copies of the *Athlone and District Visitors Guide* (open Easter-Oct. M-Sa 10am-6pm). The **phone code** is 0902.

Undoubtedly, the best place to stay in Athlone is the **Athlone Holiday Hostel** (tel. 73399; fax 73833; email athhostl@iol.ie), conveniently located next to the train station. (Single-sex 10-bed dorms £8, with full breakfast £11. Showers 50p. Laundry. reception 24hr. **Internet access. Bike rental** £10 per day.) B&Bs inhabit Inishtown Rd. and its continuation toward Dublin. Closer to town is Mrs. Devaney's **Shannon View,** Church St. (tel. 78411), near the church, offering crisp rooms with big beds and TVs (£16). Restaurants on the left bank are more expensive but more convenient than elsewhere in town. **Branburry's,** across the street from the church on Church St., is where locals go for cheap, delicious breakfast and lunch (scones 25p, sandwiches £1.50; open M-F 8am-5pm, Sa 9am-4pm). **The Left Bank,** Bastion St. (tel. 94446), serves delicious meals and homemade desserts in a bohemian atmosphere on the winding medieval streets by the Seine—no, wait, that's Paris (entrees £5-7; lunch served M-Sa 10:30am-5:30pm, dinner M-Sa 6-10pm). Venerable **Sean's Bar,** Main St. (tel. 92358), behind the castle, goes trad five nights per week. The only club in town is **BoZo's,** at Conlon's on Dublingate St. (cover £5; open Th-Su 11:30pm-2am). *The Westmeath Independent* has entertainment listings.

■ Clonmacnoise

Isolated 14 mi. southwest of Athlone and surrounded by the intense green of fields and marshes, Clonmacnoise (clon-muk-NOYS) is one of the few monastic ruins yet to be devoured by tourism. St. Ciaran (KEER-on) founded the monastery in 545 overlooking the eastern shore of the Shannon, and his settlement grew into a city and important scholastic center. The precious *Book of the Dun Cow* was written here by monks around 1100, supposedly on vellum (skin) from St. Ciaran's cow, which traveled everywhere with St. Ciaran and miraculously produced enough milk for the whole monastery. The site itself is impressive for its lonely grandeur, with crumbling buildings rising amid hills, bog, river, and sheep. The **cathedral** was destroyed by Vikings and rebuilt several times; the current structure dates from about 1100. **O'Connor's Church,** built in 1000, still has Church of Ireland services on the fourth Sunday of the month at 10am. Peaceful **Nun's Church,** left off the path through the main site about a quarter mile away, features some of the best Romanesque architecture in Ireland. One of the doorways of the cathedral is known as the **whispering arch.** By standing on either side of the arch and whispering into the hollowed-out space, lovers can discreetly convey their steamiest private thoughts. Paddy Kavanaugh's **Minibus Service** (tel. (0902) 74839 or (087) 407706) departs daily at 11am from the Athlone Castle and will pick up from the hostel or any of the B&Bs with advance notice. *(£15, students £11, includes admission.)* Tours run to both Clonmacnoise and the **Clonmacnoise and West Offaly Railway** and return around 4pm. The **visitors center** (tel. (0905) 74195) craves attention for its wheelchair-accessible displays. Entrance to the ruins is through the visitors center. *(Open daily in summer 9am-5pm; in winter 10am-5pm. £3, students and seniors £1.50.)* The **tourist office** (tel. (0905) 74134), at the entrance to the car park, gives local information. *(Open daily in summer 9am-6pm; in winter 9am-5pm).*

COS. WEXFORD, WATERFORD, KILKENNY, AND TIPPERARY

■ Wexford City

The sidewalks of densely populated Wexford are so narrow that everyone mills around on Main St. or in the numerous alleys that twist upward from the quays. The Twin Churches punctuate the skyline of the huddled harbor city. Excellent pubs and restaurants now fill the stone passageways built in the 12th century.

ORIENTATION AND PRACTICAL INFORMATION The quays hum with the construction of the town's new **marina.** North and South **Main St.,** a block north of the harbor, are joined by the **Bull Ring** at the town's center. Just off the water on the northern edge of town is the bus and rail station. The Franciscan Friary stands at the top of the hill, surveying the older city and train station to its right. **Trains** come into **North Station,** Redmond Sq. (tel. 22522), a five-minute walk along the quays from Crescent Quay. Buy tickets on the train when the office is closed. Information available from 7am until last departure. Trains hustle to Connolly Station in **Dublin** (3hr., M-Sa 3 per day, Su 2 per day, £11) and to **Rosslare Harbour** (30min., M-Sa 4 per day, Su 3 per day, £3). **Buses** run from the train station to **Dublin** (2½hr., 6 per day) and to **Rosslare Harbour** (20min., M-Sa 7 per day, Su 5 per day, £1.25). Buses to and from **Limerick** (2 per day) connect with Irish Ferries and Stena-Sealink sailings. From mid-July to August, buses run directly to **Galway** (6hr.) and other western points via **Limerick** (3½hr.) and **Waterford** (1hr.). **Hayes Cycle Shop,** 108 S. Main St. (tel. 22462), has Raleigh touring bikes. (£7 per day, £35 per week; £40 or ID deposit. Open M-Sa 9am-6pm.) **Hitchhikers** to **Dublin** (N11) stand at the Wexford Bridge off the quays; those bound for **Rosslare** head south along the quays to Trinity St. Hitchers heading to **Cork** or **Waterford** continue down Westgate and turn left onto Hill St. then right onto John St. Upper (N25). Take note: N11 and N25 merge near the city, so be sure to specify either the Dublin Rd. (N11) or the Waterford Rd. (N25). Hitching is rarer these days; as always, *Let's Go* does not recommend hitching. The **tourist office,** Crescent Quay (tel. 23111), is in the Chamber of Commerce building. The free, ad-packed *Wexford: Front Door to Ireland* and *Welcome to Wexford* offer handy maps. (open July-Aug. M-Sa 9:30am-6pm, Su 11am-5pm; Sept.-June M-Sa 9:30am-6pm). **AIB,** South Main St., has a 24-hour **ATM. Pharmacies** along Main St. rotate Sunday and late hours (all open M-Sa 9am-1pm and 2-6pm). The **post office** (tel. 22587) is on Anne St. (open M and W-F 9am-5:30pm, Tu 9:30am-5:30pm). The **telephone code** is 053.

ACCOMMODATIONS, FOOD, AND PUBS
There are a number of nice B&Bs in town as well as a hostel. If the B&Bs listed are full, ask the proprietors for recommendations or look along N25 (Rosslare Rd.). **Kirwan House Hostel,** 3 Mary St. (tel. 21208; email kirwanhostel@tinet.ie), has a small common room, nifty sleeping quarters, and internet access (dorms £7.50-8; doubles £20). **Abbey House,** 34 Abbey St. (tel. 24409), flaunts a fantastic location and comfy quarters (doubles with bath and TV £34). **The Selskar** (tel. 23349), on the corner of N. Main and Selskar St., has a double and twin on each floor sharing a bathroom, kitchen, and sitting area with TV (doubles £30). **The Yacht B&B,** 2 Monck St. (tel. 22338), offers clean, cushy rooms above the Yacht Pub overlooking the River Slaney (singles £19; doubles £30).

   Dunnes Store, Redmond Sq. (tel. 45688), has a wide selection of meats and sells clothes (open M-Tu and Sa 9am-6pm, W-F 9am-9pm, Su noon-6pm). **The Sky and the Ground,** 112 S. Main St. (tel. 21273), serves superb sandwiches. (Most main courses £4-5. Food served noon-9pm. Music most nights: trad M, Th; blues Tu; acoustic W, Su; DJ F-Sa.) **Tim's Tavern,** 51 S. Main St. (tel. 23861), has won national awards for dishes like avocado, pear, and crab, stuffed loin of pork, and bacon and cabbage. (Served Su-Th. Entrees £5-6.50. Lunch served daily noon-5pm, dinner 6-10pm. Trad W and Sa 9:30pm.) Muted voices, soft pine, and friendly people sometimes spill out of **The Tackroom,** Bull Ring, on cool evenings. **O'Faolain's** (oh FWAY lawns), 11 Monck St. (tel. 23877), is the most raucous of Wexford's pubs. The *bodhrán* and *uilleann* appear on Sundays (12:30-2pm) and Monday nights. (Mixed music Tu, Su.) **The Centenary Stores,** Charlotte St. (tel. 24424), a.k.a. "The Stores," is a pub and dance club housed within the brick walls and soaring ceilings of a former warehouse and caters to a classy crowd of twentysomethings. (Excellent trad Su mornings and Tu-W nights. Blues and folk M nights. Dance music and top 40 Th-Su nights 11pm-2am. Cover £5.)

SIGHTS
The historical society (tel. 22311) runs free **walking tours** departing from White's Hotel at 8:15pm. Tours depend on weather and interest—it's best to call around 6pm for availability. The remains of the Norman **city wall** run the length of High St. **Westgate Tower,** at the intersection of High and Westgate St., is the only one of the wall's six original towers that still stands. The tower gate now holds the **Westgate Heritage Centre** (tel. 46506), where an audio-visual show that recounts the history of Wexford with fire and canon special effects will blow your mind. *(Open July-Aug. M-Sa 10am-2pm and 2:30-5:30pm, Su 2-6pm; Sept.-June M-Sa 10am-2pm and 2:30-5:30pm. £1, children 50p.)* The center also offers walking **tours** of Wexford. *(1½-2hr. Call ahead to book or join a group. £2.50.)* Next door, the **Selskar Abbey,** site of King Henry II's extended penance for Thomas à Becket's murder, now acts as a windowbox for lush wildflowers. *(Same hours as the center.)*

   An open area between North and South Main St. marks the **Bull Ring.** Bull baiting was inaugurated in 1621 by the town's butcher guild as a promotional device. The mayor got the hide while the poor got the meat. "The Pikeman," a statue of a stalwart peasant fearlessly brandishing a sharp instrument, commemorates the 1798 uprising. Get your stuffed "Harvey the Friendly Rebel," a smiling bunny holding a pike and draped in the tricolor, at the tourist office, the exclusive distributor. The **Friary Church** in the Franciscan Friary, School St., houses the "Little Saint," a creepy effigy of young St. Adjutor that shows the wounds inflicted by his Roman father. Franciscan monks have lived in town since 1240—keep a lookout for peaceful fellows in brown.

■ Rosslare Harbour

Rosslare Harbour refers to the over-equipped village from which the ferries to France and Wales depart; Rosslare is the less important town between Rosslare Harbour and Wexford on N25. **Trains** (tel. 33114 or 33592; office open daily 6am-9:30pm) run from the ferry port to **Dublin** (2hr., M-Sa 3 per day, Su 2 per day, £10.50), **Limerick** (2¼hr., M-Sa 2 per day, £12), **Waterford** (1¼hr., M-Sa 3 per day, £6), and **Wexford** (20min., M-Sa 3 per day, Su 2 per day, £2). **Buses** stop at the Catholic church and run twice per day to **Galway via Waterford** (£16), **Killarney** (£15), and **Tralee** (£16), as well as to **Cork** (M-Sa 3 per day, £13), **Limerick** (M-Sa 2 per day, Su 3 per day, £12), **Waterford** (3 per day, £8.80), **Dublin** (3hr., M-Sa 6 per day, Su 5 per day, £9), and **Wexford** (20min., M-Sa 9 per day, Su 8 per day, £2.50). **Bus Éireann** and **Irish Rail** have desks in the terminal (tel. 33592; open daily 6:30am-9:45pm). The **ferry port** is open daily 7am to 10pm, has a bureau de change, and is served by **Stena Sealink/Sea Lynx** (tel. 33115, recorded info 33330; fax 33534; office open daily 7am-10pm) and **Irish Ferries/Britain and Ireland line** (tel. 33158; fax 33544). The manic-panic **ferry tourist office** (tel. 33623) offers free, photocopied maps covered with strange, meaningless numbers and **TravelSave** stamps (open 10am-8pm). Currency is exchanged at the **Bank of Ireland** (tel. 33304), on Kilrane Rd. (open M-F 10am-12:30pm and 1:30-4pm; **ATM**). The **post office** (tel. 33207) in the SuperValu between produce and check). The **telephone code** is 053.

Weary ferry passengers fill both good and mediocre beds, while the better places to stay in Wexford go untenanted. B&Bs swamp N25 just outside of Rosslare Harbour. There is a noticeable difference between approved and non-approved B&Bs on N25. **Rosslare Harbour Youth Hostel (An Óige/HI),** Goulding St. (tel. 33399; fax 33624), offers decent showers, cramped bunks, cinderblock walls, and a collection of continental youth. Take a right at the top of the steps on the hill opposite the ferry terminal, then head left around the far corner of the Hotel Rosslare; the hostel is down the street across from the supermarket (dorms £6.50-7.50; sheets £1.50; midnight curfew). **Marianella B&B** (tel. 33139), off N25 across from the pharmacy, lacks a great view but welcomes you with tea and cookies in each room (singles £19; doubles £32, with bath £36; spacious family room available). The restaurants in Rosslare Harbour tend to be expensive. The **SuperValu supermarket** (tel. 33107) is opposite Rosslare Harbour Youth Hostel (open M-W and Sa 8am-6pm, Th-F 8am-7pm, Su 9am-1pm). The pub in **Devereux Hotel** (tel. 33216), just up from the ferry terminal, has good pub grub for reasonable prices (large lunch about £4).

■ Waterford City

Huge metal silos and storage facilities greet the first-time visitor to Waterford. Fortunately, behind this industrial facade lies a wonderfully complex city. Waterford dates back to 1003, when Vikings built Reginald's Tower to defend their longships. The town remains a commercial center, although massive freighters have since replaced the longships and shops and amiable pubs have filled the winding, narrow streets.

ORIENTATION AND PRACTICAL INFORMATION

Waterford is a mix of narrow Viking streets and broad English thoroughfares. The various quays on the River Suir and Barranstrand St. (through its many name changes) form a crooked T where most activity takes place.

Airplanes: tel. 875589. Served by **British Airways** and **Suckling Airlines.** Follow The Quay and turn right at Reginald's Tower then left at the sign. 20min. from town.

Trains: Plunkett Station (tel. 873401, after hours 873402 or 873403), across the bridge from The Quay. Train station staffed M-Sa 9am-6pm, Su at departure times. John F. Kennedy's ancestors grew up in Waterford, and the city is still well connected. Trains chug to **Limerick** (2¼hr., M-Sa 2 per day, £11.50), **Kilkenny**

(40min., M-Sa 4 per day, £6), **Dublin** (2½hr., M-Sa 4 per day, Su 3 per day, £12), and **Rosslare Harbour** (1hr., M-Sa 3 per day, £7.50).

Buses: Plunkett Station (tel. 879000). Office open M-Sa 9am-5:30pm, Su 2-5:30pm. To **Dublin** (3½hr., M-Sa 5 per day, Su 3 per day, £8.50), **Kilkenny** (1hr., 2 per day, £5), **Limerick** (2½hr., 4 per day, £9.70), **Cork** (2½hr., M-Sa 8 per day, Su 6 per day, £8), **Galway** (4¾hr., M-Sa 4 per day, Su 3 per day, £13), and **Rosslare Harbour** (1¼hr., 3 per day, £8).

Local Transportation: City buses leave from the Clock Tower on The Quay. 75p for trips within the city. Check the tourist office for details.

Hitching: The rare hitchers place themselves on the main routes, away from the tangled city center. To reach N24 (Cahir, Limerick), N10 (Kilkenny, Dublin), or N25 (New Ross, Wexford, Rosslare), they head over the bridge toward the train station. For the N25 (Cork), they continue down Parnell St.; others take a city bus out to the Waterford Crystal Factory before they stick out a thumb.

Tourist Office: 41 Merchant's Quay (tel. 875788), between Hanover and Gladstone St. Ask for a map of Waterford and the free *Ireland's South East* guide. *The Waterford Touring Guide* (£2) has good county-wide info. Open July-Aug. M-Sa 9am-6pm, Su 11am-1pm and 2-5pm; June and Sept. M-Sa 9am-6pm; Oct.-Feb. M-F 2-5pm; Mar.-Apr. M-Sa 9am-1pm and 2-6pm.

Budget Travel: USIT, 36-37 Georges St. (tel. 872601; fax 871723). Near the corner of Gladstone St., 1 block east of Barronstrand St. ISICs, **Travelsave** stamps, student deals for daily flights and bus/ferry packages from Waterford to London. Open M-F 9:30am-5:30pm, Sa 11am-4pm.

Financial Services: 24hr. **ATM at AIB,** just off The Quay on Barronstrand Rd. Banks abound.

Luggage Storage: Plunkett Station. £1 per item. Open M-Sa 7:15am-9pm.

Bike Rental: Wright's Cycle Depot, Henrietta St. (tel. 874411). £7 per day, £30 per week; deposit £40. Open M-Th and Sa 9:30am-1pm and 2-6pm, F 9:30am-1pm and 2-9pm.

Launderette: Rainbow Launderette, Thomas St. (tel. 855656). No self-service. Serviced wash and dry £5.90. Open M-F 8:45am-6pm, Sa 9am-5:30pm.

Emergency: Dial 999; no coins required.

Hotlines: Samaritans, 13 Beau St. (tel. 872114). 24hr. hotline. **Rape Crisis Centre** (tel. 873362). Open M 10am-noon, Tu-W and F 10am-noon and 2-4pm, Th 10am-noon, 2-4pm, and 8:30-10pm.

Hospital: Ardkeen Hospital (tel. 873321). Follow The Quay to the Tower Hotel; turn left, then follow signs straight ahead to the hospital.

Post Office: The Quay (tel. 874444), the largest of several. Open M-Tu and Th-F 9am-5:30pm, W 9:30am-5:30pm, Sa 9am-1pm.

Internet Access: Voyager Internet Café, in Parnell Court Shopping Center (tel. 843843). Follow Barronstrand St. up from The Quay through its name changes to John St. Voyager is on the left opposite Eddie Rockets before John St. crosses Parnell St. Keep your eyes peeled; the shopping center is almost invisible. £1.50 per 15min., students £1.25. Open M-Sa 11am-11pm, Su 3-11pm.

Telephone Code: 051.

ACCOMMODATIONS

Most B&Bs in the city are unimpressive; those on Cork Rd. are a better option.

Viking House Hostel (IHH), Coffee House Ln. (tel. 853827; email pjreddy@iol.ie). Follow The Quay east past the Clock Tower and another block past the post office; the hostel is on the right, behind another building. Spacious lounge, clean kitchen, and a friendly staff. June-Sept. 14-bed dorms £8; 4- to 6-bed dorms £9.50-12; doubles £27. Add £1 for room with bath and £2 for TV. Prices £1-2 less off season.

Waterford Hostel, 70 The Manor (tel. 850163). From the Quay, walk down John St. and turn right onto The Manor. The hostel is on your right before the traffic lights. Not as big or as nice as Viking House, but clean and comfortable. Dorms £8.

Derrynane House, 19 The Mall (tel. 875179). Walk down the Quay away from the bridge. When it swings into The Mall, so should you. High ceilings and bright, spacious rooms. £15.

Mayor's Walk House, 12 Mayor's Walk (tel. 855427). A 15min. mayoral walk from the train station. Simple, quiet rooms. Singles £15; doubles £28. Open Mar.-Nov.

Beechwood, 7 Cathedral Sq. (tel. 876677). From the Quay, go up Henrietta St. A charming home on an ideal quiet pedestrian street. Singles £17; doubles £30.

FOOD

You might want to try Waterford's contribution to Irish cuisine, the *blaa* (BLAH), a floury white sausage roll of Huguenot origins. Besides the *blaa,* Waterford gave the world the modern process of bacon curing. To pick up some cheap groceries, visit **Dunnes Stores** in the City Square Mall (open M-W and Sa 9am-6pm, Th-F 9am-9pm). **The Late, Late Shop** (tel. 855376), farther up The Quay, gives you an extra, extra hour to shop but a smaller, more expensive selection (open daily 7:30am-midnight).

Sizzlers Restaurant (tel. 85211), on The Quay toward Reginald's Tower. Chat with the locals sharing your table over delicious fried entrees (£3-5). Open 24hr.

Café Luna, 53 John St., offers cheap food with a trendy touch. Open Su-Th until 2:30am and F-Sa until 4am.

Haricot's Wholefood Restaurant, 11 O'Connell St. Most entrees £3.50-5.50. Open M-F 9:30am-8pm, Sa 9:30am-5:45pm.

Chapman's Pantry Restaurant, 61 The Quay (tel. 873833). Homefare served in a friendly, casual atmosphere. Sandwiches £2. Open M-Sa 8:30am-5:30pm.

The Reginald, The Mall (tel. 855087). A faux castle facade nestled behind the real Reginald's Tower. Rich, delicious lunches in a classy environment. Lunch special £5, vegetarian specials £5.50. Served daily noon-3pm.

Crumbs, Michael St. (tel. 854323). Good food served quickly in a coffee shop atmosphere. Entrees about £4. Open M-Sa 9am-6pm.

PUBS

The Quays are loaded with pubs, and there are even more as you travel up Barronstrand St. into town. The pubs, however, constitute the extent of the town's nightlife.

T&H Doolan's, George's St. (tel. 841504). Waterford's oldest and best drinking establishment. Trad nightly. No cover.

The Pulpit, John St. (tel 879184). Grab a seat and a pint and enjoy the hip crowd. **Preachers,** the upstairs nightclub, opens at 10:30pm, playing tunes from the 70s, 80s, and 90s. Amen! Cover £3 before 10:30pm, £6 after.

Geoff's Pub, 9 John St. (tel. 874787). Bring a cell phone—even if it doesn't work—to enhance your hipness as you sip your pint and laugh a bit too loudly.

The Jazbah (tel. 858128), at Parnell and John St. This swanky new bar with 1920s decor is a classy joint, ideal for a mellow pint with friends. Live jazz F-Sa nights.

Muldoon's, John St. (tel. 873693). The late bar hours (Th-Su until 2am) and cheap food (£1.95 daily specials) make it worthwhile. Free food 11pm-1am.

Mullane's, 15 Newgate St. (tel. 873854), off New St. Famous for its hard-core trad sessions. Call ahead.

SIGHTS

The **Waterford Crystal Factory** (tel. 373311), 1 mi. out on N25 (Cork Rd.), is the city's highlight. Forty-minute tours allow you to witness the transformation of molten glass into polished crystal. The least expensive item is a crystal heart (£16). *(Tours and audio-visual shows every 10min. Apr.-Oct. daily 8:30am-4pm, showroom open 8:30am-6pm; Nov.-Mar. tours daily 9am-3:15pm, showroom open 9am-5pm. £3.50, students £1.75. Tours wheelchair accessible. Book ahead via telephone or through the tourist office.)* City bus #1 (Kilbarry-Ballybeg) leaves across from the Clock Tower every 30 minutes and passes the factory (75p). The City Imp also stops at the factory by request. **Reginald's Tower** (tel. 873501), at the end of The Quay, has guarded the entrance to the city since the 12th century. *(£2, children 75p.)* Just down the street, the **Waterford Heritage Centre,** Greyfriars St. (tel. 871227), off The Quay, displays a wealth of Viking artifacts snatched from the jaws of bulldozers. *(Open July-Aug. M-F 9am-8:30pm, Sa-Su 9am-5pm;*

Mar.-June and Sept.-Oct. M-F 10am-5pm, Sa 2-5pm. £1.50, students £1, children 50p, 25% off with walking-tour ticket.)

Many of Waterford's more recent monumental edifices were the brainchildren of 18th-century architect John Roberts. The **Theatre Royal** and **City Hall,** both on The Mall, are his secular masterpieces. He also designed both the Roman Catholic **Holy Trinity Cathedral** on Barronstrand St. and the Church of Ireland **Christ Church Cathedral** in Cathedral Square up Henrietta St. from the Quay, making Waterford the only Irish town to have the faiths united by a common architect.

■ Kilkenny City

As as the money rolls in, Kilkenny, already touted as the best-preserved medieval town in Ireland, has launched a historical preservation campaign to draw more visitors. Visitors find both excitement and history in Kilkenny, where ancient architecture houses rocking nightlife and nine churches share the streets with 78 pubs.

ORIENTATION AND PRACTICAL INFORMATION

From McDonagh Station, turn left on John St. and continue straight to reach The Parade, dominated by the castle. Most activity takes place in the triangle formed by Rose Inn, High, and Kieran St. Hitchhikers take N10 to Waterford, Freshford Rd. to N8 toward Cashel, and N16 toward Dublin.

Trains: McDonagh Station, Dublin Rd. (tel. 22024). Open M-Sa 8am-8pm, Su 10am-noon, 3-5pm, and 6:30-8:30pm. Kilkenny is on the main Dublin-Waterford rail route (M-Sa 4 per day, Su 3 per day). To **Dublin** (2hr., £10) and **Waterford** (45min., £5.50). Connections to western Ireland at the Kildare station 1hr. north.

Buses: McDonagh Station, Dublin Rd. (tel. 64933), and on Patrick St. in the city center. Buses leave for **Cork** (3hr., 3 per day), **Dublin** (M-Sa 5 per day, Su 4 per day), **Galway** (daily mid-June to mid-Sept.), **Rosslare Harbour** (daily mid-June to mid-Sept.), and **Waterford** (5 per day).

Tourist Office: Rose Inn St. (tel. 51500; fax 63955). Open June-Sept. M-Sa 9am-6pm, Su 11am-5pm; Oct.-May M-F 10am-5:30pm, Sa 10am-2pm.

Banks: AIB, The Parade (tel. 22089), at the intersection with High St. Open M 10am-5pm, Tu-F 10am-4pm; 24hr. **ATM.**

Bike Rental: J.J. Wall Cycle, Maudlin St. (tel. 21236). £7 per sentimental day, £30 per effusive week; tear-jerking deposit £30. Open M-Sa 9am-5:30pm.

Laundry: Brett's Launderette, Michael St. (tel. 63200). Wash and dry £6. Open M-Sa 8:30am-8pm; last wash 7pm.

Pharmacy: Several on High St. All open M-Sa 9am-6pm; Sunday rotation system.

Emergency: Dial 999; no coins required.

Police/Garda: Dominic St. (tel. 22222).

Hospital: St. Luke's, Freshford Rd. (tel. 21133). Continue down Parliament St. to St. Canice's Cathedral, then turn right and take the first left to Vicars St. and then another left on Gowran Rd. The hospital is down and on the right.

Post Office: High St. (tel. 21879). Open M-Sa 9am-5:30pm.

Telephone Code: Oh my god, 056 killed Kenny! You bastards!

ACCOMMODATIONS

B&Bs average £17; call ahead in summer, especially on weekends. Waterford Rd. and more remote Castlecomer Rd. have the highest concentration of beds.

Kilkenny Town Hostel (IHH), 35 Parliament St. (tel. 63541). Directly across from popular pubs and next to the brewery. Clean, light, and bare rooms. Friendly, non-smoking environment. 6- to 8-bed dorms £8; doubles £18. 50p discount to *Let's Go* users Sept.-June. Check-out 10:30am. Laundry £3.

Ormonde Tourist Hostel, Johns Green (tel. 52733), opposite the train station. This enormous hostel is a 10-15min. walk from the best nightlife and attractions. Dorms around £8.50; doubles £22. Laundry £4. Check out 10:30am. Curfew 3am.

Bregagh House B&B, Dean St. (tel. 22315). Handsome wood furniture, floral comforters and pristine rooms. Singles £20-25; doubles with bath £36; Nov.-May £34.

Daly's B&B, 82 Johns St. (tel. 62866). Quiet, plain, tidy rooms. £17. Breakfast £2.

Fennelly's B&B, 13 Parliament St. (tel. 61796). Large, orderly rooms and an ideal location. Singles £22; doubles £32, with bath £36.

Camping: Nore Valley Park (tel. 27229), 6mi. south of Kilkenny between Bennetsbridge and Stonyford, signposted from Kilkenny. 2-person tent £5. Open Mar.-Oct.

FOOD AND PUBS

The biggest grocery selection is at the mothership **Superquinn** (tel. 52444), in the Market Cross shopping center off High St. (open M-W and Sa 9am-6pm, Th-F 9am-9pm). **Butterslip Restaurant,** Butterslip Ln., between Kieran and High St., cooks fresh food to order at great prices with daily specials. **Edward Langton's,** 69 John St. (tel. 65133), was voted the country's best pub food 3 times and perpetually expanding (lunch £4-6, served daily noon-3pm). **Lautrec's Wine Bar,** 9 St. Kieran St. (tel. 62720), serves Tex-Mex and other cuisines as well as wine even after pubs have closed (open M-Th 5:30pm-midnight, F-Sa 5:30pm-1am).

Matt the Miller's, John St., is across the river half a block before the rail station. Huge, thronged, and friendly, it'll suck you in and force you to dance to silly Euro pop. **Caisleán Uí Cuain** (cash-LAWN ee COO-an), 2 High St. (tel. 65406), at The Parade, plays music Monday nights and Sunday afternoons as a local crowd settles in. **Pump House Bar,** 26 Parliament St. (tel. 63924), is loud, easy to find, and always packed (live rock M-Th). **Cleere's Pub,** 28 Parliament St. (tel. 62573), hosts thespians from the theater across the street (trad Mondays). At **Kyteler's Inn,** St. Kieran St. (tel 21064), mixed ages gather for food and craic in a relaxed atmosphere (late night Th-Su), transfer yourself next door to **Nero's,** a nightclub that's burning down the house (cover £5; open 11:30pm-2am). **Maggie's,** St. Kieran St. (tel. 62273), is busy, with an older group than Pump House or Cleere's (trad Tu, live contemporary W).

SIGHTS

All of central Kilkenny is a sight, since most of the buildings have preserved their medieval good looks. **Tynan Walking Tours** (tel. 65929) offers a brief introduction, departing from the tourist office on Rose Inn St. *(Tours mid-Mar. to Oct. M-Sa 6 per day, Su 4 per day; Nov.-Feb. Tu-Sa 3 per day. 1-1½hr. £3, students and seniors £2.)* Thirteenth-century **Kilkenny Castle,** The Parade (tel. 21450), housed the Earls of Ormonde from the 1300s until 1932. Many rooms have been restored to their former opulence. *(Castle and gallery open June-Sept. daily 10am-7pm; Oct.-Mar. Tu-Sa 10:30am-5pm, Su 11am-5pm; Apr.-May daily 10:30am-5pm. Access by guided tour only. £3, students £1.50.)* The formal **flower garden** and park adjoining the castle are beautifully maintained. *(Open daily 10am-8:30pm. Free.)* The internationally known **Kilkenny Design Centre** (tel. 22118) fills the castle's old stables with fine but expensive Irish crafts. *(Open Apr.-Dec. M-Sa 9am-6pm, Su 10am-6pm; Jan.-Mar. M-Sa 9am-6pm.)*

Kilkenny is well endowed with religious architecture. The finest example is 13th-century **St. Canice's Cathedral** on Dean St. The stone-step approach from Inishtown is lined with fragments of old sculpture from the cathedral itself, which was sacked by Cromwell's merry men(aces). For an additional £1, you can climb the series of six steep ladders inside for a panoramic view of the town and its surroundings. *(Open daily 10am-6pm, except during services. Donation requested.)* The **Black Abbey,** off Abbey St., was founded in 1225 and got its name from the black habits of its Dominican friars. Nearby **St. Mary's** stands testament to the incredible religious faith of the Irish people, who built the cathedral in 1849 during the darkest of the Famine days. It is rumored that crafty 14th-century monks brewed a light ale in **St. Francis' Abbey** on Parliament St.; the abbey is in ruins but its industry survives in the abbey's yard at the **Smithwicks Brewery.** *(Tours July-Aug. M-F 3pm. Tickets free at the tourist office.)* Smithwicks Brewery offers an audio-visual show and ale tasting. Smithwicks itself, called Kilkenny in Ireland, is a tasty brew naturally best in Kilkenny and easier on the palate than Guinness, but the company profanes the abbey by brewing Budweiser there.

■ Cashel

The town of Cashel lies inland, halfway between Limerick and Waterford, tucked behind a series of mountain ranges on N8 from Cork to Dublin. The **Rock of Cashel** (also called **St. Patrick's Rock**) is a huge limestone outcropping topped by a stunning complex of medieval buildings. The one-hour tour explains the legends in detail but threatens the magical potential of the Rock through its dearth of humor and excess of self-importance. On the Rock stands the two-towered **Cormac's Chapel,** consecrated in 1134. The 13th-century **Cashel Cathedral** survived the Earl and remains unequalled in its grandeur, whether because of or despite the fact that its vaulted Gothic arches no longer buttress a roof. *(Rock open daily mid-June to mid-Sept. 9am-7:30pm; mid-Sept. to mid-Mar. 9:30am-4:30pm; mid-Mar. to mid-June 9:30am-5:30pm. Last admission 45min. before closing. £3, students £1.25.)* Far from the madding crowd and down the cow path from the Rock, the ruins of **Hore Abbey,** the last Cistercian monastery established in Ireland, put out a striking view of the Rock. *(Always open. Free.)* The small but brilliantly executed **Heritage Centre,** Main St. (tel. 35362), features permanent and temporary exhibitions. *(Open July-Aug. daily 9:30am-8pm; Sept.-Feb. M-Sa 9:30am-5:30pm, Su noon-5:30pm; Mar.-June daily 9:30am-5:30pm. £1, students 50p.)*

Bus Éireann (tel. 62121) leaves from Bianconi's Bistro on Main St., serving **Dublin** (3hr., 4 per day, £9), **Cork** (1½hr., 4 per day, £8) and **Limerick** (4 per day, £8.80). Bus transport to **Waterford** is available via Cahir (15min., 4 per day, £2.40). Cashel's efficient **tourist office** (tel. 62511) is in the recently renovated Cashel City Hall, Main St. (open daily May-Sept. 9am-8pm; Oct.-Apr. 9:30am-5:30pm). **AIB,** Main St., has a **bureau de change** and an **ATM** (open M-W and F 10am-12:30pm and 1:30-4pm, Th 10am-12:30pm and 1:30-5pm.) The **post office** (tel. 61418) is also on Main St. (open M and W-F 9am-1pm and 2-5:30pm, Tu 9:30am-1pm and 2-5:30pm, Sa 9am-1pm). The **telephone code** rocks the Cashel at 062.

Cashel is graced with two excellent hostels. The plush **Cashel Holiday Hostel (IHH),** 6 John St. (tel. 62330; email cashel@iol.ie), just off Main St., has spacious bedrooms. (4- to 8-bed dorms £7; 4-bed dorms with bath £8; private rooms £10 per person. Laundry £3.50. Key deposit £3. Internet access £2.50.) **O'Brien's Farmhouse Hostel** (tel. 61003), a five-minute walk from Cashel on Dundrum Rd., has spotless rooms, fluffy beds, and a great view. (6-bed dorm £8; private room from £10 per person. **Camping** £4 per person. Laundry £5.) The high quality (and high price) of local B&Bs reflect the number of tourists drawn to the Rock. **The Bake House** (tel. 61680), by the Heritage Centre on Main St., is the town's best spot for scones, coffee, and light meals (open M-Sa 8am-9pm, Su 10am-7pm). Good craic and nightly music entice locals to the most popular pub in Cashel, **Feehan's,** Main St. (tel. 61929; trad 3 nights a week). The bartenders at the staid and well-appointed **Dowling's,** 46 Main St. (tel. 62130), make it their business to pour the best pint in town.

COS. CORK AND KERRY

■ Cork City

As Ireland's second largest city, Cork (pop. 146,000) is the center of the southwest's sports, music, and arts. Unfortunately for the visitor, behind every cultural site is its ugly but dependable twin, commerce.

ORIENTATION AND PRACTICAL INFORMATION

Downtown Cork is the tip of an arrow-shaped island in the River Lee. Downtown action concentrates on **Oliver Plunkett, Saint Patrick, and Paul St.,** and the north-south streets that connect them. City buses crisscross the city and its suburbs. From downtown, catch the buses (and their schedules) at the bus station on Merchant's Quay or on St. Patrick St., across from the Father Matthew statue.

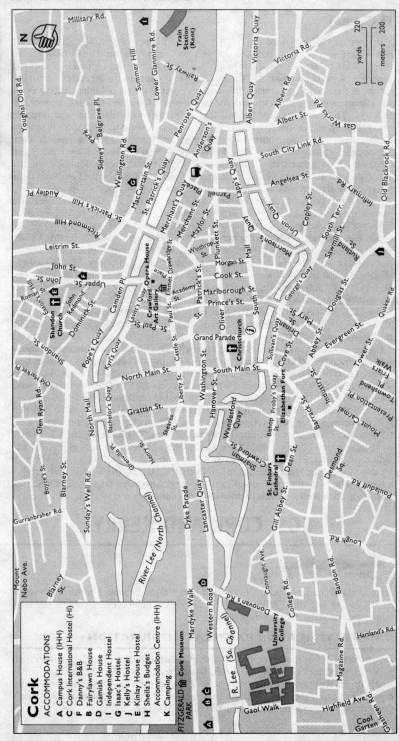

Cork

ACCOMMODATIONS

A Campus House (IHH)
C Cork International Hostel (HI)
F Danny's B&B
B Fairylawn House
D Gamish House
I Independent Hostel
G Isaac's Hostel
J Kelly's Hostel
H Kinlay House Hostel
E Sheila's Budget
   Accommodation Centre (IHH)
K Camping

Transportation

Airplanes: Cork Airport (tel. 313131), 5mi. south of Cork on Kinsale Rd. **Aer Lingus** (tel. 327155), **Manx Airlines** (tel. (01) 260158), **British Airways** (tel. (800) 626747), and **Ryanair** (tel. 313091) connect Cork to Dublin, the Isle of Man, various English cities, and Paris. A taxi (£5-6) or bus (18 per day, £2.50) will deliver you from the airport to the bus station on Parnell Pl. in Cork City.

Trains: Kent Station, Lower Glanmire Rd. (tel. 506766), across the river from the city center in the northeast part of town. Open M-Sa 7am-8:30pm, Su 7am-8pm. Lockers £1. Trains to **Dublin** (3hr., M-Sa 9 per day, Su 6 per day, £32), **Limerick** (1½hr., M-Sa 8 per day, Su 4 per day, £15.50), **Killarney** (2hr., M-Sa 5 per day, Su 3 per day, £13.50), and **Tralee** (2½hr., M-Sa 5 per day, Su 3 per day, £18).

Buses: Parnell Pl. (tel. 508188), 2 blocks east of Patrick's Bridge on Merchants' Quay. Inquiries desk open Apr.-Sept. M-F 9am-6pm, Su 9am-5pm; Oct.-Mar. M-F 9am-6pm. **Luggage storage** 80p-£1.30. Open M-F 8:35am-6:15pm, Sa 9:30am-6:15pm. Bus Éireann goes to **Bantry** (2hr., M-Sa 3 per day, Su 2 per day, £8.80), **Galway** (4hr., M-Sa 5 per day, Su 4 per day, £12), **Killarney** (2hr., M-Sa 7 per day, Su 5 per day, £8.80), **Limerick** (2hr., M-Sa 6 per day, Su 5 per day, £9), **Rosslare Harbour** (4hr., M-Sa 3 per day, Su 2 per day, £13), **Tralee** (2½hr., M-Sa 7 per day, Su 5 per day, £9.70), **Waterford** (2¼hr., M-Sa 6 per day, Su 5 per day, £8), **Dublin** (4½hr., M-Sa 4 per day, Su 3 per day, £12), **Belfast** (7½hr., M-Sa 2 per day, Su 1 per day, £17), **Sligo** (7hr., 3 per day, £16), and **Donegal Town** (9hr., 1 per day, £17).

Ferries: 24hr. info (tel. (01) 661 0715). Ferries to England dock at **Ringaskiddy Terminal** (tel. 378111), 9mi. south of the city. The 30min. bus ride from the terminal to the bus station in Cork costs £3.

Local Transportation: Downtown **buses** run every 20-40min. (reduced service Su), from about 7:30am-11:30pm. Fares from 70p. Bus Éireann Kiosk, Patrick St., near the bridge (open M-Sa 7:30am-11:15pm, Su 9:30am-11:15pm).

Car Rental: Great Island Car Rentals, 47 MacCurtain St. (tel. 503536). £40 per day, £90 for 3 days, £160 per week for subcompact standard. Min. age 23. **Budget Rent-a-Car,** Tourist Office, Grand Parade (tel. 274755). £39 per day, £175 per week. Min. age 21.

Bike Rental: Irish Cycle Hire (tel. 551430) rents hybrids and mountain bikes at £6 per day, £30 per week; deposit £30. One-way rental system (tel. (800) 298100) to Irish Cycle Hire depots in Killarney, Dingle, Ennis, and others.

Tourist and Financial Services

Tourist Office: Tourist House, Grand Parade (tel. 273251), near the corner of South Mall and Grand Parade downtown. Offers a Cork city guide and map (£1.50), booking, car rentals, and advice. The office runs an open-top bus tour of the city (£7, students £6). Open in summer M-Sa 9am-6pm; in winter M-Sa 9:30am-5pm.

Budget Travel: USIT, 10 Market Parade (tel. 270900), in the Arcade off Patrick St. Large, helpful travel office sells **TravelSave** stamps, Rambler tickets, and Eurotrain tickets. Open M-F 9:30am-5:30pm, Sa 10am-2pm.

Banks: TSB, 4-5 Princes St. (tel. 275221). Open M-W and F 9:30am-5pm, Th 9:30am-7pm. **Bank of Ireland,** 70 Patrick St. (tel. 277177). Open M 10am-5pm, Tu-F 10am-4pm. 24hr. **ATM.**

Local Services

Launderette: Duds 'n' Suds, Douglas St. (tel. 314799), around the corner from Kelly's Hostel. Provides dry-cleaning services, TV, and even a small cafe. Wash £1.50, dry £1.80. Open M-F 8am-9pm, Sa 8am-8pm. **College Launderette,** Western Rd. by the university. Large load, full service £5.20. Open M-F 8am-5:30pm, Sa 10am-5pm.

Gay, Lesbian, and Bisexual Information: The Other Place, 8 South Main St. (tel. 278470), is a resource center for gay and lesbian concerns in Cork and hosts a gay mixed disco (F and Sa 11pm-2am) and a gay coffeehouse (open M-Sa 10am-6pm). **Gay Information Cork** (tel. 271087). Helpline W 7-9pm and Sa 3-5pm. Lesbian line Th 8-10pm.

Emergency and Communications

Emergency: Dial 999; no coins required.

Police/Garda: Anglesea St. (tel. 313031).

Hotlines: Samaritans (tel. 271323) offers a 24hr. support line for depression. **AIDS Hotline,** Cork AIDS Alliance, 16 Peter St. (tel. 276676). Open M-F 10am-5pm. **Rape Crisis Centre,** 5 Camden Pl. (tel. (800) 496496). 24hr. counseling.

Hospital: Mercy Hospital, Grenville Pl. (tel. 271971). £20 fee for access to emergency room. **Cork Regional Hospital,** Wilton St. (tel. 546400), on bus #8.

Post Office: Oliver Plunkett St. (tel. 272000). Open M-Sa 9am-1pm and 2-5:30pm.

Internet Access: Cyberstation (tel. 273000), at Jumpin' Jacks Pub on unmarked Sheare St., one block west of Liberty St. £1.40 per 15min., £5.60 per hr. Open M-F 10am-8pm, Sa 10am-9pm, Su 4pm-9pm.

Telephone Code: is all grown up at 021.

ACCOMMODATIONS

Cork's eight hostels range from the drearily adequate to the brilliantly beautiful. B&Bs are clustered along Western Rd. near University College and across the Lee on Mac-Curtain St. and Lower Glanmire Rd., near the bus and train stations.

⊛**The Cork City Independent Hostel,** 100 Lower Glanmire Rd. (tel. 509089). From the train station, turn right and walk 100yd. A multicolored interior gives this place the most character of any hostel in Cork. Dorms £6; doubles £17. Laundry £3.50.

Sheila's Budget Accommodation Centre (IHH), 3 Belgrave Pl. (tel. 505562), by the intersection of Wellington Rd. and York St. Positively packed with perks (and generally packed tight). Sauna, anyone? 6-bed dorms £6.50; 4-bed dorms £8; singles £18; doubles £20. Rooms available with bath. Free luggage storage. Sheets 50p. Key deposit £5. 24hr. reception. Check-out 10:30am.

Kinlay House (IHH), Bob and Joan Walk (tel. 508966), down the alley to the right of Shandon Church. Located in less-than-luxurious but convenient Shandon, Kinlay House is large, welcoming, and clean. Dorms £7.50; singles £11; doubles £25. ISIC discount. Continental breakfast included. Internet access £5 per hr.

Cork International Hostel (An Óige/HI), 1-2 Redclyffe, Western Rd. (tel. 543289), a 15min. walk from the Grand Parade, or take bus #8. Immaculate bunkrooms in a stately Victorian townhouse. Dorms £8.50; doubles £12.50. All rooms with bath. Continental breakfast £2. Check-in 8am-midnight. **Bikes** £5 per day, £30 per week.

Isaac's (IHH), 48 MacCurtain St. (tel. 500011). Second right off Patrick St. after the North Channel. Conveniently located near the bus and train stations. 9- to 16-bed dorms £7; 4- to 8-bed dorms £8.50. Continental breakfast £1.75, Irish £2.50. 24hr. reception. Dorm lockout 11am-5pm.

Garnish House, Western Rd. (tel. 275111). Prepare to be pampered. Singles from £20; doubles from £40, with jacuzzi (!) from £50. Free laundry service.

Bienvenue Ferry Camping (tel. 312711), near the airport, 5mi. south of town on Kinsale Rd. Airport buses (18 per day) will take you there from the bus station. Tent £5 plus £1 per person. Open year-round.

FOOD

The **English Market,** accessible from Grand Parade, Patrick St., and Prince St., hops with fresh fruit, meat, fish, and cheese (open M-Sa 9am-5pm; W and Sa are the best days to visit). **Tesco,** Paul St. (tel. 270791), is the biggest grocery store in town (open M-W and Sa 9am-6pm, Th-F 9am-9pm).

⊛**The Gingerbread House,** Paul St. (tel. 276411). Huge windows, cool jazz, and heavenly breads, pastries, and quiche. Open in summer M-Th 8am-10:30pm, F-Sa 8am-11pm, Su 8am-6pm; in winter M-Th 8am-9:30pm, F-Sa 8am-10:30pm, Su 8am-6pm.

Kafka's, 7 Maylor St. (tel. 270551). After one taste of these cheap dishes, you'll undergo a metamorphosis. Sandwiches £3-4. Open M-Sa 8am-6pm. Breakfast served 8am-noon.

Polo's Gourmet Café, Washington St. (tel. 277099). Innovative Irish foods, great breakfasts, and coffee to keep you buzzing. Open M-W 8am-1am, Th-Su 9am-4am.

Scoozi, Winthrop Ave. (tel. 275077). Follow the tomato signs to this airy brick-and-wood lined establishment. Most entrees £6. Open M-Sa 9am-11pm, Su 4-10pm.

Quay Co-op, 24 Sullivan's Quay (tel. 317660). A cow's delight: nary a creature was sacrificed for the scrumptious vegetarian delights served in this classy establishment. Open M-Sa 7-10:30pm; M-Sa 9am-9pm for take-away.

PUBS

Cork's pubs have all the variety of music and atmosphere you'd expect to find in Ireland's second-largest city. Cork is the proud home of **Murphy's,** a thick, sweet stout that sometimes, and especially in Cork, tastes as good as Guinness. **Beamish,** a cheaper stout, is also brewed here.

An Spailpín Fánach, 28 S. Main St. (tel. 277949). One of Cork's most popular pubs and probably the oldest (it opened in 1779). Live music (Su-F) ranges from bluegrass to traditional. Pub grub (Irish stew £3.75) served M-F noon-3pm.

The Lobby, 1 Union Quay (tel. 311113). The Lobby has given some of Ireland's biggest folk acts their start. Live music nightly at 9:30pm, ranging from trad to acid jazz. Occasional cover £4-5.

Charlie's, Union Quay (tel. 965272). Art by local student artists decks the walls of the smallest of the Quay pubs. Live music ranging from acoustic blues to rock/pop nightly in summer, 3-4 times per week during the rest of the year.

The Old Oak, Oliver Plunkett St. (tel. 276165). The hardwood floors and stained-glass cathedral ceilings strain to contain the huge mixed crowd that files in here nightly. Live music 3-4 times per week.

Loafer's, 26 Douglas St. (tel. 311612). Cork's sole gay and lesbian pub is jam-packed nightly by people of all ages. Good conversation makes this bar a cozy spot.

SIGHTS

Cork has a smattering of sights that can be reached easily by foot. For guidance, pick up *The Cork Area City Guide* at the tourist office (£1.50). A good beginning is the center of the old city—Christ Church Ln. off Grand Parade, just north of Bishop Lucey Park. Steeple-less **Christ Church** is an emblem of the persistence of Catholicism in Cork: it has been burned to the ground three times since its 1270 consecration but rebuilt each time. Crossing South Gate Bridge, turn right onto Proby's Quay and then left onto obscure Keyser Hill. At the top of the stairs is **Elizabethan Fort,** a star-shaped, ivy-covered remnant of English rule. *(Always open. Free.)* Farther down Proby's Quay, **St. Finbarr's Cathedral,** Bishop St. (tel. 963387), testifies to Victorians' love of bombast. *(Open daily Apr.-Sept. 10am-5:30pm; Oct.-Mar. 10am-1pm and 2-5pm.)*

On the other side of the Lee, N. Main St. becomes Shandon St., heart of the **Shandon** neighborhood. It's less affluent than the rest of Cork and has more neighborhood pride. **St. Anne's Church** (tel. 505906) is Cork's most famous landmark. *(Open in summer M-Sa 10am-5pm; in winter M-Sa 10am-4pm.)* Most people call it **Shandon Church,** since the steeple is Shandon Tower. Four clocks grace the four sides of the tower. Notoriously out of sync with each other, the clocks have been held responsible for many an Irishman's tardy arrival at work and have earned the church its endearing nickname, "the four-faced liar."

West of the river, **University College Cork (UCC),** built in 1845, is on Western Rd. Gothic windows, grassy expanses, and long, stony corridors make for a secluded afternoon walk or picnic along the Lee. *(Campus always open for self-guided touring. Tours by prior arrangement £15 for group.)* Across the street from the college entrance, signs point to the **Cork Public Museum** (tel. 270679), set in the splendid gardens of **Fitzgerald Park.** *(Open June-July M-Sa 8:30am-10pm, Su 10am-10pm; May-Aug. M-Sa 8:30am-9pm; Apr. and Sept. M-Sa 8:30am-8pm; Oct.-Mar. M-Sa 8:30am-5pm. M-Sa free, Su 75p, students free.)* If time's tight in Cork, you might go directly to the **Cork City Gaol.** The museum is a reconstruction of the jail as it appeared in the 1800s. It's an easy walk from Fitzgerald Park; cross the footbridge at the western end of the park, turn right on Sunday's Well Rd., and then follow the signs. A tour of the jail tells the story of individual Cork prisoners and the often miserable treatment they endured. *(Open in* *summer daily 9:30am-6pm; in winter M-F 10:30am-2:30pm, Sa-Su 10am-4pm. £3.50, students and seniors £2.50, children £2, families £9. Last tour 1hr. before closing.)*

Blarney Castle (tel. 385252) and its **Blarney Stone** are a pilgrimage site for those seeking mastery of smooth-talking b.s. You might consider kissing a scone instead (tastier, less saliva exchange with German tourists, etc.), but the castle is impressive. *(Open June-Aug. 9am-7pm, Su 9:30am-5:30pm; Sept. M-Sa 9am-6:30pm, Su 9:30am-sundown; Oct.-Apr. M-Sa 9am-sundown, Su 9:30am-sundown; May M-Sa 9am-6:30pm, Su 9:30am-5:30pm. £3, students and seniors £2, children £1.)* **Bus Éireann** runs from **Cork** to Blarney (M-Sa 16 per day, Su 10 per day, return £2.60). Blarney is a short bike ride from Cork.

ENTERTAINMENT

Cork's nightlife is rocking, but fashions and hip bands change nightly. Check out *List Cork,* a free weekly schedule of music available at local stores. The **Lobby** and **Charlie's Bar** (see **Pubs**) are consistently sound choices for live music. **Nancy Spain's,** 48 Barrack St. (tel. 314452), is one of the city's most popular venues, often featuring live rock and blues. *(DJ Th-Sa, nightclub upstairs. Call for live music schedule. Cover £3-8.)* Dance wildly at **Club FX** and **The Grapevine,** Gravel Ln. (tel. 271120). From Washington St., make a right on Little Hangover St. and then a left onto Gravel Ln. *(Cover £3-6. Open W-Su 10:30pm-2am.)* **Sir Henry's,** S. Main St. (tel. 274391), is arguably the most popular club in Cork and also the most intense. *(Cover £2-11. Raging techno and house W-Sa.)* **The Other Place,** S. Main St. (tel. 278470), Cork's gay and lesbian disco, rocks every Friday and Saturday 11:30pm to 2am. **The Half Moon Club** (tel. 274308), tucked behind the Opera House on Half Moon St., delights with jazz, blues, and trad (Th-Sa). **An Sráidbhaile** (uhn SRAIJ-why-luh), Grand Parade (tel. 274391), jams with traditional Irish set dancing. (Cover £4. June-Sept. 9:30pm-midnight.)

Cork is sporting mad. Be cautious when venturing into the streets on game days (especially during championships), where screaming, jubilant fans will either bowl you down or, worse, force you to take part in the revelry. For information on hurling or Gaelic football matches, call the GAA (tel. 385876) or consult *The Cork Examiner.*

■ Cape Clear Island

Before the Famine, Cape Clear Island (Oileán Chléire) supported a completely self-sufficient population of 1200. Today, the population stands at approximately 150. During the summer, however, the island's population nearly quadruples with students who come here to brush up on their Irish, the island's native tongue. About a 25-minute walk up a steep hill from the pier is the island's **Heritage Centre,** half a room containing everything from an O'Driscoll family tree to a deck chair from the equally ubiquitous *Lusitania. (Open June-Aug. daily 2-5:30pm. £1.50, students £1, under 18 50p.)* On the road to the center, **Cleire Goats** (tel. 39126) sells goat's milk ice cream (65p). A right turn past the heritage center leads to the **windmills** that until recently generated three-quarters of the island's electricity. Cape Clear also shelters gulls, stormy petrels, cormorants, and ornithologists. The **bird observatory,** the white farmhouse on North Harbour, is one of the most important in Europe.

Cléire Lasmuigh (An Óige/HI; tel. 39144), the Cape Clear Island Adventure Centre and Hostel, is about a 10-minute walk from the pier (keep left on the main road). The hostel resides in a drafty but picturesque stone building only steps from the south harbor. (June-Sept. £7; Apr. and Sept.-Oct. £6; sheets 60p.) The hospitable **Cluain Mara B&B** (tel. 39153) is adjacent to the pub (£15, with bath £16; self-catering apartment across the road £25). The island's **campsite** (tel. 39136), on the south harbor, is a five-minute walk from the harbor and has breathtaking views: go up the main road, turn right at the yellow general store, then bear left (£2.70 per person, under 15 £1.50; open June-Sept.). What the Cape Clear pub scene lacks in variety it makes up for in stamina. The island has no resident authorities to regulate after-hours drinking, and if any have the impudence to sail over from the mainland, their lights give publicans plenty of time to close up shop. **The Night Jar** (tel. 39102) opens at noon and is liveliest in the afternoon and early evening, while **Club Chléire** (tel. 39184), above the cafe, has live sessions most weekend nights, often lasting until 4am or later.

Ferries run to and from the tiny fishing village of Baltimore (July-Aug. M-Sa 3 per day, Su 4 per day; June and Sept. 2 per day; Oct.-Apr. M-Th and Sa-Su 1 per day, F 2 per day; May M-F 2 per day, Sa-Su 1 per day; return £8). Call Capt. Conchúr O'Driscoll (tel. 39135) for more information.

■ Beara Peninsula

Untold numbers of visitors traveling up and down Ireland's southwest coast skip the Beara altogether. This region has a more wild and romantic majesty than the Ring of Kerry and a more profound sense of tranquility. For unspoiled scenery and solitude, the Beara is superb; if you're looking for pubs and people, head elsewhere.

■ Bantry

According to the *Book of Invasions,* the first human beings landed in Ireland just a mile from Bantry. The town still serves as a gateway to Sheep's Head to the west and the Beara Peninsula to the northwest. Impressive **Bantry House** (tel. 50047), a Georgian manor with an imposing garden overlooking Bantry Bay, is worth a visit. *(Open mid-Mar. to Oct. daily 9am-6pm. House and garden £5.50, students £4. Garden £1.50.)* Next door is the **1796 Bantry French Armada Exhibition Centre** (tel. 51796), which focuses on Theobald Wolfe Tone's attempts to foment an Irish revolution. *(Open Mar.-Nov. daily 10am-6pm. £3, students £1.75.)*

The **tourist office** (tel. 50229) is at Wolfe Tone Sq. (open M-Sa June-Sept. 9am-7pm; Oct.-May 9am-6pm). **Buses** stop outside of Lynch's in Wolfe Tone Sq., several doors from the tourist office toward the pier. **Bus Éireann** heads to **Cork** and **Bandon** (M-Sa 3-5 per day, Su 2-4 per day, £8.80) and **Glengarriff** (M-Sa 3 per day, Su 2 per day, £2.25). From June through September, buses go **Killarney** via **Kenmare** (2 per day). **Kramer's,** Glengarriff Rd., Newtown (tel. 50278), rents **bikes** (£7 per day, £42 per week; open M-Sa 9am-6pm).

Bantry Independent Hostel (IHH), Bishop Lucey Pl. (tel. 51050), not to be confused with the "small independent hostel" on the square, has adequate bunks and a pretty common room. Head away from town on Glengarriff Rd. (Marino St.), take the left fork, and walk a quarter mile. (6-bed dorms £6.50; private rooms £9 per person. Open mid-Mar. to Oct.) **O'Siochain,** Bridge St. (tel. 51339), serves well-prepared food in a comfy, if kitschy, coffeehouse (sandwiches £1.50; open daily 9am-10pm). **The Wolfe Tone,** Wolfe Tone Sq. (tel. 50900), has music (in summer Tu and Th-Su) and cooks excellent pub grub (sandwiches £1.30-4). **SuperValu** sells its stuff on New St. (open M-Th 8:30am-6:30pm, F 8:30am-9pm, Sa 8:30am-6:30pm). Bantry nightlife has kicked into overdrive thanks to **1796** (The Bantry Folk Club; tel. 52396), Wolfe Tone Sq. (food served noon-9pm).

■ Castletownbere

The largest town on the Beara Peninsula reverberates with the sounds of ferry engines, cars, and wind over the world's second-largest natural harbor, Berehaven Bay. Two miles southwest of Castletownbere on Allihies Rd., **Dunboy Castle** shelters two separate ruins. Cows roam the crumbling Gothic-style halls of its 18th- and 19th-century mansion. Three quarters of a mile past the gate stand the ruins of the 14th-century **O'Sullivan Bere** fortress (50p). The summer culminates with the regatta at the **Festival of the Sea** during the first weekend in August. In winter the town reverts to its true calling—plucking the fruits of the sea.

Bus Éireann runs a summer service between Castletownbere and **Killarney via Kenmare** (June 26-Sept. 2 M-Sa 2 per day, £8.80). **Berehaven Bus Service** (tel. 70007) goes from the parking lot next to O'Donoghue's to **Bantry via Glengarriff** (M 2 per day, Tu-Sa 1 per day; Glengarriff 45min., £2.70; Bantry 1½hr., £4) and to **Cork**

(3hr., Th only, £8). The bathroom-sized **tourist office** (tel. 70054), by the harbor, gives away maps (open June-Sept. M-Sa 10:30am-5pm). The **phone code** is 027.

Two miles west of town on Allihies Rd., the **Beara Hostel** (tel. 70184) has a pleasantly rural location and adequate rustic rooms (dorms £7; private rooms £8 per person; **camping** £3.50 per person). **Castletown House,** Main St. (tel. 70252), offers lovely rooms and lots of info (£15, with bath £17). **The Old Bakery,** Main St. (tel. 70901), has an extensive menu of sandwiches and pasta (£4-6; live trad and jazz most Saturday nights; open daily 9am-7pm). **SuperValu,** Main St. (tel. 70020), sells foodstuffs (open M-Sa 9am-9pm, Su 9am-6pm). **MacCarthy's,** Main St. (tel. 70014), the most popular pub in town and a well-stocked grocery, serves food all day (all sandwiches under £2) and belts out live trad and ballads on the weekends.

▓ Killarney

With something for everyone, Killarney seems to have just about everyone at once. And with an economy based on tourism, Killarney sometimes celebrates tourism itself rather than its extraordinarily beautiful national park or well-preserved heritage.

ORIENTATION AND PRACTICAL INFORMATION

Killarney packs into three crowded major streets. **Main St.,** in the center of town, begins at the Town Hall then becomes High St. **New** and **Plunkett St.** both intersect Main St. New St. heads west to the Knockreer Estate toward Killorglin. Plunkett St. becomes College St. and then Park Rd. on its way east to the bus and train stations. **East Avenue Rd.** connects the train station back to town hall and then bends, becoming Muckross Rd. on its way to the Muckross Estate and Kenmare.

Trains: Killarney Station (tel. 31067), off East Avenue Rd. near the intersection with Park Rd., past the Great Southern Hotel. Open M-Sa 7:30am-12:30pm and 2-6:20pm, Su 30min. before train departures. Trains run until 6:20pm to **Cork** (1½hr., 5 per day, £13.50), **Dublin** (3½hr., 4 per day, £33.50), **Galway** (6hr., 3 per day, £30), and **Limerick** (2hr., M-Sa 4 per day, Su 3 per day, £15).

Buses: (tel. 34777), off East Avenue Rd., across from the Great Southern Hotel. Open M-Sa 8:30am-5:45pm. Buses rumble to **Cork** (2hr., 6-7 per day, £8.80), **Dingle** (2hr., 3-6 per day, £8.80), **Dublin** (6hr., 3-4 per day, £14), **Galway** (7hr., 5-7 per day, £13), **Limerick** (2hr., 4-5 per day, £9.30), and **Sligo** (7½hr., 2-3 per day, £17). Buses leave daily June-Sept. for the **Ring of Kerry Circuit.** £8 if booked at a hostel; return with 1-night stop £12 for students. **Bus Éireann** also runs a no-frills Ring of Kerry circuit in the summer (2 per day).

Bike Rental: Crafts and Curios Rent-a-Bike, Bishop's Ln. (tel. 31282), next to Neptune's Hostel. £6 per day, £30 per week. Open M-Sa 9am-7pm, Su 9am-6:30pm.

Tourist Office: Beach St. (tel. 31633), off New St. Exceptionally helpful and deservedly popular. Open July-Aug. M-Sa 9am-8pm, Su 9am-1pm and 2:15-6pm; June and Sept. M-Sa 9am-6pm, Su 10am-5pm; Oct.-May M-F 9:15am-5:30pm, Sa 9:15am-1pm.

Banks: Bank of Ireland, New St. (tel. 31050). Open M-Tu and Th-F 9am-4pm, W 9am-5pm. Their **ATM,** at the corner of Main and New St., accepts most major cards.

American Express: International Hotel, East Avenue Rd. (tel. 35722). Open June-Sept. M-F 9am-8pm, Sa-Su 10am-7pm; Oct.-May M-F 9am-5pm, sort of.

Launderette: J. Gleeson's (tel. 33877), next to Spar Market on College St. £4.50 per load. Open M-W and Sa 9am-6pm, Th-F 9am-8pm.

Emergency: Dial 999; no coins required.

Police/Garda: New Rd. (tel. 31222).

Hospital: District Hospital, St. Margaret's Rd. (tel. 31076). Follow High St. 1mi. from the town center. Nearest emergency facilities are in Tralee.

Post Office: New St. (tel. 31288). Open M and W-F 9am-5:30pm, Tu 9:30am-5:30pm, Sa 9am-1pm.

Internet Access: PC Assist (tel. 37288), at the corner of High St. and New Rd. (not New St.). £1.50 per 15min., £5 per hr.

Telephone Code: 064.

ACCOMMODATIONS

The Súgán (IHH), Lewis Rd. (tel. 33104), 2min. from the bus or train station. Make a left onto College St. and take the first right. Stone common room with glowing turf fire and groovy music create ambience. Small, ship-like bunk rooms blur the distinction between intimacy and claustrophobia. 4- to 8-bed dorms £8.

Neptune's (IHH), Bishop's Ln. (tel. 35255), the first right off New St. Large and clean with good showers and solid mattresses. 8-bed dorms £7; 4- to 6-bed dorms £8.50; doubles £20. 10% ISIC discount. Breakfast £1.50-3.50. Luggage storage; £5 locker deposit. Laundry £4.50. **Bike rental** £5 per day.

The Railway Hostel (IHH), Park Rd. (tel. 35299), across the street from the bus and train stations. Big building with skylights, a modern kitchen, and a pool table. 4- to 9-bed dorms £7.50-8.50; doubles £20. Breakfast £2-3. **Bike rental** £6 per day.

The Four Winds Hostel (IHH), 43 New St. (tel. 33094). Close to the National Park entrance. Well located, but cinder-block architecture makes it a bit dreary. Large dorms £8; small dorms £9; doubles £18. Breakfast £2. **Camping** £3.50 per person.

Orchard House, Fleming's Ln. (tel. 31879), off High St. Tasteful, immaculate, friendly, and centrally located. Hard to beat. A goldfish pool—what more could you want? Singles £16; doubles £32; most rooms with bath.

Fossa Caravan and Camping Park (tel. 31497), 3½mi. west on Killorglin Rd. Kitchen, laundromat, tennis courts, shop, and restaurant. £4 per person. Showers 50p. Wash £1.50, dry 50p per 20min. Open mid-Mar. to Oct.

FOOD, PUBS, AND CLUBS

Food in Killarney is affordable at lunchtime, but prices skyrocket in the evening. **Quinnsworth,** in an arcade off New St., is the town's largest grocer (open M-W and Sa 8am-8pm, Th-F 8am-10pm, Su 10am-6pm). Battalions of jig-seeking tourists have influenced Killarney's pubs, but plenty have managed to withstand the rising tide of shamrock-mania.

Teo's, 13 New St. (tel. 36344). Salads, pasta, fresh fish, and flamenco dancing in this marvelous Mediterranean restaurant. Open noon-4:30pm and 5:30-11pm.

The Green Onion Café, Flemings Ln. (tel. 34225), off High St. Sandwiches and plentiful salads are served up in this small, skylit restaurant. Open daily noon-5:30pm.

O'Meara's Restaurant, 12 High St. (tel. 36744), above O'Meara's Bar. Lunch or dine on eclectic and high-quality cuisine from around the world. Lunch £6-8; 3-course early bird dinner 6-7:30pm £12. Open Tu-Su noon-10pm.

Yer Mans, Plunkett St. (tel. 32688). Uncontestedly the best pub in town and frequented by a young, mixed crowd actually from Killarney. The only pub in Ireland licensed to serve Guinness in jam jars (£1.25). Trad nightly in summer, singer/songwriter nights every other Friday.

Fáilte Bar, College St. (tel. 33404). A large, relaxed crowd gathers at this dark and woody pub. Singer/songwriter sessions every night, DJ on weekends.

In mid-March, Killarney hosts the **Guinness Roaring 1920s Festival,** in which pubs, restaurants, and hostels bust out in jazz, barbershop singing, and flapper regalia. In mid-May and mid-July, horses run in the **Killarney Races** in the racecourse on Ross Rd. (tickets available at gate; £3-5). The **Killarney Regatta,** the oldest regatta in Ireland, draws rowers and spectators to Lough Leane in early to mid-July. **Gaelic football matches** are held in Fitzgerald Stadium on Lewis Rd. most Sunday afternoons and some weekday evenings (tickets £2-5). Kerry's fanatical rivalry with Cork comes to a head when Cork's team comes to town.

■ Killarney National Park

The Ice Ages had a dramatic impact around Killarney, scooping out a series of glens and scattering ice-smoothed rocks and precarious boulders. The 37 sq. mi. park, stretching west and south of Killarney toward Kenmare, incorporates a string of forested mountains and the famous **Lakes of Killarney:** huge **Lough Leane (Lower**

Lake), medium-sized **Middle (Muckross) Lake,** and small **Upper Lake,** 2 mi. southwest and connected by a canal. Ireland's last indigenous herd of red deer, numbering about 850, roams the glens that surround the lakes. The park's treasures are only a few miles apart and are connected by hundreds of paths. Maps are available at the Killarney tourist office or the **Information Centre** (tel. 31440) behind Muckross House, but serious hikers should buy the 1:25,000 Ordnance Survey map. *(Open daily June-Sept. 9am-7pm.)* You can drive or walk out to **Ross Castle** (tel. 35851), a right on Ross Rd. off Muckross Rd. 2 mi. from Killarney, but the numerous footpaths from Knockreer are more scenic (15min. walk). *(Admission by guided tour only. Open daily June-Aug. 9am-6:30pm; May-Sept. 10am-6pm; Oct. 9am-5pm. Last admission 45min. before closing. £2.50, students £1.)* Other frequented destinations include **Muckross House** on Middle Lake and the **Gap of Dunloe** just west of the park area, bordered on the southwest by **Macgillycuddy's Reeks,** Ireland's highest mountain range (most of the peaks are under 3000ft.). The Gap of Dunloe is a full-day excursion, but the others can be managed in several hours or stretched over a full day, depending on your mode of transport. Hikers and bikers should take the necessary precautions whether alone or in groups. The park is also a perfect starting point for those who plan to walk the 129 mi. **Kerry Way**—essentially the Ring of Kerry (see below) on foot. Do not attempt the Kerry Way from October to March, when rains make the uneven terrain dangerous. The excellent 1:50,000 Ordnance Survey maps of the Iveragh include minor roads, trails, and archaeological points of interest (£4.60).

■ Ring of Kerry

The Southwest's most celebrated peninsula has been a visitor attraction for so long that the history of tourism can be easier to grasp than the tough, romantic spirit the visitors hope to see. A lucky few travelers spend days out on the peninsula, soaking up the great sea spray, grand views, and pervasive quiet. The term "Ring of Kerry" is often used to describe the entire Iveragh Peninsula, but it more correctly refers not to a region but to a set of roads: N71 from Kenmare to Killarney, R562 from Killarney to Killorglin, and the long loop of N70 west and back to Kenmare. If you don't like the prepackaged private bus tours based out of Killarney, try **Bus Éireann's** summer circuit through all the major towns on the Ring (2 per day), which allows you to get off anywhere and anytime you like.

■ Kenmare

A bridge between the Ring of Kerry and Beara, Kenmare has adapted to a continuous stream of visitors. Everything to be seen in a classic Irish town is here in spades, with travelers' amenities as well. There are plenty of good hikes in the country around Kenmare, but few sights in the town itself. The ancient **stone circle,** a two-minute walk from The Square down Market St., is the largest of its kind in southwest Ireland (55ft. diameter). *(Always open. £1.)* **Buses** leave from Brennan's Pub on Main St. for **Killarney** (1hr., M-Sa 3 per day, Su 2 per day), **Tralee** (2hr., M-Sa 3 per day, Su 2 per day), **Sneem** (35min., June-Sept. M-F 2 per day), and **Cork via Bantry** (4hr., June-Sept. 2 per day). The **tourist office** (tel. 41233) is on The Square (open July-Aug. daily 9am-7pm; May-June and Sept. M-Sa 9am-6pm). **Fáilte Hostel** (IHH; tel. 41083), at the corner of Henry and Shelbourne St., is a stately house featuring a common room with a VCR (dorms £7.50; doubles £20; curfew 1am). You can camp at the **Ring of Kerry Caravan and Camping Park,** Sneem Rd. (tel. 41648), 2½mi. west of Kenmare (£3.50 per person; open May-Sept.). **SuperValu** (tel. 41037) is on Main St. (open M-Th 8am-8pm, F 8am-9pm, Sa 8am-7pm, Su 8:30am-5pm). The **phone code** is 064.

■ Sneem

Tourists make Sneem their first or last stop along the Ring, and the town has adapted to please them. Canned Irish music rolls out of the Irish music shop, entertaining both those shopping at Quills and those heading off to expensive dinners. With its two public squares and its unique **sculpture park,** Sneem has a quirky charm. The closest hostel to Sneem, the **Harbour View Hostel** (tel. 45276), a quarter mile from town on Kenmare Rd., used to be a motel and still looks like one, with ranch-style units in a gravel lot (4-bed dorms £8; doubles or twins £20; **camping** £3). **The Green House** (tel. 45565), next to the bridge on The South Square, has well-decorated, light-filled rooms with TV (£15 with breakfast). For the best fish and chips (£2.75) on the Ring, gallop down to **The Hungry Knight,** The North Square (tel. 45237). The **Blue Bull** (tel. 45382), next to the wool shops, is a pub noted for its seafood (pub grub £4-6, served noon-8:30pm) and ballad sessions (M, Th, and Sa). The Ring of Kerry **bus** leaves for **Killarney** via **Kenmare** (1hr., June-Sept. 2 per day, £5.50). Sneem's **tourist information center** (tel. 45270) is across the street from Murphy's (open daily 11am-6pm). The **phone code** is 064.

■ Caherdaniel

There's delightfully little in the village of Caherdaniel to attract the Ring's drove of travel coaches, but this hamlet (2 pubs, a grocer, a restaurant, and a take-away) has the benefit of proximity to one of Ireland's best beaches and one of the region's finest hostels. Derrynane Strand, 2 mi. of gorgeous beach ringed by picture perfect dunes, is 1½ mi. from Caherdaniel in Derrynane National Park. The pre-Christian **Staigue Fort** (tel. 75288), 6 mi. west of town, is the largest and one of the best-preserved forts in Ireland. In town, the **Traveller's Rest Hostel** (tel. 75175) looks and feels more like a B&B than a hostel, with its turf fire in the sitting room and tasteful flower boxes (dorms £7; private rooms £8.50 per person). Campers get their beauty sleep 1 mi. east on the Ring of Kerry road at **Wave Crest Camping Park** (tel. 75188), overlooking the beach (£3 per person; showers 50p; laundry £4; shop open 8am-10pm; open Apr.-Sept.). The **bus** stops in Caherdaniel twice per day at the junction of the Ring of Kerry road and Main St. for **Sneem** (1½hr., June-Sept. 2 per day, £2.90) and **Killarney** (1½hr., June-Sept. 2 per day, £7.30). The new **tourist office** is 1 mi. east of town at the Wave Crest Camping Park (open daily 8am-10pm). The **phone code** is 066.

■ Cahersiveen

Good hostels, decent food, and an eminently explorable surrounding countryside make Cahersiveen (car-si-VEEN) an enjoyable place to put down your pack. And with nearly 30 pubs, there's certainly no shortage of nightlife. The Ring of Kerry **bus** stops in front of Banks Store on Main St. (June-Sept. 2 per day) and continues on to **Waterville** (25min., £2.70), **Caherdaniel** (1½hr., £3.10), **Sneem** (2hr., £6.30), and **Killarney** (2½hr., £9). One route heads directly east to **Killarney** (M-Sa 1-2 per day). Cahersiveen's official **tourist office** (tel. 72589) is housed in the former barracks on the road to Ballycarbery Castle (open June to mid-Sept. M-Sa 10am-6pm, Su 1-6pm). The **phone code** is 066.

The friendly **Sive Hostel (IHH)** (rhymes with "hive"), 15 East End, Main St. (tel. 72717), has magnificent views from its third-floor balcony (dorms £7-7.50; doubles £18; **camping** £4 per person). At the west end of town, the **Mannix Point Caravan and Camping Park** (tel. 72806), one of the best camping parks in the country, adjoins a waterfront nature reserve and faces the romantic ruins of Ballycarbery Castle across the water (£3.25 per person; open mid-Mar. to mid-Oct.). **Au Cupán** (tel. 73011), across from the bank, has Irish breakfasts for £4, a slightly cheaper vegetarian option, and plenty of sandwiches and salads. **Shebeen** (tel. 72361), near the Sive on Main St., gives great pub grub (entrees £4-6; open daily 9:30am-10:30pm). Cahersiveen's long Main St. still has several **original pubs.** Common in rural Ireland during the first half of this century, these establishments were a combination of watering hole and the proprietor's "main" business, general store, blacksmith, leather shop, and farm goods store. The **Anchor Bar** (tel. 72049), toward the west end of Main St., is one of the best. Don't come before 10pm, and take your drink into the kitchen for an unforgettable night.

■ Dingle

For now, the craic in Dingle is still home-grown, but foreigners are talking about the fabulous pubs, smart cafes, and gregarious dolphin, Fungi, who charms the whole town from his permanent residence in Dingle Bay.

ORIENTATION AND PRACTICAL INFORMATION

Dingle dangles in the middle of the southern coast of Dingle Peninsula. The R559 heads east to Killarney and Tralee and west to Ventry, Dunquin, and Slea Head. A narrow road running north through Connor Pass leads to Stradbally and Castlegregory. The streets of downtown Dingle approximate a grid, although it's just more confusing than you'd expect. The lack of street signs in English complicates matters. **Strand** and **Main St.** run parallel to Dingle Harbour. **The Mall, Dykegate St.,** and **Green St.** run perpendicular to the shore uphill from Strand St. to Main St. On the eastern edge of town, Strand St., The Mall, and **Tralee Rd.** converge in a roundabout.

Buses: Buses stop on Ring Rd., behind Garvey's SuperValu. Information available from the Tralee bus station (tel. 23566). **Bus Éireann** runs to Dingle Peninsula destinations, **Killarney** (1½hr., June-Sept. 3 per day, Su 2 per day, £7.30) and **Tralee** (1¼hr., June-Sept. 6 per day, Su 5 per day, Oct.-May 6 per day, Su 4 per day, £5.90). Additional buses tour the south of the peninsula (June-Sept. M-Sa 2 per day).

Bike Rental: Paddy's Bike Shop, Dykegate St. (tel. 52311), rents the best bikes in town. £5 per day, £25 per week. Open daily 9am-7pm.

Tourist Office: Corner of Main and Dykegate St. (tel. 51188). Open July-Aug. M-Sa 9am-7pm, Su 9am-1pm and 2:15-7pm; Apr.-June and Sept.-Oct. daily 9:30am-6pm.

Financial Services: AIB, Main St. (tel. 51400). Open M 10am-12:30pm and 1:30-5pm, Tu-F 10am-12:30pm and 1:30-4pm. **Bank of Ireland,** Main St. (tel. 51100). Same hours; **ATM.**

Launderette: Níolann an Daingin, Green St. (tel. 51837), behind El Toro. Medium wash and dry from £5.50. Open M-Sa 9am-5:30pm.

Emergency: Dial 999; no coins required.

Police/Garda: The Holy Ground (tel. 51522), across from Tig Lise.

Post Office: Upper Main St. (tel. 51661). Just the place for mailing Fungi postcards. Open M-F 9am-1pm and 2-5:30pm, Sa 9am-1pm.

Telephone Code: 066.

ACCOMMODATIONS

There are good hostels in Dingle, although some are a fairly long walk from town. B&Bs along Dykegate and Strand St. and hostels in town tend to fill up fast in summer.

Ballintaggart Hostel (IHH) (tel. 51454), a 25min. walk east of town on Tralee Rd. Gloriously renovated with enormous bunk rooms and an enclosed cobblestone courtyard. Free shuttle to town. 10- to 12-bed dorms £7; 4-bed dorms £8; private rooms from £13 per person. **Bike rental** £7 per day. **Camping** £3.50 per person.

Rainbow Hostel (tel. 51044), 15min. west of town on Strand Rd. and worth the hike. Bear right and inland at the corner of Dunquin Rd. Free lifts to and from town. July-Aug. dorms £7; doubles £18. June-Sept. £6; £16. Laundry £4. **Bike rental** £6 per day. **Camping** £3.50.

Grapevine Hostel, Dykegate St. (tel. 51434), off Main St. Smack in the middle of town and just a short stagger from Dingle's finest pubs. Close but comfortable bunk rooms with baths. Dorms £8-9.

An Caladh Spáinneach (un KULL-uh SPINE-uck; the Spanish Pier), Strand St. (tel. 52160). This comfortable hostel offers basic and friendly lodging across from the marina. Dorms £8. Open June-Aug.

Old Mill House, Dykegate St. (tel. 51120; email verhoul@iol.ie). The comfort of the new pine beds in this charming house can be outdone only by its vivacious owner and her magnificent breakfast menu. Crepes suzette, anyone? From £15.

Kirrary House (tel. 51606), across from Old Mill House. Mrs. Collins puts guests up in her delightful rooms. £16 with bath. **Bikes** £6 per day.

FOOD AND PUBS

SuperValu supermarket, The Holy Ground (tel. 51397), stocks a SuperSelection of groceries and juicy tabloids (open M-Sa 9am-9pm, Su 9am-6pm). Although only 1500 people live in Dingle permanently, the town maintains 52 pubs. Every inhabitant could hoist a pint simultaneously without anyone having to scramble for a seat.

Greany's, Bridge St. (tel. 52244). Hearty, well-prepared breakfasts (£2.50-4.50) and seafood and meat dishes (dinner £8-11) in a crowded but pleasantly modern cafe. Open daily 9am-10pm.

An Café Liteartha, Dykegate St. (tel. 51388), across the street from the Grapevine. One of the first Irish language cafes, and Irish speakers still frequent the place. Open M-F 10am-5:30pm, Sa-Su 11am-5:30pm; bookstore open until 6pm.

The Oven Door, The Holy Ground (tel. 51056). Crispy pizzas (£3.50-7) and a gleaming counter of light food lure crowds to this simple cafe. Open daily 10am-11pm.

An Droichead Beag (The Small Bridge), Lower Main St. (tel. 51723). The most popular pub in town is nearly always crowded but still unleashes the best trad around—401 sessions a year.

O'Flaherty's Pub, The Holy Ground (tel. 51983). Memorable, varied jam sessions most nights in this well-decorated pub. Be here by 9pm if you want a seat.

McCarthy's, Upper Main St. (tel. 51205), across the street and a few doors up from the post office. Good craic when there's music (Th-Sa). Also features Irish drama on Thursdays in a venue behind the pub—stop in to ask.

SIGHTS

Fungi the Dolphin swam into Dingle Bay one day in 1983 with his mother, and the pair immediately became local celebrities. Mom has taken the Big Plunge, but egomaniacal Fungi remains and is fond of humans. **Boat trips** to see the dolphin leave from the pier constantly in summer. Most cost around £6 and guarantee that you'll see the dolphin. A cheaper option (it's free) is to watch Fungi from shore as he chases the boats in a little cove east of town. To get there, walk two minutes down Tralee Rd., turn right at the Skellig Hotel, and then follow the beach away from town. You can rent a **wetsuit** from **Flannery's** (tel. 51967), just east of town off Tralee Rd. (£14 per 2hr., £22 overnight). **Dingle Ocean World,** Strand St. (tel. 52111), features 160 species of fish, a huge tank with a walk-through tunnel, and a petting-zoo tank where rays swim up to have their fins scratched or poked in disbelief. *(Open daily July-Aug. 9am-9:30pm; Apr.-July and Aug.-Sept. 10am-6pm; Oct.-Mar. 10am-5pm. £4.50, students £3.50.)* For the history buff in us all, **Sciúird Archaeology** (tel. 51606) leads three-hour whirlwind bus tours of the area's ancient spots from the pier. *(2 per day. £7. Book ahead.)* They also coordinate historic walking tours of Dingle Town. *(2 per day. £2.50.)*

■ The Dingle Peninsula

Glorious **Slea Head** inspires with jagged cliffs and crashing waves. *Ryan's Daughter* and parts of *Far and Away* were filmed around here, and it's easy to see why. The road from horseshoe-shaped **Ventry Beach** out to Slea Head passes several Iron Age and early Christian stones and ruins. **Dunbeg Fort** (£1, students 80p) and the less impressive **Fahan Group** of oratories (£1), beehive-shaped stone huts built by early monks, cluster on hillsides over the cliffs. The scattered settlement of **Dunquin** (Dún Chaoin) consists of stone houses, a pub, and plenty of spoken Irish. Along the road to Ballyferriter, the **An Óige Hostel (HI)** (tel. 56121) provides clean, adequate bunkrooms. (June-Sept. dorms £7-8; doubles £18; Oct.-May £6-7; £16. Breakfast £1.75. Sheets 80p. Lockout 10:15am-5pm. Midnight curfew.) Two miles past Dunquin, **Tig Áine** (tel. 56214) charms visitors with a gallery, a cafe, and views of the cliffs. The architecture of the **Blasket Centre** (tel. 56444), across the road from the hostel, enhances the museum's outstanding exhibits on the Blasket writers. *(Open daily July-Aug. 10am-7pm, Easter-June and Sept. 10am-6pm; last admission 45min. before closing. £2.50, students £1.)*

Evacuated in 1953, the Blasket Islands were once inhabited by poet-fishermen, proud but impoverished and aging villagers, and memoirists reluctantly warning that "after us, there will be no more." Blasket writers themselves helped produce and publicize the story of their isolated *gaeltacht* culture in English and Irish and its memorable decline. The buildings from the well-chronicled village still stand. Mists, seals, and occasional fishing boats may continue to pass the Blaskets, but the simpler ways of life once exemplified there are gone forever. **Boats** (tel. 56455) for the Blaskets depart from Dunquin May to September daily, every half-hour from 10am to 3pm, weather and ferry operator's mood permitting (return £10).

▓ Tralee

While tourists tend to identify Killarney as the core of Kerry, residents correctly see Tralee (pop. 20,000) as the county's economic center. Despite the presence of industry and traffic that make Tralee the hub it is, stately Georgian architecture and a surprisingly cosmopolitan flair provide energized atmosphere that doesn't pander only to tourists, although there's plenty for tourists to do here these days.

ORIENTATION AND PRACTICAL INFORMATION

Tralee's main street, variously called The Mall, Castle St., and Boherboy, is a good reference point, but the streets are hopelessly knotted. Find the tourist office and arm yourself with a free map.

Airplanes: Kerry Airport (tel. 64644), off N22 halfway between Tralee and Killarney. **Manx Airlines** (tel. (01) 260 1588) flies to London.

Trains: Edward St. and John Joe Sheehy Rd. (tel. 23522). Ticket office open sporadically. Phone inquiries taken M-F 9am-12:30pm and 1:30-5:30pm. Trains to **Cork** (2½hr., M-Sa 5 per day, Su 3 per day, £17), **Killarney** (40min., M-Sa 5 per day, Su 4 per day, £5.50), **Galway** (3 per day, £33.50), **Dublin** (4hr., M-Sa 4 per day, Su 3 per day, £33.50), **Waterford** (4hr., M-Sa 2 per day, £33.50), and **Rosslare Harbour** (5½hr., M-Sa 1 per day, £33.50).

Buses: Edward St. and John Joe Sheehy Rd. (tel. 23566). Station open in summer M-Sa 8:30am-6pm, Su 11am-6pm; in winter M-Sa 8:30am-5:10pm, Su 11am-5:10pm. Buses to **Cork** (2½hr., M-Sa 6 per day, Su 4 per day, £9.70), **Dingle** (1¼hr.; July-Aug. M-Sa 9 per day, Su 6 per day; Sept.-June M-Sa 4 per day, Su 2 per day, £6), **Killarney** (40min., June-Sept. M-Sa 14 per day, Su 8 per day; Oct.-May M-Sa 5 per day, Su 6 per day, £4.40), **Limerick** (2¼hr., M-Sa 5 per day, Su 4 per day, £9), and **Galway** (M-Sa 5 per day, Su 4 per day, £13).

Taxis: Kingdom Cabs, 48 Boherboy (tel. 27828), or **Call-A-Cab** (tel. 20333). Cabs stand on Denny St. at the intersection with The Mall.

Bike Rental: O'Halloran, 83 Boherboy (tel. 22820). Sometimes, you've just got to ride. £6 per day, £30 per week. Open M-Sa 9:30am-6pm.

Tourist Office: Ashe Memorial Hall (tel. 21288), at the end of Denny St. From the station, go into town on Edward St., and turn right on Castle St. and then left onto Denny St. Open in summer M-Sa 9am-7pm, Su 9am-6pm; in winter Tu-Sa 9am-5pm.

Banks: Bank of Ireland, Castle St., and **AIB,** corner of Denny and Castle St. Both open M 10am-5pm, Tu-F 10am-4pm. Both have **ATMs.**

Launderette: The Laundry, Pembroke St. (tel. 23214). 50p per lb. Open M-F 9am-6pm.

Emergency: Dial 999; no coins required.

Police/Garda: High St. (tel. 22022).

Hotlines: Samaritans, 44 Moyderwell (tel. 22566). 24hr. hotline.

Hospital: Tralee County General Hospital (tel. 26222), off Killarney Rd.

Post Office: Edward St. (tel. 21013), off Castle St. Open M and W-Sa 9am-5:30pm, Tu 9:30am-5:30pm.

Telephone Code: by any other name would still be 066.

ACCOMMODATIONS

Tralee has a remarkable supply of good hostels. A number of pleasant B&Bs line Oakpark Rd., while a smattering of others sit on Boherboy by the traffic circle. At the end of the city's most dignified street, **Finnegan's Hostel (IHH),** 17 Denny St. (tel. 27610), contains part of the old town castle. Spacious, wood-floored bunk rooms are named after Ireland's literary heroes (dorms £7.50; doubles £18). **Collis-Sandes House (IHH)** (tel. 28658) is near-perfect but far from town. Follow Edward St.-Oakpark Rd. 1 mi. from town, take the first left after Halloran's Foodstore, and follow signs another half mile to the right. This stately stone mansion, built in 1857, has beautiful high ceilings and impressive Moorish arches and sits right next to a golf course and tennis courts. (Free lifts to town and pub runs. Dorms £6.50; doubles from £18. Laundry £3. Wheelchair accessible.) **Lisnagree Hostel (IHH),** Ballinorig Rd. (tel. 27133), is 1 mi. from town center and close to the bus-train station. This small, pretty hostel is perfect for families or couples but a bit remote for anyone who wants to hit the pub at night. (4-bed dorms with bath from £7.50; doubles from £17. Bike rental £7 per day, £30 per week; deposit £40.) Pamper yourself at **Dowling's Leeside,** Oakpark Rd. (tel. 26475), about half a mile from town center, with gorgeous Irish pine antique furniture, cushy chintz chairs, and fresh flowers. Glass-enclosed dining room makes breakfast bright. (Singles £18; doubles £32.)

FOOD AND PUBS

For the chefs, there's a **Quinnsworth Supermarket** (tel. 22788), in The Square (open M-Tu 9am-7pm, W-F 9am-9pm, Sa 9am-6pm, Su 10am-6pm) and a health food store/bakery, **Sean Chara** (tel. 22644), across the street (open M-W and Sa 9am-6pm, Th 9am-8pm, F 9am-9pm). **The Old Forge,** Church St. (tel. 28095), just down from the hostel, is a Tralee institution, with fine Irish fare (open July-Sept. M-Sa 9am-10pm; Oct.-June M-Sa 9am-6pm). **Finnegan's** (tel. 27610), a candle-lit bistro on Denny St., serves unbelievably tasty delicacies (entrees £9-15). **Brat's Place,** 18 Milk Market Ln., off The Mall, conscientiously prepares vegetarian food with mostly local and organic ingredients (entrees £4.50; open M-Sa 12:30-2:30pm, perhaps later if food lasts). The mellow **Baily's Corner Pub** (tel. 23230), at Ashe and Castle St., has music Sundays through Thursdays and an especially great session on Tuesdays. **Paddy Mac's,** The Mall (tel. 21572), has the only old-style pub decor around and hosts many a trad session. Extremely popular among locals, **Val O'Shea's,** Bridge St. (tel. 21559), draws in a mixed crowd for craic but has no live music.

SIGHTS AND ENTERTAINMENT

Tralee is home to Ireland's second-largest museum, **Kerry the Kingdom,** Ashe Memorial Hall, Denny St. (tel. 27777). Named one of Europe's top 20 museums in 1994, the Kingdom marshals all the resources of display technology to tell the story of Co. Kerry from 8000 BC to the present. *(Open daily July-Aug. 9am-7pm, Su 10am-6pm; Mar.-June and Sept.-Oct. 9am-6pm; Nov.-Mar. 9am-5:30pm. £5.50, students £4.75.)* Across from the museum, the **roses of Tralee** bloom each summer in Ireland's second-largest town park. The stained glass in **St. John's Church,** Castle St., is worth a look. Just down Dingle Rd. (N86/R559) whir the arms of the **Blenneville Windmill and Visitor Centre** (tel. 21064). Blenneville's is the largest operating windmill in the British Isles, and you can climb to the top. A small **museum** focuses on the "coffin ships" that left Ireland during the Famine. *(Open Apr.-Oct. daily 10am-6pm. £2.75, students £2.25.)*

The **Siamsa Tire Theatre** (tel. 23055), at the end of Denny St. next to the museum, is Ireland's national folk theater. *(Productions July-Aug. M-Sa; May-June and Sept. M-Th and Sa. Shows start at 8:30pm. Box office open M-Sa 9am-10:30pm. £9, students £8.)* If you're ready to boogie, head down to the Brandon Hotel's club **Spirals,** Prince's Quay (tel. 23333), for discos (W and F-Su). **Horan's,** Boherboy (tel. 21933), blasts country-western and disco (Th-Su). Both stay open until 1:45am. *(Cover £4-5.)*

Lovely Irish lasses from around the world come to town during the last week of August for the **Rose of Tralee International Festival.** A maelstrom of entertainment surrounds the main event, a personality competition to earn the coveted title "Rose of Tralee." Call the Rose office (tel. 21322), in Ashe Memorial Hall, for more information. For other local goings-on, check *The Kerryman* (85p).

COS. LIMERICK AND CLARE

Even Dubliners will tell you that the West is the "most Irish" part of Ireland. Yeats agreed: "For me," he said, "Ireland is Connacht." For the less privileged, Connacht has sometimes meant poor soil, starvation, and emigration. When Cromwell uprooted the native Irish landowners in Leinster and Munster and resettled them west of the Shannon, he was giving them a raw deal. The West was hardest-hit by the potato famine—entire villages emigrated or died. Today, every western county has less than half of its 1841 population. But from Connemara north to Ballina, hikers, cyclists, and hitchhikers enjoy boggy, rocky, or brilliantly mountainous landscapes.

■ Limerick City

Despite a flourishing trade in off-color poems, Limerick has never had much status as a tourist town. While a sagging economy and its buddies "dirt" and "crime" gave Limerick a bad name in the past, the lack of tourists today seems both surprising and refreshing. The republic's third-largest city sports a top-notch museum and a developing art scene, truly fantastic food, and pubs with all of the diversity of character that a city of this size demands.

ORIENTATION AND PRACTICAL INFORMATION

Limerick's streets form a grid pattern, bounded by the River Shannon on the west and by the Abbey River on the north. A few blocks of **O'Connell St.** fosters most of the city's activity. The city is easily navigable by foot, but catch a **city bus** (75p) from Boyd's or Penney's on O'Connell St. to reach the suburbs.

> **Trains: Colbert Station** (tel. 315555), off Parnell St. Inquiries desk open M-F 9am-6pm, Sa 9:30am-5:30pm. Trains to **Dublin** (2hr., M-Sa 10 per day, Su 8 per day, £25), **Waterford** (2hr., M-Sa 2 per day in summer, 1 per day in winter, £17), **Rosslare** (3½hr., M-Sa 1 per day, £23), **Ennis** (M-Sa 2 per day, £5.50), **Cork** (2½hr., M-Sa 7 per day, Su 6 per day, £13.50), **Killarney** (2½hr., M-Sa 4 per day, Su 3 per day, £15), and **Tralee** (3hr., M-Sa 6 per day, Su 3 per day, £15).
>
> **Buses: Colbert Station** (tel. 313333 or 418855; 24hr. talking timetable tel. 319911), off Parnell St. Open June-Sept. daily 8:45am-6pm; Oct.-May M-Sa 8am-6pm, Su 3-7pm. Most buses leave from the station, but some depart from Penney's or Todd's on O'Connell St. Buses to **Cork** (2hr., 6 per day, £9), **Dublin** (3hr., M-Sa 8 per day, Su 5 per day, £10), **Galway** (2hr., 7 per day, £9), **Ennis** (1hr., 7 per day, £5), **Killarney** (2½hr., M-Sa 6 per day, Su 3 per day, £9.30), **Sligo** (6hr., 4 per day, £14), **Tralee** (2hr., 6 per day, £9), **Waterford** (2½hr., M-Th and Sa 5 per day, F 6 per day, Su 5 per day, £9.70), and **Wexford** and **Rosslare Harbour,** with some departures timed to meet the ferries (4hr., 4 per day, £12).
>
> **Bike Rental: Emerald Cycles,** 1 Patrick St. (tel. 416983; email emarldalp@tinet.ie). £7 per day, £30 per week; deposit £40. £12 for return at other locations. Open M-Sa 9:15am-5:30pm.
>
> **Tourist Office:** Arthurs Quay (tel. 317522), in the space-age glass building. From the station, walk straight down Davis St., turn right on O'Connell, then left just before Arthurs Quay Mall. Handy city maps £1. Open July-Aug. M-F 9am-7pm, Sa-Su 9am-6pm; Mar.-June and Sept.-Oct. M-Sa 9:30am-5:30pm; Nov.-Feb. M-F 9:30am-5:30pm, Sa 9:30am-1pm.
>
> **Budget Travel: USIT,** O'Connell St. (tel. 415064), across from Ulster Bank. Open M-F 9:30am-5:30pm, Sa 10am-1pm.
>
> **Launderette:** (tel. 312712), on Mallow St. Wash, dry, and fold £5. Open M-F 9am-6pm, Sa 9am-5pm.
>
> **Emergency:** Dial 999; no coins required.
>
> **Police/Garda:** Henry St. (tel. 414222), at Lower Glentworth St.

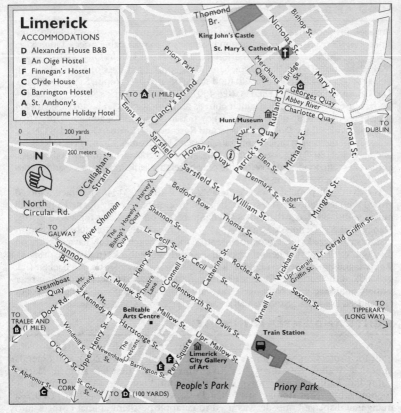

Limerick
ACCOMMODATIONS

D Alexandra House B&B
E An Oige Hostel
F Finnegan's Hostel
C Clyde House
G Barrington Hostel
A St. Anthony's
B Westbourne Holiday Hotel

Post Office: Main office on Lower Cecil St. (tel. 315777), just off O'Connell St. Open M and W-Sa 9am-5:30pm, Tu 9:30am-5:30pm.

Internet Access: Webster's, Thomas St. (tel. 312066). Full web and email access costs £2.50 per 30min. Bring your *Let's Go* and get 30min. free. Food and cider from the adjoining pub. Open M-Sa 10am-10pm, Su 2pm-10pm.

There once was a **phone code** *named 061*...Damn, nothing rhymes with 061.

ACCOMMODATIONS

Although Limerick is not the place to find cozy cottage hostels with peat fires, several hostels take advantage of the very lovely city architecture. For those seeking refuge from the bustle of the city, Ennis St. is a B&B bonanza, most priced around £16 per person. **Finnegan's (IHH),** 6 Pery Sq. (tel. 310308), in a grand old Georgian mansion overlooking People's Park, boasts elegant high-ceilinged common rooms, bright and spacious dormitories, and positively torrential showers (dorms £7.50; private rooms £10 per person). Far from the train and bus station, but very close to sights, restaurants, and pubs, **Barrington Hostel (IHH),** George's Quay (tel. 415222), compensates for its large size by offering relatively private dorms (4-bed dorms £7.50; 3-bed dorms £8.50; singles £10; doubles £20; laundry £5). At **An Óige Hostel (HI),** 1 Pery Sq. (tel. 314672), around the corner from Finnegan's, splendid views of People's Park and a cheerful staff help ease the usual An Óige restrictions and dreariness. (June-Sept. dorms £8.75; Oct.-May £7.75; £1.25 less for HI members. Sheets £1. Midnight curfew.) Pleasant rooms at **St. Anthony's,** 8 Coolraine Terr., Ennis Rd. (tel. 452607), 1 mi. from city center, look out onto a flourishing garden (£16, with bath £17, but the friendly proprietress usually gives a *Let's Go* discount).

FOOD AND PUBS

Limerick probably has more fast-food joints than all the truck stops in Ohio combined, but there are also some top-notch eateries with reasonable prices. Otherwise, stock up at **Quinnsworth Supermarket** (tel. 412399), in Arthurs Quay Mall (open M-W 8:30am-7pm, Th-F 8:30am-9pm, Sa 8:30am-7pm), or at **Eats of Eden,** Henry St. (tel. 419400), a well-stocked health food store (open M-F 9am-6pm, Sa 9am-5:30pm). **The Green Onion Café,** 3 Ellen St. (tel. 400710), just off Patrick's St., serves elite bistro fare at egalitarian prices. (Lunch entrees and sandwiches £4-6; prices skyrocket after 6pm. Open daily noon-10pm.) Enjoy massive portions of admirably prepared Irish specialities at the **Dolmen Gallery and Restaurant,** Honan's Quay (tel. 417929), across from the tourist office (entrees £5; open M-Sa 10am-5:30pm). **Java's,** 5 Catherine St. (tel. 418077), pleases a steady stream of Limerickites with flavored coffees, herbal teas, cafe food, and possibly the only bagels available in Limerick (sandwiches £1.20-3.20; open M-Su 8am-8pm).

The extremely popular dockside **Dolan's,** Dock Rd. (tel. 314483), attracts a mixed crowd with its nightly trad sessions. Its keen proprietor recently opened a beautiful music venue out back that hosts big-name bands on weekend for a £3-5 cover. **Nancy Blake's,** Denmark St. (tel. 416443), is one of the better pubs in town. A mature crowd packs itself into the large store rooms, which actually have sawdust on the floor, while the younger set revels in the outdoor "outback" (trad inside every M-W, rock and blues outside nightly). In a former warehouse, **Doc's,** Michael St. (tel. 417266), at the corner of Charlotte's Quay in the Granary, has a large outdoor beer garden, complete with palm trees and waterfalls and packed with rollicking youth (Tu and Th live music; Saturdays DJ).

SIGHTS AND ENTERTAINMENT

A few decades after the Normans invaded Ireland, King John ordered a castle built for protection. **King John's Castle,** Nicholas St. (tel. 411201), still defends Limerick. Walk across the Abbey River and take the first left after St. Mary's Cathedral. Exhibits survey town history from the Vikings to the present. Easily recognizable from its use in *Monty Python's Quest for the Holy Grail,* a **mangonel** displayed outside was used to catapult pestilent animal corpses into enemy cities and castles. Do not lick it. *(Open daily 9:30am-6pm; last admission 5pm. £3.80, students £2.10.)* The rough exterior of nearby **St. Mary's Cathedral** (tel. 416238) was built by the O'Briens in 1172. Fold-down seats, built into the wall on the side of the altar, are covered with elaborate carvings that depict the struggle between good and evil. *(Open M-Sa 9am-1pm and 2-5pm.)*

Modern and abstract art decks the walls at the very small and very busy **Belltable Arts Centre,** O'Connell St. (tel. 319866). *(Open M-Sa 9am-7pm. Free.)* The fascinating **Hunt Museum,** Custom House, Rutland St. (tel. 312833), houses the largest collection of medieval, Stone Age, and Iron Age artifacts outside Dublin. *(Open Tu-Sa 10am-5pm, Su 2-5pm. £3.90, students £2.50.)* Should you venture to the university, stop by the **National Self-Portrait Collection** (tel. 333644) that exhibits itself in Plassey House. *(Open M-F 10am-5pm. Free.)*

The **Theatre Royal,** Upper Cecil St. (tel. 414224), hosts any large concerts that come to town. The free *Calendar of Events and Entertainment,* available at the tourist office, has details on events and entertainment. Limerick also has a respectable club scene. **Doc's** (see **Pubs,** above) revels in a rave-like disco Thursday through Sunday nights. **The Works,** on Bedford Row next to the Cinema, opens its club seven nights a week. **Ted's,** O'Connell St. (tel. 417412), provides a classier alternative nightly. *(No sneakers. Cover £3-6.)* Watch for concession stubs in the pub.

■ Doolin

Ireland sees Doolin much as Europe views Ireland—as a small, beautiful, windy, rural, musical, depopulated, over-touristed place where life revolves around

McCourt Mania

Until recently, the only thing that most people knew about Limerick was its reputed penchant for raunchy poetry. Now anyone who knows nothing about Limerick can comment on its unfortunate days, thanks to Limerickian-Frank McCourt's bestselling novel *Angela's Ashes*. Although some Limerick residents have taken a dim view of McCourt's humorous, terrible account of his childhood during the 30s and 40s, the work has launched Limerick into the limelight. Some residents are proud to have grown up with McCourt (a treat, no doubt) or to see their heritage gain international recognition. Many others, however, resent the dreary depiction of Limerick and all the money McCourt's made off it. For better or worse, McCourt mania continues to grow; in addition to countless fan clubs, a movie version is in the works. The path of the "Angela's Ashes Tour" is not yet marked, but walking tours of the city will gladly show you all you want to see.

pubs. The 8 mi. paved and bicycle-friendly segment of the **Burren Way** links Doolin to the Cliffs of Moher. The steep climb along the road from Doolin to the Cliffs earns you the thrilling glide back down and the anticipation of another night of carousing at the pubs.

PRACTICAL INFORMATION Doolin is shaped like a barbell, made up of two villages about a mile apart from each other. **Fisherstreet,** the **Lower Village,** is closer to the shore than **Roadford,** which is farther up the road and separated from Fisherstreet by a stretch of farmland. A traveling **bank** comes to Lower Village every Thursday from 11am to 2pm, but there's a permanent **bureau de change** at the post office. The nearest **ATM** is in Ennistymon, 5 mi. to the southeast. The **Doolin Bike Store** (tel. 74260), outside the Aille River Hostel, will set you up with a bike (£7 per day; open M-Sa 9am-8pm). Doolin's **phone code** is 065.

ACCOMMODATIONS AND FOOD Tourists pack Doolin in the summer, so book ahead for hostels. B&Bs are common, but those along the main road tend to be expensive. The small, relaxed **Aille River Hostel (IHH)** (tel. 74260), halfway between the villages, is in a cute cottage by the river with groovy ambience. (Dorms July-Aug. £7, Sept.-May £6.50; doubles £16; triples £24. Camping £3.50. Open mid-Mar. to mid-Nov.) The brand-new **Flanaghan's Village Hostel** (tel. 74564), a half mile up the road from the Upper Village, boasts spacious sunny rooms, a modern kitchen, mammoth leather couches, and floors with a story (dorms £6.50-7; laundry £1.50). Quentin Tarantino stayed at the **Westwind B&B** (tel. 74227), Upper Village, behind McGann's, just before making *Reservoir Dogs*. The sane find it relaxing, pleasant, friendly, and clean, and they report no threats to their ears (£12).

Doolin has many excellent but costly restaurants, and all three pubs serve excellent grub. The **Doolin Deli** (tel. 74633), in the Lower Village, packs overstuffed sandwiches (£1.30) and stocks groceries (open June-Sept. M-Sa 8:30am-9pm, Su 9:30am-9pm). The pubs of Doolin are well known for their musical brilliance. Both O'Connor's and McGann's have won awards for the best trad music in Ireland. **McGann's** (tel. 74133), Upper Village, has music nightly at 9pm in the summer, weekends at 9pm in the winter, and figgety Irish stew year round (£5). **McDermott's** (tel. 74328), Upper Village, ranks right up there with McGann's (entrees around £5; music nightly in summer; weekends in winter). Most summer standing-room-only sessions start at 9:30pm. **O'Connor's** (tel. 74168), Lower Village, is the busiest of the three, with drink, song, and music nightly and Sunday afternoons all year.

SIGHTS The **Cliffs of Moher** are justifiably one of Ireland's most famous sights. The view from the edge leads 700 ft. straight down into the open sea. These cliffs are so high that people actually see gulls whirling below them. Tour groups cluster where the road ends at the cliffs, although better views await a bit farther off the road. Three miles south of Doolin, the Cliffs brush against R478; cars pay £1 for use of the parking lot. **Bus Éireann** clangs by on the summer-only Galway-Cork route (M-Sa 3 per day).

The 26-mile **Burren Way** and several non-linear bike trails more elusively weave through raised limestone and beds of wildflowers from Doolin (3hr.). The **tourist office** (tel. (065) 81171) houses a bureau de change (open Apr.-Oct. daily 9:30am-5:30pm), and a tea shop rejuvenates weary travelers.

COS. GALWAY AND MAYO

■ Galway City

In the past few years, the city's reputation as Ireland's cultural capital has brought young Irish flocking to Galway (pop. 60,000) like Elvis freaks to Graceland. Mix in the over 13,000 students at Galway's two major universities, a large transient population of twentysomething Europeans, and waves of international backpackers, and you have a small college town on craic. Numerous theater companies and proximity to the Connemara *gaeltacht* make it a center of Irish artistic tradition. Sightseers find Galway a convenient base for trips to the Clare coast or the Connemara.

ORIENTATION AND PRACTICAL INFORMATION

Any transport to Galway will deposit you in **Eyre Sq.,** a central block with the train and bus station on its east side. The real town—or, rather, the part you'll want to visit—spreads out south and west of the square. **Hitchhikers** abound in Galway; dozens at a time wait on Dublin Rd. (N6) scouting rides to Dublin, Limerick, or Kinvara. Most catch bus #2, 5, or 6 from Eyre Sq. to this prime thumb-stop.

Transportation
  Airport: Carnmore (tel. 755569). 3 small Aer Lingus planes jet to Dublin daily.
  Trains: Eyre Sq. (tel. 561444). Open M-Sa 7:40am-6pm. Trains to **Dublin** (3hr., M-F 5 per day, Sa-Su 3-4 per day, M-Th and Sa £15, F and Su £21) stop in **Athlone** (M-Th and Sa £7.50, F and Su £11); transfer at Athlone for all other lines.
  Buses: Eyre Sq. (tel. 562000). Station open July-Aug. M-Sa 8:30am-7pm, Su 8:30am-6pm; Sept.-June M-Sa 8:30am-6pm, Su 8:30am-noon and 1:40-6pm. Private bus companies specialize in the run to **Dublin. P. Nestor Coaches** (tel. 797144) leaves from Imperial Hotel, Eyre Sq. (M-Th and Su 2 per day, F 7 per day, Sa 5 per day, single or day return £5, open return £8). **Citylink** (tel. 564163) leaves from Supermac's, Eyre Sq. (5 per day, last bus at 5:45pm, same prices as Nestor's). A **West Clare Shuttle** to **Doolin, Lisdoonvarna,** and **Fanore** leaves various Galway hostels on request (June-Sept. 1 per day, £5). **Michael Nee Coaches** (tel. 51082) drives from Forester St. through **Clifden** to **Cleggan,** meeting the **Inishboffin** ferry (M-Sa 2-4 per day, £5, return £7). **Bus Éireann** heads to **Belfast** (2-3 per day, Su 1 per day, £16.30), **Cork** (5 per day, £12), **Dublin** (8-9 per day, Su 7-8 per day, £8), and the **Cliffs of Moher** (May 24-Sept. 19 3-4 per day, Su 1-2 per day, £8.20) by way of **Ballyvaughan** (£5.90).
  Local Transportation: City buses (tel. 562000) leave Eyre Sq. every 20min. (70p). Buses go to each area of the city: #1 to **Salthill,** #2 to **Knocknacarra** (west) or **Renmare** (east), #3 to **Castlepark,** and #4 to **Newcastle** and **Rahoon.** Service M-Sa 8am-9pm, Su 11am-9pm. Commuter tickets £8 per week, £29 per month.
  Taxis: Big O Taxis, 21 Upper Dominick St. (tel. 585858).
  Car Rental: Budget Rent-a-Car, Eyre Sq. (tel. 566376).
  Bike Rental: Europa Cycles, Hunter Bldg., Earls Island (tel. 563355). £3 per day, £5 per 24hr., £25 per week; deposit £30. Open M-F 9am-6pm.

Tourist and Financial Services
  Tourist Office: Victoria Pl. (tel. 563081). A block southeast of Eyre Sq. Open July-Aug. daily 8:30am-7:45pm; May-June and Sept. daily 8:30am-5:45pm; Oct.-Apr. M-F and Su 9am-5:45pm, Sa 9am-12:45pm.

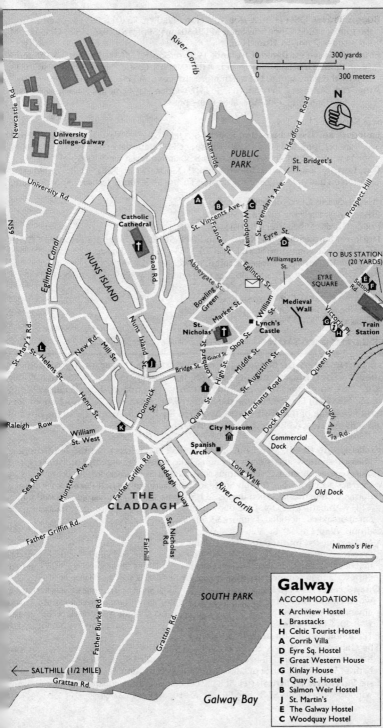

Galway

ACCOMMODATIONS

K Archview Hostel
L Brasstacks
H Celtic Tourist Hostel
A Corrib Villa
D Eyre Sq. Hostel
F Great Western House
G Kinlay House
I Quay St. Hostel
B Salmon Weir Hostel
J St. Martin's
E The Galway Hostel
C Woodquay Hostel

Budget Travel: USIT, Kinlay House, Victoria Pl., Eyre Sq. (tel. 565177), across from the tourist office. Open May-Sept. M-F 9:30am-5:30pm, Sa 10am-3pm; Oct.-Apr. M-F 9:30am-5:30pm, Sa 10am-1pm.

Financial Services: Bank of Ireland, 19 Eyre Sq. (tel. 563181). Open M-W and F 10am-4pm, Th 10am-5pm. **ATM. AIB,** Lynch's Castle, Shop St. (tel. 567041). Exactly the same hours, but much more attractive. **ATM.**

American Express: 7 Eyre Sq. (tel. 562316). Open May-Sept. M-F 9am-9pm, Sa 9am-7pm, Su 10am-7pm; Oct.-Apr. M-Sa 9am-5pm.

Local Services

Launderette: The Bubbles Inn, 18 Mary St. (tel. 563434). Wash and dry £4. Open M-Sa 9am-6:15pm; last wash 2pm. **Prospect Hill Launderette,** Prospect Hill (tel. 568343). Wash and dry £4. Open M-Sa 8:30am-6pm; last wash 4:45pm.

Gay, Lesbian, and Bisexual Information: P.O. Box 45 (tel. 566134). Recorded information on meetings and events; gay line Tu and Th 8-10pm, lesbian line W 8-10pm.

Emergency and Communications

Emergency: Dial 999; no coins required.

Police/Garda: Mill St. (tel. 563161).

Hotlines: Samaritans, 14 Nuns' Island (tel. 561222). 24hr. phones. **Rape Crisis Centre,** 3 St. Augustine St. (tel. (1 850) 355355). Limited hours.

Hospital: University College Hospital, Newcastle Rd. (tel. 524222).

Post Office: Eglinton St. (tel. 562051). Open M and W-Sa 9am-5:30pm, Tu 9:30am-5:30pm.

Internet Access: Cyberzone, Eyre Sq. (tel. 561415), above Supermac's. £2 per 30min., £3 per hr. Open daily 7am-midnight.

Phone Code: 091.

ACCOMMODATIONS

In the last few years, the number of hostel beds in Galway has nearly tripled to almost a thousand. Nevertheless, most of them sag under sleeping backpackers during July and August, so reserve a room before you arrive. **Woodquay** hostels cluster about five minutes from Eyre Sq. around the Salmon Weir. **Dominick St.** hosts its own fleet on the west side of the River Corrib, and **Eyre Sq.** hostels are closest to the bus and train stations. Most B&Bs are 1 mi. away in **Salthill.**

Kinlay House (IHH), Merchants Rd. (tel. 565244), across from the tourist office. Modern, spotless, and friendly, though a little sedate. Washcloths, blue duvets, and closet space in uncrowded rooms approach luxury. **Bureau de change.** 24hr. internet access £5 per hr. July-Sept. and special events 8-bed dorms £8.50; 6-bed dorms with bath £10; 4-bed dorms £11.50, with bath £12.50; singles £20; doubles £28, with bath £32. Oct.-June dorms 50p-£1 cheaper, private rooms £2 cheaper. Small breakfast included. Laundry £3.50. Wheelchair accessible.

Salmon Weir Hostel, St. Vincent's Ave., Woodquay (tel. 561133). Newcomers are quickly sucked into the fun-loving, comfortable atmosphere of this small hostel. Free tea, coffee, washing powder, and peace of mind. No smoking. June-Aug. 4-6 bed dorms £7.50; doubles £20. May dorms £7; doubles £18. Laundry £3. In summer curfew 3am, in winter 2am. **Bike rental** £5 per day, £3.50 per half day.

Quay Street Hostel (IHH), Quay St. (tel. 568644). Shop St. becomes Quay St. A dark wood common room with a fireplace, tidy dorms, and a peerless location in the city center make this hostel the place to be, especially for pub-crawlers. Big dorms £7-8.50; 8-bed dorms £7.50-9; 6-bed dorms £8-9.50; 4-bed dorms with bath £9.50-12; doubles with bath £24-29. Laundry £3.50.

The Galway Hostel, Eyre Sq. (tel. 566959). Attractive, airy dorms with super-clean bathrooms. June-Sept. 14-bed dorms £8; 8-bed dorms £8.50; 4-bed dorms £11, with bath £13; doubles £28. Sept.-May dorms £1 cheaper, doubles £2 cheaper.

Eyre Sq. Hostel, 35 Eyre St. (tel. 568432). A cozy, centrally located hostel with giant windows. Big dorms £7-8; 4-bed dorms £9-10; doubles £22-24.

St. Martin's, 2 Nuns' Island (tel. 568286), on the west bank of the river at the end of Dominick St. (visible from the Bridge St. bridge). Gorgeous riverside location with a grassy lawn. Singles £18; doubles £32.

Camping: Salthill Caravan and Camping Park (tel. 523972 or 522479). On the bay, ½mi. west of Salthill. Crowded in summer. £3 per hiker or cyclist. Open May-Oct.

FOOD

The east bank has the greatest concentration of restaurants; Abbeygate St. has a large selection, and the short blocks around Quay, High, and Shop St. are filled with good values. The **SuperValu** (tel. 567833), in the Eyre Sq. mall, is a chef's playground (open M-W and Sa 9am-6:30pm, Th-F 9am-9pm). **Evergreen Health Food,** 1 Mainguard St. (tel. 564215), offers food from its shelves as well as from a menu (open M-Th and Sa 9am-6:30pm, F 9am-8pm). On Saturday mornings, a **market** sets up in front of St. Nicholas Church on Market St. (open 8am-1pm). Fishermen sell cups of mussels fresh from the bay (about £1). Buy. Eat. Go mussel mad.

Java's, Upper Abbeygate St. (tel. 565086). 20 varieties of cappuccino jolt clubgoers unwilling to go home. Baps £4. Busiest at 2:30am but doesn't close until 4.

Anton's (tel. 582067). A bit off the beaten path, a 3min. walk up Father Griffin Rd. over the bridge near the Spanish Arch. Salads, vegetables, fruits, and meats all right on target. Salad and bread £3; sandwiches £2.50. Open Tu-Sa 11am-6pm.

The Long Walk (tel. 561114), next to the Spanish Arch and a hell of a lot more interesting. This cafe and wine bar magically creates a warm and relaxed atmosphere on the first floor of a medieval battlement. The food is as epic as the setting. Food served M-Sa 12:30-4pm and 7-10:30pm, Su 7-10:30pm.

Get Stuffed Olive, Saint Anthony's Pl., Woodquay (tel. 564445). Wholefood vegetarian and vegan dishes. Sandwiches under £2. Open daily 11:30am-10pm.

Pierre's, Quay St. (tel. 566066). The 3-course meal (£10.90) may be slightly out of range for most budget travelers, but if you are going to break the bank, it ought to happen at this Quay St. favorite. Delicious lunches under £5.

Food for Thought, Lower Abbeygate St. (tel. 565854). Coffeeshop and wholefood restaurant serves an interesting variety of vegetarian dishes (£2.50) and mind-bogglingly big baps (from £2.50). Open M-Sa 8am-6pm.

PUBS

Galway's pub scene is exploding along with its population. Dominick St. is the best place to hear music, Quay St. is where all the fabulously beautiful pubs are, and Eyre Sq. pubs are bigger and badder. Fabulous trad usually blazes from a few pubs a night.

La Graal, 38 Lower Dominick St. (tel. 567614). This candle-lit wine bar and restaurant draws a crowd of beautiful continentals and other sophisticates. Salsa dancing Th, disco (gay friendly) Su, and a married priest reading mass Su mornings. Open daily until 1am.

The Crane, 2 Sea Rd. (tel. 587419). The place to hear trad in Galway. Enter in the side and hop up to the 2nd-floor loft. Trad "whenever."

Buskar Browne's/The Slate House (tel. 563377), between Cross St. and Kirwin's Ln. A perfect compromise for guilty drinkers, the Slate House was a nunnery for 300 years before it became a pub. Its fantastic 3rd-floor Hall of the Tribes is the most spectacular lounge in Galway.

The Quays, Quay St. (tel. 568347). Popular with the younger crowd and scamming yuppies. The massive, multi-floored interior was built with carved wood taken from the balconies and stained-glass windows of an old church. Cover bands electrify the equally impressive upstairs extension nightly 10pm-1:30am. Cover £5.

McSwiggin's, Eyre St. (tel. 568917), near Eglinton St. A sprawling mess of small rooms and stairwells spanning 3 stories. The craic is good and so is the food.

The Skeffington Arms, Eyre Sq. (tel. 563173). A grand, splendidly decorated, newly converted, multi-storied hotel with 6 different bars.

SIGHTS

The commerce and culture of Galway overshadow its historic aspects. The tourist office sells the *Medieval Galway Map*, which discusses local history (£3.50). Galway's Catholic Cathedral, officially known as the **Cathedral of Our Lady Assumed into Heaven and St. Nicholas,** looms above the Salmon Weir Bridge where Gaol and University Rd. meet across the river from most of the city. The boring exterior reveals none of the controversy that assailed its eclectic design 25 years ago, centering around the great bare walls of Connemara stone intersecting with elaborate mosaics in the impressive interior. *(Excellent tours M-F 9:30am-4:30pm. Mood-setting organ practice M-F 3:30-5:30pm. Open Su for mass.)* Closer to the center of town near the Church of St. Nicholas, the tiny **Nora Barnacle House,** 8 Bowling Green (tel. 564743), exposes a few letters and photos relating to James Joyce and his wife. *(Open mid-May to mid-Sept. M-Sa 10am-1pm and 2-5pm. £1.)*

Shop St. runs past **Lynch's Castle,** an elegant stone mansion originally constructed in 1320. In the late 1400s, Lynch Jr. killed a Spaniard whom he suspected of liking his girlfriend. The son, sentenced to hang, was so beloved by the populace that not one man would agree to be the hangman. Lynch Sr., the lord of the castle, was so determined to administer justice that he had to hang his own son. The window from which Lynch lynched Lynch Jr. is supposedly the one behind St. Nicholas Church. A skull and crossbones commemorate the deed. The castle now houses the Allied Irish Bank. *(Exhibit room open M-W and F 10am-4pm, Th 10am-5pm. Free.)* Many Lynches lie together in their family tomb in the **Church of St. Nicholas,** Market St., behind the castle. The church, full of oddities from many sources, also devotes attention to a heritage project. *(Open May-Sept. daily 9am-5:45pm. Free. Unnecessary tour £1, students 50p.)*

By the river, the Long Walk makes a pleasant stroll to the **Spanish Arch,** the only surviving gateway to the old trading town. The **Galway City Museum** (tel. 567641), in Tower House next to the arch, can show you up the stairs to the top of the arch. *(Open May-Oct. daily 10am-1pm and 2:15-5:15pm; check at the tourist office for Nov.-Apr. opening times. £1, students 50p.)* Across the river, the neighborhood called the **Claddagh** spreads out from Dominick St. Until the 1930s, the area was an independent, Irish-speaking, thatched-cottage fishing village. The cottages were long ago replaced by stone bungalows, but a bit of the small-town appeal persists. From the Claddagh, the waterfront road leads west to Salthill. The coast here alternates between pebbles and sand perfect for beach frolicking.

ENTERTAINMENT

Culture crowds into Galway proper, and music of all varieties barrages pubs and clubs. The *Advertiser* and *Galway Guide* (free) provide listings of events and are available at most pubs and newsagents. The **Galway Arts Centre,** 47 Dominick St. (tel. 565886), will give you a good idea of what's going on in town (open M-Sa 10am-5:30pm). The **Town Hall Theatre,** Courthouse Sq. (tel. 569777), hosts everything from the Druid Theatre Company's Irish-themed plays and original Irish films to *Little Shop of Horrors*. *(Programming daily in summer. Tickets £5-15; student discounts for most shows. Most performances 8pm.)* The **nightclub** population is densest in Salthill, but Galway's action can suffice. **GPO,** Eglinton St. (tel. 563073), may not be attractive but draws a high-energy crowd nonetheless. It hosts Murphy's Comedy Club on Sunday evenings. *(£5 includes nightclub cover.)* **The Alley,** behind the Skeff, draws a young local crowd with its unimaginative music and decor. *(Cover £3-6.)* The more adventurous and mobile head out to the **Liquid Club,** King's Hill (tel. 522715), in Salthill. Expect a provocative mix of dance and odd indie that should fire your rage until well into morning. *(Cover £6. Open Th-Su.)*

■ Coole Park and Thoor Ballylee

Located west off N18 1 mi. north of Gort, the **Coole Park** nature reserve was once the estate of Lady Augusta Gregory, a friend and collaborator of Yeats (see **Literary Traditions,** p. 617). Although the house was ruined by the 1922 Civil War, the yew walk and garden have been preserved. The famous great copper beech "autograph tree" in the picnic area bears the initials of some important Irish figures: George Bernard Shaw, Sean O'Casey, Douglas Hyde (first president of Ireland), and Yeats himself. The **Coole Park's Visitors Centre** (tel. (091) 631804) eschews Yeats in favor of local rocks, trees, and furry wildlife. *(Open mid-Apr. to mid-June Tu-Su 10am-5pm; mid-June to Aug. daily 9:30am-6:30pm; Sept. daily 10am-5pm. Last admission 45min. before closing. £2, students £1.)* **Coole Lake,** where Yeats watched nine-and-fifty swans "all suddenly mount/And scatter wheeling in great broken rings/Upon their clamorous wings," is about a mile from the garden. The swans are still here in winter. Three miles north of Coole Park, a road turns off Galway Rd. and runs a mile to **Thoor Ballylee.** In 1916, Yeats bought this 13th- and 14th-century tower for £35, renovated it, and lived here with his family off and on from 1922 to 1928. A film on Yeats's life informs visitors in the **Visitors Centre** (tel. (091) 631436) while a coffee shop feeds them. *(Open Easter-Sept. daily 10am-6pm. £3, students £2.50.)*

▓ Aran Islands

The three Aran Islands (Oileáin Árann)—Inishmore, Inishmaan, and Inisheer—rise up out of Galway Bay 15 mi. southwest of Galway City. Visitors are amazed by their stark limestone landscapes plunging straight into the sea, ancient ruins, and islanders, many of whom maintain traditional lifestyles. The **phone code** for the islands is 099.

GETTING THERE

Three ferry companies—**Island Ferries, O'Brien Shipping/Doolin Ferries,** and **Liscannor Ferries**—operate boats to the Aran Islands. **Island Ferries** (tel. (091) 561767, after hours 72273) serves all three islands year-round from Rossaveal (35min., return £15). A bus connects the tourist office in Galway with the ferry port (departs 1½hr. before sailing time, return £4). The Sea Sprinter connects Inishmore with Inisheer via Inishmaan (return £10). **O'Brien Shipping/Doolin Ferries** (tel. (065) 74455 in Doolin, (091) 567283 in Galway; after hours (065) 71710), connects Doolin and Galway to the Aran Islands year-round (Galway to any island return £12; Galway-Aran-Doolin £25). **Liscannor Aran Ferries** (tel. 065) 81368) depart twice per day from Liscannor and stop at Inishmaan and Inisheer (return £17).

◀ Inishmore

Exactly 437 kinds of wildflowers rise from the stony terrain of Inishmore (pop. 900), the largest and northernmost of the Arans. The landscape is dotted with stone walls, stark cliffs, ruins, forts, and churches, in addition to holy wells and kelp kilns. The island's most impressive monument, dating from the first century BC, is **Dún Aengus,** 4 mi. west of the pier at Kilronan. One of the better-preserved prehistoric forts in Europe, its walls are 18 ft. thick and form a semi-circle around a sheer drop. Down the side of the cliff, **Worm Hole** is a saltwater lake filled from the limestone aquifer below the ground. Three miles west of Kilronan on the way to the fort lie the **Seven Churches.** This scattered grouping of religious remains stimulate speculation about the island's former inhabitants. In Kilronan, the **Aran Islands Heritage Centre** (Ionad Árann; tel. 61355) displays *curraghs,* soil and wildlife exhibits, old Aran clothes, and a cliff rescue. *(Open Apr.-Oct. daily 10am-7pm. £2, students £1.50.)* The **Black Fort** (Dún Dúchathair), 1 mi. south of Kilronan over eerie terrain, is even larger than Dún Aengus and a millennium older.

Ferries land in Kilronan. **Aran Bicycle Hire** (tel. 61132) rents bikes; just don't lose your receipt (£5 per day, £21 per week; deposit £9; open Mar.-Nov. daily 9am-7:30pm). Strangely enough, bike theft here is a problem—lock it up, hide it, or don't ever leave it. The **tourist office** (tel. 61263) in Kilronan changes money, holds bags (75p), and sells several maps (open Feb.-Nov. daily 10am-6:45pm). The **post office** (tel. 61101), up the hill from the pier, past Spar Market, has **bureau de change** (open M-F 9am-5pm, Sa 9am-1pm). **Internet access** is sometimes available at the heritage center.

Hostels on the other islands are less crowded: it's not a bad idea to see Inishmore as a daytrip. **Mainistir House (IHH)** (tel. 61169) offers a common room and huge dinners just half a mile from Kilronan (dorms £8; singles £11; doubles £24; laundry £4; **bikes** £5). **Dún Aengus Hostel** (tel. 61318) hides 4 mi. west in Kilmurvey; take the first turn-off to the right from the beach. This hostel, a 10-minute walk from Dún Aengus, is a great outpost for outdoorsy types (dorms £7; laundry £2). **Spar Market** (tel. 61203), past the hostel in Kilronan, seems to be the island's social center (open M-Sa 9am-8pm, Su 10am-6pm). **Teach Nan Phaidt** (tel. 61330), the thatched restaurant at the turn-off to Dún Aengus, specializes in home-cooked bread with home-smoked fish. (Smoked salmon sandwich £4.50. Open daily July-Aug. 10am-9pm; Mar.-June and Sept.-Dec. 10am-5pm.) For organic lunches and desserts in an historic setting, try **The Man of Aran Restaurant** (tel. 61301), located just past Kilmurvey Beach (open daily 12:30-3:30pm for lunch). **Joe Watt's Bar,** the **American Bar** (tel. 61303), and **Tí Joe Mac** (tel. 61248) attract locals and tourists and often have trad in summer.

■ Inishmaan

The seagulls on Inishmaan (Inis Meáin; pop. 300) plead with you to stay a little longer on the cliffs, while goats stand on stone walls looking for signs of life in the nearby fields of limestone. The *Inishmaan Way* brochure (£1.50) describes a 5 mi. walking route to all of the island's sights. To the left of the pier, 8th-century **Cill Cheannannach** church left its remains on the shore. One mile north of the pier is Inishmaan's safest beach, **Trá Leitreach. Dún Chonchúir,** a 7th-century fort, looks over the entire island. Halfway across the island on the main road hunches what's left of **Synge's cottage,** where the Anglo-Irish author wrote much of his Aran-inspired work from 1898-1902. The trek out **Synge's Chair** pays off with a view of splashing waves.

An Cora (tel. 73010), a small coffeeshop inside an old Irish cottage at the pier, dispenses food and **tourist information** on one plate (open July-Aug. daily 9am-6pm). The **post office** (tel. 73001) is in Inishmaan's tiny village, which spreads out along the road west of the pier to divide the island in half. The **An Dún Shop** (tel. 73067) sells some food at the access to Dún Chonchúir. The center of life on the island, **Padraic Faherty's** thatched pub, serves pub grub all day.

■ Inisheer

The Arans have been described as "quietness without loneliness." Only Inisheer (Inis Oírr, pop. 300), the smallest Aran, best fulfills the promise of the famous phrase. Islanders and stray donkeys seem to be present in even proportions on this island less than 2 mi. in diameter and traced by labyrinthine stone walls. The **Inis Oírr Way** covers the island's major attractions in 4 mi., stopping first at **Cnoc Raithní,** a bronze-age tumulus (stone burial mound) 2000 years older than Christianity. Walking along the An Trá shore leads to the romantic overgrown graveyard of **St. Kevin's Church** (Teampall Chaomhain). Farther east along the beach, a grassy track leads to **An Loch Mór,** a 16-acre inland lake where wildfowl prevail. The stone ringfort **Dún Formna** is above the lake. Continuing past the lake and back onto the seashore is the **Plassy wreck,** a ship that sank offshore and washed up on Inisheer in 1960. The walk back to the center leads through Formna Village and on out to **Cill na Seacht nIníon,** a small monastery with a stone fort. The remains of the 14th-century O'Brien castle razed by Cromwell in 1652, sit atop a nearby knoll. On the west side of the island **Tobar Einne,** St. Enda's Holy Well, is said to have healing powers.

Rothair Inis Oírr (tel. 75033) rents **bikes** (£5 per day, £25 per week). A list of Inisheer's 19 B&Bs hangs on the window of the small **tourist office** (tel. 75008) next to the pier (open July-Aug. daily 10am-6pm). The **post office** (tel. 75001) is farther up the island to the left of the pier in the cream house with turquoise trim (open M-F 9am-1pm and 2-5:30pm, Sa 9am-1pm). The **Brú Hostel (IHH)** (tel. 75024), visible from the pier, is clean and spacious. Upper-level rooms have skylights for stargazing. Call ahead in July and August. (4- to 6-bed dorms £7; private rooms £9 per person, with bath £10. Continental breakfast £2, Irish breakfast £3.50. Sheets £1. Laundry £2.) The **Ionad Campála Campground** (tel. 75008) stretches its tarps near the beach for campers who don't mind chilling ocean winds (£2 per tent, £10 per week; showers 50p; open May-Sept.).

■ Cong

Cozy little Cong (pop. 300), a pastoral, romantic village in the lake-filled hills of Co. Mayo, has all one could ask of rural Ireland. Bubbling streams and shady footpaths criss-cross the surrounding forests, a ruined abbey crumbles on the edge of the forests, and a majestic castle towers over Lough Corrib. Numerous sights commemorate Cong's brief moment in the spotlight, when John Wayne and Maureen O'Hara filmed *The Quiet Man* here in 1951. The movie was shot on the grounds of impressive **Ashford Castle**, home of the Guinness heirs from 1852 to 1939 (closed, but you can see the gardens for £3). The sculpted head of its last abbot keeps watch over the ruins of the 12th-century **Royal Abbey of Cong,** near Danagher's Hotel in the village. *(Always open. Free.)* Across the abbey grounds, a footbridge spans the River Cong. Past the Monk's Fishing House and to the right, the footpath leads to **Pigeon Hole, Teach Aille,** and **Ballymaglancy** caves and to a 4000-year-old burial chamber, **Giant's Grave.**

Buses leave for **Westport** (M-Sa 1 per day) from Ashford gates, **Clifden** (M-Sa 1 per day) from Ryan's Hotel, and **Galway** (M-Sa 1-2 per day) from both (all £6). The **tourist office,** Abbey St. (tel. 46542), will point you toward Cong's wonders (open Mar.-Oct. daily 9:30am-6pm). The **post office** (tel. 46001) is on Main St. (open M-Tu and Th-Sa 9am-1pm and 2-5:30pm, W 9am-1pm). The **telephone code** starred in *The Quiet 092*.

The **Quiet Man Hostel (IHH),** Abbey St. (tel. 46511, reservations 46089), across the street from Cong Abbey, is central, spotless, sociable, and spacious (dorms £6; continental breakfast £2.50; **camping** facilities £3). **The Cong Hostel (IHH)** is run by the same family. Locals down mammoth meals (roast of the day, vegetables, and potatoes £6) and countless pints at **Danagher's Hotel and Restaurant** (tel. 46494). **The Quiet Man Coffee Shop,** Main St. (tel. 46034), is obviously obsessed (soup and sandwich £2.70; open mid-Mar. to Oct. daily 10am-6:30pm). Cooks can go crazy at **O'Connor's Supermarket,** Main St. (tel. 46008; open daily 8am-9pm).

■ Connemara

The Connemara is composed of a lacy net of inlets and islands along the coast, a rough gang of inland mountains, and some bogs in between. This thinly populated but geographically varied western arm of Co. Galway, which harbors some of the country's most breathtaking and solitary scenery, seldom fails to impress. Ireland's largest *gaeltacht* stretches along this coast. Squishy old bogs spread between the coast and two major mountain ranges, the **Twelve Bens** and the **Maamturks.**

Cycling is a particularly rewarding way to absorb the Connemara. **Hiking** through the boglands and along the coastal routes is also popular. The **Western Way** footpath offers dazzling views as it winds 31 mi. from Oughterard to Leenane through the Maamturks. **Buses** regularly service the main road from Galway to Westport, with stops in Clifden, Oughterard, Cong, and Leenane. N59 from Galway to Clifden is the main thoroughfare; R336, R340, and R341 make more elaborate coastal loops. **Hitchers** report that friendly locals are likely to give tours of the region.

■ Clifden

Clifden slumbers in the winter but explodes in peak season as crowds of international visitors fill its five hostels, tourbuses bring traffic to a standstill, and musicians shake the town's pubs nightly. There are no cliffs in Clifden itself, but 10 mi. **Sky Road,** looping around the head of land west of town, paves the way to some dizzying cliffs and makes an ideal cycling route. One mile down Sky Rd. stand the ruins of **Clifden Castle,** once home to Clifden's founder, John D'Arcy. One of the nicer ways to acquaint yourself with Connemara is by hiking south to the Alcock and Brown monument, 3 mi. past Salt Lake and Lough Fadda. An archaeologist from the **Connemara Walking Center,** Market St. (tel. 21379), leads inspiring tours that explore the history, folklore, geology, and archaeology of the region. *(Open Mar.-Oct. M-Sa 10am-6pm. 1 full-day or 2 half-day tours per day from Easter to Oct.; call for a schedule. £8-24.)*

The **Clifden Town Hostel (IHH),** Market St. (tel. 21076), has great facilities, spotless rooms, near-pub location, and a friendly, quiet atmosphere (dorms £7; doubles £20; triples £27; quads £32). At **Leo's Hostel (IHH),** Sea View (tel. 21429), a turf fire, good location, and astounding "loo with a view" outweigh the fact that the house is feeling its age. (Dorms £7; private rooms £8. Laundry £3. **Bike rental** £5 per day. Camping £3 per person.) **An Tulan,** Westport Rd. (tel. 21942), offers wonderful homecooked meals at down-to-earth prices (sandwiches from £1.20, entrees around £4; open daily 10am-6pm). Cozy, candlelit **Mitchell's Restaurant,** The Square (tel. 21867), serves hearty plates for all palates (open daily noon-10:30pm). Dark wood adds class to the **Derryclare Restaurant,** The Square (tel. 21440), where lunch specials are a particularly good value (6 oysters £4.50). Dinner is pricier (pasta around £7; open daily 8am-10:30pm). Bring your own instruments to **Mannion's,** Market St. (tel. 21780), which has music nightly in summer (F-Sa in winter). **King's,** The Square (tel. 21800), is the town's best pint by consensus; locals vote with their feet. **Malarkey's,** on Church Hill, is perpetually packed and jiggity jammin' on Thursdays.

Bus Éireann rolls from Cullen's Coffeeshop on Market St. to **Galway via Oughterard** (2hr., June-Aug. M-Sa 6 per day, Su 2 per day; Sept.-May 1 per day, £6.50) and **Westport via Leenane** (1½hr., late June to Aug. 1-2 per day). **Michael Nee** (tel. 51082) runs a private bus from The Square to **Galway** (June-Sept., £5, return £7) and **Cleggan** (June-Sept. 1-2 per day, Oct.-May 2 per week, £3, return £4). **Mannion's,** Bridge St. (tel. 21160, after hours 21155), rents **bikes.** (£5 per day, £30 per week; deposit £10. Open M-Sa 9:30am-6:30pm, Su 10am-1pm and 5-7pm.) The friendly **tourist office** (tel. 21163) is on Market St. (Open July-Aug. M-Sa 9:45am-5:45pm, Su noon-4pm; May-June and Sept. M-Sa 9am-5:45pm.) An **AIB** (tel. 21129) with an **ATM** is in The Square (open M-Tu and Th-F 10am-12:30pm and 1:30-4pm, W 10am-5pm). The **post office** (tel. 21156) is on Main St. (open M-F 9:30am-5:30pm, Sa 9:30am-1:30pm). The **telephone code** is *ólta* after 095 pints.

■ Inishbofin

Seven miles from the western tip of the Connemara, the island of Inishbofin (pop. 200) keeps time according to the ferry, the tides, and the sun, and visitors easily slip into a similar habit. Each of the four peninsulas usually warrants a two- to four-hour walk. Most items of historical interest are on the southeast peninsula. A conservation area stretches east past the abbey and harbors long pristine beaches and a picturesque village. The ragged northeast peninsula is fantastic for bird watchers. A dramatic group of round seastacks called **The Stags** towers offshore. The tidal causeway that connects The Stags to the mainland during low tide is **extremely dangerous**—do not venture out onto it.

Ferries leave for Inishbofin from **Cleggan,** a tiny village 10 mi. northwest of Clifden (see above). Two ferries service the island: the **Island Discovery** (tel. 44642) is larger, steadier, faster, and more expensive (30min., July-Aug. 3 per day, Apr.-June and Sept.-Oct. 2 per day, £12), but the **M.V. Dun Aengus** (Paddy O'Halloran; tel. 45806) runs year-round (45min., July-Aug. 3 per day, Apr.-June and Sept.-Oct. 2 per day, Nov.-Apr.

1 per day, £10). Both ferries carry bikes for free. Tickets are most conveniently purchased on the ferry itself. Stock up at the **Spar** (tel. 44750) before you go (open daily 9am-10pm). The **phone code** is Day's 095.

Kieran Day's excellent **Inishbofin Island Hostel (IHH)** (tel. 45855) is a 10-minute walk from the ferry landing; take a right at the pier and head up the hill. Visitors are blessed with pine bunks, a large conservatory, and entertaining views. (Dorms £6.50; private rooms £9-10 per person. Sheets £1. Laundry £4. **Camping** £4 per person.) **Remote Horseshoe B&B** (tel. 45812) sets itself apart on the east end of the island (£13). The **Emerald Cottage** (tel. 45865), a 10-minute walk west from the pier, offers gracious B&B living (£13). There is no camping allowed on the east end beach or the adjacent dunes. **Day's Pub** (tel. 45829) by the pier serves food from noon to 5pm.

■ Connemara National Park

Outside Letterfrack, Connemara National Park (tel. (095) 41054) occupies 7¾ sq. mi. of mountainous, bird-filled countryside. The far-from-solid terrain of the park is composed of bogs thinly covered by a screen of grass and flowers. Be prepared to dirty your shoes and pants. Guides lead free two-hour walks over the hills and through the bogs and give lectures on the region's history and ecology. (*Open daily June 10am-6:30pm; July-Aug. 9:30am-6:30pm; May and Sept. 10am-5:30pm. £2, students £1. Walks July-Aug. M, W, and F 10:30am; talks July-Aug. W 8:30pm. Free*). The **visitors center** excels at explaining blanket bogs, raised bogs, turf, and heathland. The **Snuffaunboy Nature Trail** and the **Ellis Wood Trail** are the perfect routes for easy hikes and pony-rides. Thirty-minute walks (50p) starts at the visitors center, where the staff helps plan longer hikes. Experienced hikers often head for the **Twelve Bens** (*Na Benna Beola*, a.k.a. the Twelve Pins), a rugged range that reaches 2400 ft. heights and is not recommended for single or beginning hikers. There are no proper trails, but Josh Lynam's guidebook (£5) meticulously plots out 18 fantastic hikes through the Twelve Bens and the Maamturks. Hikers often base themselves at the **Ben Lettery Hostel (An Óige/HI)** (tel. (095) 51136) in Ballinafad; the turn-off from N59 is 8 mi. east of Clifden (June-Aug. £6.50; Easter-May and Sept. £5.50).

■ Westport

In the summer, Westport draws more visitors than it knows what to do with. Some stay in its four excellent hostels, others heartily contribute to its thriving pub life, and some spend their days strolling along its four crowded streets, drinking tea in dapper cafes, shopping for commemorative keychains, and admiring the fresh coats of paint on the newest rash of B&Bs.

ORIENTATION AND PRACTICAL INFORMATION The tiny Carrowbeg River runs through Westport's Mall with Bridge and James St. extending south. Shop St. connects Bridge St. to James St. on the other end. Westport House and ferries to Clare Island are on Westport Quay, a 45-minute walk west of town. The N60 passes through Clifden, Galway, and Sligo on its way to Westport. **Trains** (tel. 25253 or 25329 for inquiries) arrive at the Altamont St. Station, a five-minute walk up on North Mall (open M-Sa 9:30am-6pm). The train goes to **Dublin via Athlone** (M-Th and Sa 3 per day, £15; F and Su 2 per day, £20). **Buses** leave from The Octagon and travel to **Ballina** (M-Sa 1-3 per day, Su 1 per day, £6.70) and **Galway** (M-F 2 per day, £8.80). The **tourist office** (tel. 25711) is on North Mall (open Apr.-Oct. M-Sa 9am-12:45pm and 2-5:45pm, Su 10am-6pm). **Bank of Ireland**, North Mall (tel. 25522), and **AIB**, Shop St. (tel. 25466), have **ATMs** (open M-W and F 10am-4pm, Th 10am-5pm). **O'Donnell's**, Bridge St. (tel. 25163) farms pharmaceuticals (open M-Sa 9am-6:30pm). Rotating Sunday (12:30-2pm) openings are posted on the door. The **post office** (tel. 25475) is also on North Mall (open M-Sa 9am-noon and 2-5:30pm). **Dunning's Cyberpub**, The Octagon (tel. 25161), thinks different (£5 per 30min; open daily 9am-11:30pm). The **phone code** gives props to the class of 098.

ACCOMMODATIONS Westport's B&Bs are easily spotted on the Castlebar and Alta-mont Rd. off North Mall. Most charge £16-18. Firm pine beds line up in **Old Mill Holiday Hostel (IHH),** James St. (tel. 27045), a renovated mill and brewery between The Octagon and the tourist office (dorms £6.50; sheets 50p; laundry £3). **Club Atlantic (IHH),** Altamont St. (tel. 26644 or 26717), is a five-minute walk up from The Mall across from the train station. The beds in this massive institution are quiet and comfortable (dorms £5.50-6.50; singles £9; doubles £11.80-13.80; laundry £2; **camping** £4). **Slí na h-Óige (HYI),** North Mall (tel. 28751), is appropriately named "the way of the young." This family-run hostel features comfortable timber beds, free internet access, and two small kitchens (dorms £7; open June-Sept.). A garden and conservatory flank **The Granary Hostel** (tel. 25903), 1 mi. from town on Louisburgh Rd., near the main entrance to Westport House. If you don't mind the cramped quarters or the short walk to the outdoor (enclosed and hot) showers, you're guaranteed to enjoy a night within its rugged walls (dorms £6; open Jan.-Nov.). **Altamont House,** Altamont St. (tel. 25226), is the culmination of 30 years of B&B. The garden is a modern Eden (£16; open Mar.-Dec.).

FOOD Country Fresh (tel. 25377) sells juicy produce (open M-F 8am-6:30pm, Sa 8am-6pm; closes early on W during winter). The **country market** by the Town Hall at The Octagon vends farm-fresh vegetables, eggs, and milk (open Th 10:30am-1:30pm). Processed foods are abundant at **SuperValu** supermarket (tel. 27000), on Shop St. (open M-W and Sa 8:30am-7:30pm, Th-F 8:30am-9pm, Su 10am-6pm). Praised by locals as an exemplary teahouse, **McCormack's,** Bridge St. (tel. 25619), serves pastries, teas, and simple meals on floral tablecloths (open July-Sept. M-Sa 10am-6pm; Oct.-June Tu-Sa 10am-6pm). Eat-in or take-away, the food at **Cafolla,** Bridge St. (tel. 25168), is incredibly cheap. (Open June-Sept. M-Sa 11am-1am, Su noon-11pm; Oct.-May M-Sa 11am-11pm, Su 5-11pm.) **Bernie's High Street Café,** High St. (tel. 27797), soothes with soft light, ecru walls, and comfortingly healthy plants (open daily noon-10pm).

PUBS AND CLUBS Westport is blessed with good craic. Search Bridge St. to find a scene that suits you. The only disco in town is in the **Castlecourt Hotel** on Castlebar St. *(Ages 18+. Cover £5. Open F-Su.)* **Matt Molloy's,** Bridge St. (tel. 26655), is owned by the flautist of the Chieftains. All the cool people, including his friends, go here. A run-down exterior hides vibrant **Henehan's Bar,** Bridge St. (tel. 25561). Twentysome-things fight eightysomethings for space at the bar. Techno blares and Guinness flows at **O'Malley's Pub,** Bridge St., across from Matt Molloy's. Old, dark, and smoky, **Pete McCarthy's,** Quay St. (tel. 27050), uphill from The Octagon, attracts regulars (trad on weekends in summer.)

SIGHTS The grounds of **Westport House** are beautiful and free. To get there, take James St. above The Octagon, bear right, and follow the signs to the Quay (45min.). The **Clew Bay Heritage Centre** (tel. 26852), at the end of the Quay, crams together fascinating historical and literary minutia. *(Open July-Sept. M-F 10am-5pm, Sa-Su 2-5pm; Oct.-June M-F noon-3pm. £1.)*

Conical **Croagh Patrick** rises 2510 ft. over Clew Bay. The summit has been revered as a holy site for thousands of years. St. Patrick prayed and fasted here for 40 days and nights in AD 441 before banishing the snakes from Ireland. The deeply religious climb Croagh Patrick barefoot on the last Sunday in July, also Lug's holy night, Lugh-nasa. Others climb the mountain just for the exhilaration and the view. It takes about four hours total to climb and descend the mountain. Be warned that the ascent can be quite steep and the footing unsure. Well-shod climbers start their excursion from the 15th-century **Murrisk Abbey,** several miles west of Westport on R395 toward Louisburgh. Buses go to Murrisk (July-Aug. M-F 3 per day, Sept.-June M-Sa 2 per day), but a cab (tel. 27171) is cheaper for three people and more convenient. On September 19-28, 1999, Westport celebrates the annual **Westport Arts Festival** (tel. 28833) with dozens of free concerts, poetry readings, and theatrical productions.

■ Achill Island

Although its popularity as a holiday refuge has inexplicably dwindled, Ireland's biggest island is still one of its most beautiful. Ringed by glorious beaches and cliffs, the interior of Achill (AK-ill) Island consists of bog, mountain, bog-like surface, bog, bog, spam, and bog. The town Achill Sound, the gateway to the island, has its nicest hostel, while the island's life centers around the old-school seaside resorts of Keel, Pollagh, and Dooagh, which form a flat, connected strip of buildings along Achill's longest beaches. Visitors will find it easiest to travel by bike or car. The spectacular Atlantic Drive, which roams along the craggy south coast past beautiful beaches to Dooega, makes a fantastic bike ride. Achill hosts the **Scoil Acla** traditional music and art festival (tel. 45284) during the first two weeks of August. **Buses** run infrequently over the bridge from Achill Sound, Dugort, Keel, and Dooagh to **Westport, Galway,** and **Cork** (in summer M-Sa 5 per day, in winter M-Sa 2 per day, £6 return), and to **Sligo, Enniskillen,** and **Belfast** (in summer M-Sa 3 per day, in winter 2 per day). Hitchers report relative success during July and August, but cycling is more reliable. The island's **tourist office** (tel. 45385) is next to Ted Lavelle's Esso station in Cashel, on the main road from Achill Sound to Keel (open 10am-5:30pm M-Sa). True island explorers will pay £3.35 for Bob Kingston's map and guide, but there's a freebie for the rest. There's no bank on the island. Achill Sound holds a **post office** and **bureau de change** (tel. 45141; open M-F 9am-12:30pm and 1:30-5:30pm, Sa 9am-1pm); a **SuperValu** supermarket (open daily 9am-7pm), and a **pharmacy** (tel. 45248; open July-Aug. M-Sa 9:30am-6pm; Sept.-June Tu-Sa 9:30am-6pm). The **phone code** is 098.

Achill Sound Hotel (tel. 45245) rents **bikes** (£6 per day, £30 per week; deposit £40; open daily 9am-9pm). The **Wild Haven Hostel** (tel. 45392), a block left past the church, glows with polished floors, antique furniture, and a turf fire in the sitting room. (Dorms £7.50; private rooms £10 per person. Breakfast £3.50; candle-lit dinner £12.50. Sheets £1. Laundry £5. Lockout 11am-3:30pm, except on rainy days. **Camping** £4.) The **Railway Hostel,** just before the bridge to town, is a simple, multi-kitchened, casual affair in the old station (the last train arrived in the 1930s). The proprietors can be found at Mace Supermarket (tel. 45187) in town. (Dorms £6; private rooms with bath £7 per person. Sheets £1. Laundry £1.50.) Opposite the Railway Hostel, **Alice's Harbour Inn** (tel. 45138) does more than its share for the tourist industry. The owners allow **camping** and provide tourist info if the office is closed. The inn also feeds hungry souls (10am-10pm).

The sandy Trawmore Strand of **Keel** sweeps 3 mi. eastward, flanked by cliffs. Encouraged by a government tax scheme, hundreds of holiday developments have popped up like zits across the forehead of the valley within the past three years. Two miles north of Keel on the road looping back to Dugort, the self-explanatory **Deserted Village** is populated only by stone houses closely related to early Christian *clocháns.* A grueling bike ride over the cliffs to the west of **Dooagh** leads to the blue-flag **Keem Bay** beach, the most beautiful spot on the island, wedged between the seas and great green walls of weed, rock, and sheep. Basking sharks, earth's second-largest fish, were once fished off Keem Bay, but bathers who don't look like plankton have nothing to fear. The **Croaghaun Mountains,** climbable from Keem Bay, provide bone-chilling views of the Croaghaun Cliffs.

■ Ballina

What Knock is to the Marian cult, Ballina (bah-lin-AH) is to the religion of bait and tackle. The town, however, has non-ichthyological attractions as well, including its lovely vistas of river walks and a raging weekend pub scene. Almost everyone in a 50 mi. radius, from sheep farmers to college students, packs into town on Saturday nights. Former Irish President Mary Robinson grew up in Ballina and refined her political skills in the town's 40-odd pubs.

ORIENTATION AND PRACTICAL INFORMATION Ballina's commercial center is on the west bank of the river Moy. A bridge crosses over to the cathedral and tourist office on the east bank. The bridge connects to Tone St., which turns into Tolan St. This strip intersects Pearse and O'Rahilly St., which run parallel to the river, to form Ballina's navel. **Trains** (tel. 71818) come in to Station Rd. (open M-F 7:30am-6pm, Sa 9am-1pm and 3:15-6pm) and provide service to **Dublin via Athlone** (M-Su 3 per day, £15). From the station, go left, bear right, and walk four blocks to reach the town center. Buses from the nearby **bus station** (tel. 71800 or 71825; open M-Sa 9:30am-6pm) go to **Athlone** (1 per day, £11), **Dublin via Mullingar** (4hr., 3 per day, £8), **Galway** (3hr., M-Sa 9 per day, Su 5 per day, £9.70), **Donegal** (M-Sa 3 per day, Su 1 per day, £10), **Sligo** (2hr., M-Sa 3-4 per day, £7.30), and **Westport** (1½hr., M-Sa 3 per day, Su 1 per day, £6.30). From the bus station, turn right and take the first left to head toward the city center. The **tourist office,** Cathedral Rd. (tel. 70848), is on the river by St. Muredach's Cathedral. The **phone code** is 096.

ACCOMMODATIONS, FOOD, AND PUBS Ballina's only hostel closed in 1998 to make way for a new Catholic University, sending rumors of a new hostel flying around. They haven't landed, but it's worth checking to see if they've reached the tourist office. **Hogan's American House Hostel** (tel. 70582), a comfy, family-run place with a dated but dignified interior, has low rates and a convenient location just up from the bus station (singles £15; doubles £25 for *Let's Go* readers; breakfast £5). Dozens of nearly identical B&Bs line the main approach roads into town; turn right from the station for one such trove.

Pubs and restaurants tend to go hand in hand in Ballina; get the same food for half the price by sitting in the pub. **Cafolla's** (tel. 21029), just up from the bridge, is fast, cheap, and almost Italian (open M-Sa 10am-12:30pm). **Tullio's,** Pearse St. (tel. 70815), exudes elegance, with pleasantly surprising prices (restaurant open daily noon-3pm and 6-10pm; bar serves food noon-10pm). **Gaughan's** has been pulling the best pint in town since 1936; ask for the house special natural Guinness. There's no music or TV—just conversation, snugs, great grub, and homemade snuff. Jolly drinkers are fixtures of **The Parting Glass** (tel. 72714), on Tolan St., where they cheerfully sing along to music provided by proprietor David McDonald himself (Tuesdays trad). Down by the river on Clare St., the **Murphy Bros.** (tel. 22702) serve pints to twentysomethings settled into the dark wood furnishings and dish out superb pub grub. **An Bolg Bui** (tel. 22561) calls itself a "young fisherperson's pub" and sells tackle and licenses along with pints. Of Ballina's four clubs, **Longneck's** (tel. 22702), behind Murphy's, is the most attractive and the most popular, both perhaps due to its adobe and sombrero motif (ages 21+; cover £3-5; open July-Aug. Th-Su), **The Pulse,** behind the Broken Jug, is a close second (cover £3-5; open W and F-Su).

SIGHTS Behind the railway station stands the **Dolmen of the Four Maols,** locally called "Table of the Giants." The dolmen, which dates back to 2000 BC, is said to be the burial site of four Maols who murdered Ceallach, a 7th-century bishop. They were hanged at Ardaree then commemorated with a big rock. To reach the bird-rich **Belleek Woods** entrance, cross the lower bridge near the cathedral on Pearse St. and keep Ballina House on your right. Belleek Castle is an expensive hotel, but its **Armada Bar,** built from a 500-year-old Spanish wreck, is accessible and affordable.

From July 11 to 19, 1999, catch the annual **Ballina Street Festival** (tel. 70905), which has been swinging since 1964. All of Co. Mayo is hooked for the festival's **Heritage Day** (Wednesday, July 15, 1999) when the streets are closed off and life reverts to the year 1910. All aspects of traditional Irish life are staged: greasy pig contests, a traditional Irish wake, and donkey-driven butter churns.

COS. SLIGO AND DONEGAL

■ Sligo Town

William Butler Yeats spent extended summer holidays here with his mother's family, the Pollexfens, who owned a mill over the Garavogue River. It was those early visits, and the exposure they provided to the superstitions of the local people, that first interested Yeats in the supernatural world. Most of Sligo can (and does) boast some connection to Yeats. Now busy streets flow with a steady stream of people during the day and with the beer from some 70 pubs and discos in the evening. *The Sligo Guardian,* available at newsagents, has local news and useful listings.

ORIENTATION AND PRACTICAL INFORMATION

Trains and buses pull into McDiarmada Station on Lord Edward St. To reach the main drag from the station, take a left and follow Lord Edward St. straight onto Wine St., and then turn right at the post office onto O'Connell St. More shops, pubs, and eateries beckon from Grattan St., left off O'Connell St.

Airplanes: Sligo Airport, Strandhill Rd. (tel. 68280). Open daily 9am-8pm.

Trains: McDiarmada Station, Lord Edward St. (tel. 69888). Open M-Sa 7am-6:30pm, Su 20min. before each departure. Trains to **Dublin** (3 per day, £13.50).

Buses: McDiarmada Station, Lord Edward St. (tel. 60066). Open M-F 9:15am-6pm, Sa 9:30am-5pm. Buses fan out to **Belfast** (4hr., 1-3 per day, £12.40), **Derry** (3hr., 3-6 per day, £10), **Dublin** (4hr., 3 per day, £9), **Galway** (2½hr., 3-4 per day, £11), and **Westport** (2½hr., 1-3 per day, £9.70).

Taxis: Cab 55 (tel. 42333) or **Finnegan's** (tel. 77777, 44444, or 41111 for easy dialing when you're drunk). At least £3 in town, 50p per mi. outside.

Bike Rental: Flanagan's Cycles (tel. 44477, after hours tel. 62633), Connelly and High St. £7 per day, £30 per week; deposit £35. Open M-Sa 9am-6pm, Su by prior arrangement.

Tourist Office: Info booth on O'Connell St. in Quinnsworth arcade. Open M-Tu 10am-7pm, W-F 10am-9pm, Sa 10am-6pm.

Financial Services: AIB, 49 O'Connell St. (tel. 41085). **ATM.** Open M-W and F 10am-4pm, Th 10am-5pm.

Launderette: Pam's Laundrette, 9 Johnston Ct. (tel. 44861), off O'Connell St. Wash and dry from £5. Open M-Sa 9am-7pm.

Emergency: Dial 999; no coins required.

Police/Garda: Pearse Rd. (tel. 42031).

Pharmacy: E. Horan, Castle St. (tel. 42560), at Market St. Open M-Sa 9:30am-6pm. Local pharmacies post schedules of rotating Sunday openings.

Hotline: Samaritans (tel. 42011). 24hr.

Hospital: The Mall (tel. 42161).

Post Office: Wine St. (tel. 42593), at O'Connell St. Open M and W-Sa 9am-5:30pm, Tu 9:30am-5:30pm.

Internet Access: Futurenet, Pearse Rd. (tel. 50345). £6 per hr., students £5. Open M-Sa 10am-10pm.

Phone Code: The unpurged images of day recede to 071.

ACCOMMODATIONS

There are plenty of hostels in Sligo, but they fill quickly, especially during the Yeats International Summer School weeks in mid-August. Contact the tourist office for info on group cottages. Over a dozen B&Bs cluster on Pearse Rd. on the south side of town; others are near the station.

Harbour House, Finisklin Rd. (tel. 71547). Big pine bunks with custom mattresses, skylights in the upstairs rooms, sitting rooms with TVs in each dorm, and more showers than an Irish afternoon. **Bike rental** £7. Dorms £8; private rooms £10 per person. Irish breakfast £3, continental £1.50.

The White House Hostel (IHH), Markievicz Rd. (tel. 45160 or 42398), first left off Wine St. after a bridge. A fine choice. Dorms £6.50. Sheets £1. Key deposit £1.50.

The Ivy Hostel, 26 Lord Edward St. (tel. 45165), left from the bus station. Pleasant, cozy doubles £13. Free laundry. Open June-Aug.

Yeats County Hostel, 12 Lord Edward St. (tel. 45165), across from the bus station. Spacious rooms, friendly company, and backyard. Dorms £6.50. Key deposit £2.

Eden Hill Holiday Hostel (IHH), Pearse Rd. (tel. 43204). Entrance via Marymount or Ashbrook St., 10min. from town. Cozy rooms and a Victorian sitting parlor in a grand but aging house. Dorms £6.50, private rooms £8. **Camping** £3.50.

Renaté House, Upper Johns St. (tel. 62014). From the station, go straight one block and left half a block. Singles £23, with bath £25; doubles £32, with bath £36.

FOOD, PUBS, AND CLUBS

"Faery vats / Full of berries / And reddest stolen cherries" are not to be found in Sligo today. Good dinners are expensive; the best values tend to end around 6pm. Sip coffee amid paper butterflies one flight up from busy Castle St. at **The Cottage,** Castle St. (tel. 45319; open M-Sa 9am-6pm). Tucked away upstairs on Quay St., cute **Lyon's Café** (tel. 42969) brews Bewley's coffee and bakes a selection of cakes. (Lunch special of soup, entree, and cake £4.35. Open M-Sa 9am-6pm; lunch served 12:30-2pm.) **Kate's Kitchen,** Market St. (tel. 43022), is not quite a restaurant, but this combination deli-wholefood shop varies its take-away menu each day (homemade soups £1; open M-Sa 9am-6:30pm). **Abracadabra,** Grattan St., serves up fried goodies until 3:30am.

Over 70 pubs crowd the main streets, filling the town with live music during the summer. Events and venues are listed in *The Sligo Champion* (75p). At **Hargadon Bros.,** O'Connell St. (tel. 70933), one can enjoy philosophical conversations and contemplate the perfect pint unfettered by the modern audio-visual distractions found elsewhere. This is pub the way it ought to be, just as it was when it first opened in 1868. **Shoot the Crows,** Castle St., but clean up after yourself (music Tuesday and Thursday 9:30pm). Eighteenth-century lanterns light the cave-dark wooden interior of **McGarrigle's,** O'Connell St. (tel. 71193). Upstairs is just as dark, but the new-age walls and ceilings enclose blaring techno (live trad Thursday and Sunday). The *International Pub Guide* ranks **McLynn's,** Old Market St. (tel. 60743), as the best pub for music in Sligo. Enter through the unmarked door on the left of the building and tear down social barriers (music Friday). Clubbers shake it at **Toff's** (tel. 62150), on the river behind the Belfry, which pumps out disco beats (21+; cover £4.50-5; £1 discount card from the Belfry; open Th-Su). Up Teeling St., sprawling **Equinox** is darker, with newfangled neon lights, zebra-striped stools, and identical club music (cover £4.50; open W-Su).

Sink or Sin

Stand by the shore of Lough Gill and listen carefully. What do you hear? The lapping of the waves? The wind rustling in trees? The soft peal of a pure silver bell, sounding distantly from the bottom of the lake? No? That's because you're a sinner. When Sligo's Dominican Friary was wrecked during the Ulster rebellion of 1641, worshippers saved its bell and hid it on the bottom of Lough Gill. Legend insists that only those free from sin can still hear it. Don't worry, neither can we.

SIGHTS

> Under Bare Ben Bulben's head
> In Drumcliffe churchyard Yeats is laid
> An ancestor was rector there
> Long years ago, a church stands near,
> By the road an ancient cross.
> No marble, no conventional phrase;
> On limestone quarried near the spot
> By his command these words are cut;
> > Cast a cold eye
> > on life, on death.
> > Horsemen pass bye!

Yeats composed this poem a year before his death in France in 1939. The road Yeats refers to is the N15; the churchyard is 4 mi. northwest of Sligo. His grave is to the left of the church door. On summer Sunday evenings, the church sponsors concerts (tel. 56629). **Buses** from Sligo toward Derry stop at Drumcliff (10min.; in summer M-Sa 3 per day, Su 1 per day; in winter M-Sa 3 per day; return £2.60). Hitching is reportedly painless. A few miles northeast of Drumcliff, **Glencar Lake,** mentioned in Yeats's "The Stolen Child," is the subject of more literary excursions. Stunning views of Knocknarea and Benbulben and the smashing Glencar Falls add natural beauty to literary genius. The lake is marked by a sign about 1 mi. north of Drumcliff on N15.

Farther north of Drumcliff, eerie **Benbulben,** rich in mythical associations, protrudes from the landscape like the keel of a foundered boat. The climb up the 1729 ft. peak is rather windy, and the summit can be downright gusty. However, if you can keep from being blown away, standing at the very point of Benbulben, where the land inexplicably drops 5000 ft., can be a watershed experience for even the most weathered of hikers. Ask at the gas station in Drumcliff for directions to trailheads. Four miles west of Drumcliff is **Lissadell House** (tel. 63150), where poet Eva Gore-Booth and her sister Constance Markiewicz, second in command in the Easter Rising and later the first woman elected to the Dáil, entertained Yeats and his circle. Take the first left after Yeats Tavern Hostel on Drumcliff Rd. and follow signs. *(Open June to mid-Sept. M-Sa 10:30am-12:15pm and 2-4:15pm. £2.50. Grounds open year-round. Free.)*

In town, the 13th-century **Sligo Abbey,** Abbey St., is very well preserved. The Dominican Friary boasts cloisters and ornate coupled pillars that, though old, can hardly be called ruins. *(Open daily in summer 9:30am-6:30pm; last admission 45min. before closing. If it's closed, ask for the key from Tommy McLaughlin, 6 Charlotte St. £1.50, students 60p.)* Next door, the 1874 **Cathedral of the Immaculate Conception,** John St., is best visited at dawn or dusk, when the sun streams through 69 magnificent stained-glass windows. Farther down John St., the **Cathedral of St. John the Baptist,** designed in 1730, has a brass tablet dedicated to Yeats's mother, Susan Mary.

The Yeats Art Gallery, Stephen St., houses one of Éire's finest collections of modern Irish art, including a number of works by Jack Butler Yeats. Among the museum's other treasures are some first editions by William Butler Yeats and the original publications by the Dun Emer Press and Cuala Press. *(Open Tu-Sa 10am-noon and 2-5pm. Free.)* The **Sligo County Museum** preserves small reminders of Yeats, including pictures of his funeral. *(Open June-Sept. M-Sa 10:30am-12:30pm and 2:30-4:30pm; Apr.-May and Oct. M-Sa 10:30am-12:30pm. Free.)* A monthly *Calendar of Events,* available and free at the tourist office, describes the festivals and goings-on in the Northwest region. The **Sligo Arts Festival** (tel. 69802) takes place May 27 to June 7, 1999. Along with its usual fantastic events, the final weekend will focus on world music.

■ Donegal Town

Donegal Town's name comes from the Irish *Dun na nGall,* meaning "fortress of the foreigners." Like the invaders then, many travelers now begin their tour of Co. Donegal here, and some turn the town into a base for exploring the county due to the helpful tourist office and many bus routes. Marvelous trad sessions, the peaceful setting on Donegal Bay, and majestic ruins of past kingdoms that still define the town's landscape are other attractions of Donegal.

ORIENTATION AND PRACTICAL INFORMATION The center of town is The Diamond, a triangular area bordered by Donegal's main shopping streets. At the top of the hill lies Main St., which leads to Killybegs Rd. The bottom point of The Diamond leads to the tourist office along Sligo Rd. **Bus Éireann** (tel. 21101) runs to **Dublin** (4hr., 6 per day, M-Sa 6 per day, Su 3 per day, £10), **Galway** (4hr., M-Sa 3 per day, Su 2 per day, £13), and **Sligo** (1hr., M-Sa 6 per day, Su 4 per day). Buses stop outside the Abbey Hotel on The Diamond, where timetables are also posted. **McGeehan Coaches** (tel. (075) 46150) go to **Dublin** (Tu-Th at least 1 per day, F-M 2 per day); they also drive to **Killybegs, Ardara, Glenties,** and **Dungloe. Feda O'Donnell** (tel. (091) 761656 or (075) 48114) leaves for **Galway** from the tourist office (M-Sa 9:45am and 5:15pm, additional stops F and Su). The **tourist office,** Quay St. (tel. 21148), south of The Diamond on Sligo Rd., has brochures galore on Co. Donegal, reservations for accommodations throughout the Republic, information on the North, and a free map of the city. (Open July-Aug. M-F 9am-8pm, Sa 9am-6pm, Su 9am-5pm; Easter-June and Sept.-Oct. M-F 9am-5pm, Sa 10am-2pm.) **AIB** (tel. 21016), **Bank of Ireland** (tel. 21079), and **Ulster Bank** (tel. 21064) are in The Diamond (all open M-W and F 10am-4pm, Th 10am-5pm; all have 24hr. **ATMs**). The **post office** (tel. 21007) delivers on Tirconaill St. past Donegal Castle and over the bridge. (Open M 9:30-10:30am and 3:30-4:30pm, Tu 11:30am-12:30pm and 3:30-4:30pm, W 11:15am-12:15pm and 3:30-4:30pm, Th 9:45am-10:45am and 3:30-4:30pm, F 3:30-4:30pm, Sa 9-10am and 2:30-3:30pm.) The **telephone code** is 073.

ACCOMMODATIONS Donegal Town Hostel (IHH) (tel. 22805), half a mile out on Killybegs Rd., has bright rooms (some with murals) and a large kitchen. (Dorms £7; doubles £16. Sheets 50p. Laundry (wash and powder) £4.50. **Camping** £4. Separate kitchen and showers for campers.) **Ball Hill Youth Hostel (An Óige/HI)** (tel. 21174), 3 mi. from town, is an old coast guard station on a cliff with airy, spacious rooms. Go 1½ mi. out of Donegal on Killybegs Rd., turn left at the sign, and head another 1½ mi. toward the sea. Buses leaving from the Abbey Hotel (£1) often go as far as Killybegs Rd. (June-Aug. dorms £6.50; Sept.-May £5; youth discounts. 3-course dinner available for £6 at nearby Mountcharles Hotel.) **Cliffview,** Coast Rd. (tel. 21684), a two-minute walk along the Killybegs Rd., is a hybrid of Irish B&B aesthetics and Highway 66 motels. (July-Aug. dorms £9; doubles £15. Sept.-June dorms £7.50; doubles £13. Continental breakfast included. Laundry £4.) Despite being on the busiest street in town, 17-room **Atlantic Guest House,** Main St. (tel. 21187), offers the undisturbed privacy of a fancy hotel (£14, with bath £17.50; single prices negotiable).

FOOD, PUBS, AND CLUBS A good selection of £4-5 cafes and take-aways occupy The Diamond and the streets nearby. Other than that, your best bet is at the **Foodland Supermarket,** The Diamond (tel. 21006; open M-W 9am-7pm, Th-F 9am-8pm, Sa 9am-7:30pm). **Simple Simon's,** The Diamond (tel. 22687), sells fresh baked goods, local cheeses, and homeopathic remedies (open M-Sa 9am-6pm). The justifiably popular **Blueberry Tea Room,** Castle St. (tel. 22933), makes sandwiches, daily specials, and all-day breakfast (entrees around £4; open daily 9am-6pm). "Donegal's most famous chipper," **Errigal Restaurant,** Main St. (tel. 21428), has the cheapest dinner in town. Take-away or sit down in their retro blue-and-white interior. (Open in summer daily 11:30am-11pm; in winter M-Sa 11:30am-11pm and Su 3-11pm.)

Donegal puts on a good show at night, especially in the summertime. Almost every bar has live music nightly, and many pubs host Irish dancing and big name bands during the late June International Arts Festival. The best trad and contemporary sessions in town happen at **Schooner's,** Upper Main St. (tel. 21671)—and they happen every night. Schooner's also dishes out exquisite pub grub (mussels and Guinness £4). **The Voyager Bar,** The Diamond (tel. 21201), keeps its patrons happy. "Everyone has a voyage to make in life." Celebrate yours here. (Live music on weekends.) The multi-talented Folk Cabaret and a lively disco (cover £5; Su 10:30pm-2am) at **The Abbey Hotel,** The Diamond (tel. 21014), draw tourists and locals to the Abbey lounge nightly. Fifteen hundred people join in the dancing each week—why not be number 1501? **Nero's Nite Club,** Main St. (tel. 21111), plays the fiddle while Donegal burns. This club is known for its excellent dance floor, late hours, and good pick-up scene (cover £3-4; open Th-Su).

SIGHTS During the daylight hours, Donegal Town's main tourist attractions are the ruins from the tumultuous 15th and 16th centuries. Evidence of English-Irish turmoil remains in **Donegal Castle,** Castle St. (tel. 22405), the former residence of the O'Donnell clan (and, later, of various English nobles). The ruins of the O'Donnell clan's castle of 1474 stand adjacent to the recently refurbished manor built by English rulers in 1623. *(Guided tours on the hr. Open Apr.-Oct. daily 9:30am-5:30pm. £2, students and children £1, families £5.)* Gorgeous scenery, old grave slabs, and still-standing stairways are only a few of the delights that remain at **Old Abbey,** just a short walk from the tourist office along the river south of town.

■ Letterkenny

Several years ago, residents lamented the arrival of a traffic light at the intersection of Main St. and Port Rd., the first in Co. Donegal. Most tourists come to Letterkenny as a connection point for buses to various places in Donegal, the rest of the Republic, and Northern Ireland.

PRACTICAL INFORMATION

Buses: At the junction of Port and Derry Rd. in front of the Quinnsworth Supermarket. **Bus Éireann** (tel. 21309) makes tours of Inishowen Peninsula and Giant's Causeway (£7; call to book). They also run regular service to **Derry** (40min., 3 per day, £3), **Dublin** (5hr., M-Sa 5 per day, Su 3 per day), **Galway** (5hr., 3 per day, £10), and **Donegal Town** (50min.) on the way to **Sligo** (2hr., 3 per day, £6). **Feda O'Donnell Coaches** (tel. (075) 48114 or (091) 761656), **Lough Swilly Buses** (tel. 29400 or 22863), **John McGinley Coaches** (tel. 35201), **Northwest Busways** (tel. (077) 82619), and **Doherty's Travel** (tel. (075) 21105) run to destinations in Donegal, the Republic, and Northern Ireland.

Local Transportation: Letterkenny Bus Service (Handy Bus; tel. (087) 414714). Extensive city routes (70p).

Bike Rental: Church St. Cycles (tel. 26204), by the cathedral. £7 per day, £30 per week; deposit £40. Open Tu-Sa 10am-6pm.

Tourist Offices: Bord Fáilte (tel. 21160), ¾mi. past the bus station and a good bit out of town on Derry Rd. Pamphlets on Co. Donegal and accommodations booking. Open July-Aug. M-Sa 9am-8pm, Su 10am-2pm; Sept.-June M-F 9am-5pm. **Chamber of Commerce Visitors Information Centre,** 40 Port Rd. (tel. 24866 or 25505), has a much closer though slightly smaller selection of info on Letterkenny and the rest of Co. Donegal. Open M-F 9am-5pm.

Financial Services: AIB, 61 Upper Main St. (tel. 22877 or 22807). Open M-W and F 10am-4pm, Th 10am-5pm. **Bank of Ireland,** Lower Main St. (tel. 22122). Open M-W and F 10am-4pm, Th 10am-5pm. Both have 24hr. **ATMs.**

Emergency: Dial 999; no coins required.

Hotlines: Samaritans, 20 Port Rd. (tel. 27200). 24hr. Drop-in Th-Su 7-10pm.

Post Office: Main St. (tel. 22454), about halfway down. Open M and W-F 9am-5:30pm, Tu 9:30am-5pm, Sa 9am-5:30pm.

Telephone Code: 074.

ACCOMMODATIONS

The Manse Hostel (IHH), High Rd. (tel. 25238). From the bus station, head up Port Rd. toward town and turn right up the lane marked "Covehill House B&B." Continue past the playground, through the parking lot, and 50yd. up the road. The hostel is across the street. The beds and couches are as comfy as a traveler could desire. 3-, 4-, and 6-bed dorms £6; private doubles and twins £14. Dorm sheets 50p.

Riverside B&B (tel. 24907), off Derry Rd. 1mi. past Letterkenny. Turn left after the Clan Ree Hotel; signs point the way. Huge rooms with views. £15, with bath £17.

White Gables, Mrs. McConnelogue, Lower Dromore (tel. 22583). Lower Dromore is the third exit from the roundabout 1mi. out on Derry Rd.; the house is ½mi. along Lower Dromore around a bend. Call for pick-up from town. £15.

FOOD AND PUBS

Quinnsworth (tel. 22555), in the Letterkenny Shopping Center behind the bus station, is all you could ask for in a grocery store (open M-W 9am-7pm, Th-F 9am-9pm, Sa 9am-6pm, Su noon-6pm).

The Beanery, Main St., next to the Courtyard Shopping Centre. Calls itself a cappuccino and sandwich bar, but offers so much more. 4-course meals £3-5, sandwiches around £2. Open M-Sa 9am-5:30pm.

Galfees, Main St. (tel. 27173), in the basement of the Courtyard Shopping Centre, assumes different guises throughout the day. It's a carvery 12:15-3pm, a fresh food bar 8:30am-5pm, and a bar-restaurant 5-10pm. Most evening entrees £4-5.

Café Rico, Oliver-Plunkett Rd. (tel. 29808), at the end of Main St. away from the bus station, offers full breakfasts and heaping sandwiches (£2-4) in a mod coffee shop.

McGinley's, 25 Main St. (tel. 21106). A hugely popular student bar. The mixture of styles creates a pleasingly hectic ambience. Live rock, pop, and blues Th-Su.

McClafferty's, 54 Main St. (tel. 21581). Modern ballads and rock Thursdays and Sundays.

Cottage Bar, Main St. (tel. 21338). A kettle on the hearth, animated conversation around the bar, and nuns drinking Guinness in the corner. Trad Tuesdays and Thursdays.

The Old Orchard Inn, High Rd. (tel. 21615), less than ½mi. past the Manse Hostel in a parking lot. The 3 floors are always busy. Disco £4. Open W and F-Sa until 2am.

■ Inishowen Peninsula

It would be a shame to leave Ireland without seeing the Inishowen Peninsula, an untouristed mosaic of mountains, forests, meadows, and beaches that reaches farther north than "the North." You can have its white beaches to yourself all day and then be welcomed at night by crowds of locals in the pubs, which are filled with trad almost nightly. The peninsula is dotted with many villages and two larger towns, Buncrana and Cardonagh. It takes two to three days to see the whole shebang properly without a car, and even with a car one would hardly want to spend less time. The clearly posted **Inish Eoghin 100** road takes exactly 100 mi. to navigate the peninsula's perimeter. Cycling, however, can be difficult around Malin Head due to ferocious winds and hilly terrain. The map published by the Inishowen Tourism Society, available at the Cardonagh tourist office, is the most comprehensive. The **telephone code** for the peninsula is 077.

Ten miles south of Buncrana at the bottom of the peninsula and 3 mi. west of Derry, the hilltop ringfort **Grianán Ailigh** (GREEN-in ALL-ya) is an excellent place to start or finish a tour of Inishowen. This site has been a cultural center for at least 4000 years. From Buncrana, the Inish Eoghin 100 runs through Dunree Head and the Mamore Gap, while R238 cuts through the interior directly to Clonmany and Ballyliffen. **Fort Dunree** and Mamore Gap were the last area occupied in the Republic of Ireland by the British, who passed the fort to the Irish army in 1938. **Dunree Head** pokes out into Lough Swilly 6 mi. northwest of Buncrana. Salt-and-peppered peaks rise up against the ocean buffered by the occasional bend of sandy, smooth beach. At the tip of the head, Fort Dunree hides away in the jagged architecture of sea cliffs. *(Open June-Sept. M-Sa 10am-6pm, Su 12:30-6pm. Fort and walks £1.80, students, seniors, and children £1; walks only £2 per car.)* Farther north along the Inish Eoghin 100 toward Clonmany, a sign points left to the edge of the **Mamore Gap.** This breathtaking pass teeters 800 ft. above sea level between Mamore Hill and Urris. The road descends from the Gap onto wave-scoured northern beaches, proceeding to Urris, **Lenan Head,** and inviting **Lenan Strand.** Once, known for its prodigious (even for Donegal) *poitín* production, Urris was the last area in Inishowen to still speak Gaelic. North of the Gap, two tiny villages, **Clonmany** and **Ballyliffen,** are separated by 1 mi. Their combined forces make a wonderful spot to spend the night on a leisurely exploration of the Inishowen peninsula: Clonmany provides the pubs and food, while Ballyliffen has plenty of accommodations and long stretches of sandy beach kissed by crystal-clear, though rough, ocean water.

From the southeastern coast, R240 cuts straight up the middle of the peninsula to commercial Carndonagh, a good stop for amenities. Travelers flock to the Inishowen Peninsula to reach the northernmost tip of Ireland, **Malin Head,** although you won't feel anyone's presence among the rocky, wave-tattered coast and sky-high sand dunes of the area. The scattered town of Malin Head includes **Banba's Crown,** the northernmost tip of Ireland, a tooth of dark rock rising up from the ocean spray.

From Inishowen Head, the road leads south to **Greencastle,** a village that throws some spice (or sea salt, at least) into the one-street Irish-village mix. A few miles farther south is the grassy, forested seaside promenade of **Moville.** The **Moville Holiday Hostel (IHH)** (tel. 82378), off Malin Rd. about 350 yd. past Main St., was lovingly converted from stone-walled farm buildings and now emits warmth (dorms £36).

APPENDIX

■ Holidays

Government agencies, post offices, and banks (hence the term "Bank Holiday") are closed on the following days, and businesses—if not closed—may have shorter hours. Transportation in particular grinds to a halt, so be sure to check schedules carefully. Holidays in European countries are listed daily in the International Herald Tribune. In addition, each town's tourist office can provide specific information about bank holidays and local festivals.

Date	Holiday	Countries
January 1	New Year's Day	U.K. and Republic of Ireland
March 17	St. Patrick's Day	Republic of Ireland and Northern Ireland
April 2	Good Friday	U.K. and Republic of Ireland
April 5	Easter Monday	U.K. and Republic of Ireland
May 3	First Monday in May	U.K.
May 31	Last Monday in May	U.K.
June 7	First Monday in June	Republic of Ireland
July 5	Tynwald Fair Day	Isle of Man
July 12	Orange Day	Northern Ireland
August 2	First Monday in August	Republic of Ireland and Scotland
August 25	Last Monday in August	U.K. except Scotland
October 25	Last Monday in October	Republic of Ireland
November 5	Guy Fawkes Day	U.K.
December 25	Christmas Day	U.K. and Republic of Ireland
December 26	Boxing Day/St. Stephen's Day	U.K. and Republic of Ireland

■ Telephone Codes

City Codes	
London	0171 and 0181
Birmingham	0121
Manchester	0161
Edinburgh	0131
Glasgow	0141
Cork	06
Dublin	021

International Calling Codes	
Australia	61
Canada	1
Ireland	353
New Zealand	64
South Africa	13
United Kingdom	44
United States	1

Northern Ireland can also be reached from the Republic of Ireland by dialing 08.

■ Time Zones

Britain and Ireland are on Greenwich Mean Time (GMT), which sets its clocks one hour earlier than (most of) continental Europe; five hours later than Billerica, Massachusetts (EST); six hours later than Topeka, Kansas (CST); seven hours later than Crested Butte, Colorado (MST); eight hours later than Seattle, Washington (PST); nine hours later than Kodiak, Alaska; ten hours later than Nanakuli, Hawaii; eight, nine and a half, and ten hours earlier than various spots in Australia; and twelve hours earlier than Auckland, New Zealand. The British do, however, have their own seasonal time system; Winter Time is GMT, but British Summer Time (late Mar. to late Oct.) is one hour later than GMT. British time is usually 5 hours ahead of Eastern Standard Time.

■ Measurements

Although there is a British system of measurement, Americans are the only ones who use it. The rest of the world operates on the metric system, including Great Britain itself. The following is a list of U.S. units and their metric equivalents.

1 inch = 25 millimeters (mm)	1mm = 0.04 inch (in.)
1 foot (ft.) = 0.30 meter (m)	1m = 3.33 feet (ft.)
1 yard (yd.) = 0.91m	1m = 1.1 yards (yd.)
1 mile = 1.61kilometers (km)	1km = 0.62 mile (mi.)
1 ounce = 28.350 grams (g)	1g = 0.04 ounce (oz.)
1 pound (lb.) = 0.45 kilogram (kg)	1kg = 2.21 pounds (lb.)
1 quart = 0.94 liter (L)	1 liter = 1.06 quarts (qt.)

It should be noted that gallons in the U.S. are not identical to those across the Atlantic; one U.S. gallon equals 0.83 Imperial gallons. Pub aficionados will want to note that a U.S. pint likewise equals 0.83 Imperial pints.

In Britain and Ireland, electricity is 220 volts AC, enough to melt your favorite 110V American curling iron. See **Packing,** p. 24, for specific information.

■ Language

Contrary to expectation, English speakers around the world do *not* speak the same language. The following is a list of British words and phrases that will help travelers understand what on earth the Brits are saying.

"English"	English	"English"	English
aubergine	eggplant	caravan	trailer, mobile home
bangers and mash	sausage and mashed potatoes	car park	parking lot
bap	a soft bun	cheeky	mischievous
barmy	insane, erratic	cheers, cheerio	thank you, goodbye
bed-sit, or bed sitter	one-room apartment	chemist	pharmacist
biro	ballpoint pen	chips	french fries
biscuit	a cookie or cracker	chuffed	happy, or passed gas
bobby	police officer	circle	theater balcony
give a bollicking to	shout at	coach	inter-city bus
bonnet	car hood	concession, "concs"	discount on admission
boot	car trunk	courgette	zucchini
boozer	pub	crisps	potato chips
braces	suspenders	crumpets	like English muffins, only different
brilliant	nifty, "cool"	dicey, dodgy	problematic, sketchy
bubble and squeak	cabbage and mashed potatoes	dinner	lunch
busker	street musician	the dog's bollocks	the best
cashpoint	ATM or cash machine	dosh	money

APPENDIX

dual carriageway	divided highway	**props**	pub regulars
dust bin	trash can	**pudding**	dessert
fag	cigarette	**pull**	to "score"
faggot	edible, round sausage	**public school**	private school
fanny	female sexual organs	**punter**	average person, customer
first floor	second floor	**quid**	pound (in money)
geezer	man (no elderly connotations)	**queue up, Q**	line up
full stop	period (punctuation)	**return ticket**	round-trip ticket
gob	mouth	**riding**	parliamentary district
grotty	grungy	**ring up**	telephone
high street	main street	**roundabout**	rotary road interchange
hire	rental	**rubber**	eraser
hoover	vacuum cleaner	**sack**	to fire someone
I felt a great tit	I felt like an idiot	**self-catering**	with kitchen facilities
iced lolly	popsicle	**self-drive**	car rental
interval	intermission	**serviette**	napkin
"in" a street	"on a street"	**sesh**	drinking session
jam	jelly	**single carriageway**	non-divided highway
jelly	Jell-O	**single ticket**	one-way ticket
jumble sale	yard sale	**snogging**	casual or serious kissing
jumper	sweater	**sod it**	forget it
kip	sleep	**spotted dick**	steamed sponge pudding with raisins
knackered	tired, worn out	**stalls**	orchestra seats
knob	penis, or awkward person	**sultanas**	raisins
lavatory, "lav"	restroom	**sweet(s)**	candy
lay-by	roadside turnout	**swish**	swanky
leader (in newspaper)	editorial	**ta, ta-ta**	thank you, goodbye
legless	intoxicated	**tariff**	cost of a stay
to let	to rent	**toilet**	restroom
lift	elevator	**torch**	flashlight
loo	restroom	**trainers**	sneakers
lorry	truck	**trunk call**	long-distance phone call
mate	pal	**Tube/Underground**	London subway
motorway	highway	**vest**	undershirt
naff	shabby or cheap	**waistcoat (weskit)**	men's vest
petrol	gasoline	**way out**	exit
phone box, call box	telephone booth	**W.C. (water closet)**	toilet, restroom
take the piss out of	make fun of	**wellies**	boots
pissed	drunk	**yob**	prole
prat	stupid person	**"zed"**	the letter Z

British Pronunciation

Berkeley	BARK-lee	**Leicester**	LES-ter
Berkshire	BARK-sher	**Maryleborn**	MAR-lee-born
Beauchamps	BEECH-am	**Magdalen**	MAUD-lin
Birmingham	BIRM-ing-um, not "ham"	**Norwich**	NOR-idge
Derby	DAR-bee	**quay**	key
Dulwich	DULL-idge	**Salisbury**	SAULS-bree
Ely	EEL-ee	**Southwark**	SUTH-uk
Gloucester	GLOS-ter	**Woolwich**	WOOL-idge
Greenwich	GREN-idge	**Worcester**	WOO-ster
Holborn	HO-burn		

Welsh Words and Phrases

Consult **Llanguage,** p. 394, for the basic rules of Welsh pronunciation. Listed below are a number of words and phrases you may encounter on the road.

allan	ahl-LAN	exit
ar agor	ahr AG-or	open
ar gau	ahr GUY	closed
bore da	boh-RA DAH	good morning, hello
cyhoeddus	cuh-HOY-this	public
diolch yn fawr	dee-OLCH uhn VOWR	thank you
dydd da	DEETH dah	good day
dynion	dihnion	men
Ga i peint o cwrw?	gah-EE pint oh coo-roo?	Can I have a pint of beer?
hwyl	huh-will	cheers
ia	eeah	yes (sort of—it's tricky)
iawn	eeown	well, fine
llwybr cyhoeddus	hlooee-BIR cuh-HOY-this	public footpath
merched	mehrch-ED	women
nage	nahgah	no (sort of—it's tricky)
nos da	nos dah	good night
noswaith dda	nos-WAYTHE tha	good evening
os gwelwch yn dda	ohs gwell-OOCH uhn tha	please
perygl	pehr-UHGL	danger
preifat	like English "private"	private
safle'r Bus	savlehr boos	bus stop
stryd Fawr	strihd vahor	High Street
Sut mae?	sit my? or shoo my?	How are you?

Irish Words and Phrases

The following bits of the Irish language are either used often in Irish English or are common in Irish place names. Spelling conventions do not always match English pronunciations: for example, "mh" sounds like "v," and "dh" sounds like "g."

aerphort	AYR-fort	airport
aisling	ASH-ling	vision or dream, or a poem or story thereof
An Lár	on lahr	city center
Ar aghaidh linn: Éire	uhr EYE linn: AIR-ah	Let's Go: Ireland
Baile Átha Cliath	BALL-yah AW-hah CLEE-ah	Dublin
bodhrán	BOUR-ohn	traditional drum
Bord Fáilte	bored FAHL-tshuh	Irish Tourist Board
Conas tá tú?	CUNN-us thaw too?	How are you?

céilí	KAY-lee	Irish dance
craic	krak	good cheer, good pub conversation, a good time
Dáil	DOY-il	House of Representatives
Dia dhuit	JEE-a dich	good day, hello
Dia's Muire dhuit	JEE-as MWUR-a dich	reply to "good day"
dún	doon	fort
Éire	AIR-uh	Ireland; official name of the Republic of Ireland
fáilte	FAWLT-cha	welcome
feis	fesh	an assembly, Irish festival
Fianna Fáil	FEE-in-ah foil	"Soldiers of Destiny;" political party
Fine Gael	FINN-eh gayl	"Family of Ireland;" political party
fir	fear	men
fleadh	flah	a musical festival
gaeltacht	GAYL-tokt	a district where Irish is the everyday language
garda, Garda Siochána	GAR-da SHE-och-ANA	police
go raibh maith agat	guh roh moh UG-ut	thank you
inch, innis, ennis	inch, innis, ennis	island; river meadow
kil	kill	church; cell
knock	nok	hill
lei thras	LEH-hrass	toilets
lough	lohk	lake
mná	min-AW	women
mór	more	big, great
ní hea	nee hah	no (sort of—it's tricky)
oíche mhaith dhuit	EE-ha woh ditch	good night
ogham	AG-um	early Irish, written on stones
Oifig an Phoist	UFF-ig un fwisht	Post Office
poitín	po-CHEEN	moonshine; sometimes-toxic homemade liquor
rath	rath or rah	earthen fort
sea	shah	yes (sort of—it's tricky)
seanachaí	SHAN-ukh-ee	storyteller
Seanad	SHAN-ud	Senate
Sinn Féin	shin fayn	"Ourselves Alone;" the political wing of the IRA
sláinte	SLAWN-che	cheers, to your health
slán agat	slawn UG-ut	goodbye
slieve, sliabh	shleev	mountain
sraid	shrawd	street
Taoiseach	TEE-shukh	Prime Minister
teachta dála (TD)	TAKH-ta DAH-lah	member of Irish parliament
telefón	TEL-eh-fone	telephone
Tír na nÓg	cheer na nohg	Land of Youth
trá	thraw	beach
uilleann	ILL-in	"elbow;" bagpipes played with the elbow

Index

A

Abbadabba 335
Abbey of St. Edmund 295
Abbey Theatre Movement 617
Abbotsford 483
Aberconwy House 450
Abercrave 414
Aberdaron 435
Aberdeen 531–533
Abergavenny 408–409
Aberystwyth 425–428
Access 12
Accommodations 39–41
Achill Island 681
Achiltibuie 562
Act of Union 392, 613
Adam, Robert 484, 501
Adams, Gerry 581
Adams, Richard 60
adapters 25
Adoration of the Magi 278
Advanced Purchase Excursion Fare. See APEX
advisories 14
Æthelbert 52
Æthelflæd 323
Agincourt, Battle of 53
Ahern, Bertie 582, 616
Airhitch 28
Air-Tech, Ltd. 28
Albert Dock 333
Albert, Prince 55, 175
ales 620
Alfred the Great. See Kings
Alfriston 183
Alice's Adventures in Wonderland 60
alkaline water 252
Allah 278
Allasdale 559
allergies 15
Alloway 500
Alma-Tadema, Lawrence 110
Alnwick 372
alone, travel 24
Alpes Pennina 348
Alston 339
Alternatives to Tourism 18–20

Alum Bay 175
Ambergate 312
Amberly 184
Ambleside 381
American Association of Retired Persons (AARP) 21
American Express 11
American Museum 242
Amhuinnsuidhe Castle 556
An Lanntair Gallery 554
Anatomy of Melancholy 58
Aneirin 393
Angles 52, 458
Anglesey Abbey 283
Anglo-Irish Agreement 581
Anglo-Irish Treaty 614
Anne Hathaway's Cottage 266
Anstruther 514
anti-Semitism 354
Antrim 597–601
Antrim Coaster 598, 599
Antrim, Glens of 598
Aonach Gagach 543
APEX 31
Apollo Theatre 230
Appin 522
Apprentice Boys 593, 603, 606
Apted, Michael 63
Aquae Sulis 241
Aran Islands 675
Archer, Jeffrey 283
Archers, The 61
Archibald the Grim 488
Arden, Mary 266
Ardgartan Forest Park 510
Ardrossan 502
Argyll. See Central Scotland and Argyll
Arisaig 546
Armada 525
Armadale Castle 551
Armagh 595
Co. Armagh 594
Arnol Black House 555
Arnold, Matthew 59, 152, 229
Arnside 378
Arran 501–504

Highland Games 503
Arsenal 68
Arthur's Seat 475
Arun, River 164
Arundel 164–167
Ashbourne 310, 312
Ashmolean Museum 229
Asquith, Herbert 55
Assembly Rooms 241, 474
Athlone 643
ATMs 12
Aubrey Holes 235
Auden, W.H. 59, 98, 227
Audley End 283
Augustine 52
auks 422
Austen, Jane 59, 142, 159, 173, 176, 179, 180, 192, 193, 236, 242, 314
Australia 359
autos 34
Avalon 250
Avebury 236
Aviemore 535
Avon and Somerset 236–250
    Bath 236–243
    Bristol 243–245
    Glastonbury 248–250
    Wells 245–248
Avon, River 242
Ayr 500
Ayr Gold Cup 500
Ayrshire 500–501
Aysgarth Falls 345, 348

B

Ba' 568
backpacks 24
Bacon, Francis 60, 110
Baden-Powell, Lord 98
Bafinn 553
bagpipes 462
Bakewell 311, 314
Baldersdale 339
Ballina 681
Ballinafad 679
Balliol, John 459, 486
Balloch 509
ballroom dancing 329
Ballycastle 599
Ballyliffen 689

Ballymoney 583
Balranald Reserve 558
Bangor 443–445
Bank of England 107, 108
Bannockburn 508
Bannockburn, Battle of 459
Bantry 657
Barber Institute of Fine Arts 269
Barbican Theatre 131
Barbican, the 150
Barbour, John 461
Barclaycard 12
Bardsey Island 432
Barker, Thomas 242
Barnard Castle 342
Barnstaple 199
Barra 559
Barry Island 402
Barry, Sir Charles 98
Bath 236–243
    Abbey 241
    Pump Room 241
bathing machine 191
Battle 157
Battle of the Boyne 612
BBC 61
Beachy Head 183
Bealach-na-Bo Pass 561
Beamish 620
Bear Steps 300
Beara Peninsula 657
Beatles, the 62, 64, 65, 334
Beaufort, Lady Margaret 279
Beaumaris 446
Beaumont, Francis 96
Beccles 291
Becket, Thomas à 143, 147, 226
Beckett, Samuel 617, 633
Bede, Venerable 52
Beefeaters 112
Behn, Aphra 289
Belas Knap 258
Belfast 585–593
    black cabs 592
    Albert Memorial Clock Tower 591
    Cathedral 590
    City Hall 590
    Crown Liquor Saloon 591

docks 590
Falls, the 592
Giant's Ring 591
Golden Mile, the 591
Linen Hall Library 590
murals, the 591
peace line 591
Shankill 592
West Belfast 591
Belgium 152, 296
Bell, Alexander Graham 534
Bell, Clive 164
Bell, Vanessa 116, 164, 183
Bellingham 370
Beltane Festival 481
Beltane Fires 477
Ben A'an' 511
Ben Arthur 510
Ben Bulben 685
Ben Golomstock 518
Ben Heavel 560
Ben Macdui 537
Ben Nevis 457, 543, 545
Benbecula 557
Benedictine Abbey 527
Bentham, Jeremy 228
Ben-y-Vrackie 519
Benz, Karl 497
Beowulf 57
Berkeley Castle 259
Berkeley, George 612
Berneray 559
Berwick-upon-Tweed 370, 484
Bethnal Green Museum of Childhood 119
Betws-y-Coed 451–452
Bevis Marks Synagogue 119
Bharpa Langass 558
Bidean nam Bian 543
Big Ben 99
Big Brum 269
Big One, the 328
Big Strand 524
Biggest Liar in the World 386
Bill of Rights (English) 54
Billerica 690
Billy Liar 62
Birdoswald Roman Fort 375
Birmingham 268–270
Birnam 517
birth control 17

bisexual travelers 21
Bishop Auckland 343
Bishop Poore 231, 234
Bishop's Palace 247
Bishop's Throne 196
Bitches, the 422
Bite of Sandwich 150
blaa 619
Black Mountains 408, 414
Black Plague 53, 190
Black Prince, the 147
Black Watch 516
Blackmoor Gate 199
Blackpool 327–329
Tower 329
Blackshaw Head 341
Blackwell's Bookstore 221, 229
Bladon 231
Bladud 236
Blaenavon 409
Blair Athol Distillery 519
Blair Castle 520
Blair, Tony. See Prime Ministers
Blake, William 58, 110, 166, 281, 297
Blarney Castle 656
Blashaval Hill 558
Blast! 59
Bleaklow 313
Blencathra 386
Blenheim Palace 231
Bloody Sunday 581, 603, 606
Bloomsbury Group 59, 164, 283
Bloomsday 637
Blorenge 409
Blue Guides 4
Blue John Cavern 313
Blur 65
boats 30
Bodmin 206
Bodmin Moor 206–207
Body Shop, The 166
Boggle Hole 358
Bolingbroke, Henry 53
Bolton, Castle 348
Bon Voyage! 4
Bond, James 62
Bonnie Prince Charlie 54, 311, 372, 460, 483, 497, 507, 541, 545, 546, 552
Book of Invasions 616
Book of Kells 633
Book of the Dun Cow 644
Booker prize 60
Booth, Richard 407

border checkpoints 580
Borders, the 457, 478–484
Borrow, George 436
Ború, Brian 609
Borve 559
Boscobel House 300
Boston 306
Boswell, James 461, 552
bottling 547
Boulogne 154
Bourton-on-the-Water 257
bout 74
Bowmore 523
Bowness 380
Boyne Valley 641–643
Bradin 174
Braemar 533
Braids, the 477
Brains Brewery 401
Brampton 372
Branagh, Kenneth 63, 118, 266
Brantwood 383
Braveheart 391, 459, 506
breatheamh 616
Brecon 412
Brecon Beacons National Park 402, 408, 409–414
Brecon Jazz Festival 413
Bressay 571
Bretton 311
Brideshead Revisited 355
Bridge of Sighs 279
Bridgewater Hall 321
Brig o' Doon 500
Brighton 159–164
Royal Pavilion 162
Bristol 243–245
Britain in Bloom 535
Britain, Battle of 55, 334
British Broadcasting Corporation. See BBC 61
British Golf Museum 514
British Library 116
British Open 511
British Rail 71
BritRail Pass 32
British rule 581
British Tourist Authority 1
British Universities Accommodation Consortium 41

British-Irish Council 583
Britons of Strathclyde 458
Britten, Benjamin 64, 267
Broadford 550
Broadlands 180
Brockhole 376
Brodick 502
Brodie 531
Brontë, Charlotte 315, 341, 355
Brontë, Emily 59, 341, 355
Brooke, Rupert 282
Brooks, Mel 124
Brough of Birsay 567
Brougham Triptych 373
Brown Willy 206
Brown, Capability 123, 166
Brú na Bóinne 642
Bruce, The 461
Brum 268
bubble bath 150
Buckfast tonic wines 597
Budget Travel Agencies 25
building society 44
Bull Ring 645
Bunyan, John 58
Burges, William 400, 402
Buriton 184
Burke, Edmund 612, 633
Burnett, Frances Hodgson 295
Burns, Robert 98, 461, 472, 485, 488, 500
Burpham 184
Burray 567
Burrell, William 498
Burren Way 669
Burton, Robert 58
Bury St. Edmunds 293
buses 30, 33
Bute Park 396
Butt of Lewis 556
Butt, Isaac 613
Butterfly Jungle 451
Buttermere 386, 387
Butts, the 150
Buxton 310, 311, 312
Byrd, William 63
Byrness 371
Byron, Lord 103, 278, 302

C

Cabinet War Rooms

100
Cadbury World 269
Caedmon 359
Caerlaverock Castle 486
Caernarfon 441
Caerphilly Castle 402
Caesar, Julius 52, 142, 150
cafe-bars 321
Caherdaniel 661
Cahersiveen 661
Caine, Michael 62
Cairngorm Mountains 535
Cairns of Clava 541
Calais 152
calculus 306
Caldey Island 419
Cale, John 394
Callanish Stones 555
Calling Codes 690
Calton Hill 474
Calvinism 557
Camasunary 551
Cambrensis, Giraldus 388
Cambridge 272–282
Cambridge University 277–281
  Botanic Gardens 281
  Christ's College 280
  Clare College 279
  Corpus Christi College 280
  Downing College 280
  Emmanuel College 280
  Jesus College 280
  King's College 278
  Magdalene College 280
  Mathematical Bridge 279
  Museum of Zoology 281
  Pembroke College 280
  Pepys Library 280
  Peterhouse College 280
  Queens' College 279
  Robinson College 280
  Round Church 281
  School of Pythagoras 279
  Senate House 278
  St. John's College 279
  Trinity College 278
  Wren Library 279

Cambridgeshire 272–285
  Cambridge 272–283
  Ely 283–285
Cambuskenneth Abbey 508
Camelford 206, 207
Camelot 207
camera obscura 428, 485
campanologist 353
Campbell 508
Campbell, Colin 103
camping 44
Campion, Jane 133
Canary Wharf 119
Canmore 458
Canna 548
Canongate Tolbooth 473
Canterbury 52, 142–149
  Castle 148
  Cathedral 147
  Greyfriars 148
  Marlowe Theatre 149
  Norman crypt 147
Canterbury Tales, The 57, 143, 428
Cantley 291
Cape Clear Island 656
Captain Cook 359, 360
car insurance 9
Cardiff 396–402
  Bay 400
  Castle 400
Cardiff Bus 388
Cardigan 428
Cardron 481
Caredigon Heritage Coast 428
Carew Castle 419
Carfax 220
Carfax Tower 226
Carinish 558
Carisbrooke Castle 175
Carlisle 372–373, 375
Carloway 555
Carlyle, Thomas 115
Carrick-a-rede Island 600
Carroll, Lewis 60, 219, 226, 359
cars 34
carseats 14
Carson, Edward 580
Carte Bleue 12
Carter, Helena Bonham 63
Carvoan 375
cash cards 12

Cashel 651
Castell Coch 402
Castle Douglas 488
Castle Howard 355
Castle Museum 354
Castlebay 559
Castlehead Walk 386
Castlekirk 504
Castlerigg Stone Circle 386
Castleton 311, 313, 360
Castletownbere 657
Caswell Bay 417
Cat Bells 386
Cat of Nine Tails 573
Cathay's Park 400
Cathedral Church of St. Andrew 247
Catherine Howard 112
Causeway Coast 599–601
caves 302
Cawdor Castle 542
cawl 394
ceasefire, Northern Ireland 582
Cefn Bryn 416
ceilidhs 462, 540
Celts 52, 185, 391, 445
Central England 297–335
Central Library 320
Central Scotland and Argyll 505–528
Ceunant Mawr 440
Cézanne, Paul 127, 168
Chained Library 406
Chambers Institute 481
Chambers, Sir William 106
Chanctonbury Ring 184
changes 353
Changing of the Guard 101
Channel Tunnel 30, 152, 155
Chaplin, Charlie 62
Chariots of Fire 63, 514
Charlbury 255
Charles, Prince of Wales 57, 60, 109, 196, 279, 427, 441, 559
Charleston Farmhouse 164
Charleston, the 156
charters 29

Chartist movement 54, 392
Chatsworth House 315
Chaucer, Geoffrey 57, 142, 143, 231, 305
Chawton 180
cheap adolescent thrills 311
Cheap Tickets 28
Cheddar 247
Chedworth 258
cheese 248
Chelsea FC 68
Cheltenham 250–254
Chemical Brothers 65
Chepstow 404–405
Cherwell River 230
Chester 322–327
Cheviots 371, 478
Chichester 167–168
Chieftains, the 618
Child of Our Time, A 64
Child's Christmas in Wales, A 393
children, travelers with 23
Chipping Campden 257
Christ Church 119
Christ, Jesus 248
Christianity 52, 391
Christie, Agatha 59
Christie, Julie 168
Christmas Carol, A 59
Christmas Market 306
Chronicles of Narnia, The 225
Chunnel. See Channel Tunnel
Church of Ireland 612
Church of St. Martin 148
Church of the Holy Rude 507
Churchill Barriers 564
Churchill, Winston. See Prime Ministers
Chysauster 215
cider 67, 406
Cilgerran Castle 429
Cille Bharra Cemetery 559
Cinque Ports 149
Cirencester 258
Cirrus 12
Cistercians 419, 480, 486
Citicorp 12
Clapham 345
Clapton, Eric 64
Co. Clare 666
Clarinda 473

clarsach 462, 540
clean-shaven ape with a tie 280
Clearances, the 460
Cleese, John 280
Cleveland Way 358
Clickimin Broch 570
Clifden 678
Clifford's Tower 354
Cliffs of Moher 669
Clifton Suspension Bridge 245
climate 1
Clink Prison Museum 121
Clinton, William 227
Clive, Robert 298
Clockwork Orange, A 62
Clonmacnoise 644
Clonmany 689
Clovelly Village 214
Co. Louth 640
Coast-to-Coast Walk 347
Cobb 193
Cockburnspath 457
Cockermouth 379
cock-fights 213
Cocking 184
coddle 619
Coe Gorge 543
Coe, River 542
Coláiste Dara 19
Cold War 60
Coleford 403
Coleridge, Samuel Taylor 384
College Connection, Inc., The 4
Collins, Michael 614
Colman's Mustard Shop 289
Colsterworth 306
Common Sense 164
Commonwealth, the 53
commote 429
condoms 17
Confederation of Kilkenny 612
Cong 677
Coniston 383
  Coppermines 383
Connacht 609
Connemara 677
Connemara National Park 679
Connery, Sean 62
Connolly, James 613
Conrad, Joseph 148
consolidators 27
Constable, John 60, 110, 285

Constantine the Great 353
constipation 15
converters 25
Conwy 448–451
Conwy, River 449
Coole Park 675
Cooper, Ivan 581
Copinsay 564
Coquet, River 371
Co. Cork 651
Cork 651–656
  Christ Church 655
  University College Cork 655
Cormoran 185
Corn Ddu 413
corncrake 556
Cornish language 185
Cornwall 205–218
  Bodmin Moor 206–207
  Falmouth 208–210
  Land's End to St. Ives 214–215
  Newquay 216–218
  Penzance 211–214
  St. Ives 215–216
Cornwall Coast Path 187
Coronation Street 61
Corrieshalloch Gorge 562
Costner, Kevin 315
Cotswold Way 256
Cotswolds 254–259
Council 3, 19
Council Charter 26
couriers 29
Courtauld Collection 106
Coventry 267
cover photo 521, 522
Coverdale, Miles 353
Coward, Noel 104
Cowes 174
Crafnant, River 453
Cragg Vale 341
Craig Cerrig-gleisaid 414
Craig, James 580
Craignure 525
Craigower 519
Craig-y-nos 411
Crail 514
Cramond 477
cranberries 619
Crathes 531
credit cards 12
crempogen 394
Crested Butte 690
Criccieth 434
Crick, Francis 277
cricket 69

Crickhowell 414
crisps 66
Croaghaun Mountains 681
Cromwell, Oliver 53, 278, 285, 428, 459, 534, 612
  bustin' up cathedrals 650
crop circle 235
Cross Kirk 481
Crosses Walk 358
Crowden 311
Crown Jewels 112
Crown Jewels, Scottish 472, 534
Crown Prince Narvhito 227
crubeen 619
Crunchies 66
crwth 394
Cuckolded Cobbler. See Ben Arthur
Cuillin Hills 551
Culbone 214
Culla Bay 558
Culloden, battle of 460, 541
Culrain 563
Culzean Castle 501
Cumbria Cycle Way 377
curling 474, 516
currency exchange 10
currents 25
Cushendall 599
customs 6, 7, 8
cute sea animals 422
Cutty Sark Tall Ships Race 210
Cyclists' Guide to North Wales 390
cymanfa ganu 394
cynfeirdd 393

D

da Vinci, Leonardo 227, 229
Dáil 615
Daily Mirror 61
Daily Telegraph 61, 106
Daimler Company 267
Dale Head 386
Dales Barns 346
Dales Way 347
Dalí, Salvador 162
Dalmeny House 477
Danby 357, 360
Dante 269
Dan-yr-Ogof Showcaves 414
Dark Peak 309, 313
Darnley, Lord 482

DART 621
Dartmoor National Park 199–202
Darwin, Charles 280, 298
day returns 31
de Lacy, William 409
de Montgomery, Roger 298, 299
de Quincey, Thomas 384
de Valera, Éamon 614
Deal 150–152
Dean 474
Deane, Seamus 618
Dee, River 323, 453, 488, 532
Degas, Edgar 290
dehydration 15
Denmark 568
Dentdale 345
Derby, the 69
Derry 603–607
  black cabs 603
  Bogside 606
  Fountain 606
  Waterside 606
Derry and Fermanagh 603–608
Derrynane National Park 661
Derwentwater, Lake 375, 379
Design Museum 121
Devenish Brewery 191
Devil's Arse 314
Devil's Bridge 428
Devil's Dyke 184
Devil's Kitchen 438
Devil's Pulpit 405
Devil's Punchbowl 428
Devon 193–205
  Dartmoor National Park 199–202
  Exeter 193–196
  Exmoor National Park 197–199
Dewa 326
Diamond Jubilee 234
Diana, Princess of Wales 57
diaphragm 17
Diaries of Adrian Mole 60
Dickens House 117
Dickens, Charles 59, 98, 117, 118, 119, 142, 173, 236, 343
Dido and Aeneas 63
dietary concerns 23
Dimmingsdale 311
Dingle 662

Dingle Peninsula 663
diplomatic missions 31
disabled travelers 22
discounts 14, 29
distillation 547
Ditchling Beacon 183
Docklands Visitors Centre 120
Documents and Formalities 5–10
Dodgson, Charles. See Carroll, Lewis
Dolbadarn Castle 440
Dolmen of the Four Maols 682
Domesday Book 53, 176, 181
Donan Castle 549
Co. Donegal 683
Donegal Town 686
Donne, John 58, 110
Dooagh 681
Doolin 668
Dorchester 188–190
Dorset Coast Path 187
Dorset Coast, The 188–193
   Dorchester 188–190
   Lyme Regis 192–193
   Weymouth 190–192
Douglas 576–578
Dove Cottage 384
Dover 152–155
   Shakespeare Cliff 155
Dover Beach 152
Dow Gray 383
Down and Armagh 594–597
Downing Street Declaration 581
Downing, Sir George 99
Doyle, Sir Arthur Conan 59, 199, 202, 355
Dr. Faustus 58
Dr. Jekyll and Mr. Hyde 465
Dr. No 62
Dracula 359, 360
Dragon Guards 400
Drake, Sir Francis 195, 202, 280
Dream of the Rood, The 486
driving permits 9
Drogheda 642
Drogo, Castle 202
Druids, the 235
Drum 531
Drumcree 583
Drummore 491

Dryburgh Abbey 483
Dryden, John 58, 96, 278
Duart Castle 525
Co. Dublin 621–640
Dublin 624–638
   Accommodations 627
   Clubs 632
   Entertainment 636
   Food 629
   Gay, Lesbian, and Bisexual 637
   Getting There 624
   Practical Information 625
   Pubs 630
   Sights 633
   Bloomsday 637
   Grafton Street 630
   Guinness Brewery 635
   Temple Bar 632
   Trinity College 625, 633
   Writers' Museum 635
Duddingston 475
duffel bags 24
Duke of Nelson 110
Duke of Wellington 103, 110, 151, 454
Dumfries 485–487
Dumfries and Galloway 484–491
Dún Carloway Broch 555
Dún Cuier 559
Dún Laoghaire 639
Dunbar, William 461
Dunbeg Fort 663
Duncansby Head 564
Dunkeld 517
Dunkirk 154
Dunnet Head 564
Dunnotar Castle 533
Dunollie Castle 521
Dunrobin Castle 563
Dunskey Castle 489
Dunster 199
Duntulm Castle 552
Dunvegan Castle 552
Dunyveg (Dun-Naomhaig) Castle 522
Durham 55, 362–365
   Bishop of 112
   Cathedral 364
   Regatta 365
Duthie Park 532

E

Earl of Essex 112
Earth Station

Goonhilly 210
Easdal 522
East Anglia 271–296
East Beach 535
East Grampian Coast 533
East Neuk 514
Eastbourne 183
Eastenders 61
Easter Rising 614
Ecclesiastical History of the English People 53, 364
Economist, The 61
Edale 311, 313
Eday 568
Edge, The 254
Edinburgh 465–478
   Arthur's Seat 475
   Castle 472
   Edinburgh International Festival 463, 476
   Fringe Festival 476
   Gardens and Parks 475
   New Town 473
   Royal Mile 472
   Zoo 475
Education Reform Act 392
Edwards Bros. 388
Eel Crags 386
eggnog 620
Egyptian House 213
Eigg 548
eighth natural wonder 600
Eights Week 230
Eildon Hills 480
Eisenhower, Dwight 501
Electric Brae 501
electrical current 691
electricity 25
electronic banking 12
Elegug Stacks 422
Elgar, Edward 63, 259, 261
Elgin 534
   Cathedral 534
Elgol 551
Eliot, George 59, 115, 118
Eliot, T.S. 59, 64, 109, 116, 117
Elizabethan Walls 370
Elton 311
Elvis freaks 670
Ely 283–285
embassies 31
emergency number 14, 16
Emergency, the 615

Emma 180
Emmett, Robert 633
Empire 55
en suite 39
Enclosure Acts 54
Engels, Frederick 317
English Channel 152, 191
English Civil War 53, 154, 166, 226, 259, 267, 302, 404, 406, 459
English language 53
Ennerdale 379
Enniskillen 607
   castle 608
Eoligarry 559
Eriskay 559
Escher, M.C. 247
Esha Ness 571
Esk Valley Trail 358
Esk, River 517
Eskdale 379, 386
Eton College 279
EU Summit 396
Eurailpass 33
EuroCard 12
Eurolines 30
European Community 55
European Union (EU) 56, 615
Excalibur 185
Exclusion Crisis, the 54
Exe, River 192
Exeter 193–196
   Cathedral 196
   Exeter Book 196
Exmoor National Park 197–199
Eyam 311, 317

F

Face, The 61
Fair Isle 572
Falklands 56
Falls of Glomach 560
Falls of Lora 521
Falmouth 208–210
Falstone 371
Family Pass 33
family vacations 23
Fan Frynych 414
fanny pack 15
Faraday, Michael 119
fare brokers 29
Faroe Islands 563
favorite Scottish romance novel 482
Fawkes, Guy 99, 112, 118
Fayed, Dodi 57
Federation of

International Youth Travel Organizations (FIYTO) 3
Felixstowe 296
fell running 345
Fergusson, J.D. 516
fermentation 547
ferries 30
Festivals
    Bath Int'l Festival of the Arts 243
    Bath Int'l Music 243
    Birmingham Jazz Festival 270
    Boddington Manchester Festival of the Arts and Television 321
    Brecon Jazz 413
    Canterbury 149
    Chaucer Spring Pilgrimage 149
    Cheltenham Festival of Literature 253
    Cheltenham Int'l Festival of Music 253
    Chepstow 404
    Chester Summer Music Festival 327
    Edinburgh Book 477
    Edinburgh Int'l 476
    Edinburgh Int'l Film 477
    Edinburgh Int'l Jazz and Blues 477
    Exeter 196
    Fringe 476
    Gower 417
    Hay-on-Wye 407
    International Music Eisteddfod 454
    Inverness Tattoo 541
    Llangollen International Eisteddfod 395
    Military Tattoo 477
    Pontardwe International Music 415
    Robin Hood 303
    Rose of Tralee 665
    Royal National Eisteddfod 395
    Salisbury 234
    Scotland 463
    Stour Music 149
    Swansea 415
    Wales 395
    wine-tasting 234
Ffestiniog Railway 436
Fforest Fawr 413
Fielding, Henry 236

Fiennes, Ralph 266
Fife Seaside 514
50 Most Beautiful People 57
film 62, 619
Financial Times, The 61
Fingal's Cave 528
Firle Beacon 183
first-aid kit 15
fish and chips 66
Fishbourn 173
Fishguard 423
Fistral Beach 218
FitzGerald, Garret 581
Fitzherbert, Maria 159
Five Sisters of Kintail 560
Flake 66
fleadh 618
Fleet Street 106
Fleming, Ian 60
Flexipass 33
Floors Castle 483
flower festival 285
Folkestone 155
Food
    Britain 65–67
    Ireland 619
    Scotland 462
    Wales 394
football (soccer) 68
football, Gaelic 619
Footdee 532
Forest of Harris 556
Forres 535
Forster, E.M. 59, 93, 116, 142, 278
Forsyth Travel Library 4
Fort Charlotte 570
Fort William 543–545
Forth, River 508
Fortingall 518
Fortnight Festival 508
Forty Acre Lane 184
Forty-Five, the 460
Fowles, John 192
Foxy Old Woman's Guide to Traveling Alone, A 20
Francis of Assisi 148
Franciscans, the 148, 596
Franey, Ena 229
Fraser 531
Freake, Bishop 261
Free Derry 581
Freshwater 174
Freud, Lucian 60
frilly lips 335
frostbite 17
Fry, Roger 116, 164
fugginell 335

Full Monty, The 307
funerals 507
Fungi the Dolphin 663
Future Sound of London 65
Fyvie 531

G
Gaelic 529
Gaelic Athletic Association (GAA) 613, 619
Gaelic League 613
Gainsborough, Thomas 60, 242, 285, 295
Gairloch 561
Galashiels 480–481, 484
Galloway Forest Park 457, 491
Co. Galway 670
Galway 670
Gandhi 63
Gandhi, Indira 229
Gandhi, Mohandas K. 383
Gap of Dunloe 660
Garrick, David 98
Gatehouse of Fleet 488
Gatwick Airport 70
Gawain and the Green Knight 57
gay rights 151
gay travelers 21
Gazen Salts Nature Reserve 150
Gelert 439
Geoffrey of Monmouth 405
Geordie 365, 368
George, Terry 619
Getting There 25–31
Giant's Causeway 600
giardia 16
Gibbon, Edward 228
Gibbons, Grinling 108, 110
Gibbs, James 106
Gilbert and Sullivan 63
Gillaval Glas 556
Girthgate 479
Glaisdale 360
Glaisdale Riggs 360
Glamaig 551
Glamis Castle 517
Glasgow 491–500
    Art Gallery and Museum 497
    City Center 496
    George Square 496
    Glasgow Cathedral 497

Glasgow International Jazz Festival 499
Glasgow School of Art 498
Glasgow University 497
    Kelvingrove Park 497
    McLellan Galleries 498
    Museum of Transport 497
    People's Palace 497
    St. Mungo Museum of Religious Life and Art 497
    West End 497
Glastonbury 248–250
    Thorn 250
Glastonbury Tor 250
Glen Coe 457, 542–543
Glen Meavaig 556
Glen More Forest Park 535
Glen Valtos 555
Glenariff 598
Glencoe, Massacre of 542
Glenfiddich distillery 535
Glenluce 491
Glentrool 491
Glentross 481
Glimps Holm 567
Globe Theatre 266
Glorious Revolution, the 54
Glyders 438
Glyndŵr, Owain 298, 391, 415, 429, 450
G-Mex 321
Go Blue Banana 34, 457
GO25 Card (International Youth Discount Travel Card) 9
Goatfell 503
Goathland 361
Goch, Iolo 393
Godiva, Lake 267
Gododdin 393
Godrevy Lighthouse 215, 216
Godwin, Mary 116
Golden Hinde 121
Golden Mile 329
Golden Road 556
Golowan Festival 213
Gone with the Wind 224
Goonhilly Downs 210

Gordale Scar 348
Gore-Tex® 25
Gospel Pass 414
Gower Peninsula 416
Gradbach Mill 311
Grafton Street 625
Grampian Mountains 518, 533
Grand Shaft 155
Grandy, Nick 266
Grant, Cary 62
Grant, Duncan 164
Grant, Hugh 63
Grantchester 282
Grantham 306
Grasmere 384
Grassholm Island 422
Grassington 347
gravity 306
Gray, Thomas 280
Gray's Inn 105
Great Bernera 555
Great Exhibition, the 54
Great Fire of 1666 107, 109, 110
Great Gable 386
Great Ouse 291
Great Plague 176, 289
Great Skuas (Bonxies) 571
Great Yarmouth 291
Greek Cross 109
Green Gable 386
Greenaway, Peter 63
Greencastle 689
Greendale Valley 386
Greenhead 370
Greenwich Mean Time 690
Greenwich Observatory 151
Gregory, Lady Augusta 617
Gregynog Gallery 428
Grey, Lady Jane 112
Grey's Monument 365
Greyfriars Bobby 471, 473
Greyfriars Kirk 472
greyhound racing (the dogs) 69
Griffiths, Ann 394
Grinton 346
Grizedale 384
Grizedale Forest 383
Groesffordd 412
Grosvenor Museum 326
Guest, Lady Charlotte 393
Guid Nychburris Festival 484
guide dogs 22

Guildhall of St. George 292
Guinness 620
in jam jars 659
nuns drinking 688
Guinness Book of World Records 567
Guinness, Sir Alec 62
Guy Fawkes Day 690
Gwaun Valley 419
Gwilym, Dafydd ap 393
Gwydir Castle 453
Gyffin River 449

H

Haddon Hall 315
Hadrian 458, 478
Hadrian's Wall 52, 370, 372, 373, 373–375
haggis 462, 463
Haggis Backpackers 34, 457
Hall of Welsh Heroes 400
Hall, Radclyffe 115
Hallé Orchestra 321
Halley, Edmund 228
Hamilton, Ian 98
Hamlet 58
Hampshire 169–184
Portsmouth 169–173
South Downs Way 180–184
Winchester 176–180
Hampstead Heath 118
Handel, G.F. 98, 234
handfasting 517
Harcastle Crags 341
Hardrow Force 348
Hardy, Thomas 59, 98, 188
Harefoot, Harold 106
Hareshaw Linn Waterfall 371
Harlech 431
harlot's hut 386
Harp 620
Harris 556
Harrods 138
Hartington 311
Harvard, John 280
Harwich 296
Hastings 157
Hathaway, Anne 266
Hathersage 312, 314, 315
Haverfordwest 419
Hawes 346, 348
Hawkshead 384
Hawksmoor, Nicholas

109
Haworth 341
Hay Tor 202
Hay-on-Wye 407
Haystacks 387
Health 15–17
Heaney, Seamus 253, 267, 618
Heart of England 219–270
Heathrow Airport 70
heat-stroke 16
Hebden Bridge 340
Hebrides Overture 528
hedge schools 612
Heel Stone 235
Helm Cragg 385
helmets 37
Helmsley 357, 358, 361
Duncombe Park 361
Rievaulx Abbey 361
Walled Garden 361
Helston 210
Henley Royal Regatta, the 69
Henley, W.F. 110
Henrietta Park 242
Henry IV Part I 371
Hepste, River 414
Hepstonstall 341
Hepworth, Barbara 216
Herbert, George 278
Hereford 406
herodom, certified 600
Herriot, James 59, 337
Hertford, Earl of 483
Hexham 370, 375
Hickory Dickory Dock 196
High Altar 110
High Cragg 387
High Force Waterfall 343
High Kirk of St. Giles 473
High Stile 387
High Willhays 202
Highland Clearances 529
Highland Games 549
Highlands and Islands 529–572
Highlands Boundary Fault 509
highways 34
hiking boots 24
Hill of Tara 641
Hippodrome Theatre 269
hiring 35, 37

Hirst, Damien 60
Historia o Uuched Dewi 424
History
Britain 52–57
Ireland, Republic of 609
Northern Ireland 580–585
Scotland 458–460
Wales 390–393
History of the Kings of Britain 405
Hitchcock, Alfred 62, 227
hitchhiking 37
Hitler, Adolf 55
HMS Belfast 121
HMS Victory 172
HMS Warrior 172
Hobbit, The 225
Hockney, David 60
Hoddinott, Alun 394
Hoe, the 204
Hogarth, William 60, 130
Hogg, James 461
Holbein, Hans 125
holidays 690
holly-beating 444
Holme Bird Observatory 293
Holmes, Sherlock 116, 185, 202
Holst, Gustav 63, 253
Holy Grail 248, 250
Holy Island 370
Holy Roman Emperor Charles V 179
Holyhead (Caergybi) 447
Holyrood Park 475
home exchange 41
home rental 41
Home Rule 613
Honddu, River 413
Honister Pass 380, 386
Hopetoun House 477
Hopkins, Anthony 63
Hopkins, Gerard Manley 59, 229, 529
Hornel, E.A. 487
Horning 291
Horringer 295
horseracing 69, 327, 500
Horseshoe Falls 382
Horseshoe Pass 453
Horton-in-Ribblesdale 348
Hostelling International-American Youth Hostels (HI-AYH) 39

Hostelling
International-Canada
(HI-C) 40
Houghton Hall 293
Hound of the
Baskervilles, The 199,
202
Hound Tor 202
House of Lords 99
House of Pain 618
House of Tudor 53
House on the Bridge
382
Housman, A.E. 278
Hove 159
Howard, Castle 355
Howards End 59
Howth 638
Hoy 567
Hughes, Ted 267, 280,
341
Huguenots, the 148
Hume, David 460
Hume, John 581
Hunstanton 293
hurling 637
Huxley, Aldous 125,
229
hypothermia 17

I

Iarnród Éireann 33
Ickworth 295
Idle, Eric 280
Illumination 329
immunizations 15
imps 305
In Memoriam 253
Independent Holiday
Hostels (IHH) 39
independent travelers
24
Independent, The 61
Industrial Revolution
392, 460
Ingleborough 348
Ingleton 346, 348
Ingram 371
Inis Oírr Way 676
Inishbofin 678
Inisheer 676
Inishmaan 676
Inishmore 675
Inishowen Peninsula
688
Inns of Court 105
Institute of
Contemporary Arts
(ICA) 101
Insurance 18
driving 10
International Driving
Permit (IDP) 9
International Horse

Trials 231
International Music
Eisteddfod 453, 454
International Planned
Parenthood
Federation 17
International Pop
Underground 64
International Schools
Services 19
Internet Resources 4
Inveraray 508
Inverness 537–542
Iona 527
Irish coffee 620
Irish dancing 618
Irish Literary Revival
617
Irish pound 11
Irish Republican Army
(IRA) 580, 614
Irish Tourist Board 3
Iron Age 413
Ishiguro, Kazuo 60,
192
ISIC (International
Student Identity
Card) 9
Islay 522
Isle of Anglesey 445
Isle of Arran Folk
Festival 503
Isle of Islay 522
Isle of Man 573–578
Isle of Man Purchase
Act 573
Isle of Wight 173–175
Italian Renaissance
372
Itchen, River 179
ITIC (International
Teacher Identity
Card) 9
Iveragh Peninsula 660

J

Jack the Ripper 119
Jackson, Michael 155
Jacob's Ladder 428
Jacobite Rebellion 368
Jagger, Mick 115
jail 15
James Boswell 107
James, Henry 156, 235
James, P.D. 253, 407
Jane Eyre 315
Jarlshof 571
Jarman, Derek 133
Jedburgh 482
Jeeves 59
Jethart 482
Jew of Malta, The 305
Jewel Tower 98
Jewellery Quarter 269

Jewish community
119
John O'Groats 563
John Rylands Library
320
Johnson, Samuel 58,
70, 106, 552
Jones, Inigo 100, 104,
235, 280
Jones, Tom 394
Jonson, Ben 58, 96, 98
Jordan, Neil 619
Jorvik Viking Centre
354
Joseph of Arimathea
248, 250
Joyce, James 617, 639,
674
James Joyce Centre
636
Jude the Obscure 189
Juliana of Norwich
289
Julius Caesar. See
Caesar, Julius
Jura 524
Jutes 52

K

Karloff, Boris 104
Kavanaugh, Patrick
618
Keats House 118
Keats, John 58, 118,
176, 179
Keb' Mo'. See Mo',
Keb'
Keel 681
Keem Bay 681
Kelso 483, 484
Kelvin, Lord 98
Kelvingrove Park 497
Kendal 380
Kendoon 485
Kenmare 660
Kent 142–155
Canterbury 142–
149
Deal 150–152
Dover 152–155
Sandwich 149–150
Kerrera 522
Co. Kerry 651
Keswick 385
Kettlewell 346
Kew Palace 123
Keynes, John Maynard
116, 164
Kidnapped 524
Kielder 371
Water 371
Kilchurn Castle 521
Kildalton High Cross
523

Kildonan 558
Co. Kilkenny 644
Kilkenny 649
Kilkenny ale 620
Killarney 658
Regatta 659
Killarney National
Park 659
Killarney, Lakes of 659
Killigrew 208
Killigrews 208
Killin 518
Kilmallie Hall 545
Kilnsey Crag 347
Kilt Rock 552
Kinder Scout 313
King John Cup 292
King Lear 155
King's College Chapel
532
King's Lynn 291–293
King's Theatre 475
Kings
Alexander II 459
Alexander III 459
Alfred the Great 53,
176, 179, 227
Arthur 185, 206,
207, 250, 391, 393,
405, 409, 480
Bendigeidfran 431
Charles I 53, 226,
302, 459, 562
Charles II 54, 155,
176, 300, 459
Christian I 568
David 482, 483
Duncan 458
Edgar 241
Edmund 293
Edward I 293, 391,
427, 443, 448, 450,
459, 508
Edward III 534
Edward IV 111
Edward the
Confessor 96
Edward V 111
Edward VIII 55
Edwin 353, 355
Ethelbert 148
Ethelred 257
François II 482
George II 228, 558
George III 190, 252
George IV 159, 162,
499
George V 234, 293
Harold 53, 157
Henry II 53, 143,
226
Henry III 179
Henry IV 147, 183,
298

Henry V 53, 179, 405
Henry VI 111, 278
Henry VII 53, 111, 392, 423
Henry VIII 53, 147, 150, 151, 157, 164, 171, 172, 192, 209, 210, 249, 250, 278, 392, 405, 419
James I 53, 57, 111, 235, 459, 482, 507
James II 54, 459, 460, 483, 488, 612
James III 484, 508
James IV 459
James V 459
James VI 53, 506, 507
John 53, 234, 259, 289, 668
Kenneth I 458
Lear 236
Offa of Mercia 391
Phillip II 526
Richard I 53, 155
Richard II 53, 450
Richard III 53
Robert II 517
William 592, 606
William II 373, 403
William III 54, 110, 459, 519, 542, 580, 612
William the Conqueror 53, 111, 142, 148, 157, 176, 179, 180, 193, 196, 202, 299, 302, 314, 349, 368, 391, 403, 404
Kingston 183
Kinloch Castle 547
Kipling, Rudyard 98, 164, 181
kippers 573, 578
Kirk Yetholm 371
Kirkby Stephen 346
Kirkcudbright 487–488
Kirkmadrine Stones 489
Kirkwall 565
Kisimul Castle 559
Knox, John 459, 473, 507
Kodiak 690
kosher 23
Kryptonite locks 37
Kubrick, Stanley 62
Kyle of Lochalsh 549
Kyleakin 549

L

Labour Party 54, 56
Ladies Rock 507
Lady of the Lake, The 511
lager 67
lagers 620
Lairig Ghru 534
Lake Crafnant 453
Lake District 375–387
Lake Windermere 380
Lakeside and Haverthwaite Railway 376
Lamb Holm 567
lambada 156
Lammermuirs 478
Lanark 499
Land's End 214
Landseer, Edwin 60
Langland, William 57
Langmoor Gardens 193
Langsett 312
Language
  Britain 52
  Celtic 394, 461
  Scotland 461
  Wales 394
Lanhydrock 206
Lanyon Quoit 215
Lanyon, Charles 591
Larkin, Philip 59, 168
Larne 597
Last Minute Travel Club 29
Latin 391
Laugharne 419
Lauriston Castle 477
Lavenham 293, 295
laver bread 394
Lawrence of Arabia 110
Lawrence, D.H. 181, 298, 303
lazybeds 556
Leakey's Secondhand Bookshop 541
Lealholme 360
Lean, David 62
LeCarré, John 60
Leeds 335
Leeds Castle 149
Leek 312
leek 424
Leigh, Mike 63
Leigh, Vivien 62, 104
Leinster 609
Leonardo. See da Vinci, Leonardo
leprechauns 617
lesbian travelers 21
Let's Go editors 57
Let's Go researchers,

puerile 261
Letterkenny 687
Leverburgh 556
Lewes 164, 183
Lewis 554
Lewis Chessmen 555
Lewis, C.S. 60, 219, 225
Lewis, Cecil Day 190
Lews Castle 554
Leyburn 348
Libanus 411
Liberty of the Clink 121
Liffey, river 625
Lilla Cross 355
Lilt 66
Co. Limerick 666
Limerick 666
  King John's Castle 668
Limestone Way Trail 314
Linby 302
Lincoln 303–306
  Cathedral 305
Lincoln's Inn 105
Lindisfarne Priory 370
Lingwood 291
Linton 346
Literature
  Britain 57–60
  Ireland 616
  Scotland 461
  Wales 393
Little John 315
Little Princes 111
Littlehampton 166
Littleton Down 184
Liverpool 329–335
  Cathedral 333
Liverpool FC 68
Livingstone, David 242
Lizard Peninsula 210
Llanallgo 447
Llanberis Lake Railway 436
Llandaff Cathedral 402
Llandeilo 409
Llandovery 409, 411
Llanfaes 413
Llanfairpwllgwyngyllogerychwyrndrobwllllantysiliogogogoch (Llanfair P.G.) 425, 446
Llangadog 411
Llangannith Beach 417
Llangollen 453–454
Llanrwst 453
Llanthony Priory 409
Llanystumdwy 434

Lloyd's of London 108
Llŷn Peninsula 432
Llyn Cwm Llwch 413
Llyn Ogwen 438
Llywarch Hen 393
Llywelyn ap Gruffydd 112, 391, 427
Loch an t-Sailein 523
Loch Awe 521
Loch Coriusk 551
Loch Etive 521
Loch Katrine 510
Loch Leven 542
Loch Lomond 457, 494, 505
Loch Long 510
Loch Moidart 546
Loch Morar 546
Loch Morlich 534, 535
Loch Ness 541
Loch of the Lowes 517
Loch Sligachan 551
Loch Stockinish 556
Loch Tay 517
Lochaber Highland Games 545
Lochailort 546
Lochboisdale 557
Lochmaddy 557
Lochranza 503
Locke, John 96, 227
Lockton 358
Lona 293
London 70–141
  Accommodations 78–84
  Bisexual, Gay, and Lesbian London 140–141
  Entertainment 131–137
  Food and Drink 84–94
  Getting About 74–76
  Getting In and Out 70–74
  Museums 126–130
  Orientation 71
  Practical Information 76–78
  Shopping 137–140
  Sights 94–125
  ballet 134
  Belgravia 113
  Bloomsbury 116
  Bridge 109
  British Museum 126
  Camden Town 117
  Chelsea 114
  City of London 107
  clothing 138
  department stores 138

Docklands 119, 122
Dungeon 121
East End 119
emergency services 77
film 132
Fleet Street 105
Greenwich 122
halls of residence 82
Hampstead and Highgate 122
Hampton Court Palace 124
Harrods 138
Highgate 118
Holborn 119
Houses of Parliament, the 98
Hyde Park 114
Inns of Court, the 105
Islington 117
Kensington 113
Kensington Gardens 114
Kew Gardens 123
Knightsbridge 113
Mall, The 100
Marylebone 114, 116
Mayfair 113
Monument 110
music 133
National Gallery 127
National Portrait Gallery 127
nightclubbing 136
Notting Hill 115
opera 134
police 78
Primrose Hill 110
pubs and bars 92
recommended collections 129
record stores 139
Richmond 122
St. Paul's Cathedral 109, 110
South Bank 120
Southwark 121
sports 137
Strand, the 105
street markets 140
Tate Gallery 128
tea 94
theater 131
tourist offices 76
tours 94
Tower of London 111
Transport Museum 129
Underground 74
Victoria and Albert

Museum 128
Westminster Abbey 96
loners 24
Long Man 183
Long Melford 296
Longer Stays 41
Longest Journey, The 278
Longshanks 391
Longthwaite 378
Lord Hill 298
Lords Warden 151
Lossiemouth 535
Lost Valley 543
Loughrigg 383
lovespoons 417, 423
Lowestoft 291
Lucifer 58, 438, 523
luggage 24
Luing 522
Lusitania 656
Lyke Wake Walk 358
Lyme Regis 192–193
Lymington 173
Lynch's Castle 674

M

Maamturks 677, 679
Maastricht Treaty 56
Mabinogion 393
Macarena 156
Macbeth 517, 535
Macbeth 540
MacDiarmid, Hugh 461, 568
MacDonald, Clan 542
MacDonald, Flora 552, 558
MacGregor, Ewan 63
machair 556
Machars peninsula 484
Machynlleth 429
Mackintosh, Charles Rennie 495, 497, 498
MacLellan's Castle 487
MacNeice, Louis 618
Macneil, Robert Lister 559
Macpherson, James 461
Mae West's Lips 162
Maeshowe tomb 567
Magna Carta 53, 234, 259, 261, 289, 295, 305
Maiden Castle 190
Maiden Moor 386
Maidstone 149
mains 213
Malahide 639
male strippers 225
Malhamdale 348

Malin Head 689
Mallaig 546
Mallyan Spout 361
Malmesbury House 234
Malt Whisky Trail 535
Malthus, Thomas 241
malting 547
Malton 355, 357
Malvern 261
Mam Tor 313
man. See clean-shaven ape with a tie
Manchester 317–322
Museum of Science and Industry 320
Manchester United 68, 320
Manderston House 484
Manet, Edouard 229
Manorbier Castle 419
Mansion House 108
Manx cats 573
Manx Museum 577
Mappa Mundi 406
marching season 580, 582, 583, 591
Marco's An Aird 545
Mardi Gras 321
Marlowe, Christopher 58, 280, 305
Marmite 66
Marsalis, Branford 412
Marx, Karl 118
Mary Arden's House 266
Mary Rose 172
mashing 547
Massive Attack 65
Mathias, William 394
Matisse, Henri 229
Matlock 312
Matlock Bath 310
maturation 547
Maumbury Rings 190
Maurice 278
Mavis Grind 571
May 515
Co. Mayo 670
Mayor of Casterbridge 189
McAleese, Mary 616
McCaig's Tower 521
McCourt, Frank 618, 669
McLellan Galleries 498
measurements 691
Co. Meath 640
Melford 293
Mellerstain House 484
Mellte, River 413
Melody Maker 61
Melrose 479–480,

483, 484, 485
Mên-an-Tol 215
Mendelssohn Festival 526
Mendelssohn, Felix 528
Merchant Ivory 63
Merlin 207, 235, 393, 405
Merrion Square 634
Merthyr Tydfil 409, 412
methods 353
metric system 691
Michelangelo 227, 229
Middleham Jewel 354
Middlemarch 59
Middlesbrough 355
Middleton-in-Teesdale 343
midges 1
Milford Haven 420
Milne, A.A. 181, 279
Milton, John 58, 95, 278, 279, 280
Minchmoore 479
Minehead 199
Minghella, Anthony 63
Mingulay 559
Minnigaff 491
minority travelers 22
mint cakes 382
Mitchell principles 582
Mo', Keb' 412
Moil, Castle 550
Monet, Claude 98, 127, 229
Money 10–14
moneybelts 11, 14
Moniack Castle 541
Monk's House 183
Monmouth 405
Monnow, River 405
Monty Python and the Holy Grail 522
Monty Python's Flying Circus 62
Monument 109
Moore, G.E. 279
Moore, Henry 60, 110, 290
Moore, Thomas 633
Moorfoots 478
Mordred 185, 206
More, Sir Thomas 99, 114, 148
Morris, William 280
Morrison, Toni 407
Morrison's Bowmore Distillery 524
mosquitoes 16
Mossyard Beach 488

Moulin 519
Mount Fuji 309
Mount Snowdon 438
Mourne Mountains, the 594
Mousa 571
Moville 689
Mowlam, Mo 582
Muck 548
Muldoon, Paul 618
Mull 524–528
　Highland Games 526
　Music Festival 526
Mull of Oa 522
Mumbles 416
Munro Bagging 458
Munster 609
Murdoch, Rupert 61
Murphy's 620
Museum of British Road Transport 267
Museum of Childhood 473
Museum of London 129
Museum of the Moving Image (MOMI) 130
Museum of Welsh Life 402
Music
　Britain 63
　Ireland 618
　Scotland 461
　trad 636
　Wales 393

N
Nanakuli 690
Nanmor, Dafydd 393
Napoleon 154
Napoleon III 172
Narrow-gauge railway lines 436
Nash, John 101, 103, 162, 429
National Express 34
National Gaelic Mod 463
National Gallery of Modern Art (Scotland) 475
National Gallery of Scotland 474
National Library of Wales 425, 428
National Marine Aquarium 205
National Maritime Museum 130
National Museum (Ireland) 634
National Museum of

Wales 400
National Orchestra of Wales 401
National Parks
　Brecon Beacons 402, 408, 409–414
　Connemara 679
　Dartmoor 199–202
　Derrynane 661
　Exmoor 197–199
　Killarney 659
　Lake District 375–387
　North York Moors 355–362
　Northumberland 369–372
　Peak 309–314
　Pembrokeshire Coast 419–424
　Snowdonia 425
　Yorkshire Dales 313, 343–348
National Rugby Stadium 402
National Trust 3
Nationalists 580
Natural History Museum 130
Navan Fort 597
Near Sawrey 384
neck pouch 14
Needles 175
Neeson, Liam 619
Neidpath Castle 481
Nelson Monument 474
Nelson, Horatio 202
Ness Islands 541
Ness, River 541
Nessie 541
Nest 429
Nether Wasdale 380
Nevis Range 545
New 499
New Forest 180
New Lanark 494, 499
New Statesman, The 61
New Town 473
Newcastle (Northern Ireland) 595
Newcastle-Upon-Tyne 365–369
Newgrange 642
Newport 174, 403, 420
Newquay 216–218
newspapers 61
Newstead Abbey 302
Newton Stewart 491
Newton, Sir Isaac 98, 279, 306
Newtondale Forest

361
Newtondale Gorge 361
Nicholas Nickleby 173, 343
Nicholas, Jemima 420
NICRA 581
Nightingale, Florence 110
1984 59
Norfolk and Norwich Festival 290
Norfolk and Suffolk 285–296
　Bury St. Edmunds 293–296
　Harwich and Felixstowe 296
　King's Lynn 291–293
　Norwich 285–291
Norfolk Broads 290
Norfolk Coast 293
Norman crypt 179
Normans 185, 272, 391
North Devon Coast Path 214
North England 337–387
North Inch 516
North Sea oil 531
North Uist 557
North Wales 425–454
North York Moors National Park 355–362
　Castleton 360
　Danby 360
　Helmsley 361
　North Riding Forest Park 359
　Pickering 360
　Railway 355, 360
　Whitby 359
Northanger Abbey 180
Northern Ireland 579–608
Northern Ireland (Sentences) Bill 583
Northern Ireland Assembly 583
Northern Ireland Civil Rights Association (NICRA) 581
Northern Ireland Tourist Board 3
Northernhay Gardens 196
Northgate 326
North-South Ministerial Council 583

Northumberland 369–372
Norwich 285–291
Noss 571
Notting Hill Carnival 115
Nottingham 300–303
nuns drinking Guinness 688
Nunton 558
Nynex Arena 321

O
O'Connell, Daniel 613
O'Connor, Sinéad 619
O'Neill, Hugh 612
Oasis 65
Oban 520–522
O'Brien, Flann 618
Observer 61
Ochil Hills 507
off season 1
Offa's Dyke Path 390, 403, 405, 414
Ogwen Valley 438
Okri, Ben 60
Olaf, Llywelyn 388
Old Bailey 108
Old Coffin Trail 384
Old Course 514
Old Man 383
Old Man of Storr 552
Old Sarum 235
Old Trafford 319, 320
oldest
　pub in Ireland 589
Olivier, Sir Laurence 62, 168
Omagh 585
Once Brewed 370
100 Years' War 53
Oostend, Belgium 152
opium-eaters 384
Orange Day 580, 582, 591, 690
Orange Order 580
Orcadians 564
Orchard 283
Ord of Caithness 563
Order of the Garter 125
Orkney Islands 529, 563, 564–568
Orlando 59
ornithology 564
Orwell, George 59, 125
Osmotherley 358
Ossian 461
Other Place, the 267
Oulton Broad 291
Ouse, River 183
outdoors 44
Outer Hebrides 529,

553–560
Owen, Robert 499
Owen, Wilfred 298
Oxford 219–231
Oxford Playhouse 230
Oxford University
226–229
  All Souls College 228
  Ashmolean
    Museum 229
  Balliol College 229
  Bates Collection of
    Musical
    Instruments 227
  Bodleian Library 228
  Botanic Garden 227
  Carfax Tower 226
  Christ Church 226
  Corpus Christi
    College 227
  Great Tom 227
  Keble College 229
  Magdalen College
    227
  Merton College 227
  Museum of the
    History of Science
    228
  New College 229
  Old Library 228
  Oriel College 227
  Queen's College 228
  Radcliffe Camera
    228
  Sheldonian Theatre
    228
  Somerville College
    229
  Trinity College 229
  University College
    227
Oxfordshire 219–236
  Oxford 219–231
  Salisbury 231–235
  Stonehenge 235–
    236
Oxfordshire Way 256
Oxwich Bay 417

P

Packing 24–25
Paine, Thomas 164
Paisley, Rev. Ian 581
Palace of
  Holyroodhouse 473
palm trees 193
Pannett Park 360
panniers 35
Papa Stour 572
Papa Westray 564,
  568
paparazzi 57
Paradise Lost 58
paragliding 438

Parc Padarn 439
Parnell, Charles
  Stewart 613
Parracombe 199
Pass of Killiecrankie
  519
Passage to India, A 59
passports 6
pasties 66, 209
Patterdale 380
Paxton House 484
Peace Agreement,
  Northern Ireland 582
peacocks 400
Peak Cavern 314
Peak District National
  Park 309–317
peal 353
Pearse, Padraig 614
Peebles 481
Peel 578
Peel, John 61
Pembroke 422
Pembroke Dock 422
Pembrokeshire Coast
  National Park. See
  National Parks
Pembrokeshire Coast
  Path 390
pence 10
Pendennis Castle 208,
  209
Penicuik 478
penis envy 183
Penn, William 227,
  245
Pennine Way 313,
  338–343, 347
Penrhyn Castle 445
Pentland Firth 563
Pentland Hills 478
Pentland Skerries 564
Pen-y-Fan 413
Pen-y-ghent 348
Penzance 211–214
People's Democracy
  (PD) 581
People's Palace 497
Pepys, Samuel 95, 109
Percy, Henry 298, 450
period returns 31
Personal Identification
  Number (PIN) 12
Persuasion 180, 193
Perth 515–517
Petticoat Lane 119
Petworth House 166
Pevensey 157
Peveril Castle 314
Phantom Piper 501
pharmacies 16
Pharos 154
Philosophical
  Investigations 279

phrasebook 691
Picasso, Pablo 127,
  168, 290
Pickering 355, 357,
  360
Picts 52, 458, 461
Picture This 290
Piers Plowman 57
Pilgrim's Progress 58
Pilgrim's Way 484,
  491
Pilgrims, the 202, 204
Pinter, Harold 407
Pirates of Penzance,
  The 63
Pitlochry 518–520
Pitt, William 242
Plantagenet, House of
  391
Plas Mawr 450
Plas Newydd 454
Plath, Sylvia 341
Pleasure Beach 328
Plockton 549
ploughman's lunch 66
PLUS 12
Plymouth 202–205
Plymouth Sound 202
Poe, Edgar Allen 115
Poetry Festival 267
Poets' Corner 97
poitín 620
Police, the 236
poll tax 56
polo 69
Pontius Pilate 518
Pontsticill 413
Pont-y-Pair Bridge 452
pony trekking 409
Pope, Alexander 58
Poppit Sands 421
porcelain 261
Port Askaig 522
Port Charlotte 523
Port Ellen 522
Port Erin 578
Porthmadog 433
Porth-yr-Ogof 413
Portinscale 386
Portishead 65
Portland 191
Portland Castle 192
Portmeirion 434
Portnalong 551
Portobello Market 115
Portpatrick 457, 484,
  489
Portree 552
Portrush 601
Portsmouth 169–173
Postbridge 201
Potato Famine, the
  613
Potter Heigham 291

Potter, Beatrix 381,
  384, 517
pound sterling 10
Powys, Prince of 429
prenuptials 517
Preseli Hills 419, 428
Pride and Prejudice
  59, 159, 180, 314
Prime Ministers
  Blair, Tony 56, 61,
    226, 582
  Chamberlain,
    Neville 55
  Churchill, Winston
    55, 95, 151, 169,
    231, 392
  Gladstone, William
    54, 55
  Heath, Edward 55
  Lloyd George, David
    54, 392, 434
  Macmillan, Harold
    55
  Major, John 56, 581
  Palmerston, Lord
    180
  Peel, Robert 54
  Thatcher, Margaret
    56, 61, 162, 229,
    306, 581
  Walpole, Sir Robert
    99, 293
  Wilson, Harold 55
Prince Charles. See
  Charles, Prince of
  Wales
Princes St. Gardens
  475
Princess Augusta 123
Princess Bride, The
  315
Princetown 201
Prioress's Tale, The
  305
Prodigy, The 65
pronunciation 693
Proust, Marcel 383
Provos 581
pub grub 66
Pubs and Beer
  England 67
  Guinness Brewery
    635
  Ireland 619
puffins 422
Pugin, A.W.N. 98
Pump Room, The 240,
  241, 243
punt 11
punting 230
Punts 281
Purcell, Henry 63
Pwllheli 435

Q

Q 61
Quadrophenia 64
Quarry Park 300
Queen Mary's dolls' house 125
Queen Mum 151
Queen Victoria, the 450
Queens
　Anne 231, 236, 474
　Anne Boleyn 112
　Anne of Cleves 164
　Catherine Howard 112
　Elizabeth 395
　Elizabeth I 53, 166, 229, 373
　Elizabeth II 234
　Isabella 293
　Joan of Navarre 147
　Katherine Parr 257
　Margaret of Anjou 279
　Mary, Queen of Scots 166, 372, 373, 459, 473, 482, 483, 507, 514, 562
　Parr, Catherine 171
　Victoria 55, 162, 173, 175, 234, 238, 241, 510
quid 10
Quiet Man, The 677
Quirang 552

R

Raby Castle 343
Rae, John 566
Raglan Castle 406
Rail Europe Inc. 32
railways, narrow-range 436
Rake's Progress, A 60
Raleigh, Sir Walter 95, 99, 247
Ramsey Island 423
random sexual encounters 481
Ranndale Knotts 387
rarebit 394
Rathlin Island 599
Ravenglass 386
Ravenglass and Eskdale Railway 376
Recreational Equipment, Inc. (REI) 46
Red Hand, the 593
Red Pike 387
Reeth 345
Reformation 459
Reformation, Scottish 516

refund 13
Regatta Carnival 193
reindeer 537
Release 15
Rembrandt 125, 127, 235
Republic of Ireland 609–689
Resources at Home 1
Retail Export Scheme 13
return 31
Reuters 106
Reynolds, Albert 295, 581
Reynolds, Joshua 60
Rhins of Galloway peninsula 484
Rhossili Beach 417
Ribena 66
Richard III 111
Richards, Keith 115
Richardson, Tony 62
Richmond, William 110
Rights of Man 164
Ring of Brodgar 567
Ring of Kerry 660
Rising, Castle 293
Riverdance 618
rivers
　Douglas 576
Road to the Isles 545
Robert the Bruce 372, 459, 480, 484, 485, 504, 506, 507, 508, 533
Roberts, Kate 393
Robin Hood 302, 315
Robin Hood's Bay 355
Robinson, Mary 615, 681
Rock of Harlech 431
Rodel 556
Rodin, Auguste 110, 229
Rodmell 183
Rolling Stones, the 64
Rollright Stones 258
Roman Army Museum 375
Roman Baths 241
Roman Catholicism 557
Roman Museum 148
Roman Wall 190
Romsey 180
Roodee 327
Roseberry Topping 360
Rosetta Stone 126
Roslin 478
Rossetti, Dante Gabriel 60

Rosslare Harbour 422, 646
Rosslyn Chapel 478
Rothbury 371
Rothesay 501
Rottingdean 164
Rougemont Castle 196
Rough Tor 206, 207
Round Table 179, 207
Rowardennan 510
Rowen 453
Rowley's House Museum 300
Roxburghe, Duke of 483
Roy, Arundhati 60
Royal Academy 130
Royal Air Force (RAF) 106
Royal Air Force Museum 130
Royal Botanic Gardens 123, 475
Royal Courts of Justice 105
Royal Exchange Theatre 321
Royal Forest of Dean 403
Royal Liverpool Philharmonic Orchestra 335
Royal Lyceum Theatre 475
Royal Mile, the 472
Royal Museum of Scotland 473
Royal National Eisteddfod, the 395
Royal National Theatre 132
royal oak 300
Royal Observatory 477
Royal Opera House 104
Royal Shakespeare Company 266, 335, 369
Royal Shakespeare Theatre 266
Royal Ulster Constabulary (RUC) 580
Royal Victoria Park 242
Royal Windsor Cup 69
royalty 57
Rubens, Peter Paul 125, 235
Ruby Bay 515
Rudolf Hess 112
Rufus Stone 180
rugby 68
Rugby League 68

Rugby World Cup 68, 396, 402
Rum 547
Rushdie, Salman 60, 278, 407
Ruskin, John 227, 309, 317, 383
Russell, Bertrand 115, 279
Russell, John 104
Russell, Richard 162
Rutherford, Ernest 279
Ruthwell 486
Rydal Mount 384
Ryde 174
Rye 155–156

S

Safety and Security
　Britain 14–15
　Northern Ireland 580
Saffron Walden 283
St. Andrews 511–514
　Cathedral 513
St. Augustine 148
St. Briavel's Castle 404
St. Catherine's Island 418
St. Catherine's Point 175
St. Ciaran 644
St. Clement's Church 556
St. Columb's Cathedral 606
St. Columba 527
St. Cuthbert 364
St. Cuthbert's Way 370, 479
St. David's 423
St. David's Day 424
St. David's Hall 394
St. David's Head 422
St. Dogmael's Abbey 429
St. Dunstan 283
St. Edmundsbury Cathedral 295
St. Fagan's Park 402
St. Findbar 559
St. George 250
St. Giles Fair 230
St. Govan's Chapel 422
St. Ives 215
St. Just 214
St. Justinian 423
St. Lawrence 175
St. Magnus 565
St. Margaret's Chapel 472
St. Mary Redcliffe 245

St. Mary's Abbey 354
St. Mawes Castle 208, 210
St. Michael's Mount 213
St. Nicholas Priory 196
St. Ninian 491
St. Ninian's Isle 571
St. Oran's Chapel 527
St. Patrick 250, 595, 609, 680
St. Patrick's Isle 578
St. Paul's Cathedral 109, 110
St. Peter 196
St. Stephen's Day 444, 690
St. Stephen's Green 634
St. Swithun 179
St. Werburgh 326
St. Winefride 300
Salhouse 291
Salisbury 231–235
 Cathedral 234
Salisbury Stake 231, 289
salmon ladder 519
Samaritans 109
Samuel Johnson's House 106
San Juan de Sicilia 526
Sandhead 489
Sandown 174
Sandringham 293
Sands, Bobby 581
 grave 592
Sandwich 149–150
Santon Bridge 386
Sargent, John Singer 115
Saucy Mary 550
Saundersfoot 420
Saunton Sands 214
Saxons 52, 185
Sayers, Dorothy 59, 229
Sayers, Peig 617
Scalloway 571
Scalpay 556
Scapa Flow 567
Scarborough 355, 357, 358
Scarp, Isle of 556
Schlesinger, John 62
Science Museum 130
Scolpaig 559
Scolt Head Island Reserve 293
Scone Palace 516
Scotland 455–572
Scotland Yard 100
Scots 458, 461
Scots Gaelic 461

Scots Wha Hae 488
Scott, Sir Walter 373, 454, 461, 472, 483, 510
Scottish Citylink 457
Scottish Grand National 500
Scottish National Party (SNP) 460
Scottish National Portrait Gallery 474
Scottish Wars of Independence, the 459
Scotus, Duns 558
Scouse 335
Scrabster 563
scree 413
SDLP 581
Seafell Pike 386
Seal Bay 559
seals 422
Seanad 615
Seathwaite 386
Seattle 690
Secret Bunker 515
Section 28 151
Sedbergh 345
Seil 522
self-defense 14
senior citizens 21
Senior Railcard 33
Seti I 130
Seven Hills of Abergavenny 408
Seven Sisters 183
Severn, River 259, 298
Sex Pistols 64, 114
sexually transmitted diseases 17
Sgurr nan Gillean Corrie 551
Sgwdyr Elra 414
shake holes 346
Shakespeare, William 53, 57, 97, 105, 262, 265, 292, 371, 517, 540
Shanklin 174
Sharp Edge 386
Shaw, George Bernard 617, 675
Shawbost 555
Shawl of Leyburn 348
Sheffield 307
Sheldonian Theatre 228
Shelley, Percy Bysshe 116, 125, 227
Sheridan, Jim 619
Sherwood Forest 302
Shetland Islands 529, 568–572
She-Wolf of France

293
shin-kicking 257
Shrewsbury 298–300
 Castle 299
shrimp vodka 498
Sidney, Sir Phillip 227
Siege of Derry 606
Sierra Design 45
Simpson, Tony 104
Simpson, Wallace 55
"The Simpsons" 589
single 31
Sinn Féin 581, 613
Skara Brae 566
skiing 537
skinheads 64
Skip, the 474
Skipton 347
Skirrid Fawr 409
Skokholm Island 422
Skomer Island 422
Sky TV 62
Skye 548–553
Slaughters 257
Sleat Peninsula 550
sleepsacks 25
Slieve Donard 594
Sligachan 551
Co. Sligo 683
Sligo 683
Slimbridge 256, 258
Slow Coach 34
Smallest House 450
Smith, Adam 229, 460, 473
Smith, Dame Maggie 168
Smith, John 56
Smithwicks 620
Smollett, Tobias 236
sneakers 24
Sneem 660
Sng, Daryl 333
Snowdon Mountain Railway 436
Snowdonia National Park 436–441
Soane, Sir John 108
Soldier's Leap 519
Sollas 559
Somerset and North Devon Coast Path 187, 197
Sons and Lovers 300, 303
Sour Milk Gill Falls 387
South Devon Coast Path 187
South Downs Way 180–184
South England 142–184
South Queensferry 477

South Ronaldsay 567
South Uist 557
South Upland Way 484, 489
South Wales 396–424
South Wales Transport (First Cymru) 388
South West Coast Path 199
Southampton 174
Southease 183
Southern Midlands 250–270
 Birmingham 268–270
 Cheltenham 250–254
 Cotswolds, the 254–259
 Stratford-upon-Avon 262–267
 Worcester 259–262
Southern Scotland 464–504
Southern Upland Way 457, 478
Southgate-on-Pennard 417
Southsea 173
Southwark Cathedral 121
Southwest England 185–218
South-West Peninsula Coast Path 187
Spanish Armada 53
Speedwell Cavern 314
Spencer, Diana 109
Spencer, Herbert 118
Spender, Stephen 253
Spenser, Edmund 280
Speyside Way 535
Spice Girls, the 65
Spooner, Warden 229
spooning 432
sports 619
Sports and Leisure Fortnight 327
S.S. Great Britain 245
S.S. Politician 559
Staffa 528
Staffin Bay 552
Stagecoach Red and White 388
Staigue Fort 661
Stainforth 346
stainless steel 307
Staithes 355
Stalker, Castle 522
Standard, The 61
stand-by 28
Standing Stones of Stenness 567
Stanford's 139

Stansted Airport 71
Star Trek 267
Statutes of Kilkenny 612
STDs. See sexually transmitted diseases
sterling bank account 43
Stevenson, Robert Louis 461, 465, 472, 524
Stewart, Earl Patrick 565, 571
Stewarts of Scotland 483
Sting 236, 365
Stinsford Church 189
Stirling 506–508
Stirling Bridge 507
Stirling, James 280
Stoker, Bram 355, 359, 360
Stone of Scone 97, 98, 516
Stonehenge 233, 235–236
Stoppard, Tom 59
Storey Arms 413
Stornoway 554
Stour, River 150
stout 620
Stow-on-the-Wold 256, 257
Strachey, Lytton 116, 164
Stranraer 488
Strata Florida Abbey 428
Stratford Festival 267
Stratford-upon-Avon 262–267
Stromness 565
Strongbow 612
study abroad 18
Stump Cross Caverns 347
Sudbury 293, 296
Sudeley Castle 257
Suffragettes 54
Sugar Loaf 409
suitcases 24
Sumburgh Head 571
Sun, The 61
sunburn 17
Supabus 30
Super APEX 31
surfing 216
Sussex 155–168
    Arundel 164–167
    Brighton 159–164
    Chichester 167–168
    Rye 155–157
Swaledale 348
Swallow Falls 452

Swan Theatre 266
Swansea 414–415
Swedish meatballs 350
Sweetheart Abbey 486
Swift, Graham 271
Swift, Jonathan 596, 612, 617, 633
Swinburne 229
Swiss Cottage 175
Symonds Yat 403
Synge, John Millington 617

T

Taff Trail 402
Taff, River 396, 402, 419
taig 593
Tale of Peter Rabbit, The 517
Taliesin 393
Tam o' Shanter Experience 500
Tamar, River 202
Tamburlaine 58
tango 156
Taoiseach 615
Tarbert 556
Tarka Trail 197
tartan 480, 499
Tate Gallery 333
Tate, General 420
Tavistock 202
Tay, River 517
Teapot Museum 451
Techniquest 401
telephone codes 690
television 62
Temple 105
Temple Bar 632, 634
Temple of the Four Winds 355
Tenby 417–419
Tenniel, John 60
tennis 69
Tennyson, Alfred Lord 59, 98, 175, 253, 278, 305
Tentsmuir Point Nature Reserve 515
Tess of the D'Urbervilles 189
Tewkesbury 254
Texas 65
Thames River 219, 230
Theatre Royal 104, 290
Thirlestane Castle 484
Thixendale 358
Thomas, Dylan 393, 414, 415, 419
Thomas, R.S. 393
Thompson, Emma 63,

118
Thoor Ballylee 675
Thorpe, Jeremy 125
Threave Castle 488
Three Cliffs Bay 417
Three Peaks Walk 348
Thurso 563
ticks 16
Tigharry 559
Tijou, Jean 110
Time Out 61
Time Walk 191
time zones 1, 690
Timeball Tower 151
Times, The 61
Timsgarry 555
Tintagel 207
Tintern 405
Tintoretto 227
Tioram, Castle 546
Co. Tipperary 644
Tippett, Michael 64
tipping 13
Titian 372
To the Lighthouse 59, 215
Tobermory 525
toilet, two-seat 488
Tolbooth Art Centre 487
Tolkien, J.R.R. 60, 219, 225, 227
Tolstoy, Leo 383
Tom Jones 62
Tomb of the Eagles 567
Tombland 289
Tommy 64
Tone, Theobald Wolfe 612
Tongue 562
tongue-scraper 423
Tongwynlais 402
Topeka, the grand city of 690
Torosay Castle 525
Torridon 561
Tory Party 54, 56
Totland Bay 175
Tower Bridge 112
Tower Hill 111
Tower Museum 606
Tower of London 111
Townsend, Sue 60
Toy Museum 326
trad 636
Traigh Mhor 559
trails
    Kerry Way 660
    Western Way 677
trains 30, 33
Trainspotting 63, 462
Traitors' Gate, 112
Tralee 664

Kerry the Kingdom 665
Transitions Abroad 20
Traquair House 483
Travel Avenue 28
Travel Organizations 3
Travelcard 74
traveler's checks 11
traveling alone 24
TravelSave stamps 33, 604, 624, 646, 653
Travesties 59
TrawsCambria 388
Tre'r Ceiri 435
Treak Cliff Cavern 314
Treaty of Limerick 612
Trefriw 453
Treshnish Isles 528
trifle 66
Triforium Gallery 179
Trimble, David 582
Trimontium Exhibition 480
Trinity College Dublin 612, 625, 633
Trollope, Anthony 117
Trooping the Colour 102
Trossachs 510
Trothy, River 405
Troubles, the 581
trunks 24
Tryfan 438
Tudor, Welsh House of 392
Tu-Hwnt-i'r-Bont 453
Turner, J.M.W. 60, 110, 115, 127, 166, 234
Turner, Kathleen 168
Tweed Cycleway 479
Tweed, River 478, 481, 483
Tweedsmuirs 478
Twelve Bens 677, 679
Twining's Teas 106
twist, the 156
Twister the Water Slide 180
Tyndale, William 57
Tyndall, Humphrey 284
Tyne Bridge 368
Tynwald 573
Tynwald Fair Day 690

U

U.S. Citizens Emergency Center 13
U2 618
Uig 553
Uists 557
UKCOSA/United Kingdom Council for

International
Education 19
Ulaid of Ulster 609
Ullapool 561
Ulster 609
Ulster American Folk
Park 607
Ulster Folk and
Transport Museum
593
Ulster Plantation 580
Ulster Protestant
Volunteers (UPV)
581
Ulster Unionist Party
(UUP) 582
Ulster Volunteer Force
(UVF) 580
Ulsterbus 34
Ulysses 637
Underground 22
Unionists 580
Universities and
Colleges
Aberdeen 532
Admissions Services
19
California at
Berkeley 259
Cambridge. See
Cambridge
University
College of Wales
425
Edinburgh
University 473
Exeter 195
Oxford. See Oxford
University
Queen's University
Belfast 591
St. Andrews 514,
515
Trinity College 633
University College
Cork (UCC) 655
Winchester College
179
Up-Helly-A' Festival
570
Upper Beeding 184
UPV 581
Urquhart Castle 541
Useful Publications 4
Ustinov, Peter 168

V

Vacation Work
Publications 20
Vale of Conwy 451–
453
Vale of Rheidol
Railway 428
Valle Crucis Abbey

454
Valley Villages 452
value-added tax. See
VAT
Van Dyck, Anthony
125, 166, 235, 372
van Gogh, Vincent
229
Van Morrison 412,
618
Varah, Chad 109
VAT 13
Vatersay 559
Veasta 192
vegetarians 23
Venerable Bede 364
Ventnor 174
Ventry Beach 663
Vermeer 227
Vestiarium Scotium
499
Victoria Park 532
Victoria Tower 98
Vikings 53, 272, 419,
570
Vindolanda 375
Visa 11, 12
volunteering 20

W

wakes 507
Walcott, Derek 267
Wales 53, 388–454
Walk Scotland 458
Walking Festival 479
Wallace Monument
508
Wallace, William 459,
483, 499, 506, 508
Walmer Castle 151
Walrus and the
Carpenter, The 359
Walter Scott
Monument 474
Walton, William 64
waltz 156
Wanlockhead 485,
486
War of Independence
614
War of Spanish
Succession 459
Ward of Bressay 571
Warden's Way 257
Warkworth Castle 371
warming trend 1
Wars of the Roses 53,
111, 350
Warwick Castle 267
Wasdale 386
Washington 184
Washington, George
110
Waste Land, The 59

Wastell, John 278
Wastwater, Lake 375,
380
Water of Fleet 488
Waterfall District, the
413
Co. Waterford 644
Waterford 646
Crystal Factory 648
Waterloo Bridge 452
Waterloo, Battle of
180
Watership Down 60
Watson, James 277
Waugh, Evelyn 355
Waun Fach 414
Wayne, John 677
Wear, River 362
Weaver's Way 272,
291
Wells 245–248
Wells-next-the-Sea 293
Welsh Industrial and
Maritime Museum
400
Welsh Language Act
392
Welsh National Opera
230, 401
Welsh Nationalist
Party (Plaid Cymru)
393
Welsh Regiment 400
Wembley Arena 135
Wensleydale 348
West Beach 535
West Highland Way
457, 509
Western Galloway 489
Westminster Abbey
109
Westport 679
Westray 564
Co. Wexford 644
Wexford 644
Weymouth 190–192
whaling industry 360
Whalsay 572
Wharfedale 347
What's New Pussycat
394
wheelchair facilities
22
Wheeldale 358
Whernside 348
Whig Party 54
Whin Rigg 386
whiskey
a guide to 643
hot 620
Irish 620
whisky (Scottish) 519,
547, 643
Whispering Knights

258
Whistler, James 115,
192
Whitby 357, 358, 359
White Peak 309
White Rose Walk 358
White Tower 111
Whitechapel 119
Whitechapel Art
Gallery 119
Whitepark Bay 600
Whithorn 491
Whiting, Richard 250
Who, the 64
wickets 68
Co. Wicklow 640
Wicklow Town 640
Wicklow Way 640
Wide World Books
and Maps 4
Wife of Bath 147
Wight Link 173
Wilde, Oscar 97, 114,
115, 228, 617, 633
wilderness 47
William of Wykeham
179
William, Prince 57
Williams, Ralph
Vaughan 64
Williams, Shirley 229
Wilmington 183
Wilton House 235
Wimbledon 69, 137
Wimpole Hall 283
Winchcombe 257
Winchester 176–180
Cathedral 179
Winchester Bible 179
Windermere 380
Windsor Great Park
125
Windsor Palace 57
Wine Festival 306
Winnie the Pooh 279
Winslet, Kate 63
Winter Gardens 329
Winter Gardens
Hothouse 532
Winter of Discontent
56
Winterson, Jeanette
59
Wittgenstein, Ludwig
279
Wodehouse, P.G. 59
Wolds Way 358
Wolf of Badenoch 534
Wollstonecraft, Mary
116
Wolsey, Cardinal 99,
245
Wolvesey Castle 179
women travelers 20

women's movement 615
Wood, John 242
Woodford Valley Route 236
Woodstock 231
Woodville, Elizabeth 279
Wookey Hole 247
Wooler 371
Woolf, Leonard 164, 183
Woolf, Virginia 59, 116, 142, 164, 183, 215, 548, 573
Woolsthorpe Manor 306
Worcester 259–261
Worcestershire Way 262
Wordsworth Walk 385

Wordsworth, William 58, 278, 384, 403, 405, 454
work abroad 19
work permits 19, 43
World Pipe Band Championships 499
World War I 55, 154, 460
World War II 142, 154, 181, 192, 202, 236, 242, 243, 302
world's smallest house, the 450
Worms Head 417
Wren 106
Wren, Christopher 96, 101, 105, 106, 107, 108, 109, 110, 114, 168, 228, 234
Writer's Museum 472
Wroxham 291

Wuthering Heights 59
Wycliffe, John 57
Wye Valley 403–409
Wye Valley Walk 403
Wye, River 403, 405, 406
Wyn, Hedd 393

Y

Y Beridd Newydd 393
Y Wladfa 392
Yarmouth 173, 174
Yeats, William Butler 617, 675, 683
Yell 571
Yelverton 202
Yeomen 112
yew 518
Yewdale Fells 383
York 349–355
  Central Tower 353
  Great East Window 353

Minster Library 354
  York Minster 353
Yorkshire Dales Cycleway 347
Yorkshire Dales National Park 343–348
Youlgreave 312
Young Person's Railcard 33
Your Trip Abroad 5
Youth Hostel Association of Northern Ireland (YHANI) 587
Youth Hostels Associations 39
Youthpass 33
Ystradfellte 413

Z

Zefferelli, Franco 315
Zennor Quoit 214

INDEX

Researcher-Writers

Christa Franklin
South & Southwest England,
Heart of England, East Anglia

Hailing from West Virginia and ultimately seeking her roots in Ireland, Christa managed to take on the whole of southern England in six weeks. She hitched and hiked the breadth of the country, breezing through sights—from venerable institutions to surfer hangouts. Braving the World Cup crowds and the summer sniffles, Christa came through with effusive copy and cheery phone calls. At times she covered three towns in a day, armed with boundless enthusiasm and no-nonsense road hair.

Nick Grandy
Heart of England, Central & North England,
Southern & Central Scotland

Raised in London, Nick began his travels in Oxford and ran north to the small isles of Scotland. He proved an enormous boon to the book; writing intelligent revisions, sprinkling his notes with local curses, and offering a native's inside tips. Nick was popular with hostelers in Glen Coe and Oxford, B&B owners in Bath and Stratford, and dogs everywhere. Though he must tear himself away from the beautiful Lake District and his mother's home-baked cookies, we welcome Nick back with thanks.

Daryl Sng
Wales, Central & North England

A Singapore whiz kid, Daryl tackled the wilds of Wales and the urban sprawl of Central England with equal gusto, armed only with backpack, notebook, and supply of hair gel. His research—thorough, dependable, and savvy—greatly expanded nightlife coverage in England's larger cities, and his linguistic expertise helped demystify the Welsh language. His urban sophistication attracted throngs of admirers and earned him the ecstatic gratitude of his editors. Daryl, you were, in one word, brilliant.

Adriane Giebel
Scotland

Chunneling from France, Adriane arrived determined to conquer Scotland. Her thorough copy detailed her travels, which took her from festival-mad Edinburgh to the pleasantly contented Isle of Skye. One taste of haggis, and she was hooked forever.

Ben Jackson
Scotland and London

Originally from Scotland, Ben used his thick Scottish accent and bright red hair to get the scoop on the northern reaches of his homeland, but nevertheless took a fresh look at the landscape, covering mountains, lush islands, and cosmopolitan Inverness.

Justine Sadoff
Scotland

Justine braved a taxing itinerary, sending back pristine copy laced with razor-sharp wit and managing to do a little sight-seeing on her own. She was our most experienced and mature traveler.

Rachel Greenblatt	*London*
Tobie Whitman	*London*
Chanya Dingle	*Editor, London*
Kathleen Conroy	*Republic of Ireland*
Daniel Horwitz	*Northern Ireland, Republic of Ireland*
Christopher Leighton	*Republic of Ireland*
Deirdre O'Dwyer	*Northern Ireland, Republic of Ireland, Isle of Man*
Jenny Weiss	*Editor, Ireland*
Brina Milikowsky	*Associate Editor, Ireland*
Lisa Nosal	*Managing Editor, Ireland*

Acknowledgments

Our first thanks go to Christa, Nick, and Daryl, whose six weeks of hard work are the flesh and blood of *B&I '99*. Our knowledgeable ME, Derek McKee, smoothed out the wrinkles and proved an invaluable source of information about the far-flung reaches of the Empire. Lisa kept an eye on *B&I* and took on the *I* as well. Thanks to Jenny, Brina, and Shanya, whose company kept our spirits up and whose text gave us a firm stand in London and a warm hug from Ireland. Thanks to the MEs, maps, production, Tom, Jeremy, and Anne for their labor, and congratulations to Anna and Caroline on the birth of a new series. Last, but not least, thanks to Ben and Adriane for sending back healthy doses of Scotland.   **B&I**

Thanks to those who made it easier, better, or just plain fun. To my terrific AE, Alex Leichtman, whose sharp eyes and wit made *B&I* a better book and whose *Pulp Fiction* kept me sane many many times. To Derek for cleaning up the copy, baking shortbread, and pushing through the final nights. To Lisa for taking on vast chunks of *B&I* as well as the general sanity of the pod, to Jenny for the Chair Butterfly, to Brina for being money, and to Shanya for RW-gossip. To Mr. Giroux and Mr. Bull, who continue to shape my *Let's Go* experiences from beyond the pod. To Jaime for breakfast, lunch, dinner, and everything in between. To Aileen, my confidant and fellow-smack-talker. Finally, to Mom, Dad, and Leona, who are simply the best.   **OSC**

First and foremost, thanks to Olivia Choe, dancing queen, whose frightening efficiency, expertise, and accents kept us from 11th-hour panic. To Derek for his keen eyes and encyclopedic knowledge. To Shanya for serenity, Jenny for energy, and Brina for domestic violence. To Dan, Maryanthe, and Heath for making the computers go, and to Jeremy for stellar research. To all former B&Iers who passed down a great book. A special thanks to Lisa for all sorts of weird looks and tremendous help. Thanks, eh, to Jamil, Steve, and Slapshot Steph. To Adam for the advice, to Matt, who has come to pick a fight, and to Prince W for being cute. Thanks to Danny, Judy, Josh, and Jake for the hospitality. And thanks to Mom, Dad and Max for everything.   **AML**

Editor	Olivia Choe
Associate Editor	Alexandra M. Leichtman
Managing Editor	Derek McKee
Publishing Director	Caroline R. Sherman
Publishing Director	Anna C. Portnoy
Associate Production Manager	Dan Visel
Production Manager	Maryanthe Malliaris
Cartography Manager	Derek McKee
Design Manager	Bentsion Harder
Editorial Manager	M. Allison Arwady
Editorial Manager	Lisa M. Nosal
Financial Manager	Monica Eileen Eav
Personnel Manager	Nicolas R. Rapold
Publicity Manager	Alexander Z. Speier
New Media Manager	Måns O. Larsson
Map Editors	Matthew R. Daniels, Dan Luskin
Production Associate	Heath Ritchie
Office Coordinators	Eliza Harrington, Jodie Kirschner, Tom Moore
Director of Advertising Sales	Gene Plotkin
Associate Sales Executives	Colleen Gaard, Mateo Jaramillo, Alexandra Price
President	Catherine J. Turco
General Manager	Richard Olken
Assistant General Manager	Anne E. Chisholm

Thanks to Our Readers...

Mano Aaron, CA; Jean-Marc Abela, CAN; George Adams, NH; Bob & Susan Adams, GA; Deborah Adeyanju, NY; Rita Alexander, MI; Shani Amory-Claxton, NY; Kate Anderson, AUS; Lindsey Anderson, ENG; Viki Anderson, NY; Ray Andrews, JPN; Robin J. Andrus, NJ; L. Asurmendi, CA; Anthony Atkinson, ENG; Deborah Bacek, GA; Jeffrey Bagdade, MI; Mark Baker, UK; Mary Baker, TN; Jeff Barkoff, PA; Regina Barsanti, NY; Ethan Beeler, MA; Damao Bell, CA; Rya Ben-Shir, IL; Susan Bennerstrom, WA; Marla Benton, CAN; Matthew Berenson, OR; Walter Bergstrom, OR; Caryl Bird, ENG; Charlotte Blanc, NY; Jeremy Boley, EL SAL; Oliver Bradley, GER; A.Braurstein, CO; Philip R. Brazil, WA; Henrik Brockdorff, DMK; Tony Bronco, NJ; Eileen Brouillard, SC; Mary Brown, ENG; Tom Brown, CA; Elizabeth Buckius, CO; Sue Buckley, UK; Christine Burer, SWITZ; Norman Butler, MO; Brett Carroll, WA; Susan Caswell, ISR; Carlos Cersosimo, ITA; Barbara Crary Chase, WA; Stella Cherry Carbost, SCOT; Oi Ling Cheung, HK; Simon Chinn, ENG; Charles Cho, AUS; Carolyn R. Christie, AUS; Emma Church, ENG; Kelley Coblentz, IN; Cathy Cohan, PA; Phyllis Cole, TX; Karina Collins, SWITZ; Michael Cox, CA; Mike Craig, MD; Rene Crusto, LA; Claudine D'Anjou, CAN; Lizz Daniels, CAN; Simon Davies, SCOT; Samantha Davis, AUS; Leah Davis, TX; Stephanie Dickman, MN; Philipp Dittrich,GER; Tim Donovan, NH; Reed Drew, OR; Wendy Duncan, SCOT; Melissa Dunlap, VA; P.A. Emery, UK; GCL Emery, SAF; Louise Evans, AUS; Christine Farr, AUS; David Fattel, NJ; Vivian Feen, MD; David Ferraro, SPN; Sue Ferrick, CO; Philip Fielden, UK; Nancy Fintel, FL; Jody Finver, FL; D. Ross Fisher, CAN; Abigail Flack, IL; Elizabeth Foster, NY; Bonnie Fritz, CAN; J. Fuson, OR; Michael K. Gasuad, NV; Raad German, TX; Mark Gilbert, NY; Betsy Gilliland, CA; Ana Goshko, NY; Patrick Goyenneche, CAN; David Greene, NY; Jennifer Griffin, ENG; Janet & Jeremy Griffith, ENG; Nanci Guartofierro, NY; Denise Guillemette, MA; Ilona Haayer, HON; Joseph Habboushe, PA; John Haddon, CA; Ladislav Hanka, MI; Michael Hanke, CA; Avital Harari, TX; Channing Hardy, KY; Patrick Harris, CA; Denise Hasher, PA; Jackie Hattori, UK; Guthrie Hebenstreit, ROM; Therase Hill, AUS; Denise Hines, NJ; Cheryl Horne, ENG; Julie Howell, IL; Naomi Hsu, NJ; Mark Hudgkinson, ENG; Brenda Humphrey, NC; Kelly Hunt, NY; Daman Irby, AUT; Bill Irwin, NY; Andrea B. Jackson, PA; John Jacobsen, FL; Pat Johanson, MD; Russell Jones, FL; J. Jones, AUS; Sharon Jones, MI; Craig Jones, CA; Wayne Jones, ENG; Jamie Kagan, NJ; Mirko Kaiser, GER; Scott Kauffman, NY; John Keanie, NIRE; Barbara Keary, FL; Jamie Kehoe, AUS; Alistair Kernick, SAF; Daihi Kielle, SWITZ; John Knutsen, CA; Rebecca Koepke, NY; Jeannine Kolb, ME; Elze Kollen, NETH; Lorne Korman, CAN; Robin Kortright, CAN; Isel Krinsky, CAN; George Landers, ENG; Jodie Lanthois, AUS; Roger Latzgo, PA; A. Lavery, AZ; Joan Lea, ENG; Lorraine Lea, NY; Phoebe Leed, MA; Tammy Leeper, CA; Paul Lejeune, ENG; Yee-Leng Leong, CA; Sam Levene, CAN; Robin Levin, PA; Christianna Lewis, PA; Ernesto Licata, ITA; Wolfgang Lischtansky, AUT; Michelle Little, CAN; Dee Littrell, CA; Maria Lobosco, UK; Netii Ross, ITA; Didier Look, CAN; Alice Lorenzotti, MA; David Love, PA; Briege Mac Donagh, IRE; Brooke Madigan, NY; Helen Maltby, FL; Shyama Marchesi, ITA; Domenico Maria, ITA; Natasha Markovic, AUS; Edward Marshall, ECU; Rachel Marshall, TX; Kate Maynard, UK; Agnes McCann, IRE; Susan McGowan, NY; Brandi McGunigal, CAN; Neville McLean, NZ; Marty McLendon, MS; Matthew Melko, OH; Barry Mendelson, CA; Eric Middendorf, OH; Nancy Mike, AZ; Coren Milbury, NH; Margaret Mill, NY; David H. Miller, TX; Ralph Miller, NV; Susan Miller, CO; Larry Moeller, MI; Richard Moore, ENG; Anne & Andrea Mosher, MA; J. L. Mourne, TX; Athanassios Moustakas, GER; Laurel Naversen, ENG; Suzanne Neil, IA; Deborah Nickles, PA; Pieter & Agnes Noels, BEL; Werner Norr, GER; Ruth J. Nye, ENG; Heidi O'Brien, WA; Sherry O'Cain, SC; Aibhan O'Connor, IRE; Kevin O'Connor, CA; Margaret O'Rielly, IRE; Daniel O'Rourke, CA; Krissy Oechslin, OH; Johan Oelofse, SAF; Quinn Okamoto, CA; Juan Ramon Olaizola, SPN; Laura Onorato, NM; Bill Orkin, IL; K. Owusu-Agyenang, UK; Anne Paananen, SWD; Jenine Padget, AUS; Frank Pado, TX; G. Pajkich, Washington, DC; J. Parker, CA; Marian Parnat, AUS; Sandra Swift Parrino, NY; Iris Patten, NY; M. Pavini, CT; David Pawielski, MN; Jenny Pawson, ENG; Colin Peak, AUS; Marius Penderis, ENG; Jo-an Peters, AZ; Barbara Phillips, NY; Romain Picard, Washington, DC; Pati Pike, ENG; Mark Pollock, SWITZ; Minnie Adele Potter, FL; Martin Potter, ENG; Claudia Praetel, ENG; Bill Press, Washington, DC; David Prince, NC; Andrea Pronko, OH; C. Robert Pryor, OH; Phu Quy, VTNM; Adrian Rainbow, ENG; John Raven, AUS; Lynn Reddringer, VA; John Rennie, NZ; Ruth B.Robinson, FL; John & Adelaida Romagnoli, CA; Eva Romano, FRA; Mark A. Roscoe, NETH; Yolanda & Jason Ross, CAN; Sharee Rowe, ENG; W. Suzanne Rowell, NY; Vic Roych, AZ; John Russell, ENG; Jennifer Ruth, OK; William Sabino, NJ; Hideki Saito, JPN; Frank Schaer, HUN; Jeff Schultz, WI; Floretta Seeland-Connally, IL; Colette Shoulders, FRA; Shireen Sills, ITA; Virginia Simon, AUS; Beth Simon, NY; Gary Simpson, AUS; Barbara & Allen Sisarsky, CA; Alon Siton, ISR; Kathy Skeie, CA; Robyn Skillecorn, AUS; Erik & Kathy Skon, MN; Stine Skorpen, NOR; Philip Smart, CAN; Colin Smit, ENG; Kenneth Smith, DE; Caleb Smith, CA; Geoffrey Smith, TX; John Snyder, NC; Kathrin Speidel, GER; Lani Steele, PHIL; Julie Stelbracht, PA; Margaret Stires, TN; Donald Stumpf, NY; Samuel Suffern, TN; Michael Swerdlow, ENG; Brian Talley, TX; Serene-Marie Terrell, NY; B. Larry Thilson, CAN; J. Pelham Thomas, NC; Wright Thompson, ITA; Christine Timm, NY; Melinda Tong, HK; M. Tritica, AUS; Melanie Tritz, CAN; Mark Trop, FL; Chris Troxel, AZ; Rozana Tsiknaki, GRC; Lois Turner, NZ; Nicole Virgil, IL; Blondie Vucich, CO; Wendy Wan, SAF; Carrie & Simon Wedgwood, ENG; Frederick Weibgen, NJ; Richard Weil, MN; Alan Weissberg, OH; Ryan Wells, OH; Jill Wester, GER; Clinton White, AL; Gael White, CAN; Melanie Whitfield, SCOT; Bryn Williams, CAN; Amanda Williams, CAN; Wendy Willis, CAN; Sasha Wilson, NY; Kendra Wilson, CA; Olivia Wiseman, ENG; Gerry Wood, CAN; Kelly Wooten, ENG; Robert Worsley, ENG; C.A.Wright, ENG; Caroline Wright, ENG; Mary H. Yuhasz, CO; Margaret Zimmerman, WA.

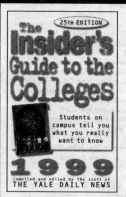

★Let's Go 1999 Reader Questionnaire★

Please fill this out and return it to **Let's Go, St. Martin's Press**, 175 Fifth Ave., New York, NY 10010-7848. All respondents will receive a free subscription to **The Yellowjacket**, the Let's Go Newsletter. You can find a more extensive version of this survey on the web at http://www.letsgo.com.

Name: _____

Address: _____

City: _____ **State:** _____ **Zip/Postal Code:** _____

Email: _____ **Which book(s) did you use?** _____

How old are you? under 19   19-24   25-34   35-44   45-54   55 or over

Are you (circle one)   in high school   in college   in graduate school   employed   retired   between jobs

Have you used Let's Go before? yes no   **Would you use it again?** yes no

How did you first hear about Let's Go? friend   store clerk   television   bookstore display   advertisement/promotion   review   other

Why did you choose Let's Go (circle up to two)? reputation budget focus   price   writing style   annual updating   other: _____

Which other guides have you used, if any? Fodor's   Footprint Handbooks   Frommer's $-a-day   Lonely Planet   Moon Guides   Rick Steve's   Rough Guides   UpClose   other: _____

Which guide do you prefer? _____

Please rank each of the following parts of Let's Go 1 to 5 (1=needs improvement, 5=perfect). packaging/cover   practical information   accommodations   food   cultural introduction   sights   practical introduction ("Essentials")   directions   entertainment   gay/lesbian information   maps   other: _____

How would you like to see the books improved? (continue on separate page, if necessary) _____
_____

How long was your trip?   one week   two weeks   three weeks   one month   two months or more

Which countries did you visit? _____

What was your average daily budget, not including flights? _____

Have you traveled extensively before? yes   no

Do you buy a separate map when you visit a foreign city? yes   no

Have you used a Let's Go Map Guide? yes   no

If you have, would you recommend them to others? yes   no

Have you visited Let's Go's website? yes no

What would you like to see included on Let's Go's website? _____
_____

What percentage of your trip planning did you do on the Web? _____

Would you use a Let's Go: recreational (e.g. skiing) guide   gay/lesbian guide   adventure/trekking guide   phrasebook   general travel information guide

Which of the following destinations do you hope to visit in the next three to five years (circle one)? Canada   Argentina   Perú   Kenya   Middle East   Caribbean   Scandinavia   other: _____

Where did you buy your guidebook?   Internet   independent bookstore   chain bookstore   college bookstore   travel store   other: _____

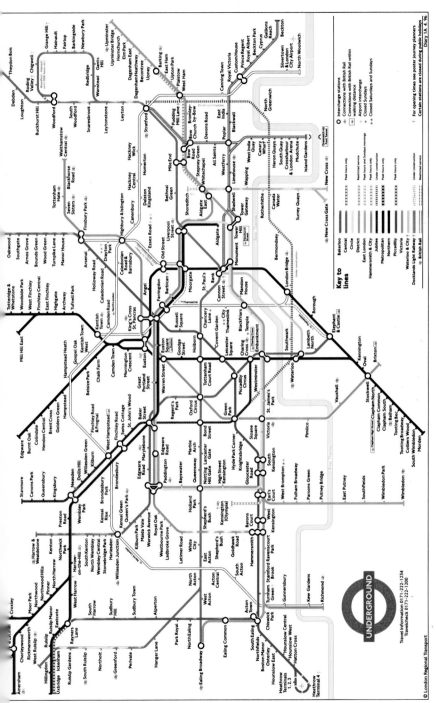

Key to
lines

| Bakerloo |
| Central |
| Circle |
| District |
| East London |
| Hammersmith & City |
| Metropolitan |
| Northern |
| Piccadilly |
| Victoria |
| Waterloo & City † |
| British Rail |

Docklands Light Railway †

○ Interchange stations
⊖ Connections with British Rail
＋ Connections with British Rail within walking distance
✈ Airport interchange
✢ Closed Sundays
✢✢ Closed Saturdays and Sundays

† For opening times see poster journey planners
Certain stations are closed during public holidays

╫ Peak hours only
╫ Restricted service
╫ Peak hours and Sundays mornings
╫ Peak hours only
╫ Peak hours only
╫ Peak hours only
╫ Under construction
╫ Restricted service

Travel Information 0171-222-1234
Travelcheck 0171-222-1200

© London Regional Transport

UNDERGROUND

Diary 1A 4.96

LRT Registered User No. 97/2726

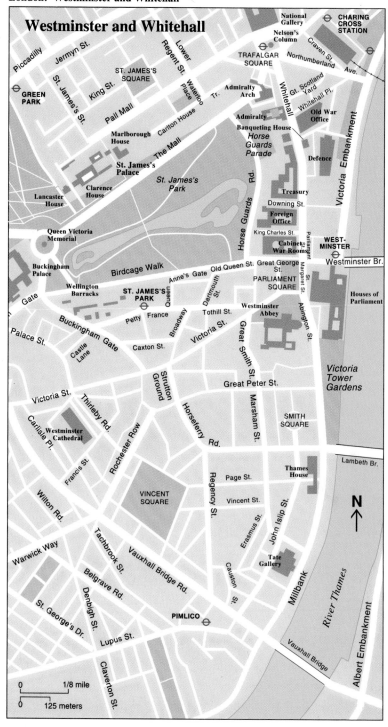

Westminster and Whitehall

Piccadilly

Jermyn St.

St. James's St.

King St.

ST. JAMES'S SQUARE

Lower Regent St.

Waterloo Place

Carlton House Tr.

Pall Mall

GREEN PARK

Marlborough House

Carlton House

The Mall

St. James's Palace

Lancaster House

Clarence House

St. James's Park

Queen Victoria Memorial

Buckingham Palace

Wellington Barracks

Birdcage Walk

ST. JAMES'S PARK

Anne's Gate

Old Queen St.

Queen

Dartmouth St.

Petty France

Broadway

Tothill St.

Victoria St.

Gate

Buckingham Gate

Palace St.

Castle Lane

Caxton St.

Victoria St.

Thirleby Rd.

Carlisle Pl.

Westminster Cathedral

Francis St.

Strutton Ground

Rochester Row

Horseferry Rd.

VINCENT SQUARE

Wilton Rd.

Warwick Way

Tachbrook St.

Belgrave Rd.

Denbigh St.

St. George's Dr.

Vauxhall Bridge Rd.

Lupus St.

PIMLICO

Claverton St.

National Gallery

Nelson's Column

CHARING CROSS STATION

Craven St.

TRAFALGAR SQUARE

Northumberland Ave.

Admiralty Arch

Whitehall

Gt. Scotland Yard

Whitehall Pl.

Admiralty

Banqueting House

Horse Guards Parade

Old War Office

Victoria Embankment

Defence

Horse Guards Rd.

Treasury

Downing St.

Foreign Office

King Charles St.

Cabinet War Rooms

Parliament St.

WEST-MINSTER

Westminster Br.

Great George St.

PARLIAMENT SQUARE

Margaret St.

Abingdon St.

Houses of Parliament

Westminster Abbey

Great Smith St.

Great Peter St.

Marsham St.

Victoria Tower Gardens

SMITH SQUARE

Page St.

Regency St.

Vincent St.

Erasmus St.

John Islip St.

Caxton St.

Thames House

Lambeth Br.

Millbank

Tate Gallery

Causton St.

River Thames

Vauxhall Bridge

Albert Embankment

N ↑

0 ____ 1/8 mile

0 ____ 125 meters

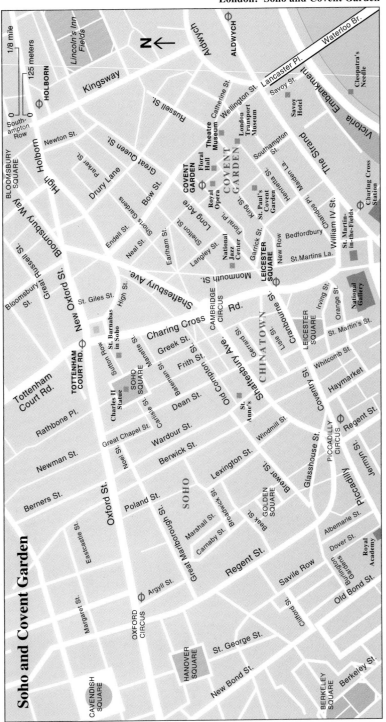

London: Soho and Covent Garden

Soho and Covent Garden

London: Buckingham Palace and Mayfair

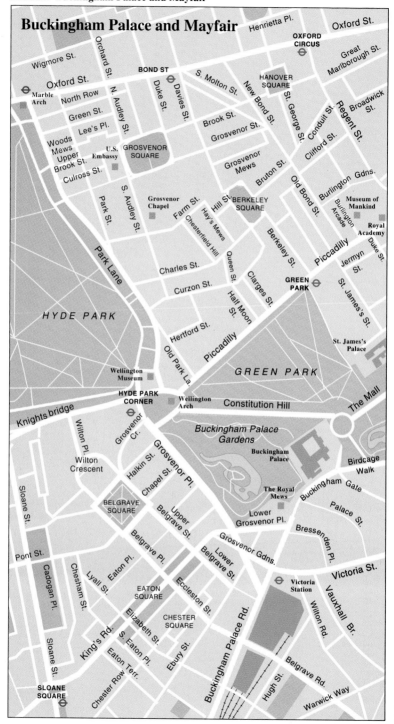

Buckingham Palace and Mayfair

Henrietta Pl.

OXFORD
CIRCUS

Oxford St.

Great
Marlborough St.

Wigmore St.

Orchard St.

BOND ST

S. Molton St.

HANOVER
SQUARE

Regent St.

Broadwick St.

Oxford St.

Marble
Arch

North Row

Duke St.

Davies St.

New Bond St.

St. George St.

Conduit St.

Clifford St.

N. Audley St.

Green St.

Brook St.

Lee's Pl.

Grosvenor St.

Woods
Mews

U.S.
Embassy

GROSVENOR
SQUARE

Grosvenor
Mews

Burlington Gdns.

Museum of
Mankind

Upper
Brook St.

Culross St.

Bruton St.

Old Bond St.

Burlington
Arcade

Royal
Academy

Park St.

S. Audley St.

Grosvenor
Chapel

Farm St.

Hill St.

BERKELEY
SQUARE

Piccadilly

Duke St.

Chesterfield Hill

Hay's Mews

Berkeley St.

Jermyn
St.

Charles St.

Queen St.

Clarges St.

GREEN
PARK

St. James's St.

Park Lane

Curzon St.

Hall
Moon
St.

HYDE PARK

Hertford St.

Old Park La.

Piccadilly

GREEN PARK

St. James's
Palace

Wellington
Museum

HYDE PARK
CORNER

Wellington
Arch

Constitution Hill

The Mall

Knights bridge

Grosvenor
Cr.

Wilton Pl.

Buckingham Palace
Gardens

Wilton
Crescent

Halkin St.

Chapel St.

Grosvenor Pl.

Buckingham
Palace

Birdcage
Walk

Sloane St.

BELGRAVE
SQUARE

Upper
Belgrave St.

The Royal
Mews

Buckingham Gate

Palace St.

Pont St.

Belgrave Pl.

Lower
Belgrave St.

Lower
Grosvenor Pl.

Bressenden Pl.

Cadogan Pl.

Chesham St.

Lyall St.

Eaton Pl.

Eccleston St.

Grosvenor Gdns.

Victoria
Station

Victoria St.

Vauxhall Br.

EATON
SQUARE

Elizabeth St.

CHESTER
SQUARE

Ebury St.

Buckingham Palace Rd.

Wilton Rd.

Sloane St.

King's Rd.

S. Eaton Pl.

Eaton Terr.

Belgrave Rd.

SLOANE
SQUARE

Chester Row St.

Hugh St.

Warwick Way

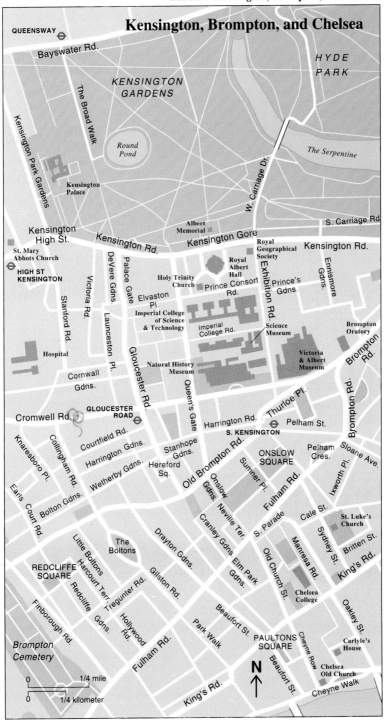

Kensington, Brompton, and Chelsea

London: City of London

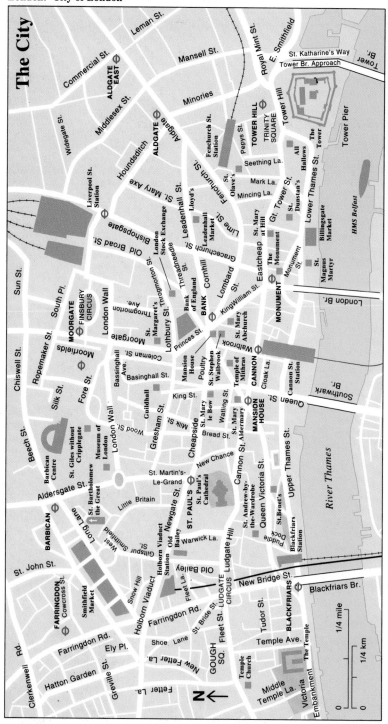

The City